ENCYCLOPEDIA OF
Homosexuality

ENCYCLOPEDIA OF
Homosexuality

EDITED BY WAYNE R. DYNES

ASSOCIATE EDITORS WARREN JOHANSSON
WILLIAM A. PERCY

WITH THE ASSISTANCE OF STEPHEN DONALDSON

St J
St James Press

Chicago and London

VOLUME 1
A - L

Published in the United Kingdom by
St. James Press
2-6 Boundary Row
London SE1 8HP
England

Originally published in the United States by
Garland Publishing, Inc., New York.

British Library Cataloguing-in-Publication Data

Encyclopedia of homosexuality.
    1. Homosexuality
    I. Dynes, Wayne *1934-*
    306.766

      ISBN 1-55862-115-6 vol. 1
      ISBN 1-55862-116-4 vol. 2
      ISBN 1-55862-147-4 set

*Book and cover design by
Renata Gomes*

Printed on acid-free, 250-year-life paper.
Manufactured in the United States of America.

Contents

Acknowledgments

he editor gratefully acknowledges a grant from the American Association for Personal Privacy, Princeton, New Jersey. The advice of the Association's president, Dr. Arthur C. Warner, was continuously helpful. Dr. Paul Hardman (San Francisco), a director of the Association, has also been generously supportive. The editor wishes to recognize the inspiring example and advice over the years of Barbara Gittings, longtime Director of the Gay Task Force of the American Library Association, and of W. Dorr Legg, Dean of the ONE Institute in Los Angeles.

The interdisciplinary, transcultural, and transhistorical scope of this enterprise rests on a tradition of pioneering scholarship initiated in the nineteenth and early twentieth centuries by Heinrich Hoessli, Magnus Hirschfeld, and Ferdinand Karsch-Haack. Many concepts utilized in the *Encyclopedia of Homosexuality* were developed at meetings of the Scholarship Committee of the Gay Academic Union, New York, during the decade 1976–85. The Scholarship Committee also began a program of exchange with foreign scholars which has been invaluable in broadening our international coverage. Among those especially helpful in this regard have been Javier Aroz (Euskadi/Spain), Massimo Consoli (Italy), Giovanni Dall'Orto (Italy), Jürgen Geisler (Germany), Júlio Gomes (Portugal), John Grube (Canada), Gert Hekma (Netherlands), Manfred Herzer (Germany), Paul Knobel (Australia), João Antônio de S. Mascarenhas (Brazil), Alan V. Miller (Canada), Luiz Mott (Brazil), and G. S. Simes (Australia). In the early stages of planning Claude Courouve of Paris gave important advice and encouragement. The editor acknowledges with gratitude the training he received as an encyclopedist at the Istituto per la Collaborazione Culturale in Rome, especially the help of Theresa C. Brakeley and Mamie Harmon.

To all the contributors, whose names appear in a separate list, we owe a special debt for sharing their expertise. The following authors have been so generous, individually and collectively, that they deserve the status of contributing editors: Giovanni Dall'Orto, Daniel Eisenberg, Stephen O. Murray, and Kathy D. Schnapper. The Index and Reader's Guide were created by Stephen Donaldson, who has been an indefatigable researcher and whose eagle-eyed editing has benefited the language and often the content of most of the major entries.

A long-standing debt is owed to Jim Kepner, International Lesbian and Gay Archives, West Hollywood, and to Don Slater, Homosexual Information Center, Los Angeles and Bossier City, Louisiana.

From his vantage point as Editor of the *Journal of Homosexuality*, Professor John De Cecco provided a heartening example. Professor Eugene Rice of Columbia University offered sage advice. In Boston, Richard Dey of the International Homophilics Institute and Pedro J. Suárez rendered editorial help and research assistance. John Lauritsen generously offered technical advice, while Professor David F. Greenberg of New York University was an unfailing source of references. At Garland Publishing our editors Gary Kuris and Kennie Lyman have worked tirelessly and efficiently to ensure that no necessary step in the complex process of editing and production was neglected.

Finally, no acknowledgment would be complete without a tribute to the thousands of unsung heroes in and out of academia and the homophile movement, whose courageous and often lonely efforts to battle the prevailing taboos against research into, and open discussion of, homosexuality have at last succeeded in making this work possible.

Preface

he love that dared not speak its name is now, in spite of or because of AIDS, shouting it from the rooftops, and in many voices. Almost as much scholarship on homosexuality has appeared since 1969 as in the previous hundred years, even in the wake of Freud and Hirschfeld, and with each passing year the volume increases. This encyclopedia is the first attempt to bring together, interrelate, summarize, and synthesize this outpouring of controversial and often contradictory writings and to supplant the pseudoscholarship, negative or positive propaganda, and apologetics that are still appearing.

As recently as the 1960s, dearth of research and the widespread Western taboo on public discussion of homosexuality even in the world of academia would have prevented publication of such a work as this. A society that sought for many centuries to suppress the very existence of homosexuality, and to exclude all mention of it from literary and historical documents and from public discourse, could not have welcomed the issuance of this encyclopedia. Indeed, even now some may seek to entomb it in silence because remnants of that taboo still persist.

As anyone who has sought information from them knows, general encyclopedias and histories offer only meager information on homosexuality, usually couched in outdated clinical or judgmental terms. Biographies of gay men and lesbian women discuss their orientation only when unavoidable, as with Oscar

Wilde. There have been several encyclopedias and dictionaries of sexuality (beginning with a German one of 1922, the *Handbuch der Sexualwissenschaft*), but this work is the first to treat homosexuality in all its complexity and variety.

In presenting the encyclopedia to the world, the editors urge the educated public to reflect upon the hidden threads that this work has followed through many areas of human endeavor, a pattern that traces the covert sexuality of figures in public life and in the arts and sciences as the clue to otherwise incomprehensible acts and events. So much effort has gone into censoring and suppressing this subject that extensive investigation has been required to bring it back to the light of day. Even so, vast areas of inquiry—historical eras, whole countries, entire disciplines of scholarly thought—remain to this day blank pages awaiting the patient detective work of future generations of scholars. That so much has already been uncovered, as this work demonstrates, is a monumental tribute to the courage, fortitude, research skills, and the sheer dedication to the difficult search for truth shown by the scholars whose findings form the heart of the encyclopedia.

How and for Whom the Work Can Be Useful

This encyclopedia is not just for academic readers. While a variety of styles and vocabulary levels coexist in the work, the editors have generally sought to make the articles accessible to all likely users, while germane to highly educated scholars. Thus a high-school student should be able to gain valuable information from the article COMING OUT even as the social psychologist finds a rigorous critique of various theoretical concepts of the "coming out" process. No advanced degree is needed to interpret BEACHES, SLANG WORDS FOR HOMOSEXUALS, PIRATES, and CATHER, WILLA; on the other hand, SOCIAL CONSTRUCTION and CANON LAW may prove a challenge for those with no previous acquaintance with related materials.

The encyclopedia should be of great practical use to a wide variety of professionals, from social workers to clergymen, from lawyers to wardens, from pediatricians to drug counselors, and from travel agents to novelists.

In addition, these volumes will aid heterosexual readers in understanding friends, co-workers, and family members who are involved in or afraid of homosexual experiences or relationships or who are simply trying to clarify and communicate their own outlook to others whom the subject baffles.

The editors hope that the encyclopedia will furnish enlightenment for the debates now unfolding in books, articles, the audio–visual media, religious bodies, courts, and legislatures about gay and lesbian rights. We trust that the data assembled will refute misconceptions and falsehoods and contribute to more accurate polemics and to a just resolution of these complex issues.

To the individual struggling to come to terms with his or her own homosexuality, the encyclopedia furnishes a wealth of points of comparison, of historical figures with whom to feel kinship, and the knowledge that all the efforts of church and state over the centuries to obliterate homosexual behavior and its expression in literature, tradition, and subculture have come to naught, if only because the capacity for homoerotic response and homosex-

ual activity is embedded in human nature, and cannot be eradicated by any amount of suffering inflicted upon hapless individuals.

WHAT THE WORK IS ABOUT

The unifying subject of this encyclopedia is ostensibly "homosexuality." But this matter is not so simple as it appears. First of all, it includes both male and female homosexuality (lesbianism), though there is a good deal more information about the former because the latter has been even more thoroughly censored from the historical record along with other aspects of the history of women. Indeed, some have suggested that the two gender aspects of same-sex behavior should be completely segregated and that the present work should restrict itself to males. The editors, however, are persuaded that the phenomenology of lesbianism and that of male homosexuality have much in common, especially when viewed in the cultural and social context, where massive homophobia has provided a shared setting, if not necessarily an equal duress.

Second, a discussion of homosexuality is incomplete without taking into account those who, for whatever reasons, have combined erotic behavior with their own sex and with the other, to whatever degree. Hence, though the term "homosexual" is often perceived as a dualistic one, standing in stark contrast to its opposite term, "heterosexual," this encyclopedia encompasses bisexuality as well. Moreover, not every person who has received a biography is gay, lesbian, or bisexual; heterosexuals have made important contributions to the subject and to this work.

Third, homosexuality cannot properly be understood if it is restricted to genital sexuality. The terminology here is difficult, but the passionate love of one male for another or of one female for another has not always found physical expression, or the evidence of genital expression has not been preserved, while the passionate feelings are perpetuated in literature and history.

Fourth, homosexuality has had great significance for all of humanity through the role that both it—and opposition to it—have played in the evolution of world culture. In this aspect, the encyclopedia must reach far beyond questions of physical sexuality to examine the effects of homophilia and of homophobia on literature, the arts, religion, science, law, philosophy, society, history, and psychology—indeed, on virtually every field of human endeavor. It is perhaps here that the reader new to this field will discover the greatest surprises, for general literature has obscured most of these effects.

The encyclopedia is concerned not simply with homosexual behavior as such, but with the hopes and aspirations, the longing and dread, with which the subject has been invested. Homophobia itself cannot be omitted, because it has played—at least in Western society—and still does play a large role in shaping popular attitudes. By way of compensation, the *Encyclopedia of Homosexuality* presents a rich banquet of novels and poems, paintings and sculptures, plays and films which have permanently recorded homosexual feelings and aspirations.

Perhaps the most difficult obstacle to a simple focus on "homosexuality" is the growing realization that what has been lumped together under that term since its coinage in 1869 is not a simple, unitary phenomenon. The more one works with data from times and cultures other than contemporary middle-class American and northern European ones, the more one tends to see a multiplicity of homosexualities. A current conception, which focuses on a sense of homosexual identity or personality, interacting with a "gay" subculture set apart from the general society, is only one of a number of paradigms or models of homosexuality, and there is far from a consensus that it is necessarily "better" or more accurate or more universal than others. A male who has sex with

another male can be seen by one society as feminine, by another as all the more masculine; his act can be accounted customary for all males or a rare monstrosity; his behavior, if limited to the insertor role, is not even considered homosexual by many cultures. He may be considered especially evil or especially sacred for his conduct, or it may not even be thought worth mentioning. In some cultures his act will be approved only if he does it with a boy, in others boy love will draw the fiercest wrath upon him. It is this variety of patterns and conceptions, on all of which the tag "homosexuality" is applied by one writer or another, that makes the study of same-sex eroticism both so difficult and so fascinating. Most of all, it adds to the great diversity the reader will find in this work.

THE EDITORS' APPROACH

In the over 770 articles included herein, the editors have ventured to survey the entire field of homosexuality *sine ira et studio*, without anger and partisanship. In selecting contributors to the encyclopedia, they have sought competence and availability rather than adherence to any particular doctrine. They have endeavored to alert the reader to such controversies as divide even well-informed scholars. With the growth of knowledge some topics boast four or five experts, often with conflicting theoretical perspectives and sometimes with different conclusions. In some areas where topics overlap, such as FREUDIAN CONCEPTS and PSYCHOANALYSIS, the contributors—in this case, two of the editors—present clearly varying positions. In most instances only one of the several experts could be chosen for representation here. In addition to this factor, space limitations and other commitments have made it impossible to include every deserving scholar—indeed their ranks swell almost daily. Nonetheless, some fields, notably non-Western disciplines, remain neglected and coverage is consequently less rich than we would wish. No conclusion should be drawn regarding the sexual orientation of any author from his or her appearance in this work.

The encyclopedia is extraordinarily interdisciplinary in nature, transhistorical, and insofar as could be done at this time, cross-cultural. Discarding limited visions which might confine attention to the recent past and to the Western world, the present work traces countless connections across space and time. The Greeks who institutionalized pederasty and used it for educational ends take a prominent role, as does the Judeo-Christian tradition of sexual restriction and homophobia that prevailed under the church Fathers, Scholasticism, and the Reformers, and—in altered form—during the twentieth century under Hitler and Mussolini, Stalin and Castro. Avoiding the Eurocentrism of many earlier attempts at synthesis, the encyclopedia provides full treatment—as far as present knowledge allows—of Africa, Asia, Latin America, and the Pacific, and of pre-literate as well as literate peoples. It is rare to encounter among these non-Western peoples anything approaching the intense homophobia found in the West.

One reason why this work is so multidisciplinary is that the phenomena of homosexuality represent an outstanding theoretical problem for all those conceptual frameworks which seek to promote a comprehensive and cohesive accounting for human behavior. Whether evolutionary biologist, Marxist, theologian, anthropologist, psychoanalyst, ancient historian, literary critic, demographer, legal scholar, folklorist, feminist, or futurologist, one must either attempt to account for these phenomena and their influence on human life, or admit to an embarrassing gap in one's theory. Here homosexuality enters a sort of "theory prism," to take a term from Stephen Donaldson: the general phenomenon is passed through the refracting lens of grand theory like a beam of light, and either it emerges in coherent fashion, if in a spectrum of variegated facets, after such passage, or the prism is revealed to be opaque

and in need of recasting. The way in which grand theories are serving as this theory prism, with mixed and often unexpected results, is one of the intriguing results of the emergence of homosexuality into the light of academic scrutiny.

How the Work Is Constructed

While the articles in this encyclopedia have not been forced into a rigid straitjacket of typology, the vast majority of them are either thematic, topical, or biographical. Thematic entries may be at a very general level (such as SOCIOLOGY) or more differentiated (such as LABELING; ROLE; SUBCULTURE); they often cross-reference and present different intellectual perspectives. Topical entries deal with particular times and places, such as ROME, ANCIENT; SPAIN; and CHICAGO, or phenomena like BARS and ORAL SEX, where themes mix and cross; they tend to be more descriptive and less theoretical. Representative biographies emphasize the interface between the homosexual activity or orientation and the creative achievement of the subject. In this way the life history treats homosexuality not as something external and negative, but as an integral and meaningful part of the personality. A careful perusal of these biographies will demonstrate to the unbiased reader the rich personalities and the importance of homoerotic tendencies and liaisons in the lives of many who inspired, formed, directed, and interpreted civilization.

The number of biographical entries could be multiplied several times. A complete roster of even historically notable gay men and lesbians is probably unattainable. The editors' concern, however, is to present figures from all walks of life. For reasons of space, the editors decided not to include biographies of living people. They are often discussed in thematic or topical articles, e.g., Leonard Bernstein in MUSICIANS, Adrienne Rich in POETRY, Harry Hay in MOVEMENT, HOMOSEXUAL, and Michel Tremblay in QUEBEC. Usually when disagreement persists about the homosexuality or bisexuality of such figures as Catalina Erauso, Langston Hughes, and Sarah Orne Jewett, the *Encyclopedia* provides no separate biographical entry, though these individuals may be discussed in other contexts.

References to other articles in this encyclopedia are indicated by **bold type** in the text, or are listed at the end of the article under "See also...." For syntactical reasons, the grammatical form of the bolded word may differ slightly from that of the article, so that **psychiatric** refers to PSYCHIATRY and **Japanese** to JAPAN. Sometimes only the first word of the full title appears in bold type; thus **prisons** refers to PRISONS, JAILS, AND REFORMATORIES. The absence of such a cross-reference does not mean there is no article on the subject, just that it is not supplementary to the present piece. It has also been felt unnecessary and distracting to highlight some of the most general entries, such as HOMOSEXUALITY itself. The Index has been constructed so as to provide a maximum of correlation.

At the end of most articles will be found a list of readings under the heading "BIBLIOGRAPHY." This is not intended to be a complete list of sources, but a general guide for the reader wishing to delve further into the subject at hand, and not knowing where to start. With a few exceptions, original works by the subjects of biographies are not listed, only works about them; complete books have been favored over scattered articles. The reader seeking a more comprehensive bibliography is advised to consult Wayne R. Dynes' *Homosexuality: A Research Guide*, also from Garland Publishing. In most cases unsigned articles were written by the editor.

CONCLUSION

Firmly convinced that homoerotic feeling and behavior—and the homophile movement and gay and lesbian literature of modern times—are here to stay, the editors offer this encyclopedia to the public in the hope that it will find readers broad-minded enough to accept its unconventional choice of subject, impartial enough to assess its strengths as well as its weaknesses, and informed enough to correct its omissions and errors. They hope for a second, expanded edition sometime in the future drawing on the assessments of readers and reviewers and also on the ever broader and deeper stream of new scholarship. Their profoundest wish is that future generations of scholars will revise, correct, and enlarge the volumes from decade to decade, so that it may serve as a trusted reference for all who seek enlightenment on the topic of homosexuality.

A Reader's Guide

Readers who wish to use the encyclopedia as an instrument or text for a systematic study of homosexuality may consult the asterisked (*) articles in the following lists as suitable points of entry. Two methods are recommended:

(1) For those interested primarily in one or a small number of areas or disciplines, begin in each grouping with any articles bearing three asterisks, then read any with two, then any with one, and finally the remainder. A good starting place before selecting a particular topic or discipline group is the grouping ORIENTATIONS AND MODES, which will familiarize the reader with basic concepts and terminology.

(2) For those wishing to undertake a more comprehensive approach, read all the entries with three asterisks from all the groupings, then turn to those with two asterisks from all the groupings, and so on. Sometimes a given article will have different numbers of asterisks when listed in different groupings; in such cases one should be guided by the higher number. This approach, however, should also start with ORIENTATIONS AND MODES. (For the convenience of those choosing this method, a suggested reading order for the three-asterisked entries is given at the end of this guide.) After the asterisked entries, the non-asterisked articles may be read by those wishing a truly "encyclopedic" education.

Biographies have not been asterisked, on the understanding that readers will gain a sense of the importance of particular individuals from the thematic and topical articles and will thus be able to follow up with their own choice of biographies.

. For tips on using cross-references within the articles, see the Preface. The reader is also directed to the **Index** for follow-up on any topics of particular interest; often additional information or a different perspective may be found in articles other than those listed. The Index is also useful for inquiries into any subjects not covered by articles of their own; the curious reader will find that a browsing perusal of the Index will suggest many interesting topics for examination.

Overview of Groupings

ENTRIES GROUPED BY MAJOR TOPIC
AND DISCIPLINE

Clement of Alexandria
Crete **
Dionysus
Ephebophilia
Epicureanism *
Etruscans **
Eunuchs *
Ganymede *
Gnosticism
Greece, Ancient ***
Greek Anthology **
Gymnasia *
Hadrian
Heliogabalus
Hellenism
Hellenistic Monarchies *
Hippocratic Corpus
Homer *
Horace
Inventor Legends *
Jesus
Josephus
Judeo-Christian Tradition*
Lucian of Samosata
Manichaeanism *
Martial, Marcus Valerius
Mediterranean Homosexuality *
Mythology, Classical **
Narcissus
Nero
Olympic Games *
Orpheus
Patristic Writers *
Pederasty **
Petronius
Philo of Alexandria
Pindar
Plato *
Plautus
Plutarch
Renault, Mary
Roman Emperors *
Rome, Ancient ***
Sappho *
Scythians
Sicily *
Slavery *
Socrates
Solon *
Sparta **

Stoicism *
Suetonius
Symposia
Tacitus
Thebes *
Theocritus
Theognis
Tibullus
Vase Painting, Greek *
Vergil
Zeno of Citium

(Communications, see MEDIA AND
COMMUNICATIONS)

CONCEPTS, TERMS, AND
THEORIES (see also
HOMOPHOBIC CONCEPTS)

Active-Passive Contrast **
Activist, Gay
Adhesiveness
Ageism
Anarchism
Androgyny *
Androphilia **
Berdache **
Bisexuality ***
Bohemianism
Boston Marriage
Buggery *
Butch-Fem Relationships *
Calamus
Camp *
Catamite *
Celibacy
Class
Clone *
Closet *
Color Symbolism
Coming Out **
Community, Gay *
Consciousness Raising
Consent
Constitutional Homosexuality **
Counterculture *
Cruising
Dandyism
Deviance and Deviation*
Dictionaries and Encyclopedias *
Dyke *
Dysphoria, Gender

Pederasty
Pedophilia
Prisons, Jails, and Reformatories
Prostitution
Rape of Males
Role **
Sadomasochism *
Slavery
Typology ***

RELIGION AND MYTHOLOGY

Abomination
Abrahamic Religions **
Achilles
Alan of Lille
Anglicanism *
Aquinas, St. Thomas
Asceticism *
Astrology
Augustine
Bailey, Canon Derrick Sherwin
Beloved Disciple *
Bèze, Théodore de
Buddhism **
Canaanites *
Canon Law*
Celibacy
Circumcision
Chrysostom, St. John
Clement of Alexandria
Clergy, Gay **
Christianity **
Churches, Gay **
Damian, Peter
David and Jonathan *
Dionysus
Ethics *
Ganymede *
Gilgamesh, Epic of *
Gnosticism
God, Homosexuality as a Denial of*
Heresy *
Homer
India **
Inquisition **
Intertestamental Literature
Inventor Legends
Islam ***
Jesus *
Judaism, Post-Biblical **
Judaism, Sephardic

Judeo-Christian Tradition ***
Kadesh *
Kadesh-Barnea
Leadbeater, Charles Webster
Manichaeanism *
Middle Ages
Monasticism *
Mythology, Classical **
Narcissus
Neoplatonism
New Testament **
Old Testament **
Orpheus
Papacy **
Patristic Writers **
Penitentials
Philo Judaeus
Protestantism **
Racha
Rumi
Shamanism **
Sodom and Gomorrah *
Sufism **
Talmud *
Witchcraft **
Zoroastrianism **

ROLES (see also GENDER)

Active-Passive Contrast ***
Berdache **
Bisexuality
Butch-Fem Relationships *
Catamite
Couples
Eunuchs
Hoboes
Lover
Macho *
Mediterranean Homosexuality **
Minions and Favorites *
Orientation, Sexual
Pederasty *
Prisons, Jails, and
  Reformatories *
Public Schools
Punk
Rape of Males
Role ***
Rome, Ancient *
Sadomasochism *
Shamanism *

Rape of Males
Sadomasochism *
Safe Sex *
Urination, Erotic

SEXUAL SITES
Bars *
Bathhouses *
Beaches
Brothels *
Geography, Social
Guides, Gay
Mardi Gras and Masked Balls
Molly Houses
Prisons, Jails, and Reformatories
Public Schools
Resorts *
Seafaring
Toilets *
Travel and Exploration

SOCIOLOGY (see also ANTHRO-
POLOGY; COMMUNICATIONS;
GROUPS; LIFESTYLES; MOVE-
MENT, GAY AND LESBIAN; RE-
LATIONSHIPS; ROLES; SEXUAL
SITES)
Activist, Gay
Advertisements
Ageism
Aging
Beatniks and Hippies
Bohemianism
Censorship and Obscenity
Circles and Affinity Groups **
Class **
Clone
Coming Out*
Community, Gay ***
Counterculture **
Cruising
Deviance and Deviation
Discrimination
Education
Ethnophaulism
Exiles and Emigrés
Folklore, Gay Male
Folklore, Lesbian
Friendship, Female Romantic
Friendship, Male
Geography, Social *

Gesture and Body Language
Ghettos, Gay *
Government
Graffiti
Guides, Gay
Hoboes
Homosociality **
Identity *
Immigration
Incidence, Frequency, and the Kinsey
    0-6 Scale **
Labeling **
Language and Linguistics
Lifestyle **
Military
Minority, Homosexuals as a **
Movement, Homosexual *
Parents, Lesbian and Gay
Pirates*
Police
Pornography
Prejudice *
Press, Gay
Prisons, Jails, and Reformatories *
Prostitution *
Public Schools*
Role **
Samurai*
Seafaring*
Semiotics, Gay *
Separatism, Lesbian
Sex-negative, Sex-positive
Shamanism
Situational Homosexuality *
Slavery*
Social Work *
Sociobiology **
Sociology ***
Stonewall Rebellion
Subculture, Gay ***
Taste
Trade *
Twins *
Typology *
Working Class, Eroticization of **
Youth **

SYMBOLISM AND SEMIOTICS
Advertisements
Calamus
Censorship and Obscenity

SUGGESTED READING ORDER FOR *** ARTICLES THROUGH-OUT THE ENCYCLOPEDIA:

Contributors

Barry D. Adam, University of Windsor (Canada)

Rudi Bleys, Catholic University, Leuven (Belgium)

Alan Bray, London (England)

Vern Bullough, State University of New York, Buffalo

David Cameron, ONE Institute, Los Angeles

Peter Christensen, State University of New York, Binghamton

Daniël Christiaens, Antwerp (Belgium)

Siong-huat Chua, Boston

Randy Conner, San Francisco

Louis Crompton, University of Nebraska, Lincoln

Giovanni Dall'Orto, Milan (Italy)

Richard Dey, International Homophilics Institute, Boston

Stephen Donaldson, New York City

Wayne R. Dynes, Hunter College (CUNY), New York City

Daniel Eisenberg, Florida State University, Tallahassee

Lillian Faderman, California State University, Fresno

Lucy J. Fair, New Orleans

Stephen Wayne Foster, Miami

Peter Gach, San Francisco

Bruce-Michael Gelbert, New York City

Joseph Geraci, Amsterdam (Netherlands)

Evelyn Gettone, New York City

Antonio A. Giarraputo, Boston

Júlio Gomes, Lisbon (Portugal)

Joseph P. Goodwin, Ball State University, Muncie, IN

Edward F. Grier, University of Kansas, Lawrence

J. S. Hamilton, Old Dominion University, Norfolk, VA

Gert Hekma, University of Amsterdam (Netherlands)

Gregory Herek, Graduate Center, City University of New York

Manfred Herzer, Berlin (German Federal Republic)

Bret Hinsch, Harvard University, Cambridge, MA

Tom Horner, New Bern, NC

Robert Howes, University of Cambridge (England)

Ward Houser, New York City

Warren Johansson, Gay Academic Union, New York City

Jim Jones, Central Michigan University, Mount Pleasant

Simon Karlinsky, University of California, Berkeley

Marita Keilson-Lauritz, Amsterdam (Netherlands)

Hubert Kennedy, San Francisco

George Klawitter, Viterbo College, LaCrosse, WI

Paul Knobel, Sydney (Australia)

Jan Laude, Bloomington, IN

John Lauritsen, New York City

John Alan Lee, University of Toronto (Canada)

Jim Levin, City College (CUNY), New York City

Steven L. Lewis, Fort Wayne, IN

Lingananda, New York City

Phoebe Lloyd, Philadelphia

Donald Mader, Amsterdam (Netherlands)

Dolores Maggiore, East Northport, NY

Theo van der Meer, Vrije Universiteit, Amsterdam (Netherlands)

Dietrich Molitor, University of Siegen (German Federal Republic)

Luiz Mott, University of Bahia Salvador (Brazil)

Stephen O. Murray, Instituto Obregón, San Francisco

Peter Nardi, Pitzer College, Claremont, CA

Joan Nestle, Lesbian Herstory Archive, New York City

Eugene O'Connor, Irvine, CA

Michael Patrick O'Connor, Ann Arbor, MI

William Olander, The New Museum of Contemporary Art, New York City

William A. Percy, University of Massachusetts, Boston

Michel Philip, University of Massachusetts, Boston

Brian Pronger, Toronto (Canada)

Geoff Puterbaugh, Cupertino, CA

Michel Rey, Paris (France)

Ritch Savin-Williams, Cornell University, Ithaca, NY

Paul Schalow, Rutgers University, New Brunswick, NJ

Maarten Schild, Utrecht (Netherlands)

Jan Schippers, Schorer Stichting, Amsterdam (Netherlands)

Kathy D. Schnapper, School of Visual Arts, New York City

Udo Schüklenk, Waltrop (German Federal Republic)

Laurence Senelick, Tufts University, Medford, MA

Charley Shively, University of Massachusetts, Boston

Rodney Simard, California State University, San Bernardino

Frederik Silverstolpe, Lund (Sweden)

G. S. Simes, University of Sydney (Australia)

Pedro J. Suárez, Boston

Clark L. Taylor, San Francisco

John Taylor, Angers (France)

David Thomas, University of California, Santa Cruz

C. A. Tripp, Psychological Associates, Nyack, NY

Randolph Trumbach, Baruch College (CUNY), New York City

Arthur C. Warner, American Association for Personal Privacy, Princeton

James D. Weinrich, University of California, San Diego

Frederick L. Whitam, Arizona State University, Tempe

Walter L. Williams, University of Southern California, Los Angeles

Leslie Wright, Hamilton College, Clinton, NY

The Encyclopedia

ABERRATION, SEXUAL

The notion of sexual aberration had some currency in the literature of **psychiatry** during the first half of the twentieth century. Although the expression encompassed a whole range of behaviors regarded as abnormalities, it is probably safe to say that it was used more with reference to homosexuality than for any other "disorder." In due course it yielded to deviation, and then to **deviance**—somewhat less negative concepts.

The term derives from the Latin *aberrare*, "to go astray, wander off." It is significant that the first recorded English use of the verb "aberr" (now obsolete), by John Bellenden in 1536, refers to religious **heresy**. For nineteenth-century alienists and moralists, the word aberration took on strong connotations of mental instability or madness. Thus, in its application to sexual nonconformity, the concept linked up with the notion of "moral **insanity**," that is to say, the nonclinical manifestation of desire for **variant** experience. The notion of departure from a presumed statistical norm, and the prefix ab-, connect with the concept of abnormal. The proliferation of such terms in the writings of psychiatrists, physicians, moralists, and journalists in the first half of the twentieth century reveals a profound ambivalence with regard to human variation, in which prescriptive condemnation struggles with, and often overcomes, descriptive neutrality.

ABNORMALITY

The lay public remains much concerned about the question of whether homosexual behavior is abnormal. In medical pathology the term "abnormal" refers to conditions which interfere with the physical well-being and functioning of a living body. Applied to social life, such an approach entails subjective judgments about what the good life is. Moreover, insofar as homosexual and other variant lifestyles can be considered "maladjusted," that assumption reflects the punitive intrusion of socially sanctioned prescriptions rather than any internal limitations imposed by the behavior itself. In other words, once the corrosive element of self-contempt, which is introjected by the social environment, is removed, homosexual men and lesbian women would appear to **function** as well as anyone else. Another difficulty with the concept is that the pair normal/abnormal suggests a sharp dichotomy. **Kinsey's** findings, however, suggest that sexual behavior is best understood as a continuum with many individuals falling between the poles and shifting position over the course of their lives.

It is true but trivial that in a purely statistical sense homosexual behavior in our society is abnormal, since it is not practiced by most people most of the time. But the same is the case with such behavior as opera singing, the monastic vocation, medicine—all of which are valued occupations, but ones practiced only by small segments of the population. Labeling sopranos, monks, or physicians abnormal would be tautological—it amounts to saying that a member of a group is a member of a group. Needless to say, we are not accustomed to refer to such pursuits as abnormal because they do not, as a rule, incur social disapproval. Sometimes the matter is referred to biology, by enquiring as to whether animals practice it . (*See* animal homosexuality.) Once again, such cultural activities as religion and medicine are not practiced by animals, but this lack does not compel us to condemn them as abnormal. Because of the negative freight that has accumulated over the years, augmented by numerous courses in "abnormal psychology," it is best that the term be used very sparingly—if at all—in connection with sexual behavior.

The history of the word itself reveals an interesting, if obscure interchange between linguistic development and judgmentalism. As the *Oxford English Dictionary* noted (with unconscious irony) in 1884, "few words show such a series of pseudo-etymological perversions." The process that occasioned this unusual lexicographical outburst is as follows. Greek *anomalos* ("not even or level") produced Latin *anomalus*—and eventually our word anomalous. Then, through confusion with *norma*, "rule," the Latin word was corrupted to *anormalis*, hence French and Middle English *anormal*. The parasitic "b" crept in as the second letter of the modern word through scribal intervention rather than the natural evolution of speech. (Compare the intrusive "d" and "h" in "adventure" and "author" respectively.)

It is true that classical Latin had *abnormis*, "departing from the rule," but it did not possess *abnormalis*. The presence of the "b" in our word abnormal serves to create an unconscious association with "aberrant," "abreaction," etc. To summarize, the pejorative connotations are enhanced by the intrusion of two consonants, "b" and "r," which—the etymology shows—do not belong there.

Two rare anticipations of modern usage may be noted as curiosities. In a harangue against sodomites, the French thirteenth-century *Roman de la rose* (lines 19619–20) refers to those who practice "exceptions anormales." In 1869 the homosexual theorist Károly Mária **Kertbeny** coined a word, *normalsexual* (= heterosexual), in contrast with *homosex-* ual (which by inference is not normal). Although Kertbeny's first word, in striking contrast to the second, gained no currency, it did anticipate the twentieth-century contrast of normal and abnormal sexuality.

BIBLIOGRAPHY. Alfred Kinsey et al., "Normality and Abnormality in Sexual Behavior," in P. H. Hoch and J. Zubin, eds., *Psychological Development in Health and Disease*, New York: Grune and Stratton, 1949, 11–32.

Wayne R. Dynes

ABOMINATION

In contemporary usage the terms abomination and abominable refer in a generic way to something that is detestable or loathsome. Because of **Old Testament** usage, however—Leviticus 18:22, "Thou shalt not lie with mankind as with womankind: it is abomination" (cf. Leviticus 20:13; Deuteronomy 22:5 and 23:19; and I Kings 14:24)—the words retain a special association as part of the religious condemnation of male homosexual behavior. In Elizabethan English they were normally written "abhomination," "abhominable" as if they derived from Latin *ab-* and *homo*—hence "departing from the human; inhuman." In fact, the core of the Latin word is the religious term *omen*.

In any event the notion of abominatio(n) owes its force to its appearance in Jerome's Vulgate translation of the Bible, where it corresponds to Greek *bdelygma* and Hebrew tō'ēbāh. The latter term denotes behavior that violates the covenant between God and Israel, and is applied to **Canaanite** trade practices, idolatry, and polytheism. The aversion of the religious leaders of the Jewish community after the return from the Babylonian captivity to the "abominable customs" of their heathen neighbors, combined with the **Zoroastrian** prohibition of homosexual behavior, inspired the legal provisions added to the Holiness Code of Leviticus in the fifth century before the Christian era that were to be normative for Hellenistic

Judaism and then for Pauline **Christianity**. The designation of homosexual relations as an "abomination" or "abominable crime" in medieval and modern sacral and legal texts echoes the wording of the Old Testament.

The complex web of prohibitions recorded in the Book of Leviticus has defied full explanation from the standpoint of comparative religion. Recently influential among social scientists (though not among Biblical scholars) has been the interpretation of the anthropologist Mary Douglas (*Purity and Danger*, London, 1967), who views the abominations as part of a concern with the boundaries of classification categories, strict adherence to which attests one's purity in relation to divinity.

ABRAHAMIC RELIGIONS

According to the French Catholic Orientalist Louis Massignon (1883–1962), the Abrahamic religions are the three major faiths—**Judaism**, **Christianity**, **Islam**—that look to the patriarch Abraham as their spiritual father. In their belief systems, Abraham ranks as the first monotheist who rejected the pagan divinities and their idols and worshiped the true God who revealed himself to him. (Modern scholars have concluded that the book of Genesis is a historical novel written only after the return of the exiles from the Babylonian captivity, and that monotheism in fact began with Akhenaten, the heretical pharaoh of **Egypt** in the fourteenth century B.C. But completely eradicated in Egypt itself after his death, Akhenaten's innovations left no resonance except for their possible survival in the neighboring Israelite monarchy, which began its rule under Egyptian cultural hegemony.)

All the Abrahamic religions proscribe homosexual behavior, a taboo that derives from the Holiness Code of the book of Leviticus and the legend of **Sodom** as these were received in Palestinian and then Hellenistic Judaism between the fifth

century B.C. and the first century, when the writings of such Jewish apologists as **Philo** Judaeus and Flavius **Josephus** show it in a fully developed form. Thus the negative attitude of all three faiths has a single **Old Testament** source; its reception in Christianity is secondary and in Islam tertiary, the Islamic tradition having mainly been shaped by Nestorian Christianity of the early seventh century. All three contrast in the most striking manner with the role that homosexual behavior and the art and literature inspired by homoerotic feeling played in Greco-Roman paganism—a legacy that the medieval and modern world has never been able fully to suppress or disavow, but which has driven scholars and translators to acts of censorship and artful silence when confronted with texts and artifacts bequeathed by the ancient civilizations.

The claim of homophobic propagandists that the prohibition of homosexuality is universal rests essentially upon its proscription in the Abrahamic religions, which have primarily condemned male homosexuality. Lesbianism is nowhere mentioned in the Old Testament, the **New Testament**, or the Koran. The passage in Romans 1:26 that has often been interpreted as referring to lesbian sexuality actually concerns another Old Testament myth, the sexual union of the "sons of God" and the "daughters of men" in Genesis 6:1–4. The association of Sodom's twin city of Gomorrah with lesbianism is an accretion of the later Middle Ages and confined to Latin Christianity.

As for the texts in Leviticus 18:22 and 20:13, modern critical scholarship has identified them as part of a legal novella from the Persian period, and the entire Mosaic Law as a document compiled by Ezra and the "men of the Great Assembly" in the years 458–444 B.C., hence long after the return of the exiles from the Babylonian Captivity. The account of the destruction of Sodom is a geographical legend inspired by the salinization and aridity of the shores of the Dead Sea, a result of the lowering of the prehistoric water level that exposed the barren vicinity to full view. The book of Genesis and its later elaboration in Christian and Islamic legend have in their totality been dismissed from history, as modern scholars with access to Egyptian and **Mesopotamian** sources now conclude that the authors of the Old Testament had no knowledge of any historic event earlier than 1500 B.C. and that there was no urban culture in Palestine in the so-called patriarchal age.

While Jewish communal life in Palestine laid the foundations, the prohibition on homosexual behavior could not be enlarged into a Kantian imperative for all humanity without a Hellenic supplement. Some Greek thinkers had independently formulated a condemnation of homosexuality on philosophical and ethical grounds, the chief of which was that sexuality was intended by nature solely for the purpose of procreation. But this view remained a philosopher's dictum with no support in religion or mythology. It was Judaism that brought to the question the uncompromising prohibitions of Leviticus and the accompanying death penalty, a sanction exemplified by the myth of the destruction of Sodom. The four lines of attack—philosophical, ethical, legal– religious, and mythical—converged in Philo Judaeus (ca. 20 B.C.–ca. A.D. 45), who formulated in flawless Attic prose the arguments that Christianity was to adopt as the basis for the intolerance of homosexuality in its own civilization.

The enforcement of the taboo in the three Abrahamic religions is quite another matter. For most of its history Judaism lacked the state power with which to impose the Levitical death penalty, but could resort to ostracism and exclusion from the Jewish community. Christianity, and above all Latin Christianity, succeeded in creating not just a fearsome legal prohibition, but also an intolerant public opinion that mercilessly ostracized not just those guilty of "unnatural vice," but even those accused or merely suspected of it,

and so burdened even exclusive homosexuals with the mask of a heterosexual identity. Islam, even after adopting this part of the Abrahamic tradition, never effectively superimposed it upon the more tolerant folkways of the Mediterranean societies which it conquered and won to its faith, but even allowed homoerotic literature to flourish in the languages cultivated by its adherents, though plastic art celebrating male beauty was restricted by dogmatic opposition to image-making.

Louis Massignon composed a work entitled *Les trois prières d'Abraham, II, La prière sur Sodome* (1930), inspired by Abraham's intercession for the Sodomites in Genesis 18, in which he professed to have discovered the "spiritual causes of inversion." It is the most sophisticated piece of theological homophobia the twentieth century has produced. A summary of his ideas appears in "Les trois prières d'Abraham, père de tous les croyants," *Dieu Vivant*, 13 (1949), 20–23.

However deep-seated and tradition-hallowed the prohibition of homosexuality in the Abrahamic religions may be, it stems in the last analysis from pre-scientific ignorance and superstition and not from beliefs accredited by modern science and philosophy. The contemporary gay liberation movement may be regarded as a rejection of the Abrahamic tradition in regard to homosexuality and a return to the more tolerant and accepting attitude of Greco-Roman paganism, even though some gay activists seek to sanction their beliefs in the guise of pseudo-Christian or pseudo-Jewish communities. On the other hand, the unanimity of the three religions authorizes their adherents to collaborate in good faith against gay liberation and other goals of sexual reform, however much they have hated, shunned, and even persecuted one another over the centuries because of their mutually exclusive claims to be the sole revealed religion.

BIBLIOGRAPHY. Guy Harpigny, *Islam et christianisme selon Louis Massignon*, Louvain-la-Neuve: Université

Catholique de Louvain, 1981, pp. 79–106; F. E. Peters, *Children of Abraham: Judaism, Christianity, Islam*, Princeton: Princeton University Press, 1982.

Warren Johansson

ABU NUWAS
(CA. 757–CA. 814)

Arab poet. One of the greatest of all Arab writers, Abu Nuwas was the outstanding poet of the Abbasid era (750–1258). Abu Nuwas al-Hasan ibn Hani al-Hakami was born in Al-Ahwaz; his father was from southern Arabia and his mother was Persian. His first teacher was the poet Waliba ibn al-Hubab (died 786), a master who initiated him into the joys of pederasty as well as poetry.

Abu Nuwas continued his education in theology and grammar, after which he decided to try his luck as an author in the capital city of Baghdad. Here he soon acquired great fame as a poet who excelled in lyrical love poetry (*ghazal*), in lampoons and satire, and in **mujun**—frivolous and humorous descriptions of indecent or obscene matters. He became the boon companion of the Caliph Al-Amin (ruled 809–813), son and successor of the illustrious Harun ar-Rashid (ruled 786–809). His irresistible humor and irony made him a favorite figure in popular stories of the Arab world, where he played the role of court jester. (He makes several appearances in *The Thousand and One Nights*.)

Abu Nuwas's favorite themes were wine and boys. He was one of the first Arab poets to write lyrical love poetry about boys, and his genius brought the genre to great heights. His preferred type of youth was the pale gazelle, whose face shone like the moon, with roses on his cheeks and ambergris in his long curly hair, with musk in his kisses and pearls between his lips, with firm boyish buttocks, a slender and supple body, and a clear voice. Beardless boys held the greatest attraction—the growth of hair on the cheek was likened to that of apes—but

here also Abu Nuwas flouted social norms by describing down on the cheek as erotically appealing, since it preserved beauty from indiscreet glances and gave a different flavor to kisses.

The only woman who played an important part in his life was Janan, a slave girl, but, because of his libertine conduct, she never trusted the sincerity of his love. When she asked him to renounce his love of boys, he refused, saying that he was one of the "people of Lot, " with reference to the Arab view that the Biblical Lot was the founder of homosexual love. Abu Nuwas was sexually interested in women or girls only when they looked like boys, but even then he considered their vagina too dangerous a gulf to cross. As he said (symbolically): "I have a pencil which stumbles if I use it on the front of the paper, but which takes great strides on the back." Lesbianism he derided as pointless: "It is fat rubbed up by fat, and nothing more. And rub as one may, when down to bare skin, there is nothing to rise in response. There is no wicked shaft that is smooth at the tip to drive itself home and sink into place."

Abu Nuwas was notorious for his mockery and satire, in which the sexual intemperance of women and the sexual passivity of men were favorite themes. A lot of people, even those in high places, were verbally "buggered" by him: "Your penis would not be soft if you did not widen your anus!" Such verbal abuse landed him in prison twice; he was also jailed once for drinking wine.

He liked to shock society by writing openly about things which transgressed the norms and values of Islam. For example, he was probably the first Arab poet to write about the taboo subject of masturbation, which he declared to be inferior to the love of boys, but preferable to marriage. He did not hide his "sinful" behavior behind a cloak of silence, as was expected in Islam; instead he openly boasted of his love of boys and wine: "Away with hypocrisy ... discreet debauchery means little to me. I want to enjoy everything in broad daylight." Social blame only served as an enticement, and regrets were not to be expected.

At the very end of his life, Abu Nuwas underwent a sudden reformation, and devoted his final days to the composition of verses in favor of Islamic holiness. Yet it is not these verses which brought him his fame.

See also **Ghulamiyya; Islam.**

BIBLIOGRAPHY. Jamel Bencheikh, "Poésies bachiques d'Abu Nuwas," *Bulletin d'Etudes Orientales*, 18 (1963–64), 7–75; William Harris Ingrams, *Abu Nuwas in Life and Legend*, Port Louis: La Typographie Moderne, 1933; Ewald Wagner, *Abu Nuwas: Eine Studie zur Arabischen Literatur der frühen Abbasidenzeit*, Wiesbaden: Steiner, 1965.

Maarten Schild

ACHILLES

Greek mythological hero. Achilles was the son of Peleus and Thetis, usually represented as their only child. All the evidence suggests that the Greeks thought of him as a man, real or imaginary, and not as a "faded" god, and that his widespread cult resulted mainly from his prominence in the *Iliad*. His portrait was drawn once and for all by **Homer**, and later writers supplied details from their own imagination or from local traditions of obscure origin.

In the *Iliad* he appears as a magnificent barbarian, somewhat outside the sphere of Achaean civilization, though highly esteemed for his personal beauty and valor. Alone among the figures of Homer, he clings to the archaic practice of making elaborate and costly offerings, including human victims. His furious and ungovernable anger, on which the plot of the Iliad turns, is a weakness of which he himself is conscious. When not aroused by wrath or grief, he can often be merciful, but in his fury he spares no one. He is a tragic hero, being aware of the shortness of his life, and his devoted friendship for

Patroclus is one of the major themes of the epic. Later Greek speculation made the two lovers, and also gave Achilles a passion for Troilus.

The homoerotic elements in the figure of Achilles are characteristically Hellenic. He is supremely beautiful, *kalos* as the later vase inscriptions have it; he is ever youthful as well as short-lived, yet he foresees and mourns his own death as he anticipates the grief that it will bring to others. His attachment to Patroclus is an archetypal male bond that occurs elsewhere in Greek culture: Damon and Pythias, Orestes and Pylades, Harmodius and Aristogiton are pairs of comrades who gladly face danger and death for and beside each other. From the Semitic world stem **Gilgamesh** and Enkidu, as well as **David and Jonathan**. The friendship of Achilles and Patroclus is mentioned explicitly only once in the Iliad, and then in a context of military excellence; it is the comradeship of warriors who fight always in each other's ken: "From then on the son of Thetis urged that never in the moil of Ares should Patroclus be stationed apart from his own man-slaughtering spear."

The Homeric nucleus of the theme of Achilles as homosexual lover lies in his relationship with Patroclus. The friendship with Patroclus blossomed into overt homosexual love in the fifth and fourth centuries, in the works of **Aeschylus**, **Plato**, and **Aeschines**, and as such seems to have inspired the enigmatic verses in Lycophron's third-century *Alexandra* that make unrequited love Achilles' motive for killing Troilus. By the fourth century of our era this story had been elaborated into a sadomasochistic version in which Achilles causes the death of his beloved by crushing him in a lover's embrace. As a rule, the post-classical tradition shows Achilles as heterosexual and having an exemplary asexual friendship with Patroclus.

The figure of Achilles remained polyvalent. The classical Greek pederastic tradition only sporadically assimilated him, new variations appeared in pagan writings after the Golden Age of Hellenic civilization, and medieval Christian writers deliberately suppressed the homoerotic nuances of the figure. But in the world of Greek gods and heroes, Achilles remains the supreme example of the warrior imbued with passionate devotion to his comrade-in-arms.

BIBLIOGRAPHY. W. M. Clarke, "Achilles and Patroclus in Love," *Hermes*, 106 (1978), 381–96; Katherine Callen King, *Achilles: Paradigms of the War Hero from Homer to the Middle Ages*, Berkeley: University of California Press, 1987.

Warren Johansson

ACKERLEY, JOSEPH RANDOLPH (1896–1967)

British writer and editor. In 1918 Ackerley wrote a play "The Prisoners of War" about the cabin fever and repressed homoerotic longings of his own stint in a German camp during World War I. It was produced in 1925, by which time Ackerley had become a protégé of E. M. **Forster**. Forster arranged for him a nebulous position with the Maharajah of Chhatarpur, whose misadventures in pursuit of homosexual love Ackerley mercilessly lampooned in his travel book *Hindoo Holiday* (1929).

The frustrations of Ackerley's own inhibited sexual encounters with working-class men and men in uniforms led him to concentrate his affections on his dog, an Alsatian named Queenie, who is the main romantic interest of *My Dog Tulip* (1956), and of his one novel, *We Think the World of You* (1960), which juxtaposes the pleasures of owning a dog with the difficulties of having a lower-class beloved. After Queenie's death and Ackerley's retirement from the BBC (where he had been an editor of *The Listener*, 1935–59), he journeyed to Japan, where he had a modicum of sexual gratification. Ackerley wrote an obituary of Forster and sold Forster's letters to the University of Texas, then predeceased him by three years.

Just before his death, Ackerley completed a memoir (*My Father and Myself*) in which he fantasized that as a youth his guardsman father had prostituted himself to rich patrons, thereby securing the financial stability that was eventually to afford his son the opportunity to rent later generations of guardsmen for mutual masturbation. Unfortunately, many of his admirers have taken this account to be established fact.

BIBLIOGRAPHY. Neville Braybrooke, ed., *The Ackerley Letters*, New York: Harcourt, Brace, Jovanovich, 1975; Peter Parker, *Ackerley: A Life of J.R. Ackerley*, London: Constable, 1989.

Stephen O. Murray

ACQUIRED IMMUNE DEFICIENCY SYNDROME
See AIDS.

ACTIVE–PASSIVE CONTRAST

Common usage divides homosexual behavior into active and passive roles. These terms are ambivalent and often confusing.

A truism of physics is that bodies may be either at motion or at rest. Inert objects, however, can only respond to external attraction and repulsion. It is the property of living things that they can initiate activity as well as respond (or refuse to respond) to stimuli. This last distinction is the basis of commonsense notions of active personalities as against passive ones. Some individuals seem to expend energy freely while others conserve it. In addition to this expend–conserve model, the active–passive contrast corresponds in large measure to those of lead–follow and command–obey.

Around such notions the popular morality of ancient **Greece** and **Rome** constructed a sexual dichotomy that classified participants in sexual acts not so much according to the male–female difference, based on body build and genitalia, or the heterosexual–homosexual contrast of object choice, both of which are familiar to modern thinking, but in a stark opposition of the doer and the one who is done to. The doer (agent) is the phallic male, his receiving partner (patient or pathic) either a female or a pubescent boy. (Sometimes older males could enact the passive role, but they were generally disprized in consequence, for the paradigm admits of only one role for the adult male.) The active–passive contrast largely corresponds to the penetrator–penetratee dichotomy. In modern sexual encounters, the penetrator can be, with respect to overall body movement, largely passive, amounting to a contradiction. The ancients avoided this problem by their tendency to analyze oral–phallic activity as irrumation, that is, where the penetrator engages his partner with vigorous buccal thrusts. A common belief in this system is the notion that only the active partner experiences pleasure; the role of the passive is simply to endure. It is easy to see how such a model of dominator and dominated would accord with the mindset of a slave-owning society.

This contrast of active vs. passive is abundantly illustrated in Greek and Latin sexual texts, and as these are the foundation of the Western tradition their formulae have often been echoed, though changed—consciously or unconsciously— to fit new social norms. The contrast is also found in medieval **Scandinavia**, in our **prisons, jails, and reformatories**, and to a large extent in contemporary **Latin America**.

All these manifestations stem from popular modes of thought which tend to privilege the active, even predatory male. Other trends were found, however, in more cultivated spheres of Greco-Roman thinking. Self-restraint is a quality much praised in ancient ethical **philosophy**, and insofar as this ideal filtered down it tended to

mitigate the notion that the more rapacious copulation the active male could engage in the better. The Platonic tradition also reserved a special place for contemplation, a preference which passed into **Stoicism**, where it even may take the form of commendation of nonaction. These contemplative and Stoic trends migrated into **Christianity**, which however did break with classical tradition by excluding the adolescent youth from the category of licit sexual objects, thus clearing the way for the male–female dichotomy that has been dominant in Western culture ever since. Nonetheless, the pederastic ideal never completely died out, despite the winds of theological disapproval. Many medieval and **Renaissance** texts attest to the survival of pederastic patterns, at least among a cultivated few.

In modern heterosexual practice the identification of the male with the active and the female with the passive was sealed by the repressive norm of the passionless female and the standard injunction of the "missionary position," in which the penetrating male lies atop his partner. Feminism has sought to combat such restrictions and today a variety of sexual positions are noted in every sex manual. With respect to male and female homosexual conduct, however, the notion lingers that sexual activity, and indeed the whole relationship, must be structured around the active–passive contrast. Thus gay men and lesbians are often asked: "Are you active or passive?" It is frequently difficult to persuade the interlocutor that the two roles are assumed alternately, or that one pattern may prevail in bed while the opposite occurs in everyday life. That is to say, a "butch" lesbian accustomed to take the lead in social encounters may be responsive rather than aggressive in bed. For a time "politically correct" gay and lesbian thinking condemned sex-role differences in couples, claiming that they were a reactionary mimicry of heterosexual norms, but it is now generally recognized that whether these patterns are to be honored or overcome should be a matter of individual choice.

See also **Pederasty; Slavery.**

Wayne R. Dynes

ACTIVIST, GAY

Familiar in the 1970s, the expression "gay activist" has become less common owing to the ebbing of the more strenuous and **utopian** aspects of the gay liberation **movement**. It served to denote someone choosing to devote a major share of his or her energies to the accomplishment of social change that will afford a better life for homosexual men and lesbian women. Its most famous institutional embodiment, subsequently imitated in many parts of the world, was the Gay Activists Alliance (GAA), formed in New York City in the wake of the 1969 **Stonewall Rebellion**. The group took as its symbol the Greek letter **lambda**, apparently because of its association with energy transformation in physics. Unlike the New Left, GAA was expressly a "one issue" organization, refusing to submerge the cause of gay rights in a network of social change groups, what came to be known as the Rainbow Coalition. In Europe the term "gay militant" is sometimes found as a variant, but in North America the word militant is generally eschewed because of its Old Left connotations and limitations.

The history of the idea of gay activism displays a complicated pedigree. The concept is rooted ultimately in the perennial contrast between the active and the contemplative life—the latter being traditionally preferred. In 1893, however, the French Catholic philosopher Maurice Blondel in essence turned the tables in his book *L'Action*. Blondel, in keeping with the vitalist currents of the day, held that philosophy must take its start not from abstract thought alone but from the whole of our life—thinking, feeling, willing.

Shortly thereafter, in Central Europe Rudolph Eucken, who received the Nobel Prize for literature in 1906, developed his own philosophy of Aktivismus. At this time many figures of Germany's political and literary-artistic avant-garde were drawn to Franz Pfemfert's periodical *Die Aktion* (1911–32). Further permutations occurred with the Flemish nationalist Activists in Belgium and the Hungarian artistic movement, Aktivismus, that arose in the aftermath of World War I. As early as 1915, however, Kurt **Hiller**, a political theorist and journalist, as well as an advocate of homosexual rights, drew several strands together in his broader concept of Aktivismus, urging the intelligentsia to abandon ivory tower isolation and participate fully in political life. How the term activist in its political (and gay movement) sense reached North America in the 1970s can only be surmised. The mediation of German refugee scholars is likely, as is suggested by this 1954 quotation by Arthur Koestler: "he was not a politician but a propagandist, not a 'theoretician' but an 'activist'." (The reference, from *The Invisible Writing*, is to Willi Münzenberg, an energetic Communist leader in Paris in the 1930s.)

Wayne R. Dynes

ADELSWÄRD FERSEN, BARON JACQUES D' (1880–1923)

French aristocrat and writer. Descended from Marie Antoinette's lover Axel Fersen, the wealthy young baron wrote several volumes of poetry and fiction in the first decade of the century, including *Hymnaire d'Adonis, Chansons légères, Lord Lyllian,* and *Une jeunesse.* In addition, he edited and contributed to twelve monthly numbers of a literary periodical, *Akademos* (1909). At the age of twenty-three he was arrested for taking photographs of naked Parisian schoolboys, but was allowed to go into exile on the island of Capri for several years, later returning to France after having visited Sri Lanka and China.

The great love of his life was the boy Nino Cesarini, who lived with him in the Villa Lysis on Capri, which was filled with statues of naked youths and which is now overrun by weeds and stray cats. Adelswärd Fersen also wrote poems to a thirteen-year-old Eton schoolboy. He was the model for Baron Robert Marsac Lagerström in Compton Mackenzie's amusing novel *Vestal Fire* (1927), and was the hero of Roger Peyrefitte's historical fiction *L'exilé de Capri* (1959). He died of a drug overdose in 1923, having for years been an opium and cocaine addict. He had modeled his life on that of Count Robert de **Montesquiou**, but the latter refused to have anything to do with him, for even in Capri Adelswärd Fersen had caused scandals. He was even associated with Essebac (as the novelist Achille Bécasse was known), Norman **Douglas**, and Baron von **Gloeden**. The story of his sexual life is to be found in his own books, in the works of Norman Douglas, and in Peyrefitte's novel, which is spoiled by a mixture of fact and fiction.

BIBLIOGRAPHY. Bruce Chatwin, "Self-Love Among the Ruins," *Vanity Fair*, 47:4 (April 1984), 46–55, 102–6.
Stephen Wayne Foster

ADHESIVENESS

The concept of adhesiveness was introduced into English by the phrenologist Johann Gaspar Spurzheim (1776–1832) in the meaning of "the faculty that causes human beings to be attached to one another." It derived ultimately from the Latin verb *adhaerere*, as in Genesis 2:24, where St. Jerome's equivalent of "Therefore shall a man . . . cleave unto his wife" is "Quam ob rem . . . homo . . . adhaerebit uxori suae." Diffusion of the concept of adhesiveness by the (pseudo-)science of phrenology enabled it to became part of the special vocabulary of the emerging homosexual subculture of the nineteenth century. Phrenologists themselves grounded this passionate friendship—which could exist between members of opposite sexes as well as between those of the same sex—in the brain, giving it a material base and a congenital origin. Walt **Whitman** self-consciously narrowed the reference of the term "adhesive love"—which he also named "comradeship"—to homosexual relationships, and in so doing coded his writings for the initiated reader.

Permutations of the Concept. George Combe (1784–1858), a middle-class lawyer from Edinburgh, met Spurzheim in 1815, and soon thereafter became a leader of British phrenology. His *Constitution of Man Considered in Relation to External Objects* (1828) became the basis of orthodox phrenology. His major contribution to the understanding of adhesiveness was his complex sense of the working of the "organ" and his additions to the iconography. He also contrasted the selfish side of adhesiveness with the nobler ends that had to be directed "by enlightened intellect and moral sentiment." Excess of adhesiveness could, however, amount to a disease.

At least two of the European contributors to the definition of adhesiveness may themselves have been homosexual: Spurzheim himself, and his younger Scottish contemporary Robert Macnish (1802–1837). In discussing women with small amativeness and large adhesiveness, he said that they "prefer the society of their own sex to that of men." Amativeness thus applied to relations between the sexes, while the other term was discreetly given the implicit meaning of "homoerotic attachment." Romantic passions between young people of the same sex Macnish deemed an "abuse of adhesiveness." He went so far as to describe a male couple whose mutual attachment was so excessive as to be "a disease."

There is no indication that Walt Whitman knew Macnish's writings. His own acquaintance with the phrenological tradition came from the Americans associated with "Fowler and Wells," the "phrenological cabinet" that distributed the first edition of *Leaves of Grass* and later hired Whitman to write for their publication *Life Illustrated*. Owen Squire Fowler (1809–1887) took up phrenology with great gusto after hearing Spurzheim's lectures during his student days at Amherst College. In 1840 he published an *Elemental Phrenology* in which adhesiveness was defined as "Friendship; sociability; fondness for society; susceptibility of forming attachments; inclination to love, and desire to be loved. . . ." When he treated adhesiveness at length, as he did repeatedly in journal articles in the following years, he was strong on repetitive rhetoric but weak in analysis. Little of his sermonizing derived from exact observation or rigorous debate.

Franz Joseph Gall (1758–1828), the founder of phrenology, had classified excessive adhesiveness as a "mania," which meant that it could fall within the scope of the physician's interest. However, in the middle of the nineteenth century medical science had not gone beyond defining *quantitative* (as opposed to qualitative) changes in the sexual drive as pathological. Homosexual tendencies were either dismissed as "excesses of friendship" or relegated to the category of "revolting moral **aberrations**."

Walt Whitman. Under the influence of Fowlerian phrenology Whitman developed his own ideas on the role of adhesiveness in his universal scheme of things. Whitman's self-conception was powerfully shaped by the reading of his head done by Lorenzo Fowler, which showed him to have immense potential, and in the wake of this event Whitman underwent a self-transformation that made him the bold prophet of a new vision of democracy.

In the 1856 edition of *Leaves of Grass* Whitman wrote:

Do you know what it is, as you pass,
to be loved by strangers?
Do you know the talk of those
turning eye-balls?
Here is adhesiveness—it is not
previously fashioned—it is apropos.

The restriction to love between members of the same sex—which was not borrowed from the phrenologists—was Whitman's initial adaptation of the term. When later in *Democratic Vistas* he came to elaborate his new vision of society, he spoke of "the adhesive love, at least rivalling the amative love." For the phrenologists amativeness and adhesiveness had been distinct, but had not been so polarized, simply because the opposition heterosexual: homosexual did not yet exist in their minds, although they could recognize adhesiveness as "the fountain of another variety of mental symptoms."

Whitman can be seen in this light as a forerunner of Hans **Blüher**, who, in the second decade of the twentieth century, from an openly elitist and conservative standpoint exalted the role of homoeroticism and of male bonding in the maintenance of the state. For Whitman the core of social organization was same-sex comradeship, which he set at least potentially on a par with heterosexual marriage. He could now celebrate the equalizing effects of his version of adhesiveness, developing it as the basis of social reform in *Democratic Vistas* (1871). His ideal of comradeship linked both his early enthusiasm for the promiscuous anonymity of Manhattan and his later, more or less serial monogamy with his hopes for the future of American democracy.

Aftermath. In the remaining decades of the century, the few surviving phrenologists became painfully aware of the moral dangers of adhesiveness and of the injurious effects of the "excessive desire for friends." In 1898, three years after the disgrace of Oscar **Wilde**, the *Phrenological Journal*, now edited by Orson Fowler's younger sister, published a two-part article that dwelt as never before on the excesses of friendship, which "causes its possessor to seek company simply for the sake of being in it, whereby their time is wasted and they become a natural prey to the dishonest, tricky, unscrupulous, and vicious, who may take advantage of and link them into all sorts of obligatory concerns ruinous to their pockets and their morals."

Today discredited and forgotten, phrenology retains a historical interest as one of the disciplines that sought to analyze the causal factors in personality before a scientific psychology had emerged from philosophy. As such, it brought Whitman and perhaps others involved in the homosexual subculture of that day to a better understanding of themselves and of the potential of homoerotic urges for the positive task of nation-building. The notion of adhesiveness as related to male comradeship linked it to the *paiderasteia* of Greek antiquity, with its emphasis on loyalty to one's comrade in arms and on duty to the state of which one was a citizen—the latter being one of the sources of the modern democratic ideal.

BIBLIOGRAPHY. Michael Lynch, "'Here Is Adhesiveness': From Friendship to Homosexuality," *Victorian Studies*, 29 (1985), 67–96.

Warren Johansson

ADLER, ALFRED (1870–1937)

Austrian psychiatrist, founder of Individual Psychology, commonly known as the Adlerian School. Like Sigmund **Freud**, Adler came from a lower middle-class Jewish family in Vienna. A central figure in Freud's psychoanalytic circle from 1902 to 1911, his heated disputes with the master in the latter year led to his seceding with several other members to form an independent group.

Adler's theories are technically less complex than those of Freud, and draw more directly on his experiences with patients of humbler social origin. As a result they have a commonsense quality that earned them considerable popularity in the middle decades of the twentieth century, a popularity that has since ebbed. Alfred Adler's thinking emphasized the individual's striving for power and **self-esteem** (with the inferiority complex often arising as an unwanted byproduct) and the patient's **lifestyle**—a concept that, much modified over the decades, was to play a notable role in the ideology of the gay movement.

Although he attained a qualified approbation of the goals of the women's movement, he insisted on classifying homosexuals among the "failures of life"—together with prostitutes and criminals. His writings on homosexuality began with a 52-page brochure in German in 1917 and continued sporadically through most of the rest of his life. Possessing little independent explanatory power, Alfred Adler's views on homosexuality are now chiefly of historical interest, as instances of stereotyped judgmentalism and reified folk belief of a kind not uncommon among professionals of his day. Beginning in the 1970s some adherents of (Adlerian) Individual Psychology proposed a less negative approach to homosexual behavior, but their revisionism was opposed by others.

BIBLIOGRAPHY. Alfred Adler, *Cooperation Between the Sexes: Writings on Women, Love and Marriage, Sexuality and Its Disorders*, H. L. and R. R. Ansbacher, eds., Garden City, NY: Anchor Books, 1978; Paul E. Stepansky, *In Freud's Shadow: Adler in Context*, Hillside, NJ: Analytic Press, 1983.

Ward Houser

ADULT–ADULT SEXUALITY

See **Androphilia**

ADVERTISEMENTS, PERSONAL

In the years before World War I insertions by homosexuals began to appear in the personal columns ("petites annonces") of mainstream newspapers in France and Germany. Unlike contemporary **graffiti**, they avoided sexual explicitness and were couched in the guise of seeking friendship. No counterpart is known in English-speaking countries of the time. In the 1920s the homophile press of Germany became even bolder, but it was soon snuffed out by the Depression and the rise of the Nazis.

In the United States in the 1960s, the underground press represented by such **Counterculture** organs as *The Berkeley Barb* and *The East Village Other* began to push farther the boundaries of accepted expression—as seen in the printing of four-letter words and graphic descriptions of sexual acts in news stories. In order to enhance revenue, these papers ran personal ads soliciting sexual partners. This custom was taken over by the gay newspapers, some of which have quite extensive listings. Although they are explicit and often raunchily detailed as to the activities desired, to save space they tend to employ a code of abbreviations recalling that used by real-estate ads. The existence of these ads has enlarged the sexual marketplace beyond the usual sphere of face-to-face meeting. These ads are generally separate from those placed by "entrepreneurs of the body," models, masseurs, and escorts; for their services payment is expected (generally at a specified rate).

Analysis of the ads reveals different styles for men and women. Women's ads are less explicit and are more likely to turn upon qualities of personality such as one might seek in a friend. Male ads tend to show remarkable narrowness in somatic tastes—height, weight, hairiness, race, etc. Age restrictions in the desired partner are common, with parameters generally going considerably below the age of the person who places the ad, but rarely much above

it. The coming of the **AIDS** crisis in the 1980s led to a decline in certain appeals (as for rimming), as well as more positive indications, such as the notation that the advertiser is "health conscious."

As a rule American and English mainstream newspapers do not accept personal ads for sex. In Europe, however, as a striking token of recent changes, they even appear in middle-class, "family" newspapers.

BIBLIOGRAPHY. John Preston and Frederick Brandt, *Classified Affairs: A Gay Man's Guide to the Personal Ads*, Boston: Alyson, 1984.

AESCHINES (CA. 397–CA. 322 B.C.)

Athenian orator. His exchanges with Demosthenes in the courts in 343 and 330 reflect the relations between Athens and Macedon in the era of **Alexander the Great**. Aeschines and Demosthenes were both members of the Athenian *boule* (assembly) in the year 347/46, and their disagreements led to sixteen years of bitter enmity. Demosthenes opposed Aeschines and the efforts to reach an accord with Philip of Macedon, while Aeschines supported the negotiations and wanted to extend them into a peace that would provide for joint action against aggressors and make it possible to do without Macedonian help. In 346/45 Demosthenes began a prosecution of Aeschines for his part in the peace negotiations; Aeschines replied with a charge that Timarchus, Demosthenes' ally, had prostituted himself with other males and thereby incurred *atimia*, "civic dishonor," which disqualified him from addressing the assembly. Aeschines' stratagem was successful, and Timarchus was defeated and disenfranchised.

The oration is often discussed because of the texts of the Athenian laws that it cites, as well as such accusations that Timarchus had gone down to Piraeus, ostensibly to learn the barber's trade, but in reality he was a hustler for the sailors landing at the port. The prosecution is one of the earliest instances of the attempt to destroy a political opponent in a democracy by attacking his sexual past. The offense of which Timarchus was guilty was that by prostituting himself he had in effect put himself in the power of another male, which was not a crime per se, but an act that disqualified a free citizen from speaking before the assembly, and had no relevance to a slave or a foreigner. Nothing in the oration suggests that a general reprobation of *paiderasteia* prevailed in Athenian society at the end of the Golden Age; Aeschines even says expressly that both he and the members of the jury have been honorable boy-lovers, but that the ignoble ("passive") and notorious conduct of which Timarchus had been guilty rendered him unfit to participate in public life. The oration contrasts Timarchus' behavior with the ideal of pederasty that the Greeks derived from the comradeship in arms depicted in the Homeric poems.

BIBLIOGRAPHY. K. J. Dover, *Greek Homosexuality*, Cambridge: Harvard University Press, 1978, pp. 13–57, 75–76.

AESCHYLUS
(525/4–456 B.C.)

First of the great Attic tragedians. Aeschylus fought against the Persians at Marathon and probably Salamis. Profoundly religious and patriotic, he produced, according to one catalogue, 72 titles, but ten others are mentioned elsewhere. He was the one who first added a second actor to speak against the chorus. Of his seven surviving tragedies, none is pederastic. His lost *Myrmidons*, however, described in lascivious terms the physical love of **Achilles** for Patroclus' thighs, altering the age relationship given in Homer's *Iliad*—where Patroclus is a few years the older, but as they grew up together, they were essentially agemates—to suggest that Achilles was the lover (*erastes*) of Patroclus.

Plato had Phaedrus point out the confusion, and argue that Patroclus must have been the older and therefore the lover, while the beautiful Achilles was his beloved (*Symposium*, 180a).

Among Attic tragedians Aeschylus was followed by Sophocles, Euripides, and Agathon. Sophocles (496–406 B.C.), who first bested Aeschylus in 468 and added a third actor, wrote 123 tragedies of which seven survive, all from later than 440. At least four of his tragedies were pederastic. Euripides (480–406 B.C.) wrote 75 tragedies of which nineteen survive, and the lost *Chrysippus*, and probably some others as well, were pederastic. Euripides loved the beautiful but effeminate tragedian Agathon until Agathon was forty. The latter, who won his first victory in 416, was the first to reduce the chorus to a mere interlude, but none of his works survive.

All four of the greatest tragedians wrote pederastic plays but none survive, possibly because of Christian homophobia. The tragedians seem to have shared the pederastic enthusiasm of the lyric poets and of **Pindar**, though many of their mythical and historical source-themes antedated the formal institutionalization of *paiderasteia* in Greece toward the beginning of the sixth century before our era.

William A. Percy

AESTHETIC MOVEMENT

The origins of this trend are usually sought in the concept of "art for art's sake," a concept that arose in France in the middle years of the nineteenth century, when a tendency to deny all utilitarian functions of art gained favor. However, the full development of the aesthetic movement would not have been possible without the background in England, for it was here that the movement in the specific sense arose. In such writers as A. W. N. Pugin (1812–1852) and John Ruskin (1819–1900) disgust with the squalor and alienation brought by the coming of the industrial revolution went hand in hand with a demand for thoroughgoing reform of society, religion, and art. This agitation called forth such diverse results as Christian socialism; the Oxford movement and Anglo-Catholicism; the Gothic revival in architecture; Pre-Raphaelitism in painting and poetry; and the arts and crafts movement. As this catalogue suggests, these trends melded a nostalgic yearning for a supposed organic society of bygone days with utopian hopes for a new social and aesthetic order. The arts and crafts movement in particular sought to transform the domestic environment. The homosexual contribution to the rise of this trend has not been adequately documented, but clearly it foreshadowed the enthusiasm of so many cultivated gay people today for furniture and antiques.

By common consent, the high priest of the aesthetic movement in the literary sphere was a homoerotic Oxford don, Walter **Pater**. His *Studies in the History of the Renaissance* (1873) was the bible of the arty young man of late Victorian times, and his novel *Marius the Epicurean* (1885) offered further detail, in a nostalgic Roman setting. By 1881 the type had become familiar enough to be satirized by W. S. Gilbert in his musical comedy *Patience*. The trend attained triumph and tragedy in the meteoric career of Oscar **Wilde**, whose trials and conviction for gross indecency tarnished the whole tendency. Many aesthetes, to be sure, were not homosexual, yet like Algernon Swinburne and Aubrey Beardsley they could be accused of cognate sexual sins. In the public perception, there was also an interface between the homosexual aesthetes and those who were merely sissified or wimpish. The overelegant, foppish type has a history stretching back to the dandy of the early nineteenth century and forward to the **sissy** of Hollywood **films**.

Another manifestation lay in the sphere of religion. Many British homosexuals were attracted to the "aesthetic" emphasis of high **Anglicanism** with its elaborate ritual and lavish vestments.

Others were attracted to esoteric novelties, such as spiritualism and theosophy. These two trends, historic ritualism and the occult, were combined in the eccentric figure of Charles Webster **Leadbeater**.

BIBLIOGRAPHY. J. E. Chamberlin, *Ripe Was the Drowsy Hour: The Age of Oscar Wilde*, New York: Seabury Press, 1977; Ian Small, ed., *The Aesthetes: A Sourcebook*, Boston: Routledge and Kegan Paul, 1979.

Wayne R. Dynes

AFGHANISTAN

A mountainous Islamic nation in central Asia, Afghanistan is inhabited by warlike tribes and their descendents. Various empires rose and fell before the nation of Afghanistan emerged from the ruins of Nadir Shah's empire in 1747. The royal dynasty of the Durranis ruled until 1973, when a republic was declared. A war between the Soviet Union and Afghan guerrillas began in 1978 and extended over the next ten years, devastating the country. Previous invasions by the British from India took place in 1839, 1879, and 1919.

Three quotations may serve to introduce a survey of homosexuality in Afghanistan. The first is from C. A. Tripp: "almost 100 percent homosexuality in Afghanistan" (*Gay News*, London, issue 118). The second is from a British soldier who fought there in 1841: "I have seen things in a man's mouth which were never intended by nature to occupy such a position." The third is an opening stanza from the Afghan love song, "Wounded Heart" ("*Zekhmi Dil*"): "There's a boy across the river with a rectum like a peach, but alas, I cannot swim."

Although there is as yet no evidence of lesbianism in Afghanistan, it is safe to assume that, as in many Islamic lands, the harems were rife with it.

A number of Afghan poets wrote about beautiful boys, including Sana'i Ghaznavi, Husain Baiqara of Herat, Badru'd-din Hilali, and Abu Shu'ayb of Herat—

the last-named famous for his love for a Christian boy (presumably a slave).

In the tenth century, the Ghaznavid empire was founded by Subuktagin, who got started as a king's boyfriend. The great Sultan Mahmud the Ghaznavid (died 1030) loved a slave-boy named Ayaz, a relationship comparable in Islamic literature to the oft-cited love of the Roman Emperor Hadrian and Antinous in Western culture.

Huseyn Mirza, who ruled from Herat (1468–1506), and his vizier (prime minister) Hasan of Ali, both had harems of boys. Babur (1483–1530), a poet who ruled from Kabul, became infatuated as a seventeen-year old with a boy known as Baburi; Babur went on to found the Mughal Empire in India and eastern Afghanistan, while Herat fell to the Persians.

During a war of the early nineteenth century, Dost Mohammed Khan fled to the Amir of Bukhara, the pederast Nasrullah, who kidnapped his guest's fourteen-year-old son, Sultan Djan. Dost Mohammed Khan went back to Afghanistan, where he captured Kabul and annihilated a British army east of there in 1842. This was the background for the "things in a man's mouth" quotation.

Herat once again became capital of a kingdom under the pederast Kamran (ruled 1829–1842). King Abd al-Rahman (ruled 1880–1901) and his sons were pederasts. King Amanullah Khan (ruled 1919–1929) was also homosexual.

Page boys had been executed for sodomy, however, and the Penal Code of 1925 established the death penalty for sodomy. If the culprit was under 15, however, he was not executed. These laws were not applied to the royal family.

In those days, Afghan soldiers of the regular army were in the habit of gang-raping boys and sometimes foreign diplomats. In later decades, more fortunate foreigners could find willing boys at a certain restaurant on the aptly-named Chicken Street.

During the late nineteenth and early twentieth centuries, Western sexologists and pornographers discovered an audience for lurid tales of sexual hijinks in Asia, yielding a good deal of gamey material about Afghanistan and other places that may or may not be true; there are few footnotes which might allow for verification of this material. This accumulation started with Sir Richard Burton (1821–1890) and culminated in 1959 with what has been called "a prurient wank book" (by the writer of a letter to *Gay News*), Allen Edwardes' *The Jewel in the Lotus*. Possibly referring to Abd al-Rahman, Edwardes quotes from an anonymous book a mention of "the Ameer of Afghanistan, insane for rare handsome white youths." The reader is unable to determine the author, the book's title, the name of the "Ameer", nor the date of the reference. The scholar is tempted to dismiss all such data, but then one finds authentication in other works for such items as the "boy across the river" song.

From various reliable and dubious sources, we can construct a picture of pederasty in Afghanistan over the past hundred years. Homosexuality was common in early adulthood. The aristocrats and frontier chiefs had harems of dancing boys and eunuchs dressed as women. Camel caravans included "traveling wives" (*zun-e-suffuree*) who were boys dressed as women.

There was a street in Kabul, the original "gay ghetto," known as Bazaar-e-Ighlaum, "the bazaar of male lust." Edwardes states without attribution that "Greek" (probably Circassian) boys with blond hair and blue eyes were especially prized by pederasts in Kabul. The popular writer James Michener mentions the dancing boys in his novel *Caravans*, which is set in 1946. More recently, the long war against Soviet troops has probably led to an increase in homosexuality, as large numbers of women fled to Pakistan.

See also **Islam**.

BIBLIOGRAPHY. Annette S. Beveridge, trans., *The Babur-Nama in English*, London: Luzac, 1922; Allen Edwardes, *The Jewel in the Lotus*, New York: Julian Press, 1959.

Stephen Wayne Foster

AFRICA, NORTH

This term generally denotes Libya, Tunisia, Algeria and Morocco, a region which the Arabs term the Maghrib, or "West." Formerly the Maghrib also embraced Muslim **Spain**—including the kingdom of **Granada**—which are discussed separately.

General Features. **Pederasty** was virtually pandemic in North Africa during the periods of Arab and Turkish rule. **Islam** as a whole was tolerant of pederasty, and in North Africa particularly so. (The Islamic high-water points in this respect may tentatively be marked out as Baghdad of *The Thousand and One Nights*, Cairo of the **Mamluks**, Moorish Granada, and Algiers of the sixteenth and seventeenth centuries.) The era of Arabic rule in North Africa did, however, witness occasional puritan movements and rulers, such as the Almohads and a Shiite puritanism centered in Fez (Morocco). This puritanism continues with the current King Hassan II of Morocco, who is, however, hampered by an openly homosexual brother.

Islam was a slave society, and one of the chief commercial activities of North Africa was the vast trade in slaves from sub-Saharan Africa. **Slavery** dated back to Roman times, but during this era it reached very large proportions—sometimes assuming almost the character of a mercantile trans-Saharan kingdom.

The Ottoman Turks, who followed the Arabs, were even more notorious as adepts of pederasty. If one is to trust the reports of scandalized European visitors, the "vice" was everywhere, and no social class was "uninfected." The simple tolerance of same-sex eroticism was a source of endless Christian horror.

The Christian horror was not universal. Some Europeans captured by the Turks saw no reason to return to the fold of Christendom; other Europeans simply emigrated (or fled the law). These "renegades" became an important subclass in North Africa. It was frequently remarked that some of the "renegades" became the worst enemies of Christianity; frequently better educated than the local citizenry, they often held the reins of power. When Moorish Spain fell in 1492, a large number of new recruits joined the "renegades." Four hundred Franciscan friars left the Spain of Isabel the Catholic and embraced Islam rather than "mend their ways," as she had commanded them to do.

During the Turkish period, the bazaars or suqs of North Africa had special sections devoted to the sale of Christian slaves, both male and female, who had been captured by pirates on the Mediterranean to face the proverbial "fate worse than death"—consignment to the seraglios of the ruling classes of the notorious Barbary Coast (the most beautiful captives were frequently reserved for the harems of Constantinople). This trade in white Christians, kidnapped and raped on the Mediterranean, gradually supplanted the previous trade in Negro slaves.

Universal throughout pre-colonial North Africa was the singing and dancing boy, widely preferred over the female in cafe entertainments and suburban pleasure gardens. A prime cultural rationale was to protect the chastity of the females, who would instantly assume the status of a prostitute in presenting such a performance. The result was several centuries of erotic performances by boys, who were the preferred entertainers even when female prostitutes were available, and who did not limit their acts to arousing the lust of the patrons. A North African merchant could stop at the cafe for a cup of tea and a hookah, provided by a young lad, listen to the singing, and then proceed to have sex with the boy right on the premises, before returning to his shop.

The French conquest of the area drove much of this activity underground. Although the French penal code, since the time of **Napoleon**, had no legal sanction for same-sex activity, and the colonists were thus largely restricted to shocked horror and verbal scorn when confronted with the behavior of the "natives," the French did put a stop to slave-trading, piracy, and much prostitution, which effectively eliminated the old romance and terror of the Barbary Coast.

Its apparent benefits notwithstanding, colonialism seems to have had an immensely destructive effect throughout much of the world, as people everywhere suddenly desired to be modern, Western, and European—certainly not to be "backwards." The European superstitions about homosexuality were swallowed entire, and adopted as if they had always been in force. The present writer has spoken with a Tunisian supervisor of schools who firmly believes in the death penalty for all homosexuals. Thus, in their rush to modernism, Third World leaders often adopt the sexual standards of medieval Christendom, even as Europe and America are moving toward legalization and tolerance of same-sex activity. Such, at least in part, is also the plight of modern North Africa.

Libya. Libya is almost entirely desert: the Sahara takes up at least 90% of the country's surface area. The coastal towns support some agricultural production, but the major export comes from the desert—oil.

Early reports from Libya include the famous oasis of **Siwa** located near the Libyan–Egyptian border, but since the accession of Mu'ammar Gaddafi and his purportedly revolutionary regime, the country has not been generally accessible to foreigners. However, numerous and independent travelers' reports indicate that at least one highly-placed Libyan authority is addicted to blond European lads, whom he flies in for weekend trysts and decorates with gold and silver. There is

also, for the general populace, a quasi-clandestine pederastic trade, with the older males in automobiles and the younger on the sidewalks, where money is exchanged for quick satisfaction of lust. Neither Libya nor its neighbor, Egypt, has a strong tradition of hedonism.

Tunisia. A small and impoverished country of some four million, Tunisia's high birthrate keeps the country very young—about half the people are under eighteen. Although it is common to see men walking hand-in-hand (as in all Islamic countries), it would not be wise for a foreigner to adopt the practice with a male lover. Tunisians can easily tell the difference between two friends of approximately equal status (where hand-holding is expected) and a sexual relation (which is "officially" disapproved of and therefore not to be made public). The "official" disapproval means that hotels will frequently not allow Tunisian visitors in hotel rooms occupied by foreigners. In the heartland of homosexual tourism (the Hammamet-Nabeul area), when summer is at its peak, squads of police have occasionally been posted to keep the boys out of the luxury beach hotels. They are not always successful.

Homosexual behavior in Tunisia goes back for hundreds or even thousands of years. In the days of Carthage, the city was known for its perfumed male prostitutes and courtesans. After Carthage was destroyed in the Punic wars, Tunisia became a Roman colony. The country did not regain its independence until modern times. The Romans were supplanted by the Vandals, who in turn surrendered the country to the Byzantine Empire. The rise of the followers of Muhammad swept Tunisia out of Christendom forever, and the country eventually passed into the Turkish Empire, where it remained until the French protectorate. In the Islamic period, Tunisia was centered on the town of Kairouan and known as "Ifriqiya."

Algeria. Algeria is different from Tunisia, principally because of the savage war of independence against the French, and the subsequent drift of Algeria into the socialist camp. Marxist societies abominate homosexuality, and this influence has had a chilling affect on Algeria. The passing tourist will see nothing of such activity, although residents may have a different experience. Another fact is that Algerians do not like the French (because of the war) and this dislike is frequently extended to all people who look like Frenchmen, though they may be Canadian or Polish. It is a strange country, where you can spot signs saying "Parking Reserved for the National Liberation Front" (the stalls are filled with Mercedes Benzes), and also the only place in all of North Africa where the present writer has even seen a large graffito proclaiming "Nous voulons vivre français!" ("We want to live as Frenchmen!").

The adventures of Oscar **Wilde** and André **Gide** in Tunisia and Algeria before the war are good evidence that this modern difference between the two countries was in fact caused by the trauma of the war. There is better evidence in the history of Algiers long before. During the sixteenth and seventeenth centuries, Algiers was possibly the leading homosexual city in the world. It was the leading Ottoman naval and administrative center in the western Mediterranean, and was key to Turkey's foreign trade with every country but Italy. Of the major North African cities, it was the furthest from the enemy—Europe. It was the most Turkish city in North Africa, in fact the most Turkish city outside **Turkey**.

Morocco. Almost nothing is known of homosexuality in Morocco prior to the end of the fifteenth century. It is possible that the Carthaginians introduced the religious prostitution of boys to the indigenous Berbers. In the impressive remains of the Roman/Moroccan city of Volubilis, a large bas-relief stone phallus testifies to a phallic cult. When Morocco does appear in written history, however, it has the same guise as the rest of North Africa: Europeans report the omnipresence of behavior which was thought to be an act against nature, or a temptation of the Devil. The loss of Azzamur on the Moroccan coast was blamed on "the horrible vice of Sodomie," in a parallel to the original tale of the destruction of Sodom itself. The **bathhouses** (*hammams*) of Fez were the object of scandalous comments around 1500.

Two factors assume a bolder relief in Morocco, although they are typical of North Africa as a whole. One is a horror of masturbation. This dislike, combined with the seclusion of good women and the diseases of prostitutes, leads many a Maghrebi to regard anal copulation with a friend as the only alternative open to him, and clearly superior to masturbation. It also leads to such behavior being regarded as a mere peccadillo.

The other, more peculiarly Moroccan tradition is that of *baraka*, a sort of "religious good luck." It is believed that a saintly man can transmit some of this baraka to other men by the mechanism of anal intercourse. (Fellatio has traditionally been regarded with disgust in the region, although the twentieth century has been changing attitudes.)

The Frenchman responsible for establishing the French protectorate over Morocco in 1912, Resident General Louis-Hubert-Gonzalve Lyautey, was an aristocratic pederast, who in his youth was already working with clubs of Catholic working men, and always paid attention to the welfare of his men. It is universally reported that Lyautey showed great respect for local Moroccan institutions. A member of the French Academy and a Marshal of France, Lyautey was a soldier/pederast of great distinction. (His own love was directed toward his aristocratic French aides.)

The city of Tangier was notorious during the period 1950–1980, when numbers of American and European celebrity homosexuals made the city their second home. (They had the same motivations as the composer Camille Saint-Saëns, who spent his declining years in Tangier.) Visitors and residents included Jane **Bowles**, Paul Bowles, William Burroughs, Truman **Capote**, Allen Ginsberg, Jean **Genet**, Tennessee **Williams,** and other notorieties. The British playwright Joe **Orton's** Moroccan vacation was shown with great panache in the biographical film *Prick Up Your Ears*, and was fully described in his diaries (published posthumously). In more recent years, there have been some indications of a puritan backlash developing, and the city has lost much of its celebrity glitter, although pederasty remains a constant of the Moroccan cultural scene.

BIBLIOGRAPHY. Malek Chebel, *L'Esprit de sérail: Perversions et marginalités sexuelles au Magreb*, Paris: Lieu Commun, 1988.

Geoff Puterbaugh

AFRICA, SUB-SAHARAN

Africa south of the Sahara presents a rich mosaic of peoples and cultures. Scholarly investigations, which are continuing, have highlighted a number of patterns of homosexual behavior.

Male Homosexuality. Recurrent attempts have been made to deny any indigenous homosexuality in sub-Saharan Africa, at least since Edward Gibbon wrote, in *The Decline and Fall of the Roman Empire* (1781), "I believe and hope that the negroes in their own country were exempt from this moral pestilence." Obviously, Gibbon's hope was not based on even casual travel or enquiry. Sir Richard **Burton**, who a century later reinforced the myth of African sexual exceptionalism by drawing the boundaries of his **Sotadic Zone** where homosexuality was widely practiced and accepted to exclude sub-Saharan Africa, was personally familiar with male homosexuality in **Islamic** societies within his zone, but had not researched the topic in central or southern Africa, where there were "primitive" hunter/gatherer socie-

ties and quite complex state formations before European conquest. In a number of the latter, such as the Azande of the Sudan (*see* Evans-Pritchard), the taking of boy-brides was well-established.

Clearly, gender-crossing homosexuality also existed from Nubia to Zululand on the East Coast of Africa (and offshore on Madagascar as well). In many societies it was related to possession cults in which women have prominent roles and male participants tend to transvestitic homosexuality. Cross-gender homosexuality not tied to possession cults has been reported in a number of East African societies. Folk fear of witches is widespread in Islamic cultures, although a link between witchcraft and **pederasty** is unusual in existing ethnographic reports of Islamic cultures.

Nadel (1955) did not mention any such link in contrasting two other Sudanese peoples: the Heiban in which there is no expected corollary of homosexual acts (i.e., no homosexual **role**), and the Otoro where a special transvestitic role exists and men dress and live as women. Nadel (1947) also mentioned transvestitic homosexuality among the Moro, Nyima and Tira, and reported marriages of Korongo *londo* and Mesakin *tubele* for the bride-price of one goat. In these tribes with "widespread homosexuality and transvestiticism," Nadel (1947) reported a fear of heterosexual intercourse as sapping virility and a common reluctance to abandon the pleasures of all-male camp life for the fetters of permanent settlement: "I have even met men of forty and fifty who spent most of their nights with the young folk in the cattle camps instead of at home in the village." In these pervasively homoerotic societies, the men who were wives were left at home with the women, i.e., were not in the all-male camps." Among the Mossi, pages chosen from among the most beautiful boys aged seven to fifteen were dressed and had the other attributes of women in relation to chiefs, for whom sexual intercourse with women was denied on Fridays. After the boy reaches maturity he was given a wife by the chief. The first child born to such couples belonged to the chief. A boy would be taken into service as his father had as a page, a girl would be given in marriage by the chief (as her mother had).

Among the Bantu-speaking Fang, homosexual intercourse was *bian nku'ma*, a medicine for wealth, which was transmitted from bottom to top in anal intercourse, according to Tessmann, who also mentioned that "it is frequently heard of that young people carry on homosexual relations with each other and even of older people who take boys." Even more remarkable than Fang medical benefits of anal intercourse is Gustave Hultsaert's report that among the Nkundo the younger partner penetrated the older one, a pattern quite contrary to the usual pattern of age-graded homosexuality.

Besmer discussed a possession cult among the (generally Islamic) Hausa strikingly similar to New World possession cults among those of West African descent. As in the voudou(n) of **Haiti**, the metaphor for those possessed by spirits is horses "ridden" by the spirit. In patriarchal Hausa society, the *bori* cult provides a niche for various sorts of low status persons: "women in general and prostitutes in particular . . . Jurally-deprived categories of men, including both deviants (homosexuals) and despised or lowly-ranked categories (butchers, night-soil workers, menial clients, poor farmers, and musicians) constitute the central group of possessed or participating males" plus "an element of psychologically disturbed individuals which cuts across social distinctions."

Herskovits reported the native view in Dahomey (now Benin) that homosexuality was an adolescent phase: when "the games between boys and girls are stopped, the boys no longer have the opportunity for companionship with the girls, and the sex drive finds satisfaction in close friendship between boys in the same

group. . . . A boy may take the other 'as a woman,' this being called *galglo*, homosexuality. Sometimes an affair of this sort persists during the entire life of the pair." Of course, this last report shows the insufficiency of the native model. Among the nearby Fanti of Ghana and Wolof of Senegal there are also gender-crossing roles for men and for women.

Among the Bala (sometimes referred to as the Basangye in older literature) in Kasai Oriental Province of the Democratic Republic of the Congo, there is a role at variance with the conventional male role in that culture (particularly patterns of dress and of subsistence activity) with expectations of unconventional sexual behavior. Although it seems *kitesha* is a gender-crossing role, rather than a primarily homosexual role, a possible reconciliation of the seemingly contradictory views that there is no homosexual behavior among Bala men and that bitesha are homosexuals is that the Bala do not consider bitesha to be men, i.e., that the Bala afford another example (compare the North American **berdache**, South Asian hijara, Polynesia mahu) of a folk model of third sex given by nature rather than volition.

In an earlier report on another Kongo tribe, the Bangala, mutual masturbation and sodomy were reportedly "very common," and "regarded with little or no shame. It generally takes place when men are visiting strange towns or during the time they are fishing at camps away from their women."

In the old kingdom of Rwanda, male homosexuality was common among Hutu and Tutsi youth, especially among young Tutsi being trained at court. In the neighboring kingdom of Uganda, King Mwanga's 1886 persecution of Christian pages was largely motivated by their rejection of his sexual advances. Junod (1927: 492–3) vacillated between attributing elaborately organized homosexuality among the South African Thonga to the unavailability of women and to a homosexual preference. The *nkhonsthana*, boy-wife, "used to satisfy the lust" of the *nima*, husband, received a wedding feast, and his elder brother received brideprice. Junod mentioned that some of the "boys" were older than 20, and also described a transvestitic dance, *tinkonsthana*, in which the nkhontshana donned wooden breasts, which they would only remove when paid to do so by their nima.

Female Homosexuality. Controversy continues about the purported chastity of woman/woman marriage in three East African and one West African culture. Other mentions of lesbian sex from the East Coast of Africa include discussion of a woman's dance, *lelemama*, in Mombassa, Kenya (which variously serves as a cover for adultery, prostitution, and recruitment into lesbian networks without the husband's knowledge) and the *wasaga* (grinders) of Oman. An Ovimbundu (in Angola) informant, told an ethnographer, "There are men who want men, and women who want women. . . . A woman has been known to make an artificial penis for use with another woman." Such practices did not meet with approval, but neither did transvestic homosexuals of either sex desist. Among the Tswana (in addition to homosexuality among the men laboring in the mines), it was reported that back home, "lesbian practices are apparently fairly common among the older girls and young women, without being regarded in any way reprehensible." Use of artificial penises was also reported among the Ila and Naman tribes of South Africa. Among the much-discussed Azande of the Sudan, sisters who are married/retained by brothers were reported to have a reputation for lesbian practices.

BIBLIOGRAPHY. Fremont E. Besmer, *Horses, Musicians, and Gods*, South Hadley, MA: Bergin & Garvey, 1983; E. E. Evans-Pritchard, "Sexual Inversion Among the Azande," *American Anthropologist*, 72 (1970), 1428–34; Melville Herskovits, *Dahomey*, New York: Augustine, 1937; Henry Junod, *Life of a South African Tribe*, London: Macmillan, 1927; S. F. Nadel, *The Nuba*, London: Oxford University Press, 1947; idem, "Two Nuba Religions," *American Anthropologist*, 57 (1955), 661–79; Günter Tessmann, *Die Pangwe*, Berlin: Wasmuth, 1913.

Stephen O. Murray

AFRICAN-AMERICANS
See **Black Gay Americans**.

AGEISM

This new term encompasses a cluster of attitudes that have become increasingly common in modern industrial societies. Ageism is prejudice of young people against the old expressed in the perpetuation of stereotypes; ridicule and avoidance of older people; and neglect of their social and health needs. Such attitudes frequently appear among male homosexuals, much less among lesbians. The word ageism, which came into use about 1970, is modeled on the older terms racism and **sexism**.

Cultural Analogues. The ancient Greeks divided the course of human life into stages, the simplest scheme being one that still lingers: childhood, maturity, and old age. Although one may assign precise boundaries to these stages—and add intermediate ones such as adolescence that may seem needed—age may also be viewed relatively and subjectively. A youth of 21 may regard someone who is 38 as old, while the latter considers himself still young.

Tribal cultures and traditional societies usually valued age as a repository of experience. This custom of honoring the elderly balanced the tendency, found among males through most of the world, to experience sexual attraction toward younger people. In an era in our own society when social security income was not yet the rule, the younger, productive members of a family acknowledged a duty to look after elderly retirees. Now younger people, with the assurance that their parents are provided for economically, often feel free to neglect them socially. Another factor upsetting the traditional balance is the fact that the virtues of youth itself came to be idealized and celebrated, beginning in the nineteenth century. Thus in 1832 Giuseppe Mazzini (1805–1872) rallied his supporters in the campaign for Italian independence under the banner of Giovane Italia (Young Italy). Hence Young Ireland, Young Poland, the Young Turks, and so forth. At the turn of the century innovative artists in Germany created the Jugendstil (literally "Youth Style"; a variant of art nouveau), while Russian painters formed the Union of Youth, echoing the title of a play by Hendrik Ibsen (De unges forbund [The League of Youth]; 1869). Increasingly, youth was identified with political change and artistic innovation, and journalists habitually contrasted its energy with the inertia of the old fogies. Beginning at the end of the nineteenth century, the enormous growth of interest in competitive **athletics** made young bodies the image of strength and accomplishment, a notion relentlessly promoted by Madison Avenue in the interests of consumerism. In a period of rapid social change youth became synomous with progress, age with reaction.

Homosexual Aspects. The youth cult among homosexuals has deep roots. In classical Greek **pederasty**, the characteristic dyad was an adult man and an adolescent. Yet this youth–age nexus is less significant for the origins of ageism than it seems, because in such couples the relative (though temporary) inferiority of the boy partner was always recognized. It was precisely to promote his education and training in manly virtues that the relationship existed. In pederasty the youth was not an equal partner; when he became so, the liaison ended. With the rise of **androphilia** (homosexual unions of two adults) in Europe in the eighteenth and nineteenth century, this pattern shifted, for both partners were adults in the sense that both had attained puberty. But age differentials did not vanish. A glance at the **advertisements** (personals columns) of today's gay press will show that most gay men seek younger partners. Indeed the advertisers often place an upper limit—40, 30 or even as low as 21 years of age—on partners they are willing to accept. Gay **slang** stigmatizes older men as "aunties," "dogs," "toads," and "trolls," who congregate in "wrinkle rooms."

Eroticization of youth produces various secondary manifestations among gay men: preference for youthful clothing styles; adhesion to the latest trends in pop music; dieting and exercising so as to maintain a slim body; and adoption of voguish hair styles, including bleaching to keep a boy's towhead look. Indisputably, the erotic imagination of the gay male community privileges youth; gerontophilia, attraction to older men, is relatively rare. This pattern of preference contrasts with that of the lesbian community where older persons are more likely to be prized. The difference between gay men and lesbians may mirror that of the larger (heterosexual) society, where older men typically marry younger women.

In the 1960s and 70s the cult of youth that had long flourished in the gay male community was reinforced through symbiosis with the **Counterculture**. As a mass movement the Counterculture was made possible by post-World War II prosperity, which gave younger people a disposable income in amounts that could only be dreamed of by their forerunners. The confidence born of such newfound economic power, and the reaction against rule by the old that was perceived as tolerating racism and war, led to open proclamations of ageist prejudice, witness the slogan "Don't trust anyone over thirty."

As a result of the confluence of all these factors, psychological counselors report seeing gay men, some as early as their mid-thirties, who have internalized ageism, regarding themselves "as over the hill." As would be expected, this subjective phenomenon of "accelerated ageing" is not common among lesbians, though it is found among heterosexual women, who are subjected to a barrage of commercial messages for products that purport to keep them looking young.

The negative effects of ageism have not been ignored in today's gay community. In the 1980s some younger gay men and women, recognizing that in due course old age awaits them as well, joined such social organizations as San Francisco's GLOE (Gay and Lesbian Outreach to Elders) and New York's SAGE (Senior Action in a Gay Environment), in order to befriend and assist older people. Over the years gay **churches** and synagogues have also done much to achieve interaction of people of various age groups.
Wayne R. Dynes

AGING

Gerontology, the social science of aging, began well before World War II, experienced rapid growth after the war, and has recently become a major field, as an ever larger proportion of the population reaches sixty. For many years, gerontological research assumed that all older people were heterosexual, even though upwards of three million North Americans over sixty are lesbian or gay. This scientific blindness was hardly accidental. The social science of "deviant behavior" knew that older homosexuals existed, but it propagated the myth that "old aunties" and "aging dykes" lived lonely, miserable lives, shunned by a homosexual subculture obsessed with youth. Not until the year of **Stonewall** (1969) did Martin Weinberg publish the first study showing that homosexuals adjust well to age. Only in the late 1980s did gay gerontology become established as a field of research.

A major theme of gay **liberation**, as of black liberation and feminism, was a new positive emphasis ("gay pride") which pushed the pendulum of gay gerontology to the opposite extreme. Some research in the 1970s argued that homosexuals actually enjoyed "advantages" over heterosexu-

als, in adjusting to midlife and old age. More recently, a middle position has been taken: homosexuals obviously differ in some aspects of aging, but on such key issues as psychological health, income, friendships, satisfaction with life they do not differ significantly from heterosexuals (Brecher; Lee).

This article supports the middle position—that homosexual elders are no less likely to live happy, healthy and comfortable lives than their nongay neighbors. The focus is on interesting aspects of contemporary homosexual aging, especially those which provide generally useful insights, whatever the person's sexual orientation.

Accelerated Aging. For many years it was argued that homosexuals experienced the effects of aging sooner than nongays. Homosexual culture was considered "obsessed with youth," thus the loss of youthful appearance made thirty the threshold of "middle age." Recent studies indicate that most homosexuals do not feel or act older at 30 or 40 than their nongay peers. However, they do think that *other* homosexuals view them and treat them as if they were further advanced in age. Thus, while feeling young and active at 40, homosexuals may lie about their age because they fear other homosexuals consider 40 "over the hill." It appears that homosexuals still suffer a mutual misunderstanding, rather like that of a male teenage virgin who lies about his sexual conquests because he concludes from his peers' boasts that they are already sexually experienced.

Earlier Socialization and Later Adjustment to Aging. A young person "growing up gay" faces much the same learning tasks as a nongay classmate, but there is an essential difference, which the gay youth has in common with other minority groups: how to handle stigmatized status. Unlike most minority stigmas, the young homosexual can decide to remain secret ("in the closet") yet enter a subculture ("the gay world") which provides numerous facilities and opportunities for contact with others of the same minority. Prior to "gay liberation" this was the only attractive option for all homosexuals except the few who deliberately chose a "flaunting" role (e.g., Quentin Crisp) or found work and friends in a tolerant, low-status occupation (e.g., restaurant waiter; hairdresser).

One of the major themes of gay liberation is "taking pride in one's chosen lifestyle." In this light, gerontology now distinguishes several forms of adjustment in gay/lesbian aging: (1) the stereotypic or self-oppressing gay/lesbian elder, who has internalized the heterosexual world's hatred of homosexuals, and is ashamed and guilt-ridden; (2) the passing elder, who at least partially accepts the validity of homosexuality as a lifestyle, but fears those who do not, so admits to being gay/lesbian only among those who can be trusted not to betray the secret; (3) the gay-positive elder, who has "come out of the closet" to at least some nongay persons in the family, workplace, and other social contexts, participating in the gay community without fear of being discovered.

There is no agreement yet among gerontologists about the ways and extent to which each of these forms of adjustment affects psychological health or happiness of the gay/lesbian elder. At least some fearful and self-oppressing gay elders lead successful and productive lives and enjoy satisfying friendships, both gay and nongay. There is certainly no evidence to persuade any homosexual, whether very open or very hidden, that the elder years must be less satisfying merely because of sexual orientation.

Older Gays/Lesbians in Their Community. Variations in socialization and adaptation to homosexual stigma pose serious problems for organizations attempting to develop a place for elders in the new gay communities. These groups must cope with the tension between public and politically active members, and those who wish gay social contact without

disclosing their private lives, which they regard as "nobody else's business."

Even a decision to invite a speaker from, or cooperate with, nongay senior citizens groups, or government agencies for the aged, may be opposed by closeted gay elders. Older homosexuals who have been married for many years to unaware spouses, or who have prestigious positions in the work world, are especially fearful that someone who believes them to be heterosexual, may see them at a gay meeting. Thus, groups tend to attract more homosexuals who have little or nothing to lose by being there, and have less resources to contribute to the group's growth.

In spite of these special problems, the number of organizations of older gay men and lesbians is slowly growing in North America. The most successful and enduring organization, SAGE of New York City, has contact with about 60 other elder gay/lesbian organizations in the USA and Canada. Many gay community listings (such as *The Gay Yellow Pages* in Los Angeles), now include one or more gay elders' groups. There is a National Association of Lesbian and Gay Gerontology at 1290 Sutter St., San Francisco.

The Gay Generation Gap. Differences in adaptation to stigma among gay elders have contributed to a "generation gap" in the gay world different from that between young and old in the nongay population. Even if not active in the gay community and gay liberation, many younger lesbians and gay men have grown up in a society which tolerates, and in some cases legislatively protects, their lifestyle. This profound difference in experience adds to the difficulty of younger and older gays understanding each other.

The "generation gap" affects gay individuals and communities by restricting the supply of suitable role models of aging for younger gays and lesbians. Most heterosexual young people have at least some positive images of middle and old age among their family, or in the media, but there are very few models of happy homosexual aging available to the younger gay/lesbian. Even within the best-developed urban gay communities there is still little contact, and often a good deal of deliberate avoidance, between younger and older gays, and this is often true even within gay liberation organizations officially opposed to "ageism" (Berger). Indeed, the generation gap has probably contributed to the sometimes passionate disputes between "essentialists" and "social constructionists" over the history of gay people. (*See* **social construction**.)

Age-Stratified Relationships. Many human societies are age-stratified; they portion out roles and rewards according to the individual's age, with appropriate markers ("rites de passage" like puberty and retirement) to indicate that the individual has successfully passed from one age strata to another. Although there remain many social distinctions between age levels, North American society has tended to emphasize equal liberty of each individual; it now opposes most forms of **discrimination**, including "ageism."

One of the least predictable consequences for the homosexual minority has been the decline of age-stratified intimacy as a key structure in the gay community. From ancient times to the Victorian era, a familiar pattern of relationship in the gay/lesbian subculture was the partnership of an older and a significantly younger person. This pattern provided stability, resources and leadership in the gay underworld. It had its most eloquent defense by Oscar **Wilde** at his second trial, as the partnership of youthful beauty, vigor and hope, with mature intellect, confidence, and social resources.

The age-stratified pattern also provided upward social mobility in the gay world, by which a young man or woman of poor economic and educational background could acquire polished manners, dress and language, and favorable economic opportunities. The reference here is not to the "kept boy" and "sugar daddy," though these also existed and continue to exist,

but rather to the classic mentor/protégé relationship as epitomized by the 33-year partnership of Christopher **Isherwood** and Don Bachardy, who met when Christopher was 48, Don 18.

Gay liberation has tended to undermine the age-stratified pattern, both through its emphasis on social equality (the mentor/protégé partnership must begin with some recognition of inequalities), and through the development, in urban gay communities, of facilities where young gays and lesbians can easily meet each other without requiring (or wanting) the mediation or resources of older homosexuals. Many gay/lesbian elders who grew up in a pre-liberation gay subculture largely organized and financed by their elders, looked forward to a time when they would take over leadership positions, and hopefully find their own young protégé. The new gay communities have reduced or eliminated these opportunities, and many gay elders are finding it difficult to adjust to a gay life largely restricted to age-peers.

Intimacy and Sexuality in Gay/ Lesbian Old Age. In an era which first made sexual pleasure practically equivalent to the enjoyment of life itself, and then (since **AIDS**) almost synonymous with the courtship of death, any consideration of happiness in homosexual old age must include sexuality. One should begin with great scepticism of self-reported data such as that of Berger's respondents who claimed not to experience a decline in sexual opportunity and outlet with the onset of old age. Elders are no more likely than teenage male virgins to openly admit that sexual gratification is lacking.

More reliable studies, such as observed behavior in gay baths, studies of advertising for partners, and participant observation in gay communities, all suggest that sexual happiness in the gay older years, *as in heterosexual old age* (Brecher), involves learning to cope with changing circumstances. Lesbians, who tend to place more emphasis on nonorgasmic intimacy from the onset of a relationship, are more likely to make sexual adaptations to age, including more frequent celibacy than reported by gay male elders.

Coping mechanisms among gay males include willingness to validate sexuality as pleasurable without orgasm; an increased reliance on **pornography** as stimulant to release (an important factor in both gay and nongay populations, as all moralists and censors should be reminded), and an improved ability to use purchased sex safely.

At least until the possibly reduced income of retirement, seniority in our society generally brings rising income, and thus resources to purchase sexual gratification. But a particularly dangerous form of ageism may be found among gay hustlers. It is built into the social structure of the hustler, who reaches occupational obsolescence long before a hockey player, and is translated into disdain, exploitation, and sometimes violence directed at the older customer.

Another notable adaptation more typical of gay males than lesbians (but this is changing in recent years) is the elaboration of sexual foreplay, and reduced emphasis on genital contact and orgasm, through such means as sexual toys, bondage, uniforms, and scenarios. In most large urban gay communities, there is a marked difference in average age between the "twinkie" or "disco" gay crowds, and the "leather and denim" places. As beauty fades, older homosexuals may learn to continue attracting partners by conveying messages of sexual self-confidence and experience through leather, accessories, and body stance.

It is quite possible to be single and happy in heterosexual old age, but overall, satisfaction with life (and even life expectancy itself) is generally correlated with intimate and enduring partnership. Likewise, gay gerontology indicates that having an intimate partner (not necessarily a "lover" or even a gay person) in homosexual old age is a reliable predictor of general adjustment and satisfaction with life.

Sharing old age with a partner "doubles the joys and halves the sorrows."

BIBLIOGRAPHY. Marcy R. Adelman, *Long Time Passing*, Boston: Alyson, 1986; Raymond M. Berger, *Gay and Gray: The Older Homosexual Man*, Urbana: University of Illinois Press, 1982; Edward M. Brecher, et al., *Love, Sex and Aging*, Boston: Little, Brown, 1984; John A. Lee, "What Can Homosexual Aging Studies Contribute to Theories of Aging?" *Journal of Homosexuality* 13:4 (1987), 43–71.

John Alan Lee

AIDS

Acquired Immunodeficiency Syndrome is a medical condition that produces a radical suppression of the human immune system, permitting the body to be ravaged by a variety of opportunistic diseases. It is believed to be caused by the Human Immunodeficiency Virus (HIV), which can exist in the body indefinitely before symptoms emerge. In advanced industrial countries and in Latin America, AIDS occurs mainly among male homosexuals and intravenous (IV) drug users; in Africa it is found primarily among heterosexuals.

The Emergence of an Epidemic. The as-yet-unnamed syndrome first came to the attention of the medical community through a report released in June 1981 by the Centers for Disease Control, a Federal agency, concerning five California cases. Because the first cases studied were in homosexual men, the syndrome became associated with homosexuality itself. In fact one of the first suggestions for a name was GRID (Gay-Related Immunodeficiency). Although this was shortly changed to AIDS, a ceaseless flow of media reports about gay men affected by the disorder served to fix the connection in the public mind.

For the first few years the number of cases in the United States doubled annually, and about half as many of those already infected died. Not only was the disease spreading very quickly but it was highly lethal. While it appears that the earlier idea that it is invariably fatal is mistaken, it is a very difficult disease for a patient to cope with, and even with the most determined and successful strategy no cure is effected—the disease is simply kept at bay. At first the American cases were largely confined to New York City and environs, the San Francisco Bay Area, greater Los Angeles, and Miami. Although AIDS subsequently was found in nearly every state, this pattern of concentration in these metropolises on the two coasts has continued. Foreign physicians found AIDS in Canada, Europe, and Latin America, though the incidences are generally lower than in the United States. (In most countries the American acronym has been used, but French-speaking nations prefer SIDA [Syndrome d'Immunodéficience Acquise]; SIDA is also the Spanish acronym.) By 1988 over 65,000 AIDS cases had appeared in the United States, 64% of the reported total world-wide. However, reliable figures for incidence in Africa are not available; they are said to be high in a number of countries of equatorial Africa.

Transmission and Symptomatology. AIDS cannot be transmitted by any form of casual contact, but must go from blood to blood or from semen to blood. Blood-to-blood transmission occurs when intravenous-drug users share narcotics needles, or occasionally through accidental needle-sticks among health-care givers. It may also occur that a surgeon will nick him or herself with a scalpel, which may cut through gloves. Sexual transmission occurs when a seminal discharge of an infected person passes into the bloodstream of another. The sexual contact that is most at risk is anal penetration; oral and vaginal contacts are unlikely to transmit AIDS unless there is a lesion in the affected part of one or both partners. If it is believed that infection may have occurred, tests can be performed for the presence of the HIV virus in the blood, though they are not absolutely reliable.

A few medical experts have expressed doubts that the HIV virus is the culprit, but they are in a great minority. If not a cause, HIV is at least a good indicator of exposure to whatever is the cause. There has also been discussion of a variety of potential "cofactors," but none has been convincingly isolated.

The majority of persons infected with HIV show no symptoms, and it remains uncertain how many will develop AIDS itself. The emergence of the condition is signaled by night sweats, loss of weight, and other signs of physical distress. In some cases a diagnosis of ARC (AIDS-Related Complex) is made; many of these patients will progress to full-blown AIDS. The patient will usually develop either Kaposi's sarcoma—a previously rare type of cancer producing numerous lesions on the outside or inside of the body—or pneumocystis carinii (PCP), a form of pneumonia that is devastating to the patient. PCP usually requires hospitalization with intensive care and the administering of a variety of drugs prescribed by the physician. However, many patients can return home after the first crisis has been met—if there is a home to return to.

Response. Members of the gay community have charged government agencies with inadequate response to the epidemic. An expression of genuine concern, these complaints are valid only in part. It was the first time in many years that advanced countries had to deal with the outbreak of a hitherto previously unknown disease, and the initial recognition of the problem could not have occurred immediately. Moreover, a few decades earlier, when prudery and censorship kept the whole issue of homosexuality from being discussed publicly at all, the official response would have been either helpless or schizophrenic, as the social locus of the epidemic would have been a taboo subject. Still, there is no doubt that bureaucratic red-tape, as well as jealousies among physicians and officials eager for the glory of being identified with break-throughs, have been a handicap. Again, because the disease was new and because there was no treatment, it inspired a whole set of amateur, politically motivated, at worst paranoid explanations of its etiology—and corresponding quack methods of treatment by special diets and medical regimes of the kind held out as a last resort to dying cancer patients. By contrast, the self-medication movement, which has placed possibly effective drugs in the hands of people with AIDS, bypassing government tests that can take years, may be a positive development. Patients abroad, where much of the research and testing was being done, had access to drugs that Americans did not. Here too dangers exist, but the situation has highlighted a serious dilemma of public policy.

Locally some communities handled the crisis better than others. Nonetheless, real progress was made in the middle years of the 1980s against a very cunning viral adversary. The gay press carried warnings of the lethal consequences of unsafe sex practices, and others were reached by leafletting and word of mouth. These campaigns had a noteworthy effect as measured by the decline in cases of all **sexually transmitted diseases**, including syphilis and gonorrhea, among gay men. The climate of the 1970s, characterized for some by a seemingly limitless horizon of sexual experimentation, yielded to a new sense of caution, and many sought long-term, essentially monogamous relationships.

Gay self-help groups specifically concerned with AIDS sprang up, involving many people who in the previous decade had turned a deaf ear to the call for movement work. By the end of the 1980s there were several hundred of these organizations in North America, and many others in Europe. Other groups were formed of people with AIDS (PWAs, the term preferred by those who have the condition). Gay and lesbian lawyers mobilized to meet a host of legal problems triggered by the

spread of the epidemic. This manifold response contrasted with the apathy of the IV-drug user community, which remained unorganized, without media of its own, and therefore almost entirely dependent on public health advocates and facilities.

Gay men and lesbians (the latter little affected by AIDS) rallied to apply pressure on politicians for more funding and to deal with some of the backlash that was developing. In the panic-laden years of the mid-1980s some religious and right-wing leaders obtained support in their calls for quarantine or drastic treatment of those who might be infected. Although these calls generally fell on deaf ears, the general public, which had previously been showing increasing tolerance of homosexuals as measured by opinion polls, now registered a moderate tendency to move in the other direction. Often insensitive reports on the nightly television news, supplemented by rumor and a flood of malicious AIDS jokes, served to spread dismay even among those who had formerly offered a modicum of support for gay rights. The publicity had the side effect of acquainting otherwise cloistered souls with some explicit realities of oral and anal sex. People even suspected of having AIDS found themselves harassed on the job and denied insurance coverage, while dentists and doctors became wary of treating persons with the disease. On the whole, however, the late 1980s showed a decline of these pressures as better information became available and gay organizations showed that they would not bow to hostile pressure.

Cultural Responses. Several plays, notably *As Is* (1985) by William Hoffman and *The Normal Heart* (1985) by Larry Kramer, an early passionate advocate of group action by the gay community to stop the disease, have been successfully presented in the United States and abroad. Fictional responses are more numerous and varied, ranging from the serio-comic fable *Tweeds* (1987) by Clayton R. Graham to the probing stories in *The Darker Proof*

(1988) by Adam Mars-Jones and Edmund White. The poet and novelist Paul Monette has written *Borrowed Time: An AIDS Memoir* (1988), an eloquent account of a decade of living with Paul Horowitz, who died in 1986. Other memoirs include a mother's story, *The Screaming Room* (1986) by Barbara Peabody, that of a wife, *Good-bye, I Love You* (1986) by Carol Lynn Pearson, and those of several persons with AIDS, including *Mortal Embrace: Living with AIDS* (1988) by the Frenchman Emmanuel Dreuilhe. In 1985 NBC Television presented a drama, *An Early Frost*, with Aidan Quinn, which offered a sensitive exploration of the emotional effects of the disease on a person with AIDS and his family. Bill Sherwood's independently made film *Parting Glances* (1986) focused on a relationship between two men, one of whom has AIDS. Several leading contemporary photographers, including Nicholas Nixon, Rosalind Solomon, and Brian Weil, have produced moving portraits of people with AIDS.

The Names Project Quilt began early in 1987 with a single cloth panel to commemorate one person who died of AIDS. In a little over a year the project grew to over 5000 panels, which were exhibited in a national tour. The colorful panels are rectangular and contain the name of the deceased which is painted on or appliqued. The victim's survivors who make the quilts often add other appliques of cloth, sequins, and the like to suggest favorite residences and avocations of the departed. The quilt, which takes up a long-established American folk tradition, constitutes a collective work of anonymous art. Not only has it provided a moving experience for visitors, it may serve as a salutory challenge to existing elitist notions of art itself.

None of this cultural activity can be construed as a "silver lining" that in any way compensates for the enormous suffering that AIDS has caused, but it gives evidence of a real effort to confront the problem rather than to hide it or to hide from it.

BIBLIOGRAPHY. Ronald Bayer, *Private Acts, Social Consequences: AIDS and the Politics of Public Health*, New York: Free Press, 1989; Douglas Crimp, ed., *AIDS: Cultural Analysis/Cultural Activism* (October, 43, Winter 1987); Harlon L. Dalton and Scott Burris, eds., *AIDS and the Law: A Guide to the Public*, New Haven: Yale University Press, 1987; Elizabeth Fee and Daniel M. Fox, eds., *AIDS: The Burden of History*, Berkeley: University of California Press, 1988; Victor Gong, ed., *AIDS: Facts and Issues*, New Brunswick, NJ: Rutgers University Press, 1986; H. Robert Malinowski and Gerald J. Perry, *AIDS Information Sourcebook*, Phoenix: Oryx Press, 1988; Eve K. Nichols, *Mobilizing Against AIDS: The Unfinished Story of a Virus*, Cambridge, MA: Harvard University Press, 1986; Sandra Panem, *The AIDS Bureaucracy*, Cambridge, MA: Harvard University Press, 1988; Cindy Ruskin, ed., *The Quilt: Stories from the NAMES Project*, New York: Pocket Books, 1988.

Ward Houser

ALAN OF LILLE (CA. 1120–1203)

French theologian and poet. A prolific writer in Latin, Alan was a leading figure in the "Renaissance" of the twelfth century. His surviving works include disquisitions in practical and speculative theology; sermons; a preaching manual; a theological dictionary; a guide for confessors; an attack on heretics; a book of versified parables; and two substantial poetic allegories, *Anticlaudianus* and *The Complaint of Nature*.

In the last-named work Alan offered original variations on the Early Christian polemic against homosexual behavior as a sin against **nature**. These animadversions were prompted by the prevalence of sodomy among the **clergy** of his day, which Alan opposed. In a series of ingenious, if bizarre comparisons, Alan likened sexual inversion to grammatical barbarism. This allegory of grammatical "conjugation," licit or illicit, was to have many successors throughout the Middle Ages. In a more general sense, Alan is a link in a chain of antihomosexual argument based on the claim that it is unnatural.

BIBLIOGRAPHY. Richard H. Green, "Alan of Lille's De Planctu Naturae," *Speculum*, 31 (1956), 649–74; Jan Ziolkowski, *Alan of Lille's Grammar of Sex*, Cambridge, MA: Medieval Academy of America, 1985.

Wayne R. Dynes

ALBANIA

Until recent decades, remoteness and a distinctive language permitted this Balkan country to retain, more than its neighbors, cultural traits from the past. Travelers in the nineteenth and early twentieth century noted that Albanian men showed a particular passion for handsome youths, so much so that they would even kill one another in disputes over them. Albanians would also contract male–male pacts which were blessed by priests of the Orthodox church; these, it was claimed, were Platonic. Yet this assertion of purity seems to be contradicted by a common term for the pederast, *büthar*, literally "butt man." Among the Muslim **Sufis** some held a belief in reincarnation; having lived a previous life as women, they believed, it would be natural for some men to be attracted to male sex objects. It is tempting to regard these customs as a provincial relic of Greek institutionalized **pederasty**, or even (following Bernard Sergent) of some primordial "**Indo-European**" homosexuality. Sometimes the Albanians attributed the custom to a Gypsy origin. Yet Turkish Islamic influence is a more likely source, supplemented by the Byzantine custom of brotherhood pacts. Of further interest is the fact that many Janissaries and **Mamluks** were recruited among the Albanians.

Since 1945 Albania has been ruled by a puritanical and repressive Marxist regime. Although homosexuality is not mentioned in the Penal Code, elementary prudence requires that relations between "friends" be conducted with the utmost discretion. Foreign tourists report sexual contacts—but only with other tourists.

BIBLIOGRAPHY. Paul Näcke, "On Homosexuality in Albania," *International Journal of Greek Love*, 1:1 (1965), 39–47.

ALBERTINE COMPLEX

In *Remembrance of Things Past*, Marcel **Proust's** female character Albertine contains elements taken from the personality of the novelist's chauffeur Agostinelli, with whom Proust was in love. Accordingly, it has been suggested that the habit of gay and lesbian novelists—once a necessity—of "heterosexualizing" relationships by changing the sex of the characters be called the "Albertine complex." In W. Somerset **Maugham's** *Of Human Bondage* (1915) the waitress with whom the main character is in love is surely a man in disguise. A different device appears in Willa **Cather's** *My Ántonia* (1918), where the choice of male authorial persona, Jim, allows the writer to express interest in various female characters.

It must be granted that this critical procedure can be reductive if it simply seeks to "restore the true sex" to a character that is a composite product of the literary imagination. It may also falsely imply that gay and lesbian novelists are incapable of creating convincing characters of the opposite sex. Nonetheless, E. M. **Forster** gave eloquent testimony of his dissatisfaction with the procedure by abandoning writing novels in mid-career. After writing five published books simulating heterosexual relationships (and one, *Maurice*, on a homosexual's quest for love, which Forster believed was unpublishable), he declined to play the game any longer.

A related, though different phenomenon appears in the disguise dramas of the Renaissance. *La Calandria* (1513), by Bernardo Dovizi da Bibbiena, concerns two twins, one male, one female. The twins appear on stage four times, once both dressed as women, once both dressed as men, once in reverse attire, and once (at the end) in the appropriate dress. These permutations allowed the dramatist to explore for comic effect the confused emotions induced in other characters who are attracted to them. In less complete form the device spread into Spanish and Elizabethan drama, including **Shakespeare**'s familiar *As You Like It*. At the end of these plays the sexual ambiguities are resolved, to the relief of the audience—or at least of the censor. Thus the effect of such dramas contrasts with that of the later novelistic Albertine complex where the device is not meant to be detected. In both cases, however, preservation—or apparent preservation—of normality is the aim.

BIBLIOGRAPHY. Justin O'Brien, "Albertine the Ambiguous," *PMLA*, 64 (December 1949), 933–52.

ALCIBIADE FANCIULLO A SCOLA, L'

According to the notation on the title page, this spirited dialogue in defense of **pederasty** ("Alcibiades the Schoolboy") was published anonymously at "Ginevra [Geneva], 1652"—though it was probably actually printed in Venice. In 1862 a new limited edition of 250 copies appeared in Paris; it is almost as rare as the original. However, an Italian critical edition appeared in 1988 (Rome: Salerno).

The identity of the author long remained mysterious. The title page of the first edition bears the initials "D.P.A," which has been interpreted as "Divini Petri Aretini"—an unlikely attribution to **Aretino**. In 1850 Antonio Basseggio gave it, on stylistic grounds, to to Ferrante Pallavicino (1616–1644), a freethinker who was a member of the Accademia degli Incogniti in Venice. Finally, an article of 1888 by Achille Neri solved the puzzle. Neri included the text of a letter by Giovan Battista Loredan, founder of the Accademia degli Incogniti, which revealed that the author was Antonio Rocco (1586–1652), a "libertine" priest, Aristotelian philoso-

pher, and a member of the Academy. The initials on the title page could be resolved as "Di Padre Antonio." It is likely that Loredan, a noble Venetian, had a hand in the printing of the little volume.

While the obscenity of the story is quite explicit, it must be understood in the context of similar texts of the trend of **libertinism**, using the term in its original sense of a sceptical philosophical tendency. The colloquy is conventionally set in ancient Athens and the teacher is modeled on **Socrates**, as suggested also by the derivation of the literary form from the Platonic dialogue. Having conceived a unquenchable passion for his pupil, the instructor resolves to overcome his charge's every objection to consummation of the relationship. Through astute marshalling of argument, as well as rhetorical skill, the preceptor is successful, thus demonstrating also the value of education. The persuader uses examples from Greek mythology and culture, which had become familiar to many Italians through the **Renaissance** revival of classical antiquity. He rebuts counterarguments of later provenance, such as the **Sodom** and Gomorrah story. Anticipating the eighteenth century, he appropriates the argument from naturalness for his own ends, saying that **Nature** gave us our sexual organs for our pleasure; it is an insult to her to refuse to employ them for this evident purpose.

BIBLIOGRAPHY. Laura Coci, "L'Alcibiade fanciullo a scola: nota bibliografica," *Studi secenteschi*, 26 (1985), 301–29; Giovanni Dall'Orto, "Antonio Rocco and the Background of His 'L'Alcibiade fanciullo a scola' (1652)," *Among Men, Among Women*, Amsterdam: University, 1983, pp. 224–32.

Giovanni Dall'Orto

ALCIBIADES (CA. 450–404 B.C.)

Athenian general and statesman. Reared in the household of his guardian and uncle Pericles, he became the *erom-*

enos and later intimate friend of **Socrates**, who saved his life in battle. His brilliance enabled him in 420 to become leader of the extreme democratic faction, and his imperialistic designs led Athens into an alliance with Argos and other foes of **Sparta**, a policy largely discredited by the Spartan victory at Mantinea. He sponsored the plan for a Sicilian expedition to outflank Sparta, which ended after his recall in the capture of thousands of Athenians, most of whom died in the salt mines where they were confined, but soon after the fleet reached **Sicily** his enemies recalled him on the pretext of his complicity in the mutilation of the Hermae, the phallic pillars marking boundaries between lots of land. He escaped, however, to Sparta and became the adviser of the Spartan high command. Losing the confidence of the Spartans and accused of impregnating the wife of one of Sparta's two kings, he fled to Persia, then tried to win reinstatement at Athens by winning Persian support for the city and promoting an oligarchic revolution, but without success. Then being appointed commander by the Athenian fleet at Samos, he displayed his military skills for several years and won a brilliant victory at Cyzicus in 410, but reverses in battle and political intrigue at home led to his downfall, and he was finally murdered in Phrygia in 404.

Though an outstanding politician and military leader, Alcibiades compromised himself by the excesses of his sexual life, which was not confined to his own sex, but was uninhibitedly bisexual, as was typical of a member of the Athenian aristocracy. The Attic comedians scolded him for his adventures; **Aristophanes** wrote a play (now lost) entitled *Triphales* (the man with three phalli), in which Alcibiades' erotic exploits were satirized. In his youth, admired by the whole of Athens for his beauty, he bore on his coat of arms an Eros hurling a lightning bolt. Diogenes Laertius said of him that "when a young man, he separated men from their wives, and later, wives from their husbands,"

while the comedian Pherecrates declared that "Alcibiades, who once was no man, is now the man of all women." He gained a bad reputation for introducing luxurious practices into Athenian life, and even his dress was reproached for extravagance. He combined the ambitious political careerist and the bisexual dandy, a synthesis possible only in a society that tolerated homosexual expression and even a certain amount of heterosexual licence in its public figures. His physical beauty alone impressed his contemporaries enough to remain an inseparable part of his historical image.

BIBLIOGRAPHY. Walter Ellis, *Alcibiades*, New York: Routledge, 1989; Jean Hatzfeld, *Alcibiade: Etude sur l'histoire d'Athènes à la fin du Ve siècle*, Paris: Presses Universitaires de France, 1951.
Warren Johansson

ALCOHOLISM

The linkage of alcoholism and homosexuality has produced a long and fascinating body of literature. Both share similar characteristics: they are stigmatized behaviors, are subject to legal and moral sanctions, have etiologies that are not completely understood, are often concealed from others, have inconsistent definitions, and are dealt with in a variety of conflicting ways. How homosexuality and alcoholism are perceived is typically a function of the theoretical position taken. The shifts from a more psychoanalytic model, to a learning theory approach, to a sociocultural viewpoint illustrate the varied attitudes toward these stigmatized behaviors by the dominant culture. Each school, however, seems to accept that the rate of alcoholism among homosexuals is significantly higher than in the rest of the population.

The Psychoanalytic Model. The earliest connections evolved from the school of **psychoanalysis** founded by Sigmund **Freud.** Emphasizing the idea of latent homosexuality as the etiology of problem drinking, neo-Freudians sought a causal model to explain what they perceived as sexual pathologies. Alcohol use was seen as the cause of regression to a level of psychosocial development in which latent homosexuality, sadistic and masochistic tendencies, and lewdness are released (Israelstam and Lambert). Excessive alcohol use, therefore, was the means of overcoming the repression of homosexuality and other sexual inhibitions.

The connection between homosexuality and alcoholism stressed the oral dimensions. Using such phrases as "oral neurotics" and "oral diseases," the psychoanalytic school focused on only certain aspects of drinking behavior and homosexuality. Alcoholics were seen to be fixated in the oral stage, to be anxious about masculine inadequacy and incompleteness, to have experienced traumatic weaning, or to have an irrational fear of being heterosexual (Nardi). Similar phrases were used to describe the etiology of homosexuality. Oral frustrations were linked to both homosexuality and alcoholism. Tennessee **Williams'** play *Cat on a Hot Tin Roof* (1955) reflects the prevalence of the psychoanalytic argument: Brick's alcoholism is linked to his frustrating relationship with his wife Maggie and his repressed homosexual feelings about his dead friend Skipper.

Much of the early empirical research on the linkage between homosexuality and alcoholism emphasized the psychoanalytic assumptions. However, rather than studying alcoholism among homosexual populations, researchers tended to look for homosexuality among alcoholics. Unfortunately, their definitions about what demonstrated homosexuality were faulty. Numerous studies used masculinity–femininity scales with the belief that high femininity scores indicated homosexuality in the male.

Clearly, then, a problem with these early studies is the faulty assumptions underlying the empirical and theoretical models. There is an overemphasis on oral aspects of homosexuality, thereby ignoring the range of sexual practices and the emotional-love dimensions of same-sex relationships. It is also assumed that only homosexuality has these oral dimensions to it, while implying that heterosexual practices do not. Furthermore, the psychoanalytic approach does not account for lesbians, for the repressed homosexuals who are not alcoholic, for the open gays and lesbians who are not alcoholic, and for the open gays and lesbians who are alcoholic (Small and Leach).

While repression of fundamental characteristics of self can often lead to destructive behavior, the focus of psychoanalytic perspectives is of particular relevance here. The relationship between latent homosexuality and alcoholism assumes that learning to overcome one's repressed homosexual feelings and to love heterosexually is the best "cure" for alcoholism. Thus, the focus of therapy is on one's sexuality, not on the drinking or the repression. The pathology is the homosexuality, not just the alcoholism.

During the 1960s and 1970s, however, the psychoanalytic models started losing favor. With the introduction of humanistic Rogerian psychology, the existential models of R. D. Laing, and the sociological approaches of **labeling** theory, the link between homosexuality and alcoholism took on different emphases (Israelstam and Lambert). With the rise of gay and lesbian rights movements, research began to look at a newer link: the relationship of **homophobia** and alcoholism. The tone was no longer on sexual repressions and regressions to oral stages, but on the social contextual dimensions of gay lifestyles. The theories now emphasized behavior and the role drinking played in integrating people into a subculture or in reducing stresses caused by hostile social settings. Alcoholism was seen as a response to situational factors, not as a correlate of homosexuality. While some argue for the dominance of biological and genetic explanations for alcoholism (and homosexuality as well), most researchers believe that the social context plays an important part in understanding the connections.

The Learning-Theory Approach. Social learning theory has contributed much to our understanding of the link between context and deviant behaviors. Alcoholism is seen as a learned behavior resulting from reinforcement of pleasurable experiences and the avoidance of negative ones. Tension reduction, relaxation, peer approval, and feelings of power have all been connected to alcohol consumption. Thus, a learning model explanation of excessive drinking among gay men and lesbians stresses tension-reduction and the positive reinforcement of participation in an open gay lifestyle of bars and other alcohol-related social events. The tension, anxiety, and guilt feelings generated in the context of a society which does not condone homosexual behavior are reduced by increased alcohol use. For some, the resultant feelings of power allow gay people to make sexual contacts and overcome social resistances.

The role of the gay **bar** becomes an important component of this approach. The emergence of gay bars as a common institution for introduction into a gay community derives from their history of permissiveness and protectiveness. Gay bars provide some anonymity and segregation from the dominant culture while contributing to and maintaining a gay identity for its patrons. The positive aspects of belonging to a gay community tend to reinforce drinking patterns. Heavy drinking, in this model, is not used to escape from some latent fears or to fulfill oral needs, but as a way to participate in a group. Initial socialization into a gay social network often occurs by attending gay bars, cocktail parties, and meals involving alcohol. Achieving a gay identity, for some people, necessitates learning roles which include an alcohol component.

Since there are many different types of homosexuals and many forms of alcoholism, searching for a single link to explain all drinking by homosexuals is a misguided task. For some open gays, a pleasure-seeking explanation is probably a more accurate learning model. For others just **"coming out,"** a tension-reduction approach may serve as a clearer explanation. For those still "in the **closet"** and repressing their identity, alcohol may serve as a means to disinhibit their feelings or to deny them further. Whichever is used, all illustrate a learning model, stressing the importance of the situation for understanding problem drinking. The shift away from pathologies and oral fixations represented a major step in the theoretical understanding of the linkage between homosexuality and alcoholism.

Sociocultural Perspectives. The approach to studying the linkage took another direction with the growing emphasis in the 1970s of a gay **lifestyle** and **subculture**. From this viewpoint, drinking patterns are a function of a group or subculture's norms, values, and beliefs. How a culture defines drinking and drunkenness, what meanings are construed for behavior while "under the influence," and what situational factors are relevant, all affect drinking rates. The whole lifestyle must be taken into account: the connections between **drug** use, alcohol consumption, and sex; the value placed on attending bars; the laws and norms directly related to alcohol consumption in that geographic area; and the attitudes of the larger social context toward the stigmatized group.

This theoretical approach focuses on the social context in which gay people find themselves, how they define reality and perceive their situation, and what symbols and values they hold with respect to alcohol use. Understanding the linkage between homosexuality and alcoholism, thus, requires understanding how certain gay individuals manage and control their feelings in an oppressive social context. In other words, homophobia is seen as a contextual explanation as to why some gay men and lesbians drink excessively. Being a homosexual is not the pathology leading to alcoholism; alcoholism is the response to a homophobic environment. Alienation, low **self-esteem**, and morally weak labels are maintained by the social system, thereby increasing vulnerability to addictive behaviors. To study alcoholism and homosexuality now means researching the subculturally approved responses to perceived and actual homophobic situations. Gay men and lesbians become the focus of study; their thoughts, behavior, and perceptions are the data. Rather than looking at alcoholics and assessing whether they are latent homosexuals or high scorers on a femininity scale, current research, under the sociocultural model, goes directly to gay alcoholics and studies their views and responses to their social situations.

Research Problems and Prospects. Unfortunately, the reliability about the extent of alcoholism problems in the gay community has suffered from faulty research methodology. Small sample sizes, lack of control groups, non-random samples, inconsistent definitions of alcoholism and homosexuality, and anecdotal information typify much of the recent research in this area. Generalizations to the diversity of homosexuals are very difficult to make. Not only are those "in the closet" impossible to study, but generating non-middle-class samples of open gays and lesbians is not an easy task. In addition, asking people to relate their drinking patterns with honesty and accuracy becomes problematic the more they drink excessively.

Despite these problems with current research, the move away from the neo-Freudian, psychoanalytic models is an important step in understanding the linkages between alcoholism and homosexuality. Results from many of the recent studies seem to indicate an alcoholism rate at two to three times that of the rest of the population. While some of this is due to the same factors that affect other alcoholics (such as low self-esteem, difficulty in expressing one's feelings, having an alcoholic parent, ethnic and religious background, and other drug use), it is the unique aspects of establishing and maintaining a gay identity in a generally hostile environment that has become the focus of attention in recent research.

The theoretical approaches discussed (psychoanalytic, learning theory, and socio-cultural perspective) represent specific sociological and psychological viewpoints. Other models can, and have, been developed to assess alcoholism using economic, political, biological, and genetic variables, and explanations. Each of these can be used to further an understanding of the linkage between homosexuality and alcoholism.

Treatment and Prevention. Which model one adopts can have important implications for the development of treatment and prevention programs. Some people define alcoholism as a disease, thereby invoking a medical model with very different consequences from a learned behavior model adopted by others. Those stressing the psychoanalytic approach focus on curing the pathology of homosexuality, while the socio-cultural model leads to the emphasis on getting the client to act on one's homosexual feelings. In general, most practitioners today believe that treating the alcoholism is the first priority. This, however, typically requires a climate in which the patients can feel comfortable about discussing their identity openly. Being honest about oneself and one's feelings is essential for recovery. This cannot be attained in a homophobic context. Some, therefore, strongly encourage homosexual clients to seek treatment in gay and lesbian facilities. When these are not available, it is very important that treatment programs and therapists can accept and encourage gay and lesbian clients to be themselves. While the techniques for treatment may be the same for everyone, the importance of establishing a climate in which the clients can express themselves openly becomes of prime importance.

Similarly, while prevention and education programs have messages relevant to all people, some specific tailoring to the needs, issues, and language of gays and lesbians is essential. For example, recent evidence on the role alcohol and drugs play in lowering immune system functioning has important prevention implications for **AIDS**. There are also some indications that excessive alcohol use can lead to higher risk taking, especially in sexual situations, thereby increasing the possibilities of engaging in practices with a higher probability of contracting the AIDS virus. Prevention and education programs aimed at the gay and lesbian populations must, therefore, take into account the unique dimensions of their lifestyles and sexuality. It is in prevention and treatment programs that the link between homosexuality and alcoholism becomes an important aspect.

BIBLIOGRAPHY. Stephen Israelstam and Sylvia Lambert, "Homosexuality as a Cause of Alcoholism: A Historical Review," *International Journal of the Addictions*, 18:8 (1983), 1085–1107; Peter M. Nardi, "Alcoholism and Homosexuality: A Theoretical Perspective," *Journal of Homosexuality*, 7:4 (1982), 9–25, reprinted in Thomas Ziebold and John Mongeon, eds., *Gay and Sober*, New York: Harrington Press, 1985; Edward Small and Barry Leach, "Counseling Homosexual Alcoholics," *Journal of Studies on Alcohol*, 38:11 (1977), 2077–86.

Peter M. Nardi

ALETRINO, ARNOLD (1858–1916)

Dutch criminal anthropologist and literary figure. Of Sephardic Jewish ancestry, Aletrino published works on homosexuality in Dutch and French. A follower of the school of Cesare **Lombroso**, who had sought to explain criminality with reference to inherited degeneracy of the central nervous system, Aletrino broke sharply with his teacher by asserting in a Dutch article of 1897 that homosexuality ("**uranism**") could occur in otherwise perfectly normal and healthy individuals, and in later works he campaigned for the end of the legal and social intolerance that still oppressed the homosexuals of early twentieth-century Europe.

At the fifth congress of criminal anthropology in Amsterdam in 1901, his defense of the homosexual brought a storm of abuse on his head from the psychiatrists and criminal anthropologists who accused him of "defending immorality"—the first harbinger of the later antipathy of the medical profession to the gay rights movement. Down to the end of his life he continued to collaborate with the initial pioneers in enlightening the general public on the subject, and was involved in the founding of the Dutch branch of the **Scientific-Humanitarian Committee** in 1911. His literary compositions still keep his memory alive in the Dutch-speaking world.

BIBLIOGRAPHY. Maurice van Lieshout, "Stiefkind der Natuur: Het Homobeeld bij Aletrino en Von Römer," *Homojaarboek*, 1 (1981), 75–106.

Warren Johansson

ALEXANDER THE GREAT (356–323 B.C.)

King of Macedonia and conqueror of much of the civilized world of his day. The Hellenizing aspirations of his father Philip II caused him to summon **Aristotle** from Athens to tutor his son. On his succession to the throne in 336 Alexander immediately made plans to invade Asia, which he did two years later. In a series of great battles he defeated the Persian king and took possession of his vast empire. Unwisely extending his expedition into India in 327–325, he returned to Babylon where he died.

Historians still debate the significance of Alexander's plans for the empire: it now seems unlikely that he intended a universal culture melding the diverse ethnic components on an equal footing.

His concessions to his new subjects were probably intended to secure their loyalty, while preserving Greek supremacy. His romantic figure has exercised an unceasing fascination over the centuries, though usually with minimal acknowledgement of his bisexual appetites, which supreme rule allowed him to gratify to the full.

Although he entered into a state marriage with the Sogdian Roxane and had relations with other women, all his life Alexander was subject to unbounded passions for beautiful boys (Athenaeus, *Deipnosophists*, XIII, 603a). From childhood Alexander had been closely bonded with his friend Hephaistion, whose death in 324 he mourned extravagantly, reportedly devastating whole districts to assuage his grief. His relationship with a beautiful eunuch Bagoas, formerly the favorite of king Darius, is the subject of Mary Renault's novel *The Persian Boy* (New York, 1972).

BIBLIOGRAPHY. Roger Peyrefitte, *Alexandre le Grand*, Paris: Albin Michel, 1981; idem, *Les conquêtes d'Alexandre*, Paris: Albin Michel, 1979; idem, *La jeunesse d'Alexandre*, Paris: Albin Michel, 1977.

Warren Johansson

ALEXANDRIA

Ptolemy I, **Alexander the Great's** successor in Egypt, transferred the capital from Memphis to the city near the Nile's western mouth, which had been founded by Alexander after he conquered Egypt to accommodate large fleets and thus secure his communications with Europe. Ptolemy II and Ptolemy III made Alexandria the center of Hellenic learning by endowing (1) the Museum, where Herophilus and his younger contemporary Erasistratus conducted vivisection on condemned slaves to advance surgery, anatomy and physiology, while Eratosthenes calculated the circumference of the globe; and (2) the Library, arranged by Aristotle's pupil Demetrius of Phalerum according to the Master's cataloguing system, which grew to contain over 100,000 (perhaps even 700,000 scrolls) where Callimachus, Apollonius, and Theocritus vied with one another in editing classical Greek texts and in composing pederastic verses. From 300 B.C. until 145—when Ptolemy VII Physcon expelled the scholars—and again after order was restored, Alexandria was also the literary center of Hellas. The golden age of Alexandrian poetry lasted from ca. 280 to ca. 240 with an Indian summer in the early first century B.C., when Meleager produced his *Garland*, so important a part of the **Greek Anthology**, and his contemporaries wrote other works that soon became popular in Rome and influenced Latin literature.

Imitating the elegists and lyricists who had flourished in the Aegean ca. 600 B.C., the Alexandrians of the golden age enthusiastically composed pederastic verse. The seven greatest Alexandrian tragedians were dubbed the Pleiad. In the second century B.C. Phanus, Moschus, and Bion continued the traditions of Callimachus, Apollonius, and **Theocritus** with archaic fastidiousness and recondite allusions of the earlier librarians there. Big city inconveniences produced a longing for the rural life expressed in pastoral poetry. Whether ideal or sensual, love—especially pederastic—held a central position.

The luxurious **gymnasia**, temples, and baths erected by the Ptolemies, of whom the seventh kept a harem of boys, surpassed those of the homeland. A local peculiarity was the Serapeum, a temple which attempted to fuse Dionysiac with Egyptian religion.

This commercial port linked Europe with Africa, and via the canal built by the ancient Pharaohs that the Ptolemies reopened between the Mediterranean and the Red Sea, also with India, for the Greeks learned to follow the monsoon to complete the periplus there and back. Its great Pharos (lighthouse) symbolized its maritime dominance, and Ptolemaic fleets often ruled the Aegean. Alexandria, whose synagogues overshadowed those in

Palestine, attracted diaspora Jews even before the Seleucid Antiochus IV began to persecute them and the Diaspora began in earnest, continuing during and after the Maccabean uprisings. In Alexandria seventy Jewish scholars were believed in later legend to have translated the Pentateuch into the *koine*, as the Hellenistic Greek of the newly acquired colonial regions was styled. Riots often occurred among the ethnic groups, especially against the Jews, who had their own quarter in the capital. Resembling New York, with a true cacophony of languages, Alexandria became the largest Greek as well as the largest Jewish city and certainly the richest in the world. **Philo** Judaeus, who clearly judged the homosexual behavior of the Sodomites responsible for the destruction of the Cities of the Plain, synthesized Old Testament homophobia with Greek philosophical condemnation: the Mosaic prohibition with **Plato**'s notion of "against nature," while the Ptolemies married their sisters and nude Greek men chased *eromenoi* in gymnasia or hired poor boys in the teeming streets or bazaars.

Lavishing the wealth for which the Ptolemies were famous, Cleopatra married first three of her brothers (Ptolemy XIII, XIV, and XV), then Julius **Caesar** (if she was not merely his mistress), and finally Mark Antony. She committed suicide to avoid gracing the triumph of Octavian, who annexed Egypt for Rome, as Augustus, administering it as a special, incomparably valuable province. Trade with India via Alexandria reached such a height during the Pax Romana (31 B.C.–A.D. 180) that the Empire was drained of specie to pay for Eastern luxuries. The later "Alexandrian" Latin poets of the first century B.C., of whom **Catullus** is the only surviving exemplar, wrote bisexual verses, like those of their models. In the early Empire, even more than in the last century of the Republic, things Egyptians were the rage. **Athenaeus** of Naucratis, another seaport at a mouth of the Nile, ca. A.D. 200 wrote of an elaborate symposium where scholars discussed pederasty as well as fine foods and wines, and pagan learning continued in Alexandria until Hypatia, a female mathematician and Neo-Platonist, was torn limb from limb by a mob of Christian fanatics incited by their bishop St. Cyril in 415, after which pagan learning declined. The neglected Library repeatedly suffered from fires, book burnings, and other catastrophes, perishing in the Arab conquest of 641.

Christianity, too, flourished in Alexandria from the time the Apostle Mark introduced it there. Combining Platonic with Biblical homophobia in the tradition of Philo Judaeus, **Clement**, Origen, Arian, and Athanasius and other **Patristic** writers shaped Orthodox dogma.

As the center of learning of the Hellenistic world and the rival of Rome for wealth and population, it was naturally the home of the most erudite Christians. They were as shocked as the Jews by the lasciviousness of the pagans with whom they rubbed shoulders in the cosmopolitan streets of the metropolis. "Nothing," it was said, "was not available in Alexandria except snow." This applied to sex where the vices, like the merchandise, of Asia, Africa, and Europe met and were exchanged amid great wealth and extreme poverty. The Patriarch of Alexandria, like that of its Hellenistic competitor Antioch, rivaled the one Constantine appointed at the new capital in 330 and the one at Jerusalem—all of whom vied with the bishop of Rome.

Alexandria was scarcely affected by the Germanic occupation of the West. Arab hordes newly inspired by the religion of Islam, however, invaded Egypt in 638 and captured Alexandria in 641, the grief of the loss causing the death of the Emperor Heraclius (610–641). Although the Moslems removed the capital to Fustat (Old Cairo), near ancient Memphis, Alexandria remained a vital port as long as they dominated the Mediterranean, a Moslem lake from about 700 to about 1100, when the crusaders regained dominance of that sea for Christendom. With its women secluded even more than in the Ptolemaic and Byzantine epochs, Moslem Alexandria, now called al-Iskandariya, continued the tradition of pederasty.

Dynasties followed one another, the Shiite Fatimids (965–1171), the Sunnite Ayyubids (1171–1250), whose Saladin fought **Richard** I the Lionhearted, followed by the **Mamluks**, a group of unmarried, often castrated Slavic bodyguards known for pederasty, one of whose number was chosen Sultan from 1250 to 1519. Under the Mamluks Cairo completely outshone Alexandria, which declined to little more than a fishing village.

In 1881 the British established a protectorate over Egypt, Turkish sovereignty being purely nominal. Thereafter Alexandria became the center of a cosmopolitan blend of Eastern and Western civilization known as Levantine. With its languid sensuousness and sexual promiscuity, Alexandria, like other Levantine ports, attracted gay writers and expatriates in the nineteenth and twentieth centuries. The modern Greek poet **Cavafy**, the Russian writer Mikhail **Kuzmin**, Lawrence Durrell and others put the city permanently on the literary map of the world. In his lyric poems Constantine Cavafy (1863–1933) evoked the moods and memories of Hellenistic Alexandria at its zenith—as the capital of the cosmopolitan civilization his ancestors had created. E. M. **Forster** had a love affair with an Egyptian tram-conductor, Mohammed el-Adl, in 1917, during World War I. He also wrote a guide to the city, and introduced Cavafy's poems to English-speaking readers.

The resurgence of Arab and Egyptian nationalism spelled the death of the "colonial," Levantine Alexandria by forcing most of the permanent foreign residents to emigrate. Now the premier beach resort of Egyptians, the city abounds in summer with homosexual activity in spite of the revival of Moslem puritanism.

BIBLIOGRAPHY. E. M. Forster, *Alexandria: A History and a Guide*, London: Whitehead Morris & Co., 1922; P. M. Fraser, *Ptolemaic Alexandria*, 3 vols., Oxford: Clarendon Press, 1977; Jane Lagoudis Pinchin, *Alexandria Still: Forster, Durrell, and Cavafy*, Princeton: Princeton University Press, 1977.

William A. Percy

ALGER, HORATIO, JR. (1832–1899)

American novelist. The son of a clergyman, he sought to emulate his father's career in a church in Brewster, Massachusetts. In 1866, however, he abruptly left the ministry and went to New York City, where he devoted the rest of his life to grinding out an enormous number of books for boys, most of which have the same plot, the legendary "rags to riches" tale about a poor boy who makes good. The most famous of these books were *Ragged Dick* (1868) and *Tattered Tom* (1871). The total number of Alger books sold, both before and after his death, is estimated at being anywhere from one to four hundred million. Alger became known as the inspiration for many of the American boys who in real life went from poverty to wealth, and even today it is said in obituaries that a man's "life was like a Horatio Alger story."

Alger's status as a wholesome legend was ironically the cause of his eventually being found out. In *The American Idea of Success* (1971), Richard Huber told how he had discovered in the archives of the church in Brewster evidence that Alger had "been charged with gross immorality and a most heinous crime, a crime of no less magnitude than the abominable and revolting crime of unnatural familiarity with boys." Alger had gone to New York to escape the wrath of the parents of Brewster. This bombshell lay dormant until a journalist read Huber's book and broadcast the news across the United States.

Alger was included in Jonathan Katz' *Gay American History* (1976) and is now a standard member of everybody's list of famous homosexuals. The story of Alger's life has been the subject of several biographies both before and after the Huber bombshell, and this is a story in itself. One early biography was a pack of lies in which Alger has relationships with various women, and other early biographies had also invented episodes here and there, and these false "facts" were repeated innocently by later biographers. Even in these early biographies, however, it was possible to read between the lines—or between the lies—to see that Alger was attracted to boys. He spent a lot of time around the Newsboys Lodging House in New York, a sort of hotel for homeless boys and a paradise for any pederast who could succeed, as Alger did, in winning the confidence of the owner and the young residents. The greatest love of Alger's life was a ten-year-old Chinese boy named Wing, who was later killed by a street-car. All of this information was reported by the early biographers, but nobody seemed to understand what it meant until Huber found the evidence.

BIBLIOGRAPHY. Michael Moon, "'The Gentle Boy from the Dangerous Classes': Pederasty, Domesticity, and Capitalism in Horatio Alger," *Representations*, 19 (Summer 1987), 87–110; Gary Scharnhorst and Jack Bales, *The Lost Life of Horatio Alger*, Bloomington: Indiana University Press, 1985.

Stephen Wayne Foster

ALLSTON, WASHINGTON (1779–1843)

American artist. The slave-owning Allstons of South Carolina enjoyed a life of near baronial splendor. Traditionally families such as his have demonstrated their appreciation of art only through patronage, since artists, like all craftsmen, must work with their hands. Allston chose to deny his family's inculcated values when, having graduated from Harvard, he insisted on pursuing his muse.

In 1801 Allston sailed for England to study for several years at the Royal Academy with Benjamin West and Henry Fuseli. They imbued the aspiring artist with the spirit of romantic classicism which was to become his stylistic hallmark. During his first European sojourn, Allston traveled extensively, settling by 1804 in Rome. There he first met Samuel Taylor Coleridge and Washington Irving. He insinuated himself into the circle of Rome's German colony, which centered around the Prussian consul, Wilhelm von Humboldt, and the habitués of the Caffè Greco. There he got to know Wilhelm's homosexual brother, Alexander von **Humboldt**, and such neoclassical sculptors as Thorvaldsen and Canova, together with the artists Asmus Jakob Carstens, Gottlieb Schick, and Joseph Anton Koch. Then in 1808 he left Rome precipitously, sailing for Boston, where he married Ann Channing, a socially prominent New Englander who had been affianced to Allston for nine years.

With his new wife, Allston traveled to England again in 1811. This time he secured the patronage of the influential Sir George Beaumont. His painting of "The Dead Man Revived" won a prize of two hundred guineas at the British Institution. In the *Annals of the Fine Arts* in 1816, he was listed as one of the principal history painters in England. The illness and death of his wife, in 1815, was the one ostensibly disturbing interlude of these very successful years. But a second time, giving his friends no warning, he decamped for America in 1818.

Back in Boston, Allston fixed his attentions on a Boston Brahmin spinster, Martha Dana, whom he married in 1830, after a courtship strung out over ten years. The course of his professional life matched that of his private life in its failure to find a focus and locate a goal. Ensconced in a studio in the suburb of Cambridgeport, the artist manifested behavior we would now perceive as highly neurotic. He habitually abandoned major, multifigured canvases—by his own report of 1836, five in 18 months. Over the years, he managed to disappoint the Boston Hospital, the Pennsylvania

Academy, the State of South Carolina, the United States government, and private individuals as highly placed as the Duchess of Sutherland. None of his undertakings, however, provided him with a better excuse for a dilatory performance than the never-to-be-finished "Belshazzar's Feast." After a visit to his studio in 1838, the English art critic Anna Jameson observed that his sensitivity on the subject of his unfinished "Bel" did "at last verge on insanity."

Why did Washington Allston live in a state of psychic imprisonment which paralyzed his will to create and made him guilt-ridden? To cast his dilemma into perspective, we must acknowledge that some of the most puzzling moments of his life begin to make sense only on the hypothesis that he was a closeted homosexual. During his lifetime, family and friends shielded him or pretended not to know, as evidenced in his official biography written by his reverential nephew, Jared Flagg. Scholars in this century have perpetuated the subterfuge when they failed to evaluate the documented evidence.

In chronological sequence, the first document—omitted in the modern biographies—is a letter of Allston's, quoted in the first comprehensive history of American art. Here Allston reminisced about his earliest patron, a South Carolinian named Bowman. The latter offered to the handsome scion of the Allston family an annual stipend of 100 pounds for the period of his study abroad. The stipend declined, Bowman upped the ante by volunteering to send him away with "a few tierces of rice." "His partiality was not of the everyday kind," the mature artist observed. And in truth Bowman's partiality was not, since the gift of a "few tierces of rice" was a highly negotiable commodity of great value. Not surprisingly, in Flagg's recycling of the incident, the word "partiality" was suppressed, leaving the inserted pronoun without antecedent: "it was not of the everyday kind." In context, the suppressed word would not have raised

eyebrows; but since Allston's adoring nephew removes the word, and so ineptly, we may conclude that family tradition wanted something hushed up.

Next, there is the matter of those courtships of unusual length even for the nineteenth century. Collectively, they provided a cover for a total of nineteen years. But the most telling circumstance involves the cause for Allston's second departure from England.

The period of Allston's sojourn in England followed years in which England instituted harsh penal measures against homosexuals. Nobles were exiled, members of the working class hanged. Under these conditions, **blackmail** became a common practice; and we have it from Allston himself that he was continuously importuned by beggars who were literate, since they petitioned through the mails. Accordingly, he wished his new address in America kept secret. After his return, he instructed his pupil, C. R. Leslie, to forward no more correspondence: "I know, my good fellow, you will excuse this, for you know what I have already suffered. . . . There are letters of this unpleasant kind I have had from Bristol and other places. Tell Mr. Bridgen never to take out any letter to me from the Dead-Letter Box. If any should be there let them remain; for I do not want them." Leslie would be just the person to sympathize with his teacher's predicament, since his own sexual orientation made him equally susceptible. His liaisons with some of the London actors whose portraits he painted fell short of discretion. Flagg, who was probably ignorant of Leslie's proclivities, applied to this former pupil for further information about his uncle's seemingly inexplicable decision. Leslie, in his written reply, elided the truth; and his explanation, as redacted by Flagg, reads like a fairytale: "Leslie gives as his belief that one cause for his leaving England was the result of his open-handed charity to street beggars in London"—as though Allston were a soft-hearted American, helpless to resist out-stretched palms and needing to put an ocean between unlettered beggars and his own purse.

BIBLIOGRAPHY. William H. Gerdts and Theodore E. Stebbins, Jr., "A Man of Genius": The Art of Washington Allston (1779–1843), Boston: Museum of Fine Arts, 1979; Phoebe Lloyd, "Washington Allston: American Martyr?" Art in America (March 1984), 145–55, 177–79; E. P. Richardson, Washington Allston, New York: Thomas Y. Crowell Co., 1948.

Phoebe Lloyd

AMAZONIA

In addition to holding the world's largest tropical rainforest, the Amazon basin of South America has remained until recently the home of many tribal peoples scarcely touched by Western civilization.

Initiation and Joking Behavior. As in the Melanesian cultures of the Pacific, initiation, more than marriage, is indispensable in northwest Amazonia to the transition from the asexual world of childhood to the sexual world of adults. In these customs, anthropologists have been struck by the commonness of joking sexual play among initiated but unmarried men. "Missionaries working in the Piraparaná are frequently shocked by the apparent homosexual behavior of Indian men. However, the Barasana distinguish between this playful sexual activity and serious male homosexuality. This play, rather than stemming from frustration of normal [sic] desire, is regarded as being normal behavior between brothers-in-law, and expresses their close, affectionate, and supportive relationship" (Hugh-Jones). Claude Lévi-Strauss, who had reported "reciprocal sexual services" by classificatory "brothers-in law" among the Nambikwara in 1943, added: "It remains an open question whether the partners achieve complete satisfaction or restrict themselves to sentimental demonstrations, accompanied by caresses, similar to the demonstrations and caresses characteristic of conjugal relationships." Although maintaining that "the brother is acting as a temporary substitute" for his sister, he admits: "On reaching adulthood, the brothers-in-law continue to express their feelings quite openly." Stephen Hugh-Jones similarly reported, "A young man will often lie in a hammock with his 'brother-in-law,' nuzzling him, fondling his penis, and talking quietly, often about sexual exploits with women." About the Yanamamo, Chagnon wrote: "Most unmarried young men having homosexual relations with each other have no stigma attached to this behavior. In fact, most of these bachelors joked about it and simulated copulation with each other in public." Alves da Silva reported public mutual masturbation by boys, although officially, homosexuality only occurs in the puberty rites for boys.

Other Aspects. Nimuendajú and Lowie noted formalized, intense, but apparently non-sexual friendships among another Ge tribe, the Ramko'kamekra. Wagley's 1939 ethnography of the Tapirape—a southern Amazon tribe with a Tupi-Guarani rather than Ge language, who were therefore likely pushed from the coast rather than being traditionally jungle dwellers prior to 1500—included reports of males in the past who had allowed themselves to be used in anal intercourse by other men. "They were treated as favorites by the men, who took them along on hunting trips. Kamairaho gave me the names of five men whom he had known during his lifetime or about whom his father had told him 'had holes.' Some of these men were married to women, he said, but at night in the *takana* [men's house] they allowed other men to 'eat them' (have anal intercourse). His father told him of one man who took a woman's name and did women's work. . . . Older men had said that the "man-woman" had died because she was pregnant. 'Her stomach was swollen but there was no womb to allow the child to be born.'" None of

Wagley's informants could recall a case of a woman who had taken the male role or who preferred sex with another female.

Gregor added a muddled account of conceptions of homosexuality as (1) inconceivable, (2) situational, and (3) forgotten for the Mehinaku of the Xingu River. Soares de Souza asserted the Tupinamba were "addicted to sodomy and do not consider it a shame. . . . In the bush some offer themselves to all who want them." In the upper Amazon, Tessmann found that "while there are no homosexuals with masculine tendencies, there are some with extreme effeminacy. My informants knew of two such instances. One of them wears woman's clothing. . . . [The other] wears man's clothing, but likes to do all the work that is generally done by women. He asked one member of our expedition to address him with a woman's name and not with his masculine name. He lives with a settler and prostitutes himself as the passive partner to the settler's workers. He pays his lovers. He never practices active sexual intercourse." A more extended description of widespread homosexual play and of fairly-enduring but "open" relationships is provided by Sorenson: "Young men sit around enticingly sedate and formal in all their finery, or form troupes of panpipe-playing dancers." Occasional sex is regarded as expectable behavior among friends; one is marked as nonfriendly—enemy—if he does not join, especially in the youth 'age group' (roughly 15–35)." Homosexual activity was limited neither to within an "age group" nor to unmarried men. Moreover, inter-village homosexuality was encouraged and some "best friends" relationships developed. That the "best friend" is more likely later to marry a sister of his "best friend" is implied in Sorenson's report.

Some of the denials that homosexual behavior among "my people" is "really homosexuality" say more about the observer than the observed. In other cases, denials of what can be observed come from natives. In such cases, it is difficult to know whether the concern that imputations of accepting homosexuality will stigmatize their tribe are the result of Western acculturation or more venerable cultural concerns.

BIBLIOGRAPHY. Alcionilio B. Alves da Silva, *A Civilisação Indígena do Uapes*, São Paulo: Centro de Pesquisas, 1962; Napoleon A. Chagnon, *Yanomamo Warfare, Social Organization and Marriage Alliance*, Ph.D. dissertation, University of Michigan, 1967; Thomas Gregor, *Anxious Pleasures: The Sexual Life of an Amazonian People*, Chicago: University of Chicago Press, 1985; Stephen Hugh-Jones, *The Palm and the Pleiades*, Cambridge: Cambridge University Press, 1979; Claude Lévi-Strauss, *Tristes Tropiques*, New York: Atheneum, 1974; Curt Nimuendajú and Robert H. Lowie, "The Social Structure of the Ramko'kamekra (Canella)," *American Anthropologist*, 40 (1938), 51–74; Gabriel Soares de Souza, "Tratado Descriptivo do Brasil em 1587," [Instituto Histórico e Geográfico do Brasil] *Revista*, 14 (1851, [1587]); Arthur P. Sorenson, "Linguistic Exogamy and Personal Choice in the Northwest Amazon," *Illinois Studies in Anthropology*, (1984), 180–93; Günter Tessmann, *Die Indianer Nordost-Perus*, Hamburg: De Gruyter, 1930; Charles Wagley, *Welcome of Tears*, New York: Oxford University Press, 1977.

Stephen O. Murray

AMAZONS, AMERICAN INDIAN

A distinct gender role for masculine females was accepted in many American Indian tribes of North and South America. This role often included a marriage between such a female and a woman. Though sometimes mistakenly referred to by anthropologists as "female **berdache**s," this term historically was applied only to males and does not account for the special character of the amazon role. Even though the Indians did not live in separate all-female societies, the earliest historic references to such masculine females referred to them as "amazons" rather than as "berdaches," and the Portugese explorers in northeastern Brazil named the large river there the River of the Amazons after the female warriors of the Tupinamba Indians.

The extent to which this gender role was socially accepted in aboriginal cultures is unclear, owing to the lack of attention paid to women in the male-written documents of the early European explorers. It is also unclear to what extent these females were "gender-crossers" who were accepted as men, or as "gender mixers" who combined elements of masculinity and femininity with some other unique traits to become an alternative gender. There was probably variation between tribes and among individuals.

Such females were noted for their masculine interests from early childhood, and as adults they often famed for their bravery as warriors and skill as hunters. In some tribes, parents who had no son would select a daughter to raise as a hunter, and this child would grow up to do all the roles of a man, including the taking of a woman as a wife. The amazon's avoidance of sex with a man would protect her from pregnancy, and thus insure her continued activity as a hunter. Kaska Indians of the western Canadian subarctic explained that if such a female had sex with a man, her luck in finding game would be destroyed. Her sexual affairs and marriage with a woman were the accepted form.

Some tribes, like the Mohave, held the view that the true father of a child was the last person to have sex with the mother before the baby's birth. This meant that an amazon would easily claim paternity to the child of her wife, if this wife had been previously impregnated by a man. Therefore, these marriages between an amazon and a woman were socially recognized with their children as families.

Because of their uniqueness, amazons often had the reputation for spiritual power and a gift of prophesy. This was sometimes shared by another form of female gender variance among Plains tribes, known as Warrior Women. Here, women would sometimes participate in male occupations on the hunt or in warfare, but this did not imply an alternative gender role since they continued to be defined as women. Still, there were some amazons on the Plains, the most famous of which was Woman Chief, a leader of the Crow Indians in the nineteenth century. She was the third highest ranked warrior in her tribe, and was married to four women.

For those who were socially defined as women, it was more important that they reproduce the population than that they be exclusively heterosexual. Motherhood was highly valued, and a woman's status was usually related to her role as a mother more than as a wife. As long as a woman had children, to whom she was married was of less concern to society. Since the amazon was not seen as feminine, and was not socially defined as a woman, she was able to gain status based on her hunting and military abilities.

BIBLIOGRAPHY. Paula Gunn Allen, *The Sacred Hoop: Recovering the Feminine in American Indian Traditions*, Boston: Beacon Press, 1986; Evelyn Blackwood, "Lesbian Behavior in Cross-Cultural Perspective," M.A. thesis in Anthropology, San Francisco State University, 1984; idem, "Sexuality and Gender in Certain Native American Tribes: The Case of Cross-Gender Females," *Signs*, 10:4 (1984), 27–42; Walter L. Williams, *The Spirit and the Flesh: Sexual Diversity in American Indian Culture*, Boston: Beacon Press, 1986.

Walter L. Williams

AMAZONS, CLASSICAL

Greek mythology includes references to a legendary race of female warriors. Homer's *Iliad* offers only scanty indications of them, and the name given to them is *antianeirai*, later interpreted as "man-hating" or "man-like." The main features of the later Greek Amazon legend are as follows. Coming from the east, they founded a commonwealth of women in the northeast of Asia Minor on the Thermodon, between Sinope and Trapezus, with Themiskyra as its capital. They honor Ares as their ancestor and Artemis. For breeding purposes they live during two months of the spring with a neighboring people. The male children are killed (or rendered unfit for military service or returned to the fathers). The girls are brought up as warriors; they remain virgins until they have slain three foes. Their weapons are bow and arrow and a sword hanging from a band that runs over the breast; they are mostly mounted. In their genealogies they do not count the father. The major sources of this legend are Didorus Siculus and the geographer Strabo of Alexandria. Herodotus connects the Amazons with the Scythians and makes the Sauromates (Sarmatians) descend from them. There is a pseudo-etymology that derives the name from *a*-privative and *mazos*, "breast," with the explanation that they cut off one of their breasts so as better to aim their arrows; the artistic depictions of them always show both breasts.

The legend is sometimes interpreted as the echo of historic combats with matriarchal Asiatic tribes combined with fairy tale motifs such as the abduction of women. The Amazons were a favorite theme of ancient art and sculpture; particularly renowned were statues of the wounded Amazon by four artists of the fifth century B.C.: Polycleitus, Cresilas, Phidias, Phradmon.

The Amazon legend both tempted and intimidated the explorers of Latin America; societies of Amazons were reported from Brazil, whence the name of the Amazon River; Guiana; the western part of the Peru of the Incas; Colombia; Nicaragua; the Western Antilles; Mexico, Yucatan, and Lower California. Modern scholarship tends to discredit these accounts as reverberations of the classical myth or as fictions invented by the natives to discourage the Europeans from proceeding farther inland. Some lesbian writers of modern times have reinterpreted J. J. Bachofen's conception of matriarchy (1861)

in the direction of a primitive, predominantly female and matrilineal society, but admit that Amazonism and lesbianism are distinct phenomena, however they may coincide in time and space.

Warren Johansson

AMERICAN INDIANS
See **Indians, American.**

ANAL SEX

The anus is the posterior opening of the alimentary canal. The actual closing and opening is effected by a muscle known as the sphincter, beyond which lies the rectum, leading to the sigmoid colon. For many in our society, the anus is either a neutral part of the body, or one that can induce pain, through hemorrhoids or other disfunctions. While a majority of the population seems to have experimented in some way with anal stimulation, many decline to practice anal sex regularly, whether heterosexually, homosexually, or autoerotically. It has been asserted that this reluctance reflects deep-seated cultural taboos, which is undoubtedly part of the explanation for avoidance. It is also likely, however, that many people simply find other sexual practices more rewarding.

Techniques. For those who derive erotic stimulation from them, anal activities fall into two main categories, external or internal. The former may consist of either digital stimulation or anilingus, that is, tongue-to-anus stimulation, known in street language as "rimming" or "rear French." While it is very ancient, the practice of tonguing the anus has been shown to hold serious risks for hepatitis and parasitic infections. External stimulation of the anus may constitute foreplay, to be followed by some other activity, including anal penetration.

Internal stimulation of the anus may be effected through the insertion of the penis (anal copulation or anal intercourse), the fingers, or through the introduction of some inert but flexible implement, such as a dildo. In all these practices lubrication of the inserting agent is required. In older writings penile penetration of the anus is sometimes termed pedication (from the Latin *pedico*), not to be confused with pederasty. The most common positions for penile penetration are standing, with the receptive partner usually bending forward; lying, with both partners prone, the penetrator reclining with his abdomen on the receptor's back; and lying, with the receptive partner supine on his back with his legs drawn up against the other's chest so that the two are face to face. In this last position the seeming discomfort is balanced by the resultant elevation of the anal opening, facilitating entry, and the ease of kissing. A nonpenile variant, apparently introduced relatively recently in our society, is fisting or **handballing**. In this practice the hand, with nails carefully trimmed, is the inserting implement. Because of the danger of puncturing the colon, which may lead to fatal peritonitis, fisting should be avoided.

Folk belief holds that in male couples practicing anal intercourse one, the "active" partner, will always take the insertor role, while the other, the "passive" partner, will always be the penetratee. Surveys show that this role polarization is not in fact common in advanced industrial countries such as the United States, though it lingers in **Latin America** and among **prison** populations.

Recent medical studies have indicated that use of a condom is indispensable in anal intercourse. For the receptive partner unprotected anal copulation with an infected companion has been shown to be a high-risk practice for Acquired Immune Deficiency Syndrome (**AIDS**). This risk may be primarily due to the fact that the rectal mucosa is easily torn, with resultant bleeding and access of AIDS-virus-infected sperm to the receptive partner's bloodstream. Moreover, it is possible that the virus may directly infect the cells of the colonic mucosa (the inner lining or

wall of the colon, which includes the anus and the rectum). In the case of dildos and other anal toys, care must be taken that they are not inflexible, contain sharp angles, or are provided with internal wires that could emerge and tear the lining of the passageway. No small objects that are capable of being "lost" should be inserted. Dildoes should be carefully washed before use, especially if shared. Finally, engaging in such activities while under the influence of drugs is doubly risky. As a general rule, the riskier the activity, the fewer chemicals are advisable.

Popular perception holds that in anal sex only the insertor derives pleasure, while the receiving partner simply agrees to bear it to please his or her partner. If this were the case, autoerotic stimulation would not be practiced. In fact the walls of the lower alimentary canal are lined with nerve endings, or proprioceptors, which transmit the pleasurable sensations. In the male, stimulation of the prostate is often found to be enjoyable, and may lead to ejaculation on the part of the receptor.

Historical Aspects. Descriptions of homosexual anal copulation are abundant from ancient Greece. In Greek society, as to a large extent in traditional China, Japan, and Islam, the practice was age graded, with the older man penetrating his adolescent partner. Adult men who took the insertee role tended to be scorned. Among the North American Indians the **berdache** commonly was the receptor in anal intercourse. In medieval and early modern British texts, anal copulation is sometimes termed **buggery** or **sodomy**, but these terms are confusing as they can also refer to other forbidden modes of sexual gratification such as bestiality and oral-penile sex, which were also subject to criminal sanctions. Some of the conceptual confusion is probably grounded in the horror that the practices engendered, inasmuch as they were associated in the popular mind with diabolism, **heresy**, and uncleanness in general. In the view of some, these acts were crimes that could not even be named, at least in the vernacular. In more recent legal texts the two major criminalized practices are commonly designated more precisely by the Latin terms "per os" (oral) and "per anum." Modern methods of sanitation, and the influences of other cultures, made the Anglo-Saxon world more tolerant of anal sex in the twentieth century.

From early times anal copulation has also been practiced heterosexually, the male penetrating the female. This has been done mainly for contraceptive reasons, though some men also hold that it is more pleasurable because the anal sphincter is tighter than the vulva. Recently, some heterosexual men have discovered that dildo stimulation by their female partner produces a pleasant sensation in the prostate.

BIBLIOGRAPHY. Jack Morin, *Anal Pleasure and Health: A Guide for Men and Women*, 2nd ed., Burlingame, CA: Yes Press, 1986.

Ward Houser

ANARCHISM

The Russian thinker Peter Kropotkin (1842–1921) defined anarchism as "a principle or theory of life and conduct under which society is conceived without government—harmony in such a society being obtained, not by submission to law, or by obedience to any authority, but by free agreements concluded between the various groups, territorial and professional, freely constituted for the sake of production and consumption, as also for the satisfaction of the infinite variety of needs and aspirations of a civilized being." While anarchists agree in abhorrence of government, there are many schools of anarchism, with some emphasizing the rights of private property and individualism (**libertarianism**), others the necessity for voluntary cooperation and community self-control.

Anarchists agree in opposing the regulation of sexual behavior by governments and other powerful organizations

(such as the church). State power has frequently been used to persecute homosexuals: thus homosexuals and anarchists have often shared a common enemy. Anarchism as a philosophy and as a movement has offered legitimation to homosexuals and homosexuals have contributed much to anarchism.

Forerunners. Etienne de la Boétie (1530–1563) and William Godwin (1756–1836) wrote two proto-anarchist classics. Boétie's *Discours de la servitude voluntaire* (1552–53) (translated as *The Politics of Obedience* and as *The Will to Bondage*) is still read by anarchists. **Montaigne** dedicated his essay on friendship to Boétie after the young man's death.

William Godwin's *Inquiry Concerning Political Justice* (1793) provided a philosophy for his circle which included Mary Wollstonecraft (his wife), Mary Wollstonecraft Shelley, and Percy Bysshe Shelley (who translated Plato's *Symposium*); another daughter of Godwin's bore a child of **Byron**'s. Their whole circle deviated wildly from conventional sexual standards. Among the followers of Godwin's philosophy was Oscar **Wilde**.

Diffusion of Anarchism. Pierre-Joseph Proudhon (1809–1865) first used the term *anarchie* to designate a political philosophy (rather than a form of disorder); like his famous "property is theft," Proudhon's anarchism challenged convention. His *De la Justice dans la Révolution et dans l'Eglise* (1858; untranslated) celebrated the Greeks and denounced the Roman Catholic Church. He interpreted **Anacreon**'s poems as gay and praised **Socrates** for his link with **Alcibiades**. "We all want to see," he wrote, "to caress attractive young boys. Pederasty comes not so much from lack of marriage bed as from a hazy yearning for masculine beauty."

Max Stirner's individualist classic *Der Einzige und sein Eigentum* (1845; The Ego and His Own) awakens a cry of recognition in every lesbian or homosexual who has ever felt she or he was the only one. The boy-lover John Henry **Mackay**

(1864–1933), who wrote widely on both pederastic (under the pseudonym "Sagitta") and anarchist topics, prepared the first (and only) biography of Stirner in 1898.

Mikhail Bakunin (1814–1876) and Sergei Nechaev (1847–1882) are the most famous anarchist pair of friends. After leaving Russia, Bakunin agitated across Europe in the revolutions of 1848, was captured, shipped to Siberia, escaped (via San Francisco, London, New York, and Paris) and played a major role in organizing the First International (a federation of working-class political organizations, 1864–76), where he engaged in a prolonged struggle with Karl **Marx**. Using a word learned in San Francisco, Bakunin nicknamed Nechaev "boy." George Woodcock maintains that the fascination that Nechaev "wielded over Bakunin reminds one of . . . Rimbaud and Verlaine, or Lord Alfred Douglas and Oscar Wilde" (*Anarchism: A History of Libertarian Ideas and Movements*, New York: Meridian, 1962).

Karl Marx and Frederick Engels had a personal disgust for homosexuality (Engels told Marx to be grateful that they were too old to attract homosexuals). Marx published full-length diatribes against Proudhon, Stirner, and Bakunin. He used Bakunin's relationship to Nechaev as an excuse for expelling the anarchists from the International in 1872. Lenin later denounced anarchists as politically "infantile," just as Freudians argued that homosexuality was an arrested infantile (or adolescent) development.

In the late nineteenth and early twentieth centuries, anarchism became popular among painters, poets, and **bohemians** as it likewise spread among workers and farmers in Italy, Spain, Greece, and other countries where homosexuality was less persecuted than in Germany, England, and the United States. In England, Oscar Wilde went to prison for his "love that dare not speak his name," but his anarchist leanings are less publicized. Besides writing the *Soul of Man Under*

Socialism in 1891, Wilde signed petitions for the Haymarket Martyrs (1886) and publicly identified himself as an anarchist. Thomas Bell, a gay secretary of Frank Harris and a trick of Wilde's, has written a book on Wilde's anarchism, available only in Portuguese.

During the Third Republic (1871–1940), **Paris** became a center for those celebrating their political, artistic, and sexual unorthodoxy. Stuart Merrill (who had met Walt **Whitman**) wrote Symbolist poems and supported the anarchist paper *Les Temps Nouveaux*. Apollinaire's sexuality was as boundaryless as his poetry, his nationality, and his politics. The Surrealists have a real but unclear tie to anarchism and to homosexuality, but they welcomed **Sade**, **Lautréamont**, and Jean Lorrain into their pantheon.

In Spain during the Civil War (1936–39), anarchists fought against both the fascists and the communists, and for a time dominated large areas of the country. Many gay men and lesbians volunteered to fight in the war, while others worked as ambulance drivers and medics. Jean **Genet**, who was in Barcelona in 1933, described a demonstration of queens ("Carolinas") after their favorite *pissoir* fell in a battle: "in shawls, mantillas, silk dresses and fitted jackets" they deposited on the fallen urinal "a bunch of red roses tied together with a crepe veil."

American and Contemporary Developments. In the United States, Emma Goldman (1869–1940) and Alexander Berkman (1870–1936) both supported homosexual freedom. Goldman herself preferred passive cunnilingus with either a man or woman to other forms of sexual intercourse. She is unquestionably the first person to lecture publicly in the United States on homosexual emancipation; she firmly supported Wilde against his persecutors. Berkman wrote appreciatively in his *Prison Memoirs* (1912) of men who loved men. Whether from choice or necessity, anarchists have written extensively against prisons and in favor of prisoners, many of whom either from choice or necessity have experienced prison homosexuality. William Godwin opposed punishment of any kind and all anarchists have opposed any enforced sexuality.

Among the American anarchists, Paul **Goodman** wrote prolifically on anarchism and homosexuality. Robert **Duncan** published his 1944 essay on homosexuality in *Politics*, an anarchist publication, and he first met Jack **Spicer** at an anarchist meeting. Goodman, Duncan, and Spicer had reservations about the **Mattachine Society** because of its conservative positions during the late fifties and early sixties.

While not always formally recognized, much of the protest of the sixties was anarchist. Within the nascent women's movement, anarchist principles bcame so widespread that a political science professor denounced what she saw as "The Tyranny of Structurelessness." Several groups have called themselves "Amazon Anarchists." After the **Stonewall Rebellion**, the New York Gay Liberation Front based their organization in part on a reading of Murray Bookchin's anarchist writings. The Living Theater embodied many of the countercultural drives of the sixties. Julian Beck, who directed the group with his wife, Judith Malina (both active in anarchist organizations), had a male lover; the theater collective included people of every gender and sexual orientation.

During the seventies, Tom Reeves and Brett Portman were active both as anarchists and as homosexuals. Ian Young of the Catalyst Press in Toronto combined poetry and anarchism in his speeches and writing. In New York, Mark Sullivan edited the gay anarchist magazine *Storm* and organized the John Henry Mackay Society, which has undertaken publication of Mackay's out-of-print works. Both anarchists and gays can be found in the **Punk Rock** movement. Since many anarchists do not really believe in organizations, they can often be as hard to identify as homosexuals once were. During the early eighties at the New York Gay Pride marches,

gay anarchists, S/M groups, gay atheists, NAMBLA, *Fag Rag* and others all marched together with banners as individual members drifted back and forth between all the groups.

Enlivened by the nascent French gay liberation movement, Daniel Guérin (1904–1988) showed the interconnections between *Homosexualité et révolution* (Paris: Le Vent du Ch'min, 1983); Guérin also advanced the notion that interclass homosexuality promoted revolutionary consciousness. In 1929 he wrote a novel, *La vie selon la chair* (Life According to the Flesh), in which he mocks the apostle Paul; in 1983 (in an article in *Gai Pied*) he attacked a Communist party official and poet who publicly denounced homosexuality but privately maintained a harem of boys.

A major question is whether homosexuals are inherently attracted to anarchism or whether homosexuals have been equally attracted to democracy, communism, fascism, monarchy, nationalism or capitalism. Because of the secrecy, no one can ever figure what percentage of homosexuals are anarchists and what percentage of anarchists are homosexual. But only among anarchists has there been a consistent commitment, rooted in basic principles of the philosophy, to build a society in which every person is free to express him- or herself sexually in every way.

Charley Shively

ANDEAN CULTURES

The northwestern coast of South America was notorious for "shameless and open sodomy" according to the chroniclers of the Inca and Spanish conquests (fifteenth and sixteenth centuries, respectively). The Inca empire and those conquered by and absorbed into it lacked writing, so that what is known about earlier societies derives from chronicles of the conquerors' conquerors, supplemented by archeological and linguistic evidence.

Chroniclers' Reports. The conquistador historian Pedro de Cieza de León's *Chronicle*, written between 1539 and 1553, mentions that Guayaquil men "pride themselves greatly on sodomy." Continuing south, Cieza recorded cross-dressing males on the island of Puna, reported that both there and on the mainland (Tumbez or Puerto Viejo) sodomy was rife, and related a Manta myth of the origin of an all-male world. Cieza reported personally punishing male temple prostitutes in Chincha (south of modern Lima near Pisco on the coast) and in Conchucos (near Huánuco in a highland valley). The Incas and other mountain peoples (serranos), specifically including the Colla (Aymara) and Tarma, he judged free of the nefarious sins so common on the coast, especially in what had been the Chimu empire, conquered by the Incas less than a half century before the arrival of the Spaniards. (Pedro Pizarro is the only chronicler who claimed that Cusco's nobility ever engaged in sodomy—during times of drunken celebrations in the precincts of Inca gravesites or *huecos*.)

Half a century later Garcilaso de la Vega in his *Comentarios reales* (written between 1586 and 1612 and drawing on oral history from his Inca relatives and considerable invention of his own) aimed to show the virtuousness in Christian terms of Inca society. Counter-Reformation Catholicism and the Inca theocracy apparently concurred in their abhorrence of sodomy and attempts to extirpate sodomites. Speaking of coastal peoples (Yungas), Garcilaso wrote that before Inca conquest they had prostitutes available for sodomy "in their temples, because the Devil persuaded them that their gods delighted in such people." Clearly there was a sacred role for sodomites in the coastal tribes the Incas conquered. In contrast, sodomy was "so hated by the Incas and their people that the very name was odious to them and they never uttered it." This formulation seems to be a projection of "the sin not named among Christians,"

especially since Garcilaso could not have known directly what words were in common use more than a century before.

Attributions of sodomy to particular tribes or areas conquered by Inca armies are more reliable than the resemblances Garcilaso adduced between Catholic and Inca ideology. The practice of sodomy was not attributed to all conquered tribes, and open practice of sodomy was attributed to still fewer, so charges of sodomy do not appear to be a general purpose rationale for Inca conquests. One should not assume that sodomy only occurred in the areas in which explicit mention is made, but can accept that it was recognized rather than invented in the areas for which mention was made. The tenth Inca, Capac Yupanqui, who reigned from 1471 to 1493, vigorously persecuted sodomites, according to Garcilaso. His general Auqui Tatu burned alive in the public square all those for whom there was even circumstantial evidence of sodomy in the [H]acari valley (south of Nazca), threatening to burn down whole towns if anyone else engaged in sodomy. Again in Chincha, Yupanqui burned alive large numbers, pulling down their houses and any trees they had planted. Unlike Cieza, Garcilaso attributed sodomy to the Tarma and Pumpu, but followed Cieza in mentioning the notorious and (embarrassingly) serrano sodomites of Callejón de Huaylas. Capac Yupanqui's son, Huayna Capac, who reigned from 1493 to 1525, appears to have been less zealous in attempting to extirpate sodomy from the lands he added to the Inca empire. He merely "bade" the people of Tumbez to give up sodomy. Garcilaso did not record any measures taken against the Manta, who he said "practiced sodomy more openly and shamelessly than all the other tribes."

The giants of Santa Elena, whose legend fascinated the conquistadors, also purportedly practiced open/public sodomy. According to Garcilaso, this all-male race was destroyed in a fire while everyone was engaged in a society-wide orgy of sodomy.

This legend is clearly a parallel to that of the destruction of **Sodom**. In the indigenous myth "a youth shining like the sun" descended from the sky and fought against the oppressors of the Indians, throwing flames that drove them into a valley where they were all finally killed, and where what were believed to be their bones were found by a Spanish captain in 1543 (Zárate).

Other Evidence. In addition to mention of sodomy in the chronicles, archeological excavations have produced evidence of coastal homosexuality, especially Mochica ceramics. Modern anthropologists have also attributed tolerance for male and female homosexuality to the modern Aymara on the basis of vocabulary relating to masculine women, effeminate (castrated?) men, and fellatio in an early seventeenth century dictionary. Although there are no reports of homosexual behavior or roles among the contemporary Aymara, most of the vocabulary has survived (Murray).

South of what was the southern end of the Inca Empire (and south of the modern Chilean capital of Santiago), socially respected third gender (gender-crossing homosexual) shamans have been reported among the Araucanians from the report of "the happy captive," Núñez de Pineda, in 1646 through fieldwork done in the early 1950s (Murray). Hardly anything is known about the social structures and cosmologies of the indigenous peoples who lived between the Aymara and the Araucanians (such as the Atacameno, Chango, Lipe and the Chilean Diaguita), whose cultures did not survive for twentieth-century fieldwork, and whose populations were not as large and concentrated as those on the northwest coast of South America. Late marriage ages for the Argentine Diaguita probably indicate elaborate initiation rites, but nothing is known of their content, homosexual or otherwise.

BIBLIOGRAPHY. Pedro Cieza de León, *The Incas*, Norman: University of Oklahoma Press, 1959; Garcilaso de la Vega, *The Royal Commentaries*, Austin: University of Texas Press, 1966; Stephen O. Murray, ed., *Male Homosexuality in Central and South America*, New York: Gay Academic Union, 1987 (Gai Saber Monograph 5); Pedro Pizarro, *Relación del descubrimiento y conquista de los Reinos del Perú*, Lima: Pontificia Universidad Católica, 1986; John H. Rowe, "The Kingdom of Chimor," *Acta Americana*, 6 (1948), 26-59; Augustín de Zárate, *The Discovery and Conquest of Peru*, London: Penguin, 1968.

Stephen O. Murray

ANDERSEN, HANS CHRISTIAN (1805–1875)

Danish writer of fairy tales. The son of a shoemaker and an almost illiterate mother, Andersen came to Copenhagen at the age of 14, and there found protectors who sent him to grammar school and then to University. His fame rests upon the 168 fairy tales and stories which he wrote between 1835 and 1872. Some of the very first became children's classics from the moment of their appearance; the tales have since been translated into more than a hundred languages. Some are almost childlike in their simplicity; others are so subtle and sophisticated that they can be properly appreciated only by adults.

A lifelong bachelor, Andersen traveled extensively in almost every country in Europe. He considered Italy his second homeland, but his ties with German culture were much closer. He developed an intense affection for Edvard Collin that peaked in the years 1835–36, when he wrote a letter to Collin asserting that "Our friendship is like 'The Mysteries,' it should not be analyzed." To describe his feelings for Collin he used expressions like "my half-womanliness," "as tender as a woman in my feelings," "I long for you as though you were a beautiful Calabrian girl," and "The almost girlish in my nature." The letters reflect the farthest acceptable limit to which a tender friendship between two males could extend at that time. Collin himself did not reciprocate the affection, and after Andersen's death he wrote that his inability to do so "must have inflicted suffering on a man of Andersen's nature."

In the novel O.T., written in the autumn of 1835, Andersen seems to have attempted to escape his frustrations in the relationship with Collin by describing a tender friendship between two students, one of whom consents to intimacy with the other and joins him on a long trip abroad. His own feminine qualities are transferred to the character modeled on Collin, while his alter ego is a capable and wealthy student who nevertheless has a self-perception as a deviant and stigmatized person—to a far greater degree than warranted by his actual social background and by the attitudes of the people surrounding him.

An attempt has been made to deny Andersen's homosexuality with reference to the fact that the concept appeared only late in his lifetime, yet a crucial component of the homosexual "identity," particularly after the trial of Oscar Wilde in 1895, was the feeling of membership in a stigmatized and ostracized minority. While it is impossible to look into the mind of the novelist to determine whether he understood that the physical consummation of his passion was socially unacceptable, it is remarkable that the villain of the novel uses the secret of the hero's (Andersen's) childhood for blackmail—a Damocles' sword over the head of every homosexual in those days—and is made to drown "accidentally" on the last page of the work. It has also been speculated that the the fairy tale "The Little Mermaid," completed in January 1837, is based on Andersen's self-identification with a sexless creature with a fish's tail who tragically loves a handsome prince, but instead of saving her own future as a mermaid by killing the prince and his bride sacrifices herself and commits suicide—another theme of early homosexual apologetic literature. In lines deleted from the draft of the story, the mermaid is allowed to say: "I myself shall strive to win an immortal soul . . . so that in the world beyond I may be reunited with the one to whom I gave my whole heart." The "Little Mermaid" was thus a monument to his unconsummated friendship with Edvard Collin, which still probably rested upon his homosexual love for a heterosexual who had no way of returning it. Thus if Andersen was not an "overt homosexual" in the modern sense, he seems to have been aware of his orientation and the insoluble conflict with nineteenth-century sexual morality that it entailed.

BIBLIOGRAPHY. Wilhelm von Rosen, "Venskabets mysterier" [Mysteries of Friendship], Anderseniana, 3d ser., 3:3 (1980), 167–214 (with English summary).
Warren Johansson

ANDERSON, MARGARET (1886–1973)

American publisher, editor, and memoirist. With her lover Jane Heap, Anderson edited the *Little Review* in New York (1915–27), which—despite its tiny circulation—was one of the best literary journals of the time. Under the banner of "Life for Art's sake," she charted a course of "applied Anarchism, whose policy is a Will to Splendor of Life." With Ezra Pound as its foreign editor, the magazine published James Joyce's *Ulysses* in installments. In July 1920, however, a reader complained about a section of the novel containing Leopold Bloom's erotic musings. The editors were arrested but, undaunted, they continued with the series. Later when she had moved to Paris with the magazine, Anderson concluded that Pound was lacking in understanding for women, especially lesbians. Clearly the continuing success of the *Little Review* depended on the close bond between Anderson and Heap. As Anderson later remarked, "my greatest ambition in [the magazine] was to capture her talk, her ideas. As she used to say, I pushed her into the arena and she performed to keep me quiet."

In France Anderson and Heap—together with Heap's ward Fritz Peters, who later became a homosexual novelist—became adherents of the mystic George Ivanovich Gurdjieff, who was then at the height of his influence. Anderson spent most of her later years in semi-seclusion in London, where she wrote her memoirs, which are an important source for the literary history of the period.

BIBLIOGRAPHY. Margaret Anderson, *The Fiery Fountains*, New York: Hermitage House, 1930; idem, *My Thirty Years' War*, New York: Covici Friede, 1930; idem, *The Strange Necessity*, New York: Horizon, 1970; Hugh Ford, *Four Lives in Paris*. San Francisco: North Point Press, 1987, pp. 227–86.

Evelyn Gettone

ANDROGYNY

An androgynous individual is one who has the characteristics of both sexes. Ideally, this quality should be distinguished from **hermaphroditism** in the strict sense, whereby the fusion of male and female is anatomically expressed through the presence, or partial presence, of both sets of genital organs. There is a tendency to consider androgyny primarily psychic and constitutional, while hermaphroditism is anatomical. In this perspective most (psychic) androgynes are not strictly hermaphrodites in that anatomically they are no different from other men and women; some hermaphrodites may not be androgynous, that is to say, despite their surplus organ endowment, they behave in an essentially masculine or feminine way.

The term androgyne stems from the Greek *androgynos*, "man-woman." The famous myth recounted in **Plato's** *Symposium* presents three primordial double beings: the man-man, the woman-woman, and the man-woman. The first two are the archetypes of the male homosexual and lesbian respectively; the third, the *androgynos*, is—paradoxically from the modern point of view—the source of what we would now call the heterosexual. Other ancient writers use the term to refer to an anatomical intermediate between the two genders, synonymous with *hermaphroditos*. From this practice stems the modern conflation of the meaning of the two terms, which is unlikely to disappear.

Basic Concepts. Modern languages use "androgynous" in a variety of senses. First, identifying it with the hermaphrodite category, it may denote a somatic intermediate. In fact, the pure type with fully developed genitals of both sexes is clinically so rare as to be virtually nonexistent in the human species. The individuals known as (pseudo-) hermaphrodites generally have *incompletely* formed genitals of one of their two sexes or both. That is to say, an individual may have a fully formed vagina together with a stunted, unfunctioning penis, or a well developed penis with a shallow, nonuterine vagina. Of course, in the plant and animal kingdoms there are many fully hermaphroditic species that are androgynous in this sense. Secondly, nineteenth-century writers extended the physiological concept to apply to those whose genitals are clearly of one sex but whose psychic orientation is experienced as primarily of the other: Karl Heinrich **Ulrichs'** "female soul trapped in a male body." Since Ulrichs and others were primarily interested in same-sex behavior, the term often carries the connotation of "homosexual," even though such usage begs several questions. Thirdly, with reference to male human beings "androgynous" implies effeminacy. Logically, it should then mean "viraginous, masculinized" when applied to women, but this parallel is rarely drawn. Thus there is an unanalyzed tendency to regard androgynization as essentially a process of softening or mitigating maleness. Stereotypically, the androgyne is a half-man or incomplete male.

In addition to these relatively specific usages there is a kind of semantic halo effect, whereby androgyny is taken to refer to a more all-encompassing realm. Significantly, in this broader, almost mystical sense the negative connotations fall away, and androgyny may even be a prized quality. For example the figures in the Renaissance paintings of **Botticelli** and **Leonardo** are sometimes admired for their androgynous beauty. It comes as no surprise that these aspects of the artists were first emphasized by homosexual art critics of the nineteenth century.

Permutations of the Androgynous Ideal. Cross-cultural material bearing on androgyny is very extensive, especially in the religious sphere. In Hinduism and some African religions there are male gods who have female manifestations or avatars. A strand of Jewish medieval interpretation of Genesis holds that Adam and Eve were androgynous before the Fall. If this be the case, God himself must be androgynous since he made man "in his own image." Working from different premises, medieval Christian mystics found that the compassion of Christ required that he be conceived of as a mother. Jakob Böhme (1575–1624), the German seer, held that all perfect beings, Christ as well as the angels, were androgynous. He foresaw that ultimately Christ's sacrifice would make possible a restoration of the primal androgyny. Contemporaneously, the occult discipline of alchemy presented androgyny as a basic cosmic feature.

After a period of neglect, interest in the theme resurfaced among the German romantics. Franz von Baader (1765–1841), who interpreted the sacrament of marriage as a symbolic restitution of angelic bisexuality, believed that primordial androgyny would return as the world neared its end. In France the eccentric Evadist (Eve & Adam) thinkers advocated the equality of man and woman; one of their leaders, Ganneau, styled himself Mapah. The occultist and decadent writer Josephin **Péladan** (1858–1918) was a tireless propagandist for androgyny; through his Rose + Croix society he had a considerable influence on Symbolism in the visual arts.

In the twentieth century the psychologist Carl Gustav **Jung** (1875–1961) was preoccupied with androgyny, which he illustrated through his ingenious, but eccentric interpretations of alchemical imagery. Some of his followers have suggested that androgyny is a way of overcoming dualism and regaining a primal unity; the half-beings of man and woman as we know them must yield to the complete man-woman. Thus androgyny points the way to a return to the Golden Age, an era of harmony unmarred by the conflict and dissension of today which are rooted in an unnatural polarization.

Contemporary Perspectives. In the field of academic **psychology**, the researches of Sandra L. Bem and others have sought to present empirical evidence that the androgynous individual enjoys better mental health and can function better socially. Significantly, it is usually "androgynous" women who score higher on such psychological tests than men. Thus these findings may be an artefact of the strategic situation in which a career-minded women finds herself: to succeed in a male-defined professional world an ambitious woman will find it expedient to incorporate some male qualities.

The androgynous ideal had considerable appeal for feminist and homosexual thinkers in the 1970s. It was pointed out, no doubt correctly, that the straitjacket of the masculine role tended to keep men from expressing their feelings, as through kissing or crying. Men can practice a wider range of expressiveness, and therefore lead more satisfying lives, if they will discard the extreme polarization inherent in the traditional masculine role. **Science fiction** writings, notably the *Left Hand of Darkness* (1969) by Ursula LeGuin, explored what complete androgyny might mean. In popular culture there was a kind of "androgyne chic," as exemplified by such rock stars as David Bowie and Boy George.

As the initial enthusiasm cooled, however, it was perceived that, applied to present day society, the androgynous ideal might lead to a disregard of the inherent strengths of male and female, whether these be culturally or biologically determined. Thus some feminist thinkers today emphasize nurturing and cooperative behavior as distinctive and desirable female traits. Despite some exaggerations, recent discussions have had the merit of helping bring into question earlier popular negative dismissals of androgyny, promoting a more supple concept of the relation between sex roles and gender.

BIBLIOGRAPHY. *Androgyn: Sehnsucht nach Vollkommenheit*, Berlin: Reimer, 1986; Sandra L. Bem, "The Measurement of Psychological Androgyny," *Journal of Counseling and Clinical Psychology*, 42 (1974), 155–67; Mircea Eliade, *Mephistopheles and the Androgyne*, New York: Harper and Row, 1965; L. S. A. M. von Römer, "Ueber die androgynische Idee des Lebens," *Jahrbuch für sexuelle Zwischenstufen*, 5 (1903), 709–940; June Singer, *Androgyny: Toward a New Theory of Sexuality*, Garden City, NY: Anchor Press/ Doubleday, 1976.

Wayne R. Dynes

ANDROPHILIA

This rarely used term serves to focus attention on those homosexuals who are exclusively interested in adult partners rather than adolescents and children. In our society such a focus would seem self-explanatory, inherent in the definition of homosexuality itself. Yet in other societies, such as ancient **Greece**, **China**, and **Islam**, and in many tribal groups, age-graded differences were or are the norm in same-sex conduct in contradistinction with androphilia, which is most familiar to us. Because of the prevalence of androphilia in modern Western culture, its assumptions are sometimes unwittingly or deliberately imported into other settings; some discussions of homosexual behavior in ancient Greece, for example, tend to gloss over the fact that it was predominantly **pederastic** (though not **pedophile** in the narrow sense of attraction to prepubertal boys).

In the early years of the present century, the great German sexologist Magnus **Hirschfeld** offered a three-fold classification of homosexuals: (1) **ephebophiles**, who prefer partners from puberty to the early twenties (in current usage, from about 17 to about 20); (2) androphiles, who love men from that age into the fifties; and (3) gerontophiles, who seek out old men.

Contemplating this scheme from the standpoint of an individual of, say, thirty years of age, it is evident that the first and third categories of sex object constitute differentiation, the second relative similarity.

The shift to dominance of androphilia, in which the two partners are of comparable age, occurs only with the rise of industrial society in Europe and North America in the eighteenth and nineteenth centuries; in **Mediterranean** countries the shift remains incomplete, and in much of the world has barely begun or has not occurred at all.

Attempts at explaining the new homosexual pattern include keying it to a change in heterosexual marriage, which led the way by becoming more companionate and less asymmetrical; to the rise of the democratic ideal; to demographic changes such as increased life expectancies; and to changes in the social treatment of **youth** which made the young less available as sexual partners. Nevertheless, the dynamics behind this fundamental transition remain historically mysterious, a major challenge to any attempt to draw up a reasonably comprehensive history of homosexuality.

Wayne R. Dynes

ANGLICANISM

Anglicanism, or Episcopalianism as it is also termed, is a worldwide Christian religious fellowship, stemming from the state-supported Church of **England**. Generally regarded as a form of **Protestantism**, Anglicanism (especially in its High Church variety) may also claim to represent a third path between Catholicism and Protestantism in the strict sense.

The Church of England and homosexuality began on an antagonistic footing, stemming not only from the inherited homophobia of **Christianity** as a whole, but from the reformers' polemical critique of Catholic monasteries as dens of corruption and sexual indulgence. It has also been argued, though the matter is disputed, that Henry VIII's law of 1533 on buggery was linked to his "smear campaign" against the monasteries. In ensuing centuries it was a commonplace of English antihomosexual propaganda to attribute the presence of sodomy to the complaisant customs of Catholic Europe, whence the infection is supposed to have spread to the otherwise untainted British Isles. Several notable scandals, including those of John Atherton, Bishop of Waterford and Lismore (1640), Reverend John Fenwick (1797), Reverend V. P. Littlehales (1812) and Percy Jocelyn, bishop of Clogher (1822), show that members of the Anglican clergy were by no means exempt from the "vice."

In the latter decades of the nineteenth century a more comfortable relationship developed, at least de facto, between homosexuals and the Church of England. This rapprochement was due to the High Church or Oxford movement, which favored an aesthetic approach to religious ceremonial. This atmosphere appealed to homosexual aesthetes, who were welcomed, as long as discretion was observed, to the churches practicing the High Church liturgy. Conversely, adherents of the opposing faction, the Broad Church, were tempted to pillory their ritualist opponents as sissies or worse.

In 1955 Canon D. S. **Bailey's** book *Homosexuality and the Western Christian Tradition* appeared, influencing both secular and ecclesiastical thinking. Bailey was a member of the Church of England's Moral Welfare Council, the predecessor of the Board for Social Responsibility. This work of these bodies was part of the background of the successful decriminalization of male homosexuality in Britain and Wales in 1967, a legal change strongly supported by the archbishop of Canterbury, Michael Ramsey. At the pastoral level, Anglican clergy offered counseling and support to British gay people. In 1979 a Board for Social Responsibility working party, chaired by the bishop of Gloucester, produced *Homosexual Relationships*, a report that acknowledged the possibility of permanent gay relationships. The appearance of the report was indicative of a new atmosphere in which many homosexuals in the church felt free to proclaim their identity.

Yet counterforces were gathering. A new breed of militant evangelicalism regarded homosexual behavior as a corrupting influence. This kind of religious intolerance accorded with the rise of Margaret Thatcher within the Conservative Party and the growth of New Right economic and political ideas. Local councils in Britain's cities that were seeking to promote positive images of gay people came under heavy attack from the right and from the tabloid press. In this context the 1987 General Synod was presented with a motion by Tony Higton, leader of the Alliance for Biblical Witness to Our Nation, calling in effect for the removal of "practicing" gay clergy. Although the resolution was rejected in favor of a compromise one, no serious theological debate took place. The popular press seized the occasion to run stories under such headlines as "Holy Homos Escape Ban" and "Pulpit Poofs Can Stay." Under these circumstances Anglican gay clergy felt intimidated. Then in May of 1988 the Lesbian and Gay Christian Movement was evicted from its home in St. Botolph's church in London, where it had been located since 1976.

Gay Anglicans have fared better in the United States. In the era of gay liberation, the lay Episcopal group Integrity was formed, encountering the benevolent support of many Anglican clerics. In 1976 the General Convention of the Protestant Episcopal Church in the U.S.A. passed a resolution stating that "homosexual persons are children of God, who have a full and equal claim with all other persons upon the love, acceptance, and pastoral concern and care of the Church." Reverend Paul Moore, bishop of New York, has been outspoken in his defence of gay people, whom he has also ordained. To be sure, his positive attitude is not universally shared among American Episcopalians, but on the whole their church has borne the stress of the age of **AIDS** with calmness and compassion

BIBLIOGRAPHY. David Hilliard, "'Unenglish and Unmanly': Anglo-Catholicism and Homosexuality," *Victorian Studies*, 25 (1982), 181–210; James Wickliff, ed., *In Celebration*, Oak Park, IL: Integrity, 1975.
Wayne R. Dynes

ANGLO-SAXONS

Our information about homosexual behavior in Anglo-Saxon **England** is chiefly linguistic. The word *baedling*, a diminutive of *baeddel*, occurs in an Old English glossary as the equivalent of the Latin terms effeminatus and mollis, designating the effeminate homosexual. A synonym is the word *waepenwifstere* (approximately: "male wife"). Evidently, these words reflect an Anglo-Saxon stereotype of the homosexual as an unwarlike, womanish type. In all likelihood, this negative concept derives in part from a common Germanic archetype, attested by a passage in *Germania* (12) by the Roman historian **Tacitus**—where death by drowning is stipulated for such individuals—but probably modified in the early **Middle Ages** by Mediterranean-Christian influences.

Similar in form to baedling is *deorling*, the source of the modern English darling. While the Old English word had a general sense of a beloved person or thing, it was also used more specifically to label a minion, a youth favored because of his sexual attractiveness.

At the present stage of research further data about homosexual behavior in Anglo-Saxon times (that is, from ca. 500 to 1066) remains elusive. For its part, however, the word baeddel survived, turning eventually—through a process of semantic expansion—into the general English adjective of pejoration, "bad." The word also forms part of two place names in England: Baddlesmere ("baeddel's lake") in Kent and Baddlinghame ("the home of the baedlings") in Cambridgeshire.

The broadening of the meaning of the word baeddel in the direction of general disparagement ("bad") has several historical parallels. The first, from another Germanic sphere, is the shift from old Scandinavian *argr*, cowardly, effeminate, to modern German *arg*, bad, wicked. Then early medieval France seems to have witnessed the creation of *felo/felonis*, evil person (the etymon of our legal term felon) from Latin *fellare*, to fellate. It is also possible that Russian *plokhoi*, bad, is cognate with Greek *malakos* (with change of the initial labial from *m* to *p*), as the Polish *plochy* has the meaning of "timid, fearful," another of the nuances of *argr*.

ANIMAL HOMOSEXUALITY

A body of evidence has accumulated showing homosexual behavior among many species of animals— behavior that has been observed both in the wild and in captivity. While this evidence suffices to dispel the old belief that homosexuality is unknown among animals, more extended comparisons with human homosexual behavior remain problematic.

Examples and Characteristic Features. In the 1970s the well-publicized reports of the German ethologist Konrad Lorenz drew attention to male–male pair bonds in greylag geese. Controlled reports of "lesbian" behavior among birds, in which two females share the responsibilities of a single nest, have existed since 1885. Mounting behavior has been observed among male lizards, monkeys, and mountain goats. In some cases one male bests the other in combat, and then mounts his fellow, engaging in penile thrusts—though rarely with intromission. In other instances, a submissive male will "present" to a dominant one, by exhibiting his buttocks in a receptive manner. Mutual masturbation and fellatio have been observed among male stump-tailed macaques. During oestrus female rhesus monkeys engage in mutual full-body rubbing.

Those who have observed these same-sex patterns in various species have noted, explicitly or implicitly, similarities with human behavior. It is vital, however, not to elide differences. Mounting behavior may not be sexual, but an expression of social hierarchy: the dominant partner reaffirms his superiority over the presenting one. In most cases where a sexual pairing does occur, one partner adopts the characteristic behavior of the other sex. While this behavioral inversion sometimes occurs in human homosexual conduct, it is by no means universal. Thus while (say) Roman homosexuality, which often involved slaves submitting to their masters, may find its analogue among animals, modern American **androphilia** largely does not. This difference suggests that the cultural matrix is important. Human sexual behavior, whether heterosexual or homosexual, has a vast expressive dimension which has both sociological (group) and psychological (individual) aspects. Cross-cultural study reveals wide variations in the social organization of homosexual behavior. In the psychological realm, we know of persons, such as some members of monastic orders, who—because of their erotic fantasy life—regard themselves as completely homophile yet have never had a homosexual experience. Such a thing is possible among animals, of course, but it is very unlikely—and in any case there is no way of studying an animal's consciousness except on the basis of its overt behavior.

Human homosexuality is a complex interaction of physiological response, social patterning, and individual consciousness. For many, homosexuality in human subjects demands the complete suppression of the dialectic of sexual polarity—it involves the masculine in the male seeking the masculine in another male, or the feminine in the female seeking the feminine in another female. It can be doubted that homosexuality, by this definition, ever occurs in animals; the mechanisms that trigger sexual arousal and activity would not allow it.

In the light of this complexity, a simple identification of human homosexual behavior with same-sex interactions among animals is reductive, and may block or misdirect the search for an understanding of the remaining mysteries of human sexuality. Still, for those aspects to which they have relevance, animal patterns of homosexual behavior help to place human ones in a phylogenetic perspective—in somewhat the same way as animal cries and calls have a relation to human language, and the structures built by birds and beavers anticipate the feats of human architecture.

Classical Antiquity and Animalitarianism. The observational powers of the Greeks encompassed the question of same-sex behavior among animals, which some affirmed and others denied. There were also folkloric beliefs, such as the notion that males of the partridge species are so highly sexed that in the absence of females they readily assault each other sexually. Early Christian writers associated the hare with pederasty because of the fantastic belief that it grows a new anus each year. More radically, the hyena symbolized gender ambiguity because it changed its sex each year. Finally, the weasel, which was supposed to conceive through the mouth, stood for the practice of fellatio. To be on the safe side, the author of the Epistle of Barnabas forbade eating the flesh of any of these creatures.

These "bad examples" from the animal kingdom, are exceptional and atypical. The contrasting notion that the conduct of animals is in key respects superior to that of human beings, and therefore serves as a yardstick to determine our "naturalness," has been dubbed "animalitarianism" by the historian of ideas George Boas. The Greek writer **Plutarch** (second century of our era) has a fanciful essay, "Gryllos," in which a talking pig asserts that animals are better than human beings because they do not practice pederasty. (This idea was in fact adumbrated by **Plato** in the fourth century B.C.) As been noted, recent evidence shows that in fact animals do engage in homosexual behavior, but of a circumscribed kind: perhaps animalitarians could now argue that less is better ("A little homosexuality is acceptable, but . . .").

Since the Greeks, the animalitarian gambit has enjoyed a long run of popularity, answering to a sentimental hankering for a pastoral life without pressures and ambiguity, for a never-never land of the "state of nature," which the life of animals—guided solely by instinct—is supposed to preserve. The beast standard is, of course, selective, inasmuch as its advocates are not apparently willing to discard a host of conveniences—from clothing to computers—not available to animals. Nor are these persons inclined (as Aristophanes pointed out when the thesis was first broached) to perch on roosts at night like birds, or to throw feces as a friendly way of gaining attention like apes. Human beings use a wide variety of soaps and deodorants to reduce or mask smells which their bodies produce. The argument that animal ways are best, then, rests on a kind of selective amnesia which makes it possible to ignore some types of human departure from the animal model, while focusing moral indignation on others.

In statements by contemporary antihomosexual propagandists, it is revealing that they will sometimes first insist that homosexuality must be unnatural, since "even the lowest animals don't do it," and then when confronted with ethological evidence to the contrary exclaim with outrage that same-sex relations drag man down to the subhuman level. "behaving like a filthy swine." Such dodges suggest that moral distinctions are first posited and then superimposed on interspecies comparisons, instead of being derived from them in any consistent way. From time immemorial human beings have used animal comparisons as criticism (dumb as an ox, scared as a rabbit) and as praise (bold as a lion, far-sighted as an eagle); the choice depends upon the presuppositions of the speaker.

Every species has patterns of sexual behavior unique to itself, so that claiming on supposedly moral grounds that man should imitate the lower animals is absurd. Moreover, social control of human sexual activity can only be justified on the grounds that the policy promotes the higher interests of mankind—including the evolutionary progress of the species—rather than following the lead of the instinctual life of creatures far lower on the evolutionary scale. All living things exist in a world in which—as Darwin showed—they must compete for scarce resources; but while nature confronts scarcity with redundance, man confronts scarcity with foresight. That is to say, lower forms of organic life survive by engendering such myriads of young that at least a minimal number will reach adulthood and the reproductive stage; but man survives by economic and demographic measures that seek to proportion his numbers to the resources available for consumption. Especially given the absence of superfetation in the human female, the notion that "homosexuality means race suicide" is preposterous. All human sexual activity, homosexual and heterosexual, occurs in a context of economic and social values that removes it entirely from the genetically programmed coupling of animals, even though such behaviors as competition and courtship anticipate the sexual rivalry and mating of human beings. Finally, the prolonged phase of education through which members of civilized society must pass—with the need for mentoring and initiation into the world of adulthood—lends a significance to homosexual bonds between adult and adolescent that could find no parallel in the social life of animals.

BIBLIOGRAPHY. Frank A. Beach, ed., *Human Sexuality in Four Perspectives*, Baltimore: Johns Hopkins University Press, 1977, pp. 306–16; James D. Weinrich, *Sexual Landscapes*, New York: Charles Scribner's Sons, 1987, pp. 282–309.

Ward Houser

Anonymous Sex
See **Impersonal Sex.**

Anthologies

An anthology is a collection of selected literary pieces or passages, usually by several authors. The selection may be determined by considerations of quality, period, or subject matter. The first homosexual example is Book XII of the collection known as the **Greek Anthology**, a collection of poetry that spans a thousand years.

With the establishment of Christianity as the state religion such same-sex gatherings became impossible—at least none is known until after the French revolution. Heinrich **Hoessli**, the pioneering homosexual scholar, included a good many selections from ancient and Islamic verse in his *Eros: die Männerliebe der Griechen* (Glarus, 1836–38), which makes him a forerunner. However, the first true anthology of male homosexuality was created during the efflorescence of homosexual studies that occurred in Germany by the artistically inclined Elisàr von **Kupffer** (*Lieblingminne und Freundesliebe in der Weltliteratur*, Berlin, 1900). This collection, with its interspersed commentary, was almost immediately imitated by Edward **Carpenter** in his *Ioläus: An Anthology of Friendship* (London, 1902), which had many subsequent editions. Despite Carpenter's cautious discussion of the matter in terms of friendship, this volume was dubbed the "bugger's bible."

After Carpenter's time the custom largely lapsed. On the European continent periodicals, some of which published contemporary and older fiction, largely took up the slack, while in the English-speaking world the subject became more taboo than ever. In 1961, however, Carpenter found a successor, albeit a timid one, in *Eros: An Anthology of Friendship*, edited by Alistair Sutherland and Patrick Anderson (London, 1961). This had been preceded by the American Donald Webster Cory's short story collection *Twenty-one Variations on a Theme* (New York, 1953). With the easing of censorship in the United States, however, pulp publishers undertook to produce various soft-core specials—some aimed at gay men, others seeking to exploit a broader interest in lesbianism; since they include little that is now hard to find, they are now justly forgotten.

The rise of militant gay liberation after 1969 created a need for new collections such as those edited jointly by Karla Jay and Allen Young, as well as the two *Gay Liberation Anthologies*, mainly of nonfiction, made by Len Richmond and Gary Noguera (San Francisco, 1973–79). The importance of periodicals was recognized by anthologies assembled from the pages of *The Ladder*, *Christopher Street*, *The Body Politic*, and *Der Kreis*. Ambitiously, David Galloway and Christian Sabisch created an international anthology of male homosexuality in twentieth-century literature: *Calamus* (New York, 1982). A wide span of mainly French material appeared in *Les Amours masculines* (Paris, 1984), while Joachim S. Hohmann issued several useful anthologies of German material. Other collections gather Dutch, Italian, and Latin American writings. Another development of this period is the creation of anthologies on a particular sector of gay experience and writing, as black gays, Chicano lesbians, lesbian nuns, older people. Genres were also singled out: poetry, plays, science fiction and fantasy. Some of these new anthologies, especially those produced by lesbians, tend to emphasize personal experience rather than "fine writing" in the usual sense.

ANTHROPOLOGY

According to an old, but serviceable tradition, anthropology has two main branches, physical and cultural. Interfacing with biology, physical anthropology focuses on reconstructing the evolution and structure of the material embodiment of humanity. Cultural anthropology, the discipline of interest in the understanding of sexual behavior, studies the lifeways and belief systems of human groups. Cultural anthropology comprises both ethnography, the examination and recording of specific cultures, and ethnology, the comparative and historical analysis of culture. In the United Kingdom the field has usually been termed social anthropology in keeping with the traditional British emphasis on social structure in contrast to the American emphasis on the concept of culture. Although in principle cultural anthropology addresses all human societies, in fact it tends to be restricted to the preliterate or tribal peoples of the third world, leaving the study of industrial society and its past to **sociology** and history respectively. Since the 1960s, there has appeared a welcome crossing of this tacit boundary in urban anthropology, which studies groups within the modern city.

The accumulating body of research in cultural anthropology has gradually dissolved the deeply rooted belief that any single culture offers an ultimate or absolute standard of value, the view known as ethnocentrism. To be sure, even today a few diehard absolutists maintain that homosexual behavior has been despised and condemned everywhere, but comparative studies have shown this notion to be utterly false: it tells us something of the wishes of those who propound it, but nothing about humanity. Cultural attitudes toward homosexuality run the gamut from outright condemnation to mandatory participation in same-sex rituals. The cultural relativism inherent in the anthropological enterprise has served not only to enhance our understanding of the range of human capabilities, but has fostered the growth of tolerance in our own society.

Historical Precedents. The Greek traveler and historian Herodotus (ca. 480–ca. 420 B.C.) is rightly regarded as the founder of a comparative approach to human societies. Avoiding overt ethnocentrism—the kind of parochial glorification of their own culture that was rife among the ancient Greeks—he examines the cultural patterns of a number of peoples in the Eastern Mediterranean and beyond. Yet recent studies have shown that he does not examine them with the objectivity cherished by modern anthropology, but rather viewed them in a "mirror" of **Greece**, emphasizing the very oddity (and therefore bizarreness) of traits that most differed from the Greek ones. Because he took same-sex behavior for granted, Herodotus rarely mentioned it—except among the Persians (his central subject) and the **Scythians**, where a still mysterious phenomenon, that of the asexual Enarees, prevailed. Other Greek and Roman writers actually professed to prefer the customs of primitive groups to their own as less corrupted by luxury. In his idealized picture of the ancient Germanic tribes, **Tacitus** notes, with his usual dry concision, the aspect of their military ethos that required the execution of cowards and effeminates. Later the Christian Salvian, a **Patristic** writer, was to transform this perception into a true homophobic pro-Germanism.

Medieval travel writers and proto-ethnologists believed that remote parts of the world were inhabited by races with strikingly different physical characteristics and correspondingly bizarre customs (the "monstrous races"). John Mandeville, for example, claimed that a region of Asia was actually inhabited by a race of **hermaphrodites** possessing the physical organs of both sexes, a myth that has reverberated in later times. When the Spanish conquistadors took possession of the New World they tended to assimilate the practices and beliefs of the indigenous peoples to archetypes inherited from their ancient and medieval past. Thus the weaknesses of pre-Columbian **Mexico** and the **Andean cultures**, according to some Spanish writers, was bound up with their toleration of sodomy. The **Amazon** takes its name from the belief that it was dominated by tribes of viraginous women, as in the classical legend.

The Rise of Cultural Relativism. Eighteenth-century **Pacific** voyages engendered a European idealization of Polynesian societies as a kind of earthly paradise. Montesquieu used the device of a set of fictitious *Persian Letters* (1721) to criticize European customs. Toward the end of the century Johann Gottfried von Herder (1744–1803) gave an impetus to the emerging discipline of folklore, by emphasizing the need to listen to the "many voices of the peoples." The interest in differences between peoples ultimately paved the way for attention to differences *within* peoples—including difference of sexual orientation. These trends fostered ethical relativism and diversitarianism, the appreciation of variety for its own sake. While they helped to erode chauvinistic prejudices, they bore within them the seeds of a contrary exaggeration, the ethnoromanticism that sees only harmony and virtue in remote primitive societies.

These developments notwithstanding, even travelers tended to see non-European cultures in the mirror of classical civilization: the lure of **Hellenism**. In time the comparison rebounded on the study of classical philology itself. A striking example is the career of the Swiss scholar Johann Jakob Bachofen (1815–1887), who formulated the hypothesis of primitive matriarchy, a prehistoric stage of society preceding the establishment of patriarchy. This fantasy—for little conclusive evidence has been offered for a universal horizon of matriarchy in humanity's past—has returned today among some anthropologists, who search for traces of a lost system of social organization which probably never existed.

Modern Anthropology. The extension of European domination throughout the globe helped to create a much larger pool of data about tribal cultures. Armchair scholars such as Adolf Bastian, Lewis Henry Morgan, and Edward Burnett Tylor then sought to synthesize this material, creating the foundations for modern cultural anthropology. This trend culminated in Sir James Frazer's massive *The Golden Bough* (1890–1936), a work that was more influential in literary quarters than among anthropologists. There also developed a popular genre of sensationalized reporting of "the strange customs and practices of savages," that sometimes included sexual data. Although it is commonly asserted that there is little information about same-sex behavior from nineteenth- and early twentieth-century travelers and anthropologists, the great survey of Ferdinand Karsch-Haack, *Das gleichgeschlechtliche Leben der Naturvölker* (Munich, 1911) shows that in fact much was observed and recorded. But since the recorders were often European government agents and missionaries, due allowance must be made for professional bias.

After some impressive nineteenth-century amateur efforts—especially with regard to the American Indians—American anthropology was put on a firm footing by the practical work and teaching of Franz Boas (1858–1942), a German immigrant. Although Boas professed methodological agnosticism, most of his followers rallied to some form of Hegelian holism. Seeing cultures as homogeneous units dominated by a single "modal" personality type, they were inattentive to subgroups who might engage in homosexual behavior. However, the reception of European psychoanalytic ideas, embodied in the "culture and personality" trend, produced some manifestations of interest in same-sex behavior, as by Ruth **Benedict** and Abraham Kardiner. Yet on the whole American anthropologists continued to neglect the subject until the 1950s, perhaps tacitly holding that indigenous peoples—at least those unpolluted by acculturation—were exempt from this typically Western vice.

Flushed with confidence in a newly emerging discipline, a few anthropologists became pundits and sages, commenting on the problems of American life. In the case of Margaret Mead (1901–1978), the "lesson" she drew from her less-than-perfect research in Pacific island cultures—namely, that gender roles are essentially malleable rather than fixed—may have been on balance salutory. Yet the sense that scientific findings were being bent to serve sociopolitical ends caused unease. Not surprisingly, Mead was eventually dislodged from her popular standing as the virtual personification of the anthropological discipline. Gradually, however, the relativistic message sank in. Even if most lay people did not accept the idea that Kalahari bushmen are on the same level as, say, modern Danes, the idea that cultures were valuable for their own sake promoted tolerance. Whether intentionally or not, by "destabilizing" the conventional ethnocentric wisdom of American culture, anthropology prepared the way for the social experiments of the 1960s.

At midcentury a major scholarly instrument emerged in the Human Relations Area Files at Yale University. This vast compilation of world culture traits, though it has rightly been faulted for crudity and errors in coding, did yield information of a substantial number of societies in which homosexual behavior was tolerated as a matter of course, thus eroding one aspect of the "homosexuality is unnatural" argument.

A new positive element appeared in the 1950s, as professional anthropologists took up again the **berdache** phenomenon among the American Indians (*see* W. L. Williams, for details). A further step was taken in the 1970s with the formation of the Anthropological Research Group on Homosexuality. The *Newsletter* of this group (now termed the Society of Lesbian and Gay Anthropologists) serves as an instrument of comunication among serious researchers.

Problems and Prognostics. Twentieth-century cultural anthropology has not been able to shake free of its earlier dilemma. In principle value-free, individual researchers find it hard in practice to steer a completely even course between the Scylla of overattachment to their own cultural norms and the Charybdis of ethnoromanticism. Until recently many cultures were known essentially from one ethnography produced by a single investigator, who may have leaned to one or the other side in the "our values/their values" contrast. More disturbingly, when second and third opinions became available, the portraits drawn of the cultures were often very different. Although this so-called "Rashomon effect" can often be explained by the fact that different field workers have been looking at different aspects of the society under study, discrepancies point up the need for fuller confirmation of many assertions. Then too, questions have been raised about the limits of ethical neutrality: is it appropriate to observe, say, slavery or clitoridectomy ("female circumcision"), and to conclude that such practices are simply a valid part of a culture different from ours? It is hard not to grant that in a universal horizon of human rights, some behavioral patterns are simply unacceptable.

Many cultures are being contaminated by acculturation or simply disappearing, and anthropologists must scramble. In many cases, however, tribal informants have learned to tailor their responses to what they believe the investigator expects—or else to make a fool of him for their own amusement. Such informant self-editing may include denial of homosexual practices, which in any event are often associated with tribal rituals closed to outsiders. Institutions thought to be dead, such as the North American berdache, are sometimes surviving marginally—but for how long? At the same time urban anthropology has extended its methods to more developed environments, especially in the third world. Acknowledging criticisms of subjectivism and lack of cross-checking, a few anthropologists have proposed simply to "write novels," a trend that is unlikely to become dominant, as it would seriously erode the scientific credentials of the discipline.

Despite these continuing problems, enough data have accumulated to essay a tentative world map of male homosexual behavior in tribal societies. There appear to be two main types. In the first, common in Sub-Saharan **Africa** and Melanesia in the **Pacific**, age asymmetry predominates, with an older man pairing with a boy or adolescent youth. In the second type, one of gender-role variation, some men depart from gender norms to become berdaches. This type predominates among the North American **Indians**, in Polynesia, and on Madagascar. In addition to this typology, anthropologists are beginning to discern regularities within a culture area, as the initiatory homosexuality of Melanesia.

BIBLIOGRAPHY. Evelyn Blackwood, ed., *Anthropology and Homosexual Behavior*, Binghamton, NY: Haworth Press, 1986; Stephen O. Murray, *Social Theory, Homosexual Realities*, New York: Gay Academic Union, 1984; Walter L. Williams, *The Spirit and the Flesh: Sexual Diversity in American Indian Culture*, Boston: Beacon, 1986.
Wayne R. Dynes

ANTINOUS

Adolescent favorite of the Roman Emperor **Hadrian** (ca. 111–130), who won his lover's affection by his beauty and grace. During a trip up the Nile in which he accompanied Hadrian, he was drowned. Contemporary gossip enveloped his death in romantic legend; some even alleged that he had given his life for his master. Hadrian's grief was such that he ordered the boy deified as god and hero and even promoted the belief that Antinous had entered the firmament as a new star; at the end of the sixteenth century Tycho Brahe assigned the name to a particular star on his stellar map.

In Egypt Hadrian founded a new city named Antinoopolis in his honor, and elsewhere he was commemorated by cult, festivals, and statues. Numerous inscriptions in his honor survive, and poems on him were written by Pancrates and Mesomedes. The Early Christians reacted to the cult as one inspired by an "impure" passion, contrasting it with their own reverence for the saints.

The Antinous type appears on scores of coins and statues. The extant statues found today in museums in Italy and elsewhere display the neo-Greek manner that flourished under Hadrian, and have been much admired in modern times by students of the classic style. The influential homosexual archaeologist J. J. **Winckelmann** (1717–1768) went into raptures over two of these works as "the glory and crown of art in this age as well as in all others." In these depictions his somewhat full features correspond to the late-adolescent type of the ephebe rather than those of the *pais* or boy. The mystery surrounding his career and death has inspired a number of literary works in modern times, some with an explicitly homosexual theme, such as Marguerite **Yourcenar's** much admired

Hadrian's Memoirs (New York, 1954). The great Portuguese writer Fernando **Pessoa** published an English poem on the theme in 1918. Antinous remains synonymous with the beauty of late adolescence, forever preserved from decay by premature death.

BIBLIOGRAPHY. Royston Lambert, *Beloved and God: The Story of Hadrian and Antinous*, New York: Viking, 1984.
Wayne R. Dynes

ANTI-SEMITISM AND ANTIHOMOSEXUALITY

Social scientists have isolated several common features in **prejudice** directed against human groups. The prejudiced individual tends to view all members of the targeted group in terms of a **stereotype**; despite empirical counterevidence, he stoutly resists any abandonment of his views. Prejudiced persons are likely to act out their feelings through **discrimination** toward and avoidance of members of the disliked groups.

Several features link Jews and homosexuals as targets of prejudice. Unlike, say, Asian-Americans, both Jews and homosexuals have the option of passing, that is, not acknowledging their difference publicly and allowing those they meet to assign them tacitly to the majority group. However, just as many Jews in recent decades have been asserting ethnic pride through resuming their original "Jewish" surnames (when Anglo-Saxon ones had been adopted by the parents or ancestors) and wearing evident markers such as the Star of David and the yarmulka, so homosexuals and lesbians are now more assertive through "coming out" to colleagues, friends, and relatives, and wearing the pink triangle and the **lambda** symbols. Yet there is another side of the coin: both Jews and homosexuals seem to have more than their share of individuals who are afflicted with self-contempt—Jewish anti-Semites and antigay homosexuals. Just as some Jews restrict themselves to non-Jewish sexual partners and spouses, some homosexuals find their erotic ideal only in the person of a heterosexual (or one presumed to be so). Both Jews and homosexuals have created mordant versions of ingroup **humor**, which serve as safety valves for such feelings, but do not suffice to exorcise them. One of the functions of advocacy and service organizations for both groups is to address such kinds of psychological self-oppression so that the victims may overcome them.

Our society also shows historical parallels of anti-Semitism and antihomosexuality. In the eleventh century in Western Europe, for reasons that are still not clearly understood, the majority society began actively to persecute heretics, lepers, Jews, and sodomites, as the Christian emperors had done by the time of Justinian. The first two social categories are no longer in the line of fire, but the latter two have continued to remain the object of prejudice, discrimination, persecution, and (ultimately) genocide. At various times Christian denominations have focused their ire on Jews (or Marranos [crypto-Jews]) and homosexuals. Even among some secularists, as the **Enlightenment** thinkers Diderot and **Voltaire**, a distaste for both groups has been freely vented. Popular opinion tends to attribute a conspiratorial clannishness to both Jews and homosexuals, the former ostensibly owing allegiance to the mythical organization described in the scurrilous *Protocols of the Elders of Zion*, the latter supposedly adherents or agents of a nonexistent "Homintern." Both Jews and homosexuals have attracted envy through their appearance of easy financial circumstances. While the economic advantages of both groups (which are relative, not absolute, as there are many poor Jews and many poor homosexuals and lesbians) reflect self-discipline and industry, they also stem from the fact that Jewish middle-class families are statistically more likely to have few children or even remain childless, while homosexuals (though more of them have children than would be expected) have considerably fewer than the average. Reduction of investment in the nourishment and education of offspring yields an economic dividend that can be applied to other purposes.

The year 1895 saw the dramatic staging of what amounted to show trials, the Oscar **Wilde** prosecutions in England and the Alfred Dreyfus case in France. These highly publicized events revealed vast reservoirs of antihomosexual feeling and anti-Semitism respectively. They also enhanced the political identity and solidarity of both groups, leading to the formation of the first homosexual rights organization in Berlin, Germany, in 1897 (the **Scientific-Humanitarian Committee**), and the convening of the First Zionist Congress in Basel, Switzerland, in the same year. In the Nazi **holocaust**, homosexuals (the pink-triangle men) were sent to concentration camps along with Jews and gypsies.

Individual Jews have been in the forefront of the modern study of sex and in the campaign for more enlightened attitudes toward it, a prominence that has served as an additional rationalization for antisemitism: Arnold **Aletrino**, Iwan **Bloch**, Sigmund **Freud**, Norman Haire, Kurt **Hiller**, Magnus **Hirschfeld**, Albert **Moll**, and Marc-André Raffalovich. As victims of prejudice, enlightened Jews have shown special sensitivity to the disadvantages of other minorities. To be sure, there are antigay Jews, who can find no persuasive analogy between the situation of the two groups, as well as anti-Semitic homosexuals, some of whom claim to ground their animosity in the antihomosexual passages of the **Old Testament**. There are also anti-Semites who vehemently defend the Biblical injunctions against homosexual behavior while denouncing all Jewish influence on modern civilization as the subversive activity of a racially alien segment of the population. This was paradoxically enough the mentality of the Nazi leaders who called for increased repression of homosexuals and even a gay holocaust.

As measured by public opinion polls, recent decades have shown a significant lessening of stereotypical prejudices directed against both Jews and homosexuals. Yet both have reason for concern about countervailing trends which suggest that bigotry is on the rise again. Unpredictable factors may lie at the root of such disconcerting reversals. In the case of the Jews it appears to be the continuing Arab–Israeli dispute and the Palestinian independence struggle that are the major sources of tensions. For homosexuals the **AIDS** crisis, especially in the sensationalized and selective presentation offered by the media, has negatively impacted progress toward full toleration. Some observers, such as the American playwrights William Hoffman and Larry Kramer, have seen an analogy between the fate of homosexuals in the AIDS crisis and the fate of the Jews in Hitler's holocaust. The analogy is imperfect, however, since the National Socialist persecution was the malevolent action of an ideology that singled out whole ethnic communities for extermination, while AIDS is a viral disease that has disproportionately affected several human groups, but (on present evidence) has not been engineered by a human agency expressly to destroy them. Nonetheless, there may well be similarities in the effects on the victims, and these parallels in the fate of otherwise dissimilar stigmatized groups merit insightful and sympathetic study.

BIBLIOGRAPHY. Barry Adam, *The Survival of Domination: Inferiorization and Everyday Life*, New York: Elsevier, 1978.

Ward Houser

APOLOGETIC, HOMOSEXUAL

For some centuries Christians have engaged in a systematic effort to analyze and defend their faith to nonbelievers, such defenses being termed apologias. An analogous tendency has surfaced among some homosexual and lesbian scholars. Conceived as an effort to cleanse the Augean stable of the accumulated detritus of homophobic **myths and fabrications**, the procedure is understandable and laudable. Sometimes, however, the undertaking may cross over into apologetic in the bad sense, distorting or glossing over the truth in an effort to create a favorable image for the cause. One instance is the claim made by modern defenders of **pederasty** that such relationships, in keeping with their purported Greek model, are always noble and character-building. Some undoubtedly are, but others are surely less so. Conversely, some students of ancient Greece, Islam, and other societies where pederasty has been the norm, claim to find only their own preferred **androphilia** there.

Another gambit is the posthumous "naturalization" of individuals such as Pontius Pilate or George Washington as gay. Of course, in many instances it is necessary first to raise the question of the homosexuality of a past figure so that the evidence may be weighed; where it is lacking, however, stubbornness should yield to agnosticism.

These matters raise broader issues of method. A dispute has long raged between those who uphold the ideal that scholarship must strive to be objective and value neutral and their opponents (many, but not all on the political left), who believe that scholarly work is always conducted in the service of a political or ideological position. The former view, that of classical European rationalism and natural science, has been eloquently defended by the great sociologist Max Weber, who held that while the choice of a research problem is shaped by interests, the conduct of the investigation itself can and must be objective. Conversely, Martin Heidegger and Jean-Paul **Sartre** insisted that the intellectual must become committed or engaged in a cause. (They differed sharply on what that cause should be, Heidegger flirting—for a time at least—with Nazism, and Sartre involving himself with a variety of left-wing tendencies from Castroism to Maoism.) Another version of this demand for commitment appeared among the New Left thinkers of the 1960s who stipulated that only "emancipatory" scholarship should be supported, while Herbert Marcuse went so far as to authorize in theory forceable suppression of "harmful" (i.e., nonprogressive) enquiry (in his 1967 essay "Repressive Tolerance").

Applied to history, selective research of the kind that has been discussed is sometimes called "advocacy scholarship." Many practitioners in this mode display what may be called a "shopper's approach" to their material. That is, they sift through the mass of data available to them, extracting only the items that are attractive and leaving the rest behind. This procedure yields a highly selective view of the past, but one which the amateur is often unable to distinguish from genuine work informed by integral understanding and judgment. In extreme cases, this selective approach, fueled by the tyro's enthusiasm and unchecked by training in method, may even resemble the industry of the magpie: the "researcher" collects attractive baubles and heaps them together, little knowing that his treasures are mostly of trifling value. Regrettably, some writings publicized as restorations of our "hidden heritage" are of this sort.

Concededly, these methodological shortcomings are part of the growing pains of research in a sphere that, until recent decades, had been largely taboo. Also, because of the lack of funding and university chairs, much of the work on the history of homosexuality and lesbianism has of necessity been conducted by private scholars, who have volunteered their own time and money, often having to content themselves with the meagerest recognition for their toil. Untrained in the strict canons of evidence and argument, their errors are often innocent ones. Having suffered from the profusion of negative stereotypes that our culture offers, it is perhaps understandable that they should attempt to redress the balance by advancing a positive, apologetic view of homosexuality. Nonetheless, the increasing depth and breadth of research should enable homosexual and lesbian scholarship to ascend to a higher plane in which these failings are obsolete. Human history is one seamless fabric, and the credibility of the growing and impressive body of research on homosexuality vitally depends on its universality.

See also **Famous Homosexuals, Lists of; Gay Studies**.

Wayne R. Dynes

AQUINAS, THOMAS, SAINT (1225–1274)

Italian theologian and philosopher, the most important exponent of the medieval system of thought known as Scholasticism. Born to a noble family in southern Italy and cousin of the Holy Roman Emperor **Frederick** II, he studied at St. Benedict's monastery of Monte Cassino and at the University of Naples, and as a young man entered the Dominican order. Trying to dissuade him from joining that new and radical order of friars, his brothers supposedly brought a prostitute to his room to tempt him, but he drove her out with a burning brand he took from the hearth. At twenty, having graduated from Naples he traveled to Paris and later to Cologne to study under Albertus Magnus, who set him on the path of fusing Aristotle with Christian thought, an innovatory combination which became his life's work. Aquinas was a copious writer whose works in their modern edition fill scores of folio volumes, and who sought to combine encyclopedic breadth with precision and systematic presentation. He called for the capital punishment of heretics, witches, and sodomites.

In his sexual views he adhered to the restrictivist approach laid down by the **Patristic** writers, interweaving, however, some elements taken from his extensive study of **Aristotle**. A sense of his approach emerges from his classification of "unnatural vice." After first condemning masturbation, he distinguishes three types of improper sexual contact: with the wrong species (bestiality), with the wrong gender (homosexuality and lesbianism), and with the wrong organ (oral and anal sex) (*Summa Theologiae*, II–II 154, 11). This threefold schema became normative for Christian thought.

In another passage (I–II 31, 7), Aquinas asserts that some pleasures are unnatural to man but become connatural for physical or psychological reasons or because of habit, and among these is intercourse with males or with brute animals. This text, however, was adapted from Aristotle's *Nicomachean Ethics* (1148b), in which the Master held that sexual intercourse with males could be pleasurable owing to the innate constitution (in the medieval Latin translation *natura*) of the individual. Aquinas reiterated this crucial point in his own commentary, the *Sententia Libri Ethicorum* (VII, 5), but suppressed it in the *Summa*. By this act of intellectual dishonesty, Aquinas made true, innate homosexuality an "insoluble problem" for Christian theologians who are obliged to maintain that erotic attraction to one's own sex is acquired and therefore abnormal and pathological.

Some modern scholars have deplored the views of Aquinas and his contemporaries as representing a turn toward a negative view of sexual nonconformity in contrast to the ostensibly more tolerant attitude that had preceded him—though they must grant that he was less hostile than Peter **Damian**. In this realm, however, Aquinas is a codifier, innovative only in his characteristically systematic approach, and not in any substantive enhancement of the negative content, which represented a fusion of the prohibitions of the Mosaic Law with an anti-homosexual tradition in the Hellenic world that went as far back as **Plato**. Even before Christianity, the synthesis of the two traditions had already been realized by **Philo** Judaeus, continued by **Clement** of Alexandria and John **Chrysostom**, and reformulated for the Latin West by St. **Augustine** in the early fifth century. What Aquinas did was to give the condemnation a proper scholastic context, thus assuring its normative status for the moral theology and the **Canon Law** of the Roman Catholic Church to this day and making the "**sodomy** delusion" a hallmark of Western civilization. His theologically and philosophically reasoned stance precludes acceptance of the premises of the gay liberation movement.

The Council of Trent recognized Thomas as a "doctor of the Church." Regrouping after the assault of the French Revolution, the Catholic restoration put great emphasis on the work of Aquinas, which had been neglected since the seventeenth century. In 1879 Leo XIII went so far as to declare Neo-Thomism the official philosophy of the Roman Catholic church. In recent decades this hegemony has ebbed in Catholic universities and seminaries, which are now in touch with a broader range of currents of thought. Official Thomism still has its survivals here and there, as seen, for example, in elements of the thinking of the radical feminist (and ex-Catholic) Mary Daly. Thomism always had a strong element of social moralism, so that it is not surprising to find traces of its influence in the liberation theology of the Third World.

Warren Johansson

ARCADIA

Arcadia is a predominantly rural area of ancient Greece that has become a byword for an idealized pastoral existence. In an important study, Byrne R. S. Fone has shown that a number of homosexual writers—from **Vergil** through Richard **Barnfield**, Walt **Whitman** and the English Uranians to Thomas **Mann** and E. M. **Forster**—drew upon the image of Arcadia to evoke "that secret Eden" that offers solace "because of its isolation from the troubled world and its safety from the arrogant

demands of those who would deny freedom, curtail human action, and destroy innocence and love." In the vision of these writers Arcadia is a sylvan retreat where it is safe to live in accord with one's feelings, while at the same time providing the author with a device to present a quasi-allegorical image of homosexual happiness during times in which such sentiments could not be openly avowed. It could serve as a vehicle for the implication that "homosexuality is superior to heterosexuality and is a divinely sanctioned means to an understanding of the good and the beautiful." In such an idyllic setting the quest for the Ideal Friend could find its term and consecration.

The Latin tag "Et in Arcadia ego" has often been translated (according to some wrongly) as "I too was in Arcadia," and thus held to encapsulate the yearning for a Golden Age. Denis Diderot, for example, rendered it "Je vivais aussi dans la délicieuse Arcadie" ["I too lived in delightful Arcady."]. In the broader perspective this tradition fits within the overall framework of the pastoral tradition stemming from **Theocritus**, the great poet of **Alexandria**.

The concept was also significant in the context of the French homosexual **movement**. With his classical training, the novelist Roger Peyrefitte suggested the name "Arcadie" for what was to become the major French homosexual organization after World War II. In fact the group began by putting out a magazine, itself called *Arcadie* (from January 1954), on the model of the Swiss *Der Kreis*. The membership society followed in 1957. André Baudry, the director dissolved the organization in 1982, when the monthly, which had been noted for the quality of its scholarly articles, also ceased.

The Arcadie group was a typical product of the "homophile" phase of the renascent gay movement as it rose from the ashes of war and the desolation of Nazi occupation. Members of Arcadie, and by extension sympathizers with its relatively conservative goals, were termed Arcadiens. It has been claimed that a high proportion of the actual membership consisted of priests and ex-priests.

BIBLIOGRAPHY. André Baudry, et al., *Le regard des autres*, Paris: Arcadie, 1979 (Actes du Congrès international); Byrne R. S. Fone, "This Other Eden: Arcadia and the Homosexual Imagination," *Journal of Homosexuality*, (1983), 13–34.

Wayne R. Dynes

ARCHIVES
See **Libraries and Archives.**

ARETINO, PIETRO (1492–1556)

Italian writer. Known as the "scourge of princes," Aretino occupies a place all his own in Italian literature, both for his erotic writings (which were for centuries considered among the most "outrageous") and for his extraordinary rapport with the powerful. He made use of his journalistic flair to sell his benevolence in exchange for monetary gifts. Of humble origins (though not bereft of education), he in fact succeeded in becoming rich and famous thanks to his literary works which oscillated between adulation of notables and libel. Among his best known works—apart from such erotic classics as the *Sei giornate* (Dialogues of the Courtesans) and the *Sonetti lussuriosi*—are comedies and six volumes of *Letters* addressed to major figures of the period.

Despite the grave charges leveled by Niccolò Franco (1515–1570)—who in his *Priapea* and *Rime contro Pietro Aretino* (1541) treats him simply as a prostitute—and by the libelous *Vita di Pietro Aretino* of 1537, there is no doubt that Aretino's erotic interest was gallantly directed toward women. Domenico Fusco, who analyzed the accusations of homosexuality directed against the writer by his contemporaries, concluded that they amounted to unfounded gossip of a type common at the time.

Nonetheless, Aretino seems to have made some forays into the realm of homosexuality. Alessandro Luzio has published two curious letters of Federico Gonzaga (of February 1528) who writes from Mantua to Aretino of having failed to convince a certain Roberto "son of Bianchino" to accept the advances of his correspondent.

In "L'Aretino e il Franco" (*Giornale storico della letteratura italiana*, 29 [1897], 252) Luzio published a 1524 letter to Giovanni de' Medici, in which Aretino playfully declared that he had decided to give up sodomy, because the ardent love he was experiencing for a lady had made him change his tastes.

As these instances show, Aretino's attitude toward homosexuality was one of amused complacency, similar to that of many contemporaries. This fact explains the presence in his work of many homosexual allusions and double entendres.

The work of Aretino in which homosexuality is most prominent is the comedy *Il marescalco* (1533). The protagonist, the duke of Mantua's farrier, dislikes women. To tease him the duke decides to force him to take a wife, which very much upsets the poor fellow. At the marriage, however, he learns that his "bride" is a beardless page dressed in women's attire, and he cannot contain his happiness. Nowhere in the play is the farrier's homosexuality openly stated, but the double entendres and various indirect references aptly serve to convey that the reason why he hates women is that he prefers boys.

The work entitled *La puttana errante* (1531), long attributed to Aretino, depicts both male and female homosexual conduct, but it is now attributed to Lorenzo Veniero.

BIBLIOGRAPHY. Domenico Fusco, *L'Aretino sconosciuto ed apocrifo*, Turin: Berruto, 1953; Alessandro Luzio, *Pietro Aretino nei primi suoi anni a Venezia e alla Corte dei Gonzaga*, Turin: Loescher, 1888.

Giovanni Dall'Orto

ARISTOCRATIC VICE, HOMOSEXUALITY AS

Little meaningful study has been accomplished on **class** differences in the incidence of homosexual behavior. The findings of the first **Kinsey** Report (1948), which appeared to show greater prevalence of homosexuality among the less educated, must be disregarded in as much as this cohort in the Kinsey survey had a disproportionate number of prisoners.

If data are lacking, stereotypes have flourished—in particular the notion that homosexual behavior is more prevalent among the upper classes. This perception accords with the broader working-class belief that the upper classes are over-educated, effete, and effeminate.

The notion of homosexuality as a distinctively aristocratic vice has a considerable history. In the seventeenth century Sir Edward Coke attributed the origin of sodomy to "pride, excess of diet, idleness and contempt of the poor." The noted English jurist was in fact offering a variation on the prophet Ezekiel (16:49). This accusation reflects the perennial truism that wealth, idleness, and lust tend to go together—a cluster summed up in the Latin term *luxuria*. Sometimes the view is expressed that the confirmed debauchee, having run through virtually the whole gamut of sexual sins, turns to sodomy as a last resort to revive his jaded appetite.

A forerunner of this thought complex appears in the comedies of **Aristophanes** (ca. 450–385 B.C.), who satirized the pederastic foibles of Athenian politicians and dandies. In the first century of our era, the Jewish writer **Philo** of Alexandria regarded **Sodom** as the archetype of the link between homosexuality and luxury: "The inhabitants owed this extreme licence to the never-failing lavishness of their sources of wealth. . . . Incapable of bearing such satiery, plunging like cattle, they threw off from their necks the law of nature and applied themselves to deep drinking of strong liquor and dainty feeding and forbidden forms of intercourse."

The scholastic theologian Albertus Magnus (d. 1280) held that the vice of sodomy was "more common in persons of high station than in humble persons." This impression reflects in part the greater visibility of the doings of the privileged, and also the fact that, through their status or influence, the nobility could frequently escape with a reprimand for the commission of crimes which were subject to capital punishment when committed by commoners. This aspect of class justice has fueled social envy, leading to the demand on the part of the straitlaced middle class that the aristocracy be disciplined and required, for its part, to adhere to the narrow canons of petty bourgeois morality.

In **England** the claim that homosexuality was an aristocratic weakness fell together with the prejudice that it was ultimately of foreign derivation; the fondness of the noble lords for the Grand Tour of the continent brought them into contact with the vice which they then conveyed to England, where it was supposedly not native. A curious episode of this phase of British social history was the Macaroni Club, an association of cosmopolites formed in London about 1760 to banquet on that then-rare food. Their foppish, extravagant dress was regarded as bordering on transvestism. This fashion explains an otherwise mysterious allusion in an American song of the period: "Yankee Doodle came to town/upon a little pony;/ he stuck a feather in his hat/and called it macaroni" (1767). The colonial hero's attempt to play the exquisite exposed him to the danger of ridicule as a milktoast—or worse.

The stereotype of aristocratic vice has a sequel in the early twentieth-century Marxist notion that the purported increase of homosexuality in modern industrial states stems from the decadence of capitalism; in this view the workers fortunately remain psychologically healthy and thus untainted by the debilitating proclivity. In the Krupp and von Moltke-

Eulenburg scandals in Germany in 1903–08, journalists of the socialist press did their best to inflame their readership against the unnatural vices of the aristocracy, which were bringing the nation to the brink of ruin.

During the late nineteenth century, homosexual vanguard writers such as Edward **Carpenter** and John Addington **Symonds** advanced an opposing thesis. They held that it was precisely the fact that homosexual contacts tended to link the rich and the poor, the educated and the uneducated, that made them suited to advancing democracy and the social integration of previously antagonistic classes. Class and homosexuality are sensitive issues for modern society, and the zone of their intersection is fraught with emotion.

See also **Working Class, Eroticization of.**

Wayne R. Dynes

ARISTOPHANES (CA. 450–CA. 385 B.C.)

The greatest of the comic playwrights of ancient Athens. Aristophanes composed a series of plays performed between 427 and 388 B.C. The texts of eleven comedies have survived, together with fragments from others. Little is known of his life other than what can be learned from the plays, which reveal a much-read and educated personality, fond of nature and of country life, and conservative by inclination.

His plays satirize contemporary Athenian society, with a verbal dexterity and wordplay that are difficult to convey in translation. The object of his wit is often the real or alleged **effeminacy**, passive homosexuality, or prostitution of the male characters—failings if not vices in the eyes of his fellow Athenians—in which the resources of Attic colloquial speech are exploited to the full. Aristophanes gives effeminate men feminine names, Sostrate instead of Sostratos, Cleonyme instead of Cleonymos (*Clouds*, 678, 680), or uses nicknames that allude to their "swishy" gestures and manner of walking, and especially the feminine dress which they affected. Similarly reproached are boys who sell their bodies for gifts or payment. In the *Plutus*, 153, a character declares: "And they say that the boys do this very thing, not for their lovers, but for the sake of money. Not the better types, but the catamites, since the better types do not ask for money."

The positive side of Greek pederasty is mentioned only in passing: the praise of boyish beauty, the wall inscriptions with the boy's name and the word *kalos*, "handsome," and the memory of the heroism of the past inspired by male comradeship and fidelity. The world of lust and venality which the comedians depict is the baser side of Greek pederasty, not the nobler, though it is the aristocrat who is depicted as the boy-lover par excellence. The allusions and innuendoes in regard to the institution are legion. An element of jealousy is present, provoked by the preference which a boy would naturally show to a nobleman over a middle-class burgher, but the significant phenomenon is the role which pederasty played in the life of the upper class in the Golden Age of Athens. Nowhere do the plays suggest that an Athenian gentleman would find intercourse with a handsome boy anything but agreeable, and even the opportunity to scrutinize boyish beauty is a source of delight (*Wasps*, 568).

The ideal cherished by the conservative Aristophanes is the smooth-skinned, muscular, shy, serious boy of the past, not the avaricious hustler or effeminate youth of the present. There is a longing for values that have been lost or submerged in the Athens of the playwright's own day. So while humor is an essential component of the treatment of homosexuality in Aristophanes, it serves to set in relief the idealized *paiderasteia* that served an educational function in Greek civilization; never does Aristophanes express indignation or disgust at the institution, he rather criticizes the debased form to which (in his view) it had sunk in his day. It is as satire of the lower and ignobler manifestations of boy-love that the humorous and sarcastic passages in his plays are to be interpreted, not as condemnation in the vein that Christianity was to adopt in later centuries.

BIBLIOGRAPHY. K. J. Dover, *Aristophanic Comedy*, London: B. T. Batsford, 1972; Hans Licht, *Sexual Life in Ancient Greece*, London: Routledge and Kegan Paul, 1932.

Warren Johansson

ARISTOTLE (384–322 B.C.)

Major ancient Greek philosopher. Aristotle's thinking was formed at the Academy in Athens, where in 366–347 he studied under **Plato**. Aristotle tutored the bisexual Alexander the Great in Macedonia (343–336), and then returned to Athens, where he opened a school. His habit of lecturing in the covered walking place (*peripatos*) of the Lyceum gave his school the name of Peripatetic. As a thinker Aristotle is outstanding for the breadth of his interests, which encompassed the entire panorama of the ancient sciences, and for his efforts to make sense of the world through applying an organic and developmental approach. In this way he departed from the essentialist, deductive emphasis of Plato. Unfortunately, Aristotle's polished essays, which were noted for their style, are lost, and the massive corpus of surviving works derives largely from lecture notes. In these the wording of the Greek presents many uncertainties: hence the differences in the various translations, which in sexual matters are often marred by euphemistic evasion or anachronistic modernization. Dubious points can only be settled by wrestling with the Greek.

Although Aristotle is known to have had several male lovers, in his writings he tended to follow Plato's lead in favoring restraints on overt expression of homoerotic feelings. He differs, however, from Plato's ethical and idealizing approach to male same-sex love by his stress on biological factors. In a brief, but important treatment in the Nicomachean Ethics (7:5) he was the first to distinguish clearly between innate and acquired homosexuality. This dichotomy corresponds to a standard Greek distinction between processes which are determined by nature (*physis*) and those which are conditioned by culture or custom (*nomos*). The approach set forth in this text was to be echoed a millennium and a half later in the Christian Scholastic treatments of Albertus Magnus and Thomas **Aquinas** (*Summa Theologiae*, Ia IIa, 31:7). In The History of Animals (9:8), Aristotle anticipates modern ethology by showing that homosexual behavior among birds is linked to patterns of domination and submission. In various passages he speaks of homosexual relations among noted Athenian men and boys as a matter of course. His treatment of **friendship** (Nicomachean Ethics, books 8 and 9) emphasizes its mutual character, based on the equality of the parties, which requires time for full consolidation. He takes it as given that true friendship can occur only between two free males of equal status, excluding slaves and women. Aristotle's ideas on friendship were to be echoed by **Cicero**, Erasmus, Michel de **Montaigne**, and Sir Francis **Bacon**.

The *Problems* (4:26), a work attributed to Aristotle but probably compiled by a follower, attributes desire for anal intercourse in men to the accumulation of semen in the fundament. This notion derives from the common Greek medical view that semen is produced in the region of the brain and then transferred by a series of conduits to the lower body.

In England and America a spurious compilation of sexual and generative knowledge, *Aristotle's Masterpiece*, enjoyed a long run of popularity. Compiled from a variety of sources, including the Hippocratic and Galenic medical traditions, the medieval writings of Albertus Magnus, and folklore of all kinds, this farrago was apparently first published in

English in 1684. A predecessor of later sex manuals, the book contains such lore as the determination of the size of the penis from that of the nose.

BIBLIOGRAPHY. William Keith Chambers Guthrie, *Aristotle: An Encounter*, Cambridge: Cambridge University Press, 1981 (A History of Greek Philosophy, 6).

Wayne R. Dynes

ARMY
See **Military**.

ART, VISUAL

Homosexuality intersects with the visual arts of painting, sculpture, and **photography** in two ways: through subject matter (iconography) and through the personal homosexuality or bisexuality of artists.

Despite the fact that until recently most of the relevant images were inaccessible—relegated to museum basements or hidden in private collections—it is no secret that the world's heritage of the fine arts includes much homoerotic material. To be sure, the project of a comprehensive history of "gay art" seems problematic. In some areas where there is reason to believe that the material is abundant—as in China and the Islamic countries—the essential studies and publications needed to form the basis for a synthesis have not been produced. More fundamentally, it is hard to extract a common denominator from the varied material itself, which ranges from explicit scenes of copulation, through simple portraits of figures known to be homosexual, to homophobic depictions of the persecution of homosexuals. Large gaps exist. Lamentably, through many centuries of Christian domination in Europe, the ban on the making of such works was effective. Then there has been vandalism. In the New World much was destroyed by the Spanish conquistadores and the fanatical churchmen who accompanied them. As recently as the early twentieth century some Moche pieces from pre-Columbian Peru showing same-sex acts were destroyed by their finders as "insults to national honor." The situation for lesbian art is even more difficult. Because until recent times works of art have generally been commissioned by men for their own purposes, sympathetic depictions of lesbian love are sparse. Before the sixteenth century, we find only representations of friendship between women; then in the Venetian school there begins an imagery of lesbian dalliance—but only for male entertainment. Only in recent decades has there been a substantial production of lesbian art by lesbians and for lesbians. This raises the final problem: how are we to consider the work of an artist known to be homosexual or bisexual, but whose subject matter—through lack of commissions or reticence—does not extend to his or her own sexuality?

Classical Antiquity. A comparison of Greek homoerotic literature and art is instructive. Since the time of their composition, Greek texts of male–male love have always been known to those who cared to seek them out, and they provided continuity through the whole subsequent literary development. Parallel works in the visual arts passed unrecognized, languished in museum storerooms, or remained hidden in the ground to be discovered only through recent excavations. Not being known to homosexual artists of later times, they could not form the signposts of a recognized perennial tradition. And the lack of a continuous tradition is the main reason why one cannot rightfully speak of a "history of gay art."

Still ancient **Greece** supplies a considerable amount of material. The explanation for this flowering lies in the fact, that unlike its predecessors in the ancient Near East, Greece was a secular society in which the priestly caste was relatively unimportant. Even in statues dedicated in temples and placed on tombs the wishes of the patron are paramount. In antiquity the Greeks were noted for their national peculiarity of exercising in the nude. Out of this custom grew the monumental **nude** statue, a genre that Greece bequeathed to the world. The tradition began a little before 600 B.C. with the sequence of nude youths known as *kouroi*. (Monumental female nudes did not appear until ca. 350 B.C.) Although archeologists have maintained a deafening silence on the matter, it seems clear that the radiance of these figures can only be explained in the light of the Greek homoerotic appreciation of the male form. Whatever else they may have been, the *kouroi* were the finest pinups ever created. Studying them in chronological order, one can observe an evolution of the ideal somatic type, from the sturdy, almost burly archaic figures, through the classical "swimmer's body" ones, to a kind of graceful dancer type in the fourth century B.C. A special variation on the kouros is the pair of figures dedicated in Athens in 477 B.C. to the memory of the homosexual lovers, the tyrant-slayers Harmodius and Aristogiton.

The recovery of masses of decorated **vases** in modern times has revealed a particularly forthright category of Greek art: the scenes of homoerotic courtship. In these depictions, which begin about 570 B.C., an older bearded man approaches a youth, clearly indicating his intent by placing one hand in entreaty against the boy's chin while the other touches his genitals. Often these scenes of courtship are accompanied by gifts of hares, cocks, and other animals to help persuade the boy. In contrast to to the occasional depictions surviving from earlier civilizations, these scenes are not merely renderings of same-sex acts or lifeways, but vivid emblems of homoerotic *desire*. Little of the monumental painting for which the Greeks were famous has survived. A spectacular exception is the fifth-century Tomb of the Diver at Paestum in southern Italy, which preserves a banquet scene of two male lovers embracing.

As Greek literature attests, the gods had their own homoerotic loves. Some vases and other works show them in pursuit of their beloveds. A special place belongs to the depictions of Zeus and **Ganymede**, as represented for example by a monumental terracotta of ca. 460 B.C. from Olympia. An essential part of the legacy of Greece is **mythology**, and we find that over the centuries artists did dare to evoke again and again the Greek homoerotic figures of Ganymede and Hyacinth, Ampelos and **Orpheus**.

The Romans did not share the Greek fondness for nude exercise and their attitude toward homosexual behavior was more ambiguous. Perhaps it is not surprising that they favored the old religious subject of the **hermaphrodite**, the doublesexed being, but now reduced largely to a subject of titillation. They also were capable of depicting scenes of peeping toms that recall the atmosphere of **Petronius's** *Satyricon*. Standing far above the general Roman contribution to the subject are the idealized portraits of **Antinous** commissioned by the emperor **Hadrian** after his Bithynian favorite drowned in the Nile in A.D. 130. In his honor the emperor founded the Egyptian city of Antinoopolis; excavations have revealed something of its magnificence.

After the reign of Hadrian, who died in 138, the great age of ancient homoerotic art was over. Consequently, the adoption of Christianity cannot be said to have killed off a vibrant tradition, but it certainly did not encourage its revival. Medieval Christian art did have nudes and scenes of classical mythology, but significantly no homoerotic ones. Liberal toward some aspects of classical culture, for centuries Christianity stifled the reemergence of positive homoerotic art. It also fostered the creation of antihomoerotic iconography, as in the scenes of the burning of the city of Sodom found at Monreale, Canterbury, and elsewhere.

The Renaissance Tradition. When homosexuality in art again became significant, as it did under the humanistic auspices of fifteenth-century **Florence**, it is through our knowledge of the biographies of the artists, rather than from their subject matter. **Botticelli, Donatello, Michelangelo**, and **Sodoma** are all known to have been predominantly homosexual in orientation, but with rare exceptions (as Donatello's bronze David and Michelangelo's drawings for Tommaso de' Cavalieri) their works give little hint of it. Still the biographical information we have is fascinating for the reconstruction of the connection between sexuality and the creative process. Since **Freud**'s essay of 1910 the enigmatic figure of **Leonardo** has offered a special appeal. A less well known Florentine figure, Jacopo Pontormo, left behind a diary which chronicled not only his troubled mental state, but also (laconically) his relations with boys. The onset of the Counter-Reformation in the later sixteenth century made life harder for Italian homoerotic artists, though the stormy career of the bisexual Michelangelo Merisi da **Caravaggio** (1571–1610) is well documented. From Flanders comes the tragic case of the Baroque sculptor Jérôme Duquesnoy, who was caught with two boys and executed in 1654.

During the Renaissance and Baroque periods the status of artists rose, and they became proud of their creativity. The image of the artist "born under Saturn" flourished, that is to say painters and sculptors were expected to be moody, melancholy, and withdrawn, but not effeminate. Homosexual artists of this time fulfilled the expectations of the stereotype. As the public's concept changed, however, the type went out of production so to speak. When in later times homosexual artists became visible they were measured according to different standards. Because of such shifts one cannot speak of any single dominant character type of the "gay artist" any more than purported continuities of style and subject matter permit the recovery of a single aesthetic of "gay art."

It is not surprising that the rococo art of the eighteenth century, so concerned with heterosexual dalliance, should have little to show that is relevant. Yet with the rise of Neoclassicism toward the end of the century this situation changed. For one thing the theorist and prophet of the new movement J. J. **Winckelmann** (1717–1768) was a homosexual bachelor whose rhapsodic descriptions of male nudes had an impact on countless artists. Regardless of the orientation of their creators, the great male nudes of such masters as Jacques-Louis David (1748–1825) and Bertell Thorwaldsen (1768–1848) are inseparable from Winckelmann's evocations. And other artists, including Jean Broc, Claude-Marie Dubufe, and Benjamin West, boldly revived the Greek themes of the homoerotic loves of the gods.

Academics and Moderns. French nineteenth-century art witnessed a significant production of lesbian scenes by heterosexual artists, including such masters as Gustave Courbet. One major artist who was lesbian, Rosa **Bonheur** (1822–1899), did not leave behind works directly related to her orientation. The same is true of the American sculptor Harriet Hosmer (1830–1908). In a number of male artists—Washington **Allston**, Thomas Couture, Thomas Eakins, Aleksandr Ivanov, Frederick Lord Leighton, John Singer Sargent, and Henry Scott Tuke—the work and other evidence points to a homosexual or bisexual orientation, but full confirmation tends to be elusive. A special place in this group belongs to the lonely German idealist, Hans von **Marées** (1837–1887), who produced evocative male nudes in an Arcadian setting. The fate of the English painter Simeon Solomon (1840–1905), disgraced after a wild party in 1873, must have given many pause. Symbolists such as Jean Delville and Gustave Moreau flirted with homoerotic subjects which were accepted as contributions to the "decadent repertoire." A similar vein of poetry runs through the practitioners of a new technique, that of photography: the German Wilhelm von **Gloeden** (1856–1931) specialized in langorous Sicilian youths while Fred Holland **Day** (1864–1933) created evocative tableaux vivants of New Testament and other exotic subjects. By the turn of the century magazines began to appear in Germany presenting, by means of photographic reproduction, works appealing exclusively to male homosexual taste; lesbian magazines were only to emerge after World War I. Exceptionally, the American George Platt **Lynes** (1907–1955) pursued a career in both mainstream and gay media (the latter in his extensive work for the Swiss magazine, *Der Kreis*).

A chief characteristic of the avant-garde art of the twentieth century is international exchange. Even when they stayed at home, artists sought to free themselves from parochial restrictions. When traveling, they tended to stop in the **Bohemian** quarters of large cities, where sexual freedom was long the rule. For the first forty years of the century, Paris was the great magnet. In the city's international lesbian colony the most formidable figure was the American experimental writer Gertrude **Stein**. Through her remarkable art collection, and her influence on her lover the major collector Etta Cone and others, Stein was able to play a formative role in the reception of advanced modernist art in English-speaking countries. Unfortunately, the only homosexual artist she promoted was the mediocre Englishman Sir Francis Rose. Paris was also the home of the American painter Romaine **Brooks** (1874–1970), whose often forceful works are executed in a somewhat old-fashioned style, recalling that of James McNeil Whistler. Also dwelling mainly in Paris, the Polish-born heterosexual Tamara de Lempicka (1898–1980), whose work became synonymous with art deco, produced lush images of women interacting that played, teasingly but sometimes powerfully, on the city's image as a modern Lesbos. Her German contemporary Jeanne Mammen (1890–1976) created a more candid and direct iconography of the lesbian cabaret culture in her country, in which she participated. The "Fur-Covered Cup, Saucer, and Spoon" (1936) of Meret Oppenheim, a Swiss woman artist, is a stark proclamation of lesbian (vaginal) symbolism; ironically it has become one of the chief icons of the Surrealist movement, which was generally hostile to homosexuality.

The trajectory of avant-garde art from post-impressionism through fauvism and cubism to non-objectivism and constructivism saw progressive abandonment of representational subject matter. This meant the exclusion of all types of sexual allusion, though these were to make a temporary comeback with the para-Freudian preoccupations of the Surrealism of the 1920s. The enigmatic, germinal figure of Marcel Duchamp (1887–1968) cherished a female persona, "Rrose Sélavy," going so far as to have himself photographed as her in drag. Inasmuch as homosexual attachments are not documented for Duchamp, this experiment in gender malleability and double personality is probably to be attributed to a personal penchant made possible by the freedom of Bohemia.

Two Americans illustrate the possibilities of the gay modern artist. Marsden **Hartley** (1877–1943) resided in Berlin at the start of World War I, where he created emblematic expressionist portraits of his lover Karl von Freyburg, a soldier who was killed in the first days of the war. The work of Charles **Demuth** (1883–1935) is hard to classify, though it has affinities with Georgia O'Keeffe and the precisionism of Charles Sheeler. Demuth did a series of evocations of New York's gay baths, as well as groups of sailors (who were important gay icons in the period). Paul Cadmus (b. 1904) deliberately chose to work in a style derived from the early Italian Renaissance. Frequently a subject of controversy, he exposed a seamy, vulgar side of American sexuality that some would prefer to forget.

Although the Surrealists sought to explore sexuality, the homophobia of their leader André Breton placed a ban on gay subjects—or at least male ones. Two related figures did explore in this realm, however, the writer Jean Cocteau (1889–1963), with his drawings of sailors, and the Argentine-born painter Leonor Fini (b. 1908), with enigmatic scenes of women. The ambitious Russian-born Pavel Tchelitchew (1898–1957), connected with several avant-garde circles in Europe and America, also belongs in this company. The gay art of southern Europe in this period is just beginning to become known, as seen in the Italians Filippo De Pisis (1869–1956) and Gulgielmo Janni (1892–1958), as well as the Spaniard Gregorio Prieto. To this group should be added the Dominican Jaime González Colson, who resided in Europe for many years.

The Contemporary Epoch. The better atmosphere of the period since 1960 has allowed artists of stature to be open about their homosexuality. The Englishman Francis Bacon (b. 1909) has created phantasmagoric scenes of two men wrestling which convey a powerful sense of existential angst. David Hockney (b. 1937), also English-born, but California–Parisian in his choice of domiciles, pleases by his agile recycling of major modernist themes. Finally, Andy **Warhol** (1928–1986) was a kind of presiding spirit over New York's chic art scene. It is possible that the popular acceptance of these artists has been achieved at the cost of pigeonholing them in steretypical categories that the straight public can assimilate: Bacon is the unhappy neurotic, Hockney the stylish, facile designer, and Warhol the arch-priest of **camp**. The restricted role categories permitted by our art world contrast with the more generous possibilities vouchsafed to artists in the Renaissance, however difficult that era may have been in other ways.

Other openly gay and lesbian artists have been less successful at securing fame, though a monographic series published by Gay Men's Press serves to make the work of some of them widely available. The somber works of the late Mario Dubsky (1939–1985) are somewhat in the Bacon mold. Others, such as the Chilean Juan Davila, Philip Core, and the London couple known as Gilbert and George, explore the byways of camp. A gentle and romantic vision is projected by the Englishman David Hutter. The major burst of neo-Expressionism that appeared in Berlin during the 1970s saw the emergence of a number of artists, including Rainer Fetting and Salome, who treat gay subject matter in a frank, often ironic way.

Lesbian art parallels the great upsurge of women's art in our time, as exemplified by the collective work "The Dinner Table" coordinated by Judy Chicago. The Scottish-born June Redfern fuses ancient myths from the goddess sphere with modern imagery. The American Harmony Hammond, who is also active as a critic, has worked in several late modern and postmodern styles. The new interest in women's art has also helped to revive painters of the recent past, such as the bisexual Mexican Frida Kahlo.

In male photography the "old master" Bruce Weber's achievement was commemorated at a retrospective at the Whitney Biennial in 1987. The photographs of Duane Michals are poetically yet disturbingly enigmatic, while Tress and Robert Mapplethorpe capture the blunt starkness of the 1970s scene. Lesbian photography has concentrated on portraiture, as seen in the work of JEB (Joan E. Biren), or evocative, nonsexual scenes.

In the late 1970s art entered a phase defined first as "pluralism" and, increasingly, as "postmodernism." It may be doubted that the long-standing premises of the modernist aesthetic—its sense of discontinuity, irony, and high seriousness—have been definitively overcome, but there is no doubt that the boundaries of the acceptable have been broadened. This enlargement creates opportunities for gay and lesbian artists. At the same time, however, the tyranny of the market and of critical stereotypes is as great as ever, so that artists are under great pressure to settle into niches that have been prepared for them. It should be remembered that many painters, sculptors, and photographers whose personal orientation is homosexual are as reluctant to be styled "gay artists" as they are to be called neo-expressionist, neo-mannerist, or some other label.

BIBLIOGRAPHY. Cécile Beurdeley, *L'Amour bleu*, New York: Rizzoli, 1978; Emmanuel Cooper, *The Sexual Perspective: Homosexuality and Art in the Last 100 Years in the West*, London: Routledge & Kegan Paul, 1986; Kenneth J. Dover, *Greek Homosexuality*, Cambridge: Harvard University Press, 1978; James M. Saslow, *Ganymede in the Renaissance: Homosexuality in Art and Society*, New Haven: Yale University Press, 1986; idem, "Homosexuality in Art," *Advocate*, 429 (Sept. 17, 1985), 40–42 (continued in issues 436, 457, 467, and 480).

Wayne R. Dynes

ARTEMIDORUS (LATE SECOND CENTURY OF OUR ERA)

Greek writer. Although Artemidorus resided in Ephesus he is sometimes termed "of Daldis" because the latter was his mother's native city. He traveled widely in the Mediterranean world to collect material for his extant major work *The Interpretation of Dreams*. This book, which incorporates much ancient folklore, influenced Byzantine and Islamic dream books, not to mention the magnum opus of Sigmund **Freud**, *Traumdeutung* (On the Interpretation of Dreams, 1900).

Artemidorus takes a favorable view of homosexuality, which he says is "natural, legal, and customary." Consequently, whenever the dream symbol involves same-sex relations Artemidorus' interpretation presages good events. The only exceptions are symbols pertaining to incestuous relations between father and son and those in which a slave takes an aggressive role in relation to his master. The interest in sexual dreams probably derives from **Egyptian** dynastic dream books, which freely note such incidents.

In his accepting attitude toward homosexual behavior, Artemidorus is fully in accord with popular Greek ethics. Significantly, however, when the body of his teaching passed to Byzantine authors of dream books, they subjected the homosexual material to a Christian filtration process so that it is either omitted altogether, or (in two rare instances where it survives) treated negatively.

BIBLIOGRAPHY. Artemidorus, *The Interpretation of Dreams: Oneirocritica*, translated by Robert J. White, Park Ridge, NJ: Noyes Press, 1975.

ASCETICISM

Sexual asceticism may take the form of total abstinence—lifelong virginity—or it may imply infrequency of sexual congress and abstinence during specified periods. In some individuals sexual asceticism is reinforced by chastisement and mortification of the body through flagellation, fasting, and denial of sleep.

Comparative studies reveal a number of motives for these restrictions. The priestesses in sanctuaries of ancient **Greece** were required to avoid sexual contact with any human being in order faithfully to serve the god whose consort they were. Widespread throughout the Mediterranean world—and elsewhere— was the idea that sexual contact makes one unclean and therefore unworthy of setting foot on holy ground without purification and a specified period of abstinence. Finally, chastity was believed to bring strength to the one who practiced it, and sometimes to others as well. In ancient **Rome** the purity of the Vestal Virgins was thought to safeguard the city from harm.

In later Greek times and under the Roman empire this cluster of beliefs underwent a sharpening, whose effects left a permanent impress on Western civilization. In some **Stoic** thinkers the shift was relatively conservative: a modification of the traditional Greek commendation of temperance in eating, drinking, and sex in the direction of a more active self-denial, which should not be pressed to extremes. Still this change is significant: the older concept had enshrined an even-handed balance between appetite and renunciation—enlightened self-management—while the newer trend tilted toward renunciation. Along these lines, the physician Musonius Rufus discouraged homosexual intercourse because of its "violence," which led to fatigue.

Set apart at first from the Greco-Roman mainstream, a number of religious and philosophical sects arose that regarded the human body as one's enemy, to be mortified and humiliated. The Galli, priests of the Eastern goddess Cybele, could be witnessed ritually castrating themselves. In the Jewish world, the Qumran sect known to us from the Dead Sea Scrolls seems to have insisted on "spiritual eunuchism"—total continence—for the inner core of believers. At the heart of **Christianity** lay a Holy Family that was cordoned off from sex. From the fourth century onwards, Mary was regarded as not simply a virgin at the time of Jesus's birth, but perpetually a virgin. Jesus, though fully capable of sexual relations, never—in the view of the Early Christian Fathers—chose to exercise the option. As for Joseph, if he had once been capable of sexual activity, he was safely beyond it by the time of his marriage. It is not surprising that these exemplary figures were imitated in various ways. Virgins had great prestige in the Early Christian communities, as did married couples who had ceased to have sexual relations. The sect of the Encratites held that semen must be conserved in the body at all costs. (Even such a respected medical authority as Soranos of Ephesus taught that every emission of the male seed was injurious to health.) And the monks of the Egyptian and Syrian deserts not only practiced chastity, but subjected the body to an unremitting regime of mortification. It is against this background that the Early Christian prohibition of homosexuality must be seen. Marriage itself was a lesser

option, justifiable only to provide offspring. Some historians have concluded that the depopulation of the later Roman empire was a direct consequence of countless numbers of individuals declining to participate in the procreation cycle.

Needless to say, in those times and in ensuing centuries the flesh made demands that were not to be denied. But their exercise was henceforth to be accompanied by a gnawing guilt. The eleventh-century papal imposition of celibacy on the priesthood meant that the whole of the clergy, held up as the fullest embodiment of the Christian ideal, was condemned to lifelong abstinence. In every walk of life transgressors of the narrow sexual ethic were exposed to ridicule and punishment. The notion that sexual uncleanness could bring divine retribution on a nation frequently recurs in sermons against homosexuality in the early modern period. At the end of the fifteenth century the appearance of syphilis in Western Europe seemed to set a terrible seal on this complex of fears. The way in which such feelings of guilt could be manipulated is evident in the great **masturbation** scare, which began in the early eighteenth century and reached its zenith in the Victorian period. In fact the horror of self-pollution was but a new avatar of the Early Christian Encratite fear of loss of semen. The commercial mind of the Victorians also linked emission of seed with monetary expenditure; hence sexual mismanagement led to sexual bankruptcy. In Britain and North America the late nineteenth century saw the rise of the Sexual Purity Movement, which effectively propagandized for continence.

In recent decades the importation of elements of Indic religions—Hinduism and **Buddhism**—into Western industrial countries does not seem to have led to any sustained emulation of the ascetic traditions cherished by those faiths in their homelands. A more powerful persuader in the direction of sexual continence has been the **AIDS** crisis, a factor that has served to enhance (and probably exaggerate) an in-

cipient reaction to the emancipated sixties and seventies.

See also **Celibacy.**

BIBLIOGRAPHY. Peter Brown, *The
Body and Society: Men, Women, and
Sexual Renunciation in Early Christian-
ity*, Berkeley: University of California
Press, 1988; Eugen Fehrle, *Die kultische
Keuschheit im Altertum*, Giessen: Alfred
Töpelmann, 1910; Aline Rousselle,
*Porneia: De la maîtrise du corps à la
privation sensorielle, IIe–IVe siècles de
l'ère chrétienne*, Paris: Presses Universi-
taires de France, 1983.
Wayne R. Dynes

Asian-Americans,
Gay and Lesbian

Asian Americans who are gay or
lesbian live within the same social constraints as their heterosexual counterparts,
facing many of the prejudices and cultural
exclusions of modern North America.
Among identifiable ethnic peoples, Asians,
even those of the third, fourth, or fifth
generation, are most likely to be considered foreign, illegal aliens, unable to speak
English and so forth. This perpetual state
of being foreign—not being part of the
American cultural milieu—stems from
multiple historical roots.

An initial wave of immigration
from **China** and **Japan** in the late nineteenth century to meet labor demands in
the railroad industry was followed by the
Chinese Exclusion Acts which explicitly
aimed at stopping immigration from Asian
countries. These obstacles to Asian immigration were not eased until the 1960s,
when a new wave of immigrants from
Asian countries, mostly middle-class and
professional people, was allowed into the
United States. Continuity and growth of
viable Asian ethnic communities were also
hampered during World War II by the mass
internment of Japanese Americans (and
Japanese Canadians), resulting in massive
dislocation and dispersion of Japanese
American families and communities who
had settled in the Western states.

Gay Men and Lesbians. In the gay
community, Asian gay men and lesbians
experience the same alienation, being
perceived as "The Other": the foreign, the
exotic, the non-American. The preoccupation of modern gay male culture with the
sexual images and physical types of the
fifties and sixties—the short-haired blue-
eyed all-American boy who symbolized
the United States in its empire-building,
expansionist phase—has also resulted in
the exclusion of Asian men from the sexual and romantic interchange of modern
gay male life in the United States. Among
both gay men and lesbians, popular stereotypes of Asians as being subservient,
passive, and eager to please inform many
of their relationships with their non-Asian
counterparts.

Within their ethnic communities
many Asian gay men and lesbians keep
their homosexuality hidden from families
and friends. While Asian traditionalists
may tolerate instances of homosexuality
if discreet and surreptitious, an open avowal
of gayness is often condemned as a Western corruption. Asian gay people with more
traditional families also have to contend
with intense social and cultural pressures
to marry, to reproduce the family line, not
to disgrace the family name and so on. For
those who have immigrated more recently
there are other pressures: immigration laws
that exclude homosexuals and that
threaten HIV testing and dependence for
cultural support on ethnic communities
which are largely homophobic.

Organizing. To provide support
and to air and resolve many of their common problems, Asian gay men and lesbians have organized in many of the largest
cities of the United States. Through their
activism, many of the groups also challenge the exclusive identification of
American gay culture and gay communities with Caucasian men.

A major impetus to organizing
began with the first National Third World
Lesbian and Gay Conference (October
12–15, 1979) held in conjunction with the

First National Lesbian and Gay March on Washington. The handful of Asian lesbians and gay men who met at the conference, many for the first time, lobbied hard to have an Asian gay person (Michiyo Cornell) speak at the March rally. Tana Loy, an Asian lesbian from New York City, also addressed the Third World Conference. The energy and support generated as a result of this first meeting led many to see the value of support and organizing in their local areas. The Boston Asian Gay Men and Lesbians (BAGMAL), the first Asian gay group in the United States, was already a few months old at the time of the conference. The Gay Asians of Toronto was formed shortly afterwards by a participant at the conference.

Throughout the eighties other groups appeared in major cities. Some are of the more social club variety with leadership and participation by both Asian and non-Asian gay men. These clubs, modeled after the Black and White Men Together groups, sprang up in such cities as Chicago, Washington, San Francisco, Los Angeles, and New York. Other groups have agendas determined more directly for and by gay Asian men and Asian lesbians themselves. Included among these are the Alliance of Massachusetts Asian Gay Men and Lesbians, the Gay Asians of Toronto, and the Gay Asian Pacific Alliance (based in San Francisco and formed in 1988). Among Asian lesbian groups there is the Asian Lesbians of the East Coast (based in New York and formed in 1983), while on the West Coast the group called Asian Women organized in 1984 around the journal *Phoenix Rising*, then regrouped as Asian Pacific Sisters in August, 1988.

The First West Coast Asian/Pacific Lesbian and Gay Conference was held July 18, 1987 in West Hollywood, California, and the first North American Conference for Lesbian and Gay Asians was held August 19–21, 1988, in Toronto, Canada. The year 1988 also saw the formation of new groups for lesbians in San Francisco and Washington (D.C.) and the inaugura-

tion of Asian gay men's groups in San Francisco, Philadelphia, and Washington.

A distinctive feature of the North American gay Asian movement is its international perspective. Many individual activists and organizations maintain ties with gay groups and activists in East and South Asia—the political and cultural exchanges that have developed have enriched the movement on both sides of the Pacific. Of note is the gay South Asian newsletter *Trikone* (formed as *Trikon* in January, 1986) based in Palo Alto, California, which has inspired chapters in the Indian subcontinent as well as throughout North America.

Communities. With the rise of local groups and the building of local communities the climate for coming out for Asian gay men and lesbians improved throughout the 1980s. Asian gay communities in most cities are a diverse mix of North American-born and foreign-born men and women from a variety of East and South Asian cultural backgrounds with a substantial proportion of persons of mixed cultural heritage. These communities vary substantially from city to city. For example, groups in San Francisco with its high incidence of AIDS concentrate on AIDS-related issues while providing support and services for infected Asian people. In Toronto where a high proportion are Hong Kong-born Chinese, a lively gay Chinese culture based on the Cantonese dialect has developed. All communities were enlivened by the influx of Southeast Asian refugees into North American cities during the eighties.

Siong-huat Chua

ASTROLOGY

The history of astrology, the pseudoscience which claims to divine events from the positions of the heavenly bodies, has attracted considerable recent scholarship, but the sexual aspects have been neglected. In a passage in the *Confessions* (4:3), **Augustine** condemns astrology because it could excuse sin as under the control not of the will but of the stars ("the cause of thy sin is inevitably determined by heaven"). For those who accepted the astrological systems, and many did in late Greek and Roman antiquity, the stars could explain attraction to members of one's own sex. The astral mechanism is detailed by Ptolemy of Alexandria (ca. A.D. 100–178) in the classic treatise on Hellenistic-Roman astrology: "Joined with Mercury, in honorable positions, Venus makes them . . . in affairs of love restrained in their relations with women, but more passionate for boys, and jealous." (*Tetrabiblos*, 3:3). The interpretation of this particular pairing of the planets was probably suggested by their Greek names Hermes and Aphrodite, which join to produce Hermaphroditos.

Babylonian astrology was the source of Greek astrology. Not surprisingly, then, a neo-Babylonian text of ca. 500 B.C. says that "love of a man for a man" is governed by the constellation Scorpio. The Greeks personalized astrology by developing the notion that each individual's character and destiny are determined by the position of the planets at his birth. Hellenistic-Roman Egypt saw astrological interpretation take the form that it was to retain through the **Renaissance**, though the intervention of Christianity and Islam caused the homoerotic readings of certain planetary dispositions to be suppressed and disappear from standard works. Ultimately, as has been seen in the case of Augustine, Christian scorn of astrology succeeded in driving the discipline underground, though it survived in Islamic lands.

During the Renaissance, as part of the overall program of revival of classical antiquity, the Florentine **Neoplatonist** Marsilio **Ficino** (who was homosexual) created a vision of the cosmos linking humanity with the heavenly bodies through emanations of love. At the same time the actual techniques of astrology enjoyed a remarkable resurgence, though with complicated readjustments to take account of shifts in the position of the heavenly bodies in the intervening centu-

ries. In the sixteenth century, for example, **Michelangelo**—whose horoscope showed just the conjunction of Mercury and Venus noted by Ptolemy—seems to have assuaged his guilty conscience with the belief that his attraction to his youthful assistants (*garzoni*) had been decreed by celestial forces beyond his control. François Rabelais, in the *Pantagrueline Prognostication* of 1532, spoke of "Those whom Venus is said to rule, as . . . Ganymedes, Bardachoes, Huflers [fellators], Ingles." Some planets were held to be androgynous, because they are sometimes hot and sometimes cold. Thus Mercury was accounted hot and dry when near the sun, cold and moist when near the Moon. Clearly, then, the concept of sexual inclination as guided by the stars helped some of the system's adherents to grasp that their sexual interests were not a mere caprice or vicious deviation, but were essentially natural, being defined by cosmic imperatives.

In the seventeenth century, under attack by rationalism, astrology went underground again. The late nineteenth-century crisis of faith, however, engendered a compensatory upsurge of occult and esoteric beliefs, notably Theosophy (founded by Helena Petrovna Blavatsky in 1875). Theosophy, which had an attraction for some homosexuals (e.g., C. W. **Leadbeater**), incorporated **Buddhist** and Hindu elements, which henceforth played their role in some astrological systems. As the emerging homophile movement made it possible to discuss homosexuality in public, the long-suppressed erotic interpretation of certain signs reappeared in the literature. The first thoroughgoing modern attempt to correlate astrology with homosexual behavior was made in the 1920s by the German occultist and right-wing theorist Karl-Günther Heimsoth. Independently, the American homophile Gavin Arthur discovered the occult tradition in Paris in the 1920s. In 1960, having settled in San Francisco, he published a book, *The Circle of Sex*, which correlates character types with astrological influences. Arthur is credited with having launched the idea of the coming of the Aquarian Age, which was to become celebrated through the musical *Hair*.

In twentieth-century America astrology has exercised an enduring hold on the popular imagination, witness the newspaper columns devoted to the subject. Thanks in large measure to the symbiosis with the **Counterculture**, astrology gained a foothold in gay circles, and several paperbacks have appeared explaining the role of the stars in homosexual and lesbian destinies. Significantly, however, astrological explanations (based, as it were, on the cosmic environment) play no part in the current debate over acquired vs. constitutional factors in the etiology of sexual orientation. Today's astrology, the debased descendant of a millennial tradition, holds an essentially personal, often superficial significance for its adherents. Before dismissing its contribution entirely, however, one should note that man, unlike the lower animals, has no fixed mating season but copulates at all times of the year, a fact that may play an as yet undetermined role in the characterological variation of which homosexual orientation is but one aspect. In a sense, then, astrology, though rightly divested of its own credentials, may yet rank as the precursor of the emerging science of biometeorology that may shed unexpected light on the causes of homosexuality.

BIBLIOGRAPHY. Franz Cumont, *L'Egypte des astrologues*, Brussels: Fondation Egyptologique Reine Elisabeth, 1938; Michael Jay, *Gay Love Signs*, New York: Ballantine, 1980; Helen Lemay, "The Stars and Human Sexuality," *Isis*, 71 (1980), 127–37.
Warren Johansson

ATHENAEUS OF NAUCRATIS (FLOURISHED CA. A.D. 200)

Author of the *Deipnosophistai*, or "Banquet of the Learned," of which 15 of some 30 books survive. It is a specimen of "**symposium** literature" in which guests at a banquet discuss philosophy, belles lettres, law, medicine, cuisine, and other subjects. The framework, while occasionally tinged with humor, serves as a vehicle for the collections of excerpts that are introduced into the dialogue. Athenaeus cites some 1,250 authors, gives the titles of more than 1,000 plays, and quotes more than 10,000 lines of verse.

The significance of his work lies in showing that in cultivated pagan society at the close of the second century **pederasty** and all that related to it could be discussed freely and casually with no tone of reproach such as Christian apologists would like to trace back to the Golden Age of Hellenic civilization and beyond. The passions of legendary and historic figures for boys are mentioned, and famous boy-lovers are named: **Alcibiades**, Charmides, Autolycus, Pausanias, and Sophocles. Books and plays on pederasty are named and cited: *The Pederasts* by Diphilus, a play entitled *Ganymede*, a treatise *On Love* by Heraclides of Pontus, the play *The Effeminates* by Cratinus, and allusions to boy-love in Aeschylus and Sophocles. The creation of the Sacred Band of Theban warriors is ascribed to Epaminondas. The fondness of particular cities and ethnic groups for homosexual pleasures is mentioned: the Cretans, the Chalcidians of Euboea, the Medes, the Tuscans, the inhabitants of Massilia (Marseilles). Some individuals who were exclusively homosexual, such as Onomarcus and the philosopher **Zeno**, are named, with no implication that their conduct was deemed pathological or reprehensible.

The extant portions of the work—Book XIII is the most relevant—are a goldmine for the study of the homosexual side of classical civilization and the cultural expression of pederasty in the ancient world. Even when the compositions quoted have not survived, the titles and fragments preserved by Athenaeus give an idea of the volume of literature and art which male love inspired when it was an accepted part of the everyday life of all classes of society, individual differences in erotic taste notwithstanding.

Warren Johansson

ATHLETICS

Athletics is the broad field of physical activity in which strength is called into play and increased. Homosexual men and women have been and are active in both mainstream and gay community athletics. Their experience in athletics is, in many respects, the same as that of their heterosexual counterparts: experiences such as physical exertion, team membership and competition.

Athletics and the Male Image. Since the ancient **Olympic Games**, athletics has been considered a sign of masculinity. Women, until the twentieth century, have been excluded from athletics; they were prohibited from participation in the Sacred Games of Olympia and from the activities of the **gymnasia** of Ancient Greece. (There is evidence, however, that in ancient China, upper-class women played a version of soccer with men.) With the emancipation of Western women in the twentieth century, some became athletes. The modern Olympics prohibited the participation of women until 1928. At the 1984 Los Angeles Olympics less than a quarter of the athletes were female.

In the nineteenth century, theories of homosexuality were developed which saw it as a symptom of gender confusion; in conjunction with that, there developed a common belief that homosexual men were essentially feminine and lesbians masculine.

The nineteenth-century expansion of the British Empire and its sphere of cultural influence, the ascendancy of the bourgeoisie, the rise of the British "public school" system, and the central role that sports played in that system have made a cumulative contribution to the twentieth-century Western conception of sports. Athletics became the quintessential ex-pression of masculine values, the values of model citizenship: aggression, competition, racism, elitism, militarism, imperialism, sexism, and heterosexism. Many writers have suggested that athletics and healthy heterosexual masculinity are popularly equated. That athletic image is dramatically unlike the dominant religious, medical, and legal models of homosexuality which categorized homosexuals as sinful, pathological, and criminal. Because the popular images of the athlete and the homosexual are virtually antithetical, model healthy citizen and degenerate pathological criminal respectively, many athletes, especially professionals, have found it difficult publicly to acknowledge their homosexual orientation. Consequently, it is difficult to know who in professional sports is homosexual. Some famous athletes are known to be homosexual, among them John Menlove Edwards (mountaineering), Billie Jean King (tennis), David Kopay (football), Martina Navratilova (tennis) and Bill **Tilden** (tennis).

Lesbian and Gay Athletes. The masculine signification of athletics, in conjunction with the popular belief that lesbians are more masculine than their heterosexual counterparts, has led to the notion that many athletic women are lesbian. It seems likely that there is a concentration of lesbians in athletics, but the factual truth of this assumption cannot be determined. Statistical research on the presence of homosexuals in athletics is inevitably flawed; fear of negative repercussions mitigates against athletes identifying themselves as homosexual. There has been a concerted effort by individual athletes, sports organizations, administrators, coaches and scholars in the history and sociology of sport to disguise the substantial participation of lesbians in sport. Many lesbian athletes have been denied participation on teams and been fired from positions as national coaches when their lesbianism became known. Research on lesbians in athletics is minimal and proposals for research are frequently dismissed by academic juries. Many lesbian athletes try to downplay lesbian participation, saying that if the extent of lesbianism in athletics were known "it would give women's sports a bad name."

Whereas in this century athletics has been a popular occupation for lesbians, until the development of the "modern" gay liberation movement, many homosexual men avoided athletics. It could be that they have been aware of the masculine heterosexual signification of athletic participation and wanted no part of it. Standard athletic insults refer to fags, pansies, or sissies. To avoid such derision, finding athletics socially and psychically traumatic, many homosexuals eschewed sports. Male homosexual oral history research projects reveal few references to athletic activity; when it is mentioned, it is usually with considerable distaste.

Gay Sports. The modern gay liberation movement fostered a strong reaction to the old medical definition of homosexuality which associated it with gender confusion. Gay writers of the 1970s saw gay liberation, in some measure, as liberation from the oppressive restrictions which society exercised over homosexuals through the effeminate stereotype of the homosexual. The popular gay conception of the homosexual has changed from degenerate effeminacy to "normal" masculinity. Consequently, gay men who want to look "masculine and normal" by developing athletic bodies have taken up exercise. Whereas before the **Stonewall Rebellion** (1969), the representation of urban homosexual men in athletics was probably equal to or less than their representation in society as a whole, gay men now comprise either a very substantial minority or, in some instances, a majority of the population of urban athletic facilities. For example, YMCAs in major North American and European cities have large homosexual memberships. Many North American cities now have athletic clubs which are almost exclusively gay male.

Since athletics offers a subjective feeling of physical power, homosexual men who have felt powerless because of the low social position of their sexual orientation, can find athletics especially significant. They can derive intense satisfaction from excelling in a sport knowing that as "faggots" they are beating "macho men" at their own game. Gay liberation encouraged gay athletes to come out. **Coming out** has made it possible for some to become athletes.

Although there have been "respectable artistic treatments" of the "jock" in gay literature, for example *The Front Runner* (1974) by Patricia Nell Warren, the most prominent position the jock has in gay culture is probably in gay pornography. One of North America's earliest and most prolific gay pornographers was the Athletic Model Guild of Los Angeles, which has produced soft-core gay pornography since 1945. Other examples of sporty soft-core gay pornography can be found in Scott Madsen's *Peak Condition* (1985) and in the photos of athletes by Bruce Weber and Christopher Makos which frequently appear in Andy Warhol's magazine *Interview*. Athletes are often featured in hardcore pornographic publications and videos with titles such as "Jocks," "Spokes," and "These Bases are Loaded."

One of the products of the gay liberation movement has been the creation of specifically gay political and social organizations. Gay athletic clubs, which can be found in major cities across North America, constitute an important aspect of gay community life. The common purpose of gay sports groups is essentially twofold: to promote social interaction, and to provide athletic opportunities for people who share a way of life. The roster of gay community sports clubs is extensive; space affords only a brief sampling of this significant facet of gay culture. In many North American cities the largest gay organizations are sports clubs. There are outing clubs affiliated with the International Gay and Lesbian Outdoor Organization; they have names like the "Out and Out Club" and organize activities such as bicycle tours, cross-country and down-hill skiing, hiking, camping, canoeing, parachuting and white-water rafting. Included in the list of organized North American gay community sports groups are: Spokes, a cycling club in Vancouver; The San Francisco Gay Women's Softball League; and the Judy Garland Memorial Bowling League in Toronto. The Ramblers Soccer Club of New York City is one of nine teams in the United Nations Soccer League; it is the only non-UN member and the only openly gay team.

There are gay sports governing bodies for many sports. The North American Gay Amateur Athletic Alliance is a non-profit organization dedicated to promoting amateur softball for all persons with a special emphasis on gay participation; it also establishes uniform playing rules and regulations. The International Gay Bowling Association has 65 local affiliates across North America with over ten thousand members. The National Gay Volleyball Association has clubs in over 60 North American cities. Many cities have umbrella sports organizations which interact with other gay community groups and help to coordinate local, national and international competitions. There is the Metropolitan Sports Association in Chicago, the San Francisco Arts and Athletics and the Metropolitan Vancouver Athletic and Arts Association which is a Registered Society and has offices in the Sports British Columbia Building, a provincially funded facility. Although there are gay sports groups in other parts of the world, Australia being an important example, most gay community sports activity at the present takes place in North American cities.

The ideological signification of gay athletics is important. Over the last ten years or so, there has been a shift in focus in the gay liberation movement from the dialectic of oppression and liberation to the experience of gay pride. An impor-

tant expression of gay pride can be found in gay athletics; in New York City, a major event in the gay pride festivities, one which attracts athletes from all parts of North America, is the five mile Gay Pride Run in Central Park. A prestigious international gay pride event is the Gay Games. Gay liberationists have seized upon athletics as an ideological instrument of gay politics. Athletic events are promoted by gay community organizers to counteract the frequently negative image of homosexuals by emphasizing a picture of health and good citizenship.

Gay community sports have been used for overt political ends. The relations between urban gay communities and police forces are notoriously poor. Many cities, including Vancouver, New York, and San Francisco, have annual competitions between police and gay all-star teams in an effort to improve relations.

Conclusion. The participation of homosexual men and women in athletics is extensive. Their presence in mainstream athletics is often not visible because of the fact that they frequently pass as straight. Their experience in that milieu can be unique and is intimately related to the history of sexuality and popular conceptions of masculinity and athletics. Gay liberation has brought with it a flourishing of gay culture which has produced a plethora of gay teams, clubs, and sports governing bodies across North America, a trend which is spreading to other parts of the world.

BIBLIOGRAPHY. R. Coe, *A Sense of Pride: The Story of Gay Games II*, San Francisco: Pride Publications, 1986; Betty Hicks, "Lesbian Athletes," *Christopher Street* 4:3 (October–November 1979), 42–50; Billie Jean King and Frank Deford, *Billie Jean*, New York: Viking, 1982; David Kopay and Perry Young, *The David Kopay Story: An Extraordinary Self-Revelation*, 2nd ed., New York: Donald I. Fine, 1988; Brian Pronger, *Irony and Ecstasy: Gay Men and Athletics*, Toronto: Summerhill Press, 1989; idem, "Gay Jocks: A Phenomenology of Gay Men in Athletics," in *Critical Perspectives on Men, Masculinity and Sports*, Michael Messner and Don Sabo, eds., Champaign, IL: Human Kinetics Publishing, 1988; D. Sabo and R. Runfola, *Jock: Sports and Male Identity*, Englewood Cliffs, NJ: Prentice-Hall, 1980; Michael J. Smith, "The Double Life of a Gay Dodger," in *Black Men/White Men*, San Francisco, Gay Sunshine Press, 1983.

Brian Pronger

AUDEN, WYSTAN HUGH (1907–1973)

Anglo-American poet and critic. The child of cultivated, upper-class parents, Auden profited from a traditional British elite schooling. As a student at Christ College, Oxford, he first excelled in science, but shifted to English with the intention of becoming a "great poet." A quick study, Auden acquired an undergraduate reputation as an almost oracular presence, and he began to assemble around him a group of young writers that included Christopher **Isherwood** (whom he had met at preparatory school), C. Day Lewis, Louis MacNeice, and Stephen Spender. After leaving Oxford in 1928 Auden decided to spend a year in Berlin learning German. He then held a series of school-teaching jobs that allowed time for writing.

Like the other members of his group—who came to be known as "the poets of the thirties"—Auden broke with the pastoral placidity of the Georgian trend in English poetry, seeking to encompass such modern technology and such trends in thought as Freudian **psychoanalysis** and **Marxism**. Although he later repudiated their ideological commitments, Auden's early poems have a numinous ambiguity that unfortunately was largely lost in his later more pellucid but often facile work. In his early poetry the exaltation of the figures of the Airman and the Truly Strong Man represents a continuation of the adolescent aesthete's admiration for the "hearty." His work in the 1930s had both the exuberance and the limitations of youth.

In 1937 he expressed his sympathy for the loyalist cause by visiting Spain, and the following year he traveled to China with Isherwood. In 1940, having become disillusioned with left-wing causes, he converted back to **Anglicanism**, a change that profoundly affected the character and tone of his writing. With the outbreak of World War II in Europe, he settled in New York, where he met and fell in love with a young man, Chester Kallman, who was destined to be his lifelong companion. This relationship was celebrated in a series of poems to an anonymous and ungendered lover, and also in a deliberately outrageous composition, "The Queen's Masque." This unpublished dramatic composition, intended to be performed for Kallman's twenty-second birthday on February 7, 1943, was not rediscovered until 1988. In 1941 Auden collaborated with the gay composer Benjamin Britten in a chamber opera, *Paul Bunyan*. Through Kallman, whose knowledge was expert and unflagging, Auden expanded his interest in opera, and the two collaborated on a libretto for Igor Stravinsky's *The Rake's Progress*, as well as other works. Although actual sexual relations between them ceased after the first years, the two men made a life together based on mutual trust and affection. Auden took charge of earning a living, while Chester excelled in cooking and homemaking. Despite some asperities, their relationship survived not only in New York, but in Ischia on the Mediterranean and in Kirchstetten in Austria, where they spent the summers.

Auden's later work is marked by ambitious cycles, such as *A Christmas Oratorio* (1945) and *The Age of Anxiety* (1947), which are technically expert but, for many readers at least, lacking in the charisma of truly great poetry. Partly to make ends meet, Auden produced a considerable body of prose criticism, and this sometimes deals movingly with other homosexual authors. His most explicit homosexual poem is a piece of doggerel called "The Platonic Lay" or "A Day for a

Lay," which is not included in authorized editions of his works. Late in life he had some contacts with the emerging American gay movement, though to some his attitudes seemed old-fashioned and not devoid of self-contempt.

Auden's works are still being edited and published, and consensus on his ultimate status has not been achieved. A recent attempt to show that his work anticipated the feminist and ecology movements is unconvincing. Often courageous in his outspokenness, Auden no doubt suffered at the hands of critics who were uncomfortable with his sexuality. His poetry and prose, which were wide-ranging and copious, retain a strong sense of period: they tell us much of what the thirties were like in Britain, and the forties and fifties in America.

BIBLIOGRAPHY. *Works: Collected Poems*, New York: Random House, 1976; *The English Auden: Poems, Essays, and Dramatic Writings, 1927–1939*, New York: Knopf, 1977; *Forewords and Afterwords*, New York: Vintage, 1974. *Studies:* Humphrey Carpenter, *W. H. Auden: A Biography*, Boston: Houghton Mifflin, 1981; Dorothy J. Farnan, *Auden in Love*, New York: New American Library, 1985; Martin E. Gingerich, *W. H. Auden: A Reference Guide*, Boston: G. K. Hall, 1977.

Wayne R. Dynes

AUGUSTINE, SAINT (354–430)

Bishop of Hippo and one of the Doctors of the Church. Born at Thagaste in North Africa, he was raised as a Christian. As a young man Augustine seems to have been deeply troubled by the strength of his sex drive. Later he recalled how "in the sixteenth year of my flesh . . . the madness of raging lust exercised its supreme dominion over me." In the course of his studies of rhetoric at Carthage he gradually abandoned his Christian faith. Augustine was drawn instead to **Manichae**-anism, which held that man was a product of a primal struggle between the high god and his Satanic opponent, whose powers were almost equally great. Although he later abandoned this dualistic belief, important residues of its dark coloration remained with him.

During his youth he formed a very deep bond with another male student. After the premature death of this beloved friend, Augustine movingly remarked: "I still thought my soul and his soul to have been but one soul in two bodies; and therefore was my life a very horror to me, because I would not live by halves. And even therefore perchance was I afraid to die, lest he should wholly die, whom so passionately I had loved." (*Confessions*, 4:6).

In his thirties Augustine came under the influence of Ambrose, Bishop of Milan, and was baptized in 387. He then returned to North Africa, where he became a priest in 391. Four years later he became bishop of Hippo, where he led a demanding life of church administration, theological controversy, and serious writing. His best known works are his autobiography, *The Confessions*, and his lengthy meditation on Christian history, *The City of God*, which was occasioned by the news of the sack of Rome in 410.

In keeping with the mainstream views of the Greek and Latin theologians who had preceded him, the mature Augustine maintained that sexual intercourse was lawful only within marriage with the aim of producing offspring—thus excluding birth control. Even within marriage he denied that sexual pleasure could ever be approved as an end in itself. Somewhat exceptionally, he held that, despite the cleansing efficacy of baptism, some taint of the sin of Adam lingered in the very act of procreation through semen which ascended genealogically to our first parent. From such premises Augustine concluded that the individual free will is radically circumscribed, seeing in the capacity of the male member for unsought-after erection a signal example of the capacities of rebellion found within our own being.

His eloquent advocacy of these rigorist views, grounded as it was in his personal ambivalence toward sexuality, has been widely influential in the Western tradition. That Augustine cannot be considered uniquely responsibly for the intensification of Christian sex negativism is shown by the parallel triumph of **asceticism** in the Eastern Church where his writings were little known.

If the consequences of Augustine's view for individual self-development have been regrettable, the political conclusions that he drew from them were perhaps more salutary. Government is at best a necessary evil. Since rulers are subject to the same character flaws as other human beings, he warned against the kind of personality cult that has been endemic from **Alexander** and Augustus to Stalin and Castro. By the same token, he placed no exaggerated faith in popular rule, since the people also are made up of fallible individuals. There can be no political utopia on earth, he counseled, and the best that can be done is to check arbitrary exercise of power through foresight and realism.

BIBLIOGRAPHY. Peter Brown, *Augustine of Hippo*, Berkeley: University of California Press, 1967; Elaine Pagels, *Adam, Eve, and the Serpent*, New York: Random House, 1988.

Wayne R. Dynes

Australia

An affluent, highly urbanized nation with a population of less than twenty million of largely European and minority indigenous (Aboriginal and Torres Strait Island) stock, Australia has a significant number of citizens who lead their lives as openly homosexual men and women. This phenomenon and the associated growth of a homosexual subculture, highly developed in the largest cities, Sydney and Melbourne, has emerged since 1970. In that year, for the first time, homosexuals established an open organization, the purpose of which was to demand recognition, equal and just treatment before the law, and an end to discrimination. When one considers the almost taboo nature of homosexuality and the social invisibility of the homosexual before 1970, the progress toward achievement of these goals has been remarkably rapid. Yet it has also been uneven, with male homosexual acts remaining illegal in Tasmania, Western Australia, and Queensland, while only two states, New South Wales and Victoria, have enacted legislation outlawing discrimination. The advent of **AIDS**, still perceived by some as a "gay disease," has created new problems, apart from the medical issues, which have been only partially resolved.

The Convict Era. White settlement of Australia began in January 1788, as a British penal colony, and the transportation of convicts continued until 1840 in eastern Australia, 1852 in Tasmania, and 1868 in the west. Throughout the transportation period there was a severe imbalance between the sexes, convict and free, and of course large numbers of convicts were kept in relative or complete isolation from the other sex. Ample evidence exists of the prevalence of homosexual behavior, then referred to as "unnatural or abominable crimes"; it is intermittent in the early years but more abundant after the term of Governor Lachlan Macquarie (1810–21).

After five years of settlement Captain Watkin Tench was pleased to note in his memoirs that the convicts' "enormities" did not include "unnatural sins." This state of affairs did not last, and in 1796 Francis Wilkinson became the first man to be charged with buggery (he was acquitted). Many more such charges were to follow. In 1822 an official inquiry into the sexual scandal that resulted from the movement of thirty female prisoners to the (male) prison farm at Emu Plains, west of Sydney, reported the rumor current that the women had been placed there to prevent "unnatural crimes" on the part of the men. Lesbianism occurred among women prisoners in the female factories. In a secret dispatch of 1843 the Lieutenant-Governor of Van Diemen's Land (Tasmania), Sir Eardley Wilmot, stated that women in the Hobart female factory have "their Fancy-women, or lovers, to who they are attached with quite as much ardour as they would be to the opposite sex, and practice onanism to the greatest extent."

Select committees of the British Parliament inquiring into transportation in 1832 and 1837 heard much evidence of the prevalence of sodomy in the colonies. Occasionally we find suggestions that it was not a sporadic occurrence but was structured to the extent of involving role-playing and mutual affection. Major James Mudie testified that prisoners called each other "sods" and that at Hyde Park Barracks in Sydney boy prisoners went by names such as Kitty and Nancy. Thomas Cook, a chain-gang prisoner laboring on roadworks in the Blue Mountains west of Sydney in the 1830s, lamented that his gangmates were "so far advanced . . . in depravity" that they openly engaged "in assignations one toward the other" and "kicked, struck or otherwise abused" anyone who dared to condemn "their horrid propensities."

The fullest evidence comes from Norfolk Island, a recidivist penal settlement. A magistrate, Robert Pringle Stuart, sent to investigate conditions on the island in 1846, made it his business to burst unannounced into the prisoners' barracks one night. "On the doors being opened, men were scrambling into their own beds from others, concealment evidently being their object." He continued: "It is my painful duty to state that . . . unnatural crime is indulged in to excess . . . I am told, and I believe, that upwards of 100—I have heard that as many as 150—couples can be pointed out, and moral perception is so completely absorbed that they are said to be 'married,' 'man and wife,' etc. [This in

a prisoner population of 600–800.] In a word, the association is not unusually viewed by the convicts as that between the sexes; is equally respected by some of them; and is as much a source of jealousy, rivalry, intrigue and conflict."

Colonial Mateship. The early economic development of the colonies was heavily dependent on pastoralism, and the opening-up of new, unfenced lands for grazing required the use of shepherds. As solitude in the bush tended to produce insanity, the shepherds worked in pairs (or threes), one (or two) tending the sheep, the mate looking after the hut and cooking. This situation is the origin of the Australian tradition of mateship, which later took other forms. Modern writers on it have made much of its quasi-marital nature but have at the same time insisted that it was nonsexual. Yet, while most early witnesses are silent on this score, a few, such as Bishop Ullathorne and Jemas Backhouse, a Quaker missionary, explicitly deprecate the prevalence of sodomy among shepherds and stockmen. In 1848 J. C. Byrne, deploring the absence of women in the "backwoods," stated expressly that "where black *gins* [women] are unobtainable, there is reason to believe, that the sins for which God punished 'the doomed cities' prevail among the servants of the squatters."

Law. English law came with the colonists, and so **buggery** (hetero- or homosexual anal intercourse and bestiality) was a felony from the outset. The Offences Against the Person Act (1861) reduced the penalty for buggery to life imprisonment and created new offences of attempted buggery and indecent assault upon a male person, and these provisions were extended to the colonies by an Imperial Act of 1885, the **Criminal Law Amendment Act**. Around the time of the Federation in 1901 the States all enacted similar laws for themselves. They also enacted statutes—N.S.W. as late as 1955—along the lines of the British Labouchere amendment of 1885, which criminalized consensual "gross indecency between males" even when performed in private.

All such offences were indictable and so tried before a judge and jury. The laws have never been dead-letter laws, though in recent decades there has been a tendency for "offences" not involving violence or coercion or abuse of authority to be prosecuted under various non-criminal statutes having to do with offensive behavior, indecent exposure, soliciting, and the like. Such lesser charges are dealt with summarily by magistrates, and convictions are easier to obtain. There is evidence that in the 1950s and 1960s the New South Wales police used *agents provocateurs* to induce the commission of offenses.

Following a gay-bashing murder in which police were involved, South Australia became, in 1972, the first state partially to decriminalize homosexual acts between consenting adults, and in 1975 introduced statutory equality for all sexual offenses, gay or straight. Decriminalization followed in the Australian Capital Territory and the Northern Territory in 1973, in Victoria in 1980, and in New South Wales in 1984. Unsuccessful attempts at law reform were made in Western Australia in 1977 and in Tasmania in 1979 and 1987; only in Queensland has no attempt been made.

Religion and the Churches. Australian anti-gay laws were the legal manifestation of the traditional Christian antipathy to the sodomite. As elsewhere, the Australian churches continued to abominate a sin that seemed all too prevalent. Yet, as elsewhere in the Anglican communion, each Australian capital city has long had at least one High **Anglican** church with a traditional toleration of homosexuality in the congregation.

In the 1960s, in line with progressive thinking, mainstream Protestant churches moved cautiously toward a less condemnatory attitude and began to support limited law reform. The Roman Catholic and parts of the Anglican church remain unreceptive to revisionist theological trends, and consequently have movements of disaffected homosexual believers working for change from within. Other gay Christians turned to the Metropolitan Community Church established in 1975 as an offshoot of the U.S. gay church of the same name.

Medicine and Psychiatry. In the nineteenth century Australian medicine did not concern itself with homosexuality per se: "It is beyond the range of medical philosophy to divine the special causes for its existence," Dr. J. C. Beaney declared in his *Generative System* (1872, 1883). In this century, although doubtless many have accepted the psychopathological explanations usual in psychiatric literature, there does not seem to have been any systematic effort to submit homosexuals to medical treatment until the late 1950s when some psychiatrists began to apply aversion therapies and psychosurgery in this area. The issue was one of the first to be addressed by the new gay movement of the 1970s, and the application of these practices to homosexuals has ceased. Although Australia avoided the fashion for sexual psychopathy laws that afflicted the United States from the 1940s to the 1960s, some cooperation between the courts and psychiatrists claiming to be able to cure so-called sex offenders occurred informally.

In its public utterances, represented by editorials and articles in *The Medical Journal of Australia*, the medical profession has, on the whole, been in advance of general community opinion in calling for reform of social attitudes and the law as they affect homosexuals.

"Camp" Life Before Gay Liberation. Given social attitudes and the legal position, it is hardly surprising that in the latter half of the nineteenth century homosexuality remained secretive, and indeed evidence of it before World War I is adventitious, court records being the most consistent source.

Dr. Beaney told with astonishment of a "respectable" Melbourne wife who "decoyed into her acquaintance young married women, and compelled them, by her influence, to entertain the same unnatural feelings toward men and women [as she had]." Other lesbians passed as men, as we learn from two cases that have come to light of transvestite women marrying and apparently satisfying their wives. In 1879 the thrice-married Edward De-Lacy Evans was revealed in the Bendigo Lunacy Ward to be a woman and in 1920 Eugenia Falleni, alias Harry Leo Crawford, was convicted of the murder of the woman she had legally married while passing as a man.

For men as well as women, friendship must have been the most common locus of homosexual relations, but of this and more extended friendship-networks we know little before World War I. A hint of what was possible emerges from a Sydney household of male couples that the police raided in 1916 because neighbors complained about the mysterious comings and goings of "women"—it transpired that some of the men cross-dressed.

The other main "institution" of male homosexual life was the *beat*, a public place, such as a park, toilet, baths, or beach, where one could expect to encounter sexual partners. Hyde Park in Sydney was a beat from at latest the 1880s until the early 1960s. The importance of the beat, indicated by the creation of a **slang** term for it, lay not simply in the opportunities for sex it afforded. For some men it was, for good or for ill, what homosexuality meant to them; for others it led to friendships and perhaps entry to a world that would otherwise have remained closed to them.

After World War I, in Sydney and Melbourne, a few cafés, restaurants, and bars were frequented by gays and/or lesbians, who never, however, constituted the exclusive clientele. Such places usually had a reputation for bohemianism. By World War II Sydney had an annual drag-ball called the Artists' Ball, of which Jon

Rose gave an hilarious account in his autobiography *At the Cross* (1960). By the 1950s social clubs had emerged in Sydney but to avoid unwanted attention from the police and the tabloid press elaborate secrecy was necessary. By the late 1960s Sydney had several exclusively gay clubs and wine bars; gay pubs emerged in the 1970s.

Homosexual Emancipation. Australia had no homophile **movement**, an absence that was regretted by a liberal social critic shortly after the first homosexual law reform organization was founded in 1969. However, a short-lived lesbian group calling itself Daughters of **Bilitis** was apparently formed in that same year. In July 1970 in Sydney, inspired by the newly emerged gay liberation movement in the United States, John Ware and Christabel Poll formed the first widely-publicized gay-run group. The Campaign Against Moral Persecution or CAMP (*camp* being then the usual Australian homosexual slang term for "homosexual") soon had branches in most states. In 1971 groups using the name gay **liberation** emerged, and some gay liberationists dismissed CAMP as "reformist." However, both CAMP and gay liberation groups organized social events and consciousness-raising sessions for their members, and both participated in demonstrations intended to assert gay pride, demand gay rights, and protest against instances of **discrimination**, which now for the first time victims were prepared to make public.

As public awareness and acceptance of homosexuals grew (in the first public opinion survey on the issue in 1967 only 22% of respondents supported homosexual law reform, but in 1976 68% did so), the gay movement found less need to employ confrontationist tactics and became increasingly involved in the mainstream political processes. Gay groups made submissions to the Royal Commission on Human Relationships whose final report in 1977 made many recommendations to improve the legal and social position of homosexuals, and began to deal directly with politicians and governments.

At the same time, the number and complexity of homosexual institutions increased and a distinct subculture emerged in the largest cities. A gay press was vital in this development. The first gay magazine, *Camp Ink*, was produced in Sydney in November 1970 by CAMP and lasted some four years. The first truly commercial magazine appeared in 1972. There are now two national monthlies, the older founded in 1975, and a number of free community newspapers, professionally produced and paid for by advertising. Gay publishing of books has been slower to develop and remains embryonic.

In 1975 the first national gay and lesbian conference was held, and for eleven years these gatherings provided a useful forum for political, cultural, and social exchange. They helped to boost morale among activists who were now increasingly involved in lobbying for law reform and anti-discrimination legislation. After failures in Western Australia and Tasmania, this process finally had a significant success in Victoria in 1980.

An unprovoked police attack on peaceful Gay Pride marchers in 1978, arrests then and at subsequent demonstrations against police brutality, and the long but successful defense against the charges led to a revival of the flagging movement in New South Wales. The police were humiliated and the political and legal skills of gays clearly demonstrated. Nevertheless, the struggle for law reform took another six years. The march acquired in the process a new symbolic meaning and, moved from wintry June to late-summer February, became the Sydney Gay **Mardi Gras**, which is now the city's largest annual street parade.

Perhaps the most striking sign of the changed situation of homosexuals in Australian society is the extent to which gays and lesbians are involved in the official structures created to respond to the AIDS crisis. Since in Australia the majority of the AIDS cases are homosexual men, this involvement is appropriate and desirable; yet it would have been as unimaginable twenty years ago as the disease itself.

BIBLIOGRAPHY. *Discrimination and Homosexuality*, Sydney: New South Wales Discrimination Board, 1982; Robert Hughes, *The Fatal Shore: The Epic of Australia's Founding*, New York: Knopf, 1987; Denise Thompson, *Flaws in the Social Fabric: Homosexuals and Society in Sydney*, Sydney: Allen and Unwin, 1985; Paul Wilson, *The Sexual Dilemma*, St. Lucia: University of Queensland Press, 1971; Gary Wotherspoon, ed., *Being Different. Nine Gays Remember*, Sydney: Hale and Iremonger, 1986.

G. R. Simes

AUSTRIA

This European country traces its existence to 1180 when Frederick Barbarossa convicted Henry the Lion of treason and confiscated his estates, dividing Bavaria proper from its eastern extension which became Austria. Defeating Otokar I of Bohemia in 1278, the Emperor Rudolf I granted Austria as a fief to his son Albert I, the first Habsburg to rule there. From 1278 until 1918 Habsburgs reigned in Austria, adding to their domain more by astute and fortunate marriages than by conquest.

Joseph II (1741–1790), great-great-grand nephew of the emperor Rudolf II (possibly homosexual) and son of Maria Theresa, was one of the most admired of Austrian monarchs. Inspired by **Voltaire** and the Encyclopedists and by the example of **Frederick the Great** of Prussia, he began in 1761 (after his mother associated him into the government) to draw up memoranda, many of which he put into effect after her death. Joseph was the first monarch in Europe to emancipate the Jews (in 1791). In reforming the penal code, he followed the humane principles of Count Cesare **Beccaria**, eliminating torture and cruel and unusual punishments, reducing the number of capital offenses, and decriminalizing many activities. He reduced the penalty for homosexuality from death at the stake to life imprisonment.

In Joseph II's time, Vienna emerged as the musical capital of Europe with such giants as Mozart and Haydn. Franz **Schubert**, the only major composer of the group actually to have been born in Vienna, was probably homosexual. Suspicions that have been voiced about Beethoven's interest in his nephew are hard to substantiate.

The Habsburg Empire that Maria Theresa and Joseph II had solidified endured the revolutions and Napoleonic wars and rose under Metternich during the Congress of Vienna to dominate European diplomacy until his overthrow by the Revolution of 1848, during which the 18-year old Franz Joseph succeeded upon his father's abdication. This grand-nephew of Joseph II reigned until 1916, trying to patch together the old system against the rising tides of nationalism and socialism, and to hold together his dominion served by three armies—a standing army of soldiers, a sitting army of bureaucrats, and a creeping army of informers. The decadence of Franz Joseph's reign contrasted with the brilliant intellectual and artistic life of his capital, which became one of the gay centers of Europe.

In the field of sex research, the first major figure of modern times was Richard Freiherr von **Krafft-Ebing** (1840–1902), called from Germany to Graz and then to Vienna, which had become the world's leading medical school. His *Psychopathia Sexualis* (first edition 1886) disclosed to the educated public the existence of homosexuality and other sexual "perversions," of which he assembled a picturesque dossier on the basis of his own and others' observations mainly in prisons and insane asylums that left the public with the conviction that all who engaged in forbidden sexual activity were in some way "mentally ill." At a symposium he criticized **Freud**'s presentation of his se-

duction theory. Also, Moritz Kaposi (1837–1902) was professor of dermatology at Vienna from 1875 until his death; in 1872 he had published the article that first described Kaposi's sarcoma, which later became significant in **AIDS**.

The misogynist and Jewish anti-Semite Otto Weininger, who committed suicide in 1903 on discovering too much of the feminine in his own personality, invented the modern concept of **bisexuality**—or perhaps borrowed it from the Berlin physician Wilhelm Fliess, who had not published it. Anna Freud seems to have had a long-term lesbian relationship with an American woman in the Vienna of the 1920s. The leading modernist writer Robert Musil described in *Young Törless* (1906) how two older boys at a preparatory school he attended forced a younger boy to have sexual relations with them. The witness, presumably the author, had a nervous breakdown. Hermann Broch's *The Death of Vergil* (1945), which he completed after his emigration to America, relates **Vergil**'s musings about the boys he loved.

The Austrian penal code of 1852, which criminalized lesbianism, reduced the penalties imposed by the Josephine code for male homosexuality, and generally came closer to the provisions of the Prussian code of the same year. But the existence of the law did not prevent Vienna from having a lively homosexual subculture at the turn of the century, with its cafés, restaurants, bathhouses, and places of rendezvous all under the surveillance of the police, who like their counterparts in Berlin kept systematic lists of those who engaged in homosexual activity.

The **Scientific-Humanitarian Committee** founded in Berlin in 1897 acquired a branch in Vienna in 1906 under the leadership of the engineer Joseph Nicoladoni and the psychoanalyst Wilhelm Stekel. Freud is reported to have made small donations to it, and Isidor Sadger used the periodical of the Committee to locate subjects for his (not particularly sympathetic) psychoanalytic studies. Among the minor gay literary figures of this time were Emil Mario Vacano, Karl Michael Freiherr von Lewetzow, Joseph Kitir, and Emerich Graf Stadion, who published in the journal *Poetische Flugblättern*, edited by Kitir.

In 1901 the writer Minna Wettstein-Adelt published under the pseudonym Aimée Duc a novel entitled *Sind es Frauen!* [Are They Women?] that depicts a circle of self-consciously lesbian women in Geneva, the center of which is a Russian named Minotschka Fernandoff. The feminist Marie von Najmajer (1844–1904), born in Hungary, saluted the new century with a "Hymn to the Daughters of the Twentieth Century" that had strong lesbian overtones. Yet the lesbian subculture of Vienna took little interest in the literary treatment of the natives of the city; it preferred works showing the Viennese lesbian abroad or the foreign lesbian drawn to the Austrian capital. Compared with the network of enterprises catering to the male homosexual the lesbian subculture remained small and marginal.

One of the myths that later circulated abroad was that the Viennese of the early decades of the century were sexually repressed to the point of neuroticism, when in fact the capital had much the same ambiance in contrast with the provinces as did Paris in relation to the rest of France. As the focal point of the homosexual emancipation movement, Berlin garnered more than its share of attention, but Vienna until 1918 was the cosmopolitan center of a multi-national empire where erotic pleasure was always sought—and frequently found. Ludwig **Wittgenstein** cruised the Prater, where the ferris wheel is located, during the 1920s, and often went to a classy café, a chess club with newspapers by day and a flaming gay club at night. After the 1938 Anschluss, which joined Austria to Hitler's Reich, a number of the country's homosexuals became victims of the **holocaust**.

The strength of the Catholic church in Austria, particularly the state that remained after the Treaty of Saint-Germain, kept law reform from occurring until 1971, two years after the Federal Republic of **Germany** amended **Paragraph 175**. There is a higher age of consent for male homosexuals (18) than for heterosexuals and lesbians (14). Moreover, article 220 of the 1971 penal code provides for up to six months imprisonment for anyone who advocates or states approval of homosexuality, while article 221 stipulates the same penalty for anyone belonging to an organization that "favors homosexual lewdness." These provisions have never been enforced. The major gay organizations Homosexuelle Initiative (HOSI) operate quite successfully under the shadow of this legislation, while gathering data about gay people in the Warsaw pact nations of Eastern Europe. From 1979 this information has been recorded in the quarterly *Lambda Nachrichten* (HOSI Wien), which even received an official press subsidy in 1987. Vienna also has a gay and lesbian community center, Rosa Lila Villa.

BIBLIOGRAPHY. Neda Bei, et al., eds., *Das lila Wien um 1900*, Vienna: Promedia, 1986.

William A. Percy

AUTHORITARIAN PERSONALITY

The concept of the authoritarian personality was introduced to social psychology by the work of Theodor Wiesengrund Adorno and his associates in a major study published in 1950. According to this model the authoritarian personality accepts middle-class conventionality because it enjoys widespread acceptance and support, but has not internalized the meaning of the accompanying social norms; is hostile and aggressive toward outsider groups, especially ethnic minorities and relatively powerless, marginalized deviant groups; and glorifies its own authority figures. Adorno had been a member of the Frankfurt school of sociology which the Nazi seizure of power exiled to the United States, and the formulation of the notion had begun in Germany through analysis of the mass psychology of the fateful years of the early 1930s, when authoritarian and democratic creeds contended for rule. Originally the contrasting democratic personality type was labeled the "socialist personality," revealing the leftist bias that hovered over the creation of the antinomy. And indeed one problem with the idea of the authoritarian personality is the difficulty that many researchers have in acknowledging that authoritarianism is found as much on the left as on the right. Put another way, the notion of the authoritarian personality, though not devoid of content, bonds all too easily with the left-liberal prejudices and folklore of the contemporary intelligentsia, serving to confirm its disdain of conservatives of every stripe and to suggest that beliefs linked with the right stem from a character disorder that occludes a "correct" perception of reality.

Academic **psychology** had until the 1950s failed to discover any correlation between personality structure and political attitudes. The contribution of Adorno and his associates was to trace a common denominator between ethnic chauvinism, political and economic **conservatism, anti-Semitism**, and authoritarianism. As an indirect measure of prejudice and a measure of "prefascism" in the personality, they developed the F scale soliciting expressions of agreement or disagreement with 29 broadly phrased assertions. Continuing review and criticism of the early work and its theoretical presuppositions have led to the development of new scales and also to debates among professional psychologists. For example, there has even been academic controversy over whether left-wing authoritarianism exists, when any insightful observer of the left knows that this is the watershed between Communists and So-

cial Democrats. The overarching problem is to determine how it is that **myths and fabrications** and **stereotypes** come to be entertained in *sets*, so that if one or two are acquired the others are likely to follow.

A hallmark of the authoritarian personality is preoccupation with deviations from the norm of sexual conduct and advocacy of harsh penalties for "perverts" and the like. While certain issues that elicited sharp contrasts between authoritarian and democratic personality types in the 1940s have become irrelevant because the political controversy surrounding them has faded, the rise of a militant gay liberation movement after 1969 has made one's tolerance of homosexuality a clear index of personality. A recently developed tool called the Attitudes Toward Homosexuals (ATH) scale asks agreement or disagreement with such statements as "Homosexuals should be locked up to protect society" and "In many ways, the AIDS disease currently killing homosexuals is just what they deserve." Authoritarianism accounted for 29% of the variation in the subjects' hostility toward homosexuals; fear and self-righteousness supplied nearly all the rest. Fear of a dangerous world—and of homosexual assertiveness in it—and self-righteousness justifying punitive sanctions are what trigger the authoritarian's rage and vindictiveness. The growing role of anti-homosexual themes in the propaganda of conservative and clerical social movements attests to the significance of **homophobia** for the mass psychology of the present day.

BIBLIOGRAPHY. Theodor W. Adorno, et al., *The Authoritarian Personality*, New York: Harper & Row, 1950; Bob Altemeyer, "Marching in Step: A Psychological Explanation of State Terror," *The Sciences*, March/April 1988, 30–38.

Warren Johansson

AUTOBIOGRAPHY
See **Biography and Autobiography**.

AUTOEROTICISM
See **Masturbation**.

AVERSION THERAPY

This type of modification of human conduct is grounded in a basic principle of behaviorism, the stimulus–response mechanism. If pleasant experiences continue to be regularly associated with a particular stimulus the behavioral response is said to be positively reinforced; unfavorable experiences cause negative reinforcement or deconditioning. Thus Pavlov's dogs came to salivate at the ringing of a bell when this sound regularly preceded feeding; substituting electric shocks for the feeding would cancel the response of salivation, replacing it with symptoms of fear. Applied to homosexuality, it is posited that if the favorable associations evoked by the same-sex bodies are displaced by unpleasant ones (in the form of electric shocks or a nausea-inducing drug), while a pattern of pleasant feelings is brought into play with respect to the body of the opposite sex, the subject will shift from a homosexual orientation to a heterosexual one. In its negative-reinforcement aspects aversion therapy amounts to a routinization of punishment. The therapy known as Behavior Modification is similar in its reliance on the principle of conditioning, but it tends to emphasize rewards more than punishments.

When imposed involuntarily—as in a **prison** or hospital setting—aversion therapy raises strong moral questions. As a result of unfavorable publicity it is rarely applied today to any but pedophiles, regarded as a danger to society. Even here, however, the ethical questions subsist. In fairness, one should note that many proponents of these techniques have protested their involuntary use, asking that such interventions cease.

Most practitioners of aversion therapy maintain that they act only at the request of the patient. Yet here, despite claims of "cures" on the part of some advocates, doubts as to efficacy of the treatment arise. While aversion therapy may succeed for a time in causing the subject to feel revulsion toward his or her homosexuality, it has failed to instill heterosexual desire where a basis for this was lacking. Thus the "cured" clients were almost always bisexuals with a strong preexisting heterosexual component; the therapeutic intervention simply deleted the homosexual component. Even here it is by no means certain that the effect will prove lasting, inasmuch as the deconditioning has a tendency to fade over time so that the homosexual side may eventually return.

Some behavioral therapists assert that they would use such techniques only to help the homosexual to adjust to his condition. Here the problems addressed would be from the realm of daily conduct (as seen, for example, in excessive timidity that would prevent the client from finding partners) and from the area of sexual functioning. Once again, because of the fading principle, one may doubt that the results are permanent. It may be that, however, in a larger program designed to achieve the patient's self-actualization, aversion procedures may have a specific instrumental value. The harnessing of the techniques to a broader, humanistic endeavor would help to address the criticism of depth psychologists and others, who assert that aversion techniques and behavior modification affect only the surface, neglecting the inner life of the client.

BIBLIOGRAPHY. William O. Faustman, "Aversive Control of Maladaptive Sexual Behavior: Past Developments and Future Trends," *Psychology*, 13 (1976), 53–60; Michael W. Ross, "Paradigm Lost or Paradigm Regained? Behaviour Therapy and Homosexuality," *New Zealand Psychologist*, 6 (1977), 42–51.
Ward Houser

AZAÑA, MANUEL
(1880–1940)

President of Spain, 1931–33 and 1936–39. Azaña was a man of letters before entering politics. With his long-time companion, the theater director Cipriano Rivas Cherif, whose sister he was to marry in 1929, he edited the literary magazine *La Pluma* (1920–23), and then joined the board of the more political *España* (1923–24). In the late 1920s he published a novel, *Garden of the Monks*, dedicated to Rivas Cherif, and much literary scholarship. Elected president of the influential Athenaeum of Madrid in 1930, Azaña emerged as a national leader with the proclamation of the Second Republic in 1931. It was he who declared that Spain was no longer Catholic, and an opposition to Catholicism, support for personal liberty, and a belief in the power of the intellect were at the center of his political philosophy.

BIBLIOGRAPHY. *Azaña*, Madrid: Edascal, 1980; Frank Sedwick, *The Tragedy of Manuel Azaña*, Columbus: Ohio State University Press, 1963.

Daniel Eisenberg

BACON, FRANCIS, SIR (1561–1626)

English statesman, philosopher, and essayist. After a somewhat shaky start in the service of Queen Elizabeth, during the reign of James I Bacon advanced from knight (1603) to the offices of attorney general (1613) and lord chancellor (1618). In 1621, however, his position collapsed when he was forced to plead guilty of charges of taking bribes; he then retired to study and write. In the philosophy of science Bacon has become identified, sometimes simplistically, with the method of induction, the patient accumulation of data to reach conclusions. Recent research, however, has shown that this stereotypical picture of a skeptical, essentially modern figure is distorted and anachronistic; Bacon's interest in experiment is in fact rooted in magical, alchemical, and esoteric traditions. Although the notion that he wrote Shakespeare's plays is now discounted, his aphoristic *Essays* (1597–1625) are a stylistic achievement in their own right.

Evidence for Bacon's erotic predilection for young men in his employ comes from two seventeenth-century writers, John Aubrey and Sir Simonds D'Ewes. The latter even states that there was some question of bringing him to trial for buggery. A letter survives from Bacon's mother chastizing him for his fondness for Welsh boys. His marriage, which was childless and probably loveless, took place at the mature age of 46. Sir Francis Bacon seems to have moved entirely in a masculine world. In accord with Greco-Roman and Renaissance predecessors, his essay "Of Friendship" confines itself to relations between men. "Of Beauty" discusses the matter exclusively in terms of male exemplars. Also significant is his Machiavellian commendation of dissimulation; the best policy is "to have openness in fame and opinion, secrecy in habit, dissimulation in seasonable use, and a power to feign if there be no remedy." The need to "edit" one's persona thus recognized is of course one facet of the closeted life, though Bacon's caution may have been reinforced by sensitivity regarding his occult and magical interests, which were scarcely popular among the masses.

BIBLIOGRAPHY. Fulton Henry Anderson, *Francis Bacon: His Career and His Thought*, Los Angeles: University of Southern California Press, 1962; Paolo Rossi, *Francis Bacon: From Magic to Science*, London: Routledge, 1968.

BAILEY, DERRICK SHERWIN (1910–1984)

British theologian and historian; Canon Residentiary of Wells Cathedral from 1962. After World War II Bailey joined a small group of Anglican clergymen and physicians to study homosexuality; their findings were published in a 1954 Report entitled *The Problem of Homosexuality* produced for the Church of England Moral Welfare Council by the Church Information Board. As part of this task Bailey completed a separate historical study, *Homosexuality and the Western Christian Tradition* (London: Longmans, 1955). Although this monograph has been criticized for tending to exculpate the Christian church from blame in the persecution and defamation of homosexuals, it was a landmark in the history of the subject, combining scrutiny of the Biblical evidence with a survey of subsequent history. Bailey's book drew attention to a number of neglected subjects, including the **intertestamental** literature, the legislation of the Christian emperors, the **penitentials**, and the link between **heresy** and **sodomy**. The author's interpretation of Genesis 19, where he treats the **Sodom** story as essentially nonsexual—an instance of violation of hospitality—has not been generally accepted. The work of Bailey and his colleagues prepared the way for the progressive **Wolfenden Report** (1957), which was followed a decade later by Parliament's **decriminalization** of homosexual conduct between consenting adults in England and Wales.

BALDWIN, JAMES (1924–1987)

American novelist, essayist, and playwright. Born in New York City's **Harlem**, his experiences as a child evangelist in the ghetto provided a rich store of material, as well as contributing to his sometimes exhortatory style. His first novel, *Go Tell It on the Mountain* (1953), which derives from this world, gave him immediate fame. Following the example of fellow black author Richard Wright, Baldwin had moved to Paris at the age of 24; he was to live in France for most of the rest of his life, though most of his concerns and work continued to center on the United States.

The acclaim that he had garnered in the 1950s emboldened him to publish *Giovanni's Room* (1961), an honest novel about homosexuality sent out into a literary world that was scarcely welcoming. This book recounts the story of David, an athletic, white American expatriate who discovers his homosexuality in a relationship with a working-class Italian in Paris; although it ends tragically with the death of Giovanni, the lean, yet intense style of this book, and its candor, left a lasting impression. At the time, to be sure, critics urged Baldwin to abandon such "exotic" subject matter and return to native themes. Baldwin responded with his most ambitious work yet, *Another Country* (1962), in which the sexual and racial themes are inextricably interwoven. Only partially successful, this novel presents the lives of a number of New Yorkers of varying sexual persuasions, who are linked by their friendship with a black musician.

Having successfully withstood the homophobia of the immediate postwar years, the emergence of the Civil Rights movement gave Baldwin the chance to play a role at the center of the stage. His prose work *The Fire Next Time* (1963) effectively captures the moral fervor of the Kennedy years, and Baldwin seemed the Jeremiah that the country needed. Although he continued to publish after this point, the writer seemed unable to find a balanced viewpoint, and his later novels and plays are sometimes diffuse and strident. Some of his former admirers felt that he had become too much wrapped up in the rhetoric of black liberation, with its angry indictment of white injustice; conversely, some black critics found him insufficiently militant. Try as he might, he could not convince the younger black radicals that he had not sold out to whitey. Baldwin's estimate of the urgency of the racial crisis led him to downplay the homosexual theme. Yet as a commentator on the continuing "American dilemma" of race, Baldwin failed to deliver a message that could carry full conviction for any group. Despite his best efforts, in the view of many readers he never recaptured the crystalline precision of his earlier works. These suffice, however, to assure his reputation as a writer of compelling power, a sensitive observer not merely of blackness and gayness, not merely of America and Europe, but of the inherent complexities of the human condition.

BIBLIOGRAPHY. Fred L. Standley, *James Baldwin: A Reference Guide*, Boston: G. K. Hall, 1980; Carolyn Wedin Sylvander, *James Baldwin*, New York: Frederick Ungar, 1980; W. J. Weatherby, *James Baldwin: Artist on Fire*, New York: Donald I. Fine, 1989.

Wayne R. Dynes

BALLET
See **Dance.**

BALZAC, HONORÉ DE (1799–1850)

French novelist. Balzac is best known as the creator of the *Comédie humaine*, a vast collection of interlocking novels and stories of which about ninety were written in less than twenty years. The *Comédie humaine* displays both unity and diversity: if a number of narratives are set in **Paris** in the 1820s, the bold stratagem of letting characters from one book know characters from another fosters the reader's growing conviction of the reality of the world evoked by the novelist. The literary complex also carries conviction because of the interplay of critical attitudes that express Balzac's intuitive analysis of modern society: even the more obscure private dramas are linked with the life of **France** at a particular moment in its history—the Restoration and the July Monarchy. The stresses and conflicts between thought and instinct, between Paris and the provinces, between those who cling to the past and those who move with the times—all these mirror Balzac's need to compensate for what life had failed to give him and the truth of his own experience. Balzac transformed the novel into a vehicle for reflective commentary on modern society and so to an incalculable degree influenced succeeding generations of writers in many tongues.

While there is no evidence that Balzac was overtly homosexual, he has been suspected of a latent and sublimated bisexuality in the paternal "friendships" which he cultivated with the handsome young men with whom he surrounded himself. At the same time, the homosexual theme flourishes in his work, in either an open or a veiled fashion, even if Balzac was always considered the author who specialized in woman and marriage.

In *Splendeurs et misères des courtisanes* (1844–46) Balzac describes the world of the *tantes* ("queens") in prison, where the prisoners, of the same sex but of different ages, are crowded together under conditions that favor homosexuality. Vautrin is the symbol of imprisoned sexuality, incarcerated because he took the blame for the crime of another, "a very handsome young man whom he greatly loved." The novelist's depiction of prison homosexuality goes beyond any mere documentary treatment; it does not hide the sexual dimension of prison friendships, but shows them as a form of love with values all their own. The homosexual element is present everywhere in the prison, yet unutterable and unmentionable. Vautrin's secret is that he does not love women, but when and how does he love men? He does so only in the rents of the fabric of the narrative, because the technique of the novelist lies exactly in not speaking openly, but letting the reader know indirectly the erotic background of the events of his story. The physical union of Vautrin with Lucien he presents with stylistic subtlety as a predestined coupling of two halves of one being, as submission to a law of nature. The homosexual aspect of the discourse must always be masked, must hide behind a euphemism, a taunting ambiguity that nevertheless tells all to the knowing reader.

The pact struck between Vautrin and Lucien is a Faustian one. Vautrin dreams of owning a plantation in the American South where on a hundred thousand acres he can have absolute power over his slaves—including their bodies. Balzac refers explicitly to examples of the pederasty of antiquity as a creative, civilization-building force by analogy with the Promethean influence of Vautrin upon his beloved Lucien. Vautrin is almost diabolical as a figure of exuberant masculinity, while Lucien embodies the gentleness and meekness of the feminine. The unconscious dimension of their relationship Balzac underlines with magnificent symbolism. He characterizes Vautrin as a monster, "but attached by love to humanity." Homosexual love is not relegated to the margin of society, as in the dark underworld of the prison, but expresses the fullness of affection with all its physical demands and its spiritual powers. Homosexuality is not the whole of Vautrin's existence, but he is incomprehensible without it, it stylizes his will to power and invests it with its driving force.

There is also a political aspect to homosexuality in Balzac: in it he saw a defiance of the society that proscribed and marginalized it and a challenge to prevailing moral values. By virtue of living outside the French bourgeois society of his day, Vautrin gains insight into its hypocrisy and expresses his contempt for its sham values. He declares that in reality honesty is useless, money is everything, the sole moral principle is to maintain a façade of propriety, justice is corrupt. The poor are no better than the rich, and it has always been this way. In such an ethical context homosexuality is the practice of those who have gauged society and perceived its hollowness, liberating themselves from the social contract, while the world of heterosexuality is a world of false anti-values maintained by shameful and covert means. The affirmation of the erotic is the negation of the legitimacy of the respectable and so-called honorable.

In 1835 Balzac published his extravagantly plotted *La fille aux yeux d'or*, which concerns a beautiful young woman kept in seclusion by a lesbian who, after an absence, discovers her ward's infidelity with a man and kills her. Again, the writer sought to use the theme to illustrate the corruption of contemporary society, but was less successful in empathizing with his characters.

Elsewhere in his work, in *Séraphita* (1834), Balzac took up the theme of the androgyne under the influence of Emanuel Swedenborg. He asserted that he had begun to write the story at the age of nineteen and that he had long "dreamed of the being with two natures." The underlying myth is that all the angels were once human beings who earned their elevation to this celestial dignity. The personage after whom the story is named appears to the main characters, Wilfrid and Minna, as Séraphita and Séraphitus respectively. But while Minna is an insignificant and dreamy romantic heroine, Wilfrid is a mature hero with a stormy past and aspirations for a glorious future, who nevertheless is ready to sacrifice all his ambitions to obtain Séraphita "who should be a divine woman to possess." Balzac represents both as in love with one and the same person, a chosen being endowed with a mysterious power. The androgyne does not symbolize bisexuality, but nature in its wholeness, in its original purity, "the diverse parts of the Infinite forming a living melody." Having revealed to the hero and heroine an ideal love, Séraphitus–Séraphita departs for a heaven free of the earthly misery that human beings must endure.

Recently, the story "Sarrasine" (1830) has attracted scholarly attention, notably from the homosexual critic Roland **Barthes**. This short, but resonant narrative concerns the ambiguities of a family whose fortunes are founded on the achievements of a castrato.

Balzac confronted the mysteries of homosexuality and intersexuality in their forms both real and ideal, not just as a chronicler of the France of his time, but also as a visionary whose imagination relived myths of pagan antiquity.

BIBLIOGRAPHY. Philippe Berthier, "Balzac du côté de Sodome," *L'Année balzacienne* (1979), 147–77; Marie Delcourt, "Deux interprétations romanesques du mythe de l'androgyne: Mignon et Séraphita," *Revue des langues vivantes*, 38 (1972), 228–40, 340–47.

Warren Johansson

BANG, HERMAN (1857–1912)

Danish novelist and short story writer. Associated with the theatre for much of his life, Bang was also active as a journalist and critic in opposition to Georg

Brandes. He died during a tour of the United States.

Bang internalized a negative view of homosexuality from the pathological theories current in his youth. Fearful of **blackmail** and ridicule, he guarded his expressions of what meant most to him, even in letters, so that his inner life must be read between the lines. Declaring that people were not ready for the truth about homosexuality, he withheld his essay on the subject. This study, "Gedanken zum Sexualitätsproblem," deliberately written in a neutral and objective tone, was published posthumously in Germany in 1922. Nonetheless, Bang believed that his homosexuality was a gift, linked to his creativity as a writer and permitting him to see both the masculine and the feminine side of human nature.

His first novel, *Haablose Slaegter* (1880; Generations without Hope) focuses on the decadent scion of an ancient family, who is evidently homosexual. His novella *Mikaël* (1904) presents a much more joyous picture of life and love, including special friendships in artistic circles. In 1916 the Swedish director Mauritz Stiller made *Mikaël* into a **film** under the title *The Wings;* this work is regarded by some as the first gay motion picture. Although Bang today enjoys the status of a major writer in his own country, understanding of his work has until recently been hampered by imposition of **Freudian** schemas, which ignore the complexities of his self-understanding.

BIBLIOGRAPHY. Pål Bjørby, "The Prison House of Sexuality: Homosexuality in Herman Bang Scholarship," *Scandinavian Studies*, 58 (1986), 223–55.

BANNEKER, BENJAMIN (1731–1806)

American mathematician and astronomer. The son of free blacks who were landowners in Baltimore County in tidewater Maryland, he received a brief education at a one-room country school that ended when he was old enough to work full-time with his father on the farm, but like most intellectuals of the colonial period he continued to learn through private reading for the rest of his life. By his method of self-instruction he emerged a competent mathematician and amateur astronomer. Proficient enough to calculate an almanac, he devised one for the year 1791 but was unable to see it through to press. However, *Banneker's Almanack* for the years 1792 through 1797 was published in a number of editions. It reflected a new trend in that its contents were devoted to national events and local causes; also by popularizing the theme of antislavery, it contributed substantially to the abolitionist cause. Banneker assisted Major Andrew Ellicott during the preliminary survey of the ten-mile square and in establishing lines for some of the major points in the future capital of Washington. In his time he was the emblematic figure of black achievement in the sciences, and as such received considerable attention from the abolitionist societies.

Banneker remained a bachelor all his life, and no evidence can be found for any romantic attachment or for illegitimate offspring. He led a casual, rather solitary existence, and since his father died when Benjamin was twenty-eight, he had to assume full responsibility for his mother and the farm. His leisure time was given by preference to his studies. A trace of self-revelation may have escaped in a short essay in his first published almanac which declared that poverty, disease, and violence inflict less suffering than the "pungent stings . . . which guilty passions dart into the heart." Benjamin Banneker deserves to be remembered as a homosexual who played a significant role in the intellectual life of the young American Republic.

BIBLIOGRAPHY. Silvio A. Bedini, *The Life of Benjamin Banneker*, New York: Charles Scribner's Sons, 1972.

Warren Johansson

BANQUETS
See **Symposia**.

BARNES, DJUNA (1892–1981)

American novelist, playwright, and journalist. She was born in Cornwall-on-Hudson, NY, the daughter of a cultivated Englishwoman and an unsuccessful artist. In her twenties she worked in New York City as a journalist and illustrator. With her tall, dashing figure, she was able to obtain colorful interviews that sold to major papers, her earnings contributing to the support of her impecunious family. The bohemian life of Greenwich Village was then at its height, and Barnes had entree into the salon of Mabel Dodge, the "den mother" of the avant-garde. She also became friends with the homosexual artist Marsden **Hartley**; throughout her life, Barnes was to have important gay-male friends.

In New York's milieu of feminist assertion her literary horizons widened, and at the end of World War I she went to **Paris**, where she became friends with James Joyce. Supporting herself with her journalism, she blended with the lesbian and homosexual life of what later came to be called the "Lost Generation" in the French capital. With Thelma Wood, a sculptress from Missouri, Barnes began a stormy affair that lasted until 1931. She also published her first serious work, a collection of poems, stories, plays, and drawings, entitled simply *A Book*, in 1923. Five years later her *Ryder*, a bawdy retelling of the history of the Barnes family, appeared briefly on the bestseller lists, the only approach to popularity she was to enjoy in her lifetime. Published anonymously, her lesbian *Ladies Almanack* (1928) was hawked on the streets of Paris by Barnes and others.

By the early thirties her drinking and nervous breakdowns had become serious, and she sought refuge first in Tangiers and then at the home of Peggy Guggenheim in England. The security that she finally found under Guggenheim's protection enabled Barnes to complete her masterpiece, *Nightwood*, which was published with an introduction by T.S. **Eliot** in London in 1936. This novel, which focuses around the bizarre figure of the homosexual Dr. O'Connor, stands in a class of its own: an incomparable evocation of one writer's view of Paris and Berlin during the interwar years.

Barely escaping from Paris at the start of World War II, Barnes returned to New York, where she found a tiny apartment in Patchin Place in Greenwich Village. Here she was to live in increasing seclusion for forty years, supported mainly by a tiny allowance from Guggenheim. Although she wrote less and less, Barnes did manage to publish a second major work, the bitter play *Antiphon*, in 1958. In her last years a few determined lesbian activists and scholars managed to penetrate her isolation, while the sale of her papers to the University of Maryland gave her a financial security that had long eluded her.

A link between the avant-garde of Paris and New York, as well as the worlds of male and female homosexuality, Barnes had a literary voice all her own that will guarantee her a place in the annals of twentieth-century sensibility.

BIBLIOGRAPHY. Andrew Field, *Djuna: The Life and Times of Djuna Barnes*, New York: Putnam, 1983.

Evelyn Gettone

BARNEY, NATALIE CLIFFORD (1876–1972)

American writer and patron of the arts. Born into a wealthy family of Dayton, Ohio, Barney had been to Europe several times, before she settled in **Paris** in 1902 at the height of the belle époque. Living a public life, she made her home in the Rue Jacob a prominent literary salon for over a half a century. While this salon attracted many famous men of letters, it was also outstanding as a focus for the international lesbian colony in Paris. With her affluence, self-assurance, and accomplishments as a writer, Barney provided a role model for many women, then and now. Always candid about her lesbianism, she nonetheless elicited the devotion of such figures as Remy de Gourmont, Gabriele D'Annunzio, Bernard Berenson, and Ezra Pound.

Her first book, *Quelques portraits-sonnets de femmes*, was published in Paris in 1900. Like most of her works it was written in classic French. Influenced by Greek literature, Barney was not stylistically an experimental writer. After her affair with the celebrated courtesan Liane de Pougy, Barney established a literary liaison with the doomed Anglo-French writer of decadent themes, Renée **Vivien** (Pauline Tarn), who died in 1909, despite Barney's ministrations. Her most long-lasting relationship, amounting to a marriage, was with the American painter, Romaine **Brooks**.

Influenced by her friend Pound, Barney's political opinions became more conservative in the 1930s. Although she was partly of Jewish descent, she chose to spend World War II in Italy, where she expressed her admiration for Mussolini. Her outspoken memoir of this period has not been published. Her luck held up, however, and she was able to resettle in her home in Paris without incident.

BIBLIOGRAPHY. Karla Jay, *The Amazon and the Page: Natalie Clifford Barney and Renée Vivien*, Bloomington: Indiana University Press, 1988; George Wickes, *The Amazon of Letters; The Life and Loves of Natalie Barney*, London: Allen, 1977.

BARNFIELD, RICHARD (1574–1627)

English poet. Born in Norbury, England, Barnfield graduated from Oxford in 1592. Among his friends were the Elizabethan poets Thomas Watson, Michael Drayton, Francis Meres, and possibly **Shakespeare**. He published his first volume of poetry in 1594, *The Affectionate Shepherd*, a sonnet sequence based on Virgil's second eclogue and using as main characters an older man in love with a younger. The volume was dedicated to Penelope Rich who was Sir Philip Sidney's "Stella" and eventually the mistress of Charles Blount, a minor court figure. Hudson reads the Ganimede character in Barnfield's poems as Blount, but Morris attacks the suggestion. No further attempts have been made to identify historical figures behind *The Affectionate Shepherd*.

The unmistakably homosexual theme in *The Affectionate Shepherd* poems may have prompted Barnfield to claim in the preface to his next volume (*Cynthia*, 1595) that readers had misinterpreted his first poems, but the disclaimer is ambiguous and suggests that Barnfield was in trouble for political reasons, not for the sexual love portrayed in his poems. Barnfield's sonnets are not graphically sexual and may best be described as "homoerotic," but they treat more obviously of an emotional infatuation between an older man and a younger than do the sonnets of Barnfield's contemporary William Shakespeare. Of his "Poems in divers Humours" (1598), two were reprinted in the 1599 *Passionate Pilgrim* and were attributed to Shakespeare until the twentieth century. Barnfield retired from public notice soon after his last book and possibly lived as a gentleman farmer.

BIBLIOGRAPHY. Scott Giantvalley, "Barnfield, Drayton, and Marlowe: Homoeroticism and Homosexuality in Elizabethan Literature," *Pacific Coast Philology* 16:2 (1981), 9–24; H. H. Hudson, "Penelope Devereux as Sidney's Stella," *Huntington Library Bulletin* (April, 1935), 89–129; Henry Morris, *Richard Barnfield, Colin's Child*, Tallahassee: Florida State University Press, 1963.

George Klawitter

Bars

In contemporary American English, a bar is a premises licensed to sell liquor by the glass to the public. In addition food may be served and entertainment offered. From ca. 1935 to 1970 the "gay bar" was the premier institution of the male homosexual **community**. There were no homosexual enclaves without at least one. Unlike other commercial establishments, crossing the threshold of a gay bar brought the patron immediately from neutral or hostile territory into "gay space," where only the rules of one's own community applied. The pivotal role of the bars was affirmed by the dubious accolade of **police** raids and shakedowns. Their positive functions notwithstanding, the popularity of the bars is linked to the high rates of **alcoholism** among gay men and lesbians.

Several reasons for the pivotal role of the bars in the male homosexual community may be noted. There is the well-known effect of alcohol in reducing inhibitions, which tend to rise to a higher threshold in those of deviant sexuality than in others. Also, in the Anglo-Saxon world drinking itself carries overtones of taboo, reinforced by recurrent temperance campaigns, which achieved a complete though ephemeral victory in the United States Prohibition (1920–33). Finally, bars have traditionally played a role in male culture as a whole.

It has been said that the bar itself is an institution limited to the English-speaking world. But if we alter the terms of the inquiry slightly to include *taverns* and *cabarets*, we can see that this is not so. Of course, public houses where liquor is served will vary in atmosphere and amenities according to national traditions, regulations, and customs.

Historical Perspectives. The first memorable association of male group drinking with homosexuality takes us back to Plato's dialogue, *The Symposium*, though this event, like other **symposia**, took place (presumably) in rented premises and only invited guests were present. The origins of the word tavern lead back to Roman shops, including wine shops, with open counters on the street. A more immediate source is the taphouse of late medieval Europe, where one could not only purchase drink but linger in the company of others. That patrons often became rowdy and licentious is shown by the common charge that such places were the "Devil's school." At the beginning of the sixteenth century Niccolò Machiavelli seems to have frequented a homosexual (or mixed) tavern in **Florence**. At the end of the century the English dramatist Christopher **Marlowe** presented his subversive views in a place which must have tolerated homosexual custom, if not actually soliciting it. In these two cases it is difficult to be certain about the actual character of the places; they belong to the general realm of the criminal underworld. In the early eighteenth century the nature of the London **molly houses** becomes very clear: they were private places of homosexual entertainment and assignation. After their unmasking, however, the various vigilance societies seem to have prevented a recurrence. In the middle of the nineteenth century the curtain lifts again, with the continental **Bohemia**n cafés, with their mixed clientele of artists, would-be artists, prostitutes, and sexual nonconformists.

Toward the Present. Scholars can first monitor an ecology of gay bars as such in **Berlin** after 1900, where a host of them, operating more or less openly, was surveyed by Magnus **Hirschfeld**. In the 1920s lesbian bars and cabarets flourished in Germany, alongside the male ones. At this time American gay bars appeared, but as part of the speakeasy underworld, because of Prohibition. Their atmosphere has been recorded in such period **novels** as Lew Levinson's *Butterfly Man* (1934), Blair Niles's *Strange Brother* (1931), and Robert Scully's *A Scarlet Pansy* (1933).

Once Prohibition was ended, the states established boards to control licencing, and these could be used to harass operators of gay bars. Places that succeeded in staying open had to maintain a low profile, being located oftentimes in unfreqented warehouse areas and with little in the way of a sign. More elegant establishments were sometimes found in the interior of hotels. Thus it was necessary to know someone to discover the "special" bars. Many patrons were regulars, attending night after night, and an informal pecking order grew up among them. Needless to say, the loyalty of the regulars was assiduously cultivated by the owners. Some patrons would seek advice from bartenders, though this habit was less common than in straight bars because the gay bartenders, chosen for their looks, tended to function as sex objects enveloped in an atmosphere of narcissistic aloofness. Partly for protective camouflage, straight couples out for a "different" evening were welcomed. Some male bars had one or more regular heterosexual women patrons, much treasured counselors who served as unofficial "den mothers." In small localities bars would cater to both men and women, but in large places they could be quite specialized, some for a younger, others (the "wrinkle bars") for an older crowd, some admitting only an elegant clientele, others hosting "rough trade." As a general rule, the bigger the city, the more specialized were the types of bars found there. Large cities also displayed a contrast between cozy neighborhood bars, with a social emphasis, and high-intensity places attracting a crowd from a broad radius.

Prices were high to take care of bribes and payoffs that were regularly required. Hitches in this system led to raids, as a result of which the patrons would be carted off to the police station and their identities taken—which could be disastrous for some. Hence an atmosphere of clandestinity and danger was always present, heightening the attraction for some patrons. The more ambitious places provided live entertainment, including semiprofessional performances by drag queens. The chief functions remained socialization and cruising, both of which were promoted by milling patterns. While it was the aim of patrons in search of a quick pickup to have one drink, find a partner, and go home, the bar owner's interest dictated causing him to linger, drinking more and more. Some of this "stay a while" effect was achieved through positive attractions, such as a pool table, but often loud music inhibited conversation, while floor layout, dim lighting, and decor discouraged speed. In this respect the gay bar stood at the opposite pole from the fast-food outlet, where lights were bright and everything was done to encourage quick eating and departure. Some bar owners maximized patronage by having one clientele, usually heterosexual, during the day, and another, the gay crowd, at night.

Gay Liberation. Much of this atmosphere disappeared in the 1970s, when bars became more open and friendly. These changes were made possible by the heightened activity of the gay liberation movement in the phase which began, significantly enough, with the 1969 raid on New York City's **Stonewall** Inn and the ensuing riot. Bar owners were quick to take advantage of the increased commercial possibilities, and a few created huge discos noted for their elaborate sound systems. In addition to their legal sales of liquor, these places saw considerable consumption and trading of drugs by patrons. Some of the more ordinary bars took on a greater civic responsibility helping to distribute movement literature and newspapers, and permitting their premises to be used for charity dances in support of **AIDS** victims and other causes. Unlike the pre-1970s bars where sexual activity was strictly forbidden, some bars had "back rooms" where a full range of sexual acts was consummated in the dark. In the era of AIDS, however, most of this orgiastic gratification ceased.

Comparative Perspectives. In Europe the gay bar was a characteristic of northern countries, especially Germany and Scandinavia. Somewhat different was the homosexual pub in Britain, which tended to retain the homey comforts of the national tradition. The tourist trade of the 1960s helped to promote the spread of the gay bar to southern Europe, while Japan continued to evolve its own distinctive variation, which had existed for a number of decades.

Lesbian bars have always been relatively few. This paucity is only partly attributable to the fact that lesbians have less spending money. Historically, the virtual monopoly of homosexual bar culture by men reflects the fact that women were at one time not welcome in most bars in general, or had to be accommodated in special rooms adjacent to the rough-and-tumble of the bar itself. Although feminist pressure has removed the rules that excluded women, the custom of social drinking retains vestiges of male culture in our society.

BIBLIOGRAPHY. Sherri Cavan, *Liquor License: An Ethnography of Bar Behavior*, Chicago: Aldine, 1966; John Alan Lee, *Getting Sex*, Don Mills, Ont.: Musson, 1978; Kenneth E. Read, *Other Voices: The Style of a Male Homosexual Tavern*, Novato, CA: Chandler and Sharp, 1980.

Wayne R. Dynes

BARTHES, ROLAND (1915–1980)

French literary critic and social commentator. Barthes introduced into the discussion of literature an original interpretation of semiotics based on the work of the Swiss linguist Ferdinand de Saussure. His work was associated with the Structuralist trend as represented by Claude Lévi-Strauss, Julia Kristeva, Tzvetan Todorov, and others. Attacked by the academic establishment for subjectivism, he formulated a concept of criticism as a creative process on an equal plane with fiction and poetry. Even those favorable to his work conceded that this could amount to a "sensuous manhandling" of the text. The turning point in his criticism is probably the tour de force *S/Z* (Paris, 1970), analyzing **Balzac**'s novella about an aging castrato, *Sarrasine*. Here Barthes turns away from the linear, goal-oriented procedures of traditional criticism in favor of a new mode that is dispersed, deliberately marginal, and "masturbatory." In literature, he emphasized the factor of *jouissance,* a word which means both "bliss" and "sexual ejaculation." Whether these procedures constitute models for a new feminist/gay critical practice that will erode the power of patriarchy, as some of his admirers have asserted, remains unclear.

Using the concept of dominant ideology of **Marxist** provenience, Barthes also wrote perceptive analyses of advertising and fashion. Apart from a study of contemporary Japan (*L'Empire des signes*, Paris, 1970), he addressed French literature and culture almost exclusively. Nonetheless, he won many adherents in the English-speaking world, in large measure because his works convey an indomitable verve and infectious relish of the subjects he discussed. These qualities, rather than any finished system, account for his continuing influence.

Barthes, who never married, was actively homosexual during most of his life. Although his books are often personal, in his writing he excluded this major aspect of his experience, even when writing about love. Because of the attacks launched against him for his critical innovations, he was apparently reluctant to give his enemies an additional stick with which to beat him. Barthes' postumously published *Incidents* (Paris, 1987) does contain some revealing diary entries. The first group stems from visits he made, evidently in part for sexual purposes, to North Africa in 1968–69. The second group of entries records restless evenings in Paris in the autumn of 1979 just before his death. These jottings reveal that, despite his great fame, he frequently experienced rejection and loneliness. Whatever his personal sorrows, Barthes' books remain to attest a remarkable human being whose activity coincided with an ebullient phase of Western culture.

BIBLIOGRAPHY. Sanford Freedman, *Roland Barthes: A Bibliographical Reader's Guide*, New York: Garland, 1983.

Wayne R. Dynes

BATHHOUSES

As a result of the general expansion and commercialization of male homosexual life after World War II, the institution of the gay bathhouse became a fixture of major cities of Europe and North America. In these establishments only a small area of the premises is devoted to immersion tubs and sauna rooms; the bulk of the floor space consists of cubicles which are used for resting and for consensual sexual encounters. Other rooms are given over to nonsexual entertainment (television, billiards, music).

Historical Perspectives. Today's gay bathhouses stem ultimately from a cultural tradition that can be traced back over two millennia. In every society in which public baths flourished, the institution was shaped not only by its specific characteristics, but also by the values and norms of the larger community.

In ancient **Greece** the baths formed part of the highly developed practice of physical culture and athletics. Archeologists have uncovered bath buildings adjoining the palaestras or training grounds of athletes. By attaching the bath to the athletic (and to some extent military) function of physical fitness, the Greeks broke with the sacral and ritual tradition of Near Eastern lustration—the religious bath—which nonetheless has a successor in the continuing Jewish custom of the *mikva* or ritual bath.

The Romans attached far more importance to public baths than did the Greeks, creating imposing structures known as *thermae* for the purpose throughout their empire. Originating under the Roman republic, the bath as an institution reached its height when **Rome** had extended its dominion throughout the Mediterranean. Amounting almost to secular cathedrals, the baths served a variety of individual and social requirements. Thermae fulfilled a need for personal cleanliness in an era when private baths were all but unknown. In addition to care of the skin, they fostered physical culture in the broader sense through exercise and massage facilities. Baths whose waters had a high sulfur content served medicinal purposes, anticipating modern spas. Then the baths were indoor arcades, permitting strolling patrons to meet friends and business associates, exchanging pleasantries and information. Some of the more imposing Roman baths embraced cultural and educational functions by offering public lectures and making libraries available to clients. Finally, Roman baths offered a convenient gathering place for those in quest of sexual release. Initially, such contacts were necessarily homosexual, since only men were admitted to the baths. Later, under the Roman Empire, some baths were open to women, for the most part female attendants who also served as prostitutes. Thus the Roman baths offered a kaleidoscopic variety of disparate, yet related functions.

As part of its inheritance from the Roman empire, the civilization of **Islam** continued the custom of offering bath facilities for health and pleasure, alongside the ritual baths required by Koranic law. Medieval Islamic sources indicate that baths of the former class were used not only for health reasons, but for socialization and homosexual contacts. Significantly, modern bathhouses of Europe and America have been termed "Turkish Baths," and sometimes boast tiled decor recalling this Muslim institution.

Strongly discouraged by Christian moralism in the early **Middle Ages**, public baths nonetheless reappeared in medieval cities as an essential aspect of sanitation, beginning in the twelfth cen-

113

tury. These locales were notoriously places of sexual dalliance. In the fourteenth century the English poets Chaucer and Langland attest the use of the word "stews" as meaning both a bathhouse and a place of prostitution, a notion that recurs somewhat later in the term "bagnio" derived from Italian *bagno*. It was in fact the outbreak of syphilis in Europe after 1493 that caused the decline of the medieval baths as loci of heterosexual intimacy.

In early modern Europe baths became less general in character and more institutions appealing to special interests. There is information on baths frequented by a homosexual clientele during the French Second Empire (1852–70) and the German Empire (1871–1918). While the details of the development require further elucidation, it was this specialized European homosexual bathhouse that was transferred in the late nineteenth century to North American cities. An informant describing the United States in the early years of the present century mentions baths patronized by homosexuals in **New York City, Boston, Chicago**, Philadelphia, and "a small city in Ohio." Contemporaneously, they are also documented in **San Francisco**, while in southern California outdoor bathing facilities frequented by homosexuals gained favor. During this period security was uncertain and police raids were always a possibility. Small wonder then that many patrons preferred to take their tricks home rather than risk detection—and possible blackmail—in the bathhouse.

Toward the Present. With the more open American society after World War II these conditions began to change. Ethnographic studies of the bathhouses in the 1970s revealed a number of salient features. Mindful of the older history of raids and continuing general social disapproval, patrons continued to rate security and protection as important. The establishments kept a low profile by having obscure entrances, sometimes being located on the upper floors of nondescript office buildings—or by being situated in warehouse districts with little traffic at night. Admission was controled by a booth where, after payment the client could deposit valuables in a small lockbox. He would then proceed to a cubicle or locker, exchanging his clothing for a towel, the only garment usually worn. The layout of a successful bathhouse would facilitate encounters so that the desirable sexual contacts could be made through the characteristic milling activity in the often labyrinthine halls. Some patrons preferred to remain mostly in their rooms with the door open, indicating by body position the type of activity required. Should a potential partner regarded as undesirable enter, he would usually be gently rebuffed, as with the words "I'm just resting." One of the more attractive features of the baths was the mildness of turndowns; the rejected person, for his part, knew that other potential partners were available.

Many bathhouses possessed "orgy rooms" for group activity, though these are now mainly a thing of the past. Physically, the bathhouse should assure a certain level of comfort and cleanliness, possibly boasting a snack bar, gymnasium, and television room. However, older, deteriorating establishments were able to conceal their dilapidation by dim lighting. In a very few cases, as in the old Continental Baths of New York City, live entertainment was provided. In any event, recorded music relaying the latest hits—and sometimes pieces meant solely for a gay audience—enhanced the sexual atmosphere throughout the premises. Many patrons were repeat visitors, basking in a known, shared reality. In an era of soaring hotel prices, some tourists would use bathhouses for cheap overnight accommodation. Usually, however, an extra fee was charged for a stay of over eight hours. It was not common to find male prostitutes (hustlers) there plying their trade—few would be willing to pay for what they could get for free—but hustlers would sometimes be brought in by a client they had met outside in order to use a room. Despite strong disapproval on the part of the management, some surreptitious drug dealing took place among patrons; consumption of mind-altering drugs, often taken just before arriving, was certainly common. As a rule, alcohol was not served, but could be brought in. Stereotypically, sexual encounters in the baths were completely anonymous; however, a few clients report having begun love affairs or friendships as a result of meetings there. A curious dynamic is that during off-hours, when few people were present, contacts could generally be made quickly, while when the building was crowded patrons could become quite choosy, in hopes that the continuing intake would produce more desirable individuals. Some patrons would have ten or more contacts, but the majority seem to have restricted themselves to two or three, or even one.

In the 1980s, with the unfolding of the **AIDS** crisis in the United States, the bathhouses came under attack because the promiscuous sexual encounters that took place there were held to promote the spread of the disease. Although this charge was denied, and many bathhouses began to distribute **safe sex** information and condoms as a positive contribution, it was clear that their days of glory were over. Many bathhouses in smaller localities were forced to close for lack of business. The owners of some establishments tried to change them into health clubs, but with mixed success. In San Francisco, as a result of pressure from public officials, the last bathhouse closed its doors in 1987. In Europe, however, bathhouses—usually termed saunas there—continue to flourish, and new ones even open from time to time.

BIBLIOGRAPHY. Joseph Styles, "Outsider/Insider: Researching Gay Baths," *Urban Life*, 8:2 (July 1979), 139–52; Martin S. Weinberg and Colin J. Williams, "Gay Baths and the Social Organization of Impersonal Sex," *Social Problems*, 23:2 (1975), 124–36.

Wayne R. Dynes

BEACH, SYLVIA (NANCY) (1887–1962)

American expatriate bookseller, publisher, and intellectual. The daughter of a Presbyterian minister in Princeton, NJ, Beach settled in France during World War I. In 1919 she established Shakespeare and Company, an English-language bookstore and lending library in **Paris** that was to become one of the chief gathering places of the international avant-garde. Beach's companion, Adrienne Monnier, whose own bookshop was located only a short distance away, played a similar role in French letters. A kind of arbiter and confidant of the whole "Lost Generation," Beach was associated with such figures as Djuna **Barnes**, Natalie **Barney**, Bryher (Winifred Ellerman), Ernest Hemingway, Robert McAlmon, Ezra Pound, and Gertrude **Stein**. Her greatest accomplishment was her two decades as publisher for her close friend, the mercurial James Joyce.

A member of the influential lesbian colony in Paris in the years between the wars, Beach nonetheless led a discreet, almost closeted life, supported by her "marriage" with Monnier. Electing to stay on during the German occupation of Paris, where she saved her books from confiscation, she emerged trimphantly after the war as a senior figure in the world of letters.

BIBLIOGRAPHY. Noel Riley Fitch, *Sylvia Beach and the Lost Generation*, New York: Norton, 1983.

BEACHES

Most North American (and many European) cities located near water have a gay (male) beach. If geography permits, it is typically more remote or difficult to reach than the beach serving heterosexuals. Only those "in the know" will go the extra distance, or negotiate the natural barriers, to get there.

Where there are no natural barriers, one portion of a large public beach may become known among homosexuals as gay territory. Original proximity to a tea-room (public **toilet** frequented for sexual purposes) may generate a tradition that a section of beach is gay, and the tradition can survive long after the tearoom is gone. In any event, the sight of hundreds of men, and no women or children, across a stretch of beach, readily leads most heterosexuals, especially with families, to stay clear. Those who unwittingly or stubbornly invade may be offended or subjected to "grossing out." This behavior (one form of camp among gays) is a deliberate enactment of a stereotype attributed to homosexuals that embarrasses the heterosexuals into moving.

A gay beach may be more capable of defense against intruding or threatening heterosexuals than other territories such as a park or main cruising street. Teenagers intent on harassment at a crowded gay beach are likely to find themselves surrounded by a silent but menacing group of gay men. This added element of safety, even if only tacitly understood, often encourages gay men and lesbians to more outrageous behavior for their own entertainment on a gay beach than in other public spaces. This in turn helps establish the beach in heterosexual minds as a gay place.

Gay beaches are favorite places for **cruising** for several reasons: a large number of potential partners is concentrated in a small area, and they are likely to be above average in attractiveness, since the tanned and well-built are readier to show the body; there are readily manufactured excuses for introducing oneself to strangers (just let the frisbee fly too far); what you see is almost what you get, since modern beach costumes leave little for the imagination; and in many cases, the gay beach is isolated by bush or rock outcroppings which serve as cover for impersonal sex.

Holiday weekends are obviously prime time, but depending on the prevailing gay occupations in the city, certain weekdays (e.g., Mondays for waiters and bartenders, Wednesday for hair stylists) may find the gay beach more occupied than other beaches. Cruising is not necessarily limited to the beach; if access is by public transport or ferry, this may also offer numerous opportunities. Offshore, gay men with sailboats or yachts may anchor, rowing to shore to offer attractive strangers a tour in their craft.

Social skills are as important as an attractive body in cruising a beach. Some men set up alone on a blanket, signalling their possible availability, while others prefer to gather in groups, hoping that mutual friends will facilitate introductions. In either case, it is common to periodically go for a stroll along the beach, winding one's way through the complex of towels and blankets, exchanging smiles or glances. The slimmest acquaintance or familiarity of faces may be used to strike up conversation (which may actually be directed not to the person conversed with, but to a total stranger on the next blanket).

Social visiting between blanket-based groups, whether by couples or singles, is easy and common. A picnic lunch increases socializing and lowers inhibitions against introducing oneself to strangers ("Are you hungry? There's lots here."). Ironically, the greater exposure of flesh in a public place often makes encounters more conversational, and less limited to an agenda of impersonal sex, than a dark park or gay baths.

Lesbians appear less likely to establish a beach and very few cities have a lesbian beach. The reasons undoubtedly include less cruising behavior in general among lesbians, less traditional social power (as women) to establish and hold territories, and lesbian preference for a proper social introduction and some prior acquaintanceship before intimate encounter. When a lesbian community develops beach-going social life, lesbians may establish some section of the existing gay male beach as their own. Covert gay men, or lesbians, may use a nearby heterosexual section of beach, but wander through the gay beach on apparent errands (trips to the washroom, water fountain, and so on).

Police—mounted on horse, or more recently in all-terrain vehicles—often attempt to discourage or harass gay beachers, or to surprise or entrap those using "the bushes." Heterosexual resentment of gay male impersonal sex opportunties may lead to political decisions to eliminate gay beaches (e.g., by constructing a promenade, or supervised swimming pool). But an experienced gay man who knows how to search is likely to discover some portion of beach frequented by gays, even in foreign lands.

See also **Geography, Social;** **Resorts; Tourism.**

BIBLIOGRAPHY. J. A. Lee, *Getting Sex*, Toronto: General, 1978, chapter 4.
John Alan Lee

BEAT GENERATION

The origins of this trend in American culture can be traced to the friendship of three key figures in New York City at the beginning of the 1940s. Allen Ginsberg (1926–) and Jack **Kerouac** (1922–1969) met as students at Columbia University, where both were working at becoming writers. In 1944 Ginsberg encountered the somewhat older William Burroughs (1914–), who was not connected with the University, but whose acquaintance with avant-garde literature supplied an essential intellectual complement to college study. Both Ginsberg and Burroughs were homosexual; Kerouac bisexual. At first the ideas and accomplishments of the three were known only to a small circle. But toward the end of the 1950s, as their works began to be published and widely read, large numbers of young people, "beatniks" and "hippies," took up elements of their **lifestyle.**

The beat writers and their friends were only sporadically resident in **San Francisco,** but the media played up this connection, especially during the "flower-

child" era in the mid-1960s. This reputation is not without relation to the Bay City's emerging status as a gay capital. To be sure the beat writers placed little stress on developing a fixed abode—their pads were never photographed for *House Beautiful.* Seminomadic, they traveled extensively not only in the United States, but in Latin America, Europe, North Africa, and Asia. Significantly, one of the most widely read beat texts was Jack Kerouac's novel *On the Road* (1957).

The word beat was sometimes traced to "beatific," and sometimes to "beat out" and similar expressions, suggesting a pleasant exhaustion that derives from intensity of experience. Its appeal also reflects the beat and improvisation of jazz music, one of the principal influences on the trend. Some beat poets tried to match their writings with jazz in barroom recitals, prefiguring the more effective melding of words and music in folk and rock. The ideal of spontaneity was one of the essential elements of the beat aesthetic. These writers sought to capture the immediacy of speech and lived experience, which were, if possible, to be transcribed directly as they occurred. This and related ideals reflect a new version of American folk pragmatism, preferring life to theory, immediacy to reflection, and feeling to reason. Contrary to what one might expect, however, the beat generation was not anti-intellectual, but chose to seek new sources of inspiration in neglected aspects of the European avant-garde and in Eastern thought and religion.

In the view of many, the archetypal figure of the group is William Burroughs. Born into a wealthy business family in St. Louis, Burroughs drifted from one situation to another during his twenties and thirties; only after meeting the younger writers did he find his own voice. First published in Paris in 1959, his novel *Naked Lunch* became available in the United States only after a series of landmark obscenity decisions. With its phantasmagoric and sometimes sexually explicit subject matter, together with its quasi-surrealist techniques of narrative and syntactic disjunction, this novel presented a striking new vision. This novel was followed by *The Soft Machine* and *The Ticket That Exploded* to form a trilogy. *Nova Express* (1964) makes extensive use of the "cut-up" techniques, which Burroughs had developed with his friend Brion Gysin.

A keen observer of contemporary reality in several countries, Burroughs has sought to present a kind of "world upside down" in order to sharpen the reader's consciousness. One of his major themes has been his anarchist-based protest against what he sees as increasingly repressive social control through such institutions as medicine and the police. Involved with drugs for some years, he managed to kick the habit, but there is no doubt that such experiences shaped his viewpoint. His works have been compared to pop art in painting and **science fiction** in literature. Sometimes taxed for misogyny, his world tends to be a masculine one, sometimes exploiting fantasies of regression to a hedonistic world of juvenile freedom. Burroughs's hedonism is acerbic and ironic, and his mixture of qualities yields a distorting mirror of reality which some have found, because perhaps of the many contradictions of later twentieth-century civilization itself, to be a compelling representation.

BIBLIOGRAPHY. Ann Charters, ed., *The Beats: Literary Bohemians in Postwar America*, Detroit: Gale Research, 1983 (Dictionary of Literary Biography, 16); Ted Morgan, *Literary Outlaw: The Life and Times of William Burroughs*, New York: Henry Holt, 1988; John Tytell, *Naked Angels: The Lives and Literature of the Beat Generation*, New York: McGraw-Hill, 1976.

Wayne R. Dynes

BEATS AND HIPPIES

This social trend in mid-twentieth-century American life was constituted by groups of alienated youths and younger adults, recognizable by their counterculture enthusiasms and defiance of then accepted norms of dress, deportment, and relation to the work ethic. Beat is the older term and it came into use to designate a self-marginalized social group of the late 1950s and early 60s that was influenced by existentialism and especially by the writers of the **Beat Generation**. The journalistic word "beatnik" is a pseudo-Slavic coinage of a type popular in the 1960s, the core element deriving from "beat" (generation), the suffix -*nik* being the formative of the noun of agent in Slavic languages. The term "hippie" was originally a slightly pejorative diminutive of the beat "hipster," which in turn seems to derive from 1940s jivetalk adjective "hep," meaning "with it, in step with current fashions." The original hippies were a younger group with more spending money and more flamboyant dress. Their music was rock instead of the jazz of the beats. Despite differences that seemed important at the time, beats and hippies are probably best regarded as successive phases of a single phenomenon.

Although the media, which incessantly sensationalized the beats and hippies, did a great deal to foster recruitment, the phenomenon has older roots, stemming not only from its immediate prefiguration in the small circle of beat writers and their friends, but also from the established Bohemian lifestyle of Western Europe and North America. **Bohemianism** is typically the product of the confluence of outcast groups in inner cities. Yet beats and hippies, as part of the whole **Counterculture** trend, had also a rural contingent, manifested in the establishment of farms run communally. Here a striking forerunner is the English utopian socialist Edward **Carpenter** (1844–1929), a bearded, sandalwearing man who lived with his male lover and other associates working a market garden and practicing various arts and crafts. Significantly, Carpenter, who had been almost forgotten, was revived during this period by homosexuals attracted to hippie ideals. These roots notwithstanding, there was much that was distinctively American about the phenomenon, and to the degree that it spread to Western Europe and Japan it was identifiable as part of the general wave of Americanized popular culture.

Attracted by the prestige of the beat writers, many beats/hippies cultivated claims to be poets and philosophers. In reality, once the tendency became modish only a few of the beat recruits were certifiably creative in literature and the arts; these individuals were surrounded by masses of people attracted by the atmosphere of revolt and experiment, or just seeking temporary separation—a moratorium as it was then called—from the banalities of ordinary American life. At its height the phenomenon supported scores of underground newspapers, which were read avidly by curious outsiders as well. As part of their general defiance of convention these papers published explicit personal **advertisements**, including those of homosexuals. Many journalists got their start in these now defunct publications, carrying with them into the mainstream media significant traces of the values they had upheld in their former careers.

Seekers after "cosmic consciousness," beats and hippies became known for their efforts at mind expansion through the use of **drugs**, alcohol, and sex. Group smoking of marijuana ("grass," "pot") became universal, a kind of secular sacrament which served as a collective bond. Grass was not only a bond of pleasure but one of danger, since stiff criminal penalties imposed by often-overzealous lawmen, led to numerous busts. Part of the appeal of rural communes lay in their suitability as sites for growing the plant. The clandestine comradeship engendered by the ever-present custom of smoking grass—the legally proscribed marijuana—created an outcast's tie with homosexuals, themselves subject to legal sanctions for their deviation. Significantly, the street term for the Other, "straight," could refer either

to non-drug users or heterosexuals. In the 1960s psychedelic substances generated in the chemical laboratory, notably LSD, enjoyed considerable popularity. LSD trips were said to aid creativity, and a type of visual art, characterized by swirling lines and lurid colors and used mainly in underground newspapers and posters, was sometimes termed LSD art. Experimentation with drugs was also popular among the political radicals of the New Left, though they were inclined to criticize hippies for their apathy and lack of social conscience.

Mysticism exerted a potent influence among beats and hippies, and some steeped themselves in Asian religions, especially **Buddhism**, Taoism, and **Sufism**. This fascination was not new, inasmuch as ever since the foundation of Theosophy as an official movement in 1875, American and other western societies had been permeated by Eastern religious elements. Impelled by a search for wisdom and cheap living conditions, many hippies and beatniks set out for prolonged sojourns in **India**, Nepal, and North **Africa**. Stay-at-homes professed their deep respect for American Indian culture.

Ignoring the deeper aspects of these exotic trends, Middle America continued to fix its disapproving gaze on the more superficial aspects of the beat–hippie lifestyle. Abundant facial hair and a preference for casual, "funky" clothing set these **deviants** off from the squeaky-clean look of mainstream America, which professed its disgust at "dirty hippies." Most hippies were heterosexual, but their long hair exposed them to jibes of **effeminacy**. In this way they could experience something of the rejection that had always been the lot of homosexuals.

The lure of unconventional behavior and experience exercised a siren call on American youth, which was chafing restlessly under the reign of the "uptightness" of the Eisenhower years. Paradoxically, it was the new prosperity of postwar America that allowed young people to drop out and "do their own thing" for a time, secure in the knowledge that—unlike members of racial minorities—they could safely rejoin the mainstream when the time came. For much smaller numbers of people, of course, historic Bohemias had offered similar attractions. Here, as in the decaying inner cities of America, a small core of creative individuals was surrounded by a large mass of outcasts and the urban poor. Even though their travels in beatdom might only be temporary, graduates of the experience developed a degree of lasting estrangement from, or at least scepticism toward, the conventional pieties of the American Establishment. Among the views that were now brought into question was the automatic pigeonholing of sexual minorities as "sick."

In a larger sense, beat attitudes, with their stress on feeling instead of reason, are a manifestation of the perennial appeal of the Romantic reaction against Classical norms. The vagabond ideal of traveling lightly, with few possessions, has affinities with **hobo** life, with the gypsies, and ultimately with the "wandering scholars" of the Middle Ages. With its adoption of a variant of jive talk, largely derived from black urban speech, the movement has left a lasting impression on the English vernacular, as seen in such expressions as "cool," "spaced out," and "rip off." As has been noted, the stress on experiment and social unconventionality created a natural affinity with homosexuality, which had been marginalized by Anglo-Saxon culture. Because of this perceived link—and the vogue of such seductive slogans of the **polymorphous perverse** as "If it feels good, do it" and "Copulate, don't populate"—it is likely that many apprentice beatniks permitted themselves to delve into aspects of sexual variation that would otherwise have remained a sealed book to them.

In the 1970s hostile critics, and some who had outgrown their earlier enthusiasm, proclaimed with relief the demise of the hippie movement. Its themes of rejection of worldly goods and the more materialistic aspects of the American dream seemed to be reversed by the yuppy trend. Yet insofar as hippiedom was only the latest manifestation of a recurring strand in Western civilization, celebration of its obsequies is unwarranted.

BIBLIOGRAPHY. Charles Perry, *The Haight-Ashbury: A History*, San Francisco: Rolling Stone Press, 1984; Marco Vassi, *The Stoned Apocalypse*, New York: Trident, 1972.

Wayne R. Dynes

BEAUTY COMPETITIONS

As a rule the heterosexual norms of the modern world have affirmed a dichotomy of physical contests: women may compete on the basis of beauty and charm, while men match their brawn and muscle development. The reason for this separation seems to be a fear of the consequences that could ensue if men were publicly adulated as sex objects. Ordinary language, for example, permits women to be called "beautiful," while men must be styled "handsome." Recently these distinctions have broken down, but only partially.

Ancient Greece. Greek mythology shows a number of competitions among women, notably the Judgment of Paris, which was won by Aphrodite, the goddess of love. In the daily life of ancient **Greece**, however, competitions among males were more important. There were three categories of these. The first, the *kallisteia*, were connected with cults and the winner had to perform a ritual for a deity. While character and deportment were significant, these contests seem to have been decided on the basis of physical beauty. The *euandria* focused on athletic prowess where strength was important. Finally, the *euexia* stood somewhat between the two, emphasizing balance of form rather than physical strength as such. These events must be understood against the backdrop of several lasting features of Greek civilization: its agonic (competitive) character, the familiar display of the nude male body in the gymnasia, and the positive evaluation placed on the institution of pederasty in which the beauty of the beloved youth is a key component. The Romans seem to have had no equivalent, and the rise of Christianity, which prized modesty and prudery, put a stop to any public admiration of the body, whether male or female.

Modern Times. The Renaissance version of the medieval tournament seems to have sometimes given handsome young men a chance to impress powerful patrons, and even to gain the favor of such an exalted monarch as James I of England. However, these events were exceptional. In the nineteenth century the rise of athletics and the desire to escape the constrictions of Victorianism led to the physical culture movement. Among the first superstars of body building was Eugene Sandow, who seems to have been as notable for good looks as for muscles. As the rituals of this subculture developed, however, a simultaneous parallel and contrast emerged between physical culture events for men and beauty contests for women. A woman became, say, "Miss Norway" for comeliness and charm, while "Mr. Norway" was selected (or so it was maintained) exclusively on the basis of his hypertrophied muscles.

In due course several cracks in this edifice appeared. In the 1940s publishers of muscle magazines discovered that they could attract a homosexual clientele by emphasizing more sexy, somewhat less muscular models. In its own sphere the homosexual subculture had drag contests in which success in simulating the female was the criterion. With the coming of open gay liberation in the 1970s, "groovy guy" contests were sponsored by bars and gay organizations, but somehow the custom never went beyond the bar milieu. Male stripping ("burlesque") became common both for gay men and straight women patrons—though the purveyors of the latter entertainment have tried to keep men out, at least during certain hours, lest the event "turn queer." At the same time the all-male domain of the muscle contest has been invaded by women body builders; how many of them are lesbians is unknown. The ambiguity that continues to envelop all these social phenomena seems to be rooted in the late-modern utopian longing for egalitarianism, with its characteristic difficulty in accepting the fact that human beings recognize a hierarchy of brain and beauty among their fellows, and in fact enjoy doing so.

Wayne R. Dynes

BECCARIA, CESARE BONESANA, MARQUIS (1738–1794)

Italian criminologist, economist, and jurist. Though of retiring disposition, he held several public offices in the Austrian government in Milan, the highest being counselor of state. Through the offices which he occupied and the books which he wrote he stimulated reforms throughout Europe, but especially in the sphere of penal law. His classic work on this subject was a small treatise entitled *Dei delitti e delle pene* (1764). This book aroused such interest that further editions, translations, and commentaries appeared within a short time throughout Europe, and by the end of the eighteenth century the number of editions had climbed to sixty. Beccaria's critique of the criminal law and criminal procedure of the Old Regime was inspired by opposition to arbitrary rule, to cruelty and intolerance, and by the belief that no man had the right to take away the life of another human being.

His treatment of the sodomy laws is limited to a single paragraph in the chapter entitled "Delitti di prova difficile" (Crimes Difficult to Prove); in some editions it is Chapter XXXI, in others XXXVI. He introduces the subject as "Attic love, so severely punished by the laws, and so easily subjected to the tortures that overcome innocence," which implies that suspects were cruelly tortured to exact confessions of guilt. He goes on to reject the notion that satiation with pleasure is the cause of this passion, but ascribes it to the practice of educating the youth at the moment when their sexual drive is mounting in seminaries that isolated them from the opposite sex.

Beccaria thus had no notion of the modern concept of homosexuality, nor was he greatly interested in the crime of sodomy. The importance of the work lies in the tremendous impetus that it gave to the campaign for reform of the archaic and barbarous criminal laws. Of all the leading intellectuals of that day, the one who took the greatest interest in Beccaria's work was **Voltaire**, who in 1766 published an anonymous *Commentary* on the book. In it he endorsed almost all of Beccaria's principles, adding to many of the book's chapters anecdotes exemplifying the faults and contradictions in the existing penal system. Other translators and commentators expanded Beccaria's concise arguments by appending their own notes and comments, so that a full collection of these would illustrate the reception of the book. England revealed the faults of its own system during the very period that reform was on the march in Europe: it was not until 1816 that exposure in the pillory to the hatred and violence of the mob was abolished as a penalty for buggery, and when Sir Robert Peel undertook a major revamping of the criminal laws in 1828 he not only let the death penalty stand but even made it easier to obtain a conviction.

In the United States Beccaria was popular at an early date: John Adams alluded to him in his speech in defense of the British soldiers on trial for what came to be known as the "Boston Massacre." But the greatest influence of Beccaria by far was on the Bill of Rights, as the part of it which refers to criminal law and procedure cannot be understood apart from Beccaria's demands for reform. The Fifth, Sixth, and Eighth Amendments to the American Constitution may be called the Lex Beccaria, since they guarantee the rights of the accused in a criminal proceeding, provide that no person "shall be compelled in any criminal case to be a witness against himself," and prohibit "excessive fines" and "cruel and unusual punishments." In adopting the Bill of Rights the founding fathers accepted and ratified Beccaria's thinking, and it is therefore a major error to assume that homosexual law reform has no history in the United States before the State of Illinois repealed its sodomy statute.

Had the principles of the treatise *On Crimes and Punishments* been followed, all the laws prohibiting consensual homosexual behavior in private would have been stricken from the books in the first decade after the adoption of the Bill of Rights—as they were in France in 1791. The **Enlightenment** thinkers held that the basic principles of justice are the same everywhere, as all human beings respond to the same fundamental drives and aspirations. If a society that is tolerant of homosexual expression remains a distant goal, Beccaria was one of those pioneers who started the movement in its direction.

BIBLIOGRAPHY. Mitchell Franklin, "Roman Law and the Constitution of the United States," *Synteleia Vincenzo Arangio-Ruiz*, Naples: Jovene, 1964, pp. 315–23; Marcello Maestro, *Cesare Beccaria and the Origins of Penal Reform*, Philadelphia: Temple University Press, 1973.

Warren Johansson

BECKFORD, WILLIAM (1760–1844)

English author, art collector, and patron. The only legitimate child of one of the richest men in England, Beckford had a spoiled, cosseted childhood. At school in Switzerland he already gave signs of a special sensitivity to male beauty. On his return to England he met and fell in love with a nobleman, William Courtenay, then eleven years old. Powerful residues of this infatuation accompanied him on his grand tour of the European continent (1780–82), and they were transmuted into the manuscript of his Gothic novel *Vathek*, which was published in French only in 1787. On his return to England he resumed seeing Courtenay, and the simmering scandal was only partly effaced by his marriage in 1783. Beckford judged it advisable to spend a number of years in exile abroad, in Portugal, Spain, and Paris, where he witnessed the French Revolution.

After his return to England he commenced construction, in 1796, of a remarkable architectural folly, his Gothic revival country seat of Fonthill Abbey, which he embellished with frescoes, stained glass and objets d'art. Financial reverses forced him to sell Fonthill in 1821, which was fortunate as it fell into ruin shortly thereafter. Beckford lived the rest of his life in Bath and London, taking a lively interest in homosexual gossip. Having survived several scandals and the repressive atmosphere of the era of the Napoleonic wars, his homosexual interests were prudently reduced to those of an epistolary voyeur. Despite his irregular life and his dilettantism, Beckford made contributions in two areas. His novel *Vathek*, with its exotic oriental setting and androgynous characters, formed part of the pre-Romantic literary movement. Fonthill Abbey, though only a portion of it survives, was one of the first major secular constructions of the Gothic Revival trend in British architecture.

BIBLIOGRAPHY. Brian Fothergill, *Beckford of Fonthill*, London: Faber, 1979.

BELGIUM

The kingdom of Belgium, though a relatively small country, enjoys a pivotal geographical position in Europe. The lands that are now Belgium, together with northern Italy, saw the emergence of European urban society at the end of the Middle Ages. As yet insufficiently explored, the history of homosexuality in Belgium promises to offer important insights. In our present state of knowledge, however, the beginnings are melancholy, since the first execution for sodomy documented anywhere in Europe took place in Ghent in 1292.

Late Medieval and Early Modern Periods. The fourteenth and fifteenth centuries show a considerable increase of prosecutions of the criminal act of *vuyle faicten* (buggery). In 1373, Willem Case and Jan van Aersdone were executed in Antwerp. In Mechelen, one person was burned at the stake, and in 1391 the same city witnessed a mass trial of seventeen people, among them two women. Yet only one confessed and was executed. In Ypres, the death penalty was imposed on two men in 1375. Twenty-two executions were recorded in Antwerp, Brussels, and Louvain during the fifteenth century.

The occurrence of these trials, though only a few led to executions in medieval Flanders, raises the question of whether there is a link between urbanization and the regulation of sexuality from above, especially since homosexual behavior continued to go largely unnoticed between farmers and male servants in the countryside. In the view of Geert Debeuckelaere, the cities witnessed more homosexual acts because of the anonymity of the urban environment. Yet medieval cities were relatively small and anonymity could only be assured from the eighteenth century onward, when urbanization had increased. Probably—but more research remains to be done and generalization is very risky—the persecution of sodomy was also inspired by a general policy of social control, launched by the small urban economic and political elite, and thus a forerunner of the "civilizing process" in modern Europe.

In the sixteenth and seventeenth centuries the persecution of sodomy was intertwined with a radical and intolerant campaign of Protestants against Catholics and, more precisely, their religious orders. In Ghent, the Church hierarchy yielded to a new political Committee of Eighteen, which favored Protestantism. After the execution of some Franciscan friars in Bruges in 1578, eight Franciscans and six Augustinians were burned at the stake in Ghent. But only a few trials occurred after 1579, when the Low Countries, until then part of the Spanish Empire, were divided into the largely Calvinist Northern Provinces, now the **Netherlands**, and the almost exclusively Catholic Southern Provinces, now Belgium. In 1601 a Jesuit was burned in Antwerp; in 1618 two women were tried for sodomy in Bruges; in 1654 the sculptor Jérôme Duquesnoy was strangled and burned at the stake after having seduced two boys aged 8 and 11; finally, in 1688, two men who had "raped" a 17-year-old boy fled the country before the actual trial could take place.

In 1713 the Southern Provinces became part of the Austrian Empire. In 1781, the Antwerp trial of Jan Stockaert, who admitted having had sex with more than a hundred boys, indicates that an important change was taking place. Contrary to practice in the previous centuries, the authorities were very careful in judging the nature of the crime and even more in determining the appropriate punishment. The court of Antwerp did not sentence Stockaert to death, but asked the Secret Council in Brussels for advice. As a result the court decided to execute Stockaert secretly within the prison walls. In the future, similar cases were to be punished by banishment or, sometimes, by execution in prison—punishment enough even without the theatrical show of public burning. This veil of secrecy contrasts with the mass sodomy trials occurring at about the same time in Holland, but it is hard to explain why. Perhaps the Church did not want to be compromised by witnesses saying that Stockaert also had sex with clergymen, but it is more probable that repression through the spread of fear and guilt was considered a better

strategy against the gradually growing gay subcultures in Brussels, Antwerp, Ghent, and Liège.

Legalization. In 1795 the French invaded and introduced the *Code Pénal* of 1791 on Belgian territory: sexual activity between people of the same sex was no longer a crime as long as it was pursued among adults and in private. The temporary reunion of the Northern and Southern Provinces in the United Kingdom of Holland from 1815 until Belgium became independent in 1830 did not bring about any change.

The control and regulation of sexuality was gradually shifted to a medical model of homosexuality and confined to personal communication within the walls of the physician's office. Still, Belgian experts assumed different positions during the International Conference on Criminal Anthropology in Brussels in 1892. Léon de Rode distinguished congenital and acquired *inversion*, but the Catholic Lefebvre warned against the "corrupting" activities of pederasts and advocated punishment. A preliminary survey reveals that prison sentences remained very common until the early twentieth century, but an enlightened elite did not share Lefebvre's plea for police repression. The trial in 1900, for example, against Georges Eekhoud's gay novel *Escal-Vigor* (1899), provoked by a conservative, was considered a ridiculous matter and the author was acquitted.

Gay Activism. In the absence of systematic research, it is impossible even to sketch the evolution between 1900 and the emergence of a gay liberation movement in the late 1960s in Brussels, Antwerp, Ghent, and Louvain. In 1968, the Gespreks-en Ontmoetingscentra (G.O.C.) were established after the model of the Dutch C.O.C. Meanwhile, gay student groups were organized at universities. In 1975 the Federatie Werkgroepen Homofilie (FWH) was to coordinate gay activism and started publishing *Infoma*, later the *Homokrant*. But soon more radical groups were founded, such as the Rooie Vlinder (Red Butterfly;

leftist) and the Roze Aktie Front, while gay subculture organized itself, setting up gay periodicals (*De Janet van Antwerpen, Zonder Pardon, Link, Antenne Rose-Info, Tels Quels, Anderzijds*), radio programs, film festivals, and other gay-defined activities, alongside the commercial circuit of gay bars, discos, coffeeshops, and restaurants.

A success of gay activism in Belgium was the repeal in 1986 of the article 372bis of the penal code, which had been introduced in 1965 stipulating eighteen instead of sixteen as the age of consent for homosexual contact.

The relative decline of gay activism in the 1980s showed its vulnerability in an age of health crisis and rising moral judgment. Yet, an AIDS-prevention campaign sponsored by the Department of Health warned against the scapegoating of homosexuals and actually discussed the campaign with FWH and the Roze Dinsdag Beweging, a recent gay activist group. Also, the acquittal of Professor Michel Vincineau, the owner of two gay bathhouses who was prosecuted for "organizing male prostitution," reveals a fairly enlightened public opinion toward the gay community.

Pedophile organization is rather limited; an Antwerp workshop on pedophilia is still active, but a police crusade was launched in February 1987 against CRIES, the Centre de Recherche et d'Information sur l'Enfance et la Sexualité in Brussels.

BIBLIOGRAPHY. Bob Carlier, et al., *Homostudies in Vlaanderen*, Antwerp: Federatie Werkgroepen Homofilie, 1985; Geert Debeuckelsere, "Verkeerd zijn in beroerde tijden," *Homokrant*, 7:3 (March 1981); ibid., "Omme dies wille dat gij, Hieronymus Duquesnoy . . . ," *Tijdschrift voor Homogeschiedenis*, 1 (1984), 5–22.

Rudi Bleys

BELOVED DISCIPLE

This mysterious figure of the New Testament, sometimes identified with John the Evangelist, has attracted the attention of some homosexuals as an "affectional ancestor." According to Christian tradition, the Apostle John is the author of the Fourth Gospel, the Book of Revelation (also known as the Apocalypse of St. John), and three of the Catholic Epistles. All these ascriptions have been questioned by modern Biblical criticism, and the consensus is that this group of writings, so different from one another, cannot be by one author. It is traditional to identify as John the unnamed disciple "whom **Jesus** loved" and who reclined on his bosom at the Last Supper (John 13:23). Again this identification has been denied by some modern scholars.

Depictions of the college of the Apostles in medieval art generally distinguish John as a youthful beardless man, in contrast to his older bearded associates. A special theme of late medieval German sculpture is the Christ–John pair, in which these two figures are excerpted from the Last Supper context with John, identified as the Beloved Disciple, asleep with his head in Christ's lap. These sculptural groups belong to a broad category of devotional imagery, intended for meditation; the groups are probably not homoerotic in any primary sense. It has been shown, however, that they generated a group of mystical texts in which John is spoken of as enjoying the milk of the Lord. This motif may relate to the imagery of Christ as mother.

However this may be, explicit mentions of a physical erotic relationship between the two New Testament figures appear in our documents only in the sixteenth century. According to the playwright Christopher **Marlowe** (1564–1593), as reported by the informer Richard Baines, "St. John the Evangelist was bedfellow to Christ and leaned always in his bosom, that he used him as the sinners of Sodoma." This blasphemous assertion has a precedent in the confession of a libertine of Venice who was tried about 1550 for believing, among other heresies, that St.

John was Christ's catamite ("cinedo di Cristo"). Thus present research suggests that the idea was diffused from Italian heterodox currents, which are still, however, insufficiently known. In the post-**Stonewall** years in New York—in the 1970s—the most successful gay religious organization was the Church of the Beloved Disciple. Although the ascription of the orientation is doubtful and unproven, some would place St. John at the head of a host of "gay saints," including St. Sebastian, Sts. Sergius and Bacchus, and St. Aelred of Rievaulx. But the erotic activities and sentiments of these figures are also shadowy, and as yet the ranks of the beatified, as determined by the Roman Catholic church, contain no absolutely bona fide, certified homosexual individual.

Historical research reveals a complex dialectical trajectory of the particular matter in question: first, the identification of John with the anonymous Beloved Disciple; followed by tentative, perhaps largely unconscious medieval hints of a kind of mystical marriage between Christ and his favorite. The carnal element comes into the open in the sixteenth century, but in a scoffing, heretical context. Finally, some modern homosexuals have sought to give a positive interpretation of the presumed relationship as a religious warrant for the dignity of gay love. All these developments reflect a legendary embellishment of laconic scriptural texts. The true relationship of Jesus Christ and his mysterious Beloved Disciple will probably never be known.

BENEDICT, RUTH F. (1887–1948)

American anthropologist. Benedict became known to a large public through her popularized characterizations of whole cultures as having particular personalities. Unsatisfied with a marriage contracted in 1914, she enrolled in the New School for Social Research in 1919 and was influenced by students of Franz Boas (1858–1943) to study with the master himself at Columbia University. She earned her Ph.D. in 1923 with a dissertation on the distribution of the concept of the "guardian spirit" in native North America. In subsequent years as Boas's "right-hand" administrative subordinate and chosen successor she did fieldwork among the Zuñi and Cochiti in the American Southwest.

Although her collections of folklore are known to specialists, *Patterns of Culture* (Boston, 1934), her book applying the "Apollonian" character to the Zuñi and contrasting them to the "Dionysian" Kwakiutl studied by Boas, and the "treacherous" Dobu studied by Reo Fortune, made her famous. This book introduced simplistic characterizations of primitive cultures to a wide audience as a means of demonstrating the variability (and thus malleability) of "human nature"—with passing mention of different conceptions of homosexuality (pp. 262–65). Benedict was noted for a lack of sympathy for male students. She had a coterie of younger women around her, including her most famous student, Margaret Mead (1901–1978), with whom she was sexually, intellectually, and politically involved during the last two decades of her life (both had relationships with other women as well, and Mead with several men, including her three husbands). Aiming to contribute to psychological war efforts, the two pioneered "the study of culture at a distance" during the Second World War, working with persons in New York who had been raised in cultures of strategic interest. Benedict wrote about Romanian and Thai culture, as well as her famous discussion of militarism and aestheticism in Japanese "national character," *The Chrysanthemum and the Sword* (Boston, 1946). As with her characterization of Zuñi as free of conflict, her interpretation of Japan has had numerous specialist critics—and many readers.

BIBLIOGRAPHY. Mary Catherine Bateson, *Through a Daughter's Eyes*,

New York: Morrow, 1984; Margaret M. Caffrey, *Ruth Benedict: Stranger in This Land*, Austin: University of Texas Press, 1988; Margaret Mead, *An Anthropologist at Work*, Boston: Houghton-Mifflin, 1959; Judith Schachter Modell, *Ruth Benedict*, Philadelphia: University of Pennsylvania Press, 1983.

Stephen O. Murray

BENTHAM, JEREMY (1748–1832)

English philosopher and law reformer. Bentham was the founder of the Utilitarian school of social philosophy, which held that legislation should promote the greatest happiness of the greatest number. As a law reformer, he attacked statutes based on what he perceived as ancient prejudices and asked instead that laws justify themselves by their social consequences, that is, the promotion of happiness and diminution of misery. His *Principles of Morals and Legislation* (1789) was eventually extremely influential in England, France, Spain, and Latin America where several new republics adopted constitutions and penal codes drawn up by him or inspired by his writings.

Bentham's utilitarian ethics led him to favor abolition of laws prohibiting homosexual behavior. English law in his day (and until 1861) prescribed hanging for sodomy and during the early nineteenth century was enforced with, on the average, two or three hangings a year. Bentham held that relations between men were a source of sexual pleasure that did not lead to unwanted pregnancies and hence a social good rather than a social evil. He wrote extensive notes favoring law reform about 1774 and a fifty-page manuscript essay in 1785. In 1791, the French National Assembly repealed France's sodomy law but in England the period of reaction that followed the outbreak of the French Revolution made reforms impossible. In 1814 and 1816 Bentham returned to the subject and wrote lengthy critiques of traditional homophobia which he regarded as an irrational prejudice leading to "cruelty and intolerance." In 1817–18 he wrote over 300 pages of notes on homosexuality and the Bible. Homophobic sentiment was, however, so intense in England, both in the popular press and in learned circles, that Bentham did not dare to publish any of his writings on this subject. They remained in manuscript until 1931 when C. K. Ogden included brief excerpts in an appendix to his edition of Bentham's *Theory of Legislation*. Bentham's manuscript writings on this subject are excerpted and described in detail in Louis Crompton's 1985 monograph on Byron. Bentham's views on homosexuality are sufficiently positive that he might be described as a precursor of the modern gay liberation **movement**. Bentham not only treats legal, literary, and religious aspects of the subject in his notes, but also finds support for his opinions in ancient history and comparative anthropology.

BIBLIOGRAPHY. Louis Crompton, *Byron and Greek Love: Homophobia in 19th-Century England*, Berkeley: University of California Press, 1985.

Louis Crompton

BERDACHE

Though mostly applied to the **Indians of North America**, this word was originally a Persian term, *bardag*, that spread to Europe by the sixteenth century (Spanish *bardaxa* or *bardaje*; French *bardache*). It meant a boy or young man who was kept by a man as his male courtesan. This term clearly referred to the passive partner in male/male anal intercourse, while the name applied to the active partner was *bougre* (French) or *bugger* (English). When French explorers came to North America, they referred to individual Native Americans as "berdaches."

While the emphasis of the Europeans was clearly on the homosexual aspects, in their references to sodomy and the more neutral word berdache, American Indian cultures focused on the gender role of the androgynous male. Before the

127

coming of the Europeans, many aboriginal societies, in almost all areas of the Americas, accepted the reality of sexual diversity and incorporated into their lifestyle more than two gender possibilities. Their acceptance came as a result of their religion's appreciation for people who are different from the average. They believed that all persons were the way they were because the spirits made them that way. In their view, there were certain individuals who were created by the spirit world as different from either men or women. Such individuals belonged to an alternative gender, and their guiding spirit—what we would call a person's basic character—was seen as more important than their biological sex in determining their social identity.

In contrast to many societies, where such people have been derided, American Indians often respected berdaches as especially gifted. Since women had high status in most of these cultures, and the spirit of women was regarded just as importantly as the spirit of men, a person who combined the spirits of both the masculine and the feminine was seen as having an extraordinary spirituality. Such sacred poeple were often honored with special ceremonial roles in religious ceremonies, and were often known as healers and shamans. They had the advantage of seeing things from both the masculine and the feminine perspective, and so were respected as seers and prophets.

With such a respected view, a family with a berdache in it was considered fortunate. Along with **Amazons**, females who took on a more masculine role, berdaches were known as creative people who worked hard to help their family and their community. They often served as teachers of the young, and as adoptive parents for orphaned children. In this way, their society did not have home-less children, and there was no need for orphanages because of the common acceptance of adoption by both berdaches and other adults.

The berdache often remained single, but in some tribes his marriage to a person of the same sex was accepted just as a heterosexual marriage was, and their homosexual behavior was not stigmatized. Since the emphasis of marriage was to pair up people in different genders, a berdache would not marry another berdache. The husband of the berdache, or the wife of the Amazon, was not considered different in any way from a heterosexually married person.

Both the Spanish in Latin America, and the English in North America, heavily suppressed berdaches, and the tradition had to go underground. In many tribes it has disappeared, but in others it has continued to be a recognized social and sexual role among traditionalist American Indians today.

While "berdache" is usually applied strictly to American Indians, considering the history of the term, it is also proper to apply it to other areas of the world. Similar traditions of an alternative gender role, with a homosexual component as part of its acceptance, exist in many culture areas: Siberian Arctic, Polynesia, India, Southeast Asia, and some areas of East Asia, Africa, and the Middle East. Some interpretations suggest close parallels with the "drag queen" concept in Europe and North America, although that role is not institutionalized as a distinct gender as much as it is in these other cultures.

The berdache role seems to be one of the most common forms in which homosexual relationships are socially recognized. In contrast, there are other cultures that are not accepting of androgynous males, for example the super-masculine warrior societies of Melanesia, medieval Japan, and ancient Greece. In this type of society, homosexual relationships are more likely to be institutionalized in the form of intergenerational pairings between men and boys.

BIBLIOGRAPHY. Walter L. Williams, *The Spirit and the Flesh: Sexual*

Diversity in American Indian Culture,
Boston: Beacon Press, 1986.
Walter L. Williams

BERGLER, EDMUND
(1899–1962)

American psychoanalyst. Periph-
erally associated for a time with **Freud** in
Vienna, he emigrated in 1938 and thereafter practiced in New York City. Perhaps
the most vocal of the homophobic "experts" who courted the attention of the
American public in the years after World
War II, Bergler promoted the notion of
"**injustice collecting**" as a key feature of
the allegedly inevitable unhappiness of
homosexuals. In his book *Homosexuality:
Disease or Way of Life?* (1956) he asserted
that all homosexuals harbor an unconscious wish to suffer (psychic masochism)
but can be cured if willing to change,
tormented by "conscious guilt" over their
homosexual activity. But at the same he
accused homosexuals of "trying to spread
their perversion" and of seducing adolescent boys who would then be "trapped in
a homosexual orientation." Bergler also
maintained that women's fashions are a
masculine invention secondarily foisted
upon the female sex to alleviate man's
unconscious "masochistic fear of the
female body," and that women's fashions
are designed by male homosexuals, "their
bitterest enemies." Although Bergler had
entrée into leading magazines and journals of opinion, he was dismayed by the
success of the **Kinsey** Reports and their
implicit tolerance of same-sex relations
which he sought to combat. His major
theoretical positions rejected by his colleagues even in his lifetime, his influence
waned precipitously after his death, so
that his writings are now of interest solely
as a classic document of psychoanalytic
rationalization of moralizing prejudice.
Warren Johansson

BERLIN

Berlin rose to prominence first as
the capital of Brandenburg and then of
Prussia. It became capital of **Germany** in
1871, retaining this status through the
Weimar republic and the Third Reich until
its occupation by the victorious Allies in
May of 1945. Currently its three million
inhabitants are divided between East Berlin, capital of the Communist German
Democratic Republic, and West Berlin, an
enclave of Western life surrounded by the
Berlin Wall.

No trace of homosexual life has
been found in the chronicles of the first
three hundred years of the city (founded in
the thirteenth century), since the legal
prosecution of homosexuality that was
usual elsewhere did not exist in Berlin
before the introduction of the *Constitutio
Criminalis Carolina* in 1532. The Saxon
penal code, which Eike von Repgow had
codified in 1225 in the *Sachsenspiegel* and
which was in force in Berlin with some
modifications, knew no penalty for "lewd
and lascivious acts against nature." In the
seventeenth and eighteenth centuries the
Berlin Municipal Court pronounced
numerous death sentences for sodomy.

Only with the rise of Prussia to
the status of one of the great powers of
Europe under King **Frederick** II (the Great;
1712–1786) can any information other than
legal sanctions be discovered on homosexuality in Berlin. In 1753 there appeared
the first of many anonymous pamphlets
accusing Frederick II and his brother, Prince
Henry, of homosexuality. These allegations are probably justified, and under the
regime of Frederick II an extensive homosexual subculture developed in the Prussian capital. In 1782, in his *Letters on the
Gallantries of Berlin*, Johann Friedel describes homosexual street prostitution, a
brothel-like inn (*Knabentabagie*), secret
signs by which the homosexuals recognized one another, and the name given the
Berlin pederasts, *warme Brüder* ("warm
brothers"). By this account persecution by
the police seems not to have been especially intensive at that time, and in 1794 a
new penal code which retained the inspiration of Frederick II came into force that

abolished the death penalty for sodomy and replaced it with imprisonment and flogging.

In 1750 Berlin had some 90,000 inhabitants, by 1800 170,000, and by 1880 over 1 million. This vigorous population growth was accompanied by a steady development and extension of the homosexual subcultures. The most frequent and extensive accounts of homosexual life in the big city that figure in the writings of Karl Heinrich **Ulrichs** pertain to Berlin. Although homosexual acts (since 1851 only between males, since 1853 only anal intercourse) remained criminal, the police seem actually to have tolerated the flowering of homosexual life: after approximately 1870 public balls for homosexuals were held, and for the first time in the world an organized gay movement emerged. In the suburb of Charlottenburg (officially incorporated into Berlin only in 1920), on May 15, 1897, Magnus **Hirschfeld**, together with E. Oberg, M. Spohr, R. Meienreis, H. von Teschenberg and F. J. von Bülow, founded the Wissenschaftlich-Humanitäre Komitee (**Scientific-Humanitarian Committee**), whose main goal was to abolish the antihomosexual **Paragraph 175** of the Imperial Penal Code. But this goal, which was to be achieved through influence on public opinion and petitions to the German Reichstag meeting in Berlin, was down to the very end (the Commitee dissolved itself on June 8, 1933 to forestall being banned by the **Nazis**) unattained.

In 1898 the anarchistic Berlin periodical *Der Eigene* (The Exceptional) converted itself into the first long-lasting gay publication (down to 1931). (Its predecessors, Ulrichs' *Uranus* of 1870 and Raffalovich's *Annales de l'unisexualité* of 1897 appeared in only a single issue each.) *Der Eigene* was edited by the Berlin writer Adolf **Brand**, who in 1903 founded the Gemeinschaft der Eigenen (Community of the Exceptional), after the Scientific-Humanitarian Committee the second gay organization in Berlin. These two organizations embody a significant part of the

gay history of Berlin, but the majority of Berlin's homosexuals never had any contact with either one.

After World War I numerous gay and lesbian periodicals appeared in Berlin, and even in films and in the theatre homosexuality could no longer be fully taboo, as after the fall of the monarchy considerably more liberal censorship rules were in force. In 1932 Berlin had some 300 homosexual bars and cafés, of which a tenth were for lesbians. During the Nazi era between 1933 and 1945 virtually all homosexual life was driven underground, and a persecution without parallel in history began. Many gay Berliners suffered as inmates with the **pink triangle** in the concentration camp established north of Berlin at Oranienburg/Sachsenhausen, and not a few of them were killed there.

After the liberation in 1945 Berlin was divided and in the Western part of the city after approximately 1948 new gay organizations developed, periodicals were founded, bars opened, and gay balls tolerated, although thanks to the conservative regime under Konrad Adenauer in Bonn the even more punitive version of Paragraph 175 inserted in the Penal Code by the Nazis remained in force until 1969. In the eastern part of the city the regime applied Paragraph 175 in its pre-Nazi wording (only "acts similar to coitus" were punishable, but not mutual masturbation and prostitution), but on the basis of the Stalinist notions of morality gay men and lesbians were forced underground and threatened with prosecution.

Only in the 1970s did an increasingly liberal climate facilitate the emergence of a gay **movement** in both halves of Berlin on the Anglo-American model. There was no continuity with the tradition of the pre-1933 organizations, the Scientific-Humanitarian Committee and the Community of the Exceptional. In East Berlin, moreover, up until the 1980s periodicals and organizations for gay men were forbidden. Whereas West Berlin today exhibits a homosexual subculture that with its numerous autonomous institutions (communications centers, journals, publishing houses, sports and choral societies, religious, political and trade union groups, a gay member of the city council, and so forth) is comparable to other Western metropolitan areas, in East Berlin the corresponding development has proceeded much more slowly because of the obstacles imposed by the Communist government in that part of Germany.

BIBLIOGRAPHY. Berlin Museum, ed., *Eldorado, homosexuelle Frauen und Männer in Berlin 1850–1950*, Berlin: Frölich & Kaufmann, 1984; Bruno Gmünder, ed., *Berlin von hinten*, Berlin: Gmünder, 1988 (annual); Magnus Hirschfeld, *Berlins drittes Geschlecht*, 1904, reprint: Berlin: Rosa Winkel Verlag, 1989; Manfred Herzer, "Schwule Preussen, warme Berliner," *Capri*, 2/1 (1988), 3–25; James Steakley, "Sodomy in Enlightenment Prussia: From Execution to Suicide," *Journal of Homosexuality*, 16: 1/2 (1988), 163–75.
Manfred Herzer

BERNESQUE POETRY

This type of Italian poetry may be regarded as an outgrowth of burchiellesque poetry; it also continues the tradition of obscene carnival songs (*canti carnascialeschi*). The genre takes its name from Francesco Berni (1496/8–1535), the best known of the poets who were engaged in softening the original obscurity of the burchiellesque trend so as to make it more accessible—while retaining the essentials of its coded language.

Bernesque poetry relies on double meanings—which are often deployed in a masterful way—characteristically incarnated in food items (round ones such as apples symbolize buttocks, phalliform ones such as eels stand for the penis) or objects of daily use (the chamber pot represents the anus; the needle symbolizes the penis).

While the Bernesque poet gave the appearance of choosing everyday objects so as to produce comic effects by heaping excessive praise on trivial things, in reality he constructed a subtle net of double meanings in order to exalt sexual relations.

Unlike the burchiellesque poets, however, who often delighted in cobbling together tangles of words that seemed to lack any coherent meaning, the Bernesque poets always made compositions that were fully meaningful, in a colloquial, humorous, and (at first sight) simple tone. This aspect permits the reader to enjoy their works as humor, even if he misses the double meanings.

In the Bernesque genre, homosexual themes (generally having to do with anal contacts) often occur. The poets sometimes took great pains to compose seemingly innocuous poems for boys (such as Berni's directed to "young abbés" of the Cornari family), which when decoded reveal highly obscene senses.

Berni also wrote serious love poems in Latin, which were fairly explicit, in praise of boys. A priest, he was shut up for a year and a half in an Abbruzzi monastery for a homosexual scandal, the full details of which are not known (1523–24). Moreover, some private letters have survived containing innocent requests to friends, but which read with the code of burchiellesque language reveal requests for the sending of boys (examples are those to Vincilao Boiano of May–August 1530).

Many authors wrote Bernesque poetry with homosexual themes. Among them are Angelo Firenzuola (1493–1543), Andrea Lori (sixteenth century) Matteo Franzesi (sixteenth century), Giovanni Della Casa (1503–1556), Benedetto Varchi (1503–1565), Lodovico Dolce (1508–1568; he also wrote a long work "For a Boy"), and Antonio Grazzini, known as "Il Lasca" (1503–1584).

With the Counterreformation, and the more repressive climate that came to prevail in Italy as a consequence, practitioners of the Bernesque genre found it prudent to abandon erotic double entendres, and the mode gradually ebbed, coming down to a series of rhetorical exercises on harmless subjects, such as the death of a cat, baldness, and the like.

A final, unexpected offshoot of the genre appeared in the amusing satires of Giuseppe Giusti (1809–1850), who revived the spent Bernesque tradition, neglecting the erotic double meanings in favor of a patriotic commitment to Italian unification.

BIBLIOGRAPHY. *Works: Opere di Francesco Berni*, Milan: Sonzogno, 1928; *Il primo (secondo) libro delle opere burlesche di M. Francesco Berni, di M. Gio. Della Casa, del Varchi, del Mauro, del Bino, del Molza, del Dolce e del Firenzuola*, 2 vols., "London: Pickard" (actually Milan), 1721; *Il primo (secondo, terzo) libro dell'opere burlesche del Berni, del Bino, del Casa, del Molza, del Varchi, del Dolce, del Mauro, del Firenzuola e d'altri autori*, 3 vols, "Utrecht: Broedelet" (actually Milan), 1760.

Giovanni Dall'Orto

BÈZE, THÉODORE DE (1519–1605)

Leading Calvinist Reformer. Born in Vézelay in Burgundy he was the son of the Royal Bailiff, a member of a wealthy and powerful noble family. From the age of nine onward he was educated at Orléans and Bourges in the house of the German philologist Melchior Weimar, who indoctrinated the boy in the principles of Protestantism. In 1539 Bèze received a law degree from the University of Orléans, and at the same time fell in love with Marie de l'Etoile, but she died after a year and a half. Bèze settled in Paris, where he enjoyed the company of prominent and literary circles, while his literary talents unfolded at the expense of the career in law for which his father had destined him. After violent inner struggles he broke with his past and moved to Geneva, renouncing the Roman Church for Calvinism. For ten years he taught Greek in Lausanne and completed the metrical translation of the Psalms begun by Clément Marot that afterwards was

incorporated in the French Protestant liturgy; his polemic and theological writings converged with those of Calvin. In 1558 he became a preacher and professor of theology in Geneva, and thereafter was one of the intellectual champions of French Protestantism (his enemies called him "the Huguenot Pope") until his retirement at the end of the century.

Although twice married, Bèze was openly attacked and vilified for his supposed homosexual liaison with his friend Audebert, the evidence for which was an epigram in the collection of poems officially entitled *Poemata*, unofficially *Juvenilia* (first edition: Paris, 1548). Admired by many when they were published, the poems were strongly influenced by the classical authors with their pederastic interests and allusions, so that the evidence for Bèze's homosexuality is uncertain at best. What is certain is that the Catholic party joined in vilifying him after a writer named François Baudouin, who had changed sides several times and been nicknamed Ecebolius by Bèze himself, in 1564 denounced him as a vice-ridden *cinaedus*. Two years later a Catholic theologian named Claude de Sainctes, embroiled in a polemic with Bèze, gave vent to a personal attack in which Bèze's sodomitical union with Audebert is likened to his spiritual embrace of Calvin and Bèze himself is branded as unworthy of a holy office. In 1582 Jérôme Bolsec, a Catholic physician and theologian, further reproached Bèze in a pamphlet addressed to the magistrates of Geneva, saying that many scoundrels and lawbreakers had taken refuge there in the guise of adhering to the Reform, including felons apprehended in the crime of sodomy; that in Paris and Orléans Bèze had in his youth freely pursued sensual pleasures and debauchery of all kinds. The opponent added that a Latin poem had been composed in which Bèze is termed a pathic and an effeminate and lustful poet who became a teacher of sacred eloquence at the instigation of Satan. Others joined in the chorus of abuse even after Bèze's death, while the Protestant party defended him as the victim of malicious misinterpretation on the part of his foes. Even from the standpoint of the twentieth century, the sources do not sustain the allegation that Bèze's friendship for Audebert amounted to a homosexual liaison. His life is more an emblem of the web of insult and countercharge that characterized the first century of the Reformation.

BIBLIOGRAPHY. Ferdinand Karsch-Haack, "Quellenmaterial zur Beurteilung angeblicher und wirklicher Uranier. 1. Theodor Beza, der Reformator," *Jahrbuch für sexuelle Zwischenstufen*, 4 (1902), 291–349; Alexandre Machard, "Recherches sur la querelle des 'Juvenilia,'" in *Les Juvenilia de Théodore de Bèze*, Paris: Isidore Liseux, 1879; Anne Lake Prescott, "English Writers and Beza's Latin Epigrams: The Uses and Abuses of Poetry," *Studies in the Renaissance*, 21 (1974), 83–117.

Warren Johansson

BIBLIOGRAPHY

Bibliographical control of published material on homosexuality encounters several problems. First, there is the inherent vastness of the subject itself: to paraphrase Goethe, the history of homosexual behavior is virtually coterminous with that of the human race. Accordingly, serious study must be cross-cultural, interdisciplinary, and transhistorical. Secondly, the taboo in which the theme has been enveloped means that until recently subject bibliographies often had no entry for it, or when they did would relegate it to some negative umbrella category, such as "perversion" or "sexual deviation." Even today the indexes and tables of contents of books often fail to mention the topic. Finally, the difficulty of establishing gay studies courses and programs in universities—blocked as they have been by tradition, inertia, and simple prejudice—has starved the field of money, personnel, and prestige. Standing against these hindrances is the devotion of countless individual gay and lesbian scholars, who have not only amassed a vast amount of primary data, but sought to display them in works of reference.

Origins. Greek literature rejoices in extensive discussions of homosexuality, or to be more accurate of *paiderasteia*. [For modern listings of this accumulated heritage, *see* Félix Buffière, *Eros adolescent: la pédérastie dans la Grèce antique* (Paris, 1980), and Claude Courouve, *Tableau synoptique de references à l'amour masculin: auteurs grecs et latins* (Paris, 1986).] The Greeks themselves had no discipline of bibliography proper; however, for an anthology of passages on homosexuality, *see* **Athenaeus** (fl. ca. A.D. 200), *Deipnosophists*, Book 13.

The tradition of erudition that emerged in early modern Europe after the invention of printing saw some hesitant assemblage of references to homosexual behavior. These data are found scattered in Latin tomes in the fields of theology, law, medicine, and classical studies. In the eighteenth and nineteenth centuries some of this information was digested for more popular consumption in admittedly meager encyclopedia articles in the vernacular. It was these sources that had to be patiently combed by such pioneers of homosexual scholarship as Heinrich **Hoessli** and Karl Heinrich **Ulrichs**, John Addington **Symonds**, and Havelock **Ellis**.

The emergence of systematic bibliographical control had to await the birth of the first homosexual emancipation **movement** in Berlin in 1897. This movement firmly held that progress toward homosexual rights must go hand in hand with intellectual enlightenment. Accordingly, each year's production was noted in the annual volumes of the *Jahrbuch für sexuelle Zwischenstufen* (1899–1923); by the end of the first ten years of monitoring over 1000 new titles had been recorded. Although surveys were made of earlier literature, up to the time of the extinction of the movement by National Socialism in

1933, no attempt had been made to organize this material into a single comprehensive bibliography of homosexual studies. Nonetheless, much valuable material was noted in the vast work of Magnus **Hirschfeld**, *Die Homosexualität des Mannes und des Weibes* (Berlin, 1914).

The American Phase and Its Influence. The nascent American homophile movement, which began about 1950, took cognizance of the need for a comprehensive bibliography. Donald Webster Cory's *The Homosexual in America* (New York, 1951), a landmark of the early movement, had as appendices lists of both non-fiction and fiction on the subject. By the late 1950s small-scale efforts toward this end had begun to coalesce in Los Angeles and the San Francisco Bay area, two of the movement's strongest centers. After many delays, the Los Angeles endeavors resulted in the most ambitious project attempted up to that point: Vern Bullough et al., *Annotated Bibliography of Homosexuality* (2 vols., New York, 1976), which was prepared in the Los Angeles offices of **ONE**, Inc. This work provides about 13,000 entries arranged in twenty broad subject categories. Some notion of the enormousness of the whole subject is conveyed by the fact that, even at that date, the number of entries could probably have been doubled. Unlike most of the other American bibliographies, this work is international and multilingual in scope; unfortunately the set is marred by thousands of small errors and lacunae, especially in foreign-language items. The title notwithstanding, annotations are very few, and uncertain in their critical stance. Full subject indexes, which would have served to offset some of these shortcomings are lacking; instead each volume has its own author indexes. The shortcomings of this major work, undertaken largely by volunteer staff working under movement auspices, illustrate the problems that have, as often as not, been made inevitable by the social neglect and obloquy in which the subject has been enveloped. Unfortunately,

plans for a completely revised edition of the ONE bibliography have had to be shelved, at least for the present.

In San Francisco in the 1960s William Parker began gathering material for a one-person effort. His first attempt was *Homosexuality: Selected Abstracts and Bibliography* (San Francisco, 1966); this publication, and a number of other earlier lists, are now most easily accessible in the Arno Press reprint: *A Gay Bibliography: Eight Bibliographies on Lesbianism and Male Homosexuality* (New York, 1975). Parker's more definitive work is *Homosexuality: A Selected Bibliography of over 3,000 Items* (Metuchen, NJ, 1971), followed by two supplements (published in 1977 and 1985), which carry coverage up through 1982. These volumes arrange the material (English-language only) by types of publication; there are helpful subject indices. Although some note is taken of films, television programs and audiovisual materials, the coverage of print items is almost entirely restricted to nonfiction.

Parker's two supplements cover six- and seven-year periods respectively, but there is no current annual bibliography. *Gay Books Bulletin* (later *The Cabirion*), issued by the Scholarship Committee of the New York Chapter of the Gay Academic Union (1979–85), concentrated on in-depth reviews, but ceased after twelve issues. The best way of monitoring current production is through the "Relevant" section of the scholarly Dutch bimonthly *Homologie* (Amsterdam, 1978–).

In San Francisco the lesbian monthly *The Ladder*, published by the Daughters of **Bilitis** organization, included notices of books from its inception in 1956 (the full set was reissued with a new index in New York in 1975). Eventually these notices were coordinated on a monthly basis by Gene Damon (Barbara Grier), whose later columns have been recently collected in a handy, indexed volume: *Lesbiana: Book Reviews from the Ladder, 1966–1972* (Reno, 1976). Utilizing input from Marion Zimmer Bradley and others,

Damon and Lee Stuart produced the first edition of *The Lesbian in Literature: A Bibliography* (San Francisco, 1967). This work subsequently appeared in an expanded, third edition: Barbara Grier, *The Lesbian in Literature* (Tallahassee, 1981), with about 3100 items, including some nonfiction. The entries are coded by an unusual rating system, which correlates both relevance and quality.

The complement to Grier in the male sphere is Ian Young, *The Male Homosexual in Literature: A Bibliography* (Metuchen, NJ, 1982), with 4282 items, interpretive essays by several hands, and title index. While there are no annotations, Young sweeps the field: fiction, poetry, drama, and autobiography. Like Grier, the volume is limited to works written in English and translations of foreign works.

Apart from the general bibliographies just discussed, which claim to cover at least the whole-English language production in their chosen domains, there are also a number of works defined by country of production. William Crawford (ed.), *Homosexuality in Canada: A Bibliography* (Toronto, 1984), contains a good deal of material, in French as well as English, that has been overlooked elsewhere. Manfred Herzer, *Bibliographie zur Homosexualität* . . . (Berlin, 1982) is an exemplary compilation of nonfiction items published in German from 1466 to 1975. A similar work, annotated, is Giovanni Dall'Orto, *Leggere omosessuale* (Turin, 1984), which covers Italian publications from 1800 to 1983. Still to be covered is the rich Italian material before 1800. Claude Courouve's work on French bibliography has been privately published.

Almost from the beginning homosexual organizations have created their own periodicals to supplement the mainstream journals which tend to scant, or even exclude altogether research on sexual variation. A detailed roster of no less than 1924 publications existing (or believed to exist) in the 1980s is Robert Malinowsky, *International Directory of Gay and Lesbian Periodicals* (Phoenix, 1987). By definition, this work does not include older journals that had ceased (309 of these are listed in Bullough, et al., cited above), nor does it provide, for obvious reasons, a listing of the contents of these publications. Gay and lesbian journals are covered only sporadically in current bibliographies, and even copies of the less familiar newspapers are hard to find once they leave the stands; here the gay and lesbian archives are doing an essential job of preservation, since public and university libraries usually do not preserve these materials.

A summation of bibliographical work appears in Wayne R. Dynes, *Homosexuality: A Research Guide* (New York, 1987). In addition to the bibliography section proper, each of the approximately 170 subject groups contains an introduction outlining the strengths and problems of the topic in its current state of development (or lack of development). This volume is conceived as interdisciplinary, cross-cultural, and transhistorical, and may be consulted for a sense of the complexity of the overarching field. In some respects it is the complement to the present *Encyclopedia of Homosexuality*, where space for citations is necessarily limited.

Electronic Retrieval. In due course the bibliographical situation will be transformed by electronic systems of retrieval of material from data-base sources. For financial reasons, this shift began first in the natural and biological sciences. An early exemplar is the MEDLARS medical database, which traces its origins to 1964. A facility of considerable use to the study of homosexual behavior is the PsychLIT Database, which offers citations and summaries in **psychology** and related disciplines published from January 1981 on. It is compiled from material published in *Psychology Abstracts* and the PsychINFO Database. PsychLIT covers about 1400 journals in 29 languages from approximately 54 countries. The *Lexis* system, available mainly in law libraries, goes back to the early 1970s. Geared mainly to the practice of law in North America, *Lexis* also offers access to British and French libraries. As these examples show, the time frame of such enterprises tends to restrict the items collected to recent years, so that exclusive use of such sources narrows the focus of material at the researcher's disposal by date of origin of the material.

Large public and university libraries are beginning to record their acquisitions—though not usually extending to older holdings—in on-line systems, which are gradually being "hooked up" into larger systems. One such computerized catalogue lists the recent acquisitions of 25 major American research libraries, with terminals and print-out facilities in all of them. These retrieval systems are commonly linked to printers, so that users can with minimal effort obtain a permanent record of what they have found. In using all these instruments, it must be remembered that they are only as good as what has been entered in them. Classifiers may lack sophistication, so that entries under "Georgian" may mix indiscriminately the American state, the Soviet republic, the Caucasian language, and English architecture. Also, books and periodical articles tend to live in two different universes as far as on-line systems go. For a number of reasons (including the inherent convenience of the book format), conventional, hard-copy materials will probably continue to be used for a long time to come. Of course, the two modes are not incompatible, and the ideal situation is probably that of simultaneous access to most collections of material through both channels.

Whatever systems may be used, the compilers must face the problem of the enormous proliferation of material. In 1910, say, a one-page item would be worth noting, while by 1980 the output has increased so markedly that selectivity is imperative. Today no one would aspire to collect every piece of writing with some relevance to homosexuality in any given year: too much would simply be redundant. Like all else in human affairs, the problems are in part a function of the time matrix. Yet when all is said and done, our knowledge of homosexuality is increasing. Masses of material that in former decades would have been ignored are being recorded and classified by state-of-the-art techniques.

See also **Libraries and Archives.**

BIBLIOGRAPHY. Wayne R. Dynes, *Homosexuality: A Research Guide*, New York: Garland Publishing, 1987.

Wayne R. Dynes

BILITIS

The name Bilitis is one of the Hellenic forms of Ba'alat, the female counterpart of Baal in Northwest Semitic mythology. In the writings of Philo of Byblos, Baaltis is equated with Dione, one of the three daughters of Uranos and consorts of Kronos, who receives the city of Byblos as her domain. The significance of Bilitis for lesbianism stems not from antiquity proper, but from the work of Pierre Louÿs, *Les Chansons de Bilitis, traduites du grec*, first published in 1894, although clandestine editions with the erotically explicit lesbian passages appeared only after the author's death, with the title *Les Chansons de Bilitis inédites* (1929), and as *Les Chansons secrètes de Bilitis* (1931). Louÿs originally offered the collection of texts to the world as translations from a classical source; it made the author's reputation in France and was never surpassed by his later writing. The heroine of the work is described as "born at the beginning of the sixth century before our era, in a mountainous village located on the banks of the Melas, in the eastern part of Pamphylia.... She was the daughter of a Greek and a Phoenician woman." Leaving her homeland, she settled in Mytilene on the isle of Lesbos, "then the center of the world," which "had as its capital a city more enlightened than Athens and more corrupt than Sardis." Here she became part of the circle around **Sappho**, the poetess who taught her the art which she expressed in some thirty elegies devoted to her attachment to a girl of her own age named Mnasidika.

This product of the decadent school of the fin-de-siècle has, though written by a man, became one of the classics of lesbian literature, and was to give its name to the American organization The Daughters of Bilitis, founded in San Francisco in October 1955. The name was chosen just because it "would sound like any other women's lodge," but convey an esoteric meaning to lesbians everywhere.

This first lesbian political organization in the United States was founded some five years after the **Mattachine Society**. The leaders of the group were Del Martin and Phyllis Lyon, who had settled in San Francisco as lovers in 1953. Their desire was to socialize with other lesbian women. When one of their acquaintances invited them to a meeting to discuss the start of a social club, the two accepted with enthusiasm. On September 21, 1955 eight women—four couples—gathered and within a few weeks had formed the Daughters of Bilitis (DOB). Before long Martin and Lyon were arguing that DOB should broaden its activities to include the political task of changing the public's attitude toward lesbianism. The model for the new endeavor was the Mattachine Society of San Francisco.

The group split over the suggestion, and the six women who remained joined forces with the Mattachine Society and with ONE, Inc. in what was then called the homophile movement. In April 1956 the group participated in its first public event, a forum cosponsored by Mattachine on the differing problems faced by lesbians and homosexuals. DOB then resolved to hold its own "public discussions," where lesbians could attend without fear as the "public." In October of the same year the organization published the first issue of its monthly publication, *The Ladder*, in a printing of 200 copies that was mailed to "every lesbian whom any of its members knew" and to professionals in the Bay Area.

For the most part, the Daughters of Bilitis worked closely and cooperatively with its male homosexual counterparts throughout the 1950s, since in an era of intolerance, the tiny movement had to close its ranks for self-protection. The full support of the Mattachine Society mitigated the growing pains of DOB, and the shared outlook—the belief that dispelling myth, misinformation, and prejudice was the primary means of bettering the status of their members—bound the organizations together. But DOB also existed to provide self-help for lesbian women, a haven where they could experience a sense of belonging instead of the rejection that they encountered elsewhere, and where they could reorient their lives so that they could face the larger society with renewed strength.

The pages of the *Ladder* reflected the priority that DOB attached to personal problems of the individual lesbian, especially the one living in isolation far from the subculture of the large cities. The magazine reported political news, but was never meant to be a political journal, and so the publishers shunned advocacy, devoting space instead to poetry, fiction, history and biography. It was also a soundingboard for the experience that society distorted and denied. The special concerns of lesbians were debated on its pages, such as the rearing of children in a lesbian household, the problems of the still married lesbian, and the low salaries and restricted job opportunities of women in Eisenhower's America. Published continuously for sixteen years, this journal remains a major source for the period's activism; it was reprinted by Arno Press (New York) in 1975 with a new index by Gene Damon.

Some male attitudes, such as the notion of the homosexual organizations that this was a "ladies' auxiliary," created tension between DOB and its allies. The promiscuity of many homosexual men and the police harassment which they encountered struck the lesbians as an encumbrance and a stigma unjustly attached to them by society. At jointly sponsored events the men even questioned the need for a separate women's group, to which the DOB members replied by asserting their need for autonomy and their identification with a larger movement for the emancipation of women—foreshadowing the far more radical feminism of the 1960s.

On the whole, DOB attracted significantly fewer members than did the male organizations, in part because the pool of potential constituents was smaller, in part because women had a more precarious economic position in American society. Professional women who had been successful felt that they did not need the group, and those who benefited from its nurturing efforts achieved independence and "graduated." The founders and leaders were white-collar semi-professionals who could not identify with the blue-collar bar subculture of working women, reflecting the fact that women are generally more sensitive to class identity than are men. The lesbian patronage of the bars belonged to a different subculture with its own well-defined identity—one that the membership of DOB generally did not share. But during the initial phase of the American homosexual movement, the Daughters of Bilitis were the rallying point for lesbian interests and aspirations.

BIBLIOGRAPHY. Del Martin and Phyllis Lyon, *Lesbian/Woman*, new ed., New York: Bantam, 1983.

Evelyn Gettone

BIOGRAPHY AND AUTOBIOGRAPHY

The appeal of biography is multi-faceted, ranging from a desire to elevate one's imagination by dwelling on the accomplishments of great figures to an all-too-human love of gossip and muckraking. Moreover, the form of a human life, from birth to death, provides a readily comprehensible narrative structure in which the reader can identify with the subject as the moving center. Homosexual autobiographies, uncommon before modern times, are the external embodiment of a process of internal self-examination; in writing autobiography and publishing it, one willy-nilly creates an apologia for oneself. Problems of concealment are common in the biographies and autobiographies of homosexuals; lengthy tomes have been compiled about such figures as Walt **Whitman** and Willa **Cather** without a mention of their sexuality. Determining the sexual orientation of noted figures of the past is significant for its own sake: the establishment of historical truth in its fullness. This aim of truth usually accords (though it occasionally conflicts) with the psychological need that members of any minority group have for heroes. And homosexuals and lesbians, so often stereotyped en masse as hopelessly neurotic if not deranged, understandably yearn for reassurance that all have not been cases in the medical waxworks museum of **Krafft-Ebing**'s *Psychopathia Sexualis*. Although such psychological needs are normally met by candid and accurate biographies, there is also a temptation to provide "gay hagiography," works which extol an individual because he or she is homosexual, not to mention the "reclamation" of figures whose sexual orientation is uncertain.

Classical Antiquity. The first hesitant emergence of biography as a genre about 500 B.C. is grounded in Greek individualism, the idea that the uniqueness of the human personality stands over against and must not be subsumed by one's public persona as fixed by official or class standing. This awareness allowed the Greeks to maintain biography as a genre distinct from **history**, which is concerned more with the general and typical. The Theban poet **Pindar** (518–438 B.C.), whose writings are suffused with homoerotic sentiment, eulogized great athletes in brief odes. Broadly speaking, the funeral oration, one of the sources of Greek biography, tends to fall into the trap of "de mortuis nil nisi bonum," the stipulation that only admirable aspects of the deceased should be displayed. Another type of skewing is the novelized biography, as seen in Xenophon's (ca. 434–ca. 355 B.C.) *Cyropaedia*. In later variants the temptation to invent details is freely indulged, a temptation fostered by increasing demand for "juicy bits." On the whole these faults are remarkably avoided in the portraits of **Socrates** by his school: the writers candidly reveal the faults as well as the stature of this lover of men. Relatively few lives of women were produced; here, however, the career of the Lesbian poet **Sappho** (who flourished ca. 600 B.C.) provided a focus, though one afflicted to some extent with romantic invention.

While much has been lost, we know that Greek biographies concentrated on two types of people: public figures (statesmen, law givers, rulers, and generals) and intellectuals (poets and philosophers). A remarkable collection of biographies of public men survives: the *Parallel Lives* of **Plutarch** (ca. A.D. 46–ca. 120), who portrays an equal number of Greek and Roman subjects, preparing the way for international biography in contrast to the nationalistic (and even localistic) restriction of earlier Greeks. Although Plutarch was keenly interested in psychological motivation, his mentions of homoerotic aspects in some of his subjects are totally matter-of-fact: he takes his subjects' interest in boys as almost routine. Diogenes Laertius and Philostratus wrote lives of the philosophers replete with pederastic revelations.

The Romans, who regularly eulogized their ancestors, had a more ambivalent attitude toward homosexual behavior. They also savored the eccentricities and scandals that might be associated with it. Such gossipy preoccupations come to the fore in **Tacitus'** *Annals* and *Histories*, arranged around the lives of emperors, and even more in **Suetonius'** *Lives of the Twelve Caesars*, written in the early second century, where the foibles of one **Roman emperor** after another are set forth with a relish that anticipates a modern supermarket scandal sheet. The most outrageous life of a homoerotic Caesar stems from the late empire: that of **Heliogabalus** (reigned 218–222), attributed to Lampridius, one of Suetonius' continuators. Oddly, the first major surviving autobiography, except for the inscription erected by Augustus Caesar, came later. In his *Confessions*, St. **Augustine** (354–430) contrasts his life before and after he became a Christian; here we see a life transformed by a shift from one set of ideals to the other. Although Augustine wrote his memoir after his conversion, he nonetheless saw fit to include in it an account of his deep **friendship** with a fellow student. His immensely popular autobiography, which long remained unique, thus preserved a moving account of special friendship that was to reverberate through the centuries.

Medieval and Modern Times. The Gospels are echoed in Philostratus' *Life of Apollonius of Tyana*, a homosexual philosopher. Biographically, the early and high medieval eras are notable for the lives of the saints. One, that of St. Pelagius/Pelagia, gives an account of an attempted homoerotic seduction and the saint's heroic resistance. The letters and lives of monks often attest to **particular friendships**, though the conventional aspect of such effusions makes it difficult to use them as direct historical evidence.

The Italian **Renaissance**, with its emphasis on the idea of fame, gave renewed life to the art of secular biography. In 1550, for example, Giorgio Vasari (1511–1574) published his monumental *Lives of the Architects, Sculptors, and Painters*, providing, in addition to serious assessments of the art works, many piquant details of the artists' personal lives. Then in 1562, the flamboyant bisexual sculptor Benvenuto **Cellini** (1500–1571), completed his *Autobiography*. In France, Michel de **Montaigne** (1533–1592), though he published no autobiography as such, devoted much of his writing to introspection and to musing on the nature of his own intense male friendships.

At the end of the sixteenth century the repressive influence of the Council of Trent, coupled with the new standards of decorum dictated by literary classicism, caused self-censorship to eliminate details that would previously have been permitted. One has to wait until the *Autobiography* of Jean-Jacques Rousseau (1712–1778) for a new standard of candor and authenticity. In this account of his life, devoted to a search for the truth about himself, Rousseau describes his involvement in a youthful homosexual episode in Turin.

The Nineteenth and Twentieth Centuries. The Victorian period counts as the high water mark of prudery and censorship. Yet in this era scholars began to uncover material from the archives that had been neglected before. The *Life of Michelangelo* (1893) by the English homosexual John Addington **Symonds** (1840–1893), with its hints of the artist's abnormal sexuality, is an example of the fruits of this new research. At the same time, regrettably, the late nineteenth century was obsessed with a purported link between genius and insanity championed by such psychiatrists as Cesare **Lombroso**, leading to the popular genre of "psychopathographies," in which the torments and inadequacies of literary and artistic figures are highlighted. Related to this trend is Sigmund **Freud**'s 1910 essay on the homosexuality of **Leonardo** da Vinci. Despite the expectations it awakened, psychoanalytic method did not contribute much in the ensuing decades to the deep analysis of historic figures.

The rise of the homophile **movement** in Germany at the turn of the century fostered a diligent scrutiny of the current production of biographies for indications of homosexuality and lesbianism.

At this time the sexual orientations of such varied figures as Helena Petrovna Blavatsky (founder of Theosophy), François de **Boisrobert**, **Christina** of Sweden, Heinrich von **Kleist**, August von **Platen**, and Walt **Whitman** came out of the shadows. Subsequently several of the major figures of the German Movement, including Kurt **Hiller** and Magnus **Hirschfeld**, wrote their own memoirs.

Because the trials of Oscar **Wilde** in 1895 mercilessly exposed the intimate details of his sexual activities, his life could not be sanitized. The first sympathetic accounts were the memoirs of friends, such as Robert Ross and André **Gide**. Almost a century had to pass before we got the fuller biographies of H. Montgomery Hyde and Richard Ellmann. It may be, however, that the best life of Wilde is his inadvertent autobiography, the *Letters* as edited by Rupert Hart-Davis (1962). The memoirs of Wilde's scholarly contemporary John Addington Symonds could be published only in 1985.

Twentieth-century French writers excelled in self-examination as set forth in diaries intended for publication. Best known of these works is the extensive *Journal* of André Gide (1869–1951), covering the years 1889–1949, and Marcel **Jouhandeau**'s (1888–1979) colossal *Journaliers* in 26 volumes. Jean **Cocteau** (1891–1963) also wrote a number of memoirs and diaries, some of which are being published posthumously.

Michael Holroyd's full biography (1967–68) of Lytton **Strachey** (1880–1932) provided both candor and balanced detail; it succeeded in reviving the reputation of the subject as well as contributing to the expanding industry of **Bloomsbury** scholarship. Subsequently a number of large biographies have appeared on such Bloomsbury figures as Lord **Keynes**, E. M. **Forster**, and Virginia **Woolf**. An unusual contribution is Nigel Nicolson's *Portrait of a Marriage* (1973), treating the homosexuality of both his parents: Harold **Nicolson** and Vita **Sackville-West**. Attention to the expatriate writers and artists of that generation in Paris has focused especially on noteworthy lesbians, including Natalie **Barney**, Romaine **Brooks**, and Gertrude **Stein** and Alice B. Toklas.

A distinguished recent biography of a major figure of the past is Louis Crompton's *Byron and Greek Love* (1985). Not seeking to replace other biographies of the poet, Crompton highlights the periods of **Byron's** known homoerotic infatuations; he also shows the problems engendered by the homophobia of his contemporaries, as well as Jeremy **Bentham's** efforts to argue against it. The continuing fascination with such romantic figures as William **Beckford**, Queen Christina of Sweden, T. E. **Lawrence** ("of Arabia"), and King **Ludwig** II of Bavaria has led to numerous biographical works, but establishing the truth tends to prove elusive. Adequate studies of the homosexuality or bisexuality of a number of kings of England and France are still lacking, though the record is somewhat better with military commanders.

The post-Stonewall gay movement after 1969 has been commemmorated in a number of activist reminiscences, most of them slight. Perhaps coincidentally, Tennessee **Williams** decided to make a clean breast of things in his *Memoirs* (1975), while William Somerset **Maugham** was finally dragged completely out of the closet in the lengthy biography by Ted Morgan (1980). The homosexuality of the English dramatist Joe **Orton** was revealed in the lurid circumstances of his murder by his lover in London in 1967; Orton has now been profiled not only in the biography by John Lahr (1978), and in the writer's *Diaries*, but also in an explicit film, *Prick Up Your Ears* (1987), based on both these sources and directed by Stephen Frears. Needless to say, Hollywood films on the lives of public figures who were homosexual or bisexual typically black out unconventional sexual aspects. In 1986 ex-Congressman Robert Bauman published a rare example of an autobiography of a gay po-

litical figure; its existence, however, is probably owing to his public exposure.

The lives of ordinary male homosexuals and lesbians of the past are for the most part hidden from us. Representing turn of the century American life, however, are the memoirs of Claude Hartland (1901) and Ralph Werther ("Earl Lind," 1918; 1922). The four volumes of the diaries of Donald Vining cover a third of a century: 1936–75. Lesbian scholars have begun to emphasize collective records, as seen in Margaret Cruikshank, ed., *The Lesbian Path* (1980), and Julia Penelope Stanley and Susan J. Wolfe, eds., *The Coming Out Stories* (1980). A much-noticed contribution to this genre is a collection of the reflections of some fifty Catholic religious: Rosemary Curb and Nancy Manahan, eds., *Lesbian Nuns: Breaking the Silence* (1985). Mostly unpublished are the tape-recorded reminiscences of older homosexuals gathered by oral-history projects in several cities of North America; an exception is Keith Vacha's *Quiet Fire* (1985), in which older gay men tell their own story.

Research Challenges. The problems confronting any scholar who would attempt an in-depth study of the personality of a subject believed to be homosexual or lesbian are serious. Where same-sex practice is documented through autobiographies or police records, there remains the task of situating the individual's sense of self within the larger context of prevalent attitudes toward homosexuality. In many cases, however, a self-protective instinct caused the individual to lead a closeted life. In individual cases it may be hard to establish whether the subject is a deeply closeted individual, whose secrets will nonetheless emerge with determined effort, or whether contemporary gossip or later speculation has labeled someone homosexual who in fact was not. In the past some overenthusiastic researchers have, in effect, "shanghaied" historic figures for enshrinement in the homosexual pantheon.

In order to proceed with the investigation of some person of the past believed to have been homosexual, one should ascertain the presence of several of the following indicators: the subject is unmarried (even, as sometimes happens, to the point of vehemently resisting marriage); the subject belonged to a circle other members of which are known to have been gay; the subject had interests or pursuits prevalent at the time among gay people; and the subject adopted unusual turns of phrase (say the use of pronouns appropriate to the opposite sex). Once the scholar has attained familiarity with the period, a cluster of such signs triggers a bell. One need scarcely add that the absence of one of the others should not bring the investigation to a halt. Many almost exclusively homosexual figures, for example, have been married; the giveaway is the taunting phrase "the marriage was a failure."

Above and beyond these endeavors of detection, sexual orientation needs to be fitted into larger contexts that will show how it molded the individual's own personality, and in turn what are the social functions of the orientation in the host society. The task is formidable, but conscientiously pursued it will yield substantial rewards in understanding the inner life of the subject of the biography.

Wayne R. Dynes

BIOLOGY
See **Animal Homosexuality;** **Sociobiology.**

BIRDS AND AVIAN SYMBOLISM
Human interest in birds, both wild and domestic, and study of their behavior impinge on sexual concerns in several ways. From ancient Greek times onwards, barnyard fowls have provided a ready source for the observation of behavior, including sexual acts. Principles drawn from study of these birds have sometimes been transferred to other species, including the human. **Aristotle** noted homosexual behavior in fowls, and in the eighteenth century the French naturalist Georges Louis Leclerc de Buffon reported his own independent observations in birds. In the present century, the social hierarchy of the barnyard formed the starting point for the concept of the pecking order in psychology.

In 1977 a considerable stir took place in the American media over the reports by George and Molly Hunt (University of California, Irvine) of female–female pairs of gulls. As early as 1885 a female–female swan pair had been reported from England, and there is now documentation of preferential same-sex patterns among a number of species of birds living in the wild.

Birds figure in erotic metaphor and symbolism in a variety of ways. In contemporary North America the term "chicken" circulates among pederasts to denote an attractive teenage boy. This usage should not be confused with the clipped form "chick"—occasionally found in older sources in the full form, "chicken" showing the origin—meaning woman. The general derivation from slang *chicken* = child is clear (attested from the eighteenth century onwards). The homoerotic sense may be traced back as far as the late nineteenth century: "The Affection which a sailor will lavish on a ship's boy to whom he takes a fancy, and makes his 'chicken,' as the phrase is." (*Congressional Record*, April 21, 1890). In another bird metaphor, the pursuer of adolescents is called the *chicken hawk* in today's street language.

Curiously, this semantic development had a forerunner in Latin, where *pullus*, chicken, was a general term of endearment, especially for handsome boys. *Pullarius* (literally "poulterer) meant a "kidnapper of boys" or "boy stealer"; more generally it signified "pederast."

The male fowl, the *cock*, has provided a slang term for penis, by way of the watercock or faucet (an evolution paralleled in other languages). Once the metaphor was created, however, it was reinforced by a natural similarity: "The extreme erectness of the cock, straining upwards, has suggested to many besides the Greeks the erectness of a tumid penis" (Smith and Daniel). There is also evidence of a broader association of birds with the penis, as seen in Italian, *uccello*, bird, penis, and German *vögeln*, to copulate (from *Vogel*, bird). Somewhat unusually, contemporary Spanish street language uses the female form *polla*, hen, to designate the penis. Contrast the established French *poule*, hen, whore. In older American slang, the word *capon*, a castrated rooster, served as an abusive epithet for an "effeminate man, a homosexual."

Confusingly, in a few parts of the English-speaking world, as in the southern United States, the slang word cock refers to the female pudenda. There is no doubt, however, that in the compounds cocksucker and cockteaser the male organ is meant (though the former term is usually limited to male homosexuals, the latter to flirtatious heterosexual women).

In seduction scenes depicted on ancient Greek **vases**, roosters are the most common gift presented to youths by older male suitors. In the mythological realm the cock was associated with the bisexual god **Dionysus**. The noblest bird of all, the eagle, sometimes deputizes for father Zeus in depictions of the rape of **Ganymede**. A common emblem for homosexual lust in classical writing was two male partridges, who were said to be so highly sexed they turned to each other as easily as to the female. Another bird, the kite was linked to homosexual behavior because of a fanciful association of its Latin name *milvus* with *mollis*, a passive homosexual. Ancient folklore held that ravens conceived through their beaks; hence the Roman satirical poets **Martial** and **Juvenal** styled fellators "ravens." Finally, the ibis, a bird well known to the Egyptians, figured as a symbol of anal preoccupations because it

was reputed to employ its long beak to clean its own bowels.

See also **Animal Homosexuality.**

BIBLIOGRAPHY. Page Smith and Charles Daniel, *The Chicken Book*, Boston: Little Brown, 1975; Beryl Rowland, *Birds with Human Souls: A Guide to Bird Symbolism*, Knoxville: University of Tennessee Press, 1978.
Wayne R. Dynes

BISEXUALITY

Human bisexuality may be defined as the capacity to feel sexual attraction toward, and to consummate sexual performance with, members of the opposite and one's own sex. The concept needs to be distinguished from **androgyny** and **hermaphroditism**, with which, however, it is historically affiliated.

History of the Concept of Bisexuality. Modern thinking about bisexuality stems in part from medical investigations in the middle decades of the nineteenth century, which found that during the first few weeks after conception the urogenital system of the human embryo is undifferentiated as to sex. (Bisexuality in plants had been recognized since the beginning of the ninetenth century.) Determination of the anatomical gender of the organs of the originally neutral being is triggered by the intervention of mechanisms later identified as chromosomal. This embryological discovery suggested that human maleness and femaleness is in some sense secondary, and the puzzling duality of our natures could be restored, at least on the level of ontogeny, to a primal unity. Almost inevitably, these modern findings called to mind ancient Greek and Near Eastern mythological thinking about primordial androgyny. From this fertile mix of ideas it could be concluded that human sexual attraction should also be undifferentiated as to gender, since our postnatal gender dimorphism is but a secondary process superseding, but not completely effacing, an original oneness. The result of such research and speculation was to offer two complementary models, one of primordial unity, the other of a comprehensive triad: neutral, male, and female. Both the unitary and the triadic themes were to exercise their influence on the concept of sexual **orientation**.

Before this medical and mythological amalgam could be applied to the psychodynamic sphere, a conceptual apparatus had to be invented and diffused that assigned human sexual orientation to two distinct poles—heterosexual and homosexual—a polarity which is distinct from, yet analogous to the gender dimorphism of male and female. In classical antiquity and the Middle Ages, as well as in many non-Western cultures today, no such dichotomy was recognized. The medieval sodomite was viewed as a departure, sinful it is true, from universal human standards which form the abiding context. Thus, although the Middle Ages had to all intents and purposes its own notion of the homosexual (the sodomite), it lacked a concept of the heterosexual as such. The polarity of heterosexual and homosexual attraction was formulated in Central Europe in the 1860s by Karl Heinrich **Ulrichs** and Károly Mária **Kertbeny**, who developed the **homosexual concept**. By the end of the century it had become widely familiar, and in the work of such writers as Richard von **Krafft-Ebing**, Otto Weininger, Wilhelm Fliess, and Sigmund **Freud**, the heterosexual–homosexual contrast melded with the previously discussed medical concept of primordial gender neutrality. Hence the Freudian idea of the "**polymorphous perverse**," in which the individual's attraction is freeform and undifferentiated (though in mature individuals this state yields to full heterosexuality). From this family of ideas descends the contemporary popular notion that "we're all bisexual."

In the 1940s growing dissatisfaction with such notions of bisexuality led to significant critiques. Sandor Rado's paper of 1940 signaled their abandonment by the **psychoanalytic** community. In 1948 Alfred

C. **Kinsey** faulted the then-current concept of bisexuality on two grounds. First, in view of its historical origins, reliance on the term bisexuality fosters confusion between the categories of gender and orientation, which must be kept quite distinct. Second, Kinsey averred, the triad of heterosexuality, bisexuality, and homosexuality is too rigid, and should be replaced by his own more supple 0-6 scale. While Kinsey effectively attacked the prevailing exclusivism, his numerical scale presented its own problems and failed to gain widespread popular recognition. Its legacy was to leave the term "bisexual" with a somewhat amorphous and controversial claim to all those who could not be classified as exclusively heterosexual or homosexual.

The **countercultural** and social-utopian currents of the 1960s and 70s stimulated attempts at revision and partial restoration of the paradigm among many innovative (or would-be innovative) thinkers, who viewed the inherited "gender system" of fixed roles for men and women as an albatross which kept women inferior and hindered the full self-realization of both men and women. There was thus a trend to regard the anatomical differences of men and women as a minor matter. If this be so, it makes little sense to be overly concerned about the gender of the individual to whom one is attracted, and we are all free to be simply "humansexuals."

Also in this period the vocal assertion of homosexual rights, often cast in the minority mold, suggested to some that bisexuals too were a neglected and victimized minority, suffering from the invisibility which had once characterized homosexuality, and who should join together to fight for recognition and rights (Klein, 1978). Adoption of this "bisexual activist" view would lead to full-fledged recognition of three orientations, as seen, for example in the 1986 New York City gay rights ordinance, which explicitly protects heterosexuals, homosexuals, and bisexuals.

Contrasting with this triadic scheme is a unitary futurist **utopian** model which posits bisexuality as the eventual human norm, superseding both exclusive heterosexuality and exclusive homosexuality which would be regarded as forms of sexual restrictiveness, and even bigotry.

In support of their contention, the advocates of bisexuality point to earlier civilizations and contemporary tribal societies where, they claim, bisexual response is the norm. This would be true also in advanced industrial societies, which, it is held, would be also bisexual were it not for their sophisticated apparatus of sexual repression. Here one should interject the caveat that since the concepts of heterosexuality, homosexuality, and bisexuality are themselves of recent Western origin, it may not be wise to impose them insouciantly on cultures other than one's own. Still, with all due caution, one can observe that some societies, such as ancient **Greece** and some contemporary Melanesian tribes, do exhibit a serial bisexuality, in which the maturing male does undergo homosexual experience as part of initiatory rites, assuming the heterosexual roles of husband and father afterwards. This seriality is far, however, from the ideal of nonorientation propounded by some theorists, that is to say, the notion that an individual is free to chose objects of sexual attraction in total disregard of their gender.

Bisexual Liberation Movement. In the 1970s (and to a lesser extent in the 1980s) a number of organizations were active in support of "bisexual liberation," modeled on the gay liberation and the other sexual freedom movements. While these groups did not establish a consensus definition of bisexuality, they tended toward a broad conceptualization in which bisexuality was thought of as a basic capacity to respond erotically and emotionally/romantically to persons of either gender, either simultaneously or serially; the response did not have to be equal but had to be sufficient for a bisexual to feel somewhat alienated from identification as either homosexual or heterosexual.

Bisexuals, according to the leaders of this movement, were discriminated against by homosexuals as well as by heterosexuals, and much of the discussion revolved around a critique of homosexuals' attitudes toward bisexuality, and the exclusion of recognition of bisexuals in the gay **movement**, which was seen as dedicated to the fostering of an exclusively homosexual **identity**. Other topics were the implications of bisexuality for such institutions as marriage and the ghettoization which leaders decried in homosexual circles at the time. Bisexuals, it was held, should be allies in a common struggle with gays against discrimination, but should function as a bridge to the heterosexual world rather than being submerged in an exclusivist subculture.

Many bisexual spokespeople advocated bisexuality as superior (for various reasons) to either form of "exclusivism" (heterosexual or homosexual); they also held it to be much more threatening to the prevailing sexual norms, precisely because it potentially involved everyone rather than a small minority which could be ghettoized.

With the **AIDS** crisis in the 1980s, bisexuals were targeted as the most serious source of infection for the heterosexual majority, and "bisexual chic" passed as quickly as it had arisen. With it, for the most part, went the bisexual liberation movement. Its self-description as threatening had been realized all too quickly, but in a way none of its leaders had foreseen.

Bisexual Patterns. Examination of the biographies in this Encyclopedia reveals that many of the individuals chronicled displayed behavior patterns which today might be labeled "bisexual," whether a wide or a narrow definition is used. It is difficult, however, to analyze and categorize data from such a wide spectrum of eras and cultures.

Contemporary American society exhibits a number of behavior types which may be classified as bisexual. There are, for example, **macho** men, basically heterosexual, who become to some degree habituated to achieving occasional gratification—employing the inserter role only—with men who would define themselves as gay. Among women, the sense of sisterhood engendered by the women's movement, accompanied in some cases by a wariness toward men, has led to lesbian contacts involving women whose previous experience was essentially heterosexual.

The United States, together with other advanced industrial societies, reveals a number of versions of serial patterns of other- and same-sex behavior. In what is sometimes termed **situational** homosexuality, inmates of total institutions, typically men's and women's **prisons**, form homosexual liaisons, only to resume their heterosexual patterns on release. Some young men follow a career of male **prostitution** for a time, and then, as their looks fade or other circumstances supervene, settle into a completely heterosexual lifestyle. Yet another type of serial experience appears in "late blooming" individuals, that is, men and women who have entered into heterosexual marriages or relationships, and then find, sometimes as late as their forties, that they are strongly attracted to members of their own sex. It should be noted that self-reports of persons' sexual orientation are not always fully reliable; for understandable reasons, some men and women who are essentially homosexual will say that they are bisexual, in the belief that this label is less stigmatizing.

It seems that there are few individuals in today's society who have attained the posited ideal of "gender-blindness," choosing their partners solely on the basis of personal qualities, so that they will go with a man one day and a woman the next. It is hard to say how many come close to this ideal, with gender playing a relatively small role. If they are comparable with the Kinsey "3's" (those who "accept and equally enjoy both types of contacts, and have no strong preferences for one or the other"), they are a substantial group, Kinsey's "3's" representing somewhere between 4 and 5 percent of all males for at least three years of their life.

Those persons who are bisexual under the definition cited at the beginning of this article, but who have a definite preference for one side or the other, may be compared to Kinsey's "2's" and "4's", described by him as "predominantly" one way but "rather definitely . . . more than incidentally" the other way. Added together, these represent about 10.5 percent of the male population at age 25, divided between 7 percent predominantly heterosexual and 3.5 percent predominantly homosexual. Add the "3's" and we see why it is said that, using a broad definition, about 15 percent of the American male population is bisexual for a significant part of their lives.

As the types selectively reviewed above and the Kinsey figures suggest, most people fall more strongly on the one side than the other, and when all is said and done may be classified as predominantly heterosexual or homosexual with at least as much justification as bisexual. Moreover, there seems to be a kind of funnel effect, whereby as an individual grows older he or she tends to focus more and more exclusively on one sex or another. Thus the number of Kinsey "3's" declines from 4.7 percent at age 25 to 2 percent at age 45. This trend is particularly evident if one contrasts adolescent "sexual experimentation" with the more settled patterns of later life. The risk, perhaps, is in sliding easily from the description "*predominantly* homosexual" (or heterosexual) to just plain "homosexual" (or heterosexual), thereby picking up the connotations of exclusivity often associated with those terms.

Conclusion. All in all, the present status of the concept of bisexuality is far from satisfactory. As has been noted, both learned discussions and popular thinking display a recurrent tendency to confuse bisexual orientation with anatomical or psychic androgyny. Further, the assembling of useful ethnographies of contemporary groups requires a careful delimitation of the specific type or variety of bisexual behavior to be studied. With respect to individual psychodynamics, it is essential to pay careful attention to the depth and quality of the experience, rather than relying on a mere quantitative assessment of "sexual outlets." It is to be hoped that with further well-planned research, the present chaotic amalgam of "bisexuality" will yield to a more rational spectrum of "bisexualities," perhaps in parallel to a comparable phalanx of "homosexualities."

BIBLIOGRAPHY. Sandor Rado, "A Critical Examination of the Concept of Bisexuality," *Psychoanalytic Medicine*, 2 (1940), 459–67; Fred Klein, *The Bisexual Option*, New York: Arbor House, 1978; Fritz Klein and Timothy J. Wolf, eds., *Bisexuality: Theory and Research*, New York: Harrington Park Press, 1985 (with bibliog. by C. Stear, pp. 235–48).

Wayne R. Dynes

BLACK GAY AMERICANS

Thus far the social profile and achievements of black gay Americans have not received their due. This neglect stems from several sources. White Americans tend to view blacks almost monolithically, through a lens of stereotypes, one of which is that the black male is typically a **macho** heterosexual. The slighting of black lesbians is part and parcel of the relative invisibility of lesbians as a whole. Until recently, most socially conscious black gays chose to put their energies in the civil rights movement, rather than in the gay movement. Finally, there is the view that homosexuality is somehow alien to the black experience. Some black nationalists claim that same-sex behavior was unknown in Sub-Saharan **Africa** until European colonialists imposed it. Although abundant evidence now exists for a variety of homosexual social patterns in black Africa, the notion that the behavior is somehow distinctively white lingers.

Earlier History. For countries such as **Brazil** and **Haiti** there is evidence of direct transfer of forms of homosexual life as part of the African cultural diaspora. For North America such evidence is lacking, perhaps because the slave masters, observing Protestant norms of opposition to "sodomy," ruthlessly sought to stamp the phenomenon out. Oral tradition suggests, however, that just as white masters engaged in sexual relations with black women, so some white men would seek the sexual company of attractive young black slaves. After Emancipation, at the turn of the century, there is evidence of large-scale black dance events in such centers as St. Louis and **Washington**, D.C. These gatherings probably lie at the origin of the drag balls in Harlem in the 1920s, which attracted both blacks and whites. Not altogether dissimilar is the still surviving tradition of **Mardi Gras** in **New Orleans**—though a more visible black–white gay presence is evident in the carnivals in Brazil.

New York City's Harlem, originally developed as housing for the white middle class, emerged at the end of World War I as a vital center of black culture (the **Harlem renaissance**). A number of black gay writers contributed to this flowering, including the poet Countee Cullen (1903–1946), and the prose writers (Richard Bruce Nugent (1906–) and Wallace Thurman (1902–1934). Other writers such as Langston Hughes (1902–1967) were very discreet and ambiguous in their sexuality but occasionally displayed homoerotic sensitivities. More tolerant than Greenwich Village, Harlem's vibrant nightclub scene attracted many white gays from other parts of the city. Here they were regaled by such bisexual and lesbian entertainers as Ma Rainey, Bessie Smith, "Moms" **Mabley**, and Gladys Bentley (1907–1960). Of these, Bentley was most easily identifiable, with her male attire and tough, butch behavior; eventually she married her white lesbian lover in a highly publicized ceremony. Her recording career spanned the two decades after 1928. During the heyday of **McCarthyism** she was forced to conform and denounce her lesbianism, but even that could not save her singing career.

While the Depression of the 1930s put an end to the special brilliance of Harlem, black gay and lesbian life continued as before. There is increasing evidence of bars and nightspots in many American cities that were largely and completely black. More frequently than their heterosexual counterparts, blacks and whites entered into homosexual coupled relationships—though such "salt and pepper" couples could attract the particular ire of white bigots and also the disapproval of black relatives.

Toward the Present. In the 1960s James **Baldwin** achieved national—and international—renown with his depiction of blacks and gays in such books as *Another Country* (1962) and *Tell Me How Long the Train's Been Gone* (1968). In a more subdued way the playwright Lorraine Hansberry lent her support to the nascent lesbian movement. Black gays such as Bayard **Rustin** made important contributions to the civil rights movement.

In the years of gay liberation after the **Stonewall Rebellion** relatively few black gays and lesbians participated. This reflected in part their sense of the greater urgency of the black civil rights movement, as has been noted, as well as the feeling of many who did attend that they were not comfortable. Heterosexual black leaders, even radicals, tended to keep their distance from the cause of gay liberation well into the 1980s. In 1983, after a stormy battle over gay participation in the 20th anniversary March on Washington, a group of prominent black leaders endorsed the national gay rights bill and put a speaker, Audre Lorde from the National Coalition of Black Gays, on the agenda; the following year the Reverend Jesse Jackson included gays in his "Rainbow Coalition."

The largely white and middle class gay subculture sometimes openly discriminated against blacks, as in the practice of "carding" whereby black patrons of nightclubs were singled out by being required to present personal documents to be admitted.

These and other problems led to the formation of such organizations as Black and White Men Together (renamed Men of All Colors Together in some cities) and the National Coalition of Black Lesbians and Gays (1978). Several little magazines appeared featuring black writers, and such black lesbian and gay authors as Michelle Cliff, Anita Cornwell, Larry Duplechan, Audre Lorde, and Anne Allen Shockley took their place in America's gay bookstores. Samuel R. Delany came to be recognized as one of the four or five most distinguished **science fiction** writers of America. New York's Blackheart Collective brought together and published gay black poets. Other black gays became known in the worlds of music, sports, and the church. Black gay self-affirmation in turn stimulated similar movements among Asian-American and American Indian gays. Meanwhile, organized black homosexuals continue to wage a two-front battle against both racism in the gay community and homophobia in the black community.

Black Perspectives on Homosexuality. While a substantial portion of black Americans share the dominant modern industrial-world model of homosexuality, the majority of the black population, perhaps reflecting class differences as well as a different ethnic tradition, seems to accept a different, more **"Mediterranean"** conception. For these blacks, homosexuality tends to be equated with effeminacy, and the penetrator is less likely to view himself as homosexual. Thus, there are fewer inhibitions preventing a "macho" black male from engaging in sexual activity with another male, as long as he himself retains the "male role" and his partner restricts himself to the "female role," than for his white counterpart. The high proportion of young black males who pass through American confinement institutions and absorb models of homosexuality which are normative in **prisons, jails, and reformatories** may contribute to this perspective.

Complicating the American black perspective on homosexuality is the perception that slavery represented an attack on black *manhood* and that continued white (economic, political, legal) control over black men is an extension of that attack. Thus behavior which is seen as undermining black manhood, such as taking what is perceived as a feminine sexual role, is seen by many as a betrayal of the race, imposing a burden on black gays which whites do not ordinarily share.

Nonetheless, the black community, having long commiserated in the face of common oppression and misfortune, seems to have developed an ethos which is somewhat more tolerant of individual eccentricities, including sexual ones, and cognizant of the pernicious effects of discrimination of all kinds. Black culture seems to have been spared much of the anti-sexual heritage of the white Puritans and their successors, and the sort of organized witchhunt which white heterosexual society has from time to time inflicted on white homosexuality has apparently been absent from black American history. It is on this community ethos of relative tolerance that black gays must build in the future.

Kinsey Statistics. The **Kinsey** Institute study of homosexuality in the San Francisco Bay Area, published by Alan Bell and Martin Weinberg in 1978, sought to measure differences between white and black homosexuality; the original Kinsey surveys had restricted themselves to whites. Among the findings of this survey (which has undergone some methodological criticism) is that homosexual blacks were more likely to be "out" with their families than whites, were more sexually active but had fewer partners, were more likely to cruise at private parties and on the street, were less likely to worry about public exposure of their orientation, were less likely to have sex with strangers, more likely to accept older partners, more likely to engage in anal sex, less likely to belong to a homophile organization, and were less likely to have been arrested (in contrast with the heterosexual blacks in the study, who were more likely to have been arrested than the heterosexual whites).

Interracial Homosexuality. Given a perspective which frequently interprets homosexual relations as signifying dominance and submission, interracial sexuality must often deal with racial politics. For many heterosexual black men, it is more acceptable to take a dominant, controlling sexual role with a white male who takes a "female" role because this is seen as reversing and compensating for the historic political dominance of white men, a white dominance which has frequently been expressed (hetero)sexually, not only in slave society when white men freely appropriated black women, but in the contemporary world where black prostitutes are seen as having been appropriated by finaincially more powerful white male clients. This dynamic is expressed in the most extreme form in prison **rape**, which often follows racial lines.

Some gay blacks, on the other hand, being more comfortable in the submissive role, generalize from their experience of whites as holding the major power positions of American society to perceive white males as particularly sexually powerful, and so are attracted to them.

Whites, too, can get caught up in this situation, seeking out black transvestites and effeminate gays because they feel more comfortable dominating them or placing them in roles which elicit contempt from such white males. In the other direction, there are whites who are drawn to more "macho" black men because they are responding to a popular belief which depicts blacks as more virile, sexually uninhibited and forceful, with larger organs and without the supposedly weakening qualities of cultivated white civilization. Certainly the images of black men presented in written, photographic, and cinematic gay **pornography** do nothing to dispel such notions.

Having outlined such situations, it must also be noted that there is widespread interracial homosexuality which does not follow such lines, but which may be affected more by the attractiveness of the "different," curiosity, **class** differences, rebellion against social custom, or a belief that race should not be a factor in discriminating between potential sexual partners.

The San Francisco Kinsey survey found that 22 percent of white but only 2 percent of black homosexual males had never experienced interracial sex; none of the whites reported more than half their partners to be black, while two-thirds of the blacks reported more than half their partners to be white. For lesbians, only 28 percent of the whites had interracial experience, while 78 percent of the blacks did, and 30 percent of those had a majority of white partners.

Interracial **couples** seem to be rarer than the frequency of interracial sex would lead one to expect, probably because the dynamics of an ongoing relationship are more likely to trigger hostility from a society which is both homophobic and racist than would isolated encounters.

BIBLIOGRAPHY. Alan P. Bell and Martin S. Weinberg, *Homosexualities*, New York: Simon & Schuster, 1978; J. R. Roberts, *Black Lesbians*, Tallahassee: Naiad Press, 1981; Michael J. Smith, *Colorful People and Places*, San Francisco: Quarterly Press of BWMT, 1983; idem, ed., *Black Men, White Men*, San Francisco: Gay Sunshine Press, 1983.

Ward Houser

BLACKMAIL

Blackmail is the popular term for what criminal law designates as extortion, which is defined as the making of a demand for some action (the handing over of money or secret information, or the commission of some official act) with a threat (to reveal some compromising action committed by the victim) for one's own gain or to the detriment of the victim. Until quite recent times the fear of blackmail in homosexual circles was intense. Most overt homosexuals were obliged by the moral attitude of society to lead a double life, posing as heterosexuals in public view and engaging in forbidden sexual acts clandestinely. By contrast, the professional criminal often cannot be blackmailed simply because he has no façade of respectability, or else lives in a subculture in which such a demand would be promptly met with violence against the would-be informer.

History. The origins of blackmail lie in the practice of delation that was widespread in antiquity. Before a modern police and detective force existed, the state power had to rely on informers who were characteristically rewarded for the information which they conveyed to the authorities. But if they could obtain a far greater sum from the delinquent party than the state would pay for the information, cost-benefit analysis pointed in the direction of extortion. It has been established that by the end of the thirteenth century, the moral teaching of the Western Church had succeeded in outlawing homosexual behavior, for which the Bible and the Code of Justinian prescribed the penalty of death. This meant that the individual who defied the ban on sodomitical acts exposed himself to capital punishment, and had besides to conceal even his interest in the forbidden conduct. In practice the fact that sexual behavior tends to be relegated to the most intimate sphere of private life, one to be hidden from all except the participants, made it nearly impossible for the state power to uncover and punish the culprits. But the potential blackmailer, if he discovered the homosexual propensities of his victim, could extort major sums of money from him for his silence.

The lifelong hypocrisy and concealment that Christian morality imposed upon the homosexual meant that in early modern times, for the criminal underworld blackmail of covert sex offenders was to be a lucrative source of income, as the morals squads of nineteenth-century Europe quickly discovered. Even in countries like **France**, where the Constituent Assembly had abolished the laws against sodomy in 1791, the social ruin that would befall the homosexual whose conduct became widely known was basis enough for the practice of *chantage* (although French law prefers the term *extorsion*). Léo Taxil even alleged that every government from that of **Napoleon** I to the Third Republic had used homosexuality as grounds for political blackmail. A third use of blackmail—after money and social control—was for purposes of **espionage**, as in the case of the Austrian Colonel Alfred **Redl**, who was supposedly compelled by the Russians to reveal his country's military secrets.

Arguments of the Homosexual Rights Movement. The early homosexual rights movement made much of the danger of blackmail in its propaganda for repeal of the notorious **Paragraph 175**. The threat of extortion exacerbated the fear and misery of the homosexual who already exposed himself to imprisonment and social ruin every time he sought sexual gratification. The situation of the victim was made even worse by the legal practice of allowing the blackmailer, even if found guilty in court, to testify against the other party in turn, so that the homosexual who was subjected to extortion had every reason to fear any judicial inquiry. English law, by contrast, confined the proceeding against the blackmailer to the simple question of whether the extortion had been committed. The blackmailer could be a male prostitute, but more often a young criminal who knew that he could entice a homosexual into a compromising situation and then obtain either money or valuable objects as the price for his silence. The actual demand could be expressed in a letter which stated or implied that if the recipient did not pay the sum demanded, his conduct would become public knowledge or would be disclosed to the authorities. If the victim or his family were wealthy, the sums extorted annually could run into thousands of dollars. On the other hand, a petty criminal desiring only a small sum might merely threaten the homosexual with physical violence on the spot. More subtle forms of blackmail could turn upon the conduct of a businessman or politician in his professional life, or take the form of threats to reveal an individual's conduct on the pages of a newspaper or magazine. This latter practice was a lucrative source of income for the yellow press of the early twentieth century.

In the face of an intolerant public opinion, the homosexual threatened with blackmail rarely attempted to seek aid from the **police**, and there were cities in which the police force itself, or individuals on the margin of law enforcement, engaged in regular shakedowns of homosexuals whom they either entrapped or observed in known trysting places. The invention of instantaneous photography provided the blackmailer with a convenient tool, since an unsupported allegation of behavior that left no physical trace could far more easily be refuted than the evidence of the culprit in flagrante delicto. Even if the victim sought the aid of an attorney, he would find that no respectable member of the bar would touch the case, and he would be referred to a criminal lawyer on the fringe of the profession who for his services would demand fees that amounted to an indirect mode of extortion. Some masochistic individuals were unable to break out of the blackmailer's clutches, others sought to escape by fleeing to another country, some were driven to suicide when they saw no way out of their plight. Only rarely would a particularly strong or aggressive individual find the courage to intimidate or even kill the blackmailer. Of Magnus **Hirschfeld**'s ten thousand subjects only a small number had ever been imprisoned, but more than three thousand had been blackmailed. A study made in Austria in the early 1970s, when homosexual conduct was still illegal, came to a similar figure: approximately one-third of a sample group of homosexuals had been victims of extortion.

Official Response. The arguments mounted by Hirschfeld and other supporters of the early homosexual rights movement were compelling enough to persuade even the National Socialist lawmakers who in the legislation of June 28, 1935 increased the penalties for male homosexuality, but at the same time amended the Code of Criminal Procedure to allow the district attorney to refrain from prosecuting an individual whose criminal conduct had subjected him to blackmail. In contrast, the subcommittee of the United States Senate that was appointed in 1950 to investigate Senator Joseph R. McCarthy's charges that the administration was harboring "sex perverts in government" found that the danger of blackmail made homosexuals security risks; and since the penal laws of the District of Columbia had no provision against homosexual acts the subcommittee urged that the code be amended in this direction. In other words, it created a situation in which a homosexual employee of the Federal Government could be dismissed from his job and even prosecuted for his sexual activity, and then used the risk of blackmail to justify the policy it was advocating. This is a classic instance of how arguments formulated as an appeal for toleration could be maliciously turned into justifications for further intolerance.

Current Situation. In the debate over the recommendations of the **Wolfenden** Committee in England after 1957, the issue of blackmail played a considerable role, and the **Criminal Law Amendment Act** of 1885 was even dubbed "The Blackmailer's Charter" because of the opportunity that it had given the criminal underworld to prey upon otherwise respectable, law-abiding members of society. As the

threat of prosecution faded with the reform of the criminal laws, beginning in England in 1967, and even more with the education of law enforcement officials in regard to homosexuality, the danger of blackmail receded. In retrospect, blackmail was the tribute which fear paid to intolerance. It will end only when the social stigma attached to homosexual behavior has been eradicated. The rallying cry of the gay **liberation** movement "Come out!" is an appeal for candor and courage on the part of the homosexual community that will relegate the eventuality of blackmail to the dark annals of history.

BIBLIOGRAPHY. Magnus Hirschfeld, *Die Homosexualität des Mannes und des Weibes,* Berlin: Louis Marcus, 1914; Konrad Schima, *Erpressung und Nötigung: Eine kriminologische Studie,* Vienna and New York: Springer-Verlag, 1973.

Warren Johansson

BLOCH, IWAN (1872–1922)

German physician, historian, and sex researcher. One of an extraordinary group of investigators active in Wilhelmine **Berlin,** Bloch perhaps surpassed all the others in learning. Omnivorously curious, he is said to have possessed a personal library of 80,000 volumes. In addition to the medical approach in which he had been trained, Bloch directed his full attention to historical, literary, sociological, and ethnographic evidence, so as to create a multidisciplinary concept of Sexualwissenschaft (sexual science). In his own time he viewed the problem of venereal disease as emblematic, holding that this once overcome, humanity could look forward to a bright future.

Rejecting the degeneration theory, Bloch first held that homosexuality could be acquired in a multiplicity of ways, but then—on the basis of first-hand observation—accepted Hirschfeld's doctrine that "true homosexuality," of congenital origin, was not morbid, but rather healthy in that it was spontaneous and occurred in individuals who were able to function as well as other members of society. He distinguished homosexuality per se from pedophilia, pederasty, hermaphroditism, misogyny, and "pseudo-homosexuality" (the latter largely corresponding to bisexuality).

Some of the English translations of Bloch's works, especially those dealing with anthropological and historical subjects, are so heavily abridged as to be no true measure of his erudition.

BIBLIOGRAPHY. *Works: Das Geschlechtsleben in England*, by Eugen Dühren [pseud.], 3 vols., Berlin: Barsdorf, 1901–03; *Beiträge zur Ätiologie der Psychopathia sexualis*, 2 vols., Dresden: H. R. Dohrn, 1902–03; *Die Prostitution*, 2 vols., Berlin: L. Marcus, 1912–25; *The Sexual Life of Our Time*, trans. M. Eden Paul, London: Heinemann, 1908; *Der Ursprung der Syphilis*, 2 vols., Jena: G. Fischer, 1901–11.

BLOOMSBURY

Taking its name from the district of London where many of the members lived, the Bloomsbury coterie influenced British thought and letters during the first half of the twentieth century. Broadly cultural rather than academic in their interests and affiliations, its members practiced and favored several arts, standing for civilized tolerance as against the competitive ethic of official Britain. Adherents were socially cohesive, but sexually varied: the salons of Bloomsbury hosted heterosexual, bisexual, and homosexual members.

The group began in March 1905, when the Stephen family launched their "at homes" at 46 Gordon Square. Many of the recruits were young men who had just been graduated from **Cambridge**, where they had absorbed, in an atmosphere of wide-ranging enquiry, the ethical precepts of the philosopher G. E. Moore. At Cambridge most had belonged to a secret society, The Apostles, which was suffused with homoeroticism (the "Higher Sodomy"). Although Bloomsbury was not secret, the smugness and self-satisfaction stemming from belonging to an exclusive coterie clung to members—and repelled outsiders such as D. H. **Lawrence** and Wyndham Lewis. For those who had been scarred early by life's rough-and-tumble, Bloomsbury offered a refuge. Within the protected redoubt they freely cultivated opinions, modes of speech and conversation, and clothing styles that struck outsiders, to the extent that they could comprehend them, as aberrant and bizarre. The character and doings of members and friends were tirelessly chronicled in arch and informed gossip. Blasphemy and bawdiness flowed unstintingly. In a 1914 letter Vanessa Bell wrote: "One can talk of fucking & sodomy & sucking & bushes all without turning a hair." Social gatherings, the life support of the group, featured more than just talk: opportunities for sexual encounters—indeed of a sexual merryground—were ever present. Homosexuality was "in." As Virginia **Woolf**, a member of the Stephen family, bluntly remarked: "The society of buggers has many advantages—if you are a woman. It is simple, it is honest, it makes one feel . . . in some respects at one's ease." A sign of their sexual adaptability was the fact that some members settled into a ménage à trois.

After Clive Bell—who stood out for his "special charm of normality"—married Vanessa Stephen in 1907, a second salon was established in which the visual arts were favored. Later Roger Fry was to promote avant-garde modern art through his writings, exhibitions, and above all through a collaborative atelier, the Omega Workshops, which employed a number of "Bloomsberries." By international standards, however, the Bloomsbury painters—Vanessa Bell, Duncan **Grant**, and Fry himself—were second-rate, never enjoying the prestige of the novelists E. M. **Forster** and Virginia Woolf, not to speak of the economist John Maynard **Keynes**.

The public image of the group was already forming before World War I, and the mutual support that adherents could rely on helped to advance their individual careers. The group was generally hostile to the war, and a number of members became conscientious objectors. In 1918 a homosexual Bloomsberry, Lytton Strachey, published his *Eminent Victorians*, which poured scorn on the icons of official Britain. Bloomsbury discounted religion as something that educated people could not take seriously, while politics was generally dismissed as coarse and life-diminishing. The values of the group were frankly hedonistic: they appreciated modernist painting largely for its "retinal" qualities, cultivated French cuisine, and engaged in the kinds of sex that appealed to individual taste. Although members were individualistic, their headquarters in London gave them a cohesion that no group of academics, scattered among provincial universities, could hope to attain. They used their access to the media to project what they sincerely believed were the ideals of civilization and tolerance.

To its enemies Bloomsbury stood for superficiality and self-indulgence, a prolongation in a new guise of the **aestheticism** and **decadence** of the 1890s. In art and literature, the Bloomsberries sacrificed content to form, and indeed their aesthetic ideas belonged to the international context of Formalism. For their highbrow tastes "proletarian culture" was as repulsive as "capitalist culture": both were hopelessly vulgar. For all their dislike of the degradation brought by the industrial system, their revolt against Victorianism seemed to depend, all too crucially, on the maintenance of the stability secured by the sacrifices of earlier generations—not to mention their social position and income. At Bloomsbury gatherings, servants always hovered in the background and **class** privilege was taken for granted. The coming of the international depression in 1929 and World War II seemed to lend substance to this critique,

and Bloomsbury faded in public awareness, though individual members continued to produce.

The revival of interest in Bloomsbury coincided with the new prosperity of the 1950s, which made its **lifestyle** preferences available to a larger segment of society. A further stimulus was the fascination with the early phases of **modernism**. Then there was the sexual revolution of the 1960s, which Bloomsbury was rightly seen as having anticipated. For the first time Michael Holroyd's massive study, *Lytton Strachey: A Critical Biography* (London, 1967–68) revealed to a larger public the centrality of homosexuality to the group. All these factors turned writing about Bloomsbury into an academic growth industry, and there was much uncritical acclaim. Books poured from the presses, and on the art market prices of even the shabbiest Omega workshop items increased enormously. Inevitably, a reaction followed, but not so sharp as to exclude the consolidation of a more balanced picture of the group's accomplishments.

BIBLIOGRAPHY. Leon Edel, *Bloomsbury: A House of Lions*, New York: Avon, 1980; J. K. Johnstone, *The Bloomsbury Group: A Study of E. M. Forster, Lytton Strachey, Virginia Woolf and Their Circle*, New York: Noonday, 1954; S. P. Rosenbaum, *The Bloomsbury Group: A Collection of Memoirs, Commentary and Criticism*, Toronto: University of Toronto Press, 1975.

Wayne R. Dynes

BLÜHER, HANS (1888–1955)

German homophile leader and scholar. His early, controversial studies on the German youth movement (Wandervogelbewegung) emphasized the positive function of male eroticism in the initiation of the young to collective life. Blüher was strongly influenced by the psychoanalytic theories of Sigmund **Freud**, and radically opposed to the "third sex" theory of Magnus **Hirschfeld**, the leader of the German homophile movement. In a two-volume work of 1917–19, *Die Rolle der Erotik in der männlichen Gesellschaft* [The Role of the Erotic in Male Society], he divided homosexuals into three types: the "heroic male," the effeminate invert, and the suppressed homosexual. Society was in his view organized around two institutions, the family and the state. The first was by its very nature heterosexual, the second had its basis in male bonding—with homoerotic overtones. He was also an anti-Semitic thinker who played a part in the right-wing politics of homosexual paramilitary cliques under the Weimar Republic. In later years, increasingly departing from his earlier concerns, Blüher evolved a somewhat murky metaphysics of Christianity and nature. He was twice married and had two children. Despite his fame as the author of two major books on homosexuality the **Nazis** left him alone. At the close of his life he composed his memoirs under the title *Works and Days*.

BODY LANGUAGE
See **Gesture and Body Language.**

BOHEMIANISM

The expression *La Bohème* first emerged in **Paris** in the 1840s, where it denoted a segment of urban life characterized by a mixture of semiunderground figures—mountebanks, fixers, petty criminals, and prostitutes along with struggling, impoverished writers and artists—and the free use of alcohol and other stimulants. The term derives not from the Bohemia (Bohème) that is now a part of Czechoslovakia, but from the gypsies, to whom that geographic origin was erroneously ascribed. The fame of the Parisian Bohème led to the detection of others (which had probably been in existence for some time) in the major cities of Europe and North America. A typical feature of bohemia was emancipation from the family with its values and constraints. Contrary to outsiders' impression of its being disorganized, bohemia had its fixed meeting places—the café being of central importance—and its press.

This urban phenomenon is obviously older than the name itself. A text by Richard of Devizes pertaining to **London** in the twelfth century shows homosexuals living in the company of other denizens of the urban demimonde. At the end of the **Middle Ages** a Cologne text of 1484 points to the existence of a homosexual **subculture** with regular meeting places, known habitues, and the like. A group of difficult jargon poems of François Villon (b. 1431) has been given an interpretation which would reveal their author as a homosexual situated in just such a milieu in mid-fifteenth-century Paris. Most Italian cities, including **Venice** and **Florence**, had such groups.

The gay side of Paris under the early Third Republic is illuminated by the classic relationship of the poets **Rimbaud** and **Verlaine**. Francis Carco's novel *Jésus-la-Caille* (1910) paints a convincing picture of the life of a bisexual hustler in the French capital during the Belle Epoque. In the United States the archetypal bohemias were in **New York City**: the Greenwich Village and **Harlem** of the 1920s. The Greenwich Village poet Maxwell Bodenheim (1893–1954) openly admitted his bisexuality in his autobiography, and popular journalism affords occasional glimpses of cafes and bars frequented by homosexuals in the interwar period. Outside New York City, the most fertile ground for imitation of the "bohemian" lifestyle was the elite college campus, where students (and ex-students) emancipated from the surveillance of their families could revel in the freedom of late adolescence without adult responsibilities. Bohemian cafés, though their patrons may have been "mixed," were clearly the ancestors of today's gay and lesbian establishments. The nationwide Prohibition of alcohol as a result of the passage of the Eighteenth Amendment in 1919 caused speakeasies to spring up in every city, but with a particular concentration in the bohemian quarters. While attracting a more varied and upscale clientele, these mob-protected bars created a new interface between bohemia and crime. Then, when Prohibition was repealed in 1933 much of the acquired aura of clandestinity—and the need for payoffs—lingered in gay **bars** in the bohemian quarters, where the effects of sleazy, specious glamor and the aura of the forbidden were not to disappear until the 1960s.

The **beatniks and hippies** of this period sanctioned sexual experimentation along with the use of consciousness-expanding drugs and similar avenues of secession from the constraints of American middle-class life. To a considerable extent, the post-1969 phase of the gay movement was launched from the social base of an "alternative" culture in the metropolitan bohemias whose residents were not threatened by the ostracism and economic boycott that would have befallen known activists in Middle America.

BIBLIOGRAPHY. Jerrold Seigel, *Bohemian Paris: Culture, Politics and the Bourgeois Life, 1830–1930*, New York: Viking Press, 1986; Caroline F. Ware, *Greenwich Village 1920–1930*, Boston: Houghton Mifflin, 1935.

Wayne R. Dynes

BOISROBERT, FRANÇOIS LE METEL DE (1592–1662)

Courtier of Cardinal Richelieu and founder of the French Academy. Born in Caen, he practiced law briefly in Rouen, but after some legal troubles in that city he left for **Paris** with letters of recommendation to highly placed personalities. In the French capital he soon gave proof of his lifelong talent for insinuating himself in to circles of pretty and educated women whom he flattered and entertained. In time a sexual interest in the handsome pages who adorned the court of Louis XIII awakened in him, and he exhibited a feminine delight in appearing publicly in elegant and luxurious clothing. But at the same time he evinced a wit and humor, a gift for storytelling, that made him a favorite of Cardinal Richelieu. He knew how to wound and stigmatize some, to flatter and cajole others. Though not high-born or brilliant, he gained access to the highest circles thanks to the Cardinal's protection, and in spite of his undisguised sexual proclivities. "He could have given the Greeks lessons in how to make love," said a contemporary, and he even earned the sobriquet of "the mayor of Sodom." His position at court he also used to intercede on behalf of less talented and needy men of letters. As a token of his favor Richelieu conferred the title of canon at Rouen on Boisrobert, but this in no way changed his lifestyle.

At this time a group of writers assembled weekly in a remote corner of Paris to discuss matters of language and literature, and out of this Boisrobert created an association with formal membership and statutes—the French Academy, admission to which became a coveted symbol of recognition as a littérateur of the first rank; and at the outset it was Boisrobert's personal recommendation that mattered, and he presided over the Academy with elegance and refinement. An incident at the theatre cost him the favor of the monarch, and he was exiled to Rouen, but returned as Cardinal Richelieu was dying (1642). In favor again, he encountered hostility from the grammarian and lexicographer Gilles Ménage, who railed at him as "Cet admirable Pathelin/Aimant le genre masculin" [That admirable pathic/Loving the masculine gender]. After a further mishap that led to a second exile in Rouen, the courtier returned to bask in the favor of the ladies of the court, with whom he had a feminine identification that made them overlook or forgive his own erotic proclivity for pages and manservants. With a physique reminiscent of a fragile statuette he combined a charm that enabled him to empathize with the female sex and to play the role of courtier with skill and audacity. The French Academy with its forty immortals remains a monument to his incarnation of the homosexual affinity for literature and art.

BIBLIOGRAPHY. Emile Magne, *Le plaisant abbé de Boisrobert, Fondateur de l'Académie française, 1592–1662*, Paris: Mercure de France, 1909; Numa Praetorius (pseudonym of Eugen Wilhelm), "Der homosexuelle Abbé de Boisrobert, der Gründer der 'Académie française,'" *Zeitschrift für Sexualwissenschaft*, 9 (1922), 4–7, 33–43.

Warren Johansson

BONDAGE
See Sadomasochism.

BONDING
See Friendship; Homosociality.

BONHEUR, ROSA (1822–1899)

French painter. Born into a family of artists, Bonheur was encouraged early on by her father, who sent her to the Louvre to copy old-master canvases and urged her to visit farms and stables to sketch. She was only nineteen when she entered her work for the first time in the official Salon. In her twenties she frequented the slaughterhouses and horse fairs for material. For these visits she obtained a permit to wear male costume. At the age of twenty-six she won her first Gold Medal, awarded by a jury that included Corot, Delacroix, and Ingres. Five years later, her reputation reached its height in France with the display of *The Horse Fair*, an imposing tour de force which today adorns The Metropolitan Museum of Art in New York.

Prosperity enabled her to acquire a chateau near Fontainebleau, where she kept a menagerie of exotic animals. She traveled frequently and hobnobbed with royalty. Claiming that the duties of her craft required her full attention, Bonheur never married.

At the age of fourteen Rosa Bonheur began a friendship with Nathalie Micas, a sickly child whom she protected. In their blossoming relationship (which Bonheur described as "sisterly"), Nathalie looked after the clothes and the studio, freeing Bonheur for her work. Although it was never openly acknowledged as a love affair, this intimate connection lasted until Nathalie's death in 1889.

Her last years were illuminated by a passionate friendship with a young American artist, Anna Elizabeth Klumpke, whose mother had brought her daughters from San Francisco to Paris so that they might take advantage of European culture. Although they had met in 1889, the very year of Micas' death, it was not until 1898, in an imperious letter to Mrs. Klumpke, that Bonheur announced that she and Anna had decided to share their lives. Klumpke's writings leave little doubt of the nature of her relationship with Bonheur. In a few letters to intimate friends the aged painter referred to her companion as "my wife." Despite family opposition, Bonheur made Klumpke her sole heir.

Although there had been notable women painters in earlier centuries, Bonheur's career flourished in an era of increasing assertion of women's rights and creativity, as seen in the careers of such writers as Flora Tristan and George Sand. Bonheur also took advantage of the interest in androgyny then current to paint "men's" subjects, while adopting, however guardedly, a male role in her personal relations as well. After her death Bonheur's reputation declined, but it revived again with the late twentieth-century resurgence of interest in academic painting.

BIBLIOGRAPHY. Dore Ashton and Denise Browne Hare, *Rosa Bonheur: A Life and a Legend*, New York: Viking Press, 1981; Albert Boime, "The Case of Rosa Bonheur: Why Should a Woman Want to Be Like a Man?" *Art History*, 4 (1981), 384–409.

Kathy D. Schnapper

BOSTON

The capital of Massachusetts was founded in 1630 by John Winthrop and other Puritans as "the city on a hill" to be a beacon to show the world how true Christians should live. The religious convictions of the colonists naturally entailed a hatred of all forms of sexual "depravity." As early as 1636 the General Court of Massachusetts Bay asked Rev. John Cotton to draft a law code for the colony, which included the death penalty for "unnatural filthiness, whether sodomy, which is carnal fellowship of man with man, or woman with woman." Although this proposal was not accepted, another law—providing for the death penalty for male homosexuality only—was adopted in 1641.

Because of its exceptional harbor and enterprising merchants and shipowners, Boston achieved wealth and sophistication in the eighteenth century. Profits from the sordid triangle trade—molasses, rum, and slaves—were not disdained by these mercantile aristocrats. Secularizing merchants won their prolonged struggle against dour ministers, but the Puritan strain has never been completely eradicated. Boston's aggressive patriots, like the Adamses, remained more puritanical than the Southern deists with whom they were allied. After 1830 clipper ships and China trade brought new wealth and power to the Boston Brahmins, who gave the city the particular cachet it has long retained. The flowering of New England lifted the city—now called the Athens of America—to the front rank of American culture. Bostonians profited in the mid-nineteenth century from speculation in railroads, textile and leather manufacturing, banking and profiteering from the Civil War, while abolitionists, wrapping themselves in the mantle of moral superiority that their Puritan forebears had worn, berated both Southern slaveowners and Northern robber barons. President Charles William Eliot (1834–1926) raised Harvard to a leading position among American universities and, by adopting the German Ph.D. system, turned it into a world center of scholarship.

Prominent homosexuals as well as bars and an emerging gay subculture can be traced to this period. The Imagist poet Amy **Lowell** smoked cigars and had a long-term relationship with a lesbian lover. Katherine Lee Bates, who wrote "America the Beautiful" in 1893 and was a professor at Wellesley (1885–1925), was also gay. In 1907 the *Monatsberichte* of the Berlin **Scientific-Humanitarian Committee** printed a letter which said that "Boston, this good old Puritan city, has homosexuals by the hundreds," Yankees being the most numerous, but French Canadians also well represented. Homosexuality extended into all social classes, from the North End teeming with immigrants to the fashionable Beacon Hill and Back Bay. The grapevine carried word of homosexual figures in the highest stratum of Bostonian life. However, the anonymous correspondent believed that the American homosexuals were "astonishingly ignorant about their own true nature"—which amounted to saying that while they were conscious of their physical desires, they had not yet been exposed to European concepts of homosexual identity and militancy. The political emancipation of the American gay subculture lay decades in the future.

With the coming of the subway, street-car, and electric tram, suburbs developed. World War I increased the cosmopolitanism of Bostonians and loosened their sexual mores. During Prohibition certain speakeasies, including the Napoleon Club and the Chess Room in the Hotel Touraine, attracted a gay clientele. Irish politicians such as James Michael Curley broke the power of the Brahmins who retreated to Beacon Hill or the suburbs, though they still held power in the financial district. One governor was reputedly gay, as were the son of another and two cardinals. A gay ghetto developed on St. Botolph Street, on the border between the Back Bay and the South End, the once-fashionable district where George **Santayana** lived. Italians occupied the North End and blacks were displaced from the back of Beacon Hill to Massachusetts Avenue where they had their own speakeasies and jazz places, their numbers swollen by emigrants from the South.

World War II saw more black immigration and more sexual experimentation in the military by all classes of males and females. After the war, as the elite and upper-middle class fled the city to the automobile suburbs, the gay movement began with the formation of Boston's Daughters of **Bilitis** and the founding of the **Mattachine Society** of Boston in the late 1950s by the erratic and picturesque figure of Prescott Townsend, a scion of one of the great Brahmin families, who summered in nearby Provincetown, now a major gay resort. Gay bars in and near the "combat zone" and in Scolly Square continued the prosperity they had gained during the war.

Boston declined in the 1950s and 1960s for economic and social reasons. Later, a bitter dispute over school busing pitted Irish in South Boston and Italians in East Boston intent on protecting their ethnic neighborhoods against blacks and Hispanics, now the fastest growing element in Boston's mix. Economic recovery and urban renewal began in the late 1960s and have since accelerated. Homosexuals arrived in great numbers on elegant Beacon Hill and Back Bay and subsequently gentrified the South End and the Fenway.

After the **Stonewall Rebellion** in New York City in 1969 Boston's gay **movement** developed. The Mattachine Society had been replaced by the Homophile Union of Boston (HUB).

In 1977 the Boston Boise Committee organized to demand fair trials for a group accused of child pornography. The District Attorney was thrown out of office, and only two of the defendants were convicted. Out of the Committee grew GLAD (Gay and Lesbian Advocates) and the North American Man–Boy Love Association (NAMBLA), founded in 1978 and now a national group, although the Boston chapter disbanded subsequently.

Fag Rag, the second oldest gay periodical still published in North America, was founded in 1970 by an editorial group that included Charley Shively. Three years later appeared the *Gay Community News*, a lesbian/gay weekly unique in being a collective equally balanced between men and women. A successful gay book publisher, Alyson Press, was created by Sasha Alyson, who also founded a pro-religious paper *Bay Windows*.

Though deeply divided and often cantankerous, Boston's gay community ranks as one of the most important in North America. Its annual Gay Pride March has been held each year since 1971 in mid-June, before the one in New York. The Good Gay Poets was organized in 1972 and has continued to publish. If Boston has less of a **Bohemia** and is more discreet in its gay life than **New York** or **San Francisco**, as an educational center each year it attracts thousands of the brightest American youth. With over 200,000 students in numerous colleges and universities, large numbers of faculty, and outstanding medical and legal institutions, the city vies with **Paris, London**, and New York as one of the leading cultural centers of the world. Increasingly, it is also a tourist mecca that lures the gay vacationer in search of erotic pleasures.

BIBLIOGRAPHY. Joseph Interrante, "From the Puritans to the Present: 350 Years of Lesbian and Gay History in Boston," *Gay Jubilee: A Guidebook to Gay Boston—Its History and Resources*, Boston: Lesbian & Gay Task Force of Jubilee 350, 1980, pp. 7–29.
Antonio A. Giarraputo and William A. Percy

BOSTON MARRIAGE

The term "Boston marriage" was used in late nineteenth-century New England to describe a long-term monogamous relationship between two otherwise unmarried women. The women were generally financially independent of men, either through inheritance or because of a career. They were usually feminists, New Women, often pioneers in a profession. They were also very involved in culture and social betterment, and these female values formed a strong basis for their life together. Their relationships were in every sense (as described by a Bostonian, Mark DeWolfe Howe, the nineteenth-century *Atlantic Monthly* editor, who had social contact with a number of these women, including Sarah Orne Jewett who had a Boston marriage with Annie Fields), "a union—there is no truer word for it." Whether these unions sometimes or often included a sexual relationship cannot be known, but it is clear that these women spent their lives primarily with other women, they gave to other women the bulk of their energy and attention, and they formed powerful emotional ties with other women. If their personalities could be projected to our times, it is probable that they would see themselves as "women-identified women," i.e., what we would call lesbians, regardless of the level of their sexual interests.

Henry **James** intended his novel *The Bostonians* (1885), which he characterized as "a very *American* tale" (the italics are James'), to be a study of just such a relationship—"one of those friendships between women which are so common in New England," he wrote in his *Notebook*. James' sister Alice had a Boston marriage with Katharine Loring in the years before Alice's death.

BIBLIOGRAPHY. Lillian Faderman, *Surpassing the Love of Men: Romantic Friendship and Love Between Women from the Renaissance to the Present*, New York: William Morrow, 1981.
Lillian Faderman

BOTTICELLI, SANDRO (ALESSANDRO DI MARIANO FELIPEPI; CA. 1444–1510)

Italian painter of the early **Renaissance** in **Florence**. Botticelli's art matured in the cultural efflorescence fostered by the Medici family—a milieu that was shattered by the turbulent events of the end of the century, including the theocratic dictatorship of Savonarola. After this break there developed the different artistic ideals that were to crystallize in the high Renaissance.

Botticelli's paintings capture perfectly the essence of a transient era. The remarkable beauty of the artist's style stems from a thoroughgoing fusion of the older linear manner known as the International Style with the new sense of formal rigor demanded by Renaissance ideals. Although most of Botticelli's surviving works were religious—responding to standard patterns of patronage—he also excelled in portraiture as well as mythological allegory of classical derivation. Paintings in the latter category, above all the celebrated *Primavera* (Spring) and the *Birth of Venus*, were created in an atmosphere of philosophical syncretism generated by the Neo-Platonic movement. The chief figure in this trend, Marsilio **Ficino**, advocated a concept of Socratic love, a cautious and high-minded rationalization of his own homoerotic leanings. Moreover, the influence of another closeted homophile Humanist, the poet and philologist Angelo **Poliziano,** has been detected in Botticelli's works.

More concrete evidence of Botticelli's sexual orientation is available. On November 16, 1502, someone dropped a denunciation in the box of the sinister Uffiziali di Notte, a municipal committee concerned with morals charges. According to this anonymous informant, the artist had been engaging in sodomy with one of his young assistants. Perhaps because of the painter's venerable age and high professional standing, no further action was taken. In view of the fact that Botticelli never married, and that such liaisons with pupils (*garzoni*) were common, as shown by similar accusations lodged, among others, against **Donatello** and **Leonardo**, it seems unwise to dismiss the incident, as some modern scholars, in their zeal to preserve Botticelli's "purity," have done.

In the last decade of his life Botticelli had the misfortune of seeing his art come to be regarded as old fashioned, and he painted little. On his death his artistic reputation fell into a decline that lasted some 250 years. The triumphant revival of Botticelli, which was made possible in the light of more inclusive nineteenth-century taste, owes much to two homophile writers: the aesthete Walter **Pater**, who included an essay on the painter in his immensely popular *The Renaissance* (1868), and the scholar Herbert Horne, who published his great monograph on Botticelli in 1908.

Wayne R. Dynes

BOTTO, ANTONIO
See **Pessoa, Fernando**.

BOWLES, JANE
(1917–1973)

American writer. Born Jane Auer to a middle-class Jewish family of New York City, she early had a sense of a powerful imagination together with a awareness of standing apart from others. A childhood brush with tuberculosis resulted in an operation that made her lame, increasing her alienation. In 1937, at a party in Harlem, she met the bisexual American writer and composer Paul Bowles. They soon traveled to Mexico together, and in the following year were married. Jane began work on her novel *Two Serious Ladies*, which was published by Knopf in 1943. In 1947 Paul left for Morocco, where Jane joined him the following year. Tangiers was to be her home for the rest of her life.

Jane had had lesbian relationships before her marriage and was to have a number afterwards, often with Europeans

visiting Morocco. In 1948 Paul introduced her to an illiterate, but charismatic young woman of Fez, Cherifa, with whom Jane was to have a stormy relationship over the years. She suffered intermittently from a writing block, complicated by troubles with drinking. During their stay in Morocco Jane and Paul Bowles became acquainted with many visiting gay literary figures, including William Burroughs, Truman **Capote**, Allen Ginsberg, and Tennessee **Williams**.

Jane Bowles' last years were difficult, and she converted to Catholicism. She was hospitalized on several occasions in a clinic at Málaga, where she died on May 4, 1973. Her husband Paul continued to live and work in Morocco, devoting himself to translating the work of local writers.

In the view of the poet John Ashbery, Jane Bowles was "one of the finest modern writers of fiction, in any language." Her work stands outside the mainstream of American fiction, and some have likened it to the Jewish mystical tradition of the Kabbala. She had a powerful sense of women's independence from men, which she strove to incarnate in the force and quality of her writing.

BIBLIOGRAPHY. Millicent Dillon, *A Little Original Sin: The Life and Work of Jane Bowles*, New York: Holt, Rinehart and Winston, 1981.

Evelyn Gettone

BRAND, ADOLF
(1874–1945)

German book dealer, publisher, and writer. Brand is chiefly remembered for editing *Der Eigene: Ein Blatt für mannliche Kultur* [The Exceptional: A Magazine for Male Culture] between 1896 and 1931— a publication that has been claimed as the world's first homosexual periodical. It began to appear in April 1896 with the subtitle *Monatsschrift für Kunst und Leben* [Monthly for Art and Life], and only in July 1899—that is to say, after the founding of the Berlin **Scientific-Humanitarian Committee**—did it assume the subtitle which openly identified it as a homoerotic publication. Unlike the *Jahrbuch für sexuelle Zwischenstufen* [Yearbook for Sexual Intergrades], *Der Eigene* was devoted to literature and art, publishing short stories on homosexual themes and drawings and photographs of male subjects in a style that represented the best of the printer's art of that day. The volumes for 1903 and 1906 are magnificent productions, with illustrations in sepia and in color. In contrast with Magnus **Hirschfeld** and his followers, Brand gravitated more to the faction of the homosexual movement represented by Benedict **Friedlaender**, John Henry **Mackay** ("Sagitta"), and Gustav **Wyneken**, who sought to revive the pederastic traditions of antiquity and the cult of the *eros paidagōgikos*, the handsome adolescent as protégé and love object of an older man.

To a certain extent Brand inclined politically to the right, though he qualified himself as an "anarchist and pederast"; his interests overlapped with the cult of the youthful athlete and with the Wandervogelbewegung, the German youth movement, as well as with a certain aristocratic idealization of the past and of the exclusive male bonding that had been a feature of warrior societies. For all these reasons Brand and his collaborators scorned Hirschfeld's notion of the homosexual as a "**third sex**" and of the male homosexual as an effeminate "intergrade." Although *Der Eigene* did not survive the early years of the great Depression, the volumes scattered in libraries and private collections are a legacy of what the early twentieth century could accomplish in explicit male homoerotic art and literature.

BIBLIOGRAPHY. Joachim S. Hohmann, ed., *Der Eigene: Das Beste aus der ersten Homosexuellenzeitschrift der Welt*, Frankfurt am Main and Berlin: Foerster Verlag, 1981.

BRAZIL

This vast country, with its 140 million inhabitants, is unique in **Latin America** in deriving its language and much of its culture from **Portugal**. It enjoys the enviable distinction of being known internationally as the New World country with perhaps the greatest freedom for homosexuals. Visitors concur in praising the beauty and vivacity of Brazilian gays who may be easily encountered in the streets, squares, and places of public accommodation. Historical and anthropological factors underlie this phenomenon. The vibrant multiracial character of Brazil, which blends large components of native Indians, Africans imported as slaves, and Portuguese colonists—all groups that had their own homosexual traditions—explains the strong presence of male and female homosexuals in Brazilian society.

The Colonial Era. When the Portuguese reached Brazil in 1500, they were horrified to discover so many Indians who practiced the "unspeakable sin of sodomy." In the Indian language they were called *tivira*, and André Thevet, chaplain to Catherine de Medici, described them in 1575 with the word *bardache*, perhaps the first occasion on which this term was used to describe Amerindian homosexuals. The native women also had relations with one another: according to the chroniclers they were completely "inverted" in appearance, work, and leisure, preferring to die rather than accept the name of women. Perhaps these *cacoaimbeguire* contributed to the rise of the New World Amazon myth.

In their turn the blacks—more than five million were imported during almost four centuries of slavery—made a major contribution to the spread of homosexuality in the "Land of the Parrots." The first transvestite in Brazilian history was a black named Francisco, of the Mani-Congo tribe, who was denounced in 1591 by the **Inquisition** visitors, but refused to discard women's clothing. Francisco was a member of the brotherhood of the *quimbanba*, homosexual fetishists who were well known and respected in the old kingdom of Congo–Angola. Less well established than among the Amerindians and Africans, the Portuguese component (despite the menace of the Tribunal of the Holy Office [1536–1621]) continued unabated during the whole history of the kingdom, involving three rulers and innumerable notables, and earning sodomy the sobriquet of the "vice of the clergy." If we compare Portugal with the other European countries of the Renaissance—not excluding England and the Netherlands—our documentation (abundant in the archives of the Inquisition) requires the conclusion that Lisbon and the principal cities of the realm, including the overseas metropolises of Bahia and Rio de Janeiro, boasted a gay subculture that was stronger, more vital, and more stratified than those of other lands, reflecting the fact that Luso-Brazilian gays were accorded more tolerance and social acceptance. Thirty sodomites were burned by the Inquisition during three centuries of repression, but none in Brazil, despite the more than 300 who were denouced for practicing the "evil sin." They were referred to as *sodomitas* and *fanchonos*.

Independence. With Brazilian independence and the promulgation of the first constitution (1823) under the influence of the Napoleonic Code, homosexual behavior ceased to be criminal, and from this date forward there has been no Brazilian law restricting homosexuality—apart from the prohibition with persons less than 18 years of age, the same as for heterosexuals. Lesbianism, outlawed by the Inquisition since 1646, had always been less visible than male homosexuality in Brazil, and there is no record of any *mulher-macho* ("male woman") burned by the Portuguese Inquisition. In the course of Brazilian history various persons of note were publicly defamed for practicing homosexuality: in the seventeenth century two Bahia governors, Diogo Botelho and Camara Coutinho, both contemporaries of the major satirical poet, Gregôrio de

Matos, author of the oldest known poem about a lesbian in the Americas, "Nise." He himself was brought before the Inquisition for blasphemy in saying that "Jesus Christ was a sodomite." In the nineteenth century the revolutionary leader Sabino was accused of homosexual practices. A considerable surviving correspondence between Empress Leopoldina, consort of the Brazil's first sovereign, Dom Pedro, with her English lady in waiting, Maria Graham, attests that they had both a homosexual relationship and an intense homoemotional reciprocity. Such famous poets and writers as Álvares de Azevedo (1831–1852), Olavo Bilac (1865–1918), and Mário de Andrade (1893–1945) rank among the votaries of Ganymede. The list also includes the pioneer of Brazilian aeronautics, Alberto Santos-Dumont (1873–1932), after whose airship the *pommes Santos-Dumont* were named.

At the end of the nineteenth century homosexuality appears as a literary theme. In 1890 Aluízio Azevedo included a realistic lesbian scene in *O Cortiço*, and in 1895 Adolfo Caminha devoted the entire novel *O Bom Crioulo* (which has been translated into English) to a love affair between a cabin boy and his black protector. In the faculties of medicine of Rio de Janeiro and Bahia various theses addressed the homosexual question, beginning with "O Androfilismo" of Domingos Firmínio Ribeiro (1898) and "O Homosexualismo: A Libertinagem no Rio de Janeiro" (1906) by Pires de Almeida—both strongly influenced by the European psychiatrists **Moll**, **Krafft-Ebing**, and Tardieu. From 1930 comes the first and most outspoken Brazilian novel on lesbianism, *O 3° Sexo*, by Odilon Azevedo, where lesbian workers founded an association intended to displace men from power, thus setting forth a radical feminist discourse.

The Contemporary Gay Situation. It was only at the end of the 1970s that gays were able to realize the dream of the *terceiristas* of Azevedo's novel. In 1976

appeared the main gay journal of Brazilian history, *O Lampião* ("The Lantern"), which had a great positive effect on the rise of the Brazilian homosexual movement. By 1980 twenty-two organized groups had been formed and two national congresses had been held. Such a promising start was succeeded by inevitable setbacks, caused mainly by the lack of political discipline of the gay activists who had founded the groups and the material and intellectual poverty of the participants. Four gay groups remain (Bahia, Rio de Janeiro, and two in São Paulo), all of them legally recognized. Among the main victories of the Brazilian gay movement is the freeing of homosexuals from the role of "sexual deviants and inverts" and the ratification of several resolutions on the part of scientific bodies protesting antigay discrimination and calling for financial support for research on homosexuality. One of the chief battles of gay activists is to denounce the repeated murders of homosexuals—about every ten days the newspapers report a homophobic crime.

Recently the transvestite Roberta Close appeared on the cover of the main national magazines, receiving the accolade of "the model of the beauty of the Brazilian woman." In the mid-1980s more than 400 Brazilian transvestites could be counted in the Bois de Boulogne in **Paris**; many also offer themselves in Rome. When they hear the statistics of the **Kinsey** Report, Brazilian gays smile, suggesting through experience and "participant observation" that in Brazil the proportion of predominantly homosexual men is as high as 30 percent.

Since 1983, with the death of the first Brazilian **AIDS** victim, the "epidemic of the century" has caused much concern in the homosexual community. Situated in the third place in the world, after the United States and France, Brazil was tardy in mounting a public information campaign aimed at the prevention of AIDS. Given the general bisexuality, the spread of the disease was particularly worrisome among less prosperous youth, who constitute half of the population. Brazil, once the paradise of gays, has entered a difficult path.

BIBLIOGRAPHY. Peter Fry, "Male Homosexuality and Afro-Brazilian Cults," in S. O. Murray, ed., *Male Homosexuality in Central and South America*, New York: Gay Academic Union, 1987, pp. 55–91; Luiz Mott, *O Lesbismo no Brasil*, Porto Alegre: Mercado Aberto, 1987; João Silverio Trevisan, *Perverts in Paradise*, London: Gay Men's Press, 1986; Frederick Whitam, *Male Homosexuality in Four Societies*, New York: Praeger, 1986.

Luiz Mott

BRITAIN
See **England.**

BRITTEN, BENJAMIN (1913–1976)

English composer. His works, written in a variety of media, achieved both popular and specialist success, though with the passage of years they came to be labeled "traditionalist" by some. Britten shared much of his life with the tenor Peter Pears, who frequently interpreted his works. In the late 1930s he began several collaborations with the poet W. H. **Auden**, including incidental music to two plays, songs, and the operetta *Paul Bunyan* (1941). Words have always been an important stimulus for Britten: he has set to music poems by **Michelangelo** and **Rimbaud**, among others. In 1976 he was named a life peer (Baron Britten of Aldeburgh) by Queen Elizabeth.

In his dramatic compositions Britten worked with the idea of "parable" as a means of effecting changes in existing patterns of human relationships. The opera *Peter Grimes* (1945) is loosely based on a poem by George Crabbe. Grimes, a fisherman accused of involvement in the death of two apprentices, cannot face social pressure and commits suicide. In this choice of subject it has been argued that Britten was presenting, perhaps unconsciously, a parable of his own homosexuality. The libretto of *The Turn of the Screw* (1954) derives from a famous story by Henry **James**, which it follows closely. Two orphaned children are placed in the care of a new governess, who must struggle for control of the boy Miles with the ghost of Quint, a former valet. Although she persuades Miles to repudiate Quint, the effort is too much and he falls lifeless beside her. In the story one could assume that the ghost is a figment of the characters' imagination—a collective delusion—but in the opera he must appear in the flesh. Hence the relationship takes on a more clearly pederastic character than it otherwise would have done.

The Turn of the Screw remains shrouded in a certain amount of ambiguity, which disappears in the case of *Death in Venice* (1976). Thomas **Mann**'s novella, which the opera faithfully follows, concerns a Central European bourgeois, the image of respectability, who falls precipitously in love with a teenage boy. The Britten setting, which has been successfully staged in a number of major opera houses, offers an adroit, sometimes moving version of a subject that at first sight would seem difficult for audiences to accept. *Death in Venice* is not only a fitting climax to a brilliant career, but an example of the work of a homosexual artist who made creative use of the opportunities that a changing social climate provided.

BIBLIOGRAPHY. Alan Blyth, *Remembering Britten*, London: Hutchinson, 1981; Donald Mitchell, *Britten and Auden in the Thirties*, London: Faber, 1981; Christopher Palmer, ed., *The Britten Companion*, London: Faber, 1984.

Wayne R. Dynes

BROOKS, ROMAINE GODDARD (1874–1970)

American artist. Born in Rome to a wealthy American family, Romaine had a childhood marred by her mother's preferring her sickly brother to her. At the age of seventeen she was sent to a girls' finishing school in Geneva, where she had crushes on several other students. She showed a talent for both art and music, and was able to transfer to **Paris**. She was briefly married to the homosexual pianist John Ellingham Brooks, and had a stormy relationship with the predatory Italian writer Gabriele d'Annunzio. In 1905, after study in Italy, Romaine Brooks began a serious career as an artist in Paris, capped by her successful show in 1910. Her specialty was portraiture, where she showed the influence of James McNeil Whistler, though she never studied with him. Her finest single work is probably her self-portrait, which captures a magnificent brooding figure set against a ruined landscape (Washington, DC, National Collection of Fine Arts). Many of her female portraits, including one of Una Lady Troubridge, the companion of Radclyffe **Hall**, have an androgynous quality.

On the eve of World War I Brooks met Natalie **Barney**, a wealthy lesbian expatriate. Their relationship was to last for fifty years. The two women collaborated on Barney's book *One Who Is Legion*, for which Brooks produced a series of quirky drawings of impossibly thin figures. Some have detected a humorous side in this aspect of her work, complementing the high seriousness of her portraiture.

The last thirty years of Brooks' long life were passed in obscurity, and she did not live to see the revival of interest in women artists that emerged in the 1970s (including a posthumous retrospective of her work in 1971). Brooks stood apart from **modernism** and abstraction, pursuing a humanistic art that gradually opened a gulf with the avant-garde. Her importance is secured, however, by her place in the constellation of creative expatriate lesbians in Paris in the first half of the twentieth century, which included not only Natalie Barney, but Djuna **Barnes**, Gertrude **Stein**, and Alice B. Toklas.

BIBLIOGRAPHY. Meryle Secrest, *Between Me and Life: A Biography of Romaine Brooks*, Garden City, NY: Doubleday, 1974.

Kathy D. Schnapper

BROTHELS

Because of the clandestinity in which they have been shrouded, it is difficult to essay a history and typology of houses of male prostitution. Where demand was present, however, generally means would be found to satisfy it. Often male prostitutes would be included—as they are today in Mexico—as a sideline of the female brothel, men being the clients of both. Secular houses of prostitution must be distinguished from locales where sacred prostitutes were available.

Historical Perspectives. In fourth-century Athens houses existed in which attractive boys were readily available. There seems to have been no need for concealment, as their owners paid a special tax. Attractive slaves were freely traded for use in such establishments. Athenian law strictly insisted that only slaves or metics (foreigners resident in the city), not free-born citizens, could be inmates. Occasionally, as in the case of the handsome Phaedrus, a well-born war captive who became a member of **Socrates'** circle, a boy would catch the fancy of a client who would buy and free him.

While male prostitutes existed in medieval Europe, their situations are hard to assess, in part because the category of house of prostitution merged, as it had often done in the Roman Empire and still does in many countries, with that of the bathhouse (the "stews" or "bagnio"). The institution flourished in medieval and later Islam, though what connections it had with Europe is uncertain. In **China** boy brothels were known to exist in profusion from Sung (960–1279) times. In the late nineteenth century, European travelers report visiting a then-characteristic type of brothel situated on a junk.

Nineteenth-Century Paris. From early nineteenth-century Paris we have an exceptionally detailed report of a male brothel in the Rue du Doyenne, which even had its own resident physicians. This establishment was closed by the police in 1826. François-Eugène Vidocq, in his *Voleurs* (1837), mentions an establishment run by a certain Cottin for the benefit of pederasts in the Paris of the July Monarchy. The ex-police chief Louis Canler reported in his *Mémoires* that an individual nicknamed *la mère des tantes*, "the mother of the queans," kept a house of male prostitution that attracted a varied clientele. Under the Second Empire Paris had a world-renowned male brothel kept by an elderly proprietor who had been a hustler in his youth but was left destitute by the Revolution of 1848. Toward 1860 he organized his establishment in such a manner that clients of every social and economic class could frequent its premises. The room corresponded in price to the degree of luxury that it afforded, and could be rented by the hour or by the day, as well as reserved by correspondence in advance. Likewise a customer with a particular sexual preference could arrange to have his desires satisfied by an appropriate partner, and if he was not pressed for time, even without advance notice he could have a prompt search made for the hustler of his choice. The proprietor energetically managed the affairs of the brothel, aided by the pan-European notoriety which it enjoyed among both potential clients and aspiring employees. Thus modern capitalist methods of business administration filtered down to the market for illicit sexual pleasures in the prosperous France of Napoleon III.

The Cleveland Street Affair. Victorian London was to be scandalized by the discovery on July 4, 1889 of a male brothel at 19 Cleveland Street in the West End. This aspect of the sexual underworld of London had been familiar to Henry Spencer Ashbee, who had written that if discretion did not forbid it, "it would be easy to name men of the very highest positions in diplomacy, literature and the army who at the present day indulge in these idiosyncrasies, and to point out the haunts they frequent." What particularly alarmed the British authorities was that messengers from the General Post Office were being recruited as hustlers for a brothel that catered to "the most abominable of all vices." For the British press of that day the sordid facts of the case were virtually unmentionable, even by way of euphemism, and only the peripheral aspects were publicized at the time, thanks to Henry Labouchere, who had also been responsible for the provisions on **"gross indecency"** in the **Criminal Law Amendment Act** of 1885. The proprietor of the house from the latter part of that year until the scandal broke was Charles Hammond, who fled the country on July 6, 1889, and a few months later took up residence in Seattle, joining a long list of British **exiles and émigrés**. He had kept a roster of his clients that fell into the hands of the police when the premises were raided. The conduct of the case revealed the inequity of class justice in the prosecution of sexual offenses, as the wealthy and powerful figures compromised by the disclosures found underlings in the field of law enforcement who did their best to obstruct the investigation.

The Contemporary Scene. The male house of prostitution continues to exist at the present day. Its raison d'être is the same as that of a legitimate enterprise, that is, to make a profit by satisfying the demands of customers who will patronize the establishment again and again. The brothel offers the client the assurance of full protection against being cheated, robbed, assaulted, or blackmailed during or after the sexual encounter; furthermore, the client, who may be socially prominent or in a sensitive position in political life or in the diplomatic or intelligence community, is shielded from public exposure of his homosexuality, which would make his existence impossible. In one typical estab-

lishment, the brothel owner carefully screens applicants to exclude those with criminal records or a history of hepatitis or venereal disease. The would-be male prostitute is usually a model, sometimes an aspiring actor, who takes on the trade to supplement his income. The owner interviews the candidate to determine the character of his own preferences; to have qualms is perfectly acceptable, as he is not disqualified for not desiring a partner of another race or refusing to participate in sadomasochistic activities. The versatile applicant is preferred, but one who is extremely attractive will be accepted even if he takes the active role only. The owner asks the candidate whether he objects to having nude photographs of himself appear in magazines or motion pictures; such exposure usually precludes a further career as a commercial model. The applicant is finally required to perform in a situation approximating one with a client; if he proves impotent under these conditions he is disqualified. If he passes the test he is photographed in the nude with his penis both relaxed and erect. The owner carefully records the exact dimensions of the virile member. The photographic and other data are, with additional vital statistics, then entered in a book which is shown to prospective clients. The owner warns his new employee not to have sexual contact with others in the house, as this causes conflicts and undesirable attachments among the staff.

The financial arrangement consists of a fixed fee for a stated period of time, which in certain establishments is split on a prescribed basis between the management and the prostitute, who retains any tips that he receives from the client. Minimum fees for first-class establishments have risen with inflation, and may be as high as $225 for a single encounter. Prostitution is characterized by the commercialization of the entire relationship: emotional indifference to the customer, barter, and promiscuity. The employees of the brothel rarely use their real names, only assumed ones; they are cautioned not to become emotionally involved with their clients or to see them outside the business context, and also not to give customers their real names, addresses, or telephone numbers. For economic reasons, the house seeks to control the channels of contact between the client and the prostitute.

The prostitute is expected to maintain a youthful and attractive exterior. The hair must be carefully groomed and not too long, while body hair is shaved off or removed with depilatory creams. The clothing worn by the male prostitute must correspond to the image that he desires to project, whether as an escort for dinner in an exclusive restaurant or as an habitue of leather bars. At the outset the employment can be financially rewarding and emotionally gratifying, but as time goes by it looms more and more as a dead end, financially and emotionally, as age and the strain of the sexual routine take their toll. The prostitute often needs drugs or alcohol or both in order to perform on demand, and these stimulants are ruinous to the peak of physical attractiveness that the successful provider of sexual services must maintain. The time span of a career in this field is seldom more than three years, but as the house has a steady supply of new applicants, it can always find replacements for those who retire.

See also **Kadesh; Prostitution.**

BIBLIOGRAPHY. David J. Pittman, "The Male House of Prostitution," *TransAction*, 8/5–6 (1971), 21–27.

BUDDHISM

A spiritual tradition founded in northern India in the sixth to fifth century B.C. by Siddhartha Gautama (known as "the Buddha," or "Awakened One"), Buddhism places emphasis on practicing meditation and following a spiritual path that leads from a state of suffering, viewed as the result of attachment, to a state of enlightenment, transcendence and bliss called nirvana. This path is seen as extending over many lifetimes. Buddhism has exerted a major influence on the cultures of **India**, Nepal, **China**, **Japan**, Tibet, **Korea**, Mongolia, **Thailand**, Burma, Sri Lanka, Laos, Cambodia, and Vietnam, and in the current century has gained a foothold in Western countries as well. Among world religions, Buddhism has been notable for the absence of condemnation of homosexuality as such.

Early and Theravada Buddhism. For an account of the earliest form of Buddhism, scholars look to the canonical texts of the *Tipiṭaka* preserved in the Pali language and transmitted orally until committed to writing in the second century B.C. These scriptures remain authoritative for the Theravada or Hinayana school of Buddhism, now dominant in Southeast Asia and Sri Lanka.

The Pali Canon draws a sharp distinction between the path of the layperson and that of the *bhikkhu* (mendicant monk, an ordained member of the Buddhist *Sangha* or Order). The former is expected primarily to support the *Sangha* and to improve his karmic standing through the performance of meritorious deeds so that his future lives will be more fortunate than his present one. The *bhikkhu*, in contrast, is expected to devote all his energies to self-liberation, the struggle to cast off the attachments which prevent him from attaining the goal of nirvana in the present lifetime.

The layperson's moral code pertaining to sexuality consists of the resolution to avoid *kāmesu micchacāra*. As a "training rule" or resolution it does not have the absolute prohibitive nature of Western religious codes (e.g., the Ten Commandments), and is promulgated not as the desire of a God but as a practical guide toward improving one's karma and so (eventually) attaining nirvana. The Pali phrase cited is literally translated as "wrongdoing in the sense-desires," and thus is thought originally to have covered misuse of all the senses (for example, gluttony). In most current English translations, under the influence of Victorian missionaries who did the early translations, this has been rendered, however, as "sexual misconduct."

The lay moral code (*Pañcasīla*) leaves it up to the individual to interpret what such misconduct might be, but the supplementary texts spell out such offenses as adultery, rape, and taking advantage of those over whom one exercises authority. What is *not* included even in the supplementary canonical texts is any condemnation of pre-marital sex or of homosexuality as such. In short, the unmarried Buddhist layperson is free to engage in consentual homosexual acts. This had led to a great deal of tolerance of homosexuality in modern Buddhist countries.

The monastic code of discipline or *vinaya*, however, is aimed at curtailing all passions, including sexual ones. "Is not the Law taught by me for the allaying of the fever of pleasures of the senses?" explains the Buddha in a canonical *vinaya* text. Thus all acts involving the intentional emission of his semen are prohibited for the monk; the insertion of the penis into a female or male is grounds for automatic expulsion from the *Sangha*, while even masturbation is a (lesser) offense. On the other hand, the *vinaya* is silent on matters which presumably were not thought to arouse the sense-pleasures; thus there is no law against a monk receiving a penis into his own body. While a monk is prohibited by lesser rules from even touching the body of a female (even a female animal), no such rule pertains to other males, and the physical expression of affection is very common among the Buddhist monks.

The full rules of the *vinaya* are not applied to the *sāmanera* or novice monk, who may be taken into the *Sangha* as early as seven years old and who is generally expected though not obligated to take the Higher Ordination by the age of 21. In this way the more intense sexual drive of the male teenager is tacitly allowed for. A *sāmanera* may masturbate without committing an offense. Interestingly, while a novice commits a grave offense if he engages in coitus with a female, requiring him to leave the *Sangha*, should he instead have sex with a male he is only guilty of a lesser offense requiring that he reaffirm his *samanera* vows and perform such penance as is directed by his teacher. This may be the only instance of a world religion treating homosexual acts more favorably than heterosexual ones.

While there is very little secondary Theravada literature (at least in English) pertaining to homosexuality, it has been speculated that homosexual orientation may arise from the residual karma of a previous life spent in the opposite gender from that of the body currently occupied by the life-continuum. This explanation contains no element of negativity but rather posits homosexuality as a "natural" result of the rebirth cycle.

The Mahayana and Japanese Buddhism. The form of Buddhism which spread northward into Tibet, China, Japan, Korea, and Mongolia from its Indian heartland came to be known as the *Mahayana.* It de-emphasized the dichotomy between monk and layperson and relaxed the strict *vinaya* codes, even permitting monks to marry (in Japan). The *Mahayana* doctrinally sought to obliterate categorical thinking in general and resolutely fought against conceptual dualism. These tendencies favored the development of positive attitudes toward homosexual practices, most notably in Japan.

Homoeroticism was introduced to Japan, legend has it, by the Buddhist monk Kukai, also known as Kobo Daishi, in 806 upon his return from studying with a spiritual master in China. According to Noguchi Takenori and Paul Schalow, while "homosexuality surely existed in Japan before then . . . the traditional account of its origins helps explain why homosexuality became a preferred form of sexual expression among the Buddhist priesthood."

When Father Francis Xavier arrived in Japan in the mid-sixteenth century with the hope of converting the Japanese to **Christianity**, he was horrified upon encountering many Buddhist monks involved in same-sex relationships; indeed, he soon began referring to homoeroticism as the "Japanese vice." Although some Buddhist monks condemned such relationships, notably the monk Genshin, many others either accepted or participated in same-sex relationships. Among Japanese Buddhist sects in which such relationships have been documented are the Ji-shu, Hokke-shu, Shingon, and Zen.

Practitioners of Ji-shu revered Amida, the "Buddha of the Pure Land" or of "the Western Paradise." Many of its devotees were warriors, and Father Xavier reported that Ji-shu monks acted as teachers, spiritual masters, and lovers to the sons of samurai. Practitioners of Hokke-shu (or Nichiren) Buddhism, the "black" or "lotus" sect, revered Shakyamuni (Siddhartha Gautama). They were well known for their sacred mantra, *Namu-myohorengekyo*, "homage to the lotus of the good law." While Hokke-shu monks officially disapproved of all forms of sexual intercourse, relationships between monks and novices often appear to have been both pedagogic and amatory. According to Xavier, despite their official disapproval of intercourse, the monks "openly admitted" their sexual preference for other males; moreover, Xavier reports that "the vice was so general and so deeply rooted that the bonzes [monks] were not reproached for it."

Shingon Buddhism is traditionally linked to homoeroticism by way of its founder, Kukai (mentioned above). The Japanese manifestation of Tantric Buddhism, Shingon may also have included homoerotic sex-magical practices which are now lost to us.

Zen, that form of Buddhism perhaps most familiar to Westerners, emerged during the ninth century. In the Zen monasteries of medieval Japan, same-sex relations, both between monks and between monks and novices (known as *kasshiki* and *shami*), appear to have been so commonplace that the shogun Hojo Sadatoki (whom we might now refer to as "homophobic") initiated an unsuccessful campaign in 1303 to rid the monasteries of same-sex love. Homoerotic relationships occurring within a Zen Buddhist context have been documented in such literary works as the *Gozan Bungaku*, *Iwatsutsuji*, and *Comrade Loves of the Samurai*.

The blending of Buddhism and homoeroticism has continued to figure prominently in the works of contemporary Japanese writers, notably Yukio **Mishima** and Mutsuo Takahashi.

Although not specifically linked to homoeroticism, at least one Japanese response to **AIDS** should be noted. In 1987, Wahei Sakurai reported that at a fertility shrine in Kawasaki City where elements of Shinto and Buddhism are blended, a local priest, Hirohiko Nakamura, displayed two paintings, one of a samurai, the other of a deity in meditation, both in the process of destroying AIDS, in the hope that these paintings, when combined with prayers, would protect practitioners from the disease.

Tibet. Although four major traditions of Buddhism emerged in Tibet, only one, the Gelug or d Ge.lugs.pa sect, has been traditionally associated with same-sex love. The Gelug, or "yellow hat," tradition was founded in the early fifteenth century by Tsongkhapa Lozang, and it is to this tradition that the Dalai Lama (spiritual head of Tibetan Buddhism) belongs. "Among the Gelugpas," Lama Anagarika Govinda explains, "intellectual knowledge . . . including history, logic, philosophy, poetry . . . medicine and astrology, was given particular prominence . . . the Gelugpas had to qualify themselves through a long course of studies in one of the monastic communities (like Drepung, Ganden, or Sera)."

It is most probably in its adoption of the strictest *vinaya* rules regarding females that the Gelug tradition has become linked to homoeroticism. According to these rules, no woman may stay overnight within the monastery walls. Moreover, the Gelugpas (at least in the past) condemned heterosexual intercourse for monks, believing that the mere odor resulting from heterosexual copulation could provoke the rage of certain deities. Such misogynistic and anti-heterosexual notions may have encouraged same-sex bonding. A number of writers have suggested that homoerotic relationships were until recently quite commonplace in Gelug monasteries, especially those relationships between so-called "scholar" and "warrior" monks. In the early twentieth century, E. Kawaguchi, describing the monks of the monastery at Sera as "descendents of the men of Sodom," reported that the monks "scarcely fight for a pecuniary matter, but the beauty of young boys presents an exciting cause, and the theft of a boy will often lead to a duel. Once challenged, no priest can honorably avoid the duel, for to shun it would instantly excommunicate him from among his fellow-priests and he would be driven out of the temple."

Buddhism in America. Among those who may be credited with introducing the West to Buddhism are Walt **Whitman** and Henry David Thoreau, both of whom are thought to have loved members of the same sex and both of whom blended elements of Buddhism with elements of other spiritual traditions in their work. In the latter half of the twentieth century, many American gays are practitioners of Buddhism, and the blending of homoeroticism and Buddhism may be found in the work of a number of gay American writers and musicians including Allen Ginsberg, Harold Norse, Richard Ronan, Franklin Abbott, and Lou Harrison. Of these, Ginsberg has perhaps been the most vocal in terms of claiming Buddhism, especially in its Tibetan manifestation as taught by the late Chögyam Trungpa Rimpoche, as a source of inspiration. A number of Buddhist organizations

have also begun to focus on the specific concerns of gay people, as, for example, the Hartford Street Zen Center of San Francisco, whose co-founder, Issan Dorsey, is a gay Zen monk. Other organizations, like the Buddhist AIDS Project of Los Angeles, while not addressing the specific concerns of gays, have been established to provide services for persons with AIDS.

While some practitioners of Buddhism maintain that the practice of same-sex love runs counter to the moral precepts set down long ago by Buddhist monks, many others, both gay and non-gay, maintain that if one accepts one's gayness and attempts to dwell in harmony with and to care for one's fellow creatures, then one is indeed following in the steps of the Buddha.

BIBLIOGRAPHY. Ron Bluestein, "Zen and the Art of Maintenance in Mecca," *The Advocate*, April 2, 1985; Martin Colcutt, *Five Mountains: The Rinzai Zen Monastic Institution in Medieval Japan*, Cambridge: Harvard University Press, 1981; Saikaku Ihara, *Comrade Loves of the Samurai*, E. Powys Mathers, trans., Rutland, VT: Tuttle, 1972; Matsuo Takahashi, *Poems of a Penisist*, Hiroaki Sato, trans., Chicago: Chicago Review Press, 1975; Noguchi Takenori and Paul Schalow, "Homosexuality," in *Kodansha Encyclopedia of Japan*, Gen Itasaka, ed., Tokyo and New York: Kodansha Ltd., 1983, vol. 3, pp. 217–218; Allen Young, *Allen Ginsberg: Gay Sunshine Interview with Allen Young*, Bolinas: Grey Fox Press, 1974.

Randy P. Conner and
Stephen Donaldson

BUGGERY

By the early eighteenth century buggery had become the universal signifier in English law for intercourse regarded as criminally unnatural, whether man with man, man with woman, or man or woman with beast. That is to say, it had come to encompass male homosexuality (anal and oral), deviant heterosexual conduct (anal and oral), and bestiality. Lesbianism, which was never criminalized in **England**, is not included in this list. Curiously, after homosexual offenses between consenting adults were decriminalized in 1967 in England and Wales, a few cases were still prosecuted subsequently for male–female buggery.

Although the legal definition is broad, attention tends to focus on anal relations, as shown by the verb "to bugger," which almost always refers to anal penetration. Once invested with an aura of taboo—the word bugger was considered unprintable outside of legal statutes and commentaries—it has undergone considerable banalization in popular speech, as seen in such expressions as "the old bugger" = "the old guy." Note also "bugger up" (mess up) "buggered out" (tired), and "bugger-all" (nothing). All these expressions are much more common in Great Britain than in North America, where the word family is obsolescent. There is no etymological link with "bug" or "bogeyman," though these words may enter into the outer zones of the term's semantic penumbra.

Historical Background. The history of the word bugger displays a number of revealing bypaths of popular prejudice. Ultimately it stems from the Old Bulgarian *bŭlgarinŭ*, the ethnic name of the Slavic people inhabiting the southeastern part of the Balkan peninsula. Although the Bogomil and Paulician (dualist) **heresies** emerge in Bulgaria—on the periphery of the Byzantine empire—as early as the tenth century, it was only in the wake of the Fourth Crusade (1204) that medieval Latin *bulgarus* (and its vernacular congeners) came to be associated with these heresies. In the West the principal reflex of the dualist systems was the Cathar or Albigensian heresy in southern France.

And so in the thirteenth century *bougre* appeared in Old French with two meanings: (1) Albigensian heretic; (2) sodomite. Sexual depravity had, in fact, been charged to certain Gnostic sects as early as the time of Irenaeus of Lyon (late second century). In the Middle Ages heresy and "unnatural" sexual activity were both traced to the instigation of the Devil, since neither could presumably have occurred to anyone spontaneously. At all events the ascription of sexual irregularity to the Albigensians seems wholly unfounded, albeit the *perfecti*—the inner circle of rigorists—did abstain from all types of intercourse. Thus what might at most be termed a case of sexual exceptionalism, chastity, was slanderously converted into its opposite, sexual licence. Such accusations no doubt helped to rationalize the bloody suppression of the Albigensian heretics.

The English derivative of *bougre* is *bugger*, which in the medieval texts has the sole meaning of "heretic." The first occurrence of "buggery" in the legal sense of "sodomy" is in the fateful law of 1533 (25 Henry VIII c. 6). In his commentaries on the laws of England, Sir Edward Coke (1552–1634) defined buggery as "a detestable and abominable sin amongst Christians not to be named, committed by carnal knowledge against the ordinance of the creator and order of nature by mankind with mankind or with brute beasts, or by womankind with brute beast" (*Third Part of the Institutes of the Laws of England*, 1644, pp. 58–59). All that is lacking in this catalogue of **capital crimes** (for which the penalty specified was execution by hanging or drowning) is heterosexual buggery. That is supplied in the comprehensive definition found in G. Jacob's *Law Dictionary* of 1729: "Buggery . . . is defined to be *carnalis copula contra Naturam et hoc vel per confusionem Specierum, sc.* a Man or Woman with a brute Beast; *vel sexuum,* a Man with a Man, or Man with a Woman."

An additional factor is the Old French use of *bougre* to mean "**usurer**," a moneylender who profits from interest. This association (heretic = sodomite = usurer) derives from the ancient notion that interest is "unnatural" because money, unlike land, is intrinsically sterile, just as homosexual activity is doomed to sterility. Lexicographers have noted the curious fact that the three areas of human experience that generate the greatest amount of slang are money, sex, and inebriation. Though it is now obsolete, the sodomite–usurer link united the first two.

In France the word *bougerie* never gained status as a term of art in law codes, though it sometimes makes its way into reports of executions ("sin of buggery"). In the seventeenth and eighteenth centuries a contrast developed between *bougre* for the active homosexual partner as against *bardache* for the passive one. Modern French retains the old word, together with the female counterpart *bougresse*, mainly as a jocular term of pity or mild abuse; the sexual content has almost entirely faded away. As has been noted, the English enshrined the term buggery in the statute books and legal commentaries, tying the meaning to the sexual aspect, but broadening it to include a whole spectrum of carnal offenses (excepting only lesbianism and masturbation).

In southern Europe forms prevailed in which the second consonant is soft; hence Spanish *bujarrón* and Italian *buggerone* (cf. the French variant *bougeron*). At the end of the fifteenth century the Italian word was carried northwards to German-speaking countries by travelers and mercenaries in the adapted form *puseran(t)*, with devoicing of initial 'b.' Thus Albrecht Dürer labels his 1504 drawing of the Death of Orpheus "Der erst puserant" (the first bugger). Although the word has disappeared in modern German, variants linger as loan words in several neighboring Slavic tongues. Thus when the American gay poet Allen Ginsberg visited Prague in 1965 his popularity among Czech students provoked the ire of the Communist authorities and he was roughed up by a plainclothesman who yelled the epithet *buzerant* at him (see "Kral Majales," *Collected Poems, 1947–1980*, 1984, p. 353).

BIBLIOGRAPHY. Claude Courouve, *Vocabulaire de l'homosexualité masculine*, Paris: Payot, 1985.

Wayne R. Dynes

BURCHIELLESQUE POETRY

This term denotes a type of Italian poetry (*alla burchia*; "haphazardly") utilizing "Aesopic" or coded language, and bristling with obscene double meanings which offer a certain parallel to the famous poems in *jargon* of François Villon (1431–ca. 1463). Burchiellesque poetry flourished from the early years of the fifteenth century through the sixteenth. The leading practitioner of the mode was Domenico di Giovanni, known, because of his facility, as "Il Burchiello" (1404–1449).

Among the followers and successors of Il Burchiello, one should note Antonio Cammelli (1436–1502) and Bernardo Bellincioni (1452–1492), who wrote many compositions on homosexual themes. Various other writers also wrote *alla burchia*, notably Domenico di Prato (ca. 1370–ca. 1432), Rosello Roselli (1399–1451), and the great architects Filippo Brunelleschi (1377–1446) and Leon Battista Alberti (1404–1472).

Burchiellesque language also appeared in prose: for Tuscan Renaissance writers it was standard practice—when they wrote euphemistically on sex (as in private correspondence, for example)—to have recourse to Burchiellesque "cypher," as did Niccolò Machiavelli and Francesco Berni.

Burchiellesque poetry faded away in the sixteenth century, giving life to the less exuberant variant of burlesque known as **Bernesque**. Yet elements of Burchiellesque language lingered for a long time, for example in the Roman pasquinades satirizing the popes.

Often innocent nonsense, foreshadowing the later limericks, Burchiellesque language consists entirely in double meanings, which usually stem from riddles or puns; these are almost always obscene, and often homoerotic. To the uninitiated burchiellesque poems can seem complete in themselves in terms of their surface meaning, so that they seem harmless if somewhat eccentric. In other instances they are hermetic at the surface level also, and indecipherable to anyone who does not possess the key.

Interpreting burchiellesque language is difficult, inasmuch as often the solution is a riddle leading to another riddle. For example, it is possible to read the verb *tagliare* (meaning "to cut" in standard Italian) as "to sodomize" because it echoes the word *tagliere*, "chopping board." In former times these boards were round, not square; hence the meaning "anus." The metaphorical meaning of *tagliere* parallels that of *tondo* ("round" and, by extension, a round sculpted or painted relief), which also means "anus."

Burchiellesque jargon is generally constructed through symmetrical contrasts: *asciutto*, "dry" = "sodomy" vs. *umido*, "humid" = "heterosexual coitus"; *valle*, "valley" = "vulva" vs. *monte*, "mountain" = "anus." In other comparisons the counterpart of the penis is not the vagina, but usually the anus.

Penetration is not usually expressed in the heterosexual sense, but commonly in terms of anal copulation with a man as object. This prominence of sodomitical coitus probably reflects the "transgressive" intent of burchiellesque poetry, for which anal relations are more suited than "banal" heterosexual contact.

The difficulty of burchiellesque language, and the "scandalous" subject matter, have combined to discourage scholarship. Even today there is no critical edition of the works of Il Burchiello, the founder of the trend, nor has a key been worked out that would enable one to recover all the hidden meanings.

BIBLIOGRAPHY. *Works: Sonetti del Burchiello, del Bellincioni e d'altri poeti fiorentini alla burchiellesca,* "London" (actually Lucca and Pisa), 1757; Il Burchiello, *Sonetti inediti,* M. Messina, ed., Florence: Olschki, 1952.
Giovanni Dall'Orto

BURMA

A southeast Asian republic of about 40 million people, Burma is an agricultural, mountainous country. Conquered by Great Britain in the nineteenth century, it achieved independence in 1948. Knowledge of homosexuality in Burma is complicated by the fact that the country has been largely closed to tourists since independence (except for brief tourist visas of up to seven days), by the dominant language, Burmese (which is tonal and part of the Sino-Tibetan group), by the Burmese script (which derives from south Indian scripts), and by the plurality of cultures and cultural influences. More than one hundred indigenous languages are spoken in Burma. Besides Burmese, Mon, Shan, Karin, Chinese, and Kachin are spoken by large numbers of people, though at the time of the British occupation only Burmese, Mon, and Shan had written alphabets.

Animism, which preceded **Buddhism**, introduced in the fifth century, is still practiced by the hill tribes in the northeast such as the Shans, Karins, and Kachins. Among the Kachin, the Gashadip, according to Joel M. and Ester G. Maring, is "conceptualized as a bisexual human being who controls the fertility of the soul and of human beings. The Kachin chief makes periodic offerings to the *gashadip*." Such bisexual mythic beings appear widely across southeast Asia, in **Indonesia** and in northern Australia.

Burmese Buddhism, like that of **Thailand**, is of the Theravada School dominant in Sri Lanka and in Southeast Asia and has been compulsory in large parts of the country since King Anawaratha conquered Thaton in the south in 1044 and forcibly removed the entire population, including Buddhist monks, to Pagan in the north. It has been tolerant of homosexuality. Monks are said to be highly sexed and tourists are warned to be careful of sexual advances—though such reports may be exaggerated. Transvestism is also known. The first Western report of homosexuality in Burma stems from Jan Van Linschoten's (1563–1611) visit to Pegu.

Homosexuality is said to be portrayed in puppet plays in a comic way as in Indonesian puppet theatre, in Asia as far west as Turkey and in Europe. Homosexuals no doubt existed and exist in Burmese theatre—especially probably in Burmese dance—as they certainly do in the closely related dance traditions of East Java. Dance in Burma is largely based, as in Indonesia, in East Java and Bali, on the epics of **India**, the *Ramāyana* and *Mahabhārata*. The greatest oil painter of modern Burma, U Thein, was almost certainly homosexual; for example, in the painting "Best Friend" in the National Museum in Rangoon, the artist's Friend is portrayed as the Loving Buddha, an icon suggestive of homosexuality.

Homosexual references or writings have not been found in Burmese; but as Burmese literature is based on Indian literatures—which are highly erotic without, especially in south India and in Tantrism, distinguishing between hetero- and homoeroticism—it seems reasonable to look for them. Homosexual writing in **Thai**—also tonal and written in a similar script with a common south Indian origin—has been reported; so, given the close interrelationship of the two bordering cultures (the Burmese conquered Thailand in the eighteenth century and sacked the capital Ayutthaya), this also points to the fact that homosexual references and homoerotic writings may exist in Burmese. The issue is complicated by the massive destruction of Burmese culture both by wars (such as the British conquest in the nineteenth century and scorched earth policies in World War II) and by nature (a ferociously hot climate in the north which led to the destruction of the wooden palace of Burmese rulers and its contents in Mandalay after it survived World War II—and high humidity in the south). Manuscripts in Rangoon and in London at the British Library and the University of London, School of Oriental and African Studies (the main repositories outside Burma) have not been assessed for homosexuality so far as is known.

With over 2,000 monuments, the great archeological site of Pagan sacked by the Mongols in 1287 (but not destroyed), should be examined (particularly its wall reliefs and frescoes) by someone familar with Buddhist iconography and its possible homosexual references. The erotic symbolism of the stupa and the spire needs to be considered—especially in regard to the great Shwedagon pagoda in Rangoon and such masterpieces as the Ananda pagoda in Pagan and also in relation to Tantric Buddhism which is highly influential in Burma. The underplaying of eroticism is a serious handicap. I. B. Horner in translating the Pali scriptures in the early twentieth century left out many references to sexuality at the time of Christ, including the split among Buddhists in Sri Lanka over five theses, one of which concerned nocturnal emissions by monks. The influence of Chinese culture—also tolerant of homosexuality—on Burmese culture must also be considered. For much of its history Burma, like Thailand, Vietnam, **Korea**, and **Japan** (though only culturally for Japan), was a vassal state of **China** where the ruler had absolute power until 1908. In the matter of sexuality this meant that he—or she—could do as he—or she—pleased sexually. Burmese rulers, like Thai, Korean, and Vietnamese, modeled themselves on Chinese. Their sexuality needs to be examined in detail by a competent scholar as does the art and literature, both written and oral.

BIBLIOGRAPHY. J.H. Luce, *Old Burma, Early Pagan*, Locust Vally, NY: J.J. Augustin, 1969; Maung Htin Aung, *Burmese Drama*, new ed., London: Oxford University Press, 1957; idem, *A History of Burma*, New York: Columbia University Press, 1967.

Paul Knobel

BURNS, JOHN HORNE (1916–1953)

American novelist. Born into an Irish Catholic family in Andover, Massachusetts, Burns was educated at Harvard University. He taught English at the Loomis School from 1937 to 1942. During World War II Burns served in the Army in North Africa and Italy. There he gathered the material for his book *The Gallery* (1947), a series of brilliant episodes unified by the passage of the characters through the Galleria Umberto in Naples. Many readers have regarded the section entitled "Momma" as the most vivid account of the special atmosphere of a classic gay bar that has ever been written. The characters, several of whom are campy queens, are sharply delineated, and the author showed a remarkable ear for argot and the rhythms of gay speech. Other parts of the novel contain gay allusions, but these are generally too subtle to be picked up by most readers. The overarching presence in the novel is the freedom and sensuality of Italy, and the book is thus another document in the attraction of the northerner for fabled Mediterranean lands, though in this instance refracted in the turmoil of war.

Sensing a change in the American literary climate signaled by critical attacks on writers who allegedly belonged to the "fairy Freudian" school, Burns sought to direct his talent into more conventional paths. Although the main character of *Lucifer with a Book* (1949) is heterosexual, the novel contains a number of minor gay characters. Its main purpose was to indict the hypocrisy of American secondary education, which Burns knew well. *A Cry of Children* (1952) also has a heterosexual hero, a pianist named David Murray. Although homosexuality enters into this book as well, it is much more negatively presented. This shift reflects not only the hostile climate of the Cold War years, but Burns' own confusions stemming from his growing alcoholism. The writer died of sunstroke during a visit to Leghorn, Italy.

BIBLIOGRAPHY. John Mitzel, *John Horne Burns: An Appreciative Biography*, Dorchester, MA: Manifest Destiny, 1976.

BURTON, RICHARD FRANCIS, SIR (1821–1890)

British explorer, geographer, adventurer, writer, anthropologist, translator, and sexologist. Although married unhappily to the beautiful but obtuse Isabelle Burton, by whom he had no children, he led a life that was eccentric and scandalous. In his youth, he visited boy-brothels in Karachi, which led him to have a lifelong interest in homosexuality, although this interest bore fruit only toward the end of his life. Burton was famous for his explorations in Arabia and Africa, and he traveled to every part of the globe, often being the first white man to visit the regions which he explored. He wrote a long series of thick volumes on Africa and other places, and translated several books.

The later part of Burton's life was devoted to translation of the *The Thousand and One Nights* and other works of oriental eroticism, which created a stir at a time when such writings were considered to be outrageously pornographic and unspeakable. He added insult to injury by appending a notorious "Terminal Essay" to the *Nights* which included a long article on **pederasty**, one of the first (and the first published in English) extended discussions of this taboo theme in modern times. Burton believed that there was a so-called **Sotadic Zone** in the equatorial regions of the world in which pederasty was widespread and tolerated, while the northern and southern regions tended to outlaw pederasty and limit it to a minority. He said that the hot weather was the factor which determined all of this, a theory which now appears unlikely but which was taken seriously in the early days of sexology. It now appears that this division into two zones has some validity, but is due to folkways, morality, and economic factors rather than the weather. This essay has sometimes been mistaken for a "gay lib" apology ahead of its time, but a close reading reveals that Burton looked upon sodomy as a lurid vice suitable for shocking Mrs. Grundy when Burton was in a mischievous mood. There is no proof that he ever had sexual relations with any woman (including his wife) or boy, although the visit to the brothels of Karachi has naturally led to suspicions that he did more than just look at the catamites.

The final years of Burton's life were spent in Trieste, working on a massive erotic masterpiece which supposedly included much information on homosexuality, information supplied to him by **Symonds**, **Ulrichs**, Henry Spencer Ashbee, and Guy de Maupassant. However, the manuscript was destroyed after Burton's death by his widow as part of her sanctification plans for her husband's memory. This work was supposedly an annotated translation of the *Perfumed Garden* of the Sheikh Nefzawi (or Nafzawi), but the French translation had no references to pederasty. *The Glory of the Perfumed Garden* is a recent work claiming to be the "missing" half of this work, with chapters on pederasty and lesbianism, but this may be a fraud.

BIBLIOGRAPHY. Stephen W. Foster, "The Annotated Burton," in *The Gay Academic*, Louie Crew, ed., Palm Springs, California: ETC Publications, 1978, pp. 92–103; Brian Reade, ed., *Sexual Heretics*, New York: Coward-McCann, 1971.

Stephen W. Foster

BUTCH–FEM (LESBIAN) RELATIONSHIPS

Butch–fem(me) relationships are a style of **lesbian** loving and self-presentation which can in America be traced back to the beginning of the twentieth century; historical counterparts can be found even earlier. Butches and fems have separate sexual, emotional and social identities, outside of the relationship. Some butches believe they were born different from other women; others view their identity as socially constructed.

While no exact date has yet been established for the start of the usage of the terms "butch" and "fem," oral histories do show their prevalence from the 1930s on. The butch–fem couple was particularly dominant in the United States, in both black and white lesbian communities, from the 1920s through the fifties and early sixties.

Basic Features. Because the complementarity of butch and fem is perceived differently by different women, no simple definition can be offered. When seen through outsiders' eyes, the butch appears simplistically "masculine," and the fem, "feminine," paralleling heterosexual categories. But butches and fems transformed heterosexual elements such as gender attitude and dress into a unique lesbian language of sexuality and emotional bonding. Butch–fem relationships are based on an intense erotic attraction with its own rituals of courtship, seduction and offers of mutual protection. While the erotic connection is the basis for the relationship, and while butches often see themselves as the more aggressive partner, butch–fem relationships, when they work well, develop a nurturing balance between two different kinds of women, each encouraging the other's sexual-emotional identity. Couples often settle into domestic long-term relationships or engage in serial monogamy, a practice Kennedy and Davis trace back to the thirties, and one they view as a major Lesbian contribution to an alternative for heterosexual marriage. In the streets in the fifties, butch–fem couples were a symbol of women's erotic autonomy, a visual statement of a sexual and emotional accomplishment that did not include men.

Butch–fem relationships are complex erotic and social statements, filled with a language of stance, dress, gesture, and comradeship. Both butches and fems carry with them their own erotic and emotional identities, announced in different ways. In the fifties, butch women, dressed in slacks and shirts and flashing pinky rings, announced their sexual expertise in a public style that often opened their lives to ridicule and assault. Many adopted men's clothes and wore short "DA" hair cuts to be comfortable and so that their sexual identity and preference would be clearly visible. As Liz Kennedy and Madeline Davis, authors of a study of a working-class black and white butch–fem community in Buffalo, New York, 1940–60, have pointed out, the butch woman took as her main goal in love-making the pleasure she could give her fem partner. This sense of dedication to her lover, rather than to her own sexual fulfillment, is one of the ways a butch is clearly distinct from the men she is assumed to be imitating.

The fem woman, who can often pass as a straight woman when not with her lover, actively sought to share her life with a woman others labeled a freak. Before androgynous fashions became popular, many fems were the breadwinners in their homes because they could get jobs open to traditional-looking women, but they confronted the same public scorn when appearing in public with their butch lovers. Contrary to gender stereotyping, many fems were and are aggressive, strong women who take responsibility for actively seeking the sexual and social partner they desire.

Community Aspects. Particularly in the fifties and sixties, the butch–fem community became the public face of lesbianism when its members formed bar communities across the country, and thus became targets of street and police violence.

In earlier decades, butch–fem communities were tightly knit, made up of couples who, in some cases, had long-standing relationships. Exhibiting traits of feminism before the seventies, butch–fem working-class women lived without the financial and social securities of the heterosexual world, caring for each other in illness and death, in times of economic depression, and in the face of the rampant homophobia of the fifties. Younger butches were often initiated into the community by older, more experienced women who passed on the rituals of expected dress, attitude, and erotic behavior. This sense of responsibility to each other stood the women in good stead when police raided their bars or when groups of men threatened them on the streets.

Bars were the social background for many working-class butch–fem communities and it was in their dimly lit interiors that butches and fems could perfect their styles and find each other. In the fifties, sexual and social tension often erupted into fights and many butches felt they had to be tough to protect themselves and their women, not just in the bars but on the streets as well.

Butch–fem is not a monolithic social-sexual category. Within its general outline, class, race, and region give rise to style variations. In the black lesbian community of New York, for instance, "bull dagger" and "stud" were more commonly used than the word "butch." A fem would be "my lady" or "my family." Many women of the lesbian literary world and of the upper classes also adopted this style of self-presentation. In the 1920s, Radclyffe Hall, the author of *The Well of Loneliness*, called herself John in her marriage to Lady Una Troubridge. Butch–fem style also shows the impact of changing social models and politics. Feminism, for instance, as well as open relationships and nonmonogamy, have been incorporated into butch–fem life of the seventies and eighties.

With the surge of lesbian feminism in the early seventies, butch–fem women were often ridiculed and ostracized because of their seeming adherence to heterosexual **role** playing. In the eighties, however, a new understanding of the historical and sexual-social importance of butch–fem women and communities has begun to emerge. Controversy still exists about the value of this lesbian way of loving and living, however. Members of such groups as Women Against Pornography depict butch–fem as a patriarchal, oppressive, hierarchical way of relating. The American lesbian community is now marked by a wide range of relational styles: butch–fem is just one of the ways to love, but the butch–fem community does carry with it the heritage of being the first publicly visible lesbian community.

Related Terms.

"Stone butch": a butch woman who does not allow herself to be touched during lovemaking, but who often experienced orgasm while making love to her partner. This was a sexual style prevalent in the forties and fifties.

"Baby butch": a young-looking butch woman with a naive face who brings out the maternal as well as sexual longings of fem women.

"Kiki": a term used from the forties through the sixties for a lesbian who could be either butch or fem. A publicly kiki woman in the forties and fifties was often looked upon with suspicion though in the privacy of butch–fem homes, different sexual positions were often explored.

"Passing woman": a woman who works and dresses like a man; this style of self-presentation was often used in the past to transcend the gender limitations placed on women. Many working-class women "passed" in order to hold down the jobs they wanted without harassment; in earlier decades passing women often married other women. Passing women have their own sexual identity.

(The author wishes to extend special thanks to Deborah Edel, Lee Hudson, and the New York Butch Support Group for help in preparing this article.)

BIBLIOGRAPHY. Madeline Davis and Elizabeth Lopovsky Kennedy, "Oral History and the Study of Sexuality in the Lesbian Community: Buffalo, New York. 1940–1960," *Feminist Studies* 12 (Spring 1986), 7–28; Jonathan Katz, *Gay American History*, New York: Thomas Y. Crowell, 1976; Audre Lorde, *Zami*, Trumansburg, New York: The Crossing Press, 1982; Merril Mushroom, "How to Engage in Courting Rituals, 1950 Butch Style in the Bars: an Essay," *Common Lives/Lesbian Lives* (Summer 1982), 6–10; Joan Nestle, "The Fem Question," in *Pleasure and Danger*, Carole S. Vance, ed., Boston: Routledge and Kegan Paul, 1984; idem, *A Restricted Country*, Ithaca: Firebrand Books, 1987; idem, "An Old Dyke's Tale: An Interview with Doris Lunden," *Conditions* 6 (1980), 26–44.

Joan Nestle

BYRON, GEORGE GORDON, LORD (1788–1824)

English Romantic poet, born in London. The most influential poet of his day, with a world-wide reputation, Byron became famous with the publication of *Childe Harold's Pilgrimage* (1812–18), an account of his early travels in Portugal, Spain, Albania, and Greece. The proud, gloomy, guilt-ridden, alienated Harold defined the "Byronic hero" who was to reappear in various guises in Byron's later poems, notably in "Manfred," "The Corsair," and "Lara." The type became a defining image for European and American romanticism. Forced into exile in 1816 because of the scandal caused by his wife's leaving him, Byron settled in Italy, principally in Venice. There he wrote his sparkling satire on cant and hypocrisy, *Don Juan*. He spent the last months of his life in Greece, trying to help the Greeks in their struggle to gain independence from the Turks.

Notorious in his lifetime for his many affairs with women, Byron at 17 fell in love with a Cambridge college choir boy, John Edleston, two years his junior. This love is expressed in such early poems as "To E—," "The Cornelian," and "Stanzas to Jessy," but most fully in the "Thyrza" elegies written after Edleston's death in 1811 and published (in part) with *Childe*

Harold. Because of the intense homophobia of English society these poems were ostensibly addressed to a woman, as the name "Thyrza" and Byron's use of feminine pronouns implied.

During his first journey to Greece (1809–11) Byron was involved in several liaisons with Greek boys. One of them, Nicolò Giraud, he made his heir when he returned to England. Details of these affairs appear in letters to his friend John Cam Hobhouse, sometimes in a Latin code. Rumors about Byron's homosexual adventures, circulated in London by Byron's ex-mistress Lady Caroline Lamb after Byron's wife left him, were a principal reason for Byron's being forced to go into exile; publicity about his love affair with his half-sister, Augusta Leigh, compounded the scandal. We know nothing more of the homosexual side of Byron's life until his final return to Greece. There he fell in love with the fifteen-year-old Loukas Chalandritsanos, a young soldier in the Greece resistance movement, whose family he had befriended. Byron's last three poems, "On This Day I Complete My Thirty-Sixth Year," "Last Words on Greece," and "Love and Death," poignantly describe his love for Loukas, which was not reciprocated.

Byron died at Missolonghi attempting to provide financial and military aid for the Greeks while under the spell of this "maddening fascination," as he called it.

Byron's bisexuality remained a secret from the general public until 1935, when Peter Quennel broached the subject in *Byron: The Years of Fame.* A surreptitiously published erotic poem, *Don Leon,* purporting to be Byron's lost autobiography, probably written in 1833, had set forth many of the facts about Byron's homosexuality but was dismissed as an unwarranted libel. An edition appeared in 1866 but it remained unknown to all but a few specialists. When the Fortune Press reprinted it in 1934, the publication was confiscated by the British police.

BIBLIOGRAPHY. Louis Crompton, *Byron and Greek Love: Homophobia in 19th-Century England,* Berkeley: University of California Press, 1985; Leslie A. Marchand, *Byron: A Biography,* 3 vols., New York: Alfred A. Knopf, 1957; Doris Langley Moore, *Lord Byron: Accounts Rendered,* London: John Murray, 1974 (Appendix 2: Byron's Sexual Ambivalence).

Louis Crompton

BYZANTINE EMPIRE

Like **China** and **Egypt** this Greek Empire was known for its stability and conservativism. Held together by fidelity to Orthodox **Christianity** and Roman law, the Byzantine Empire evolved over eleven centuries. This development falls into three distinct formations: 330–711, 711–1071, 1071–1453, each about half the size of the previous. Beginning in 641 the empire lost Asian and African provinces to **Islam**; in 1071 half of Anatolia fell to the Turks. Byzantium defended Europe from invaders in spite of bitter religious squabbles involving monks and heretics.

Basic Features. The beginning of the Byzantine empire, also known as the Eastern or East Roman Empire, is usually placed at A.D. 330, when Constantine the Great founded his new capital, Constantinople, on the ancient site of Byzantium (now Istanbul). From the first the new city was Christian, but many of its institutions, including the Senate and the law code, continued the traditions of ancient **Rome**. Latin was the official language until the reign of Justinian, but Greek was from the start the language of commerce and intellectual life. The imperial administration, which never wavered in its policy of antihomosexual repression, managed largely to drive same-sex love underground. Yet some of the dearth of current knowledge of Byzantine homosexuality is probably owing simply to inadequate attention by modern scholars.

Byzantine monks and scholars did copy and transmit many ancient Greek pederastic texts, including the twelfth book of the **Greek Anthology**. Although lexicographers and antiquarians recorded rare ancient terms for homosexual acts, and some original heterosexual erotica are also known from the empire, homosexual erotica of this kind have not yet come to light. From the time of Constantine nude figures disappeared from art, and nothing is heard of **gymnasia** after 380. The pre-Justinian period was nonetheless one of some ambiguity: those who overthrew him alleged that Constans, Constantine's son, was an exclusive homosexual who surrounded himself with barbarian soldiers selected more for looks than for military ability.

The Cappadocian Fathers, Sts. Basil, Gregory of Nyssa, Gregory of Nazianzen, and most of all John **Chrysostom**, harshly condemned homosexuality. Uninfluenced by Latin Christianity, they set the tone for the official attitudes of the Orthodox church.

The Byzantine terms for male homosexuality are *paiderastia, arrhenomixia* ("mingling with males"), and *arrhenokoitia* ("intercourse with males"). The general designation for sexual immorality in Byzantine law codes is *aselgeia* ("lasciviousness"). *Malakia*, which had meant "effeminacy" in Classical Greek, came to mean "masturbation," so that in the Byzantine cultural sphere the translation of I Corinthians 6:9 reads "masturbators . . . shall not inherit the kingdom of God." Homosexual behavior is also styled the "sin of the Sodomite" (e.g., Macarius the Great, *Patrologia Graeca*, 34:2243).

Justinian. The reign of Justinian (527–565) constitutes what is sometimes termed the First Golden Age of Byzantium. Justinian's military campaigns succeeded in recovering Italy and other areas of the empire that had been lost to the barbarians in the preceding century, and he adorned the cities of the empire with splendid buildings, above all the cathedral of Hagia Sophia in Constantinople. He also reorganized Roman law in the *Corpus Juris Civilis*, the ultimate basis of the civil law tradition that today dominates legal systems in a large part of the globe.

Even before assuming full power in 527, Justinian seems to have been implicated in an anti-homosexual trial of 521. The chronicler John Malalas describes the trial of two bishops, Isaiah of Rhodes and Alexander of Diospolis in Thrace; the former was exiled after being subjected to cruel tortures, the latter castrated and publicly dragged in an ignominious procession.

Not surprisingly, the *Corpus* retains the antihomosexual laws promulgated by his predecessors in 342 and 390. Justinian shrewdly perceived, however, that just as in the case of divorce, the hated practices could not by extirpated by a stroke of the pen. Initiating a more tenacious and extended series of steps, he issued two new antihomosexual laws in 538–39 and 559, which reiterated the death penalty already prescribed by the Theodosian Code 9.7.3. In the first of the novellae (no. 77) he ascribed homosexual lust to diabolical incitement and claimed that "because of such crimes there are famines, earthquakes, and pestilences," inferring that homosexual behavior endangered the very physical basis of the empire. Enough of the seismological literature of antiquity had survived into his reign to make such reasoning clearly a superstitious regression, a point conveniently ignored by Christian apologists who would have Justinian act only out of "sincere concern for the general welfare." The second (no. 141) was the first law ever to refer explicitly to **Sodom**, where the land supposedly still burned with inextinguishable fire. Seeming to combine magnanimousness with severity, Justinian appealed to such sinners to confess themselves humbly and penitently to the Patriarch of Constantinople, consigning them to the avenging flames if they did not repent. In fact Justinian and his consort Theodora conducted a kind of witch hunt among homosexuals of the city, several of whom were publicly disgraced, whether penitent or not. The rulers used the imputation of homosexuality to persecute those "against whom no other crimes could be imputed," (Edward Gibbon, *Decline and Fall of the Roman Empire*) or whose fortunes offered a tempting adjunct to the imperial treasury (Procopius, *Secret History*, 11:34–36).

Later Byzantine Times. Needless to say, these measures, though reaffirmed in later codes such as the *Basilica*, did not stop same-sex activity. A number of emperors themselves are believed to have been homosexual. Successful in military campaigns against the Arabs, Slavs, and Bulgars, the iconoclast Constantine V (r. 741–775) sought to limit the power of the monasteries. Theophanes the Confessor lists the "impious lust for males" among his crimes. A particularly tragic case, the alcoholic Michael III (r. 842–867), fell in love with a macho soldier-courtier, Basil the Macedonian, whom he made coruler in 866. Basil promptly murdered his patron, and founded the Macedonian dynasty. Also thought to be homosexual were Basil II (r. 976–1025), a great campaigner against the Bulgarians, Constantine VIII (joint ruler with his brother 976–1025, sole r. 1025–1028), and the Empress Zoe's husband Constantine IX (r. 1042–1055). Eunuchs played a major role at the imperial courts, reaching their zenith under the Macedonian dynasty (867–1057).

Accusations of homosexual vice became a standard device of Byzantine polemics. After the ninth century such charges become rarer probably after the consolidation of Christian family values and emerging masculine ideals. In the field of law the *Basilica* do not repeat the old regulations but only something of secondary importance from the Pandects, a change that might be significant in view of the foregoing circumstance. In the last centuries of the Eastern Empire, however, complaints about homosexuality again surface (e.g., in the Patriarch Athanasius I and Joseph Bryennius). The vice flourished in both male and female monasteries (*typicon* of Prodromos tou Phoberou, 80.31–82.1); the *typica* denied access to the monasteries to beardless youths and eunuchs in an effort to shield monks from temptation.

The Later Byzantine Empire. Beginning in 1071 the Comneni created a new state. After the Byzantines expelled the Latins, who ruled the Eastern empire from the time of the Fourth Crusade (which captured Byzantium in 1203–04) until their expulsion in 1261, the Palaeologi restored a decentralized state ruled by "feudal" magnates on the Western model with the commerce dominated by the Italian maritime republics. Cities shrank, Turks from the East and Bulgars, Serbs, and Franks in the Balkans encroached and barbarized the provinces, and culture declined so precipitously that by the time the capital fell in 1453 the dwindling elite had less knowledge of Plato and Homer than did the **Renaissance** Italian humanists, who had mastered as well the *Corpus Juris Civilis* and the Orthodox fathers.

An eleventh-century text offers evidence for homosexual **clergy** in the Orthodox church. The *Penitential* of pseudo-John IV the Faster instructed the confessor to inquire about the sin of *arrhenokoitia*, which in this text means "anal intercourse" in general. Ecclesiastical law punished the "sin of the Sodomite" with two or three years of *epitimion*, while civil law (the *Eclogues*) established decapitation by the sword as the penalty.

In the Orthodox church priests, the "white clergy," could marry, but not monks or bishops, the "black clergy." Still a staple of reading, the texts of the Cappadocian Fathers, whose admonitions to those who could not resist sex to marry young probably lowered the age of marriage, denounced homosexuality as the most heinous of sins, but nothing could prevent its spread in the monasteries. At the most famous monastic establishments, those on Mount Athos, from which even female animals were banished, homosexuality must have flourished from early times; certainly it became notorious there in later centuries.

In 1453 Byzantium fell at last to the Ottoman Turks, and Mehmed the Conqueror immediately sent his agents to requisition the most beautiful boys of the Christian aristocracy for his harem. Mehmed tried to rape the fourteen-year-old son of the noble Lucas Notaras; father and son both perished for their resistance. Likewise the sons of the historian George Phrantzes were killed for refusing to yield to the Sultan's lusts.

These episodes suggest a cultural contrast that was probably less acute in practice, for interface with Islamic homosexuality must have begun centuries earlier. Officially, the greater vigilance of the Byzantine authorities against "the vice" would have served to distinguish them from their adversaries; in practice, there was undoubtedly a good deal of borrowing from Islamic pederastic customs. This cultural interaction awaits further study.

BIBLIOGRAPHY. John Boswell, *Christianity, Social Tolerance and Homosexuality*, Chicago: Chicago University Press, 1980, pp. 137–66, 335–53, 359–65; Eva Cantarella, *Secondo natura*, Rome: Riuniti, 1987; Danilo Dalla, *"Ubi Venus mutatur"*: *omosessualità e diritto nel mondo romano*, Milan: Giuffrè, 1987; Phaidon Koukoules, *Byzantinon Biōs kai Politismos*, Athens, 1948–55, vol. 6, pp. 506–15; Spyros N. Troianos, *Ho "Poinalios" tu Eklogadiu* [*Forschungen zur byzantinischen Rechtsgeschichte*, 6], Frankfurt am Main: Klostermann, 1980, pp. 16–19.

William A. Percy

CABARET
See **Variety, Revue, and Cabaret Entertainment.**

CAESAR, [GAIUS] JULIUS (100–44 B.C.)

Roman politician, general, and author. Although of distinguished patrician lineage, Caesar was connected by marriage with the popular party. Accordingly, he found that his political career was hindered by the success of Sulla, who had triumphed over Marius, the leader of the popular forces. Refusing to divorce his wife Cornelia as Sulla had commanded, he found it prudent to join the military campaign in Asia Minor (81 B.C.). Exploiting his youthful good looks, together with the boundless charm for which he continued to be noted, he threw himself with relish into a scandalous liaison with king Nicomedes IV of Bithynia.

Returning to Rome, he maneuvered successfully in the treacherous Senatorial politics of the day, forming an alliance (triumvirate) with Pompey and Crassus. Beginning in 58 B.C. he undertook the nine-year conquest of Gaul, an achievement he commemorated in the *Gallic Wars*, a masterpiece of trenchant Latin prose. Eventually, unfavorable events in Rome forced him to return and, crossing the River Rubicon, he undertook the conquest of Italy itself. Becoming dictator, he initiated a vigorous program of legislation that foreshadowed the empire founded by his great-nephew Octavius, subsequently known as Augustus. On the Ides of March 44 Caesar was killed by a conspiracy headed by his associates Brutus and Crassus.

In addition to his three wives and several mistresses, Julius Caesar had a number of homosexual affairs. After serving as the catamite of Nicomedes, as mentioned, Caesar was (according to **Catullus**) the *cinaedus* or hustler to one Mamurra. Ceaseless in sexual as in every other activity, he earned the sobriquet of "Husband to every woman and wife to every man." Sex and money were essential barter for rising in the troubled period of Rome's Civil Wars. And in fact Octavius in turn was rumored to have ingratiated himself with his great-uncle through sexual availability.

BIBLIOGRAPHY. Arthur D. Kahn, *The Education of Julius Caesar: A Biography, a Reconstruction*, New York: Schocken, 1986.

Warren Johansson

CALAMUS

This word derives from the Greek *kalamos*, a reed; and by extension a flute, fishing rod, and a reed pen. From the latter usage stems the Latin *lapsus calami*, a slip of the pen. Walt **Whitman** entitled the most overtly homoerotic and self-revealing section of *Leaves of Grass*, "Calamus." He was thinking of one particular variety of plant, the sweet flag (*Acorus calamus*), as a symbol of male–male affection. It must have appealed to him also because of the the traditional association of the calamus (= reed pen) with the writer's profession. Yet, from Greek mythology he may have known the story of Calamus, the son of a river god, who was united in tender love with another youth, Carpus. When Carpus was accidentally drowned, the grief-stricken Calamus was changed into a reed.

The English poet Algernon Charles Swinburne (1837–1909), whose attitudes toward homosexuality were conflicted, dubbed John Addington **Symonds** and his associates "Calamites," with a mocking echo of "catamites" and the pejorative nuance of the *-ite* ending. In his book *Greek Love* (New York, 1964), J. Z. Eglinton employed the term to designate the broader school of minor English and American homoerotic poets who flourished under the aegis of Whitman, Edward **Carpenter**, and Symonds (ca. 1890–1930). Timothy d'Arch Smith, the author of *Love in Earnest* (London, 1970), the standard work on the English poets in this group of writers and their themes, prefers to call them **Uranians**. However, Donald Mader, in the learned introduction to his edition of the *Men and Boys* anthology (New York, 1978), speaks of the American poets as "calamites."

Just as Whitman used the calamus to symbolize male homosexual attraction, so some of the English Calamite/Uranian poets favored the plant *ladslove* (*Artemisia abrotanum*), ostensibly because the odor of its sap resembled that of semen, but more likely just because of the name.

CAMBACÉRÈS, JEAN-JACQUES RÉGIS DE (1753–1824)

Arch-Chancellor of the French First Empire and editor of the Code **Napoléon**. Born in Montpellier as the scion of an old noble family, Cambacérès became a lawyer in his birthplace and a counselor at the Cour des Comptes. Renouncing his title of nobility in 1790, he became active in the revolutionary movement. As a member of the National Assembly he did not vote for the death of Louis XVI, but did move for the execution of the death sentence. He withdrew from the murderous factional struggles of the 1790s to pursue his legal calling, with such success that following the coup d'état of 18 Brumaire (1799), he became the second consul after Napoleon Bonaparte. When Napoleon became Emperor in 1804, he named Cambacérès Arch-Chancellor and in 1808 conferred on him the title of Duke of Parma. Great as was his influence with Napoleon, he failed to persuade him not to undertake the disastrous Russian campaign of 1812. After the Restoration of Louis XVIII to the throne he was forced into exile, but restored to his civil and political rights in 1818. He lived quietly in Paris until his death.

Cambacérès' greatest achievement was the drafting of the Code Napoléon, which was not a new set of laws but a revision and codification of all the legislative reforms since 1789 into a set of 28 separate codes to which the Emperor then attached his name. He was not responsible for the silent omission of sodomy from the criminal code; this step had been taken by the Constituent Assembly in 1791, and he was not even a member of the legislative committee of the Council of State that debated the draft of the penal code of 1810. But his reputation as a homosexual was such that when the question of allowing bachelors to adopt children arose, Napoleon asked him to speak for the proposal. As early as his days as second consul, the rumors of his homosexuality had reached the ears of the agents of Louis XVIII. Napoleon was fully aware of the truth of these allegations, but was too unprejudiced and astute to attach any significance to them in his evaluation of Cambacérès' character. Various stories, witticisms, and cartoons about the Arch-Chancellor's proclivities circulated during his years of power, and a number of women prominent during the First Empire—among them Madame de Staël—were his bitter enemies. As a consequence, as late as 1859 the City Council of Montpellier refused to erect a statue in his honor. For the same reason the memoirs of Cambacérès have remained unpublished and his family has denied historians access to its private archives.

While Cambacérès was a major figure in the entourage of Napoleon Bonaparte, the reform of the penal laws on homosexuality was not his doing; this action was rather the consequence of the philosophical trends of the eighteenth century and the critique of the criminal legislation of the Old Regime by such writers as Beccaria and Voltaire. No one statesman can be credited with the merit of this advance over the barbarity of previous centuries. The prestige of Napoleon and the force of French arms fostered the spread of the code and marked the dawn of an era of toleration for the homosexuals of **France** and many other countries.

BIBLIOGRAPHY. Jean-Louis Bory, *Les cinq girouettes; ou, Servitudes et souplesses de . . . Jean-Jacques Régis de Cambacérès, duc de Parme*, Paris: Ramsay, 1979; Numa Praetorius (pseudonym of Eugen Wilhelm), "Cambacérès, der Erzkanzler Napoleons I. und sein Ruf als Homosexueller," *Jahrbuch für sexuelle Zwischenstufen*, 13 (1912), 23–42.

Warren Johansson

CAMBRIDGE AND OXFORD

Residential colleges have dominated England's two ancient universities—sometimes verbally merged as "Oxbridge"—which trace their origins to the twelfth century. Royal and aristocratic patronage, accentuated by the richly endowed, exquisite colleges in which fellows slept and dined, gave them an elite character often, though not always, conducive to academic excellence.

Early Indications. Following the clerical tradition of the Middle Ages, the dons were (until Gladstone's liberal reforms in 1877) forbidden to marry. Temptation beckoned in the form of an endless supply of highborn and attractive undergraduates. After 1500 most trained academically and (homo)sexually at the aristocratic **public** [i.e., private boarding] **schools** like Harrow and Winchester on a curriculum of Greek and Latin classics which, despite careful selection, could not be purged of pederastic motifs.

On early sodomites the curtain of silence lifts only occasionally. In 1739 the Rev. Robert Thistlethwayte, who had served as warden of Wadham College at Oxford for fifteen years, was charged with making a "sodomitical attempt" on William French, an undergraduate. As depositions to the grand jury revealed, Thistlethwayte had shown a previous pattern of homosexual activity, and he fled to France, fearing mortal consequences. John Fenwick, known to have had homosexual relations as a student at Oxford, but not charged until 1797, when he had become a clergyman, also fled to the continent. At Cambridge George Gordon, Lord **Byron**, already in love at Harrow, had a relationship with a choirboy named John Edleston and formed lifelong friendships with John Cam Hobhouse, the dissipated Scrope Berdmore Davies, and the irreverent Charles Skinner Matthews—his correspondents and defenders when, having discovered a more open homosexuality in Italy and Greece, Byron went into exile.

Reformers and Aesthetes. The Victorians (1837–1901) strove to raise the standards of Britain's decayed educational establishment. In addition to the the universities, the feeder system of the elite public schools had to be restructured. Unbeknownst to the reformers, public school boys fashioned a thriving homosexual subculture, with its social hierarchies and special vocabulary, and passed it on to the universities.

The mid-nineteenth century also saw a crisis of faith. Some like Cardinal Newman resolved this by converting to Roman Catholicism. Gravitating toward aestheticism, a creed with strong homosexual overtones, others—unlike the Oxford don Walter Pater, the pontiff of aestheticism, who was most discreet about his sexual longings—became notorious, Oscar **Wilde** met Alfred **Douglas** when the latter was a handsome undergraduate at Oxford, and the *Chameleon*—which played a fateful role in Wilde's trial—was an Oxford undergraduate magazine whose single issue, cloyingly tinged with homoeroticism, appeared in December 1894.

The Cambridge Apostles. A remarkable example of intrainstitutional continuity is the Society of Apostles founded by students at Cambridge University in 1820, whose members gathered once a week to hear papers on controversial topics. The first recruits to this distinguished intellectual club were mainly clergymen, apparently of impeccable moral character. By the 1840s, however, intimations of homosexuality begin to emerge—though sometimes only in the form of the "Higher Sodomy," that is, nonsexual male bonding.

Later in the century a picturesque, bibulous, socialite don, Oscar Browning, nourished a special homosexual atmosphere at Cambridge. In 1862 he began almost annual visits to Rome with an undergraduate in tow. As the novelist E. M. **Forster**, another Cantabrigian, was later to demonstrate, Italy played a special role for cultured Englishmen in search of sexual freedom.

The influence of the Cambridge Apostles radiated into the larger community. William Johnson, later Cory (elected in 1844), became a leading member of the Calamite group of pederastic poets. At the end of the century, the Cambridge atmosphere was determined by the philosopher G. E. Moore (who was not homosexual) and Goldsworthy Lowes Dickinson (who was). Then, in the early years of the present century, homosexual graduate Apostles, notably Lytton **Strachey** and John Maynard **Keynes**, formed a kind of adult branch in London, which became known as **Bloomsbury**. Most of the members of this literary and artistic group were connected with Cambridge through family ties if not by direct attendance.

The Oxbridge Heyday. A distinctive feature of Oxbridge is the social contact between dons and undergraduates, who daily drank sherry together and dined together in "commons" at the college where they had their rooms, on terms of familiarity that would be almost inconceivable at an American college. Until the Edwardian era, the two universities were by and large socially closed institutions that drew their student body from the cream of the upper classes, especially from the graduates of the public schools where adolescent homosexuality was rampant. Also, from the decline of medieval scholasticism until modern higher education policy opened its doors to scholarship holders from impecunious but talented families, Oxbridge offered far more a "playboy" than an intellectual setting, where the future politician, public servant, or member of the House of Lords passed a stage in his *cursus honorum*. All these circumstances, together with intense and prestigious competition in sports if not in learning, made for homosexual contact between the dons and students and for the sort of bonding among undergraduates that readied Oxbridge alumni for their life roles as builders and administrators of the British Empire.

But not all ran smoothly in the creation of future public servants. At Cambridge in the 1930s Anthony Blunt, Guy Burgess, and Donald McLean, all homosexual Apostles, converted to Marxism and became secret Soviet agents. Their unmasking during the Cold War occasioned speculation about a connection between the upper classes, homosexuality, and **espionage**. After the war, however, the homosexual complexion of the Cambridge Society of Apostles faded.

During the interwar years Oxford became more prominently identified with the homosexual sensibility. Figures such as Evelyn Waugh succumbed to it only for a time, but the poets W. H. **Auden** and Stephen Spender forged a lifetime comradeship. In the depression of the 1930s many undergraduates converted to **Marxism**, as at Cambridge. Toward the end of his life, Auden returned to live at his Oxford college but found the atmosphere too much changed for his taste. The more democratic emphasis of education after World War II, sparked by Labor governments, eroded both the privileges and mystique of Cambridge and Oxford. Moreover, gay liberation in the 1970s diffused homosexual life and the need for special redoubts of privileged homophilia at the universities and public schools receded.

Alfred L. Rowse, claiming to be unbiased, and Sir Kenneth Dover, professing that he is straight and happily married, broke the taboo against writing on homosexuality which John Addington **Symonds** thought had barred him from a chair in classical scholarship and on which Sir Maurice **Bowra** never dared write a book or even an article. After World War II British universities proliferated. At Essex and Sussex, institutions on a new model, gay studies have emerged under auspices that encourage rethinking of established gender patterns.

BIBLIOGRAPHY. Richard Deacon, *The Cambridge Apostles*, London: Robert Royce, 1985.

William A. Percy

CAMP

Camp is a type of wit common to, but by no means exclusive to male homosexuals. A definition of the concept is elusive, but it may be tentatively circumscribed by saying that camp consists of taking serious things frivolously and frivolous things seriously. Camp is not grounded in speech or writing as much as it is in gesture, performance, and public display. When it is verbal, it is expressed less through the discursive means of direct statement than through implication, innuendo, and intonation. As an art of indirection and suggestion, it was suited to the purposes of a group that found it imprudent to confront culturally approved values directly, but preferred to undermine them through send-ups and sly mockery. Because it is viewed, perhaps mistakenly, as relatively unthreatening, camp gains entree into the upscale worlds of chic and swank.

Roots of Camp. Camp has close links with the modern world of mass entertainment, and it may have found its first artistic outlet in late-nineteenth-century music halls, vaudeville, and pantomime. The word first appears in the slang of this period—the earliest printed attestation is from 1907—where it refers to outrageous street behavior. The term has been plausibly traced to the French verb *se camper*, which can mean (among other things) to posture boldly. (In **Australia**, *camp* has acquired the common meaning of "gay, homosexual" without other qualification, but this usage is rare elsewhere, where heterosexuals and bisexuals may be "camp" with little fear of loss of reputation.)

Some recognize a gamut of low to high camp, ranging from the provocative behavior of a street queen determined to "camp up a storm" to the elegant writings of Oscar **Wilde** and Ronald **Firbank**. Indeed, Wilde's tour of America in 1882 was one of the first media successes of high camp. By definition camp is a form of exhibitionism that requires an audience; it cannot be done in the privacy of one's home—except as practice.

The targets of camp are good taste, marriage and the family, suburbia, sports, and the business world. Camp is thus a less hostile continuation of the trend of nineteenth-century Bohemia to *épater le bourgeois*, to bait middle-class respectability. Undeniably, camp is subversive, but not too much so, for it depends for its survival on the patronage of high society, the entertainment world, advertising, and the media.

Antecedents and Analogues. Camp is characteristicly modern, yet examples have been noted in earlier centuries, including the Roman writer Petronius, the Italian mannerist paintings of the sixteenth century, the *précieuses* of the French salons of the time of Louis XIV, Bel Canto opera, and in fops and dandies of various periods. To a large extent camp is in the eye of the beholder, so that Charles De Gaulle's stylized speeches and appearances may have been camp to scoffing Anglo-Saxons but not to his French followers.

Camp should be distinguished from several related phenomena. Classic satire strives to reinforce social solidarity by exposing its targets to withering ridicule, while camp narrows the distance between performer and victim, suggesting that the last laugh might actually be with the latter. Kitsch is uninentional bad taste, while camp is always aware of the elements of artifice and irony. A camp collector can acquire kitsch objects, but only if they are displayed in a manner that indicates he knows what they are. Camp often employs elements of the decadent sensibility, but avoids heavy satanism and the macabre. Thus Joris-Karl Huysmans' novels are decadent, the *Rocky Horror Picture Show* is camp. Camp may employ the device of pastiche, that is, putting together components that have been "pinched" from different sources. However, not all pastiche is camp (Baroque oratorios, 1980s painting). The world of chic belongs exclusively to the affluent and fashionable, but even a guttersnipe can attempt camp. Bitchiness reflects underlying anger and a desire to wound; camp tolerantly views everyone as imperfect, but eminently salvageable. A frozen analogue of bitchiness, "attitude" requires striking a pose, but one that is too narrow and inflexible. Drag in the sense of a male impersonating a woman may be an element of camp, but ironically not if it is successful. If the transvestite's simulation is so complete that the observer is taken in, the element of conscious and detectable artifice that is essential to camp is lost. Camp is always presented with an invisible wink.

Representative Figures. Examples that would generally be recognized as camp are (in the theatre) Sarah Bernhardt, Noel **Coward**, Joe **Orton**, Tallulah Bankhead, Danny LaRue and "impressionists" generally; (in films) Fatty Arbuckle, Divine, Jayne Mansfield, Mae West, and Sean Connery (in the James Bond movies); (in literature) Wilde, Firbank, Jean **Cocteau**, Gabriele D'Annunzio, Lytton **Strachey**, the Sitwells, Stevie Smith, Evelyn Waugh, Dorothy Parker, and Truman **Capote**; (in popular music), David Bowie, Boy George, Mick Jagger, Grace Jones, and Bette Midler. By common consent the crown prince of camp in the 1960s and 1970s was Andy **Warhol**. His effect was achieved not solely through his paintings and films, but through his trademark self-stylization that used New York's media factory as its megaphone. During this period, popular culture, formerly condemned by the intellectual elite, became fashionable, though it was usually approached in an arch, ironic context. The principle of shift of context, yielding incongruity, is a basic camp procedure.

Conclusion. Perhaps it is not too much to say that camp aspires to fulfill Friedrich Nietzsche's precept of the reversal of all values. It certainly serves to bring into question established hierarchies of taste, as expressed in the scale from high brow to low brow. Proof of the accomplishment of such subversion is the delighted cry: "It's so bad it's good!" By suggesting that inauthenticity pervades the performance and the thing satirized, the camp adept puts us on notice that the line between authenticity and inauthenticity is never easy to draw; it may even be nonexistent. The world of camp then serves to deconstruct the cult of seriousness and "values" that sought to fill the gap produced by the fading of religion and traditional class society in the West. Significantly, no equivalent of camp seems to exist in the Third World. The recognition and cultivation of camp is thus a distinctively modern phenomenon, belonging to a cultural landscape of doubt, alienation, relativism, and pluralism.

See also **Humor; Variety, Revue, and Cabaret Entertainment.**

BIBLIOGRAPHY. Mark Booth, *Camp*, London: Quartet, 1983; Philip Core, *Camp: The Lie that Tells the Truth*, New York: Putnam, 1984.

Wayne R. Dynes

CANAANITES

The reference of the geographical term Canaan is complex. In ancient times "Canaan" was used to refer to an area between the Amanus Mountains in the north, the Sinai Peninsula on the southwest, the Mediterranean on the west, and, to the east, the Great Rift Valley (comprising the cleft between the Lebanon and Anti-Lebanon mountain ranges, the Sea of Galilee, the Jordan River, and the Dead Sea), corresponding to modern Lebanon and Israel and parts of Turkey, Syria, and Jordan. The **Old Testament** also uses the term Canaanite to refer to members of the merchant class, because trade and commerce remained in the hands of the older strata of the population inhabiting the coastal cities even after the Israelite landowners and peasants had occupied the interior of the country. Hence the socioeconomic opposition was paradoxically the reverse of that in some parts of early modern Europe, where Jews were merchants and traders in the midst of a rural native clientele.

Modern scholars use the term Canaanite to designate those aspects of Syro-Palestinian culture against which the religion of Moses defined itself; this usage leads to the simplified opposition of Israelite versus Canaanite. This is not a Biblical usage, since, for example, the Bible speaks of what we now call Hebrew as "the language of Canaan." The opposition does, however, reflect the dominant Biblical attitude toward the people of Phoenicia and Philistia and the non-Yahweh-worshipping elements of the population of Judah and the northern kingdom of Israel. Thus "Canaanite" is modern shorthand for what the core religious tradition of Israel opposed. There are many sources which can meaningfully be grouped together as illuminating Canaanite culture, but the Hebrew Bible is the most informative as well as one of the least reliable. Other sources include archeological remains as well as numerous texts, notably from the city of Ugarit in modern Syria (1400–1225 B.C.).

Part of the character of Mosaic religion was adversarial, and the official and popular cults of Canaan provided much to oppose. Polytheistic devotions and political appropriations of theology were among the features most opposed by Israelite prophets and priests. Sexual activities that figured in fertility rites associated with the worship of Ishtar and Tammuz were also condemned, but the character of these is harder to deduce from the extant sources. That there was some degree of sexual license in Canaanite cult is certain, as is the role of female prostitutes serving male clients, but the texts are either laconic or formulated in a poetic language that is still being deciphered. The prophets, Hosea in particular, state clearly that the kĕdē-shôth, or female hierodules, fornicated with the male worshippers, and hence make sexual infidelity a metaphor for Israel's departure from the service of Yahweh. In contrast, the role of non-Israelite male prostitutes, or kĕdēshīm, serving male clients seems to have been marginal. The institution of cultic "dogs" (attested in Deuteronomy, in one text from a Phoenician colony on Cyprus, and in a Punic inscription from Carthage) is often associated with male prostitution or homosexuality, but the institution remains obscure. (It has been associated with transvestism, which is not in itself a matter of sexuality. Although transvestism is well attested in the ancient Near East, it is notably absent from the Levant.)

Most interpretations of Canaanite religion and sexuality, from the rabbis and church fathers to the present, make up for a lack of information by fabulizing reconstruction. A few modern enthusiasts have glorified Canaan for its ostensibly permissive and celebratory attitude toward sexuality, but this view also seems unhistorical. Canaan remains the symbol of the cultural and religious tradition which Israel rejected and condemned, but whose rites and practices form the backdrop for the historical narratives of the Old Testament.

Michael Patrick O'Connor

CANADA

A vast, unevenly developed nation, Canada's culture has been significantly shaped by influences from France, Britain, and the United States. Approximately 75 percent of the population of 25 million is located in a 3000-mile long, 100-mile wide band along the top of the American border, making the development and survival of a nation-wide gay movement difficult and rendering local and provincial activity particularly important.

New France. Prosecutions of sodomy are recorded among the settlers in New France in 1648 and 1691, the latter involving three men. The death penalty was not imposed on any of the accused, perhaps because the population was too thin in the colony to permit unnecessary reductions. The French settlements on the St. Lawrence with their capital at Quebec were the base for extensive journeys by explorers and missionaries far to the west and south (where they reached the other French colony of Louisiana, established in the seventeenth century, with **New Orleans**, founded in 1718, as its capital). These trips familiarized the travelers with the North American Indian homosexual institution known as the **berdache**. Following his experience as a missionary in New France in 1711–17, Joseph François Lafitau wrote the first attempt at a synthesis of the phenomenon. Expansion of European patterns, of course, spelled the end of Indian social customs, and the berdache was not rediscovered by North American homosexuals until the 1950s.

The Nineteenth Century. English-speaking Upper Canada (largely populated by loyalist refugees from the American Revolution) was rocked by a scandal centering on Inspector-General George Herchmer Markland. This official, who was accustomed to having sexual relations with young men (usually soldiers) in his office, was forced to resign in 1838. Several other cases came to light in the 1840s.

With the coming of the Confederation in 1867, Canada required its own legislative structure. Yet in matters of sexual law, the British example was imitated almost slavishly everywhere for almost a century. Thus Westminster's 1885 **Criminal Law Amendment Act**, the law under which Oscar **Wilde** was later to be prosecuted, was dutifully copied the following year by a Canadian law against indecent assault.

During the early pioneering days the Western provinces seem to have seen a good deal of variant sexual behavior that excited little notice. As in the United States, there are cases of women dressing as men: these may or may not have been lesbian. In the latter decades of the nineteenth century Canada was swept by the social purity movement of British and U.S. derivation. Through mass-circulation pamphlets and public meetings, the latter often held at churches, they sought to combat masturbation and other forms of nonprocreative sex, as individual pollution and "race suicide." Such agitation, and the "civilizing process" in general, spelled the end of the relative sexual liberty of the Canadian West, and a number of prosecutions for buggery occurred there from 1880 to 1910.

Modern Canada. Typical urban gay subcultures emerged in major cities, with distinctive cruising grounds and places of entertainment. As with U.S. service personnel, participation in the two World Wars gave many men and women ideas of sexual freedom that they could not have otherwise obtained. In Montreal and Toronto after 1945 a more visible gay subculture focused mainly on "queen's circles," coteries formed around one or more central figures, who controled entrance to the group and set its standards. Through the mentor–protégé relations of such groups many young people were socialized into the gay subculture, in addition to a much larger number of closeted persons with more tenuous links to the subculture. Canadian homosexuals had to face the same practices of metropolitan vice squads as did their American counterparts—surveillance of cruising areas, entrapment, raids on gay meeting places. The McCarthyite witch hunt against perverts engendered a Canadian imitation, and the Royal Canadian Mounted Police began to keep personal records, a practice that continued, on a smaller scale, into the 1970s. Legislation, repealed in 1977, was also passed against homosexuals as immigrants on the model of the Walter–McCarran Act in the United States.

In due course, awareness of the American gay movement of the 1950s made its way over the border. Just as the **Mattachine** Society had begun on the U.S. west coast, the first organized Canadian gay group, the Association for Social Knowledge (ASK), began in Vancouver in 1964, generating a *Newsletter* and a social center. Later in 1964 two gay magazines began in Toronto, *Two* (imitating the Los Angeles *ONE*) and *Gay* (later *Gay International*), apparently the first periodical in North America to use the vernacular word in its title. Subsequently, several French-language periodicals appeared in **Quebec**, culminating in *Sortie* (founded 1982). There have also been books, supplementing the larger body of francophone literature from France itself. Playwright Michel Tremblay, author of the trenchant *Hosanna*, has achieved international recognition. Several novels of the lesbian writer Marie-Claire Blais have been translated into English.

Even before American developments, the official British **Wolfenden Report** of 1957 had made a significant impact on Canadian opinion. After some discussion the Ottawa parliament passed a new Criminal Code in May 1969, decriminalizing homosexual conduct in private between consenting adults. This change left gay public life still subject to harassment, but Canada only gradually adopted the

new militant model of gay liberation introduced in the United States after the Stonewall Uprising of June 1969. In February 1971 the Community Homophile Association of Toronto (CHAT) was formed, quickly becoming the country's most important gay organization. The fall of the same year saw the appearance of the first issue of the monthly, *The Body Politic*, which in its heyday was North America's finest gay paper. In Quebec, French-Canadian nationalism influenced gay organizations, and in 1977 that province passed an antidiscrimination provision, part of the Charter of Human Rights, that initially had no equal in English-speaking Canada but was followed first by several cities, and then by Ontario in 1986 and the Yukon in 1987. The 1970s saw a rapid development of commercial gay enclaves in major cities—baths and bars, bookstores and boutiques. Toronto, in particular, gained a reputation of being the "San Francisco of the North." There a magnet institution, the Canadian Gay Archives, issued several publications, and scholarship began to flourish, following—sometimes uncritically—New Left and French models.

Heralding conservative shifts in many advanced industrial nations, this climate became more adverse in the late 1970s. *The Body Politic* was subjected to several prosecutions, a form of harassment which contributed to its demise in 1986. "Pornography," meaning gay publications from abroad, was confiscated, bathhouses were repeatedly raided and charged with operating as "common bawdy houses." These attacks provoked justifiable anger and resistance on the part of Canada's gay communities. The country settled into an uneasy, but probably stable peace, but as elsewhere the **AIDS** crisis has meant changes; significantly, many communities and linkages—including artistic, religious, entertainment, interior design—have come together in support of charitable AIDS projects. Since the Third World communities in Canada are still relatively small, about 90 percent of the AIDS cases affect homosexual men.

BIBLIOGRAPHY. William Crawford, ed., *Homosexuality in Canada: A Bibliography*, Toronto: Canadian Gay Archives, 1984; Gary Kinsman, *The Regulation of Desire: Sexuality in Canada*, Montreal: Black Rose, 1987; Paul-François Sylvestre, *Bougrerie en Nouvelle France*, Hull: Editions Asticou, 1983.

Wayne R. Dynes

CANON LAW

Canon law, *jus canonicum*, is the totality of the established rules of the Roman Catholic Church: canons (the decisions of councils), disciplinary regulations, decretals, and other texts collected from local bishops and councils as well as from the **New Testament**. Like Roman civil law, canon law is divided into public—the constitution of the church and its relation to other bodies—and private—the internal discipline of members.

History. Canon law falls into three periods: (1) from the beginning to the decretum of Gratian, *Concordia discordantium canonum*, completed shortly before 1150; (2) from then to the Council of Trent (1545–63); and (3) from the Tridentine Council to the present. Gratian's collection completely superseded all earlier compilations and remained the text of the scholastics at medieval universities. In order to build a coherent system out of various precedents and writings of the Church Fathers, Gratian organized his five books on Roman law principles, thus introducing natural law, which became important in antisodomy provisions. In 1234 Gregory IX expanded the collection and created what in time came to be known as the *Corpus juris canonici*, the Five Books of Canon Law, as opposed to the *Corpus juris civilis*, the codification of Roman secular law by Justinian, to which were added the later Sextus in 1298 and the Clementines in 1317 to form seven books (to which two *extravagantes* were later added), all of which were over time glossed.

Increasingly homophobic theologians, often fanatic friars from Thomas Aquinas to Luca da Penne, continued to influence the glossators. With the aid of **philosophy** the **Inquisition** inspired **feudal, royal,** and **municipal laws** to order the fining, castration, and even burning of sodomites—all penalties that remained foreign to Canon law proper. The Council of Trent reformed doctrine and discipline, elevating Thomas **Aquinas** to the rank of the most important doctor of the church. In the twentieth century the canon law was twice recodified.

Early Antisodomy Provisions. As early as 177, Athenagoras had characterized adulterers and pederasts as foes of Christianity and and subjected them to the harshest penalty the Church, itself still persecuted by the Roman state, could inflict: excommunication. Even before Constantine had ended the Roman state's persecution, the council of Elvira (305) had severely condemned pederasts. Canons 16 and 17 of the Council of Ancyra (314), mainly concerned with defining penance for those guilty of sin rather than with prescribing legal penalties, were interpreted as inflicting lengthy penances upon those guilty of sexual intercourse with males and excommunicating them from the church. Christian Emperors when they became heads of the church meted out savage penalties for unrepentant sodomites: the sons of Constantine the sword, and Theodosius and Justinian the avenging flames.

Of the Germanic kingdoms that succeeded the Western Empire in the West, only the Visigothic in Spain (ca. 650) enacted any penalty at all, namely castration, in spite of **Tacitus'** famous remark long interpreted to mean that primitive Germans threw homosexuals into bogs. Irish and other **penitentials** treated homosexual offenses more severely than heterosexual ones, most often condemning anal intercourse, but prescribing greater severity for anal than for oral sex, whether with a partner of the opposite or of the same gender. The early canons followed them in prescribing penance despite the death penalty in Leviticus and the fulminations of the Apostle Paul, **Clement** of Alexandria, St. John **Chrysostom**, St. **Augustine**, and other **Patristic** authors. In fact, some penitentials were soon invested with canonical authority. Writers of rules for **monasticism** tried to prevent homosexual acts by keeping candles lit in the dormitories all night and having an elderly monk sleep between two young ones, each in single beds.

Heightened Repression. Repression reappeared in the eleventh century with an obsessive diatribe against all forms of "unnatural vice," the *Liber Gomorrhianus* of Peter **Damian**. Asserting that whoever practiced sodomy was "tearing down the ramparts of the heavenly Jerusalem and rebuilding the walls of ruined Sodom," his harsh denunciations presaged the attitude of the later councils and canonists. Burchard of Worms and Ivo of Chartres published collections containing canons that condemned fellation, bestiality, pederasty, and sodomy, and prescribed severe penalties. In the Latin Kingdom of Jerusalem, which created a short-lived interface between Christianity and a more tolerant **Islam**, the council of Nablus, preoccupied with sodomy, decreed in 1120 that guilty men should be burnt at the stake.

Although Gratian's *Decretum* devoted little space to "unnatural" sexuality, at the end of the twelfth century Peter the Chanter devoted a long chapter of his *Verbum abbreviatum* to sodomy, and his circle seems to have originated a fantastic addition to the legend of the Nativity according to which, at the moment when the Virgin Mary was giving birth to Jesus, all sodomites died a sudden death. From then on, canonists regularly cite Justinian's Novella 77 that disasters such as famine, pestilence, and earthquake, to which many added floods and other natural catastrophes, are divine retribution for "crimes against nature." The Third Lateran Council (1179) adopted a canon specifi-

cally prohibiting "that incontinence which is against nature" and decreed that clerics guilty of unnatural vice must either forfeit clerical status or be confined perpetually in a monastery. Somewhat paradoxically, Bernard of Pavia held that since sodomy did not create affinity, it constituted no impediment to marriage.

The High and Late Middle Ages. From the second half of the thirteenth century, savage penalties for homosexual offenses become part of Western European legislation. Not merely a cause of misfortune for the whole community, sodomy is also repeatedly linked with heresy, and accusations of it become a convenient ingredient of political invective as popes hurled it against **Frederick II**, and a weapon in power struggles within the feudal ruling class. Popular belief inclined to ascribe this vice to the clergy—probably with much justification. Like the Scholastics, canon law treated homosexuality, bestiality, and masturbation as *contra naturam*, "contrary to nature," because they excluded the possibility of procreation, which thus became the touchstone of sexual morality. Such crimes on the part of a religious constituted *sacrilege*, because his or her body was a vessel consecrated to the service of God. If publicly practiced or widely known, these offenses carried with them the sanction of **infamy** (*infamia*), a deprivation of status that involved unfitness for holding most kinds of public office or positions of trust and deprivation of the right to appear in court as a plaintiff or witness. Ironically enough, the canonist Pierre de La Palud (ca. 1280–1342) had to explain at length why the church did not allow two males to marry each other and so legitimize their relationship.

Formally beginning at least as far back as Gregory IX's commission to the Dominicans in 1232 to hunt down heretics in southern France and elsewhere, the papal Inquisition in due course in certain regions extended its jurisdiction to sodomites as well, now viewed as allied with supernatural powers, demons, devils, and witches. The convicted were handed over to the secular authorities for punishment; in time the secular governments were to act independently of the Church in prescribing and enforcing the death penalty. Before execution, confessions were wrung from victims by torture, and often the trial records were burnt together with them. St. Bernardino of Siena (1380–1444) denounced homosexual desire as a form of madness.

Modern Times. Given that secular laws already prescribed the extreme penalty, canon law provisions against sodomy, renewed in the sixteenth century as part of the Counter-Reformation, had few novelties. Considerable attention was given, however, to **masturbation** as well as to lesbianism and transvestism.

James A. Brundage poses the question: Why have medieval Christian beliefs and practices concerning sex endured so persistently? He offers three reasons: the continuity of the socioeconomic environment, the persistent identification of the erotic with the sacred, and the inertia of the law and its institutions. None of these factors fully explains why medieval beliefs survived even the cataclysm that altered the political and legal face of Europe at the end of the eighteenth century, when under the influence of deistic and freemasonic ideas the law codes were rewritten and a new, liberal ethos began to inspire ever larger strata of society. In no small measure the continuity is rather to be explained by the intolerance that forbade any criticism of Christian sexual morality and branded opponents of its norms as a "justifying their own filthy vices"—an argument reiterated as late as 1957 in a decision of the West German Constitutional Court upholding **Paragraph 175** with specific reference to the doctrines of the Church. In such a climate of opinion the sexual reform trend faced an uphill battle; and without an effective movement to change public opinion and bring pressure upon legislators, liberals were loath to expose themselves to obloquy and ridicule. In the United States it

was only toward the end of the 1960s that a few Congressmen with "safe" seats began to speak in defense of gay rights. As a result of these changes the official position of the Roman curia came to be increasingly isolated, though its champions remained obdurate.

In 1904 the reactionary Pius X appointed a commission to prepare a new codification of the canon law. Because he condemned religious modernism, it is not surprising that the results of this labor, published in 1917 as *Codex Juris Canonici,* offered no innovations in sexual morality.

The hope that the liberal measures adopted in the *aggiornamento* or "renewal" initiated by the Second Vatican Council under John XXIII (pope, 1958–63), when conditions seemed more propitious, would lead to changes in Roman Catholic policy regarding homosexual conduct, was not fulfilled. A pontifical commission charged with the revision of canon law in 1962, when it was finally promulgated in 1983, explicitly reaffirmed traditional doctrines. The "Declaration on Certain Questions Concerning Sexual Ethics," issued by the Vatican Congregation for the Doctrine of the Faith on December 29, 1975, described homosexual acts as deprived of their "essential and indispensable finality" (that is to say, having no procreative function); and being "intrinsically disordered," in no case could they be approved. Reinforcing this statement was another issued by the same body, the "Letter to the Bishops of the Catholic Church on the Pastoral Care of Homosexual Persons" of October 30, 1986, which led to the gradual expulsion from church premises in the United States of Dignity, the Catholic homosexual organization.

See also **Law, Germanic; Law, Feudal and Royal; Law, Municipal.**

BIBLIOGRAPHY. James A. Brundage, *Law, Sex, and Christian Society in Medieval Europe,* Chicago: University of Chicago Press, 1987; Michael Goodich, *The Unmentionable Vice: Homosexual-*

ity in the Later Medieval Period, Santa Barbara: ABC-Clio, 1979; Jeannine Grammick and Pat Furey, eds., *The Vatican and Homosexuality,* New York: Crossroad, 1988.

William A. Percy

CAPITAL CRIME, HOMOSEXUALITY AS A

With **decriminalization** of same-sex relations between consenting adults in many countries, and nonenforcement of existing laws in others, it may come as a shock that homosexual conduct was once judged worthy of death. Although only a few fanatics call for capital punishment nowadays, such barbarism has been a historical reality.

Judeo-Christian Sources. According to the Holiness Code of Leviticus (in its present form, probably of the fifth century B.C.), "If a man lie with mankind as he lieth with a woman, both of them have committed an abomination (tō ēbāh): they shall surely be put to death; their blood shall be upon them." (Leviticus 20:13, reinforcing the earlier prohibition in 18:22). From this dire injunction, which applies to male homosexuals only, stem all later Western laws prescribing the death penalty for sodomy. Although our sources are silent as to how frequently the Levitical sanction was enforced (the method was probably stoning), it was endorsed with new arguments by some later Jewish rigorist thinkers, notably **Philo** of Alexandria (first century of our era).

After the Roman Empire's recognition of **Christianity** as effectively the state religion (A.D. 313), capital enactments against male homosexuality made their way into the Civil Law. One statute of 342 prescribed death by the sword, another of 390 indicated burning. As in the case of the Levitical injunction, it is not known how often these capital punishments were carried out; certainly burning would have been unlikely at this point, though decapitation with the sword would not. The emperor Justinian's sixth-century legisla-tion, however severe its attitude toward sexual variation, does not seem to have insisted on death, and a Visigothic code in Spain of ca. 650 specified castration. The penitentials which appeared in the early Middle Ages prescribe only regimes of penitence ranging from a few months to some years in duration.

The Later Middle Ages. A new wave of hostile legislation emerged in the twelfth century, starting with the Nablus Council of 1120, which specified burning. The prevalence of this penalty is based in part on the **Sodom** story, but it also reflects the parallel with heretics who were usually burned. A somewhat later French law required execution only on the third offense. Unusual (and surely without effect) was the English *Fleta,* which called for death by drowning—probably a reminiscence of Tacitus' *Germania* 12, where the Roman historian says that the ancient Teutons would drown *corpore infames* ("the infamous for their sexual vices") in bogs. (The Nazi Heinrich Himmler was later to urge revival of this practice.)

During the central Middle Ages a vicious rationalization became popular, claiming that sodomy was equivalent to murder (or worse) as it threatened the survival of the human race (found in the ecclesiastical writers Peter **Damian**, Peter Cantor, and Luca da Penne. This strange notion, anticipated by **Philo** of Alexandria, was still alive as late as 1895, when the magistrate in Oscar **Wilde**'s trial repeated it in his sentence.

Available evidence suggests that capital penalties were enforced rather selectively: fewer than 1000 executions have been documented from the late Middle Ages and the Renaissance. Apparently it was thought sufficient to stage a public execution from time to time in order to discourage the practice—or at least its public display. Following the Levitical tradition, lesbians were for a long time exempt from any punishment, but the Scholastic predilection for analogy eventually brought them into the purview of some legislation. Yet fewer than ten lesbian executions are known, and some of these are doubtful, since other crimes were involved.

The Reformation and After. It might be thought that the age of Reformation would have brought some relief in this grim onslaught of lawmaking—if only because a deeply divided society was preoccupied with other problems. But not so, for the death penalty stipulated by article 116 of the Caroline Code of 1532, extending the provision of the Bambergensis of 1507 throughout the Holy Roman Empire, provided a baneful model, followed almost immediately by Henry VIII's law of 1533, of paramount importance for English-speaking, **common law** countries. This Tudor legislation anchored the prohibition of sodomy firmly in the fabric of the secular law as a felony, taking it out of the jurisdiction of the ecclesiastical courts which were believed to have become lax.

While some Enlightenment thinkers, notably the great penal reformer Cesare **Beccaria** (1738–1794), had been critical, credit for the first real break in the dismal pattern belongs to one of the emerging United States. After several earlier reform attempts, in 1786 Pennsylvania substituted hard labor for death, to be followed by Austria in 1787 and Prussia in 1794. Just as antihomosexual legislation had crossed ideological lines in the 1530s, the mitigations were the product of two very different climates: the Quaker tradition (transatlantically) and enlightened despotism (in Europe).

Decriminalization. In the wake of the French Revolution, the French National Assembly swept away the whole repressive apparatus of the ancien régime when it adopted a new criminal code in 1791. Then in 1810, the French Code Penal (as part of the Code **Napoléon**) eliminated homosexual conduct entirely from the penal law, a salutary step that has been followed in many countries since.

In Hitler's **holocaust** male homosexuals died in the concentration camps, though they were rarely officially condemned to death. In the 1970s, the Ayatollah Khomeini's **Iran** instituted execution for homosexuals (on spurious precedents derived from **Islam**). Such fanatical acts have been universally condemned by enlightened opinion.

See also **Canon Law; Law, Feudal and Royal; Law, Germanic; Law, Municipal; Sixteenth-Century Legislation.**
Wayne R. Dynes

CAPOTE, TRUMAN (1924–1984)

American novelist and journalist. Capote became famous at the age of 24 with his elegant, evocative book *Other Voices, Other Rooms,* which concerns the growing consciousness of a boy seeking to comprehend the ambivalent inhabitants of a remote Mississippi house. Dubbed "swamp baroque," this short novel was easily assimilated into then-current notions of Southern decadence. Born in New Orleans, Capote lived most of his life in New York and at the homes of his jetset friends in Europe. He cherished a lifelong friendship with fellow writer Jack Dunphy. In 1966 he published *In Cold Blood,* a "nonfiction novel" about the seemingly senseless murder of a Kansas farm family by two drifters. In preparing for the book, Capote gained the confidence of the murderers, and was thus able to make vivid their sleazy mental universe.

The controversy surrounding this book elevated him to celebrity status, and he began a series of appearances on television talk shows, where his waspish wit amused, but where he often served the function (rivaled only by **Liberace**) of reinforcing for a mass audience their stereotype of a homosexual. During this period Capote became the confidant of rich and famous people, especially women, and he gathered their stories for incorporation in a major work which was intended to rival Marcel **Proust.** Yet when excerpts from this work-in-progress were published in magazines, not only were they found to be vulgar and lacking in insight, but Capote began to be dropped by the socialites he had so unsubtly satirized. Dismayed, the writer sank more and more into a miasma of alcohol, cocaine, and valium—his only consolation the devoted love, or so he claimed, of a succession of straight, proletarian young men whom he prized because of their very ordinariness. When a fragment, apparently all that has survived, of the magnum opus appeared posthumously as *Answered Prayers* in 1986, it had little more than gossip value. In retrospect Capote was not alone among American writers in being destroyed by his addictions. He will nonetheless be remembered for his earlier work, which remains to document the style of an era.

BIBLIOGRAPHY. Gerald Clarke, *Capote: A Biography*, New York: Simon and Schuster, 1988.

CARAVAGGIO, MICHELANGELO MERISI DA (1571–1610)

Italian painter. Trained in Northern Italy, Caravaggio went to Rome as a young man where his meteoric career transformed the then-somnolent art scene and left a permanent impression on European art. Caravaggio came under the protection of Cardinal Francesco Maria del Monte, a homosexual prelate. During this period he painted several works showing ambiguous or androgynous young men, including *The Musicians* (New York, Metropolitan Museum). Efforts have been made to deny the homoerotic implications of these works, but they seem feeble. Modern heterosexual art historians have claimed that because of Caravaggio's relations with women he cannot have had a homosexual side—which not only denies **Kinsey** but what we know of dominant bisexual patterns in the era in which the artist lived.

His mature career began with a painting of *St. Matthew and the Angel* for the church of San Luigi dei Francesi in Rome, which was rejected because the figure of the saint was considered too plebeian. Although the artist produced a second, toned-down version, he continued to exploit a vein of dramatic realism that gave his work a direct impact not seen in art before, and rarely since.

Caravaggio had an adventurous, often violent life. His hot temper several times got him in trouble with the police, and in 1603 a rival artist sued him for libel. His career in Rome was terminated in 1606 when, during a game of racquets, he quarreled with a man and killed him. He fled to Naples and then Malta, where he assaulted a member of the Order. He died of fever in port near Rome, where he had hoped to obtain a pardon.

For a long time, especially in the eighteenth and nineteenth centuries, Caravaggio's reputation was in eclipse; he was considered a mere "tenebrist" who excelled only in painting shadows. He did not fit any of the accepted categories. Only after World War II did his reputation begin to climb, attaining remarkable heights in the 1980s, when even the abstract artist Frank Stella praised him. In 1986 Derek Jarman's stylish film *Caravaggio* was released, presenting the artist as bisexual, but emphasizing the homosexual side.

BIBLIOGRAPHY. Howard Hibbard, *Caravaggio*, New York: Harper and Row, 1983; Donald Posner, "Caravaggio's Early Homo-erotic Works," *Art Quarterly*, 24 (1971), 301–26.
Wayne R. Dynes

CARNIVAL

See **Mardi Gras and Masked Balls**.

CARPENTER, EDWARD (1844–1929)

English writer, mystical thinker, and utopian socialist. Educated for the clergy at Cambridge University, Carpenter resigned from the Church of England in 1873 and taught for a time in the university extension movement in northern

England, where he became increasingly attracted to socialism. Like his older contemporary John Addington **Symonds**, Carpenter was a fervent admirer of Walt **Whitman**, whom he visited in Camden, New Jersey, in 1877 and 1884. His book-length poem *Towards Democracy* (1883) reflects both Whitman's style and ideas. At the same time he became involved in Hindu and **Buddhist** thought, visiting India and Ceylon in 1890. He believed that the redemption of a deeply flawed society had less to do with external reorganization than with individual self-realization leading to the development of cosmic consciousness.

Carpenter put his ideals into practice at his market-gardening farm at Millthorpe near Sheffield, where he lived with his working-class lover George Merrill. Like Symonds, Carpenter believed that such relationships could serve as a powerful solvent to break down class barriers, and thus open the way to a new era of human happiness, which would be cooperative rather than competitive. His return to the "simple life"—which included vegetarianism and casual dress, a proto-hippie lifestyle—was part of his program of "exfoliation," a deliberate discarding of the husks of the old society in preparation for the dawning New Life. By the turn of the century his ideas, which also included support for women's rights, had achieved a broad international circulation.

Despite early discouragements from publishers and a malicious campaign of defamation that was waged against him, Carpenter produced books discussing homosexuality openly. His concept of "homogenic love" emphasized the helping role of the gentle male homosexual as an "intermediate type" between man and woman. Men of this kind were called to a special role in the inauguration of the New Life. In addition to this side of same-sex love, which had roots in the historic figures of the **berdache** and the **shaman**, Carpenter also recognized the warrior homosexual, as seen in the **Samurai**. His

1902 gay anthology *Iolāus*, modeled on a similar German work edited by Elisàr von **Kupffer**, was dubbed by the book trade "the bugger's bible." But there is no doubt that this work, and other widely distributed volumes, helped to reinforce a sense of positive self-identity in a period of profound antihomosexual backlash in English-speaking countries in the wake of the Oscar **Wilde** trials.

Carpenter's combination of utopian socialism, mysticism, and feminism made him widely influential in the years before World War I, when his ideas were taken up by such major figures as D. H. **Lawrence** and E. M. **Forster**. Yet by his death in 1929 he was largely forgotten. In the 1960s, however, his reputation was revived by the intellectual side of the Counterculture, which he strikingly prefigured. Many of his books were reissued, and his life was commemorated in a play by Noel Greig, "The Dear Love of Comrades" (1981).

BIBLIOGRAPHY. Chushichi Tsuzuki, *Edward Carpenter, 1844–1929: Prophet of Human Fellowship*, Cambridge: Cambridge University Press, 1980.
Wayne R. Dynes

CARTOONS
See **Comic Strips**.

CASEMENT, ROGER (1864–1916)
Irish diplomat and patriot. Sprung from an Anglo-Irish family, Casement studied at Ballymore Academy, then, left penniless by his father's extravagance, he settled in Liverpool as a clerk in a shipping company active in the West African trade. His first taste of Africa in 1883 drew him back to the continent which was just then being colonized by the European powers, and he spent the next twenty years of his life there. In 1903 he conducted an on-the-spot investigation of the abuses and atrocities perpetrated in the Congo Free State under the rule of King Leopold of Belgium.

In the course of the expedition he kept a journal that survived to play a fateful role at the end of his career. It consisted of quick, laconic, unreflective jottings, seldom of expressions of feeling, though there is a passage referring to the suicide of general Sir Hector **Macdonald** in Paris where homosexuality is termed "a terrible disease." But there are also elliptical records of homosexual encounters with the natives, whose genital size he particularly appreciated and coveted. The diaries reveal a man habituated like many homosexuals of that day to living a double life without undue anxiety or reflection.

At the end of 1903 he composed a report which denounced Leopold's regime in the Congo as "an infamous, shameful system," in which "cruelty toward the blacks is the basis of administration, and bad faith towards all the other states the basis of commercial policy." The next post that Casement occupied was that of British consul in Santos, Brazil, then a similar position in Pará, finally that of Consul-General in Rio de Janeiro. In 1910 he engaged in an investigation of atrocities perpetrated against the native Indians in the rubber trade in the Putumayo basin of Peru, keeping another fateful and revealing diary. Returning to England, he composed his report in the spring of 1911, and for his services he was knighted by King George V. Another trip to the Amazon basin followed, but illness forced him into early retirement in August of 1913.

At this point a new phase in Casement's life began with his attending a meeting of amateur Ulster Nationalists in Ballymoney in October 1913. He found himself caught up in the first flowering of the hopeless political conflict that plagues Ulster even today. Although Protestant and northerner by ancestry, he took up the cause of Irish independence, and invited by Eoin MacNeill to join the Irish Volunteers founded in Dublin on November 25, he sensed that it meant a major new direction in his life. The split between the north and the south gradually widened as Sir Edward Carson became ever more parochial in pursuing the interests of the Unionist North. The outbreak of World War I found Casement in the United States soliciting support for the Irish cause. The idea of a rapprochement with Germany was not strange to him; once England was defined as the enemy of Ireland, the enemy of England was Ireland's friend. In October he left for Germany, where his original intention was to persuade the imperial government to issue a declaration of friendly intentions toward Ireland. With Count Georg von Wedel, chief of the English Department of the Foreign Ministry, he discussed a scheme to organize Irish prisoners of war in Germany into an Irish legion, and subsequently he visited a prisoner-of-war camp at Limburg for recruiting purposes, but most of the prisoners proved to be violently anti-German. Undaunted by this failure, Casement wrote to Sir Edward Grey, the British Prime Minister, on February 1, 1915 renouncing all loyalty to Great Britain. A mere fifty Irishmen were recruited for the Brigade, and to the Germans Casement became less an ally than a nuisance.

On learning of the uprising planned for Easter Sunday of 1916, he resolved to return to Ireland on a German submarine so as to be in the thick of the action. After a series of mishaps Casement and two other men were put ashore at Banna Strand, but were quickly apprehended by the Royal Irish Constabulary. Convicted of high treason in the wake of the Easter Sunday Rising, Casement was sentenced to death. His only hope was an appeal for clemency backed by sympathizers and admirers who still respected him for his humanitarian deeds of the past. At this point the British intervened by circulating copies of pages from his private diaries, which—found in his lodgings— exposed his homosexual proclivities and actions. The knowledge or the rumor of the diaries alienated many potential supporters, and even turned some into bitter foes. On August 3, 1916 he was executed by hanging.

Casement's supporters denied the authenticity of the diaries for some forty years, but in 1959 the texts were finally published as *The Black Diaries*. Examination of the autograph copies proved that forgery or interpolation would not have been possible. Casement was revealed for the judgment of all succeeding generations as a homosexual—as one of those homosexuals whose patriotism, self-sacrifice, and love for humanity could be overshadowed but not obliterated by the malice of their enemies.

BIBLIOGRAPHY. Brian Inglis, *Roger Casement*, New York: Harcourt Brace Jovanovich, 1973; B. L. Reid, *The Lives of Roger Casement*, New Haven: Yale University Press, 1976.

Warren Johansson

CASTRATI

The castrati were male singers emasculated in boyhood to preserve the soprano or contralto range of their voices, who from the sixteenth century to the nineteenth played roles in Italian **opera**.

Historical Background. **Eunuchs** are attested from the dawn of civilization in the Near East, as the Bible and other ancient sources indicate; but at what point in time children began to be castrated specifically for the sake of their voices cannot now be determined. The historian Dio Cassius obscurely refers to such a practice in the reign of Septimius Severus (193–211). However, the adoption of Christianity first provided a genuine motive for their existence, as St. Paul had expressly forbidden women to sing in church (I Cor. 14:34; *"mulier taceat in ecclesia"*)—an interdiction that prevailed everywhere until the seventeenth century, and in some places until much later, so that when high voices were required, boys, falsettists, or eunuchs had to be employed. Boys are commonly mischievous, unruly, and troublesome, and by the time they have really

been trained their voices are usually on the edge of breaking; falsettists do not share these drawbacks, but their voices have a peculiar, unpleasant quality, and as a rule cannot attain as high a range as the soprano.

At Constantinople, the capital of the Eastern Roman Empire, it appears that eunuchs were constantly in use during the Middle Ages. Theodore Balsamon, tutor to the Emperor Constantine Porphyrogenitus (reigned 912–59) and possibly himself a eunuch, wrote a treatise in their defense in which he speaks of them as habitually employed as singers; while a eunuch named Manuil is recorded as having arrived at Smolensk in 1137 and having sung there. In the churches of the Byzantine capital soloists were censured for interpolating passages of coloratura into their music, as were later the castrati.

Castrati in European Music. The elaborate *a cappella* style, which began to flourish about the middle of the fifteenth century, required a much wider range of voices and a higher degree of virtuosity than anything that had gone before, and for this task the existing singers were inadequate. The first response took the form of Spanish falsettists of a special kind, but by the end of the sixteenth century these had yielded to the castrati, who also dominated the new baroque art form—the opera, which was the principal musical activity of the Italian nation in the next two centuries. Opera was unlike legitimate theatre in that it traveled well; it was the first form of musical entertainment that was both popular and to a certain degree international, so that a star system transcending national borders arose. Leading singers were discussed, criticized, and compared in fashionable drawing rooms from Lisbon to St. Petersburg. Most of the singers who attained such celebrity were castrati. If other nations had some form of native opera, this ranked lower on the cultural scale and was indifferently sung, while the Italian version enjoyed the highest standard of singing that had ever been known, and will in all likelihood never again be attained. France alone refused admission to Italian singers, and virtually banned the castrati; but Frenchmen, like other Europeans, were full of praise for the opera of Italy.

Character and Status. Since no recording devices existed in the heyday of the castrati, the modern critic has no way of judging the quality of their performance, yet six generations of music-lovers preferred the voices of these "half-men" to those of women themselves and of whole men. A practice that modern opinion would judge both strange and cruel prevailed in part because Christian society tolerated the mutilation of children who in most cases were born of humble parents, since only a family hard pressed for money would consent to such a fate. In this economic stratum, however, it was accepted that any male child who betrayed the slightest aptitude for music should be sold into servitude, just as in modern Thailand children are sold by their parents to labor in factories or serve in brothels. The successful castrato naturally tried to conceal his humble origins and pose as the scion of an honorable family. The singing-masters of that era were responsible for the perfection of the art of the castrati; no one since has rivaled them in perseverance and thoroughness, and in their perfect command of the capabilities and shortcomings of the human vocal organs. They usually worked in a conservatorio, though sometimes they had their own singing schools or tutored pupils on the side.

Since **canon law** condemned castration and threatened anyone involved in it with excommunication, which could be reinforced by civil penalties, the business had to be carried on more or less clandestinely, and everywhere prying questions brought only misleading and deceitful answers. The town of Lecce in Apulia, and Norcia, a small town in the Papal States about twenty miles east of Spoleto, are mentioned as notorious for the practice, though the castrati themselves came from all parts of the peninsula. The doctors most esteemed for their skill in the operation were those of Bologna, and their services were in demand not just in Italy but abroad as well.

The operation itself was no guarantee of future success, as sometimes the voice did not display itself, or the child proved to lack a natural aptitude for music. The educational practice of that day did not spare the rod, and the lessons were often lashed into the castrated boy. The curriculum entailed much hard work, and was thorough and comprehensive; as much attention was given to the theory of singing as to its actual practice. Between the ages of fifteen and twenty, a castrato who had retained and embellished his voice, and passed the various tests with greater or lesser distinction, was considered ready for his debut. On contract to some opera house, he would often first be seen in a female part, for which his youth and fresh complexion would particularly suit him. His looks and unfamiliarity would perhaps gain him greater success than his art would have merited, to the rage and envy of his senior colleagues. Once his name was made, he would have his clique of admirers who attended en masse his every performance and extolled him as their idol; aristocratic ladies and gentlemen would fancy themselves in love with him and manipulate a piquant interview. Backstage, the rivalry with other singers could rage with intense virulence; and a castrato who was too vain and insolent might be assassinated by the hirelings of a rival's protector. If, however, the performer did not please his audience, he would be doomed to touring small provincial opera houses, or to performing in a church choir. Dissatisfied with his situation, he could set off for Bologna, the marketplace for the musical profession in Italy, to better his fortunes.

The castrati came in for a great amount of scurrilous and unkind abuse, and as their fame increased, so did the hatred of them. They were often castigated as malign creatures who lured men into homosexuality, and there were admittedly homosexual castrati, as Casanova's accounts of eighteenth-century Italy bear witness. He mentions meeting an abbé whom he took for a girl in disguise, but was later told that it was a famous castrato. In Rome in 1762, he attended a performance at which the prima donna was a castrato, the minion of Cardinal Borghese, who supped every evening with his protector. From his behavior on stage, "it was obvious that he hoped to inspire the love of those who liked him as a man, and probably would not have done so as a woman." He concludes by saying that the holy city of Rome forces every man to become a pederast, even if it does not believe in the effect of the illusion which the castrati provoke.

The Catholic Church does not permit eunuchs, or those known to be impotent, to marry; and this rule was applied to the castrati, so that they had no hope of heterosexual married life. The principle that marriage was solely for procreation barred any concession to a husband who could not father offspring. Hence the castrati were officially stamped as asexual beings, even if they clandestinely gratified their own and others' homosexual impulses.

Opponents of castration have claimed that the practice caused its victims an early loss of voice and an untimely death, while others have affirmed that castration prolonged the life of the vocal cords, and even that of their owner. There is no solid evidence for either contention: the castrati had approximately the same life span as their contemporaries, and retired at roughly the same age as other singers. The operation appears to have had surprisingly little effect on the general health and well-being of the subject, any more than on his sexual impulses. The trauma was largely a psychological one, in an age when virility was deemed a sovereign virtue.

Aftermath. Toward the end of the end of the eighteenth century castrati went out of fashion, and new styles in musical composition led to the disappearance of these singers. Meyerbeer was the last composer of importance to write for the male soprano voice; his *Il Crociato in Egitto,* produced at Venice in 1824, was designed especially for a castrato star. Succeeding generations regarded their memory with derision and disgust, and were happy to live in an age when such products of barbarism were no longer possible. A few castrati performed in the Vatican chapel and some other Roman churches until late in the nineteenth century, but their vogue on the operatic stage had long passed.

BIBLIOGRAPHY. Angus Heriot, *The Castrati in Opera,* London: Secker & Warburg, 1956.

Warren Johansson

CASTRATION
See Eunuchs.

CATAMITE

The Latin common noun, *catamitus,* designating a minion or kept boy, is usually derived from the Greek proper name **Ganymede**(s), the favorite of Zeus. Another possible source is Kadmilos, the companion of the Theban god Kabeiros. The word entered English in the sixteenth century as part of the Renaissance revival of classical literature, and has always retained a learned, quasiexotic aura. The term could also be used as a verbal adjective, as "a catamited boy."

In modern English the termination *-ite* tends to be perceived as pejorative, as in Trotskyite (vs. Trotskyist) and sodomite. Hobo slang records a turn-of-the-century expression *gey cat,* for a neophyte or young greenhorn, of which the second element may be a truncated form of catamite, though this is uncertain. In keeping with the **Active–Passive Con-**

trast, the catamite is commonly perceived as the passive partner of the sodomite or pederast.

See also **Ingle; Minions and Favorites.**

CATHER, WILLA (1873–1947)

American novelist, short story writer, poet, and editor. Cather was born to a cultivated country family in Virginia. When she was nine the family moved to Red Cloud, Nebraska, where the ruggedness of the frontier still persisted. Arriving at the University of Nebraska in Lincoln in 1890 dressed as William Cather, her opposite-sex twin, Willa soon learned to tone down her image. Still she stood out as a brilliant eccentric. A large, ungainly girl, she was too outspoken and socially unsure of herself to adjust comfortably. She also had a habit of developing crushes on women: classmates, faculty wives, and acquaintances. The intensity of her feeling repelled its objects, and Willa would sulk. Nonetheless, her writing skills matured and she joined a Lincoln newspaper as a reviewer. In her art reviews she praised the beauty of female sitters in portraits. Later, her device of male narrators in her novels allowed her to set forth the varied charms of female characters at length.

Cather did not long remain in Nebraska. She got a better job in Pittsburgh, where she met Isabelle McClung, the beautiful sixteen-year-old daughter of a judge. Swept off her feet, Willa committed herself without reservation. In return Isabelle granted affection but not passion. Although Isabelle married in 1916, her close connection with Willa lasted for forty years.

In the meantime Cather had been sending out her short stories to New York magazines, usually with little success. In 1903, however, she met Sam McClure, the aggressive editor of *McClure's Magazine*. Summoning her to New York, he said that he would print anything she cared to submit. In 1905 he brought out her first volume of short stories, *The Troll Garden*. In turn Cather moved to New York to work for McClure as an editor. She spent six years with him, acquiring a wide variety of writing skills, while her conviction that she should write out of her experience grew. Her new friend, the New England writer Sarah Orne Jewett, urged her to leave the magazine, which she finally did in 1912. Cather settled into a Greenwich Village apartment with her companion Edith Lewis, who was a copyeditor at the magazine. Together they created an orderly life that allowed Cather to produce her masterpieces. One of her greatest pleasures was music, which meant more to her creative life than the conversation of New York intellectuals. As World War I ended, she had already written *O Pioneers!*, *The Song of the Lark*, and her best-known novel, *My Ántonia*. Successful from the first, the books allowed her to travel to the Southwest and to Europe. For forty years Lewis was her indispensable friend, companion, and secretary. To outsiders their relationship was a typical **Boston marriage**, an arrangement that suited two professional women. It is uncertain whether there was any genital aspect. Cather's heart was still pledged to Isabelle McClung.

Her novels tell little of sex and marriage. *Death Comes for the Archbishop* (1927) is the story of a French missionary priest in New Mexico, and *My Ántonia* (1918) depicts the world of immigrant settlers in Nebraska's open spaces. In each the beauty and strength of the land is central. Cather is rightly regarded as a quintessentially American writer. But she was sophisticated as well, and her novels bear comparison with the best that England and Europe could offer at the time. She did not choose to become an open lesbian, though it was always women that she loved, their support that made her work possible. Unfortunately, she decided to destroy her letters to Isabelle McClung, but there survives a revealing series to

Louise Pound, a dashing friend from her college days.

Drawing on a personal alchemy, she transmuted her feelings into the strong characters of her novels. As she put it: "Whatever is felt upon the page without being specifically named there—that, one might say, is created. It is the inexplicable presence of the thing not named, of the overtone divined by the ear but not heard by it, the verbal mood, the emotional aura of the fact or the thing or the deed, that gives high quality to the novel or the drama, as well as to poetry itself." Whether intentionally or not, the expression "thing not named" evokes an old tradition of homosexual love as unnameable. But Cather's triumph is that her need to veil her inner emotional life did not condemn her to silence, but inspired her great writing.

BIBLIOGRAPHY. Sharon O'Brien, "'The Thing Not Named': Willa Cather as a Lesbian Writer," *Signs* (1984), 576–99; James Woodress, *Willa Cather: A Literary Life*, Lincoln: University of Nebraska Press, 1988.
Evelyn Gettone

CATHOLIC CHURCH

See **Christianity; Clergy, Gay; Monasticism; Papacy.**

CATULLUS, GAIUS VALERIUS (87–54 B.C.)

Latin poet. Born at Verona, he spent most of his life in Rome, but kept a villa near his birthplace at Sirmio on Lake Garda. Often considered the best Republican poet, he imitated **Sappho** as well as other archaic, classical, and Hellenistic models, upon which he often improved, and which he combined with native Latin traditions to create stunning, original pieces. He wrote poems, 116 of which survive, of happiness and bitter disappointment. Some are addressed to his highborn, married, then widowed mistress Clodia, the sister of **Cicero**'s antagonist,

10 years his senior, whom he addressed as Lesbia (though with no insinuation of what we now call lesbianism), and who was unfaithful to him with other men. Homophobic Christian and modern schoolmasters have, however, greatly exaggerated the importance of the poems to Lesbia, which amount to no more than an eighth of the Catullan corpus.

Besides a wide variety of other verses, in some of which he criticized **Caesar** and Pompey, many of Catullus' poems were pederastic, addressed to his apparently aristocratic beloved Juventius. He was unusual among Romans in preferring an aristocratic boy to a slave but made clear that most others preferred *concubini*, that is, male slaves with whom they slept. Sophisticated and fastidious, he set the standard for the Augustan poets of love Ovid, **Horace, Vergil,** and Propertius. In the Silver Age even **Martial** acknowledged his debt to Catullus' epigrams. Like those poets, and most specifically **Tibullus,** he showed little inhibition and equal attraction to boys and women, but also shared the traditional attitude that the active, full-grown male partner degraded the passive one, and that the threat to penetrate another male symbolized one's superior virility and power. On the other hand, the accusation of having been raped by another male has a largely negative force; Catullus poses as victim in order to insult the excessively Priapic male.

In Latin erotic poetry, as in its Greek sources after the fifth century, the boys have no family, no career, and no identity other than as athletes and slaves, with the sole exception of Juventius. Like most of the Hellenistic poets, their Roman imitators often sang of boys who demanded gifts or were even outright prostitutes. The older, still beardless boy was considered superior to younger ones, so that eighteen was preferred to thirteen. Even in his wildest flights of imagination or rancor no Latin or Greek poet ever advised his listener to enjoy another adult male sexually. So Catullus' homoerotic poetry is firmly in the tradition of the Hellenistic and the fashionable Roman attitude toward the love of boys.

BIBLIOGRAPHY. Jean Granarolo, *L'Oeuvre de Catulle: Aspects religieux, éthiques et stylistiques*, Paris: Les Belles Lettres, 1967; Saara Lilja, *Homosexuality in Republican and Augustan Rome* (Commentationes Humanarum Litterarum Societatis Scientiarum Fennicae, 74 [1982]).

William A. Percy

CAVAFY, CONSTANTINE P. (1863–1935)

Leading poet in modern Greek. Cavafy was born in **Alexandria**, Egypt, in a merchant family that had long been prominent under the Ottoman Empire. His father died when he was seven and his mother took him to England where they remained for seven years. In 1887 the Cavafy export business collapsed and the family returned to Alexandria, moving to Constantinople in 1882. Here the poet had his first love affair—with a cousin, George Psilliary. In 1885 Cavafy returned with his mother to Alexandria, where he found work in the Department of Irrigation. He remained there for over thirty years. As a young man he led an active street life, some of which is recorded in his poems. When his mother died in 1899, he moved to an apartment over a brothel in the Rue Lepsius. His only known long-term relationship was with Alexander Singopoulos, whom he made his heir.

The canon of Cavafy's works is small, consisting only of about 150 lyrics—though these have been supplemented after the writer's death by several score of unpublished and rejected works. In subject matter his poetry ranges from historical episodes of **Hellenistic** and **Byzantine** times to scenes of modern life. The historical poems reveal his sense of kinship with the earlier phases of the Greek diaspora, together with the fin-de-siècle interest in late or "decadent" stages of civilization. His more personal poems in the latter mode are poignant reflections on the fleeting joys of youth, especially in the homoerotic sphere. Such poems as "In the Street" (1916), "Two Young Men, 23 to 24 Years Old" (1927), and "The Mirror in the Front Hall" (1930) present a comprehensive picture of the urban gay man's world that is easily recognizable today: street cruising, one-night stands, pressures to remain closeted, regret at growing older, ethnic and social contrasts, and nurturing friendships. The cosmopolitan city of Alexandria in which these poems are set is now completely transformed, but Cavafy's vision of it stands as an incomparable metaphor for the awareness of spiritual exile that is a key component of **modernist** sensibility.

Though concise, Cavafy's lyrics have an extraordinary staying power, an indefinable aura, which largely survives the translation process. In the Greek originals their subtle infusion of the inherited literary language with elements of the spoken vernacular has made them an important stylistic influence. Cavafy has achieved a considerable international reputation, thanks in part to such advocates as W. H. **Auden**, E. M. **Carpenter**, Lawrence Durrell, and Marguerite **Yourcenar**.

BIBLIOGRAPHY. *Works: Collected Poems*, translated by Edmund Keeley and Philip Sherrard, Princeton: Princeton University Press, 1975 (includes Greek texts *en face*); *The Complete Poems of Cavafy*, translated by Rae Dalven, expanded ed., New York: Harcourt Brace Jovanovich, 1976. *Criticism*: Carmen Capri-Karka, *Love and the Symbolic Journey in the Poetry of Cavafy, Eliot and Seferis*, New York: Pella, 1982 (with bibliography of Greek-language critical writings); Gregory Jusdanis, *The Poetics of Cavafy: Textuality, Eroticism, History*, Princeton: Princeton University Press, 1987; Edmund Keeley, *Cavafy's Alexandria: Study of a Myth in Progress*, Cambridge, MA: Harvard University Press, 1976; Robert Liddell, *Cavafy: A Critical Biography*, New York: Schocken Books, 1974.

Wayne R. Dynes

CELIBACY

The word *celibate* derives from the Latin *caelebs*, "unmarried." In modern usage celibacy generally means not only that one is unmarried but also abstaining from sexual intercourse. Celibacy may be a matter of individual choice or it may be the condition of joining an institution, as in Christian and Buddhist monasteries. Historically, Christian "total institutions" are enclaves which result from a social compromise in which a state of sexual asceticism, originally recommended as the ideal for all members of society, became mandatory for a defined minority only. Some inmates of Christian monasteries and nunneries have rationalized that homosexual conduct, not constituting marriage and not necessarily extending to intercourse, does not represent a breach of vows. Others hold that monks may experience homosexual feelings, but must not act on them.

Over the centuries many individuals have adopted sexual abstinence either for a given period or for life. This option may reflect aversion to the sexual act ("frigidity"), or a conscious decision to husband energy for the accomplishment of some other goal.

In the twentieth century psychiatrist Wilhelm **Reich** and his followers regarded frequent heterosexual intercourse as the very definition of mental health. Less extreme, other sex reformers, who seek to free those they counsel from the shackles of puritanical self-denial, seem to imply that the modern individual must fulfill a sort of quota of sexual acts. Faced with such pressures, some individuals react against what they perceive as the tyranny of the cult of the orgasm and choose celibacy. With the development of the **AIDS** crisis in the 1980s, many are adopting celibacy less as a matter of personal preference than as a precaution. Their fears may be exaggerated, but some actually find relief in being excused from participating in the "sex race."

See also **Asceticism; Buddhism; Monasticism**.

Ward Houser

CELLINI, BENVENUTO (1500–1571)

Florentine sculptor, goldsmith, and memoirist. After early success as a goldsmith, Cellini could virtually write his own ticket as an artist, and he conducted a successful and peripatetic career in a number of places in Italy and France. His autobiography (written in 1558–62, and therefore not covering his last years) gives a highly colored account of the artist's motivation in these wanderings. A fervent admirer of **Michelangelo** in art, he conspicuously departed from the austerity of his mentor in his swashbuckling life, so that his name has become a byword for the profligacy and extravagance of the **Renaissance** artist.

Cellini's sculpture *Perseus* (1545–54) was judged worthy of a place of honor in Florence's Loggia dei Lanzi near Michelangelo's superb *David*. In 1540–43 Cellini completed the daunting task for the salt-cellar of Francis I in France. This and other undertakings in that country served to consolidate the mannerist taste of Fontainebleau, with which Cellini was perfectly in tune.

During his later years he chose to reside in Florence, where his relations with grandduke Cosimo I were stormy. Once during a quarrel a rival artist Baccio Bandinelli cried out, "Oh keep quiet you dirty sodomite," an early instance of public **labeling**. In 1527 he was called before a court for sexual irregularity, but the case appears to have been quashed. In 1557 he was placed under house arrest for sodomy, using the occasion to begin dictating his *Autobiography*, which more than any of his other works has made him famous. Some years later, apparently rehabilitated, he married the mother of some of his illegitimate children. In 1571 Cellini died and was buried with full honors in the church of the Santissima Annunziata.

One of his most personal works is the marble *Ganymede* of 1545–46 (Florence, Bargello), where the Phrygian youth stands next to the eagle, a manifestation of his abductor, Zeus. In his right hand Ganymede holds a small bird, evidently a love gift from his suitor. Other works heavy with male eroticism are the *Narcissus* and *Apollo and Hyacinth* (both Florence, Bargello).

Heir to the Renaissance tradition of the artist as a special being, exempt from ordinary demands of morality, Cellini nonetheless fell afoul of changing religious currents. The Council of Trent, which began meeting in 1545 during his middle years, was the bellwether of this shift. After Cellini Italy saw only one other major artist in this grand homosexual/bisexual tradition, the painter Michelangelo Merisi da **Caravaggio** (1571–1610).

BIBLIOGRAPHY. Luigi Greci, "Benvenuto Cellini nei delitti e nei processi fiorentini," *Archivio di Antropologia Criminale*, 50 (1930), 342–85, 509–42; James Saslow, *Ganymede in the Renaissance*, New Haven: Yale University Press, 1986.

Wayne R. Dynes

CELTS, ANCIENT

In the first millennium B.C. the Celtic peoples expanded from their original homeland in Central Europe to occupy much of what is now France, the British Isles, and Northern Italy. Although Celtic languages are today confined to small areas in Scotland, Ireland, Wales, and Brittany, their heritage forms an important substratum of developing European culture, as seen, for example, in the legends of the Arthurian cycle.

In their dynamic period, bodies of Celts also moved eastward, where they encountered the ancient Greeks, who celebrated their warlike character and their attachment to male homosexuality. In his *Politics* (II, 9:7–8), **Aristotle** compares the Spartans unfavorably with the Celts: under the influence of their wives the former have fallen into luxury, while the Celts use their devotion to male love as a shield against such self-indulgence. **Athenaeus** (XIII, 603a; echoed by Diodorus Siculus and Strabo) says that although the Celts had beautiful women, they much preferred boys. Sometimes, he states, they would sleep on animal skins with a boyfriend on either side. This observation seems to reflect the fact that great warriors had two squires, each with his own horse.

Inasmuch as the ancient Celts were illiterate, we are compelled to rely on the scanty testimony of the Greeks and Romans. The wonderful specimens of Celtic art ("La Tène") found in tombs do not suffice to make up the gap. What is known suggests that homosexuality had an initiatory function among these warriors, not unlike that found among some Greek peoples. Whether all these manifestations derive in turn from a unitary primordial **Indo-European** institution of initiatory homosexuality, as Bernard Sergent has argued, must be regarded as still unproven.

In the late Roman Republic and the first century of the Empire most of the western Celtic peoples lost their independence—with which their devotion to male love had been linked—and fell under the domination of Rome, with its more ambivalent attitudes to homosexuality. The coming of Christianity finally severed the link with the old homoerotic traditions, although traces of them seem to have survived here and there in imaginative literature. The early Irish **penitentials** also show that homosexual love continued in the monasteries, while subject to continuing surveillance and repression.

BIBLIOGRAPHY. Bernard Sergent, *L'Homosexualité initiatique dans l'Europe ancienne*, Paris: Payot, 1986.

Wayne R. Dynes

Censorship and Obscenity

Censorship is the official prohibition, whether by civil or ecclesiastical authorities, of the publication and circulation of printed and visual materials.

Basic Features. While in former times the activity of censors focused primarily on the written word as the vehicle of subversive or sexually arousing discourse, in recent decades emphasis has largely shifted to visual expression. This change in emphasis is not a tribute to the power of art as such, but a recognition that in the age of **film** and **television** a large portion of the population derives its information and entertainment almost exclusively from these sources. In the case of written materials, many regimes, as in the Soviet Union today, have permitted the circulation of nonprinted (handwritten or typewritten) copies of otherwise unacceptable texts (*samizdat*). In North America in the past, some sexually explicit writings have been issued in this fashion. It has also been common to print materials abroad (*tamizdat*) and import them clandestinely—or to feign foreign issue through a false indication of place of publication.

The practice of tolerating certain hand-produced materials clearly shows that censorship is concerned not simply with the prohibition of materials, but with the size of the audience. A small elite, prepared to go to unusual trouble and to pay high prices, can be allowed materials that are denied to the masses. It is for this reason that medical and other books dealing with sexual matters formerly had the crucial details in Latin. This antidemocratic tendency, reserving sexually explicit materials to the few who can pay the monetary or linguistic entry fee, was a factor in the United States court decisions of the 1960s overturning censorship.

Historical Perspectives. The urge to censor is probably ultimately rooted in fear of blasphemy, the apprehension that if utterances offensive to the gods are toler-ated their wrath will fall on the whole society. It was impiety toward the gods for which Socrates was tried and condemned in 399 B.C. The Roman erotic poet Ovid was banished by the puritanical emperor Augustus in A.D. 8.

On the whole neither classical antiquity nor the Middle Ages had an adequate system of surveillance that would permit prior restraint, a characteristic feature of censorship of the modern type. It is true that on a number of occasions, as Peter Abelard's *Introductio ad Theologiam* in 1120, works were condemned by medieval synods to be burned. However, no centralized machinery existed for the control of books. Since the monasteries had a monopoly on producing manuscripts, it was assumed that such oversight was not necessary. In fact the abbey scriptoria not only copied erotic materials from Greco-Roman times, but created their own new genres of this type. In any event, the medieval authorities were concerned more with doctrinal deviation than with obscenity.

The introduction of printing by Gutenberg in the mid-fifteenth century changed the whole picture. There was a much greater incidence of the issuing and circulation of heretical broadsides and brochures; without printing, the Reformation, beginning in 1517, might never have taken place. Yet, in the view of the authorities, it was not too late to lock the barn door. The centralization of printing in the hands of a relatively few firms made it possible to scrutinize their intended productions before publication; only those that had passed the test and bore the imprimatur could be printed. It was then only necessary to make sure that heretical materials were not smuggled in from abroad. In Catholic countries this system was put in place by the establishment, under the **Inquisition**, of the Index of Prohibited Books in 1557. In countries where the Reformation took hold the control of books was generally assumed by the government. In England the requirement that books should be licenced for printing by the privy council or other agents of the crown was introduced in 1538. These origins explain why the activity of censors was for long chiefly concerned with the printed word. Revealingly, this system is still in force in Communist countries today.

One other area in which censorship was widely practiced was the **theatre**, where plays generally had to be licenced before being produced. In a few instances, as in England from 1642 to 1660, the theatres could be entirely shut down. Even where they were not, an antitheatrical prejudice lingered in many countries, which had the effect of limiting the range of subjects that could be safely presented lest the ax fall on all performers.

In the visual arts a similar broad attack was aimed at certain types of material. In the seventh and eighth centuries all religious imagery was banned by the iconoclastic rulers of the **Byzantine Empire**; in the sixteenth and seventeenth centuries similar attacks took place in Protestant countries of northwest Europe. Here, however, the prohibition was sacral in origin; images were said to contravene the Second Commandment.

The operation of censorship with regard to sexually explicit material may be seen in two seventeenth-century examples. The *Alcibiade Fanciullo*, a pederastic classic, was apparently written by the Venetian Antonio Rocco and published anonymously and clandestinely in 1652. Initials on the title page slyly suggested that it was written by Aretino, who was long since dead and safely beyond the reach of the Inquisition. The French author Nicolas Chorier contrived an even more ambitious ruse for his pansexual dialogues of *Aloisia Sigea* (1658?), which purported to be a translation into Latin by a Dutch author (Jan de Meurs) working from a Spanish original by a learned woman. As the censorship tightened in the course of the seventeenth and eighteenth century, recourse to apparent—and increasingly real—

foreign presses was ever more necessary. Many French books, unwelcome to throne and altar, were published in Geneva, in Amsterdam, and in Germany. With the coming of the French revolution, however, all restraints were off. Thus the large works which the Marquis de Sade had composed in prison were published, as well as two fascinating homosexual pamphlets *Les enfans de Sodome* and *Les petits bougres au manège*. Although controls were eventually tightened again, Paris gained the reputation (which lasted until about 1960) among English and American travelers as the place where "dirty books" could be obtained.

Anglo-American Censorship. England itself entered an era in which respectability at all costs was the watchword. Through his prudish editions of Shakespeare, Thomas Bowdler (1754–1825) gave rise to the term "bowdlerize." At the ports an efficient customs service kept all but a trickle of works deemed to be obscene from coming in. In the United States, the morals crusader Anthony Comstock (1844–1915) not only fought successfully for stringent new legislation, but as head of the New York Society for the Suppression of Vice he claimed responsibility for the destruction of 160 tons of literature and pictures. The restrictions on mailability proved to be particularly hard on publishers of homosexual material, and this problem was not overcome until the **ONE**, Inc. case in 1954. A landmark in freedom to read books in the United States was the 1931 *Ulysses* case. Shortly thereafter, however, Hollywood instituted a system of self-censorship known as the "Hays Office." This device effectively prevented any direct representation of homosexual love on the silver screen for decades, the only exceptions being a very few foreign films shown at art houses. During this period book publishers practiced their own form of self-censorship by insisting that novels featuring homosexual characters must doom them to an unhappy end.

Dismantling of Censorship. Only after World War II did the walls begin to come tumbling down in English-speaking countries. In Britain the publishers of *Lady Chatterley's Lover* by D. H. **Lawrence** were acquitted after a spectacular trial in 1960. In America Grove Press had obtained a favorable court decision on the mailability of *Lady Chatterley* in 1959; three years later the firm went on to publish Henry Miller's *Tropic of Cancer* without difficulty. The travails of a book containing explicit homosexual passages, William Burroughs' *Naked Lunch*, were more extended. In 1958 authorities at the University of Chicago refused to permit publication of excerpts in a campus literary review. This led to the founding of a new journal, largely to publish the Burroughs text; once this had been done, a lengthy court battle ensued. Only in 1964 was the way clear for the whole novel to be issued by Grove Press. (The book had been published in Paris in 1959.)

Subsequently, a series of United States Supreme Court decisions made censorship impractical, and for all intents and purposes it has ceased nationally, though local option is sometimes exercised. This cessation permitted the appearance and sale of a mass of sexually explicit books, films, and magazines. The only restriction that is ubiquitously enforced is the ban on "kiddy porn," photographs and films of children engaging in sexual acts. In an unlikely de facto alliance, two groups emerged at the end of the 1970s in America to reestablish some form of censorship: one consisting of fundamentalists and other religious conservatives; the other of feminist groups.

A new type of censorship has arisen in cases where public institutions become fearful of losing government funds. In June 1989 the Corcoran Gallery in Washington, DC, canceled a retrospective exhibition of the work of the late photographer Robert Mapplethorpe containing explicit homoerotic images because of concern that Congress might slash the funds of the National Endowment for the Humanities, the sponsoring body. The cancellation was, however, vigorously protested, and as a result Mapplethorpe's work became better known than it had been previously.

See also **Pornography; Private Presses**.

BIBLIOGRAPHY. David Copp and Susan Wendell, eds., *Pornography and Censorship*, Buffalo: Prometheus Books, 1983; Michael Barry Goodman, *Contemporary Literary Censorship: The Case of Burroughs' Naked Lunch*, Metuchen, NJ: Scarecrow, 1981; Felice Flannery Goodman, *Literature, Obscenity and the Law*, Carbondale: Southern Illinois University Press, 1976.

Wayne R. Dynes

CERNUDA, LUIS (1902–1963)

Spanish poet. Cernuda was an unhappy man; his only major and enduring pleasure, the writing of poetry, was the focus of his intellectual life. He scorned careers, and supported himself by working in a bookstore and by commissioned translations. During the Spanish Civil War Cernuda moved to England, later to the United States, in both of which countries he held university teaching posts, which were for him nothing more than a source of income. His last years were spent in Mexico, where he died.

Cernuda was a twentieth-century Romantic; he admired and wrote on the English and German romantic poets, and translated Hölderlin into Spanish. Timid, introspective, misogynistic, easily offended, in an isolation at least somewhat self-imposed, he permitted few to be his friends, and never had an enduring love relationship. He was obsessed with the loss of his youth and with the fugacity of sexual pleasure. His anger was expressed in withdrawal and in poetry, rather than activity in support of social change; Cernuda felt the world unworthy of efforts on its behalf.

Secure in his own gay identity, confident that he was correct and puritanical society wrong, Cernuda's primarily autobiographical poetry explores his own isolation and suffering. He sought to recapture his lost youth in that of young sexual partners, and his *Forbidden Pleasures* and *Where Oblivion Dwells* are openly pederastic; he was the first to publish on such topics in Spain. In addition to his verse, which was well received in literary circles, Cernuda was a frequent contributor of critical essays to literary magazines. He published a lengthy essay on André **Gide**, from whose writings he learned that others felt as he did and that suffering could be expressed and alleviated through literary creation.

BIBLIOGRAPHY. *Works: Poesía completa*, 2nd revised edition, Barcelona: Barral, 1977; *Prosa completa*, Barcelona: Barral, 1975; two partial translations are *The Young Sailor and Other Poems*, trans. Rick Lipinski, San Francisco: Gay Sunshine, 1986; and *The Poetry of Luis Cernuda*, New York: New York University Press, 1971. *Criticism*: Rafael Martínez Nadal, *Españoles en la Gran Bretaña: Luis Cernuda. El hombre y sus temas*, Madrid: Hiperión, 1983.

Daniel Eisenberg

CERVANTES, MIGUEL DE (1547–1616)

Spanish novelist. Cervantes, probably of Jewish ancestry, is the last major representative of the Spanish humanism that was extinguished by the Counterreformation. That Cervantes might have had homosexual desires and experiences was first suggested in print in 1982 and restated more explicitly in 1987 (Rossi). There is much to support this suggestion: his teacher Juan López de Hoyos, to whom he remained close until his death in 1583, called him "my dear **beloved disciple**"; Cervantes subsequently spent a year in Italy, of which he always kept fond memories and wished to return. For five years he was a captive in Algiers, where he was on surprisingly good terms with a homosexual convert to Islam; he refers several times in his writings to the pederasty that flourished in the Ottoman empire; on his return from Algiers he was accused of unspecified filthy acts. His marriage was unhappy, and women in his works are treated distantly. Like Manuel **Azaña**, he put a very high value on freedom.

While Cervantes presented the male–female relationship as the theoretical ideal and goal for most people, the use of pairs of male friends is characteristic of his fiction, and questions of gender are often close to the surface. In his masterpiece *Don Quixote* (1605–15), which includes cross-dressing by both sexes, the middle-aged protagonist has never had, and has no interest in, sexual intercourse with a woman. A boy servant who appears fleetingly at the outset is replaced by the unhappily-married companion Sancho Panza. The two men come to love each other, although the love is not sexual.

BIBLIOGRAPHY. Louis Combet, *Cervantès ou les incertitudes du désir*, Lyon: Presses Universitaires, 1982 (review in *MLN*, 97 [1982], 422–27); Rosa Rossi, *Ascoltare Cervantes*, Milan: Riuniti, 1987 (Spanish translation, *Escuchar a Cervantes*, Valladolid: Ambito, 1988); Luis Rosales, *Cervantes y la libertad*, 2nd ed., Madrid: Cultura Hispánica, 1985; Ruth El Saffar, "Cervantes and the Androgyne," *Cervantes*, 3 (1983), 35–49; idem, *Beyond Fiction: The Recovery of the Feminine in the Novels of Cervantes*, Berkeley: University of California Press, 1984.

Daniel Eisenberg

CHASTITY
See **Asceticism; Celibacy.**

CHICAGO
At the beginning of the twentieth century, America's chief Midwestern city achieved a remarkable economic and cultural eminence. At that time a homosexual **subculture** with its own language, dress, mores, and institutions began to take shape

on Chicago's south side. This development was owing largely to the tremendous influx of both foreign immigrants and native-born Americans from rural and small town areas who came not only for economic betterment but also to find personal freedom and anonymity by escaping from a more traditional society. Taking root in the 1910s, this diverse subculture flourished openly throughout the 1920s, went underground during the 1930s, and resurfaced in the 1940s, especially after World War II.

One of the first written descriptions of Chicago's homosexual subculture appears in the Chicago Vice Commission Report of 1910, which indicated that the increase in cases of sexual perversion was so great that the existence of whole "colonies" with their own world of meeting places had been uncovered. The report then gave a lengthy description of an investigator's visit to a local bar frequented by homosexuals who were being entertained by female impersonators performing "explicit" musical numbers! The commission also noted the alarming increase in male homosexual solicitation on Chicago's streets and in its parks, especially Grant Park which served as headquarters for a homosexual street gang known as "The Bluebirds."

This subculture was primarily located in two geographical locations: (1) the bohemian area known as "Towertown"; and (2) the hobo zone south of the Loop around West Madison and State streets. Although these areas overlapped and their physical boundaries constantly changed, each had a distinct identity and flavor to it. Chicago's **bohemia** attracted mostly persons of the middle class who were either artistically inclined or at least intellectually stimulated through association with the artists. Here one could find various restaurants, bars, studios, and cabarets that at least tolerated, if not welcomed, the sexual outcast as an equal. One important place was the Seven Arts Club owned by Ed Classy, a well-known homosexual. What little information that has been found on the Seven Arts Club points to the fact that it served as a point of entry to the homosexual underground for many people.

On the other hand, "hobohemia" attracted a transient male population, many of whom were homosexuals from the working class. Here a large amount of homosexual prostitution existed as well as Turkish **bathhouses**, cheap hotels, "pig pens" (homosexual **brothels**), and the sleazier **bars**. One peculiar and popular "hobohemia" meeting place was Jack Jones' Dill Pickle Club which sought to promote a free exchange of ideas by presenting speakers on current controversial issues. One of the most successful presentations was on the pros and cons of sexual perversion. Another colorful hobohemia "institution" was Dr. Ben Reitman, the Hobo Doctor, who freely accepted homosexuals as his clients and friends and wrote one of the first medical studies on venereal disease among homosexuals.

An important tradition in the early decades of Chicago's homosexual community was the masquerade or "drag" ball held annually on or around Halloween. Fun-filled and outrageous, these gatherings gave individuals a chance to interact with a diverse underground and thereby develop a sense of commonality and community. Although sanctioned by neither public nor private agencies, the city government gave police protection to those persons in attendance and suspended, for this occasion only, the law against crossdressing in public.

Although Chicago's homosexuals remained largely apolitical, it is Chicago that justly claims to be the birthplace of the first known homosexual organization in the United States. Inspired by the German homosexual rights movement, Henry **Gerber** and several other men formed the Society for Human Rights in 1924 in hopes of improving the life of homosexuals by drawing attention to their plight and to serve as a social group where homosexuals could find support and friendship. Short-lived due to the harassment and arrest of all its members, the Society, however, managed to produce two issues of a magazine (*Friendship and Freedom*) of which no copies are now known to exist. The ideals of these early pioneers later served to inspire the post-war homophile and gay liberation **movements**.

Although perhaps not as conspicuous as its counterparts on either coast, Chicago's gay/lesbian community began to increase rapidly in the hectic days of World War II and even more so in the postwar prosperity of the following decades. By the early 1950s, the community began to assert a quiet, low-key presence, benefitting from the fact that Illinois became the first state to decriminalize homosexual conduct between consenting adults (1961). This continuing Midwestern approach to political activism has allowed a thriving, openly gay and lesbian community to make permanent inroads in changing the political and social atmosphere in one of the America's major cities. A sign that the gay community had reached political maturity came on December 22, 1988, when the Chicago City Council adopted a gay rights ordinance, 28 to 17, over the opposition of the Catholic archdiocese, after all the major candidates for mayor had endorsed the proposal. Two of them, incumbent Mayor Eugene Sawyer (who had voted against a gay rights bill in 1986), and Cook County State's Attorney Richard M. Daley, son of the legendary mayor "Boss" Daley and eventual winner of the election, vied with each other in lobbying for the ordinance.

BIBLIOGRAPHY. Chicago Vice Commission, *The Social Evil in Chicago*, Chicago: Gunthorp-Warren Printing Co., 1910, reprinted New York: Amo, 1970.

Steven L. Lewis

CHILDREN
See **Pedophilia**.

CHINA
The civilization of China emerged from prehistory during the first half of the second millennium B.C. in the valley of the Huang He (Yellow River), spreading gradually southwards. Over the centuries China has exercised extensive influence on **Korea**, **Japan**, and southeast Asia. Inasmuch as Chinese society has traditionally viewed male homosexuality and lesbianism as altogether different, their histories are separate and are consequently treated in sequence in this article.

Zhou Dynasty. As with many aspects of Chinese civilization, the origins of homosexuality are both ancient and obscure. The fragmentary nature of early sources, the bias of these records toward the experiences of a tiny social elite, and the lack of pronouns differentiated by gender in ancient Chinese all frustrate any attempt to recapture an accurate conception of homosexuality in China's earliest periods. Only with the Eastern Zhou dynasty (722–221 B.C.) do reliable sources become available.

During the latter part of the Zhou, homosexuality appears as a part of the sex lives of the rulers of many states of that era. Ancient records include homosexual relationships as unexceptional in nature and not needing justification or explanation. This tone of prosaic acceptance indicates that these authors considered homosexuality among the social elite to be fairly common and unremarkable. However, the political, ritual and social importance of the family unit made procreation a necessity. **Bisexuality** therefore became more accepted than exclusive homosexuality, a predominance continuing throughout Chinese history.

The Eastern Zhou produced several figures who became so associated with homosexuality that later generations invoked their names as symbols of homosexual love, much in the same way that Europeans looked to **Ganymede**, **Socrates**, and **Hadrian**. These famous men included Mizi Xia, who offered his royal lover a half-eaten peach, and Long Yang, who compared the fickle lover to a fisherman who tosses back a small fish when he catches a larger one. Subsequent references to "sharing peaches" and "the passion of Lord Long Yang" became classical Chinese terms for homosexuality. Rather than adopt scientific terminology, with associations of sexual pathology, Chinese litterateurs preferred the aesthetic appeal of these literary tropes.

Homosexual Emperors of the Han Dynasty. Although the unification of China with the fall of the Zhou induced fundamental changes in China's political and social order, homosexuality seems to have continued in forms similar to those it took in the previous dynasty. In fact the Former Han dynasty (206 B.C.–A.D. 9) saw the highpoint of homosexual influence at the Chinese court. For 150 years, emperors who were bisexual or exclusively homosexual ruled China. The Han dynastic history discusses in detail the fabulous wealth and powerful influence of male favorites and their families, analogous to that of imperial consorts. The comprehensive Han history *Records of the Historian* (*Shi ji*) even includes a section of biographies of these favorites, the author noting that their sexual charms proved more effective than administrative talents in propelling them to the heights of power.

Several early Han emperors, such as Gaozu (r. 206–194 B.C.) and Wu (r. 140–86 B.C.) favored more than one man with their sexual attentions. This behavior paralleled the heterosexual polygamy popular at court and among wealthy families. Some of the imperial male favorites had special talents in fields such as astrology and medicine which originally brought them to the ruler's attention, while others obtained favor solely through their sexual charms. The desire to catch the emperor's eye at any cost, and thereby win substantial material rewards, fueled intense sartorial competition as courtiers vied with one another to dazzle the Son of Heaven with ornate clothing.

Dong Xian. The most famous favorite of the Han, Dong Xian, exemplifies the rewards and dangers which could come to one of these men. He became the beloved of Emperor Ai (r. 6 B.C.–A.D. 1), the last adult emperor of the Former Han, and rose to power with his lover. The Han dynastic history records that Emperor Ai presented him with an enormous fortune and lists an extensive array of offices he held. Since Emperor Ai lacked sons or a designated heir, he proposed during his reign to cede his title to Dong Xian. Although his councilors had firmly resisted the notion, nevertheless on his deathbed Ai handed over the imperial seals to his beloved. This unorthodox succession lacked the support of the most powerful court factions, and so Dong Xian found himself compelled into suicide. The resulting political vacuum left the kingmaker Wang Mang in control and after a short period of nominal regency through child emperors, Wang Mang declared the overthrow of the Han dynasty. Thus the homosexual favoritism which helped shape the political topography throughout the Former Han was also present in its destruction.

One incident in the life of Dong Xian became a timeless metaphor for homosexuality. A tersely worded account relates how Emperor Ai was sleeping with Dong Xian one afternoon when he was called to court. Rather than wake up his beloved, who was reclining across the emperor's sleeve, Ai took out a dagger and cut off the end of his garment. When courtiers inquired after the missing fabric, Emperor Ai, told them what had happened. This example of love moved his courtiers to cut off the ends of their own sleeves in imitation, beginning a new fashion trend. Ever since then, authors have used "cut sleeve" as a symbol of homosexuality.

The periods of disunity following the Han produced a wider range of source materials which reflect the presence of homosexuality in classes other than the uppermost elite. Famed literary figures such as the "Seven Worthies of the Bamboo Grove" admired one another's good looks quite openly, and the contemporaneous accounts in *A New Account of Tales of the World (Shishuo xinyu)* substantiate the wide diffusion of homosexuality in post-Han society. The honored poet Pan Yue and the master calligrapher Wang Xizhi both fervently admired male beauty. And the greatest intellectual force of the third century, Xi Kang (223–262), had a male lover.

Male Prostitution. During this period male prostitution also becomes evident, and is both celebrated and denigrated in verse. The Jin dynasty (265–420) poet Zhang Hanbian wrote a glowing tribute to the fifteen-year-old boy prostitute Zhou Xiaoshi. In it he presents the boy's life as happy and carefree, "inclined toward extravagance and festiveness, gazing around at the leisurely and beautiful." A later poet, the Liang dynasty (502–557) figure Liu Zun, tried to present a more balanced view in a poem entitled "Many Blossoms." In this piece he shows the dangers and uncertainty associated with a boy prostitute's life. His Zhou Xiaoshi "knows both wounds and frivolity/ Withholding words, ashamed of communicating." Although these poems take opposite perspectives on homosexual prostitution, the appearance of this theme as an inspiration for poetry points to the presence of a significant homosexual world complete with male prostitutes catering to the wealthy.

Of course homosexuality also continued among the social elite. Emperors such as Wei Wen (r. 220–227), Jin Diyi (r. 336–371), Liang Jianwen (r. 550–551) and several Tang dynasty rulers all had male favorites. These powerful men often preferred boys or eunuchs, although they sometimes also favored grown men.

By the Song dynasty (960–1280) a broadening of literary accounts makes available detailed information beyond the lives of emperors and literary figures. One source estimates that at the beginning of the dynasty in the Song capital alone there were more than ten thousand male prostitutes inhabiting a maze of **brothels** known as "mist and moon workshops." A love of sensuality continued throughout the dynasty. A source describing the fall of the Song notes "clothing, drink, and food were all that they desired. Boys and girls were all that they lived for."

The high profile of male prostitution led the Song rulers to take limited action against it. Many Confucian moralists objected to male prostitution because they saw the sexual passivity of a prostitute as extremely feminizing. In the early twelfth century, a law was codified which declared that male prostitutes would receive one hundred strokes of a bamboo rod and pay a fine of fifty thousand cash. Considering the harsh legal penalties of the period, which included mutilation and death by slicing, this punishment was actually quite lenient. And it appears that the law was rarely if ever enforced, so it soon became a dead letter.

The revival and transformation of Confucian doctrine in the movement now referred to as Neo-Confucianism had influence far beyond metaphysics. On a practical level the movement enforced a more rigid view of the status of women and of sexual morality. In general, Confucians became more intolerant of any form of sexuality taking place outside of marriage. This was all part of an attempt to strengthen the family, held by Confucians to be the basic unit of society. The Song law prohibiting male prostitution came as an early response to this new social ethos. Legal intervention peaked in the Qing dynasty (1644–1911) when the Kang Xi Emperor (r. 1662–1723) took steps against the sexual procurement of young boys, homosexual rape, and even consensual homosexual acts.

A law codified in 1690 specifically prohibits consensual homosexuality as part of an overall series of laws designed to strengthen the family. Although laws against rape of males were actively enforced, as demonstrated in a substantial body of Qing case law, it seems that the traditional government laissez-faire attitude toward male sexuality prevented enforcement of the law against consentual homosexual acts. After 1690 homosexuality continued as an open and prominant sexual force in Chinese society.

Flowering of the Ming Period. By the Ming dynasty (1368–1644) homosexuality had attained a high degree of representation in literature, erotic art, scholarship, and society as a whole. The rise of literacy and inexpensive printing generated demand for popular literature such as *Golden Lotus (Jin ping mei)*, depicting in colloquial language all forms of sexual conduct, and for erotic prints which presented homosexuality visually. A thirst for knowledge of homosexual history led to the compilation of the anonymous Ming collection *Records of the Cut Sleeve (Duan xiu pian)* which contains vignettes of homosexual encounters culled from nearly two millennia of sources. This anthology is the first history of Chinese homosexuality, perhaps the first comprehensive homosexual history in any culture, and still serves as our primary guide to China's male homosexual past.

In Fujian province on the South China coast, a form of male marriage developed during the Ming. Two men were united, the older referred to as an "adoptive older brother" (*qixiong*) and the younger as "adoptive younger brother" (*qidi*). The younger qidi would move into the qixiong's household, where he would be treated as a son-in-law by his husband's parents. Throughout the marriage, which often lasted for twenty years, the qixiong was completely responsible for his younger husband's upkeep. Wealthy qixiong even adopted young boys who were raised as sons by the couple. At the end of each marriage, which was usually terminated because of the familial responsibilities of procreation, the older husband paid the necessary price to acquire a suitable bride for his beloved qidi.

As China entered the Qing era, homosexuality continued to maintain a high profile. Besides several prominent Ming and Qing emperors who kept male favorites, a flourishing network of male brothels, and a popular class of male actor–prostitutes dominating the stage, Qing popular literature expanded on the homosexual themes explored during the Ming. The famous seventeenth century author Li Yu wrote several works featuring male homosexuality and lesbianism. The greatest Chinese work of prose fiction, *Dream of the Red Chamber (Honglou meng)*, features a bisexual protagonist and many homosexual interludes. And the mid-nineteenth century saw the creation of *A Mirror Ranking Precious Flowers (Pinhua baojian)*, a literary masterpiece detailing the romances of male actors and their scholar patrons.

Western Influences. The twentieth century ushered in a new age for all aspects of Chinese society; homosexuality was no exception. Within a few generations, China shifted from a relative tolerance of homosexuality to open hostility. The reasons for this change are complex and not yet completely understood. First, the creation of colloquial *baihua* literary language removed many potential readers from the difficult classical Chinese works which contained the native homosexual tradition. Also, the Chinese reformers early in the century began to see any divergence between their own society and that of the West as a sign of backwardness. This led to a restructuring of Chinese marriage and sexuality along more Western lines. The uncritical acceptance of Western science, which regarded homosexuality as pathological, added to the Chinese rejection of same-sex love. The end result is a contemporary China in which the native homosexual tradition has been virtually forgotten and homosexuality is ironically seen as a recent importation from the decadent West.

Communist China. In the People's Republic of China, homosexuality is taken as a sign of bourgeois immorality and punished by "reeducation" in labor camps. Officially the incidence of homosexuality is quite low. Western psychologists, however, have noted that the official reporting of impotence is much higher in mainland China than in the West. It seems that many Chinese men, unfamiliar with homosexual role models, interpret their sexuality solely according to their attraction to women. Nevertheless, a small gay subculture has begun to develop in the major cities since the end of the Maoist era. Fear of discovery and lack of privacy tend to limit the quality and duration of homosexual relationships. And for the vast majority of Chinese living in the conservative countryside, homosexual contacts are much more difficult to come by.

Hong Kong. Modern Hong Kong has adopted many aspects of British law, including the criminalization of homosexuality. Until recently, the Hong Kong police were extremely active in searching out and prosecuting homosexuals. With the 1997 return of Hong Kong to China approaching, British liberals have supported a last minute repeal of the sodomy law. This reform effort has been vigorously resisted by the colony's Chinese population. Despite official disapproval, the cosmopolitan sophistication of Hong Kong has guaranteed a relative toleration of the gay community. Gay bars and private parties provide an extensive social network for Hong Kong's homosexuals.

Taiwan. The situation for Chinese gays on Taiwan is improving. Since 1949, when Nationalist soldiers frequenting Taipei's New Park provided the nucleus of a gay community, this subculture has gradually expanded. Now it includes several bars and discos. The AIDS crisis has recently focused public attention on gay life, resulting in general public awareness of homosexuals. One of Taiwan's most well-known novelists, Pai Hsien-yung, has also raised general awareness with his successful novel about Taiwan

gay life entitled *The Outsiders (Niezi)*, which served as the basis for a 1986 film by the same title. There is no sodomy law in Taiwan, but gays still face intense social and family pressure against openly expressing their sexuality. As a result, as in Hong Kong and the mainland, Taiwan's homosexuals almost always follow the traditional Chinese custom of entering into heterosexual marriage so as to raise a family.

Lesbianism. Traditionally, Chinese people have viewed male homosexuality and lesbianism as unrelated. Consequently, much of the information we have on male homosexuality in China does not apply to the female experience. Piecing together the Chinese lesbian past is frustrated by the relative lack of source material. Since literature and scholarship were usually written by men and for men, aspects of female sexuality unrelated to male concerns were almost always ignored.

Reliable accounts of lesbianism in China only date back as far as the Ming dynasty. Sex manuals of the period include instructions integrating lesbian acts with heterosexual intercourse as a way of varying the sex lives of men with multiple concubines. And Ming erotic prints pictorially represent lesbian intercourse. Artificial devices for stimulating the vagina and clitoris also survive.

Most of our information about lesbianism comes from popular literature. Li Yu's first play, *Pitying the Fragrant Companion* ("Lian xiangban"), describes a young married woman's love for a younger unmarried woman. The married woman convinces her husband to take her talented beloved as a concubine. The three then live as a happy *ménage-à-trois* free from jealousy. A more conventional lesbian love affair is detailed in *Dream of the Red Chamber*, in which a former actress regularly offers incense to the memory of her deceased beloved.

Lesbian Marriages. The most highly developed form of female relationship was the lesbian marriages formed by the exclusively female membership of "Golden Orchid Associations." A lesbian couple within this group could choose to undergo a marriage ceremony in which one partner was designated "husband" and the other "wife." After an exchange of ritual gifts, a wedding feast attended by female friends served to witness the marriage. These married lesbian couples could even adopt young girls, who in turn could inherit family property from the couple's parents. This ritual was not uncommon in nineteenth-century Guangzhou province. Prior to this, the only other honorable way for a woman to remain unmarried was to enter a Buddhist nunnery.

In modern China, lesbian contacts are severely limited by social pressures as well as by economic dependence on family and husband. The existence of Golden Orchid Associations became possible only by the rise of a textile industry in south China which enabled women to become economically independent. The traditional social and economic attachment of women to the home has so far prevented the emergence in modern China of a lesbian community on even so limited a scale as that of male homosexuals.

BIBLIOGRAPHY. *Duanxiu pian (Records of the Cut Sleeve)*, in *Xiangyan congshu*, Shanghai, 1909–11; Bret Hinsch, *Passions of the Cut Sleeve: A History of the Male Homosexual Tradition in China*, Berkeley: University of California Press, 1990; Samshasha (Xiaoming Xiong) [Ng Siu Ming], *Zhongguo tongxingai shilu (History of Homosexuality in China)*, Hong Kong: Pink Triangle Press, 1984; Weixingshi guanshaizhu, *Zhongguo tongxinglian mishi (Secret History of Chinese Homosexuality)*, 2 vols., Hong Kong: Yuzhou chubanshe, 1964.

Bret Hinsch

CHIZH, VLADIMIR FIODOROVICH (1855–19?)

Russian psychiatrist. From a noble family from the government of Smolensk, in 1878 Chizh was graduated with distinc-

tion from the Medico-Chirurgical Academy in Saint Petersburg and entered naval service. In 1880 he was appointed resident physician in the psychiatric division of the hospital on Kronstadt and, in the following year to the Primary Asylum for the Mentally Ill and resident physician at the prison hospital in the Imperial capital. This position brought him into contact with a lesbian patient whom he described in a paper read in Saint Petersburg on February 1, 1882 and published under the title "K ucheniiu ob 'izvrashchenii polovogo chuvstva' (*Die conträre Sexualempfindung*)" [On the Doctrine of "Perversion of Sexual Feeling"] in the *Meditsinskie pribavleniia k Morskomu sborniku* [Medical Supplements to the Naval Magazine] of the same year. The 26-year-old Russian author realized what the German and Austrian psychiatrists who wrote the first clinical papers on sexual inversion had missed: that so far from being a rare phenomenon, an isolated "freak of nature," homosexuality was the explanation of many of the cases of sodomy that came before the courts every day. As late as 1886, in the first edition of *Psychopathia Sexualis*, Richard von **Krafft-Ebing** painstakingly enumerated all the individual case studies (35 in all) that had appeared in the psychiatric literature as if each one were some extraordinary discovery.

Meanwhile, Veniamin Mikhailovich Tarnovskii (1837–1906) had published a longer work entitled "Izvrashchenie polovogo chuvstva" [Perversion of Sexual Feeling] in the *Vestnik klinicheskoi i sudebnoi psikhiatrii i nevropatologii* [Herald of Clinical and Forensic Psychiatry and Neuropathology] in 1884. Two years later a German version of his work appeared as *Die krankhaften Erscheinungen des Geschlechtssinnes* [The Morbid Manifestations of the Sexual Instinct], through which Chizh's insight reached the learned public of Central and Western Europe.

Following the Russification of the University of Iur'ev (now Tartu) by the government of Alexander III in 1890, Chizh was named to the chair of nervous and mental diseases, a post he held to the end of his career. After attending the Fifth International Congress of Criminal Anthropology in Amsterdam in 1901, he wrote an unsympathetic account of Arnold **Aletrino**'s paper on "The Social Situation of the Uranist" that was published in "Piatyĭ mezhdunarodnyĭ kongress kriminal'noĭ antropologii v Amsterdame 9–14 sentiabria 1901 g." in *Voprosy filosofii i psikhologii* in 1902. His article reveals that the President of the Congress, Gerard Anton van Hamel (1842–1917), asked the representatives of the press not to print anything about the discussion of Aletrino's paper. This is an early example of how the psychiatric profession, when challenged by the homophile **movement**, took an overtly hostile stance in the hope of denying the public access to the new understanding of the subject which the experts who rallied to its support were promoting.

Warren Johansson

CHRISTIANITY

The body of beliefs and practices characterizing Christianity, a religious tradition based on the life and teachings of **Jesus** of Nazareth ("the Christ") (ca. 3 B.C.–A.D. 33), was defined by the Christian church as it took shape under the empire of **Rome**. Inasmuch as this consolidation was achieved gradually and obscurely, it is difficult to say when the church and its ideology crystalized. By about A.D. 200, however, the church had come to recognize the texts making up the **New Testament** as a single canon. After some hesitation, the Hebrew Bible, known to Christians as the **Old Testament**, was taken from **Judaism** and also accepted as divinely inspired. From this point onwards, Christian doctrines were elaborated by a group of intellectuals, known as the Fathers of the Church or the **Patristic** writers, beginning with such figures as Origen, **Clement of Alexandria** and Tertullian.

It was these theologians who pieced together the often contradictory and ambiguous scriptural statements about sex and homosexuality into a consistent doctrine. Though they based their exegesis upon the Bible, they were inevitably influenced by philosophical and religious currents of their own time, especially Greek **Stoicism** and **Neo-Platonism** and by rival mystery cults such as **Manichaeanism** and **Gnosticism**. Not all these interpreters of what the Christian message entailed agreed, and as a result there were competing Christian groups, most of which were eventually eliminated. Still today there are differences on such sexually related topics as divorce, celibacy, and so forth between Roman Catholics and members of various eastern branches of Christianity which date from the foundations of Christianity, including Coptic, Nestorian, and various Orthodox Churches. In practice, most of these churches have been more tolerant of homosexuality than the Roman Catholic Church and its Protestant offshoots.

Augustinianism. The dominant Christian attitude in the west has been what might be called the Augustinian one which essentially regarded celibacy as more desirable than marriage and only tolerated sexual activity within marriage for the purpose of procreation. St. **Augustine** (d. 430), one of the great scholars of the ancient world, had converted to the austere faith of Manichaeanism after receiving a classical education. It seemed to his mind more suited to his Neo-Platonic and Stoic ideals than the Christianity of his mother. In Manichaean belief, which drew heavily from **Zoroastrianism**, intercourse leading to procreation was particularly evil because it caused other souls to be imprisoned in bodies, thus continuing the cycle of good versus evil.

Augustine was a member of the Manichaean religion for some eleven years but never reached the stage of the Elect in part because of his inability to control his sexual appetites. He kept a mistress, fathered a child, and according to his own statement, struggled to overcome his lustful appetites everyday by praying: "Give me chastity, and continence, but do not give it yet." Recognizing his own inability to give up sexual intercourse, Augustine finally arrived at the conclusion that the only way to control his venereal desire was through marriage. He expelled his mistress and his son from his house, became engaged to a young girl not yet of age for wedlock (probably under 12 years of age), and planned a marriage. Unable to abstain from sex, he turned to prostitutes, went through a religious crisis, and in the process became converted to Christianity.

Miraculously, he found he could control his sexual desires and no longer even desired a wife. Once he managed to gain control of his own "lustful" desires, Augustine expressed hostility to the act of coitus. He reported that he knew nothing that brought "the manly mind down from the heights [more] than a woman's caresses, and that joining of bodies without which one cannot have a wife." It was through concupiscence or lust that the genitals lost the docility of innocence and were no longer amenable to the will. He accepted the Biblical statements that the Christian God had commanded human beings to multiply and propagate, and thus reproduction was to be tolerated, but he insisted that it be done without lust. He concluded that "We ought not to condemn marriage because of the evil of lust, nor must we praise lust because of the good of marriage."

Through marriage, and only through marriage, could the lust associated with coitus be transferred to a duty, and then only when the act was employed for human generation. In his mind, abstinence from sex was the highest good, but marriage was second, providing that the purpose of sex within marriage was for the purpose of procreation. All other sex was sinful including coitus within marriage not performed in the proper position (the female on her back and facing the male)

and using the proper appendages and orifices (penis in vagina).

St. Augustine's views became the views of the western church centered in Rome. Taken literally, the Augustinian view was no more hostile to homosexuality than to any other form of non-procreative sex. In general there was no extensive discussion of homosexuality by any of the early Church Fathers, and most of the references are incidental. What references do occur, however, leave no doubt as to the basic hostility of these early theologians, and homosexual activities were usually classified as on the level of adultery. The Eastern Orthodox Churches on the other hand looked upon it somewhat less seriously, classifying it as equivalent to fornication.

The Medieval Church. The Augustinian views were modified in the thirteenth century by St. Thomas **Aquinas**, who held that homosexual activities, though similar to other sins of lust, were more sinful because they were also sins against **nature**. The sins against nature in descending order were (1) masturbation, (2) intercourse in an unnatural position, (3) copulation with the same sex (homosexuality and lesbianism), and (4) sex with nonhumans (bestiality). Aquinas was willing to concede that on the surface such sins were not as serious as adultery or rape or seduction, sexual activities which injured others, but he argued that since God had set the order of nature, and these activities contravened it, they were an injury to God and therefore more serious.

Communicating these theological concepts to the believers was not easy and was not always done consistently. Sermons, homilies, illustrations, were used by the early church although there was an ambivalence over whether people were more likely to adhere to the church belief system if the rewards of heaven were emphasized or whether the punishments of hell received the greatest attention. The medieval period saw both approaches used at different times and by different groups.

In general the church took control over sexual matters until the fourteenth century, and so church teachings and laws are a key to understanding attitudes. One of the key sources in the early medieval Church is the **penitential** literature. Originally penance had been a way of reconciling the sinner with God and had taken place through open confession. The earliest penitentials put sexual purity at a high premium, and failure to observe the sexual regulations was classified as equal to idolatry (reversion to paganism) and homicide. Ultimately public penance was replaced by private penance and confession which was regulated by the manuals or penitentials designed to guide those who were hearing them. Most of the early penitentials classified homosexual and lesbian activities as equivalent to fornication. Later ones classified such activities as equivalent to adultery although some writers distinguished between interfemoral intercourse and anal intercourse and between fellatio or oral–genital contacts. Anal intercourse was regarded as being the most serious sin. There was, however, wide variation in the treatment of sexual activities in the penitentials, and this variation drew the scathing denunciation of St. Peter **Damian** (1007–1072), a homophobe, who in his *Liber Gomorrhianus* blasted the church's tolerance of homosexuality. He urged Pope Leo IX to set more rigorous standards for penitentials and to deal with the widespread homosexuality among the clergy and others. The pope accepted Peter's dedication of his work to him but emphasized that it was necessary for him as pope to season justice with mercy. Peter's treatise, however, was the beginning of growing hostility to homosexuality which also coincided with the growing power of the church.

Aiding and abetting these stronger actions against homosexuality was the growth of **canon law**. Among the earliest collections was the *Decretum* of Burchard of Worms (1000–1025), a contemporary of Damian, and Ivo of Chartres (1091–1116),

who made a more complete collection than Burchard. Both collections contain numerous canons condemning sodomy, bestiality, fellatio, pederasty, and lesbianism. Building on these pioneering efforts was the work of the jurist Gratian who in about 1140 completed his *A Harmony of Discordant Canons* which revolutionized the study of canon law and gave it the intellectual coherence which it previously had lacked. In spite of the earlier efforts of Ivo and Burchard, Gratian paid relatively little attention to homosexuality although he did indicate that such activities were far more heinous than adultery or fornication. By the late twelfth century, the hostile attitudes of Peter Damian had found their way into both the legal codes and the theological writings.

Increasingly, in fact, deviance from the church's code on sexual preference was equated with deviance from accepted church doctrine, that is homosexuals could be regarded as proponents of **heresy**. Sodomy came to be regarded as the most heinous of sexual offenses, even worse than incest, and as civil law began to take over from canon law, it could be punished as a **capital crime**. This seems to be most noticeable in the civil law enacted by various municipalities who starting from the church doctrine of heresy branded homosexuality as something which would bring divine wrath upon the inhabitants of those cities where it was widely practiced. These fears of homosexuality were particularly noticeable in the fourteenth century when the advent of the Black Death led to some homosexuals' suffering particularly grisly punishments. Increasingly, in fact, civil law became far more hostile to homosexuality than canon law although the justification for the civil law provisions was often a religious one.

Protestantism. The trend toward civil control of sexuality was accentuated by the development of Protestantism in the sixteenth century although the Protestants were not any less hostile to homosexuality than the Catholic Church. Martin Luther, for example, stated that homosexuality came from the devil and should be treated as the work of the devil. While John Calvin was not quite so hostile, he emphasized that homosexuality was a sin against nature.

In the sixteenth century accusations of sexual licence, including sodomy, became part of the lexicon of invective of the Protestant–Catholic quarrel. Catholics denounced Calvin for his supposed pederasty, a charge that was completely unfounded. In the case of Calvin's lieutenant, Théodore de **Bèze** however, a relationship with one Audebert seems to have some substance. In compensation Protestant writers repeatedly denounced the Papacy as a sink of sexual iniquity. Somewhat surprisingly, Henry VIII's investigators were unable to find much evidence of homosexual behavior in their enquiries leading to the dissolution of the monasteries in England. In 1730–31 the great Dutch persecution of sodomites occurred, and in the accompanying propaganda the old charges against Roman Catholicism were revived. In Catholic countries themselves, the dissolution of the Jesuit order in 1773 was preceded by accusations of sodomy.

The most detailed of the Anglican writers on sexual matters, Jeremy Taylor (1613–1667), did not regard homosexual behavior as any worse than any other sexual sins. He insisted in all cases that such matters as motive, occasion, and consequences of the act be considered; this perhaps is the first breakthrough in western Christian attitudes since St. Augustine. Unfortunately, English civil law did not reflect this tolerance, and it was the civil law which by this time was dominant.

Modern Developments. In nineteenth-century England, the rise of the Anglo-Catholic movement within the established Church, with its strong aesthetic component, attracted many homosexual communicants. Yet no real changes in official church attitudes took place until the twentieth century, when a number of churches, led by the Quakers, the **Angli-**cans and the Unitarian-Universalists, in the period following World War II, modified their stand on homosexuality. Their action was followed by many of the mainline Protestant Churches in the United States and elsewhere. Similar changes took place in some segments of Judaism, particularly Reform Judaism, and even Conservative Judaism.

To counter the refusal of evangelical and fundamentalist Protestants to change, the Metropolitan Community Church developed, emphasizing that Biblically, homosexuals were not anathema. Even among Churches which officially did not modify their stands, special homosexual groups and organizations such as Dignity, which has considerable support from many elements in the Catholic Church. Some religiously oriented organizations such as the Affirmation (gay Mormons), however, remain ostracized by the main religious body with which they would like to be affiliated.

Conclusion. Christian religions traditionally have been hostile not only to homosexuality but to sexuality in general. They were the dominant institutions in establishing attitudes about homosexuality which were not so much Biblical or even particularly Christian, but a reflection of undercurrents of thought in existence at the time Christianity emerged. These extraneous ideas about sex and homosexuality were incorporated into Christian teachings by theologians and canon lawyers who then erected a belief system upon them, and from the church they were communicated to the wider public at large. Only when these extraneous ideas are effectively challenged, as they have been in the last few decades, can the churches think through their attitudes and concepts about sexuality and homosexuality; this has been taking place in the last few decades, but there is still a long way to go.

See also **Churches, Gay; Clergy, Gay; Monasticism; Protestantism.**

BIBLIOGRAPHY. James Brundage, *Law, Sex, and Christian Society in Medieval Europe,* Chicago: University of Chicago Press, 1988; Vern L. Bullough, *Sexual Variance in Society and History,* Chicago: University of Chicago Press, 1976; Vern L. Bullough and James Brundage, eds., *Sexual Practices and the Medieval Church,* Buffalo: Prometheus Books, 1982.

Vern L. Bullough

CHRISTINA, QUEEN OF SWEDEN (1626–1689)

The daughter of Gustavus II Adolphus and Maria Eleonora of Brandenburg, she lost her father at the age of six when he was killed in the Thirty Years War. Until 1644 Sweden was ruled by a regency headed by the Imperial Chancellor Axel Count Oxenstierna. The talented girl received an excellent education and was reared almost exclusively under male guidance. On December 17, 1644, she assumed personal rule, but remained another two years under Oxenstierna's influence, then chose Gabriel de la Gardie as her chief counselor. More interested in science and art than in politics, she took little part in the negotiations at Bromsebro (1645) and Osnabrück (1647) that culminated in the Peace of Westphalia (1648), which redrew the political map of Europe on lines that largely remained until the French Revolution. She was a generous patron of the sciences, supported native scholars and corresponded with foreign ones, and attracted such intellects as Descartes and Grotius to her court. The former she is reputed to have asked for advice on her amorous disposition.

Her aversion to official duties, her extravagance, and the favor that she accorded to constantly changing and unworthy courtiers earned her the displeasure of her subjects, and her growing sympathies for Catholicism provoked the resistance of the Lutheran clergy. At a session of the Parliament in Uppsala in 1654 she abdicated in favor of her cousin Karl-Gustav of Pfalz-Zweibrücken and his male descendants. In Brussels she converted secretly to Catholicism, then at Innsbruck she formally adopted the new faith and journeyed to Rome, where she kept a brilliant court and soon became the center of a circle of scholars. She undertook numerous travels, and attracted attention by her political activity in papal and ecclesiastical affairs and also in French, Polish, and above all Swedish matters. The friendship of Cardinal Azzolino, her adviser in financial and economic affairs, played a great role in the last years of her life. She died in Rome in 1689.

Contemporary accounts of Christina unanimously emphasize the masculine qualities of her personality. Her deep voice and her fondness for men's clothing are particularly noted. A description of her by the Duc de Guise mentions that "her hand is white and well-shaped, but resembles a man's more than a woman's. The face is large, all the features quite pronounced. . . . The footwear resembles a man's, and likewise she has a male voice, and almost her whole deportment is male too. She sets great store on appearing as an Amazon. She is as proud as her father. She speaks eight languages, French in particular like a native Parisian." Another account of her tells that "all in all, she struck me as a handsome little boy." The ascription of her homosexuality is based on the fact that she refused marriage, even with so distinguished a suitor as the Kurfürst of Brandenburg. On the other hand she is supposed to have had a series of erotic escapades with men, in particular the Italian Monaldesco, whom she later had murdered, allegedly because he learned of her lesbian tendencies. Only one of her female partners is known, Countess Ebba Sparre, whom she met in Paris in 1654 after her abdication. Many of her letters to the Countess contain the epithet "belle." The German historian Leopold von Ranke said of her that she was "the greatest princely woman from the race of intermediate types. Women's tasks she never assumed, . . . but on the other hand she sat boldly on horseback. While hunting she hit the game with her first shot. She studied Tacitus and Plato and understood these authors at times better than did philologists by profession."

Christina of Sweden is thus a classic type of woman with a decidedly masculine intellect and personality that carried over, at least in part, into her sexual life. The film *Queen Christina* (1932), in which the heroine was played by the Swedish actress Greta Garbo in one of her memorable roles, resonated with homosexual and lesbian innuendo; it has served to reinforce the image of the queen in modern times.

BIBLIOGRAPHY. Sophie Hoechstetter, "Christine, Königin von Schweden in ihrer Jugend," *Jahrbuch für sexuelle Zwischenstufen*, 9 (1908), 168–96; Albert Moll, *Berühmte Homosexuelle*, Wiesbaden: J. F. Bergmann, 1910.

Warren Johansson

CHRYSOSTOM, JOHN, SAINT (CA. 347–407)

Greek patriarch of Constantinople, the first to claim its primacy over the eastern sees, and leading theologian of the Orthodox church. This most famous Greek father fully brought the extreme asceticism of the desert fathers into the mainstream of the church.

Chrysostom was educated at Antioch by the pagan sophist and rhetorician Libanius, more of whose works have survived than of any other pagan writer. After being baptized about 370, John retired to the desert for asceticism and study, but after ten years illness forced him to return to civilization. Ordained deacon in 381 and priest in 386, he won fame for his inspiring sermons and only reluctantly became bishop of Constantinople in 398. Having alienated many by strident criticism and fanaticism, including the empress Eudoxia and bishops in the Eastern provinces, who were resentful of his attempts to subordinate them to his see

which he deemed preeminent, he was deposed by the Synod of the Oak in 403. Banished, recalled by popular demand, and then banished again in 404, he died in exile in Armenia in 407.

For his eloquence he received the title Chrysostom, "Golden mouthed," but many Western scholars consider his theology mediocre. In the Antiochene tradition, he expounded scripture historically, practically, and devotionally, denouncing luxury and demanding alms for the poor. His numerous writings fill volumes 47 to 64 in J.-P. Migne's *Patrologia Graeca*. The people loved him for his charities and his support of hospitals, as well as for his devout and eloquent denunciations of the extravagance of courtiers. He forbade the clergy to keep "sisters" as servants, and confined wandering monks to monasteries where they could be disciplined. Upon his second deposition arranged by his numerous enemies, the populace set fire to the Cathedral of Hagia Sophia and the Senate House. In 437 the Emperor had to bring his bones back to the capital, imploring divine forgiveness for the empire's persecution of the saint. Probably the most venomous of a long line of vehement early Christians who preached against Judaism, he was also the most violent of a long series of homophobes stretching back to St. Paul.

Chrysostom's invectives against homosexual sins reveal the paradoxes and circular reasoning in which the Christian apologist was trapped by his need to justify the apodictic prohibition of the **Old Testament** in terms adequate to Greek philosophical notions of right and wrong. The **Stoic** reverence for nature and the **Manichaean** condemnation of pleasure both determined his rhetoric; on the one hand "the passions in fact are all dishonorable," but on the other homosexual acts fail even to provide pleasure: "Sins against nature . . . are more arduous and less rewarding, so much so that they cannot even claim to provide pleasure, since real pleasure is only according to nature." The later view that "excess of desire" led to homosexual depravity he expounded as the outcome of God's abandonment of those in question because of the heinous sin of—excess of desire. Aware that the Greeks had long practiced **pederasty**, he nevertheless denounced homosexuality as a loathsome invention, "a new and insufferable crime." And he was among the first to rank homosexual sins as the supreme evil than which "nothing is more demented or noxious," though in other passages he let the rhetorician in him declare that "there are ten thousand sins equal to or worse than this one." He managed to reason that the male who takes the passive role with another not only loses his maleness but fails to become a woman; he forfeits his own sex without acquiring the opposite gender.

Chrysostom thought the gravity of homosexual transgression merited God's punishment of **Sodom**: "The very nature of the punishment reflected the nature of the sin [of the Sodomites]. Even as they devised a barren coitus, not having as its end the procreation of children, so did God bring on them a punishment as made the womb of the land forever barren and destitute of all fruit." Chrysostom is thus a classic exemplar of Christian unreason in regard to homosexuality, but also the prototype of preachers and moral reformers in later centuries who from the pulpit incited the authorities and the populace to campaigns of repression against those guilty of "unnatural vice." More homophobic even than St. **Augustine**, he set the stage for the persecutions that would fill the annals of the centuries to come.

William A. Percy

CHUBB, RALPH NICHOLAS (1892–1960)

English writer and artist. His experiences connected with World War I created severe emotional stress which affected him for the rest of his life. Between the two world wars, he retired to rural England and, in the tradition of Wil-

liam Blake, he produced an astonishing series of hand-made illustrated books in limited editions. These include, among others, *The Sun Spirit* (1931), *The Heavenly Cupid* (1934), *Water-Cherubs* (1937), and *The Secret Country* (1939). There were also some earlier and later works that do not match these books for quality.

Chubb's memory was rescued by the bibliophile Anthony Reid and the bookseller Timothy Smith, and his first editions are much sought after by a limited audience of pedophile men. A mystic, Chubb created a private mythology focused on adolescent boys, especially the youngest ones, who were the erotic gods of his pantheon. Although he was a pacifist, this commitment did not stop him from sadistic fantasies about older teenagers. His books blended poetry, fiction, drawings, and paintings to create a never-never land where he was free to pursue hordes of naked boys. His real sexual life was unhappy.

BIBLIOGRAPHY. Timothy d'Arch Smith, *Love in Earnest*, London: Routledge & Kegan Paul, 1970.
Stephen Wayne Foster

CHURCHES, GAY

The emergence of **Christian** churches with predominantly gay and lesbian congregations, as well as interest groups within or allied to existing denominations, is a recent phenomenon, centered in the English-speaking world. There are records of homosexual monks, nuns, and priests, especially in the later **Middle Ages** and in early modern times, but no indication that they even thought of organizing on the basis of their sexual preference. Christian homosexuals drawn to particular parishes, where cliques occasionally even became a visible segment of the congregation, would not openly avow this shift in the church's character: they remained closeted gay Christians, so to speak.

The contemporary trend toward gay churches—and other religious organizations, including gay synagogues—is a product of the increasing visibility of the gay/lesbian **movement** in the 1960s, which in turn had its roots in the well publicized social assertion of the civil-rights and antiwar movements that preceded it. Perceived exclusion from full participation in mainstream churches impelled many gay men and lesbians to set up their own institutions.

Background. A homoerotic atmosphere enveloped the High Anglican movement as it emerged in Britain toward the middle of the nineteenth century. The emphasis on elaborate liturgy appealed to the aesthetic sense, while the revival in some sectors of clerical **celibacy** (as suggested by the alternative expression "Anglo-Catholicism," Roman Catholic clergy being always celibate) relieved homosexual priests from the traditional Protestant clerical marriage. Appalled by the goings on that they detected in some High Anglican parishes, members of the broad church attacked them as "un-English and unmanly." This disapproval notwithstanding, the alliance of **aestheticism** with aspects of **Anglicanism** was destined to endure.

Out of this ferment came Charles Webster **Leadbeater** (1854–1934), who began his career as an obscure curate in the Church of England. After many years as a leader of the Theosophical Society in Ceylon, India, and Australia, Leadbeater founded the Liberal Catholic Church in Sydney in 1916; the organization's claim to apostolic succession was assured by his receiving his orders from a man who had obtained them from an Old Catholic bishop in England. A pederast, known familiarly as the "swish bish," Bishop Leadbeater liked to surround himself with boy acolytes. Although the Liberal Catholic church has since modified its original character, the atmosphere developed in Leadbeater's Sydney establishment gives it a claim of being the first gay church.

Gay people have emerged from all denominations. For converts, however, those with rich liturgical traditions seem to have more appeal (as Ptolemy anticipated in the astrological classic *Tetrabiblos* [second century])—suggesting a parallel with the well-known homosexual attachment to theatre and opera. This aspect need not preclude a deeper concern with religious values, as in tribal societies in which the **berdache** exercised priestly functions. At all events, until the 1960s many gay men and women felt drawn to particular congregations, largely because of the sympathetic reception they received there, regardless of whether the individual pastor was homosexual. Churches of choice tended to be theologically liberal, rather than conservative Protestant or Roman Catholic. Significantly, the first convention of the **Mattachine** Society was held in 1953 at the First Universalist Church in Los Angeles, headed by the Reverend Wallace de Ortega Maxey.

In the early 1950s in England a group of Anglican clergy and physicians began to study the question of homosexuality under official ecclesiastical auspices. This work led in due course to the pioneering study by Canon Derrick Sherwin **Bailey**, *Homosexuality and the Western Christian Tradition* (1955), to the **Wolfenden Report** (1957), and to sodomy **law** reform (1967). Apart from his historical survey, Bailey sought to reinterpret some of the scriptural passages, holding, for example, that the Sodom story in Genesis 18–19 concerns not homosexuality, but inhospitality.

This controversial trend in exegesis continued in the work of such scholars as John McNeill (a Jesuit until forced out of the order in 1987) and Roman Catholic convert Professor John Boswell of Yale, first to be promoted to that rank in an Ivy League university because of a major monograph on homosexuality. Despite the fact that these scriptural reinterpretations have not commanded assent among mainstream exegetes, gay churches have eagerly embraced them as the "enabling act" for their foundation, offering assurance—

at least in their own view—that Christianity was not primordially or essentially antihomosexual. Needless to say, this optimistic supposition puzzles and even scandalizes the average Christian believer.

Gay Religious Organizations. In 1968 the charismatic Reverend Troy Perry (originally ordained in a southern Pentecostal denomination) began the first American gay church with a handful of congregants in his southern California home. This was clearly an idea whose time had come. Three years later 600 men and women gathered each Sunday for services in a downtown Los Angeles building acquired by the Metropolitan Community Church, as the organization had come to be known. Missions spread the church to other American cities and abroad, chiefly in English-speaking countries. By 1983 the Universal Fellowship of Metropolitan Community Churches (UFMCC) included 195 congregations in ten countries.

While attempting to maintain organizational unity around a broad ecumenical theology, many UFMCC pastors (including Perry) are theologically conservative, taking a fundamentalist approach to scripture. In order to maintain this hermeneutic, they generally follow gay exegetes who deny the antihomosexual character of key passages in the Old and New Testament. Some maintain that **Jesus**—an unmarried man in a Jewish milieu where marriage and procreation were de rigueur even for the religious elite—had a passionate relationship with John, the **beloved disciple**. Liturgically and sociologically the UFMCC tends to be of a "low church" character, with notable exceptions in some congregations. The evangelical-fundamentalist domination of the UFMCC may be regarded as a response to the homophobic vehemence of the mainstream fundamentalist churches, which drives gay Christians out of their fold with a vengeance and forces them into an external redoubt, in contrast to the relatively more tolerant atmosphere, hospitable to internal gay caucuses, of the more liberal churches.

Other gay churches with a generally liberal approach developed in some American cities, contributing to the rise of gay synagogues, beginning in New York in 1973 and spreading across the country and abroad. In Paris the Belgian Baptist Reverend Joseph Doucé founded the the Centre du Christ Libérateur in 1976, which branched into some other European countries, an exception to the rule that gay churches, like gay **student** groups, characterize English-speaking countries.

Although the UFMCC and the other gay churches exist outside the existing denominations, many gay people have preferred to retain their connection with their own churches, securing within them a better situation for themselves. They form study groups, typically consisting of both homosexual and heterosexual persons, to reexamine church doctrine and pressure the denomination's governing body to adopt a statement in favor of gay rights. In 1963 a group of English Quakers (Friends) privately published the first statement of this kind. In 1970 the Unitarian Universalist Association (U.S.) and the Lutheran Church in America declared support, both with full denominational backing. Many other statements have followed (*see* Batchelor, appendix). Recognition of the inherent dignity of homosexual persons has gained endorsement more readily than overt sexual relations; the latter are usually permitted only with the stipulation that lifetime fidelity be maintained. Although a particular bone of contention has been ordination of homosexual men and women, some openly gay people have been consecrated, including the lesbian priest Ellen Barrett by New York's Anglican bishop Paul Moore, Jr. (1976). At its convention in the summer of 1988, the Assembly of the United Church of Canada with 800,000 members voted after long discussion to ordain worthy homosexual men and women—a decision that provoked threats of secession.

Many denominations have gay and lesbian affiliates, seeking official recognition and sometimes holding services in established churches. Their prototype, the Catholic-linked Dignity, was founded in San Diego in 1969. It was quickly followed by an episcopal twin, Integrity (1972), and by Affinity (Mormon), Brethren/Mennonite Council on Gay Concerns, Evangelicals Concerned, the Seventh Day Adventist Kinship, and others. While they aim to function within their denominations, many have found themselves forced outside. After a long period of quasi-toleration, the publication of Cardinal Joseph Ratzinger's Vatican letter in 1986, perhaps inspired by the reactionary new American cardinals Law of Boston and O'Connor of New York, began a process of exclusion of Dignity itself, the largest group, which attracted about 7000 members at its zenith.

Rationale. Many participants hold that the purpose of the gay churches and organizations is not to set up permanent rivals to mainstream churches but to provide transitional institutions awaiting a time when the established denominations welcome homosexual persons as full members. Nonreligious and atheist gays regard the new religious organizations as an aberration, a collaborationist movement, even a kind of surrender to the enemy—a negative view that cannot be readily dismissed considering the historic role of Christian churches in persecuting homosexuals.

Nonetheless, the organizational success of the gay groups speaks for itself. Because religion has deep roots in human life and psyche, many homosexuals in spite of the historical record seek outlets for their feelings somewhere in the Western religious tradition which has dominated the culture in which they were raised. Homosexuals are hardly the first group which has sought to alleviate oppression by working from within to change the attitudes and practices of their oppressors. In this respect the gay movement has more in common with the black civil rights movement which had a deep foundation in the black churches than with the feminist movement, which made little if any appeal to traditional religion. In any event, the persistent dialogue which has ensued with the leaders of the established churches has perhaps done more to undermine, dilute, and perhaps eventually neutralize a major source of Western homophobia than all the appeals issued by homosexuals using purely secular, biologistic, and psychological value systems. Mainstream leaders and their congregations are being educated and continually forced to rethink their positions. Progress within Protestant denominations is dramatic indeed, viewed from the perspective of centuries of Christian homophobia. In recent decades clergy have routinely volunteered or been enlisted as allies in confrontations with homophobic insurgents, and provided critical support for passage of gay rights bills, the ending of police harassment, and the like. It is a long way from burnings at the stake to the ordination of an avowedly homosexual priest in a major denomination, and the gay Christian groups must be given credit for contributing to that evolution.

Gay churches have also provided the wider community with leadership, money, volunteer workers, and demonstrators, meeting space, printing facilities, and publicity when these requisites were scarce. In some smaller towns the gay church is the only social facility that homosexuals can openly attend and the only venue where gay political activity is permitted.

Unlike most bars and baths, gay churches do not discriminate on the basis of age or looks. Pastors and congregations are committed to providing understanding and support: when all else fails they are there. Filling a genuine social need for their parishioners, gay churches are likely to continue.

See also **Clergy, Gay; Heresy; Monasticism.**

BIBLIOGRAPHY. Edward Batchelor, Jr., ed., *Homosexuality and Ethics*, New York: Pilgrim Press, 1980; John Fortunato, *Embracing the Exile: Healing Journeys of Gay Christians*, New York: Seabury Press, 1982; Jeannine Grammick, ed., *Homosexuality and the Catholic Church*, Chicago: Thomas Moore Press, 1983; Robert Nugent, *A Challenge to Love: Gay and Lesbian Catholics in the Church*, New York: Crossroad, 1983; Troy Perry (with Charles Lucas), *The Lord is My Shepherd and He Knows I'm Gay*, Los Angeles: Nash, 1972; Tom Swicegood, *Our God Too*, New York: Pyramid, 1974; Jim Wickliff, ed., *In Celebration*, Oak Park, IL: Integrity, 1975.

Wayne R. Dynes

CICERO, MARCUS TULLIUS (106–43 B. C.)

Roman politician, orator, and writer, who left behind a corpus of Latin prose (speeches, treatises, letters) that make him one of the great authors of classical antiquity. Unsuccessful in politics, he was overestimated as a philosopher by the Middle Ages and the Renaissance and underestimated in modern times, but was and is ranked as one of the greatest masters of Latin style. His career as an orator began in 81 B.C., and from the very beginning his speeches revealed his rhetorical gifts. His denunciation of Verres, the proconsul who had plundered the province of Sicily, opened the way to his election as aedile, praetor, and then consul, but subsequently the intrigues of his enemies led to his banishment from Rome (58/57), followed by his triumphal return. In the civil war he took the side of Pompey and so failed again, but was pardoned by the victorious Caesar, after whose death he launched a rhetorical attack on Mark Antony. The formation of the triumvirate meant that Cicero was to be proscribed by his opponent and murdered by his henchmen.

The theme of homosexuality figures in Cicero's political writings as part of his invective. In the last turbulent century of the Roman republic in which he lived, a contrast between the austere virtue of earlier times and the luxury and vice of the present had become commonplace. Also, as we know from the slightly later genre of satirical poetry, a taste for salacious gossip had taken root in the metropolis. In his orations Cicero remorselessly flays the homosexual acts of his enemies, contrasting homosexual love with the passion inspired by women which is "far more of natural inspiration." The glorification of male dignity and virility goes hand in hand with the condemnation of effeminacy as unnatural and demeaning. Something of the Roman antipathy to Greek *paiderasteia* transpires from Cicero's condemnation of the nudity which the Greeks flaunted in their public **baths** and **gymnasia**, and from his assertion that the Greeks were inconsistent in their notion of **friendship**. He pointedly noted: "Why is it that no one falls in love with an ugly youth or a handsome old man?" Effeminacy and passive homosexuality are unnatural and blameworthy in a free man, though Cicero remained enough under the influence of Greek mores to express no negative judgment on the practice of keeping handsome young slaves as minions of their master. The right of a free man to have sexual relations with his male slaves Cicero never challenges, though he distinguishes clearly between the slave in the entourage of his master and the "hustler" whose viciousness is imputed to his keeper. The Judaic condemnation of homosexuality per se had not yet reached Rome, but the distinction that had existed in Hellenic law and custom between acts worthy and unworthy of a citizen was adopted and even heightened by the combination of appeal to Roman civic virtue and his own rhetorical flair.

Cicero's denunciation of homosexual conduct in his enemies—not of exclusive "homosexuality," which is never in question—remained in the context of effeminacy, debauchery, and other sexual offenses designated by the general term *stuprum*. He depicted the other side as living in a demimonde of vicious and corrupt associates who revel shamelessly in drunken orgies. The impudent Mark Antony had a clientele of drunkards and debauchees like himself, his house was *impudica*, "unchaste," and he himself was *impurus*, which is to be understood as the equivalent of Greek *akáthartos*, "impure," the term applied to the passive-effeminate homosexual who is defiled by the lust of others. The antithesis was the virile man who guards his honor in his relations with other men, who has not submitted to their sexual advances. Accordingly, the followers of Cataline were denounced as young men who are *impuri impudicique*, ready *amare et amari*, "to love and to be loved," hence having both active and passive homosexual relations in a promiscuous manner. At the same time Cicero defended the honor of his clients by saying that the accusations against them are no more than malicious gossip.

The character of the freeman stood in contrast to the baseness of the slave who freely lent himself to the unchaste desires of his master. According to Cicero, Verres surrounded himself with slaves whose degradation infected his whole entourage, while treating free men as if they were slaves. The same inversion of the social hierarchy attached to Clodius as the heir of Cataline. The term *patientia* used with reference to Verres implies the passivity in sexual relations that is degrading and unworthy of a free man, just as in the case of Mark Antony, charged with having "prostituted himself to all," much like the Timarchus whom **Aeschines** had denounced centuries earlier in Athens for a like failing. The other aspect of passive homosexuality was the lapse into **effeminacy**, so that Cicero's enemies were accused of delight in luxury, the adoption of women's gestures, and the wearing of feminine clothes and makeup.

Cicero's rhetoric thus had two sides: the attempt to discredit opponents by inflammatory imputations of homosexual conduct and of sexual immorality in general—a type of smear to be followed in political life down to modern times; and his rigorous demarcation between the active and the passive partner in sexual relations, the active role being the only one worthy of a man and a citizen, the passive role being equated with effeminacy and servility. This view has its roots in the primary distinction made by classical civilization between the active and the passive which, however, Cicero heightened for his own tendentious ends.

See also **McCarthyism**.

BIBLIOGRAPHY. Françoise Gonfroy, "Homosexualité et idéologie esclavagiste chez Cicéron," *Dialogues d'histoire ancienne*, 4 (1978), 219–62; Ilona Opelt, *Die lateinischen Schimpfwörter und verwandte sprachliche Erscheinungen*, Heidelberg: Winter, 1965.

Warren Johansson

CINEMA
See **Film**.

CIRCLES AND AFFINITY GROUPS

Sociologists treat the group as a plurality of individuals defined by some principle of recruitment and by a set of membership rights and obligations. Sometimes these groups may be visible, as in the case of medieval guilds and modern collegiate fraternities and sororities; in other instances, as the freemasons and the illuminati, they are more or less secret. Homosexuals and lesbians do not belong in toto to any such well-defined grouping, though outside observers, such as the French literary critic Charles Augustin Sainte-Beuve, have sometimes perceived them as forming such a fraternity. The clandestine marks of recognition whereby gay men and lesbians have communicated their nature to one another recall the more structured gestures of freemasons. Such comparisons aside, it is more useful to posit small groupings within the larger pool of homosexuals, and to employ looser concepts of association—such as circles, coteries, and cliques—as well as the contemporary notion of networking, involving patterns which are nurtured by individuals interacting with others.

During the mid-eighteenth century the University of Leiden was the center of a remarkable homoerotic student circle, as documented by G. S. Rousseau. This mainly British group included the poet and physician Mark Akenside, as well as John Wilkes and Baron d'Holbach, who were both to distinguish themselves as radicals. At the end of the century a network formed around Lord **Byron**, though this was geographically dispersed. The 1895 trials of Oscar **Wilde** served to make his London circle only too visible.

The Cambridge Apostles and Bloomsbury. A relatively well-documented instance of a secret society with strong, continuing homoerotic overtones is the Society of Apostles founded by students at **Cambridge** University in 1820. Members gathered once a week to hear papers on controversial topics. The first members of this distinguished intellectual club were mainly clergymen, and apparently of impeccable moral character. By the 1840s, however, intimations of homosexuality begin to emerge—though sometimes only in the form of the "Higher Sodomy," that is, nonsexual male bonding and a conviction of the innate superiority of men over women. In the early years of the present century the Society served as a refuge for some gifted homosexuals who were made cautious by the reverberations of the Wilde affair. In the 1920s Anthony Blunt and Guy Burgess, both Apostles, became converted to Marxism and entered a clandestine career of **espionage** for the Soviet government. Once unmasked, their activity occasioned hostile speculation about a purported connection among the upper classes, homosexuality, and spying. After World War II, however, the homosexual complexion of the Society faded.

The influence of the Apostles radiated into the larger community in several ways. William Johnson, later Cory (elected in 1844), became a leading member of the Calamite group of pederastic poets. In the early years of the present century, homosexual Apostles graduates, notably Lytton **Strachey** and John Maynard **Keynes**, formed an adult offshoot in **London**, which became known as **Bloomsbury**. The members of this more loosely constituted group of writers, artists, and thinkers were both homosexual and heterosexual (and bisexual in the case of Virginia **Woolf** and a few others), but they were united in their opposition to Victorian moralism and prescriptivism.

Expatriates in Paris. Across the channel at the same time there flourished in **Paris** an extraordinary constellation of expatriate lesbians, including Renée **Vivien**, Natalie **Barney**, Romaine **Brooks**, Margaret **Anderson**, Djuna **Barnes**, Gertrude **Stein**, and Alice B. Toklas. Sylvia **Beach** and her French lover Adrienne Monnier both ran bookstores, that were favorite gathering places of the avant-garde. These creative figures were not organized in a coherent group, but were nonetheless often perceived as such, giving Paris the reputation of a "Sapphic capital." Male homosexual expatriates were less prominent in the French capital; the publisher and writer Robert **McAlmon** was an exception. A lesser center at the same period was Florence, which attracted both male homosexuals and lesbians.

The Beat Generation. After World War II the **beat** group of American writers emerged, the central figures being William **Burroughs**, Allen **Ginsberg** (both gay), and Jack **Kerouac** (bisexual). The venue of these writers was a shifting one, beginning in New York, and moving—depending on individual choice—to Paris, Mexico City, Tangiers, and San Francisco. The last city attracted its own creative circle, including the poet Robert Duncan and the filmmaker James Broughton. In conducting research to document intellectuals and others of the past, it is important to be attentive to friendship patterns; the "birds of a feather" principle will often lead to unexpected liaisons.

General Features. Undoubtedly there are countless circles and cliques that have been lost from sight, having produced no creative figures worthy of remembrance. Indeed the pattern of the clique surrounding one or more "queens" (den-mother figures) was an almost ubiquitous feature of homosexual life before 1969. In the view of hostile outsiders, such groupings were stereotyped as "rings" on the pattern of criminal gangs. This idea need not be negative, however, as shown by the Swiss society (and magazine) *Der Kreis/Le Cercle* (1932–67), the name of which conjures up the metaphor of a ring. And when the American homophile **movement** emerged in the 1950s, most local groups were initially formed of people who had come to know each other through gay social cliques. This type of bonding also has its downside, and newcomers to activist groups, even today, may sometimes be dismayed by the invisible wall around the clique that controls the group.

Up to this point, groups have been discussed mainly in terms of interaction in single localities, cities in fact. Yet another type of linkage has existed in which individuals communicate over large distances, originally by mail, now also by telephone and computer modem. Such a pattern has often been the case in gay scholarship. In the nineteenth century the independent scholar K. H. **Ulrichs** (1825–1895) had a circle of correspondents, most of whose names remain unknown to us because of the caution that they felt obliged to observe. More public and institutional was the group formed by the Berlin **Scientific-Humanitarian Committee** (1897–1933), which had collaborators not only through much of Germany, but also in Austria, The Netherlands, Scandinavia, and the English-speaking countries. Today many gay and lesbian scholars, unable to obtain academic posts, work as private individuals from their homes, relying on contacts with like-minded individuals to assist in developing and diffusing their discoveries and writings.

BIBLIOGRAPHY. Catherine van Casselaer, *Lot's Wife: Lesbian Paris, 1890–1914*, Liverpool: Janus, 1986; Richard Deacon, *The Cambridge Apostles*, London: Robert Royce, 1985; G. S. Rousseau, "'In the House of Madam Vander Tasse': A Homosocial University Club in Early Modern Europe," *Journal of Homosexuality*, 16:1/2 (1988), 311–47.

Wayne R. Dynes

CIRCUMCISION

Male circumcision, or the cutting away of the foreskin of the penis, has been practiced by numerous peoples from remotest antiquity as a religious custom, while to some modern homosexuals it has an aesthetic and erotic significance. It has been speculated that the custom originated somewhere in Africa where water was scarce and the ability to wash was limited. Thus the Western Semites (Israelites, Canaanites, Phoenicians, Arabs, Edomites, Syrians), who lived in an area where water was never really plentiful, also observed the custom, while the Eastern Semites (Assyrians and Babylonians), in an area where water was more abundant, did not circumcise. This is true also of the Greeks and other Aegean peoples who always lived near the water.

In the fifth century B.C. the Greek historian Herodotus provided the following information about the ancient Egyptians: "They practice circumcision, while men of other nations—except those who have learnt from Egypt—leave their private parts as nature made them. . . . They circumcise themselves for cleanliness' sake, preferring to be clean rather than comely." (*Histories*, Bk. II). There is also some evidence that the Israelites learned it in Egypt (Exodus 4:24–26; Joshua 5:2–9). However, they may simply have adopted circumcision from their neighbors up to the time of their Babylonian Exile, for all those who lived around them until this time were also circumcised except for the coastal-dwelling Philistines, a people of Aegean origin who are often mentioned on the pages of the **Old Testament** quite distinctly as "the uncircumcised" or "the unclean" (Judges 14:2; I Samuel 14:6). Around 1000 B.C. the Israelite king Saul demanded of David as a bride-price for his daughter Michal one hundred Philistine foreskins (I Samuel 18:25), alluding to the practice of stripping the foreskin off a slain foe.

Jesus never mentioned circumcision, though the Jewish rite was [Luke 2:21] performed upon him on his eighth day as it was with all other males of his community of faith—hence the designation of the calendar in which the first day of the year is January 1 as "circumcision style." In the early church the party of Paul of Tarsus which opposed circumcision was victorious, and uncircumcised Greeks and Romans poured into the new faith, so that to this day the majority of European men have retained their foreskins. With the coming of the faith of **Islam**, however, in the seventh century the Middle East and North Africa became a stronghold of the practice of circumcision. Hindus and Buddhists avoid it, hence East Asians—and Amerindians—retain their foreskins.

Among Americans in general circumcision was relatively rare until Victorian times when it was thought to be a deterrent to the practice of masturbation. But it was not until World War II that it came into widespread use, supposedly to overcome soldiers' occasional infections associated with poor hygiene. Circumcision of male infants became popular in the United States, but was believed unnecessary in most of Europe.

In the late twentieth century the trend is being reversed in America as more and more medical articles—and some books—have argued that the operation in most cases is needless. In July 1986 Blue Shield of Philadelphia announced that it will no longer pay for routine infant circumcision as a part of its childbirth insurance coverage, defining the operation as cosmetic and not essential to the health of the child. Recently Rosemary Romberg has gone so far as to argue that there may be numerous negative effects of routine infant circumcision and that the practice, in general, ought to be dropped. She cites remarkable cases in which a number of American Jews—or at least those who were born into the Jewish faith—have elected to do so.

Some male homosexuals have a decided preference for an uncircumcised ("uncut" or "unsliced") or circumcised partner, as the case may be. There are even groups of men who have retained their foreskins (and others who admire them); these individuals with generous or pronounced "curtains" are in demand. In a few rare cases the overhang of the foreskin suffices partially to sheath the partner's penis during sex. A few uncut men neglect personal hygiene to the point of allowing smegma ("cock cheese") to accumulate beneath the prepuce in a manner that tends to repel the partner, but this is easily remedied.

BIBLIOGRAPHY. Bud Berkeley and Joe Tiffenbach, *Circumcision: Its Past, Its Present, &) . . . Its Future*, San Francisco: Bud Berkeley, 1983–84; Rosemary Romberg, *Circumcision: The Painful Dilemma*, South Hadley, MA: Bergin & Garvey, 1985; Edward Wallerstein, *Circumcision: An American Health Fallacy*, New York: Springer Publishing Co., 1980.

Tom Horner

CLASS

Although class is one of the most commonly used political and sociological terms today, it is not easy to define. A degree of consensus obtains that a class system is hierarchical, allocating power according to rank order. A class structure in which all classes were equal would be a contradiction in terms. Class membership may be a function of income (the traditional measure), occupation, education, residence, patterns of consumption, and even to a certain extent of ethnicity. The mix varies from one observer to another, so that class remains an "essentially contested concept"—that is, an idea whose very nature precludes final agreement, but which serves as a focal point for the disputes of various interest groups.

General Features. Apart from the debates of scholars, there is no doubt that contemporary American society (like that of other Western industrialized countries) has adopted a practical or folk classification of the concept that shows some stability. This lay model of class usually articulates in three main strata: upper, middle, and lower. Middle may be divided into upper- and lower-middle, and some recognize an "under-class" below the others. Taste preferences are generally a good index of popular judgments, so that grand **opera**, tennis, and sushi restaurants fall on one side of an invisible boundary, with country music, bowling, and fast food on the other. Of course there are "taste-crossing" individuals and occasions, but the ensemble of such choices makes up a mosaic of ever-present reminders and reinforcers of the folk distinctions, which often come to the fore when persons anchored in different strata seek to work together, as in a political campaign.

Class and Homosexuality. Because class status is so intimately associated with family identity and membership, homosexual behavior has often discounted and crossed class lines; in many cases homosexuals in search of partners—especially casual ones—need have little concern with what the family (or society) would think of the liaison, while heterosexuals must often choose their prospective spouse within narrowly prescribed limits.

For some individuals, homosexual arrangements may offer a path to mobility between class strata, or more commonly for a positional improvement within a single class. Yet like most heterosexual marriages, most gay/lesbian unions are endogamous, in that like tends to bond with like: the partners come from the same class (and relatively similar strata therein). Still gay dyads of members stemming from contrasting class backgrounds do exist, though very little study has been made on how taste preferences are negotiated in such households. How is money made and spent? What compromises are needed so that entertainment and vacations can be enjoyed together? How are the **couple's** friends chosen? Which of the two partners is more likely to compromise to "keep the peace"? Complications may ensue among lesbian couples because of the cross-cutting of the traditional **butch–fem** role contrast with class perceptions. The butch woman is supposed to be "working class," but in the actual situation it may be the fem who is.

Cross-Class Relationships. Short-term relationships are more likely to involve connections between persons of different strata and classes. Upper-class socialist gay men, such as Edward **Carpenter** and Daniel Guérin, rationalized their fondness for lower-class men by claiming that the encounters helped to promote harmony among classes. Such expectations point to a **utopian**-socialist rather than **Marxist** theoretical background, where the perception of class struggle is central. Certainly many politically unsophisticated upper- and middle-class homosexuals prefer lower-class partners whom they perceive as "more **macho**." It has been proposed that this difference—together with that of race, which often meshes with class in this arena—represents a surrogate for the missing male–female dichotomy.

Viewed in historical perspective, such seemingly unlikely conjunctions may prolong an old linkage, at least in matters of sexual enjoyment, between the "rake," the aristocrat of easy morals, and the accommodating proletarian. These transient liaisons could present a dangerous side, as suggested by the expression current in the circle of Oscar **Wilde**: "feasting with panthers." When the arrangements worked, however, both ends of the social spectrum found themselves in alliance against the straight-laced morals of the emerging middle class, for whom respectability was an ideal to be honored at all costs.

When there are no children to raise there is more discretionary income, so that adopting a homosexual lifestyle provides a margin for class enhancement. The chances are particularly favored if the novice links up with a mentor more experienced or wealthy than he or she is. An established gay man or lesbian may put resources which parents would use for raising the status of their children into helping a lover–protégé. The mentor may also provide private lessons in manners and business acumen. Conversely, two men or two women living together across class lines may provoke from outsiders subtle or not-so-subtle ostracism that hinders career advancement. And the negative reaction of one or both sets of parents may cause anguish. Curiously, some parents seem to tolerate same-sex alliances by their offspring more easily than those that cross class or racial lines.

Internalizing the folk belief that homosexuals are more "artistic," some gay men cultivate musical, theatrical, and culinary tastes that are above their "station"—and above their income. Acquisition of these refined preferences, together with "corrected" speech patterns, hinders easy communication with former peers, though there are many factors that work for geographical and psychological distance between homosexuals, on the one hand, and their families and original peer groups, on the other. Given their relative freedom, some individuals may be inclined to experiment with "class bending," sometimes with paradoxical results. Observations of the American metropolitan scene in the 1970s revealed that patrons of leather bars tended to be lawyers, physicians, and other professionals "dressing down" after a day at work, while the denizens of "fluff" establishments were likely to be clerks and stockboys flaunting elegant gear that they could not wear on the job. There is class, and there is class fantasy.

Prostitution. A study of young men beginning a career of hustling showed that lower-class recruits entered it immediately on discovering the financial rewards, sometimes suffering identity conflicts as a result. Middle-class boys, less in need of money, often began their involvement in **prostitution** casually and marginally, taking their time about making a full commitment. As for the clients or "Johns," there is a major contrast between the working-class man who pays a street transvestite for quick oral sex in his car, the middle-class man who can only afford to rent a body occasionally for a few hours, and the wealthy connoisseur who "leases" his sex object, installing him in luxury as a semi-permanent resident.

Sexual Behavior. An interesting question is whether class differences affect what is done in bed. There seem to be considerable differences in the conceptualizations of homosexuality; the older model (strict dichotomy between inserter, who is considered "normal," and insertee, who is the only one labeled "gay/feminine") is more firmly entrenched, if not dominant, among the working class, while the newer model of reciprocality among two gay men prevails in the middle and upper classes. One consequence of the older model is that there is less of a psychological barrier for lower-class males who consider themselves "straight," "normal," and "masculine" to participating in homosexual acts as long as they remain in the inserter role; for them it is not a homosexual act on their part. This is one reason why homosexuals from other classes who are content with the insertee role have frequently sought out macho partners from the working class; they are more likely to be willing than randomly-selected males from the middle class. Other factors which encourage "trade" behavior by working-class males are a more accepting attitude toward any activity done for income (such as prostitution), a greater familiarity with jailhouse sexual mores, and a lesser interest in sophisticated categorical schemes ("sex is sex; if it feels good, who cares what you call it").

In the 1940s Alfred C. **Kinsey** and his associates found significant distinctions of this kind among men based on educational level, which he found the best objective test for class status. His data indicated the highest incidence of homosexual activity among males who had attended high school but not college; at the same time he found the highest levels of **homophobia** in the same group. This may be explained by the difference in conceptual models referred to above, under which males could experience what Kinsey called a "homosexual outlet" without thinking of themselves as homosexual, and while looking down on their sexual partners. But since a substantial proportion of the lower-class male interviewees were prisoners, the data cannot be considered wholly reliable.

The Kinsey Institute data for females, which are more reliable (though not per se applicable to men as well), show that the percentage with homosexual experience to orgasm rises with educational levels; at age 30 the females without college had a cumulative experience level of 9 or 10 percent, while those who had attended college had 17 percent and females with some graduate school education had 24 percent. However, when data are limited to the period between adolescence and age 20, the girls with the lowest education show the most homosexual activity and the future college students the least.

Beginning with the sexual revolution of the 1960s (together with rising incomes) substantial changes occurred in sexual behavior in many sectors of the population, and class allegiances would have been unlikely to have deterred these shifts in the way that, say, religious conviction did. Premarital sex became more accepted among heterosexuals, while some homosexuals seemed willing to experiment in a broader range of sexual practices, even including "way out" activities such as fisting.

It has been suggested that there are some variations in preferred sexual practice among classes, with lower-class men being more likely to prefer anal over oral sex, and middle-class men the opposite, but there are few hard data to support or contradict this hypothesis, which is based on anecdotal evidence.

Some homosexuals tend to eroticize a class other than their own. In England and France, for example, many educated upper-class men have sought their partners exclusively among the **working-class** men, whose perceived overt masculinity is much prized. Conversely, some men of working-class background find great satisfaction in being accepted in jet-set circles. In white men attracted to blacks or the converse, the element of crossing class lines may be central.

Class boundaries in modern industrial societies are more fluid than in times past, and this fluidity in turn has impacted on sexual behavior, though the consequences are not always easy to assess. Further shifts may be expected.

Wayne R. Dynes and
Stephen Donaldson

CLEMENT OF ALEXANDRIA (CA. 150–CA. 215)

Greek church father. Born in Athens, probably of pagan and peasant ancestry, he is not to be confused with Clement, bishop of Rome, author of the **New Testament** epistle. After his conversion, Clement of **Alexandria** traveled widely to study under Christians, finally under the learned Pantaenus in Alexandria. Of the early Fathers, he had the most thorough knowledge of Greek literature. He quoted Homer, Hesiod, the dramatists, and (most of all) Platonic and **Stoic** philosophers. Sometime before 200 he succeeded Pantaenus, whom he praised for his orthodoxy, as head of the catechetical school at Alexandria, but in 202 he had to flee the persecution unleashed by the emperor Septimius Severus and perhaps died in Asia Minor. Although most of his works are lost, the chief ones form a trilogy: *Hortatory Address to the Greeks,* written ca. 190 to prove the superiority of Christianity to paganism and philosophy; *Tutor,* written ca. 190 or 195 about Christ's moral teaching as it should be applied to conduct in eating, drinking, dress, expenditure, and sex; and *Miscellanies,* written ca. 200–2 in eight books proving the inferiority of Greek to Christian philosophy. Minor works include *What Rich Man Shall be Saved?* which urges scorn of worldly wealth.

Although Clement's Christianity has been criticized as being too Hellenized, his serene hope and classical learning helped convert the upper classes. His pseudo-Platonic doctrine that homosexuality was particularly noxious because it was "against nature" served to combine that strand of classical philosophy with Hellenistic Jewish homophobia, most trenchantly exemplified by the Alexandrian philosopher **Philo** Judaeus (20 B.C.– A.D. 45), to justify persecution of sodomites. He thus preceded and stimulated the homophobia of the Christian emperors, from Constantine's sons to Justinian, and of the two most influential Fathers, John **Chrysostom** and **Augustine** of Hippo.

See also **Patristic Writers.**

William A. Percy

CLERGY, GAY

One of the central paradoxes of the history of homosexuality, as well as of the history of **Christianity,** has been the role of gay clergy in the government and the functioning of an institution that outwardly condemned any form of sexual expression between members of the same sex. The question of gay clergy extends beyond the bounds of Christianity (the focus of the present article) to many religions, including those of primitive peoples, as seen in the **berdache** and **shamanism.** This broad diffusion tends to confirm what Edward **Carpenter** claimed early in the twentieth century, that there is a psychological affinity between religious ministry and homophilia.

The Early Centuries. Almost from the beginning, Christian clerics have been suspected and denounced by pagans, atheists, and anticlerical propagandists for homosexuality even more than the facts themselves merit. Among Greek and Roman orators, accusations of having prostituted oneself to other males or of having taken the passive role in adulthood became standard fare—deserved or not. Although there is no confirmation of the assertion that St. John, identified as the **beloved disciple** (John 13:23), was Jesus' sexual partner (as an anonymous Venetian and Christopher **Marlowe** claimed in the sixteenth century), pagan polemicists of the second and third centuries routinely accused Christians of ritual murder and cannibalism, incest and orgies both heterosexual and homosexual, notably in connection with the mass. As **celibacy** increased, especially among the monks who seemed particularly uncouth and threatening, such charges became more common, and the writers of the **monastic** rules took care to legislate in such a way as to prevent homosexual activity (*see,* e.g., The Rule of St. Benedict, chapter 22). Indeed hermit monks, who had been accustomed to an individualistic way of life, were herded into the monasteries where they could be watched and regulated to reduce opportunities for vice and occasions for slander. Fasting and vigils were imposed to reduce libido. The space allotted to homosexual acts in the **penitentials** confirms that monks often sinned with their fellows and engaged in masturbation. The penitentials aimed at clerics ministering to Celtic and Germanic laymen indicate frequent homosexuality, onanism and in such agrarian societies, bestiality.

The Central Middle Ages. During the period of laxity that followed the Carolingian revival in the ninth century, several popes were particularly blatant. The patrician John XII (938–964) went so far as to model himself on the scandalous Roman emperor **Heliogabalus**, holding homosexual orgies in the papal palace—a practice imitated by Benedict IX (1021–ca. 1052).

These excesses helped to bring on the rigorism of the Gregorian reform movement in the middle of the eleventh century. Yet paradoxically the enforcement of celibacy on priests and even attempts to impose it on those in lesser orders increased the danger of homosexuality. Peter **Damian**, who led the attack on Nicolaitism (nepotism within the church) around 1050, also denounced what he perceived as widespread homosexuality among Italian priests. All the major canonical collections of the high **Middle Ages** from Burchard of Worms, then Gratian and the *Corpus Juris Canonici* legislated against the abuse which undoubtedly increased as the seculars had to put aside their wives, concubines, and often even female housekeepers. Friars, who unlike the monks were free to wander among the laity without much supervision, became notorious as seducers of boys as well as women, whose confessions they often heard to the disgruntlement of parish priests. Many homosexual clergy, then as now, confessed to one another and were formally absolved. Indeed, the confessional at times became the locus of seduction.

Unlike the Roman Catholic church, Greek Orthodoxy has never adopted the principle of obligatory celibacy for the entire clergy. The result is that homosexuals are tracked into careers in the "black" or monastic clergy from which the high dignitaries of the Orthodox church are chosen, while the "white" or parish clergy are allowed to marry and have children. The offspring of the latter played a great role in the formation of the Russian intelligentsia in the nineteenth and early twentieth centuries.

The military orders were drawn, like the episcopate, mainly from the insouciant lustful nobility. Many of these recruits proved wanting in serious religious conviction or were placed often unwillingly by their relatives at an early age. Sometime suspicions arose of secret rites, as with the Knights **Templars** who paid dearly by being cruelly tortured and burned.

St. John (conventionally identified with the beloved disciple) was only the most famous of a number of saints suspected by contemporaries or by modern scholars. The eastern saints Sergius and Bacchus have been interpreted as a pair of lovers, but close examination of the evidence does not support the claim. In twelfth-century England St. Aelred, abbot of Rievaulx, left behind writings saturated with deep feeling for male spiritual friendship. Yet as in the case of many other medieval monks claimed by modern homophiles as "gay," this theme of *amicitia* probably belongs more to the realm of **homosociality** than homosexuality in any genital sense. The martyr St. Sebastian has been a homosexual cult object at least since the second half of the nineteenth century, but there is no basis for assuming that he himself was homosexual. Penitential flagellation, practiced by many monks, has secondary sexual connotations.

The hypocritical visitations of the Middle Ages and the papal inquisitions periodically unearthed homosexual clergy, as did secular courts, especially those of the Italian towns. The archdeacon Walter Map observed of St. Bernard of Clairvaux unsuccessfully attempting to revive the corpse of a boy: That *was* the unhappiest monk of all. For I've never heard of any monk who lay down upon a boy that did not straightaway rise up after him. The abbot blushed and they went out as many laughed." **Heretics** accused Catholic clergy of sodomy just as the Catholics in turn accused Cathars and Fraticelli, the Beguines and Bogomils. Opponents of the popes sometimes accused them of sodomy: Philip IV of France charged Boniface VIII not only with heresy, usury, and simony, but with sodomy and masturbation as well.

The Early Modern Period. The **Renaissance** in Italy, with its revival of classical antiquity and love of art, saw a number of popes who were interested in their own sex. Among them were the antipope John XXIII (d. 1419), who began his career as a pirate. Entering the clergy he quickly acquired the reputation of an unblushing libertine. The humanist pope Pius II (1405–1464) watched boys run naked in a race at Pienza, noting a boy "with fair hair and a beautiful body, though disfigured with mud." The vain Venetian Paul II (1417–1471) toyed with adopting the name Formosus ("beautiful"). Affecting the most lavish costumes, he was attacked by his enemies as "Our Lady of Pity." His successor, Sixtus IV (1414–1482), made his mark as an art patron, erecting the Sistine chapel. He also elevated to the cardinalate a number of handsome young men. Julius II (1443–1513), another art-loving pope, provoked such scandal that he was arraigned under various charges, including that of sodomy, but he managed to survive the attempt to depose him. His successor, the extravagant Medici Leo X (1475–1521), became embroiled in intrigues to advance favorite nephews, a hobby that strained the treasury to the utmost. Julius III (1487–1555), who had presided over the Council of Trent before his pontificate, was nonetheless sometimes seen at official functions with catamites, one of whom he made a cardinal.

After the Reformation, Protestants—who rejected clerical celibacy and thereby made heterosexuality virtually obligatory for the clergy as well as the laity—undertook vigorous campaigns of slander directed at the homosexuality of the Catholic clergy. It has been claimed that Henry VIII's visitors greatly exaggerated the extent of sodomy and every other vice among English monks in order to precipitate suppression of the monasteries and confiscation of their property, but the actual text of the correspondence between him and his agent in Scotland indicates that a "covert action" was intended and that imputed to the monks were such vices as laziness with which no court, even in the Middle Ages, would have concerned itself for a moment. Thus only Orthodoxy had the wisdom to divide its clergy into two groups, one of whom would be wholly dedicated to its service, while not depriving society of the offspring of the other. Given the virtual monopoly of higher education which the clergy enjoyed in the Middle Ages and even afterwards in many places, the Orthodox solution seems more viable than the Catholic or Protestant one.

Skeptics and **libertines** from the Renaissance through the **Enlightenment** also ridiculed the sodomitical practices of the clerics and monks as an example of the hypocrisy of the church, and of the idle, vicious, parasitic way of life that its clergy led, all the while urging others to abstinence and self-denial in every form. **Voltaire** repeatedly suggested that the Jesuits liked young boys, and Pierre-Jean de Béranger (1789–1857) continued the anti-Jesuit tradition with a song about their propensity for spanking young boys.

The Nineteenth and Twentieth Centuries. During the religious revival and triumph of bourgeois morality in the nineteenth century, only leftists and eccentrics continued to emphasize the homosexuality of the clergy. The anticlerical literature of the last decades of that century delighted in exposing cases in which a clergyman had committed a sexual offense, to the point where in 1911 the Pope had to issue the *motu proprio* decree *Quamvis diligenter* forbidding the Catholic laity to bring charges against the clergy before secular courts. This step unilaterally abolished the principle of the equality of all citizens before the law established by the French Revolution, reinstating the "benefit of clergy" of the Middle Ages. The anticlerical literature of that period still needs study for the light that it can shed on the homosexual subculture of the clerical milieux. In England the **Anglican** High Church was particularly identified with effeminacy and homosexuality, a state of affairs that produced a certain amount of puritanical revulsion in the middle class.

The Communists and then the **Nazis** attacked clerics and their other enemies by charging homosexuality. The classic of Soviet anti-religious writing, *The Bible for Believers and Unbelievers* (1922), identified the "crime of Sodom" with the practices of the medieval monks, and violation of **Paragraph 175** of the Penal Code of the Reich was an accusation which the Nazis used against Catholic priests who may have been convicted solely on perjured testimony.

Because of the decline in the number of applicants for the priesthood after World War II in England and America, it has been estimated recently that more than 50 percent of Catholic priests under 40 in the United States today are gay, many of whom support Dignity (the gay Catholic organization), and also that 40 percent of Anglican priests are (in both countries). In the wake of the **AIDS** crisis in England an open attack on homosexuals in the church was mounted by conservative circles.

One aspect of the gay liberation **movement** in the United States has been the demand for ordination of openly gay and lesbian postulants as members of the clergy, and several denominations, among them the United Church of Canada, have acquiesced—to the dismay of the tradition-minded among their followers. Church organists as a professional class tend to be homosexual, for whatever denomination they practice their art, and in recent years some of them have "come out of the closet." Francis Cardinal Spellman (1889–1967) of New York was well-known in homosexual circles even while he publicly condemned every form of sexual "immorality"—and it was the only aspect of immorality about which he cared. A biography that was prepared for publication after his death intended to reveal to the world the awful truth, but the archdiocese intervened with the publisher to have the offending passages excised. In the final version Spellman's homosexuality was relegated to the category of rumor. According to the French novelist Roger Peyrefitte, pope John XXIII (1881–1963) and, more plausibly, Paul VI (1897–1978) conducted homosexual affairs before their election.

The distinction between the **androphile** and the **pederast** extends to the gay clergy as well. Some homosexual members of the clergy—androphiles—seek only other adults as partners and move freely in the gay subculture of the large cities, while others are attracted only to adolescents or at times to even younger partners. In the mid-1980s in the Cajun area of Louisiana, the Roman Catholic church was embarrassed by the revelation that there were pedophile priests who had abused children in their parishes, and the families were able to collect such large sums in civil damages that the church could no longer obtain insurance to cover its potential liability in such cases. In fairness, however, it must be acknowledged that there are homosexual and lesbian religious who take their vows of celibacy seriously and abstain from any sex, even though as members of communities of their own gender they are exposed to temptations that would have no meaning for the exclusive heterosexual.

The plight of homosexuals as clergy of a religion that condemns all homosexual expression remains unresolved, and will be a source of turbulence within the denominations for decades to come, until Christianity as a whole finds a modus vivendi with the phenomenon of attraction to one's own sex.

William A. Percy

CLIFT, MONTGOMERY (1920–1966)

American actor. Born into an ambitious nouveau-riche family, Clift responded to guidance by becoming a successful child and adolescent actor. By the age of 20 he was starring with Lunt and Fontanne in Robert Sherwood's Pulitzer Prize–winning play *There Shall Be No Night*. At the same time he had his first serious affair—with a fellow actor. Making a national splash in the film *The Search* (1948), he was for a time one of Hollywood's top romantic male leads. His brooding good looks appealed to both women and men, but some of his associates such as Frank Sinatra and the director John Huston taunted him for his homosexuality. Nonetheless, Clift's career continued meteoric until his 1956 car crash, after which his face had to be reconstructed, but without complete success.

Clift suffered from a strong sense of internalized self-contempt, referring to himself as "the fag." At times he pursued desultory affairs with women, but more frequently sought out the company of hustlers and other companions in casual male sex. His abuse of alcohol and drugs increased as the years passed. In New York City Clift found a psychiatrist who tried to help him to accept his homosexuality, but at the cost of a crippling personal dependence. The actor's tortured life reflected not only the difficulty of being a homosexual in America in the middle decades of the twentieth century, but also the stresses caused by the hypocrisy of an entertainment industry seeking to protect its investment in a talented, but "unstable" property.

BIBLIOGRAPHY. Patricia Bosworth, *Montgomery Clift: A Biography*, New York: Harcourt Brace Jovanovich, 1978.

CLIQUES
See **Circles and Affinity Groups.**

CLONE

In current general usage, the word clone has come to mean "a living organism created as a duplicate of another through genetic engineering." In addition, the word acquired a vogue use in gay circles in the late 1970s to designate an emergent male homosexual style.

First attracting attention as a definite type, it seems, in such enclaves of gaydom as San Francisco's Castro and New York's Greenwich Village, the gay clone wore short hair and a clipped moustache, while sporting (if possible) a sculpted chest with prominent pectorals. Clothing, typically flannel shirts and leather, was chosen to accentuate these features. The intent was to create a masculine, even **macho** image, while at the same time signaling one's orientation. Such signaling might be accentuated through gay **semiotics**—keys worn externally on a ring and a handkerchief, color-coded to indicate specific sexual wishes, placed in the back pocket. In public gathering places, especially **bars**, gay clones were said to be frequently observed "giving attitude," that is, assuming a scornful and haughty demeanor, and offering only laconic and surly replies when addressed.

The popularity of this style reflected several converging tendencies. On the one hand, there was a rejection by a substantial portion of the gay male community of both the **effeminate** mode (as prescribed by the traditional stereotype) and the **androgynous** mode (championed by early gay **liberation**), in favor of a markedly masculine style. Hostile observers were wont to say, of course, that the clone look was just another form of gay costuming, and therefore just as much "drag" as the looks it displaced, but this was surely not the motivation of those who adopted the trend. American culture itself had tended to promote rough-hewn, proletarian styles for men, **television**'s adaptation of the Hollywood Western being the most notable source. Then there was the national interest in physical fitness, which was surely a healthy reaction to the neglect of health and the body that the hippie style and the drug culture had fostered. Not surprisingly, the clone look was taken up in Europe and other places where local homosexuals eagerly followed changes in American gay fashions.

Jean-Paul **Sartre** has identified "seriation" as a key aspect of modern society—the tendency of individuals to assort themselves into "sets" characterized by homologous features. Sartre gives the example of passengers taking a ticket and falling into line in numerical order at a bus stop. This social trend represents, of course, a symbolic mimicry of industrial mass production. In this light the "cloning" of the male homosexual may be viewed as part of a larger social process whereby a "nonconformist" subgroup fosters conformity in its own realm. Among the members of the subgroup behavioral norms are rigidly enforced by group consensus. Similar phenomena have been observed among the pachuco ("zoot suit") youth of the 1940s, the beatniks of the 1960s, and the skinheads of the 1980s. Such phenomena are not limited to groups usually seen as marginalized; Harold Rosenberg sardonically, but perhaps not unjustly styled American intellectuals as "a herd of independent minds."

The gay clone vogue also has a psychological dimension. One made oneself over as a clone in order to attract other clones, and success in cruising meant possessing someone similar to oneself. This quest for one's double is a major recurrent aspect of homosexual consciousness. It was perhaps first set forth in the *Symposium* where **Plato** posits that all homosexuals are sundered halves of a once whole being. One's goal therefore is to find the mirror image who will dovetail with oneself and then to unite with him. To be sure, such aspirations have sometimes been stigmatized as egocentric narcissism, the wish of someone who does not truly seek an interpersonal relationship but only to mate with himself. A fascinating explora-tion of this concept appears in David Gerrold's **science fiction** novel *The Man Who Folded Himself* (1973). Yet it is essential to recognize that the quest for the double usually operates in tandem with a simultaneous search for difference—for complementation.

BIBLIOGRAPHY. Nicholas Howe, "Further Thoughts on *Clone*," American Speech, 57 (1983), 61–68.

Wayne R. Dynes

CLOSET

Until the late 1970s the term closet was restricted to gay jargon, where it meant a state of concealment in which one immured one's homosexuality. Some individuals were said to be remaining "in the closet," and thus passing for heterosexual—or so they hoped. Some were chastised for their illusions by being labeled "closet queens," the idea being that they remained what they were no matter how elaborate and seemingly successful their impersonation of heterosexuality might seem. Others emerged from the closet, or were urged to do so, by **coming out**. Then mainstream journalists appropriated and extended the usage so that they could speak of "closet conservatives" and "closet gourmets" with no sexual connotation.

Semantics of the Closet. All these connotations of *closet* depend on an underlying metaphor. In American usage, the architectural space designated in the primary meaning is typically small and confined, essentially an alcove secured by a door for the storage of clothing. Older English usage treats a closet as any private room or chamber. Through a combination of these meanings, the verb "to closet oneself" came to merge the idea of privacy and remoteness, on the one hand, with narrow confinement, on the other. For the element of secrecy occasioned by the suspect character of what is being hidden, compare the proverbial expression: a skeleton in the closet. Historians of literature also speak of a "closet drama," that is one never intended for public performance. An ecclesiastical writer of the reign of **James I** of England penned the expression "closet sins," so that the adjectival use of the word has a long history. Sometimes gay writers and speakers reactivate the metaphor, so that the expression is taken in a literal, architectural sense, as in "stifling closet" or "his closet is nailed shut." Assisting in the process of coming out has been dubbed, by Philadelphia activist Barbara Gittings, as "oiling the hinges of the closet door." It is also possible to speak of "returning to the closet" with respect to those who have come to feel uncomfortable with their homosexuality out in the open or to sense that it is imprudent to advertise their sexual orientation.

Sociology of the Closet. Sociologists, preeminently Erving Goffman, have written of seemingly analogous tendencies among other groups, as ex-prisoners and former mental patients, to "manage spoiled identity" by editing their presentation of self. It is doubtful, however, that closeted gay people think of themselves in quite the same way. Unencumbered as most of them are by stigmatizing documentation of official origin and convinced that their cover has not been blown, they rarely give consideration to their own self-concealment. When pressed, they appeal to the Anglo-Saxon tradition of the separation of public business from private lives. Many heterosexuals would agree that sexuality is a private matter.

In the view of gay **activists**, closeted persons can have a negative impact on the welfare of other homosexuals. "[A] truism to people active in the gay movement [is] that the greatest impediments to homosexuals' progress often [are] not heterosexuals, but closeted homosexuals. . . . By definition, the homosexual in the closet [has] surrendered his integrity. This makes closeted people very useful to the establishment: once empowered, such people are guaranteed to support the most subtle nuances of anti-gay prejudice. A closeted homosexual has the keenest understanding of these nuances, having chosen to live under the subjugation of prejudice. The closeted homosexual is far less likely to demand fair or just treatment for his kind, because to do so would call attention to himself." (Randy Shilts, *And the Band Played On*, New York, 1987, p. 406).

Ethical and Methodological Aspects. For a variety of reasons—which may not even be clearly known to themselves—a vast number of homosexuals and lesbians in our society can and do remain "in the closet." This is so despite frequent and fervent exhortations on the part of the leadership of the gay/lesbian movement to "come out." Their reluctance makes it hard to organize gay men and lesbians politically, to estimate their true numbers, and to collect valid samples for social science research. There has been some discussion of the ethics of "forced decloseting." For example, liberal gays asserted that the late **conservative** politician Terry Dolan was benefiting from "playing both sides of the street": participating in fund raising for causes that included antigay planks, while personally enjoying a gay life though closeted to the general public. As it happened, Dolan died in 1987, making the issue in this particular instance moot—though the general question abides. Even in obituary notices, many newspapers refuse to mention that a lover has survived, or other aspects of gayness, presumably in order to protect the privacy of relatives. This reticence would seem to go too far. Of course the restriction on information has made it difficult to make certain of the homosexuality or lesbianism of past figures who very likely were gay. Although in the present *Encyclopedia* efforts have been made to determine this status—historical decloseting, if you will—for many individuals, editorial policy has established that no living individuals should receive biographical entries of their own. This restriction has been taken not only to avoid invidious distinctions of the

"X is more important than Y" sort, but also to protect "closet rights."

The task of the biographer who is called upon to study the evidence of the sexual proclivities of a figure of the past is a challenging one. The individuals themselves may have taken great precautions to destroy or have destroyed any "incriminating" evidence. Then there is the problem of individuals, such as the painter Theodore **Géricault** and Eleanor **Roosevelt**, for whom we have good reason to believe that there were strong elements of a homoerotic sensibility, but the interpretation cannot be fixed to everyone's satisfaction. Such twentieth-century figures as New York's Francis Cardinal Spellman and FBI Director J. Edgar Hoover continue to resist any final pigeonholing. Assuredly, knowledge of the subject will advance, but it will also need to recognize many historical question marks.

Wayne R. Dynes

CLOTHING

Beyond its obvious functions of protecting and supporting the body, clothing (along with jewelry, cosmetics, tattooing, and cosmetic scarring) has been used from prehistoric times to alter bodily appearance. This has taken on two overlapping forms: to indicate social group and status, and to enhance the body's sexual appeal. Clothes are used to make the body appear more youthful, firm, and slim, or to enhance sexual characteristics. Men have used clothing to call attention to their muscles, buttocks, or "basket" (genitals; formerly the codpiece served this function); women the breasts, buttocks, and legs, formerly the abdomen, and very recently their muscles. Clothing also serves the function of retaining bodily odors, the sexual importance of which has yet to be thoroughly understood.

Gay men have often used clothing to indicate that they were potential sexual partners for other males. Of course any type of clothing associated with the opposite gender can be so used, but more subtle signals are often desired. The Roman poet **Martial**, for example (I.96; III.82), points out *galbinus* (greenish-yellow) as an effeminate color in clothing; Aulus Gellius (VI.12) similarly mentions the tunic (covering the arms) as an unmasculine style of clothing, used by men seeking the recipient role in male–male sex. Havelock Ellis, in *Sexual Inversion* (1915), reports that a red tie was "almost a synonym" for homosexuality in large American cities. Greek, Roman, or Arabic clothing was formerly used in photography to suggest homosexual identification. Styles of clothing can also be used as signals: the "dandy" of the late nineteenth century was a gay style of dress, and more recently cowboy clothing—work shirt, Levi jeans, and boots—has served the same purpose. Especially favored by and associated with American gay men in the 1970's and 1980's were Levis style 501, with a button fly, making for comfortable access to or display of the penis. An elaborate system of colored rear-pocket bandannas emerged in the 1970s to signal the desired type of gay sexual activity. It was derived from the use as signal of a visible key ring, whose presence indicated interest in leather or S/M sex, and whose position (left or right) indicated the role preferred.

In affluent times it has been possible to have special clothes for sexual purposes, clothes which are not normally worn at one's daily work. The dandy is the embodiment of the aristocratic male who is obsessed with his costume and even strives to be a leader of fashion. Within the gay male subculture leather garments are used to project an image of sexual power and nonconformity; nylon lingerie to suggest weakness, tenderness, or interest in seduction. Police or military uniforms are used in sex play to indicate authority; athletic clothing, including the quintessentially gay male jockstrap, to create an imaginary locker room; white cotton briefs to suggest innocence and youth. The variety of clothes used in sex play is large.

During the 1920s lesbians were stereotyped as affecting a severe version of male formal dress, and indeed some prominent figures such as Radclyffe **Hall** did adopt this mode, while Marlene Dietrich offered a subtle variant of it in the movies. More recently lesbians have been perceived as preferring somewhat shapeless garments and no makeup. While this look does correspond to the type sometimes known as the "granola dyke," other gay women prefer more elegant dress, of which there are several versions.

Nudism began in Europe in the early twentieth century, and is still more widespread there than in the United States. It is often thought of as being sexually provocative, but in practice nudism is ascetic. The removal of clothes, as in striptease, suggests sexual activity to follow; without clothes one lacks an important means of communication, enticement, and bodily enhancement.

See also **Dandyism**; **Transvestism**.

Daniel Eisenberg

COCTEAU, JEAN (1889–1963)

French playwright, poet, novelist, filmmaker, actor, and artist. Cocteau was one of the most famous, controversial, and perplexing of twentieth-century cultural figures.

By 1908 Jean Cocteau was corresponding with Marcel **Proust** and well on his way to self-promotion in the art world. He became an important contributor to Sergei **Diaghilev**'s Ballets Russes. Cocteau lived openly with male companions at many times in his life. Grief at the death of the young novelist Raymond Radiguet in 1923 was one cause of his famous turn to opium in the 1920s. During the period 1937–50 his creativity was spurred by his relationship with the actor Jean Marais. Later he adopted the painter Edouard Dermit. Throughout his life, Cocteau was surrounded by a coterie of gay male artists

and celebrities. His homosexuality kept him at a distance from André Breton's Surrealists, who championed heterosexuality.

Cocteau tended not to deal directly with homosexuality in his public work, generally choosing either indirect, displaced, or universal approaches to sexuality. Yet one of his first dramatic works was an adaptation of Oscar **Wilde**'s *The Picture of Dorian Gray*. In his three earliest collections of poems Cocteau treated narcissism and the "love that dare not speak its name." In 1928 he published without signing his name to it *The White Paper*, a story which begins with an open declaration of homosexuality. His first film, *The Blood of a Poet* (1930), has an overall homoerotic and autoerotic ambiance. Throughout his career, he made many drawings, including some for Jean **Genet**'s novel *Querelle of Brest* (1947). The frequent themes of doubling, monstrosity, and punishment for love in his work can be linked to his experiences as a sexual outsider, but more rigorous scholarship is needed to go beyond the old clichés.

Cocteau created one of the most extraordinary private mythologies of the twentieth century. Of his voluminous works, some of the best include the films *Beauty and the Beast* (1946) and *Orpheus* (1950), the novel *The Terrible Children* (1929), the plays *The Infernal Machine* (1934), *The Knights of the Round Table* (1937), *The Eagle with Two Heads* (1947), and *Bacchus* (1951), the poetry collections *Opera* (1927) and *Requiem* (1962), and the essay "Opium" (1930). Publication of Cocteau's multivolume diary (1951–63) is now in progress. In 1987 his letters to Jean Marais were published, as earlier his poetry for him had been appended to Marais' *Stories of My Life*. Marais continues to direct Cocteau's plays and preserve the legacy of his friend.

BIBLIOGRAPHY. *L'Album Masques: Jean Cocteau*, Paris: Persona, 1983; Lydia Crowson, *The Aesthetic of Jean Cocteau*, Hanover: University of New

Hampshire Press, 1978; Arthur King Peters, ed., *Jean Cocteau and the French Scene*, New York: Abbeville, 1984; Francis Steegmuller, *Cocteau: A Biography*, Boston: Little, Brown, 1970.

Peter G. Christensen

COLETTE (1873–1954)

French novelist. Born Sidonie-Gabrielle Colette in a small Burgundian village, she was the daughter of an army captain who had fought in the Crimea and lost a leg in the Italian campaign. Her whole literary career was to be marked by memories of her rural childhood, in which "Claudine's household" was a disorderly but sensual ambiance, with a somewhat eccentric mother, an assortment of pets, a large garden, and all the sensations of the provincial countryside. But the lost paradise of her early years caused regrets later on, when she said: "A happy childhood is a bad preparation for contact with human beings." In 1893 she married Henry Gauthier-Villars, who under the name of Willy was a celebrity of the Paris boulevards, but the marriage was ill-fated, as Willy soon reverted to the ways of a free-roving bachelor. This failure in her first marriage impressed upon the young woman the distance between love and happiness.

Some notebooks that Colette had filled with her childhood memories at Willy's behest were the starting point for her first novel, *Claudine à l'école* (1900), followed by a whole series with the same heroine which found its way to the stage. The sequel was Colette's slow conquest of her marital and literary independence. In 1906 she obtained a divorce and began to live alone in a modest apartment in Paris, soon "protected" by a strange creature, Missy, the youngest daughter of the Duc de Morny, who possessed money and a passion for the theatre. The two women appeared on the stage in daring pantomimes, a period of her life in which Colette struggled to earn her livelihood and which she recorded in *La Vagabonde* (1911) and *L'Envers du music-hall* (1913). Her second marriage in 1912, this time to Henry de Jouvenel, the editor-in-chief of the newspaper *Le Matin*, to which she contributed an article a week, was no happier than the first. For a time she abandoned both the stage and her writing career and gave birth to a daughter. World War I revived her journalistic bent, and she was sent as a reporter to the Italian front. She also composed a work entitled *La Paix chez les bêtes* (1916), which depicts her withdrawal from the world of human relations into the intimate sphere of household pets. In 1920 Colette published her masterpiece *Cheri*, whose male hero confronts Léa, a woman of fifty who has not "abandoned her search for happiness."

In 1923 she divorced her second husband, and also published *Le Blé en herbe*, whose serialization by *Le Matin* was halted so as not to offend the readers. By now a successful writer, in possession of a villa at Saint-Tropez, "la Treille muscate," she issued one novel after another on the theme of the eternal combat between the sexes. In 1935 Colette married Maurice Goudeket, her faithful admirer, and settled permanently at the Palais-Royal in Paris. In her last years she composed a few more important works, among them *Gigi* (1945), while basking in her reminiscences and her literary fame.

Colette's work was more autobiographical than anyone could have admitted when it first appeared. The Claudine series features a tomboyish girl who at fifteen develops an intense crush on a pretty assistant mistress, Aimée, who tutors her in English at home, but the affair is interrupted when the domineering headmistress herself turns fond of the assistant. Aimée abandons Claudine to become the pampered favorite of her superior. Claudine even eavesdrops one day upon an intimate moment enjoyed by the two women in their dormitory quarters while their classes are running wild in the schoolrooms. Later, the headmistress implies to Claudine that she might have replaced the junior mistress as her favorite. The second volume of the series finds Claudine in her seventeenth year in Paris, where a long illness causes her hair to be cropped and her contacts limited to her father's older sister and the latter's grandson, Marcel, a pretty and effeminate youth who is absorbed in his own affair with a male schoolmate, which has already made trouble for them at the lycée and provoked the wrathful contempt of Marcel's father. The series continues in the same vein with homoerotic as well as heterosexual interaction among the characters.

Stella Browne, in a psychological study of women authors with lesbian tendencies, mentions Colette as having been involved with two women, the film star Marguerite Moréno and an unnamed foreign noblewoman, of whom character sketches drawn with great discretion figure in *Ces Plaisirs* (1932). The entire setting of Colette's life work is the amoral, sensual world of a coterie of Parisian literati and *rentiers* in the years before World War I—an ambiance in which homosexuality was a subdued, but certainly not a major element. Colette herself enjoyed the company of male homosexuals, especially Jean Cocteau and Jean Marais, in her literary set during the years of her renown as one of the great living French authors.

BIBLIOGRAPHY. Jeannette Foster, *Sex Variant Women in Literature*, Baltimore: Diana Press, 1975; Michèle Sarde, *Colette, libre et entravée*, Paris: Stock, 1978.

Evelyn Gettone

COLOR SYMBOLISM

In addition to their aesthetic aspect, colors acquire symbolic values, which are culturally variable. In Western civilization black is the color of mourning, while in some Asian societies white is. Many men today will avoid wearing lavender or pink because of their "fruity" associations. Yet over the centuries so many hues have been linked to homosexuality that it would be almost impossible to eschew them all.

According the poet **Martial**, several colors were associated with effeminate homosexuality in imperial Rome. He limns an exquisite "who thinks that men in scarlet are not men at all, and styles violet mantles the vesture of women; although he praises native colors and always affects somber hues, grass-green (*galbinus*) are his morals" (I, 96). While scarlet and violet were the traditional colors of effeminacy, an off-green seems to have been the new, "in" color of the day. Martial even uses the *galbinus* shade metaphorically to represent the lifestyle as a whole. In late Victorian England, Robert Hichens' novel *The Green Carnation* (1894) helped to revive the association. In 1929 an American physician, John F. W. Meagher, stated flatly, "Their favorite color is green." Whether it was or not, this assertion took hold in the popular mind, and in the 1950s American high school students avoided green on Thursday, reputed to be "National Fairy Day." Another color associated with the "decadent" 1890s was yellow, because of the London periodical that was almost synonymous with the aesthetic sophistication of that era, *The Yellow Book*. A current Russian term for a gay man is *golubchik*, from *goluboy*, "blue," evidently through association with the "blue blood" of the aristocracy of the Old Regime.

Probably the most enduringly significant sector of the color wheel is, however, the red to purple range (as Martial duly noted two thousand years ago). According to Havelock **Ellis**, one could not safely walk down the streets of late-nineteenth-century New York wearing a red tie without being accosted, since this garment was then the universal mark of the male prostitute. In gay slang this fashion was referred to as "wearing one's badge." Because of the "scarlet woman," the great Whore of Babylon of the Book of Revelation, that color has acquired a strong association with prostitution and adultery (cf.

Nathaniel Hawthorne's novel *The Scarlet Letter*). During the Nazi **holocaust** homosexual inmates were made to wear a pink triangle, and subsequently gay activists have taken up this symbol as a kind of armorial badge. In Europe the words *rosa* and *rose* (= pink) are widely used. The popularity of this color seems to reflect the contrast boys/blue vs. girls/pink, suggesting gender-role reversal. In American culture the word lavender—a blend of red and blue (as in "lavender lover," *The Lavender Lexicon*, etc.)—almost speaks for itself. Gershon Legman (in his 1941 glossary published as an appendix to George Henry's *Sex Variants*) claimed to relay popular lore when he wrote of seven stages of homosexuality, "from *ga-ga* to the 'deeper tones' of lavender." This shade has a secondary association with scented powder and aromatic flowers, producing an unconscious synaesthetic effect. Beginning with the Romans, it has been customary to refer to florid passages of writing as "purple patches." Reflecting at the end of his life on his many bittersweet encounters with male prostitutes, Oscar **Wilde** saluted them as "purple hours" illuminating life's grayness.

In the 1970s some elements of gay-male society observed a back-pocket handkerchief code with colors correlating with one's specific preference. Thus yellow signified an interest in "water sports" (urolagnia), black **S/M**, and brown scatophilia. The mid-1980s saw public display at rallies and marches of a rainbow "Gay Pride Flag," consisting of six parallel stripes ranging from bright red to deep purple. The juxtaposition of colors stands for the diversity of the gay/lesbian community with regard to ethnicity, gender, and class— perhaps also connoting, in the minds of some, the coalition politics of the Rainbow Alliance headed by Jesse Jackson.

Although the color preferences ascribed to gay people are various, two features, not altogether compatible, stand out. First there is a fondness for mixed hues and off-shades, generally from the red-to-blue gamut. In keeping with the notion of the "third sex" as an intermediate entity, these hues may be associated with a particular time of day, the transition between daylight and night that is the province of "twilight men." Second, following the stereotype of homosexuals as "screaming" self-dramatizers who flaunt their identity, they are held to be irresistibly attracted to such bright colors as red and purple. These attributed motivations reveal the degree of prejudice that is involved, but over the course of time many gay people have adopted such colors, in part as a signal that can be easily understood by their peers.

See also **Flower Words**.

Wayne R. Dynes

COMEDY
See **Theatre and Drama**.

COMICS

The ultimate origins of this familiar aspect of modern popular culture lie in the illustrated European broadsheets of the sixteenth and seventeenth centuries which were, however, directed toward adults. Among these are a few stray items depicting the execution of contemporary sodomites, as well as lurid images of the conflagration that destroyed the city of Sodom itself.

The nineteenth century saw the appearance of children's books which approximate real comics, but these were not accessible to a mass audience. The first true comic strips were introduced in 1897 as a circulation-building device in the Sunday supplements of the Hearst newspapers. The now-familiar pulp comic book was a creation of the Depression: the first commercial example is *Famous Funnies* of 1934. Although these strips generally affirmed middle-class values, and certainly contained not the slightest overt indication of sex, they were regularly denounced by pundits as a pernicious influence on the young (cf. Fredric Wertham,

Seduction of the Innocent, New York, 1953).

Batman, appearing in 1939, featured the adventures of a playboy detective and his teenage ward, Robin. Although the relationship is portrayed as a simple mentor–protégé one, some teenage male readers were able to project something stronger into it. This aspect was certainly flirted with in the campy television offshoot beginning in 1966, though this series reflects a much changed cultural climate. In 1941 there appeared *Wonderwoman*, featuring an Amazon with special powers living on an all-woman island. This strip—contrary to the expressed wishes of its creators—served as a focus for lesbian aspirations. In the 1970s it was rediscovered by the women's movement as a proto-feminist statement.

In the late 1940s "Blade" drew several illustrated stories, including "The Barn" and "Truck Hiker," that can be considered predecessors of the gay comics. Circulated underground, they have been officially published only in recent years. Somewhat later the wordless strips of supermacho types created by Tom of Finland began to circulate in Europe.

It was the American **counterculture** of the 1960s, however, which first made possible the exploration of taboo subjects in a context of crumbling censorship restrictions. In 1964 a Philadelphia gay monthly, *Drum*, began serializing *Harry Chess* by Al Shapiro ("A. Jay"). Modeled on a popular television series, *Harry Chess* was both macho and campy, though explicit sex scenes were veiled. In the 1970s no-holds-barred examples appeared drawn by such artists as Bill Ward, Sean, and Stephen (*Meatman*).

Following the practice of mainstream magazines, the Los Angeles *Advocate* had a regular one-panel series by Joe Johnson named *Miss Thing*. The hero of this popular classic was an outrageous queen of a type that gay liberation was trying to make obsolete. Subsequently *Christopher Street* published a series of

New Yorker-style cartoons that capture, perhaps all too well, the sophistication of Manhattan's upper East Side.

In 1980 Howard Cruse, together with his publisher Dennis Kitchen, started a series of pulp books called *Gay Comix* that included work by both men and women. Out of this work evolved Cruse's gay-male couple, Wendell and Ollie, with whose more-or-less real-life problems many *Advocate* readers could identify.

European artists also developed strips. France's Hippolyte Romain's *Les Chéries* provides an acid portrait of older Parisian queens. In Spain Nazario's *Anarcoma*, featuring a macho transvestite, played fast-and-loose with gender categories. Probably Europe's most original contribution, however, is the work of Düsseldorf-based Ralf König. The often ludicrous situations of his homely characters highlight banal, yet touching aspects of everyday gay male life.

BIBLIOGRAPHY. Winston Leyland and Jerry Mills, eds., *Meatman*, San Francisco: G. S. Press, 1986; Robert Triptow, *Gay Comics*, New York: New American Library, 1989.
Wayne R. Dynes

COMING OUT

The cultural and psychological process by which persons relate to a particular model of homosexuality by internalizing a sense of **identity** as "homosexual" or "lesbian" in accordance with that model is called "coming out." As there are different (if any) identity models of homosexuality in different cultures, the coming out process also shows wide variation.

Conceptual Problems. In the industrialized countries of Northern Europe and North America, the process can be applied to anyone with a substantial erotic interest in others of the same gender, and its end result is identification as a "homosexual" or "lesbian." In much of the rest of the world, the process concerns primarily the sexually receptive male, not the active-insertive one, and the end result may be identification as a quasi-female; it remains unclear to what extent a corresponding process exists for females. In other cultures and at other times, and in particular in areas where **pederasty** has been popular, the identity model is lacking and the question of "coming out" does not arise.

Research into "coming out" has generally been limited to areas where the northern-industrial model of homosexuality is dominant, and this must be kept in mind in evaluating any claims to universally valid findings. Another flaw in much of the research is its assumption that a homosexual identity is somehow innate and intrinsically valuable and needs only to be uncovered or unsuppressed in order to blossom; an alternative which posits the sense of homosexual identity as something learned from the (sub- and dominant) culture, and hence views "coming out" as a socialization process, has not been sufficiently explored. Most of the research assumes that "coming out" is a necessary and in the long run beneficial (if at times difficult) process leading to an identity which is assumed to be an objective good. Both of these assumptions are culture-bound and subject to question.

Even in the northern-industrialized societies, there is considerable dispute over the question of where "coming out" ends, with minimalists holding it to be a state of internal acceptance of a homosexual self-identity (which could be completely private), gay liberationists taking it to be a state in which one's homosexuality is made known to virtually anyone with whom one has significant contact, and various writers taking intermediate positions. The latter group seems to have divided "coming out" into a multifold process in which one "comes out" to oneself, one's family, one's friends, to people in a gay social setting, to one's boss, colleagues, and others in many combinations and sequences.

Age at Coming Out. In contemporary northern-industrial countries, with their wide media exposure of homosexuality and its **subculture**, coming out is primarily a matter for **youth** from puberty through the mid-20s. Before the taboos on public exposure of homosexuality were broken, however, the process was not uncommon at much older stages of life, prompted by a chance encounter.

The best time (psychologically and sociologically) to come out is an issue few have systematically addressed. Many in the gay community simply take the view that the earlier, the better: "Out of the closets and into the streets!" This position, however, needs to assess carefully the liabilities accompanying early identification as homosexual, when an early or even pre-teenager has few resources to help him cope with social homophobia, little chance of meaningful assistance from older homosexuals, and may prematurely be closing off routes of self-exploration which would otherwise lead to bisexuality or heterosexuality. Against these disadvantages may be placed the ability to discover earlier adult role-models with which the young homosexual may feel more comfortable, and the opportunities which youth affords for an active and enjoyable sexuality.

Another perspective suggests that one might benefit by delaying the revelation of homosexual identity, if this has been internally adopted, until the environment is more positive and supportive (usually after secondary schooling is completed), or limiting it to a few "safe" persons who can give necessary social and psychological support while the teenager is learning crisis competence, self-respect and ego integrity and in various ways preparing to eventually face the reality of a homophobic society.

Some argue in favor of delaying "coming out" to a later stage, when economic independence and social status have already been secured and are not so easily jeopardized, or even later when family obligations have been met through marriage and procreation, and when middle-aged ennui can be replaced with the adventure of exploring a whole new sexual terrain.

Going Back In? The argument might also be advanced that, in view of the lesser intensity of **ageism** in heterosexual society, the midlife period would be a good time for homosexuals to "come out" into heterosexuality. Very little is known about such "reverse coming out," however, since few if any researchers have gathered study groups of former homosexuals. Despite this absence, there are indications that such a reversal can take place, especially during the teenage years, and a study of the **Kinsey** data would also suggest a substantial "drop-out" population waiting to be studied.

Coming Out as a Developmental Process. A few gays and lesbians report no memory of a coming out process; they always considered themselves homosexual and were never "in the closet." Others have reported a sudden revelation of their own homosexuality which does not fit into any theory of stages but has brought them from apparently heterosexual to comfortably homosexual virtually overnight.

Theorists of the coming out process, however, have generally characterized it as a series of milestone events whereby a person moves from a point of almost complete concealment of homosexuality to one of self-recognition or external proclamation of a homosexual identity. Perhaps the most comprehensive statement of this process is by Gary J. McDonald: "As a developmental process through which gay persons become aware of their affectional and sexual preferences and choose to integrate this knowledge into their personal and social lives, coming out involves adopting a nontraditional identity, restructuring one's self-concept, reorganizing one's personal sense of history, and altering one's relations with others and with society . . . all of which reflects a complex series of cognitive and affective

transformations as well as changes in behavior."

Most coming out models propose a linear series of developmental stages based on a particular theoretical perspective (e.g., Erikson, Piaget, Goffman). Examples of such sequences include: precoming out, coming out, exploration, first relationships, integration (Coleman); sensitization, signification-disorientation/dissociation, coming out, commitment (Plummer, Troiden); identity confusion, identity comparison, identity tolerance, identity acceptance, identity pride, identity synthesis (Cass).

Unresolved issues include the linearity of the process within the life of an individual (including backsliding and changes in the sequence of stages) and individual differences in the timing of the process, including absolute time in terms of age at reaching various set points and relative time in terms of how long the process takes.

There is some evidence that coming out is occurring earlier and that the process is becoming more compact with each new cohort of gays and lesbians, especially in urban, collegiate, and media-saturated communities. It is no longer rare for the coming out process to begin shortly after puberty and be essentially completed by the end of adolescence. This is attributable in large part to the recent visibility of gay and lesbian topics in many parts of the world.

Significant Milestones. The coming out milestones often have great significance to the individual. Many remember, and even celebrate, the anniversary of their coming out. Books devoted primarily to coming out stories document and highlight the pain, the indecision, and sometimes the violence, isolation and alienation that often accompany the coming out process. For many, however, the process is not particularly noteworthy or painful. Education, supportive friends and family, youth, gender atypicality, and a history of some homosexual but no heterosexual experiences have been cited as "facilitating factors," but few if any of these have been systematically investigated.

The self-help literature for gay and lesbian youth is quite explicit in designating parents as the crucial factor in the youth's coming out process. Those who do not come out to their family, according to G. B. MacDonald, become "half-members of the family unit: afraid and alienated, unable ever to be totally open and spontaneous, to trust or be trusted. . . . This sad stunting of human potential breeds stress for gay people and their families alike—stress characterized by secrecy, ignorance, helplessness, and distance." The scientific literature, however, has largely ignored the role of parents, having centered on gay and lesbian adults.

Obstacles and Difficulties. Many defenses are used by individuals to check the seemingly inevitable process, including rationalization ("I was drunk"), relegation to insignificance ("I only did it as a favor for a friend"), compartmentalization ("I get turned on by boys but that doesn't make me a queer"), withdrawal to celibacy or asexuality ("I'm saving myself until I get married"), and denial ("I can't be lesbian because I date boys"). Repression of same-sex desires may lead to future feelings of panic or major disruptions of established coping strategies. It may be difficult for a person going through early phases to request assistance in coping with inner turmoil because consciously there is no problem, and the issues are so nebulous and intensely personal that they constitute an existential crisis. It is not easy to recognize that social standards of behavior, attitudes, and expectations for the future that normally accompany a heterosexual identity are not relevant to one's own life. Passing as heterosexual has its own costs: loss of personal authenticity, feelings of hypocrisy, constant fear of being discovered, and generalized anxiety.

A positive outcome may provide identity integration, a lessening of feelings of guilt and loneliness, a fusing of sexuality and emotionality (such as taking a lover), and a sense of support from the surrounding gay or lesbian community.

The existence of a coming out process is usually attributed to a homophobic environment in which one must take a stance against the perceived social consensus in order to assert one's own preferences, attractions, feelings and inclinations. In this view, full social acceptance of homosexuality as a natural and common variation on a sexual theme would end most of the emotional difficulties as well as the sense of fateful significance of what is otherwise described as coming out.

BIBLIOGRAPHY. Vivienne C. Cass, "Homosexual Identity Formation: A Theoretical Model," *Journal of Homosexuality*, 4 (1979), 219–35; Eli Coleman, "Developmental States of the Coming Out Process," *Journal of Homosexuality*, 7 (1982), 31–43; G. B. MacDonald, "Exploring Sexual Identity: Gay People and Their Families," *Sex Education Coalition News*, 5 (1983); Gary J. McDonald, "Individual Differences in the Coming Out Process for Gay Men: Implications for Theoretical Models," *Journal of Homosexuality* 8 (1982), 47–60; Julia P. Stanley and Susan J. Wolfe, eds., *The Coming Out Stories*, New York: Persephone, 1980; Richard R. Troiden, "Becoming Homosexual: A Model of Gay Identity Acquisition," *Psychiatry*, 42 (1979), 362–73.
Ritch Savin-Williams (with additional material by Stephen Donaldson)

COMMON LAW

Common law is the designation for a system of **law** that relies on long-established custom and the evolving pattern of precedent established by court decisions. The law common to the whole realm—so termed originally to distinguish it from local custom—began in medieval **England**, and spread overseas with British colonization. Today, with various national modifications, the common law tradition characterizes most English-speaking nations, including the United States, and sets them apart from the so-called civil law countries (including Scotland), which derive their legal tradition from the Roman law codified by Justinian, then further refined by medieval jurists and commentators. A major feature of the common law is the role of jurisprudence, that is to say, of decisions rendered by the courts that enlarge or reduce the scope of existing laws or prior decisions and are then followed by other courts, so that they enter the body of law quite apart from the action of any executive or legislative authority. In other legal systems the courts either do not exercise this role or are formally denied the right to contravene the will of the legislature by altering an existing law or finding it unconstitutional.

The Medieval Background. The first mention of criminal punishment for homosexual behavior in the English common law tradition occurs in a somewhat eccentric treatise known as *Fleta* (ca. 1290), composed by an anonymous jurist at the court of Edward I. This text prescribes that sodomites (along with those who have sexual commerce with Jews and those guilty of bestiality) are to be buried alive. This mode of execution, which does not seem to have been adopted, is probably a reminiscence of a passage in **Tacitus**, which states that among the ancient Germans effeminate cowards were drowned in bogs. As this example suggests, early thinking was a mixture of learned and folkloric elements, grounded in Christian fear of otherness. The treatise known as *Britton* (perhaps by John Le Breton), which is only a few years later than *Fleta*, seems to have had more authority. Here sodomites are to be burned. Although there is little indication of enforcement of this punishment in England from this period, executions are known to have been carried out on the continent, where their sanction derived from an enactment of Justinian and served to link sodomites to heretics, who were

also burned. As in the case of heretics, church officials and courts were charged with finding sodomites, who were then handed over to the secular arm for punishment. However, the king's court had the power of acting independently, and thus sodomy was a crime which partook of both canon (ecclesiastical) and common law.

From the Renaissance through the Eighteenth Century. In 1533, in keeping with a wave of antisodomy legislation on the European continent, Parliament enacted a felony statute against the "detestable and abominable vice of buggery," providing for the penalty of death (25 Henry VIII c. 6). Reenacted under Elizabeth I and made perpetual, this act, which became the charter for all subsequent criminalization in the English-speaking world, secularized the crime, removing it from church jurisdiction and even denying benefit of clergy to the culprits. The language recurred somewhat later in statutes from the southern colonies in North America, though the more northerly ones, many of them under dissenter auspices, preferred to reinforce the wording with biblical language. In England only a few executions, and these by hanging, not burning at the stake, are known from the following two centuries, and Englishmen seemed content to discuss the matter as little as possible, a position taken as late as the *Commentaries* (1765–69) of William Blackstone, which says that the crime is "not to be named among Christians." However, a series of polemical pamphlets, such as John Dunton's *The He-Strumpets* (1707) and the anonymous *Satan's Harvest Home* (1749), began to stir up public opinion against the homosexual subculture that flourished in the British metropolis.

Modern Times. At the end of the eighteenth century, and into the second decade of the nineteenth, a number of executions took place, probably linked to the national malaise caused by the uncertain fortunes of the Napoleonic wars. By 1828 a series of decisions had limited the definition of the offense and imposed a greater burden of proof on the prosecution, but was offset by a new version of the statute enacted as part of the reform of the criminal law by Sir Robert Peel, prescribing that penetration alone (without emission of seed) sufficed to establish the crime. The death penalty for buggery (= anal intercourse) was not formally abolished until 1861 in England and Wales.

The reception of the common law in the newly independent United States meant that British precedent could be followed by American courts in their interpretation of existing laws, but did not bind them. Hence the individual states came to have their own definitions of the crime and penalties for it. Some ratified a British decision of 1817 that removed oral–genital sexuality from the definition of buggery, but others rejected it.

Then in 1885, in response to a wave of sensationalism in the press concerning the prostitution of teen-aged girls, Parliament adopted the **Criminal Law Amendment Act**. This contained an amendment devised by Henry Labouchere that prescribed a penalty of two years for "gross indecency" between male persons. Oscar **Wilde** was punished under this act, and the notoriety of the case, and the general hostility to homosexuals, blocked legal reform for decades throughout the English-speaking world. Further, many American states enacted their own versions of the amendment that made homosexual acts between males, and sometimes between females, criminal in a loosely defined manner, although the courts could later give more precision to the statute. By and large, courts in the common law tradition did not go beyond holding that "any penetration, however slight" was "sufficient to constitute the offense." This differed from the ruling of German courts that any "beischlafsähnliche Handlung" (act similar to coitus, such as full contact between two male bodies) was criminal under **Paragraph 175** of the Penal Code of the German Empire.

In 1957, however, the **Wolfenden Report** urged decriminalization, which was accomplished, for England and Wales, ten years later, although the age of consent was set at 21, far above the one prescribed by tradition for heterosexual intercourse. In Scotland, Northern Ireland, Canada, and New Zealand legal reform occurred subsequently. The United States and Australia are a legal checkerboard, with some states reformed and others retaining the archaic legislation.

See also **Canon Law; Capital Crime, Homosexuality as; Law: United States; Sixteenth-Century Legislation.**

BIBLIOGRAPHY. H. Montgomery Hyde, *The Love That Dared Not Speak Its Name*, Boston: Little, Brown, 1970.

William A. Percy

COMMUNICATIONS

In the broadest sense communication refers to all acts and processes of signaling from one sentient being to another. In the narrower sense, with which this article is concerned, communications embraces all aspects of human technological enhancement of information conveyance—beyond speaking, gesture, and writing. Inherent in these enhancements is the potential to reach mass audiences, far bigger than the hundreds, say, that a Demosthenes or **Cicero** was able to reach.

Print Media. It is generally agreed that the first step in this momentous development was the spread of printing from Germany in the middle years of the fifteenth century. This invention made it possible for written texts to come out of the monasteries and universities and reach middle-class audiences. Early on the authorities recognized the potential for circulation of heretical or seditious material; hence the apparatus of **censorship** set up throughout Europe. These restrictions could never be absolutely effective, and various stratagems of clandestine publication appeared. These methods were developed in the first instance by religious dissenters who smuggled their wares across hostile frontiers. In due course publishers appeared who were prepared to print and distribute erotic materials, but always with precautions to avoid detection. For example, the *Alcibiade fanciullo a scola* (1652?), an anonymous defense of pederasty now attributed to Antonio Rocco, was ostensibly printed by one "Iuann Wart" at "Oranges." Actually, it seems to have been printed at Venice where, despite the famous tolerance of that city, the publisher (whose name remains unknown) judged it wise to be cautious. The device of using false imprints became common; many books claim to be printed in Holland or by "Pierre Marteau" (and in fact some were, since that country was more liberal than most). In any event, these practices eventually gave rise to the existence of **private presses**, such as those of Carrington and the Olympia Press, based in Paris at the turn of the century and after World War II respectively. In the 1970s new methods of typesetting and printing permitted the emergence of a proliferation of small presses, some of which are gay and lesbian. The emergence of "desktop" publishing means that no author with a little money to spare need forgo the chance to publish a book.

Newer Technologies. Books, newspapers, and other printed matter still belong to the "Gutenberg galaxy" that emerged in the fifteenth century. Yet a whole series of new ways of communication appeared in the wake of the industrial revolution. Because of speed in transmission, the telegraph transformed journalism and international relations, but because the material transmitted was strictly controlled at each end, there was virtually no opportunity for clandestine use. After its appearance in the early twentieth century, radio quickly fell under the control of the state, with many countries reserving all rights of transmission to the government. In the 1970s, however, a series of constitutional decisions in Belgium, France, and Italy struck down the state

monopoly and opened the airways in those countries to a free-for-all. The opportunity was seized by many groups, including those conventionally regarded as "socially marginalized." Many of the new counterculture stations took on gay programming, and in Paris 24-hour broadcasting began on Fréquence Gaie. In North America some gay and lesbian programming has occurred, especially on the stations of the Pacifica network, but its status is precarious. Undoubtedly some "ham operators" have ventured cautiously into the gay realm, but the extent of such excursions is almost impossible to monitor. In the 1970s considerable attention was given to the colorful CB radio transmissions of long-distance truckers, where the presence of homosexuals ("three-legged beavers") on the road was apparently mentioned fairly often. Although commercial and public radio has survived, it has come to be restricted to an increasingly smaller share of the total communications pie, and this seems to be a sector that does not lend itself to a major gay presence. In fact in the United States the Federal Communications Commission has intervened more than once to warn stations about material deemed to be sexually explicit.

Films underwent a trajectory that is well known. First regarded as indecent, they came to acquire middle-class respectability in the 1920s—though only at the cost of self-regulation. During the period of Hollywood self-censorship, male homosexuals were shown only in veiled terms, as in the "sissy" stereotype. Homosexual and lesbian performers had to keep their inclinations strictly in the closet, as audiences expected to empathize with them as red-blooded heterosexual lovers. With the spread of gay liberation in the 1970s, homosexual interest groups were able to exercise leverage to reduce the prevalence of sexual stereotyping; even a few major films presenting favorable views of gay relationships were made. For much of its short life, **television** has been even more restrictive, though here, too, gay leaders and pressure groups have been able to combat stereotypes. In a few American cities cable television has permitted gay programming, in part as a response to public access legislation.

Special-Audience Applications. In communications, a general rule is that the larger the audience, the greater the filtration of the content. The other side of this principle is seen in works intended for small audiences—as the private-press book trade, with its expensive, under-the-counter editions, undoubtedly was. Almost as old as the cinema itself are **porno** movies, which were generally shown clandestinely until the 1960s, when Andy Warhol and others achieved a breakthrough to public acceptance. By the 1980s, when a repertoire of hundreds of gay-male examples had been built up, these films became widely available on VCR, where they are enjoyed by adults in the home. Such taped films are sold by mail, in porno bookstores, and also sometimes in special sections of general video stores.

The availability of mail-order items is noted in the advertisements in the gay **press**. Arising out of the "underground press" of the hippie 1960s, there are now hundreds of gay and lesbian papers worldwide. In North America these papers are, in many instances, given away free in bars so that they reach a wide segment of the socially active gay population. Most of the papers contain "personal" columns, with **advertisements** in which readers can learn of others who share their sexual tastes.

To some extent this function of meeting has been taken over by personal computers linked by modems. A number of services make available gay lines which, however, are more commonly used for chatting than for making sexual assignations. As such they are a great boon for those living in remote areas or who are otherwise social isolates. In France computer dating is even facilitated by a government-sponsored service, the Minitel. Activists have also found that the word-processing functions of computers

facilitate letter-writing campaigns to protest bigoted or demeaning treatment in the major media.

The 1980s saw a fashion for receiving recorded sexual messages by telephone, which was partly fostered by fears of actual sexual contact engendered by the AIDS crisis. In the United States the **phone sex** user dials a 976-prefix number and listens to a brief "canned" message. Precisely because it is not communication in the sense of one person talking to others, the future of this custom would appear to be limited. The telephone had been, of course, the one electronic channel open during the times of oppression, when it served as a "grapevine." Today it is used by some activist groups to form a telephone tree allowing the group to mobilize its members quickly for a demonstration.

As indicated, the tendency toward "massification," with its pressures toward conformity and potential for centralized censorship, is inimical to minority expression in communications. The microchip age, however, has seen major countertrends toward diversification and fragmentation, witness cable TV, satellite transmissions, VCRs, and desktop publishing (typically of books, but also of tapes). These changes would seem to bode well for richer and more varied communication to serve the special needs of gay men and lesbians.

Wayne R. Dynes

COMMUNITY

Debate over the existence of "gay community" stems in part from the lack of consensus about what a "community" is, and in part from a separate standard for "gay community" in contrast to other kinds of urban communities. North American gay (male) communities fit all the criteria suggested by sociologists to define "community" as well as or better than urban ethnic communities do, and lesbian communities exhibit the same features, albeit to a lesser extent.

Territory. The first, common-sense component of "community" is territory. The mythical "traditional" rural village is supposed to have been geographically distinct, internally homogeneous and harmonious, and without important external influences. Yet nowhere are rural villages entirely isolated from each other. Demands for taxes, soldiers, and labor are levied from outside, and even in extremely mountainous regions, there are usually some persons oriented beyond the immediate locale to larger entities. Internal variability and conflict are more common than anthropologists once supposed.

To make communities out of geographical aggregates, people must experience spatial boundaries as important, and differences which occur as dividing kinds of people. That is, geography must be supplemented by endogamy, restriction of trade, local cults, and other such social creations to make socially salient boundaries. Isolation and propinquity alone do not automatically produce solidarity, while seemingly trivial commonalities (such as living in a gray housing project rather than a green one) may come to symbolize distinction salient to collective action.

There are no walled-in ghettoes in North American cities, nor checkpoints to prevent the flow of persons between perfectly segregated areas. Thus, one can travel from a predominantly Italian territory to a predominantly Chinese one to a predominantly gay one to a predominantly black one in San Francisco. None of these areas is inhabited exclusively by Italians, Chinese, gays, or blacks; yet residents of a city are able to report where such communities are—at least to report where the centers are, the boundaries often being fuzzily conceived.

Community Institutions. There may be several neighborhoods with lesbian and/or gay residential concentrations in a large city. Clustering of recreational facilities, particularly nocturnal ones, such as **bars**, foster in-group perception of a gay

or lesbian territory. The existence of distinctive institutions is more salient to identification of a community—both for insiders and outsiders—than residential segregation or concentration. Over the course of the 1970s, gay men in European and North American cities developed a fairly complete set of basic social services beyond gay bars. These included bookstores, churches, travel agencies, periodicals, political clubs, charities, a savings and loan, and whole Gay Yellow Pages directories listing gay businesses and services.

Gay Endogamy. In contrast to relatively impoverished immigrants speaking an alien language, whom sociologists expect to form distinct (ethnic) institutions, gay men were relatively integrated into a full range of occupations, and mostly had native command of the official language before the gay institutional elaboration began. Most gay persons could and did "pass." They chose to interact with their "own kind," rather than being restricted to those who spoke the same language. Given a previous homosexual exogamy (a preference for straight "trade" rather than for "sisters," or for boys rather than adults, as sexual partners), sexual endogamy (self-identified gay men coupling with other self-identified gay men) was crucial to the formation of gay pride, consciousness, and collective action. Lesbians may be relatively less affluent than gay men, but, like gay men, lesbians of all strata patronize distinctively lesbian/gay facilities, are likely to be in lesbian networks, and tend to endogamy in choosing sexual partners and to homosociality in choosing friends.

The Role of Stigma. Not everyone engaged in recurrent homosexual behavior chooses to recognize a sexual orientation as defining their **identity** or as providing a criterion for friendship and non-sexual interaction. Gay consciousness is no more automatic than class consciousness or ethnic consciousness. Some individuals fight the expectation to be part of any such "us," while others eagerly seek a sense of community. Consciousness of kind is not innate, but emerges. This is true of ethnic consciousness as much as of gay consciousness. Stigmas inhibit identification, but when a critical mass develops to challenge the stigma, either by proclaiming "We are not like that," or "The ways we are different are fine, or even valuable," societal stigmas become badges of honor and stimuli to collective organization and action challenging discrimination and affirming the value of the group's stigmatized characteristics. For lesbians and for gay men, challenging societal valuations may be more difficult than it is for some ethnic communities to affirm the value of their lifeways. However, there is also considerable ambivalence to the lifeways of previous generations within ethnic communities. In a pluralistic society, ethnic identification is an achieved status, not automatically and irrevocably established at birth or in primary socialization.

Expectations of others "that you are like us" and should therefore behave in certain ways, and societal definitions used by opportunistic politicians either to advance minorities or to organize against them, help to crystallize identification with a group, so that people defined categorically come to see themselves as having a common history and destiny distinct from others. Advocates and adversaries both foster collective identification, which is a necessary (but not sufficient) prerequisite to collective action. Gay leaders have pressed economic boycotts, political coordination, and mass demonstrations. Anti-gay leaders have promoted legal discrimination and harassment, as well as criminalization of homosexual behavior. In response to police raids and the legal acceptance of assassinating one gay leader (Harvey **Milk**), there have also been gay riots. Nonetheless, it bears stressing that even those who have the feeling of being part of a group may still not join in collective action. Collective action is rarely—if ever—characteristic of any population.

Sporadic action by a self-selected vanguard is more common for class-based or ethnic-based groups, as well as for lesbians or gays.

See also **Geography, Social; Subculture, Gay.**

BIBLIOGRAPHY. Joseph R. Gusfield, *Community*, Oxford: Blackwell, 1975; Stephen O. Murray, "The Institutional Elaboration of a Quasi-Ethnic Community," *International Review of Modern Sociology*, 9 (1979), 165–77.
Stephen O. Murray

CONSCIOUSNESS RAISING

This expression gained wide circulation in the 1970s to designate the practice of forming small groups of persons (usually from five to ten) to work collectively to increase their members' awareness of the political and ideological significance of their actions. The consciousness-raising (CR) trend, often accompanied by the slogan "The personal is the political," seems to have first emerged in the Women's Movement in the late 1960s, whence it migrated (with much else) to gay **liberation** circles.

The expression, which has been traced to Chinese Communist (Maoist) usage in the 1930s, reflects the **Marxist** contrast between true consciousness of one's situation and powers versus "false consciousness," a set of obfuscatory beliefs fostered among oppressed groups in order to preserve ruling-class interests. Only when the oppressed discard the blinkers of false consciousness, the theory goes, will they be in a position to wage a successful struggle for their rights. This discarding, and the complementary advance to higher levels of group awareness, constitute the "work" of consciousness raising.

In the gay **movement**, the formation of consciousness-raising groups was often promoted as a means to an end: a phase of strengthening and toughening in a supportive atmosphere of comradeship in preparation for more active intervention in the struggle. Yet under the influence of pop-psychology trends, such as "sensitivity training," gay groups of this kind often became an end in themselves, to all intents and purposes serving as harbingers of the self-absorption of the "me generation." In the self-improving middle classes, the period saw a shift in fashion from individual therapy to group therapy, a model which the consciousness raising groups all too easily adopted—the difficulty being that the new **psychotherapy** (like the old) fostered adjustment to the prevailing mores of society, while the gay/lesbian groups fitted their members for participation in a heterodox, dissident movement. By the end of the 1970s the CR vogue, part of the period's general enthusiasm for "doing things collectively," was effectively spent.

Whatever the weaknesses of consciousness raising in practice, it did address a pervasive problem in modern society, that of social atomization which frustrates the aspiration for solidarity with like-minded others. Modern consumer society engenders social isolation, and this can only be combatted by forming intermediate structures of group affinity. Moreover, homosexuals tend to meet only for sexual purposes: the consciousness-raising groups, together with coffee houses and community centers, were a laudable attempt to create an alternative. The consciousness-raising process served to spread the new ideology of the insurgent gay movement to broad circles of individuals who until then had been exposed only to the hostile indoctrination of the mass media; it initiated them into the beliefs and mores of the political community they were joining, following the original model of consciousness raising which in its homeland had functioned to incorporate the peasant masses into the fighting force whose victory founded the People's Republic of China. Historical hindsight, of course, reveals pitilessly the romantic illusions of such attempts at replaying a revolution, and once this incongruity was

perceived, consciousness raising as such was doomed.

CONSENT
Consent is broadly defined as "voluntary agreement to or acquiescence in what another proposes or desires." For the purpose of this article, however, it will to be taken to mean "willingness to engage in sexual activity with a partner of the same sex." Consent to a course of action does not imply a mature understanding of the consequences of that course of action, but merely a willingness that it should take place. Homosexual offenses are classified as consensual or non-consensual. The legal application of this distinction is not as clearcut as it would at first seem. The law is not obliged to recognize consent as a defense (for example, in incest cases); moreover, when it does, the persons must be over a certain age.

Homosexual behavior is criminal when it occurs without the consent of the other party. **Rape** is by definition non-consensual and so always satisfies this condition, as does indecent assault except in some cases involving minors; buggery (anal intercourse) may fall under this heading.

Homosexual behavior is criminal with a person under the age of consent, a demarcation which varies considerably from one jurisdiction to another, and may be higher than the age of consent for heterosexual intercourse. Likewise homosexual behavior is criminal if included in a category of sexual behavior that is globally prohibited, such as incest or intercourse with a mental defective. Finally, homosexual acts committed in public or in a place of public resort are criminal even with the consent of both partners.

That no one, even a hustler or a prostitute, should be compelled to engage in sexual activity against his or her will is a sound and unchallenged principle of law. The borderline cases are those in which consent was given grudgingly or promises or enticements were utilized to secure the consent at first withheld. The legislator has directed the concern of the law mainly to adolescents thought to be in need of protection ("corrupting the morals of a minor"). In some jurisdictions the adult who engages a minor for homosexual prostitution is subject to prosecution, even if the consensual act was not in and of itself a crime.

In some jurisdictions (approximately half of the United States, and several Australian states) all male homosexual acts are illegal; in these areas consent is no defense, since the behavior is criminal under all circumstances, whether committed in public or in private.

The issue of consent arose when the first proposals were made to abolish the laws criminalizing sodomy and other homosexual offenses. One of the arguments for repeal was that when the partners to a sexual act consent to its performance, no wrong is committed which the state would have an interest in redressing. Only intrusive enforcement practices—prying and entrapment—can hope to ferret out such offenses. The opponents of reform argued that society has an interest in enforcing its moral code, even if the authorities seldom learn of consensual sexual activity. A further argument was that there is such a thing as public consent, which differs from the consent of private individuals to relationships between them. In this view consent cannot legitimate behavior which public opinion regards as morally wrong and injurious to the best interests of society. On the other hand, a pluralistic society that recognizes the moral autonomy of the individual as a cardinal principle does not have the right to impose the moral standards of one part of the community upon another which flatly rejects them.

In all legal systems rape, that is, sexual gratification obtained with the use of force or of threats against the non-consenting party, is a criminal offense. (At present, however, some states do not rec-ognize male rape as a statutory offense.) The issue of the age at which an individual can give valid consent to a sexual act is a disputed one, and in the course of decriminalizing homosexual behavior between adults some jurisdictions set a higher age of consent for homosexual activity than for heterosexual. Equal justice would require that the age of consent, and the other conditions establishing consent, be the same for both classes of acts.

Warren Johansson

CONSERVATISM

Setting aside significant national differences and viewing the phenomenon as a whole, the political philosophy known as conservatism has several main features. First, there is a belief in the natural hierarchy of society which must be defended against the onslaughts of egalitarianism and demagogic populism. Then conservatives display a strong attachment to the time-honored, traditional elements of civilization, together with an abhorrence of sudden revolutionary change and social "experimentation." This reverence for tradition marks the sexual sphere in particular, where the norm is lifelong monogamous heterosexual marriage—the antithesis of the "gay lifestyle" with its tolerance of casual unions that can be terminated at the wish of either party. Many conservatives, though not all, look to organized religion and its moral codes as a bulwark against unwanted social shifts. The final hallmark of the conservative mentality is an idealization of the past as contrasted to the "**decadent**" and "corrupt" present, with the recurrent, even obsessive notion that homosexuality is increasing and that "something has to be done" to stop the spread of the vice before it leads to the moral ruin of society, if not to outright race suicide. This attitude is documented over so many centuries and in so many countries that it is a virtual cliché of conservative lament over the loss of the righteousness and innocence of former times.

Homosexuality and conservatism would therefore seem totally antithetical. Stereotypically, conservatives are viewed as the chief reservoir of antihomosexual bigotry and the most determined opponents of gay rights. However, antihomosexual attitudes have been common—and even fostered by the regime—in such **Marxist**, state-socialist societies as the USSR, the People's Republic of China, and Cuba. Moreover, as a result of centuries of virtually unchecked virulence, antigay views are widely diffused in many industrial countries; they have been documented, for example, among liberal writers in North America. Nor are antihomosexual motifs necessarily to be traced ultimately to conservative ideologies; the religious circles in ancient Iran and Israel that developed the most potent early forms of homophobia might justly have been regarded as progressive in their day.

Historically, conservatism has even favored some forms of homosexual expression. In ancient **Greece** the institution of initiatory **pederasty** was an instrument of the aristocracy in training neophytes to uphold its values. Adolf **Brand's** German gay periodical *Der Eigene* (1896–1930) printed articles with an idealized vision of the erotic relationship between knight and page in medieval European society. Tokugawa **Japan** shows a similar phenomenon among the **samurai**—the feudal warrior class. And in some traditional Third World countries, like **Afghanistan**, tribal leaders have clung to pederastic customs, while fiercely resisting the incursions of Western liberalism and Soviet Communism alike.

In the United States and similar countries conservatives tend to fall into two main groups. The first is a traditional command conservatism which favors the deployment of state power, including the military establishment, to achieve policy aims. The second adheres to laissez-faire or **libertarian** ideas, and proposes a reduc-

tion in the role of government and greater reliance on the working of private initiative and the free market. Conservative parties are aware of the tension that divides the traditionalists and the libertarians in their ranks. It is the second group, which has shown some receptivity to the idea of excluding the state from the bedroom, that has had some affinity for homosexuals. Gay Republicans are generally of this second stripe.

In Britain the Conservative Group for Gay Equality argues that legislation is needed to end the second-class citizenship of homosexuals. As ordinary citizens and taxpayers—the group's chair Peter Campbell notes—"they contribute to society by work and voluntary efforts in the same ways as heterosexuals, and are no more likely than heterosexuals to commit crimes against persons, property, and the public interest."

The far right has had little attraction for homosexuals. In France a few gay men have indicated qualified support for the neo-fascist party of Jean-Marie Le Pen, the National Front. Other French homosexuals have formed a conservative group of their own, Gaie France, which favors the cultivation of "Indo-European" values. Such ideas seem to enjoy little international currency.

BIBLIOGRAPHY. Robert Bauman, *The Gentleman from Maryland: The Conscience of a Gay Conservative*, New York: Arbor House, 1986.

Wayne R. Dynes

CONSTITUTIONAL HOMOSEXUALITY

The question of whether homosexual conduct is the result of inborn or constitutional factors, on the one hand, or is the product of environmental influences, on the other, is part of the larger nature–nurture debate. While animal behavior is essentially the result of genetic and hereditary mechanisms, human beings are subject to a vast amount of cultural conditioning, representing a layer standing over and above the biological substratum, though not necessarily in conflict with it. Regardless of which solution one chooses, the constitutional-biological or the environmental, the etiology of homosexual behavior remains a conundrum. Adopting the first perspective (the constitutional), one has to explain how nature would continue to replicate, generation after generation, a trait that does not contribute to procreative fitness and, to the extent that an individual is exclusively homosexual, is not genetically transmitted at all. Yet if environment, through cultural conditioning, is king, one may still ask why homosexuals exist, since the glorification of heterosexuality and love of offspring is an ever present drumbeat in all societies. To be sure, human psychosexual development is probably the result of the interaction of innate and environmental factors, but the problem of explaining their deployment, separately and conjointly, remains.

The prestige of Darwinian evolution in the later nineteenth century, together with growing understanding of the actual mechanisms of heredity, gave constitutional ("congenital") theories great appeal during this period. Magnus Hirschfeld, whose conclusions were based on the study of thousands of individuals, was a firm believer in the idea that sexual orientation is innate. In support of this view he pointed out that many individuals manifest marked homosexual tendencies before puberty (when they are unaware of any peers), that they maintain them with the greatest tenacity against all internal and external pressures for change, and that they insist that their sexual interests bond with the inmost core of their being. He also held that homosexuals are found in families in greater numbers than chance would suggest, and that same-sex behavior occurs in an astonishing range of human societies, past and present. Nonetheless, Hirschfeld and his colleagues were unable to suggest any transcendent biological

reason for the recurrence of this trait in one generation after another. The belief that homosexuality is in some sense innate nonetheless provided a political argument for toleration and decriminalization: individuals whose behavior is not the result of choice should not be subjected to coercive procedures aimed at changing that which cannot be changed.

Sigmund **Freud**'s theory of psychodynamic development postulates a common origin for both sexual orientations in the **polymorphous perverse** stage, though heterosexual development represents the outcome of full maturity, homosexuality being an arrested or retarded pattern. This theory, which was widely diffused after World War I, has sometimes been misunderstood as one of "universal **bisexuality**." While it has the seeming advantage of combining constitutional and environmental factors, it still leaves unexplained why there should be a homosexual component at any stage, or why homosexual subjects exhibit such a range of adult personality types.

The rise of Nazism, which preached racial determinism in theory and embraced a coercive form of population control in practice, served to discredit all theories of constitutional-biological conditioning. In the case of homosexuality, the dominance of environmentalism lead to a search for all sorts of putative factors, from the "close-binding mother" to a notion that society itself is somehow antiheterosexual. A study produced by the Kinsey Institute of Indiana University (*Sexual Preference*, Bloomington, 1971) examined the various environmental theories and found them all wanting, opting for an (unspecified) biological solution through a process of elimination.

In the 1950s evidence became available that identical **twins** raised apart showed a remarkable correlation for sexual orientation, though these data have been largely ignored. Only the controversial discipline of **sociobiology** has produced a tentative reconstruction of a biological rationale for homosexuality. The sociobiologists hypothesize that homosexuality contributes to the "inclusive fitness" of a gene pool, by permitting a childless, but energetic individual to devote efforts to the advancement of his or her nieces and nephews. While sociobiology has achieved considerable success in animal studies, its applicability to human beings is hotly contested, and the future of such explanations remains in doubt.

As a final element of caution, it should be recognized that the possible isolation of a body of individuals whose homosexual behavior, exclusive or not, is essentially conditioned by biological-constitutional factors, does not preclude the existence of another body of individuals capable of homosexual response whose modalities are not so determined. That is to say, the range of behavior and character types among individuals of a predominantly homosexual orientation is extremely varied, and one of the elements of variation may be the fact that the larger pool subsumed under the rubric of homosexual represents a confluence of "innate" and environmentally produced streams.

Ward Houser

CONTAGION

The notion of contagion as applied to disease originated only in the Middle Ages, when it was associated with plague and leprosy—both objects of intense dread. Almost from the beginning, however, the notion of moral contamination became attached to the word in the modern languages, so that it could be applied to deviant practices or heretical beliefs that threatened to "infect" society.

Hence the emergence of the **medical** concept of sexual **inversion** or homosexuality led to the belief that same-sex conduct could manifest an "infectious disease" and that the "innate homosexual" was a source of contagion who could "spread his perversion" to previously healthy heterosexuals. The term "moral leprosy" (from medieval Latin *lepra moralis*) applied to homosexuality appears at the beginning of the twentieth century, signaling the rise in **homophobic** circles of a new mythology that to some extent counteracted the pleas then beginning to be heard for toleration of the "born invert."

Underlying the notion of the contagiousness of homosexuality is the macroevolutionary capacity of human beings for sexual response to members of their own sex—as distinct from an exclusive homosexual orientation which occurs in a small minority at most. Hence the peculiar fear that homosexual activity can "spread like wildfire" if the criminal and social sanctions against it are relaxed "for even a moment." This apprehension figures in much of the twentieth-century polemic (such as that in **Nazi** Germany) which calls for increased penalties for homosexual conduct in order to forestall so rapid a spread of non-procreative sexuality as to raise the specter of race suicide. The widespread if transient homosexuality of adolescence also contributes to this delusion, usually fortified by the claim that unsuspecting adolescents are seduced by the adult homosexual and then "fixated in a lifelong pattern" of exclusive orientation to their own sex. There is also the accusation that homosexuals, since they cannot reproduce, must ceaselessly proselytize for their aberrant lifestyle.

Obviously there is no virus or germ that can account for homosexual response, and a pattern of exclusive homosexual activity that is inborn or acquired in early childhood could hardly be spread to other adults by mere contact, yet the belief that homosexuality is a contagious disease serves to reinforce patterns of legal discrimination and ostracism, all the more as it cannot be proven that the average member of the population is incapable of homosexual activity, even if the preference for such gratification remains confined to a demonstrable minority. The alliance of moral condemnation with the late-nineteenth-century notion of homosexuality as disease has given the ambiguous notion of contagion a new lease on life and contributed to the persistence of homophobic attitudes which the gay movement has had to work patiently to dispel—thus far not with entire success. The recent association of homosexual activity with the spread of a pathological and usually fatal condition such as Acquired Immune Deficiency Syndrome (AIDS) has the side-effect of reviving the paranoid aspect of this belief system in the unconscious depths of the mass mind.

Warren Johansson

CONTEST LITERATURE

In Greek literature a subgenre—sometimes known under the rhetorical term *syncrisis*—developed in which two characters debate opposing points of view. Thus in **Aristophanes'** *Frogs* the characters Aeschylus and Euripides argue the merits of their poetry, while his *Clouds* verbally pits Just Reasoning against Unjust Reasoning. In later Greek writing several pieces of contest literature appeared debating the relative merits of boys and women as love objects. Such a debate is featured in the novel *Leucippe and Clitophon* by Achilles Tatius (perhaps second century A.D.). An anonymous specimen is the so-called *Affairs of the Heart* by pseudo-Lucian.

Together with much else in the Greek heritage, this tradition of arguing the merits of pederasty vs. the love of women passed to Islam, where the first known example seems to be by al-Jāhiz of the ninth century. A more accessible instance occurs in the *Arabian Nights* (419th night and following in the Burton translation). In the mid-seventeenth century a specimen appeared in Japan, the *Dembu monogatari* (Story of a Boor), perhaps derived ultimately from an Islamic source.

In the medieval literature of Western Europe the boy–woman contest flourished, the most salient instance being the twelfth-century "Ganymede and Helen." In this **medieval Latin poem**, Helen offers herself to Ganymede only to find that he would rather assume the passive role with another man. A violent quarrel breaks out, to settle which they appoint Nature and Reason as arbiters. Traveling to "the world's eastern edge, the house of Nature," they argue their respective positions before their judges, who are not exactly impartial. Ganymede praises love between man and boy, Helen champions the passion of man and woman. Although Ganymede makes several telling points, in the end he is vanquished by the argument that intercourse between males is sterile, that it wastes potential human lives. "The old heresy is abandoned by the gods," and the teaching of the church is vindicated. Parallels to this literary genre of debate were the public controversies between Jewish and Christian theologians that typically ended in a decision in favor of the church, and often in woe for the Jewish communities in the cities where the debates were staged.

After the church had imposed obligatory heterosexuality upon the population of Western Europe, all debate on the issue ceased, and it became impossible to defend male love publicly. But in cultures where a significant part of the male population is actively bisexual and intercourse with a boy is a viable social option, the choice is posed in life quite as much as in literature—and not always to Ganymede's disadvantage. With the gradual rehabilitation of the homosexual option in today's pluralistic world, the notion of victory in such a contest has become moot.

Wayne R. Dynes

CONTRARY SEXUAL FEELING

This expression is the English rendering of the overarching term adopted by the German physician Karl Friedrich Otto Westphal (1833–1890) for the condition that he had abstracted from two case histories under his observation, one of a lesbian, the other of a male transvestite. A colleague in classical philology suggested to him the expression *die contraire Sexualempfindung*, which he then used in the title of an article published in *Archiv für Psychiatrie und Nervenkrankheiten* in 1869 that is regarded as the first medical paper in modern times on what came to be designated as homosexuality. Westphal himself judged the condition inborn, a symptom of a neuropathic or psychopathic state, as an alienation from the feeling proper to the anatomical sex of the subject. He drew the forensic distinction between exclusive and occasional homosexuality, but his failure to separate the two psychological entities that he had encountered was not corrected until fifty years later, when Havelock **Ellis** formulated the differential concept of *eonism* and Magnus **Hirschfeld** that of *transvestism*, the latter on the basis of 17 cases of heterosexual transvestism that he had isolated from the 7,000 homosexual case histories he had taken until that time.

The English abstractors and translators of psychiatric literature from the Continent were never able to decide upon a uniform equivalent for the awkward German expression (in which the adjective is, strictly speaking, a French word), but "contrary sexual feeling" or "contrary sexual instinct" does figure in the writing of some British and American alienists at the close of the nineteenth century. To the English-speaking lay public, of course, the word "contrary," like "perverse" conveyed a notion of the rebellious, refractory, and antithetical, though such connotations were not overtly recognized by specialists. In any event the expression was not destined to survive. As early as 1870 an American psychiatrist preparing an abstract of Westphal's article had used "inverted sexual feeling," and eight years later the Italian Arrigo Tamassia invented the far more satisfactory *inversione dell'istinto sessuale* in an article published in *Rivista sperimentale di freniatria e medicina legale*. With appropriate modifications this term, simplified to sexual **inversion**, was adopted in all the Romance languages and in English as the *medical* designation for what journalistic style was later to dub **homosexuality,** a term invented by the apologist Károly Mária Kertbeny in 1869 and taken up by Gustav Jaeger in the book *Entdeckung der Seele* in 1880. Since the last of these fitted perfectly into the international nomenclature of Greek–Latin expressions and allowed for a triptych with **bisexual** and **heterosexual**, it drove the clumsy and eccentric coinages that had been proposed in earlier decades out of use. So "contrary sexual feeling" is the linguistic remnant of the first, uncertain psychiatric attempt to grapple with the problem of homosexuality.

Warren Johansson

COUNSELING

The concept of counseling, as it was introduced at the beginning of the twentieth century, referred to the way students were helped to deal with problems in the areas of study and choice of a professional career. The counselor gave information and advice, expecting the student to act accordingly.

Since then the meaning of the word "counseling" has changed considerably. It is now widely used in the sense of a more or less professional way of helping people with relatively uncomplicated emotional or social problems, by way of conversation (listening and talking). More complicated psycho-social problems, necessitating an intrapsychic personality change or complex and difficult behavioral changes, are the realm of **psychotherapy**.

Over the years counseling techniques have changed considerably as well, especially as a result of the work of Carl R. Rogers. In his view, people can, under the right circumstances, find the answers to their problems themselves. Instead of giving ready-made advice, counselors should help clients to explore their difficulties and assist them in the process of solution-finding. Rogers developed a non-directive or client-centered way of counseling, which has become influential among the helping professions all over the western world. It stresses the importance of counselors following the client's lead, as well as developing important listening-skills. Rogers also formulated the most important conditions under which effective counseling can take place:

1. the counselor should experience an unconditional positive regard toward the client;
2. the counselor should experience an empathic understanding of the client's internal frame of reference;
3. the counselor should be congruent (himself/herself) in the relationship with the client;
4. the counselor should be able to communicate his or her unconditional positive regard, empathic understanding and congruency to the client.

Recently more directive approaches to counseling have been developed. The basic value of the conditions mentioned above, however, remains unchallenged.

Counseling and Homosexuality. Homosexuality has been called a terrible sin, a crime and a disease. Irrational fear and disgust of homosexuality and homosexuals (**homophobia**) are still firmly rooted in society. The practice of counseling has been deeply influenced by these views and emotions. Changing attitudes toward sexuality in general and a growing sensitivity for the rights of minorities, however, have made many counselors aware of the position of their gay and lesbian clients as members of an oppressed minority. At the same time a host of new research has shown, among other things, that homo-sexuality is not uncommon or restricted to certain societies and cultures, that there is no essential difference between homosexuals and heterosexuals as far as the distribution of psychological health or illness is concerned, that it is almost impossible and often damaging to try to change a person's sexual orientation, and that homosexuals share a sexual preference for members of their own sex, but do not share a single personality profile or fit any general stereotype.

Due to these changes, most counselors have abandoned efforts toward sexual reorientation of their homosexual clients. Instead the focus has shifted toward helping gay men and lesbians to accept and appreciate their sexual feelings and to find a fulfilling and satisfying lifestyle. Taking into account the four Rogerian conditions for effective counseling, it becomes quite clear that a positive attitude toward homosexuality is necessary, if the counselor wishes to help homosexual clients to attain these goals.

Homosexual men and women can have all kinds of problems that require counseling. Often these difficulties are not very different from those of the heterosexual population and include sexual dysfunctions, relationship problems, substance abuse, neurotic and psychotic symptoms.

There are, however, some specific topics and problems that are of special interest for counselors working with homosexual clients. The most important ones are the following.

Acceptance and "Coming Out" Process. The stigmatization of homosexuality in Western society is mainly responsible for the fact that most people go through a difficult phase upon discovering their same-sex attraction. This phase, which usually takes two to six years or even much longer, is commonly referred to as the acceptance and **coming out** process. It can be subdivided into several stages, the first one being repression or denial of homosexual impulses sometimes accompanied by aggressive feelings toward self and others (especially other homosexuals). Here the anti-homosexual attitude of the environment is reflected in what might be called an internalized homophobia.

In the second stage, the feelings are given a name, "I must be gay," but they remain a secret. Characteristic of this period are feelings of anxiety and depression. The following stage is one of experimentation and testing. The company of other homosexuals is sought, first sexual contacts are made, and the person involved "comes out" to one or more significant figures in his or her environment. At this stage, fear of rejection may play an important role. If all goes well, the fourth stage is reached in which homosexual feelings become an integral part of the personality, and a fitting and affirmative lifestyle evolves. The coming out is as complete as the circumstances permit.

Homosexual Identity. In Western society a distinction is made between homosexual acts and homosexuality. Since exclusive erotic interest in the same or opposite sex prevails only for a minority of people, committing homosexual acts apparently does not always lead to a self-identification as a homosexual. This is particularly true in a number of non-western cultures. For the counselor, it is important to take into account that the category or "construction" of homosexuality is in fact a fluid one, taking different forms in different cultures. At the same time, the formation of a strong homosexual identity adds, in many cases, to the individual's sense of belonging and security.

Socialization. Homosexual men and women are usually socialized as heterosexuals. For them there are very few positive role-models with whom to identify. This standard socialization as traditional men and women can cause problems in later life. In Western society, men are expected to be strong, competitive, active and unemotional, while women are trained to be submissive, passive, caring and expressive. Homosexual women are, there-

fore, faced with different issues from those of homosexual men. Cultural norms and values can become especially problematic in the relationships between men and between women. Homosexual men, for example, may find it difficult to deal with intimacy in their affectional and sexual relationships, while lesbians may have trouble maintaining a fair amount of autonomy in contacts with other women.

Discrimination. Most homosexual men and women sooner or later have to deal with discriminatory remarks, anti-homosexual violence, rejection by family, friends or colleagues and, in some countries or states, legal prohibitions. Taking these facts into account, it is quite astounding that many seem to manage by themselves, without any form of professional help. Counselors should be aware of this oppression, for it is the only way to gain insight into the defense mechanisms homosexuals have had to develop in order to survive psychologically.

Health. **AIDS** has become an important factor in the lives of homosexual men. Changes in sexual behavior, adoption of "safe sex," has become a matter of life and death. Many have been confronted with the loss of close friends and lovers, or may have been infected with HIV themselves. For seropositive men, uncertainty about their future health and fear of death and dying may cause a number of serious problems. Men with AIDS or ARC (AIDS Related Complex) are confronted with a host of medical, psychological, social, and material difficulties.

Conclusion. Changing attitudes toward homosexuality have transformed the practice of counseling gay men and lesbian women. Gay-affirmative counseling methods have been developed; many of them by the homosexual community itself. Most larger cities in Europe and the United States now have counseling services that cater exclusively to the needs of homosexual men and women. Apart from individual and relationship counseling, these services usually offer opportunities to participate in various groups, such as coming out groups, **consciousness-raising** groups, groups for people with AIDS-related problems, and so forth. Sometimes workshops are organized covering topics such as self-defense, intimacy and autonomy, or (homo)social skills.

Most homosexuals manage to lead positive and fulfilling lives without the intervention of counselors. Some, however, do need help. It is clear that such help must be given by counselors who have acquired a positive attitude toward homosexuality. Familiarity with the literature on homosexual psychology and with the (local) gay community, its activities and establishments, is also a prerequisite.

BIBLIOGRAPHY. A. Elfin Moses and Robert O. Hawkins, *Counseling Lesbian Women and Gay Men*, St. Louis: C. V. Mosby Co., 1982; W. S. Sahakian, ed., *Psychotherapy and Counseling*, Chicago: Rand McNally, 1970; Natalie Jane Woodman and Harry R. Lenna, *Counseling with Gay Men and Women*, San Francisco: Jossey-Bass, 1980.

Jan Schippers

COUNTERCULTURE

The term counterculture came into wide use in North America in the late 1960s to designate a lifestyle then popular among young people and characterized by open rejection of mainstream values—materialism, sexual conformity, and the pursuit of career success, in short what was widely known as the "Protestant ethic." The abandonment of these "square" values was blatantly announced by such markers as experimentation with **drugs**, rock music, **astrology** and other aspects of the occult, as well as flamboyant styles of dress and coiffure. Opposed to atomistic individualism, many counterculturists attempted collective living arrangements in communes, urban at first and then increasingly rural.

Apparently the term counterculture is an adaptation of the slightly earlier "adversary culture," an expression coined by the literary critic Lionel Trilling (1905–1975). In many respects the counterculture constituted a mass diffusion—fostered by diligent media exploitation—of the prefigurative **beat**/hippie phenomenon. As American involvement in the Vietnam War increased, in the wake of opposition to it the counterculture shifted from the gentle "flower-child" phase to a more aggressive posture, making common cause with the New Left, which was not, like the radicalism of the thirties, forced by economic crisis to focus on issues of unemployment and poverty. Of course radical political leaders were accustomed to decry the self-indulgence of the hippies, but their followers, as often as not, readily succumbed to the lure of psychedelic drugs and the happy times of group togetherness accompanied by ever present rock music. The watchword in all these interactions was **liberation**, a term usually left undefined as it served a multitude of interests. All too soon, however, the violence endemic to the times seeped in, and the 1967 "summer of love" yielded, two years later, to the Altamont tragedy and the revelation of the Manson killings.

Apart from the revulsion against violence, why did the decline set in so quickly? The counterculture shamelessly embraced **ageism**: "Don't trust anyone over thirty." Observing this precept cut young people off from the accumulated experience and wisdom of sympathetic elders. Moreover, it meant that the adherents of the movement themselves quickly became back numbers as they crossed over the thirty-year line. In regard to gay adherents, the distrust of older people tended to reinforce the ageism already present in their own subculture. To be sure, the full force of such problematic effects has become evident only in retrospect. Although outsiders, and some insiders as well, exaggerated the fusion of the counterculture and the New Left, still the convergence of massive cultural innovation with hopes for fundamental political change gave the young generation a heady sense of imminent revolution.

Discarding (or so they believed) the judgmental hangups of their elders, many counterculture recruits became sexually experimental, willing to try homosexual activity a time or two "for kicks," even if they were predominantly heterosexual. Massive arrests for marijuana possession created a new understanding for the plight of others—sexual nonconformists—who were being persecuted by victimless crime laws. The psychiatrist Thomas Szasz and others correctly perceived the link between the campaign to decriminalize marijuana and the efforts to reform sex laws.

Because the gay movement became visible only in 1969 after the **Stonewall Rebellion**—at the crest of the counterculture wave, many assumed that homosexuals were essentially counterculturist, leftist, and opposed root and branch to the established order. Subsequent observation has shown, not surprisingly perhaps, that a majority of gay men and lesbians were (and are) **liberal**-reformist and even **conservative**, rather than revolutionary in their overall political and social outlook. Nonetheless, the counterculture fostered a mood of defiant unconventionality that made possible a quantum leap from a score of timid, semi-clandestine organizations to a national movement that openly challenged one of the most deep-seated taboos in Western civilization. It left its mark on the gay lifestyle in terms of dress and music, use of hippie expressions and street talk, the diffusion of at least a nominal communitarian ideal, an eagerness to question the shibboleths of the establishment, a lessening of guilt, and (for gay men at least) a more open acknowledgment of the legitimacy of "promiscuity" or sexual pluralism. Significantly, while the **AIDS** crisis of the 1980s has caused a reexamination of some precepts of sexual freedom, other counterculture lifestyle traits have persisted, albeit overlaid by new trends to-ward elite consumerism and career professionalism.

BIBLIOGRAPHY. Theodore Roszak, *The Making of a Counter Culture*, Garden City, NY: Doubleday, 1969.
Wayne R. Dynes

COUPERUS, LOUIS (1863–1923)

Dutch novelist. Couperus was born in The Hague to a family of leading colonial administrators. For a decade of his youth he lived in the capital of the Dutch East Indies, Batavia (now Jakarta). It made a strong impression on the boy, who was to become famous because of his novels about society life in Indonesia and The Hague. Young Couperus was not the manly youngster destined for the administration of the Dutch colonies his parents would have preferred, but was frail and feminine. In the circle of the women of his family he was beloved, and later he married one of his cousins.

He started writing poetry in a delicate style which was not very successful. By contrast his first novel, *Eline Vere* (1889), stood out. It was naturalist with a decadent theme: the sensuous woman. In his semi-autobiography, *Metamorfoze* (1897), he stated that Eline was a self-portrait. His second novel, *Noodlot* (1891, Destiny), resembles Oscar Wilde's *Dorian Gray* of the same year (translated into Dutch by Couperus' wife). Bertie, a weakling, and Frank, a straight man, are friends, but to Bertie the friendship is love. When Frank gets acquainted with a young woman and is on the verge of marriage, Bertie sabotages the arrangement with a forged letter. When he admits this many years later, Frank kills him. After his release from prison, Frank meets his fiancee again; they wed, but their marriage is doomed to unhappiness, and they commit a double suicide. The third novel, *Extaze* (1893), has a homoerotic undertone which continued in subsequent works.

From 1900 onwards, Couperus wrote classical novels such as *Dionyzos* (1904) and his most gay *De berg van licht* [Mountain of Light] (1905–06), on the androgynous, bisexual Roman emperor **Heliogabalus**. Eastern decadence is shown to corrupt western morals. In the struggle of east and west, of female sensuousness and male rigidity, Couperus favors the sensual perspective. For his interpretation of Heliogabalus, Couperus made use of L.S.A.M. von Römer's work on homosexuality and androgyny. Critics came down hard on this book. For many years Couperus wrote no further novels; he considered writing a pamphlet on the critics' attitudes toward homosexuality, but did not do so. His later novels *De komedianten* (1917), on two Roman boy actors, and *Iskander* (1920), on Alexander the Great, also had strong homoerotic undertones.

Before World War I, Couperus lived mostly in Nice and Italy because of his dislike of the northern European climate. Returning to The Hague in 1914, he became a successful lecturer, although the press considered him too much the dandy. Most of his books sold well, with the exception of *De berg van licht*, which today is considered one of his best.

When Couperus died in 1923, he was probably a virgin, as his decadent successor Gerard Reve maintains.

Couperus was the foremost Dutch novelist of the turn of the century. In 1987, a new critical edition of his complete works began to appear.

BIBLIOGRAPHY. Frédéric Bastet, *Louis Couperus, een biografie*, Amsterdam: Querido, 1987.

Gert Hekma

COUPLES

The familiar term "couple" here denotes two persons, not closely related by blood, usually but not always living together, forming an ongoing sexual partnership, whether married or unmarried, heterosexual or homosexual. It serves to efface the older sharp distinction between fornication and matrimony, thereby fostering a more objective scrutiny of human relationships. Because this conceptual change is recent, serious research in the field is not far advanced; unfounded stereotypes linger, and generalizations based on present knowledge may in time be superseded.

Role Models. Intensely devoted same-sex couples who have been taken as inspirational models include **Gilgamesh** and Enkidu, Damon and Pythias, **Achilles** and Patroklos, **David and Jonathan**, **Jesus** and the **Beloved Disciple**, Han Ai-ti and Dong Xian, **Hadrian** and **Antinous**, Gertrude **Stein** and Alice B. Toklas, Christopher **Isherwood** and Donald Bachardy. The sexuality in several of these relationships remains controversial, though those for whom these couples are models assume there were genital relations. In the legendary and ancient-world cases, the intensity of the loves was not challenged by the stresses of a long life together. The modern role models exemplify durability as well as intensity of same-sex love. Such models reassure lesbians and gay men that long-term relationships are possible, despite the obstacles posed by social arrangements and by social conceptions of homosexual relationships as necessarily transitory due to an essential promiscuity. Less widely known role models are influential in small communities or social circles among more recently formed couples, who look to them for advice and factors which promote durability and amicability. As such they frequently find themselves in leadership positions in the social clique to which they belong.

Pressures Against Coupling. Homophobes and the Roman Catholic Church have regarded homosexual relationships as more serious (sinful, neurotic) than fleeting anonymous sexual encounters, because a relationship entails greater acceptance of homosexuality—"living in sin" rather than distinct "sinful acts." As John De Cecco observed, "That two men who have sex together can also love each other symbolizes the ultimate detoxification of homosexuality" in homophobic societies.

Because commitment to homosexuality is a greater affront to homophobic opinion than is homosexual behavior (where the transitoriness of individual acts offers reassurance that such liaisons are "unstable"), the kind of social pressure on married couples which urges them to stay together is exerted on gay and lesbian couples to break up. Both institutions (church and state) and social groupings (the natal family) provide positive sanctions for heterosexual relationships while denying legitimation and rewards to same-sex couples. Thus, traditionally religious and socially conservative families may mourn and punish divorces of heterosexually married children, but celebrate and reward the dissolution of lesbian or gay offspring as marking a return to normalcy, or as at least opening the possibility of "growing out of a homosexual phase." Although there are commonalities among all kinds of relationships, gay and lesbian couples must routinely cope with obstacles not generally encountered by those in heterosexual relationships.

Role-Playing. Given the importance of gender as an organizing principle, the assumption in many cultures that a relationship requires replication of distinct gender roles, so that one partner must play the part of the wife (fem) and the other the part of the husband (butch), is rife even among "professional experts" on individual differences, psychiatrists. Although there are instances of such replication, most Western industrialized-world contemporary gay relationships do not conform strictly to traditional "masculine" and "feminine" roles; instead, role flexibility and turn-taking are more common patterns. Only a minority of homosexual couples in this part of the world engage in clearcut **butch–fem** role-playing. In this sense, traditional heterosexual marriage is not the predominant model or

script for current homosexual couples (Peplau, in De Cecco). Indeed, with a historical change in the functions of the family from economic production to companionship and with feminist challenges to traditional female roles, heterosexual relationships increasingly have come to resemble the companionate dyad of gay relationships, even including experimentation with sexually "open" relationships during the 1970s in North America.

The increased visibility of gay enclaves provided a larger pool of potential passive partners than in earlier eras in which only cross-gender appearance or behavior publicly signalled homosexual availability of a partner willing to be passive. The chances of finding an approximation to one's conception of a desirable partner are better in a larger pool, and, specifically, a preference for butch–butch relationships was increasingly realized for North American urban gay men. Joseph Harry found that North American gay men who value masculinity in themselves also tend to seek masculine-appearing partners. It is debatable, however, whether the relative size of the potential partner pool is larger today than it was and is in pederastic cultures, non-homophobic cultures, or cultures featuring a heavily skewed gender ratio. He also found that those living in cities with gay communities were more likely to cohabit with their partners and were more interested in emotional intimacy than those living in suburbs and small towns, where the chances of meeting a partner and being able to live together with the approval of neighbors were also less.

Formation of Gay Couples. Although there are reports of enduring same-sex pairs from many locales, there is a dearth of systematic data on homosexual couples even in North American cities, so that it is not possible to estimate whether the age and status disparities of the examples listed above are typical of relationships. Many gay writers assert that homosexual relationships cross racial, class, and age discrepancies more often than do heterosexual relationships. "Opposites attract" is the predominant folk wisdom—except when "birds of a feather flock together." How often lesbian and gay relationships cross social discrepancies is a question deserving of systematic research.

Currently, what little empirical evidence exists finds choice of long-term partners in homosexual relationships to be based on similarity of social characteristics (homophily) and opportunities for contact (propinquity), just as the choice of heterosexual marriage partners typically but not always is (Laner in De Cecco; Harry). Undoubtedly, racial and cultural differences often enhance sexual attraction. The same differences that initially intrigue and attract may become problematic when an affair becomes a marriage. Long-term gay and lesbian relationships in which there is not the friction between male expectations and female expectations may thrive relatively better than heterosexual relationships with conflicting cultural expectations, but there remains the tendency observed in heterosexuals to marry their "own kind" despite being attracted to and even sexually involved with persons of other classes, races, and/or ethnicities. The attributes of those with whom one wants to have sex and those with whom one would consider settling down (marrying) are often quite distinct for homosexual as for heterosexual men and women. Similarly, the kinds of relationships someone wants and seeks are not necessarily the kinds he or she has.

Statistics on Couple Formation. Most self-identified lesbians and gay men have some experience of being in a relationship. In their survey of black and white male and female homosexuals in San Francisco during the late 1960s, Bell and Weinberg found 51 percent of white homosexual men, 58 percent of black homosexual men, 72 percent of white homosexual females and 70 percent of black homosexual females saying they were currently in a relationship. As in most surveys, most of the rest reported having at some time in their lives been in a relationship of some duration.

There were no significant age discrepancies in 5, 10, 10, and 3 percent of the couples, respectively, and differences of more than five years in 51, 40, 35, and 47 percent of the couples. Sixty-four percent of white gay male respondents judged their social position to be the same as their partner's, compared to 39 percent of black males, 56 percent of black lesbians, and 72 percent of white lesbians. Equal income was reported for 3 percent of black homosexual couples, 17 and 18 percent of white female and male couples, although negative effects of income disparity were reported by only two percent of the gay white men, four percent of black gay men and women, and six percent of white lesbians. Blacks in the sample were substantially younger than whites when they began their relationship.

Power in Relationships. In a large-scale survey of contemporary American couples, Blumstein and Schwartz found that couples in which both people felt they were genuine partners with equal control over economic assets were more tranquil. Peplau and Cochran (1982), and De Cecco and Shively (1978) also found decision-making equality the central concern; Harry (1982) found age to predict power in decision-making within gay male relationships, especially among those couples living together, but also suggested that "in gay relationships it is more likely that partners will be more similar to each other in the possession of bases of power than in heterosexual relationships."

Other studies with smaller samples of lesbians and gay men also found perceived equality in making important decisions central to relationships judged successful by those in them. Perceived equality in decision-making is not necessarily lacking in couples who differ substantially in age, status, or income; but the older and/or more affluent partner tends to dominate such relationships. Greater sex-

274

ual marketability may also be a factor. That is, if one partner is more desirable by conventional standards of beauty, he or she may be able to use this "capital" within relationship decision-making. Yet another complication in predicting power within relationships is "the power of the least interest": the partner least concerned about preserving the relationship can deter opposition to his or her choices by being more willing than the other partner to leave the relationship.

These same factors operate in heterosexual relationships. The person who brings into a relationship the most resources valued by the other partner tends to make decisions when the two disagree. In heterosexual relationships the man typically has the power of higher status and economic resources and often that of the least interest as well. Moreover, in many cultures, including North America, women are raised to support relationships and to be defined by them, while men are socialized to and defined by what they do outside the domestic sphere. Despite recent social changes, North American women continue to defer to partners' career contingencies while men pursue their careers, either ignoring a partner's preferences or jettisoning partners unwilling to go along with their choices. Some of the differences in duration of lesbian and gay male relationships result from such differences in primary socialization.

Stages in Relationships. McWhirter and Mattson (in De Cecco) outlined a natural history of predictable stages of (gay) relationships: blending, nesting, maintaining, collaborating, trusting, and renewal. The stages are labels for recurrent patterns, not causal models of what every relationship must pass through and in what order. Moreover, their model does not take any account of different kinds of love (contrast Lee in the same volume). Despite its limitations, a model of stages does draw attention to the changes with time that affect relationships. In particular, the initial romance and mutual

discovery tend to give way to everyday coexistence and reduced frequency of sex in relationships that endure.

Financial Disparities. The gay white southern California males McWhirter and Mattson studied did not merge money and possessions until the trusting stage, which they estimate as ten or more years into the relationship, after some resolution of questions about individual autonomy have been resolved to both partners' satisfaction. Whether or not it usually takes so long, as relationships endure, lesbian couples and gay male couples (even more so) tend to pool assets. Such pooling reinforces decision-making equality among those making differing economic contributions to the relationship and maintains the stability of the relationship. Very few same-sex couples (five percent) believe that one partner should routinely support the other. Fewer still (Harry reported one percent) do so. Yet, even unequal income in couples both of whose members work is a major source of stress in same-sex couples (but not in male–female ones in which the man has greater income). Male socialization to competitiveness and a tendency to measure success in monetary terms make economic inequality particularly problematic in male–male couples. Blumstein and Schwartz suggest that the egalitarian ideology of two strong women holding their own against each other may become an unconscious solvent of relationships between women of unequal income, propelling the more economically successful partner out of the relationship. Their study reaffirmed the truism that it is difficult to be poor and happy in a consumer society.

Whether or not one can buy happiness, relative wealth generally establishes a balance of power within relationships for gay male couples, as for heterosexual couples (married or not). Monetary comparisons are less predictive of relative power in lesbian couples (in part because large income differences between women are less common). The more affluent partner has more control over the couple's recreational activities for lesbian and gay male couples (this differs from the pattern found in married heterosexual couples, where this is often the domain where the wife makes choices). Because same-sex couples share more activities outside work than do heterosexual couples, this aspect is probably more important to satisfaction within the couple for lesbian and gay men in relationships than for men and women in heterosexual relationships. (Most social life of heterosexual men and women is homosocial in most cultures. To the extent that primary socialization shapes interests differentially depending upon the sex of the child, same sex couples are likely to have more compatible interests than mixed-sex couples.)

Cohabitation. Various studies have found lesbian couples more likely to live together than gay male couples. The extent to which this is a result of temperament, differing levels of social acceptability for unmarried same-sex roommates, or a difference of economic resources is not clear from the available data. Partners who have gay and/or lesbian friends are also more likely to cohabitate. Probably integration into gay/lesbian circles cannot be separated from self-acceptance as gay or lesbian, and both individual and social acceptance of homosexuality make living together more conceivable for those who are sexually involved with someone of their own sex.

Sex. Blumstein and Schwartz found that relationships with at least one partner more concerned with the relationship than with his or her career are more likely to endure. They also reported that the relationship-centered partner usually initiated sex, and the more powerful one, who was more likely to be career-oriented and to have relative power due to greater economic success, was more likely to refuse sexual intercourse. The frequency of sex decreased with the duration of all types of relationships, but especially with homosexual ones. Forty-five percent of

married heterosexual couples had sex three times a week or more often, compared to 67 percent of gay male couples, and 33 percent of lesbian couples. For couples who had been together ten or more years the percentages fell to 18 for married couples, 11 for gay male couples, and one percent for lesbian couples.

At least prior to the devastation of **AIDS**, men in gay couples were relatively casual about extra-marital sex, outside sex often replacing sex between partners without being conceived as a threat to the relationship (*also see* Kurdeck and Smith in De Cecco). In contrast, non-monogamous sex was associated with dissatisfaction and lack of commitment to their relationship by lesbian lovers. Given female socialization against casual sex (socialization based on sex-specific dangers, notably pregnancy), women, including lesbians, tend to have affairs more than the one-time "tricks" with little emotional investment sought by men (gay or not). Affairs represent a greater threat to a relationship than casual encounters, so that lesbian non-monogamy is more serious than male sexual encounters outside relationships. Of course, gay men sometimes had affairs as well as or instead of tricks, and possessiveness is not a monopoly of women. All these differences are statistical, not absolute.

In regard to sexual acts, lesbians, in common with gay men and straight men, are happier both with their sex lives and with their relationships the more they engage in oral sex. Roles in both oral and anal sex raise sensitive issues of dominance and reciprocity in gay couples. Traditionally, anxieties were settled and sexual incompatibilities compensated for outside the relationship. Reciprocity also mutes anxieties about seeming to be "submissive." Blumstein and Schwartz found that "the partner who performs anal sex is no more 'masculine' or powerful than the partner who receives it," but that "for both partners, anal intercourse is associated with being masculine: in couples where both partners are forceful, outgoing, and aggressive, there is more anal sex."

BIBLIOGRAPHY. Alan Bell and Martin Weinberg, *Homosexualities*, New York: Simon and Schuster, 1978; Betty Berzon, *Permanent Partners: Building Gay and Lesbian Relationships That Last*, New York: E. P. Dutton, 1988; Philip Blumstein and Pepper Schwartz, *American Couples*, New York: Morrow, 1983; John De Cecco and Michael C. Shively, "A Study of Perceptions of Rights and Needs in Interpersonal Conflicts in Homosexual Relationships," *Journal of Homosexuality*, 3 (1978), 205–16; John De Cecco, ed., *Gay Relationships*, New York: Harrington Press, 1988; Haydn Curry and Dennis Clifford, *A Legal Guide for Lesbian and Gay Couples*, San Francisco: Nolo Press, 1988; Joseph Harry, *Gay Couples*, New York: Praeger, 1984; Lawrence A. Kurdek, "Relationship Quality of Gay and Lesbian Cohabiting Couples," *Journal of Homosexuality*, 15:3/4 (1988), 93–118; Letitia Peplau and Susan D. Cochran, "Value Orientations in the Intimate Relationships of Gay Men," *Journal of Homosexuality*, 8 (1982), 1–8; Rolf Pringel and Wolfgang Trautvetter, *Homosexuelle Partnerschaften: Eine empirische Untersuchung*, Berlin: Verlag Rosa Winkel, 1987; Donna Tanner, *The Lesbian Couple*, Lexington, MA: Lexington, 1978.

Stephen O. Murray

CORVO, BARON
See Rolfe, Frederick.

COWARD, NOEL, SIR (1899–1973)

British playwright, songwriter, and entertainer. Born at Teddington near London in 1899, Noel Coward made his debut on the stage as Prince Mussel in Lila Field's *The Goldfish* in January 1911. For several years a highly popular boy actor, he began his own career with his first comedy, *I'll Leave It to You* (1920). His succeeding plays were marked by a frivolity and a gift for exploiting the moment to the fullest that catered to the disenchantment, the lack of concern with meanings and essences, of the interwar generation. *Fallen Angels* and *Easy Virtue* (1925) exploited the public's fascination with sex, scandal, and pseudo-sophistication. His reputation as a playwright rests on *Hay Fever* (1925), *Private Lives* (1930), *Design for Living* (1933), *Hands Across the Sea* (1936), *Blithe Spirit* (1941), and *Present Laughter* (1943). In all these comedies the characters are adults living in the male adolescent's fantasy world where there is no family life to speak of, no children to care for, no commitment except to pleasure. The characters do no real work; and money—in a decade of depression, hunger marches, and then war—is simply taken for granted. Incarnations of vanity and selfishness, they appeal to the audience because their frivolity has a kind of stoic dignity. Written in a few days each, his best plays exhibit the aggressive edge of a performer on the stage of life who as a homosexual had mastered the disguise crucial for survival.

Two less remembered plays, *Cavalcade* (1931) and *This Happy Breed* (1942), appealed to the political chauvinism of the day and were even considered serious patriotic statements about England and her fighting spirit. Many of his plays were subsequently filmed, from *The Queen Was in the Parlour* (1927) to *Tonight at 8:30* (1952).

When, in the 1950s, his plays had lost public favor, he took his message of frivolity to the audience in person as a cabaret performer, mocking the conventions of the theatre with such impish songs as "Why must the show go on?" and "There are bad times just around the corner." Once, when asked how he would be remembered by future generations, Coward shrewdly replied "By my charm."

Coward was homosexual, but his private life was unsensational. Rebecca West wrote of him: "There was impeccable dignity in his sexual life, which was reticent but untainted by pretense." He enjoyed sex as much as anyone, and made no secret of the fact, but a list of his sexual partners would be uninteresting. When he fell in love, he was in the state of agitation which the ancient Greeks had called *aphrosyne*, a total loss of self-control that left him unable to write, obsessively jealous, and driven to verbal cruelty at the expense of the loved one.

Noel Coward is the classic example of the British "man of the theatre" of the twentieth century. His plays do not make pleasurable reading: they need to be seen and heard. Rich in wit and feeling, they reveal the author's talent above all in the design of the scenes and the scintillating dialogue. They are always more entertaining than profound, appealing to the element in the Anglo-Saxon character that rejects anything intellectual and wants only to spend an evening in the theatre to be relieved of the cares of the day. Unlike such authors as **Wilde** and **Firbank**, he rarely attempted the epigram or toyed directly with ideas in his plays. He shared the homosexual sense of living for the moment and not for the posterity that would never be. His comedies are masterful less for the situations in which the characters find themselves than for the dialogue by which they extricate themselves from them. But however wanting in ideas his comedies may have been, they captivated audiences for a generation, and made the author a phenomenon, a beloved theatrical personality. While Coward could not openly reveal his homosexuality to an Anglo-American public that had not reached the level of sophistication needed to accept it, his sexuality tinted the image of life that his plays projected onto the stage and screen.

BIBLIOGRAPHY. John Lahr, *Coward the Playwright*, New York: Avon Books, 1982; Cole Lesley, *Remembered Laughter: The Life of Noel Coward*, New York: Alfred A. Knopf, 1977.

Warren Johansson

CRANE, HART (1899–1932)

American poet. Born in Ohio, Crane lived mainly with the family of his mother after his parents' separation when he was three. From his mother's Christian Science beliefs (which he formally abandoned) he distilled a kind of "home-brew" neo-Platonism in which true reality was remote, and when glimpsed, evanescent. His poetry tends to recall epiphanic moments of ecstasy, which have occurred fleetingly in the past or can be hoped for, rather than exhibit the fruits of any steady vision. Because of syntactic and other uncertainties, the poems are often hard to interpret. Undoubtedly these difficulties of resolution were linked to his double sense of alienation as a homosexual and an artist coming to maturity in an America that prized "normalcy."

After failing to find satisfactory employment in his father's businesses, Crane moved to New York City where he worked as a copy writer in an advertising agency. The intensity of life in the metropolis was both a creative goad and an intolerable strain. In 1923 he fell in love with the heterosexual Slater Brown; since Brown only wanted friendship, Crane sought sexual satisfaction in the speakeasies and with sailors, who then ranked as major homosexual icons. For most of his life Crane was troubled by the fact that his intellectual friends did not sympathize with his sexual nature. In 1924, however, Crane fell in love with a Danish publisher, Emil Opffer, and his feelings were reciprocated. The wonder of this event gave him the energy to envision his ambitious cycle *The Bridge*, which he was never able to carry out as he had intended.

Crane's poetry was influenced by the Elizabethan writers and the French symbolists, as well as living modernists, such as T. S. **Eliot**. By the time he began *The Bridge*, however, **Whitman** had emerged as the dominant influence; the older Brooklyn poet was important to Crane both for his sense that America itself was an epic subject and because of his sexual orientation. Employing a kind of musical structure as a unifying element, *The Bridge* (1930) took the arc of the Brooklyn Bridge, which the poet could see from his room in Brooklyn Heights, as a symbol of the dynamism of America. The successive sections of the poem recount major elements of the American experience, including Columbus, Pocahontas, Rip Van Winkle, Melville, Poe, Whitman, and even the subway.

Crane was granted only about eight years of full maturity as a poet. Troubled by alcoholism and difficulty in achieving self-esteem, he traveled restlessly. Returning from Mexico, where he had gone to write a poem on Montezuma, Crane threw himself overboard from a ship and was drowned.

BIBLIOGRAPHY. Robert K. Martin, *The Homosexual Tradition in American Poetry*, Austin: University of Texas Press, 1979.

Wayne R. Dynes

CRETE

Lying almost halfway between Greece and Egypt, Crete like Cyprus, the other large island in the Eastern Mediterranean, received writing, urban culture, and other elements of civilization from Egypt, Syria, and Palestine.

Minoan and Mycenean Society. Minoan civilization takes its name from the legendary Minos, king of the city of Cnossus, in whose labyrinth the Minotaur, son of a bull and Minos' wife Pasiphae, lurked to devour human sacrificial victims sent as tribute from Greece until it was killed by the legendary Athenian hero Theseus. On his return trip to Athens Theseus abandoned Ariadne, Minos' daughter who had helped him find his way through the labyrinth to the Minotaur, and took a boy as his *eromenos*. Modern archeologists divide Minoan civilization into three stages: early (ca. 3000–2200 B.C.), middle (ca. 2200–1500), and late (ca.

1500–1000), decline setting in about 1200 B.C. owing to earthquakes, fires, and invasions by sea peoples including Greeks. Artistic depictions suggest that Minoan religion included the worship of snakes, leaping bulls, and other sensual symbols and practices. Nudity was the exception in their art, and no unusual evidence of pederastic activity occurs in it. Because of the bare-breasted female figurines, including the so-called "snake goddesses," some feminists have hailed Minoan civilization as matriarchic, but this claim has no real support.

Although the tablets written in Minoan script (Linear A) remain undeciphered, in 1956 Michael Ventris published his decipherment of those in Linear B (an early form of Greek), many of which were also found on the mainland, particularly the Peloponnesus, to which their script had been imported by Achaean Greek invaders from there who conquered the island ca. 1400 B.C. Linear B tablets also show no evidence of pederasty, although they mention almost all the major Greek gods and goddesses, with the gods dominating the goddesses, being mainly tribute lists, inventories, and other financial records. Mycenean art was less sensuous than Minoan, perhaps because unprotected by the sea, Myceneans, having unlike Minoans to wall their cities and stand on the alert, could less enjoy leisure and sensuality.

The Question of Pederastic Origins. The absence of any indication of pederasty in Minoan and Mycenean records and remains indicates that pederasty had not yet been institutionalized in Greece, despite myths written later assigning pederasty to Minos and to Zeus. Beginning in the Archaic period (800–500 B.C.), when the first evidence becomes available (just before 600) with the introduction of writing among Greeks, this time in an adaptation of the Phoenician script after a 400-year illiterate "dark age" from 1200 to 800, during which barbarous Dorian Greeks seized the island, most

Greeks and Romans associated the institutionalization of pederasty with Crete. Born in the cave of Harpagos in Crete, Zeus supposedly stole **Ganymede**, son of Tros, king of Troy, to replace the lame girl Hebe as his cupbearer (and bedmate) on Olympus. Minos and his brother Rhadamanthus, heroes in **Homer's** *Iliad*, had had, according to later mythmakers, squires who acted as their charioteers, to be described in later times as their beloveds. By the end of the classical period (500–323 B.C.) almost every god had his boy or boys, Apollo more than twenty.

Did these pederastic myths form an older core written down and depicted only after 600, or did the Greeks thereafter project back relationships among the gods in order to explain their institutionalization of them? Certainly in the fifth century **Pindar** took great pride in ascribing pederasty to Zeus' brother Poseidon.

Although other locales were sometimes said to be the birthplace of pederasty (Thebes, with Laius, and Thrace, with Orpheus, being the commonest), Crete generally held pride of place, with such figures as Zeus, Minos, and Rhadamanthus.

From the destruction of Mycenean civilization on Crete and on the mainland by catastrophes about 1200, a dark age ensued until the rebirth of writing in Greece with the importation of a new alphabetical script from Phoenicia ca. 725. This invention came, along with other Semitic influences by way of Cyprus, a source which may have led the Cretans first among the Greeks to seclude women. While the Homeric epics took shape, art remained primitive, often geometric, with the result that it gives no clue to sexual practices. In such times of insecurity, warriors banded together in the closest bonds of intimacy, and many hold that pederasty became institutionalized then, but the writings and art of the period 800–600 B.C. do not document pederasty.

Cretan Pederasty in Reality. After 600 B.C., however, it became customary for Greek hoplites, the upper-class warriors who fought in the phalanx, each to take a twelve-year-old boy as a beloved to train until he could hunt and fight, i.e., until at about the age of eighteen he sprouted a beard. In Crete the relationship had a distinctive feature: a ritual kidnapping (*harpagmos*) consecrated the pairing. After two months of living together in the wild, the mentor returned his protégé to his family laden with rich gifts, symbolizing his coming of age: armor, a drinking cup, and a bull.

The overwhelming majority of later Greeks believed that the Cretans had institutionalized pederasty in order to curb the population explosion which had begun in the tenth century, leading to the colonization of southern Italy, Sicily, and other western outposts as far as the Iberian peninsula, and in the east of most of Anatolia, the southern shores of the Aegean, and much of the Black Sea coast with emporia in Syria and Egypt between the eighth and the sixth centuries. By 550 most desirable colonial sites had been occupied, and Persians and Carthaginians began pushing the Greeks back from east and west. Another means of controlling population growth (for Plato the usual one) was female infanticide, which caused an imbalance in the sex ratio that effectively denied wives or even women to slaves and many lower-class free males.

Crete was the first Greek area to stop sending out colonists. According to such late sources such as Plato, Aristotle, Herodotus, Thucydides, Strabo, Diogenes Laertius, and Athenaeus, the Cretan "musicians" or statesmen Onomacritus and Thaletas, after about 650 developed a system to limit the expansion of the upper classes by postponing the marriage of males until thirty, giving the young warrior in his early twenties a boy of twelve to train and love. The males after the age of seven lived and messed together, the boys roaming in "herds" until they entered the barracks (*andreia*) at about 18. Men in this society began to exercise nude, in sharp contrast to Homeric practice. High-born women were segregated. Thus the estates of the nobles would not be overly subdivided, resulting in their impoverishment. When Sparta entered a crisis, "Lycurgus" visited Crete and imported along with the adviser Thaletas most of its institutions: a concatenation of interlocking institutions—segregation of women, institutional pederasty, athletic nudity, messes for males, late marriages, and herd membership for boys. Thereafter the Spartans became invincible in battle and athletics. Soon other lawgivers imitated the system in a less rigorous fashion. Solon imported a modified version of it to Athens with the aid of the Cretan Epimenides. Then, it seems, poets and artists began to ascribe pederasty to the gods and heroes. Perhaps under Solon's beloved and successor Peisistratus and his pederastic sons the *Iliad* was emended to include its two brief references to Ganymede, for those tyrants certainly had the text altered to stress the early importance of Athens, since they had Homer recited at the annual Panathenaic festival. Plato set his last major dialogue *The Laws* on Crete, where ironically an Athenian instructed a Cretan and a Spartan on how to make a good constitution which would bar pederasty as unnatural.

The brief revival that Crete enjoyed in the archaic period ended before the beginning of the classical era, perhaps in part because the Persian Empire's seizure of the eastern coast of the Mediterranean, cutting off Greek trade with Egypt and the Levant, which had made Crete central, rendered it instead peripheral.

No Cretan works are extant before the third century B.C., so that the scholar must rely on mainlanders for information, but they are virtually unanimous that pederasty was first institutionalized in Crete, either in the Minoan period by gods and legendary heroes, or in the archaic period as a device against overpopulation. A nineteenth-century German hypothesis that Dorian warriors on the steppes of Central Asia institutionalized pederasty and introduced it, iron, cremation, and other institutions when they overran and settled the peninsula ca. 1200, a theory now discredited, rests on the observation that most Greeks thought that their ancestors borrowed the institution from Crete and Sparta, but proponents of the "Dorian" origin cannot show that it also existed from the time of their first settlements in other Dorian areas. Early Spartan poets such as Tyrtaeus (b. ca. 650 B.C.) show no trace of it; rather Tyrtaeus ridicules "an effeminate." In fact all the earliest pederastic writing that survives is non-Dorian.

After being under **Rome**, the **Byzantine Empire**, **Venice** and Ottoman **Turkey**, Crete gained independence and joined Greece as a consequence of the First Balkan War in 1912. The strong survival of pederasty and other forms of homosexuality in modern Crete, subject of novels such as Nikos Kazantzakis', may perhaps best be traced to the long Turkish occupation.

William A. Percy

CREVEL, RENÉ (1900–1935)

French novelist and essayist. His mother encouraged him in his education after his father's suicide in 1914. While writing a Sorbonne doctoral dissertation on Diderot, Crevel rejected the eighteenth-century Enlightenment and embraced **Paris** of the twenties.

In 1921, Crevel founded the short-lived literary review, *L'Aventure* (chance, surprise, adventure, or love affair), which was followed by *Dés* (Dice). In 1924 he joined the surrealists after they disrupted a Dada play in which he was acting. Crevel introduced automatic writing, interpretation of dreams, hypnotism, and other novelties into the surrealist circle. He pursued chance, spontaneity, luck, the unconscious, dreams, sex, revolution, love, unintended consequences, and other ruses in order to transcend common sense and definition.

Crevel put great hopes in the Association of Revolutionary Artists and Writers. The Stalinist iron of socialist realism, however, shattered the effort to reconcile revolutionary art and politics. At the Congress meeting in Paris in 1935, a Russian poet denounced the surrealists as pederasts; André Breton, the pope of surrealism, expelled Crevel from his circle for being a homosexual; Crevel put his head in a Paris oven and expired in the arms of Salvador Dali.

In his sexual life, René faced equally great contradictions. He had a passionate love affair with Eugene Mac-Cown, an expatriate American painter, of whom Crevel wrote, "He was sent to punish me by the people I have hurt." Crevel celebrated the promiscuous homosexuality of working class bars, parks, quays, and the back alleys of Paris—what he called an "anonymous continent." At the same time he was jealous when his lover turned from him to a tattooed hustler. He nonetheless believed that every erotic activity was subversive which rebelled against "the reproductive instincts."

An example of the political sexual contradictions Crevel faced can be seen in the matter of Louis Aragon (himself a closet pedophile), arrested after he published a revolutionary poem, "Front Rouge" (Red Front) (1931), celebrating communism. Confronted by Crevel, André **Gide** refused to sign a petition against Aragon's arrest. Gide responded, "When I published *Corydon*, I was prepared to go to prison. Ideas are no less threatening than actions. We are dangerous people. To be convicted under this government would be an honor. However, if Aragon were convicted, he would deserve prison no less than Maurras" (a fascist). Gide talked of working behind the scenes; Crevel called for public protest against great infamy.

René Crevel's obscurity in the English-speaking world arises from multiple causes. Because he was a Trotskyist, the communists have suspected him; because he was an outspoken homosex-ual, the surrealists have avoided him; because he was a communist, academics have red-listed him; because he celebrated promiscuity, gay liberationists have neglected him. His works have recently been reprinted; two of his sex novels have been translated into English, and gay liberation publications (*Masques, Christopher Street*, and Boston's *Gay Community News*) have devoted critical attention to his work. What his closest friend Salvador Dali wrote in 1954 remains true: "René Crevel offers a new bombshell in the genre of confrontation."

Charley Shively

CRIMINAL LAW AMENDMENT ACT

This was an act of the British Parliament (48 & 49 Victoria c. 69) which in its eleventh clause provided a term of imprisonment not exceeding two years, with or without hard labor, for any male person guilty of an act of gross indecency with another male person in public or in private. This clause had been introduced into a bill directed against prostitution and white slavery by Henry Labouchere late on the night of August 6, 1885. Accepted without debate, the clause became part of a bill that was rushed through the third reading the following night, August 7, and passed.

Under the existing Offenses against the Person Act of 1861 (24 & 25 Victoria cap. 100) only buggery = anal intercourse was punishable in English law, though in 1828 Sir Robert Peel in his reform measures had made "any penetration, however slight" sufficient for conviction, contrary to the earlier holding of the courts that proof of penetration and emission was required. The effect of the new statute was that any and every form of male homosexual expression, if only "filthy and disgusting" enough to offend the feelings of a jury, became criminal. It was under this law that Oscar **Wilde** was convicted in May 1895, spending a full two years in Reading Prison and being socially disgraced and ruined as well. Not until 1957 did the **Wolfenden** Committee recommend repeal of this statute, which had inspired many similar innovations in the penal codes of other jurisdictions in the English-speaking world. Even at the time, when the first articles on homosexuality were appearing in the psychiatric press in the wake of appeals by homosexual apologists for toleration, the law was a retrograde measure. But it was part of the "moral purity" trend of the time in which Victorian humanitarianism interacted with Victorian prudery to put a new set of statutes on the lawbooks to enable the police to combat "vice and immorality" in which women and children were often the exploited victims. The law, dubbed the "blackmailer's charter," cast the shadow of criminality over British homosexual life until its repeal in 1967—82 years after its enactment.

BIBLIOGRAPHY. F. B. Smith, "Labouchere's Amendment to the Criminal Law Amendment Bill," *Historical Studies*, 17 (1976), 165–175.

CROSS-DRESSING
See Transvestism.

CROWLEY, ALEISTER (1875–1947)

English writer and occultist. By his own account, as an adolescent he was initiated into homosexual practices by a clergyman. As a wealthy undergraduate at Trinity College, Cambridge, Crowley—who had changed his given name(s) from Edward Alexander to Aleister in order to have the metrical value of a dactyl followed by a spondee—had his first book published at his own expense (*Aceldema, or a Place to Bury Strangers in: A Philosophical Poem*, London, 1898). In another book of the same year, *White Stains*, he extolled the joys of pederasty in verse. During this period he announced that "he wished to get into contact with the devil." Crowley's occult interests took a quantum leap with his participation in 1898–1900 in the Order of the Golden Dawn, an offshoot of Theosophy. Under the tutelage of several members of the order he became adept in "Ceremonial Magick." In London he established himself in a flat in Chancery Lane, styling himself Count Vladimir Svareff. Two rooms of the apartment became temples dedicated respectively to the twin pillars of Light and Dark.

After the turn of the century Crowley's public career began, and he was regularly attacked in the press as "The Great Beast" and "The Wickedest Man in the World." In 1904 Crowley was visited—so he claimed—by his Holy Guardian Angel, Aiwass, who dictated to him *The Book of the Law*, which became the charter for his later activities. Among its precepts are "The word of Sin is Restriction" and "There is no law beyond Do what thou wilt." In a 1910 memoir he proclaimed, "I shall fight openly for that which no Englishman dare defend, even in secret—sodomy! At school I was taught to admire Plato and Aristotle, who recommend sodomy to youths. I am not so rebellious as to oppose their dictum; and in truth there seems to be no better way to avoid the contamination of woman and the morose pleasures of solitary vice."

In the United States during World War I he experimented with the mind-altering properties of mescaline. He then established a kind of commune or Abbey at Cefalù in Sicily, where (in 1921) he advanced beyond the grade of Magus to the supreme status of Ipsissimus. His earlier misogyny notwithstanding, the abbey also sheltered two mistresses and their children, placing a severe strain on Crowley's finances. He also had a male lover, the poet Victor Neuburg, whom he dominated ruthlessly. With the dissolution of the Abbey in 1929, he began to publish the volumes of his "autohagiography," the final text of which was not issued until

1969 as *The Confessions of Aleister Crowley*. In 1945 Crowley went to live in a shabby room in a boarding house near Hastings, where he died two years later. Scarcely known today outside occult circles, Crowley is an extravagant instance of the concern with heterodox religion that has flourished among some male homosexuals who could find no peace within established Christianity, and more recently among female adherents of "the craft." Through his voluminous writings Crowley foreshadowed the emergence of the "Age of Aquarius."

BIBLIOGRAPHY. Israel Regardie, *The Eye in the Triangle: An Interpretation of Aleister Crowley*, St. Paul: Llewellen Publications, 1970.

Wayne R. Dynes

CRUISING

Cruising is the deliberate, active, and usually mobile search for sexual partner(s) in a social setting. One may cruise on foot, by bike, car, even by boat. The searcher watches for potential partners, and for signs of interest from others, while displaying a choice of signs (body language, **gesture**, **clothing**, even systematic color and key codes that may be regarded as social **semiotics**) to indicate that the search is on. Cruising is a way of avoiding the social inhibition that requires "proper introduction" or other mediation by third parties when seeking intimate encounter with a stranger.

Searching for sexual partners in social settings is not original with modern gay men; earliest published advice on cruising came from the poet of ancient **Rome**, Publius Ovid (*Art of Love*, ca. A.D. 1). His favorite cruising places were the market, temple, and race track. No sexist, he cruised both genders, and his poem includes advice for women seeking male partners. English gay men refer to cruising as "trolling." A quasi-equivalent among heterosexuals is "picking up."

Gay male cruising was traditionally a more systematic activity than heterosexual "flirting" because the gay searcher was taking serious risks—assault by a heterosexual who resented sexual approach, entrapment by undercover **police**, "queer bashing" by teenagers looking for "thrills," and the like. Gay cruisers who survive take precautions and master cruising skills. These include well-informed choice of locale, safety of entry and exit, subtle use of glances, and well-informed use of signs and code words to establish sexual understanding. Most urban centers have "cruisy" gay places—favored streets, parks, **beaches**, and the like—where the searcher is most likely to find a partner. Those not wanting to take an active searching role, but willing to be "cruised" or "picked up," could hang around these places.

Traditional gay male skill in covert cruising led to a myth that total strangers who were homosexual had some sixth sense to recognize each other. In recent years, as public knowledge and tolerance have increased, gay cruising has become less covert, and many cruising techniques are now used by heterosexual men and women. However, the threat of **AIDS** has increasingly inhibited cruising for casual sex partners by both sexes and sexual orientations. Potential partners are now more likely to want a "proper introduction" and background information.

Cruising today ranges from the most blatant—staring, openly following a desired partner for blocks, making comments ostensibly to a third party but intended to be overheard by a desired stranger—to the most covert, where third parties present do not even suspect a sexual liaison is being negotiated. Overt cruising uses imagination to find any excuse for introducing oneself to a stranger, and many of its techniques are similar to those of the male or female prostitute seeking clients. In covert cruising, skilled use of the eyes is critical. Eye contact must be less than a stare, but more than a casual glance, and is especially effective when each simultaneously "catches the other offguard" (e.g., turning around after passing), and exchanges a knowing smile.

If the time is opportune (both partners are searching, the situation does not compromise other commitments, and so forth), cruising can lead promptly to **impersonal sex**. If not, skilled searchers will find a means, even without alerting others present, to exchange information for future contact. Cruising is most often a brief search for a one-time, unpaid sex partner (**trick**), but it may also be a lengthy search for a candidate long-term **lover**.

BIBLIOGRAPHY. Nicole Ariana, *How to Pick up Men*, New York: Bantam, 1972; Mark Freedman and Harvey Mayes, *Loving Man*, New York: Hark, 1976, chapter 2; J. A. Lee, *Getting Sex*, Toronto: General, 1978.

John A. Lee

CUBA

The largest island of the Antilles chain, home to ten million Spanish-speaking people, Cuba separates the Gulf of Mexico from the Caribbean Sea. At its closest point, it is 90 miles south of Florida.

The Colonial Period. Cuba was discovered by Christopher Columbus in 1492 and colonized by Spain beginning in 1511. Overwork and disease brought from the Old World caused the death of most of the native Caribs, who were replaced by Africans imported as slaves beginning in 1518. The Spanish *peninsulares* normally intended to return to Europe and rarely brought women with them.

During the seventeenth century **pirates** and privateers roamed boldly throughout the Caribbean. The British, French, and Dutch seized islands from the Spanish or colonized vacant ones as naval bases or sugar plantations; like the pirates they seldom brought women along. All three European powers were involved in the notorious triangular trade, shipping molasses or rum to Europe, guns and trinkets from there to Africa, and slaves back to the West Indies. Many maintain that the common economies and social systems thus evolved rendered Caribbean islands and indeed parts of the adjoining mainland, including **New Orleans**, Vera Cruz, and Caracas, and their hinterlands more alike than different. **Slavery** and exploitation promoted a low regard for life and labor and set up situations for institutional and situational homosexuality, with males outnumbering females by a great margin. The varieties of language, politics, topography, size, and history, however, created differences, some islands having received great numbers of East Indian (Trinidad, for example) or Chinese immigrants (Cuba).

Cuba began to excel in sugar production after 1762. Havana became a glittering metropolis, rivaling New York and Rio de Janeiro, by 1800. The slave population, including huge numbers of males imported for work in the cane fields or molasses manufacturing, grew from fewer than 40,000 in 1770 to over 430,000 seventy years later. The census of 1841 reported that more than half the population was non-white (black and mixed blood) and that 43 percent were slaves. Males outnumbered females by 2 to 1 in the center and west and were just equal in the east. Other islands in the Caribbean had even greater sexual imbalances. Documentation for the homosexuality that must have abounded is scarce but the earlier prevalence can be assumed from attitudes and customs that still survive.

When most of Spain's colonies in the Americas gained independence in the early nineteenth century, Cuba remained Spanish. By the 1840s, however, the slave trade became more difficult as the British energetically pursued smugglers and after 1850 the Spanish authorities cooperated more earnestly. With Spain's adoption of the Napoleonic Code in 1889, homosexuality was decriminalized three years after the abolition of slavery.

Independence. Cuba gained its independence from Spain in 1898 as a consequence of the Spanish–American War, but became a virtual American protectorate until the Platt Amendment (1902) was repealed in 1934, by which time Americans had come to own over one third of the sugar mills, producing over half of Cuba's sugar.

During World War I, Europe was closed to North Americans and Cuba, especially Havana, became a resort for the more adventurous. Prosperity increased with a rise in commodity prices. Also, Prohibition in the United States after 1920 left Cuba as an oasis where liquor still flowed freely. Casino gambling and prostitution were also legal. A favorite port of call of cruise ships, Havana flourished as a mecca for pleasure-seekers.

Havana was also a center for Spanish-speaking culture, as Federico García **Lorca** discovered to his delight when he visited the city in 1930. In the late 1930s, José **Lezama Lima**, who was to become one of Latin America's greatest novelists, began his literary career there.

The postwar collapse of commodity prices was to some extent offset by tourism. Everything was for sale in Havana under the dictator Fulgencio Batista, whose 1952 coup ousted an outwardly democratic but venal and nepotistic predecessor.

Old Havana had gay bars. Moral laxity, characteristic of the slave-rooted Caribbean economy, the Napoleonic Code, and the weakness of the Catholic Church (which was mainly Spanish, urban and upper class) produced an environment where gays were only mildly persecuted and could buy protection from corrupt officials. Drugs, especially marijuana, which flourished throughout the Caribbean, were available in Cuba long before they won popularity in the United States.

The Castro Regime. Exploiting popular revulsion against continuing political corruption as well as resentment of the diminishing but still important American domination, Fidel Castro led an ill-assorted group of liberals, patriots, and Marxists, including some gays, to victory over Batista in 1959. Only after he came to power did the United States realize that Castro was an avowed Communist. The American Central Intelligence Agency then tried and failed to assassinate him. Hatred of the Colossus of the North and of the upper classes, some of whom had by corruption shared the spoils of foreign exploitation, as well as implacable American opposition to his regime, drove Castro to ally with the Soviet Union. His triumph was sealed by the missile crisis of 1962 when Khrushchev agreed to withdraw the missiles in return for Kennedy's promise never to try to invade Cuba. Since then the situation has been a stalemate.

Castro closed all gambling casinos, houses of prostitution, and gay bars. Not only are all the male brothels and bars where boys could be bought gone, but so also are all other gay establishments. Two million people have fled, including almost all of Havana's 15,000 Jews.

Soviet hostility toward homosexuality since 1934, when Stalin restored the penal laws against male homosexuals, combined with traditional Latin American machismo and Catholic homophobia, to make the existence of Cuban homosexuals wretched and oppressive. To prevent their "contamination" of youth, thousands of gays in the 1960s were placed in work camps known as Military Units to Increase Production (UMAP). Although the camps were abolished by the end of the decade, other forms of discrimination continued. Article 359 of the Cuban penal code prohibits public homosexuality. Violations are punished with a minimum of 5 and a maximum of 20 years. Parents must discourage their children from homosexuality or report their failure to officials as Articles 355–58 mandate. Articles 76–94 punish with 4 years imprisonment sexual deviation regarded by the government as contrary to the spirit of Socialism. Cuban gays are left undisturbed only if they abstain from practicing, but even then they are not permitted to hold jobs which involve contact with foreigners or to attend university.

The gifted playwright and fiction writer Virgilio Piñera (1912–1967) returned from Argentina in 1957 and after Castro's triumph worked for several of the newspapers of the regime. On October 11, 1961, he was arrested and jailed for homosexuality. Che Guevara personally denounced him. The novelist Reinaldo Arenas, an authentic son of the proletariat, was subjected to constant restriction by the Castro government. An early exile, the gay satirical writer Severo Sarduy has chosen to live and work in Europe.

Between 10,000 and 20,000 gay men and lesbians were among the 125,000, which included an indeterminate number of criminals and insane people, who chose to leave (or were forced to leave) in the boatlift from Mariel in 1980. Among the refugees was Reinaldo Arenas, who resumed a productive career in New York City.

Cuba is the only country that imposes AIDS tests on all its people, and the only one that confines for life anyone carrying the HIV virus. In a 1989 report, the independent human rights group Americas Watch described Cuba as a tightly controlled society in which people are restrained from speaking freely and holding meetings and most are forbidden to leave the country. According to the report, the regime has perfected a system of monitoring "almost every aspect" of private life, beginning with neighborhood committees that collect information, opinions, and gossip and determine who is admitted to day-care centers and universities, who may purchase consumer goods, and whether a job change is appropriate. People's lives "are shaped by judgments about how their conduct and their views conform to officially prescribed doctrines." The report concluded that "Cuba's practices on human rights are sharply at odds with international standards." Despite intensive persecution, closeted gays still serve in political and cultural institutions.

BIBLIOGRAPHY. Allen Young, *Gays under the Cuban Revolution*, San Francisco: Grey Fox Press, 1982.
Pedro J. Suárez

CULT PROSTITUTION
See Ḳādēsh.

CUNNILINGUS
See **Oral Sex**.

D

DAMIAN, PETER, SAINT (CA. 1007–1072)

Italian prelate and ecclesiastical writer. Originally of Ravenna, by dint of rigorous austerity and solitary prayer he reluctantly became superior of the hermitage of Fonte Avellana (1043) and corresponded with emperor Henry III. As a trusted counselor of three popes, he became cardinal bishop of Ostia in 1057, and then papal legate to France, to Florence, and finally to Germany, where in 1072 he persuaded Henry IV not to divorce his wife Bertha. (Henry IV was perhaps bisexual and has been analyzed as unstable because of a troubled childhood during which an archbishop kidnapped him from his mother.)

Along with the fanatic Humbert—soon to be made a cardinal—whose mission to Constantinople in 1054 resulted in permanent schism between the Orthodox and Catholic churches, Peter Damian was an ally of Hildebrand, the leader of the papal reform movement. Hildebrand, as pope Gregory VII (1073–1085), challenged lay control of the Church, particularly the domination by the German emperors, which initiated a two-hundred-year-long struggle that weakened both. Gregory VII claimed supremacy in Western Christendom, denying the old Gelasian doctrine that emperors were of equal power and dignity with popes. In his *Dictatus Papae* (1076), the uncompromising Gregory insisted that popes could make and unmake kings and emperors, judge everyone but be judged by no one, and that anyone who defied them could not gain entrance to Heaven.

Although he is often described as less fanatic than Humbert and Gregory, Damian, an informal member of the papal circle, was actually more fierce than they about several matters. He was vigorous in denouncing Nicolaism, the sin of clerical marriage, for he believed that wives and children would distract priests from serving the church with all their heart and also might incline them to skim church funds for their families and to pass on their offices to their sons. It was largely owing to his influence that the higher secular clergy—priests and bishops—had to give up their wives and concubines. Until then most of them, like those in lower orders, deacons, exorcists, acolytes, and so forth, often had female "housekeepers" or even wives, as priests in the Orthodox church still today may marry. Once the papal reformers demanded and began to enforce chastity for secular clergy, as popes did from the mid-eleventh century (just when they also began to insist that kings not divorce or abandon their wives), homosexuality became as great a problem for the secular clergy in the outside world as it had been for monks from their earliest days. This happened when monks fled the company of women to the Egyptian desert and were later cloistered in monasteries, that is, walled into areas from which women and often other outsiders were excluded. The eleventh-century reform movements, under the banner of a return to the selfless *vita apostolica* of the first Christians, attempted to restore the full rigor of monastic life after it had fallen into desuetude as a result of unsettled political conditions. The monks henceforth lived only with one another, under strict rules designed to discourage sexual contact and under the watchful eye of the abbot who was empowered to flog them when other coercive measures failed.

Secular clerics were far harder to control than monks. They mingled freely with the laity, heard their confessions, and often visited them or received them alone. Their opportunity for homosexual as well as for heterosexual contact was far greater than that of monks, and bishops' supervision was more distant and generally much laxer than that of abbots. Many seculars attained their posts as the younger sons or brothers of nobles or, in the case of poor priests, through less exalted family connections. Not a few bought their offices—the sin of simony, named for Simon Magus, who tried to buy his way into heaven, a sin Peter Damian denounced bitterly. But homosexual sodomy became a greater problem once celibacy was demanded of the secular clergy. Although some always cohabited with women (which the Protestant reformers in the sixteenth century were to allow again if they married), secular clerics after the eleventh century increasingly had to live apart from women, and as they did, sodomy among them probably increased, though Protestant propaganda exaggerated its frequency among the Catholic clergy.

The whole issue of clerical **celibacy** raises psychological, biological, and philosophical issues which the apologists for Roman Catholicism have never fully faced. Can an instinct exist in human beings only to be denied and suppressed? If procreation is the sole legitimate end of sexual activity, why should any part of the population be forbidden to procreate, all the more as the church condemned castration on the ground that the reproductive powers of a human being should never be abolished? It has been maintained that administrative convenience underlay the whole policy: a celibate clergy would have no wives and children to maintain, could be moved from one locale to another with a minimum of burdens, and so forth. It is probably also true that a sexually inhibited and frustrated clergy would be more prone

to implement the antisexual policies of the church out of envy and resentment for those who sought—in defiance of the Church's teaching—to obtain illicit sexual gratification. On the other hand, the eccentric Russian social critic Vasilii Vasil'evich **Rozanov** maintained that homosexuals instigated the church to adopt ascetic policies as a way of separating men from women, and also to provide themselves with a cozy haven in which they would not be encumbered with the obligations of heterosexual marriage and family life. However, in an age when the clergy had a virtual monopoly on higher learning, such policies, with the intelligentsia as a class doomed not to reproduce itself, might in the long run result in the genetic impoverishment of the population.

In 1059 in his almost hysterical *Liber Gomorrhianus*, addressed to Pope Leo IX, Peter Damian denounced clerical sodomites. Although the Pope refused the extreme punishments Damian recommended, and expressly and firmly proclaimed that there was no need to depose sodomitical clerics, persecution increased with the growing organization of the church. In 1045 a local synod excommunicated sodomites along with heretics. In 1104 Guibert de Nogent noted that heretics near Soissons were accused of homosexual acts. At the same time the scholastic Anselm of Laon condemned heresy and sodomy as forms of sacrilege and deserving of death. The council of Nablus in 1120 enacted into law the death penalty for heresy and sodomy which it saw as two aspects of the same offense.

Peter Damian thus ushered in the period of intensified condemnation and repression of sodomy that culminated in the total outlawry of homosexual expression in the late thirteenth century.

See also **Christianity; Clergy, Gay; Monasticism.**

BIBLIOGRAPHY. Peter Damian, *Book of Gomorrah: An Eleventh-Century Treatise Against Clerical Homosexual Practices*, ed. Pierre J. Payer, Waterloo,

Ont.: Wilfrid Laurier University Press, 1982; Michael Goodich, *The Unmentionable Vice: Homosexuality in the Later Medieval Period*, Santa Barbara: ABC–Clio, 1979.

William A. Percy

DANCE

The impulse to execute patterned rhythmic movements that are different from simply walking or running lies deep in the human constitution. Dancelike forms are employed by some animal species for courtship and communication. As it has evolved, human dancing may be divided into social, ritual, folk, and art dance.

Early Forms. In ancient Greece dance events were associated with the sexually ambivalent god Dionysus. In many cases dance festivals that began as religious were transformed into opportunities for lasciviousness. In Athens at the Cotyttia festival dance performances took place by men in women's clothes in which the ceremonies, which at first had referred only symbolically to sex, gradually passed into homosexual orgies. During Roman times the castrated priests of Cybele were alleged to use religious dances as a prelude to the seduction of young men. In Islam, with its rigid segregation of the sexes, a long tradition has existed of boy dancers for the entertainment of adult men. The popularity of masked balls in eighteenth-century Europe permitted some revelers to dress as members of the opposite sex and to engage in amorous dalliance with members of their own.

Modern Social Dancing. In a remarkable description in *Sodome et Gomorrhe*—the encounter of Charlus and Jupien—Marcel **Proust** analyzed the separate segments of a male–male cruising episode in terms of dance. From the end of the nineteenth century homosexual balls have been given in which some male attendees dress up in glamorous women's attire. These events, frequently held on Hallowe'en, were tolerated as social oddi-

ties. Generally speaking, however, the law banned homosexuals and lesbians from ballroom dancing in which the couples hold one another. Changes in legal climate in most Western countries eliminated this barrier, and gay **bars** began holding "tea dances," sometimes to raise money for charities. The phenomenon of disco, which began in the early 1970s, was particularly associated with male-homosexual patronage. Opposed to disco is the **punk rock** trend, which has its own dance forms, most notably the "slam dance," which features turbulent mass body contact in a usually all-male context; the participants, however, are generally unaware of the implicit homosexuality involved.

Modern Art Dance. Familiarity with the world of classical ballet and modern dance reveals a disproportionate number of male homosexuals among the performers. Anton Dolin, who had his own company in England, and John Cranko, former director of the Stuttgart Ballet, stand out among dance figures who were straightforward about their sexuality. Despite great advances in the standing of dance in the middle decades of the twentieth century, the notion lingers among the general public that, in contradistinction to **athletics**, dance is not a truly masculine activity.

The explanation for these facts lies in part in the history of dancing. Before the French Revolution men dominated the dance, usually also assuming women's roles since respectable women were generally barred from the medium. Even kings such as Louis XIV performed in ballets. After 1800 the status of dancing declined, while at the same time women began to dominate, even dancing men's roles on occasion. The ballet girl as the plaything of the libertines became almost a stereotype in Victorian times. It is difficult to recover the biographical details of male ballet dancers during this period; many married women, but no small number of them were probably gay.

In the early twentieth century a remarkable upgrading of the status of ballet occurred. A remarkable group of innovative women, including Loie Fuller, Ruth Duncan, Mary Wigman, Ruth St. Denis, and Martha Graham, created modern dance. The homosexual impresario Sergei **Diaghilev** introduced the Russian ballet to the West. Inspired by his love, Diaghilev repeatedly shaped his erotic protégés into world-class dancers: Vaslav Nijinsky, Léonide Massine, Anton Dolin (born Patrick Healey Kay), and Serge Lifar. Ironically, in Russia, perhaps because boys were sent to ballet schools for economic reasons, most dancers remained heterosexual. It is perhaps of interest that of the two great male dancers to have left the Soviet Union after World War II, one is gay, the other heterosexual.

Several homosexual composers achieved notable success in writing ballets, including Jean-Baptiste **Lully**, Peter Ilitch **Tchaikovsky**, and Aaron Copland. Tchaikovsky's *Sleeping Beauty* (1890) and *Swan Lake* (1877) are particular favorites of gay audiences.

A pivotal figure in American ballet was Ted **Shawn**, who formed the Denishawn company with Ruth St. Denis. Perhaps because he himself was bisexual, Shawn went to considerable lengths to dispel dance's sissy reputation. He employed athletes to provide an aggressive show of masculinity. Hollywood dancers—at least those who became famous as distinct from the chorus boys—were heterosexual, but belonged to different genres: tapdancers and jazz dancers.

In the more liberal climate of the 1960s all-male dances began to be common. The avant-garde Merce Cunningham, who has shared his life with the composer John Cage, was the inspirer of the unisex trend in "postmodern" dance. In Brussels Maurice Béjart innovated with shifts in sex roles in his company at the Théâtre de la Monnaie in Brussels; in 1987 he was succeeded there by Mark Morris, who continues the tradition, though in an entirely different way. A documentary film, *Nik and Murray*, tells the story of dance-world luminaries Alwin Nikolais and Murray Louis, treating their long-term relationship simply as a matter of fact.

Understandably, dancers are anxious to protect their reputation from imputations of homosexuality, which would make their performances in classic male–female roles less credible. One group which has no such problem is New York's transvestite Les Ballets Trockadero de Montecarlo, which spoofs not only gender roles, but art dance itself.

Conclusion. What are the reasons for the affinity of gay men and dance? In part they are economic: the poor income can be borne by a single man more easily than a married one with children (women dancers are often married to a male breadwinner). Then there is the appeal of a "chameleon" role, a successful simulation before a demanding audience; the satisfaction that is gained in this way is not unlike that of the actor, the diplomat, and the spy. Professional dancing allows gay men to indulge a love of colorful costume and makeup during periods of gray social conformity. It may be also that the exhibitionism inherent in the profession is sexual sublimation. The performances are suffused with eroticism and emotion in a setting of simulated and unconsummated heterosexuality. This profession may be regarded as a haven from the harsh worlds of commerce and masculine competition, a haven in which one may nonetheless show one's excellence. Finally there is the social magnetism inherent in stereotyping itself: because dance was thought to be "faggy," impressionable young gay men were drawn to it.

BIBLIOGRAPHY. Judith Lynne Hanna, "Patterns of Dominance: Men, Women, and Homosexuality in Dance," *The Drama Review*, 31 (1987), 22–47.

Ward Houser

DANDYISM

The dandy has been since antiquity the man who prides himself on being the incarnation of elegance and of male fashion. The word itself stems from the Romantic period in the nineteenth century, when the character type reached its apogee; England and France were the principal countries in which it flourished. Charles Baudelaire (1821–1867) was one of the first to perceive that the type was not limited to the age just preceding his own, but had emerged across the centuries in some celebrated historical figures. Jules Barbey d'Aurevilly (1808–1889) wrote an *Essay on Dandyism and George Brummel* (1845), dealing with Beau Brummell (1778–1840), the most famous English representative of the dandy in the London of George IV.

History of the Type. Ancient Greece saw two classical specimens of the dandy: Agathon and **Alcibiades**. In **Plato's** *Symposium* Agathon is a poet and tragedian, not merely handsome, but obsessed with the most trivial details of his wardrobe. **Aristophanes** shows him using a razor to keep his cheeks as smooth and glistening as marble, wearing sumptuous clothing in the latest Ionian fashion. Later in the same dialogue Alcibiades also enters the stage, the most dazzling figure of the *jeunesse dorée* of Athens, richer and more influential than Agathon, and never sparing any expenditure that would enhance his renown.

In the Renaissance the aristocratic male sported colorful and ostentatious clothing that paralleled the brilliant plumage of the peacock or the flowing mane of the male lion—as can be seen from the portraits of that era. Somewhat later, the Macaroni Club in the London of George III united members of the upper class who became proverbial for their elaborate costumes—which earned them the reproach of effeminacy; it is to this assemblage that the line of "Yankee Doodle" alludes: "Stuck a feather in his cap/And called it macaroni." It was in the period when the costume of the bourgeoisie—the merchant class—was becoming ever more somber that the dandy reached full flower. During the first quarter of the nineteenth century dandyism was a characteristically English phenomenon, then with the mounting influence of the British aristocracy and gentry on the upper classes of the continent it spread there as well. Outfitted by the renowned tailors of the English capital, the dandy made his mark on elegant society. A Frenchman, Alfred de Grimaud, Count d'Orsay, dazzled a London struck by both his physical beauty and his stylish dress, yet a biographer of his noted that "Nature had lavished all her gifts on him but denied him the virility that enables one to conquer the fair sex." Having become the lover of Lady Blessington, he accompanied her to Italy where they encountered Lord **Byron** at Genoa.

A later incarnation of the dandy was Robert de **Montesquiou**-Fezensac (1855–1921), the "professor of beauty," as he was styled by Marcel **Proust**, for whom he was the model of the Baron de Charlus in *A la recherche du temps perdu*, as he had earlier suggested Des Esseintes to Joris-Karl Huysmans in *A Rebours*. He adorned and perfumed his person in a style worthy of a *fin-de-siècle* decadent scion of the nobility. Another **aesthete** of this era, Oscar **Wilde**, affected a particularly striking costume when he made a lecture tour of the United States, capitalizing on a character featured in the Gilbert and Sullivan opera *Patience* (1881).

In the Britain of the 1960s, newly affluent youth reacted against the drabness of the postwar years and began to experiment with dress, first recycling fancy Edwardian castoffs and then donning made-to-order Carnaby Street gear. While these trends, which migrated from "swinging London" to the United States and elsewhere on a crest of enthusiasm for British popular **music**, were largely heterosexual, leather fashions began with gay men—originally those in the **S/M** subculture—and penetrated all advanced Western societies in the 1980s.

Rationale. The relation of the dandy to male homosexuality is complicated. As a rule the homosexual—more than the male who is attracted to women—feels the need to distinguish his person in some way, is more conscious of the world of male fashion and more likely to be narcissistically preoccupied with his image. Naturally not all the dandies of the past were homosexual or bisexual, and an element of leisure class self-demarcation and snobbery enters into the picture. Since it is usually the male of the species whom nature makes physically more noteworthy, the male–female antithesis in style of dress that has prevailed in Western culture since the French Revolution reverses the immemorial state of affairs. The notion that only a woman may be preoccupied with her wardrobe and that a man should dress simply and even unobtrusively is of recent date.

The dandy is also relevant to the role of the homosexual subculture in determining male fashion. Not a few of the idols of stage and screen, and of course professional models, have been attracted to their own sex, whatever façade they maintained in deference to the prevailing heterosexual mores. In these individuals, and particularly in their public image, the perceptive eye can often discern a homoerotic element, a subtle blending of the masculine and feminine which the heterosexual cannot easily capture.

Originally a paragon of leisure-class ostentation, the dandy toward the end of the nineteenth century took on a new social identity as a type of the aesthete, of the bearer of a culture that flaunted its scorn for the humdrum way of life of the staid middle class. The convention that a gentleman could wear only custom-made clothing, never ready-made and hence mass-produced garments, also played into the hands of the dandy who could order a costume that would be his very own, shaped to stress the elegance of his figure, and even able to determine fashion.

The dandy exemplifies the symbolic value of **clothing** in European civilization, the use of costume for self-defini-tion and self-affirmation, and also an expression of the aesthetic in private life, where clothes merge with the personality of the wearer and confirm his status in the eyes of others. In this scheme the homoerotic element lies chiefly in the narcissism, the attention to one's own male beauty, the pleasure in holding a mask between one's true self and the gaze of others.

See also **Theatre and Drama; Transvestism.**

BIBLIOGRAPHY. Françoise Coblence, *Le Dandysme, obligation d'incertitude*, Paris: Presses Universitaires de France, 1988; Patrick Favardin and Laurent Bouexière, *Le Dandysme*, Paris: La Manufacture, 1988; Simone François, *Le Dandysme et Marcel Proust: de Brummell au baron de Charlus*, Brussels: Palais des Académies, 1956.

Warren Johansson

DANTE ALIGHIERI (1265–1321)

Italian poet, critic, and political thinker. A Florentine patrician, Dante was an active member of the Guelph party. As a youth he had a profound spiritual experience in an encounter with the young Beatrice Portinari; after her death he submerged himself in the study of philosophy and poetry. In 1302 Dante was banished from Florence, pursuing his literary career in various other cities of Italy. He died and was buried in Ravenna.

Dante's masterpiece, written in exile, was the *Divina Commedia*, divided into the three major parts, the *Inferno*, the *Purgatorio*, and the *Paradiso* that relate his imaginary voyage through Hell, Purgatory, and Heaven. The presence in both the *Inferno* and the *Purgatorio* of groups of "sodomites" has given rise to a series of debates over the centuries. These passages must be interpreted in the larger context of the great poem's situations and personnel. In his imaginary travels Dante encountered many persons of note, including one whom he named as his master: Brunetto Latini (ca. 1212–1294).

The sodomites of the *Inferno* (cantos 15 and 16) are seen running under a rain of fire, condemned never to stop if they wish to avoid the fate of being nailed to the ground for a hundred years with no chance of shielding themselves against the flames. Having recognized Dante, Brunetto Latini called him to speak with him, voicing an important prophecy of Dante's future. In describing his fellow sufferers, Latini mentioned a number of famous intellectuals, politicians, and soldiers.

In the *Purgatorio* (canto 26) the sodomites appear in a different context—together with lustful heterosexuals. The two categories travel in opposite directions, yelling out the reason for their punishment.

How can one account for the striking deference and sympathy that Dante shows for the sodomites? This matter began to puzzle commentators only a few years after the poet's death.

Dante's education took place in the thirteenth century when Italy was beginning to change its attitudes toward homosexual behavior. Conduct which had been a transgression condemned by religion but viewed with indulgence by everyday morality assumed increasing seriousness in the eyes of the laity. For Dante it was still possible—as it had commonly been through the first half of the thirteenth century—to separate human and divine judgment with respect to sodomy. As a Christian Dante placed those who were guilty of that crime in Hell, but as a man of his time he did not deem the behavior grave enough to blot out the admiration that he retained for some of those guilty of it. Hence Dante vouchsafed to the sodomite Latini, and not to others, the prophecy that has been mentioned.

This approach became simply incomprehensible only a generation after the poet's death. For Dante's commentators sodomy was a sin of such gravity that it was inconceivable for them to treat with respect men seared with such "infamy."

How then could Dante's own attitude to be understood? How could one explain his placement of a man he respected and admired, Brunetto Latini, in such a circle of infamy?

There were few who, like Francesco da Buti (1324–1406), one of the most esteemed of the older commentators of Dante, saw that for Dante "the vicious man who is guilty of some sin may have virtue in himself, for which he merits honor and respect," and that Dante, with regard to Brunetto, had "honored the virtue that lay within him, disregarding the vice."

Over the centuries, in an effort to reconcile what appeared to later readers irreconcilable the commentators set forth a series of very odd explanations. That Dante had spoken of Brunetto Latini and the sodomites with too much sympathy because he too shared their feelings was the conclusion of one anonymous commentator of the fourteenth century. Another wild suggestion is that the shameless Latini had made an attempt on Dante's own virtue, and that hence Dante's gentle words are in reality sarcasm that must be understood "in the opposite sense" (Guiniforto dei Bargigi; 1406–after 1460?). Then, foreshadowing a thesis that would be favored by medical opinion in the twentieth century, it was suggested that there were two types of sodomites, those by "choice" and those who are such by "necessity." The latter were less savage that the former, having sinned only because they had no other possibility of having sex, and it is of these that Dante speaks in the *Inferno*. (This last is the thesis of an anonymous commentator who wrote between 1321 and 1337.)

The debate on Dante's motives has continued until our own day. In 1950 André Pézard devoted a whole book, *Dante sous la pluie de feu*, to an effort to show that the sin for which Brunetto and his companions were being punished was sodomy not in the usual sense, but in an allegorical one: *sodomie spirituelle*, which in Brunetto's case meant having used the French language as a medium for one of his works.

Opposed to this attempt to "cleanse" the *Inferno* of homosexuals was Giuseppe Aprile. His 1977 book, *Dante, Inferni dentro e fuori*, offers a "psychoanalytic reading" of Dante's poem that takes up the old thesis of Dante's personal homosexuality: it was their common predilection that made the poet treat the sodomites so gently.

The authoritative *Enciclopedia Dantesca* has sought to bring the conflict to an end, taking adequate account of Dante's indulgent judgment as the correct key for solving the supposed "enigma" of the band of sodomites. As regards the reason for Brunetto Latini's presence among the sodomites, Avalle D'Arco's recent confirmation of the attribution to him of a long love poem directed to a man, "S'eo son distretto inamoramente," shows that it was probably on the basis of facts that were publicly known in Dante's time that he was consigned to Hell.

BIBLIOGRAPHY. Giuseppe Aprile, *Dante, Inferni dentro e fuori*, Palermo: Il Vespro, 1977; Silvio Avalle D'Arco, *Ai luoghi di delizia pieni*, Milan: Ricciardi, 1976; Giovanni Dall'Orto, "L'omosessualità nella poesia volgare italiana fino al tempo di Dante," *Sodoma*, 3 (1986), 13–35 (with further bibliography); *Enciclopedia Dantesca*, Rome: Istituto della Enciclopedia Italiana, 1976, vol. 5, pp. 285–87; André Pézard, *Dante sous la pluie de feu*, Paris: Vrin, 1950.
Giovanni Dall'Orto

DAUGHTERS OF BILITIS
See **Bilitis.**

DAVID AND JONATHAN

The biblical story of David (ca. 1012–972 B.C.) and his loving friend Jonathan has long been a source of inspiration for Western homoerotic art and literature, and has been construed as the one episode in the Judeo-Christian scriptures which affirms at least passionate attachment between two males, if not an outright homosexual relationship. The nature of this friendship, however, can only be glimpsed through a veil of legend.

David himself ranks as a central figure in the Judeo-Christian tradition, revered by Christians as an ancestor of **Jesus** Christ. Jesus is described as of the "House of David," in accordance with an **Old Testament** prophecy regarding the Messiah, and his title "Christ" means "the Anointed One," reflecting back on David who was anointed King of Israel. Thus Jesus is given royal ancestry in addition to his divinity. Jews admire him as Israel's greatest king and national hero, ruler of an impressive Near Eastern empire at the turn of the first millennium B.C., and (putative) author of the Psalms.

Sources. The earliest sources about David are often judged to stem ultimately from the reign of his successor Solomon and in any case probably predate the Babylonian Exile of the sixth century B.C. The key early material on David's life, a compilation of sometimes conflicting narratives, appears in the Old Testament books of Samuel; a later version treating only his reign is found in the books of Chronicles. Later Jewish and Christian traditions magnified his role as a cultural, political, and spiritual hero.

The youngest son of a wealthy Bethlehem landowner, David is first seen as a shepherd, a cunning musician, and valiant, if underage, warrior, who rose to the position of armor-bearer and soothing harpist for Israel's first king, Saul, who "loved him greatly" (I Samuel 16:21) at first sight. In combat with the giant Goliath, the boy vanquished the champion of the Israelites' arch-enemies, the Philistines, with a stone from a slingshot. This deed caused Saul, who in this text seems unacquainted with David, to bring the boy into the royal household, where he came to enjoy a close relationship with Saul's son, Jonathan. They forged a compact of some sort, and Jonathan doffed his clothes and gave them to David. Although Saul resented David's popularity, he rewarded further martial deeds (bringing him the foreskins of 200 Philistines) by giving him his daughter Michal in marriage. David's star continued to rise, until Saul resolved to kill him. Both Michal and Jonathan took David's side against their father, helping him escape. After various adventures in hiding, David learned that both Saul and Jonathan were killed in battle with the Philistines, and he became king of Israel, having numerous wives and concubines, and sons by them. His otherwise glorious reign is marred by his passionate heterosexual adultery with Bathsheba, which led him to connive at the death of her husband Uriah, and a revolt by David's fratricidal son Absalom.

David's Beauty. The biblical description of David as "ruddy, and withal of a beautiful countenance, and goodly to look to" (I Samuel 16:12; repeated at 17:42) has made David an icon of sensuous male attractiveness not unlike Greek Apollo and **Ganymede**, or Roman **Antinous**, but within the Judeo-Christian sacred tradition, and hence a more legitimate subject for European Christian artists and writers during periods when religious-based cultural inhibitions surrounded the theme of male beauty. "Goodly to look to," it has been suggested, signifies that he had beautiful eyes, a quality much prized in ancient **Mesopotamia**.

David often appears in medieval and Renaissance art, though usually without Jonathan. The teen-aged bronze David figure (ca. 1435) of **Donatello**, now in the Bargello at Florence, radiates homoerotic sentiment. In 1501–04, **Michelangelo** created his heroic marble David as a symbol of the city of Florence, but doubtless also reflecting his interest in youthful male beauty.

Jonathan. A careful review of the sources suggests that in the relationship between David and Jonathan, it was Jonathan who was the desiring partner, submissive and perhaps somewhat effeminate, while David appears less committed (there are many references to Jonathan's love for David, but in no text is David said to "love" Jonathan) and more macho, perhaps something of a political opportunist. Establishment scholars and churchmen have insisted that there is no sign of an erotic link betwen the two men, denying that there is any evidence that would afford the basis for an interpretive context for such a link. The narrative of their relationship, however, is highly charged: "The soul of Jonathan was knit with the soul of David, and Jonathan loved him as his own soul. . . . Jonathan, Saul's son, delighted much in David. . . . Then said Jonathan unto David, Whatsover thy soul desireth, I will even do it for thee. . . . They kissed one another, and wept one with another, until David exceeded." (I Samuel 18:1, 19:1, 20:40–41). After Jonathan's death, David laments: "I am distressed for thee, my brother Jonathan: very pleasant hast thou been unto me: thy love to me was wonderful, passing the love of women." (II Samuel 1:26). In retrospect, the great womanizer David compared Jonathan's love favorably to that bestowed by men on women.

Ward Houser

There are, in addition, two other passages that deserve close scrutiny. The first of these is I Samuel 20:30, in which the irate Saul hurls at Jonathan a series of epithets which the King James version renders: "Thou son of the perverse rebellious woman, do not I know that thou hast chosen the son of Jesse to thine own confusion, and unto the confusion of thy mother's nakedness?" There is no indication in Samuel of any reason for Saul to cast aspersions on Jonathan's royal mother, so the text in the Rabbinic Bibles may be corrupt. The first clause in the standard versions of the received Hebrew text reads essentially as rendered above, but following the Septuagint it could be read and interpreted as: *ben nă'arōt ha-mōrdōt,* "Thou son of the man-crazy harlot!" Saint

Jerome, who was usually sensitive to erotic nuances of his original, translates as *fili mulieris virum ultro rapientis*, "son of a woman pursuing the man of her own desire." The second part of the quotation in Hebrew (amending *haber* for *boher*, in conformity with the Greek of the Septuagint), could then be rendered as: "do I not know that thou art the *darling* of the son of Jesse, to thine own shame and the shame of thy profligate mother?" John **Chrysostom** paraphrased the passage as "son of man-crazy harlots running after the effete, thou enervated and effeminate and having nothing of a man." This reading suggests that Saul was reproaching Jonathan for homosexuality, or at least that the virulently homophobic Chrysostom (A.D. 347–407) so understood it. If this interpretation is correct, what Saul is denouncing is probably not homosexuality as such, but rather the politically unacceptable subordination of the prince to his dangerous rival (in Saul's eyes) David; for Jonathan was David's "liege lord" and should have taken the masculine/dominant role with him, while the final words of the exclamation show that Saul suspected David's political ambitions on the throne.

The second passage is I Samuel 20:41, which depicts the meeting of David and Jonathan in the field, where the prince warns the soldier to flee for his life. They kissed, they wept, "until David exceeded" (*'ad higdīl*). The question here is the meaning of the Hebrew verb *higdīl*, which the King James translators rendered literally, following the second-century Greek version of Aquila. Yet the analogy of a root of similar meaning in the cognate Arabic language, a type of comparison of recognized value among Biblical scholars, offers a much better interpretation. *Higdīl* is derived from the adjective *gādōl*, "large," which has an exact parallel in Arabic *akbara*, "to have an erection; to ejaculate," alongside the adjective, *kabīrun*, "large." The variant readings of the Septuagint and of a some Hebrew manuscripts also suggest that the Hebrew originally had *'ad hagdēl*, rendered in Greek as *heôs tēs synteleias*, "until the ejaculation." Of course, with such a rendering one is left wondering how David could weep to the point of an ejaculation, behaviors not normally associated with each other. Or perhaps they first wept, then kissed, then David ejaculated, and the compiler got the sequence wrong as well. Still another possibility is that the physical contact left David with an erection, that he "grew large," at which point the narrative drew a discreet veil over the subsequent events. In any event, there is no suggestion that Jonathan was active; if there is an erotic element in this passage, then David was the active partner and Jonathan the passive.

Warren Johansson

Subsequent Interpretations. Although the philological points just reviewed represent a new understanding of the text, the popular interpretation of Jonathan and David as lovers has become relatively well-established in recent times, and some would take it as a transcultural gloss on the biblical story. In previous centuries it was often used as a coded reference to homoerotic relations when the mention was socially discouraged or even punished.

Abraham Cowley's "Davideis" (1656) is an epic poem with abundant treatment of the friendship motif. In the world of music, George Frideric Handel's oratorio "Saul" (1739) contains a moving setting of David's lament upon the death of Jonathan. The erotics of the battle between David and Goliath feature in Richard Howard's poem "The Giant on Giant-Killing: Homage to the Bronze *David* of Donatello, 1430" in his book *Fellow Feelings* (1976).

Contemporary American literature shows two attempts at fictionalization of the David narrative. Gladys Schmitt's 1946 novel *David the King* gives only veiled and unfavorable references to homosexual attractions. However, Wallace Hamilton's 1979 book *David at Olivet* not only glamorizes David's homosexual affairs but makes them central to the book, depicting the young harpist as soothing the king with more than music. Thus, when David becomes involved with Jonathan, the king is jealous not of his military prowess and popularity, but of his son. James Levin, in *The Gay Novel* (1983), criticizes Hamilton for not understanding the sexual rituals of ancient Palestinian ethnic groups, but retrofitting David with a twentieth-century sexual perspective instead.

Throughout its history the David and Jonathan legend shows a constantly changing interplay between ancient texts and modern interpretations, an interplay that will doubtless persist in the future.

Ward Houser

DAY, F. HOLLAND (1864–1933)

American photographer. With, and perhaps even before Alfred Stieglitz, F. Holland Day was America's first advocate of photography as an art form, as opposed to a mere technique for recording reality. Day was a key figure in developing the pictorialist aesthetic which is today associated with the Photo-Secession movement. Between 1895 and 1910 Day's prints were well known and influential both in America and Europe, making him the first American photographer with an international reputation.

The only child of a wealthy **Boston** manufacturer, Day had money to indulge his tastes: assembling a notable collection of Keats material; publishing fine books as a partner of Copeland and Day; providing educational expenses and personal instruction for boys from the Boston slums, such as the poet Kahlil Gibran, who was Day's most famous discovery and pupil; and, of course, his photography. Following his meteoric rise and almost equally steep descent as the leader of the new American photography, Day retired in 1917 to his bedroom on the third floor of the family mansion, spending the fifteen years before his death as a self-proclaimed invalid.

Day's homosexuality was never openly acknowledged, but may be inferred from the circumstances of his life, the circle of known homosexuals with whom he associated, and his work. A number of his finest photographs are male nudes or Greek themes involving young boys, adolescents or men. Unlike his contemporary Baron von **Gloeden**, Day's fall from photographic grace was largely not because of the sexual undertones of his work. Bostonians were sufficiently cultured to accept male nudes as "art," though they were scandalized when Day had himself lashed to a cross on a local hillside and photographed as the dying Christ for a "sacred series." More important causes were a 1904 fire which destroyed his studio and much of his work, his own dilettantism and willful withdrawal from the photographic scene, and his quarrel with Stieglitz, who simply wrote Day out of photographic history.

BIBLIOGRAPHY. E. F. Clattenberg, *The Photographic Work of F. Holland Day*, Wellesley, MA: Wellesley College Museum, 1975; J. and K. Gibran, *Kahlil Gibran: His Life and Work*, Boston: New York Graphic Society, 1974, chapters 3–8; Estelle Jussim, *Slave to Beauty*, Boston: Godine, 1981.

Donald Mader

DECADENCE

A historic phase of decline or deterioration of a society or nation is sometimes called decadence. The term is also used more narrowly to denote certain facets of literature and art in France and England during the last decades of the nineteenth century, when some of the creative figures of the fin-de-siècle were homosexual.

Belief in historical decline is probably rooted in the psychological fact that, as they grow older, human beings tend to recall earlier phases of their own lives in rosy terms, while deprecating the present. Projected onto peoples and societies, this experience suggests that the "good old days" were better than the present, while the future is likely to be worse yet. In some **conservative** modes of thinking this comparison is elevated to an archetypal pattern.

Classical Models. The Greeks and Romans had two chief models of epochal decline. According to the first, as outlined by the seventh-century poet Hesiod, human society began in an Edenic time of harmony and abundance, termed the Golden Age. In due course, however, this utopia yielded in turn to Silver and Bronze ages of increasing barbarism—until society plunged into the final bleak Iron Age. This pessimistic historical scheme presents a grim picture of successive stages of decline, the only consolation being the memory of the happiness of the Golden Age. According to some poets like **Vergil** and **Horace** in the entourage of the emperor Augustus (ruled 27 B.C.–A.D. 14), this age of bliss could return, starting the cycle anew.

The other model of decline cherished by classical antiquity begins with the idealization of a primitive past in a rural setting with a low level of technology, when human society was happy precisely because of scarcity. Since there was little to steal, theft was rare, and hardship caused people to work together instead of against each other. "Sweet are the uses of adversity," as Shakespeare was later to put it. This idealized picture of a stern but virtuous past held particular appeal for such Roman moralists as **Cicero** and **Juvenal**, who evoked the early days of the Republic as a foil to denounce their own age. A variation was to locate primitive virtue not in the remote past but in contemporary tribal societies. **Tacitus** lauded German uprightness, condemning in contrast Roman decadence, luxury, covetousness, and self-indulgence. Revealingly, not until the Christian Salvian, who wrote during the collapse of the Empire in the fifth century, does homosexual conduct per se figure in the catalog of vices.

Because of the pessimism (or pessimistic realism) of the classical mind these two models—that of decline from the Golden Age and that of corruption of primitive virtue—were dominant. A few Greek thinkers, however, did adopt a more hopeful view, pointing to the triumphs of technology as evidence that humanity had progressed after all. Moreover, with the official adoption of Christianity in the fourth century, Eusebius and other **Patristic** writers elaborated a new concept of progress, that of advancing states of moral perfection. Thus in **Old Testament** times, polygamy and even incest (Lot and his daughters) had under certain circumstances been permissible, but are so no longer. A great signpost on this road of human moral advance was of course the Incarnation of Christ, which will lead in due course to the Second Coming and the restoration of all things. Before the longed-for consummation can be secured, however, there will be a period of frightful apocalyptic turmoil. This prospect of sudden reversal—of decline *after* progress—was to prove a haunting vision.

The victory of the Moderns in their quarrel with the Ancients in late seventeenth-century France, as well as the scientific revolution completed at the same time in Sir Isaac Newton, prepared the way for the **Enlightenment** belief in human progress through science and institutional reform for a mankind that was basically good.

Evolutionary Concepts. The publication of Charles Darwin's *Origin of Species* in 1859 set the doctrine of evolution on its triumphant march, seeming to demonstrate scientifically and conclusively that in the larger scheme of things progress was inevitable. Even here, however, there were dark patches. Evolutionists recognized a regressive potential in organisms, the so-called atavisms. Thus the Italian criminologist Cesare **Lombroso** lumped homosexuals together with criminals as throwbacks to a more primitive phase of human existence. Still humanity could maintain progress by blocking these anachronisms and accelerate it by eugenics.

The overall atmosphere of optimism and uplift notwithstanding, nineteenth-century political considerations led to a more somber view in some quarters. The countries of southern Europe were compelled to recognize that the pacesetters of material progress were found in northwestern Europe, and that they seemed to be falling inexorably further and further behind. Even in a British Empire "on which the sun never set" doubts began to be voiced. How secure were society's foundations? Were savages noble after all? Was Nietzsche right in *Beyond Good and Evil*? Was the Boer War humane?

Historical and Literary Permutations. It was in France, however, that the theory of decadence emerged most fully and influentially. The word *décadence* had figured in the title of Montesquieu's *Considérations sur les causes de la grandeur des Romains et de leur décadence* (1747), and then of the French translation of Edward Gibbon's masterwork, and was thus redolent of the perennial problem of the reasons for Rome's decline. Gradually it came to indicate not simply a historical phase, but also a qualitative judgment on the state of civilization.

The word *décadence* was given a new twist by the French critic Désiré Nisard in 1834 as a pejorative term for certain literary trends of his own day. Nisard, whose professional interest was Latin literature, compared the mannerism and affectation of the Silver Age with certain aspects of the romanticism of his own day.

The defeat of France in the Franco–Prussian war (1870) induced a profound undertaking of national self-examination, accompanied in some quarters by a mood of resignation. In the 1880s the label *décadence* was actively embraced by the bisexual poet Paul **Verlaine** ("Langueur"), the novelist Joris-Karl Huysmans (*A Rebours*), and their followers. Joséphin **Péladan**, an advocate of androgyny, wrote a series of novels under the umbrella title "La Décadence latine," implying that the whole of the Romance world was on the downward path. Others were fascinated by the regressive history of the **Byzantine Empire** and the perverse figure of Salome. While the "decadent" writers and artists soon found that it was more expedient to march under the banner of Symbolism, the association of their work with hot-house sophistication and rarified excess—in short the fin-de-siècle—did not immediately vanish.

England, much influenced by nineteenth-century French cultural exports, had her own decadent writers and poets. The disgrace of the most notable of them, Oscar **Wilde**, in the three trials of 1895, which had repercussions throughout Europe, served for many to link the literary concept of decadence with the image of a perverted lifestyle.

In due course, with the dawning of the new century and especially after the drama of World War I, much of the old thinking faded away. In the Soviet Union today, however, the official line still treats every kind of literary and artistic experiment as *dekadentnyĭ*, occasionally labeling its creators as "pederasts."

Degeneration. In a parallel development, biological and pseudobiological thought spread the concept of degeneration. The French physician Bénédict-Auguste Morel held that the insalubrious conditions and relentless pressures of modern urban life caused the emergence of degenerate types who inevitably bequeathed their afflictions to their descendants (*Traité des dégénérescences . . .*, 1857). In his insidious *L'uomo delinquente* of 1889, Lombroso claimed to have isolated a whole cluster of physical traits characterizing congenital criminals, including male homosexuals and lesbians. The English Darwinian E. Ray Lankester linked biological degeneration with the fall of empires (*Degeneration*, London, 1880). It remained for the journalist Max Nordau to fuse the literary and biological trends in his widely read diatribe *Entartung* (Degeneration) of 1891. He held that sexual psychopaths would gain power to compel society to adapt to them, and even predicted that sexual inverts would become numerous enough to elect a majority in the imperial German parliament that would vote persons of the same sex the right to contract legal marriage. Even sadists, zoophiles, and necrophiliacs, he anticipated, would find regulated opportunity to gratify their cravings.

His contemporary Friedrich Nietzsche castigated the nineteenth century for its pervasive decadence, which he likened to the biological decline of an organism, but saw a possibility of renewal through the cultivation of "Dionysiac art." Hitler was later to assert that homosexuality had destroyed ancient Greece—in which **Sparta** represented for National Socialism the ideal "Aryan civilization"— and that his Reich must avoid this fate.

Modern Offshoots. A recent variation on the decadence concept is the notion circulating in some quarters of Afro-American opinion that sub-Saharan **Africa** was originally exempt from homosexuality, this perversion being forced on its inhabitants and their descendants in the New World as an instrument of colonial subjugation. In this perspective, homosexuality figures as part of the pathology of the declining white race. However this may be, there is abundant evidence for homosexuality in Black Africa both before and after colonization. Ironically it is the fear of homosexuality as a purported obstacle to progress and modernity that was forced on Africans by "enlightened" western opinion, not the practice itself. The ultimate origin of the myth of the sexual exceptionalism of Black Africa is probably Chapter XLIV of Edward Gibbon's *Decline and Fall of the Roman Empire* (1781): "I believe, and hope, that the negroes, in their own country, were exempt from this moral pestilence."

Appraisal. Two final points remain to be considered: the components of the decadence model, and the question of whether the sexual side of it can be aptly applied to Greece and Rome. The symptoms of decadence frequently mentioned are economic recession and dislocation, population decline, corruption, excessive luxury, widespread neurasthenia, social alienation and unrest, moral licence, and collapse of trust and honesty. Insofar as homosexuality has been regarded as a negative factor it has been added to this list. More specifically, it has been claimed, as among National Socialists perpetrating the **Holocaust**, that the homosexual person, by withdrawing from the procreative pool, contributes to population decline, which has (as now, for example, in Western Europe) often provoked anxiety in the pro-natalist camp. Let us try to enter somewhat further into the mindset which entertains this mode of thinking. Are the factors cited in this catalogue mere symptoms or are they causes? To the extent that homosexuality, say, is simply—in this view—merely a sign of an underlying malaise, would it make sense to combat it? It might seem that in this context antihomosexual measures are the equivalent of slaying the messenger who has brought unwelcome news. As these questions show, thinking about decadence tends to be emotionally fraught, and in practice symptoms and causes are thrown together helter-skelter.

These varied aspects notwithstanding, the popular mind still seeks to inculpate homosexuality in the fate of **Greece** and **Rome**, and especially to see its indulgence as a major cause of the decline and fall of the Roman Empire, which crumbled in the face of the invading barbarian hordes of the fifth century, and later lost what had been three-fourths of its territory to the expansionist zeal of Islam. Can this charge be sustained? The expansive age of Greece from the seventh through the third century was, according to our documentation, their age of idealized **pederasty**. Far from causing a decline in population, this flowering of same-sex love accompanied an almost explosive increase in population, requiring the foundation of colonies throughout much of the Mediterranean world and later the conquests of **Alexander the Great** in western Asia. Conversely, the period of Greek decline— the second and first centuries B.C.—corresponded to an incipient sexual puritanism and a glorification of heterosexual married life.

As for Rome, most of the homosexual scandals reported by such writers as **Suetonius** and **Tacitus** belong to the great age of the first and second century; according to Gibbon the latter century ranks as one of the greatest ages of human happiness. Only in the fourth century, under the Christian emperors, did the Roman state take legal action against consensual male same-sex conduct. Thus, if the legitimacy of this general line of macrohistorical moralism be allowed—and probably it should not be—the unwise suppression of homosexuality failed to revive the might of the Roman empire, and may even have hastened its decline. To be sure, as we have seen, Roman writers were given to rhetoric about decadence, including denunciations of homosexual behavior as early as Cato the Elder (234–139 B.C.), but historical evidence provides no warrant for the truth of their assertions. The issue is injected into contemporary discourse solely as a tactic of homophobes, not as a causal factor debated seriously by historians.

BIBLIOGRAPHY. J. Edward Chamberlain and Sander L. Gilman, eds., *Degeneration: The Dark Side of Progress*, New York: Columbia University Press, 1985; Louis Crompton, "What Do You Say to Someone Who Claims That Homosexuality Caused the Fall of Greece and Rome?" *Christopher Street* (March 1978), 49–52; Alexander Demandt, *Der Fall Roms: Die Auflösung des Römischen Reiches im Urteil der Nachwelt*, Munich: Beck, 1984.

Wayne R. Dynes

DECRIMINALIZATION

The repeal of the sodomy laws which had been inherited from the late **Middle Ages** and the **sixteenth century** came in two distinct phases. First, there was the wave of decriminalization generated by **Enlightenment** criticism of the penal legislation and practice of the Old Regime, characterized by harsh and barbarous penalties for trivial or purely sacral offenses, the use of torture to elicit confession, and the like. The second major phase developed as a product of the social reform movement that began late in the Victorian era.

The Enlightenment Tradition. The thinkers of the eighteenth century— Montesquieu, **Beccaria**, **Voltaire**—paved the way for the law reforms that came in the period of the French Revolution. In September–October 1791 the French Constituent Assembly adopted a new criminal code which embodied the principle that offenses against religion and morality, insofar as they did not harm the interests of third persons or of society as a whole, should not be the object of prosecution by the secular authorities. This law became the basis of the Penal Code which forms part of the so-called Code **Napoléon**, a comprehensive set of laws for the First Empire adopted in 1810.

The influence of this code was enormous, particularly in the Catholic countries of the Old and New Worlds. Thanks to the spread of the Napoleonic model, virtually all the Catholic states of Western Europe abandoned the medieval statutes against sodomy. But in the Protestant sphere it was only the **Netherlands** that benefited from decriminalization, for the simple reason that Napoleon annexed the entire country to his Empire in 1811, and when independence was regained in 1815, the new code remained.

A few other jurisdictions saw major changes in the law. The colony of Pennsylvania founded by William Penn in 1681 reduced the penalty for sodomy to the minimum that public opinion would allow, and the criminal code of Catherine the Great of **Russia** in 1769 did likewise. But reaction was to restore far more severe penalties in due course.

In other countries the only change during this first major phase was the abolition of the death penalty in favor of life imprisonment at hard labor or some other enormous sentence comparable to the punishment for the worst crimes of violence. Such was the reform introduced by the Josephine Code in **Austria** in 1787, and the statute of 1861 in England and 1887 in Scotland.

Modern Sexual Reform. Toward the end of the nineteenth century social reformers began to take up such questions as contraception, prostitution, and women's equality. Within this framework arose a sexual reform **movement** that led to further decriminalization as a result of effective propaganda and lobbying for repeal. In particular, the anthropological concept of the homosexual as an individual attracted solely by members of his own sex created a justification for demanding the end of the archaic laws. The **Scientific-Humanitarian Committee** founded in Berlin in 1897 made repeal of **Paragraph 175** of the Penal Code of the German empire its major objective, and similar goals were enunciated by the World League for Sexual Reform on a Scientific Basis in the 1920s and later, down to its dissolution in 1935.

The first country to respond to the new approach was **Denmark**, which reformed the laws against homosexual behavior in 1930. The uniform code adopted in Poland in 1932 followed the example of the Code Napoléon, although all four of the codes (German, Austrian, Russian, Hungarian) that had been in force at the end of the country's partition still had penalties for homosexual sodomy. Switzerland chose the example of the French cantons under Napoleonic influence when it adopted a penal code for the entire country in 1941, and **Sweden** followed Denmark in 1944.

After World War II. In the postwar period it was Great Britain that took the lead, beginning with the Report of the **Wolfenden** Commission in 1957, which recommended decriminalization of homosexual acts between consenting adults on grounds essentially deriving from classical liberalism. The report provoked a debate between two legal authorities, Hart and Devlin, in which the latter argued that if "the man in the Clapham omnibus" considered a sexual act abominable he should not have to give a logical reason for his feelings. But some ten years later, in 1967, a Labor Parliament voted passage of a private member's bill to repeal the law against homosexual buggery and gross indecency in England and Wales.

The United States, in which each state of the Union still has its own penal code, posed a far greater challenge to the advocates of reform. In 1962 the American Law Institute, after some ten years of deliberation over earlier versions, published an official draft of a Model Penal Code that omitted homosexual acts from the list of crimes. The state of Illinois had in 1961 already enacted a new code with these provisions, and a few other states followed its lead. Effective lobbying for reform was conducted by such groups as the National Committee for Sexual Civil Liberties, which also attempted a second route: that of appeal to the courts to strike down the survivals of pre-Enlightenment penal law as unconstitutional. Such a course was made possible by the specifically American tradition that the appellate courts could declare acts of the legislature unconstitutional on the ground that they violated provisions of the fundamental law of the commonwealth. In most European countries the judiciary has no such power to review acts of the legislature which simply took over the prerogatives of the sovereign. The precedent for this was, in particular, the decision of the United States Supreme Court (1954) outlawing racial segregation. Successful actions were subsequently brought in states such as Pennsylvania and New York where the legislature, under the influence of the Catholic Church and of fundamentalist Protestant sects, had refused to act.

A similar appeal to the European Commission of Human Rights against a decision of the Constitutional Court in Karlsruhe in 1957 had failed because the court accepted the view that the Federal Republic of Germany had the right to prohibit homosexual activity in the interest of health and morals. A Social Democratic majority in the Bundestag did, some 12 years later, modify Paragraph 175 of the Penal Code to exclude homosexual acts in private between consenting adults. But in 1981 the European Court of Human Rights, in response to a case brought by a citizen of Northern Ireland, Jeff Dudgeon, found that the statute in that country violated the right to privacy contained in Article 8 of the European Convention on Human Rights. However, when an appeal was brought to the United States Supreme Court in 1986 to test the constitutionality of the sodomy law of the State of Georgia, a 5–4 majority upheld the law, principally on the ground that there was nothing in the Anglo-American legal tradition that extended the right of privacy to homosexual activity (Bowers v. Hardwick). So the option of deciding to retain or abandon the existing laws was left with the individual states. The enormous problem of confronting the prejudice and ignorance of legislatures intimidated by conservative religious denominations thus endures. A similar situation prevails in Australia, where each state also has its own criminal code in the common law tradition.

Even when the basic law making homosexual activity illegal has been stricken from the books, there is still the further task of reeducating the law enforcement authorities and the public to the notion that homosexuals have certain rights in the exercise of which they should be protected, and of invalidating statutes such as those against solicitation which were based on the primary ones. More-

over, it is necessary to remove the sundry forms of discrimination that had made their way into civil and administrative law beginning with the second decade of this century, once the psychiatric concept of homosexuality as a "disease" had filtered down to the courts and legislatures. Individuals who, through prosecution under the old laws, had lost the right to pursue the profession of their choice or still languished in prison needed to be rehabilitated. Complete equalization of the laws pertaining to homosexuality and heterosexuality, including the age of **consent**, therefore still lies in the future. The elimination of **police** harassment and of a multitude of forms of private discrimination and intolerance will be a challenge for the decades ahead.

Conclusion. A world-wide survey of the situation presents a varied picture. In the first world, that of the advanced industrial countries of the West and the Asian rim, decriminalization has largely succeeded, with some exceptions. In a few countries, it has been followed by enactments of positive statutory protections for homosexuals and lesbians. In **Marxist** countries of the second world de facto change has been largely secured which has halted most prosecutions, but no actual rights are accorded to homosexuals, who are not permitted to form their own independent organizations and are obliged to meet clandestinely and unobtrusively. (In Poland and Hungary, where fledgling organizations have appeared, the change must be regarded as a sign of the incipient withdrawal of those countries from the Communist world.) The Third World has shown itself actually to be retrograde: not only have countries formerly under British rule, such as **India** and Kenya, retained the old colonial laws, but nations that were formerly French possessions, where the Napoleonic Code tradition had been implanted, have introduced new bans. On almost the whole of the African continent homosexual activity is now illegal, though it continues to be widely practiced. This reversal has varied motives. To some extent it results from the influence of fundamentalist religion, whether Christian or Islamic. In other instances, prohibition of same-sex behavior reflects a misguided notion that modernization requires a ban on "**decadence**" and "perversion." Another problem is that the World Health Organization continues to list homosexuality as an illness. Beginning in 1984, the International Lesbian and Gay Association undertook to monitor the situation on a worldwide basis, and to encourage renewed momentum toward decriminalization.

BIBLIOGRAPHY. International Lesbian and Gay Association, *Second ILGA Pink Book 1985: A Global View of Lesbian and Gay Liberation and Oppression*, Utrecht: Interfacultaire Werkgroep Homostudies, 1988.

Warren Johansson

DELLA CASA, GIOVANNI (1503–1556)

Italian prelate and author. Della Casa served as archbishop of Benevento in 1544, papal nuncio to the Venetian republic (1544–49), and papal secretary of state under Paul IV (1555–56). He wrote a manual of polite conduct, *Il Galateo, ovvero dei costumi* (1558), which enjoyed great success after its posthumous publication.

Before undertaking a clerical career in 1537, Della Casa wrote various compositions in the **Bernesque** vein, which are typically full of double entendres. Among his juvenilia it is conventional to mention a text in Latin prose entitled *In laudem pederastiae seu sodomiae* or *De laudibus sodomiae* (in praise of buggery). In reality this work never existed, as was demonstrated by Gilles Ménage (1613–1692) in his *Anti-Baillet* (The Hague, 1682). In this study Ménage traced the attestations for the supposed work, showing that they all go back, directly or indirectly, to propagandistic pieces spread by Protestants in order to discredit Della Casa and Roman Catholicism with which he was prominently connected.

Much of the responsibility lies at the door of Pier Paolo Vergerio, a heterodox prelate whom Della Casa harassed by bringing him to trial; after loudly adhering to **Protestantism**, Vergerio composed a harsh indictment of his persecutor. In reality the young Della Casa had written only a small satire, the *Capitolo del forno*, in which he pretended to praise, in a Bernesque vein, bread and the oven, while extolling the sexual act through double entendres. Although this composition was mainly heterosexual, a few lines do speak of homosexuality. From this slender foundation arose the legend of the pretended *In laudem . . . sodomiae*. In his own lifetime Della Casa defended himself of the charge in the short Latin work *Ad Germanos* in which he declared of himself: "We did not praise men, but clearly women." Nonetheless, some have held that the charge cost the learned prelate a cardinal's hat.

Other references to homosexual behavior that appear here and there in the *Galateo* serve, however, to confirm that, like many intellectuals formed before the Counter-Reformation, Della Casa held a detached and tolerant attitude toward same-sex love. This attitude drew Protestant attacks aimed at an educated class that was considered excessively lax and tolerant toward homosexual conduct.

Giovanni Dall'Orto

DEMOGRAPHIC FACTORS

Demography is the study of populations. Sex ratios, marriage ages, life expectancies, and prevalence of polygamy may tell us much about the relative frequency of homosexuality, or perhaps more strictly speaking, of **bisexuality**.

Theoretical Basis. Such deductions follow from a theoretical framework which sees the prevalence of homosexual behavior as somewhat plastic, responsive to **situational** factors, rather than fixed at birth or in infancy, and particularly sensitive to the relative lack or abundance of opportunity for heterosexual behavior, rather than being a phenomenon associated for the most part with exclusive "homosexuals." Demographically-oriented theorists take reports of increased homosexual behavior in such contemporary populations as those situated in **prisons, seafaring,** and **public schools,** where access to the opposite sex is difficult, and reason that when heterosexual opportunities are relatively scarce, more and more of the general population will turn to homosexuality.

Applied historically, this method must take into account different social conceptions of homosexuality. Arguably, societies that tolerate homosexuality openly expect few social obstacles to such "surrogate" behavior, which Ancient **Greece,** overpopulated in the seventh century B.C., encouraged.

Until recent times, the absence of a folk model of exclusive homosexuality made it much easier for males to switch back and forth from penetrating the opposite sex (or desiring to) to penetrating the same sex (especially if the receptor was not perceived as equally masculine, such as was the case with boys, slaves, captives, the poor, or those of inferior social rank) without facing either an **identity** crisis or massive social opprobrium. At the most, such an opportunistic switcher had made himself guilty of a vice considered minor except by **Abrahamic religions;** his marriage or financial prospects remained unimpaired.

On the other hand, without available passive partners, or the willingness by actives to switch roles on demand, such a possibility would be of only theoretical interest. Reciprocity was by all accounts historically rare until recent times, but an overabundance of boys, passive partners in relation to adult males, has normally existed. Late ages of marriage, widespread slavery, resident non-citizens, prolonged warfare, and an overabundance of paupers favored the development of **pederasty.** Sufficient evidence for lesbianism in harems and other situations without males such as nunneries sustains demographic theorizing without further elaboration.

Prehistory. Before the breakthrough to agriculture—which terminated the Paleolithic Age—cave-dwellers averaged well under 20 years of life, primarily because of high infant mortality. Those who survived infancy, if often sick and frail by 40, had a good chance to reach 50. Active females who suffered from early pregnancies thus did not survive their peak sexual drive, which is currently estimated to occur at 27, by more than a decade or so. High death rates from pregnancy and childbirth may have reduced the number of women even more than deaths from hunting and warfare reduced the numbers of adult males. Women capable of reproduction were taken by men upon whom they depended for game, their major protein supply. Thus lesbianism would have been relatively infrequent. On the other hand normal males did not live into such old age that they became impotent, as so many do now.

The hypothesis that females dominated society by putting the young males outside the horde, as do baboons and gorillas, greatly stimulating homosexual contacts among the outcast adolescent males as it does among such primates, may have been realized occasionally in certain human groups. If so, lesbianism may have flourished among such "Amazons," but the surviving evidence, largely the widespread existence of "mother goddesses" on neolithic sites, is too scanty for proof.

Early Civilizations. Beginning in **Mesopotamia** and **Egypt,** about 3500–3100 B.C., the earliest writings depict a male-dominated society with a pantheon ruled by males. In most societies adolescents married shortly after puberty, and polygamy predominated as it has done throughout most of history—there have been hardly any polyandrous and relatively few monogamous societies. One survey reports that monogamy prevails in 24 percent of societies, polyandry in 1 percent, and polygamy in 75 percent. Even in Egypt, where considerable evidence exists for monogamy, the wealthy certainly kept concubines and sexually used slaves and prisoners of war of both sexes. Mesopotamia and all the civilizations outside Europe practiced polygamy, replete with harems such as King Solomon's. Such institutions assured that many slave, poor, or young men could not have women for themselves, with a consequent probability of widespread homosexuality among the lower classes who could rarely have afforded prostitutes.

As life expectancy increased in these archaic civilizations that developed irrigation and storage facilities along with the plough, infanticide, especially of females, seems to have increased. Only Egyptians, who married relatively late, and Jews seem to have prohibited it, but even they greatly preferred male offspring. As a result of much more frequent female infanticide, males greatly outnumbered females in most societies. A 4:3 ratio was perhaps not uncommon, although among especially warlike nomadic societies like those of the Arabian Peninsula, men were in such short supply that Mohammed may have been recognizing actual conditions when he transmitted Allah's command that a man might have four wives and as many concubines as he can afford.

Even in monogamous societies such as those of the **Indo-Europeans** who settled in Europe, upper-class males married at very different ages. After about 600 B.C., copying a custom begun on **Crete**, Greek warriors waited until the age of 30 when they married girls from 15 to 18, getting an aristocratic boy of 12 when they were 22 to train and love until they married. Aristocratic Roman boys, on the other hand, married in their teens girls of 12 or 13 as arranged by their *patres* (male heads of families). Middle-class males who predominate on tombstones married later, in their mid-twenties to women as old as twenty. Practically no women, who may have composed little more than one-third

of society because of excess female infanticide, failed to find husbands, and virtually all upper-class males married, at least before the times of the **Roman emperors**. In Greece and **Rome** when a baby was born, the husband would decide whether to raise the infant or expose it—as contraception was ineffective and abortion dangerous, infanticide remained the usual method of birth control. **Christianity**, which took over the Empire and banned other religions with the sole exception of Judaism during the fourth century, outlawed infanticide and had the emperors decree death for sodomites.

The Medieval Period. During the Dark Ages (roughly A.D. 500–1000), after the Germans overran the depopulated Western provinces of the Roman Empire, little central control in the church or state survived. Among the barbarian laws, only those of the Visigoths condemned sodomy. The Celtic **penitentials** punished it harshly, but never with death. Many Merovingians and Carolingians had several wives and most had concubines, and evidence of excessive female infanticide continues. Knights and squires bound together by the closest ties in all-male (except for the lord's women and the serving wenches) castles often loved each other. Some poor in such an underpopulated society as Europe in the early **Middle Ages** could earn a sufficient living at an early age to marry or rather cohabit with a woman. Life expectancies decreased from classical times but upper class males at least married in their teens.

From the end of the invasions about 1000 to the arrival of the Black Death in 1347, the population grew from thirty to seventy million as life expectancies improved again to 40 or 50. As it became more difficult to get a farm or a position in a guild, commoners began to marry later in life. Merchants and professionals postponed marriage to accumulate capital or education. The marriage age for males went up from 20 to 30, but as they preferred women of 18 or even 16, a gap developed in the population pyramid. Lots of rowdy, lusty young bachelors must often have lapsed into homosexual acts. Moreover, when the smaller age-group of 30-year-old men married 18-year olds, many unwed women became spinsters or nuns, often cloistered against their will, vastly increasing the allure of lesbianism. Catholic authorities and even **canon law** condoned female prostitution so that unmarried males would avoid the worse evil of sodomy.

The Black Death, wars, and famines decreased the population by one-third, from seventy to fifty million. Wages rose and food prices fell. Men could establish a living for themselves earlier and their marriage age, except for merchants and professionals, dropped. As the number of young bachelors and of spinsters decreased, homosexual activity probably declined. Demographics may have been more important than clerical persecution or municipal houses of **prostitution** and **municipal laws** or **royal laws**, which became quite severe, often ordering castration before hanging or burning, in reducing sodomy and lesbianism during the late Middle Ages—just when documentation of it (such as there is) becomes more plentiful. On the other hand, urbanization not only provided anonymity and other opportunities to escape family control but produced a secular **gay subculture** outside monasteries.

Early Modern Europe. The economic boom of the Renaissance and following period could not keep up with population expansion so that real wages fell. Bullion from the New World spurred inflation. Those unmarried increased, reaching almost 20 percent of the population in Spain. **Pirates,** sailors, merchants, and soldiers in the longer, more distant wars and voyages lived in male societies with only occasional contact with females, often through prostitution and rape, with a resultant increase in homosexuality. In the demographic boom that began in 1740 wages fell and males delayed marriage in

the lower as well as in the upwardly mobile middle classes.

In England between 1550 and 1800 the age of marriage rose to 26 for males and 23 for females. The percentage of unmarried males rose to 22 but fell by 1800 to about 17; that of females rose to the low 20s. Other European countries displayed similar patterns. Between 30 and 50 percent of peasants in preindustrial Europe never married. Sons could often not afford to marry until their father retired or died, leaving one of them land.

The Nineteenth Century. In nineteenth-century agrarian Ireland overpopulation meant that many "boys" (so called until marriage), could never secure and support a wife and hence did not marry. The society became obsessed with homophobia, taking that fear with them wherever they emigrated. Sicily and Southern Italy in a similar situation, however, continued the ancient **Mediterranean** tolerance of homosexuality, a common Catholicism notwithstanding, but the Italians tended to emigrate to American and other overseas areas after the Irish and ranked beneath them in the Church in these areas. Catholicism in English-speaking overseas areas became more homophobic than Catholicism in Latin areas.

Immigration usually loosened family and church ties. Often the first generation delayed marriage so that overseas immigrants engaged in homosexual acts as in Carolina plantations or early Virginia, and even more so in penal colonies like Georgia and Australia where males greatly outnumbered females. Puritans, however, took wives and children with them to the promised land where the unchallenged church was strengthened.

Easy access to western land and the constant labor shortages even in the eastern cities, however, lowered the marriage ages in comparison with Europe, where increasing numbers in both Catholic and Protestant countries remained lifelong celibates. Upper and middle class men married in Victorian England at age

30. The American frontier, however, was populated by young males with few females in the initial phase of settlement.

Among these nineteenth-century urban celibates the homosexual emerged and was named in 1869, exclusive as opposed to the earlier sodomites who, it was assumed, would normally be married.

Reaching their sexual peak later than men, women had opportunities to become lesbian at various stages of their increasingly long lives. Most men long outlived their sexual peak (in their late teens), more and more living into the slackening of sexual potency attendant on middle and old age. No wonder one hears so much of lesbianism after the eighteenth century and so little before.

The application of demographic principles to the study of sexual patterns is still in a pioneering stage; further investigation may shed considerable light, not only on the periods discussed above, but also on contemporary developments in the Third World and elsewhere. In the absence of literary and other documentation for sexual mores in the broad mass of the population, demographic analysis may open a window into these little-known areas.

William A. Percy

DEMUTH, CHARLES (1883–1935)

American painter. Born into a well-to-do family in Lancaster, Pennsylvania, Demuth was a sickly child who was educated largely at home. After art school in Philadelphia, he made two trips to Europe, absorbing modernism at its source in Paris. During the second of these, in 1913, he met another gay American artist, Marsden Hartley, a friendship that was to last all his life. After returning to the United States at the beginning of World War I, Demuth began to spend more and more time in New York's Greenwich Village, where new ideas of aesthetics and sexuality effervesced in equal measure. In the company of Carl Van Vechten he began to frequent nightclubs in Harlem, then considered off-limits by bourgeois society. He also visited bathhouses, producing frank watercolors of scenes of sexual solicitation. Always strongly interested in literature—a connection enhanced by his friendships with such figures as Eugene O'Neill and William Carlos Williams—Demuth began to illustrate works of fiction, including books by Honoré de **Balzac** and Frank Wedekind concerned with sexual variation. Also emerging at this time was his continuing predilection for flower subjects, into which sexual meanings were read in the then-prevailing Freudian mode. To the extent that Demuth himself shared these readings (a matter that is uncertain), they are not without validity.

In the later 1920s and 1930s, suffering from diabetes and under his mother's care in the family home in Lancaster, Demuth summoned himself to produce major works evoking the American scene, which have much in common with the precisionism of Charles Sheeler. At the same time, he produced for private viewing a series of watercolors that are even now striking in their frankness. These show street cruising, blatant sexual display, and even episodes of male group sex. These works feature military men, especially sailors, and "rough trade."

Demuth worked at a time of transition in American art, as it was abandoning the certainties of the academy and the realism of the Ashcan School, but before it fully embraced the modernist aesthetic. This historical position, and the unusual range of his subject matter, make his ultimate standing hard to determine. Certainly the 1980s rediscovery of his sexually explicit works—achieved at a time when critics are questioning the conventional distinctions between high and low art, between erotic painting and pornography—makes a reassessment mandatory. Significantly, as a major retrospective of his oeuvre was mounted in four American cities in 1987–88 some critics still expressed distaste for Demuth's more overt works. In an art world characterized by increasing pluralism and an attitude that "anything goes," this lasting power to shock is an achievement.

BIBLIOGRAPHY. Barbara Haskell, *Charles Demuth*, New York: Whitney Museum of American Art, 1987.

Wayne R. Dynes

DENMARK

This small country, which occupies the Jutland peninsula and neighboring islands, is the home of a people who roamed far and wide in the medieval period. Denmark was converted to Latin Christianity just before the year 1000 and became Lutheran in the sixteenth century. Since World War II it has been both admired and excoriated for its liberal atttitudes toward sex and pornography.

The Middle Ages and the Early Modern Period. Pagan **Scandinavia** knew no generalized taboo on homosexuality, certainly no laws against it, but there was a folk belief that the man who took the passive role with another in a sexual relationship had forfeited the respect owed his sex. **Christianity** at first brought only moral condemnation and religious penance. On February 2, 1227 pope Honorius III wrote a letter to the Danish archbishop in reply to his request for advice on how to deal with a number of individuals guilty of incest or homosexual sodomy. As they could not very well make the long trip to Rome, the pope gave the archbishop the authority to decide for himself on a penance which should be neither too hard nor too lenient.

With the influence of the Reformation and its revived interest in the **Old Testament**, the Danish Lawbook (*Danske Lov*) of King Christian V (1683) prescribed burning at the stake for sodomy. In point of fact, however, little is known of prosecutions for homosexual intercourse, and they were probably rare. An isolated case of pederasty is recorded in which a married weaver was in 1744 sentenced to two years'

hard labor followed by banishment from the province of Jutland for having had sexual connection with a boy. The attitude of that time was expressed by a professor at the University of Copenhagen, Ludvig Holberg, in his *Introduction to Natural and International Law* (1716). Admitting that "we must condemn the evil vice," he went to say that "the authorities cannot punish vices which are practiced by so many, and which are so firmly embedded that to eradicate the evil would be to cause the disintegration of the whole state. And if they are but works of darkness and are not generally noticed and of little consequence, why trouble the authorities by calling their attention to them?"

Toward the Present. This attitude, however, changed after 1866 when the death penalty was rescinded and replaced by imprisonment. After this time a considerable number of prosecutions and convictions occurred. It is likely also that the introduction of modern police methods of surveillance and entrapment contributed to the new situation. Just as in the penal code of the **German** empire, the provisions of the law applied only to male homosexuality.

The first Danish author to address the plight of the homosexual from the standpoint of the literature produced by the inchoate homophile movement and by responsive psychiatrists wrote under the pseudonym "Tandem." Himself a layman, he published in the medical journal *Bibliotek for Laeger* (1892), an article of some fifty pages surveying everything that had been written in Western Europe and Scandinavia on the subject, concluding with a plea for toleration. This was not to come, however, until the sexual reform movement in Germany had placed the issue on the agenda. In 1928 the World League for Sexual Reform on a Scientific Basis held its second congress in Copenhagen, at which Magnus Hirschfeld read the text of an "Appeal on Behalf of an Oppressed Variety of Human Being" composed by the activist Kurt **Hiller**. Two years later, in 1930, the Danish parliament did reform the law—the first country in Scandinavia to do so.

The Contemporary Situation. After World War I Denmark acquired a reputation as a country with unusually liberal attitudes toward sexuality, and Copenhagen became a mecca for the sex-starved tourist from the rest of the world. The Forbundet af 1948 was founded by Axel Axgil and Hjelmer Fogedgaard, and in 1949 it began a periodical, *Vennen* (Friends). The Forbundet stimulated similar organizations in Norway and Sweden. In Denmark it grew into the major national gay and lesbian organization and recognized by the authorities as such. Active today on many fronts, it not only counsels homosexuals on their personal problems in all spheres of life, but also conducts education and propaganda meant to enlighten the general public and undo the legacy of defamation from the past, and collaborates with foreign homophile organizations. All its activity is conducted by a staff of volunteers.

A particular notoriety accrued to the Danish capital as the venue of the male-to-female sex change operation performed on Christine Jorgensen (who died in 1989 after living as a woman for almost forty years). Gay tourists flocked to Copenhagen, though the city later lost its primacy in this regard to Amsterdam. The effect of Denmark's liberal laws on pornography has been disputed, some claiming that free availability reduced demand. Some of the pornography offered for sale in Denmark contains photographs of quite young children. In any event, Denmark and Sweden played major roles as laboratories for the sexual revolution of the 1970s, while the United States took the lead in the gay liberation movement.

In 1976 the legal age of consent to homosexual relations was reduced to 15; consensual sexual activity with a boy under 15 but not less than 12 years old is a misdemeanor. The sentence is usually—

but not always—suspended, but a foreigner found guilty is fined and immediately deported. The burden of proof in such cases rests with the police, who do not investigate on their own initiative but only in response to a complaint.

In 1989 the Danish parliament approved a far-reaching law granting legal sanction, except the right of adoption, to same-sex unions; however, its benefits are not extended to foreigners.

See also **Andersen, Hans Christian; Bang, Herman.**

BIBLIOGRAPHY. Axel Axgil and Hjelmer Fogedgaard, *Homofile kampar: Bøsseler gjennom tiderne*, Ridkobing: Grafolio, 1985; Wilhelm von Rosen, "Sodomy in Early Modern Denmark: A Crime Without Victims," *Journal of Homosexuality*, 16:1/2 (1988), 177–204.
Ward Houser

DETECTIVE STORIES
See **Mystery and Detective Fiction.**

DEVIANCE AND DEVIATION
Sociologists and criminologists have adopted the term deviance to refer to behavior that is prohibited, censured, stigmatized, or penalized by the normative structures of a society. The boundaries of the concept, and its appropriateness for homosexuality, have not been settled; it originated in the wish for a neutral term that would not imply approval or disapproval of the activity, whatever the attitude of the host society might be. Critics of the approach assert that it offers little more than a jumble of "nuts, sluts, and perverts." For the study of homosexuality, however, its value may lie in the fact that it does make one think of analogies (and differences) between homosexuals and other groups.

The words deviation and deviant, while designed to be neutral and statistical terms, are related to a system of concepts centered on alterations in direction which have an extensive historical background of inherited judgmentalism. The legacy of these ideas facilitated the acceptance of the terms, but at the same time undermined the attempt to keep them value free.

Historical Semantics. Some of the background is Judeo-Christian. A rabbinical exegete, Bar Kapparah, glossed the term *tōʻēbāh*, "**abomination**"—a word of importance because of its occurrence in the prohibitions of the Holiness Code of Leviticus—as meaning *tōʼeh attāh bāh*, "you are going astray because of it". Another scripturally rooted instance occurs in Jerome's rendering of *Exodus* 23:2: "Non sequeris turbam ad faciendum malum; nec in judicio, plurimorum acquiesces sententiae, ut a vero devies." ("Do not follow the mob in doing evil; nor in your thinking yield to views of the many, so that you deviate [go astray] from the truth.") This application of *devio*, "to turn from the straight road, to go aside," is rooted in the ancient metaphor of human life as a journey.

There is also a contrast between **perversion** and *conversion*, both from the Latin *verto*, "to turn (round)." Moreover, there is a Hebraic background to this idea of turning around = reform of one's life.

Until early modern times, this complex of meanings does not seem to have been brought into use in connection with homosexuality. Then there is Sir Simonds D'Ewes' usage: "He [James I] had his vices and deviations." (1625).

Another variation on the *verto* root, the modern term **inversion**, was introduced by Arrigo Tamassia in 1878. Unconsciously this coinage takes up the late medieval idea of "the world upside down." French medical writers (Paul Moreau, 1880; Valentin Magnan, 1885) are responsible for introducing another directional term, *aberration* (from *ab* + *erro*, "wander off"), for certain types of sexual conduct, including same-sex relations.

Medical writers of the late nineteenth century show some statistical use of the term *deviation*. The word seems to have been introduced into the social sciences by the anthropologists Margaret Mead and Ruth **Benedict** in the 1920s. In her discussion of Samoa, Mead contrasts deviation upward, a kind of withdrawal, with deviation downward, delinquency. The locution did not become popular outside of professional circles until after World War II, when it absorbed some of the connotations of Durkheim's *anomie*. The term *deviant* hovers between a covertly pejorative meaning and a value-free use ("A character structure which is normal among us may be deviant among the Kwakiutl." Gregory Bateson, 1944). The term **variant** enjoyed some popularity among lesbians in the 1950s and 60s.

Slang Analogues. While deviance and deviation are terms used by scholars, colloquial speech indicates that the directional metaphor was adopted by the deviant groups themselves. In order to understand this point it is useful to focus on the contrast between straight, on the one hand, and crooked or bent, on the other. The *Oxford English Dictionary* records a colloquial use of straight as "honest, honorable, frank," in 1864. During the same period the word meant "chaste" (of a woman). Some contamination from the Biblical "strait is the gate" is likely.

Since at least 1914, criminal argot has applied *bent* both to individuals (thieves) and things (e.g., a bent ["hot"] car). The secondary usage of bent, "homosexual," has been current in British slang since the fifties. The term crooked, which parallels bent in the criminal sense, does not seem to have a sexual use. The origins of the sexual use of "straight" (as an antonym to "bent"?) are problematic, though it clearly was widespread in homosexual circles before it became a part of the general vocabulary as an equivalent for "heterosexual" during the 1970s. During the sixties straight had acquired a new meaning: "not using drugs" or "not under the influence of drugs at the moment" (paralleling sober). Later expansions included "not inebriated" or "teetotaler." The term is semantically greedy, and new usages are appearing; thus in reference to employment, it may mean "normal/reportable to the government/taxable." Nonetheless, there remain three main layers to the colloquial meaning of straight: (1) honest or respectable; (2) heterosexual; (3) drug-free/sober. As with many argot terms this polysemy (multiplicity of meanings) serves the purpose of the deviant user group in confusing eavesdropping outsiders, even though this effect fades as the term seeps into general usage. From a sociological point of view, one can also note the testimony of the word about the propinquity of populations brought together by the maintenance of the victimless-crime laws. These groups are "birds of a feather" because society has made them so.

Built along lines similar to "bent" is the term "kinky," which originated as a directional term, developed a reference to criminality, and in recent times, perhaps in reaction to the growing sexual use of "straight," gained a non-pejorative sexual sense as a reference to erotic eccentricity, whether heterosexual or homosexual.

BIBLIOGRAPHY. Erich Goode and Richard Troiden, *Sexual Deviance and Sexual Deviants*, New York: William Morrow, 1975; Edwin M. Schur, *The Politics of Deviance: Stigma Contests and the Uses of Power*, Englewood Cliffs, NJ: Prentice-Hall, 1980.

Wayne R. Dynes

DIAGHILEV, SERGEI PAVLOVICH (1872–1929)

Russian cultural figure and ballet impresario. Diaghilev came from a family of provincial nobles whose fortune derived from ownership of a vodka distillery. In 1890 he went to St. Petersburg to pursue a career while living in the household of his aunt and uncle. Their son Dmitri ("Dima") integrated the young man into a preco-

cious set that had formed at his gymnasium, including the artists Alexander Benois, Konstantin Somov, and Leon Bakst. The newcomer soon established a sexual relationship with his handsome cousin Dima, and they traveled on holiday to Italy together. Diaghilev, who eventually discovered that he lacked the talent to become either a singer or a composer as he intended, began to look for another area in which to make his mark. He found it in the burgeoning artistic and cultural activity of what has come to be known as Russia's Silver Age. Russian symbolist poets and artists were casting off the narrow constrictions of aesthetic utilitarianism in favor of new trends that were both cosmopolitan and at the same time in touch with Russia's historic past.

The first great phase of Diaghilev's impact on the arts lasted from 1899 to 1909. He became the animator of Mir Iskusstva ("The World of Art"), which was both a group of intellectuals and artists and a sumptuous magazine. Although this work of editing and promotion brought Diaghilev into contact with ballet, at this time he was concerned with all the arts, for the program of cultural renovation proposed by Mir Iskusstva was all-embracing: painting, poetry, drama, dance, even architecture and the crafts. Unfortunately for Diaghilev, Mir Iskusstva was to lead to his breakup with his cousin–lover, for Zinaida Gippius, an ambitious writer and member of the group, succeeded in taking Dima away from him in 1904.

From 1906 to 1909 Diaghilev was engaged in organizing a series of exhibitions of Russian art in Paris, as well as performances of Russian concerts and operas. In 1908, in the course of organizing a ballet company, he had his fateful meeting with Vaslav Nijinsky, a promising young dancer at the Imperial Ballet. At that time Nijinsky was being kept by a wealthy aristocrat, Prince Pavel Lvov, who seemed, however, willing to part with his protégé. In their five years together, Diaghilev was able to shape Nijinsky into one of the finest dancers the world has ever seen, a figure who is inseparable from such masterpieces as Stravinsky's *Rite of Spring* and Debussy's *Afternoon of a Faun*—ballets that Diaghilev organized. However, on an ocean voyage to South America, Nijinsky deserted him for a Hungarian ballerina. Diaghilev replaced him with the sixteen-year-old Léonide Massine, who, though heterosexual, was willing to go along with the relationship to learn what Diaghilev could teach him.

In the meantime Diaghilev's first efforts at establishing the ballet were difficult, though he did present the world with the genius of Igor Stravinsky through *The Firebird*. In 1911 he formed his own company, which from its base in Paris reached other Western European cities. World War I caused problems, but Diaghilev was nonetheless able to keep things going from Rome. Throughout his career as an impresario Diaghilev had the ability—through his matchless self-confidence—to rescue triumphs from seemingly impossible situations.

The last decade of his life was the time of achievement that has made his name virtually synonymous with ballet. He had not only a sure instinct for dancers, but also for conductors, composers and artists. He was able to utilize avant-garde artists such as Pablo Picasso, André Derain, and Georges Rouault in such a way as to make them accessible to a middlebrow public. In this way he made a decisive contribution to the emergence of modernist painting from its earlier constricted environment. During his last years Diaghilev had non-exclusive affairs with three young men: the English dancer Patrick Healy Kay (who became known by the name that the impresario gave him, Anton Dolin); the Russian dancer Serge Lifar; and the Russian conductor Igor Markevitch. In August 1929, after completing twenty years of ceaseless creativity in Western Europe, Diaghilev died suddenly in Venice, his favorite city, where he was buried.

BIBLIOGRAPHY. Richard Buckle, *Diaghilev*, New York: Atheneum, 1984; Simon Karlinsky, "Sergei Diaghilev: Public and Private," in *The Christopher Street Reader*, New York: Coward-McCann, 1983, pp. 265–73.

Ward Houser

DICKINSON, EMILY (1830–1886)

American poet. After brief periods at Amherst Academy and Holyoke Female Seminary, she settled into an outwardly uneventful life keeping house for her family. Dickinson never married. The real events in her life are her writings, which have assumed classic status in American literature.

Emily Dickinson's letters to several of her female acquaintances convince us that throughout her life she had strong emotional attachments, which may be described as love relationships, with other women. A comparison of such love letters with letters which she wrote at about the same time to women who were merely good friends indicates that her impassioned language was not simply sentimental rhetoric of the period, and that these involvements, while probably non-genital, were clearly homoerotic. Those letters help to explain the forty or fifty poems in the Dickinson canon which cannot be understood unless recognized as love poems from one woman to another.

Certainly Dickinson had heterosexual interests as well—the Master letters, those to Judge Otis Lord, and many of her poems are irrefutable proof. But it is impossible to doubt the intensity of her involvement with women when one reads letters such as those to Emily Fowler:

I cannot wait to be with you . . . I was lonely without you, and wanted to write you a letter MANY times, but Kate [Hitchcock] was there too, and I was afraid you would both laugh. I should be stronger if I could see you oftener—I am very puny alone.

You make me so happy, and glad,
life seems worth living for, no
matter for all the trials.—early 1850
But another spring, dear friend, you
must and shall be here, and nobody
can take you away, for I will hide
you and keep you—and who would
think of taking you if I hold you
tight in my arms?—spring 1854

and to Kate Anthon:

Distinctly sweet your face stands in
its phanthom niche—I touch your
hand—my cheek, your cheek—I
stroke your vanished hair. Why did
you enter, sister, since you must
depart? Had not its heart been torn
enough but YOU must send your
shred?—summer 1860

and especially those to the woman who
became her sister-in-law, Sue Gilbert, with
whom, if her letters and notes are any
proof, she ostensibly had the most intense
and enduring emotional relationship of
her life:

Oh my darling one, how long you
wander from me, how weary I grow
of waiting and looking, and calling
for you; sometimes I shut my eyes,
and shut my heart towards you, and
try hard to forget you because you
grieve me so, but you'll never go
away.—February 1852
To miss you, Sue, is power. The
stimulus of Loss makes most
possession so mean. To live lasts
always, but to love is firmer than to
live.—September 1871

The sentiments, and sometimes
even the imagery, of such letters are occasionally adopted in Dickson's poems and
may help in the explication of those poems.
For example, the poem: "The Day she
goes/ Or Day she stays/ Are equally supreme—/ Existence has a stated width/
Departed, or at Home." (Poem 1308,
Johnson edition) is more easily understood

in the context of a brief note to Sue: "To
the faithful Absence is condensed presence" (about 1878). The poem "Wild
Nights—Wild Nights!" (poem 249), which
caused many critics to observe a puzzling
"reversal of the lover role," becomes clearer
in the light of an early letter to Sue (about
February 1852):

The wind blows and it rains. . . . I
hardly know which falls fastest, the
rain without, or within—Oh Susie, I
would nestle close to your warm
heart, and never hear the wind blow,
or the storm beat, again. Is there any
room there for me, or shall I wander
all homeless and alone?

While the language of the letter
lacks the poetic energy and sophisticated
imagery of the poem which was written
nine years later, both seem to suggest the
same thing: "If I were moored in you, I
would not be lost or lonely or afraid of the
storm." When understood as a love lyric in
which the principals, both being women,
have no pre-defined roles or set sexual
functions, the poem no longer contains
the puzzling role-reversal that has so often
been observed.

Several biographers, most notably Rebecca Patterson, John Cody, and
Richard Sewall, have dealt with Emily
Dickinson's homosexuality. Patterson, in
fact, suggests as a major thesis in her book,
The Riddle of Emily Dickinson, that Dickinson had a love affair with Kate Scott
Anthon which, at its conclusion in the
1860s, crushed Dickinson and accounted
for her "peculiarities" during the remaining twenty-odd years of her life.

Cody adopts a Freudian approach
and argues that while Dickinson's Puritan
heritage would not have permitted her to
indulge in homosexual love-making, she
had no wish to fulfill a female role since
she despised her weak mother and feared
her tyrannical father; thus well into adulthood she experienced "pre-pubescent"
crushes on other women, particularly Sue

Gilbert, who served as a mother-surrogate to Emily.

Sewall, while seeming at first to reject Cody's suggestion that Emily was in love with Sue and hurt and upset when she lost her to Austin, later refers to Emily's letters to Sue as "nothing less than love letters."

All of these writers cite ostensibly lesbian poems to support their biographical narrative. Dickinson's homoerotic poetry seems to span the entire length of her literary career, from one of her first poems, written in 1854 ("I have a Bird in spring") to one of her very late poems, written in 1883 ("To see her is a picture" in the third variant). While the subject of these poems is sometimes identifiable (it is frequently Sue), most often she is not. This is not surprising since, as several scholars have observed, we probably have only about one tenth of the letters Dickinson wrote and less than a thousandth of those written to her. But, while we may have no idea who the persons were who evoked some of Dickinson's most moving love lyrics, of one thing we may be certain: many of them were women.

The speaker in Dickinson's homoerotic poems is usually the lover and pursuer in the relationship. Such a relationship is often represented by the symbol of a nest in which the speaker finds (or at least expects to find) comfort and "home" with the other. But she recognizes that she cannot expect permanence in her love, not because it is an inherently flawed kind of love, but generally because the beloved other woman will eventually marry, as it was assumed most women would in the nineteenth century, being without an independent source of income or a profession that would make them self-sufficient. The speaker accepts the reality of this situation, but not without difficulty. What is much more difficult for her to accept, of course, is a beloved woman's cruelty which has no basis in custom or pragmatism. In such a situation the speaker usually cries out bitterly against the other woman, but she is willing to return to her and apparently to be hurt again. She is frequently self-pitying. Only occasionally does she perceive herself victorious in love, and then it is a poor victory, having conquered the other woman by arousing her pity. These homoerotic poems are never joyous, but that is to be expected in a society where heterosexual marriage was virtually believed inevitable and there was little possibility of two unrelated women establishing a life together if they were not wealthy through independent inheritance.

BIBLIOGRAPHY. John Cody, *After Great Pain: The Inner Life of Emily Dickinson*, Cambridge: Harvard University Press, 1971; Rebecca Patterson, *The Riddle of Emily Dickinson*, Boston: Houghton Mifflin Company, 1951; Vivian R. Pollak, *Dickinson: The Anxiety of Gender*, Ithaca: Cornell University Press, 1984; Richard Sewall, *The Life of Emily Dickinson*, New York: Farrar, Straus and Giroux, 1974.

Lillian Faderman

DICTIONARIES AND ENCYCLOPEDIAS

Because of the knowledge explosion of recent decades, there has been an increasing demand for works of reference, both generalized and specialized, which will serve not only the interested lay public but also those engaged in primary research who would otherwise be unable to keep up with advances in neighboring fields.

The history of the great reference book enterprises goes back to the eighteenth-century Enlightenment. Stimulated by several lesser British exemplars, the great French *Encyclopédie ou dictionnaire raisonné des sciences, des arts et des métiers* began to appear in 1751. Edited by Denis Diderot and Jean d'Alembert, this work strove not only to provide a storehouse of factual information, but also to bring to readers the latest conceptual advances. It comes as something of a shock to find that the major article on "Sodomie" largely concerns masturbation, having been taken over from an earlier work by S. A. D. Tissot, a physician obsessively concerned with that subject. Clearly the attempt to move beyond traditional religious ideas into a realm of unbiased secular information had not even begun at this point. Better informed is the article on "Socratic Love" in the more personal *Dictionnaire philosophique* of **Voltaire** (1764). Incidentally, this tradition of the sometimes idiosyncratic one-person dictionary has been revived in recent years by such scholars as Mary Daly, Wayne Dynes, and Monique Wittig.

The eighteenth century also saw the beginning of a more informed tradition of treatment in medical reference works, of which the first notable example is Robert James, *A Medical Dictionary* (1743–45). This tradition continued into the nineteenth century, as seen in the French multivolume *Dictionnaire des sciences médicales* and *Encyclopédie des sciences médicales*.

Dictionaries of sexual information did not appear until the twentieth century. The *Handwörterbuch der Sexualwissenschaft* (1923), edited by Max Marcuse, combines articles derived from the mainstream German tradition of sex research with newer psychoanalytic viewpoints. The first example in English is *The Encyclopedia of Sexual Knowledge* (1934), edited by the Australian homophile Norman Haire, though this volume is largely based on German materials assembled by Arthur Koestler. In the post-World War II period, the *Encyclopedia of Sexual Behavior* (1961), of Albert Ellis and Albert Abarbanel, attempted to be truly cross-cultural with much material on non-Western cultures, even though the coverage may seem thin or dated today.

When not subject to censorship, slang dictionaries often contain considerable lexicographical material on homosexuality, though the terms included are usually culled from the usage of heterosexuals, often from the argot of the urban lower classes or members of the criminal underworld. There are also erotic dictionaries of various languages; significantly, the first of these appears to be that of Pierre Pierrugues, of Latin terms and in Latin, of 1826. The classic in this genre is Alfred Delvau's *Dictionnaire érotique de la langue verte* (1864).

Homosexuality and lesbianism have not fared well in general encyclopedias in English, such as the Britannica and the Americana, perhaps because these are addressed in part to a secondary-school readership, for which extensive discussion of such matters is not deemed suitable. The general articles are relatively brief and suffer from outdated and incomplete information. Biographical articles rarely mention that the subjects are gay or lesbian, and contributions of eminent figures to the study of homosexuality are omitted from their biographies. The general rule is, the more accessible and popular a reference work is, the more uninformative it is likely to be on the topic of homosexuality.

With today's demand for more information on sexual matters, it is to be hoped that this situation will change. Yet with the increasing tempo of information build-up, it will probably be necessary to resort more and more to information stored in computer-accessed data banks.

BIBLIOGRAPHY. Edmund F. Santa Vicca, *The Treatment of Homosexuality in Current Encyclopedias*, Ann Arbor: University of Michigan, 1977 (unpub. diss.).

Ward Houser

Dionysus

Greek god associated with wine and emotional exuberance. Although the name occurs in linear B tablets from the end of the second millennium B.C., his figure absorbed additional elements from Thrace and the East in the following centuries. Dionysus, called Bacchus in Latin, was the son of Zeus and a mortal Semele. When his mother unwisely besought Zeus to reveal himself in his true form, she was incinerated, but the embryo of her son escaped destruction. Zeus then inserted it into his own thigh and carried the child to term. This quality of being "twice born," once from a woman and once from a man, points to the ambiguity of the god, who though male had effeminate traits. In literary and artistic representations, he sometimes served as a vehicle for questioning sex roles, otherwise strongly polarized in ancient Greece.

According to the late-antique writer Nonnus, Dionysus fell in love with a Phrygian boy, Ampelos, who became his inseparable companion. When the boy was killed in a bull-riding accident, the grief-stricken Dionysus turned him into a vine. As a result, the practices of vine cultivating and grape harvesting, of wine making and drinking, commemorate this deeply felt pederastic relationship: in honoring the vine (*ampelos* in Greek), one honors the god through his beloved.

In historic times Dionysus attracted a cult following consisting largely of women, the Bacchae or maenads. During the ritual followers abandoned their houses and work, to roam about in the mountains, hair and clothing in disarray, and liberally imbibing wine, normally forbidden to women. At the height of their ecstasy they would seize upon an animal or even a child, tear it to pieces, and devour the uncooked flesh, by ingesting which they sought to incorporate the god and his powers within themselves. From a sociological point of view, the Bacchic cult is a "religion of the oppressed," affording an ecstatic relief to women, whose status was low. Occurring only once during the year, or once every two years, these Dionysiac rites were bracketed off from the normal life of the Greek polis, suggesting comparison with such later European customs as the feast of fools, the carnival, the charivari, and **mardi gras**.

The maenads assume a major role in Euripides' tragedy, *The Bacchae* (406 B.C.). Accompanied by his female followers, Dionysus appears in Thebes as a missionary. Unwisely, King Pentheus insults and arrests the divine visitor; after he has been rendered mad and humiliated, the transgressor is dismembered by the maenads. Interpretations of the play differ: a warning of the consequences of emotional excess versus a reaffirmation of the enduring presence of humanity's irrational side. The subject probably attracted Euripides as a phenomenon of individual and group psychology in its own right, but it is unlikely that he intended it as a forecast of modern gay liberation in the "faery spirituality" mode, as Arthur Evans has argued. Inasmuch as the sexuality of *The Bacchae* was not pederastic, the Greek audience would not have seen the play as homosexual (a concept foreign to their mentality), but rather as challenging gender-role assumptions about men and women, whatever their sexual orientation. That the parts of the maenads were taken by men was not exceptional: women never appeared on the Greek stage.

Bacchanalian rites were introduced into Rome during the Republic. Men joined women in the frenzied gatherings, and (according to the historian Livy) there was more debauchery among the men with each other than with the women. Apart from their orgiastic aspects, the rites caused concern because they crossed class lines, welcoming citizens, freedmen, and slaves alike. Condemned as a subversive foreign import, the Senate suppressed the Bacchanalia in 186 B.C., but they evidently were soon revived. Roman sarcophagi of the second and third century of our era show Bacchic scenes, projecting hopes for an afterlife spent in Dionysic bliss. In its last phases the cult of Dionysus emerged as an other-worldly mystery religion, showing affinities with Mithraism, the religion of Isis, and Christianity. Meeting now behind closed doors, members of the sect recognized one another by passwords and signs.

Although the early Christians regarded all pagan worship as demonic, they were not averse to purloining the

Bacchic wine harvest imagery for their own sarcophagi and mosaics. Some Bacchic reminiscences recur in drinking songs of medieval goliardic poets, notably the *Carmina Burana*. As a religious phenomenon the Bacchanalia attracted discreet attention among the hermetic adepts of the Italian Renaissance, foreshadowing the latter interest of students of comparative religion. At the end of the sixteenth century the flamboyant bisexual painter **Caravaggio** created a notably provocative image of Bacchus–Dionysus (Florence, Uffizi Gallery).

The most influential latterday evocation of the god occurs in *The Birth of Tragedy* (1872) of Friedrich Nietzsche, who exalted the category of the Dionysiac as a antidote for excessive rationality in the interpretation of ancient Greece and, by implication, in modern life as well. Nietzsche's ideas were modernized and correlated with anthropology and psychoanalysis by the classical scholar E. R. Dodds, who in turn influenced the poet W. H. **Auden**. Together with his lover, Chester Kallman, Auden turned Euripides' play into an opera liberetto entitled *The Bassarids*. Set by the gay composer Hans Werner Henze, the work premiered at Salzburg in August 1966. While the opera has not gained a permanent place in the repertoire, Euripides' play—with Dionysus as the apostle of the "do your own thing" principle—found much favor in the experimental **theatre** of the 1970s and 1980s, though sometimes transformed to the point of unrecognizability.

BIBLIOGRAPHY. Arthur Evans, *The God of Ecstasy: Sex-Roles and the Madness of Dionysos*, New York: St. Martin's Press, 1988; Karl Kerenyi, *Dionysus: Archetypal Image of Indestructible Life*, London: Routledge, 1976.
Wayne R. Dynes

DISCRIMINATION

In its social dimension, discrimination refers to treatment that disadvantages others by virtue of their perceived membership in a group. Earlier studies of such patterns concentrated on economic discrimination—the denial to a group of earnings commensurate with ability. Interest focused on groups that are either ethnic or religious minorities (blacks in the United States, untouchables in India, Jews in the Soviet Union), or political or social minorities (blacks in South Africa, immigrants from North Africa in Israel, women in most countries). Even this aspect was neglected in the past because economists were reluctant to interpret any significant economic phenomena in terms of the **Marxian** concept of "exploitation." The growing concern of economists with this phenomenon has been grounded in thinking that circumvents the Marxian analysis by making an even sharper break with traditional economic theory. This approach holds that a group can be the object of discrimination if others are willing to sacrifice resources or gains of their own in order to avoid employing, working beside, lending to, training, educating, or associating in any manner with its members.

History. The attitude of Western **Christianity** toward individuals known to have engaged in homosexual activity has been one of persistent discrimination and exclusion. It was the pattern of ostracism and general intolerance that drove homosexual men and women to desperate measures of concealment and deception in order to avoid the economic and social penalties which a hostile environment sought to inflict upon them. This discrimination differed from the exclusion imposed on members of groups such as women or religious minorities who had an inferior status within the society, but still held a recognized place; these groups were not stigmatized as criminals and outcasts, even though they were until quite recent times denied access to higher education and to the exercise of certain professions.

American Developments. Until the 1940s the right of American employers, landlords and the like to discriminate on the grounds of racial or ethnic origin went unchallenged; then a movement began to declare such forms of exclusion illegal that led to the enactment of many state laws forbidding such practices and ultimately to the Civil Rights Act of 1964. But discrimination based upon the sexual orientation of the subject was upheld by the courts as a right to eliminate "immoral" persons from the work force or from housing. The judiciary consistently echoed the cultural norms of the heterosexual majority as binding upon the whole of society. Early attempts to include homosexuals within the protections afforded cultural, religious, and racial minorities met uniformly with failure. Only gradually did groups concerned with civil liberties come to believe that discrimination against homosexuals violated their civil rights. The struggle to include "sexual orientation" (= bisexuality or homosexuality) in the protected list of anti-discrimination laws began in the 1970s and has led to the passage of some 50 municipal ordinances with such guarantees.

Federal Employment. The United States federal government has since the late 1940s maintained that homosexual conduct is immoral and that homosexuality in itself establishes unfitness for employment. The argument is that homosexual conduct is scandalous and disgraceful and requires punitive policies on the part of the executive. While more recent court decisions have somewhat limited the Civil Service Commission in this area, they leave open the possibility that homosexual conduct might justify dismissal where interference with efficiency could be proved. The military establishment has almost uniformly been successful in defeating suits brought against it by homosexual and lesbian members of the armed forces threatened with discharge and often loss of benefits as well.

Public Schools. The situation of school employees is entangled in a web of contradictory and inconsistent decisions. While procedural due process is accorded public employees, there is no guarantee that a teacher's classroom performance will be the basis of the decision. Homosexual teachers and counselors often face dismissal on the basis of substantive rules that disqualify such an employee for "moral turpitude" or "immoral or unprofessional conduct." Because popular belief identifies the homosexual with the child molester, public schoolteachers face a particularly invidious type of discrimination. Revocation of the teaching credential has been a virtual rule when a teacher is convicted of a homosexual offense, even though the party with whom the act was committed may have long since passed the school attendance age. More recently, a few courts have held that an employee's private life should not be of concern to an employer unless it could be shown to affect the employee's ability to perform his duties. In practice, the criterion has often been the employee's visibility: if his sexual activity is covert and unknown to the community, the school officials can overlook it, but if it becomes publicly known, they feel obliged to "protect the reputation of the institution." Such is also the logic of court decisions that uphold the right of an employer to dismiss a gay activist whose political overtness has made him notorious.

Housing. Discrimination in housing is another barrier that homosexuals face, particularly when trying to rent apartments. Single homosexuals who "pass" are not likely to encounter difficulty; moreover, gay people are recognized by many landlords as likely to improve property. When two prospective tenants of the same sex apply, however, they may be denied at the whim of the owner or, in the case of large corporate landlords, as the result of company policy. The argument is voiced that their presence will have a "morally corrupting influence" on the children of families living in the same building or in the general area. Homosexuals are by definition single, even if in fact they are long-term, stable couples; they may have children, but they do not qualify for benefits offered to young married couples or families with children. If one of the partners in a relationship dies, the lease may not be transferable to the survivor because there is no formal marriage tie.

Public Accommodations. Restaurants, bars, and hotels do not offer the same problems for the homosexual as they once did for ethnic or religious minorities who were explicitly denied lodging or service, though an obviously gay couple may still be the object of rudeness or hostility. On the whole, however, homophile activists have not raised this issue in the courts, while for the civil rights movement of the early 1960s it was a prime concern. Similarly, the denial of voting rights that was a major issue in the drive for racial equality did not concern the gay movement, because homosexuals have never been politically demarcated even for purposes of exclusion. Also, the development of a network of guest houses, restaurants, bars, and similar establishments that welcome a gay clientele has filled the need for such places of recreation and leisure.

Economic Aspects. The **economic** dimension of discrimination against homosexuals is difficult to assess, just because it may consist in underemployment, denial of promotion, or rejection for an executive position though not an entry-level one. In fields where a significant proportion of the workers are gay (e.g., librarianship, **dance**), it is only those with a heterosexual appearance or social façade who may be chosen for advancement to the upper levels of the occupational hierarchy. Also, some homosexuals fearing discovery or dismissal may opt out of the normal career path entirely, preferring to create their own firms from which they cannot be fired at the whim of a heterosexual employer.

Private Life. Forms of discrimination in private life cannot be separated from the right of an individual to choose his associates and intimates. The private

citizen who wants no part of homosexuals cannot be taken to court on any ground, even if he engages in open rudeness. Also, there is a civil liberties issue: the freedom of association necessarily includes the right of non-association, which can be motivated by any number of idiosyncratic dislikes and aversions. Here only patient education—and diplomacy on the part of homosexuals in their dealings with unsympathetic heterosexuals—can erase the invisible barriers.

Affirmative Action. From the late 1960s onward, laws and guidelines were enacted that called for "affirmative action" to increase the numbers of women and ethnic minorities in fields from which they had traditionally been excluded or limited to low-level, menial positions. These have even included actual quotas that an employer needed to meet to comply with the law. None of these programs has contained any measure to increase the number of homosexuals in any firm or industry, indeed critics sometimes advanced the very suggestion that there should be one as the *reductio ad absurdum* of the entire scheme. It is also a fact that homosexuals are overrepresented in many areas of employment relative to their numbers in the general population, and in these fields quotas would not benefit the gay community, but rather deprive its members of their hard-earned livelihood. Then too, many homosexuals who are in no way obvious would never identify themselves as deserving preference under a quota system.

People with AIDS. In recent years, the spread of **AIDS** in the gay male population has resulted in demands for antidiscrimination measures that have enjoyed some success as part of a general movement to protect the rights of the disabled and handicapped. Courts have interpreted such statutes as meaning that an employee with AIDS cannot be fired so long as he is capable of performing competently on the job. On the other hand, efforts by insurance companies to identify homosexual men and deny them protection have in some instances been tacitly approved by the courts and legislatures. Also, forms of ostracism and social isolation inspired by fear of disease have gone so far as to deny people with AIDS seats on a commercial airliner.

Prospects and Goals. The campaign for anti-discrimination ordinances parallel to those protecting other minorities will be a major part of gay movement activity in the decades ahead, as removing the negative sanctions in the law is only the first, though necessary, step. One cannot logically ask to be protected in behavior which is per se illegal. Many homosexuals choose not to advertise their sexual orientation to an unfriendly environment, and desire only respect for their privacy. The long tradition of exclusion and ostracism of homosexuals in Western civilization has only begun to recede in the face of the organized movement for gay rights, and positive guarantees of the fundamental liberties that homosexuals need to become full-fledged members of modern society remain one of that movement's principal goals.

BIBLIOGRAPHY. Bruce Galloway, ed., *Prejudice and Pride: Discrimination Against Gay People in Modern Britain*, London: Routledge & Kegan Paul, 1983; Judith M. Hedgpeth, "Employment Discrimination Law and the Rights of Gay Persons," *Journal of Homosexuality*, 5 (1979), 67–78; Arthur S. Leonard, "Employment Discrimination against Persons with AIDS," *University of Dayton Law Review*, 10 (1985), 745–65.

Warren Johansson

DISGUST

Disgust is a physical reaction comparable to nausea that is provoked by exposure to something experienced as distasteful or loathsome. Nausea is a primary response of the gastro-intestinal system to substances rejected and expelled by it, typically in the form of vomiting. The close relationship between the oral cavity, the sense of taste, tactile sensations, and deglutition on the one hand, and the functions of the stomach, on the other, explain the existence of tastes and odors that are nauseating even to one who has never previously encountered them.

The principal reason for mentioning disgust in this encyclopedia is that it figures so frequently as an argument for the intolerance of homosexual expression. In debates on the **sodomy** laws speakers often allege that "hearing of these practices makes me sick to my stomach" or that "what I read there nauseated me to the foundations of my being." Further, this reaction is cited as a spontaneous expression of the *vox populi*, as the natural aversion of the common man to "this revolting filthiness" that justifies the perpetuation of the statutes by a democratically elected legislature.

Psychology. Modern psychology recognizes that erotic sensations are closely associated with the arousal of certain parts of the body known as erogenous zones. Among these, the buccal cavity must be regarded not merely as primary and as one of the most important, but also as one of those which retain their function into adulthood. Early in the life of the child the feeling of disgust originates as a negative reaction deriving from external conditioning that represses the erotic tendencies associated with the oral cavity. Just as the complete gratification of the hunger instinct is followed by a disgust felt for further nourishment, so the satisfaction of sexual desires can result in disdain for further activity.

A further consideration is that the sexual acts of others are capable of arousing disgust in an individual who regards his own with equanimity. This reaction is not confined to high stages of civilization, but is found among primitive peoples in an even more palpable form. It gives rise to the belief that sexual intercourse is unclean, impure, defiling, and also to the social compulsion to hide one's sexual activity from the light of day, to perform erotically only in the absence of witnesses. Hence the **privacy** of sexual behavior is a need recognized by virtually every human society, even if the criminal law in the Western world has only recently become aware of the contradiction between this norm of the "deep structure" of social control and the century-long tradition that made the law of the state coterminous with the **canon law** of the Church.

History. Of all the peoples of antiquity, the Greeks had the least collective sense of disgust at the sexual side of life. The nonchalance with which the classic authors discussed erotic matters sorely embarrassed later generations of scholars who had to prepare bowdlerized editions of their writings. The Persian religion, on the other hand, with its pronounced dualism, relegated homosexuality to the realm of darkness and evil, reinforcing the Judaic tradition that associated sexuality with ritual impurity. Christianity reinforced this negativism with its ascetic strivings that identified the flesh and sexual pleasure with sin and defilement. In the high Middle Ages this belief system evolved into a virtual compulsion neurosis with ritualized defense mechanisms that included violently punitive measures against those found guilty of "uncleanness." Homosexual sodomy became for the Christian mind the quintessence of filthiness and foul horror, a pollution that excluded the offender from Christian society and turned him into a "moral leper" and "plaguebearer."

Analysis. That homosexual activity in particular should arouse disgust in the uninitiated cannot surprise anyone given that it so often entails anal–genital or oral–genital contact, and that the opposite ends of the gastro-intestinal tract are major loci of taboos associated with cleanliness and propriety. It is even alleged that the very word "homosexual" provokes in the minds of certain individuals the image of a subject engaged in anal intercourse, with accompanying feelings of disgust and horror. The experience of another male's semen as repugnant and defiling must also enter into the negative reaction.

It is also a fact that the homosexual orientation may include a feeling of disgust for the person of the opposite sex, an inversion of the attraction experienced by the heterosexual. For some, there is not just the positive magnetism experienced for one's own sex, but a negative repulsion that magnifies the distasteful sides of the person of the other sex—the specific odor of the body, the texture of the skin and hair, the perceived disharmonies of the physique.

Concluding Reflections. To what extent should disgust figure as a motive for legislation aimed at the control of sexual activity? That such activity should be confined to private places or to ones where only other consenting adults are present is tacitly assumed by all modern legislation. On the other hand, to claim that such behavior is "abominable" and "offensive" even when committed in private, and therefore within the scope of the criminal law, is to deny the significance of privacy itself; it is the state, not the sexual partners, that is infringing the principle of privacy by invoking the sanctions of criminal law. What adults do under conditions of strict privacy for their own sexual pleasure offends the feelings of no one, even if it would cause profound indignation and disgust when committed in public. In fact, at the end of the eighteenth century, one of the chief motives for repealing the medieval sodomy statutes was desire to avoid the scandal attendant upon sensational trials and executions.

BIBLIOGRAPHY. Eugène Carp, "Quelques remarques sur la psychologie du dégoût," *L'Encéphale*, 27 (1932), 107–112; Gustav Kafka, "Zur Psychologie des Ekels," *Zeitschrift für angewandte Psychologie*, 34 (1929), 1–46; Emilio Majluf, "Fenomenología y clínica del asco en la neurosis compulsiva," *Revista de neuro-psiquiatría*, 10 (1947), 257–323; C. Theodoridis, "Sexuelles Fühlen und Werten. Ein Beitrag zur Völkerpsychologie," *Archiv für die* gesamte Psychologie, 40 (1920), 1–88; Abraham L. Wolbarst, "Sexual Perversions: Their Medical and Social Implications," Medical Journal and Record, 134 (1931), 5–9, 62–65.

Warren Johansson

DONATELLO (DONATO DI NICCOLÒ DI BETTO BARDI; CA. 1386–1466)

Florentine sculptor. Less well known today than some other Italian **Renaissance** artists of the fifteenth century, Donatello may have been the most original. His apprenticeship took place in the orbit of ongoing work on Florence Cathedral. In 1408–09 he created the marble *David;* the youthful, teasing grace of this delightful figure already shows the sculptor's homosexual tastes, which are documented from other sources. From 1416 to 1420, for Or San Michele, he created the moving figure of *St. George,* a work which later became the "boyfriend" of countless admirers of male beauty.

In 1431–33 he was in Rome with the architect Brunelleschi, studying ancient works of art which were then accepted as touchstones of quality. On his return Donatello created the bronze *David* now in the Bargello Museum. From 1433 to 1453 he was in Padua, where he made the high altar of the great church of St. Anthony, as well as the equestrian monument to the condottiere Gattamelata, which set the pattern for countless such figures in public squares throughout Europe and the Americas. On his return to Florence, Donatello explored new expressive dimensions of characterization, opening avenues which were important for the paintings of Sandro **Botticelli.**

Donatello's patrons, including Cosimo de' Medici, took an attitude of amused tolerance with regard to his homosexual escapades. On one occasion he is supposed to have chased a boy to another town with the intention of killing him, only to relent when he saw the beloved form once more. As a homosexual Donatello was fortunate to live mainly in the first half of the fifteenth century when attitudes were relatively relaxed. After his death, the authorities of **Florence**, alarmed at the city's reputation as a new Sodom, sought to take "corrective" action. Although the resulting denunciations did little to stem the overall incidence of activity, they dissolved the easy, almost carefree environment in which Donatello flourished.

BIBLIOGRAPHY. H. W. Janson, *The Sculpture of Donatello*, Princeton: Princeton University Press, 1957; Laurie Schneider, "Donatello and Caravaggio: The Iconography of Decapitation," *American Imago*, 33 (1976), 76–91.

Wayne R. Dynes

DOOLITTLE, HILDA (H.D.; 1886–1961)

American poet, novelist, and translator. A Pennsylvanian, H.D. met Marianne Moore at Bryn Mawr and Ezra Pound and William Carlos Williams at the University of Pennsylvania. Footloose after college, she formed her first lesbian attachment with Frances Gregg, a family friend. In 1911 she left America to settle in Europe. Pound introduced her to his London circle and gave her the nickname "Dryad." He also included her work in his anthology *Des Imagistes* (1914), and arranged for her poems to be published elsewhere, signed (at his suggestion) "H.D. imagiste." Her lyrics, influenced by ancient Greek poetry, were characterized by a minimalist concision and purity of language. In 1913 H.D. married the English writer Richard Aldington; while they were not officially divorced until 1938, the separation caused by his wartime service effectively ended the union.

In 1918 Annie Winifred Ellerman, daughter of one of the richest men in England, sought her out. Ellerman, better known under her pen name of "Bryher," had memorized H.D.'s volume *Sea Garden* (1918). Although she was linked to the bisexual American writer Robert McAlmon in an "unconventional" marriage, Bryher had long been aware of her lesbianism. She swept H.D. off her feet and the two embarked on a number of trips together, including visits to Greece and Egypt, a country which left a great impression, reorienting H.D.'s subject matter. They both remained on friendly terms with McAlmon, whose Contact Editions became H.D.'s publisher. The two women settled more or less permanently in Switzerland, providing mutual support in their careers as writers. They both consulted with Sigmund **Freud** in Vienna and helped to spread his fame in the English-speaking world. Another passion was films, which they made and supported with a critical journal. H.D. spent the war years in London, returning to Switzerland where Bryher was watchful over her deteriorating health.

The reputation of H.D. remained for a long time linked to her participation in the imagist movement in the teens of the century, to the detriment of her later work. In the 1960s, however, she underwent a revival, influencing a number of contemporary poets, including Robert **Duncan.**

BIBLIOGRAPHY. Barbara Guest, *Herself Defined: The Poet H.D. and Her World*, Garden City, NY: Doubleday, 1984.

Evelyn Gettone

DOUGLAS, ALFRED, LORD (1870–1945)

British writer and adventurer. The third son of John Sholto Douglas, the eighth marquess of Queensberry, Alfred Douglas was an exquisitely beautiful child. The boy was sent to various preparatory schools and then to Winchester, where he encountered a good deal of what Douglas called "public-school nonsense," which he at first resisted but then accepted. While he was at Winchester, his father took as mistress a woman so notorious that when Lady Queensberry eventually sued for divorce the proceedings took only fifteen minutes.

This episode marked the beginning of Alfred's alienation from his father, who was later to declare, "I never believed he was my son."

In the summer of 1889 young Douglas had his first affair with a woman, a divorcee whom he encountered while staying at a hotel in the south of France, but who found herself the object of indignation for having seduced "an innocent boy." In the fall of 1889 he entered Magdalen College, Oxford, where despite some faults of character—he was a poor loser—he was popular, with a dashing personality and lighthearted rebelliousness that endeared him to his fellow undergraduates. His burgeoning literary talent also won him admirers. The minor poet Lionel Johnson arranged an introduction to the celebrated litterateur Oscar **Wilde** at his house in Tite Street in London in the late summer of 1891.

Douglas later admitted that the friendship between them had some sexual expression (though of sodomy "there was never the slightest question"), which began about six months after they met and ended forever some six months before the catastrophe that terminated Wilde's career. Wilde did not generally care for sexual intimacy with young men of refinement and preferred "rough trade" from the lower depths of society, while Douglas was aggressively masculine. At the outset, moreover, each of the friends was inordinately proud of the other. It was a few nights after Douglas attended the premiere of *Lady Windermere's Fan* (February 20, 1892) that the intimacy between them began.

During the term that followed Douglas became involved in a homosexual scandal at Oxford and got out of it by paying £100 to a blackmailer. He was an aristocrat in the worst sense, indifferent to bourgeois morality, and obsessed with the belief that he enjoyed the inalienable privilege of amusing himself as he pleased. Wilde, for his part, reveled in flirting with danger, deriving much of his pleasure from the thought that his actions were branded as vices by respectable society.

In the summer of 1894 there occurred an episode, trivial at the time, which had grave consequences for the two men. A homosexual undergraduate at Oxford named John Francis Bloxam asked Douglas for a contribution to a new periodical called *The Chameleon*. Not only did Douglas contribute two poems, but Wilde submitted some "Phrases and Philosophies for the Use of the Young" originally destined for the *Saturday Review*. Bloxam published a homosexual story entitled "The Priest and the Acolyte" that was later—and falsely—attributed to Wilde.

On February 18, Queensberry began the series of events that led to Wilde's disgrace, arrest, and imprisonment by leaving a card at the Albemarle Club addressed "To Oscar Wilde posing as a somdomite" (sic). Alfred Douglas never testified at any of the three trials, yet he maintained to the end of his life that if he had gone into the witness box he could have saved Wilde, even though the presiding judge in summing up the testimony said that "the whole of this lamentable inquiry has arisen through the defendant's association with Lord Alfred Douglas." After the trial Douglas wrote furious letters in defense of Wilde and of homosexuality, although his family and its friends wanted his liaison with Wilde utterly forgotten.

In prison Oscar Wilde composed the *De Profundis*, originally as a letter of forty thousand words which he intended to send to Douglas. However it was neither published nor delivered to its addressee; it was ultimately brought out of the British Museum Library as evidence against Douglas in a civil action for libel.

The two men resumed their friendship in France, after Wilde's release from prison, despite pressure from various sources to break off the relationship. The marquess of Queensberry died half-insane in 1900, and his son received £15,000 from the estate. Of this he gave Wilde some £1000 during what was to be the writer's last year of life; he told no one and produced the evidence only years later to prove that he had not abandoned Wilde.

During the subsequent decades of his own life Douglas had an indifferent career as a writer and as the editor of several small magazines. In 1902 he married a woman named Olive Custance who deserted him in 1913. At the age of forty he converted to Catholicism and derived emotional strength from it when what he called "the years of persecution" began. In 1933 he published a book entitled *The True History of Shakespeare's Sonnets*, not an outstanding work of scholarship, but an exploration of the possible homoerotic attachment between the poet and a boy actor named Will Hughes (the "Mr. W.H."). Other trials and controversies figured in his later years, including a feud with Robert Ross, who had also been intimate with Wilde. Remembered chiefly as the companion of the ill-fated playwright, Lord Alfred Douglas was a defender of homosexuality before the cause had achieved any standing in England, and also a minor author in his own right, a personality that will continue to intrigue future generations.

BIBLIOGRAPHY. Rupert Croft-Cooke, *Bosie: Lord Alfred Douglas: His Friends and Enemies*, New York: Bobbs-Merrill, 1963; H. Montgomery Hyde, *Lord Alfred Douglas*, New York: Dodd Mead, 1985.
Warren Johansson

DOUGLAS, NORMAN (1868–1952)

British novelist and travel writer. Born in Falkenhorst, Austria, of mixed Scottish and German parentage, Douglas was educated at Uppingham, England, and at Karlsruhe, Germany. His cosmopolitan leanings were confirmed by a career in the British Foreign Service, which included residence in St. Petersburg from 1894 to 1896. He abandoned this calling, however, and went to Italy to live. Though he was married at the time, Douglas' stay in Italy brought forth his pederastic bent. It is said that during his later years he would take a different boy "muse" as inspiration during the writing of each of his books. *Siren Land* (1911) and *Old Calabria* (1915) are evocative records of his travels in southern Italy that mingle chronicle, observation, historical notes, and philosophical musings. During one of these trips he recalls spending months with Amitrano, an illiterate peasant boy of the Sorrento countryside, renewing contact with "elemental and permanent things . . . casting off outworn weeds of thought with the painless ease of a serpent." Evidently the casting off was incomplete, for he could still recognize the outlines of classical statuary in the laboring bodies of Italian fieldhands.

Douglas wrote his popular novel *South Wind* (1917) to capture the expatriate atmosphere of the Capri colony. Set against the semitropical flora and fauna of "Nepenthe" (as he calls the island), the novel evokes a gentle hedonism that softens the sharp edges of the northern visitors. The plot, such as it is, pivots on the gradual conversion of the straitlaced Anglican colonial bishop, Mr. Heard, to a kind of aesthetic paganism. Although nothing in *South Wind* is overtly homosexual, the alert reader can detect allusions to the fancies and foibles of the island's foreign gay residents. Continuously in print since its first publication, the novel owes its success to its depiction of a Mediterranean outpost of **bohemia**, whose denizens have learned to "go with the flow."

In the nineteen-twenties Norman Douglas settled down in Florence, where he lived in straitened circumstances, sometimes with the bookseller Pino [G. M.] Orioli. He spent the war years 1941–46 in England. Most of Douglas' later fiction was not successful, owing to his lack of convincing characterization and plotting. As a result he sometimes required subventions from more fortunate authors such as W. Somerset **Maugham**. His efforts to earn money not infrequently had entertaining results, as in his spoof of literary scholarship, *Some Limericks, Collected for the Use of Students, and Ensplendour'd with Introduction, Geographical Index, and with Notes Explanatory and Critical* (1928). In this little book, the point is not so much the bawdy limericks themselves, but the ingenious and improbable glosses supplied by the editor.

A renowned consumer of haute cuisine and wines, Douglas had little fondness for avant-garde literature, which he described as "rats' feet over broken glass in a dry cellar." As he grew older his interest in people became increasingly selective, and he acquired a reputation as a misanthrope. But his enthusiasm for young people never waned. "A child," he remarked, "is ready to embrace the universe. And, unlike adults, he is never afraid to face his own limitations."

In retrospect Douglas represented the milieu of the select foreign colony in Italy before the age of mass tourism. His Florentine circle included other homosexual and lesbian residents, notably Harold Acton, Vernon **Lee**, and Reggie Turner. They were seduced to their venerable surroundings by a largely illusory Mediterranean paradise of the senses. But since many of them flourished and were creative there, the illusion was a beneficial one.

Wayne R. Dynes

DRAG
See **Transvestism; Transvestism, Theatrical**.

DRAMA
See **Theatre and Drama**.

DREAMS
Since the beginning of time human beings have dreamed and have been fascinated, perplexed, and terrified by their dreams. Universal as is the experience of dreaming, the interpretation of dreams is

variable and culturally conditioned. In various traditions dreams have been understood as religious experience (divine possession); predictions of future events, good or ill; a review of the previous day's happenings; wish fulfillment; and communications, often puzzling or disguised, from the unconscious. Their elliptical, protean character suggests that dreams are messages in code. This code requires translation by an interpreter, who may be the dreamer in person, a village elder, a priestly figure, an occultist, or a psychiatrist. When a dream has homosexual content, the hermeneutic process is complicated by the ethical assumptions of the dreamer and the interpreter, which reflect the attitudes of society toward same-sex experience.

To understand their dream experiences human beings have formulated a lore to which the ancients gave the name oneirocritical. Because the ancient world accepted homosexual interest and activity as part of human sexuality, the dream interpreters of the eastern Mediterranean cultures could calmly explain the homoerotic episodes in dreams in terms of their overall system of signs and meanings and without anxiety. Such was the work of **Artemidorus** of Daldis (middle of the second century), which alludes to pederastic and homosexual dream sequences and assigns them a specific, often prophetic meaning. Not so the Christian Middle Ages; the literature of dreams became exclusively heterosexual because the taboo with which theology had tainted sexual attraction to one's own sex imposed a censorship that is only now being lifted.

The folk, the occult, and the psychoanalytic traditions offer quite varied approaches for the interpretation of dreams. Yet all work with a set of symbols which the interpreters claim to have validated through individual experience. Some begin by questioning the client about events in his life that may have activated the dream and then try to elicit his own understanding, before they proceed to an explanation or prediction on the basis of the reported dream material. Others may simply elaborate the client's own association. An interpreter with a flair for a particular set of images and symbols may tend to focus on the latent content of these, while giving only formal translation-like explanations of others. In some traditions one symbol is assigned universal significance, but another may have a polyvalent range of meaning that is pointed to the client's concrete life situation. If the interpreter ignores the latter, he may encounter justified contradiction and even rejection from the client.

The homoerotic content of dreams, in a culture where homosexuality is severely tabooed, may provoke deep, fundamental conflicts. Such dreams are dangerous to the subject, charged as they are with explosive content which the client may not be ready to accept and which may therefore greatly frighten him. The interpreter is well advised to postpone the analysis and explanation of such dreams until a time when the client is able to accept them without needless anxiety. Other dreams may be at odds with the subject's overt sexual life, and he may even wish to adapt their content to his conscious orientation. **Kinsey** mentions instances of such disparity in the subjects of his interviews.

According to the psychoanalytic tradition, the dream, by widening the avenues of perception and attention, can lift amnesia of past events in the life of the subject. The dream may reflect the role of homosexuality in psychic conflict, portraying with special clarity the ways in which it complicates the analytic relationship. The dream also exposes the homosexual conflicts of adolescence, a period often relegated to the limbo of the client's memory. Broader intellectual and social acceptance of overt homosexuality may increase rather than decrease the problems raised by its unconscious dynamics, as the subject then has to confront the possibility of having homoerotic desires that are within reach of gratification. Homosexuality becomes meaningful to a subject only when he can integrate it with his own living experience. Future studies of the role of homosexuality in the dream need to take account of the long repressed homoerotic component of human culture, as well as the value assigned specifically homosexual symbols in the traditional literature of dream interpretation. Moreover, new research on the physiology of sleep is likely to open future perspectives on the dream.

BIBLIOGRAPHY. Leon L. Altman, *The Dream in Psychoanalysis*, New York: International Universities Press, 1975; Sandor Lorand, *Technique of Psychoanalytic Therapy*, New York: International Universities Press, 1946.

Warren Johansson

DRUGS

As used in this article drugs are substances introduced into the body to produce pleasure, altered states of consciousness, or hallucinations (short-term psychosis). Not included, because they are considered neither major social issues nor gay-related, are drugs and foods which influence brain chemistry in other ways (for example, antidepressants; tranquilizers; the amino acid tryptophan; phenylethylamine, the psychoactive ingredient in chocolate).

Drugs are of diverse origins and have sharply contrasting characteristics. Some are produced by plants (alcohol, caffeine, cannabis [marijuana], coca, mescaline, nicotine, opium); some are concentrated extracts (cocaine, heroin, spirits); others are manufactured (amphetamines, barbiturates, LSD, volatile nitrites). Some drugs have a high overdose potential (heroin; PCP), others low (cannabis); some are effective in very small doses (LSD), others only at high doses (alcohol); some are highly addictive (cocaine, nicotine, opiates), others mildly so (alcohol), and others not addictive at all (cannabis, LSD). In addi-tion, drugs vary dramatically in mode of action and effects on the brain and other bodily systems. They can be divided into depressants and stimulants, with the hallucinogens a subcategory of the latter.

Policy. The degree to which society should or can tolerate recreational drug use, psychic exploration or artistic creation through drugs, or self-destructive use of drugs, is an unresolved question. There is a partial consensus that private use, which does not impede societal functioning or lead to gross neglect of health, is tolerable and can even be endorsed (the glass of wine with dinner). The use of drugs is so widespread in human history—it has been proposed that agriculture was born from a desire to easily produce **alcoholic** beverages—that their use could respond to some biological drive. There is also a consensus that society has the right to demand unimpaired capacity from those in hazardous activities with responsibility for the safety of others (surgeons, pilots, drivers of automobiles). Between those extremes there is a vast, confused area. It should be noted that there has never been a country or society in which unrestricted use of all psychoactive drugs has been permitted over any period of time.

Under ideal conditions, with controlled strengths and purities and a warm, supportive environment, there is little long-term harm to the healthy subject in infrequent use of drugs. However, drug use easily becomes frequent, and the amount used may increase because the body develops tolerance for some drugs and the desired effects decrease. Frequent use can cause bodily harm, although this varies with the drug and the user, and some bodily harm (for example, sports injuries) may be considered acceptable by society. The history of drugs reveals that while benefits are immediately evident, harmful effects may not be discovered until much later. Damage from drugs can be produced so slowly that it is hard to perceive, and sometimes it has no early symptoms at all; addiction can make the user blind to harm. Drugs can reduce the disease-fighting capacity of the body's immune system.

Illegal drugs are seldom used under ideal conditions; they vary widely in potency and are sometimes adulterated. Without quick medical treatment overdoses of the more hazardous substances, particularly those which depress respiratory function or cause vomiting, can cause brain damage or death; overdoses of stimulants can cause death from circulatory system failure. In some users hallucinogens cause terrifying experiences; psychological problems can be exacerbated, and brain damage caused. The action of stimulants is often followed by a compensatory negative experience through which the body restores its equilibrium. Injection bypasses natural protection against infection. Without supervision a person with drug-impaired capacity can injure him- or herself, or others. Even without harmful effects, there is a philosophical and sometimes spiritual opposition to the use of chemicals to influence the brain, and controversy about their value as a means of self-improvement. Some of the effects for which drugs are taken can be achieved more safely by non-chemical means (for example, yoga, meditation, sensory deprivation).

There is in addition the question of social motivation. Pleasure and spiritual enlightenment from drugs bypass social mechanisms. When these mechanisms misfunction, when people feel that something is wrong with their lives, the use of drugs to supply the missing gratification is all the more attractive. Society can tolerate drug use if it is encapsulated within an artistic, recreational, religious, or therapeutic context; while some are able to so control their usage, for many that is a daunting or impossible condition, at least in our present culture. Society can also tolerate a small proportion of voluntarily non-productive members without offending the perception of equity. However, civilization above a subsistence level

cannot coexist with widespread loss of productivity owing to drugs. While it might seem that the use of drugs is inherently anticapitalistic, in that they discourage both production and consumption, drugs can also undermine activism for social change. Repressive governments have used drug policy as a means of pacifying the population and circumventing challenges to their rule.

At the same time, legal restrictions on drug use have been spectacularly unsuccessful and counterproductive. The long-term solution to the threat posed by drugs is a fairer and more meaningful society. Meanwhile, education is more effective than prohibition. Exaggeration of drugs' harmful effects reduces respect for law, overwhelms the courts and prisons, inhibits research on and therapeutic use of drugs, makes drugs of controlled strength and purity unavailable, gives drugs the glamour of the forbidden, and encourages progression to ever more dangerous yet legally equal substances. As with alcohol during America's Prohibition (1920–33), the supply of illegal drugs has become a very profitable industry, and not a passive or benign one. Foreigners who supply drugs sometimes justify their actions to themselves and their countrymen as a means of striking back at the political and economic power of the United States. The costs of America's drug policies have not yet been fully paid.

Homosexuals and Drugs. Gay people have historically used more drugs than the population at large. The first explanation is simple hedonism. Repression of sexuality causes focus on it, and a commitment to the enjoyment of pleasure naturally brings a receptivity to other ways in which pleasure might be produced or increased. Homosexuals have been privileged to see societies' limitations and hypocrisy over sex, and this has created a skepticism about other societal policies in conflict with individual desires. Similarly, those who are in an oppressed minority have extra motivation to try to learn about themselves; drugs have been used for that purpose.

In some cases drugs which loosen inhibitions or which stimulate new and unusual perspectives on self and behavior have helped individuals become more aware and accepting of their homosexuality or bisexuality. Alcohol has often served this function, but during the 1960s, there were a considerable number of reports of people becoming aware of homoeroticism for the first time while under the influence of LSD especially. Drugs have also been used by musicians, artists, and writers who claim that the substances help them create, although this claim is controversial, perhaps because if substantiated it would be a powerful argument for drug use. Finally, homosexuals have suffered, on the average, more emotional pain and deprivation than heterosexuals, and drugs, especially alcohol, have been used to numb that pain.

History. Throughout classical Mediterranean antiquity and into the Islamic period the only widely-used drug was alcohol, in the form of wine. Wine was the drink of poets and lovers, a distinction it still retains, though somewhat weakened. A party, such as we see in **Petronius'** *Satyricon,* would often combine wine and sexual activity, and the cup-bearer Ganymede was the mythological model for the ephebe. In the *Rubaiyat* of Omar Khayyam, we find that all one needed for happiness was the beloved, a garden, poetry, bread, and wine. Wine was valued for more than hedonism, however: wine released truths ("in vino veritas"), and thus both produced enlightenment and brought one closer to the divine.

The use of hashish (cannabis), eaten in sweets rather than smoked, is found in the Bible (Song of Songs 5.1; 1 Samuel 14.25–45), and there is evidence of psychic use of hemp (marijuana), from which hashish is made, from prehistoric times. Herodotus, for example, reports its popularity among the Scythians. However, widespread use of hashish begins in **Islam** in the twelfth and thirteenth centuries. While the Koran prohibited wine, which because of distribution costs was somewhat more expensive than today, it was silent on hashish, which was also much less expensive. There was debate about whether the Koran's silence was to be taken as approval, or whether prohibition was to be inferred from the treatment of wine; still, as long as it remained a minority indulgence it was tolerated, as wine usually was. Hashish users became a subculture; in particular it is linked to the mystical **Sufis,** who made a cult and ritual of its use. However, almost every Islamic poet from the thirteenth to the sixteenth centuries produced at least some playful poems on hashish, although wine poetry is much more abundant.

A link between hashish and homosexuality is well documented in classical Islamic literature. Hashish was thought to cause effeminacy, a preference for the passive sexual role, and a loss of interest in sex. However, it was also prized as the drug of scholars and lovers of young men, and an aid in seduction of the latter. Turkish soldiers frequently ate hashish together before going into battle.

Coffee was introduced to Europe in the seventeenth century from the Turkish empire. Both within Islam and in Europe coffee was at first a similarly controversial drug, subject to occasional legal restriction or suppression. Its use in coffeehouses, later cafés, was typical of intellectuals and dissidents.

The reaction to the failure of the French Revolution and the loss of faith in the powers of human reason, associated with the Romantic movement, led to a new awareness of and interest in the nonrational and unconscious. For the first time drugs were investigated as sources of selfknowledge and stimulants for creativity, as well as for recreation. The takeover of part of the Ottoman empire by France and England led to the introduction of hashish into Europe. In addition to hashish and wine, opium was used, as were nitrous oxide and ether; the recreational use of the two latter antedates their use as anesthetics. The center of drug exploration was France, where it remained associated with poets and dissidents throughout the century.

The first half of the twentieth century was characterized by a wave of reaction against drugs and the establishment of legal controls throughout Western Europe and North America. However, the tensions of the 1960s, against a backdrop of the **Holocaust** and the invention and use of the atomic bomb, brought on a new wave of drug use. The hedonistic use of cannabis increased greatly; its enthusiasts promoted it as an aid to sensual and sexual enjoyment. The **Beat generation**, especially William Burroughs and Allen Ginsberg, had already turned to potent psychedelics as a means of self-improvement; they became part of the short-lived counterculture of the late 1960s. The discovery of psychedelics was in part due to progress in anthropology and archeology. The use by native peoples of mescaline (peyote), psilocybin (mushrooms), and other psychedelics became known, and the possible role of such substances in visions and oracles of the ancient Mediterranean world was proposed by scholars. The hallucinogenic properties of the most potent psychedelic yet known, lysergic acid diethylamine-25 (LSD), were discovered in 1943; until it became too controversial, it was manufactured by a pharmaceutical company for research in psychotherapeutic treatment.

Modern gay culture emerged in Germany, and perhaps for that reason was centered on bars and the use of alcohol; this pattern spread to the United States at approximately the time it was suppressed in Germany by the Nazis. The gay **bar** remains the only gay institution in many American communities, as it was almost everywhere until the 1970s. The visibility of gay culture in the 1970s coincided with the wave of drug use referred to above. A variety of drugs were used, at least by the more visible and hedonistic parts of the gay subculture, until the early eighties: marijuana, mescaline and other hallucinogens, the anesthetic ethyl chloride, and finally a "gay drug": poppers, so called from the sound made when opening the glass vials in which they were first sold.

Poppers are a vasodilator of transitory effect, and cause a "high" from a drop in blood pressure; users say that the intensity and/or duration of orgasm is increased, that muscles (such as throat and anal sphincters) and gag reflexes are relaxed, and that feelings of increased union or "melting" with the sex partner result. Many users report that continued use (a single inhalation produces effects only for a few minutes) inhibits erections, while other users seem unaffected. Likewise, some users say the poppers encourage passivity and complete relaxation, while others report no such effect. Headaches and dizziness are sometimes reported as side effects.

The pharmaceutical amyl nitrite, prescribed for treatment of angina, was replaced for legal reasons with butyl and other related volatile nitrites with similar effects. Under the pretense of use as a room odorizer, these were sold under such brand names as Crypt, Cum, Locker Room, Pig, Rush, and the like. "Pot and poppers" came to be in some circles a routine part of gay male sex, and poppers began to be used by heterosexual Americans, most visibly, and sexually, on disco dance floors. There has, however, been little indication of widespread sexual use of poppers by heterosexuals or by lesbians. In the early 1980s poppers were accused of being a cofactor in the development of **AIDS**, and they were made illegal in some areas, although the accusation remains unproven. The AIDS epidemic brought an increased concern with bodily and especially immune system health, and a reduction in gay drug use of all sorts.

BIBLIOGRAPHY. Edward M. Brecher, et al., *Licit and Illicit Drugs*, Mount Vernon, N.Y.: Consumers Union, 1972;

William Burroughs, "Letter from a Master Addict to Dangerous Drugs," *British Journal of Addiction*, 53 (1957), 119–31, reprinted as an appendix to *Naked Lunch*, New York: Grove, 1959, pp. 239–55; William Burroughs, "Points of Distinction between Sedative and Conscious-Expanding Drugs," *Evergreen Review*, No. 34 (December, 1964), 72–74; C. Creighton, "On Indications of the Hachish-Vice in the Old Testament," *Janus*, 8 (1903), 241–46 and 297–303; Aldous Huxley, *The Doors of Perception*, New York: Harper, 1954; Andrew C. Kimmens, ed., *Tales of Hashish*, New York: William Morrow, 1977; Martin A. Lee and Bruce Shlain, *Acid Dreams: The CIA, LSD and the Sixties Rebellion*, New York: Grove, 1985; Cynthia Palmer and Michael Horowitz, eds., *Shaman Woman, Mainline Lady: Women's Writings on the Drug Experience*, New York: Quill, 1982; Franz Rosenthal, *The Herb: Hashish versus Medieval Muslim Society*, Leiden: Brill, 1971; Frits Stall, *Exploring Mysticism*, Berkeley: University of California Press, 1975; Jay Steevens, *Storming Heaven: LSD and the American Dream*, Boston: Atlantic Monthly Press, 1987; Andrew Weil and Winifred Rosen, *Chocolate to Morphine: Understanding Mind-Active Drugs*, Boston: Houghton Mifflin, 1983.

Daniel Eisenberg

DUNCAN, ROBERT EDWARD (1919–1988)

American poet. He was born Edward Howard Duncan, January 7, 1919, in Oakland, California. His natural mother died after childbirth and the boy was adopted by Edwin and Minnehaha Symmes, whose family name he used until 1942. The Symmes maintained a prosperous middle-class household in Bakersfield, California. As members of the Hermetic Brotherhood (itself an offshoot from Helena Petrovna Blavatsky's Theosophical Society), they received a prediction that their adopted boy would embody the decadence of a civilization to be destroyed during his lifetime.

Between 1936 and 1938, Robert was a student at the University of California at Berkeley, where he became active in radical politics, explored sex with men, and published his first poems in campus papers. When his lover Ned Fahs graduated and took a job in Maryland, Duncan left school and moved to the East Coast; the two separated in 1940, but Robert lived around with both men and women as he pursued his interest in literature. Duncan circulated within the Manhattan gay circles in the 1940s and met Pavel Tchelitchew, Lou Harrison, Parker Tyler, Sanders Russell, Charles Henri Ford, James **Baldwin**, Paul **Goodman**, W. H. **Auden**, and others. Duncan published his pathbreaking essay in the anarchist magazine *Politics* (August, 1944): "The Homosexual in Society." The essay argued that, like blacks and Jews, homosexuals were an oppressed minority in a hostile society. Duncan's making a political issue of homosexuality disturbed many famous New York homosexuals. W. H. Auden later wrote begging Duncan not to publish an essay discussing Auden's sexuality: "I earn a good part of my livelihood by teaching and in that profession one is particularly vulnerable."

In 1945 Duncan returned to California and in 1946 (at the urging of a boyfriend and German exile, Werner Vordtriede) he began study under Ernst **Kantorowicz**, another exile and a member of the Stefan **George** Circle. *Heavenly City Earthly City* (1947), *Poems, 1948–49*, and *Medieval Scenes* (1949) attempted to link the world both of politics and of sexual intercourse (particularly that between men) with hermetic spiritual truths. In 1946 at an anarchist meeting Duncan met Jack **Spicer**; the two became close friends (although not lovers). They collaborated (and occasionally quarreled) on many political and poetry projects central to the **San Francisco** Renaissance.

From his earliest to his latest works, Duncan incorporated gay and lesbian themes; in one early poem, he exclaims: "I am not afraid to be a queen." Being woman-identified, he wrote a series of poems after those of Gertrude Stein and took as his lifelong work an extended commentary on H.D. His 1947 "Venice Poem," weaves the themes of love and loss with the architectural beauties of St. Mark's Square; like the Venetian empire his love was transitory, first he won the young man, Gery Ackerman, who then ran off with Paul Goodman.

Duncan's love life may be divided (like his poetry) between an earlier period of promiscuity and a later period of domesticity. One New Year's Day, 1951, he and Jess Collins, a painter, set up house together and were only separated by the poet's death on February 3, 1988. Among the domestic volumes are *Caesar's Gate* (1955), *The Opening of the Field* (1960), *Roots and Branches* (1964), *Bending the Bow* (1968), *Ground Work Before the War* (1984), and *Ground Work II, In the Dark* (1987).

In *Ground Work Before the War*, the battle is "that War which rages throughout the world today, as enormous in its crimes and madness" as the ancient wars of religion, a war including gay liberation. In 1973, Duncan wrote John Wieners about the gay liberation fronts, "With the way words have of drawing us into their depths, that term 'liberation' that is so much the jargon of the day (so that while the bosses of the U.S. . . . move in on Asia burning and exterminating as they go it is called 'liberating') does draw us deeper into searching out for ourselves true liberations." And he predicted that the word/world "gay" would "be searcht out until it rings painfully true to us."

BIBLIOGRAPHY. Robert Berthoff, *Robert Duncan: A Descriptive Bibliography*, Santa Barbara: Black Sparrow Press, 1986; Ekbert Faas, *Young Robert Duncan: Portrait of the Poet as Homosexual in Society*, Santa Barbara: Black Sparrow Press, 1983.

Charley Shively

DYKE

This word is a slang term in American English designating a female homosexual, which elements of the American lesbian community have adopted as a self-designation. It was originally a term of abuse, and only in the 1970s, with the reversal of values that accompanied the radical upsurge following the Vietnam War, did it obtain a positive, political value.

The term may stem from an earlier compound expression *bulldyke*, which is recorded from the black American slang of the 1920s in the forms *bull-diker* (with the variant *bull-dagger*) and *bull-diking woman* in the sense of "mannish lesbian."

Several theories are current concerning the etymology of *dyke* or *dike* (both spellings are found). There are a number that do not bear serious examination: the suggestion that dyke stems from the Greek word *dike*, fancifully identified with Athena, the "man–woman" who is the principle of total order; or from *hermaphrodite*, with only the last syllable retained and then mispronounced as *dyke*; or from Boadicca, the queen of the ancient Britons who fought against the Roman occupation of her country. The last is impossible on both historical and philological grounds.

More plausible is the derivation from the verb *to dike*, "to attire oneself faultlessly for social purposes," or *to be diked out*, which is recorded as American student slang as early as 1851. Somewhat later *dike* is attested in the meaning of a man so attired, or merely the set of male clothing. Since the original usage of *bull-diker* is a form denoting the agent of a verb, the meaning would thus be "a lesbian wearing male, particularly formal male attire."

However, this still fails to explain fully the compound *bulldiker*, which is all the more noteworthy as *bull* is an English word that is quite prolific in compounds in the literary language and even more in the dialects. Two of these are *bull-dog*, known from the beginning of the Modern English period (with counterparts in Dutch *bulhond* and German *Bulldogge*), and *bull-bitch* "female bull-dog," first recorded in 1681. Now in the same semantic field there is also the word *tyke*, whose primary meaning in the Germanic languages is "bitch," but which in the dialect of Yorkshire (northeastern England) came to be the usual word for dog, and in the Scottish dialects meant a dog, "generally with contemptuous force, a hulking uncouth ill-bred dog, a cur." Since the *bull* is the zoomorphic symbol of maleness par excellence, it is possible that the putative compound *bull-tyke* yielded *bull-dyke* with the notion of "a bitch who behaves like a bull" = a woman who behaves like a man in dress and mannerisms. The influence of the verb *to dike* then produced the forms which later gave the monosyllable *dyke* through such expressions as *dyking ourselves up* which for members of certain lesbian subcultures meant "dressing in a most beautiful, proud, defiant masculine manner." Thus what had been a vulgar epithet with connotations of self-hatred and shame has been adopted as a badge of rebellion against the values of a heterosexist, male-dominated culture by the militant lesbian of today. There is even an organization of lesbian mothers with the name Dykes 'n Tykes. Modern Dutch has borrowed the Americanism but in the spelling *dijk*, the same as the word meaning "sea-wall."

BIBLIOGRAPHY. J. R. Roberts, "In America They Call Us Dykes: Notes on the Etymology and Usage of 'Dyke,'" *Sinister Wisdom*, 9 (Spring 1979), 2–11.
Evelyn Gettone

DYSPHORIA, GENDER

Gender dysphoria is the feeling reported by a few individuals (sometimes labeled "preoperative **transsexuals**") that they are acutely uncomfortable in their own bodies, and that their sex organs in particular "should not be there." The concept may ultimately stem from Karl Heinrich **Ulrichs'** formulation *anima muliebris corpore virili inclusa*, "a female soul trapped in a male body," although he applied the phrase to subject homoerotics, that is to say, homosexuals who identify with the opposite sex and play the corresponding role in relations with their own. *Gender dysphoria syndrome* is a broader concept that may include homosexuality and transvestism as well as transsexualism.

From the early 1950s until recently, individuals with gender dysphoria were often guided toward transsexualizing operations in which their sex was surgically "corrected." After recovery from surgery they were resocialized and legally reassigned to the desired gender. Lothstein (1982) estimated that there are 30,000 transsexuals in the entire world, of whom 10,000 are believed to reside in the United States. Male-to-female transsexuals outnumber female-to-male ones by at least four and perhaps eight to one, perhaps suggesting a psychological origin of the problem. While such operations seemed to alleviate the gender dysphoria of the subject, follow-up studies have shown that in many cases drastic medical intervention is not the answer, and in fact approximately two-thirds of those classified as transsexuals have not undergone surgery, but are nonetheless living as members of the other gender on a full-time basis. They have assumed the role of the other gender in mannerisms and appearance in all their varied social functions and are, presumably, passing in the eyes of the rest of society as apparent members of that sex.

Although the contradiction between transsexualism and anatomy suggests to some that the condition is pathological, the real problem lies in society's dichotomization of masculine and feminine forms of behavior—in its belief that because there are only two sexes, there can be only two **genders**. The transsexual has commonly heard about sex reassignment before approaching the medical counselor and knows the questions and the "correct" answers even before they are formally posed. In other words, the individual seeking treatment has made a self-diagnosis and is simply asking the doctor as a surgical technician to perform the necessary treatment. Of historical interest is the fact that the Roman Emperor **Heliogabalus** (218–222) offered the physicians of his time great rewards if they could effect a transsexualizing operation on his person, but the task exceeded the powers of Greco-Roman medical science.

Individuals with acute gender dysphoria exhibit a great range of personality types, with a resulting legal paradox: If the subject passionately craves the surgery, he or she may be labeled insane and denied the wish, yet if the subject moderately desires the surgery, he or she is pronounced competent and granted the wish. Transsexuals tend to fall into three major clusters: (1) individuals reporting a lifelong contradiction between their core-morphologic sexual identity and their anatomy and an absence of effective socialization and sexual arousal in the role appropriate to their anatomy ("true transsexuals"); (2) males who have vacillated in their sexual identity or been ambivalent in their sexual identity since childhood, and who have experienced genital arousal in connection with cross-dressing ("transvestitic transsexuals"); (3) individuals experiencing no contradiction between their core-morphologic identity and their anatomy who have had extensive sexual activity with members of their own sex ("feminine-male and masculine-female homosexual transsexuals").

Even if transsexuals depend upon the most modern surgical and biochemical techniques for the realization of their hopes, it is improbable that the phenomenon of gender dysphoria exists solely because of medical progress or that conflicts in gender identity and gender role lack historical and anthropological precedents and parallels. Non-Western cultures offer examples of alternate gender statuses in which the individual assumes, by personal choice or by inner compulsion, the role of the other gender; the best known of these is the **berdache**. Ethnographers are still to some extent perplexed by these phenomena and their intricate psychological relationship to what modern Western society labels homosexuality. Hence the psychiatric evaluation of gender dysphoria must take account of the motives for alternate gender statuses in other cultures—which, however, may be the specific cultural mode of resolving or at least neutralizing a pathological identity crisis. In other words, gender dysphoria may express a dissatisfaction with the way in which a particular culture has defined and allocated sex roles rather than a fundamental genetic disharmony within the subject. Transsexuals are reacting to their own interpretation of the cultural meanings inherent in the concept of gender; they are seeking to resolve the conflict between gender identity and the socially prescribed role for the appropriate gender. What is obvious to the individual with gender dysphoria is that his or her identity falls on the other side of even the most tolerant line of demarcation between the sexes. **Counseling** and therapy with such patients may aid them to resolve their conflicts in a manner less damaging to their biological selves, to accept the feminine or masculine component of their personality as no longer ego-alien even if they retain the genitalia of the sex into which they were born.

BIBLIOGRAPHY. David E. Grimm, "Toward a Theory of Gender: Transsexualism, Gender, Sexuality, and Relationships," *American Behavioral Scientist*, 31 (1987), 66–85; Leslie Martin Lothstein, *Female-to-Male Transsexualism: Historical, Clinical and Theoretical Issues*, Boston: Routledge & Kegan Paul, 1983; John Money, *Venuses Penuses*, Buffalo, NY: Prometheus Books, 1986.

Warren Johansson

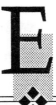

EASTERN ROMAN EMPIRE
See **Byzantine Empire.**

ECONOMICS

Economics is the systematic study of the production, distribution, and consumption of goods and services. The term may also refer to the activity itself, apart from the study of it. Non-procreative sexual behavior has generally been assigned to the sphere of leisure activity—and therefore excluded from economics proper. But there are economic aspects of homosexuality, both as overt sexual activity and as a mode of sociosexual expression.

Assets and Liabilities of Homosexuality with Respect to the Employee. Although it is usually thought of as a disadvantage, there are professions in which homosexuality can be an asset. It is an asset when it responds to a covert norm (as in interior decorating, **dance**, etc.), or provides a password to the fraternity. In the past there were professions in which **celibacy** was the rule, so that they offered the homosexual an escape from the heterosexual marriage into which he would otherwise have been forced by family pressures and social convention. In other situations it is a liability that must be hidden throughout life, as disclosure would result in dismissal or disqualification, or else block promotion beyond the entry level. Of course such dangers may be exaggerated by misperception, and many who have "come out" on the job have experienced no repercussions. Nonetheless, there are professions in which an upwardly mobile individual is virtually obliged to be married, and the spouse has a prescribed set of auxiliary functions that cannot eas-ily be performed by an associate of the same sex, even if the two are living in a quasi-marital relationship. In these settings the homosexual is pressured to find an accommodation, contracting a marriage of convenience, sometimes even a "front" marriage with a lesbian.

In some jobs, discreet homosexuality can be helpful by fostering an inclination to travel unfettered by familial bonds. The absence of a wife and children (whose place of residence and schooling must be arranged while the husband serves a tour of duty abroad or in a hardship post) favors a flexibility that the heterosexual may not be able to match.

The mentor–protégé relationship can be the locus of a homosexual liaison which is all the more advantageous for the younger party, who instead of "marrying the boss's daughter" takes on the boss himself as lover and protector. In this way working-class youths may achieve upward mobility by learning not only the elements of a business that might otherwise be closed to them, but also middle-class etiquette and speech patterns.

Homosexuality can be an obstacle to advance in bureaucracies such as the government or the corporate hierarchy where the **lifestyle** of the lower ranks is carefully scrutinized and even subjected to secret surveillance. This situation places the homosexual at a disadvantage in state socialist regimes that allow little or no opportunity for private enterprise. In capitalist countries the freedom always exists to create one's own firm where no obligation to conceal one's sexual proclivities from one's superiors can arise. This capacity explains the profusion of small businesses with homosexual proprietors—

antique dealers, florist shops, men's clothing boutiques, restaurants, bookstores—where the owner can be free to express his sexual orientation without fear of retaliation. Also, in such small firms a protégé–lover can benefit from a mentor relationship in which he learns the tricks of the trade and the other skills required for branching out on his own. In small businesses where profit margins are low, the monetary advantage to the owner of not having a spouse and children who represent a fixed and even mounting responsibility as the years pass is likewise considerable.

In recent decades, with the relaxation of gender role stereotypes in fields traditionally reserved to men, lesbians have been able to move ahead in such fields as business and law where a certain aggressiveness can be enhanced by freedom from the demands of a husband or the duties associated with child-rearing. On the other hand, the absence of a wife as auxiliary may impose a handicap on the woman who undertakes a career in a profession where such a "support system" has both social and psychological value.

Hustling. Male **prostitution** is an economic activity in and of itself, though mainly limited to those between the ages of 15 and 30. It can be practiced as a supplement to modeling or acting, or can be a way of earning money while in college or graduate school, when other opportunities of making a living would require too much time and be less remunerative as well. Finally, it can be a way of making contact with men in the upper echelons of the business and professional world and moving into a mentor–protégé relationship that will serve as a springboard for a later career. Unlike the female prostitute, the hustler is not automatically disqualified from a long-term relationship.

Economic Theory. In the field of economics as a social science, it is noteworthy that both Adam Smith and John Maynard **Keynes** were childless. It may be that their separation from the world of procreation and inheritance gave them the detachment they required to view the economic process dispassionately and analytically, as someone enmeshed in the human reproductive cycle could not have done. Keynes himself was a member of the **Bloomsbury** circle in which overt homosexuality was accepted along with other unconventional tastes and lifestyles.

The problem of the reproduction of human capital—from the genetic, not the educational standpoint—has been neglected by investigators preoccupied with the issues of capital formation at the macro- and micro-economic levels. The model of ancient Greek society suggests that while heterosexual relationships produce the raw human capital in the form of new age-cohorts, homosexual liaisons may assume the function of refining that human capital by providing the educational and initiatory experience which readies it for adult life.

Businesses Directed to the Gay Community. The advent of the gay liberation **movement** fostered the emergence of a whole range of enterprises catering primarily or exclusively to the homosexual or lesbian client. These take the form of bars, restaurants, bookshops, and bathhouses that served as social gathering places and areas of recreation. In addition, travel agencies and guest houses have taken advantage of the greater discretionary income of the childless adult and also of the wanderlust that leads many homosexuals to distant places and exotic lands in search of new partners. There are also services that provide escorts or computer dating in a manner that parallels similar enterprises with a heterosexual clientele. A **press** aimed at the homosexual or lesbian reader has taken root, with news features and personal columns oriented specifically to the needs and interests of a readership that could find nothing comparable in the establishment media. Through their **advertising**—without which they could not survive—these newspapers have established a symbiotic relationship with gay businesses, in whose premises the papers are often distributed free. Clinics and counseling services have sprung up that address themselves specifically to the needs of gay and lesbian clients.

While gay radicals decry many of these commercial activities as mere mimicry of the capitalist norms of the larger society, the strength of the gay **community** may well lie more in the economic activities that it is able to support than in the political power which it is largely unable to wield because its members are so thinly dispersed over the territory of most self-governing political units. The *Gayellow Pages* for the USA and Canada and the *Spartacus Guide* now published in West Berlin furnish a fairly reliable annual index to this growing network of enterprises and services in many countries. Organizations of gay businessmen have been formed in a number of cities as well.

This web of commercial activity also explains the failure of a gay movement to arise in countries where state socialism precludes the creation of an economic power base, and where in turn there are no independent media in which group identity and solidarity could be cultivated. In the past enterprises catering to a gay clientele often fell under the control of the underworld because respectable businessmen wanted nothing to do with them and because of the need for protection from police harassment. With the lessening of the stigma, the economic development of the gay community is only a matter of time and of the prosperity of the nation in whose midst it resides. Moreover, the ability to convert economic power into political power may well be the key to the ultimate success of the movement for homosexual emancipation.

Warren Johansson

EDUCATION

Recent perspectives have focused on the place in our educational system of students and teachers who happen to be homosexual. Responding to the emergence of a broad-based gay and lesbian movement, some of these individuals have joined organizations for mutual support and defense against **discrimination**. There is, however, an older tradition that holds that homoerotic attraction itself has a significant place in the educational experience: the pedagogic eros.

Rationale. To understand the continuing role of same-sex patterns in education, it is useful to suspend, at least for the sake of argument, initial objections. In this light the rationale for a homoerotic component in education may be set forth in the following terms. The adolescent often has a homosexual phase of development that precedes the heterosexual one—a kind of "dry run" for the sexuality of adulthood that permits him or her to experience erotic stimulation and pleasure without incurring the danger of pregnancy. This homosexual phase may have as its object an adult who is not just the lover of the adolescent, but also a role model—appropriately of the same sex. A heterosexual liaison, apart from the unwanted reproductive aspect, would be discordant because the male youth can only mature into an adult man, the female into an adult woman.

If this reasoning is valid, the homosexual character of the initiatory process thus flows from biological and social constraints quite as logically as does the heterosexual character of the reproductive process. Every society has an objective need for the biological reproduction of its members—its **demographic** base—that far transcends the ephemeral attraction of a man and a woman for one another. In the same way it has an objective need for the reproduction of its traditions and values—its cultural base—that far transcends the ephemeral attraction of an adult and an adolescent of the same sex for each other. The shorter time-span of the pederastic attachment—conditioned as it is by biological stimuli—as compared with the heterosexual one is justified by its role in the service of the *eros paida-*

gogikos (the child-educating eros), which if successful must end in the maturing of the younger party and his or her emancipation from the transitory homoerotic and educational phase to enter the world of adulthood as a full-fledged member of society; while the heterosexual attachment serves the *eros paidopoios* (the child-begetting eros), which is followed by responsibility for rearing the children from infancy to adulthood. The two expressions of the sexual drive are thus complementary and non-antagonistic in character; they represent the evolutionary underpinning of the social relationships obligatory for the twofold continuity of the human community, the biological and the cultural.

That the Judeo-Christian tradition has defamed the homoerotic urge and driven it underground does not alter the evolutionary legacy which is intimately linked with man's survival as a time-binding animal—one that does not simply reproduce its kind as the consequence of an irrational compulsion to procreate, but also must in each generation recapitulate the acquisition of the cultural heritage which must be *learned*, as much by the genius as by the mediocre or even talentless student.

The effort to suppress the homosexual component of education is unlikely ever completely to succeed, no matter what the means employed or the amount of pain and sorrow inflicted on those who violate the taboo. If the above reasoning be true, an educational program cognizant of the findings of modern **psychology** would do well to accept this phenomenon as a potentially serviceable part of the process of learning. Yet even if modern opinion were able to discard its prejudices, rehabilitation of the pedagogic eros would still face obstacles. To be sure, many would concede that the teacher requires some special appreciation of his or her pupils to muster—year in, year out—the instructional fervor needed to overcome their natural recalcitrance to learning. Yet, with

the best will in the world, introduction of erotic bonds may conclude by retarding the process of maturation that for the student is the essential dynamic of the educational endeavor. While over the years the teacher has become accustomed to transfering his interest from one pupil cohort to another, the student—as a "first-timer"—may become fixated in the pattern of a relationship, which by its own character can only be transitory. It is also said that the pedagogic eros is asymmetrical, since the teacher is more powerful than the student. Yet many, perhaps most, human relationships are asymmetrical. This is true of education itself, whether one views it as a process of introjection— that is, the teacher helping the student progress by inspiration—or of elucidation, the Socratic midwifery whereby the teacher encourages the student to bring forth knowledge from inner resources.

Antiquity. The ancient Greeks were the first to practice and explore the full range of relations between homophilia and education. Although the origins of the institution of **pederasty** are lost in the mists of early Hellenic society, when it first emerges into view it is essentially initiatory, the paradigm being that of the older man who takes an adolescent under his wing to train him in military and manly virtues. In the course of time, and depending on the locality, this relationship became simplified into a merely erotic one. **Sappho**'s school on the island of Lesbos shows that in some communities of ancient **Greece** a parallel pedagogic-erotic tradition existed for women and girls.

In Athens in the fifth century, however, with its high regard for education in the modern sense, the initiatory process was retained and reshaped so as to focus no longer on purely military virtues but on education in the modern sense, including—for the most gifted—**philosophy**. It is this conception that is recorded in **Plato**'s dialogues. These writings also idealize a chaste kind of pederastic guidance in which the beauty of the boy is cherished, but physical expression of the admiration is resisted. Nonetheless, it seems clear that many pederastic teachers did not resist. The direction of Plato's Academy was itself conducted for several generations according to a succession from erastes to eromenos—lover to beloved—and these relationships do not seem all to have been without sexual expression. The heritage was taken up by the Stoic thinkers who recommended not so much total abstinence as moderation.

Eclipse of the Pedagogic Eros. The link between pedagogy and pederasty, which had become almost second nature to the Greeks, was not indigenous to the Romans; where it emerged among them it was thanks to philhellenism. It was **Christianity**, however, that finally severed the connection—or so it would seem. For by developing monasticism, by definition a same-sex community consisting of individuals of different ages, Christianity created a new set of temptations. The texts of the various Rules and **penitentials** contain instructions on how to avoid temptations. Nonetheless, it seems clear that in monasteries and nunneries there developed deeply rooted traditions of "particular friendships" that were passed on, in due course, to the same-sex elite schools of modern Europe.

The Italian **Renaissance** restored classical culture to a place of honor, and some thinkers, such as the Florentine Marsilio **Ficino**, began to advance cautious arguments in favor of restoring the link between pedagogy and eros. In the sixteenth century Camillo Scroffa wrote his *Cantici di Fidenzio* about the unrequited love of a Paduan pedant for his student, while in the *Alcibiade fanciullo a scola* (ca. 1652) Antonio Rocco set forth a bold plea for sexual enjoyment as the culmination of the student-teacher relationship.

Educational reformers of the eighteenth century recognized that segregating adolescents in same-sex schools created a hot-house climate for homosexual sentiments and actions, and in time these were replaced by the "healthier environment" of today's coeducational schools. The nineteenth-century English **public school** remained sex-segregated and, in conjunction with the reading of the Greek classics, led to the "higher homoeroticism" as found, for example, among the **Cambridge** Apostles.

The Twentieth Century. In the two decades preceding World War I, Central Europe was the scene of several important trends for social and sexual change. The youth movement known as the Wandervogelbewegung generated, as a byproduct, the book of Hans **Blüher**, *Die deutsche Wandervogelbewegung als erotisches Phänomen* (1912), a work that forthrightly defended erotic relationships between men and boys as a positive contribution to the consolidation of social bonds. More elitist was the contemporary Stefan **George** circle, which sought to recruit a small group of highly gifted young men, who were also notable for their good looks. Educational in the more narrow institutional sense was the Free School Community founded at Wickersdorf near Weimar in 1906 by Gustav **Wyneken** (1875–1964). Wyneken advocated a new version of Greek *paiderasteia* as an educational procedure for the initiation of privileged youth into art and culture. Unfortunately, Wyneken's experiment was shattered by a series of charges and countercharges in 1920.

It is significant that the free-school movement of the Anglo-Saxon world—as seen, for example, at the famous Summerhill in England—never dared permit any sexual component. And in the United States, the "life adjustment" trend, which was not to peak until the 1940s, was strictly an adjustment to the heterosexual norm. In the 1940s and 1950s American teachers and college professors whose homosexuality was exposed were subject to instant dismissal in mid-semester, even if there had been no overt sexuality with students. Academic freedom or no, any academic who dared to write about homosexuality had to assume a posture of stern disapproval, or else conceal his identity behind an impermeable pseudonym.

The Ferment of Change. Change was not to come until the 1960s when demographic and social trends, catalyzed by the growth of the **Counterculture** and opposition to the Vietnam War, caused a loosening of traditional attitudes. The new educational theories seemed to bring life into the placid—sometimes almost comatose—purlieus of educational theory. Yet this shakeup was less novel than it was assumed, going back to Jean-Jacques Rousseau's eighteenth-century critique of authoritarianism in education. A number of the 1960s reformers were themselves gay. The most notable of these was Paul **Goodman** (1911–1972) who, largely self-educated, sought to bring an **anarchist** perspective to the theory of education.

In 1966 Stephen Donaldson founded the first gay **student** organization on the campus of Columbia University in New York City. Despite much opposition on the part of administrations, similar organizations sprang up in hundreds of North American college campuses. Shortly therefter, but more cautiously, gay and lesbian teachers' associations, usually comprising those in the primary and secondary schools rather than college teachers, appeared in a number of localities.

In 1973 the Gay Academic Union (GAU) was formed in New York City to bring institutional change and foster the development of gay studies programs in academia. In keeping with the liberationist ideas of the time, GAU expected that many faculty members would "come out" by acknowledging their homosexuality, and that some of these would offer courses in gay and lesbian studies. Yet by the end of the eighties there were probably fewer than fifty openly gay and lesbian tenured professors in an American university system that boasted more than 2000 campuses. Moreover, these faculty members tend to be concentrated in schools of second rank rather than in the Ivy League and the great state universities. The caution of many established teachers, combined with a covert "tracking system" that tended to shunt overtly gay faculty to the sidelines, served to reduce the number of "out" teachers. The situation with gay studies has been even more discouraging. No coordinated programs, such as those for women's studies and black studies, took root, and there was even a dearth of individual courses. Much research and teaching has had to be organized in parallel, private institutions, such as Los Angeles's **ONE**, Inc. Finally, in the 1980s the emergence of a more conservative social climate and the **AIDS** crisis have caused gay and lesbian students, especially in secondary schools, to assume a lower profile.

In short, the bottle is half empty, but it is also half full. It is unlikely that there will be a return to the atmosphere of clandestinity and open contempt with which gay members of the college community had to contend in the 1950s. Many university administrations acknowledge the need to support gay and lesbian student organizations, and few are willing to tolerate antigay violence on campus. Gay studies courses may be scarce, but special campus events in what is often termed "gay pride week" offer informative lectures. Although faculty still find little encouragement in their efforts to expand teaching and research in this realm, an increasing number of serious scholars are writing and publishing on homosexuality in their own disciplines.

BIBLIOGRAPHY. Wayne R. Dynes, *Homosexuality: A Research Guide*, New York: Garland, 1987; J. Lee Lehman, ed., *Gays on Campus*, Washington, DC: National Students Association, 1975; Henri-Irenée Marrou, *A History of Education in Antiquity*, New York: New American Library, 1956.

Ward Houser

EDWARD II (1284–1327)

Plantagenet king of **England**. Born at Caernarvon, Edward was the first English Prince of Wales. Said by one fourteenth-century chronicler to have "particularly delighted in the vice of sodomy," Edward's open homosexuality was a contributing factor in his overall lack of success as king.

Following in the footsteps of Edward I, the "Hammer of the Scots," was no easy task, and it was one for which Edward II seems to have been singularly unfitted. From his youth he showed himself to be rather irresponsible; he was an habitual and extravagant gambler, and on one occasion he precipitated his own exile from his father's court by recklessly breaking into a park belonging to the bishop of Chester.

In order to provide the prince with a role model of courteous martial behavior, Edward I introduced a young Gascon, Piers Gaveston, into his son's court in 1300. Ironically, Gaveston was to become Edward II's lover and a focal point of the baronial discontent that was to last throughout his reign, culminating in the king's deposition and murder in 1327.

In the spring of 1307 Edward I exiled Gaveston in an effort to restrain his son's behavior, but within a few months the aged monarch was dead, and Edward of Caernarvon had ascended to the throne. Gaveston was immediately recalled and elevated to the peerage as Earl of Cornwall. Soon thereafter he married the king's niece, Margaret de Clare, sister of the Earl of Gloucester. This sort of lavish display of patronage was ultimately to be the undoing of both Gaveston and Edward.

Dissatisfaction with the king's rule—and Gaveston's influence—surfaced as early as January 1308 in a statement of baronial grievances known as the Boulogne Agreement, drafted at the wedding of Edward II to Isabella of France, daughter of Philip IV ("the Fair"). But this warning went largely unheeded.

Indeed, upon his return to England from his marriage in France, Edward his reported to have ignored the other magnates and run to Gaveston, hugging him repeatedly while smothering him with kisses. A similar, and even more public, scene was played by the two at the banquet following the coronation of Edward and Isabella. Gaveston, resplendent in royal purple trimmed with pearls—looking like the god Mars according to one contemporary—was the center of attention. Indeed, the fact that Edward spent more time on the favorite's couch than on that of the queen was taken as an insult not only to the English nobility, but to the French royal house, represented at the banquet by the queen's uncles Charles d'Orléans and Louis d'Evreux and her brother, the future Charles IV.

The ultimate result of the banquet was Gaveston's second exile in as many years and Edward's assent to the appointment of a body of reformers, the Lords Ordainers. Gaveston spent the year between June 1308 and June 1309 as king's lieutenant in Ireland, and Edward spent the year working to restore his favorite. He achieved this, perhaps at the expense of more urgent concerns such as Robert the Bruce's rising power in Scotland, but learned little in the process.

Within months baronial discontent had resurfaced yet again, perhaps hastened by Gaveston's scurrilous nicknames for his fellow earls. A third exile for Gaveston ensued, followed by another swift but ill-conceived return. This time the favorite was hunted down and executed by the barons. A particularly vivid image of Edward's attachment to his favorite is presented by the ruby found on Gaveston's person when he was taken by the barons; "la Cérise" was valued at the phenomenal sum of one thousand pounds in 1312!

Edward's relations with the barons did not improve after Gaveston's death, but the king was not linked with another individual favorite until the emergence of Hugh le Despenser the younger in around 1320. There is less evidence of a sexual relationship between them, yet one has generally been presumed. If we are to believe the chronicler Jean Froissart, following her successful coup in 1326, Isabella ordered that Despenser's genitals be cut off and burned before his eyes prior to his hanging.

As for Edward himself, the red-hot poker which is said to have ended his life has virtually become a symbol of his unfortunate reign. However, regardless of the exact nature of his death, it is incorrect, as has sometimes been suggested, to claim that Edward was deposed and murdered *because of* his homosexuality. His sexual behavior was used as a means of justification for events after his death, as part of what can only be called a propaganda campaign on behalf of Isabella and her paramour Roger Mortimer. Nevertheless, Edward II's example was subsequently held up as a pointed warning to later kings—homosexual and/or ineffective—and their favorites, not only in England, but in France as well.

BIBLIOGRAPHY. Natalie Fryde, *The Tyranny and Fall of Edward II, 1321–26*, Cambridge: Cambridge University Press, 1979; J. S. Hamilton, *Piers Gaveston, Earl of Cornwall, 1307–1312*, Detroit: Wayne State University Press, 1988; Hilda Johnstone, *Edward of Carnarvon, 1284–1307*, Manchester: Manchester University Press, 1946.

J. S. Hamilton

EFFEMINACY

Effeminacy is any of various forms of feminine or female-like behavior in a man. It tends to be disliked if not condemned in virtually every society—though, like other anxiety-arousing behavior, it can be the focus of wit and **humor**. In a few tribal societies where it is associated with **shamanism** it has been respected or feared.

By a kind of "opposites attract" reasoning, the effeminate man is generally assumed to want male partners in sex, and thus to be homosexual—a double error since effeminate men are sometimes notably heterosexual while, as the **Kinsey** research found, most homosexuality is not marked by effeminacy; in fact, a very considerable amount of same-sex behavior "is found among ranchmen, cattlemen, prospectors, lumbermen, . . . groups that are virile, physically active." (Kinsey et al., p. 457).

Similar and worse confusions have arisen in various descriptions of what effeminate behavior actually is. The psychoanalysts, noting certain exaggerations in effeminacy, have interpreted its gestures as take-offs or as caricatures of women or of femininity (Bieber). Less abusive interpretations have simply noted the similarities between effeminacy and femininity, usually concluding that female-like mannerisms in a man must originate from "identity" problems, such as a profound uncertainty about his maleness, or an overt identification with women, or with his "overclose" mother. The appeal of such insufficiency theories is remarkable. They are in line with popular notions of a homosexual's "impairment" and "inadequacy" but fly in the face of important contradictions—not only from Kinsey but from a few perceptive clinicians: almost forty years ago Karen Machover demonstrated that, far from being "sexually confused," effeminate males frequently have a sharper-than-average awareness of male/female differences, even when they identify more with women than with men.

But if effeminacy is not impaired maleness, if it does not spell male insufficiency, and is not necessarily homosexual, if it is not a fixation on one's mother, nor a caricature of women, then what *is* it and where *does* it come from? Exactly where it comes from is too hard a question. (Like trying to say precisely why one person is more aggressive, or fussy, or good-natured than another, the answer is invariably multifaceted—too scattered among a maze of social, genetic and physiologic biases to permit confident answers.) But accurate and useful descriptions can be given.

No matter which effeminacy is involved—nelly, swish, blasé, or camp—it is a set of mannerisms quite like equivalent movements and gestures seen in women. Nelly and blasé movements are similar enough to be virtually identical in femininity and effeminacy. But the gestures of swish and **camp** are clearly more forceful in effeminacy, probably due to the higher muscularity of males, thus inviting interpretations of their being "caricatures" of femininity. Similar gestures and high-animation movements seen in both women and effeminate men have been shown to come about in the same way, that is, they reflect particular attitudes toward just how, and how directly, to engage the environment. Just as a relatively aggressive, straight-line mode of affronting and engaging the environment is a hallmark of male movement, the rounded, relatively curvaceous movements of femininity pull away from so directly or aggressively engaging the environment.

For instance, when a man walks with a quick step but slightly pulls back from fully extending each stride, the result is a mincing gait—a set of movements that is decidedly softer, faster, and less brusk than is typical of men. Or, in various arm movements seen in swish and camp, a fast-moving outgoing gesture may at the last moment suddenly be pulled back or stopped from completing its path by the twist of a bent wrist, thus producing one of the high-speed, high-animation curves of swish, or one of the exaggerated stack-ups of emphasis seen in camp. The roundness of such moves is typical of femininity, while their energy and sharpness is decidedly male—the very combination that most characterizes the difference between femininity and effeminacy.

Thus it is not that effeminate movements copy or caricature feminine ones, but that both styles arrive at their curves and their relatively high animation from the same source: that is, the mental set of both femininity and effeminacy share the kinds of attitudes and the particular kinds of aggressive-readiness that cause them to select very similar styles of engaging the environment.

BIBLIOGRAPHY. Irving Bieber, et al., *Homosexuality: a Psychoanalytic Study of Male Homosexuals*, New York: Basic Books, 1962; Alfred C. Kinsey, et al., *Sexual Behavior in the Human Male*, Philadelphia: Saunders, 1948; Karen Machover, *Personality Projection in the Drawing of the Human Figure*, Springfield, IL: Charles C. Thomas, 1949; C. A. Tripp, *The Homosexual Matrix*, second ed., New York: New American Library, 1987.

C. A. Tripp

EFFEMINACY, HISTORICAL SEMANTICS OF

Containing as its core the Latin word *femina* ("woman"), the adjective *effeminate* has been used to mean womanish, unmanly—and by extension enervated, self-indulgent, narcissistic, voluptuous, delicate, and over-refined. Applied to sexual orientation it has had two opposed senses: (1) seeking the company of women and participating in their lifeways (heterosexual) and (2) adopting the woman's role (homosexual). In reading older texts it is important to bear these differences in mind, for the term effeminate can be used slightingly of a womanizer as well as of a "womanish" man.

Classical Antiquity. The ancient Greeks and Romans sharply differentiated the active male homosexual, the *paiderastes* (in the New Testament *arsenokoites*, literally "man-layer"), from the passive partner, the *cinaedus* or *pathicus* (New Testament Greek *malakos*; Hebrew, *rakha*). The Greeks also sometimes used the term *androgynos*, "man-woman," to stigmatize the passive homosexual. Beginning with the Old Attic comedies of **Aristophanes**, the passive is a stock figure of derision and contempt, the active partner far less so. Because of the military ideals on which ancient societies were founded, passivity and softness in the male were equated with cowardice and want of virility. A seeming exception is the god **Di-onysus**—whose effeminate characteristics are, however, probably an import from the non-Greek East.

In ancient **Rome** the terms *mollis* ("soft") and *effeminatus* acquired special connotations of **decadence** and enervating luxury. By contrast the word *virtus* meant manliness. The Roman satirists took sardonic delight in flagellating the vices of luxury that were rampant among the upper classes of a nation that, once rude and warlike, had succumbed to the temptations that followed its successful conquest and plunder of the entire ancient world. The classical notion of effeminacy as the result of luxury, idleness, and pampered self-indulgence is thus far removed from the claim of some gay liberationists today to kinship with the exploited and downtrodden. **Juvenal**'s Second Satire (ca. A.D. 100) ridicules several types of effeminate homosexuals: the judge attired in a filmy gown who hypocritically upbraids a female prostitute, the male transvestites who infiltrate a female secret society, and the degenerate scion of a venerable family who marries a horn-player in a lavish travesty of a wedding.

The Middle Ages. The old Icelandic literature stemming from medieval **Scandinavia** documents the condemnation of the *argr*, the cowardly, unwarlike effeminate (compare Modern German *arg*, "bad"). The Latin term *mollities* ("softness") entered early Christian and medieval writings, but often with reference to masturbation. It may be that the eighteenth-century English term *molly* for an effeminate homosexual is a reminiscence of Latin *mollis*.

Ordericus Vitalis, a historian chronicling the England of William Rufus (1087–1100), denounced "foul catamites" who "grew long and luxuriant locks like women, and loved to deck themselves in long, over-tight shirts and tunics." Writing about 1120, William of Malmesbury recalled these courtiers with their "flowing hair and extravagant dress. . . . [T]hen the model for young men was to rival women in delicacy of person, to mince their gate, to walk with loose gestures and half naked. Enervated and effeminate, they remained unwillingly what nature had made them; the assailers of others' chastity, prodigal of their own."

Modern Times. In the sixteenth century the French monarch **Henri III** assembled an entourage of favorites whose name *mignon* connotes effeminacy and delicacy. In French also the original meaning of *bardache* was the passive partner of the active *bougre*. English writings of the seventeenth and eighteenth century frequently denounced foppery, sometimes homosexual but more often heterosexual. Particular objects of scorn were the "Macaronis" of the 1770s, with their bright coats decked out with big bunches of ribbon, huge wigs, and betasseled walking sticks. In the view of Susan Shapiro such elegants attracted scorn because they were believed to threaten the very foundations of civilization. "They negate[d] the assumption that sex and gender identity are immutable, for their androgynous dress [was] constantly blurring, overlapping, and tampering with the supposedly fixed poles of masculinity and femininity."

Restoration times also witnessed the popularity of the self-referencing habit of male homosexuals adopting **women's names**: Mary, Mary-Anne, Molly, Nance or Nancy, and Nelly. The habit occurs in other languages as well—Janet in Flemish; Checca (from Francesca) in Italian; Maricón (from María) in Spanish; and Adelaida in Portuguese.

Nineteenth-century English witnessed a semantic shift of a number of terms originally applied to women to provide opprobrious designations of male homosexuals. Thus **gay** had the meaning of a loose woman, prostitute; **faggot**, a slatternly woman; and **queen** (or *quean*), a trollop. Even today the popular mind tends to the view that gay men seek to imitate women, or even become women; the considerable number of unstereotypical, masculine homosexuals are not taken into account.

The term "mannish woman" had some currency for lesbians in the 1920s. In general, however, such terms redolent of sex-role reversal do not have the same significance for men as for women. *Termagant* and *virago*, though pejorative, do not suggest variance of sexual orientation. The girl who is a tomboy has always been treated more indulgently than the boy who is a **sissy**. This difference between "womanly men" and "manly women" probably reflects the fact that our society clings to the notion that it is degrading for a man to be reduced to the status of a woman, while it is a step up for a women to be credited with the qualities of a man. In fact some studies of the "androgynous personality" suggest that even in today's changing social situation there is more practical advantage (in the business world and in politics) for a woman who "gets in touch with the other side of her personality" than a man who does so. Nonetheless, the men's movement has helped to break down some taboos, and men now feel less reluctance to cry or show strong affection.

Men who cross-dress as women are of two kinds. Some go to great lengths to make the simulation credible, an effort that may be a prelude to transsexualism. In other instances the simulation is imperfect, a kind of send-up. Although some feminists have interpreted such cross-dressing exercises as mockery of women, it is more likely that they signify a questioning of gender categories. In any event, **transvestism** is not normally held to lie within the province of effeminacy, which is thought to be the adjunction of feminine traits in a person otherwise fully recognizable as masculine.

BIBLIOGRAPHY. Hans Herter, "Effeminatus," *Reallexikon für Antike und Christentum*, 4 (1959), cols. 620–50; Susan Shapiro, "'Yon Plumed Dandeprat': Male 'Effeminacy' in English Satire and Criticism," *Review of English Studies*, new series, 39 (1988), 400–12.

Wayne R. Dynes

Ego-Dystonic Homosexuality

This neologism for a purported disorder was officially adopted by the American Psychiatric Association in the third edition of its widely respected *Diagnostic and Statistical Manual of Mental Disorders* (Washington, D.C., 1980). "The essential features are a desire to acquire or increase heterosexual arousal, so that heterosexual relationships can be initiated or maintained, and a sustained pattern of overt homosexual arousal that the individual explicitly states has been unwanted and a persistent source of stress." The *Manual* assures that the disorder does not refer to all homosexuals and lesbians: "This category is reserved for those homosexuals for whom changing sexual orientation is a persistent concern...." (302.00). Even though it has some history of previous use in psychiatry, the term "dystonic" seems inappropriate to denote a psychic state, as it can only meaningfully refer to the impaired tonicity of tissues or muscle. Following a custom that goes back to **Freud** himself, **psychiatry** has borrowed medical-physical terminology in order to simulate a precision that is not warranted. Another point that is made in the definition is that the condition must be self-certified to warrant treatment. In true mental illness one could scarcely say that the need for treatment does not exist simply because the patient denies it.

As these observations suggest, the quoted definition was the outcome of a compromise. It brought to a temporary end a struggle that had begun several years before, when homosexuals had invaded psychiatric meetings charging the practitioners with making the situation of homosexuals worse, rather than better, because their pronouncements gave a spurious rationalization to official and popular **homophobia**. These confrontations triggered a period of professional self-examination, leading to a 1973 Association vote against defining homosexuality as an illness, which seemed to clear the way for banishing the suspect category from the *Manual* altogether. Yet bitter reactions suggested that a majority of psychiatrists remained opposed to "normalizing" homosexual behavior. Their critics in turn alleged that client fees played a part in the opposition: if a whole category were to be deleted, a significant cohort of patients would disappear. However, this observation probably underestimates the deeply rooted character of American psychiatrists' opposition to homosexuality. A committee was formed under Robert Spitzer to decide the practical management of the problem. To the disgust of gay psychiatrists, the definition excerpted above found its way into the third edition of the *Manual*.

Although the following years seemed to effect little change in the attitudes of many psychiatrists, gay professionals both within and without the organization continued to lobby for deletion of 302.00. Somewhat to their own surprise, this was achieved during the first half of 1986, again through the work of a committee headed by Robert Spitzer. (Another section of the new version of the manual says, with seeming neutrality, that some may wish to change sexual orientation, so that this type of client need not entirely disappear.) While pleased at the outcome, those critical of psychiatry as currently established held that the protracted maneuverings had shown unmistakably the political and value-ridden character of the discipline. Nonetheless, the American Psychiatric Association is now far ahead of the World Health Organization, which retains the classification of homosexuality as an illness.

BIBLIOGRAPHY. Ronald Bayer, *Homosexuality and American Psychiatry: The Politics of Diagnosis*, new ed., Princeton: Princeton University Press, 1987.

Ward Houser

EGYPT, ANCIENT

Egyptians of dynastic times were inclined to regard with equanimity a wide variety of sexual practices. Traditionally the pharaohs married their half-sisters, a custom that other peoples considered curious. Self-confident in their cherished habits and customs, the Egyptians nonetheless cherished a distinct sense of privacy, which restrictred discussion of erotic themes in the documents that have come down to modern times. Most of our evidence stems from temples and tombs, where a full record of everyday life could scarcely be expected. Unfortunately, Egypt had no law codes comparable to those known from ancient **Mesopotamia**.

The realm of mythology provides several instances of homosexual behavior. In order to subordinate him, the god Seth attempted to sodomize his brother Horus, but the latter foiled him, and tricked Seth into ingesting some of his (Horus's) own semen. Seth then became pregnant. In another myth the ithyphallic god Min anally assaulted an enemy, who later gave birth to the god Thoth. Both these stories present involuntary receptive homosexuality as a humiliation, but the act itself is not condemned; in the latter incident the god of wisdom is born as a result. (In another myth the high god engenders offspring parthenogenetically by masturbation.) While it is sometimes claimed that the ancient Egyptians were accustomed to sodomize enemies after their defeat on the battlefield, the evidence is equivocal.

The "negative confessions" of the Book of the Dead contain a sentence that may be translated as "I have not had sexual relations with a boy." This precept should not be generalized, and may be a reference to a need for maintaining ritual purity in the temple precincts in which it is found.

In what is surely history's first homosexual short story, King Pepy II Neferkare (Phiops II; 2355–2261) makes nocturnal visits to have sex with his general Sisinne. This episode is significant as an instance of androphilia—sex between two adult men—rather than the pederasty that was dominant in the ancient world. From a slightly earlier period comes the Tomb of the Two Brothers at Thebes, which the excavators have explained as the joint sepulcher of two men, Niankhnum and Khnumhotep, who were lovers. Bas reliefs on the tomb walls show the owners embracing affectionately.

A dream book from a later period attests to the presence of male prostitutes of the ordinary kind; yet the institution of male temple prostitution, well established in Western Asia, seems to have been lacking. A woman's dream book contains two casual mentions of lesbian relations, which may have been common, though the evidence is scanty. Wall paintings frequently show women in "homosocial" postures of touching, grooming, and other nongenital expressions of affection. Queen Hatshepsut (reigned 1503–1482 B.C.) adopted male dress and even wore a false beard; these male attributes probably stem from her decision to reign alone, rather than from lesbianism.

A figure of particular interest is the pharaoh Akhenaten (Amenhotep IV; reigned ca. 1372–1354 B.C.), who was a religious and artistic reformer. Although this king begat several daughters with his wife, the famous Nefertiti, in art he is often shown as eunuch-like, with swollen hips and feminine breasts. According to some interpreters these somatic features reflect a glandular disorder. Other scholars believe that they are a deliberate artistic stylization, so that the appearance of androgyny may convey a universal concept of the office of kingship, uniting the male and the female so as to constitute an appropriate counterpart of the universal god Aten he introduced. Scenes of Akhenaten caressing his son-in-law Smenkhkare have been interpreted, doubtfully, as indicating a homosexual relation between the two.

Later Greek observers stressed the sexual exceptionalism of the Egyptians, especially the custom of brother-and-sister marriage. Some Egyptian figurines show a grotesque emphasis on the phallus, which was circumcised, while texts reveal an unusual inventiveness in devising hedonistic and medical enemas. In the area of homosexual behavior, however, our evidence does not suggest any radical departure from the broad Near Eastern pattern that homosexual relations might incur disapproval under certain conditions, but were not globally condemned. Most frequently they seem to have been simply aspects of daily life.

BIBLIOGRAPHY. Terence J. Deakin, "Evidence for Homosexuality in Ancient Egypt," International Journal of Greek Love, 1:1 (1961), 31–38; Lise Manniche, Sexual Life in Ancient Egypt, London: Kegan Paul International, 1987.
Wayne R. Dynes

ELIOT, THOMAS STEARNS (1888–1965)

Anglo-American poet and critic. Helped at first by his friend Ezra Pound, Eliot surpassed him in public esteem; during the last decades of his life, Eliot attained the position of a kind of aesthetic dictator of English and American literary standards. After his death his reputation fell somewhat, but he remains a formidable figure in the annals of literary modernism.

Raised in a St. Louis family of New England origin, Eliot received his major formation at Harvard and in postgraduate study in France, Germany, and Oxford, originally intending to become a teacher of philosophy. In 1910 in a rooming house in Paris he met a medical student, Jean Verdenal, who was to be his closest friend during his continental wanderings. A number of letters survive from Verdenal, though none of Eliot's to him; in one the Frenchman speaks of the "undefinable influence and emotional power" that two close people have over one another. Their mutual friend, the aesthete Matthew Stuart Prichard, was almost certainly homosexual. Although several Verdenal transcripts were published in the 1988 edition of the *Letters* by Eliot's widow, there are said to be others, which are perhaps franker. Eliot's first masterpiece, *The Waste Land* (1922), is dedicated to Verdenal, who was killed on military service not long after the start of World War I. For a long time critics viewed the poem as an impersonal commentary on the sorry state of Western civilization, but it is now known to derive from personal experience, especially Eliot's unhappy relations with his unstable first wife, Vivien. In view of this personal emphasis, the dedication to his deceased male friend may have been more telling than has usually been thought. In any event, the poem contains a homosexual reference, when a levantine merchant invites the narrator to a "weekend at the Metropole," that is, to a homosexual encounter.

Vehemently opposed in principle to any biography of him, Eliot succeeded in wrapping his inner self in a cloud of enigma. Ostensibly this reticence is grounded in his espousal of the doctrine of poetic impersonality. It may, however, have more personal roots. Eliot's first marriage with Vivien Haigh-Wood was undertaken quite suddenly in 1915, ostensibly on the rebound from an unrequited love for an American woman. There were no children, and Vivien spent much of the remainder of her life in mental homes. For many years Eliot shared bachelor quarters with another literary man, John Hayward. The "secret" of Eliot's personality, if such there be, may reside chiefly in his *fear* of being taken as homosexual, since he was not given to manly pursuits such as athletic sports and hunting and the profession of poetry itself tends to be regarded with suspicion in the English-speaking world. Time will tell whether this is the case, or whether there is something more that has been held back by the official guardians of Eliot's reputation.

BIBLIOGRAPHY. James E. Miller, Jr., *T.S. Eliot's Personal Wasteland*, University Park: Pennsylvania State University Press, 1977; John Peters, "A New Interpretation of The Waste Land," *Essays in Criticism*, 19 (1969), 140–75.

Ward Houser

ELLIS, HAVELOCK (1859–1939)

Pioneering British writer on sexual psychology. Descended from a family with many generations of seafarers, Henry Havelock Ellis was named after a distinguished soldier who was the hero of the Indian Mutiny. Early in life he sailed twice around the world and spent some years in Australia. In boarding school he had some unpleasant experiences suggesting a passive element in his character, and his attachments to women were often more friendships than erotic liaisons. At the age of 32 he married Edith Lees, a lesbian; after the first year of their marriage all sexual relations ceased, and both went on to a series of affairs with women. By nature an autodidact, Ellis obtained in 1889 only a licentiate in Medicine, Surgery, and Midwifery from the Society of Apothecaries—a somewhat inferior degree that always embarrassed him. More interested in his literary studies than in the practice of medicine, he nevertheless collected case histories mainly by correspondence, as his autobiography makes no mention of clinical practice.

One of his early correspondents was John Addington **Symonds**, who discussed with him the possibility of a book on sexual inversion, in which the case histories were the core and empirical foundation. Ellis recognized two conditions: "complete inversion" (= exclusive homosexuality) and "psychosexual hermaphroditism" (= bisexuality). In the midst of the writing Symonds died suddenly, and the book first appeared in German under the title *Das konträre Geschlechtsgefühl* ("Contrary Sexual Feeling"; 1896) with both names on the title page. In the atmosphere that prevailed after the disgrace of Oscar **Wilde** (May 1895), publication in England was problematic, but under doubtful auspices the English edition was released in November 1897.

Sexual Inversion was the first book in English to treat homosexuality as neither disease nor crime, and if he dismissed the current notion that it was a species of "degeneracy" (in the biological sense), he also maintained that it was inborn and unmodifiable—a view that he never renounced. His book, couched in simple language, urged public toleration for what was then regarded as unnatural and criminal to the highest degree. To a readership conditioned from childhood to regard homosexual behavior with disgust and abhorrence, the book was beyond the limits of comprehension, and a radical publisher and bookseller named George Bedborough was duly prosecuted for issuing "a certain lewd wicked bawdy scandalous and obscene libel"—Sexual Inversion. In his defense Ellis maintained that the work aimed at "remedial treatment"—a hypocritical line that was to be followed for many decades thereafter by defenders of the homosexual. The trial caused Ellis and his wife much anxiety, though it ended without a prison sentence for Bedborough.

The book was to appear in two later editions as the second volume of Ellis' Studies in the Psychology of Sex, which in its final format extended to seven volumes covering the whole of sexual science as it existed in the first three decades of the twentieth century. The most iconoclastic stance in the entire work remained the calm acceptance of homosexuality. Ellis never endorsed the explanations offered by Freud and the psychoanalytic school, so that the third edition of Sexual Inversion (1915), which was supplemented by material drawn from Magnus Hirschfeld's Die Homosexualität des Mannes und des Weibes, published a year earlier, presented essentially the standpoint of 1904. The next in radical character was the measured discussion of masturbation, which Victorian society had been taught to regard with virtual paranoia as the cause of numberless ills. The message of all his writings was that sex was a joy and a boon to mankind that should be embraced with ardor but also with knowledge. If many of the views expressed in his work are dated, the frame of mind in which the author approached his subject, tolerant and condoning rather than vindictive and condemnatory, served to move educated opinion in the English-speaking world in the direction of the reforms that were to be realized only in the wake of the Wolfenden Report of 1957.

Parallel with Magnus Hirschfeld in Germany, Ellis further distinguished transvestism from the homosexuality with which it had been confounded since Westphal's paper of 1869, except that he proposed the name "eonism," from the Chevalier d'Eon, a French nobleman of the eighteenth century who habitually dressed as a woman. Man and Woman, first published in 1894, continued to be revised down to 1927; it was a study of "secondary sexual characters," in contemporary terms the problems of gender, of women's rights, and of woman's place in modern society, again in a spirit of sympathy and toleration that has not lost its relevance to the issues debated at the close of the twentieth century.

In addition to his own insights and research, Havelock Ellis helped to diffuse the findings of continental scholars, making accessible to a broad audience—one that hitherto had been subjected to a literature meant to inspire shame and fear—a comprehensive body of knowledge of human sexuality. His enlightened approach to homosexuality marked the first step toward overcoming the Victorian morality that had shrouded the subject in ignorance and opprobrium.

BIBLIOGRAPHY. Phyllis Grosskurth, Havelock Ellis: A Biography, New York: Alfred A. Knopf, 1980.

Warren Johansson

EMPLOYMENT
See Discrimination; Economics.

ENCYCLOPEDIAS
See **Dictionaries and Encyclopedias**.

ENGLAND

The history of homosexual behavior in England between the eleventh and the twentieth centuries can be divided into two periods, the traditional and the modern, with the break occurring around 1700. The evidence for the earlier period is slender until the seventeenth century, but the evidence after 1700 eventually becomes overwhelming. The two periods are distinguishable by differences in the dominant mode of homosexual behavior. The behavior of men is always more easily documented than that of women, but roughly the same patterns can be found in both genders, even if the changes after 1700 were differently timed for men than for women.

Basic Features of the First Paradigm. Between 1100 and 1700 sexual relations between males were usually between an active man and a passive boy. The man was usually attracted to women as well, and it is an error to suppose that such men were *really* interested only in boys. The boys were valued for their feminine characteristics: slight bodies and smooth skin. They were often encouraged to dress in a way that was seen as effeminate.

Effeminacy could also be a characteristic of two kinds of adult males. There were, first, men who liked to take the passive role and were thought to be peculiarly corrupt for surrendering male dominance. They were consequently sometimes seen as **hermaphrodites** and confused with actual physical hermaphrodites. Some of the latter did go back and forth between genders, but they were held guilty of sodomy for doing so. There was, however, a second category of men accused of effeminacy: namely those who liked the sexual company of women so much that they were thought to have come under their power. **Sodomy** had a similar range of meaning: anal sex with women and with males, and genital sex with animals. And references to Sodom could be made simply to describe a general situation of rampant sexual irregularity.

This sexual behavior has to be seen as part of a general cultural system that emerged in the twelfth century and lasted until the seventeenth; there were only minor adjustments in the system after 1500 as a result of the **Renaissance** and the **Protestant** Reformation. This new western European culture produced its own pattern of family structures, sexual behavior, and gender roles. Aristocratic families adopted a patrilineal ideology. Marriage for men was late. Monogamy was enforced and divorce forbidden. Many in the general population never married, and priestly celibacy was promoted. Sexual relations outside of marriage were forbidden. But a regulated prostitution was tolerated for fear, as Thomas **Aquinas** said, that the world would otherwise be overrun with sodomy. Sodomy and all sexual acts which were not procreative were peculiarly sinful. But sexual acts between males nonetheless occurred. They can be documented in the royal court, in monasteries and colleges, and in the large cities like **London**, which were a part of this new world. But it is not until the seventeenth century that one can show the male peasant who had a wife and seduced the local boys.

The Medieval Development. At the end of the eleventh century the king, William Rufus, was accused of sexual irregularity, but only one writer claimed that his vices included relations with youths. Two years into the reign of his successor (1102), a church council did condemn sodomy. Anselm, the Archbishop of Canterbury, sought, however, to limit the effects of the condemnation, because many would not have known that sodomy was a grave crime. Henry's son, Prince William, was drowned in a shipwreck in 1120. This was blamed on the effeminacy and sodomy of his companions, but it is not clear what the relationship was between these two characteristics. Henry's great-grandson, **Richard I** (the Lion-Hearted), was of course a most brave and chivalrous knight, who was also observed to be passionately fond of the king of France, and who was frequently rebuked for his fondness for males. Archbishop Anselm promoted friendships between monks. Aelred of Rievaulx, another saintly abbot, also did so. It is clearer that his **friendships** were based on physical attraction, but he presumed that such relations would not be carnal, except perhaps among adolescents. The libertine Latin poems of the time which circulated in England and elsewhere always stated that the authors desired both boys and females and spoke of boy prostitutes in the towns. Richard of Devizes described these boys in late twelfth-century London—smooth-skinned, pretty and passive—and placed them among the rest of the city's low life: dancing girls, actors, beggars and magicians.

By the end of the thirteenth century the new culture of the twelfth had become a fully organized system of a kind in which most sexual activity was viewed as dangerous. The law codes now reflected this. In Edward I's reign a law was promulgated punishing with death sexual relations with Jews and with beasts, as well as between sodomites. Edward's successor, **Edward II**, was hounded by his enemies, in part because of his lovers. He was killed by having a red-hot poker thrust up his anus. But it is unclear whether many men were actually tried for sodomy, as they were in the contemporary Italian cities. At the end of the fifteenth century there was sodomy in London: one man publicly boasted that he had committed sodomy with another; and a married man was called "a woman" because he grabbed priests between their legs. But both of these involved sex between two adults. It may have been that relations of men with boys were not much noticed.

The Reformation and After. In the sixteenth and the seventeenth centu-

ries England went through the upheavals associated with the Reformation, but these do not seem to have made much difference for sodomy, except that a statute in Henry VIII's reign took jurisdiction over sodomy with "mankind or beast" away from the ecclesiastical courts. The common law courts interpreted the statute as condemning anal intercourse and bestiality, but not sexual relations between women.

In the seventeenth century, when the evidence grows more detailed, one can observe patterns of behavior rather similar to those of the twelfth century. The royal court had a bad reputation under **James I** and **William III** who had their male favorites, as well as wives, and in William's case, a mistress too. London had more sodomy cases than anywhere else in the country. There were boy prostitutes who, like the female ones, clustered around the theatres. A male libertine culture flourished in which men pursued women and youths. **Shakespeare** wrote his sonnets in part for a youth and in part for a woman. **Marlowe** said St. John was Jesus' boy. Lord Castlehaven watched his male servants have sex with his wife, and then had sex with them. Lord **Rochester** had wife, mistress, and page, all as sexual companions. And Captain Rigby and the other London beaux took to boys as safer when too many of the whores were infected. But it could all be dangerous: Castlehaven was executed and Rigby stood in the pillory.

In the colleges and the schools, there were fellows and masters who seduced their students. In the countryside, there were ordinary poor men who had a taste for sodomy. They were usually married. They might also be as interested in buggering the horse, or the cow, as the boy. If caught they might suffer death or public mockery. But the mockery was never on the ground that they were effeminate. They were wicked but manly. Only in the few cases of adult males who took the passive role with another man, was sodomy seen as leading to the upset of behavior proper to the two genders.

The Shift to a New Paradigm.
This system of some six hundred years
standing began to unravel in the 1690s and
in the first decade of the eighteenth century, as the culture of modern Western
society began to crystalize all over northwestern Europe, in the **Netherlands**, in
France, and in England. Like the previous
culture of the twelfth century, it produced
a distinctive familial, sexual, and gender
system. Marriage became romantic, companionate and universal, and divorce grew
more commonplace. Women and children
were in theory held equal to adult males,
but in practice the two genders were presumed to exist in separate spheres. Most
individuals were thought to desire only
the opposite gender. Adult males who
desired males were socialized to be sexually passive and effeminate, and were given
a status equivalent to those women who
became prostitutes. This new role for men
was established by 1750, but a comparable
change did not occur for women until just
before 1900.

The adult effeminate sodomite or
molly, as he was popularly called, can be
documented from the London sodomy
trials of the first thirty years of the eighteenth century. Such men met each other
in the parks, latrines, and streets, much as
prostitutes met their customers. They
consummated their acts either there or in
a public house or tavern. In these molly-
houses most men adopted feminine characteristics in speech and gesture, and took
women's names. Sometimes there were
balls when they dressed as women. A few
men seem to have spent most of their time
in female dress, and to have been referred
to entirely as she and her. There were raids
by the constables, and those found guilty
were either pilloried, fined and imprisoned, or executed if anal penetration could
be proven.

It now became much more dangerous for an adult man to make a pass at
an adolescent boy than it had been under
the previous system. Boys could now tolerate only with difficulty any suggestion

that they passed through a period of sexual
passivity. Some boys ran for the constable
if they were simply touched; others would
allow themselves to be treated and perhaps fellated but would resist a continued
relationship that might compromise them
with their peers. A few boys were identified as future sodomites by their effeminacy and their affectionate ways toward
males. These boys were sometimes sexually abused by men who would themselves
have denied that they were sodomites; and
sometimes they were seduced by a fellow
sodomite. But physical affection between
most men, such as kissing in greeting, was
given up as potentially compromising.
Male clothes were increasingly differentiated from women's in sobriety of color and
cut. Some trades like making women's
clothes were avoided because sodomites
practiced them. A thriving trade in the
blackmail of seemingly effeminate men
grew up. They paid under the threat that
the blackmailer would swear sodomy
against them. In some cases they were
actually sodomites.

The old **bisexual** libertine did not
entirely disappear. But it was now said
that they simply used marriage to screen
themselves from notoriety. In some cases
this was probably true. But **seafaring** men
who were isolated on ships at sea still
seduced the cabin-boys in the old way.
And when **prisons** at the end of the century
became segregated by gender, something
similar occurred. Consequently separate
wings for boys, adult men, and sodomites
were established in the London house of
correction.

In the countryside, however, and
perhaps also in parts of working-class life,
the old and the new systems coexisted into
the early twentieth century. The upper
classes accepted the new system. Aristocrats who were discovered to have transgressed against it were separated from their
wives and sometimes had to go live abroad,
especially in **Italy** where the old system
still prevailed. Lord **Byron**'s life in the
early nineteenth century when contrasted

with Lord **Rochester**'s in the late seventeenth perfectly shows the difference between the two systems of homosexual behavior: Rochester with wife, mistress, and boy, and his social position intact; Byron ostracized, separated from his wife, and guiltily indulging his taste for males only in Italy and Greece.

The Nineteenth and Twentieth Centuries. In early nineteenth-century England, more men were hanged for sodomy than in any other period, apparently. The new system was being enforced with a brutal relish. But after 1830 the hangings ceased, and in 1861 the death penalty was repealed. Throughout the century a thriving underground of male prostitution can be documented in London. There were as well mutual acts between persons of the same social class who had met in parks, latrines and pubs; many of these were effeminate to some degree, and a few of them were transvestite. Middle-class boys in public schools often had considerable homosexual experience, and there were networks of friends among adult men, the most famous of which was revealed when Oscar **Wilde** was accused by the father of his younger, effeminate lover. London's Anglo-Catholic churches also became noted as meeting places for homosexual men, confirming every stout-hearted Englishman's worst suspicions of the connections between popery and sodomy.

At the end of the nineteenth century two important changes occurred. A lesbian role for women began to emerge which paralleled the male role of the early eighteenth century. And there appeared a new way of talking about same-gender sexuality which did not use the language of the streets but the language of psychological deviance. Both trends can be placed in a line of development which led to the repeal of the laws against consensual homosexual acts in 1967, as well as to the development of a gay rights **movement** in the two decades after 1969.

Women, like men, had before 1700 been presumed to be as capable of desiring women, as of desiring men, though it was sinful to do so. They damaged their gender standing only if they dressed as males, married women, and used an artificial penis, as a few did. This was still the case in the 1750s. By the early nineteenth century, affectionate friendships between women were allowed and protected by the presumption of female asexuality. But in the late nineteenth century there appeared female couples, one of whom was masculine in dress and manner, and neither of whom desired men. It is still unclear, however, why this should not have occurred until that point.

At the same time, men like J. A. **Symonds** who were sodomites, and others like Havelock **Ellis** who were sympathetic, set out to explain what came to be called homosexuality. They treated it as a psychological condition that could be explained either biologically or by the dynamics of individual experience. They did not see it as a social role. By the 1950s, liberal opinion had learned to speak easily enough of the phenomenon that the **Wolfenden** Committee could be appointed and the law changed in 1967. But two generations of increasing self-consciousness on the part of gay men and lesbian women led them in the following decade to openly declare their sexual orientation and to demand a fuller social acceptability. In the 1980s the reaction to the appearance of the **AIDS** virus among gay men showed the continued existence of homophobia in the general population, and was partly used to justify repressive measures by the government and in the churches.

See also **Anglo-Saxons; London; Social Construction.**

BIBLIOGRAPHY. Derrick Sherwin Bailey, *Homosexuality and the Western Christian Tradition*, London: Longmans, Green, 1955; John Boswell, *Christianity, Social Intolerance and Homosexuality*, Chicago: University of Chicago Press, 1980; Alan Bray, *Homosexuality in Renaissance England*, London: Gay Men's Press, 1982; Louis Crompton, *Byron and Greek Love: Homophobia in*

19th-Century England, Berkeley:
University of California Press, 1985;
Lillian Faderman, *Surpassing the Love of
Men: Romantic Friendship and Love
between Women from the Renaissance
to the Present*, New York: William
Morrow, 1981; H. Montgomery Hyde,
*The Love that Dared Not Speak Its
Name: A Candid History of Homosexu-
ality in Britain*, Boston: Little, Brown,
1970; Randolph Trumbach, "London's
Sodomites: Homosexual Behavior and
Western Culture in the Eigtheenth
Century," *Journal of Social History*, 11
(1977), 1–33; idem, "Sodomitical
Assaults, Gender Role, and Sexual
Development in 18th-Century London,"
Pursuit of Sodomy, K. Gerard and G.
Hekma, eds., New York: Haworth Press,
1988; idem, "Gender and the Homosex-
ual Role: the 18th and the 19th Centu-
ries Compared," *Homosexuality, Which
Homosexuality*, T. van der Meer, et al.,
eds. (in press); idem, "The Birth of the
Queen: Sodomy and the Emergence of
Gender Equality in Modern Culture,"
*Hidden from History: Reclaiming the
Gay and Lesbian Past*, M. Duberman, M.
Vicinus, G. Chauncey, Jr., eds. (in press);
Martha Vicinus, "'They Wonder to
Which Sex I Belong': The Historical
Roots of the Modern Lesbian Identity,"
Homosexuality, Which Homosexuality,
T. van der Meer, et al., eds. (in press);
Jeffrey Weeks, *Sex, Politics and Society:
The Regulation of Sexuality Since 1800*,
London: Longman, 1981; idem, *Coming
Out: Homosexual Politics in Britain
from the Nineteenth Century to the
Present*, London: Quartet Books, 1977.

Randolph Trumbach

ENLIGHTENMENT

The Enlightenment thinkers—
the *philosophes*—who flourished in the
eighteenth century sought to give practical effect to the era's fundamental advances in knowledge. The trend represented both a prolongation and a departure
from the Age of Reason of the previous
century. Continuing to rely on the application of rationality as the solution to problems, the Enlightenment shifted attention
away from pure thought and natural science to ethics and human happiness. Firm
believers in progress and the value of
education, the philosophes were strongly
secularist, viewing established religion as
a major source of continuing human ills.
The movement's two heroes were Confu-
cius and **Socrates**, the humanistic philosophers of East and West. Because of its
commitment to human betterment, the
Enlightenment has been called the "Party
of Humanity."

Basic Problems. For many today
the word "Enlightenment" retains a halo
owing to the underlying metaphor of illu-
mination and also to its social optimism
and humanism. Moreover, films and other
modern popular presentations have spread
the idea that the eighteenth century was
an era of joyous and unrestrained sexual
hedonism. Before endorsing this view, it
should be remembered that this was the
period in which the great **masturbation**
scare began—the claim that physical
weaknesses of all kinds, leading to insanity and death, were the inevitable result of
this harmless practice. The hysteria began
with an anomymous English publication,
*Onania; or, the Heinous Sin of Self-Pollu-
tion, and all its Frightful Consequences in
both Sexes, Considered* (1707–08), continued in the Swiss Dr. Tissot's *L'Onanisme;
ou dissertation physique sur les maladies
produites par la masturbation* (1760), and
was even enshrined in the great French
Encyclopédie, the pantheon of the Enlightenment, under the article "Sodomie."

Rather than taking it at its own
evaluation and that of its latter-day admirers, one should examine the Enlightenment critically and historically, and distinguish the contingent and personal views
of individual thinkers from overarching
principles. Diderot and **Voltaire** harbored
some conventional anti-Jewish prejudices,
yet the overall thrust of their rhetoric
promoted the emancipation of European
Jewry. Also, Voltaire praised enlightened
despots, but furthered the recognition
of individual rights and of political
democracy.

Individual Thinkers. In a brief,
but suggestive passage Baron Montesquieu

(1689–1755), hereditary judge of the parlement of Bordeaux, puzzled: "It is curious that we recognize three crimes, magic, heresy, and the crime against nature [homosexuality], of which one can prove that the first does not exist, that the second lends itself to an infinite number of distinctions, interpretations, and limitations, and that the third is frequently obscure; all three are punished by burning." Same-sex conduct, of which Montesquieu disapproved, he saw as being fostered by social conditions (*The Spirit of the Laws*, XII, 6; 1748). Elsewhere he charged that Christian asceticism was Malthusian in its consequences, robbing the Roman Empire of manpower for its wars and causing its decline—thus implying that sexual activity should be procreative.

Famous for his comparison of the human body to a machine, the materialist philosopher Julien Geoffroy de La Mettrie (1709–1751) advocated hedonistic ethics with an emphasis on satisfaction, including sexual gratification.

Anticipating twentieth-century media, Voltaire (1694–1778) made clever use of the press to mobilize public opinion against injustices. In the Calas case of 1762, for example, he showed how a Protestant had been wrongly executed out of religious bigotry. Tireless in his indictments of the cruelty, arbitrariness, and irrationality of the French legal system of his day, Voltaire's voice was unfortunately raised only slightly in defense of sodomites, who were still being put to death. In the article on "Socratic Love" in his *Philosophical Dictionary* (1764), he makes it clear that although he personally found homosexuality repellent, it should be regarded as an aberrant taste, rather than a crime. He also gives historical instances of famous homosexuals, anticipating a device that homophile apologists were to use abundantly during the twentieth century.

The prolific Denis Diderot (1713–1784), co-editor of the great *Encyclopédie*, wrote on virtually every topic in human affairs. In a guarded, though for its time unusually frank, discussion of the limits of sexual expression, "The Conclusion of the Conversation between D'Alembert and Diderot" (1769), he states: "Nothing that exists can be either against nature or outside nature. I don't except even voluntary chastity and continence, which would be chief crimes against nature if one could sin against nature." Diderot anticipated twentieth-century sexologists in holding to the **hydraulic metaphor** of sexual energies, which demand an outlet. His animus against chastity is also linked to his hostility to the ascetic morality of Christianity, to which he gives full sway in his novel, *La Religieuse* (1760; not published until 1796). In this melodramatic work he presents a catalogue of anguish and horrors, not excluding lesbianism, which he deems the result of involuntary collective seclusion of women in convents. To berate Europe for its unnatural restrictions, Diderot's "Supplement to Bougainville's *Voyage*" (1772) uses the device of a South Sea island paradise of heterosexual satisfactions that combined, quoting Horace, the pleasurable with the useful, so that women who had passed the childbearing age were supposed to refuse coitus. In keeping with general eighteenth-century opinion, he disliked masturbation. His reasoning on sexual morality is Janus-like: while criticizing its asceticism, he retained the procreative bias of Christian thought in fostering a naturalistic sexual morality that set definite limits on nonconformity, and so created a secular rationalization of the religious argument that homosexuality is unnatural. In this way Diderot anticipated the "social materialist" homophobia of Communist nations today.

The Italian Marquis Cesare **Beccaria** (1738–1794) sought to apply a kind of Occam's razor to laws. In his view, draconian punishments, including those against sodomy, were not achieving their aim. He also proposed a sociogenic explanation of homosexuality, which he held was fostered by the one-sex populations of total institutions, such as boarding schools and prisons. The corollary was that undesirable behavior could be lessened by altering the design of human institutions. As this example shows, the Enlightenment was concerned not only with lifting the burden of inherited irrationality, but with proposing new devices of social control, ones which, by virtue of their good intentions, might be all the more oppressive. Thus the Enlightenment is the ancestor not only of modern liberalism but also of state socialism.

Evaluation. The *philosophes* forged powerful arguments to discomfit tyrants everywhere. Yet the passage of time has revealed some weakness in their thought: an overemphasis on reason itself, to the neglect of feelings and sentiments, which have often swayed humanity. To a large extent this onesidedness was corrected and superseded by the ensuing romantic approach begun by Jean-Jacques Rousseau. There was a vital survival, however, in the work of Jeremy **Bentham**, whose carefully considered theories of homosexual emancipation were regrettably not published in his lifetime.

In political philosophy rationalism has tended to yield to the seductions of *constructivism*, as F. A. Hayek has termed it. This is the tendency to assume that one can sweep away existing habits and preferences, and then create a new society by fiat according to a deductive idea of how humanity should be. In this heady vision, the old divinities depart—but society becomes the god. In this outcome, the tyranny of the majority is scarcely avoidable. Or contrariwise, in keeping with the doctrine of self-interest, the wishes of the individual become the only criterion. The farthest reaches of this second avenue were trodden by the most radical of the Enlightenment thinkers, the Marquis de **Sade**. Without fear of punishment in an afterlife and the restraining bonds of tradition, how can we be certain that human beings will not simply abandon themselves to a mael-

strom of self-indulgence? This question, which might be tiresome in a conventional moralist, gains force in Sade's novels, with their detailed visions of cruelty. Sade was the first great creator of a dystopia, a negative vision of society in which the trends of his day found their utmost logical extension.

The mainstream, or positive utopian aspect, of the Enlightenment held that human nature is, or ideally should be, uniform. Thus present diversities will yield to a new universalist ideal of humanity and of uniformly applicable principles of law. And the Enlightenment thinkers, while deists, did not deny the need for institutions as arbiters of morality—which in practice meant the ascetic morality which was to blight Victorian society with its exaltation of "the sacred marriage bond" and the social-purity movements which relegated homosexuals to the underworld of vice that was to be eradicated. Even if **Frederick II the Great**, Joseph II, and other enlightened despots abolished the death penalty for sodomy in the eighteenth century, the Code **Napoléon** did not keep the **Paris** police under the Third Republic from establishing a vice squad.

No organized movement for homosexual rights emerged during the Enlightenment; only at the end of the nineteenth century did the earlier trend toward freeing disadvantaged groups and empowering them finally reach the despised and outlawed homosexual community. Still, to the extent that its supporters can draw on the intellectual capital of the earlier trend, the struggle for gay rights counts as part of the "unfinished business of the Enlightenment." The appeal to knowledge as the ground of human freedom has deep resonance. Yet the empirical study of homosexuality owes little or nothing to the Enlightenment; it stems from nineteenth-century innovations in the fields of biology and psychiatry. This research is often of intrinsic value, but in and of itself it clearly has not accomplished the emancipation of homosexuals.

Human beings are only in part rational creatures, and lingering **myths and fabrications** have proved hard to eradicate from the popular mind. Sober reflection indicates that Enlightenment in the sense of education and the spread of knowledge must be fused with an effective political program that can secure recognition of the innate diversity of human beings as the bulwark of fundamental rights.

BIBLIOGRAPHY. Jacob Stockinger, "Homosexuality and the French Enlightenment," in G. Stambolian and E. Marks, eds., *Homosexualities and French Literarature*, Ithaca: Cornell University Press, 1979, pp. 161–85.
Wayne R. Dynes

ENRIQUE IV
See Juan II.

EPHEBOPHILIA
The word "ephebophilia" refers to an erotic attraction to maturing male **youth**, and as such stands in contrast to terms such as **androphilia** (love of one adult male for another), gerontophilia (love of the old), **pedophilia** (whether this term is restricted to love of prepubescent children or includes adolescents as well), and "puberphilia" (love of pubescents).

Terminology. The term ephebophilia seems to have been coined by Magnus **Hirschfeld** in his *Wesen der Liebe* (1906), where he applied it to sexually mature youths from puberty up to the age of 20; in his 1914 magnum opus, *Die Homosexualität des Mannes und des Weibes,* Hirschfeld specified the range of love objects as from "the beginning to the completion of maturity, so approximately ages 14–21." The German researcher estimated that 45 percent of all homosexuals were ephebophiles. For women, he used the term "parthenophiles."

The Greek word which Hirschfeld borrowed for his compound, *ephebos,* is of various meanings, used for one arrived at adolescence or manhood (at 16 to 18, depending on locality) or at the prime strength and vigor of youth. It seems, however, to have referred to the older youths, those with bearded faces who had outgrown the stage at which they were appropriate as the younger partners in **pederasty**, but not yet old enough to marry: the prime age for military service. The ancient Greek age of puberty was likely in the mid-teens rather than the younger ages typical of contemporary Western society.

In current usage, the term seems to have dropped the youngest segment of Hirschfeld's definition, those adolescents just emerging from puberty, and focused on the later years, 17–20. In many societies, this age group is treated as adults for **consent** purposes, drawing a strong legal and practical boundary between ephebophilia as currently used and the sexual attractions to younger ages. In other societies, ephebes are legally on a par with younger children, but in practice sexual activities with them are not as harshly repressed as with the younger group.

According to Hirschfeld, two ephebes in love with each other are both ephebophiles, but as attraction of same-aged persons is not of special intrinsic interest, this article will focus on adult ephebophilia.

Popularity of Ephebophilia. Most male **prostitutes** and models for homosexual **pornography** seem to be drawn from the ranks of ephebes, supporting Hirschfeld's observation that ephebophilia is a major component of adult homosexuality (in modern Western cultures).

Aesthetic considerations (which may well have biological roots related to the best ages for childbearing) under which in most cultures males prize youthfulness in their sexual partners, whether male or female, play a role in this attraction, but other factors are also significant.

Sex researcher Alfred **Kinsey**'s 1948 finding that the statistically average white American male reaches his peak sexual activity (measured in orgasms per week) at the age of 17 points to the widely held belief that ephebes are the most sexually energetic male population group.

Seventeen also appears to be the age at which the average male attains his fully mature erect penile length. This fact, together with other observations, suggests that ephebophiles may be more interested in the late teenager's fully developed and highly energetic *maleness*, in contrast to pedophiles (here understood as those attracted to younger boys) who seem to be interested in more androgynous or even feminine features (hairlessness, smaller stature, lack of muscular development) and for many if not most of whom the greater sexual interest is in the boy's passive/receptive capabilities. In the classical Greek model of pederasty, the boy's penis played no role.

The combination of heightened sexual energy with a lack of heterosexual outlets (owing to marriage ages in the twenties and restrictions on pre-marital opportunities) and low incomes (characteristic of males still in school, military service, or just beginning to acquire work experience) has in many societies made heterosexual ephebes more available for **trade** (one-sided) relationships with homosexuals than any other group of heterosexual males.

For many ephebophiles, the naïveté of ephebes is a source of attraction, their enthusiasm for new experiences (including sexual and romantic involvements) contrasted with what is perceived to be the more jaded and sceptical attitudes of other adults.

Psychology of Ephebophilia. Almost nothing of an academic nature has been written about ephebophilia from a psychological perspective. Dr. John Money, who distinguishes the ephebophile from the pedophile, claimed, in his introduction to Theo Sandfort's *Boys on Their Contacts with Men* (New York, 1987), that "the true ephebophile has an adolescent erotosexual status and is attracted toward, and attractive to teenagers." This idea seems to harken back to the **Freudian**

concepts of arrested development which at one time were supposed to explain adult homosexuality. Certainly, there are ephebophiles who feel most comfortable in the company of ephebes and share many if not most of their tastes, attitudes, and interests. Yet many adults who are sexually attracted to ephebes, and would chose them as prostitutes, pornographic models, or occasional companions, nevertheless do not feel drawn to the social, psychological, or cultural aspects of late adolescence; they do not identify with the adolescent nor with adolescent characteristics in themselves, and hence display no interest in deep personal relationships with ephebes. Presumably, Money would not consider these men "true" ephebophiles.

Ephebophilia is quite striking in **prisons and jails**, but there the ephebes, being the youngest people present, are prized by heterosexuals as being less "masculine" than adults, and the psychological dynamics of it are quite different from homosexual ephebophilia.

History. The historical development of ephebophilia has yet to be written. The ancient Greeks acknowledged this trait with the term *philephebos* (fond of young men) and *philoboupais* (one who is fond of over-matured boys, "bull-boys" or "husky young men"), but generally slighted it in favor of the pederastic preference. Nevertheless, the athletic games of which the Greeks were so fond featured nude ephebes, the size of whose members received public acclaim, and the victors basked in adulation; **Pindar** wrote odes to them. (Contemporary **athletics**, especially at the high school and college levels, still display widespread, if sublimated, ephebophilia on the part of their adult male fans.)

The ancient Romans seem to have drawn a distinction between ephebic prostitutes, who were sexually passive, and those in their twenties (*cinaedi*), who were sexually active. By the time of the Renaissance, the ephebic ideal as seen in **Michelangelo's** classic statue of David

(1503–4) had gained wide currency. In contrast, there seems to be little evidence of ephebophilia in the literary tradition of the Islamic countries.

By the mid-nineteenth century, in America Walt **Whitman** was composing erotic poems of clearly ephebophilic nature, followed by John Addington **Symonds** with his attraction to strapping young Swiss peasants and robust gondoliers, while in England the ephebic soldiers of the Guards were prized sexual partners.

Examples of ephebophilia in literature include Herman **Melville**'s *Billy Budd* and Christopher **Isherwood**'s autobiographical works, in politics the British imperialist Cecil Rhodes, in art Marsden **Hartley**, in film *Maurice*, in popular music Pete Townsend of The Who ("Rough Boys"), in photography Bruce Weber.

Conclusion. In the twentieth century, the dominance of the androphile model of male homosexuality has tended to subsume, appropriate, and obscure the ephebophile current, and to consider it as a mode of adult–adult relationships rather than as a distinctive type of preference. As it becomes clearer to the research community, however, that the umbrella of homosexuality (and indeed, of sexuality itself) covers a wide variety of behaviors rather than a unitary phenomenon, it can be hoped that further investigation of ephebophilia will result.

Stephen Donaldson

EPICUREANISM

Knowledge of Epicureanism, the classical rival of **Stoicism**, is fragmentary because Christians, disliking its atheistic materialism, belief in the accidental existence of the cosmos, and ethical libertarianism, either failed to copy or actually destroyed the detested works. Of all the numerous works composed in antiquity, only Lucretius' philosophical poem *De rerum natura* survives intact. Diogenes Laertius reported that Epicurus wrote more than anyone else, including 37 books *On Nature.* A typical maxim: "We see that pleasure is the beginning and end of living happily."

Epicurus (341–270 B.C.), the founder of the school, served as an ephebe in Athens at 18 and then studied at the Academy, a fellow classmate of Menander, when Aristotle was absent in Chalcis. Having taught abroad, where he combatted the atomist philosophy of Democritus, he returned to Athens and bought his house with a garden in 307/6. There he taught until his death, allowing women and slaves to participate in his lessons—to the shock of traditionalists. Only a few lines of his works survive. Apparently he likened sexual object choice, whether of women or boys, to food preferences—a parallel that often recurred in later times. His beloved Metrodorus predeceased him.

The Epicurean school, consisting of scholars who secluded themselves from society in Epicurus' garden, lived modestly or even austerely. Stoics, however, libeled the secretive Epicureans because of their professed hedonism, accusing them of profligacy of every kind despite the fact that Epicurus felt that pleasure could be attained only in restraint of some pursuits that in the long run bring more pain than the temporary pleasure they seem to offer. Natural pleasures are easily satisfied, others being unnecessary. The ideal was freedom from destiny by satisfying desire and avoiding the pain of desires too difficult or impossible to satisfy. By freeing man from fear of gods and an afterlife and by teaching him to avoid competition in politics and business it liberates him from emotional turmoil. Friendship was extremely important to Epicureans.

Like its rival Stoicism, Epicureanism along with many other Greek tastes became popular in the late Roman Republic. Lucretius (ca. 94–55 B.C.) seems not to have added any ideas to those taught by Epicurus himself. But others, like the fabulously rich general Lucullus, whose banquets became proverbial, excused their gross sensuality by references to Epicurus' maxims. Julius **Caesar** proclaimed himself an Epicurean. Under the Empire Stoicism vanquished its rival and vied with Christianity, which when triumphant anathematized Epicureanism.

The text of Lucretius survived into the **Renaissance** and was disseminated in printed editions that naturally provoked intense controversy, since the author's materialism and polemics against religion called forth unmeasured attacks and subtle defenses. The author became the favorite of a small coterie of materialists, of the libertines in the seventeenth century, then of the **Enlightenment** thinkers, and finally of the Soviet Communists, who naturally ranked Epicurus above Plato as the greatest philosopher of antiquity. The rehabilitation of Epicurus was the achievement of Pierre Gassendi (1592–1655), a priest of unimpeachable orthodoxy. Acquainted with most of the leading intellectuals of his time, though not himself a great scientist or a great philosopher, Gassendi exerted enormous influence on both Newton and Leibniz.

For others Epicureanism was a respectable philosophical cloak for mocking impiety or lighthearted sensuality. The intelligent courtesan and leader of fashion Ninon de l'Enclos was of this stamp, while Molière and Cyrano de Bergerac admired Epicurus and Lucretius for their candor, their courage, and their sensible view of life. The Epicurean outlook, accepting sensual pleasure as a good and not as the necessary evil which an ascetic morality would barely allow, opened the way to a more tolerant attitude toward the forbidden forms of sexual expression that is implicit in the work of such philosophes as La Mettrie and of legal reformers such as **Beccaria**, not to speak of the Marquis de **Sade**. So Epicurus contributed to the **Enlightenment** trend toward abolition of the repressive attitudes and laws with which Christianity had burdened all forms of nonprocreative gratification.

See also **Libertinism.**

BIBLIOGRAPHY. Philip Mitsis, *Epicurus' Ethical Theory: The Pleasures of Invulnerability*, Ithaca, NY: Cornell University Press, 1989.

William A. Percy

EPISCOPALIANISM
See **Anglicanism; Protestantism.**

ESPIONAGE

In our society the role of espionage operative is one that has certain affinities with homosexuality. Because the homosexual is forced from his mid-teens— from the moment of self-discovery—to lead a double life, the normal boundaries between candor and deception, between loyalty and disloyalty, between self-concealment and self-revelation may be effaced so that a morally ambiguous existence becomes second nature. Unless he has "come out of the **closet,**" the homosexual is compelled to deceive others as to his real intents and motives in the most private sphere of his life, and he can with relative ease transfer this art of duplicity to his professional activity. The self-discipline that comes from learning not to reveal a secret but to live with it for years on end is also an asset of homosexual character that lends itself to a career in espionage. Then, too, the homosexual, typically unmarried, is free of the usual family ties— the "hostages to fortune"—that make the heterosexual loath to leave his home for prolonged service "in the field," often under the assumed identity that is crucial to his intelligence-gathering role. That is why the successful homosexual is sometimes also the best actor, diplomat, undercover agent, and spy; indeed this very skill in maintaining a façade that convinces the outside world of his "normality" was cited by psychiatric authors of the 1890s as a proof that homosexuality could not be a disease, since the mentally ill are totally unable to orient their behavior with such constant finesse.

Moreover, the homosexual may also harbor a grudge against the society that oppresses him and in rare cases feel justified in harming it as an act of retribution, so that betrayal becomes revenge for past wrongs. John Costello has argued that this motive was important for Anthony Blunt. That he is in certain respects an eternal outsider can deprive him of the final motive for identifying with the governing forces of the society in which he lives. And his involvement in a clandestine network that flourishes in spite of society's prohibitions and sanctions makes him part of a counterculture that can create its own loyalties and direct its own channels of information and influence.

A further consideration is that the sexual activity of the homosexual exposes him to pressure and blackmail if it becomes known to interested third parties. Magnus **Hirschfeld** and his supporters made this a prime argument for repealing **Paragraph 175** of the Penal Code of Germany, but the echo of their propaganda boomeranged when, during the 1950s **McCarthyism**, homosexuals were branded as security risks by the United States Government and dismissed from positions even in areas that had nothing to do with military or diplomatic functions.

The earliest instance of a homosexual's using his contacts for espionage purposes that became publicly known was that of the First Secretary of the French Legation in Berlin, Raymond Lecomte, who infiltrated the circle around Prince Philipp von **Eulenburg** and revealed to the Quai d'Orsay that Germany was bluffing in the first Morocco crisis (January–April 1906). This episode provoked open charges against Eulenburg on the part of the journalist Maximilian Harden, leading to the trial and disgrace of the Kaiser's intimate friend. Then in 1913 the Austrian authorities discovered that Alfred **Redl**, the homosexual head of the military intelligence service of the Dual Monarchy, had been acting as a double agent on behalf of Russian officials who had taken advantage of his

need for money. A contrasting case is that of the celebrated [T. E.] **Lawrence** of Arabia, who functioned on his own country's behalf in reconnaissance and subversion in the Ottoman Empire before and during World War I.

More recently, in the era of the cold war the case of two British diplomats, Guy Burgess and Donald Maclean, was paraded before the public to demonstrate that homosexuality was tantamount to sympathy for communism and proclivity for treason. The art historian Anthony Blunt was also implicated, but his part in the affair did not come to light until many years later, when he was stripped of his knighthood. It was subsequently claimed that Blunt was the ringleader, using his knowledge of the sexual proclivities of the British establishment for blackmail to advance his work for the Soviet cause.

In February 1950, Senator Joseph R. McCarthy of Wisconsin made "sex perverts in government" an issue with which to attack the Truman Administration, and a Senate subcommittee of 4 Democrats and 3 Republicans upheld his charges—even though the only case which it could cite was that of Redl in 1913—after another investigation had accused him of perpetrating a "fraud and a hoax" on the Senate by using unimportant and public information as the basis for groundless assertions, mainly that some Federal employees had been members of the Communist Party. (*See* **McCarthyism**.)

For two decades a policy of excluding homosexuals from "sensitive" positions prevailed in official circles in the United States and its allies, and it is only recently that the public position of the State Department and other administrative agencies has begun to change. Behind the scenes, however, the reality was probably little different from what it has been in the past, simply because the heterosexual cannot always acquire the art of duplicity which the homosexual must often master as a condition of survival in an unyieldingly hostile environment. The politically compromising nature of successful espionage—and the fact that records of such operations belong to a nation's most secret and inaccessible files—will keep the full truth from being known for decades if not generations. Only the breakdown of society's taboos could genuinely alter the situation—and perhaps deprive a few homosexuals of the motive for mastering an exceedingly dangerous but sometimes psychologically and financially rewarding profession.

BIBLIOGRAPHY. John Costello, *Mask of Treachery*, New York: William Morrow, 1988; Georg Markus, *Der Fall Redl*, Vienna: Amalthea, 1984; Barrie Penrose and Simon Freeman, *Conspiracy of Silence: The Secret Life of Anthony Blunt*, New York: Farrar, Straus & Giroux, 1987.

Warren Johansson

ETHICS

Ethics may be defined as a body of moral principles which are capable of application to human conduct. The term also designates the branch of **philosophy** that studies such principles.

In recent times the general ethical upheaval in Western civilization occasioned by the decline of **Christianity** and the rise of relativism has substantially eroded the earlier consensus on ethical norms. The resulting pluralism and openness has had a leveling effect, making it possible for such formerly marginalized groups as homosexuals to have their concerns addressed on the same plane of seriousness as the mainstream. Nonetheless, the lingering sense of guilt that afflicts some gay men and lesbians may foster a gnawing sense that they are somehow deficient in ethical responsibility.

It is a notable fact that homosexuals, a stigmatized minority, nonetheless remain basically law abiding and respectful of the rights of others. They scarcely live in the profligate state of "unconditional self-surrender to the immoral" that is the caricature of the hostile ignoramus.

Ethical Dilemmas of Homosexuals. Few ethical questions are pertinent to homosexuals alone, but several need to be considered as they are of frequent occurrence in daily life.

Older analyses of the matter contain discussions about whether it is right to engage in homosexual activity at all. Those who take this position almost invariably base their arguments on some particular tradition of religious rigorism or **asceticism**. In the sense that human sex organs make the behavior possible, homosexuality is not unnatural; nor is it per se injurious. It is a reasonable assumption, in view of the collapse of the earlier consensus rooted in Judeo-Christian precepts, that the censorious view that homosexual acts are in and of themselves unethical will continue to recede in prominence and plausibility.

But once this negative and antihumanistic approach is discarded, other concerns arise. For the practicing homosexual or lesbian, maintenance of the **closet**—the age-old habit of hiding heterodox sexual preferences—poses a challenge. Should one refrain from **coming out** to one's parents in order to spare them stress, or will they benefit from the disclosure in the long run? Should an individual refuse to take his lover on a holiday visit to his parents in order to save them emotional turmoil? Is the obligation to live a truthful life higher than the duty to avoid causing others distress? Should one reveal one's sexual identity to blatant homophobes, or to personal enemies who may use the fact to one's patent disadvantage? To what extent is it ethical to "pass" at all? In the heyday of gay **liberation** in the 1970s it was often maintained that every gay person's obligation is to come out. However, there is general agreement that coming out remains in the last analysis a personal decision; it is wrong to reveal someone else's homosexuality without his or her consent (this reservation is sometimes termed "closet rights").

Then there are issues of fairness to sexual partners. Some commentators grounded in conservative religious traditions hold that sexual conduct is only permissible with a partner to whom one has pledged lifelong fidelity. Such a conclusion is for the most part binding only within the context of a larger commitment to a religious tradition. Setting this restriction aside, other questions crowd in. Given the sexual pluralism to which many gay men are accustomed, are they not especially prone to sexual **objectification**? Is such objectification necessarily immoral in and of itself? What about "cheating" on partners? If one has been engaging in "extramarital" sex, what precautions must one take to protect one's regular partner from possible exposure to venereal disease? In practice questions of this kind can often be resolved by frank discussion with the partner, or in some settings by an implicit mutual agreement. Thus if two men meet at a gay **bathhouse** each can assume that the other has no reservations about sexual objectification.

It is difficult to say whether one should attempt to formulate a broader code of morality for homosexuals. Even this structure would probably be best accommodated in the larger framework of the values of the society. For example, in traditional **China** it was believed that each individual has a duty to his ancestors to produce offspring. The toleration of homosexuality that existed there reflected the fact that this precept was generally honored. Thus in China a homosexual ethic might include a concession to spending at least part of one's life in heterosexual marriage, a concession that Western homosexuals feel no obligation to make.

University courses in ethics rarely consider homosexuals and their distinctive problems, and extrapolations may be difficult. Further, homosexual writers and organizations—apart from religious groups—tend to neglect this realm. Even psychological questionnaire studies on truthfulness and honesty pose queries that make virtually every homosexual seem to be living in a world of duplicity and moral unreliability. Fusing with existing prejudice, this outcome has lead some hostile observers of the gay lifestyle to the mistaken conclusion that the homosexual is trapped in a maze of concealment and deception that makes him a dubious confidant or employee.

This neglect of ethics on the part of gay organizations is in part a legacy of the ignorance of earlier decades followed by the "anything goes" mentality of the 1960s, but it may reflect a deeper sense that morality is a matter of personal privacy and judgment, or of justifiable diplomacy in private life. Admirable as such restraint may be in principle, it tends to leave the young person in search of guidance with only slender resources. In practice one may obtain some help from a sympathetic counselor, but the value of such advice depends on the competence and insight of the giver.

Research Problems. A different set of problems arises in connection with social-science research conducted on homosexual subjects. In order to obtain optimal samples, modern techniques require random selection of the members of the survey "universe," with replies from all or almost all of those queried. In speaking to those who are planning to vote in an election for president this goal is not difficult to achieve, but with a private (even for some persons still taboo) realm such as sexuality the obstacles are almost unsurmountable. In the course of his research for a monograph on **toilet** sex, *Tea Room Trade* (Chicago, 1970), Laud Humphreys noted the licence plate numbers of the patrons (who had come by car) and, after tracing them, interviewed the participants in their homes. Although the names were not disclosed, some other scholars felt that an invasion of privacy had occurred. In the 1980s concerns were raised about the ethics of testing new drugs for **AIDS**. With increasing sensitivity among researchers to ethical practices with human subjects, inappropriate procedures are likely to be subjected to vigorous criticism and subsequent corrective action—at least in democratic societies.

Wayne R. Dynes

ETHNOLOGY
See **Anthropology.**

ETHNOPHAULISM

This rare term (coined by Abraham Roback) serves as a useful designation for the chauvinistic practice of human groups to attribute the origin—or at least prevalence—of social failings to neighboring groups or peoples. Thus we speak of German measles, of taking French leave, and of going Dutch. In former times Italians blithely dubbed syphilis the *mal francese* (or *morbus gallicus*), while Frenchmen returned the compliment with their *mal florentin* (or *mal de Naples*).

In the case of homosexual behavior, ethnophaulism is not only a type of group slander, but it also reflects a curiosity to trace the custom to its purported source, in keeping with "popular diffusionism," which overlooks the possibility that such behavior patterns are human universals. Thus, in eighteenth-century **England**, when native homosexual behavior had been documented for centuries and when important innovations seem to have been occurring in the conceptualization of homosexual acts, the fashion continued to ascribe the custom to Italy.

Divided as they were into many competing city states, the Greeks were given to ascribing unusual sexual predilections to neighboring, but distinct Hellenic groups, as well as to foreigners. Ostensibly special proficiency in fellatio obtained among the inhabitants of the island of Lesbos (its association with female homosexuality became commonplace only in comparatively recent times) and the alien Phoenicians. At various times unusual fondness for pederasty was remarked in Crete (Plato and others held that the institution began there), at Sparta, Chalcis, and the island of Siphnos. To become blatantly homosexual was sometimes called "taking ship for Messalia," after the ancient Greek colony on the site of modern Marseille, which perhaps acquired its renown through propinquity with the notoriously homosexual **Celts.** The **Scythians,** northern neighbors of the Greeks, were associated with a particular type of effeminacy. Among a basically tolerant people such as the Greeks, these ethnophaulic appellations have more the character of an amused chiding than harsh reproof, much as we would say today "X is German and likes to work hard," or "Y's Scottish background makes him thrifty."

In the first century B.C. the Roman writer Cornelius Nepos seems to have been the first to describe pederasty simply as "Greek love." The Romans themselves were often charged with special devotion to the "posterior Venus" with various wordplays on the palindrome Roma = Amor.

In later times in Europe there were various expressions associating sodomy with Italy. In 1422 the Zurich *Rat- und Rechtbuch,* a legal text, designated the practice by the verb *florenzen,* suggesting that the city of **Florence** had developed a particular reputation in this regard. Pierre de Brantôme (ca. 1540–1614) described the fashion for lesbian liaisons in sixteenth-century France with the Italian phrase "donna con donna" (lady with lady). At the courts of Louis XII and XIV male homosexual proclivities were traced to Italy, as in the Sun King's sarcastic comment "La France devenue italienne!" In England Sir Edward Coke (1552–1634) thought that Lombard bankers had introduced sodomy in the late Middle Ages, while in the eighteenth century Italian opera was held to be a source of new infection. Ironically, Mussolini was later to reject a proposal to criminalize homosexuality in his country on the grounds that its practice was limited to rich foreign tourists. The rural inhabitants of **Albania**, who until recently boasted a rich indigenous tradition of pederasty, nonetheless sometimes designated their custom as *madzüpi*, derived from *madzüp*, "Gypsy," implying that pederasty had been brought in from the outside by this wandering people.

Some French writers localized the customs in other zones of the Mediteranean littoral. French trade with Arab countries and the occupation of North **Africa** (beginning in 1830) are probably responsible for the popularity of such expressions as *moeurs levantines* and *moeurs arabes*. Just after the turn of the century, the Krupp and **Eulenburg**-von Moltke scandals contributed greatly to the popularity in a hostile France of the expression *vice allemand*, apparently reviving a notion current there in the time of **Frederick II the Great** in the second half of the eighteenth century. The temptation to hurl such charges becomes particularly great in wartime as seen in an absurd volume by Samuel Igra, *Germany's National Vice* (London, 1945), which even alleges that Hitler had been a male prostitute. A more general type of ethnophaulism, found both in Communist and some Third World countries, claims that the Western industrial nations collectively are declining because of their tolerance of "unnatural vice." As a kind of silver lining, if only that, we may be grateful that the appearance of **AIDS**, whose spread has been connected both to Africa and the United States, has not led to any general international label of origin. While such hopes must be proffered with diffidence, perhaps some degree of reason is beginning to prevail in these matters.

See also **Fascist Perversion**.

BIBLIOGRAPHY. Irving Lewis Allen, *The Language of Ethnic Conflict*, New York: Columbia University Press, 1983; Abraham Roback, *A Dictionary of International Slurs*, Cambridge, MA: Sci-Art Publishers, 1944, repr. Waukesha, WI: Maledicta, 1979.

Wayne R. Dynes

ETIOLOGY

Etiology is the study of the factors that contribute to the occurrence of a disease or abnormal condition. As such the term has been employed in inquiries and speculations regarding the causes of homosexual behavior. In medicine the significance of etiology is that it is the necessary starting point for therapy and even more for prophylaxis, to which modern public health programs owe their chief successes in the eradication of disease.

Historical Perspectives. The application of the idea of etiology to same-sex behavior stems from several judgmental perspectives. The broad outlines of their reasoning are as follows. (1) If homosexuality is mere depravity—moral failure rooted in individual caprice and self-indulgence—then society is justified in ostracizing and punishing those who engage in it. Such measures would serve as a warning to others to amend their conduct, which they can do through an exercise of free will. (2) If, however, homosexuality is a psychological condition that has arisen independent of the conscious will of the individual, then therapeutic measures of one kind or another are called for. These must be imposed for the good of the individual and that of society. (3) Yet again, the homosexual may be simply manifesting an inborn and unmodifiable condition determined by hereditary or genetic factors; then society is well advised to leave him alone as neither punishment nor therapy will change his orientation.

The Pathological Explanation. For many centuries the first interpretation—the abuse of free will—was virtually the only one admitted in Christian Europe, and accordingly habitual sodomites were seen as criminals and outcasts for whom no punishment could be too severe. The matter fell in the realm of the criminal law and the role of the forensic physician was ancillary. Only in the nineteenth century, when the early homophile apologists had drawn the attention of psychiatrists such as Karl Westphal and Richard von **Krafft-Ebing** to the existence of exclusively homosexual individuals, did the notion of sexual inversion as a pathological state raise the question of etiology, properly speaking. The psychiatrists of the late nineteenth century were inclined to organic explanations that made homosexuality a consequence of hereditary degeneration of the central nervous system—and some people even now thoughtlessly brand homosexuals as "degenerates." Little do they suspect that with the acceptance of the findings of Mendel and Weismann that acquired characteristics cannot be inherited—for good or for ill—the notion of hereditary degeneration ceased to exist for medical science.

A variant was that homosexuality resulted from the psychological vicissitudes of early childhood. This idea had a few adherents in the nineteenth century, but found much broader support in the twentieth, thanks to such psychiatrists as Albert von Schrenck-Notzing and psychoanalysts of whom Isidor Sadger and Alfred **Adler** are the most outstanding. In the view of such writers, homosexuality was a fixation in a stage of psychological development which normal individuals left behind on their way to adult heterosexuality. An assortment of fears and attachments in childhood left an indelible impression on the psyche of the individual, and this complex of factors triggered a homosexual orientation. This thinking offered a rationale for the compulsory psychotherapy imposed upon some young homosexuals by their parents and upon others by judges in lieu of a prison sentence.

The Shift to a More Positive View. During the same period a very different view emerged. As early as 1896 such defenders of homosexual rights as Magnus **Hirschfeld**, Marc-André Raffalovich, and Albert **Aletrino** held that homosexuality was a non-pathological variation within the human species, inborn and unmodifiable, occurring in all races in all epochs of history in approximately the same degree

and with roughly the same range of constitutional types. And in fact more than a century of medical and biological research has failed to discover any common denominator in exclusively homosexual subjects other than their sexual orientation. If a specific cause underlies the sexual orientation of such individuals, genetic science has thus far been unable to identify it.

Other Etiologies. Other explanations have been defended from time to time. One is that hormonal imbalance or some glandular abnormality causes homosexuality, but therapies grounded in these assumptions have had little result. The attempt of biologists such as Richard Goldschmidt to prove that all homosexuals were constitutional intersexes ("disguised" members of the opposite sex) has also found no confirmation. Moralizing psychiatrists such as Edmund **Bergler** have argued that homosexuality is the outcome of the seduction by older homosexuals of adolescents who are then trapped in an orientation into which they initiate younger males in their own adulthood—a view paralleling the interpretation offered by the second edition of the *Great Soviet Encyclopedia* published at the end of Stalin's lifetime. And simple-minded fundamentalists believe that homosexuality is the result of demonic possession or some equally malign spell cast by the evil powers of another world.

Edward O. Wilson and other advocates of **sociobiology** have offered several explanations based on the concept of "inclusive fitness." In this view homosexuals and lesbians who have no offspring of their own assure the transmission of their genes by helping siblings and their children. This factor would account for the transmission of a trait that otherwise cannot be accounted for in modern Darwinism.

A fifteen-year longitudinal study by Richard Green defined sissy boys as cross-dressing, role playing as girls, frequently playing with dolls, and avoiding rough-and-tumble sports. Such boys were found to be much more likely to become homosexual than a control group. This finding, though it has been supported by several other scholars, probably cannot be generalized, since a large proportion of adult homosexuals report no effeminacy in childhood, while others were without excessive difficulty able to suppress the traits, becoming masculine in appearance while still homosexual.

Correlations and Ulterior Motives. Whatever the etiology proposed by a given author, the political correlation has been fairly clear. With a bare handful of exceptions, those who believed in the genetic or constitutional determination of homosexuality have been supporters of gay rights. Conversely, many who upheld the theory of the neurotic or environmental origin of the condition (which they tended to regard as a "disease") have, historically, been antagonistic to the homophile movement. More recently, however, many anthropologists and sociologists, even if they profess that human behavior is by and large culturally rather than biologically conditioned, have expressed toleration for a plurality of lifestyles. The old school racked its brains to discover rationalizations for refusing to abolish the medieval laws, to recognize gay organizations, or to grant plaintiffs in court cases the rights which they sought. In not a few instances a kind of ideological shadow boxing occurs; those who insist upon the neurotic causes of homosexuality in reality think of it as depravity, while those who champion the genetic origin are obliquely dismissing the moral condemnation that derives from Christian theology with its absolute rejection of all "non-procreative" sexual activity.

Future Directions. A valid account of the causes of homosexual behavior must take account of the dialectic of sexual dimorphism. In so doing it must attempt a unified-field theory of sexual development that will account for the whole spectrum of orientation, including

shifts within a single individual's lifetime. Thus heterosexual behavior demands an explanation as much as homosexual conduct. Also, a distinction must be drawn between the macroevolutionary causes of homosexuality (Why do homosexual behavior and response occur in *homo sapiens*? Why does exclusive homosexuality occur?) and the microevolutionary causes (Why do homosexual response and behavior occur in a particular individual? Why is a given individual exclusively homosexual?). Not only must teleological conceptions of the "purpose" of sexuality be discarded in order to reach a scientific answer to the above questions, but the perspectives of different disciplines must be brought to bear to separate the phylogenetic from the ontogenetic (the species-wide phenomenon from the individual case history).

A solution to the question of causes will involve a rethinking and revision of the confusions introduced by the older concepts of etiology, fraught as they are with the insinuation that homosexual behavior is tainted with pathology. No progress can be made as long as research is hobbled with such an a priori judgment. The answer will also require integration of new scientific perspectives and findings which are still unfolding.

BIBLIOGRAPHY. Richard Green, *The "Sissy Boy Syndrome" and the Development of Homosexuality*, New Haven: Yale University Press, 1987; Noretta Koertge, ed., *Philosophy and Homosexuality*, New York: Harrington Park Press, 1985; Edward O. Wilson, *On Human Nature*, Cambridge, MA: Harvard University Press, 1978.

Warren Johansson

ETRUSCANS

The Etruscans were the dominant people in central and northern Italy from the ninth to the second centuries B.C. Their civilization stood at its prime from the sixth to the third century B.C., but the language has not for the most part been interpreted, so that our knowledge of them must rest at present on an examination of their art.

Most of what has been discovered is the contents and decorations of tombs. As the goods found in them show, the Etruscans had close cultural and commercial ties with the ancient **Greeks**. Indeed, Otto Brendel states that "Etruscan is a branch of the civilization which we call classical," going on to say that "it constitutes the only known case of a contemporary classical art apart from the Greek." The achievement of the Etruscans has been obscured by their conquerors, the Romans, whom they greatly influenced.

Etruscan civilization incorporated an unmistakeable male homosexual element, readily seen in tomb frescoes, bronze sculptures, utensils, urns (*cistae*), and mirrors. This is not to say that Etruscan art does not celebrate heterosexuality (which it does); but rather that homosexual components are strongly present, as with both the Greeks and the Romans.

The earliest homosexual image appears on the fresco of the rear wall of the so-called Tomb of the Bulls at Tarquinia (one of the earliest tombs excavated to date, from ca. 540 B.C.), showing what is almost certainly one man anally penetrating another who has horns and who is, in turn, being charged by a bull. The iconography of this tomb has not been satisfactorily interpreted but it may have religious connotations. **Symposium** scenes were popular in the fifth century; they frequently featured naked and semi-naked male dancers and musicians in an all-male setting and bring to mind similar contemporary scenes on Greek vases, which have been found massively in Etruscan graves.

Bronze sculptures celebrating the **nude** male body inaugurated an Italian sculptural tradition which continues to the present day. These statues show close links with Etruscan terracotta sculptures and with Greek sculpture. Naked males frequently appear on Etruscan candelabras and incense burners in the form of satyrs or sportsmen. They become an elaborate motif on the handles of the lids of cistae dating from the early fourth century B.C.; these were apparently toilet boxes and were buried with the owner. Some of the earliest examples feature two clothed warriors carrying a dead warrior (also wearing clothes); but later all three figures are naked. By the late third century they become even more openly homoerotic—as on a cista in the Museo Archeologico, Palestrina, which shows **Dionysus** and a satyr.

The sides of cistae were frequently engraved with scenes from Greek mythology. The Chrysippos cista (ca. 350 B.C.; Villa Giulia, Rome) features the homosexual abduction of Chrysippos by Laios. The largest and finest cista, the so-called Ficorini Cista (ca. 400 B.C.; Villa Giulia), signed Novios Plautus in Latin, is virtually a symphony to the nude male body showing it in seventeen separate poses (two other figures are clothed). One naked figure, with his back to us and one arm tantalizingly covering his anus, puts his arm around the neck of another unconcealed male, who wears only a helmet and gazes longingly at him. Another, by contrast, offers his backside to the viewer: a pose which was to be repeated in frescoes in Pompeii and later in oil paintings from the **Renaissance** on and was to become a classic motif suggesting homosexuality. The eroticism of this cista suggests that the artist was homosexual.

Engravings behind Etruscan bronze mirrors also celebrate the male body in homoerotic terms. Some, such as a mirror displaying Hercules and Atlas (ca. 460 B.C.), are little more than an excuse for depicting the naked male body. In another mirror, a naked youth reaches up to kiss a rather mannish woman while another gazes longingly at the youth's body (ca. 450 B.C.); while such a mirror may have been used by a woman, its underlying male homoeroticism is undeniable. Some bronze mirrors were cast in relief: one late-fifth-century example depicts the homosexual abduction of Cephalos by Eos; another, one of the most tantalizing objects in Etruscan art, depicts two naked winged males, one of whom holds what is apparently a dildo, flanking a naked frontal youth.

The largest collection of Etruscan art adorns the Villa Giulia in Rome, a museum entirely devoted to artifacts of this ancient people. The monograph of Otto G. Brendel discusses the major surviving objects.

BIBLIOGRAPHY. Otto G. Brendel, *Etruscan Art*, New York: Penguin Books, 1978.

Paul Knobel

ETYMOLOGY

The discipline of etymology seeks to explain the origin of words, whether they are inherited from a reconstructed parent language, borrowed from a known foreign tongue, or simply invented in historic time. The etymologist examines the earliest attestations of a word, variations in its form, explanatory glosses or comments in early texts, parallels in other languages, and terms derived from the same root or related in meaning to ascertain what was the source of the word. A secondary matter is the history of a word or word family, the changes in meaning or frequency of use over centuries or even millennia, and the role which a particular term may play in the political or cultural life of the speech community to which it belongs, or in the case of international terms, even of the entire world.

The word *lesbian*, for example, serves in all the modern languages of Europe to designate a woman erotically attracted to her own sex; it is derived from the Greek island of Lesbos, where the poetess **Sappho** lived in the sixth century before our era. *Sodomite*, the term used in medieval Europe for the sinner guilty of unnatural vice, comes from the city of **Sodom**, which according to Genesis 19 was destroyed by a rain of brimstone and fire on account of the depravity of its inhabitants. **Bugger**, a word attested in English beginning with the law of Henry VIII in 1533, stems from the Old French *bougre*, "heretic", then "sodomite" and even "usurer," which in turn came from Medieval Latin *Bulgarus*—the name of the Slavic people who called themselves *bulgarinu*—because their land was a center of the Bogomil heresy akin to the Catharism of Southern France. *Tribade*, the older word for "lesbian" in European languages, came from the Classical Greek *tribein* "to rub," hence tribades were women who obtained erotic satisfaction by friction against each other's bodies. *Homosexual*, by contrast, is a modern term invented by the German-Hungarian translator and bibliographer Károly Mária **Kertbeny** in 1869 from the Greek *homo*, "same," and Medieval Latin *sexualis*,"sexual," on the model of French *unisexuel* and *bisexuel* which had been introduced as terms of botany in the 1790s. *Pederast*, a word whose meaning differs from language to language in modern times, is the Classical Greek *paiderastes* which unambiguously denoted "boy-lover."

An ancient doctrine, now discarded, maintained that similarities in the form of words are not accidental, but offer a key to understanding. Thus Isidore of Seville (ca. 560–636) referred the Latin name of the kite, *milvus*, to *mollis*, "soft, effeminate," attesting to the supposed homosexual proclivities of the **bird**. The search for such links probably stems from a quasi-magical world view, in which knowledge of the true meanings of words gives the privileged knower control over things.

Such associative techniques, resting on foundations as old as **Plato**'s dialogue *Cratylus*, are not unlike folk etymologies, which stem from the effort of naive and uneducated speakers to explain unfamiliar terms by relating them to the lexical core of a language. At times these folk etymologies can lead to the deformation of a word in popular speech which ultimately finds its way into the literary language. A good example of this in Modern English is **faggot** for "effeminate male homosexual." The folk etymology of this word is that it derives from the male sodomites who were used as faggots (bundles of firewood) when witches were burned at the stake. Little does it matter to the folk mind that the word is attested in its homosexual meaning only in American English in 1914, that it comes from the dialectal use of *faggot* (and *fadge*) in the sense of "fat, slovenly woman," and that the penalty for buggery in English law was hanging, not burning at the stake, which was the punishment of heretics until the homosexual monarch **James** I put an end to the practice. The speaker who knows *faggot* only in its primary meaning (and does not consult such a source as Wright's *English Dialect Dictionary*) can accept such an explanation because it matches his imperfect command of the range of senses of the word with his hazy recollection that "in the Middle Ages people were burned at the stake for various crimes that offended the church."

The origin of **dyke** in the sense of "lesbian" (with the variant *bulldyke*) has inspired several folk etymologies, because the exact source of the term is unknown. One of the more fanciful interpretations is that the word is a deformation of Boadicca, the name of the British queen who fought against the Roman invaders. A more recent interpretation of the second syllable of *bulldyke* is that it comes from the American slang expression "to be diked out," presumably in male attire. A possible etymology is that the second element is the word *tyke* in the meaning "bitch," attested in English and other Germanic languages; a *bulldyke* would then be "a bitch who behaves like a bull" (the male animal par excellence). In American English *tyke* has gone its own way to become an endearing expression for a child, hence the organization of lesbian mothers Dykes 'n Tykes.

The English language may lend itself to etymological curiosity and speculation more than others because so much of its vocabulary is foreign, hence the perennial question "What does it mean?," while the native vocabulary is often opaque to the specialist because its origins are lost in the obscure centuries of Middle and Old English. Also, in the sexual realm there has been a long battle between the vulgar terms banned from literature and public life and the learned euphemisms that were created or borrowed so that certain topics could be discussed at all. It is commonly believed that the little "four-letter words" that cannot be used in polite conversation are of Anglo-Saxon origin, when in fact most of them are not attested in the Old English period, and Anglo-Saxon had its own sexual vocabulary, now lost even in the British dialects.

The etymon of a word was supposedly its "true" meaning, but to the professional linguist it is only an earlier meaning or form. In the case of the modern languages most words can be traced to sources attested in medieval and ancient writing, and recent coinages can often be assigned to a particular author who first used them in speech or print. For the general public, literature on "word origins" can be an entertaining set of anecdotes, while for the specialist the discipline of etymology is a clue to problems in cultural history, as words can preserve customs and beliefs of bygone eras even when their primary meaning is lost in the mists of time.

See also **Language and Linguistics.**

Warren Johansson

EUGENE, PRINCE OF SAVOY (1663–1736)

Austrian general and statesman. Born the son of Eugène Maurice count of Soissons and Olympia Mancini, a niece of Cardinal Mazarin, Eugene was destined for the clerical profession by Louis XIV, but in 1683 fled from Paris to the court of the Holy Roman (Austrian) emperor, as he was denied entry into the French army. In 1697 he was entrusted with the high command in the Turkish war (1683–99), and at Centa on September 11, 1697, he won a decisive victory against the sultan's forces. In the War of the Spanish Succession his victories over the French at Carpi and Chiari (1701) contributed to the conclusion of the Grand Alliance at The Hague. The victory over France and Bavaria at Höchstädt on the Danube on August 13, 1704 was the outcome of his strategic planning and collaboration with the British under the duke of Marlborough. After the death of margrave Ludwig Wilhelm of Baden, Eugene was named imperial field marshal by the Diet. Fighting alongside Marlborough once more, he won victories at Oudenaarde (1708) and Malplaquet (1709). He was commissioned by the emperor to conduct the preliminary peace negotiations at The Hague in 1709, and to represent **Austria** at the peace conference at Rastatt and Baden in 1714. In the Turkish War of 1714–18, after victories at Petrovaradin and Temesvár he besieged the fortress of Belgrade, where on August 16, 1717, he defeated an enormous Turkish relief force and by capturing Belgrade decided the outcome of the struggle. Court intrigues and a subsequent crisis in which Eugene was involved ended with his complete vindication, but led him in 1725 to renounce the governor generalship of the Austrian Netherlands which he had occupied since the War of the Spanish Succession.

Eugene of Savoy was the most talented general of his day and a far-sighted politician as well, one who replaced the dynastic outlook of the seventeenth century with the concept of raison d'état. A generous patron of the arts and sciences, he entertained relations with Montesquieu, **Voltaire**, Leibniz, and the historian Muratori; in Vienna he had the Belvedere Palace built by Johann Lukas von Hildebrandt. In nationality and character he was Italian;

although he understood German, he never wrote a sentence in that language. As a general and a statesman he served the multi-national Habsburg monarchy and the Holy Roman empire; his political horizon was still that of the feudal order based on a harmony of the estates, not the democratic outlook of the later eighteenth century. In the twentieth century German National Socialism and Italian fascism claimed him as one of their predecessors in the struggle for a "new order" in Europe— rather anachronistically, although he did acquire Hungary and the South Slavic lands for the Habsburg crown.

Eugene lived at a time when his lack of interest in the opposite sex could be lauded by naive panegyrists as meaning that he was "chaste and pure as a seraph." His long association with countess Eleonora Batthyány led to no greater intimacy than card playing, never to marriage. His enemies, however, whispered that he "does not bother with women, a couple of handsome pages are his métier." He even received the nickname "Mars without Venus." His best friend at the court of Louis XIV was also homosexual, the Prince de Turenne, who accompanied him on his flight to Austria. But while the prince repented and returned home, Eugene vowed that he would set foot on French soil again only at the head of a hostile army—and kept his word. Only a few anecdotes surfaced in regard to his sexual life, but these tell enough. One is a soldier's song in kitchen Latin that alludes to his voyage on the Rhone River with his friend, the marquis de la Moussaye. When a storm broke out, the general dreaded the worst, but the Marquis consoled him with the words: *Securae sunt nostrae vitae/ Sumus enim sodomitae/ Igne tantum perituri/ Landeriri*, "Our lives are safe/ For we are sodomites/ Destined to perish only by fire/ We shall land." A comment made by Schulenberg in 1709 should probably read that the prince enjoyed "la petite débauche et la p[ine] au dela de tout," which means that he derived his sexual gratification from the virile member—of others. So Eugene of Savoy was one of those military figures whose homosexuality freed them to devote their lives to a dangerous career without the distractions of a wife and family, and he is remembered as one of the ablest generals in Austrian history.

BIBLIOGRAPHY. Derek McKay, *Prince Eugene of Savoy*, London: Thames and Hudson, 1977; Curt Riess, *Auch Du, Cäsar . . . Homosexualität als Schicksal*, Munich: Universitas, 1981.

Warren Johansson

EULENBURG UND HERTEFELD, PHILIPP FÜRST ZU (1847–1921)

German politician and diplomat, an intimate of Kaiser Wilhelm II. A former guards officer, jurist, and owner of a vast estate, he entered the German diplomatic corps in 1877. Eulenburg formed a close personal relationship with the future Kaiser in 1886 thanks to which he was able to play a key role in German politics that far exceeded his official position as Ambassador to Austria–Hungary (1894–1903). He both reinforced the megalomania of the Kaiser and judged him critically, but also acted as intermediary between Wilhelm II and the Foreign Office.

Eulenburg was the center of a homosexual clique that was effectively penetrated by the first secretary of the French legation and later ambassador to Berlin, Raymond Lecomte (1857–1921), who used his position to reveal to the Quai d'Orsay that Germany was bluffing in the Morocco crisis of January–April 1906, which ended in a French diplomatic victory at the Algeciras Conference. This reverse for Germany inspired a bitter attack on Eulenburg and his circle in November 1906 by Maximilian Harden, the jingoist editor of *Die Zukunft*, an influential political weekly. In the series of trials that followed, Harden was victorious and Eulenburg was exposed as a homosexual and socially ruined, spending the remaining years of his life in isolation on his country estate, though he was spared the final disgrace of imprisonment. The **Scientific-Humanitarian Committee**, the homosexual rights organization headed by Magnus **Hirschfeld**, who testified as an expert witness, suffered a severe setback and loss of support, and the monarchy itself was exposed to such humiliation that the whole subject has been a "blind spot" for German historians ever since. Although this episode was the Watergate of the Second Reich, references to it in standard works are laconic and uninformative. In all likelihood, the missing piece in the picture was Wilhelm II's own homosexuality—hence the peculiar attachment that gave Eulenburg such influence over his sovereign in the shaping of German foreign policy, which Lecomte in turn intercepted to his country's advantage. Ironically enough, it was the journalistic use of the term *homosexual* in the vast contemporary coverage of this scandalous affair that confirmed it as the usual word for the subject in German and the other modern languages.

BIBLIOGRAPHY. Isabel V. Hull, *The Entourage of Kaiser Wilhelm II, 1888–1918*, Cambridge: Cambridge University Press, 1982; Marc-André Raffalovich, "Chronique de l'unisexualité," *Archives d'anthropologie criminelle*, 24 (1909), 357–81.

Warren Johansson

EUNUCHS

Eunuchs are men or boys whose testes or external genitals have been removed. This condition differs from other physical defects such as amputation of the hand or foot or removal of the eye in that, at various historical epochs it was intentionally created, so that the eunuch had not merely a physical or medical but also a social definition.

Antiquity. The practice of castrating slaves or prisoners of war began in the Ancient Near East and reached Greece as a cultural influence from the Orient. The Greeks themselves anachronistically ascribed the invention of the eunuch to the legendary Assyrian queen Semiramis. In Babylonia and Assyria (**Mesopotamia**) eunuchs played a major role both as officials of the royal court and as members of the priestly castes in the temples. Eunuchs held the highest offices as chamberlains of the sovereign and as provincial governors. The heterosexual employ of the eunuch, then and later in the Islamic Middle Ages, was as guardian of the harem. In religion the *assinnu* and *kurgaru* had both erotic and mantic functions, serving as hierodules and as practitioners of incantation and magic, particularly in connection with the cult of Ishtar, who had supposedly consecrated their status. The Akkadian texts describe the eunuch as *sinnisanu*, "effeminate," and even as a "half-man," anticipating the Latin *semivir*. The courtier served his ruler sexually much as the hierodule served the worshipper—in the passive role.

In Greece the keeping of eunuchs as slaves began gradually toward the end of the fifth century B.C., increased during the Hellenistic period, and reached Rome in the second century, becoming more frequent under the principate and then the empire. Eunuchs as costly slaves serving their masters in highly personalized functions were part of the economic stratification of Greco-Roman society: they were acquired by the wealthiest classes to perform the functions of housekeeper, valet, guard, and tutor. The political role of the eunuch was a function of the Orientalization of the Hellenistic and Roman administrations; where the Greek presence was strongest, eunuchs only exceptionally acquired power and influence at court; but where the layer of Hellenization was thin and superficial, eunuchs were able to assert their age-old position in the political hierarchy. The eunuchs' interests, while coinciding with those of the ruler, often collided with those of the upper strata of the aristocracy, so that they excellently served a centralizing monarchical power.

Castration was most often inflicted on slaves without their consent to enhance their value as merchandise. The operation was usually performed on boys in childhood; but if the object was to market the boy as a **catamite**, castration was effected at the onset of puberty so that sexual response would be present. While Roman law forbade castration, it never sought to restrict the trade in eunuchs imported from foreign lands. The wealthiest members of the Roman upper class did not shrink from paying enormous sums for particularly handsome eunuchs.

The outstanding characteristic of the eunuch in the ancient mind was his **effeminacy**, equated with physical weakness and unfitness for military service. In the sexual sphere the eunuch was supposed to behave "like a woman," that is, to take the passive-effeminate role in a relationship with a man. In this role the eunuch was deemed neither male nor female, but as a kind of third sex, *tertium genus hominum*. The effeminacy and sterility of the eunuch were a stigma even in the pagan world, and more so in Christian times. On the other hand, the social isolation of the eunuch made him ever more dependent upon his master for advancement, and this assured his loyalty—a quality praised by ancient writers.

The mentality of the eunuchs and of those who kept them must be seen against the background of the markedly transsexualizing tendencies of Hellenistic and then Roman society. The Greeks in particular were aware that the practice of keeping eunuchs as catamites differed enormously from the pederastic relationship in which the emphasis lay in developing the virile qualities of the younger partner to ready him for his duties as warrior and as citizen. It was an aspect of Eastern sensuality and servility that contradicted and undermined the social values of *paiderasteia*. But when the conquests of **Alex-**

ander the Great broke down the barriers between Hellenic and Near Eastern cultures, the sexual customs of the Orient gained ground in the **Hellenistic monarchies**. Alexander himself loved the Persian eunuch Bagoas. As Hellenistic culture spread to Rome, so did the role of eunuchs as effeminized passive partners for Roman men. The general Fabius Valens (about 69) had a retinue of "concubines and eunuchs." Titus, Domitian, Trajan, **Hadrian**, Commodus, Caracalla, **Heliogabalus**, and others were accompanied by such *exoleti*, and some emperors and other magnates even celebrated marriages with their favorite eunuchs. **Nero** went so far as to confer upon the eunuch Sporus the honors of an empress. Roman moralists criticized the practice of castrating slaves as a violation of their human dignity and as an act of cruelty, even while Roman society tacitly acknowledged the right of the owner to use the slave as he desired.

The Judaeo-Christian Tradition. Judaism, possibly abreacting to the role that eunuchs played in the Ishtar-Tammuz cult, formally excluded them from its sacral community (Deuteronomy 23:1). For that reason one of the most enigmatic utterances ascribed to **Jesus** is Matthew 19:12: "For there are some eunuchs, which were so born from their mother's womb: and there are some eunuchs, which were made eunuchs of men: and there be eunuchs, which have made themselves eunuchs for the kingdom of heaven's sake. He that is able to receive it, let him receive it." For Christian theologians and commentators this verse has been a source of endless embarrassment; one can only surmise that it found its way into the text of Matthew from an ascetic circle on the periphery of the early Church where castration was recommended if not rigorously practiced as the ultimate denial of the sexual urge, and that the otherwise Judaizing author of the Gospel was unaware of the Old Testament strictures on the matter. The usual evasion has been to interpret all three parts of the verse as

meaning "like eunuchs," and William Tyndale even translated the verse: "There are chaste, which were so born out of their mother's belly . . .," but the reputation of the eunuch in antiquity was hardly for chastity, rather for passive-effeminate homosexuality—which would leave the Church in an even greater quandary, since the plain meaning of the verse makes the eunuch an ideal of asexuality. Some modern homophile apologists have even construed the first part of the triptych as an allusion to innate homosexuality, but such an interpretation ill fits the tenor of the passage. The verse well exemplifies the extra-Judaic sources of Christian sexual morality whose ascetic tendency directly contravened the established norms of Judaism itself.

But otherwise faithful to the Judaic tradition that rejected the eunuch, the Christian Church in its **canon law** nowhere prescribed castration as a penalty for any offense, so that castration as a punishment for **sodomy** in the royal and municipal law of the late Middle Ages cannot be ascribed to ecclesiastical influence or precept. The Church did not, however, forbid the secular authorities to inflict such penalties, nor did it prevent the making of **castrati** for singing in church choirs. In principle, however, since it opposed the practice of castration as a violation of the dignity of the human subject, the policy of the Church deprived the eunuch of his political and erotic functions, and ultimately made him disappear as a social category from the Western world.

BIBLIOGRAPHY. Peter Browe, *Zur Geschichte der Entmannung: Eine religions- und rechtsgeschichtliche Studie*, Breslau: Verlag Müller & Seiffert, 1936; Peter Guyot, *Eunuchen als Sklaven und Freigelassene in der griechisch-römischen Antike*, Stuttgart: Klett-Cotta, 1980; Georg Luck, "Trygonions Grabschrift," *Philologus*, 100 (1956), 271–86; Ernst Maass, "Eunuchos und Verwandtes," *Rheinisches Museum für Philologie*, new series, 74 (1925), 432–76.

Warren Johansson

EXILES AND ÉMIGRÉS

Over the course of the centuries, political vicissitudes and, after the rise of **Christianity** and **Islam**, religious bigotry have forced gay people to leave their own countries and seek refuge abroad. The ingrained adaptability and propensity for disguise and camouflage of homosexuals have often facilitated this process, but the coercive nature of the change has tended to induce a cautious temper in those upon whom it has been forced.

Historical Examples. The earliest known homosexual refugee fled the Greek island of Samos in the late sixth century B.C. The philosopher and mathematician Pythagoras escaped the tyranny of Polycrates, himself a pederast, who had made the island a great maritime power and cultural center. Later, in 521, when the Persians crucified him and suppressed pederasty there, the pederastic poets he had attracted to his court, **Ibycus** and **Anacreon**, fled.

There are no known instances of ostracism (banishment by popular vote) in ancient **Greece** for pederasty. The Romans knew a form of voluntary self-banishment called *exsilium*. Magistrates would allow those guilty of a capital crime to escape, but they could never return to Roman territory.

In later centuries, when Christianity had influenced the **Roman emperors** to impose the death penalty for homosexual activity, the extreme penalty was sometimes commuted to banishment. Expelling the sodomite from its territory was sufficient to placate or at least deflect the divine wrath that would otherwise have spelled immeasurable woe for the state. In the great prosecution inspired by **Protestantism** of homosexuals in the Netherlands in 1730, 57 of the 250 men and boys who were convicted were put to death, while the majority were simply banished from the country. At other times culprits took to flight as a way of escaping burning at the stake, inflicted when the Inquisition "relaxed" sodomites to the secular authorities, or in England (which never allowed the Inquisition to enter) the hangman's noose—or in the eighteenth and early nineteenth centuries, when English homophobia reached an apex, exposure in the pillory.

Some sodomites fled persecution to the Italian **Renaissance** cities even before the religious and other disputes of the sixteenth century in Europe caused much displacement of individuals who, for one reason or another, could not accept the new state of affairs in their native land—or the continuation of the old one. Among these was the French philologist and professor Marc-Antoine **Muret** (1526–1585), who had to escape to Italy to elude punishment for sodomy. Many by flight avoided prison and perpetual imprisonment or the galleys—the penalties meted out by the Spanish and Portuguese **Inquisitions** more often than burning at the stake.

Conversely, the abolition of the sodomy laws in **France** in 1791 and subsequently in other countries, including all the Latin ones (except Romania) and their colonies overseas, that adopted the Code **Napoléon** made these lands an appealing haven for northern European and Anglo-Saxon homosexuals. Even before the French Revolution the very wealthy eccentric William **Beckford** had found it prudent to leave England for Portugal. In the Napoleonic period three clergymen, the Rev. John Fenwick, the Rev. V. P. Littlehales, and the Bishop of Clogher were obliged to flee England. The case of the last-named individual, a member of an aristocratic Anglo-Irish family, was so notorious that in French his name became a sobriquet for a British sodomite. Two other Hibernian figures were more fortunate. Lady Eleanor Butler (1739–1829) and Sarah Ponsonby (1755–1831) fled Ireland together in 1778; in the following year they settled in a rustic cottage near **Llangollen**, Wales, where they resided unmolested—and in fact increasingly admired—for the rest of their lives.

Two great poets of romanticism, George Gordon, Lord **Byron**, who was bisexual, and the exclusively homosexual Count August von **Platen** resided much of their lives in Mediterranean countries. The inspirational homeland of ancient Greek pederasty, Greece, not under the Napoleonic Code but under Ottoman Turkish influence, tolerated homosexuality as did all Moslem countries. Improvements in the ease and convenience of travel made expatriation an option for an increasing number, including John Addington **Symonds**, Frederick **Rolfe** ("Baron Corvo"), and the nonsense writer and artist Edward **Lear**. Karl Heinrich **Ulrichs**, the lonely German pioneer of homosexual rights, who began to protest even before in 1866 Prussian prohibitions were imposed on his native Hanover, formerly under the Code Napoleon, passed his last years in L'Aquila in Abruzzi, where he died in misery in 1895, though not before Symonds had visited him. After his release from prison in 1897 Oscar **Wilde** departed from England for France, where he died three years afterwards. A few years later the French aesthete Count Jacques d'**Adelswärd Fersen**, after a scandal involving some photographs of boys, found it wise to withdraw for a time to the island of Capri (where the emperor Tiberius had long before established a retreat replete with a swimming pool filled with boys and girls to service him). Capri was then entering its modern apogee as a place of residence of foreign homosexuals. In the last Byzantine capital in Sicily, Taormina, whose views of Etna vie with Capri's of Vesuvius, the German Baron Wilhelm von **Gloeden** produced his celebrated photographs of Sicilian boys and attracted other foreign pederasts. On the eve of World War I actual colonies of English and German homosexuals lived in Italy, where they had taken up residence after being compromised socially or legally in their own countries, scenic Venice, where **Winckelmann** was murdered, being a favorite, along with **Florence** and Rome, both beautified by **Michelangelo**.

Lesbians, even if less likely to be menaced by the law, still had to fear intolerant public opinion, particularly in Protestant lands. The Americans Natalie **Barney**, Sylvia **Beach**, Romaine **Brooks**, Gertrude **Stein**, and Alice B. Toklas preferred to reside in Paris. So too did Radclyffe **Hall**, after her novel *The Well of Loneliness* (1928) was banned in England. Vernon **Lee**, the lesbian writer on aesthetics, chose to live in Florence.

Refugees from Totalitarianism. The best known and most numerous examples of exile and emigration occurred as a result of the authoritarian and totalitarian regimes of right and left in the twentieth century. In the 1920s many talented figures fled Communist Russia and Fascist Italy, to be joined in the early thirties by refugees from Nazi Germany and at the end of the decade from the annexed or occupied countries of Europe and from Franco Spain. After 1945 a new wave of refugees from an Eastern Europe that fell under Communist domination was followed by still others from Cuba and Vietnam when these countries shared the same fate. In the 1980s the Mariel refugees from Cuba and the Sino-Vietnamese boat people are melancholy reminders of the intolerance of Communist states. It was a well-known if not well-publicized fact that many of the Mariel émigrés were homosexuals fleeing the repressive policies of the Castro regime in **Cuba**, which while proclaiming equality for women and attempting to overcome the inveterate machismo of Latin American culture made the lot of the homosexuals on the island far worse than it had been under the deposed Fulgencio Batista. Gay bars and synagogues have disappeared from Havana as from Berlin under the Nazis.

Unlike many earlier refugees who vegetated on the margin of the intellectual and cultural life of their host countries, the trans-Atlantic migrants of the 1930s bonded with American society (and English to a lesser extent) and inspired its higher culture. Before their arrival America was a provincial backwater whose third-rate academic institutions contrasted sadly with the European universities, but had in some places, richly endowed, begun to rise with the introduction of the German model of graduate study in the late nineteenth century and to catch up as Europe squandered its youth in World War I. With their help, it became a dominant force in the intellectual life of the mid-twentieth century and an exporter of the software—the ideas, innovations, trade secrets, and patents—consumed by other nations. Significantly, with the retirement of the émigrés and their immediate pupils, American supremacy began to fade.

During the 1930s and early 1940s, because the thirty or so major American universities could not absorb the influx of new talent, many went to smaller or less elite schools. This enrichment contributed to today's polycentrism of American colleges—the fact that many campuses undistinguished before 1940 have become significant centers of learning. There were, inevitably, significant concentrations. With its cosmopolitan tradition, New York drew social scientists to the New School for Social Research and painters and sculptors to Greenwich Village, where Hans Hofmann's school provided the nucleus for abstract expressionism. The gay painter Pavel Tchelitschew, earlier a refugee from Bolshevik Russia, represented surrealism, with a notable influence on film and writing as well as the visual arts. At New York University's Institute of Fine Arts Alfred Salmony, formerly of Cologne, made many converts to Oriental art, his specialty.

Near New York City was the lodestone of the highly gifted, Princeton's Institute for Advanced Study, with Albert Einstein as its presiding spirit. In Germany Einstein, though himself heterosexual, had signed Magnus **Hirschfeld**'s petition against Paragraph 175 of the Penal Code. At Princeton he was later to be joined by the distinguished medievalist, Ernst **Kantorowicz**, more or less openly gay and a former member of the Stefan **George** circle. At Berkeley Kantorowicz, along with Robert Oppenheimer who became director of the Princeton Institute, had stood out as one of a small number of faculty to lose their jobs because they had refused to sign the loyalty oath which was part of the anti-Communist furor of the late 1940s. As a homosexual Kantorowicz could have been deported for this act of defiance. Another medieval historian—the field seems to have an affinity with homosexuality—Theodor Mommsen, was affiliated with Princeton University and very attracted to the art historian A. M. Friend for a time. Princeton was also the home of the great Austrian novelist Hermann Broch, who there completed *The Death of Vergil* (1945).

Southern California was the destination of many artistically creative individuals. After a short stay in Princeton, the bisexual Thomas **Mann** settled in the Los Angeles area. His gay son Klaus also made his way to America. The Southern California scene was further enlivened by English gay exiles, including the novelist Christopher **Isherwood**, compelled to leave the Berlin he loved, and the actor Charles Laughton. The eccentric Anglo-Irish thinker Gerald Heard helped to lay the philosophical foundations for the gay **movement**. Also active in Southern California was the gay fashion designer Rudi Gernreich, who became the lover of Henry Hay, the founder of the American homophile movement. Hollywood gave refuge to many lesser figures in the entertainment world who found employment behind the scenes in the studios and were sometimes hunted by adherents of **McCarthyism**.

Not all gay émigrés went to North America. Outstanding exceptions were the Spanish poet Luis **Cernuda**, who settled in Mexico, and his compatriot the composer Manuel de **Falla**, who preferred Argentina. However, Latin American countries were generally too underdeveloped economically and intellectually for such figures to make a permanent impress. In fact some refugees whose first haven was Latin America resettled in the United States.

Still others went to England. The philosopher Ludwig **Wittgenstein**, who remained in the closet, had settled there before the rise of Hitler. Kurt **Hiller**, the leftist writer and gay activist, lived in Prague until the Munich accords made it necessary for him to flee to England, where he proved unable to adapt and returned to West Germany in 1955. Anna Freud, who had conducted a closeted lesbian lifestyle for a time in Vienna, accompanied her famous father to his exile in England, then lived and practiced psychotherapy there until her death.

Amnesty International still refuses to protest the persecution and imprisonment for reasons of sexual orientation of homosexuals in any country, despite the appalling treatment meted out to them by such diverse authorities as those of Islamic countries, notorious among them the late Ayatollah Khomeini, or secular governments such as **Turkey's** on the one hand and Communist regimes on the other. In Argentina under the military junta in the 1970s the situation of the homophile movement deteriorated so badly that its leaders had to go into exile in monarchist Spain.

Conclusion. English and American prejudices and laws against homosexuality obliged homosexual refugees to hide their proclivities in order to gain entry visas and then get and retain citizenship papers. Hence it is often difficult to obtain accurate information on persons dead or alive. It may be inferred that homosexuals succeeded less often than their heterosexual colleagues in escaping from Europe and getting into the Anglo-Saxon democracies. Even when they succeeded, they faced discrimination in academia, where even now there are barely fifty tenured professors who are openly gay on all the more than 2000 American college and university campuses, and not five in the Ivy League.

The history of oppression and totalitarianism is far from ended, and America may in the future open its doors to still other émigrés from foreign lands. Three main categories may be discerned in the ranks of gay émigrés and exiles through the ages: (1) those who had to flee their native lands to escape severe legal and social penalties; (2) those who judged it prudent to emigrate to lessen the burden of social ostracism and potential conflict with the law; and (3) those who preferred life abroad, with the sexual privileges accorded the foreigner, particularly one with independent means, to a confined existence at home. The study of émigré colonies in exotic parts of the globe may shed additional light on the lives and fortunes of the gay exiles.

BIBLIOGRAPHY. Donald Fleming and Bernard Bailyn, eds., *The Intellectual Migration: Europe and America, 1930–1960*, Cambridge: Harvard University Press, 1969.

William A. Percy

F

FAGGOT

This contemptuous slang term for male homosexual carries overtones of **effeminacy** and cowardice. Inasmuch as its use is widespread and its origins usually misunderstood, it deserves careful consideration.

One of the most persistent **myths** that have gained a foothold in the gay **movement** is the belief that "faggot" derives from the basic meaning of "bundle of sticks used to light a fire," with the historical commentary that when witches were burned at the stake, "only presumed male homosexuals were considered low enough to help kindle the fires."

The English word has in fact three forms: *faggot*, attested by the Oxford English Dictionary from circa 1300; *fadge*, attested from 1588; and *faggald*, which the *Dictionary of the Older Scottish Tongue* first records from 1375. The first and second forms have the additional meaning "fat, slovenly woman" which according to the *English Dialect Dictionary* survived into the nineteenth century in the folk speech of England.

The homosexual sense of the term, unknown in England itself, appears for the first time in America in a vocabulary of criminal slang printed in Portland, Oregon in 1914, with the example "All the fagots (sissies) will be dressed in drag at the ball tonight." The apocopated (clipped) form *fag* then arose by virtue of the tendency of American colloquial speech to create words of one syllable; the first quotation is from the book by Nels Anderson, *The Hobo* (1923): "Fairies or Fags are men or boys who exploit sex for profit." The short form thus also has no connection with British *fag* as attested from the nineteenth century (for example, in the novel *Tom Brown's Schooldays*) in the sense of "**public school** boy who performs menial tasks for an upperclassman."

In American slang *faggot/fag* usurped the semantic role of **bugger** in British usage, with its connotations of extreme hostility and contempt bordering on death wishes. In more recent decades it has become the term of abuse par excellence in the mouths of heterosexuals, often just as an insult aimed at another male's alleged want of masculinity or courage, rather than implying a sexual role or orientation.

The ultimate origin of the word is a Germanic term represented by the Norwegian dialect words *fagg*, "bundle, heap," alongside *bagge*, "obese, clumsy creature" (chiefly of animals). From the latter are derived such Romance words as French *bagasse* and Italian *bagascia*, "prostitute," whence the parallel derivative *bagascione* whose meaning matches that of American English *faggot/fag*, while Catalan *bagassejar* signifies *to faggot*, "to frequent the company of loose women."

The final proof that *faggot* cannot have originated in the burning of witches at the stake is that in English law both **witchcraft** and buggery were punishable by hanging, and that in the reign of the homosexual monarch **James** I the execution of heretics came to an end, so that by the time American English gave the word its new meaning there cannot have been in the popular mind even the faintest remnant of the complex of ideas credited to the term in the contemporary myth. It is purely and simply an Americanism of the twentieth century.

Given the fact that the term faggot cannot refer to burning at the stake, why does the myth continue to enjoy popularity in the gay movement? On the conscious level it serves as a device with which to attack the medieval church, by extension **Christianity** in toto, and finally all authority. On another level, it may linger as a "myth of origins," a kind of collective masochistic ritual that willingly identifies the homosexual as victim. It should be evident that the word faggot and the ideas that have been mistakenly associated with it serve no useful function; the sooner both are abandoned, the better.

BIBLIOGRAPHY. Warren Johansson, "The Etymology of the Word *Faggot,*" *Gay Books Bulletin,* 6 (1981), 16–18, 33.
                    Warren Johansson

FAIRY

The word *fairy,* derived from the French *féerie,* the name of the mythical realm of these supernatural beings, was one of the commonest terms for the male homosexual in America in the 1925–1960 period. In an article published in *American Journal of Psychology* in 1896, "The Fairies" of New York are mentioned as a secret organization whose members attended coffee-klatsches; dressed in aprons and knitted, gossiped and crocheted; and held balls in which men adopted ladies' evening dress. The spellings *faery* and *fary* also appear in the literature. The word designated the more stereotypical or "obvious" sort of street homosexual, with the semantic link supplied by the notion of the delicate and fastidious that had attached itself to the expression, so that it was transferred effortlessly to a dainty and effeminate type of male. The image of the "fairy" in book illustration as a winged creature flitting about the landscape probably contributed to the further evolution of *flit* as a slang term for homosexual. The semantic development of *fairy* in this sense began on the east coast and spread to the rest of the country, but not to other English-speaking areas of the world. In the 1960s the word yielded to **gay** as a positive term preferred by the **movement,** and to **faggot** or *fag* as the vulgar term of abuse.

In the late 1970s a quasi-religious movement began on the west coast of the United States under the rubric of fairy spirituality. Inspired by the ideas of gay pioneer Harry Hay, this trend emphasized the concept that male homosexuals who will acknowledge their difference ("fairies" or "faeries") have special insights and gifts for interpersonal relations. It looked to the supposed homoerotic element in **shamanism** as a prehistoric archetype. Fairy retreats held at remote country sites, with neopagan rituals, serve to affirm solidarity among the fairies. This movement, combining **counterculture** survivals with elements of the hermetic tradition, is part of a larger complex of New Age religious phenomena that are characteristic of the western United States, though they also enjoy some following elsewhere.

FALLA, MANUEL DE (1876–1946)

Spanish composer. Falla ranks as a key figure in both the renovation of Spanish classical music and the flowering of Andalusian culture in the early twentieth century. His homosexuality is not known directly, but the circles in which he moved in both Paris and Granada, his friendships, style of life, and enthusiasm for the Andalusian past, enthusiasm which was frequently associated in Spain with homosexuality, permit it to be inferred.

Falla was born in the ancient Andalusian city of Cádiz. As his compositions were received with indifference in Madrid, in 1907 Falla moved to Paris, where he was successful. He left that city at the outbreak of World War I, and influenced by his librettist Gregorio Martínez Sierra, author of *Granada, guía emocional* (1911), made his home in **Granada** from 1919 to 1939.

Andalusian civilization was already of considerable interest to Falla; Granada was the setting of his opera *La vida breve* (Life is Short; 1904–05), and his very successful *Nights in the Gardens of Spain* (1916) is an evocation of the vanished sensual and erotic world of Islamic **Spain**. He was the key figure in the effort to conserve, through a festival and competition in 1922, the dying *cante jondo* song of Andalusia's past. The festival, for reasons which are not public, marks a turning point in Falla's work, which became progressively less Andalusian and more Catholic in inspiration. His *Retablo de maese Pedro* (Master Peter Puppet's Show; 1923), based on an episode from *Don Quixote*, and the *Harpsichord Concerto* (1927), both masterpieces, were the last major compositions he would complete. He declined to set to music a one-act libretto, *El calesero* (The Coachman), written for him by Federico García **Lorca**, although, strongly urged by friends, he did set Góngora's "Sonnet to Córdoba"—Córdoba was the capital of Andalusia at its peak—to music for the tercentenary of that author in 1927.

In 1927 Falla began a composition ideologically opposed to his Andalusian-themed works, an operatic setting of Verdaguer's epic poem *L'Atlántida*. In it, Catalonia and Falla's native Cádiz are fulfilled through the discovery of America by Columbus. Falla never completed his *Atlántida*, which was completed after his death by his only student, Ernesto Halffter. It has been indifferently received.

Falla was disturbed and depressed by the anti-Catholic violence of Spain of the early 1930s. Isolated and silent during the Civil War, in 1939 he fled to Argentina, where he died.

BIBLIOGRAPHY. J. B. Trend, *Manuel de Falla and Spanish Music*, New York: Knopf, 1934.

Daniel Eisenberg

FAMOUS HOMOSEXUALS, LISTS OF

It seems that every disadvantaged social group has a need to find distinguished individuals of the past with whom it can identify. This need is nowhere more clearly illustrated than in the case of the homosexual minority in modern society. Even in the era when sexual activity between members of the same sex was branded as a "crime against nature," their conduct was extenuated by the fact that figures celebrated in the annals of war, politics, and literature had loved their own sex.

In "L'Amour nommé Socratique," an article in his *Dictionnaire philosophique* (1764), **Voltaire** gives one of the earliest of such lists, based largely on his knowledge of Greco-Roman pederasty. The anonymous author of *Don Leon* (ca. 1836) has the poet **Byron** say:

> When young Alexis claimed a
> Virgil's sigh, He told the world his
> choice; and may not I? . . .
> Say, why, when great Epaminondas
> died,
> Was Cephidorus buried by his side?
> Or why should Plutarch with
> eulogiums cite
> That chieftain's love for young
> catamite,
> And we be forced his doctrine to
> decry,
> Or drink the bitter cup of infamy? . .
> Look, how infected with this rank
> disease
> Were those who held St. Peter's holy
> keys, . . .
> How many captains, famed for deeds
> of arms,
> Have found their solace in a
> minion's arms!

The first serious attempt to draw up a list of notable homosexuals of past centuries was in the second volume of Heinrich **Hoessli**'s *Eros: Die Männerliebe der Griechen* (1838). Later in the nineteenth century other lists were assembled by Karl Heinrich **Ulrichs** and by the British writers Henry Spencer Ashbee, Sir Richard **Burton**, and Havelock **Ellis**. An entire volume entitled *Berühmte Homosexuelle* (Famous Homosexuals) was compiled in 1910 by the pioneer student of homosexuality, the Berlin physician Albert **Moll**. No fewer than 300 names appear in Magnus Hirschfeld's major work synthesizing almost two decades of research, *Die Homosexualität des Mannes und des Weibes* (1914). The early phase of the postwar homophile **movement** produced a 751-page roster in Noel I. Garde's *Jonathan to Gide* (1954), which is, however, the high-water mark for the uncritical use of sources (such as including Pontius Pilate, the Roman prefect of Judea, on the basis of a passing mention in a novel published in 1932!). The most recent specimen of this class of literature is Martin Greif's often fanciful *The Gay Book of Names* (1982).

The need for such writings is motivated by the insult and humiliation heaped upon the homosexual minority by those who defame it. The ability to identify with glorious and universally admired figures in history gives the member of the oppressed minority role models conveying a sense of inner worth. The homosexual attains the conviction that he belongs to a part of mankind with its own achievements, its own traditions, and its own right to a "place in the sun." The tendency can become so marked as to invite parody, as amusingly executed by James Joyce for the counterpart among the Irish in *Ulysses* (1922). Paradoxically, some homophobes still revere noted figures in the past of their own nation despite the unanimous testimony of impartial biographers to their homosexuality. The phenomenon is comparable to that of anti-Semites who admire Spinoza and Einstein.

Historians of homosexual behavior have found that the method of accumulating famous names has a number of inadequacies. It tends to assimilate different types—exclusive homosexuals and bisexuals, **pederasts** and **androphiles**—under one rubric, neglecting the historical ambiance of the individual's orientation. Rarely is there a concern with the nexus between homosexual behavior and interests, on the one hand, and creativity, on the other. Use of evidence is often slipshod, and famous persons are included whose homosexuality is doubtful—even unlikely. Finally, focusing on a small constellation of politicians, writers, and artists obscures the life experience of the great mass of ordinary homosexuals and lesbians. Because of these drawbacks, books containing such lists are now regarded as belonging to the realm of popular culture rather than to that of scholarship.

The term eponym refers to a person from whom something, as a tribe, place or activity, takes its name. In this way proper names become common nouns designating any practitioner of the activity in question, such as *onanist* (from the Biblical Onan), *sapphist* (from Sappho of Lesbos), *sadist* (from Donatien-Alphonse-François, Marquis de **Sade**), and *masochist* (from Leopold von Sacher-Masoch), along with such jocular expressions as a *Tilden* (from the tennis star) and *Wildeman* (from Oscar **Wilde**). Similarly, French has the verbs *socratiser* and *engider*, both meaning "to sodomize." The latter is a nonce coinage created by the novelist Louis-Ferdinand Céline from the name (André) **Gide**. One writer of the early twentieth century commented that to name sexual practices after living persons who embodied them was to invite actions for libel, but it constitutes a fascinating intersection between **biography** and social **labeling**.

Warren Johansson

FANTASIES

Fantasies are mental scenes, produced by the imagination, distinct from the reality in which the person lives. This article concerns those of sexual content.

Everyone fantasizes to a considerable extent; thinking and fantasy are inseparable. Every time one sets a goal, makes a plan, or considers the desirability of a course of action, one fantasizes. One of the ways in which human beings differ from animals is that animals, to our knowledge, do not have fantasies.

The use of fantasies to produce and enhance sexual excitement is common. Fantasies may contain activities one would like to do or repeat: sex with a highly desirable partner or partners, or under exciting circumstances. These are unproblematic as long as the fantasizer accepts that there are things one would like to do which are impossible or impractical to realize, and takes steps toward the realization of appropriate fantasies. The prospect of realizing sexual fantasies is one of the great stimuli of human activity.

Potentially more stressful are fantasies of activities one might not or definitely would not like to do. These involve every sort of situation depicted in **pornography**, among them the infliction or suffering of pain, violence, or humiliation; promiscuous or anonymous sex; unfaithfulness to a partner; the exposure of the body to harm; and activities which do not conform to one's sexual orientation (gay or straight). Such erotic fantasies are potentially in conflict with one's self-image, and may cause worry and guilt.

If fantasies cause great distress, the assistance of a competent therapist may be helpful. That such fantasies are very widespread, however, suggests that their existence is normal and even healthy; we all have within us atavistic capacities, such as that to inflict pain, which cannot be expressed directly in a civilized society. Fantasies can help discharge tensions rather than increase them. A fantasy does not produce action against one's principles or true wishes. Furthermore, fantasies need not be revealed to anyone, although sharing them can be an exciting part of love-making. Lovers with fantasies that dovetail (the dominant with the submissive, for example) are truly blessed, although this is far less frequent than pornography

would suggest. The commercial sex industry (pornography, **prostitution**, **phone sex**) is primarily devoted to providing fantasies.

Daniel Eisenberg

FASCISM

The term fascism derives from *fasces*, the bundles of rods carried by the lictors of ancient **Rome** to symbolize the unity of classes in the Republic. Fascism is the authoritarian movement that arose in **Italy** in the wake of World War I. Although Hitler admired its founder Mussolini and imitated him at first—the term Führer is modeled on Duce—one cannot simply equate his more radical National Socialist movement with the Italian phenomenon, as writers of the left are prone to do. "Fascism" was also applied to related trends in eastern Europe, the Iberian peninsula, and Latin America. Some of these regimes (especially the Horthy dictatorship in Hungary and the Falange in **Spain**) had pronounced clerical-traditional overtones, which set them apart from the more secularist regimes of Italy and Germany. Whether all these political trends constitute so many variants of a single genus of fascism, or whether they are only loosely connected, is still earnestly debated by historians.

Italy. Not essentially racist like **Nazism** or anti-bourgeois like **Marxism**, Italian fascism, with its corporative binding of workers and employers, has been less consistently hostile to homosexuals. Attracting adherents from **anarchism** and syndicalism, both of which had been strong in Italy, Benito Mussolini (1883–1945) deserted pacifist, gradualist socialism to found fascism after his exhilarating wartime experience of violence. He henceforth extolled war as purifying, progressive, and evolutionary because the strong overcame the weak. He also argued in a discussion of a draft penal code in 1930 that because Italians, being virile, were not homosexuals, Italy needed no law banning homosexual acts, which he believed only degenerate foreigners to practice. A ban would only frighten such tourists away, and Italy needed the money they spent to improve its balance of payments and shore up its sagging economy. **Napoleon** had promulgated his code, which did not penalize homosexual acts between consenting adults, in northern Italy in 1810, and thus decriminalized sodomy. It had already been decriminalized in Tuscany by Grand Duke Leopold, the enlightened brother of Joseph II. The Albertine Code of 1837 for Piedmont-Sardinia was extended to all its dominions after the House of Savoy created a united Kingdom of Italy, a task completed in 1870. Pervasive was the influence of the jurist Marquis Cesare **Beccaria**, who argued against cruel and unusual punishments and against all offenses motivated by religious superstition and fanaticism.

Thus Italy with its age-old **"Mediterranean homosexuality"** in which women were protected, almost secluded—upper-class girls at least in the South being accompanied in public by dueñas—had like other Latin countries allowed female prostitution and closed its eyes to homosexuality. As such it had become the playground par excellence during the "grand tour" of the English *milords*, and also the refuge of **exiles and émigrés** from the criminal sanctions of the Anglo-American common law and the Prussian code. The Prussian Code was extended in 1871–72 to the North and then South German territories incorporated in the Reich, including ones where the Code Napoléon had prevailed in the early part of the century. **Byron** and John Addington **Symonds** took refuge in Italy, as William **Beckford** did in Portugal and Oscar **Wilde** in Paris. Friedrich Alfred Krupp's playground was in Capri, Thomas **Mann's** in **Venice**, and Count **Adelswärd Fersen's** also in Capri.

Il Duce's rise to power did not end Italy's welcoming role. Although he emphasized the virility of Italians and the decadence of foreigners and decried homosexuality as a sign of weakness, Mussolini regarded homosexuals either in the old clerical fashion as sodomites given over to vice or in the ancient Roman fashion as effeminates—but not as a threat to the virility of the race. (Personally, Mussolini was somewhat of a sexual acrobat, in that he had a succession of mistresses and often took time out in the office to have sex with one or another of his secretaries.) Like Napoleon III under the French Second Empire, he preferred to leave same-sex conduct outside the criminal code in order to avoid sensational trials that would expose his nation to ridicule in the foreign press. Rather he decided to exile homosexuals to remote areas of Italy where they would provoke no scandal. Believing in military strength through numbers, Mussolini did more than Hitler to subsidize parents of numerous progeny, thus hoping to increase Italy's population from 40 to 60 million. Although local authorities occasionally conducted raids on gay cruising areas and the like, before 1938 he did not persecute homosexuals more than previous regimes had done.

However, after he formed the Rome–Berlin Axis with Hitler in 1936, Mussolini began, under Nazi influence, to persecute homosexuals and to promulgate anti-Semitic decrees in 1938 and 1939, though these were laxly enforced, and permitted exceptions, such as veterans of World War I. New laws were passed penalizing "offenses against race and the provisions for education of the youth of the Regime." After 1938 homosexuals thus were considered political offenders. Oppressing homosexuals more than Jews, Mussolini's regime rounded up and imprisoned a substantial number, a procedure poignantly depicted in Ettore Scola's excellent film *A Special Day* (1977). Fascists whose homosexual behavior embarrassed the regime were usually only dismissed from their posts. Notorious homosexuals without influence were punished merely with short jail sentences. Political opponents received longer sentences. Following established Italian fascist practice, homosexuals were sent into exile (*confino*) in remote places (generally islands) where they eked out a meagre existence. The actual enforcement of the laws, and in particular mass roundups of suspected homosexuals, were left to local authorities. But the bulk of Italians in town and country continued under fascism, as they had previously, the occasional homosexual practices for which Italy had been so famed. Even exclusive homosexuals, if they were not unlucky, survived fascism unscathed.

Eastern Europe. In Eastern Europe "clerical fascism" overthrew all the democratic regimes established in the wake of the Allied victory and the Paris Peace Conference of 1919, as well as those carved from the territory of the Russian Empire. The only exception was Czechoslovakia. With the encouragement of the clergy and support from the peasantry, gentry, army, and professional and business classes, Admiral Horthy seized control of Hungary from the Communist Béla Kun in 1920 and as "Regent" unleashed a "White Terror" largely directed against Jews, two years before Mussolini marched on Rome with his blackshirts. One by one the other democracies fell. In Poland the tolerant Marshall Piłsudski, who dominated Poland after seizing Russian and Lithuanian territory, actually decriminalized sodomy when a uniform penal code (*Kodeks karny*) was adopted for the whole of Poland in 1932. (This perhaps hearkened back to the days of the Grand Duchy of Warsaw when Poles lived under the Code Napoléon, or perhaps to the thwarted project to introduce the Code into "Congress Poland" after 1815.)

By contrast, most of the dictators of East Central Europe simply perpetuated the old clerical strictures; by allying with the Catholic or Orthodox Church they stiffened reactionary opposition to liberalization, just as they encouraged traditional Christian hatred of Jews. In this unfavorable climate none of these countries could develop a sexual reform movement of any significance.

Naturally amid such ethnic diversity and various dates of introduction of the Code Napoléon, differences in sexual expression were vast, and even within one country no consistent pattern existed. Fascists were less consistent and more divided among themselves than even Communists or Nazis. After all, they had no sacred text like *Das Kapital* or *Mein Kampf*, and further were not ruling only a single powerful country. Many were nevertheless influenced by Hitler, himself perhaps in part inspired by his totalitarian rival Stalin's homophobic repression in Soviet **Russia** beginning in January 1934. Being hostile to classical **liberalism** with its emphasis on toleration and the rule of law, fascism made homosexuals uneasy. However, it may be doubted whether they suffered more during the 1920s and 1930s in the fascist countries (not counting Nazi Germany) than in France and the Anglo-Saxon democracies, where premature attempts to found gay **movements** were suppressed by police action with no outcry whatsoever from the defenders of civil liberties. Czechoslovakia, the only democracy in Central Europe to survive this period, simply continued the Austrian penal code of 1852 that penalized both male and female homosexuality.

Spain and the Falange. The middle-class, ascetic, deeply Catholic Franco, who overthrew the Spanish Republic in the Civil War of 1936-39, established one of the harshest of the fascist regimes, executing many of the defeated republicans and jailing others under brutal conditions. The great homosexual poet Federico García **Lorca** was shot by a death squad near Granada in 1936; it is said that they fired the bullets through his backside to "make the punishment fit the crime." On the other hand, the Falange theoretician José Antonio Primo de Rivera, who was killed by the left at the beginning of the Civil War, was widely believed to be homosexual. Even Franco himself, rumor has alleged, had an occasional fling during his service in Morocco.

More than Mussolini, Franco resisted the theories and pressures of Hitler, whom he regarded as a despicable (and perhaps deranged) upstart. It has been argued that Franco was not a fascist at all and that he actually maintained a pro-Jewish policy, granting asylum to refugees from Nazi-occupied Europe and attempting to protect Sephardic Jews in the Balkan countries. In his last years he in fact liberalized Spain to a certain extent, allowing among other things a resurgence of gay bars, baths, and culture even before the accession of King Juan Carlos upon his death in 1975. Today **Spain** is one of the freest countries in Europe.

Latin America. Juan Perón in Argentina and other dictators in Latin America mouthed fascist doctrines without even the consistency of Mussolini's Eastern European imitators. Naturally Latins, like Slavs, being considered inferior peoples by Hitler, did not in general espouse racism (Hitler had to make the Japanese honorary Aryans to ally with them in the Tripartite Pact of 1937), so they had no reason to think of homosexuals in his terms. Rather, they looked upon them with amused contempt, in the vein of Latin machismo. This machismo reinforced clerical prejudice to keep social intolerance the rule in Latin America. As Perón was gaining power in 1943–44, there was some repression, perhaps instigated by the military, but after he consolidated his rule in 1947 there was little.

Conclusion. On the whole, fascism was too tradition-minded and lacking in innovative will to formulate a coherent policy regarding such a "modern" phenomenon as homosexuality. The twentieth-century demand of homosexuals for justice and equality, the homosexual emancipation movement, which was heralded in Germany as early as 1864, and was

first organized by Magnus **Hirschfeld** in 1897, elicited a violent and reactionary response from National Socialism and to a lesser extent from the other great totalitarian movement, Stalin's Communism. However, in countries where homosexual emancipation did not exist (and no need was felt for it in states that had adopted the Code Napoléon), a campaign of repression simply had no motive in the ideology of the rightist regimes that dominated much of the interwar period.

See also **Holocaust; Nationalism**.

BIBLIOGRAPHY. Giovanni Dall'Orto, "Le ragioni di una persecuzione," in: Martin Sherman, *Bent* (Italian trans.), Turin: Edizioni Gruppo Abele, 1984, pp. 101–19; idem, "Per il bene della razza al confino il pederasta," *Babilonia* (April and May 1986); Walter Laqueur, *Fascism: A Reader's Guide: Analyses, Interpretations, Bibliography*, Berkeley: University of California Press, 1976.

William A. Percy

FASCIST PERVERSION, BELIEF IN

Fascism and National Socialism (**Nazism**) were originally distinct political systems, but their eventual international ties (the "Rome–Berlin axis") led to the use of "fascist" as an umbrella term by Communist writers anxious to avoid the implication that "National Socialism" was a type of socialism. Neither in Italy nor in Spain did the right-authoritarian political movements have a homosexual component. Rather it was in Weimar Germany that the right-wing paramilitary groups which constituted the nucleus of the later National Socialist German Workers Party (NSDAP) attracted a considerable number of homosexuals whose erotic leanings overlapped with the male bonding of the party. This strong male bonding, in the later judgment of their own leaders, gave the Nazis a crucial advantage in their victory over the rival Social Democratic and Communist formations in the early 1930s.

The most celebrated of the homosexuals in the Nazi Party of the 1920s was Ernst **Röhm**, whose sexual proclivities were openly denounced by left-wing propagandists, but this did not deprive him of Hitler's confidence until the putsch of June 30, 1934, in which he and many of his homosexual comrades in arms were massacred. Ironically enough it was said that with Röhm the last socialist in the NSDAP died. For Communist writers as early as the mid-1920s homosexuality was an element of "bourgeois decadence," or of *le vice allemand* (the German vice), and theorists such as Wilhelm **Reich** who were opposed to homosexuality could claim that the right-wing youth were "becoming more homosexual." The victory of National Socialism at the beginning of 1933 then reinforced Communist and émigré propagandists in their resort to "fascist perversion" as a rhetorical device with which they could abuse and vilify the regime that had defeated and exiled them—and which they hoped would be transient and unstable.

In particular, the statute by which Stalin restored the criminal sanctions against homosexuality that had been omitted from the penal codes of 1922 and 1926 was officially titled the "Law of March 7, 1934"—a pointed allusion to the anniversary of the National Socialist consolidation of power one year earlier. Maxim Gorky is even supposed to have said "Destroy the homosexuals and with them destroy fascism!" During his exile in the Soviet Union, the leftist German director Gustav von Wangenheim (1895–1975) made a film entitled *Bortsy* (The Fighters; 1936), in which the Nazis are shown as homosexual. The reaction of the Hitler regime to all this was to enact a new and more stringent version of the notorious **Paragraph 175** in the legal novella of June 28, 1935. Under its provisions the number of convictions for homosexual activity rose

to many times what it had been at the end of the Weimar Republic.

While the subject of homosexuality was still largely taboo in the British and American press during World War II, allusions to the theme of "fascist perversion" are found in denunciations of Nazi Germany, and occasional echoes of the belief recur in left-wing propaganda of the recent decades. In the United States Maoists charged that the gay liberation movement of 1969 and the years following was an example of "bourgeois **decadence**" that would vanish once the triumph of socialism was achieved. Communist and Catholic organizations in coalitions of the American left have even formed ad hoc alliances for the purpose of excluding "gay rights" from the common program of the umbrella group or of keeping gay speakers off the platform at major rallies. The belief in homosexuality as a "fascist perversion" is one of the Stalinist myths of the 1930s that are belied by the historical facts but still kept alive by uncritical writings on the subject and by artistic treatments such as Luchino **Visconti**'s film *The Damned* (1970).

BIBLIOGRAPHY. Samuel Igra, *Germany's National Vice*, London: Quality Press, 1945; John Lauritsen and David Thorstad, *The Early Homosexual Rights Movement (1864–1935)*, New York: Times Change Press, 1974, pp. 43–45.

Warren Johansson

FASSBINDER, RAINER WERNER (1945–1982)

West German filmmaker, author, director, and actor. With his "anti-theatre" troupe in Munich Fassbinder set out to redefine the aesthetic experience on stage. His search quickly brought him (along with the members of this troupe who would often serve as his actors) to **film**. From his first films in 1969 to his forty-third in 1982, he explored the intricate connections between love and manipulation while also charting his vision of the path of **German** history (especially the periods of the Third Reich and the growth of a West German society he felt to be economically affluent but spiritually impoverished).

Often castigated as someone who expressed a solely subjective view, Fassbinder openly made use of a variety of sources—his own love affairs, Hollywood films, works from German literature—which he then filtered into his own entwinement of the personal and the public spheres. A relatively static camera (especially in his early films), mirrors and frames, layers of sound, a heightened sense of melodrama—these are all elements of a cinematic style which Fassbinder employs in order to speak for those who have been denied a voice.

Those films where homosexual relationships form the main theme clearly demonstrate Fassbinder's concern and his techniques. *The Bitter Tears of Petra von Kant* (1972), *Fox and His Friends* (1975), and *In a Year with Thirteen Moons* (1978) all deal with same-sex relationships in which erotic desire becomes a function of the struggle for dominance of one partner over the other. His films of two literary masterpieces, *Berlin Alexanderplatz* (1980), a television mini-series, and *Querelle* (based on a novel of Jean **Genet**; 1982), explore intense homoerotic relationships between men as well as openly homosexual ones.

Yet Fassbinder, himself homosexual, shows that the failure of the relationships he depicts to survive or even to nurture does not stem from the nature of homosexuality itself. Rather, he makes evident that such love cannot succeed in this society under conditions where human beings have lost their ability to form any relationship except one based on objectification and exploitation.

In the end, though, what Fassbinder presented is not an analysis of the futility of love, be it homosexual or heterosexual in nature. By portraying the precari-

ous existence of relationships between love and manipulation and by using the fates of individual characters to portray the path of German history and its influence in shaping everyday existences, Fassbinder's films open the possibility for change.

BIBLIOGRAPHY. Ronald Hayman, *Fassbinder: Film Maker*, New York: Simon and Schuster, 1984; Robert Katz, *Life Is Colder Than Death: The Life and Times of Rainer Werner Fassbinder*, New York: Random House, 1987; Tony Rayns, ed., *Fassbinder*, 2nd ed., London: British Film Institute, 1979 (1st ed., 1976); *Rainer Werner Fassbinder* (Reihe Filmbuch), Munich: Carl Hanser Verlag, 1983.

James W. Jones

FELLATIO
See **Oral Sex.**

FERENCZI, SANDOR (1873–1933)

Hungarian psychoanalyst. Born to a Jewish family in Miskolc in northeastern Hungary, he grew up in his father's bookstore and lending library. He studied medicine at the University of Vienna, graduating in 1894. Ferenczi met Sigmund **Freud** for the first time in 1907. He underwent analysis with Freud, and the two passed many summers together. Ferenczi became a central figure in the psychoanalytic movement and the founder of psychoanalysis in Hungary, where he played much the same role as did Karl Abraham in Berlin. He translated many of Freud's writings into Hungarian, and under the short-lived Communist regime of Béla Kun he was appointed professor of psychoanalysis at the University of Budapest.

Major Contributions. Ferenczi's reputation was established by his *Über die Entwicklungsstufen des Wirklichkeitssinnes* (On the Stages in the Development of the Sense of Reality), in which he described the feeling of infantile omnipotence. His second major book, *Thalassa:*

Versuch einer Genitaltheorie (Thalassa, an Essay on the Theory of Genitality) he began to write in 1914 and published in 1924. In it he described the "Thalassal regression," and for the first time used the word *bioanalysis*. During the same period Ferenczi developed a more active form of psychoanalytic technique, in which directives to the patient were used to provoke increasing tension that would mobilize unconscious material and overcome the patient's resistances. He urged active interference, role playing, and free expression of love and affection for the patient. While critical of some of his innovations, Freud could later say that Ferenczi "has made us all his pupils."

With Freud's British disciple, Ernest Jones, Ferenczi had an unhappy and ambivalent relationship. Jones underwent a training analysis with Ferenczi in the summer and autumn of 1913, but later composed a negative account of his analyst's last years, saying that an "unhappy deterioration of his mind" had set in and that he suffered from a "very deep layer of mental disturbance." Those who knew Ferenczi at the close of life dismiss Jones' allegations as mythical.

Publications on Homosexuality. Ferenczi's contribution to the study of homosexuality took the form of two papers, an early one in Hungarian on "Homosexualitas feminina," published in *Gyógyászat* in 1902, and a German article of 1914 entitled "Über die Nosologie der männlichen Homosexualität" (On the Nosology of Male Homosexuality), first delivered at a psychoanalytic congress in 1911. The first article described a lesbian transvestite named Roza K. who because of her sexual interests and manner of dressing had been rejected by her family and was in frequent conflict with the police. She led a pitiable existence of wandering between a charitable institution, a prison, a shelter for the homeless, and a psychiatric hospital. Ferenczi saw her as posing two problems: a clinical one and a political one; he proposed that "communal hospices" be created where homosexual persons could find sufficient freedom to work if they chose, and at the same time a refuge from the hostility which they encountered in the outside world. The patient exhibited numerous masculine traits, but also, in his view, stigmata of degeneration, in particular a repellent ugliness. He concluded that the abnormality of her sexual drive was nature's infallible way of inhibiting her reproductive activity.

In the latter article Ferenczi expounded the difference between subject and object homoeroticism, that is to say, he rejected the notion that "homosexuality" was a single clinical entity. The "active" homosexual feels himself a man in every respect, is as a rule very energetic and aggressive, and nothing effeminate can be discovered in his physical or mental type. The object of his sexual drive is his own sex, so that he is a homoerotic through transfer of the love object. The "passive" homosexual, whom Ferenczi styles "inverted," alone exhibits the reversal of the normal secondary and tertiary sexual characteristics. In intercourse with men, and in all relations of life, he feels himself a woman and thus is inverted in respect of his own ego, so that he is a homoerotic through subject inversion. The first type, the object homoerotic, is almost exclusively interested in young, delicate boys with a feminine appearance, yet feels pronounced antipathy to the adult woman. The second, the subject homoerotic, feels attracted to more mature, powerful men, but can relate to women on terms of equality. The true invert, said Ferenczi, is seldom impelled to seek psychoanalytic advice; he accepts the passive role completely, and has no wish other than to be left alone and allowed to pursue the kind of gratification that suits him. The object homoerotic, on the other hand, suffers acute dysphoria, is tormented by the consciousness of his abnormality, never satisfied by his sexual activity, plagued by qualms of conscience, and overestimates the object of his desires as well. It is he who seeks analytic help for his problems, and also is promiscuous because of repeated disappointment with his love object. Subject and object homoeroticism, concluded Ferenczi, are different conditions; the former is a developmental anomaly, a true "sexual intermediate stage," while the second is suffering from an obsessional neurosis.

Besides these articles, in April 1906 Ferenczi presented to the Budapest Medical Association a paper entitled "Sexualis átmeneti fokozatokról" (On Sexual Intermediate Stages), which was his report, as a neuro-psychiatrist, on the 1905 volume of the *Jahrbuch für sexuelle Zwischenstufen* which the **Scientific-Humanitarian Committee** in Berlin had sent to the Association, asking it to take a stand against the penal sanctions to which homosexuals were subjected. In the report, published in *Gyógyászat* the same year, Ferenczi fully endorsed the position of Hirschfeld and his supporters, saying: "I consider the repression of the homosexuals profoundly unjust and utterly useless, and I think that we should give our firm support to the petition drafted by the Scientific-Humanitarian Committee and signed, since the beginning of 1905, by some 2800 German physicians." Thus Ferenczi was one of those who even at the turn of the century spoke out against the archaic penal statutes and in favor of legal and social toleration.

BIBLIOGRAPHY. Judith Dupont, ed., *The Clinical Diary of Sandor Ferenczi,* Cambridge, MA: Harvard University Press, 1988; Sandor Ferenczi, "The Nosology of Male Homosexuality," in *The Problem of Homosexuality in Modern Society,* Hendrik M. Ruitenbeek, ed., New York: E. P. Dutton, 1963, pp. 3–16; Claude Lorin, ed., *Le jeune Ferenczi: Premiers écrits 1899–1906,* Paris: Aubier Montaigne, 1983; Claude Sabourin, *Ferenczi: Paladin et Grand Vizir secret,* Paris: Editions Universitaires, 1985.

Warren Johansson

FETISHISM

A fetish is an object or, in fact, any focal point which has come to stir irrational reverence or obsessive devotion. A sexual fetish, unlike a mere preference, usually amounts to an exclusive demand, in that full arousal cannot occur in the absence of the fetish—be it a black shoe, a particular piece of underwear, or some partner-attribute such as perhaps broad shoulders, narrow or broad hips, large breasts in women or a large penis in men, an extreme presence or absence of fat, an abundance or absence of body hair, and the like.

Fetishistic demands usually stem from an early, particularly pleasurable experience, although it can perhaps never be precisely determined how one person's pleasurable experience is transformed into a lifelong fetishistic requirement, while a similar event for someone else may hardly stand out as exceptional, let alone as an ongoing fetish. And yet the basic mechanisms of strong preference-formations *are* known.

The pre-adolescent male's sexual response tends to be extremely diverse (polymorphous) and easily triggered by virtually any exciting event—anything from fast rides, big fires, and loud noises to being called on in class, seeing animals in coitus, or imagining close bodily contact with other children or adults. The onset of puberty quickly brings a narrowing down of sexual response to a much reduced number of specifically sexual items. The range is narrowed still further by the conditioning effects of a person's individual experience and basic disposition, until only a few strong preferences prevail—preferences that tend to become narrowed to ever fewer targets as a person builds up aversion reactions to "opposite" alternatives. At the extreme end of this whole conditioning process are the narrow, intense fetishistic preferences.

And yet all this work of conditioning applies almost exclusively to males. For reasons that are still not fully understood, female sexual response is virtually non-conditionable (Kinsey, 1953, p. 642f.). Thus despite local, rewarding sex experiences of myriad kinds, women simply do not become "fixated" onto any one particular kind of sex practice or preference in the way that men do. (Nobody on record ever saw a female black-shoe fetishist and probably never will, although this and a host of equivalent male fetishes are commonplace.)

Male homosexuality affords uniquely useful insights into the whole problem of understanding fetishes. By its very nature, the male–male pairing affords a double chance of seeing a fetishistic demand revved up in intensity by being fed from both sides. By contrast, since fetishistic responses are very rare among women, they are virtually non-existent among lesbian couples.

In heterosexual couples the fetishistic male has to work out a compromise acceptable to his female partner; this may call for tact and other forms of inhibition on his part, and a degree of forbearance from her—a compromise on both sides that can greatly obscure the true reactions of each. However, there is no indication that heterosexual men, if given equally responsive partners, would be any less inclined toward fetishism than are homosexual men.

BIBLIOGRAPHY. Alfred C. Kinsey, Wardell B. Pomeroy, and Clyde E. Martin, *Sexual Behavior in the Human Male*, Philadelphia: Saunders, 1948; Alfred C. Kinsey, Wardell B. Pomeroy, Clyde E. Martin, and Paul H. Gebhard, *Sexual Behavior in the Human Female*, Philadelphia: Saunders, 1953; C. A. Tripp, *The Homosexual Matrix*, second ed., New York: New American Library, 1987.

C. A. Tripp

FICHTE, HUBERT (1935–1986)

German writer. One of the major (West) German authors of the postwar period, Fichte is rare among German authors in that he not only treated the subject of homosexuality openly but even made it his starting point and guiding force.

Born the illegitimate child of a mother who was unable to realize a longed-for career as an actress and a Jewish father who seems to have disappeared after emigrating to Sweden, Hubert Fichte grew up an "outsider." After a career as a child actor in Hamburg theatres and in the movies (and an ambivalent relationship with Hans Henny **Jahnn**), Fichte set off for France with a traveling scholarship from the French government. In that country he served for a time as a leader in the camps of Abbé Pierre. Back in North Germany and in Sweden, Fichte devoted himself—and in a completely professional manner—to farming. At the same time he worked on translations (rendering *Simplizius Simplizissimus* into French, together with Jean Giono), and on his own writings.

His first publications (1959, 1961) brought him his first successes: writing fellowships and participation in the congresses of the influential Gruppe 47. From 1965 onward his strongly autobiographical novels, beginning with *Das Waisenhaus*, appeared. In the year in which the last novel in this series, *Versuch über die Pubertät*, was published (1974), Hubert Fichte began an ambitious project: "The History of Sensibility," planned for 19 volumes, novels and books containing "glosses," on which he labored almost obsessively until his death, and which is now being edited in a fragmentary form by the administrators of his literary heritage. Some of the volumes (so far as can be judged from the extant published work and the plans for publication) derive from the autobiographical world of the earlier novels; an additional section continues a project that Fichte had undertaken alongside his novels. Closely related to the novels is a "poetic anthropology/ethnology" that focuses not just on Afro-American religions—to which two large volumes of text and parallel volumes of illustrations by the photographer Leonore Mau, who had been living and working with Fichte since 1963, are devoted (*Xango: Die afroamerikanischen Religionen: Bahia, Haiti, Trinidad*, 1978/84, *Petersilie: Die afroamerikanischen Religionen: Santo Domingo, Venezuela, Miami, Grenada*, 1980/84)—but also on traditions and phenomena of European culture with the same perspective of the ethnologist and anthropologist. In these works high culture (**Sappho**, **Homer**, August von **Platen**, **Genet**) is treated and depicted with the same attentiveness as the world of the Hamburg "Palais d'Amour." After Fichte's death there appeared *Homosexualität und Literatur: Polemiken*, vols. 1 and 2 (1987–88).

What is new, different, and rewarding in Hubert Fichte is more than his range. It is stimulating to observe how the new standpoint, which probably even without "gay consciousness," leads to new forms of verbalization and to open forms (even the format of Fichte's novels on the printed page—with much blank space—is open). His use of text collages at the macro and micro level can be read as the reflex of a process "of fragmentation and rebirth." In this process Fichte brought together a broadly conceived interpretation of "puberty" and "religion."

BIBLIOGRAPHY. Thomas Beckermann, ed., *Hubert Fichte: Materialien zu Leben und Werk*, Frankfurt am Main: Fischer, 1985; Marita Keilson-Lauritz, "Durch die goldene Harfe gelispelt: Zur George-Rezeption bei Hubert Fichte," *Forum Homosexualität und Literatur*, 2 (1987), 21–51; Wolfgang von Wangenheim, *Hubert Fichte*, Munich: C. H. Beck, 1980.

Marita Keilson-Lauritz

FICINO, MARSILIO (1433–1499)

Italian philosopher and humanist. The son of a physician, he preferred to take up the study of philosophy rather than to follow in his father's footsteps. The arrival in Italy of learned Byzantines fleeing Constantinople after it had fallen to the Turks in 1453 gave Italian humanists the opportunity of studying Greek works which had been previously unknown to them. In this way the young Ficino discovered Platonism, learning Greek in order to study its texts.

Having gained the favor of the Medici family in Florence, Ficino was protected by them for the rest of his life; they presented him with a precious gift of Greek manuscripts, which he translated. Ficino quickly became a respected personality, attracting various pupils in a kind of Platonic Academy. In 1473 he took priestly orders, while continuing his philosophical speculations and taking on the responsibility of showing that the philosophy of **Plato** was in accord with Christian doctrine, as St. Thomas **Aquinas** had done earlier with **Aristotle**.

Among his most important works is the *Theologia platonica* (published in 1482), to which must be added strictly religious works (e.g., his Commentary on the Epistles of St. Paul), and philosophical disquisitions (e.g., his Commentary on Plato's Symposium of 1469, in which he revived the form of the Platonic dialogue), as well as an impressive number of translations from the Greek of works of Plato and other ancient Greek thinkers. These translations made available to a scholarly public works that for the most part had been inaccessible up to that time in the West.

Marsilio Ficino is one of the most representative personalities of the Italian **Renaissance**. His fame is inseparable from his love and painstaking work of rediscovery, translation, commentary, and advocacy of the works of Plato.

Of special significance in this regard is his resurrection of the Platonic ideal of love, as it is known from the *Phaedrus* and the *Symposium*. In the sixteenth century Ficino's version was elaborated in countless treatises on love, becoming the prototype of a new concept of "courtly love."

Under the rubric of *amor socraticus* Ficino set forth a paradigm of a profound but highly spiritual love between two men, perhaps linked by their common devotion to the quest for knowledge. According to his statement in the abovementioned Commentary on Plato's *Symposium*, this love is caused, following Plato's conception, by the vision of beauty vouchsafed by the soul of the other individual—a beauty that reflects the supernal beauty of God. Through the physical beauty of a young man—women were incapable of inciting this rapture, being more suited to stimulate copulation for the reproduction of the species—the prudent man ascends to the Beauty which is the archetypal Idea (in Plato's sense) on which the beauty he sees depends—hence to God himself. Thus contemplating the physical and spiritual beauty of a young man through love is a way of contemplating at least a fragment of Divine Beauty, the model of every individual terrestrial beauty.

Ficino practiced this love metaphysic with the young and handsome Giovanni Cavalcanti (ca. 1444–1509), whom he made the principal character in his commentary on the *Convivio*, and to whom he wrote ardent love letters in Latin, which were published in his *Epistulae* in 1492. It is an ironic fact that the object of his love always remained (as Ficino himself laments) in a state of embarrassment.

Apart from these letters there are numerous indications that Ficino's erotic impulses were directed toward men. After his death his biographers had a difficult task in trying to refute those who spoke of his homosexual tendencies.

Fortunately the universal respect enjoyed by Ficino, his sincere and deep faith, as well as his membership in the Catholic clergy, put him outside the reach of gossip and suspicions of sodomy—which, however, such followers as Benedetto Varchi were not spared.

After Ficino's death the ideal of "Socratic love" became a potent instrument to justify love between persons of the same sex; during the high Renaissance many persons were to make use of this protective shield. Yet this use served ultimately to discredit the ideal in the eyes of the public, and with the passage of the years it was regarded with increasing distrust, until—about 1550—it became simply identified with sodomy itself. Consequently, in order to save it, from the middle of the sixteenth century the ideal was heterosexualized, and in this guise it long survived in love treatises and in Italian and European love literature in general.

BIBLIOGRAPHY. Giovanni Dall'Orto, "'Socratic Love' as a Disguise for Same-sex Love in the Italian Renaissance," *Journal of Homosexuality*, 16 (1988), 33–65.

Giovanni Dall'Orto

FICTION
See **Novels and Short Fiction.**

FIDENTIAN POETRY

This minor genre of Italian poetry originated as a vehicle for homosexual themes that within the larger context of burlesque poetry have given rise to **Burchiellesque** and **Bernesque** poetry. The initiator of Fidentian poetry was Camillo Scroffa (1526–1565), a jurisconsult of Vicenza, in his *Cantici di Fidenzio* published in 1562 (but composed about 1545–50).

The *Cantici*, which probably come from Scroffa's student days at Padua, are supposed to have been written by an "amorous pedant," one Fidenzio Glottocrisio Ludomagistro, who is hopelessly in love with the handsome Camillo Strozzi. It is possible that the *Cantici* began as a student prank at the expense of a pedantic teacher at the University of Padua, Pietro Giunteo Fidenzio da Montagnana.

In fact the author seems to have forgotten this hoax of his youth; he decided to prepare an edition only after a series of unauthorized, and often enlarged, published collections had made the material popular.

The anthology amounts in the main to an anti-Petrarchan pamphlet, poking fun at well-worn conventions of love poetry, while at the same time it is a satire on the excessive preoccupation with classical antiquity into which the humanists had fallen, both from a linguistic standpoint and in view of their exaltation of the so-called Socratic love.

In fact not only is the fictitious author of the *Cantici* "Socratically" in love with his pupil "in the ancient manner," but he composes love poetry in a language in which immoderate love for the Latin language produces a thoroughgoing bastardization of the Italian, which has to bear an endless assault of Latinisms. The effect is comically pompous.

Scroffa's literary astuteness emerges in his having created a very human character, one who is pathetically caught up in the toils of an "impossible" love, set apart from the lives of normal people, and incapable of seeing anything wrong in the overwhelming sentiment he feels for "his" Camillo. The poems are tender and very candid, to the point that, the satire notwithstanding, the reader feels great sympathy for the hapless Fidenzio.

What came to be known as Fidentian poetry—which is technically the opposite of macaronic poetry, which mixes vernacular elements into Latin, instead of vice versa—was cultivated even before the first authorized edition of the *Cantici* in 1562, and lasted until the beginning of the eighteenth century.

Scrofa's first imitators kept close to his homoerotic inspiration. The finest among them are probably the anonymous author of "Jano Argyroglotto" (who also translated an anacreontic poem) and Giambattista Liviera (1565–early seventeenth century).

With the spread of Counterreformation ideas, the tone of the compositions was prudently and prudishly changed from homoerotic to heterosexual. Incapable of maintaining the subtle balance between irony and transgression, which Scroffa had exemplified, later Fidentian poetry became a sterile and repetitive poetic exercise, the equivalent of the mannered poetry which was in fact the original target of the *Cantici di Fidenzio*.

BIBLIOGRAPHY. Camillo Scroffa, *I Cantici di Fidenzio, con appendice di poeti fidenziani*, Pietro Trifone, ed., Rome: Salerno, 1981.

Giovanni Dall' Orto

FIEDLER THESIS

In a 1948 essay widely circulated in the 1950s ("Come Back on the Raft Ag'in Honey"), the innovative literary critic Leslie Fiedler argued that interracial male homoerotic relationships (not necessarily genitally expressed) have occupied a central place in the American psyche. Citing works by Fenimore Cooper, Richard Henry Dana, Herman **Melville**, and Mark Twain, he even spoke of the "sacred marriage of males."

Whatever the ultimate verdict on this thesis may be, it is probably true that male homosexuals—and lesbians—have for a long time been more open to interracial contact than the population at large. It has been suggested that racial complementation serves as a surrogate for the absent complementation of gender. Those who hold this view find a similar pattern in relationships that cross class lines. In the case of racial dyads, as seen typically in the "salt-and-pepper **couple**," the greater frequency may also be facilitated by the fact that no children will be born from the union, a question that heterosexual couples—in view of the lingering racism of our society—cannot ignore. That interracial gay relationships have been accompanied by some self-consciousness (and hostility on the part of bigoted individuals) transpires from such slang epithets as *dinge/chocolate queen, snow queen, rice queen,* and *taco queen.*

In the late 1970s the organization Black and White Men Together appeared in a number of American cities, attracting a good deal of support. In addition to offering social opportunities, the group has sought to explore the subtler aspects of the dynamics of such relationships, as well as to oppose racism. In some cities it is called Men of All Colors Together (MACT).

See also **Black Gay Americans; Working Class, Eroticization of.**

BIBLIOGRAPHY. Leslie Fiedler, *An End to Innocence,* Boston: Beacon Press, 1952, pp. 142–51; Michael J. Smith, *Black Men/White Men: A Gay Anthology,* San Francisco: Gay Sunshine Press, 1983.

FILM

Movie making is both an art and an industry. It has drawn for inspiration on theatre, fiction, biography, history, current affairs, religion, folklore, and the visual and musical arts. Active in stimulating the fantasy lives of viewers, motion pictures also reflect, though in a highly selective and often distorted way, the texture of daily life.

History of Motion Pictures. Although the first crude efforts with a proto-movie camera were made in the 1880s, films did not begin to be shown in specially designed cinemas until the beginning of the present century. Widely regarded at the time as disreputable and not suitable for middle-class audiences, the silents were subject to pressure to make them more respectable.

By 1913 Hollywood had emerged as the center of America's film industry, and by the end of the decade it was the world's leader. This commercial success drew additional attention from the "guardians of morality" in the pulpits and the press. In 1922 Hollywood set up an office of self-**censorship**, the Motion Picture Producers and Distributors of America (popularly known as the Hays Office), to head off efforts to install government censorship. However, the Motion Picture Production Code was not promulgated until 1930; four years later, at the behest of religious groups, it was strengthened. In 1927 sound dialogue was introduced (the "talkies"), making possible, inter alia, the inclusion of suggestive dialogue of the Mae West type, though a constant running battle with the guardians of the code was required to retain even the subtlest double entendres.

In its heydey (1930–60) the motion picture industry was dominated by a small number of powerful Hollywood studios cranking out seemingly endless cycles of films based on a few successful exemplars. The focus on the stars, which had begun in the silent era, was continued, some of them now becoming (for reasons that are not always clear) gay icons: Bette Davis, Judy Garland, and James Dean. Anything that did not conform to the code had to be shown in a few "art theatres" in the large cities or in semi-private film clubs such as Cinema 16 in New York; it could find no mass audience.

By the mid-sixties **television** had begun to call the tune, and some studio lots were given over to producing standard fare for the small screen. Yet motion pictures survived and the sixties saw the rise of independent producers, who broke the stranglehold of the big studios. The demographics of the motion picture audience also changed, becoming more segmented, younger and more sophisticated. In this new climate some offbeat themes became realizable, often in films for "special audiences" such as counterculture youth and blacks. Even the rise (in the eighties) of **videos** rented in stores and played on home VCRs did not kill the movie houses. Moreover, the videos proved a boon to film scholars, who were able to reexamine older statements and theories through minute study of the films themselves.

Although the naive observer regards movies as a direct transcription of reality, technical and aesthetic considerations require transformation of the basic material. Moreover, social pressures—and the basic need to make money that is affected by them—shape choices of what is to be excluded and included. Gay and lesbian scholars have argued that their communities have never been adequately represented in mainstream motion pictures, which have been content to serve up brief glimpses and easy stereotypes. Be this as it may, there is much to be learned from a careful study of filmic images—mainstream and experimental, amateur and pornographic—that relate to alternative sexuality.

Beginnings. The first serious homosexual film appears to be Mauritz Stiller's *The Wings* (1916), based on the novel *Mikaël* by the Danish gay author Herman **Bang**. This work is an early example of the perennial practice (not of course limited to homosexual movies) of basing the story line on a successful novel. In 1919 the German director Richard Oswald produced an educational film *Anders als die Andern* (Different from the Others) with the advice and participation of the great sex researcher Magnus **Hirschfeld**. The movie portrays the difficulty of establishing a homosexual identity in a hostile environment, the expectation of marriage imposed by relatives, coming out, the tensions within gay relationships, blackmail, and the tragedy of suicide. The stormy reception accorded public showings of *Anders als die Andern* tended to discourage the otherwise innovative film industry of Weimar Germany from venturing much further into the realm of homosexuality. Probably the first explicit lesbian in film, however, was featured in G. W. Pabst's *Pandora's Box* (1929), based on a play by Frank Wedekind. In 1931 Leontine Sagan's *Mädchen in Uniform* appeared, based on a play by lesbian writer Christa Winsloe. The story, which concerns the love of a sensitive student for

her teacher, serves a broader purpose of questioning social rigidity and authoritarianism. This film, whose intense performances held audiences from the beginning, is rightly designated a classic.

Constricted by the Hays office, America produced little that was comparable. An exception is the experimental *Lot in Sodom* (1933) of James Watson and Melville Webber, which however played upon lingering fin-de-siècle ideas of decadence. In France Jean Vigo's *Zéro de Conduite* (1933), set in a boy's school, has homoerotic overtones, but these are not explicit.

Drag Films and Scenes. From the nineteenth-century tradition of theatrical **transvestism**—male and female impersonation—the movies inherited a minor but surprisingly persistent motif. Julian Eltinge, a renowned female impersonator from the vaudeville circuit, was brought to films by Adolph Zukor in 1917. The plots of his popular films generally offered some pretext for his making a transition from male to female attire. Brandon Thomas's theatre staple *Charley's Aunt* was first filmed as a silent in 1925, to be followed eventually by four sound versions. The plot concerns a young aristocrat at Oxford who comes to the rescue of two fellow students by disguising himself as the Brazilian aunt of one of them. In the German musical comedy *Viktor und Viktoria* (1933; remade in England in 1935), an aspiring actress gets her chance to replace a major male star by doing his role first as a man and then as a woman—a double disguise. In 1982 Blake Edwards remade this comedy to great effect starring Julie Andrews. Beginning with *Morocco* in 1930 Marlene Dietrich essayed a series of male impersonations—a device which became virtually her trademark. In the historical drama *Queen Christina* (1933), rich in homosexual and lesbian innuendo, Greta Garbo made a stunning appearance as the monarch disguised as a boy. Billy Wilder's *Some Like It Hot* (1959) featured Jack Lemmon and Tony Curtis as musicians compelled to disguise themselves as women because they inadvertently witnessed a gangster shootout. Although this film has remained a great favorite among gay men, only the last scene, in which Joe E. Brown insists that he still wants to marry Lemmon even though he is a man, is truly homosexual. The grossly obese transvestite Divine (who died in 1988) appeared in a number of deliberately tacky John Waters films in the 1970s and 80s. After an initially tepid audience response, the musical *The Rocky Horror Picture Show* (1976) became the focus of a cult of remarkable longevity in which members of the audience dress up as the characters, doubling the action as the film unfolds. Tim Curry plays a "sweet transvestite," Dr. Frank-N-Furter, who creates a muscle-bound monster for his own delectation. Then the French weighed in with *La Cage aux Folles* (1979), about two older gay men on the Riviera. This list could be extended for many pages. The point of the drag films is not so much whether they are explicitly homosexual, but their capacity to challenge gender role conventions. Yet the genre is so well entrenched that, unless specially charged, it has lost most of its power to shock, and thus change thinking.

The Sissy Motif. While contempt for **effeminacy** is deeply rooted in Western culture (it is already found among the ancient Greeks), the motif took on special coloration in America, where the sissy was identified with effete European culture as contrasted with the frontier-bred he-man. Thus in the film *Mollycoddle* Douglas Fairbanks is a foppish expatriate living in Europe who must win his way back to his rugged, masculine American heritage. In the comedies of Harold Lloyd, the bespectacled weakling is made to prove his masculinity over and over again.

In the 1930s, as the Hays Office code tightened its stifling hold, the sissy became a camouflage for the male homosexual, who could not be presented directly. In Lewis Milestone's 1931 version of *The Front Page*, a milktoast poet–reporter, played by Edward Everett Horton, is a foil for the tough-guy reporters. During the 1930s Ernest Truex and Franklin Pangborn made the character virtually their own. With the collapse of censorship in the late 1960s, this subterfuge became less common, but it is still resorted to occasionally when the filmmakers wish to blur the image of a homosexual character.

Buddy Films. The drag and sissy films featured individuals who were generally isolated and risible, and hence could scarcely be regarded as role models by the general public. It was quite different with the buddy films—a classic example is *Beau Geste* (1926)—which generally presented dashing specimens of manhood who bonded with others of their ilk. For this reason homoerotic overtones generally had to be more subtle than in the other two genres. Many of these films raise problems of interpretation, in that the homoerotic elements that are detected by gay viewers (and a few homophobes) are often ignored by general audiences. Is it a case of projection (on the one hand) or obtuseness (on the other)? Recent literary criticism has emphasized that each work lends itself to a multiplicity of interpretations as the reader recreates the work. Regardless of whether this principle applies to films in general, it does seem helpful in understanding the divergent interpretations of buddy films.

An early landmark of the genre is William Wellman's *Wings* (1928), not to be confused with Stiller's earlier work. As one of the two flyer heroes is dying in the arms of the other, the survivor epitomizes: "There is nothing in the world that means more to me than your friendship." A sinister example is Alfred Hitchcock's *Strangers on a Train* (1951), based on a novel by Patricia Highsmith, where two men make a double murder pact. Adolescent alienation was the theme of *Rebel without a Cause* (1955), in which, however, the delicate Sal Mineo character dies so that James Dean can be united with Natalie Wood. In

1964 *Becket* provided a medieval setting, while the popular *Butch Cassidy and the Sundance Kid* (1974) updated the long tradition of Westerns featuring male heroes and their "sidekicks" by making Paul Newman and Robert Redford equal partners.

The seventies provided a few opportunities for a franker divulgence of the subtext. In the French *Going Places* (*Les valseuses*, 1974) Gérard Depardieu and Patrick Dewaere even have sex in one scene; the next day Dewaere is remorseful and ashamed, but Depardieu tells him to forget it: it's OK among friends.

Transfers. Novels having gay and lesbian characters have received a variety of treatments. Early on, the gay character is either written out or made straight (*Young Man with a Horn*, 1950) or the gender is changed (as in *Serenade* [1956], after James M. Cain's novel, the gay-male impresario is turned into a femme fatale agent, played by Joan Fontaine). *Cabaret* (1972) made the **Isherwood** character bisexual, but the earlier *I am a Camera* passed him off as straight. *Inside Daisy Clover* made the gay movie star (Robert Redford) only bisexual, and then only through the dialogue of other people. In the book *Midnight Express* the hero admitted to a gay love affair in prison, but in the movie version (1978) he rejects a handsome fellow inmate's advances. Although William Hurt received an Academy Award in 1986 for his portrayal of a fem prisoner in *Kiss of the Spider Woman*, many gay viewers—including the book's author, Manuel Puig—found him unconvincing.

In screened plays, especially those of Tennessee **Williams**, the crucial bits of dialogue are omitted, so that one wonders what the fuss is about with Blanche and her dead friend in *Streetcar Named Desire* (1951) or the problem that keeps Brick and Maggie apart in *Cat on a Hot Tin Roof* (1958). Yet the English *Taste of Honey* (1961) retained the honesty of Shelagh Delaney's play, providing a rare instance of a sympathetic effeminate gay man.

Screen biographies of gay people have had similar fates. **Michelangelo** and Cole **Porter** appear as joyful heterosexuals; Oscar **Wilde** could not be sanitized, to be sure, but he was presented in a "tasteful" manner (three British versions, two in 1960, one in 1984). Recent screen biographies have been better; the documentary on the painter Paul Cadmus (1980) is open without being sensational; *Prick Up Your Ears*, on the life of Joe **Orton**, is as frank as one can wish, though it somehow misses the core of his personality. *Nik and Murray*, while not properly speaking a biography, told the story of dance-world luminaries Alwin Nikolais and Murray Louis, treating their long-term relationship simply as a matter of fact. *Unanswered Prayers: The Life and Times of Truman Capote* (1987) pulled few punches, and *Gian-Carlo Menotti: The Musical Magician* (1986), though it provided no intimate details, did not gloss over the relationship with Samuel Barber.

The European "Art Film." After World War II, as Europe emerged from the stultifying restraints of the Occupation, a greater freedom was sought in many areas, including the erotic. Moral guardians were still very much on the scene, however, and homosexuality had to be presented in aestheticized, "tasteful" guise. Clearly ahead of its time was Jean **Genet's** *Un Chant d'Amour*, about prison homoeroticism and its repression. In *The Third Sex* (West Germany, 1959) a sophisticated older man has an entourage of teen-aged boys. Although this film purveys dated ideas of homosexuality, it went farther in explicitness than anything that Hollywood was able to do for over a decade. Federico Fellini's celebrated *La Dolce Vita* (1960) is a multifaceted portrait of eternal decadence in chic circles in Rome. The English *Victim* (1961), which concerns the blackmailing of a young homosexual, is clearly a plea for law reform in the wake of the 1957 **Wolfenden** Report. Sidney J. Furie's *The Leather Boys* (1964) portrays a buddy relationship between two motorcyclists, one gay, one straight. In the same year a French director Jean Delannoy even showed (though in highly aestheticized form) love between two schoolboys in *Les Amitiés particulières*, based on the 1945 novel of Roger Peyrefitte.

The Sixties Thaw in America. The early years of the sixties saw the start of the civil rights movement in the United States, while at the same time a series of court decisions struck down literary censorship, signaling that restriction on films would be relaxed as well. Otto Preminger's *Advise and Consent* (1962) even brought homosexuality to the hallowed halls of the United States Senate, but presented it as a seamy reality far from the conventional life of an upright American politician, even though it was based on the suicide of Senator Lester Hunt of Wyoming in 1954. This film presented audiences with their first glimpse of a gay bar. One breakthrough came in 1967 when the legendary Marlon Brando portrayed a closeted homosexual army officer in John Huston's *Reflections in a Golden Eye*, a film which drew a "Condemned" rating from the Catholic Church. In *The Sergeant* (1968) and *Suddenly Last Summer* (1969) both protagonists meet death as the wages of their perversion. The lesbian relationship in 1968's *The Fox* is also ended through the death of Sandy Dennis. Although it was essentially a buddy movie, *Midnight Cowboy* (1969), with Jon Voight and Dustin Hoffman, offered some revealing glimpses of the Times Square hustling scene, with Voight sympathetically playing a "straight trade" type; one scene has him experiencing oral sex in an all-night movie theater.

The Underground Cinema. In 1947 Kenneth Anger, then still a southern California high school student, made *Fireworks*, a symbol-laden, quasi-surrealist portrayal of a gay sex encounter. Although his career never really took off in the commercial sense, Anger made another innovative film *Scorpio Rising* in 1963, which foretold **Counterculture** sexual freedom and the interest in the occult. Some-

what similar was Jack Smith's *Flaming Creatures* (1963), while Gregory Markopoulos achieved a more aestheticized and abstract version of the mode. These developments have been termed the "Baudelairean cinema," since they depend on some aspects of the French nineteenth-century decadent sensibility. Their immediate heir, however, was Andy **Warhol**, who branched out from painting in such deliberately crude films as *Blow Job* (1963) and *My Hustler* (1965). Neither was really pornographic but their acceptance helped speed the fall of censorship barriers.

Breakthough. Only with William Friedkin's *Boys in the Band* (1970) were audiences confronted with a Hollywood film in which all the characters are stereotypical homosexuals. The tone remained mocking and hostile, reassuring straight audiences that such people were doomed to unhappiness in "the wasteland of homosexual existence."

Also in 1970 came Michael York's portrayal of a scheming, murderous bisexual in *Something for Everyone*. York again played a bisexual as the male lead Brian in the film version of *Cabaret* (1972), based on Christopher Isherwood's *Berlin Stories*. The early seventies were also notable for two films which dealt with male rape, in each case of a heterosexual by a heterosexual. The 1971 Canadian film version of John Herbert's play *Fortune and Men's Eyes* dealt with a prison setting, and included some rather explicit footage as well as a drag-queen who turns out to be the strongest of the main characters. Burt Reynolds starred in *Deliverance* (1972), in which a white-water macho buddy trip is disrupted by some hillbillies who take advantage of an opportunity to sodomize one of the buddies at gunpoint.

Against this background, Christopher Larkin's *A Very Natural Thing* (1973) came as a wholly positive portrait of gay relationships. Sidney Lumet's *Dog Day Afternoon* (1975) followed with the real story of a bisexual bankrobber, played by

Al Pacino, and his would-be transsexual lover, sympathetically told.

Europe continued to be important with the emergence of openly gay directors. As early as 1968 Pier Paolo **Pasolini** had made *Teorema*, about the visit of a pansexual angel to the household of a Milan industrialist. Not to be outdone, his older colleague Luchino **Visconti** made *The Damned* (1969), a somewhat fanciful recreation of the massacre of Captain **Röhm** and his Nazi storm trooper comrades in the 1934 "night of the long knives," depicted as a wild orgy of blond German youths suddenly interrupted by submachine guns from the rival Nazis of the S.S. Bernardo Bertolucci's *The Conformist* (1970) made a questionable equation between childhood homosexual experience and Italian **fascism**. A year later Visconti brought out a more lyrical and successful film, a rendering of Thomas **Mann**'s novella *Death in Venice*. Britain's John Schlesinger depicted a triad of two men and a woman in which one of the men was involved with the other two in 1971's *Sunday Bloody Sunday*; this film was notable for the shock experienced by straight audiences at a kissing scene between Peter Finch and Murray Head. Perhaps the most notorious of the gay directors was Rainer Werner **Fassbinder**, whose *Fox and His Friends* (1975) deals with homosexuality and class struggle. Fassbinder's last film was his controversial version of a **Genet** novel, *Querelle* (1982). The death of Franco created the possibility of a new openness in Spanish culture, including a number of gay films. Influenced by Luis Buñuel, *Law of Desire* (1986) by Pedro Almodóvar is surely a masterpiece of comic surrealism.

The Positive Eighties. Homophobia in movie-making became a major issue in 1980, when street demonstrations called to protest and disrupt the filming of *Cruising* proved effective and the movie's showings were often targeted for further protests. As the controversial film failed to score big at the box office, Hollywood drew the lesson that blatant homophobia was no longer good business.

In 1982 Hollywood came back with *Making Love*, a high budget soap opera about two yuppie lovers, in an attempt to lure a new market; as the attempt failed, no further such excursions appeared. Also in 1982 came *Personal Best*, with Mariel Hemingway as a lesbian athlete, and in 1986, the independently produced *Desert Hearts*, after the novel *Desert of the Heart* by Jane Rule, but both films showed disappointing box-office receipts. Bill Sherwood's *Parting Glances* (1986), a sensitive story of two men, one with **AIDS**, the other not, was not intended to make money. Modest expectations also attended the British *My Beautiful Laundrette* (1985), featuring an unselfconscious love affair between two teenage boys, one white, the other Pakistani; yet it enjoyed surprisingly long runs. In 1987, however, *Maurice*, a beautifully detailed recreation of the E. M. **Forster** novel by the Merchant–Ivory team, showed that excellence, high budget commercial standards, and honesty about homosexuality could be successfully combined.

Gay and Lesbian Personalities. While actors are often thought of as homosexual or bisexual—and many are—the real gay side of Hollywood is probably to be found in those who do not appear on the screen—agents, costume designers, choreographers, and makeup artists. Already in the 1920s some major directors were known to be gay, including the German Friedrich W. Murnau and the Russian Sergei Eisenstein. Dorothy Arzner certainly projected a mannish appearance, whatever her sex life was. The English James Whale went to Hollywood, where he achieved success in directing horror movies. Pasolini, Visconti, and Fassbinder have been mentioned above; the multitalented Franco Zeffirelli (also active in the field of **opera**) should also be noted.

From an early date Hollywood had promoted the cult of the stars, with their images carefully shaped by studio public relations departments. A curious aspect of star adulation is the preoccupation, amounting almost to identification, of gay men with such heterosexual divas as Joan Crawford and Judy Garland. Of course the gossip mills turned endlessly. While Rudolph Valentino had to undergo (still unsubstantiated) gossip about his homosexuality, his successor Ramon Novarro really did it, as his tragic murder by two hustlers in 1968 finally attested. The screenwriter Mercedes de Acosta claimed to have had affairs with both Garbo and Dietrich. During their lifetimes Charles Laughton and Montgomery Clift had to suffer fag-baiting taunts from colleagues, while Rock Hudson remained largely untouched by public scandal until his death from AIDS in 1985. Tyrone Power and Cary Grant were decloseted after their deaths. The sexuality of others, such as Errol Flynn and James Dean, remains the subject of argument. In Germany the stage actor and film director Gustav Gründgens managed to work through the Nazi period, even though his homosexuality was known to the regime. In the 1970s, the English actor Dirk Bogarde, in a rare and courageous act of candor, went public about his homosexuality.

Gay-Male Porno Films. The origins of this genre are obscure, but one source is the "blue movies" made for stag parties and sold under the counter even before World War II. Another source is the nonexplicit genre of "muscle films" showing buddy relationships and wrestling, which were purchased by gay men. In the late 1960s Pat Rocco produced a series of romantic soft-core (not showing acts of sexual penetration) films of virile men in love with one another. In 1969, however, hard-core porno arrived, apparently to stay. Some fifty theatres across the United States specialized in the genre, and where the authorities were willing to turn a blind eye, sexual acts took place there, stimulated by the films.

Much of the early production was forgettable, but in 1971, in *Boys in the Sand* starring Casey Donovan (Cal Culver), the director—producer Wakefield Poole achieved a rare blend of sexual explicitness and cinematographic values. For a while New York and Los Angeles vied for supremacy, the eastern city specializing in the seamy side of gay life, whereas the California city featured wholesome west coast boys. Among those who achieved some distinction (or at least commercial success) as directors in Los Angeles are J. Brian, Fred Halsted (1940–1989), and William Higgins. Other notable American directors include Arch Brown, Jack Deveau, Francis Ellie, Joe Gage, Dave Nesor, and Christopher Rage. The French Jean-Daniel Cadinot showed that one could combine porno with convincing setting and characterization. Although they are not strictly porno, much the same can be said for the films of the late Arthur J. Bresson, who even dared to deal with boy love.

In the later eighties AIDS began to devastate porno-industry workers, gay and straight, and safe sex procedures became more rigorous on the set (it should be noted, however, that long before AIDS, by strict convention pornographic film ejaculations were always conducted outside the body, so as to be graphically visible; hence film sex was always basically "safe sex"). Video rentals for home use competed with cinema showings, and some of the sleazier houses closed.

Lesbian porno exists only as scenes within films addressed to heterosexual males, their being, thus far, no market for full-length lesbian films of this nature. A number of independent lesbian filmmakers have made candid motion pictures about lesbian life, but they are not pornographic.

Documentaries. Perhaps the first is a chapter in the life of openly gay artist David Hockney, *A Bigger Splash* (1974). *Word is Out* was a 1977 composite set of interviews providing a remarkable panorama of gay and lesbian reality. In 1978 Rosa von Praunheim, a militant German gay director, brought out *An Army of Lovers*, a record of his visits to American gay liberation leaders. *Improper Conduct* (1984) by Néstor Almendros and Orlando Jiménez featured interviews with gay exiles from Castro's **Cuba**. *The Times of Harvey Milk* (1985), concerning San Francisco's slain political leader, received an Academy Award in 1986. The availability of cheaper equipment has made documentaries of important events, such as the 1987 march on Washington, easier, and the video rental system has made them available to those who cannot attend the often brief theatrical engagements. Major cities, such as Amsterdam, Chicago, Los Angeles, and New York, now have annual film festivals in which gay and lesbian motion pictures of all sorts are showcased.

BIBLIOGRAPHY. Kenneth Anger, *Hollywood Babylon II*, New York: Dutton, 1984; Rebecca Bell-Metereau, *Hollywood Androgyny*, New York: Columbia University Press, 1965; Homer Dickens, *What a Drag: Men as Women and Women as Men in the Movies*, New York: Quill, 1984; Richard Dyer, et al., *Gays and Film*, New York: New York Zoetrope, 1984; Stefanie Hetze, *Happy end für wen? Kino und lesbische Frauen*, Frankfurt am Main: Tende, 1986; Joan Mellen, *Big Bad Wolves: Masculinity in the American Film*, New York: Pantheon Books, 1977; Bertrand Philbert, *L'Homosexualité à l'écran*, Paris: H. Veyrier, 1984; John W. Rowberry, *Gay Video: A Guide to Erotica*, San Francisco: G. S. Press, 1987; Carel Rowe, *The Baudelairean Cinema: A Trend Within the American Avant-Garde*, Ann Arbor, MI: UMI Research Press, 1982; Vito Russo, *The Celluloid Closet: Homosexuality in the Movies*, New York: Harper and Row, 1981; Parker Tyler, *Screening the Sexes: Homosexuality in the Movies*, New York: Holt, Rinehart and Winston, 1972.

Wayne R. Dynes

FIRBANK, RONALD (1886–1926)

English novelist and playwright. Firbank, an aesthete and a dandy, was the grandson of a Durham miner, whose Victorian rags-to-riches ascent provided the income for his grandson to live independently and to publish most of his books privately. A delicate child, he was educated mainly by private tutors. He attended Trinity College, Cambridge, during the height of the university's homoerotic period, but never took a degree. In 1907 he was converted to the Roman Catholic church by R. H. Benson, a closeted homosexual who had been a patron of Frederick **Rolfe** ("Baron Corvo"). Shy and retiring, Firbank spent much of his life traveling, writing his novels on the backs of large postcards. He seems to have had no long-term homosexual affairs; as he remarked with resignation, "I can buy companionship."

Characteristically, the plot of his first novel, *Vainglory* (1915), which concerns the quest of a society woman to have herself memorialized in a stained-glass window, is a slight affair. The interest lies in the social color as expressed in the dialogue, where Firbank leaves out many of the usual narrative markers, including the identity of the speakers, so that the reader is left to construct much of the background for himself. *Valmouth* (1919) concerns a nursing home for centenarians, while *Prancing Nigger* (1919) is set on a Caribbean island. In the latter novel, he introduces his own name as that of an orchid: "a dingy lilac blossom of rarity untold." His last novel, *Concerning the Eccentricities of Cardinal Pirelli*, in which the eponymous cleric chases but never quite succeeds in catching choir boys, was published just after his death in Rome from a pulmonary infection (1926).

Seemingly spun from the stuff of trivial social comedy, Firbank's novels made a significant contribution to literary modernism through their original use of the device of the "reader's share," whereby he left unstated the details of plot and characterization. Firbank's popularity waxes and wanes, but he had a major influence on such younger contemporaries as Evelyn Waugh and Muriel Spark.

BIBLIOGRAPHY. Miriam J. Benkovitz, *Ronald Firbank: A Biography*, New York: Alfred A. Knopf, 1969; Brigid Brophy, *Prancing Novelist*, New York: Harper and Row, 1973.

Ward Houser

FLANNER, JANET ("GENET"; 1892–1978)

American journalist. After settling in Paris in the 1920s, Janet Flanner began a series of reports on life in the French capital in *The New Yorker*. From 1925 onwards she wrote under the pseudonym of Genet, and the acuteness of her analyses of politics, diplomacy, and culture made the name an indispensable asset during the magazine's great phase.

Having returned to the United States as the clouds of World War II gathered, Flanner met her life companion, Natalia Danesi Murray, in New York in 1940. Of Italian birth, Murray was an editor, publisher, film producer, theatrical and bookstore manager, and Allied propagandist for the United States Office of War Information. At the time of their meeting Flanner was 48, Murray 38. The two women, who had both divorced their husbands before they met, remained linked emotionally and intellectually until Flanner's death at the age of 86. They were separated physically for much of each year: Flanner returned to live in Paris, while Murray lived in New York and Italy. They both witnessed many important events of the times, knew those who created them, and commented on what they saw in pungent prose. The evidence lies in their letters, which Murray decided to publish when she "realized how unique our relationship was," but "also as a demonstration of how two women surmounted obstacles, trying to lead their personal and professional lives with dignity and feeling."

In their comments on political events, Flanner and Murray saw male vanity and the persistence of unthinking ideological loyalties as responsible for many difficulties that could have been avoided. Much of their correspondence focuses on their friends: Margaret **Anderson**, Kay Boyle, Nancy Cunard, Ernest **Hemingway**, Carson **McCullers**, Anna Magnani, and Tennessee **Williams**. Because some aspects of the exchange do not accord with today's social conscience, it attracted mixed reviews in the 1980s. Yet the letters are an invaluable record of over thirty years of a passionate, yet honest relationship of two intensely active women.

BIBLIOGRAPHY. Flanner, Janet, *Darlinghissima: Letters to a Friend*, Natalie Danesi Murray, ed., New York: Random House, 1985.

Evelyn Gettone

FLAUBERT, GUSTAVE (1821–1880)

French novelist. The son of a surgeon, Flaubert grew up in a medical milieu preoccupied with the progress of a science to which he felt himself unequal. From his early years at the lycée onward, he preferred the pen to his father's scalpel, and singlehandedly edited a minor journal, the *Colibri*, that clumsily but clearly foretold his future talent. In Paris he read law but never took the degree for reasons of health, and there met Maxime Du Camp, with whom he formed a close friendship. Together they traveled through Brittany and Normandy in 1847, bringing back a volume of reminiscences that was to be published only after Flaubert's death (*Par les champs et par les grèves*, 1885). Between October of 1849 and May of 1851 the two traveled in Egypt and Turkey, and there Flaubert had a number of pederastic experiences which he related in his letters to Louis Bouilhet.

On his return to France Flaubert shut himself up in his country house at Croisset, near Rouen. Instead of aspiring to self-discovery in the manner of the

Romanticists, Flaubert sought to bury his own personality by striving for the goal of art in itself, and he devoted his entire life to the quest for its secrets. His ferocious will to be in his works "like God," everywhere and nowhere, explains the nervewracking effort that went into each of his novels, in which nothing is left to the free flow of inspiration, nothing is asserted without being verified, nothing is described that has not been seen. This explains the multiple versions that are periodically uncovered of almost every one of his works, with the sole exception of *Madame Bovary* (1857), which led to his being tried for offending public decency. At the trial he won acquittal but was denied the costs of the proceedings. The novel gains its power from the careful picture of the Norman town and countryside he knew so well, while the lovers with whom Emma Bovary seeks to realize her dreams are as petty as the leaders of the provincial society in which she is trapped.

In 1857 he traveled to Tunisia to collect material for a historical novel set in Carthage after the First Punic War. *Salammbô* (1862), abundantly documented, is so rich in sadistic scenes, including one of a mass child-sacrifice, that it horrified some contemporary readers. It was followed in 1869 by *L'éducation sentimentale*, which relates the life and the education in love of Frederic Moreau, and although an uneventful tale, perfectly captures a certain period and stratum of French society. In 1874 he published *La tentation de saint Antoine*, a prose poem of great power and imagination. His last work, *Bouvard et Pécuchet* (issued posthumously in 1881), is an unfinished study in male bonding.

Flaubert had an interest in homosexuality that went beyond mere voyeurism. Among his mementoes was the autograph confession of a pederast who had killed his lover out of jealousy and was eventually guillotined after confessing every detail of his passion and crime. He was also delighted by the story of a group of men surprised in a homosexual encounter in a *pissoir* in the Champs-Élysées, among them the son of a former Governor of the Bank of France. But it was in Cairo, in the winter of 1849–50, that Flaubert experienced homosexuality in its Oriental guise. A letter to Bouilhet mentions the *bardaches* (passive homosexuals): "Sodomy is a subject of conversation at table. You can deny it at times, but everyone starts ribbing you and you end up spilling the beans. Traveling for our own information and entrusted with a mission by the government, we regarded it as our duty to abandon ourselves to this manner of ejaculation. The occasion has not yet presented itself, but we are looking for one. The Turkish baths are where it is practiced. One rents the bath for 5 fr., including the masseurs, pipe, coffee, and linen, and takes one's urchin into one of the rooms.—You should know that all the bath attendants are *bardaches*." Then he relates his disappointment at not obtaining the masseur of his choice. In another letter he writes in Greek characters that "Maxime [Du Camp] tried to sodomize a *bardache* in Jeremiah's cave.—It's untrue!" Then he adds: "No! No! It's true." The experiences of the two travelers parallel in a way Sir Richard **Burton**'s adventures while on government service in India; in the exotic setting they felt free to experiment with pleasures tabooed in their home countries. Although the major themes of Flaubert's work would always be heterosexual, it is interesting that he was not repelled by "the other love," but pursued it with nonchalance and with some evident curiosity.

BIBLIOGRAPHY. Enid Starkie, *Flaubert the Master: A Critical and Biographical Study (1856–1880)*, New York: Atheneum, 1971.

Warren Johansson

FLORENCE

This city in central Italy, the capital of Tuscany, is famous as the native or adoptive home of many of the chief artistic and cultural figures of the Italian Renaissance, and for its art treasures.

Historical Background. Of Etruscan origins, it was a Roman town, but declined with the barbarian invasions until the Carolingian period (eighth century). An economic renewal took place in the eleventh and twelfth centuries, causing the city gradually to detach itself from its feudal overlords, while adding to its own territory. A merchant and manufacturing city-state, it underwent a complex political development, punctuated by internecine strife. The continuing turbulence gave the commercial Medici family the opportunity gradually to impose its domination (from 1434). Under Lorenzo de' Medici, known as "the Magnificent" (1448–1492) Florence reached the zenith of its artistic, cultural, and political development—though not in the economic realm, which had its apogee in the previous century.

After various conflicts—which saw the Medici twice expelled—the family prevailed in 1530, and in 1569 Pope Pius V named them grand-dukes of Tuscany, a title reflecting the extension of their rule over most of the province. The seventeenth and eighteenth were centuries of decline. Only with the reign of Peter Leopold of Habsburg-Lorraine (1765–1790) did Florence begin to recover culturally and economically.

Having revolted in 1859, in the following year Florence joined the new Kingdom of Italy, serving as capital from 1865 to 1871. Through the nineteenth and a large part of the twentieth century Florence was one of Italy's most important cultural centers, dense in literary, artistic, and publishing activities. Industrial development was centered in nearby Prato, permitting the historic center of Florence to be preserved.

Homosexuality in Repute and in Law. More than **Venice**, which has attracted many historians today, it was Florence that enjoyed the reputation, both in Italy and abroad, of being excessively "tolerant" of homosexual conduct. This renown is attested by the Middle High German verb *florenzen*, "to sodomize." And St. Bernardino of Siena (1380–1444), preaching on May 23, 1425 against sodomy, lamented that "You cannot leave Tuscany without being reproached twelve times a day that here we never punish such a vice."

In reality Florentine laws (beginning with that of 1325) severely punished sodomy, but in practice the authorities imposed the death penalty reluctantly, preferring fines or corporal punishments of other types (including castration). Capital punishment, as far as present knowledge goes, was reserved for cases of special gravity, such as rape, seduction of a small child, or public scandal.

How much the death penalty was viewed as excessive by the Florentines can be seen in a proposal advanced in a pamphlet of 1496 of Domenico Cecchi (ca. 1445–after 1514), who says that to make *harsher* the penalty against sodomites one should amputate one testicle for each of the first two offenses; on the third occasion the culprit should be locked up in a madhouse.

Nonetheless, Florence had a special court, that of the Uffiziali di Notte (the "Officers of the Night"), which was charged with the task of monitoring and punishing homosexual acts. Exploration of the enormous quantity of material contained in the Florentine state archives has only just begun. Nonetheless, some of the documents of the Uffiziali di Notte have been studied by the American scholar Michael Rocke. This research shows that most of the penalties exacted were fines. The relative mildness of Florentine justice helped to assure the denunciation of notorious sodomites, since the accuser knew that he was unlikely to cause a person's death.

In this way one can see how in "tolerant" Florence the accusations amounted to several thousand. Thanks to this option of mild, but systematic repression (instead of severe, but sporadic), Florentine society succeeded in keeping homosexual behavior under control, despite the existence of a popular culture that regarded it indulgently, especially if the culprits were adolescents. Among the names of famous persons accused of sodomy under this system were **Leonardo** da Vinci, Sandro **Botticelli**, and Benvenuto **Cellini** (who was twice condemned).

The Homosexual Subculture of the Renaissance. The existence of a real **subculture**, and not simply of isolated acts, is confirmed by numerous sermons preached by the above mentioned Bernardino of Siena in the years 1424–27. In these texts Bernardino mentions various privileged places where sodomites met, especially taverns and pastry shops, noting the hours of the night preferred by the sodomites, those "wild pigs," in their search for sexual partners.

Niccolò Machiavelli, in a letter of February 25, 1514, to his friend Francesco Vettori, amused himself by recalling street by street the path of a common friend in nocturnal quest of a boy. Among the locales noted are Borgo Santo Apostolo, Calimala Francesca, and Il Tetto de' Pisani.

The prevailing pattern of this subculture is the same as that known for other Italian cities of the period: the sodomite couple consists of an adult, who takes the role of the insertor, and an adolescent, who is the insertee. The availability of adolescents for prostitution was decisive for maintaining the subculture; Rocke has calculated that in the period ca. 1478–83 ten percent of all Florentine boys had to appear before the authorities charged with sodomy. The same author notes also that those accused of sodomy included a conspicuous number of bachelors and recidivists, whom it is probably correct to describe as having a "deviant lifestyle."

This phase of relative tolerance saw also the flowering of a notable amount of literature on the homosexual theme, authored by both homosexuals and heterosexuals, and written either in standard Italian or in **Burchiellesque** jargon. With Marsilio **Ficino** there was also an idealized, socially acceptable (though chaste) version of the love between two men.

Post-Renaissance Developments. The period following the **Renaissance**, in which Florence fell into decline, has not yet been the object of special study. Certainly the Counter-Reformation and the definitive return to power of the Medici dynasty fostered an atmosphere of gloomy moralism and puritanism, which discouraged writing about homosexuality so that there is a "blackout" in the written records of almost two centuries.

Still, indirect light is shed on this period by biographical gossip concerning the last two rulers of the Medici house compiled by Luca Ombrosi in the eighteenth century and published under the title of *Vita dei Medici sodomiti.* Grand-Duke Gian Gastone (1671–1737) was a notorious homosexual and he died without issue, ending the Medici line. There is also the semiserious invective, *Della Vita e costumi de' fiorentini*, of Francesco Moneti (1635–1712), who accused his fellow citizens of being too much given to unnatural love. These texts document the persistence of widespread male prostitution and a degree of tolerance for homosexual conduct.

In the eighteenth century Ferdinando III, of the new ruling house of Habsburg-Lorraine, was one of the first European sovereigns to accept the Enlightenment ideas concerning the crime of sodomy; in 1795 he abolished the death penalty.

In the nineteenth century Florence became part of the grand tour of homosexual travelers from northern Europe, though it was less popular than such cities as Venice, Naples, and Rome. Still by the end of the century a small colony of foreign gay and lesbian residents, mainly English speaking, had formed. The persisting tolerance is shown by the indulgence always enjoyed by the noted Florentine versifier Tommaso Sgricci (1786–1836), of whom Byron remarked in 1820: "He is also a celebrated Sodomite, a character by no means so much respected in Italy as it should be; but they laugh instead of burning, and the women talk of it as a pity in a man of talent."

In the twentieth century Florence saw a fervent cultural flowering, to which such homosexuals as the writers Carlo Emilio Gadda (1893–1973), Piero Santi (1912–), Aldo Palazzeschi (1885–1974), and the painter Ottone Rosai (1893–1957) contributed. The present scene in Florence is characterized by a special concentration of leather locales, which attract homosexuals from other northern Italian cities, as well as foreigners.

BIBLIOGRAPHY. Michael Goodich, *The Unmentionable Vice*, Santa Barbara, CA: Ross-Erickson, 1979; Luigi Greci, "Benvenuto Cellini nei delitti e nei processi fiorentini, ricostruiti attraverso le leggi del tempo," *Archivio di antropologia criminale*, 50 (1930), 342–85, 509–42; Michael Rocke, "Sodomites in Fifteenth-Century: The Views of San Bernardino of Siena," *Journal of Homosexuality*, 16 (1988), 7–31.

Giovanni Dall'Orto

FLOWER SYMBOLISM

In classical antiquity the theme of picking flowers represented enjoyment of life's transient pleasures, which must be gathered before they fade: the *carpe diem* motif. For many cultures the budding of plant life in spring represents nature's resplendent, but ever temporary self-renewal. Ancient pederasts wrote poignantly of the *anthos*, or "bloom" of the adolescent sex object destined to fade all too soon.

The idea that specific flowers have meanings, that there is a "language of flowers," seems to derive from Turkish eighteenth-century practice, when flowers served to make up a secret code for love messages in the harem. This concept of the *selam*, a flower code able to express a range of meanings, spread to western Europe, so that by 1820 Victor Hugo spoke of

"doux messages où l'amour parle avec des fleurs!" In 1884 Kate Greenaway summed up Victorian lore on the subject in her book *The Language of Flowers*. One dialect she did not present was the homosexual one, which was then known to a very small group. In 1894 Robert Hichens' novel, *The Green Carnation*, popularized that flower as the distinguishing mark of the aesthete, though the **Wilde** scandals in the following year led quickly to the abandonment of that particular badge. Of course flowers featured prominently in the interior-decoration schemes of the Arts and Crafts Movement and they were central to the fin-de-siècle imagery of the Art Nouveau in design and the minor arts.

The association of pansies with male homosexuals is documented in America as early as 1903. Dressing up in overelegant fashion may be called pansying up, while an effeminate boy may be called pansified. Other flowers that have been associated with male homosexuality are lilies and daffodils (the latter is jocular). The use of violets as a gift in Edouard Bourdet's play *The Captive*, a major event of the 1926 Broadway season, caused an association of this flower with lesbianism that lasted several decades.

The slang term for the act of several persons having sexual intercourse with each other simultaneously is a daisy chain. While such a gathering might be heterosexual, the usual interpretation is that of a male-homosexual orgy.

The reasons for the floral metaphor are various. Botanically, flowers have both male and female organs of reproduction. In the early nineteenth century the study of this phenomenon led to the creation of the term bisexuality, though it is doubtful whether this recognition had much direct impact on the popular imagination. Flowers assume complex shapes and colors as a means of passive sexual attraction, since they lure insects who will bear their pollen to their partners. Then too they often have a scent, something to which homosexuals are allegedly addicted.

In Greek mythology the death of heroes could give rise to flowers and other plants. Especially touching is the story of the lovers **Calamus** and Carpus. When the latter was accidentally drowned, Calamus, inconsolable in his grief, found solace in being changed to a reed. Then the beautiful youth **Narcissus**, having spurned the love of a nymph, was caused by the goddess Aphrodite to feel unquenchable love for himself. At length he gained relief by being turned into the flower that still bears his name. As noted, the ancient Greeks described the bloom of a teenaged boy as the *anthos*, "blossom, flower," a term which captures not only the rosy glow of youthful beauty but its transience.

In our society flowers, because of their delicacy and beauty, are most often given by a man to a women. Flower names, such as Blossom, Camille, Daisy, Lily, and Petunia, are given only to women (though at one time they were assumed by gay men as "camp names"). The adjective florid means ornate and excessive; it can also describe an advanced stage of disease. Finally, flowers can be raised in hothouses to assume striking, even bizarre shapes and colors. They represent the triumph of culture over nature, a principle that also serves to buttress our society's stereotype of the homosexual.

See also **Color Symbolism**.

BIBLIOGRAPHY. Philip Knightly, *Flower Poetics in Nineteenth-Century France*, Oxford: Clarendon Press, 1986.
Wayne R. Dynes

FOLKLORE, GAY MALE

Traditional aspects of culture—learned behavior—that are generally passed on orally or by example instead of through writing are usually classified as folklore. All people, regardless of education and social status, have many types of folklore. Often this is divided into such broad categories as oral tradition, nonverbal communication, and material culture. Each of these concepts can be further broken down into genres—specific types of folklore.

Homosexual men have developed a large number of traditions, including an argot (a form of language used by people who wish not to be understood by outsiders), jokes, legends, personal experience narratives, clothing and jewelry used as symbols, and a type of behavior known as "camp."

Language and Humor. The **language** used by some homosexual men is quite developed, and it is much more enduring than slang. The words and phrases cover a range of subjects; the largest group is made up of words used to describe various types of people. For example, **queen** is a standard term some homosexual men use to refer to themselves and others; it can be used derogatorily or as a term of endearment, a sort of affectionate insult. This term is frequently used in compounds, like "flaming queen"; "flaming" means "carrying on in a blatantly effeminate manner" and is probably derived from "flamboyant." Some gay expressions have entered the general vocabulary, most notably "to come out of the **closet**" and the word **gay** itself, as referring to sexual orientation. Such a colorful language commonly results in puns and other types of word play.

Humor is one of the hallmarks of the folklore of homosexual men. The most familiar genre of humor is the joke. The following riddling question shows how jokes can carry messages: "How many psychiatrists does it take to change a light bulb?—Only one, but the light bulb has to really want to change." The joke is based on the stereotype that homosexual people are mentally ill and in need of professional help, and that psychiatrists can "change" them, making them heterosexual. But the punch line carries the subject further, making the point that homosexual people are in control of their lives, and psychiatrists cannot "change" them. By implying that gays do not *want* to change, this joke offers a psychological victory over oppression.

Legends and Personal Narratives. Homosexual men also tell legends—stories that are told as actual events; sometimes the tellers believe the stories, and in fact the event described in a legend may have taken place. After countless retellings, however, the legend has been associated with so many people, places, and times that any facts it may contain cannot be verified. Often the story is told as something that happened to a friend of a friend of the teller. A common legend told by homosexual men is the following:

"This really happened to a friend of a friend of mine in Chicago. He went into a tearoom [public rest room] and stuck his dick through the glory hole [a hole cut through the partition between two stalls]. The guy on the other side stuck a hatpin through it so he couldn't get out."

This legend is a cautionary tale, warning against anonymous and semipublic sexual acts. It is ironic that this story reveals a substantial amount of internalized homophobia; the theme of punishment for homosexual activity is quite clear.

Another type of story people tell is the personal experience narrative. Stories of this sort are not traditional in themselves, but the narrators have told them so often that they have taken on a traditional structure. The most familiar type of personal experience narrative among homosexual men is the **coming-out** story, in which a man describes revealing his homosexuality to someone (usually friends or family). Most gay men have more than one coming-out story, since one comes out to different people at different times.

Nonverbal Expressiveness. Nonverbal communication involves the use of **gestures**, **clothing**, symbols, jewelry, and the like to convey messages about oneself. For example, some homosexual men wear black leather to indicate an interest in sadomasochism; others may wear the same type of outfit to project a **macho** image. A gay man might wear a necklace with a pendant in the shape of the lower case Greek letter **lambda**, a symbol of gay liberation. Another might wear a badge in the form of an inverted **pink triangle** as a symbol of the oppression to which homosexual men and women are subjected. (During the **Holocaust** the Nazis forced homosexual prisoners to wear inverted pink triangles. Many thousands of these men, like millions of Jews, ultimately died in the camps.)

Drag and Camp. Two types of gay men's folklore, drag and camp, combine verbal and nonverbal behavior. Drag, or female impersonation, although not practiced by most homosexual men, is widely associated with gays, and drag shows are a common form of entertainment in some gay **bars**.

Camp is widespread and widely misunderstood. Camp is an attitude, a style of humor, an approach to situations, people, and things. The camp point of view is assertively expressed through exaggeration and inversion, stressing form over content, deflating pomposity, mocking pretension, and subverting values. Sometimes (but certainly not always) camp behavior is **effeminate**. Like much gay humor, camp plays with stereotypes, carrying them to extremes, flouting heterosexual values. Camp can be solely playful, but often it is a serious medium, providing a weapon against oppression.

Camp is best understood through examples. In the spring of 1987, someone stomped several goslings to death in an Indianapolis neighborhood that has a large number of resident ducks and geese. Shortly thereafter, someone planted a small cross beside the canal where the goslings had been killed. Reminiscent of the crosses placed at the sites of fatal automobile accidents, the memorial in this case implied—contrary to most Christian theologies—that animals have souls and that the deaths of the goslings were the equivalent of human deaths.

Strategic Deployment of Folklore. Homosexual men demonstrate a variety of strategies in their use of folklore. Humor is pervasive. Ambiguity is also common, allowing covert messages to be conveyed through the use of double meanings. If someone receiving a message takes offense, the sender can protest innocence by insisting that the receiver misunderstood. Since gay men were brought up in the heterosexual culture, they have a background from which they can draw double meanings.

In the following *double entendre*, the ambiguity is rather obvious. Feeling his attempt at finding a sexual partner for the evening to be futile, one man said, "Well, I guess I'll go home and do something constructive, like knit." Another man responded, "But you only have one needle." The first replied, "So I'll crochet." The exchange was spontaneous and the reactions were quick; nothing was laboriously thought out. The humor goes a bit deeper than it first appears, for it plays upon the stereotype of the effeminate homosexual male: both knitting and crocheting are associated with women. A man with only one needle (or penis) cannot engage in a cooperative endeavor like knitting, which requires two needles working together. Thus he must make do with the equipment at hand: having but one needle, he must crochet (masturbate). Since this encounter took place between two men, each of whom knew the other was homosexual, and because it occurred within a gay context, both intended meanings were clear to those who heard the exchange. The two men were simply engaging in a bit of word play. Had the men continued the conversation along similar lines, the double entendres could have been used to lay the basis for a sexual proposition.

Inversion is a third stratagem used by homosexual men. In taking words like **faggot** that heterosexual people have used as tools of oppression and turning them into statements of pride and defiance, gay men state their refusal to be labeled as sick, immoral, and evil.

Conclusion. The folklore of homosexual men functions in many ways—as a means by which gays can identify and communicate with one another without other people's awareness, as a tool to help create a sense of "group" and belonging, and as a way of coping with and expressing conflict. Most of all, folklore helps homosexual men gain cultural competence, that is, to function as gay men with other gay men. As long as schools, families, churches, and other institutions fail to fulfill this role, folklore will continue to meet such needs.

BIBLIOGRAPHY. Joseph P. Goodwin, *More Man than You'll Ever Be: Gay Folklore and Acculturation in Middle America*, Bloomington: Indiana University Press, 1989; Bryan Keith Knedler, "Performance and Power in the Gay Male Community," master's thesis, Ohio State University, 1983; Venetia Newall, "Folklore and Male Homosexuality," *Folklore* 97:2 (1986), 123–47; Bruce Rodgers, *Gay Talk: A (Sometimes Outrageous) Dictionary of Gay Slang*, New York: Paragon Books, 1979.

Joseph P. Goodwin

FOLKLORE, LESBIAN

Lesbian folklore is the collection, documentation, and analysis of the traditional cultural products and experiences of lesbians learned through face-to-face interaction and through observation and imitation. The following presentation utilizes examples of contemporary American lesbian folklore collected by the author from a cross-section of the Bloomington, Indiana lesbian-feminist community during the first half of 1988. Bloomington, a small Midwestern town and home of Indiana University, is a "gay mecca" because of the large homosexual population.

Bloomington lesbians belong to three lesbian communities: national, regional, and local. Within the local lesbian community diverse groups exist such as factory dykes, academic dykes, and **bar** dykes. It is within these informally structured community networks that the majority of lesbian folklore exists. That folklore can be classified into three categories: verbal folklore (oral), customary folklore (verbal and non-verbal), and material folklore (artifacts).

Verbal Folklore. One particularly fertile area in this realm is folk speech, including a specialized vocabulary and expressions which are circulated by word of mouth within the folk group. Folk terminology utilized by lesbians is vast. **Dyke**, formerly a derogatory term, is now a reclaimed term of pride. Numerous derivations of dyke exist: "baby dyke," "blazer dyke," "psychodyke" (in therapy), "execudyke" (yuppie), "softball dyke," "back-to-the-land-dyke," and "the dyke of life" (stereotypical lesbian). Formalized phrases also make liberal use of the word dyke: "it was dykes for days" means seeing a lot of dykes, especially in unexpected places such as the grocery store. "Dyke detector" means picking out another lesbian. Another example is the term "queer," which can be comfortably spoken in a group of lesbians, thus serving as a camaraderie word. The traditional toast "cheers for queers" shows the friendly way queer can be used in an in-group context.

The lesbian lexicon contains a wealth of other folk speech items: initialized terms such as "p.i." (politically incorrect), "d.p." (dyke potential), and "p.h.d." (pretty heavy dyke); expressions to refer to outsiders (heterosexuals) such as "hets" and "breeders"; and word play such as "no homo" (when someone is not home when the phone rings), "forward gaily" (when giving directions), and "straightening up" (the house). One fascinating area of folk speech concerns coding or the way one lesbian communicates information when lesbian identity is concealed. "She goes to my church" (she's a lesbian) is a phrase of black lesbians. Folk speech demarcates the lesbian community's uniqueness and separateness. Use of folk speech helps maintain group solidarity.

Personal experience narratives are a significant part of many lesbians' repertoire. These stories are about an experience in the narrator's own life that one recounts frequently. Two types of personal experience narratives in the Bloomington lesbian community are "coming out" stories and humorous tales of lesbian life. Coming-out stories are the best known of all lesbian narratives and are so firmly ingrained into lesbian culture that a lesbian may request another lesbian to share her coming-out story. Coming-out stories are now available in printed form. Two collections are *The Coming Out Stories* edited by Julia Stanley and Susan Wolfe and *Testimonies: A Collection of Coming Out Stories*, edited by Sarah Holmes. Each lesbian's story is unique and chronicles the transitional stage of a lesbian's life when she solidifies her lesbian identity to herself and to others. Since coming-out is a process, many lesbians have several coming-out stories. Telling and retelling one's coming-out story or stories serves to reinforce one's lesbian identity.

Humorous tales of lesbian life are experiences after one has established her identity. Common themes in these humorous tales are: visiting parents, especially during holidays; asking another woman for a date; detailing of a situation where the lesbian is for the first time being open with non-lesbians failing to understand; situations in the workplace and ironic situations (e.g., a lesbian teacher of sex education meeting a lesbian worker at Planned Parenthood). More often than not the core of these humorous narratives points to the painful aspects of living day-to-day as a lesbian in a homophobic world. Telling these tales provides an avenue for the narrator and her audience to laugh at herself and lesbian life.

Customary Folklore. This area encompasses both verbal and non-verbal traditions. Customary folklore can be found within celebrations and festivals. Within the lesbian community, relationships provide a framework for the creation and perpetuation of celebratory customs. One celebration frequently observed is the anniversary, acknowledging the day a couple made love for the first time; the celebration serves as a marker for the longevity of the relationship. Anniversary celebrations are private, quiet times. Many couples go out to dinner or make a special dinner at home and exchange gifts. When a major relationship landmark has been reached, such as the fifth anniversary, a couple may have a big party.

Joinings or bondings are another relationship celebration with traditional customs which, although not legally recognized, acknowledge the couple's pairing. A local park or other natural setting is a frequently chosen site for a bonding. A couple write their own vows and may exchange rings. Following the ceremony food (including vegetarian selections), music (women's), and games (volleyball is a favorite) may complete the celebration. One relatively new addition to the lesbian community's expanding list of celebrations is baby showers, as more and more lesbian couples choose to have children. Lesbian-feminist community values are reflected in these folk celebrations and customs.

Festival season (summer) is many a lesbian's favorite time of year. Strength and energy gained during "festi's" helps one get through the rest of the year. In the Midwest, two festivals are frequented: The National Women's Music Festival and the Michigan Womyn's Music Festival. Festivals bring together diverse groups of lesbians as well as a few heterosexual women. When in progress, festivals become temporal lesbian communities. Over the years (both mentioned festivals are now in their teens) a variety of customs have developed. It is customary, for example, to make sure that the festivals are accessible to women with disabilities. Sign-language interpreters for women who are deaf or hearing impaired are provided for major concerts and for other activities upon request. At the concerts it is becoming customary for performers to recognize interpreters in a lovingly humorous way, behavior which brings loud applause from the audience. These annual music festivals with their attending customs hold special signficance for lesbians as times to escape the daily oppression of a homophobic culture and as times to celebrate one's lesbianism communally.

Material Culture. Among the tangible objects of material culture are items of folk costume. In pre-feminist days describing a lesbian folk costume was a relatively simple matter, as several older Bloomington lesbians recalled. Plaid flannel shirts or work shirts, bib overalls or jeans, and heavy work boots were standard pieces of apparel. A lesbian might wear a pinky ring (a symbol of one's lesbian identity recognized by other lesbians) and cut her hair short (Ann Bannon's novels about Beebo Brinker and Lee Lynch's novel *Swashbuckler* are excellent sources for learning about clothing styles in the 1950s and 60s). With the advent of feminism in the 1970s folk costume became more diversified. Shirts are cotton or other natural fibers commonly worn open at the neck to show off one's woman-identified jewelry (especially at lesbian community events). A more tailored style—not a lot of frills— is appropriate for shirts. T-shirts often display sayings. Lesbian sayings such as "I got this way from kissing girls" may be worn at lesbian events. For everyday wear good "lefty" sayings are usual choices. Most selected color choices are lavender, purple, or bright colors, not pastels. Pants can be jeans, tailored slacks, or baggy pants. Again, natural fibers and no pastel colors are the rule.

Shoes should be flat and comfortable, made of good quality material, especially leather. Tennis shoes, especially high-tops, are popular style choices. One comic note which points to the prevalence of comfortable shoe use can be gleaned from Robin Williams' movie *Good Morning, Vietnam.* At one point during one of his A.M. radio broadcasts he says: "We can't even use the word dyke, you can't even say the word lesbian. It's women in comfortable shoes." Much lore surrounds Birkenstocks, including the belief that there is a good chance that a woman who wears Birkenstocks is a lesbian.

Favorite jewelry choices are crystals (unpolished) and woman-identified jewelry such as a labrys (double ax) or a double women's symbol. Cowrie shells woven into the hair are favored by many black lesbians. The primary lesbian community value expressed in how and what clothing and adornments are worn is comfort.

Conclusion. There are also other forms of lesbian folklore: legends, jokes, arts, crafts, and the like. Other regions of the United States would provide additions to and variations of the examples given. Imbedded within lesbian books are wonderful samples of lesbian folklore. The grassroots newsletter *Lesbian Connection* is another rich source of lesbian folklore. On the academic side several ethnographies give descriptions of lesbian communities. Lesbian archives located throughout the United States house primary data collections (letters, diaries, photographs, and the like) which contain folkloric information. Lesbians should be encouraged to preserve their heritage by donating documents to archives and by interviewing friends and donating tapes.

Aside from a few papers read at the American Folklore Society's annual meetings in the 1980s, folkloristic analysis of lesbian material is non-existent. By not including data about lesbians within folklore scholarship, a heterocentric bias has been allowed to permeate the scholarship. When lesbian data are part of folkloric definitions and theories, they will add to a better understanding of America, its folklore, and American lesbian culture.

BIBLIOGRAPHY. Susan Krieger, *The Mirror Dance: Identity in a Woman's Community*, Philadelphia: Temple University Press, 1983; Denyse Lockard, "The Lesbian Community: An Anthropological Approach," *Journal of Homosexuality* 2:3 (1985), 83–95; Gail Sausser, *Lesbian Etiquette*, Trumansburg, NY: Crossing Press, 1986; Deborah Goleman Wolf, *The Lesbian Community*, Berkeley: University of California Press, 1979.

Jan Laude

FORSTER, E[DWARD] M[ORGAN] (1879–1970)

English novelist, short story writer, and essayist. Forster's father died less than two years after his birth, and he was raised by a group of female relatives, who were connected with a stern evangelical sect. When he was ten, a great-aunt left him a legacy, which permitted him to obtain a good private education and to attempt a career as a writer. Forster detested public school, but found King's College, **Cambridge**, by contrast almost a paradise. Among students and faculty the atmosphere was strongly homoerotic, and Forster developed an intense Platonic relationship with another undergraduate, H. O. Meredith, whom he later was to depict as "Clive" in *Maurice*. Forster's sensibility took shape under the guidance of teachers of Hellenist bent, especially Goldsworthy Lowes Dickinson, and under the influence of the ethics of personal integrity that stemmed from the philosopher G. E. Moore. In 1901 Forster was elected to the elite secret society at Cambridge, The Apostles, leading to close ties with such other members as John Maynard **Keynes** and Lytton **Strachey**.

Uncertain what course to follow after graduation, he sojourned for a year in Italy with his mother. Not only did he find his vocation as a writer there, but he came to cherish to the end of his life a somewhat idealized concept of Mediterranean tolerance and "earthiness" in contradistinction to the Protestant uprightness and commercialism of his native England.

Returning to London in 1902 he affirmed his belief in reducing class barriers by teaching a course at the Working Men's College, a part-time commitment he would retain for over twenty years. Four novels followed in quick succession: *Where Angels Feared to Tread* (1905), *The Longest Journey* (1907), *A Room with a View* (1908), and *Howards End* (1910). This brilliant debut secured him fame and membership in the exclusive **Bloomsbury** group. Critical of Edwardian pieties, the novels adhere to an individualistic ethics of psychic integration and fulfilment through interpersonal relationships. Although in retrospect elements of male-bonding are evident, all these novels deal with heterosexuality.

In July 1914 Forster completed the first draft of a homosexual novel, *Maurice*. Realizing that it was not publishable in the England that had persecuted Oscar **Wilde**, he shared the manuscript only with a few friends, including D. H. **Lawrence**, who chose it as the model for his heterosexual *Lady Chatterley's Lover*. Forster last revised *Maurice* in 1960, but it was not published until after his death, in 1971. After completing *Maurice* Forster felt that his novel writing was over, as he had exhausted his insights into heterosexual relationships and would not be allowed to publish about those that affected him most deeply.

In 1915 he went to **Alexandria** in Egypt with the Red Cross. There he came to know the great modern Greek poet Constantine **Cavafy**, whose work he helped to publicize. He also met a young tram conductor, Mohammed el Adl, with whom he enjoyed his first satisfactory sexual relationship. After Forster returned to England, El Adl died (1922).

Forster's connection with India began earlier, in 1906, when he met a handsome young Indian in England, Syed Ross Masood. Forster then visited the subcontinent in 1912–13 in the company of G. Lowes Dickinson. In 1921–22 he served as private secretary to the Maharajah of Dewas State Senior. During this period he gathered the material for his novel, *A Passage to India*, which on publication in 1924 was acclaimed his masterpiece. Offering a sharp critique of British imperialism, the novel nonetheless portrays human connections as possible even across national and class lines.

Having resettled in England for good, in 1927 he gave the Clark Lectures at Trinity College, Cambridge, which were published as *Aspects of the Novel*. He became concerned with civil liberties, and in the following year he rallied public opinion to protest the suppression of the lesbian novel of Radclyffe **Hall**, *The Well of Loneliness*. The most significant personal event of this period was Forster's friendship with the heterosexual police constable, Bob Buckingham, which lasted for the rest of his life.

In 1946, forced to leave his ancestral home at Abinger, he accepted an offer to become an honorary fellow at King's College Cambridge, where he lived for the rest of his life. After 1924 he wrote no further novels, just reviews and essays, but the five that he had published in the first quarter of the century sufficed to secure his reputation as a novelist. As he had feared, however, the posthumous appearance of *Maurice* (1971), even in the liberal climate of the "sexual revolution," caused a furor. Several critics who had formerly admired his work now began to speak of "homosexual bias," and the novel was generally relegated to an inferior place outside the canon of his major works.

These criticisms are unjustified. While *Maurice* is not flawless, it is certainly as good as his first four novels. Forster's homosexual novel falls into two parts. In the first, the impressionable hero is under the domination of the highminded, but insubstantial Platonism of his Cambridge friend, Clive; in the second, he comes to find his true destiny with a working-class boy, the gamekeeper at Clive's estate with whom he then elopes "into the greenwood." Although this ending has struck some readers as romantic and unlikely, it is modeled on the successful life of Edward **Carpenter**, who ran a farm together with his proletarian lover, George Merrill. With minimal changes, the film version released by the Ivory–Merchant–Jhabvala team in 1987 emerged as fully credible.

In his novels Forster was a conservative **modernist**, with roots in the social comedy of Victorian times, but also showing affinities with the work of his friends D. H. **Lawrence** and Virginia **Woolf**. Although the revelation of Forster's homosexuality diminished him in the eyes of some critics, his familiarity with the ideas of the early homosexual rights movement was actually a source of strength. He succeeded in translating the insights of Carpenter, John Addington **Symonds**, and others into universal terms, and for this all his readers should be grateful.

BIBLIOGRAPHY. P. N. Furbank, *E. M. Forster: A Life*, New York: Harcourt Brace Jovanovich, 1978; Claude J. Summers, *E. M. Forster*, New York: Frederick Ungar, 1983.

Wayne R. Dynes

FOUCAULT, MICHEL (1926–1984)

French historian and social philosopher. After completing his university work, Foucault was active in the French cultural services in a number of European cities. His first major book was *Folie et déraison: histoire de la folie à l'âge classique* (Paris, 1964; translated only in an abbreviated version: *Madness and Civilization*, New York, 1967). This monograph shows Foucault's characteristic ability to frame bold historical hypotheses and to give them literary form in gripping set pieces. As the audience for his work grew, however, more conventional historians began to flag gaps between evidence and inference.

Developing his ideas further, Foucault advanced the guiding concept of "archeology," the notion that western civilization had seen a succession of distinct eras, each characterized by its particular "episteme," or style of thinking. He then extended the scope of his investigation into clinics and **prisons**; as "total institutions" these sites display in concentrated form the strategies of social surveillance and subjugation that regulated the whole society. Foucault's work in the 1960s was often viewed as structuralist, but he denied this affiliation. Although he was out of France at the time, he was deeply marked by the **Paris** uprising of May 1968, which created a general climate of activism; in Foucault's case this commitment found expression in concern for prisoners, mental patients, the Afghan rebels, and human rights generally.

The 1970s saw him increasingly involved with the problem of power, which he perceived as universally diffused though not in very different measures. The modern state in particular has learned to harness to its purposes such bodies of knowledge as medicine and the social sciences, which serve to colonize and subjugate the individual. The individual can confront this phalanx of domination with only a stubborn recalcitrance. At this time the concept of archeology yielded to the more corrosive and dynamic "genealogy," derived from Friedrich Nietzsche, probably the most important influence on Foucault's later thought. His increasing iconoclasm and skepticism led him to deny that historical record yields any evidence of a stable human subject, of a human "condition," or of human "nature."

In the mid-70s he turned to the matter of sexuality, issuing a programmatic statement in 1976 (*La Volonté de savoir*, Paris, 1976; translated as *The History of Sexuality*, vol. I, New York, 1978). The five volumes that were to succeed this little book, treating the early modern period and the recent past, never appeared. Yet at the end of his life he surprised the world with two successor volumes with a different subject matter: the management of sexuality in ancient **Greece** and **Rome**.

While completing these books he was already gravely ill, a fact that may account for their turgid, sometimes repetitive presentation. In June 1984 Michel Foucault died in Paris of complications resulting from **AIDS**.

In some ways a quintessential Parisian intellectual, Foucault obtained remarkable success also in the English-speaking world. On several occasions he taught at the University of California at Berkeley. Although he was wary of being identified as a homosexual thinker *tout court*, he made no bones about his orientation, and could sometimes be found in the leather bars south of Market Street in San Francisco.

It is not surprising that scholars of homosexuality should be attracted to Foucault's work, since apart from its (nonexclusive) focus on sexuality it accorded with several aspects of the spirit of the times. Discontent with the systems of **Marx** and **Freud** and their contentious followers had nonetheless left an appetite for new "megatheories," which the Anglo-Saxon pragmatic tradition was unable to satisfy. Foucault's thought was both ambitious and critical. Moreover, he attacked the oppression model, which saw the shaping of sexual minorities as merely a function of negative social pressures, while at the same time he denied that there was such a thing as a transhistorical homosexual, an invariant building block of social typology. In particular Foucault was influential among a group of gay and lesbian historians who rallied to a program called **Social Construction**. This approach sees human beings and their sexuality as artifacts of the spirit of the age in which they live. Social Construction also detects sharp breaks, "ruptures," from one era to another. This concept of discontinuity was all the more welcome as the ground had been prepared by an influential American philosopher of science, Thomas Kuhn, whose concept of radical shifts in paradigm had been widely adopted. In vain did Foucault protest toward the end of his life that he was not the philosopher of discontinuity; he is now generally taken to be such.

As has been noted, the influence of Foucault has been complex and ramifying. Not since Jean-Paul **Sartre** had France given the world a thinker of such resonance. Yet Foucault's work shows a number of key weaknesses. Not gifted with the patience for accumulating detail that since **Aristotle** has been taken to be a hallmark of the historian's craft, he often spun elaborate theories from scanty empirical evidence. He also showed a predilection for scatter-gun concepts such as episteme, discourse, difference, and power; in seeking to explain much, these talismans make for fuzziness. Foucauldian language has had a seductive appeal for his followers, but repetition dulls the magic and banalization looms. More generally, Foucault found it hard to resist an anarchistic, "anything goes" vision of historical change, which leaves unanswered the question of why we are embedded in a temporal-cultural process from which it is useless to try to escape. Methodologically, his relativism permits no secure place from which to evaluate conflicting truth claims. Despite these criticisms, there can be no doubt of Foucault's personal sincerity, and his generosity toward those who sought to consult him. Refusing to be bound by the somewhat rigid and old-fashioned training he had received in France, he boldly sought to open new vistas of enquiry. The lesson of Foucault then is his quest, rather than the particular points at which he arrived in his relatively short creative life.

BIBLIOGRAPHY. Michael Clark, *Michel Foucault: An Annotated Bibliography*, New York: Garland, 1983; J. G. Merquior, *Foucault*, London: Fontana, 1985.

Wayne R. Dynes

FOURIER, CHARLES (1772–1837)

French **utopian** philosopher and sexual radical. Fourier spent much of his life in Lyon, trapped in a business world which he hated with a passion. Disillusioned in childhood by the dishonesty and hypocrisy of the people around him, he gradually formulated an elaborate theory of how totally to transform society in a utopian world of the future known as Harmony, in which mankind would live in large communes called Phalansteries.

Fourier hid his sexual beliefs from his contemporaries, and it was more than a century after his death before his main erotic work, *Le nouveau monde amoureux*, was first published. He was "modern" in many of his sexual attitudes, believing in the overthrow of traditional morality and universal replacement of this morality with a restrained and elegant promiscuity for everyone over the age of sixteen. He did not believe that anyone under sixteen had any sexual feelings, nor did he understand the psychology of sadism, pedophilia, or rape, so that his sexual theories are not entirely suitable for modern experimentation. Moreover, he had a bizarre belief that planets were androgynous beings that could and did copulate. He was attracted heterosexually to lesbians, and although he called pederasty "a depraved taste," he was tolerant of male homosexuals and ephebophiles. He recognized male homosexuals and lesbians as biological categories long before **Krafft-Ebing** created the modern concept of immutable sexual "perversions."

Fourier called for a "sexual minimum," the right of everyone to constant sexual gratification by means of teaching young people of both sexes to commit the "saintly" act of sexually sacrificing themselves to older people, rather like Lars Ullerstam's modern call for providing the poor with free prostitutes at the taxpayers' expense.

Fourier, however, had no sympathy for "gutter" sex or for promiscuity in the face of the threat of venereal diseases. He wanted these diseases to be done away with before sexual liberation would be allowed. He wrote some fictional episodes

in the vein of William **Beckford**, one of which describes the seduction of a beautiful youth by an older man.

BIBLIOGRAPHY. Jonathan Beecher and Richard Bienvenu, trans. and ed., *The Utopian Vision of Charles Fourier*, Boston: Beacon Press, 1971.

Stephen Wayne Foster

FRANCE

In its present basic form ("the hexagon") France emerged from the territory of the early Gauls and Franks during the central **Middle Ages** (1000–1270). Waves of repression of homosexuality by church and state have never succeeded in uprooting the homophile subculture, stifling the writing of erotic literature, or preventing homosexuals from occupying high positions. French politics and literature have exercised an incalculable influence on other countries, from **England** to **Quebec**, from Senegal to Vietnam. Whether justified or not, a reputation for libertine hedonism clings to the country, and especially to its capital, **Paris**—by far the largest city of northern Europe from the twelfth to the eighteenth centuries (when **London** surpassed it), making France a barometer of changing sexual mores.

The Middle Ages. Little of the exuberant homosexuality for which the ancient **Celts**, including the Gauls, were famed in antiquity seems to have survived the Roman occupation, Christian conversion, barbarian invasions, and finally the Frankish conquerors' adoption of Catholicism with its moral theology that pilloried as the "crime against nature" all nonreproductive forms of sexual expression. The heavy-drinking later Merovingians, descendants of the Frankish king Merovech and his grandson Clovis, who conquered all Gaul, were barbarians who indulged their sensual appetites freely. Lack of control allowed considerable sexual license to continue into the more Christianized Carolingian period (late eighth–ninth centuries), and probably to increase during the feudal anarchy that followed the Viking invasions of the ninth and tenth, but in the eleventh century the church moved to regulate private conduct according to its own strict canons.

The term *sodomia*, which appears in the last decades of the twelfth century, covered bestiality, homosexual practices, and "unnatural" heterosexual relations of all kinds. As early as the late eleventh century theologians associated what came to be called **sodomy** with **heresy** and magic. Commentators on the Scriptures grouped around Anselm of Laon, the most influential teacher of his day, linked heresy and sodomy as forms of sacrilege both punishable by death.

Before 1200 Southern France became a stronghold of heretical sects known as Cathars or Albigensians. Because of their similarity to the Bogomils of Bulgaria they came to be stigmatized as *bougres*, a term that meant first "heretic" and then "sodomite." Charges of sexual heterodoxy were brought against them by the Catholic authorities, who claimed that unrestrained sexual hedonism was part of their cult. Popes organized the **Inquisition** against them and invoked the bloody Albigensian Crusade which devastated much of Languedoc, homeland of a sensual culture tinged by Moslem influences from the south. The word itself survives to this day as English *bugger*, which in Great Britain, apart from legal usage, remains a coarse and virtually obscene expression.

Paris, already the center of French academic and political life, had its trouvères who like the troubadours of Languedoc sang of love—and its clandestine homoerotic subculture. About 1230 Jacques de Vitry denounced the students at the Sorbonne for practicing sodomy, and in 1270 the poet Guillot in his *Dit des rues de Paris* cited the rue Beaubourg as a favorite cruising area for sodomites. Again in the fifteenth century the poet Antonio Beccadelli alluded to the continued homosexual practices of the intellectual community in Paris and the still-obscure jargon

poems of François Villon (b. 1431) have also been cited as evidence for that Parisian subculture.

Some feudal customaries and municipal ordinances punished sodomy. Politics have occasioned accusations of sodomy in many epochs, none ever more notorious than the trial of the entire order of Knights **Templars**, who were blamed for the fall to the Moslems of Acre (1291), the last remnant of the crusader state in Palestine and Syria. The first charges of sexual heterodoxy against the Templars date from 1304 or 1305 in the Agen region of France. Many witnesses—some of whose testimony is suspect because they had been expelled from the order for misconduct or subjected to torture under examination—claimed that the order tolerated as sinless "acts against nature" between members. Philip IV of France pressured Pope Clement V to take action against the Templars, and by October 13, 1307, the arrest of all Templars throughout France was ordered. For the next several years, despite some conflict between secular and ecclesiastical authority, hundreds of episcopal and royal tribunals tallied the wealth of the order, gathered witnesses, heard testimony, and passed judgment. By 1314 the dignitaries of the order were placed in perpetual imprisonment by the church and executed by royal edict. The guilt of the Templars remains moot to this day; while some may have been involved in homosexual liaisons, the political atmosphere surrounding the investigation and the later controversy made impartial judgment impossible.

A persistent fear of sexuality and a pathetic inability to stamp out its proscribed manifestations, even with periodic burning of offenders at the stake and strict regulations within the cloister, plagued medieval society to the end. However, the medieval state was unable to concert the mass arrests and judicial murders of homosexuals that were to occur in the eighteenth-century **Netherlands**.

The Renaissance. If the **Italy** of the quattrocento saw the revival of the culture of classical antiquity—including its open avowal of pederasty—in France homosexuality was long deemed a caprice reserved to the nobility, the intellectual and artistic elite, and the princes of the Church. To be sure, other classes are known to have been involved, but their activity tended to be severely repressed. The notion of homosexuality as the **aristocratic vice** took root and thrived into modern times, though even this privileged minority did not enjoy absolute immunity from prosecution.

At the court both male and female homosexuality could at times flourish. The "flying squadron" of Catherine de' Medici was accused of lesbianism by such contemporaries as Brantôme. **Henri III** was celebrated for his mignons, the favorites drawn from the ranks of the petty nobility—handsome, gorgeously attired and adorned adolescents and magnificent swordsmen ready to sacrifice their lives for their sovereign. Although the king had exhibited homosexual tendencies earlier in life, these became more marked after a stay in **Venice** in 1574. Yet neither he nor the mignons scorned the opposite sex in their pursuit of pleasure, and there is no absolute proof that any of this circle expressed their desires genitally. Yet a whole literature of pamphlets and lampoons by Protestants and by Catholic extremists, both of whom disapproved of the king's moderate policy, was inspired by the life of the court of Henri III until his assassination in 1589.

The intellectual nonconformity of the last centuries of the Old Regime was accompanied, or perhaps motivated, by a sexual nonconformity that found expression in different modes. The amalgam of free thought and sodomy precisely mirrored the medieval association of heresy and sodomy. The circle of **"libertine"** poets whose work launched the great tradition of French erotic verse included Denis Sanguin de **Saint-Pavin**, who so openly proclaimed his fondness for Greek love that he earned the nickname "the King of Sodom." For centuries his poems could circulate only in manuscript, where many of them still await publication. Saint-Pavin's friend and fellow poet Théophile de **Viau** was also gay in his life and writings.

Even the entourage of Cardinal Richelieu included the Abbé **Boisrobert**, patron of the theatre and the arts, and founder of the French Academy, the summit of French intellectual life. His proclivities were so well known that he was nicknamed "the mayor of Sodom," while the king who occupied the throne, **Louis XIII**, was surnamed "the chaste" because of his absolute indifference to the fair sex and to his wife Marie de' Medici.

Under Louis XIV, who himself was strongly averse to homosexuality, the court nevertheless had its little clique of homosexuals led by the king's brother "Monsieur" (Philippe of Orléans), who may have inherited the tendency from their father Louis XIII, if indeed he was their biological father. Despite France's long history of homoeroticism, the king and his associates affected to believe that the practice had been recently introduced from Italy. About 1678 the court homosexuals formed a secret fraternity whose statutes provided for total abstinence from women other than for the purpose of obtaining offspring and whose insignia depicted a man trampling a woman underfoot in the manner of Saint Michael and the devil. In 1681 the young Count de Vermandois, the son of Louis by Louise de La Vallière, applied for admission, but so indiscreetly that the king learned of the order in 1682 and broke it up with great severity. He sent for his prodigal son, had him whipped in his presence, and then exiled him. The other members of the fraternity were in their turn disgraced and driven from the court.

The Enlightenment. In the eighteenth century France became the center of the intellectual movement that was to challenge the beliefs of the Old Regime and overthrow it. Critique of the morality and criminal legislation of the past could not fail to include the medieval attitude toward "sodomy." The very word *sodomite* faded from the usual vocabulary to be replaced by *pédéraste* or *infâme*, the latter being the designation preferred by the police. On the other hand, the **Enlightenment** philosophes could never break fully with the earlier beliefs, in part because they had no alternative sexual morality, and in part because they were aware of the large number of homosexuals in the church, which they hated as the source of the superstition and intolerance they opposed. In fact, a monastic setting characterizes one of the best erotic novels of the eighteenth century, Gervaise de Latouche's *L'Histoire de Dom Bougre, portier des chartreux* (The History of Dom Bougre, the Porter of the Carthusian Monks; 1742). In his posthumously published novel *La religieuse*, Denis Diderot indicted convents as hothouses of lesbianism.

Despite the link between theological and sexual non-conformity, the Enlightenment thinkers never perceived individuals with homosexual inclinations as their allies. When they wrote on the subject of homosexual activity and the attitude which the state should adopt toward it, it was either in terms of condemnation as "unnatural," "infamous vice," "turpitude," "filthiness," or else as a peccadillo that had lost the aura of the mephitic and diabolical in which medieval fantasy had enveloped it. At times they could treat homosexual inclinations as the result of a "bad habit" encouraged by the rigid segregation of the sexes in the educational establishments of the Old Regime, or advocate a more rigorous "police des moeurs" that would maintain the moral purity of the large cities. The practice of keeping a list of known pederasts already existed; in Paris in 1725 it had 20,000 names, in 1783 40,000. However, with the Italian Cesare **Beccaria** the task of reforming the criminal law of the Old Regime began, to be pursued by **Voltaire** and others who upheld the general principle that crimes against religion and morality, when they violated the rights of no third parties or the interests of society but were penalized solely out of superstition and fanaticism, did not fall within the purview of civil law, until the French Revolution created a new code of laws in which sodomy had no place.

This innovation, it is true, was effected quietly and almost without attracting anyone's attention; it was an act of omission rather than of commission. But the criminal code enacted by the Constituent Assembly in September – October 1791 for the first time in modern history contained no penalties for homosexual activity that did not entail the use of force or the violation of public decency; and incorporated into the Code **Napoléon** of 1810, it became the model for repeal of the medieval laws throughout the civilized world.

During the Revolution an anonymous pamphlet appeared entitled *Les Enfans de Sodome à l'Assemblée Nationale* (The Children of Sodom at the National Assembly), proposing to ameliorate the lot of the homosexuals in the name of the rights of man, and offering a Constitution in seven articles which asserted that one could be both *bougre et citoyen*, "bugger and citizen." It contained a list of all the members of the National Assembly who were accused or suspected of belonging to the special interest group to which the title of the pamphlet refers. The Revolution secured the release (though only for a time) of the imprisoned pansexual writer and thinker, the Marquis D. A. F. de **Sade**, who carried the transgressive strain in the Enlightenment to the ultimate limits of the imagination.

From the Restoration to World War I. While French homosexuals were freed from the legal burdens of outlawry and infamy which had been theirs under the Old Regime, society still forced them to lead a clandestine existence, with cruising areas known only to the initiated, secret gatherings and clubs—in short, they constituted in the nineteenth century a "freemasonry of pleasure" that unobtrusively pursued its goals but did not as yet claim to be a distinct sub-species of mankind. While conditions were scarcely ideal, in the absence of a criminal code that made their activities illegal the French homosexual subculture felt no need of a movement that would assert its rights. France became a haven for Englishmen seeking refuge from the far more intolerant law and public opinion of their own country. Also, Paris was a publishing center where books banned in England could be published and sold to British and American tourists.

Nineteenth-century France did see significant treatments of the homosexual theme in literature, from the pornographic novella *Gamiani* (1833) by Alfred de Musset to the realism of **Balzac** who included several gay characters in his panorama of the France of the July monarchy, followed by Paul **Verlaine**, the lover of Arthur **Rimbaud** and author of a number of classic poems on homosexual love and Joris-Karl Huysmans, whose 1884 novel *A rebours* (Against the Grain) depicts the decadent sensuality of the *fin-de-siècle*. Joséphin **Péladan** celebrated androgyny in a series of works under the general title *La décadence latine*. It is to France that modern art and literature owe the whole "decadent" trend that often included a display of overt homosexuality among the more bohemian-inclined sectors of the artistic elite. To the theme of lesbianism Pierre Louÿs devoted his *Chansons de Bilitis* (1894), while Paris under the Third Republic became the residence of little coteries of French and foreign intellectuals, including Oscar **Wilde**, Natalie **Barney**, Djuna **Barnes**, Robert McAlmon, and Gertrude **Stein**, and patrons of the arts who expressed their homosexuality in literature. This foreign colony was to play a significant role in spreading a more open

discussion of the matter to the cultural life of other nations. But a political movement aimed at "emancipation" of the homosexual did not develop.

The homosexual emancipation movement that began on the other side of the Rhine, in Germany, after 1864 barely reached France, where after 1871 everything German became suspect. In 1909 Jacques d'**Adelswärd Fersen** published a few issues of a journal entitled *Akademos* in Paris. The erotic literature that flourished in France in the early years of the century abounded in lesbian themes, but only rarely treated male homosexuality. Also, the psychiatric study of homosexuality that began in the German-speaking countries reached France only in the 1880s, when Julien Chevalier published first a dissertation and then (1893) a book entitled *Une maladie de la personnalité* (A Disease of the Personality). Several other French psychiatrists wrote on the subject, at times in connection with other sexual "perversions," but two foreigners, Marc-André Raffalovich, a Polish Jew resident in England, and Arnold **Aletrino**, a Dutch Jew, were responsible for the most important writings in French. The pages of the Lyon periodical *Archives d'Anthropologie Criminelle* from the years before the First World War contain numerous contributions on the subject, among them Raffalovich's eyewitness accounts of the trial of Oscar **Wilde** in London and the Harden-**Eulenburg** affair in Berlin and Munich.

From the Interwar Period to the Present. Not until after World War I did the public become aware of the extent of homosexuality in French life. The work that "broke the ice," the first part of Marcel **Proust**'s *Sodome et Gomorrhe* (1921), featured the homosexual Baron de Charlus as a member of the French aristocracy in the early years of the Third Republic. Then André **Gide**, by publishing the set of essays entitled *Corydon* (1924), made homosexuality a literary and political question that the salons could no longer ignore. Yet the attempt to create a homosexual journal *Inversions* in 1924–25 ended when the publisher was prosecuted and convicted. In the literary avant-garde Jean **Cocteau** devoted *Le Livre blanc* (1929) to an autobiographical treatment of homosexuality, albeit anonymously, and contributed poetry, plays, diaries, and drawings to the subject; beginning with *Le Sang d'un poète* (1930) he added films to his repertoire. The surrealist movement proved hostile to homosexuality, except for René **Crevel**, who was openly gay. Interwar Paris saw the number of resident foreigners multiply, and a colony of expatriates, **exiles and émigrés**, escaping the provincialism and puritanism of normalcy on the other side of the Atlantic established itself. A few minor non-fiction works on homosexuality were published, never approaching in volume the material issued in Germany under the Weimar Republic.

The fall of the Third Republic and the imposition of the Vichy regime saw a change in the laws that had scarcely been altered since 1810. A new law of 1942, promulgated by Pétain at the instigation of Admiral Darlan, made homosexual acts with an individual under the age of 21 criminal—a parallel to similar legislation elsewhere. On the other hand, in occupied France Roger Peyrefitte completed the writing of *Les Amitiés particulières* (1943), a classic novel of homosexual attachment between two boys at an exclusive Catholic boarding school that was later filmed (1959). Peyrefitte's friendship—based on their joint quest of teen-aged boys—with the closeted novelist Henry de **Montherlant** was only revealed after the latter's suicide (1971). The postwar period, in which French law retained Pétain's innovation, did not alter the general atmosphere, but witnessed significant developments.

Under the editorship of André Baudry, the homosexual monthly *Arcadie* was for many years after 1954 the most intellectual among the journals that promoted the gay cause. In the face of the hostility of the De Gaulle regime the publication stood firm and survived beyond his fall until the beginning of the 1980s. The novels of Jean **Genet**, a former professional thief, treated male homosexuality with a pornographic frankness and style rich in imagery unparalleled in world literature. Genet enjoyed the patronage of the dominant intellectual of the time, the heterosexual Jean-Paul **Sartre**, who also wrote about homosexuality in other contexts. Heartened by his example, other writers in the 1950s and 1960s broached the matter as public hostility diminished.

The sudden efflorescence of the gay **movement** in the **United States** after 1969 could not fail to affect France, which had already felt the impact of American popular culture. A whole subculture inspired by the example of **San Francisco** and **New York** sprang up, with bars, baths, political organizations, and a pictorial magazine entitled *Gai Pied* (first issue: April 1979) that outdid the Los Angeles *Advocate* in splashing homoerotic sensuality across its pages. The arrival in power of a socialist regime at the end of the 1970s spelled the end of many of the barriers which the Gaullist Fifth Republic had erected against the intrusion of such a minority as the homosexual, and soon even a gay radio station, *Fréquence Gaie* (subsequently renamed *Future Génération*), was broadcasting around the clock. In 1981 the socialist government repealed the discriminatory law that had been enacted by the Vichy regime, and the existence of a homosexual minority was accepted as an unalterable fact by even the conservative parties which regained much of their strength in the mid-1980s, if not by the church. Innovations such as a computerized gay bulletin board—the Minitel—reached France, but also the tragic incursion of **AIDS** (in French SIDA), spread in no small part from Haiti and the United States. A flood of new publications ranging from trivial and movement literature to serious investigations of the homosexual aspects of France's own past showed that the Gallic spirit had its own inimitable contribution to the homoerotic culture of the late twentieth century. Even the provincial cities began to boast their own organizations, periodicals, and rendezvous for the gay public. All are recorded in the *Gai Pied Hebdo Guide*, published annually since 1983.

The political battles that had to be waged before courts and legislatures in other countries to gain the minimum of legal toleration were spared the French movement; its principal foe was the unenlightened public opinion surviving from the recent past, but receding as the subject of homosexuality became an everyday matter in the mass media. So France joined the ranks of those nations with a politically conscious and culturally enterprising gay community.

BIBLIOGRAPHY. Gilles Barbedette and Michel Carassou, *Paris Gay 1925*, Paris: Presses de la Renaissance, 1961; Jean Cavailhes, et al., *Rapport gai: enquête sur les modes de vie homosexuelles en France*, Paris: Persona, 1984; Claude Courouve, *Vocabulaire de l'homosexualité masculine*, Paris: Payot, 1985; D. A. Coward, "Attitudes toward Homosexuality in Eighteenth-Century France," *Journal of European Studies*, 10 (1980), 231–55; Maurice Lever, *Les bûchers de Sodome*, Paris: Fayard, 1985.
Warren Johansson and William A. Percy

FREDERICK II
(1197–1250)

Hohenstaufen king of Sicily and Holy Roman emperor (1212–1250). Called *Stupor mundi* (Wonder of the World) by contemporaries, he was designated the "first modern man" by the Swiss historian Jakob Burckhardt in his *Civilization of the Renaissance in Italy* (1860). Son of the German Emperor Henry VI and Constance, the Norman heiress of the Kingdom of

Sicily, as well as grandson of the Emperor Frederick Barbarossa, he was born in the square in a small town in Southern Italy, in full public view so that no one could doubt that his mother, old in the estimation of contemporaries for a first conception, produced him. Orphaned at the age of one and entrusted to the guardianship of Innocent III (1198–1216), the most powerful of medieval popes, he actually grew up on the streets of Palermo in Sicily, where he received a most unorthodox education, learning Arabic and Greek as well as German, French, and Latin in that melting pot of cultures.

When Frederick attained his majority he broke his promises to his now dead guardian by failing to surrender the Sicilian crown, which included all of Southern Italy up to the border of the Papal States, when he received the crowns of Germany (1215) and of the Holy Roman Empire (1220), which included all of Northern Italy down to the Papal States. Innocent's successors excommunicated him when he also delayed his promised crusade. Frederick was the only leader to crusade while excommunicated, but he recovered Jerusalem, which Saladin had recaptured from the Christians, by negotiating with Saladin's sophisticated nephew al-Kamil. When he returned he completed the reorganization of Sicily, making it the first autocratic European monarchy, basing it on Arab, Byzantine, and Norman models and Roman law precedents. He issued at Melfi in 1231 the constitution known as the *Liber Augustalis*, which remained in effect until 1860. He was then drawn into the disastrous second Lombard war by the papacy that feared renewed imperial domination more than before, now that Frederick's lands surrounded the papal states. The struggle renewed the War of the First Lombard League (1162–1183) that the popes had waged against his grandfather Barbarossa and the earlier war of the Investiture Controversy (1076–1122) that Pope Gregory VII had launched against another of Frederick's relatives, Emperor Henry IV (1050–1106), who has frequently been considered bisexual.

The Guelph allies of the Papacy captured one of Frederick's sons, Enzio, and held him captive in a cage in Bologna for years, breaking the emperor's heart. Later popes ordered the extermination of "that breed of vipers." Charles of Anjou, brother of St. Louis of France, dutifully beheaded the last of the line, Frederick's grandson Conradin and his noble Austrian companion in the marketplace of Naples in 1268. Here to this date German tourists weep for the fate of these royal youths, who were still adolescents and probably lovers.

Propagandists accused Frederick of keeping a harem and also of homosexual sodomy—both Moslem practices. He supposedly blasphemed "Mankind has had three great deceivers: Moses, Jesus, and Mohammed," a legend that underlay the belief in the apocryphal *Liber de tribus impostoribus*. At his court in Sicily Frederick encouraged the beginning of Italian literature in the form of troubadours, poets who copied the Provençal lyrics and inspired the Tuscans and **Dante**. He himself composed outstanding love poems as well as what became the standard text on falconry. Many medieval poets were homoerotic and some modern scholars believe that courtly love with its unattainable ladies spurred homosexual instincts and even acts among knights and squires.

BIBLIOGRAPHY. David Abulafia, *Frederick II, a Medieval Emperor*, London: Allen Lane, 1988; Ernst Kantorowicz, *Frederick the Second, 1194–1250*, London: Constable, 1931.

William A. Percy

FREDERICK II (THE GREAT) OF PRUSSIA (1712–1786)

Prussian general and enlightened ruler of the eighteenth century. The son of the brutal, anti-intellectual, homophobic, and fanatical Friedrich Wilhelm of Prussia, Frederick was in his adolescence small and pretty, loved French literature and art, wore French clothes and curled his hair. His relationship with his father was hideous; almost every day of his life until he was eighteen Frederick was beaten and verbally abused. At that time he decided to run away from home with his dearest friend, Lieutenant Hans Hermann von Katte, who was eight years older than Frederick, well-educated, a lover of the arts, and a freethinker. Just what their sexual relationship was remains unknown, as Frederick took care to destroy the evidence. The father discovered their plot and had them both arrested; then, overruling the decision of the court-martial that had sentenced Katte to life imprisonment, he ordered him beheaded and forced Frederick to watch the execution. At the moment the sword fell on Katte's neck Frederick fainted, and after regaining consciousness he hallucinated for a day and a half.

Upon ascending to the throne of Prussia in 1740, he immediately displayed the qualities of leadership and military skill that characterized his reign, during which Prussia expanded territorially and gained the basis for its later role as cornerstone of the German empire. Frederick's officials, confidants and friends never doubted that he was homosexually oriented. Ecclesiastical Councilor Busching declared that "Frederick forewent a good deal of 'sensual pleasure' because of his aversion to women, but he made amends for it by his intercourse with men, recalling from the history of philosophy that Socrates had a great fondness for Alcibiades." Hard put to account for Frederick's unorthodox social life, historians ascribed it to misogyny, but this assumption has no other ground than his separation from his wife and the general absence of women from his court. He did have female friends and correspondents with whom he had an intellectual affinity, but his courtiers in residence were all male, and Prussian society in general had a high degree of sex segregation.

Frederick's separation from his wife is quite understandable. His father had forced him to marry her as a sign of his obedience, to produce an heir to the throne, and possibly to prove his heterosexuality. The bride, Elizabeth Christine of Brunswick, had been chosen by the Holy Roman emperor in the hope that she would influence Frederick to follow Austrian policies, but Frederick had no intention of being dominated by a woman. The wife, moreover, was a dull German hausfrau, submissive, unsophisticated, and nowhere near as intellectual as he, so that the absence of a sexual interest precluded any human relationship between them. The minute his father died, Frederick separated from his wife but never divorced her, and as compensation he gave her the palace of Schönhausen, apartments in the palace in Berlin and an income suitable for the queen of Prussia.

Frederick's brother **Henry of Prussia**, who was fourteen years younger and also homosexual, but far more open and undisguised in his erotic preferences, chose the officers in his regiment for their handsomeness rather than for their military competence. Frederick did, however, force his younger brother to marry "to save appearances."

There are allusions to homosexuality in a mock-epic which Frederick composed in French, *Le Palladion*, and in a victory poem commemorating the defeat of the French at Rossbach on November 5, 1757. Some of his poetic references to Greek love were negative on the surface, but this may have been mere literary camouflage. The male friends whom he loved deeply nearly all died of disease or in battle and left him lonely in his old age. He carefully kept his male intimates separate from the affairs of state, never allowing them to exert an undesirable influence on his regime. His relationship with the French writer and philosopher **Voltaire** was fraught with ambivalence—including

the homoerotic overtones, and the exasperated Frenchman went so far as to publish an anonymous book entitled *The Private Life of the King of Prussia* which amounted to an exposé of Frederick's homosexuality, yet in the end each acknowledged the other's greatness.

Frederick was a crowned homosexual who loved other men passionately—and sometimes suffered terribly as a result. He exercised his royal prerogative to pardon those convicted of sodomy, and never let his personal feelings override his duties as a ruler. If his life experiences made him bitter, they never robbed him of the capacity for male love.

BIBLIOGRAPHY. Susan W. Henderson, "Frederick the Great of Prussia: A Homophile Perspective," *Gai Saber*, 1:1 (1977), 46–54.

Warren Johansson

FREEDOM, SEXUAL

See **Liberation, Gay; Sexual Liberty and the Law.**

FREEMASONRY

The fraternal order of Free and Accepted Masons is a male secret society having adherents throughout the world. The order is claimed to have arisen from the English and Scottish fraternities of stonemasons and cathedral builders in the late Middle Ages. The formation of a grand lodge in London in 1717 marked the beginning of the spread of freemasonry on the continent as far east as Poland and Russia. From its obscure origins freemasonry gradually evolved into a political and benevolent society that vigorously promoted the ideology of the **Enlightenment**, and thus came into sharp and lasting antagonism with the defenders of the Old Regime. The slogan "Liberty, Equality, Fraternity" immortalized by the French Revolution is said to have begun in the lodges of the Martinist affiliate. The Catholic church became and remained an implacable foe of freemasonry and of liberalism, so that the political history of not a few countries is the chronicle of the struggle between them.

The significance of freemasonry for homosexuality is complex. By actively furthering the downfall of the Old Regime, freemasonry contributed to the massive reform of the penal codes of Europe, including the abolition of the crime of **sodomy**. And the clandestine nature of the freemasonic lodges, with their degrees of initiation, suggested to the participants in the erotic subculture of nineteenth-century Europe that they belonged to "love's freemasonry" as the unknown author of the *Leon to Annabella*, attributed to Lord **Byron**, expressed it. The great French literary critic Charles Augustin Sainte-Beuve (1804–1869) later spoke of a "freemasonry of pleasure" whose adepts recognize one another everywhere at a glance. Down to the beginning of the modern homosexual liberation movement, this was probably how most homosexuals defined themselves—not as members of a psychological or ethnic "minority." Not surprisingly, the conservative and clerical forces in retreat sought to defame the masonic lodges by claiming that their members were "vile pederasts," so that the issue of homosexuality has largely been avoided within masonic circles. A book such as Hans Blüher's *Die Rolle der Erotik in der männlichen Gesellschaft* (The Role of the Erotic in Male Society; 1917–19), which emphasized the homoerotic component of male bonding and organization-building, could create only embarrassment in masonic circles, even if the lodges practiced a considerable toleration in regard to the sexual lives of their members.

Harry Hay's original design for the **Mattachine Society** was modeled in part on the well-established hierarchical orders of freemasonry, as well as on the clandestine, anonymity-protecting structure of the American Communist Party in the 1930s and 1940s. Such a scheme risked rousing fears of an international "homin-tern" that like freemasonry exercised an invisible web of influence over the political life of the country, and in 1953 the national conventions of the Society abandoned this conspiratorial model for a simpler set of local and regional organizations. In the United States freemasonry has had the quality of a fraternal and benevolent society extending into all walks of American life rather than that of a political force engaged in sinister manipulations.

In Europe the freemasons have retained some of their former political might. A well-known French freemason, Henri Caillavet, drafted the law eliminating antihomosexual discrimination that was passed in 1981. At the same time the leading French lodge, the Grand Orient de France—despite its defense of other oppressed groups—remains uneasy about the subject of homosexuality, and gay members feel obliged to remain in the closet.

Warren Johansson

FREUD, SIGMUND (1856–1939)

Viennese physician and thinker, the founder of **psychoanalysis**. Born in Príbor in Moravia (now Czechoslovakia) of a Jewish family that stemmed from Galicia, Freud accompanied his father, a wool merchant, when he moved to Vienna in 1859. The family lived in considerable poverty, relieved only by gifts from the two sons of a previous marriage of his father's who had settled in Manchester and prospered. In school Sigmund was a brilliant student, sitting at the head of his class and mastering the classical and several modern languages.

Early Career. In 1871 Freud entered the University of Vienna as a medical student and passed his qualifying examinations as a physician in 1881. He continued research work for some fifteen months, publishing among other things a paper that entitles him to rank among the discoverers of the neurone theory, a basic concept for modern neurology. In 1882, however, his teacher Ernst Brücke advised him to abandon research and to practice medicine; and since Freud wished to marry and start a family, he took this advice. There followed three years as a resident at the Vienna General Hospital, with five months in the psychiatric division. In 1885 the University awarded him a traveling fellowship that enabled him to study in Paris under Jean-Martin Charcot, the famous neurologist who had demonstrated the value of hypnosis; this contact awakened Freud's interest in hysteria and psychopathology. In 1886 Freud began his practice as a specialist in nervous diseases, and a few months later, after a long engagement, he married Martha Bernays.

The role played by sexuality in Freud's writings has given his own sex life a certain interest for the investigator. The available evidence suggests that Martha Bernays was the only love of his life, that he had no extramarital affairs and no homosexual activity, and that he ceased having sexual relations with his wife at the age of 42, in 1898, on the pretext that he wanted no more children and that contraceptive devices were aesthetically unsatisfactory. Thus he was a preeminently Victorian figure in his private life, even if his theories helped to foster the demand for sexual liberation from the bind of Christian **asceticism**.

The Emergence of Freud's Distinctive Ideas. In the 1880s most of the patients referred to a specialist in nervous diseases were neurotics with no physical illness of any kind, while the emphasis in psychiatry on hereditary degeneration and on lesions in the central nervous system left the practitioner helpless, fostering an attitude of therapeutic nihilism. The x-ray had not yet been discovered, operations on the brain were exceedingly dangerous and usually ended in the death of the patient, and diagnostic brain imaging techniques lay many decades in the future. Freud exhibited moral courage when he adopted the hypnotic technique in 1887 and a re-

version to scientific respectability when he replaced hypnosis with "free association," advising the patient to utter whatever came into his head in the hope that such undirected thought would revive the repressed traumatic event that had caused the illness. The underlying theoretical assumption was that neurotic symptoms are physical expressions of repressed emotion that will vanish if the painful experience is recalled and the emotion belatedly expressed. Examples of this were given in the book by Freud and Josef Breuer, *Studien über Hysterie* (Studies on Hysteria; 1895), which is usually regarded as the first psychoanalytic work, since it introduced into psychiatry the concepts of trauma, the unconscious, repression, conversion, and abreaction. It should be noted, however, that the concept of the unconscious had been for some decades a commonplace of German romantic literature and philosophy.

Breuer recoiled, however, from certain of the corollaries of the technique, in that patients who benefited from this form of therapy became passionately attached to the therapist, and the pathogenic, traumatic experience often seemed to be sexual. Freud was undeterred and went on to formulate the concept of transference to explain the first phenomenon and his theory of infantile sexuality to explain the second. Breuer's withdrawal from the scene left Freud alone, and so psychoanalysis proper was his individual creation, not that of a group of collaborators. Also, in the years 1894–1902 Freud was undergoing a period of self-analysis that was in fact a creative mental illness. During this time Freud was obsessed by his own dreams and suffered from feelings of total isolation alleviated only by correspondence and occasional meetings with the Berlin physician Wilhelm Fliess, in whose eccentric numerological fantasies he was absorbed for years. He only gradually emancipated himself from them.

At the close of this ordeal he emerged with the conviction that he had discovered three great truths: that dreams are the disguised fulfillment of unconscious, mainly infantile wishes; that all human beings have an Oedipus complex in which they wish to kill the parent of the same sex and possess the parent of the opposite one; and that children have sexual feelings. At the same time Freud felt himself despised, rejected, and misunderstood. This last attitude became part of a myth which held that Freud was universally ignored and even persecuted by his psychiatric colleagues, although it is true that the lay reception of Freud's work was often far more sympathetic and positive than theirs.

Maturity. Freud's first notable publication concerning bisexuality and homosexuality was the *Drei Abhandlungen zur Sexualtheorie* (Three Essays on the Theory of Sexuality) of 1905. During the following decade Freud made other significant observations on sexuality. In 1902 he had founded the Vienna Psychoanalytic Society, to be followed, in 1910, by the International Psychoanalytic Society. Promoted by an increasing number of disciples, Freud's thought was on the way to becoming institutionalized.

In the 1920s he added two ideas to his original corpus: the tripartition of the human mind into superego, ego, and id; and the concept of the death instinct (*thanatos*). As the founder of psychoanalysis Freud attracted the rich and famous to his couch in Vienna, while a cancer of the upper jaw induced by cigar smoking undermined his health. His rise to world renown during this period was clouded by the threat of National Socialism, which finally forced him to leave Austria. Just after the outbreak of the World War II, he died in London on September 23, 1939. At this point the turmoil of world events precluded any full assessment of the value of his work.

After World War II appraisals in the English-speaking world inclined to the laudatory, following paths laid down by the psychoanalytic establishment itself;

Ernest Jones' three-volume biography is the best example of this tendency. Those who criticized Freud and his ideas were commonly accused of clinging fearfully to traditional morality and of willful resistance to his insights, while the foes of psychoanalysis branded it a mystical and dogmatic belief system that merely perpetuated in a new guise notions inherited from the idealistic thinkers of antiquity. In the 1970s and 1980s, however, more fundamental criticisms were heard, and the psychoanalytic establishment was forced on the defensive, while new therapeutic techniques took the place of prolonged and costly analyses with doubtful outcomes.

BIBLIOGRAPHY. Ernest Jones, *The Life and Work of Sigmund Freud*, 3 vols., New York: Basic Books, 1953–57; Paul Roazen, *Freud and His Followers*, New York: Alfred A. Knopf, 1976; Frank J. Sulloway, *Freud, Biologist of the Mind: Beyond the Psychoanalytic Legend*, New York: Basic Books, 1979.

Warren Johansson

FREUDIAN CONCEPTS

The following discussion reviews a number of Sigmund **Freud**'s published writings on sexuality and homosexuality, in an attempt to isolate elements of enduring value within them. Five aspects of Freud's **psychoanalytic** work are relevant to homosexuality, though by no means have all of them been fully appreciated in the discussion of the legal and social aspects of the subject. These include: (1) the psychology of sex; (2) the etiology of paranoia; (3) psychoanalytic anthropology; (4) the psychology of religion; and (5) the origins of Judaism and Christianity. In regard to the last two the psychoanalytic profession in the United States has notably shied away from the implications of the founder's ideas, in no small part because of its accommodation to the norms of American culture, including popular Protestant religiosity.

Psychology of Sex. This realm was treated in a classic manner in *Drei Abhandlungen zur Sexualtheorie* (Three Essays on the Theory of Sexuality; 1905), in which Freud polemicized against Magnus **Hirschfeld**'s theory of homosexuality as constitutionally determined, inborn, and unmodifiable. He pointed out that these characteristics could only be ascribed to exclusive inverts, as he designated them; but to accept such an explantion would be tantamount to renouncing an understanding of homosexual attraction in its totality. He stressed the continuum that extends from the exclusive homosexual to the individual who has only fleeting experiences or merely feelings in the course of adolescence. In a footnote (conveniently overlooked by many psychoanalysts since then) Freud mentioned that in the understanding of inversion the pathological viewpoints have been replaced (*abgelöst*) by anthropological ones, and that this shift was the merit of Iwan **Bloch** in his *Beiträge zur Ätiologie der Psychopathia sexualis* (Contributions to the Etiology of Psychopathia sexualis; 1902–03), which laid particular emphasis on homosexuality among the civilized peoples of antiquity.

In this study Freud also recognized that deviations of the secondary and tertiary sexual characters in the direction of the norm for the opposite sex are independent of the homosexual orientation itself. He examined the theories that related homosexuality to a primitive or constitutional **bisexuality**, and pointed out that the pederast is attracted only to the male youth who has not yet lost his androgynous quality, so that it is the blend of masculine and feminine traits in the boy that arouses and attracts the adult male; and the male prostitutes of Freud's time seem to have affected a particularly effeminate guise to lure their customers. The disturbance in the orientation of the sexual impulse, he held, must be related to its development. In all the cases that he had analyzed he found that in the early years of their childhood future inverts had an intense but short-lived phase of intense fixation on a woman (usually the mother), which after overcoming, they identify with the woman and take themselves as sexual object. So that with a narcissistic starting point they seek youthful sexual partners resembling themselves, whom they then love as the mother loved them. He also determined that alleged inverts were not indifferent to female stimuli, but transferred their arousal to male objects. This mechanism continues to function throughout their entire lives: their compulsive quest of the male is caused by their restless flight from the female.

Freud later (1915) added to these remarks the assertion that psychoanalysis is decisively opposed to any effort at separating homosexuals from the rest of mankind as a special class. If anything, psychoanalytic study has found that all human beings are capable of a homosexual object choice and have in fact made one in the unconscious. Libidinous feelings for persons of the same sex play no less a role in normal mental life, and a greater one in the pathological, than do those for the opposite sex. Independence of the object choice from the sex of the object, the freedom to pursue male and female objects that is observed in childhood, among primitive peoples, and in early historic times, is the primitive state from which both heterosexuality and homosexuality derive through a process of restriction. Thus Freud adopted the notion of universal primary bisexuality, which had earlier been propounded by Wilhelm Fliess, and made it a cornerstone of his thinking on all aspects of human sexuality.

Not long after the publication of the *Drei Abhandlungen*, Freud gave an interview to the editor of the Vienna newspaper *Die Zeit* (who as it chanced lived in the same apartment house at 19 Berggasse, although the two men were not acquainted socially) in connection with the trial of Professor Theodor Beer, accused of homosexual relations with two boys whom he had used as photographic models. In a statement printed in the issue of October 27, 1905, he asserted that "like many experts, I uphold the view that the homosexual does not belong before the bar of a court of justice. I am even of the firm conviction that the homosexual cannot be regarded as sick, because the individual of an abnormal sexual orientation is for just that reason far from being sick. Should we not then have to classify many great thinkers and scholars of all ages, whose sound minds it is precisely that we admire, as sick men? *Homosexual persons are not sick, but neither do they belong before the bar of a court of justice.* Here in Austria, and to a greater extent in Germany, a powerful movement is on foot to abrogate the paragraph of the penal code that is directed against those of an abnormal sexual disposition. This movement will gather ever more support until it attains final success." Long ignored by orthodox psychoanalysts (though noted by Hirschfeld's committee and reprinted in several publications), this opinion reflects not just Freud's judgment as the founder of psychoanalysis, but also his political liberalism as a follower of John Stuart Mill, whose essays he had translated into German early in his career.

Etiology of Paranoia. In explaining the genesis of **paranoia**, Freud purloined from Wilhelm Fliess the notion that it was dependent on repressed homosexuality, but only in 1915 did he formulate this interpretation as a general rule. He believed that the paranoic withdrawal of love from its former object is always accompanied by a regression from previously sublimated homosexuality to narcissism, omitting the half-way stage of overt homosexuality. Recent investigations have sought to confirm this insight for paranoia in male subjects only, and in all likelihood it is related not just to the phenomenon of homosexual panic but to the generally higher level of societal anxiety and legal intolerance in regard to male as opposed to female homosexuality. This

would also explain why lesbianism is invisible to the unconscious: the collective male psyche experiences no threat from female homosexuality.

Psychoanalytic Anthropology. Reading in manuscript the first part of Jung's *Transformations and Symbols of the Libido*, Freud became increasingly unhappy with the latter's tendency to derive conclusions from mythology and comparative religion and transfer them to clinical data, while his own method was to start with his analytic experience and to apply the conclusions to the beliefs and customs of man's early history. The outcome of Freud's explorations in this direction was *Totem and Taboo* (1913), which despite the break with his Swiss colleague in that year is the most Jungian of all his works.

The first section, on "The Horror of Incest," deals with the extraordinarily ramified precautions primitive tribes take to avoid the remotest possibility of incest, or even a relationship that might distantly resemble it. They are far more sensitive on the matter than civilized peoples, and infringement of the taboo is often punished with instant death. This observation is pertinent to the problem of intergenerational homosexuality, above all to the intense condemnation that Western society still attaches to pederasty—which ironically enough is the *normative* type of homosexuality in many other cultures. While Hellenic civilization could distinguish between father–son and *erastes– eromenos* relationships, Biblical Judaism could not, and expanded its earlier prohibition of homosexual acts with a father or uncle to a generalized taboo. It is perhaps pertinent that pedophilia (sex with prepubertal children), as distinct from pederasty, usually involves members of the same family, not total strangers. Also, extending this mode of thinking, the fascination which some homosexual men have for partners of other races may be owing to the unconscious guilt that still adheres to a sexual relationship with anyone who could be even remotely related to them, which is to say a member of the same ethnic or racial group.

The second section is entitled "Taboo and the Ambivalence of Feelings," whose relevance to homosexuality lies in the survival of the medieval taboo in its most irrational forms down to the last third of the twentieth century. To the believer the taboo has no reason or explanation beyond itself. It is autonomous, and the fatal consequences of violating it are equally spontaneous. Its nearest parallel in modern times is the conscience, which Freud defined as that part of oneself which one knows with the most unquestioning certainty. The tabooed person is charged with prodigious powers for good or evil; anyone coming in contact with him, even accidentally, is similarly laden. These notions are relevant for the understanding of the ostracism which Christian society has traditionally inflicted upon individuals known to have had homosexual experience, and of the belief that the homosexual constantly seeks to initiate others into his own practices—for which they then ostensibly experience an irrepressible craving.

The fourth section, the most important of all, was called "The Infantile Return of Totemism." Totems were originally animals from a particular species of which the clan traced its descent, and which the clan members were strictly forbidden to kill. From studying the attitude of young children to animals Freud had found that the feared animal was an unconscious symbol of the father who was both loved and hated. Exogamy was nothing but a complicated guarantee against the possibility of incest. Totemism and exogamy are hence the two halves of the familiar Oedipus complex, the attraction to the mother and the death wishes against the rival father.

Following a suggestion of Darwin's that early man must have lived in primal hordes consisting of one powerful male, several females, and their imma-ture offspring, Freud postulated that on the one hand the dominant male would drive away, castrate, or kill his younger challengers, on the other the growing sons would periodically band together to kill, slay, and devour the father. The clan of brothers that would be left would be ambivalent toward the slain father and prone to quarrel among themselves; this situation would lead to remorse and an internalized incest taboo. Freud then appealed to Robertson Smith's writings on sacrifice and sacrificial feasts in which the totem is ceremonially slain and eaten, thus reenacting the original deed. The rite is followed by mourning and then by triumphant rejoicing and wild excesses; the events serve to perpetuate the community and its identity with the ancestor. After thousands of years of religious evolution the totem became a god, and the complicated story of the various religions begins. This work of Freud's has been condemned by anthropologists and other specialists, yet it may throw considerable light on aspects of Judeo-Christian myth and legend that cluster around the rivalry of the father and his adolescent son—in which the homosexual aggressor is, ostensibly, seeking to destroy the masculinity of his rival by "using him as a woman."

Psychology of Religion. In the tradition of the **Enlightenment** Freud approached religion from the standpoint of a dogmatic atheism. As early as 1907 he published an essay on "Obsessive Acts and Religious Practices," showing that in both there is a sense of inner compulsion and a more or less vague apprehension of misfortune (= punishment) if the ceremonies are omitted. In obsessional neurosis the repressed impulses that have to be kept at bay are typically sexual ones; in religion they may extend to selfish and aggressive desires as well. Obsessional neurosis is thus a pathological counterpart of religion, while religion may be styled a collective obsessional neurosis.

Twenty years later, in *Die Zukunft einer Illusion* (The Future of an

Illusion), Freud returned to the problem of religion and its survival, albeit in attenuated forms, in modern society. He pursued the line of scientific criticism of religion which concluded that religion is the collective neurosis which, like inoculation against disease, saves the individual from his individual neurosis. Then in *Das Unbehagen in der Kultur* (Civilization and Its Discontents; 1929), Freud approached the problem of the conflict between instinctual drives and the demands of civilization, in particular the restrictions imposed on sexual life, which exact a heavy toll in the form of widespread neuroses with the suffering and loss of cultural energy which they entail. These writings are pertinent to the conflict experienced by many homosexuals between their religious identity acquired in childhood and the needs of the erotic side of their personality which the Judeo-Christian moral code forbids them to satisfy.

The Origins of Judaism and Christianity. The fullest treatment of this subject Freud reserved for his last major work, *Der Mann Moses und die monotheistische Religion* (Moses and Monotheism; 1938). The book has two main themes: a study of the beginnings of Judaism, and secondarily of Christianity, followed by a consideration of the significance of religion in general. From the secondary sources that he had read, Freud surmised that the lawgiver Moses was an Egyptian who had opted for exile after religious counter-revolution had undone the reforms of the first monotheist, Akhenaten. His Egyptian retinue became the Levites, the elite of the new religious community which received its law code, not from him, but from the Midianite priest of a volcanic diety, Jahweh, at the shrine of **Kadesh Barnea**. This last site, amusingly enough, presumably took its name from the bevy of male and female cult prostitutes who ministered at its shrine. The Biblical Moses is a fusion of the two historic figures.

Freud also, on the basis of a book published by the German Semiticist Ernst Sellin, posited the death of Moses in an uprising caused by his autocratic rule and apodictic pronouncements. The whole notion was based upon a reinterpretation of some passages in the book of Hosea, which because of its early and poetic character, not to speak of the problems of textual transmission, poses enormous difficulties even for the expert.

The last part of the study treats the role of Oedipal rivalry and conflict in the myths and rites of Judaism and Christianity. Judaism is a religion of the father, Christianity a religion of the son, whose death on the cross and the institution of the eucharist are the last stage in the evolution that began with the slaying and eating of the totem animal by the primal horde. However fanciful some of Freud's interpretations may have been, given that he was a layman speculating on secondary sources, in opening the supposed Judeo-Christian revelation to the scrutiny of depth psychology, he stood squarely in favor of a critical examination of the myths and the taboos of Judaism and Christianity.

Legacy and Influence. The half-century following Freud's death in exile in London in 1939 saw the controversy over the merits of his theories continue unabated. The exodus of the German and Austrian psychoanalysts to the English-speaking world greatly enhanced their influence on the culture of the countries in which they settled. At the same time, a body of experience with psychoanalytic practice and a critical literature on Freud's life and work arose that make it possible to evaluate his contribution to the problems posed by homosexuality and the Judeo-Christian attitude toward it.

In retrospect it is clear that Freud's own strictures in regard to homosexuality have been disregarded by the psychoanalytic profession, particularly in the United States, where many analysts have been almost fanatical in their insistence that "homosexuality is a disease." The particular emphasis with which Freud contradicted Magnus Hirschfeld's notion that homosexuals were a biological **third sex** led—together with a tendency (not confined to psychoanalysis) to deny the **constitutional** bases of behavior—to the assertion that homosexuality was purely the result of "fixation" in an infantile stage of sexual development provoked by the action or inaction of the parents. The corollary was that individuals with varying degrees of homosexuality were forced into prolonged therapeutic sessions, or even subjected to cruel applications of electric shock—invented only in 1938 by Ugo Cerletti—and other measures designed to "cure" them. In the popular mind the belief that homosexuality is somehow a failure of psychological development has its underpinning in the Freudian concepts.

Freud's contribution to the psychology of the intolerance of homosexuality has, on the contrary, never been fully appreciated and utilized by the psychoanalytic profession. Yet by freeing the thinking of the educated classes from the taboos that enveloped sexuality in the Victorian era, Freud strongly promoted the demystification of the whole subject and made possible a gradual onset of rationality in place of the horror, disgust, and condemnation that had been the norm until recent times. Although seldom quoted in the continuing legal debate over gay rights, his legacy has quietly worked in favor of toleration—as Freud himself would have wished.

On his eightieth birthday Freud was honored with an address composed by Thomas **Mann** and signed by some two hundred European intellectuals which congratulated "the pioneer of a new and deeper knowledge of man." It went on to say that "even should the future remould and modify one result or another of his researches, never again will the questions be stilled which Sigmund Freud put to mankind; his gains for knowledge cannot be permanently denied or obscured." The weaknesses and shortcomings of Freud's legacy were in no small part failings of the science of his own day. He had to study the final product of conscious and unconscious mental activity; future generations, thanks to new devices for sounding the brain and the central nervous system, will be able to correlate these with the underlying physiological processes. Pioneer that he was, he ventured at times into fields that were beyond his own command, but left footsteps which others, endowed with a surer perspective, would follow into the heart of the matter. To homosexuals he bore no ill-will, to religion he had no commitment, to intolerance of sexual expression he gave no sanction, and by tearing away the curtain of irrationality and superstitious fear that had for so long enveloped sexuality in general he set the stage for the forces of reason that must someday overcome the misunderstanding and injustice that homosexuals have endured in Western civilization.

BIBLIOGRAPHY. Kenneth Lewes, *The Psychoanalytic Theory of Homosexuality*, New York: Simon and Schuster, 1988; Timothy F. Murphy, "Freud Reconsidered: Bisexuality, Homosexuality, and Moral Judgement," *Journal of Homosexuality*, 9:2/3 (1983–84), 65–77.

Warren Johansson

FRIEDLAENDER, BENEDICT (1866–1908)

German natural scientist, thinker, and leader in the homosexual emancipation movement. In 1903, he cofounded the "Gemeinschaft der Eigenen" ("The Community of the Exceptional," but "eigene" also means "self," "same" [sex], and, in reference to Max Stirner's **anarchist** philosophy, "self-owner"), along with Wilhelm Jansen and Adolf **Brand**. Although also a member of Magnus **Hirschfeld's Scientific-Humanitarian Committee**, he did not agree with the Committee's exclusive emphasis on explaining homosexuals as a **third sex** who by their nature were creatures that exhibited the external attributes of one gender while possessing the

"soul" (character, emotions) of the opposite gender. Friedlaender led a move to
split the Committee in 1907, but it failed
in part due to his death in 1908 and to
Hirschfeld's successful outmaneuvering of
the "secessionists."

These men desired a renaissance
of the male–male bonds which had formed
so important a part of culture in ancient
Greece. Their ideal would be realized in a
homoerotic relationship, usually between
an adult man and an adolescent boy. The
base, animal desires were reserved strictly
for procreative purposes; thus, woman's
role in their utopia was strictly subordi-
nated to that of the male. His notion of
"physiological friendship" did, however,
lead to the assumption that male bonding
would find expression in physical acts. To
be sure, several of the Community's
members, including Friedlaender and
Brand, were married. Friedlaender expounded this philosophy at length in his
treatise *Die Renaissance des Eros Uranios*
(1904). This work greatly influenced the
theories of Hans **Blüher** as to the cohesive
and driving forces of homosexuality within
society (*see esp.* Blüher's *Die Rolle der
Erotik in der männlichen Gesellschaft*,
1917-19).

The Community's defense of
male–male "love" (i.e., friendship) evinced
an elitist character which looked longingly toward the past. It demonstrated a
decidedly hostile attitude toward the
modern era with its supposed evils of
urbanization, socialism, and women's
liberation, all of which made more difficult, if not impossible, the unity of body
and soul because they dragged all men
down to the basest level.

James W. Jones

FRIENDSHIP,
FEMALE ROMANTIC

The Renaissance interest in Platonism encouraged a revival of passionate
friendships between men, reflected in
works such as **Montaigne's** "On Friendship," Castiglione's *The Book of the Courtier*, Timothe Kendall's "To a Frende,"
William Painter's *Palace of Pleasure*, and
Thomas Lodge's *Euphues Shadowe*. Literary examples of such relationships between
women are less numerous in the Renaissance, but they may be found in work such
as Thomas Lodge's *Rosalynde*, and later,
in the seventeenth century, in many of the
poems by Katharine Philips. It is in the
eighteenth century that such relationships,
which came to be called "romantic friendships," became common. Romantic friendship between women was socially condoned, originally because it was not believed to violate the platonist ideal, and
later for more complex reasons. But while
it is true that love between women was "in
style," women's experiences of that love
were no less intense or real for their social
acceptability.

The Ladies of Llangollen. Such
passion in the eighteenth century was not
believed seriously to violate any code of
behavior, even when it was taken to such
extremes that women eloped with each
other, as did the Ladies of **Llangollen**—
Eleanor Butler and Sarah Ponsonby—in
1778. When Sarah's family discovered that
she had run off with a woman instead of a
man, they were relieved—her reputation
would not suffer any irreparable harm (as
it would have had her accomplice been
male). Her relative Mrs. Tighe observed,
"[Sarah's] conduct, though it has an appearance of imprudence, is I am sure void
of serious impropriety. There were no
gentlemen concerned, nor does it appear to
be anything more than a scheme of Romantic Friendship."

The English, during the second
half of the eighteenth century, prized
sensibility, faithfulness, and devotion in a
woman, but forbade her significant contact with the opposite sex before she was
betrothed. It was reasoned, apparently, that
young women could practice these sentiments on each other so that when they
were ready for marriage they would have
perfected themselves in those areas. It is

doubtful that women viewed their own romantic friendships in such a way, but—if we can place any credence in eighteenth century English fiction as a true reflection of that society—men did. Because romantic friendship between women served men's self-interest in their view, it was permitted and even socially encouraged. The attitude of Charlotte Lennox's hero in *Euphemia* (1790) is typical. Maria Harley's uncle chides her for her great love for Euphemia and her obstinate grief when Euphemia leaves for America, and he points out that her fiancé "has reason to be jealous of a friendship that leaves him but second place in [Maria's] affection"; but the fiancé responds, "Miss Harley's sensibility on this occasion is the foundation of all my hopes. From a heart so capable of a sincere attachment, the man who is so happy as to be her choice may expect all the refinements of a delicate passion, with all the permanence of a generous friendship."

Eighteenth-Century Fiction. The novels of the period show how women perceived these relationships and what ideals they envisioned for love between women. Those ideals generally could not be realized in life because most women did not have the wherewithal to be independent. In fiction, however, romantic friends (having achieved economic security as a part of the plot, which also furnishes them with good reasons for not having a husband around) could retire together, away from the corruption of the man-ruled "great world"; they could devote their lives to cultivating themselves and their gardens, and to living generously and productively, too; they could share perfect intimacy in perfect equality. The most complete fictional blueprint for conducting a romantic friendship is Sarah Scott's *A Description of Millennium Hall* (1762), a novel which went through four editions by 1778.

Even the mention of such a relationship in the title of a work must have promoted its sales—which would explain why a 1770 novel that uses friendship between women as nothing more than an epistolary device was entitled *Female Friendship.* Women readers could identify with the female characters' involvement with each other, since most of them had experienced romantic friendship in their youth at least. Mrs. Delany's description of her own first love (in *The Autobiography and Correspondence of Mrs. Delany,* ed. Sara L. Woolsey) is typical of what numerous autobiographies, diaries, letters, and novels of the period contained. As a young woman, she formed a passionate attachment to a clergyman's daughter, whom she admired for her "uncommon genius . . . intrepid spirit . . . extraordinary understanding, lively imagination, and humane disposition." They shared "secret talk" and "whispers" together; they wrote to one another every day, and met in the fields between their fathers' houses at every opportunity. "We thought that day tedious," Mrs. Delany wrote years later, "that we did not meet, and had many stolen interviews." Typical of many youthful romantic friendships, it did not last long (at the age of 17, Mrs. Delany was given in marriage to an old man), but it provided fuel for the imagination which idealized the possibilities of what such a relationship might be like without the impingement of cold marital reality. Because of such girlhood intimacies (which were often cut off in an untimely manner), most women would have understood when those attachments were compared with heterosexual love by the female characters in eighteenth-century novels, and were considered, as Lucy says in William Hayley's *The Young Widow,* "infinitely more valuable." They would have had their own frame of reference when in those novels, women adopted the David and Jonathan story for themselves and swore that they felt for each other (again as Lucy says) "a love passing the Love of Men," or proclaimed as does Anne Hughes, the author of *Henry and Isabella* (1788), that such friendships are "more sweet, interesting, and to complete all, lasting, than any other which we can ever hope to possess; and were a just account of anxiety and satisfaction to be made out, would, it is possible, in the eye of rational estimation, far exceed the so-much boasted pleasure of love."

American Aspects. By the mid-eighteenth century, romantic friendship was a recognized institution in America, too. In the eyes of an observer such as Moreau de St. Méry, who had just recently left Revolutionary France for America and must have been familiar with the accusations of lesbianism lodged against Marie Antoinette, the women of her court, and most of the French actresses of the day, women's effusive display of affection for each other seemed sexual. Saint Méry, who recorded his observations of his 1793–1798 journey, was shocked by the "unlimited liberty" which American young ladies seemed to enjoy, and by their ostensible lack of passion toward men. The combination of their independence, heterosexual passionlessness, and intimacy with each other could have meant only one thing to a Frenchman in the 1790s: that "they are not at all strangers to being willing to seek unnatural pleasures with persons of their own sex." It is as doubtful that great masses of middle- and upper-class young ladies gave themselves up to homosexuality as it is that they gave themselves up to heterosexual intercourse before marriage. But the fiction of the period corroborates that St. Méry saw American women behaving openly as though they were in love with each other. Charles Brockden Brown's *Ormand*, for example, suggests that American romantic friends were very much like their English counterparts.

The Female Island. So many of these fictional works were written by women, and they provide a picture of female intimacy very different from the usual depictions by men. The extreme masculine view, which is epitomized in Casanova's *Memoirs*, reduced female love to the genital, and as such it could be called "trifling." But love between women, at least as it was lived in women's fantasies, was far more consuming than the likes of Casanova could believe.

Women dreamed not of erotic escapades but of a blissful life together. In such a life a woman would have choices; she would be in command of her own destiny; she would be an adult relating to another adult in a way that a heterosexual relationship with a virtual stranger (often an old or at least a much older man), arranged by a parent for consideration totally divorced from affection, would not allow her to be. Samuel Richardson permitted Miss Howe to express the yearnings of many a frustrated romantic friend when she remarked to Clarissa, "How charmingly might you and I live together and despise them all."

Throughout much of the nineteenth century, women moved still farther from men as both continued to develop their own even more distinct sets of values. Men tried to claim exclusively for themselves the capacity of action and thought, and relegated women to the realm of sensibility alone. Women made the best of it: they internalized the only values they were permitted to have, and they developed what has been called the Cult of True Womanhood. The spiritual life, moral purity, and sentiment grew in importance. But with whom could they share these values?

Female Bonding Strengthens. In America and England during the second half of the nineteenth century, as more women began to claim more of the world, the reasons for bonding together against men who wished to deny them a broader sphere became greater. Carroll Smith-Rosenberg has amply demonstrated that deeply felt friendships between women were casually accepted in American society, primarily because women saw themselves, and were seen as, kindred spirits who inhabited a world of interests and sensibilities alien to men. During the second half of the nineteenth century, when women slowly began to enter the world that men had built, their ties to each other became even more important. Particularly when they engaged in reform and betterment work, they were confirmed in their belief that women were spiritually superior to men, their moral perceptions were more highly developed, and their sensibilities were more refined. Thus if they needed emotional understanding and support, they turned to other women. New England reform movements often were fueled by the sisterhood or kindred spirits who were righting a world men had wronged. In nineteenth-century America close bonds between women were essential both as an outlet for the individual female's sensibilities and as a crucial prop for women's work toward social and personal betterment in man's sullied and insensitive world.

What was the nature of these same-sex bonds? Margaret Fuller, an early feminist, saw same-sex love as far superior to heterosexuality. She wrote in her journal in the 1840s, "It is so true that a woman may be in love with a woman, and a man with a man." Such love, she says, is regulated by the same law that governs love between the sexes, "only it is purely intellectual and spiritual, unprofaned by any mixture of lower instincts, undisturbed by any need of consulting temporal interests."

William Alger in *The Friendships of Women* (1868) cites one historical example after another of love between women. Typically the women wrote each other, "I feel so deeply the happiness of being loved by you, that you can never cease to love me," "I need to know all your thoughts, to follow all your motions, and can find no other occupation so sweet and so dear," "My heart is so full of you, that, since we parted I have though of nothing but writing to you," "I see in your soul as if it were my own."

The Twentieth Century. In 1908 it was still possible for an American children's magazine to carry a story in which a teenage girl writes a love poem in honor of her female schoolmate, declaring:

My love has a forehead broad and
fair,
And the breeze-blown curls of her
chestnut hair
Fall over it softly, the gold and the
red
A shining aureole round her head.
Her clear eyes gleam with an amber
light
For sunbeams dance in them swift
and bright
And over those eyes so golden
brown,
Long, shadowy lashes droop gently
down . . .
Oh, pale with envy the rose doth
grow
That my lady lifts to her cheeks'
warm glow! . . .
But for joy its blushes would come
again
If my lady to kiss the rose should
deign.

If the above poem had been written by one female character to another in magazine fiction after 1920, the poetess of the story would no doubt have been rushed off to a psychoanalyst to undergo treatment of her mental malady, or she would have ended her fictional existence broken in half by a tree, justly punished by nature (with a little help from a right-thinking heterosexual) for her transgression, as in D. H. **Lawrence**'s *The Fox.* Much more likely, such a poem would not have been written by a fictional female to another after the first two decades of the twentieth century, because the explicit discussion of same-sex love in most popular American magazines by that time was considered taboo. In the early twentieth century, however, popular stories in magazines such as *Ladies Home Journal* and *Harpers* often treated the subject totally without self-consciousness or awareness that such relationships were "unhealthy" or "immoral," even for several years after French

441

novelists and German sexologists started writing voluminously about lesbianism and were published in America.

America may have been slower than Europe to be impressed by the taboos against same-sex love for several reasons: (1) Without a predominant Catholic mentality the country was less fascinated with "sin" and therefore less obsessed with the potential of sex between women; (2) by virtue of distance, America was not so influenced by the German medical establishment as other countries were, such as France and Italy and, to a lesser extent, England; (3) there was not so much clear hostility, or rather there was more ambivalence to, women's freedom in a land which in principle was dedicated to tolerance of individual freedom. Therefore, romantic friendship was possible in America well into the second decade of the twentieth century, and, for those women who were born and raised Victorians and remained impervious to the new attitudes, even beyond it.

However, that view did not continue for long in this century. A 1973 experiment conducted by two Palo Alto, California, high school girls for a family-life course illustrates the point. For three weeks the girls behaved on campus as all romantic friends did in the previous century: they held hands often on campus walks, they sat with their arms around each other, and they exchanged kisses on the cheek when classes ended. They did not intend to give the impression that their feelings were sexual. They touched each other only as close, affectionate friends would. But despite their intentions, their peers interpreted their relationship as lesbian and ostracized them. Interestingly, the boys limited their hostility to calling them names. The girls, who perhaps felt more anxiety and guilt about what such behavior reflected on their own impulses, threatened to beat them up.

BIBLIOGRAPHY. William Rounsevelle Alger, *The Friendships of Women*, Boston: Roberts Bros., 1868; Lillian Faderman, *Surpassing the Love of Men: Romantic Friendship and Love Between Women from the Renaissance to the Present*, New York: William Morrow, 1981; Carroll Smith-Rosenberg, "The Female World of Love and Ritual: Relations Between Women in Nineteenth Century America," *Signs: Journal of Women in Culture and Society*, 1:1 (Autumn 1975), 1–29.

Lillian Faderman

FRIENDSHIP, MALE

Friendship has been a basic theme in Western civilization, one which has interacted with other social and intellectual currents. As the definition of homosexuality has changed over time, so has the way of conceiving its relationship with friendship.

Themes of the Classic Texts. When the Greeks first learned to write they wrote about friendship. For more than two millennia the discussion they began continued with undiminished enthusiasm, across Imperial **Rome**, the Christian **Middle Ages** and the philosophers, poets, and dramatists of the **Renaissance**.

The essential texts on which this discussion depends are very few. One is **Cicero**'s essay *De Amicitia*. The second is **Aristotle**'s discussion of friendship in Books VIII and IX of the *Nicomachean Ethics* and Book VII of the *Eudemian Ethics*. The third is **Plato**'s *Symposium*, both in his own version and in the influential commentary written by Marsilio **Ficino** in the fifteenth century. These three texts dominated the discussion of friendship until well into the seventeenth century and one finds them woven together time and again with the supple ease of ideas which have long been companions.

One might well wonder why. For all that they appear together so frequently, these are very diverse texts. Cicero's essay breathes the clear air of humanism. For him, friendship is personal and its basis is virtue. It is thus a harmony between two people in everything, multiplying joys and dividing griefs. Such a friendship necessarily requires an equality and if it is lacking it must, Cicero tells us, be made. For Plato friendship is rather part of the philosopher's quest: a link between the world of the senses in which we live and the eternal world. In Ficino's commentary, however, there is a subtle shift from the philosopher to the lover of God. The sparks of God's glory scattered throughout the world, if the haunted lover but knew it, are what attract him in the beauty of his beloved and the love they inspire are what binds the universe together in all its myriad forms. But something which is the very knot of the universe is as likely to bind the high and the low as much as it does men of equal degree, if all these are but the shadow of the bond that binds in one the Creator and His creation. Somewhere along the way, equality has been forgotten.

But friendship is disinterested, both Ficino and Cicero agree on that: it is content to be its own reward. It is here, though, that we hear the questioning voice of Aristotle. Such friendship, he tells us, is of course the best, but it is not the most common. Why do most men love one another, he asks? They do so, he tells us, because of their usefulness to each other.

These writers had by no means the same ideas about friendship, and the lack of embarrassment with which they were later combined needs some explanation. It is odd to see the humanism of Cicero intertwined with the religious rapture of Ficino; but we do, frequently. It is also odd to find a critical comment reminiscent of Aristotle within a text which otherwise draws on either of these two; but the assiduous researcher will also find that. This ease in combining the uncombinable tells us something we ought perhaps in any case to have guessed for ourselves. It is that when medieval or Renaissance writers wrote of friendship, they were not writing of something they had discovered in the pages of Cicero or Plato. It was something that already existed in their society, and what they were

doing was presenting it in its very best clothes.

Subsequent Reflections. In the more mundane documents of their time—in the writings of a medieval chronicler or the letters of a man of affairs—there is a tacit but salutary commentary on such material. There one will frequently find "friend" or "friendship," but the kind of relationship characterized by these words is altogether more practical. It is quite likely to be the relationship a patron had with his client or a lord with his tenants: the relationship, to put it at its broadest and most characteristic, between those men who possessed power and those with whom they were willing to share it.

"Friendship" in this sense casts a revealing light on the more literary descriptions of friendship. Typical of many is John Lyly's (ca. 1554–1606) description of Euphues' friendship with his friend Philautus, written in the England of Elizabeth I:

But after many embracings and
protestations one to another they
walked to dinner, where they
wanted neither meat, neither music,
neither any other pastime; and
having banqueted, to digest their
sweet confections they danced all
that afternoon. They used not only
one board but one bed, one book (if
so be it they thought not one too
many). Their friendship augmented
every day, insomuch that the one
could not refrain the company of the
other one minute. All things went
in common between them, which
all men accounted commendable.

The description is engagingly ideal and it was meant to be, but the idealization does not lie in its details; all had their ready parallels in the England in which John Lyly was writing. Similar protestations of affection could be found in the correspondence of the hardworking secretaries of the Earl of Essex or Lord Burghley. Edmund Spenser (1552–1599), the hopeful poet of *The Shepheardes Calender*, also looked forward, as many of his contemporaries did, to the kisses and embraces of other men that would mark his success. And as Euphues slept with Philautus, so Archbishop Laud dreamt of sharing his bed, in the eyes of all the court, with the great Duke of Buckingham: in a society where most people slept with someone else in conditions which lacked privacy, with whom a powerful man shared his bed was a public fact and a meaningful one. The idealization lies rather in what John Lyly misses out: that material interest between men of which such signs were the public symbols, and the stream of coin, of New Year's gifts and ready credit that these marks of influence could produce from those who sought to make use of them.

It is such things that were apt to find themselves dressed in elegant garments drawn from Cicero's *De Amicitia* or Ficino's commentary, without, it has to be said, a very close reading of either; and one will very probably find that the immediate source is not these writings but one of those numerous treatises of love which were as common in the sixteenth century as popular Freudianism is today.

Between such friendship and homosexuality there appears at first sight a towering divide. Elsewhere John Lyly speaks of homosexuality with the same terms of fear and loathing Elizabethan writers usually used when mentioning "unnatural vice;" and to some extent there had always been anxiety about it. How could the masculinity of a youth be preserved in a homosexual relationship with an older man? That was the kernel of the problem for the Greeks. For the Romans it was the perennial anxiety that a free citizen might take a passive role in a sexual relationship with a slave. Homosexuality in itself was not the problem for either: it was in the forms that homosexuality might take that the difficulty lay.

Distinctions. In the late Middle Ages the absolute abhorrence of homosexuality took full shape, and it was a fear the Renaissance inherited in full measure. It was characteristically among the fears and anxieties of the thirteenth century that the fearful link was first made between the sodomite and the heretic and, by a transition natural to a society where state and church lay so close together, between these figures and the traitor; the polemics of the Reformation only sharpened that deadly association. Now more than ever the distinction between friendship and homosexuality had to be securely defined.

It was not, though, an easy distinction to make. A description like that of John Lyly makes that very clear. Each involved an emotional bond, each required a physical intimacy and the signs of the one were dangerously close to the signs of the other. Yet the distinction was all the more important and no light matter in a society where "friendship" in the forms of its daily use played the role it did.

In time the problem would lessen, and it is not one that the modern world has inherited. With the coming of the eighteenth century, friendship was well on the way to becoming a more individual and personal relationship. Homosexuality, too, was putting on a different mask, for it was from about this point that the sodomite began to be conceived as part of a minority of human beings for whom homosexual desire alone was a possibility. The change has meant that the tension between friendship and homosexuality which was alive for so long is apt now to elude one.

But if it does, one will have difficulty in fully understanding the history of either homosexuality or friendship before the eighteenth century, for it is here that one inevitably finds the larger world of relations between men in which homosexuality found expression; and time and again in the courts of medieval and Renaissance Europe the accusations of sodomy occur in social relations which at other times a contemporary might have called "friendship."

But there is another reason also why the historian needs to be alive to this tension. Is one so sure that on occasion some did not indeed call the one the other? The two also lay at the boundaries of each other's meaning and to see that is also to ask inexorably a more critical question about who it was that had the power to define that the one was the one and the other was the other. Here is an illustration: In 1368 a boy called Antonio appears among the court records of Renaissance Venice in a trial for sodomy along with a man called Benedicto, who was teaching him to be a herald. During the proceedings, the judges turned to the boy and asked him what *he* made of this crime. It was, the boy replied, "friendship" because Benedicto was "teaching him like a master." His judges had not asked their question out of curiosity. They had elicited his answer all the more effectively to replace it with their own. They had decided that their account should prevail, not his. But why, one is forced still to ask, should the modern investigator?

Homosexuality and friendship: they may well appear at first as two discrete histories, one of society and the other of sexuality. But if one tries to follow their subterranean currents in the Europe of the Middle Ages and the Renaissance, one will end by finding oneself drawn into writing about something larger. One will find oneself writing about power and the power not only of judges but of words.

Alan Bray and Michel Rey

Post-Renaissance Developments. Since the Renaissance the relationship between friendship and homosexuality has seen a contrast between those who sought to define friendship in a manner that would exclude the homoerotic element, and those who preferred, often for covert reasons, to make friendship encompass the phenomenon of homosexuality and serve as a code name for it. Did **homosociality**, a major aspect of modern social relations, include or exclude homoerotic feelings and rela-

tions? The distinction between friendship and love that denied the erotic component of the former and legitimized eroticism solely between men and women redrew the boundary between them in a manner which the defenders of homosexuality tended not to contest directly, but rather to modify by placing their own markers.

Marriage itself was redefined, with implicit consequences for friendship. A society that had observed the tradition of arranged marriages between unequal partners was confronted with a need for change. Under the influence of the middle-class ideology of the eighteenth century, society now accepted the principle of a marriage founded upon the affinity of equals, upon love rather than family interest. In this sense husband and wife could now be friends, and friendship was no longer invested with an exclusively homosocial character. The decisive shift in this direction occurred in England, where the Industrial Revolution and the ideology of classical liberalism went hand in hand.

In Germany political and social relations were more backward, and the period between 1750 and 1850 is often called the "century of friendship" because friendship was held in such high esteem as a bond of intimate feeling in circles where conversely, the intimacy and self-revelation of friendship were opposed to the mask that one had to wear in order to play one's role in society. That this notion corresponded to the antithesis between the homosexual's true self and the socially prescribed mask of obligatory heterosexuality subtly reinforced the fusion of friendship with homoeroticism. This type of friendship was grounded in a bond between kindred spirits, but also was an expression of social virtue that promoted the general well-being. However, because true friendship excluded the erotic, it could not exist between men and women, in whose lives it would be only the antechamber leading to a sexual relationship. Friendship with its higher and nobler ends could thus be seen as superior to the emotionally stormy and unpredictable relationship between a man and a woman. So Romanticism revived the classical model of friendship for which Hellenic antecedents could always be held up as an ideal by such homosexual admirers of antiquity as Johann Joachim **Winckelmann**, a thinker who in **Goethe**'s words "felt himself *born* for a friendship of this kind" and "became conscious of his true self only under this form of friendship."

Ambiguities of the Modern Situation. The ambivalence which the Christian attitude toward male homoeroticism introduced into the equation always made for mixed feelings on the subject. (As late as the 1930s German legal authors seeking to justify the Nazi laws against homosexuality claimed that their purpose was to keep relations between men—but not women—free of the sexual element.)

It was in this context that the first psychiatric writers on homosexuality formulated their definitions, taking as their point of departure the notion that in "normal" subjects sexual contact with members of the same sex caused aversion and disgust, while in pathological subjects it was a source of pleasure. Friendship was healthy because it remained asexual, homosexuality was diseased because it did not. This view was clearly not acceptable to defenders of homophile affection. Their rejoinder took either the form of (1) treating homosexuality as "Freundschaftseros," or (2) of openly asserting the homoerotic element in male bonding and its institutional expression. The first course was followed by Elisàr von **Kupffer** in his anthology *Lieblingsminne und Freundesliebe in der Weltliteratur* (1900), which inspired Edward **Carpenter**'s *Ioläus: An Anthology of Friendship* (1902)—two collections of texts in which the homosexual content was scarcely veiled. The second, more insightful claim was put forth by Hans **Blüher**, first in *Die Wandervogelbewegung als erotisches Phänomen* (The German Boy Scout Movement as an Erotic Phenomenon; 1912) and then in *Die Rolle der Erotik in der männlichen Kultur* (The Role of the Erotic in Male Culture; 1917–19). In these works Blüher revived the Platonic opposition between the *eros pandemos*, the lower form of erotic attraction that united man and woman and served as the basis of the family, and the *eros uranios*, the higher form that underlay male bonding and was the psychological underpinning of the state.

Controversial as this idea had to be, it has been revived in recent times by such authors as Lionel Tiger, who have analyzed at length male bonding and the advantage it gives the male sex in political and economic competition, as well as in shaping the ethos of teamwork which, even in an individualistic society, is necessary for the effective functioning of organizations. Viewed in this perspective, the inability of women either to internalize this ethos or to participate in male bonding with its ever-present, but highly subdued eroticism handicaps them in two crucial respects.

At the same time, sociologists such as Georg Simmel denied that the old forms of friendship were appropriate to modern society. In particular, the tradition of pairs of warriors fighting and dying together on the battlefield had been replaced by an ethos of the group, the military unit. It was this feeling that lingered after World War I, with its experience of comradeship in the trenches, and carried over into the paramilitary groups that fought in the streets of German cities under the Weimar Republic. But the old ambivalence remained, again finding oblique expression on both sides of the fence dividing homosexual from heterosexual. While Ernst **Röhm** could boast, late in 1933, that the homoerotic component in the SA and SS had given the **Nazis** the crucial edge in their struggle against the Weimar system, homophobic writers could call for the suppression of all forms of overt male homosexuality and the enactment of even more punitive laws—which were in fact adopted in 1935.

Contemporary America. The lingering distinction between friendship and love based upon the absence or presence of the overt erotic component also affects relations between homosexual men and heterosexual women. Certain women feel more comfortable in their dealings with gay men, just because they know that they do not have to be constantly on guard against sexual aggression, but can have close relationships, both social and professional, that attain high levels of creativity and imagination. Particularly in professions where homosexuality is no handicap, there can be friendships between gay men and women who take no offense at the male's lack of physical desire for them.

The use of "friend" or "friendship" as a euphemism for the homosexual partner (**lover**) and the liaison itself persists. Recently the compilers of newspaper obituary columns have taken to describing the lifelong companion of a deceased homosexual as his "friend," in contexts where a heterosexual would be survived by the spouse and children. And the author of a bibliography of *Freundschaftseros* published in West Germany in 1964 stoutly upheld not only the distinction between classical pederasty and modern homosexuality, but also the existence of a form of male bonding from which the erotic element is absent.

Conclusion. The overlap since time immemorial between friendship and eroticism persists in the ongoing debate over the place of homosexual feeling and homosexual activity in modern society. The advent of the gay rights **movement** has helped some individuals become more accepting of the erotic nature of their attachments to friends of the same sex—though some others have become more self-conscious and defensive. The lines of demarcation are being continually renegotiated as part of the revolution in moral values that has undermined many of the old norms without as yet formulating new ones. It will be the task of the future to resolve the antagonism rooted in the encounter of classical and Judeo-Christian attitudes toward homoeroticism/homosociality.

BIBLIOGRAPHY. Janet L. Barkas, *Friendship: A Selected, Annotated Bibliography*, New York: Garland, 1985; John W. Malone, *Straight Women/Gay Men: A Special Relationship*, New York: Dial Press, 1980; Stuart Miller, *Men and Friendship*, Boston: Houghton Mifflin, 1980; Ernst Günther Welter, *Bibliographie Freundschaftseros einschliesslich Homoerotik, Homosexualität und die verwandte und vergleichende Gebiete*, Frankfurt am Main: Dipa Verlag, 1964.

Warren Johansson

FRUIT

In general English usage, this noun designates the edible reproductive body of a seed plant, particularly one having a sweet pulp. In North American slang, especially in the second and third quarter of the twentieth century, it has been a disparaging epithet for a male homosexual—sometimes used in the vocative: "Hey, fruit!"

Unlikely as it may seem, the term belongs to that significant class of words in which a pejorative appellation at one time given to women shifted to male homosexuals (compare **gay** and **faggot**). The explanation of this transfer is as follows. At the end of the nineteenth century, fruit meant an easy mark, a naive person susceptible to influence, reflecting the notion that in nature fruits are "easy pickings." From this sense it came to mean "a girl or woman easy to oblige." The transfer and specialization to gay men was probably assisted by the stereotypes that homosexuals are soft and use scent. In the 1940s, the heterosexual counterpart was the more specific "tomato," an available woman.

In England the expression "old fruit" is a mild term of affection (compare "old bean"). The word may also be a clipped form of "fruitcake"—from "nutty as a fruitcake."

The disparaging use of the term in reference to male homosexuals is now less common, and a Los Angeles gay radio program is called (with a quaint air) "Fruit Punch."

Wholly unrelated is the "Sodom apple," a name given to a mythical fruit that is fair to the eye but, once touched, turns to ashes—hence recalling the conflagration of **Sodom** in Genesis 19. The transformation could be glossed metaphorically as the outcome of vain or illicit conduct. "Through life we chase, with fond pursuit,/ What mocks our hope like Sodom's fruit" (J. Bancks, *Young's Last Day*, 1736).

See also **Flower Symbolism.**

Wayne R. Dynes

FULLER, HENRY BLAKE (1857–1929)

American novelist. Scion of an eminent Chicago family, he gradually slid into genteel poverty and literary obscurity after enjoying early wealth and critical esteem. He used to be remembered as the author of novels which attacked the corrupt plutocrats of Chicago, and it is only in the last few years that attention has been turned to his literary treatment of homosexuality, in which he was a pioneer.

Little is known about his private life. His journals from his teenage days make it clear that he was in love with some dormitory roommates at Allison Classical Academy (1873–74). At the age of 19 he wrote an imaginary personal advertisement in which he says, "I would pass by twenty beautiful women to look upon a handsome man."

The years pass without further evidence until, at the age of 34, Fuller admits to being in love with a 15-year-old boy whose initials are "C.N.," and who had blue eyes and strawberry-blonde hair. Five years later, Fuller wrote and managed to publish a very short play, *At Saint Judas's*, about a homosexual who commits suicide at the wedding of his former lover. This was strong stuff for the period, but today this poorly-written play would be laughed at for its melodramatic absurdities. Nevertheless, it deserves credit as the first American play to deal explicitly with homosexuality.

Fuller did not return to this theme until 1919, when he published at his own expense *Bertram Cope's Year*, a novel about a homosexual love affair between Bertram Cope and Arthur Lemoyne, which ends with Cope turning heterosexual. Critics agree that Fuller lost his nerve while writing this novel and spoiled it by having his hero end up as a conformist. Four years later, the elderly Fuller began an affair with a college student named William Shepherd, with whom he went to Europe. A few years later, Fuller died after Carl Van Vechten had made an attempt to revive interest in his writings. Mention should also be made of the letters that Fuller received in 1897 and 1898 from a homosexual Canadian named Harold Curtis, which reveal the homosexual subculture of Toronto. Fuller saved these letters for future historians.

BIBLIOGRAPHY. Kenneth Scambray, *A Varied Harvest*, Pittsburgh: University of Pittsburgh Press, 1987.

Stephen Wayne Foster

FUNCTIONING

Down to the 1950s, **psychiatric** and **psychological** opinion held that homosexual behavior in an adult was symptomatic of severe emotional disorder. A detached evaluation of the homosexual personality was rendered even more difficult by the anger, revulsion, and distaste with which many clinicians reacted. The central difficulty, however, stemmed from the fact that for decades the clinical picture of homosexuality had been formed by the observation of subjects found in consulting offices, mental hospitals, or prisons. These groups did not constitute a valid sample of the homosexual population as a whole.

The Hooker Study. In the mid-1950s, recognizing this bias, Evelyn Hooker of the University of California at Los Angeles set out to investigate the adjustment of the overt homosexual. She judged it important to obtain a sample that did not derive from skewed sources. Thus there was a chance of finding individuals with an average psychological adjustment. She also believed it important to obtain a comparable control group of heterosexuals that would not only provide a standard of comparison but also assist the clinician in suspending theoretical preconceptions. Securing both was a difficult undertaking, but in the end she procured two samples of thirty individuals each who were paired for age, education, and intelligence quotient. No assumptions were made about the random selection of either group. The materials used for the comparative study of personality structure and adjustment of these two groups of men consisted of a battery of projective techniques, attitude scales and intensive life history interviews—the standard paraphernalia of the American depth psychologist of the 1950s. Experts in the assessment of personality structure were called in to evaluate the 60 sets of records. The judges knew that some of the subjects were homosexual and some heterosexual, but did not know which; their task was merely to tell as much as the data revealed about the personality structure and adjustment of each subject.

The finding of the study—epoch-making for its time—was that there were no significant differences between the number of homosexuals having a rating of average or better for each judge; two-thirds of each group of subjects received an adjustment rating of average or better. In 42 out of the 60 cases the judges agreed exactly or differed by only one step. The judges themselves commented that the records which they thought to be homosexual were unlike the ones familiar to them from clinical experience. Hooker concluded that healthy skepticism was justified in regard to many of the so-called homosexual-content signs on the Rorschach test. Moreover, no single pattern of homosexual adjustment emerged; the richness and variety of ways in which homosexuals adjust could not be reduced to a formula. Some homosexuals proved to be quite ordinary individuals, indistinguishable except in their sexual orientation and behavior from other ordinary individuals who were heterosexual. Some were even quite superior individuals, not only devoid of pathology, but capable of functioning at a superior level.

Hooker concluded that (1) homosexuality as a clinical entity did not exist, that its forms were as varied as those of heterosexuality, (2) homosexuality may be a deviation in sexual orientation that is within the normal psychological range, and (3) the role of particular forms of sexual desire and expression in personality structure and development might be less important than hitherto assumed. Even if homosexuality represents a form of maladjustment to a society that condemns it, this fact does not imply that the homosexual subject is severely maladjusted in other areas of his behavior.

Freedman and Others. This study was replicated in 1967 by Mark Freedman with lesbian subjects in a doctoral dissertation in clinical psychology at Western Reserve University in Cleveland, Ohio. He even found that the lesbians functioned better than the control group of heterosexual women; they scored higher on autonomy, spontaneity, orientation toward the present (as opposed to being obsessed with the past or anticipating the future), and sensitivity to their own needs and feelings. An earlier study using Raymond B. Cattell's 16 Personality Factor test showed the lesbian subjects as independent, resilient, self-sufficient, and "bohemian," while a third investigator, again using a control group, found the lesbians scoring higher on both goal-direction and self-acceptance.

Freedman made the further point that homosexuals and lesbians, marginalized as they are by conventional society, do not reject all its standards and mores, but choose among them and so develop new, stable patterns of behavior. The consciousness of alienation can lead to a creative adaptation within a hostile environment, even if not to it. At the same time sexual roles may be more egalitarian and sexuality more expressive than in contemporary heterosexual milieux. There is more freedom to experiment in both couple and group sexual activity. Even the need to hide one's true sexual identity may render the homosexual subject quite sophisticated about the persona of others—the tension between role-playing and covert identity. The range of self-disclosure can also be controlled, and in a friendly setting the homosexual can be more truthful and candid than his heterosexual counterpart. Others pragmatically hide their sexual orientation, adapting as best they can to the social dangers of life as a homosexual, while benefiting from the survival skills that they have internalized.

More recent studies done in a number of countries have confirmed the aforementioned findings. Not only are homosexuals no less psychologically adjusted than heterosexuals, the homosexual identity may be positively correlated with (1) psychological adjustment and (2) support of "significant others." It cannot be judged a psychopathological phenomenon, and such differences as can be demonstrated to exist are those directly related to the sexual orientation itself. The differences in mental functioning for which evidence has been found—higher verbal ability in females, higher mathematical and scientific ability in males—are not disabilities, but correlate with a different locus on the androgyny scale. They correspond to the evolutionary continuum between the sexes that Magnus **Hirschfeld** stressed in his magisterial work on grades of intersexuality, not a dichotomy divinely ordained for all time.

Anticipations. This recent work on the psychological functioning of the homosexual was anticipated by what had been learned at the end of the nineteenth century and the beginning of the twentieth. The first homosexual subjects examined by psychiatrists were seen in the setting of the mental hospital or the prison; usually they were severely disturbed and individuals in conflict with society and with themselves. But when sympathetic psychiatrists were enabled to make contact with homosexuals in everyday life, in their homes and places of work, under conditions that favored a relaxed confidentiality, they reversed their earlier judgment. At a meeting of the Berlin Psychiatric Society on June 8, 1891, the discussion following a paper concluded that homosexuality in and of itself is no mental illness for the following reasons:

(1) there is no clouding of consciousness or disturbance of the rational mind;

(2) there is no irresistible impulse;

(3) the subject has no delusion as to the character of his own sexual organs or those of the partner;

(4) the subject is aware that his sexual orientation differs from that of the majority of the population.

Papers written later in the decade, when such writers as **Moll**, Chevalier, and Raffalovich had published their monographs on the subject, argued that an individual who successfully deceives his surroundings as to his true sexual orientation and activity quite as well as does the undercover agent in a hostile milieu cannot be judged mentally ill or lacking in responsibility. The homosexual subject is as responsible, legally and morally, for his sexual conduct as is the heterosexual one. The condemnation of homosexual behavior on religious grounds does not alter the personality functioning of the homosexual in any objective manner. Whether the sexual activity of the population should be exclusively with members of the opposite sex is an issue of sexual politics that falls outside the empirical question of whether or not the homosexual functions efficiently and purposefully in his milieu and in the face of the obstacles that an intolerant society poses to his quest for sexual gratification.

Conclusion. Beginning with the pioneer study by Evelyn Hooker, modern investigators have overturned the assumption that homosexuals are less able to cope with their life tasks than are heterosexuals, or that homosexuality is in and of itself a pathological entity. The research of the future should address the question of the manner of their adjustment and the subtleties of the interaction between society and the homosexual as a paradigm of survival in a hostile environment.

BIBLIOGRAPHY. Mark Freedman, *Homosexuality and Psychological Functioning*, Belmont, CA: Brooks/Cole, 1971; Sue K. Hammersmith and Martin S. Weinberg, "Homosexual Identity: Commitment, Adjustment, and Significant Others," *Sociometry*, 36 (1973), 56–79; Evelyn Hooker, "The Adjustment of the Male Overt Homosexual," *Journal of Projective Techniques*, 21 (1957), 18–31;Paul Kronthal, Discussion of Lewin, "Ueber perverse und conträre Sexual-Empfindungen. [Forenischer Fall]," *Neurologisches Centralblatt*, 10 (1981), 378–79; Martin Willmott and Harry Brierley, "Cognitive Characteristics and Homosexuality," *Archives of Sexual Behavior*, 13 (1984), 311–19.

Warren Johansson

FUNDAMENTALISM
See **Protestantism.**

GAMES, GAY

An international festival of athletic competitions and the arts, the Gay Games are held quadrennially as a celebration of the international gay community. The first and second Gay Games were held in San Francisco in August of 1982 and 1986. The third Games are scheduled for the summer of 1990 in Vancouver, Canada.

The Gay Games at San Francisco were founded by Tom **Waddell** and organized by San Francisco Arts and Athletics, Inc. The 1982 Games involved 1,300 male and female athletes in sixteen sports; four years later the games attracted 3,482 athletes with a ratio of men to women of 3:2 in a total of 17 sports. (This may be contrasted with the 1984 Olympics in Los Angeles where the sex ratio was 4:1.) Among the events were basketball, soccer, bowling, cycling, diving, triathlon, softball, physique, track and field, marathon, power-lifting, volleyball, swimming, tennis and wrestling. The artistic festival, called "The Procession of the Arts," featured over twenty events including dance, theatre and plastic art exhibits. Although athletes came from many parts of the world, the majority were from North America.

In her opening address at the 1986 Gay Games, novelist Rita Mae Brown highlighted the meaning of the games, ". . . these games are not just a celebration of skill, they're a celebration of who we are and what we can become: . . . a celebration of the best in us."

Tom Waddell said that the Games were "conceived as a new idea in the meaning of sport based on inclusion rather than exclusion." Anyone was allowed to compete regardless of race, sex, age, nationality, sexual orientation, religion, or athletic ability. In keeping with the Masters Movement in sports, athletes competed with others in their own age group. The track and field and swimming events were officially sanctioned by their respective national masters programs. Athletes participated, not as representatives of their respective countries, but as individuals on behalf of cities and towns. There were no minimum qualifying standards in any events.

The Games have been used by gay liberationists for ideological purposes. Historically, homosexuality has been associated with pathology, and the rise of AIDS in the homosexual community has reasserted that association. Many of those who spoke at the 1986 Games said that the Games emphasized a healthy image of gay men and lesbians. Brown also said in her opening address that the Games "show the world who we really are. We're intelligent people, we're attractive people, we're caring people, we're *healthy* people, and we're proud of who we are."

The organizers of the Gay Games have experienced considerable legal difficulties. Before the 1982 Gay Games, the United States Olympic Committee (USOC) filed a court action against the organizers of the Gay Games, which were going to be called the "Gay Olympic Games." In 1978, the United States Congress passed the Amateur Sports Act which, among other things, granted the USOC exclusive use of the word "olympic." Although the USOC had allowed the "Rat Olympics," "Police Olympics," and "Dog Olympics," it took exception to the term "Gay Olympic Games." Two years later, the USOC continued its harassment of the Gay Games and filed suit to recover legal fees in the amount of $96,600. A lien was put on the house of Tom Waddell, a member of the 1968 United States Olympic Team.

Just as the Sacred **Olympic Games** and Pythian Games in ancient **Greece** were a celebration which gave expression to Hellenic values of the time, so, too, the Gay Games are a celebration and expression of the contemporary spirit of the gay community.

Brian Pronger

GANYMEDE

In Greek **mythology** Ganymede was a beautiful Phrygian shepherd boy who attracted the attention of Zeus, the king of the gods. Unable to resist the boy, Zeus seized him and carried him aloft to be his cupbearer and bedmate on Mount Olympus. While the motif of flight through the heavens is probably of Near Eastern origin, the abduction recalls the Cretan custom of older men "kidnapping" their adolescent innamorati and living with them in the wild for a time. (Plato states that the myth of Ganymede originated in **Crete**.) In any event the story is part of a large set of stories of the Olympian gods falling in love with mortal boys.

In ancient art Zeus is sometimes depicted abducting the boy in mortal form and sometimes in the guise of an eagle, his attribute. **Vase paintings** occasionally show the anthropomorphic Zeus pursuing Ganymede as an analogue to the wooing conducted by mortal pederasts. In later antiquity the motif of the beautiful youth being carried aloft by an eagle was given an allegorical significance, as the soul's flight away from earthly cares to the serenity of the empyrean.

In the medieval debate poem *Altercatio Ganimedis et Helenae* (twelfth century) Ganymede conducts an able defense of male homosexuality. The mythographers of the later Middle Ages

and the Renaissance (above all Giovanni Boccaccio in his *Genealogia Deorum* of 1375) presented a number of examples of the male amours of the Greek gods, and these texts influenced artists. In 1532 **Michelangelo** created a drawing of Ganymede Abducted by the Eagle for presentation to a Roman nobleman, Tommaso de' Cavalieri, for whom he experienced a deep, though Platonic affection. Other images of Ganymede were produced by Correggio, Parmigianino, Giulio Romano, and Benvenuto **Cellini**.

In the French language, beginning in the sixteenth century, the divine youth's name became a common noun, with the sense of "passive homosexual" or *bardache*. Joachim du Bellay (1558) speaks of seeing in Rome "Un Ganymède avoir le rouge sur la tête" ("A Ganymede with red on his head," that is, a cardinal). The *Dictionnaire comique* (1718) of P. J. Le Roux is explicit: "Ganymede: berdache, a young man who offers pleasure, permitting the act of sodomy to be committed on him."

In *As You Like It* (Act I) Shakespeare made the transvestite Rosalind assume the name of Ganymede, "Jove's own page." In 1611 the lexicographer Randle Cotgrave defined "Ganymede" as an *ingle* (passive homosexual or catamite). A pointed reference comes from Drummond of Hawthornden: "I crave thou wilt be pleased, great God, to save my sovereign from a Ganymede" (1649), referring to the tradition of royal minions at the Stuart court. Such associations notwithstanding, in the seventeenth century Simon Marius named Jupiter's largest moon after Ganymede, giving him preference over the god's female lovers who are commemorated in the names given to the smaller moons. Thus the way was paved for Ganymede to enter today's age of space exploration.

BIBLIOGRAPHY. Gerda Kempter, *Ganymed: Studien zur Typologie, Ikonographie und Ikonologie*, Cologne: Bohlau Verlag, 1980; James M. Saslow, *Ganymede in the Renaissance: Homo-*

sexuality in Art and Society, New Haven: Yale University Press, 1986.

Wayne R. Dynes

García Lorca, Federico

See **Lorca, Federico García**.

Gay

This word is often taken as the contemporary or colloquial equivalent of **homosexual** without further distinction. But there are other nuances of meaning, especially as some activists vigorously disown the latter term which they falsely believe to be of medical origin and bear the stigma of the pathological, while others would see in *gay* the designation of the politically conscious and militant supporter of the homosexual **liberation** movement, as opposed to sexual orientation which is an artifact of personal history rather than a matter of deliberate choice. To some the word has proven troublesome, and for this reason it merits extended discussion.

The word *gay* (though not its three later slang meanings) stems from the Old Provençal *gai*, "high spirited, mirthful." A derivation of this term in turn from the Old High German *gahi*, "impetuous" (cf. modern German *jäh*, "sudden"), though attractive at first sight, seems unlikely. *Gai* was a favorite expression among the troubadours, who came to speak of their intricate art of poetry as *gai saber*, "gay knowledge." Despite assertions to the contrary, none of these uses reveals any particular sexual content. In so far as the word *gay* or *gai* has acquired a sexual meaning in Romance languages, as it has very recently, this connotation is entirely owing to the influence of the American homosexual liberation **movement** as a component of the American popular culture that has swamped the non-Communist world.

Beginning in the seventeenth century, the English word gay began to connote the conduct of a playboy or dashing man about town, whose behavior was not always strictly moral but not totally depraved either; hence the popularity of such expressions as "gay lothario," "gay deceiver," and "gay blade." Applied to women in the nineteenth century (or perhaps somewhat before), it came to mean "of loose morals; a prostitute": "As soon as a woman has ostensibly lost her reputation we, with grim inappositeness, call her 'gay'" (*Sunday Times*, London, 1868). Curiously the 1811 *Lexicon Balatronicum*, attributed to Captain F. Grose, defines *gaying instrument* as "penis." Thus far, the development has an interesting forerunner in the Latin *lascivus*, which first meant "lively, frolicsome," and then "lewd, wanton."

What was to come, however, has no independent parallel in any other language. The expansion of the term to mean homosexual man constitutes a tertiary stage of modification, the sequence being "lothario," then "female prostitute," then "homosexual man." Viewed in the perspective of the saturation of nineteenth-century usage by the spectacle of the "gay woman" (= whore), this final application to homosexual men could not fail to bear overtones of promiscuity and "fallen" status. Despite ill-informed speculations, thus far not one unambiguous attestation of the word to refer specifically to homosexual men is known from the nineteenth century. The word (and its equivalents in other European languages) is attested in the sense of "belonging to the demimonde" or "given to illicit sexual pleasures," even specifically to prostitution, but nowhere with the special homosexual sense that is reinforced by the antonym *straight*, which in the sense of "heterosexual" was known exclusively in the gay **subculture** until quite recently. While the latter semantic innovation (straight) has been tacitly accepted by those to whom it applied, it has *not* spread to other languages, just as K. H. **Ulrichs'** coinage *Dioning* (= heterosexual) never gained any currency with the general public, even if its antonym *Urning* (and the English counterpart *Uranian*) were used for some decades by German authors and their British imitators. The earliest appearance of the words *gay/straight* in tandem must therefore be the term of development of the whole semantic process.

Although it has not been found in print before 1933 (when it appears in Noel Ersine's *Dictionary of Underworld Slang* as *gay cat*, "a homosexual boy"), it is safe to assume that the usage must have been circulating orally in the United States for a decade or more. (As Jack London explains in *The Road* of 1907, gay cat originally meant—or so he thought—an apprentice hobo, without reference to sexual orientation.) In 1955 the English journalist Peter Wildblood defined *gay* as "an American euphemism for homosexual," at the same time conceding that it had made inroads in Britain. Grammatically, the word is an adjective, and there has been some resistance to the use of *gay, gays* as nouns, but this opposition seems to be fading.

In the light of the semantic history outlined above, a particularly ludicrous complaint is the notion, advanced by some heterosexual writers, that the "innocent" word gay has been "kidnapped" by homosexuals in their insouciant willingness to subvert the canons of language as well as morals. As we have seen, the sexual penumbras of meaning were originally introduced by the mainstream society (i.e., chiefly heterosexuals), first to designate their own rakes and ramblers, and then the women these men caused to "fall." Quite apart from the quaint charge of verbal kidnapping (which ignores the fact that many words in English are polysemous in that they have two or more distinct meanings), there does exist a legitimate concern among homosexuals themselves that the aura of frivolity and promiscuity adhering to the word has not been dissolved. In that sense the comparison of the substitution of gay for homosexual with black for Negro is not valid, though

the two shifts were contemporary. To be sure gay has gained the allegiance of many well-meaning outsiders for the same reason as black, the assumption being that these terms are the ones preferred by the individuals they designate. Many lesbian organizations now reject the term gay, restricting it to men, hence the spread of such binary phrases as "gay and lesbian" and "lesbian and gay people." Such ukases notwithstanding, expressions such as "Is she gay?" are still common among lesbians.

Despite all the problems, brevity and convenience suggest that this three-letter word is here to stay. Significantly, in 1987, in the aftermath of negotiations with the Gay and Lesbian Alliance Against Defamation (GLAAD), the *New York Times*, which had formerly banned the use of gay except in direct quotations, assented to its use.

Wayne R. Dynes

GAY LIBERATION
See **Liberation, Gay.**

GAY RIGHTS
See **Decriminalization; Movement, Gay.**

GAY STUDIES
Gay scholarship on the subject of homosexuality has been fostered by both political and personal motives. On the political plane, it has meant the search for other cultures and societies in which the homosexual was not a criminal and an outcast, in which homosexual love was not the object of opprobrium and disgust, but both were an accepted part of the social and sexual life of the age. Above all, the homoerotic component of the glorious civilizations of the past—ancient **Greece** and **Rome**, medieval **Islam** and **Japan**— was a stimulus and a challenge to homosexual researchers seeking the roots of their own situation. At the same time they were studying themselves through the

mirror of the gay personalities and literary monuments of the past—and even the clandestine literature of the present—that shed light on their own psychological states and life situations. By demonstrating that homosexual love had enriched the cultural heritage of mankind, that homosexual experience was attested universally, gay scholars were arguing for its legitimacy and acceptance at the present day.

Origins. Heinrich **Hoessli** (1784–1864) was both the first homosexual rights advocate and the first gay scholar. His book *Eros: Die Männerliebe der Griechen* (Eros: The Male Love of the Greeks; 1836–38) was in large part an assemblage of literary materials from Ancient Greece and Medieval Islam that illustrated the phenomenon of love between males. Far more erudite than he was the jurist and polymath Karl Heinrich **Ulrichs** (1825–1895) whose *Forschungen zur mannmännlichen Liebe* (Researches on Love between Males), published from 1864 to 1870, ranged in an encyclopedic manner over the history, literature, and ethnography of past and present.

Driven into exile in Italy at the end of his life, Ulrichs was the first of a series of investigators who lived and published abroad to escape the intolerance of the Germanic world; and down to the 1960s many works that could not see the light of print in the English-speaking countries were issued in France, where publishing houses such as those of Charles Carrington at the end of the nineteenth century and the Olympia Press after World War II produced books for British and American tourists—who now and then managed to slip them back into their native lands.

Far broader in scope was the activity of the Wissenschaftlich-humanitäre Komitee (**Scientific-Humanitarian Committee**) with its journal, the *Jahrbuch für sexuelle Zwischenstufen* (Yearbook for Sexual Intergrades), whose 23 volumes, published between 1899 and 1923, cover almost every imaginable aspect of the subject, with major articles on the history, biography, and psychology of homosexuality, as well as precious bibliographical lists and surveys of the literature of past and present. For the collaborators of the Committee, working under the overall supervision of Magnus **Hirschfeld**, their scholarship was a tool for demonstrating the position that the homosexual personality was a constant and stable type throughout human history, that it was found in all strata of society, and was therefore a biological phenomenon which could not be suppressed, but was deserving of legal and social toleration. Such scholarship was all the more needed as university curricula and standard reference works alike dishonestly omitted all reference to homosexuality, even in the lives and works of individuals who were "notorious" in their lifetimes for their proclivity to their own sex.

In England John Addington **Symonds** may be considered the first gay scholar, since he composed two privately printed works, *A Problem in Greek Ethics* and *A Problem in Modern Ethics*, the latter of which introduced to the English-speaking world the recent findings of continental psychiatrists and the new vision of Ulrichs and Walt **Whitman**. Symonds was also a major contributor to the first edition of Havelock **Ellis'** *Sexual Inversion* (German 1896, English 1897). At the same time the American university president Andrew Dickson **White** quietly inserted into his two-volume *History of the Warfare of Science with Theology in Christendom* (1896) a comprehensive analysis and demolition of the Sodom legend. In the same year Marc-André Raffalovich published his *Uranisme et unisexualité* (Uranism and Unisexuality), with copious bibliographical and literary material, some from German authors of the nineteenth century, which he supplemented at intervals in a series of articles in the *Archives d'anthropologie criminelle* down to World War I. In the Netherlands L.S.A.M. von Römer, besides contributing several major articles to the *Jahrbuch*, also published a study entitled *Het uranisch gezin* (The Homosexual's Family), which argued for the genetic determination of the condition on the basis of abnormalities in the ratio of the sexes among the siblings of male and female homosexuals. Edward Irenaeus Prime-**Stevenson**, writing under the pseudonym "Xavier Mayne," published in Naples a major work *The Intersexes*, which roamed the historical and sociological scenes of past and present, collecting much of the folklore of the gay subculture of early twentieth-century Europe.

In the last decades of the nineteenth century heterosexuals began to study homosexual behavior, often from the biased standpoint of the clinician observing patients in psychiatric wards or the forensic psychiatrist examining individuals arrested for sexual offenses. The writings of **Krafft-Ebing**, notably his *Psychopathia sexualis* (first edition 1886) were of this sort, followed by those of Albert **Moll** and Albert Freiherr von Schrenck-Notzing, the last of whom did, however, achieve a good critical overview of the subject in an article published in *Zeitschrift für Hypnotismus* in 1898. In Italy Carlo Mantegazza had collected anthropological materials on the subject in *Gli amori degli uomini* (The Sexual Relations of Mankind; 1885). He was followed by Iwan **Bloch**, who early in his career as sexologist attacked the notion of innate homosexuality in his *Beiträge zur Ätiologie der Psychopathia sexualis* (Contributions to the Etiology of Psychopathia sexualis; 1902), which had the merit of giving the phenomenon an anthropological rather than a medical dimension, but later in *Das Sexualleben unserer Zeit in seinen Beziehungen zur modernen Kultur* (The Sexual Life of Our Times in its Relations to Modern Civilization; 1907) rallied to the standpoint of the Committee. Albert Moll provided homosexual apologetics with one of its favorite themes in a book entitled *Berühmte Homosexuelle* (Famous Homosexuals; 1910).

Assisted at first by John Addington Symonds, Havelock Ellis devoted the second volume of his monumental *Studies in the Psychology of Sex* to *Sexual Inversion* (third edition 1915). In the book he assembled case histories that he had collected, mainly by correspondence, and an assortment of ethnographic and historical materials from his own vast reading as well as the German literature that had accumulated since the founding of the Scientific-Humanitarian Committee in 1896. The editions and translations of his work made the subject part of the body of scientific knowledge accessible to the rather small public that was willing to accept it in the first half of the century.

The psychoanalytic study of homosexuality began with **Freud**'s *Drei Abhandlungen zur Sexualtheorie* (Three Contributions to the Theory of Sexuality; 1905), which rejected the static notion of innate homosexuality with the attendant therapeutic nihilism in favor of an approach that stressed the role of the dynamic unconscious in the formation of sexual orientation. Because this assumption played into the hands of the enemies of the homosexual emancipation movement, it has led to a good deal of intellectual dishonesty and hypocrisy, with even Catholic and Communist thinkers who reject **psychoanalysis** on philosophical grounds championing the views of depth psychologists whom they regarded as allies at least on this issue. A series of papers based mainly on psychoanalytic case histories appeared in the journals of the movement, sometimes growing into full-length books such as those of Wilhelm Stekel, who promoted the view that bisexuality was normal but that homosexuality was a "curable neurosis." These papers could also take the form of psychoanalytic biographies of famous homosexuals, a genre initiated by Freud's philologically rather weak *Eine Kindheitserinnerung des Leonardo da Vinci* (A Childhood Reminiscence of Leonardo da Vinci; 1910).

This scholarship had to be conducted almost entirely outside the walls of the university—in physicians' consulting rooms or the private libraries of independent scholars—and published in specialized journals or in limited editions "for members of the medical and legal professions." Hence an academic tradition could not be born, much less develop within the parameters of scholarly discipline, and the field continues to attract amateurs who pass off their journalistic compositions—often produced by exploiting the talent and industry of others—as works of genuine scholarship.

The interest of geneticists in twin studies led to some papers on the sexual orientation of monozygotic and dizygotic **twins**, a field pioneered by Franz Kallmann. While certain issues continue to be disputed, the study of monozygotic twin pairs has revealed concordances as marked as those for intelligence and other character traits, albeit with a complexity in the developmental aspect of the personality that earlier thinkers had not fully appreciated.

Trends in the United States. The survey method of investigating sexual behavior had been used sporadically in the 1920s and 1930s, but only in 1938 did Alfred C. **Kinsey** undertake the monumental series of interview studies that provided the material for *Sexual Behavior in the Human Male* (1948) and *Sexual Behavior in the Human Female* (1953), which astounded the world by stating (perhaps overstating) the frequency of homosexual experience in the American population, and enraged the psychoanalysts by disclosing the biased and statistically unreliable character of the population on which they based their often fanciful interpretations. However, his work has lasting merit in demonstrating that the homosexual was not an exhibit in a pathological waxworks museum, but a stable minority within the entire population and within all the diverse segments of the American nation.

The homosexual **movement** in the United States was from its outset interested in promoting the study of the phenomenon in order to prove that its followers were "like other people" as opposed to the psychiatrists who were always ready to argue that homosexuals were at least neurotic and sometimes pre-psychotic. Hence groups like the early Mattachine Society furnished the subjects for the investigations of Evelyn Hooker and others whose clinical soundings showed that homosexuals could not be distinguished from heterosexuals on the basis of the Rorschach or other standard tests. The work of the German and other continental predecessors of the American movement was used fitfully at best, and has never been fully exploited by American investigators, in some instances because they cannot even read it. A certain amount of vulgarization occurred on the pages of *Mattachine Review, ONE, The Ladder* and their counterparts *Arcadie* and *Der Kreis/Le Cercle*, which fondly revived memories of past epochs of homosexual greatness.

The new phase in the history of the American movement that began with New York's **Stonewall Rebellion** of June 1969 did not at first find an echo in the halls of learning, besieged as the elite institutions were by students vociferously demonstrating for the privilege of not being drafted to serve in Vietnam. But in time the gay "counterculture" coalesced in the Gay Academic Union, whose founding conference was held at John Jay College in New York City in November 1973. A journal named *Gai Saber* was created shortly thereafter, and went through a number of issues. Only a minority of the adherents of GAU had academic motives and goals; many more were interested only in "lifestyle politics" or in causes that began to fade from public attention once the Vietnam War ended in a stalemate in 1973. A few introductory courses made their way into college curricula, chiefly in sociology and psychology, so that the gay undergraduate could confront his identity problems with a modicum of academic guidance; but no standard textbooks or syllabi were ever produced that would compare with the advances in women's studies in the same period. Even these concessions to the radical mood of the early 1970s began to vanish as the far more conservative trend of the following decade reached the campuses.

However, it became possible for the first time to utilize and to publish vast amounts of historical and biographical material that had simply been ignored or deliberately suppressed in previous centuries. The role of homosexual experience in the lives of the great and near-great, the meanings and innuendos of obscure passages in the classics of world literature, the paths and byways of the clandestine gay subculture in the cities of Modern Europe and the United States—all these matters could now be legitimate subjects of academic concern, to be discussed as calmly as any other facet of human life, not as a subject the very mention of which demanded a profuse apology and a disclaimer of the investigator's personal involvement.

Present Situation and Outlook. After World War II the accelerating pace of specialized knowledge fostered calls for synthetic perspectives in the form of "interdisciplinary" approaches. Although their existence is partly a response to political and social conditions, black studies and women's studies are by their very nature interdisciplinary. In 1976, for example, ONE Institute, the independent Los Angeles homophile education foundation, articulated the subject in the following fields: anthropology, history, psychology, sociology, education, medicine and biology, psychiatry, law and its enforcement, military, religion and ethics, biography and autobiography, literature and the arts, the homophile movement, and transvestism and transsexualism (*An Annotated Bibliography of Homosexuality*, New York, 1976). Apart from the intrinsic

unwieldiness of such a list, many scholars have clung to their own institutional bases, so that sociologists tend to see the matter chiefly in terms of contemporary social formation, literary critics are interested mainly in reflections in novels and poetry, and so forth.

It seems, however, that three main constellations or domains of research may be identified. (1) The empirical–synchronic domain studies the behavior and attitudes of living subjects, using primarily questionnaires and interviews. This great realm comprises **sociology**, social and individual **psychology**, public opinion research, **medicine**, and **law** enforcement (including **police** studies). The advantage inherent in this range of disciplines is direct access to the groups of human beings that are being studied. Yet problems arise from researcher bias, the difficulty of obtaining adequate samples from a still largely closeted population, and (in sociology) a neglect of the biological and historical substrates. (2) The historical–comparative domain includes **history**, **biography**, and **anthropology**, together with the historical aspects of the disciplines discussed in the first category. The advantage of this method is that it permits one to view present arrangements as but one set of possibilities in a larger conspectus of documented human behavior and attitudes. Dangers arise from an anachronistic project which elides differences, seeing "gay" people everywhere. Regrettably, the attempt of the **social construction** approach to correct such present-mindedness errs on the side of an overemphasis on difference and distinction, claiming (in a few extreme examples) that there were no homosexuals before 1869. In anthropology there is a continuing temptation to "ethnoromanticism," that is overidealizing the exotic culture one is studying, viewing it as "natural," "nonrepressive," "organic," and so forth. (3) The final domain is that of cultural representation, and it studies the appearance of homosexual themes and characters in **novels**, **poetry**, the visual **arts**, **film**, and radio and **television**. Here one can see, in gay-authored works, the ways in which homosexuals have sought to image themselves, while in "straight" works the stereotypes, as well as the rare instances of honest effort toward understanding, are available for inspection. In researching this third domain one cannot neglect the constraints of publishers, producers and other cultural "gatekeepers" in shaping the material.

Apart from this suggested articulation of research in three main domains, some general desiderata should be mentioned. Narrow parochialism should yield to horizons that are as broad as the subject demands. For example, a study of the gay **subculture** in early twentieth-century New York City should show an awareness not only of other places in America, but also of the European setting, from which so many immigrants came. Moreover, a study of causal factors should be polythematic, considering a variety of conditioning factors, and not reducing them, say, to a mere matter of the socioeconomic base (historical materialism) or conversely the downward trickle of learned notions (the history of ideas approach). Researchers must be alert to lingering biases in their own makeup, as from **Christianity** or secular belief systems such as **Marxism**. Unexpected differentiations must always be watched for: for example with male **transvestites** there are at least three distinct varieties, none of which is assimilable to the model of the "gay person." Finally, there is an urgent need for the acquisition of auxiliary sciences; in this field that means first and foremost foreign languages—the standard academic languages of German and French to assimilate the older literature, plus Latin, Greek, Arabic, Persian, Chinese, Japanese, Russian, and the like according to one's particular research interest.

Having been relegated to the margin of academia for so long, it is perhaps understandable that the field developed somewhat idiosyncratic standards,

not exempt from advocacy scholarship and apologetics. Now that these studies are receiving serious academic attention, it is essential that accepted canons of evidence and exposition be observed. In this way gay studies will not only find its proper place in the constellation of knowledge, but in so doing replace homosexual behavior in its proper context as part of the mainstream of history.

BIBLIOGRAPHY. Wayne R. Dynes, *Homosexuality: A Research Guide*, New York: Garland, 1987.

Wayne R. Dynes and Warren Johansson

GENDER

In current social science usage gender denotes consciousness of sexual dimorphism that may or may not be congruent with actual genital sex in human beings. The expression *gender role* was introduced by John Money in 1955, as a relatively new use of a term that has a long history in English in other senses. In a relatively short time, however, it found acceptance in both scientific and political usage as a needed complement to the older term *sex*.

Origins in Linguistics. The concept of gender originated in linguistics, where it designates a specific grammatical category of the noun that can find expression morphosyntactically. In this function it bonds with adjectives ("agreement") and verbs and with particular suffixes limited to a single gender. There is also a syntactic aspect, expressed through combination with appropriate forms of the article and the pronoun. For the speaker of English, in which these relationships have been lost, they may be somewhat hard to understand. And indeed gender based upon analogy with the natural sex of animate beings is not universal; it is limited to the Indo-European and Semito-Hamitic families. However, of the six classical languages of the world, five have the category of sex gender: Latin, Greek, and Sanskrit have the three-gender system of Indo-European—masculine, feminine, and neuter—and Hebrew and Arabic have the two-gender system (masculine and feminine) inherited from Common Semitic. Only Chinese operates with noun classes not based upon the real or ascribed sex of the person or object. But because of the cultural diffusion and influence of the first five literary languages, the intelligentsia of virtually all civilized peoples have some familiarity with the notion in its linguistic application.

General Considerations. In social psychology gender means one's personal, social, and legal status as male or female, or mixed, on the basis of somatic and behavioral criteria more inclusive than the genital organs alone. That is to say, human beings possess a reflective consciousness that includes a perception of the masculinity or femininity of oneself and of others. Moreover, this perception is determined by a host of traits of the individual, some having to do with secondary sexual characteristics, others conditioned by the cultural typing of modes of thought and action as appropriate to one sex or the other.

Because it is impossible to know what another human being feels, personal gender identity can only be inferred from what the subject under observation expresses in speech, **gesture**, and movement. These sources of data constitute one's gender behavior or gender role. Yet gender identity remains private and subjective; it is a dimension of the personality that has been scripted in the course of the individual's lifetime in accordance with forces guiding his psychological development. Gender is more subtle and more inclusive than sex, as it embraces far more than the genitals and their functioning. But because homo sapiens is characterized by sexual dimorphism—the basic anatomical contrast—human societies have gender dimorphism as well: they operate with the dichotomy masculine/feminine in assigning behavioral traits to the phenomenon of gender.

This macroevolutionary fact—the sexual dimorphism of humanity and of its phylogenetic ancestors—predetermined the dimorphism in behavior that constitutes gender. Moreover, the accumulating evidence of animal sexology on the fetal influence of hormones on the governance of sexual behavior by way of the central nervous system precludes the ascription of gender differences to merely social and cultural determinants, even though the assignment of particular traits has an element of the arbitrary. Granted, the structure of gender in the culture of a particular society may virtually dictate what at first glance seems fortuitous; in this matter the binary logic of the differentiating process overrides the scattered distribution of a trait in real populations.

Core Gender Identity. Differentiation of a core gender **identity** probably follows the same principle as the morphological differentiation of the gonads and the internal organs of reproduction. Both systems are latent, but one alone finally becomes functional. In the case of gender identity, however, the nonfunctional schema does not become vestigial, in the true sense, but is negatively coded—marked as not to be manifested by oneself, but appropriate to members of the opposite sex and even to be demanded of them. The two-gender schema is encoded in the brain of the human subject, with one half suitable for one's personal gender identity, and the other half for use in predicting and interpreting the gender role of the opposite sex.

In the customary nuclear family, the child identifies primarily with the parent of the opposite sex, though other members of the household may be surrogates or complements for the parents. As the child grows, the models for identification and complementation extend beyond the household to include older siblings, playmates, and figures of folklore, sports, politics, the media, and even the world of learning. The latter figures require no re-

462

sponsive reaction, except in the world of fantasy, but they may offer an ideal which the individual strives to realize—or even excel—in the course of his lifetime.

With the advent of hormonal puberty, a new milestone in psychosexual development is reached, namely the ability to fall in **love**. The onset of this capacity is not simultaneous with puberty, but is triggered by a mechanism whose site is still unknown. Falling in love resembles imprinting in that a releaser mechanism from within must encounter a stimulus from without before the event can occur. That event has remarkable longevity; its echoes can last a lifetime. The stimulus, normal or pathological, that will affect a given individual will have been written into his psychosexual program, so to speak, in the years before puberty and as far back as infancy.

Broader Connotations. Beyond the sphere of sexuality in the narrow sense, a vast amount of human behavior is gender-marked in that what men do one way, women do another way. Such gender-related behavior ranges from fashions in dress to conventions at work and earning a living, from rules of etiquette and ceremony to labor-sharing in the home. These stereotypes of what is masculine and what is feminine ultimately stem from such macroevolutionary differences as stature, weight, and muscle power, menstruation, childbearing, and lactation, but the conventions themselves are defined by custom—the accumulated residue of economic and cultural processes—which may resist change or conversely be subject to sudden shifts of taste and fashion. What matters is that they exist at any given time and place, that in all societies human beings are exquisitely sensitive to the signals and cues emanating from others, and that if a collective can adapt and change the signals over time, it cannot obliterate them altogether.

Cultural tradition determines not just the criteria of behavior related to sexual dimorphism, but also sundry criteria of sexual interaction. An age (such as our own) that has undergone tremendous cultural change has also seen the traditional norms of sexual behavior rejected and openly flouted. While there has been no change of tradition in respect to the pairing of couples similar in age—with its negative implications for the man–boy homosexual relationship—the sanctions against homosexuality are being reexamined and (with much ambivalence) eased in favor of consensual activity between adults. The trend is toward greater individual freedom, though not necessarily toward a greater social good. The leading pressure point of change in the area of gender is toward a greater diversity and plurality of **roles**, for males and for females, on a basis of interchange and reciprocity. Nature and nurture interact in the determination of gender; some gender traits are common to all members of the species, while others result from the unique life history of the individual.

The genetic code does not find expression in a vacuum, it requires a permissive environment. The limits of permissiveness are prescribed for each species and must be empirically defined for each variable, including gender identity. The bulk of the available evidence points to the early years of life as very important for gender-identity differentiation. There is a parallel here with the ability to use language: by the age of five a child has an effective grasp of the grammatical and syntactic principles of his native tongue, and his gender identity is firmly imbedded. As a system in the brain, the latter programs a boy's masculine behavior and imagery while at the same time programming the feminine counterpart as the mirror image of the boy's own reactions in relationships with the opposite sex. Gender identity is not simply the effect produced by an immanent (genetic) cause; the genetic endowment interacts with the environment to yield the final effect.

The only absolutes in male and female roles are those determined by the genital apparatus: males ejaculate, females menstruate, gestate, and lactate. Other criteria of sexual dimorphism either derive from these irreducible four, or are functions of time and place—as can be learned from economic history and cultural anthropology. The optional (and optimal) content of male and female roles is changing and will change further with the evolution of technology and society. Ideally, both parents will agree on the role suitable for each child, even if the goal is not always easy to achieve. Also, the child's family will ideally not be isolated and stigmatized for the role definition it has chosen, since this societal reaction would mark a child negatively among his agemates, and could force him to choose between his parents and his peer group.

Ludic (Playful) Variations on Gender. In the seventeenth and eighteenth centuries, members of Europe's aristocracy enjoyed dressing in the clothing of the opposite sex. From the Chevalier d'Eon (Charles d'Eon de Beaumont; 1728–1810), who adopted women's dress during a diplomatic mission to Russia, stems the name that Havelock Ellis invented for **transvestism**: Eonism. In the nineteenth-century these practices trickled down to a larger public through the popular stage productions employing female and male impersonators. These performers in turn were imitated by people of working-class origin, giving rise to the modern drag queen and the mannish dyke. In the period after the **Stonewall Rebellion** (1969+), drag queens were prominent in activist circles, combining a defiance of society's gender norms with opposition to sexual conformity. This old tradition in a new guise, sometimes known as *gender bending* or *gender fuck*, is notable not only for its political awareness, but also for the fact that the illusion of assuming the opposite sex need not be convincing—indeed it is often deliberately not. Such behavior reflects an intuitive awareness of the sophisticated contemporary concept of gender. Social psychology and social activism meet.

Gender Studies. Along with women's studies, gender studies have since the early 1970s become a focus of attention in the academic world. Articles, monographs, and books are devoted to the problem of gender, and to such questions as how it can be measured by standardized tests, how it is socially defined in different historical epochs, and how it affects the functionality and the psychic health of the individual in various occupations and life stages. Crossing as they do the boundaries of conventional disciplines, gender studies and women's studies utilize a multidimensional approach to arrive at a deeper understanding of the forces that shape and maintain sexual identity in human beings. Gender studies also intersect with a reexamination of the legal status of men and women, and the effort to correct **discrimination** against women by legal enactments and their enforcement. In 1988 the University of Texas Press began to publish a journal, *Genders*, with a primarily cultural emphasis.

BIBLIOGRAPHY. Suzanne J. Kessler and Wendy McKenna, *Gender: An Ethnomethdological Approach*, New York: John Wiley, 1978; John Money, *Venuses Penises*, Buffalo: Prometheus, 1986; Marilyn Strathern, *The Gender of the Gift*, Berkeley: University of California Press, 1989.

Warren Johansson

GENDER DYSPHORIA
See **Dysphoria, Gender.**

GENET, JEAN
(1910–1986)

French poet, novelist, and playwright. The son of an unknown father, abandoned by his mother shortly after his birth, Genet was brought up by a country couple. At a very early age, Genet began to think that there was no clear-cut distinction between parent, master, and judge—a conflation that was to become the cornerstone of his philosophy. At the age of 16 he was convicted of theft and sent to a reform school. Four years later he escaped and joined the Foreign Legion but deserted after a few days. Rebelling against society, he became a drifter who lived by begging, dealing in narcotics, and prostitution. Crime became for him a ritual with religious overtones, but he was unlucky enough to be caught and sentenced several times to prison, where he wrote poems, novels, and plays.

With the encouragement and financial support of friends, Genet wrote the novels that were to launch his fame, *Notre-Dame des Fleurs* (Our Lady of the Flowers; 1944) and *Miracle de la rose* (Miracle of the Rose; 1946). In 1948, on the verge of being sentenced to prison for life, he was pardoned by president Vincent Auriol at the behest of such influential literary figures as Jean **Cocteau** and Jean-Paul **Sartre**. (The latter was to devote a huge, but not always factually accurate book to the writer, *Saint Genet, comédien et martyr* [1952].) Set free, Genet concentrated on his literary work and soon became a writer of international renown, yet still without a fixed domicile and using his publisher's address for purposes of contact.

An autobiographical work, *Le Journal du voleur* (The Thief's Journal; 1949), gave an account of the writer's earlier vicissitudes in the purlieus of the French criminal underworld and of prison. Genet also wrote a number of plays that—unlike the novels—have no overt homosexual theme. In the novels, the clarity and purity of the style contrast with the sordidness of the content. It is the world of prisons and brothels that forms the backdrop to the plot. These settings are waiting rooms for violent death, either by assassination or by legal execution, and they provoke almost insufferable scenes of passionate hatred or love—often homosexual—among the inmates. In the microcosm inhabited by Genet's characters everything comes at a high price, either in money, or in loss of ideals, of liberty, or of life. The burdensome daily routine of the prison is metamorphosed into the ceremonies of a cathedral within whose walls miracles occur. The inmates deliberately flout the rules of a society that has rejected and condemned them, and within the walls of their jail they create a new hierarchy. The reader is made to sense that any concept can yield to its opposite, that if vice is not virtue, it may equal virtue.

In the last decades of his life Genet became involved in political causes, including the defense of the Black Panthers in the United States in the early 1970s. He declined any affiliation with the gay liberation **movement** that had emerged as part of the radical upheaval of the Vietnam War era, saying that he considered homosexuality a personal rather than a political matter. His own interpretation of the homosexual experience strayed far from the precepts of a movement that set its face against much of the role-playing prescribed by the criminal and inmate milieu that forms the background of his tales. For Genet the sexual relationship is always one of power asymmetry, yet the line between promiscuity and fidelity is also effaced. The novelist remained a rebel, not a revolutionary inspired by a dream of a new sexual morality.

The homosexuality of Genet's characters is explicit, and the scenes of lovemaking attain the limit of physical and psychological detail, recounted in the argot of the French criminal underworld (which largely defies English translation) and in a style once possible only in pornographic novels sold "under the counter." If the homosexuality of the heroes of Genet's novels has a strong sado-masochistic component, their love is depicted with honesty and tenderness. The plot construction borders on free association, while the sordid and brutal aspects of male love are not suppressed or denied. Criminality and homosexuality are two sides of the personality of Genet's heroes. The novels are suffused with a poetry studded with a striking imagery in which memories, desires, and fantasies are interwoven by a creative writer who freely transmutes experience into art. The frankness of Genet's handling of the homoerotic caused no little embarrassment to the critics and literary scholars who even managed to write articles in which the homosexual component of his work went totally unmentioned. But the novels in their realism defied all conventions and shattered the last barriers against the treatment of homosexuality in literature. Since French writing shapes literary trends throughout the world, the influence of Genet on future depictions of homosexual experience is likely to mount.

BIBLIOGRAPHY. Albert Dichy and Pascal Fouché, *Jean Genet: essai de chronologie 1910–1964*, Paris: Université de Paris 7, 1989; Jean-Bernard Moraly, *Jean Genet: La Vie écrite*, Paris: Editions de la Différence, 1988; Laura Oswald, *Jean Genet and the Semiotics of Performance*, Bloomington: Indiana University Press, 1989; Richard C. Webb and Suzanne A. Webb, *Jean Genet and His Critics: An Annotated Bibliography, 1943–1980*, Metuchen, NJ: Scarecrow Press, 1982.

Warren Johansson

GEOGRAPHY, SOCIAL

Geographical distribution of homosexuals in Western industrial societies is not random. Gay men and lesbians are more likely to live in urban areas than in the countryside, in large cities rather than towns, and (in the United States) on or near the two coasts rather than in the hinterland. In many countries, regions noted for their religious conservatism are not favored by homosexuals. In North America, where mobility is common, the single homosexual is more mobile than most, and will seek new locales based not only on the expectation of tolerance, but on climate and the availability of good cultural and recreational facilities. Many gay men and lesbians deliberately move far from their home areas to escape family constraints as well as peer pressure from people with whom they grew up.

The diminished visibility that most homosexuals find it expedient to adopt (and the absence of any usable census or survey statistics) hinder an accurate estimation of these clustering patterns. On the one hand, naive observers miss almost all the identifying signals; finding homosexuals nowhere, these people assume that they must be everywhere. Others, more alert to the gay presence, register it only in such areas of concentration as those mentioned, concluding that the concentration is absolute. It is not. There are many homosexuals living isolated lives in remote and unexpected places. Just as there are village atheists, there are village gays—though most small-town homosexuals choose to maintain a low profile. In any event, this article is concerned with the concentrations, and with the social semiotic that allows the inhabitants therein to establish group identity and community.

High-Visibility Concentrations. In the United States media attention has spotlighted certain urban quarters in which homosexuals are highly visible, and even predominate, such as New York's Greenwich Village, San Francisco's Polk Street and Castro Street areas, and Houston's Montrose. These quarters are often termed "gay **ghettos**," a problematic expression, though one that would be difficult to eradicate. The word ghetto originally served to designate sections of Italian cities of the sixteenth century in which Jews were compelled to live under conditions of strict segregation. The ghettos were surrounded by walls behind which all Jews were required to withdraw at night—to prevent them from having sexual relations with Christians. In the 1920s the meaning of the term ghetto was significantly extended by sociologists of the Chicago School, who used it to to refer not only to the urban enclaves favored by various immigrant groups—the Little Italys, Little Warsaws, and Chinatowns—but also to sections populated by bohemians, hobos, and prostitutes. Since the 1960s

466

it has been common to refer to black districts, such as New York's Harlem and Bedford-Stuyvesant, as ghettos. Clearly, the expression "gay ghetto" stretches the definition, possibly misleadingly so. Since most gay men and lesbians are not stereotypically identifiable to outsiders, they cannot be forced into a strictly delimited geographical enclave; indeed in all cities a majority of homosexuals choose to live outside "their" quarter, though they will usually visit it for entertainment and commercial transactions. Moreover, the boundaries of the gay urban concentrations are porous, so that it is impossible to say that some particular street marks the dividing line. Traditionally, the denizens of the ethnic slums struggled to climb out of them; the fashionable gay person struggles to acquire enough income to move in. Finally, gay populations often overlap in a kind of patchwork with other group concentrations, such as intellectuals and drug users. In some cases the overlapping of groups is a direct descendent of the early twentieth-century **bohemias**. During this period homosexuals often lived in boarding houses and YMCAs, which were also favored by other single people who had come to the city in order to be free of restrictions. Significantly, only one gay enclave today, West Hollywood, CA, is incorporated as a city, and that is shared with other groups. Although lesbians are usually welcome, few choose to live in the enclaves, perhaps because many have small children who need appropriate space and schools. It may be, however, that we are witnessing the beginnings of specifically lesbian enclaves in such areas as New York's East Village and the zone north of the Castro in San Francisco.

Characteristic Features of the Enclaves. Typically, the enclave is located fairly centrally—not downtown, but close enough and reachable by public transportation for those who do not wish to use cars. In this way it stands at the opposite pole from the universal emporium of today's mainstream: the suburban mall.

Initially, the quarter was somewhat run down, but it contains solid residential structures with "character" so that homosexuals, using their stereotypical (but often real) interior-decorating skills, can restore the buildings to their original liveability and dignity. This process of urban reclamation and rehabilitation has sometimes been termed "gentrification." Because they lead to increases in rents, such improvements are often resented by older, more impoverished residents. Inasmuch as many of these are members of racial minorities, the refurbishment trend has caused intergroup tensions.

As the character of the newly settled urban enclave begins to emerge, a number of features become evident. There is a greater profusion of shops catering to the childless affluent: antique stores, delicatessens, ice cream parlors, and bookstores. Bars and restaurants increase in number and elegance as the old-fashioned dives are gradually forced out by rising rents. Many of these changes parallel those occurring in "yuppie" (young, upwardly mobile professional) districts, and indeed the relative affluence of both groups, and the general absence of children, creates a degree of superficial social symbiosis. In Madison Avenue jargon both are the home of SINCS (single income, no children) and DINCS (dual income, no children). To distinguish the gay enclaves one must develop a more subtle eye for social semiotic. The inhabitants themselves have little difficulty, and when gay and yuppie districts overlap as they do in San Francisco's Folsom Street, mutual hostility may occur. The dress and deportment of passersby provide good clues, as do the names of bars and other commercial establishments which reflect fashionable trends in the gay world. Cinemas are likely to favor camp classics or current films appealing to gay taste. Pedestrian traffic, interlaced with cruising, abounds at all hours, in contrast to most other neighborhoods, where traffic peaks only as residents are leaving for, or returning from, work. These signs are not lost on interested outsiders. Insurance companies and other businesses are said to pinpoint enclave locations by their particular postal ZIP codes.

Analogous Formations. These enclaves just discussed are characterized by a combination of residential and commercial use. And in fact it is possible for some residents to pass virtually their whole lives within the enclave, working, shopping, banking, and cruising there. There are, however, other more limited zones of "gay space." University districts often host a goodly share of homosexual residents, attracted by their relative tolerance and the cultural amenities. Some are simply students who stayed on, never having formed families which would require larger quarters. Old warehouses, in industrial zones where no one lives, may open at night as bars or discos that attract surprising numbers of people. These locales are chosen for their inconspicuousness, and may not even present a sign on the street, much as Christian churches in old Cairo have their entrances off obscure courtyards so as to maintain a low profile. City parks, which may lie at some distance from the residential–commercial gay enclave, are claimed after a certain hour at night as cruising grounds. In Europe a fragmentary history of such "zones of licence" may be pieced together from the late Middle Ages onwards. A church-sponsored inquiry undertaken in Cologne in 1484, for example, ascertained the presence of sodomites in several areas of the city, at least one of which corresponds to an area still frequented by homosexuals in the early years of the present century. To be sure, changes in favored spots occur for various reasons. Modern methods of transport made railroad depots and bus stations favorite places. Curiously, airport terminals do not seem to fulfill this function, in part because they are not easily reached on foot or by ordinary means of transportation and in part because security is omnipresent. Repeated raids or obtrusive sur-veillance may make some spots permanently unattractive. The need to use a car need not itself be a bar to the appropriation of "gay space," and is a positive advantage during periods of police "heat." Outside the cities certain commercial strips, highway reststops, and toilets are reachable only by automobile. All these public areas of encounter seem at first bewilderingly diverse, but reflection shows that a key common denominator is the cover rationale that they all provide for loitering. In Europe in former times, churchyards (where one could simulate contemplation of one's sins) and bridges (where fishing served as an excuse) flourished as cruising spots for similar reasons. In traditional Spain ports (Seville, Valencia, Barcelona) were meeting places, as were (probably) inland establishments serving mule drivers.

Some city neighborhoods have **bars** that serve, say, construction workers during the day, but switch to a gay clientele at night, the daytime patrons being scarcely aware of the double hat that "their" bar is wearing. This time-sharing phenomenon is found in other spheres of urban life, as in the hotels that boast "110 percent occupancy," because they rent rooms for sexual assignations for an hour or two in the middle of the day.

Social Semiotics. Although much attention has been given to the behavioral geography of cities, little work has been done on what might be termed their "gay semiotics." What determines the appropriation and modification of the built environment by male homosexuals and lesbians? How do their kinetic patterns, those of movement and loitering, serve to "stake out" and structure the parts of the city they favor? And finally what mental maps do these individuals form of landmarks and pathways that are significant to them?

Resorts. Differing significantly from the urban gay enclaves and their satellites are what might be termed "exclaves": the gay **resorts**. Some of these, located like Key West and Palm Springs in tropical climes, function the year round. Here gay residents and retirees who live there share the towns with transients. In some places the influx of gay tourists, who in their holiday mood may behave more flamboyantly than at home, causes tension with straight "townies," the regular residents; for those in business the influx of dollars is most welcome. On the East Coast, Provincetown, MA, and Fire Island near New York City are seasonal resorts, where the population shrinks to almost nothing in winter. Occupying an intermediate position with respect to seasonal use are the European islands of Ibiza and Mykonos, with their international clientele. Although Italian gay groups sponsor a summer camp each year in the south of their country, there seems as yet no homosexual equivalent of the Club Méditerranée.

Rural Gays. Far from American cities are small settlements, occasionally communes, but usually just farms run by one or two individuals. In some instances these establishments are owned by rural people on inherited family land; most, however, show the influence of the ecology and hippy movements and are worked by one-time urbanites who have fled the stress and pollution of the urban "rat race." Although a slight preference for the western states may be detected (possibly reflecting the mystique of the cowboy as a rugged individualist), these farms and communes are usually geographically isolated; residents communicate with other sympathetic people by mail, telephone, and computer modem. They also have a periodical, *RFD: A Country Journal for Gay Men Everywhere* (Bakersville, NC).

BIBLIOGRAPHY. Manuel Castells, *The City and the Grassroots: A Cross-Cultural Theory of Urban Social Movements*, Berkeley: University of California Press, 1983; Frances FitzGerald, *Cities on a Hill: A Journey through Contemporary American Cultures*, New York: Simon & Schuster, 1986; Martin P. Levine, "Gay Ghetto," in: M. P. Levine, ed., *Gay Men: The Sociology of Male Homosexuality*, New York: Harper & Row, 1979, pp. 182–204; Neil Miller, *In Search of Gay America*, New York: Atlantic Monthly Press, 1989.

Wayne R. Dynes

GEORGE, STEFAN (1868–1933)

German lyric poet. A student of languages, George traveled widely, knew Mallarmé and **Verlaine** in Paris, and was profoundly influenced by Spain. His life and work have a strongly esoteric character, as despising the mass culture of the *fin-de-siècle*, he chose to live amidst a circle of admiring disciples, with and for whom he published the journal *Blätter für die Kunst* (1890–1919). Membership in the circle was conferred on an elite group of men qualified by their handsome and aristocratic bearing. Though certain themes in his work—noble youths, exalted leaders, and a "new Reich"—were interpreted by the National Socialists as akin to their cause, George spurned their advances, going into voluntary exile at the end of his life.

The homosexual aspect of George's work is difficult to define: on the surface it is invisible, at deeper levels omnipresent. By the end of the 1890s he achieved a studied elegance, a perfection of form, a regularity of rhythm and purity of rhyme that remain the hallmarks of his best poetry. His later poems have a prophetic, quasi-mystical character, inspired by his worship of a "divine" youth, Maximin, and a longing to realize in life the vision of the ideal that permeates his poetry, together with a rapturous quality of love. The homosexual strain of the text is never expressed in conventional erotic topoi; rather it is masked by various stratagems that escape the uninitiated reader: gender-neutral language, poems in the genderless second person "Du," allusions to traditionally homosocial groupings such as military or athletic formations, setting the poem in a historical period rich in homoerotic connotations (such as the credo: "Hellas eternally our love"), even using a female persona or pretending to demean or satirize homosexual attachments. Yet in his work the passion between males is always named "love," never disguised as mere "friendship," but at the same time discreetly merged with heterosexual "love," or with the asexual "love" of Christian theology. In some passages masculine and feminine signals alternate in an androgynous pattern, leaving the reader to divine what is intended.

The taboo on overt manifestation of homosexuality in late nineteenth-century **Germany** obliged George to devise for self-expression to a discerning minority a complicated code that utilizes masks and symbols inherited from previous literary epochs, while cherishing the dream of a "new world" of male beauty and comradeship. The very notion of the "secret" is tantamount to the forbidden, the homoerotic—as it was objectively in the culture of George's time—but it is the "secret" that perceptive critics recognize as the clue to all of George's life and work, however veiled these may be to the profane reader. George remains the outstanding representative of a literary school, forbidden to express homosexual feeling and experience openly, that conveyed its message by a complex linguistic code which united form and content with enduring aesthetic mastery.

BIBLIOGRAPHY. Marita Keilson-Lauritz, *Von der Liebe die Freundschaft heisst: Zur Homoerotik im Werk Stefan Georges*, Berlin: Verlag Rosa Winkel, 1988.

Warren Johansson

GERBER, HENRY (1892–1972)

American gay rights pioneer. Born in Bavaria, Gerber arrived in the United States only in 1914, and the following year joined the U.S. Army under a provision admitting aliens. From 1920 to 1923 he served in the American army of occupation in the Rhineland, where he discovered the German homosexual **movement** in full bloom. The upshot of this experience was that on his resettlement in Chicago Gerber founded the Society for Human Rights, inspired in name and purpose by the Liga für Menschenrechte. On December 10, 1924, the State of Illinois granted a charter to the society—the first documented homosexual rights organization in the United States. It saw as its task the combatting of the "almost wilful misunderstanding and ignorance on the part of the general public concerning the nature of homosexuality," and the forging of an organized, self-disciplined homosexual community. Like its German predecessors, it focused on the repeal of the laws—in this case those of Illinois—that penalized homosexual acts. It managed to issue two numbers (now lost) of a periodical named *Friendship and Freedom*, again after the German *Freundschaft und Freiheit*, before Gerber and several of his associates were arrested, and he lost his job and his savings. Although the members of the society were finally acquitted, Gerber remembered this failure with the bitterness of one who went unaided in his hour of trial.

Between 1928 and 1930 he contributed three articles to homosexual periodicals in Germany, and in 1932, under the pseudonym "Parisex," he published what was for the time a bold defense of homosexuality. In the same period he produced two mimeographed journals in which he printed several essays on homosexuality. Through an advertisement for pen-pals in one of these he began a correspondence with Manuel Boyfrank, who had ideas, impractical at the time, for a homosexual emancipation organization. Gerber conceived its structure and purposes in a manner that notably anticipated the Mattachine Society in the earliest phase of its existence. In the 1940s his activities took the form of correspondence and of translating into English several chapters of Magnus **Hirschfeld**'s *Die Homosexualität des Mannes und des Weibes* (Male and Female Homosexuality), which were later published in *ONE Institute Quarterly*. After the founding of the **Mattachine Society** he joined its Washington chapter, but took no prominent role in its functions, fearing a repetition of the catastrophe that had befallen his first venture. Like Karl Heinrich **Ulrichs** in Germany, Henry Gerber was a lone pioneer—one of those who came before their time, but had the vision which others would later realize and bring to fulfillment.

Warren Johansson

GÉRICAULT, THÉODORE (1791–1824)

French romantic painter. Like most artists of his day, Géricault was trained in the Neo-Classic style with its didactic foundation in studies from the male nude. Unlike other artists who moved into a romantic style, Géricault never evinced a complementary interest in the sensuality of the female form. Indeed, some of his drawings and paintings show an almost torrential response to the virility and force of the male body, which in his military scenes extends to highly charged scenes of comradeship. In other works his response to the human body is more conflicted. His most important work, the vast canvas of *The Raft of the Medusa* (Louvre; 1819), shows a group of shipwrecked people in their last extremities before being rescued. Géricault had an affinity for grisly and harrowing subject matter, and toward the end his life, when he was suffering from the effects of a nervous breakdown, he painted a series of portraits of the insane, in which an element of self-identification is unmistakeable.

Speculation about his personal homosexuality has been fueled by the apparent absence of a romantic interest in the artist's life. Recently, however, it has been discovered that Géricault conducted a clandestine affair with a maternal aunt by marriage, Alexandrine-Modeste Caruel,

who became the mother of his illegitimate son. For those given to simple either–or thinking, this would seem to settle the question. But as Edward Lucie-Smith has pointed out, the matter is more complex. The question of what is homosexual **art** is still in flux, but it seems clear that it cannot be resolved by a straightforward litmus test stemming from the known facts of the artist's life. The work tells its own story, and in the case of Géricault there are strong elements of homosexual sensibility, regardless of what he may have done in bed. Admittedly, it is different from the sensibility of twentieth-century gay artists, but has more in common with such Renaissance masters as **Michelangelo** and **Cellini**. As our studies of art as expression of the complexities of **gender** identity become more subtle, greater understanding of the riddle of Géricault's powerful oeuvre is likely to emerge.

BIBLIOGRAPHY. Edward Lucie-Smith, "The Homosexual Sensibility of Géricault's Paintings and Drawings," *European Gay Review*, 2 (1987), 32–40.

Wayne R. Dynes

GERMANIC LAW
See **Law, Germanic.**

GERMANY

Since, historically speaking, there is no unambiguously defined territory named "Germany," the following article concentrates on the geographical area included in the present Federal Republic of Germany (Bundesrepublik Deutschland) and the German Democratic Republic (Deutsche Demokratische Republik).

The Middle Ages. In medieval German literature male homosexuality is seldom mentioned, lesbianism never. In the *Passion of Saint Pelagius* composed in Latin by Roswitha (Hrotswith) of Gandersheim, there is the story of the son of the king of Galicia in Spain who, captured by the Moslem invaders, was approached by Abderrahman with offers of the highest honors if he would submit to his pederastic advances but violently refused—at the cost of his life. The Latin poem on Lantfrid and Cobbo relates the love of two men, one homosexual, the other bisexual. A High German version of *Solomon and Morolf* composed about 1190 makes an allusion to sodomy, while the *Eneit* of Heinrich von Veldeke has the mother of Lavinia, the daughter of King Latinus of Italy accuse Aeneas of being a notorious sodomite to dissuade her from marrying him. *Moriz von Craun*, a verse narrative of ca. 1200, makes the emperor Nero the archetype of the mad sodomite, who even wishes to give birth to a child. In his rhymed *Frauenbuch* (1257), Ulrich von Lichtenstein presents a debate between a knight and a lady, in which the latter accuses men of preferring hunting, drinking, and boy love to the service of women. About the same time the Austrian poet Der Stricker used references to Sodom and Gomorrah in his negative condemnation.

Legal History. Down to the founding of the German Empire in 1871 there existed numerous smaller states whose penal codes had very different provisions regarding homosexuality. While in the Middle Ages there was no punishment at all for homosexual acts, in 1532 the death penalty for "Sodomiterey" (sodomy) was introduced throughout the Holy Roman Empire, as Charles V promulgated a uniform *Constitutio Criminalis Carolina* with a corresponding paragraph as part of the criminal law of his realm. The death penalty remained in force in individual German states, but was applied in a quite different manner that varied with time and place and on the whole rather inconsistently. Prussia was the first German state that in 1794 abolished the death penalty for sodomy and replaced it with imprisonment and flogging. After 1810 many states (including Bavaria, Württemberg, and Hannover) followed the model of the Code Napoléon in France and introduced complete impunity for homosexual acts, a policy reversed in 1871 in favor of the anti-homosexual **Paragraph 175** of the uniform Imperial Penal Code.

From the Reformation to Romanticism. With commentaries on the relevant passages in the Bible as their starting point, Martin Luther (*Warning to His Beloved Germans*, 1531) began a tradition of reproaching the Catholic church by claiming that the clergy and especially the monks were homosexual. This polemic became a staple of Protestant–Catholic debate. As late as the **Nazi** period, the regime conducted a campaign against the Catholic church in which numerous priests were accused of homosexuality in show trials (1937–38).

The translation and reception of ancient texts since the eighteenth century offered frequent occasion for the treatment of homosexuality (a partial translation of Petronius' *Satyricon* by Wilhelm Heinse in 1773, *Vindications of Horace* by Gotthold Ephraim Lessing in 1754, *On the Male Love of the Greeks* by Christoph Meiners in 1775 and others), as did likewise translations of **Enlightenment** texts from France and Italy (Pierre Bayle, *Dictionnaire historique et critique*, 1741–44, Cesare **Beccaria**, *Dei delitti e delle pene*, 1766).

In German poetry, however, the homosexual theme was rare before the nineteenth century. **Friendship** between men is, to be sure, a frequent subject of poetry (especially in Friedrich Gottlieb Klopstock, Johann Wilhelm Ludwig Gleim, Wilhelm Heinse, even in Hans Jakob Christoffel von Grimmelshausen and others), but the amicable feelings depicted in them are clearly demarcated from the longing of pederasts and sodomites, and the boundary between friendship and sexuality is seldom if ever crossed (though possibly in F. W. B. von Ramdohr, *Venus Urania*, 1798, Part 2, pp. 103ff.)

Homosexual Lifestyles and Their Conceptualization. All such texts, however, tell us scarcely anything of the everyday life of those who were actively involved in homosexuality. The first document that shed light on this matter is Johann Friedel's *Letters on the Gallantries of Berlin* (1782), where what amounts to a homosexual subculture in a German city is described. It is quite possible that the conditions in **Berlin** that are described as "having become fashionable only since Voltaire's time" existed in a more or less pronounced form in other German capitals such as Dresden, Munich, or Hannover.

In the nineteenth century homosexual lifestyles developed parallel to the growth of the population and the expansion of the big cities in such a manner that one increasingly finds documents of homosexual self-depiction and reflection such as had not previously occurred, for example the diaries of the poet August von **Platen** and autobiographical accounts embedded in the works of physicians and forensic psychiatrists such as Johann Ludwig Casper, Richard von **Krafft-Ebing**, and Albert **Moll**. Apologetic theories of the naturalness of homosexuality (K. H. **Ulrichs**, K. M. **Kertbeny**, and perhaps the philosopher Arthur **Schopenhauer**) were formulated, competing with a different conceptualization that was developed by the aforementioned medical authors, describing homosexuality as a congenital disease.

The Rise of the German Homosexual Rights Movement. The criminalization of male homosexuality in the German empire came about through the inclusion of a special article in the Imperial Penal Code of 1871: Paragraph 175. The article was the occasion and precondition for the emergence of a modern gay movement, the founding of the **Scientific-Humanitarian Committee** (Wissenschaftlich-humanitäre Komitee) by Magnus **Hirschfeld** in 1897, which soon became active not just in Berlin, but also in other cities such as Leipzig, Munich, Hamburg, and Frankfurt am Main, as well as abroad in the **Netherlands** and in Austria, which had their own organizations. The flowering of a gay **movement** in the first third of the twentieth century was the outstanding feature that set the homosexuals in Germany apart from those in other countries.

The movement was accompanied by major scholarly efforts, augmenting the groundswell of studies in the field of sexuality that had appeared from the mid-1880s onward. The campaign for the abolition of Paragraph 175 provoked an enormous literature of books, pamphlets, and articles pro and con, so extensive that by 1914 the criminologist Hans Gross could write that everything that anyone could ever have to say on the subject had by then appeared in print. There was also a profusion of gay and lesbian poetry, short stories, and novels. Such mainstream authors as Hans Henny **Jahnn**, Klaus **Mann**, Thomas **Mann**, Anna Elisabet **Weihrauch**, and Christa Winsloe also discussed the theme. This cultural efflorescence lent substance to the claim of Weimar Germany to be a land of cultural innovation, though to be sure the Republic had its dark side as well.

From the Thirties to the Present. This gay movement developed in a relatively straightforward course—with interruptions caused by the **Eulenburg** affair and World War I. The era also saw the beginnings of a lesbian movement, and a full panoply of homosexual subculture unfolded down to the year 1933. If until then Germany was probably unique and unparalleled in the world in terms of governmental liberalism and of opportunities for homosexual life, then the same was true in reverse for the Nazi era from 1933 to 1945: at least 10,000 homosexual men, stigmatized with the **pink triangle**, were confined in German concentration camps under the **Holocaust** during those twelve years, and many of them were killed. Apart from this fact, for the vast majority of gay men the period of Hitlerism was a time of intensified peril, of persecution and punishment, since alongside the threat of internment in a concentration camp, Paragraph 175 was made even more punitive and applied with mounting frequency.

After the victory over the Nazis the situation of the homosexuals in the two newly emerging states was different. In West Germany after about 1948 conditions returned to what they had been before 1933. Although the Nazi version of Paragraph 175 remained on the books, homosexual organizations, bars, and gay magazines were tolerated in many West German cities and in West Berlin. In East Germany, to be sure, only the milder pre-1933 version of paragraph 175 was in force, but homosexual life was subject to restrictions on the part of the state and the police, so that gay men and lesbians had scarcely any opportunity to organize and express their views freely. After the liberalization of the penal laws against homosexuality in both German states (East Germany 1968, West Germany 1969), a gay movement of a new type arose in the Federal Republic under the influence of Anglo-American models. In East Germany the beginnings of an independent gay and lesbian organization tolerated by the state appeared only in the mid-1980s.

See also **Austria**.

BIBLIOGRAPHY. Gisela Bleibtreu-Ehrenberg, *Tabu Homosexualität*, Frankfurt am Main: S. Fischer, 1978; Magnus Hirschfeld, *Die Homosexualität des Mannes und des Weibes*, Berlin: Marcus, 1914, reprint, Berlin: Walter De Gruyter, 1985; Rüdiger Lautmann, *Seminar Gesellschaft und Homosexualität*, Frankfurt am Main: Suhrkamp, 1977; Richard Plant, *The Pink Triangle*, New York: Henry Holt, 1986; James D. Steakley, *The Homosexual Emancipation Movement in Germany*, New York: Arno, 1975.

Manfred Herzer

GESTURE AND BODY LANGUAGE

Gestures can have a specific import, as (in our culture) the forefinger laid vertically against the lips, which means "silence." Contrasting with such semiotic gestures are ones expressing more general states, as drumming of the fingers on a surface displaying nervousness. Gestures of the first type are culturally determined signs and vary enormously in meaning across the world, while the latter are more the product of somatic processes and tend to be relatively uniform, though vaguer in signification. The degree of acceptance of gesticulation varies from one culture to another, so that the peoples of northwestern Europe and North America are much more sparing in its use than, say, those of Sicily or Argentina. In our culture this restraint goes together with a general reduction of affect, and a consequent magnification of its significance when enacted, so that a touch or a kiss that would be a minor matter in another society may be taken as a sexual invitation and found offensive.

In ancient **Greece**, to judge from depictions in **vase paintings**, a man's courtship of a boy was conveyed by an eloquent gesture with one hand touching the youth's genitals while the other chucked his chin in entreaty. In modern western culture, the best-known courtship gesture among gay men is less directly physical: the *eye lock* employed in **cruising**, or ambulatory sexual solicitation. This act constitutes a deliberate violation of the taboo on staring, and if the partner is uninterested or uncomprehending he will immediately break contact. A different eye gesture is *reading*, now less common than in the first half of the century, in which the gay person indicates by a knowing look that he is aware that the other individual is also homosexual. Seemingly recent is *attitude*, a bodily posture found in makeout bars conveying hauteur and disdain. The **queen** of former decades was inclined to adopt gestures associated with the gentility of upper-class drawing rooms and café society, as in the distension of the little finger when taking tea. Winks and eyebrow-raising may be common in some circles, though these are not specifically gay. In the world of entertainment, drag performers developed an elaborate repertoire of exaggerated **gender**-crossing gestures, which were imitated by other members of the gay community only on occasion, as **camp**.

One would expect that during earlier times of clandestinity self-protection would have fostered a sophisticated language of gesture to signal the suspected presence of plainclothesmen, dangerous individuals and the like, but in fact such warnings seem to have been expressed mainly in verbal form ("tilly," "dirt"), using **slang** known to the adepts but not to outsiders. The comparative study of gesture is still in its infancy and future studies are likely to discover a richer heritage of gay and lesbian gestures worldwide than the few now known. In our culture, nonverbal communication also takes the form of tokens and regalia, such as **lambda** pins and **pink triangle** buttons, as well as keys worn externally and colored handkerchiefs dangling from a back pocket.

Deprecatory gestures signaling the presence of gay people occur among heterosexuals. Widespread is the *limp wrist* posture connoting sissihood and affectation: the arm is kept close to one's side but bent sharply at the elbow, while the hand dangles helplessly aloft. Some gestures are quite culture-specific. In Latin America an "invert" may be signified by placing the arm along one's side with the thumb and forefinger forming a circle just below the belt; the implication is that the other person possesses a vagina rather than a penis. Also in Latin America, the suspected presence of a lesbian may be signaled by slapping the hands together, alluding to the word *tortillera*, "tortilla maker, lesbian." As this example shows, some gestures are parasitic on verbal language, which must be known in order to decipher them. Other hostile gestures seek to convey the notion of **effeminacy** through disposition of other parts of the body, as through swaying hips and supercilious smiles. Male homosexuals are traditionally thought to have a "mincing" gait, a stereotype that is reflected in such slang labels as *swish* and *flit*. By contrast lesbians are caricatured through heavy gestures and a stomping walk. These devices of mimicry reflect the notion that homosexual persons are irresistibly drawn to adopt the conduct of the opposite sex.

Another aspect of body language studied by scholars is proxemics, the distance that people assume from one another. In social encounters Europeans prefer greater distance than Arabs and Brazilians. To come close makes the other individual feel uncomfortable, and may even be interpreted as a sexual "pass." In straight company, therefore, many homosexuals check themselves from approching "too close" to their interlocutor—so that paradoxically the excessive distance which they maintain amounts to a giveaway.

See also **Semiotics, Gay**.

Wayne R. Dynes

GHETTOS, GAY

The term *ghetto* originated in Renaissance Italy, as the Venetian dialect form derived from Vulgar Latin *iectus* "foundry," the name of the enclosed area of Venice in which the Jews were not merely required to live, but even had to be after a certain hour in the evening, while conversely Christians were forbidden to enter the Jewish quarter after dark. The motive for the creation of the ghetto was to prevent sexual intercourse between Jews and Christians. In the nineteenth century the abolition of the ghetto was a significant part of the emancipation of the Jewish communities of Western and Central Europe.

In the 1960s, the survival of the word in English usage led to its being applied by analogy to areas in the inner cities of the United States in which racial minorities, especially blacks and Latinos, were concentrated by reason of poverty or of the collusion of real estate interests to prevent them from obtaining homes or apartments outside of designated neighborhoods. It also connoted the exclusion (or self-exclusion) of such minorities from the political and cultural life of the larger society. As early as 1942, a survey of residential patterns in New York City had found similar clusters of homosexuals in three areas of Manhattan: Greenwich Village, the East Side in the 50s, and the neighborhood around 72nd Street and Broadway. Subsequently, other cities were noted to have sections largely populated by those practicing an evident homosexual lifestyle. Along with the West Village and Chelsea in New York City, Chicago's North Side and San Francisco's Castro Street have such an ambience.

Such concentrations probably stem from the **bohemias** of the late nineteenth century, in which the sexually unconventional mingled openly with artists, writers, and political radicals, among them advocates of what was then called "free love." The gay ghettos of the present are often districts that have been reclaimed from previous decay, with neatly refurbished apartments and brownstones alongside fashionable boutiques and exotic restaurants, as well as enterprises offering wares or services specifically for a homosexual clientele. The urban homosexual can be the spearhead of gentrification in that he frequently has considerable discretionary income, no wife or children who would suffer from the initially depressed environment, and a preference for the anonymity of the metropolis over the high social visibility of the upper-middle-class suburb with its basically heterosexual lifestyle. This tendency of gay ghettos to encroach upon former working-class minority neighborhoods as part of the gentrification (and Europeanization) of American cities has at times generated social friction between the two groups. However, while the ghettos in which other minorities find themselves confined are resented as symbols of discrimination and exclusion, the gay ghetto can be a haven of toleration whose denizens enjoy liberties seldom accorded to overt homosexuals residing elsewhere.

See also **Geography, Social; Subculture.**

BIBLIOGRAPHY. Martin P. Levine, "Gay Ghettos," *Journal of Homosexuality*, 4 (1979), 363–77.

Warren Johansson

GHULAMIYYA

This rare Arabic term (plural *ghulamiyyat*) alludes to a girl whose appearance is as boyish as possible, and who therefore possesses a kind of boyish sensuality. Especially prominent in the ninth and tenth centuries, this phenomenon seems to have originated in the court of the Abbasid caliph Al-Amin (809–13) in Baghdad. It is said that his mother arranged for a number of girls to be disguised as boys in order to combat the caliph's preference for male eunuchs. The practice spread quickly, especially among the upper classes, where many female slaves and servants circulated dressed and coifed as boys.

A ghulamiyya dressed in a short tunic with loose sleeves; her hair was worn long or short, with ornamental curls across the temples. Some girls even painted a mustache on their upper lips, using a colored perfume such as musk. ("Did you perhaps kiss the rainbow? It is just as if he is drawn on your red lips.") Ghulamiyyat also tried, as much as possible, to act and speak like boys, often taking up sports or other masculine pastimes.

These girls were adept in two varieties of sexual intercourse, and therefore potentially attractive to both men who loved girls and those who loved boys. But true pederasts, naturally, would not be fooled: "But how could she, alas, plug up that deep and sombre pit, something that no boy possesses." **Abu Nuwas** once made the mistake of being attracted to a ghulamiyya, "although the love of generous breasts is not my taste," but regretted this when he nearly drowned: "And I swore that for as long as I lived I would never again choose the abundant froth, but would only travel by back."

The short-lived popularity of the ghulamiyya may have derived from androgynous ideals of beauty, which a boyish girl or a girlish boy can approximate more closely than a grown male or female. In the Middle East, male prostitutes often wear female clothing, possibly to appear more attractive. In ancient Greece, female prostitutes were obliged to wear male clothing, and in seventeenth-century Japan they dressed as boys, which made them popular with **Buddhist** monks, who were prohibited from being seen in the company of women.

The term ghulamiyya stems from an Arabic root, *ghalima*, which means "to be excited by lust, be seized by sensuous desire." Derived terms are *ghalim*, "excited by lust, lewd," *ghulma*, "lust, heat, rut," and *ghulam*, "boy, youth, lad; slave; servant, waiter." The two facets of meaning seem to be clearly pederastic in nature. Ghulamiyya in the present sense seems to be derived from ghulam, simply being the feminine form of the better-known word.

See also **Mukhannath.**

BIBLIOGRAPHY. Maarten Schild, "The Irresistible Beauty of Boys: Middle Eastern Attitudes Towards Boy-love," *Paidika*, 3 (1988), 37–48.

Maarten Schild

GIDE, ANDRÉ (1869–1951)

French novelist, diarist, and playwright. Born into a family that gave him a strict Calvinist and puritanical upbringing, Gide rebelled against his background, yet throughout his life joined a Protestant attachment to the Gospels with a profound admiration for the beauty and sensuality of the pagan classics. After his visits to North Africa between 1893 and 1896, he gave open expression to a pagan value system that was for him a self-liberation from the moral and sexual conventions of his upbringing. He became a controversial figure in the French intellectual world of the first half of the twentieth century, not least because of his public defense of homosexuality.

Life and Works. In 1891 Gide met Oscar **Wilde**, the flamboyant aesthete, who set about ridding him of his inhibitions— with seductive grace. Gide's first really striking work of moral "subversion" was *Les Nourritures terrestres* (The Fruits of the Earth; 1897), a set of lyrical exhortations to a fictional youth, Nathanaël, who is urged to free himself of the Christian sense of sin and cultivate the life of the senses with sincerity and independence. During the political turmoil of the 1930s Gide returned to the same themes and stylistic manners in *Les nouvelles nourritures* (1935).

In 1895 he married his cousin, Madeleine Rondeaux, and suffered an acute conflict between her strict Christian values and his own yearning for self-liberation, together with his awakening homosexual drives. The never-ending battle within himself between the puritan and the pagan, the Biblical and the Nietzschean, caused his intellect to oscillate between two poles that are reflected in his succeeding books. In *Les Caves du Vatican* (The Vatican Cellars; 1914), the hero, Lafcadio, "lives dangerously" according to the Gidean formula and commits a seemingly senseless murder as a psychologically liberating "gratuitous act." A further series of short novels have an ironic structure dominated by the viewpoint of a single character, while his major novel, *Les Faux-monnayeurs* (The Counterfeiters; 1926) has a Chinese-box like structure meant to reflect the disorder and complexity of real life.

In 1908 he was among the founders of the highly influential periodical *Nouvelle Revue Française.* After World War II he traveled widely, writing ever more on colonialism and communism. During the period of the popular front he joined other intellectuals in rallying to the left, but after visiting the Soviet Union in 1936, he wrote a book voicing his disillusionment with the workers' paradise, *Retour de l'U.R.S.S.* (Back from the USSR; 1936). While others were dazzled by what their Soviet hosts chose to show them, or turned a blind eye to what they preferred not to see, Gide's experience as a homosexual had taught him to look for the telltale signs of the disparity between the surface of society and the hidden reality—which he espied only too well.

His publications include an autobiography, *Si le grain ne meurt* (If It Die . . .; 1926) and his *Journal*, which ultimately covered the years 1885 to 1949. His ambivalent stand during the years of the German occupation cost him much of the influence which he had enjoyed during the height of his career, and even the Nobel Prize for literature awarded him in 1947 could not restore his prestige. He died in 1951 at a moment when his importance as a man of letters had largely waned and the homosexual liberation movement that was to vindicate a significant part of his life's work was just beginning.

Views on Homosexuality. Gide's major work on homosexuality was a set of four dialogues entitled *Corydon*. A short first version had been privately printed in 1911, the enlarged essay was issued privately in March 1920, and the public version was placed on sale in May 1924, creating a scandal in that it made a tabooed subject the talk of the literary salons of Paris. Limited in scope as they were, Gide's four dialogues constituted a remarkable achievement for their time by blending personal experience, the French literary mode of detached presentation of abnormal behavior, the traditional appeal to ancient **Greece**, and the then quite young science of ethology—the comparative study of the behavior of species lower on the evolutionary scale.

The incidents that prompted the dialogues were the Harden–**Eulenburg** affair in Germany and a debate over Walt **Whitman**'s homosexuality on the pages of the journal *Mercure de France*. Their publication followed the appearance of **Proust**'s *Sodome et Gomorrhe* (1921), with the explicit depiction of the homosexuality of the character Baron de Charlus. The essay is designed to oppose the medical point of view, as Gide thought physicians the social group most hostile to homosexuality in that era. Religion is ignored save for remarks in the fourth dialogue about the monastic suppression of the pederastic literature of antiquity and the Christian exaltation of chastity. The first two dialogues argue that homosexuality is natural because deriving from the structure of sexual polarity, the ratio between the sexes, and the independence of sexual pleasure from reproduction. The third and fourth dialogues then claim that homosexuality occurs naturally in human beings, and so far from being the unfortunate relic of an earlier stage of evolution, it is capable of inspiring a great and classic civilization.

Responding to the polemic literature of his time, Gide addressed two antithetical issues in the discussion of homosexuality. The first was the origin of homosexual response as a problem in human macroevolution; the second was the role of homosexuality as a factor in the erotic and cultural life of human society. Going against the temper of the age, he noted that the positive achievements of ancient civilization credited to the homoerotic impulse all belong to the institution of pederasty, not to the androphile homosexuality of modern times, and even less to "inversion," the passive-effeminate male homosexuality which he spurned as diseased or "degenerate." The problematic equation of the "natural" with the socially desirable he therefore left unresolved, even if his work answers some of the conventional objections to homosexuality on pseudo-biological grounds.

André Gide blazed a trail in making homosexuality a topic for literature and for literary criticism, and the capital fact of his own sexual orientation—including the narcissistic side of his personality—remains crucial to the understanding of his entire life's work as a French prose writer.

BIBLIOGRAPHY. Justin O'Brien, *Portrait of André Gide: A Critical Biography,*

New York: McGraw-Hill, 1953; André Gide, *Corydon*, with a comment on the second dialogue by Frank Beach, New York: Noonday Press, 1950.

Warren Johansson

GILGAMESH

This **Mesopotamian** figure ranks as the first tragic hero in world literature. The Epic of Gilgamesh has survived in Sumerian, Akkadian, and Hittite versions that go back to the third millennium before our era. Lost from sight until the decipherment of the cuneiform script retrieved the literatures of early Mesopotamia, the epic is a blend of pure adventure, morality, and tragedy. Only the final version, that of Assurbanipal's library in Nineveh, has survived in virtually complete form, but all the episodes in the cycle existed as separate poems in Sumerian. The setting of the story is the third millennium, and the original language was Sumerian, the Paleoeurasian speech of the first literate civilization of Mesopotamia, which continued like Latin to be copied as a dead language of past culture even after it was displaced by the Eastern Semitic Akkadian.

The epic opens with a brief résumé of the deeds and fortunes of the hero whose praises it sings. Two crucial themes are sounded: (1) that love is at the heart of the hero's character, and (2) that love (or *eros* as the Greeks later called it) is the force that provokes the transformation and development of man's nature. Gilgamesh is announced at the outset as a hero: two-thirds god and one-third man, endowed by the gods with strength, with beauty, with wisdom. His sexual demands upon the people of Uruk are insatiable: "No son is left with his father, for Gilgamesh takes them all. . . . His lust leaves no virgin to her lover, neither the warrior's daughter nor the wife of the noble." In reply to their complaints Aruru, the goddess of creation, forms Enkidu out of clay. "His body was rough, he had long hair like a woman's. . . . He was innocent of mankind; he knew not the cultivated land." To tame the wild man a harlot offers her services, "she made herself naked and welcomed his eagerness, she incited the savage to love and taught him the woman's art." At the conclusion, the transforming power of eros has humanized him; the wild animals flee from him, sensing that as a civilized man he is no longer one of them. The metamorphosis from the subhuman and savage to his new self proves strikingly how love is the force behind civilization.

Gilgamesh has two dreams with symbolism which presages the homoerotic relationship which the gods have planned for him and the challenger Enkidu. In the Akkadian text there are puns on the words *kisru*, "ball (of fire), meteorite," and *kezru*, "male with curled hair," the counterpart of the harlot, and on *hassinu*, "axe," and *assinu*, "male prostitute." Gilgamesh's superior energy and wisdom set him apart from others and make him lonely; he needs a male companion who can be his intimate and his equal at the same time, while their male bond stimulates and inspires them to action. After a wrestling match between Enkidu and Gilgamesh in which the latter triumphs, the two become comrades. Their erotic drive is not lost, but rather transformed and directed to higher objects; it leads to a homoerotic relationship that entails the rejection of Ishtar, the goddess of love. A liaison of this kind is not contingent on the physical beauty of the lover, it endures until death. Gilgamesh himself abandons his earlier oppressive conduct toward Uruk and comes to behave like a virtuous ruler who pursues the noble goals of fame and immortality through great deeds. But a dream warns Gilgamesh: "The father of the gods has given you kingship" but "everlasting life is not your destiny. . . . Do not abuse this power, deal justly with your servants in the palace."

Because the pair have slain the Bull of Heaven and have slain the demon Humbaba, the council of the gods decrees that one of the two must die, and the choice falls on Enkidu, who succumbs to illness. Gilgamesh grieves for him and orders a statue erected in his honor. To obtain the secret of everlasting life he journeys far across the sea to Utnapishtim, who tells him the Babylonian version of the story of the Deluge. On his return he carries with him a flower that has power of conferring eternal youth, but loses it to a serpent lying beside a pool and so reaches Uruk empty-handed, yet still able to engrave the tale of his journey in stone. Gilgamesh has been transformed by a love that makes him seek not the pleasures of the moment, but virtue, wisdom, and immortality, hence the motif of the epic is that male bonding is a positive ingredient of civilization itself.

BIBLIOGRAPHY. George F. Held, "Parallels between The Gilgamesh Epic and Plato's Symposium," Journal of Near Eastern Studies, 42 (1983), 133–141; Berit Thorbjørnsrud, "What Can the Gilgamesh Myth Tell Us about Religion and the View of Humanity in Mesopotamia?" Temenos, 19 (1983), 112–137.

Warren Johansson

GLOEDEN, WILHELM, BARON VON (1856–1931)

German photographer. Wilhelm von Gloeden was born near Wismar on the Baltic Sea. Though his stepfather was an advisor to the Kaiser, von Gloeden opted for the arts, and trained as a painter in the academic tradition. In his early twenties he showed signs of tuberculosis, and was advised to seek a warmer, dryer climate. In 1878 he settled in Taormina, **Sicily**. More than just the weather there proved attractive, as he was also able to explore his homosexuality more freely. It was family money and not his painting that supported him, until 1888 when his stepfather defied the new Kaiser and his family estates were forfeited.

Through his cousin, Wilhelm von Plüschow, a professional photographer in Naples, von Gloeden had become interested in photography, and a new career

was launched. Already in 1889 von Gloeden won a prize at an exhibition in Rome; other prizes followed in London, Cairo, Milan, and Paris. The male nudes for which he is best known today were not his only work; he also produced landscapes and studies of peasant life, and was perhaps the world's best-selling photographer in the first decade of this century.

His life changed abruptly again in 1914, when he was repatriated to Germany upon the outbreak of World War I. His studio and home were left in the care of his assistant, Pancrazio Bucini, who had joined him as a model years before at the age of 14. Although von Gloeden returned in 1918, and continued to photograph until 1930, cultural trends had changed and he never regained his reputation. Upon his death he was buried in his adopted village.

Bucini inherited some 3000 glass plate negatives, but five years later was forced to defend von Gloeden's work against obscenity charges brought by the **fascist** authorities. His defense was successful, but nearly two-thirds of the plates were destroyed during the proceedings or never returned.

Von Gloeden's work must be seen in the light of the artistic concerns of the mid-nineteenth century, during which he was trained. On the one hand, his studies of peasant life reflect a concern for finding a source of artistic inspiration in common life; on the other, his famous male nudes work out in photography the concern for taking classical and academic forms and naturalizing and humanizing them.

BIBLIOGRAPHY. M. F. Barbaro, Marina Miraglia, and Italo Mussa, Le Fotografie di von Gloeden, Milan: Fotolibri Longanesi, 1980; Charles Leslie, Wilhelm von Gloeden, Photographer, New York: Soho Photographic Pub., 1977; Ulrich Pohlmann, Wilhelm von Gloeden: Sehnsucht nach Arkadien, Berlin: Nischen, 1987; Bruce Russell, "Von Gloeden: A Reappraisal," Studies in Visual Communication, 9:2 (1983), 57–80.

Donald Mader

GNOSTICISM

Derived from the Greek word meaning "pertaining to knowledge," Gnosticism is a generic term mainly used of sects that broke with Christianity during the second and third centuries, though one can also speak of Jewish and other gnostics, some of whom were independent of the Jewish-Christian tradition and formed syncretistic movements in the Middle East. Simon Magus, Basilides, Valentinus, and **Manichaean** gnostics derived many of their doctrines from **Christianity**. Although gnostic groups differed more among themselves than did Christian groups because they had no "Book," most had certain beliefs in common:

(a) Rejection, as in Hellenized Zoroastrianism and late Jewish apocalyptic, of the material universe as an emanation of an evil spirit—darkness as opposed to light, which was identified with the good.

(b) A view of the universe as the creation not of the high god, but of an incompetent, perhaps even malign demiurge. Human beings ought not replicate his mischief by engaging in procreative sex; other forms might be acceptable, however.

(c) An assertion that souls in the elect are imprisoned temporarily in bodies, awaiting a redeemer to awaken them and help them to escape and ascend to heaven.

Gnostics held that all religions provided partially valid myths describing the human condition. Because the world, and not man, was evil, most sects advocated extreme asceticism. The Christian gnostic sect, the Carpocratians, however, advocated sexual license based in part on an antinomian reading of Pauline predestination and antitheses between grace and law, between soul and body. Some groups incorporated Mithraism's ascent of the soul through seven planets, and angelology and demonology from such disparate sources as the Old Testament, noncanonical scriptures, Philo Judaeus, and the Pauline epistles. Anti-Judaism and anti-nomianism often occur, even when Old Testament myths and personages are utilized as the basis for Gnostic speculations.

The account of the Naassenes in Hippolytus' *Refutation of All Heresies* asserts that the serpent in Genesis (*naas*, from Hebrew *nahas*) was the first pederast, since he had homosexual intercourse with Adam and introduced depravity into the world. The passage further ascribes to the Naassenes a text incorporated in Romans 1:18–32 that blames idolatry for departure from the sexual order of nature that provoked the deluge and the destruction of Sodom. In Gnostic thinking, the primal man was androgynous, and the intercourse of woman with man wicked and forbidden, while the restoration of **androgyny** was tantamount to the abolition of sexuality. A profound malaise in regard to the origin of sexuality and the meaning of sexual dimorphism is evident in the Gnostic thinkers, who equated sexual reproduction with prolonging the soul's enslavement in the material universe of the body, taking as their point of departure Jewish (and ultimately Babylonian) anthropogonic and cosmogonic myths.

For centuries after the end of classical antiquity, knowledge of the Gnostic systems came almost exclusively from the writings of Christian heresiologists who opposed and condemned them. In 1945, however, a cache of Gnostic manuscripts in the Coptic language came to light at Nag Hammadi in Egypt. These, together with other writings such as those in the Hermetic tradition, the Manichean literature in languages of Central Asia, and magical and astrological texts preserved in manuscript or on papyrus, have broadened the picture of the religious life of the late Roman Empire.

The *Paraphrase of Shem*, a Gnostic text from Nag Hammadi, even makes heroes of the Sodomites for having opposed the will of the Jewish creator God. "The Sodomites, according to the will of the Majesty, will bear witness to the universal testimony. They will rest with a pure conscience in the place of their repose, which is the unbegotten Spirit. And as these things happen, Sodom will be burned unjustly by a base nature. For the evil will not cease." Another such work, the *Gospel of the Egyptians*, declares: "The great Seth came and brought his seed. And it was sown in the aeons which had been brought forth, their number being the amount of Sodom. Some say that Sodom is the place of pasture of the great Seth, which is Gomorrah. But others say that the great Seth took his plant out of Gomorrah and planted it in the second place, to which he gave the name Sodom."

In the view of some scholars, Gnostic elements in Christianity helped to differentiate it from Rabbinic Judaism. Judaism developed in the following centuries, to a considerable degree, as a dialectical reaction to the spread of Pauline Christianity in the Roman Empire. What in Judaism had been concrete and national was in Gnosticism metamorphosed into the symbolic and cosmic. The legacy of Gnostic speculation framed the incarnation and death of Jesus as an event of universal import in which the whole of mankind was redeemed from the sin of Adam and offered the possibility of salvation; it also strengthened the **ascetic**, world-rejecting tendencies of primitive Christianity that led to a devaluation of sexuality and exaltation of virginity which remained foreign to Judaism in any form. In this way, Gnosticism reinforced ascetic **Zoroastrian** and **Stoic** motifs familiar to the Greco-Roman environment. As the upshot of this complex process, a radical denial of sexual expression which neither biblical Jewish law nor classical Greek philosophy had urged became for later Christian thinkers an ethical ideal, and one to which homosexual gratification was counterpoised as the ultimate moral evil.

William A. Percy

GOD, HOMOSEXUALITY AS A DENIAL OF

In the debates on the **Wolfenden Report** and later proposals for **decriminalization**, some Christian clergy asserted that "homosexuality is a denial of God" because it is "an affront to the Creator who made them male and female" (cf. Genesis 1:27). The underlying assumption is that since God divided the human race into opposite sexes, any sexual dalliance with one's own gender frustrates his express purpose and command.

The critique of this argument can take various lines. First, there is good evidence from the early text of the Septuagint (the Greek **Old Testament**) and its daughter versions, as well as from some passages in Rabbinic literature, that the original reading of Genesis 1:27 was "And God created man; in the image of God he created him male-and-female," which is to say **androgynous**, since the Semitic languages have no formal way of compounding two nouns, and must express the relationship paratactically—by juxtaposing them. The verse in question would then be a mutilated fragment of an earlier Babylonian myth in which the future heterosexual pair is a male-female, an *androgynos*. Modern evolutionary theory recognizes that man is sprung from phylogenetic ancestors who were **hermaphroditic**, and from them, even with the later sexual dimorphism, he has inherited the archaic capacity for erotic response to members of both sexes.

But a more fundamental objection to this line of thinking noted at the outset lies in the very notion of purpose (or **teleology**). Economy and purpose itself are functions of a reflective consciousness that is aware of the scarcity of the resources at its disposal. An intelligence that had at its command infinite time, infinite space, infinite matter, and infinite energy could have no notion of economy, or even of purpose, because anything and everything would be possible, anywhere and anywhen. Man is forced to organize his activity on economic principles because he lives in a world whose every resource is finite, and he must constantly reflect on how best to deploy his limited means to attain his desired ends.

The conventional Christian reply amounts to claiming that because homosexuality does not lead to reproduction, if tolerated it would lead to the biological death of mankind and thus frustrate the will of the Creator. Hence the positive injunction: "Be fruitful and multiply" (Genesis 1:28) which the homosexual implicitly violates by "wasting his semen," which is the formal evil represented by **sodomy**.

The rejoinder to this claim is that the finite character of the economic means at man's disposal—land, natural resources, capital and industrial plant, social and cultural infrastructure—itself imposes a limit upon his numbers, if distributive justice is to accord each member of the human family the irreducible minimum of worldly goods necessary for his existence. If one admits for the sake of argument that God created the planet Earth as a habitat for man, then by making its land mass and resources finite he has also implicitly set limits on the numbers which the human species could attain. Furthermore, macroevolution has severely limited the reproductive potential of heterosexuality by excluding superfetation. That is to say, once the human female has been impregnated she cannot conceive again until the end of the nine-month gestation period. Male and female have been allotted quite different roles in the reproductive process; theoretically the male can have hundreds or even thousands of offspring, the female can have only a handful, even if impregnated again and again during her child-bearing years. The principle holds true for the thoroughbred stallion and mare as much as it does for man and woman. Even the economic interest of the breeder cannot offset this reproductive disparity attendant upon sexual dimorphism.

The occurrence of homosexual activity in homo sapiens, therefore, implies nothing with reference to God or his supposed purposes. The 3 percent or so of the population that is exclusively homosexual insignificantly diminishes the birth rate of the nation—which is only one factor in the **demographic** picture. Even if a tenth of human sexual activity is homosexual, the other nine-tenths more than suffices to maintain any population in equilibrium with the economic resources at its command. Indeed, the task of the modern state is to synchronize its demographic movement with the evolution of its economy, so that not just a privileged few, but all its citizens can enjoy a rising standard of living. Family planning services will in the future have the role of guiding the citizenry in this direction.

Warren Johansson

GOETHE, JOHANN WOLFGANG VON (1749–1832)

Greatest German writer. Born in Frankfurt am Main, he studied arts at Leipzig and law at Strasbourg. His tragedy *Götz von Berlichingen* (1773) and Romantic short novel *The Sorrows of Young Werther* (1774) began the literary movement known as *Sturm und Drang*, often said to be the start of Romanticism. Settling at Weimar under the patronage of the ducal heir and elected to the Privy Council, he became leader in that intellectual center, associating with Wieland, Herder, and later Schiller. His visit to Italy recorded in *Italienische Reise* and probably involving pederastic adventures inspired him anew as did his intimate friendship with Schiller. Even after he married in 1806 he continued his frequent love affairs with women. His autobiographical *Wilhelm Meister*, a Bildungsroman or novel of character formation, and the second part of *Faust* (in 1832), exalted his reputation further, although he was already first in German literature. The nonexhaustive Weimar edition of his works extends to over 130 volumes.

Goethe often hinted at his own sympathy for bisexuality. It is perhaps in the nature of Germans to seek something that they do not have—a basic Romantic yearning. And this striving and seeking, extending to sexuality outside the bourgeois norm—not a crass sexuality but a refined sensitivity—goes into homoeroticism and at times even into homosexuality. An epigram of his reads:

Knaben liebt ich wohl auch, doch lieber sind mir die Mädchen,
Hab ich als Mädchen sie sätt, dient sie als Knabe mir noch.
[I loved boys too, but I prefer the girls,
If I have had enough of one as a girl, she still serves me as a boy.]

In the play *Egmont* (1788) the hero's enemy Alba is embarrassed by his son's intense emotional bonding with Egmont. The figure of Mignon, the waif girl in *Wilhelm Meister*, could be androgynous. In his *Travels in Switzerland* he waxed rapturous over the sight of a nude comrade bathing in the lake, and in the *West-Eastern Divan* (1819; enlarged edition, 1827), he used the pretext of being inspired by Persian poetry to allude to the "pure" love which a handsome cupbearer evokes from his master (section nine). In the last act of *Faust*, Part II, Mephistopheles freely admits the attraction that he feels for "handsome boys," so pretty that he "could kiss them on the mouth." These and other passages demonstrate that Goethe, though he may not have practiced it, had a clear and remarkably unprejudiced understanding of homosexuality in several of its forms.

In German literature Goethe's name will always be linked with that of his close friend Friedrich von Schiller (1759–1805), who left at his death the unfinished manuscript of a homophile drama, *Die Malteser*.

BIBLIOGRAPHY. "Notizen aus Goethes Werken über Homosexualität," *Zeitschrift für Sexualwissenschaft*, 1 (1908), 179–81.

William A. Percy

GOODMAN, PAUL (1911–1972)

American novelist, short story writer, playwright, psychologist, and social critic. Born in New York City, Goodman was too poor to obtain a regular college education during the Depression, but he managed to combine auditing of college courses with a program of self-education that continued throughout his life. His continuing production of fiction, though it did not result in any masterpieces, showed his tenacity and seriousness of purpose. In 1947 he coauthored, with his brother the architect Percival Goodman, the book *Communitas*, which is concerned with city planning and which foreshadowed the critical social **utopianism** of his later work. In an attempt to deal with his own personal conflicts he developed, together with F. S. Perls and Ralph Hefferline, Gestalt Therapy, an invention that did not prove to be very durable.

Goodman finally gained public attention in *Growing Up Absurd* (1960), a study of youth and delinquency which captured the mood of a country attempting to extricate itself from the conformity of the Eisenhower years. A copious flow of other writings explored alternative possibilities for American society. Not surprisingly, in view of his unwavering philosophical anarchism, Goodman emerged as one of the major gurus of the **Counterculture** movement of the late 1960s. Yet his insistence on the need for competence, carefully acquired through study and contemplation, alienated him from some younger, would-be supporters.

Goodman never hid his homosexuality, and his open propositioning of students tended to make his appointments at the various colleges where he taught controversial and shortlived. A lonely man,

Goodman never seemed to achieve in life the balance and harmony that he seemed to be seeking for society. In his work he aspired to be a Renaissance man, but his own temperament, and perhaps the times as well, worked against his realizing this ambition. He nonetheless remains a worthy exemplar of the independent gay scholar, doggedly marching to the beat of his own "different drummer," and unperturbed by changes in fortune.

GORDON, CHARLES GEORGE (1838–1885)

English general, surnamed "Chinese Gordon." In 1852 he entered the engineer corps and took part in the Crimean War and then in the war against China. After peace was concluded he traveled in China and in 1863 entered Chinese service to suppress the Taiping rebellion. In February 1874 the Viceroy of Egypt summoned him to continue the campaign to subdue the upper Nile as far as the equatorial lakes. After his success, in 1877 he was named Pasha and Governor General of the Sudan. Resigning this post in 1879, he was for a brief time Military Secretary of the Viceroy of India and then adviser to the Chinese government. In January 1884 he was dispatched to Khartoum by the British government to assert Egyptian rule in the Sudan against the Mahdi. Furnished as he was with insufficient means, he took up a military position in the city and was vigorous in pursuing his assignment; but as the Mahdi's supporters grew in number, while the Gladstone cabinet failed to send relief forces, after a ten-month siege Khartoum was captured and Gordon himself was transfixed by a spear (January 26, 1885). He was immediately recognized and honored as a national hero whose legend remains to this day.

The homosexual aspect of Gordon's personality remains obscure and disputed. From his early twenties, when he left to fight in the Crimean War, he was possessed by a longing for martyrdom, and his actions fully confirmed the desire which he repeatedly expressed in words to those closest to him. On Russian soil and in the savage hand-to-hand fighting against the Taiping rebels in China, he invited death at every step, exposing himself to wholly needless risks and unarmed except for a rattan cane. Again in the Sudan, whether tracking down slavers or suppressing a tribal rebellion, he would delight in outpacing his military escort in order to arrive alone in the enemy's lair. And in the final year of his life, in complete disregard of official instructions, he courted and met death at the hands of the Mahdi's warriors. Gordon never married and his relationships with women seem all to have been platonic. While living at Gravesend in the mid-1860s, he took a remarkable interest in the ragged urchins of the neighborhood, "scuttlers" or "kings," as he called them. He fed them and taught them, and when they were filthy, he would wash them himself in the horse trough. He preached to them, though not very well, gave them talks on current affairs, and most important, he found them jobs—in the army, in barges and warehouses, and at sea.

It seems probable that coming from a strict military family he was tormented with guilt over his homosexual impulses, and that repressing his urges was so painful to him that he sought death as a release from unbearable inner anguish. In his personality he was both conformist and rebel, one who could never reconcile his inner nature with the obligations that tradition and discipline imposed upon him. His life was one continuous conflict, and he resolved it only by service to the point of self-sacrifice and a hero's death at Khartoum.

BIBLIOGRAPHY. Anthony Nutting, *Gordon of Khartoum, Martyr and Misfit*, New York: Clarkson N. Potter, 1966; Charles Chenevix Trench, *The Road to Khartoum: A Life of General Charles Gordon*, New York: W. W. Norton, 1979.

Warren Johansson

GOVERNMENT

This subject has two main aspects: homosexuals in government and the actions of government with respect to homosexuality. The coming of modern regimes based on "the consent of the governed" would have seemed to promise improvement in this often adversarial relationship but, as the contemporary struggle for gay rights shows, this is far from the case. Insofar as the residual ignorance and hatred of homosexuality among the masses offer a tempting opportunity for reactionary propagandists and demagogues, rational arguments that can sway the educated go unheard. Conversely, earlier authoritarian regimes often allowed some room for **aristocratic** homosexuality that was subsequently lost; such "zones of licence" were particularly fostered when the rulers themselves were prone to take same-sex favorites.

Historical Perspectives. The first indication comes from a surprisingly early source. The last great pharaoh of the Old Kingdom in Egypt, Pepy II (2355–2261 B.C.), conducted an affair with his general Sisine. Much later the controversial pharaoh Akhnaten (reigned ca. 1372–1354 B.C.) has been held by some to have combined sexual variation with his better-known innovations in religion and art. Beginning in ancient Sumeria **Mesopotamia** saw the emergence of institutions of state-supported cult prostitution, male and female, attached to the temples. In some instances the inmates received a regular salary. This institution became controversial in ancient Israel, and the suppression of the male cult prostitutes (*kĕdēshīm*; sing. **kādēsh**) may be said to constitute the first state interference in homosexuality.

In ancient **Greece** the **pederastic** institution played an important role in state building, and not a few of the boys whose names appear on vases followed by *kalos* ("handsome") later became generals, admirals, and statesmen of the Athenian polis. Some **Roman emperors** were noted for their **minions**. Alongside such notorious pairs as **Nero** and Sporus, **Heliogabalus** and Hierocles, stands the noble relationship of **Hadrian** and **Antinous**.

The minion habit recurred in medieval and early modern Europe with **Edward II** and **James I** of England, **Henri III** and **Louis XIII** of France. More influential than royal minions were powerful politicians who used their office for their own purposes, including Lord John Hervey (1896–1743), who was Vice-Chamberlain to the household of George II for ten years, and Jean-Jacques Régis de **Cambacérès** (1753–1824), archchancellor under the First Empire who was responsible for the creation of the **Napoleonic** code.

Traditionally homosexuals in government service have had an affinity with the diplomatic corps, perhaps because the practice in masking their feelings to conceal their sexual orientation is good preparation for diplomatic discretion. In any event it is interesting that nineteenth-century British history provides information on two foreign secretaries. Robert Stewart, Lord Castlereagh (1769–1822), committed suicide after confessing his homosexuality to George IV. Archibald Philip Primrose, Lord Rosebery (1847–1929), who himself had a homosexual secretary, was rumored to have been involved with Lord Alfred **Douglas**.

Modern Times. Modern nations, where rumor and the media can conspire to spread sexual innuendo, have whispering campaigns to discredit politicians who are claimed to be sexually deviant. Until recent decades the favorite accusation was adultery, homosexuality apparently having been believed either unlikely in holders of high office or statistically quite rare. As homosexuality has come to be more discussed and familiar, such diverse figures as Hitler, Stalin, and Adlai Stevenson have been accused of having homosexual affairs. In the absence of evidence such claims must be dismissed as the product of smear campaigns.

In the United States, Walt **Whitman** was discharged on June 30, 1865, from a job in Washington after his supervisor discovered a book of immoral poems in his desk (*Leaves of Grass*). The ensuing gilded age is largely an era of silence, though there are reports of cruising grounds in Washington, D.C. In 1918–21 the United States Navy was involved in the suppression of a complex scandal at Newport, Rhode Island. The New Deal saw such individuals as Sumner Welles, under secretary of state, and Senator David Walsh of Massachusetts implicated. Persistent rumors have circulated about the person of J. Edgar Hoover, who was the immensely powerful director of the Federal Bureau of Investigation from 1924 to 1972. Although Hoover never married and had a life-long buddy relationship with his subordinate Clyde Tolson, it has not been possible to learn the true nature of his sexuality, and probably it never will be.

In 1950 Senator Joseph R. **McCarthy** of Wisconsin began a vociferous and unprincipled campaign against communists and homosexuals in government. A spurious legitimacy was lent to this by such cases as the Austrian double agent Alfred **Redl** before World War I and the recent Burgess-McLean-Blunt scandal in Britain. It was rarely pointed out—except by homophile activists—that the only reason that gay people in government service are subject to blackmail is the existence of archaic laws. In most advanced countries these laws have been eliminated, while (perhaps not coincidentally) the leading sex scandals in the diplomatic corps have been heterosexual. After **McCarthyism** had died down, another case made the headlines, that of an aide to President Johnson, Walter Jenkins, who had been arrested in a public restroom. No one knows how many civil servants accepted discharge in silence. However, Frank Kameny, a government astronomer, decided to fight back after his dismissal in 1957. Although Kameny never was reinstated, his experiences made him a gay **activist**, one of the most vocal and vigorous of those prominent in the 1960s.

Openly Gay Office Holders. The more militant phase of the gay **movement** (after 1969) with its demand "Out of the closets!" made possible the first openly lesbian and gay elected officials, Elaine Noble and Alan Spear, state representatives in Massachusetts and Minnesota, respectively. Somewhat later Wisconsin representative David Clarenbach was able to achieve both decriminalization and a gay rights bill in his state.

In San Francisco the 1978 homophobic murder of openly gay elected supervisor Harvey **Milk**, and Mayor George Moscone, together with the judicial treatment of their murderer, produced local riots and nationwide outrage. From this time forward, however, gay politics have been a central and irrepressible feature of the Bay City. In Southern California a newly incorporated City of West Hollywood seems to be largely, though not completely, gay.

In the 1980s a new frankness in the media regarding the sexual behavior of politicians has sometimes had unfortunate results, witness the 1987 Gary Hart affair. In the U.S. House of Representatives a closeted conservative Republican, Robert Bauman, was hounded out of office, but openly gay Democrats Gerry Studds and Barney Frank of Massachusetts seem secure in their districts.

In the British House of Commons Maureen Colquhoun and Chris Smith have both been open about their sexual orientation. In Norway the Conservative lawmaker Wenche Lowzow is lesbian. For understandable reasons, given the pressures of public office, most gay and lesbian lawmakers chose to remain in the closet everywhere, but anecdotal evidence suggests that they are numerous.

Wayne R. Dynes

GRAFFITI

Since classical antiquity, the art of writing has afforded the opportunity to record one's sexual feelings, interests, desires, and experiences in the form of inscriptions, for the most part anonymous, that were left for all and sundry to read. A few of these have survived over many centuries to be recorded by modern archaeologists. The oldest known texts of a pederastic character are from the Dorian island of Thera; stemming from the sixth century B.C. and later, they seem a record of homosexual acts performed as rites of initiation. The ruins of Pompeii and the remains of ancient **Rome** furnish a considerable number of erotic graffiti duly recorded in the Corpus Inscriptionum Latinarum; some relate sexual adventures, others are insults directed at the hapless passerby.

The word *graffito* made its appearance in Italian toward the end of the sixteenth century. The study of homosexual graffiti in modern times began shortly after the beginning of this century. The first articles in which homosexual urinal inscriptions were published appeared in 1911 in *Anthropophyteia*, the journal of sexual folklore edited by Friedrich S. Krauss. More recently whole volumes have been devoted to collections made in men's rooms from different parts of the world. Some of these locales were in effect homosexual rendezvous where the writer could expect an attentive—and responsive—public.

The graffiti may take either verbal or pictorial form, or both. The pictures are frequently obscene, often of the erect virile member or of two or more persons engaged in homosexual intercourse. Exceptionally, the texts may be narratives—diary entries as it were—of sexual encounter or experience, liberally embellished by the writer's fantasy. Others are **advertisements** that until quite recently could not be published in any periodical and so had to be inscribed on the wall. These are requests for partners for sexual encounters, with the desired physical attributes, age and the like specified in detail, followed by instructions for making

contact—time and place, telephone number, and the like. Presumably such texts were originally inspired by the more conventional personal advertisements that were printed in nineteenth-century newspapers. Then there are general comments on sexual mores, expressions of ridicule or hostility directed against classes of individuals disliked by the writer, or rhymes and sayings of an erotic nature. The significance of such graffiti is that they express notions that are taboo in the conventional media which, until quite recently, had to conform to all the restrictions imposed by society, attest the occurrence of socially condemned forms of sexual expression, and record non-literary and obscene words and phrases excluded from polite speech.

Sometimes, as during the 1968 uprising in Paris, graffiti emerge from their accustomed haunts in toilets and underpasses and appear prominently on the streets, where they make some political point. The prominence of graffiti—usually neither sexual or political—in New York City subways has prompted an effort to interpret them as an art form. However this may be, the gay artist Keith Haring, now internationally known, first attracted attention through his subway drawings, which were executed clandestinely in a deliberately simplified style.

The analysis of graffiti can yield evidence for linguistic forms unattested elsewhere, for sexual behavior not usually recorded by the participants, and for the attitudes not just of those engaging in such behavior but also of outsiders. Thus homosexual graffiti may provoke dialogues with others so inclined, or abusive and hostile comments by heterosexuals, even threats of violence to the author of the homoerotic inscription. In the 1980s the spread of AIDS in the gay community became a frequent topic of comment. Clever puns, rimes, word plays and the like may reflect a moment of lewd inspiration on the part of the author. Others are banal pieces of doggerel. Within the walls of an institution graffiti may contain bits of malicious gossip about the sexual identity or the sexual life of a wellknown individual, who cannot retaliate because of the anonymity of the writers. This function of giving vent to repressed feelings recalls the grotesque marginalia of medieval manuscripts that spill over into the crudely obscene. Political opinions and attitudes, especially ones excluded from the media by contemporary unofficial censorship, can find vivid expression in erotic graffiti that blend anger and satire, insult and defiance, reality and fantasy. Nearly all homosexual graffiti are by men; lesbian inscriptions are so far the rare exception.

Graffiti are thus in modern times, even with the freeing of the media from long-standing taboos, a precious document of the attitudes and mores of the culture that produces them and of the evolution of both homosexuals' own behavior and the attitudes of heterosexuals toward homosexual expression.

BIBLIOGRAPHY. Emilio Cantù, et al., *Il cesso degli angeli: Graffiti sessuali sui muri di una metropoli*, Milan: Gammalibri, 1979; Ernest Ernest, *Sexe et graffiti*, Paris: Alain Moreau, 1979; Peter Kreuzer, *Das Graffiti-Lexikon*, Munich: Heyne, 1986.

Warren Johansson

GRANADA

Granada is a small city, until 1492 capital of the last Islamic kingdom in **Spain**. Blessed by climate and geography, it is a striking example of the incorporation of running water into architecture and urban design. Much of the Moorish city has been lost, and visitors should be aware that for many present-day *granadinos* its Moorish heritage is only a source of tourist income. However, there remains the superlative palace, the Alhambra, with a unique esthetic which has suggested homosexuality or androgyny to many, although the topic has yet to be given proper examination in print. There is also the most important survivor of the many pleasure-gardens of Andalucía, the Generalife. The city of Fez (Morocco) is said to resemble Moorish Granada.

When the Castilian armies conquered Córdoba and Seville in the thirteenth century, Granada, with its natural defenses, reached new prominence as a center for refugees. There are great gaps in our knowledge of Granadine culture, and basic source works, such as Ibn al-Khatib's *Encyclopedia of Granadine History*, remain untranslated. The last major poets whose works survive are the fourteenth-century Ibn al-Khatib, his disciple Ibn Zamrak, whose verses adorn the walls of the Alhambra, and the king Yusuf III. Five thousand manuscripts, which would presumably have much illuminated the fifteenth century, were publicly burned by Cardinal Cisneros shortly after the conquest of the city. The best-known and most-translated Spanish source is Ginés Pérez de Hita's *Granadan Civil Wars*; it and other sixteenth-century presentations of former Granadan life include much that is deliberate falsification.

What information we have suggests that homosexuality was widely practiced in Granada, as part of a broad tapestry of hedonistic indulgence. (Wine and hashish were also widely used.) As preserver of the spirit of **Islam** in Spain, anything else would be very surprising. Granada was "an example of worldly wisdom" in which "their quest in life was to impart beauty to every object, and joy to every hour." All the major Granadan poets are linked to homosexuality to a greater or lesser extent. Various of its rulers, apparently including the last king Boabdil, openly indulged. Castilian monarchs who were sympathetic to homosexuality (**Juan II**, Enrique IV) lived in relative peace with Granada. Isabella's expensive campaign against Granada was partly motivated by fear of a Granadine alliance with **Turkey**, which had recently conquered Constantinople; it may well have had as another motive the suppression of homosexuality in Castile.

At the time of its conquest Granada was the most prosperous, cultured, and densely-populated part of Spain; its population and economy declined sharply after its conquest and did not recover. Contrary to misconception, its Moorish inhabitants were not expelled in 1492 (it was the Jews who were expelled that year); Islam was permitted in Granada until 1499 and Arabic language and dress until the 1560s, when their prohibition brought civil war, ending with the forced resettlement of the Moorish inhabitants elsewhere in Spain. They were finally expelled in 1609.

Into the seventeenth century, however, and from the mid-nineteenth century until the Spanish Civil War, the Alhambra and the legend of Moorish Granada it preserved have been an inspiration to dissidents and reformers. St. John of the Cross wrote some of his most famous works, taking the female role in a mystical union with God, in Granada. Poets of withdrawal, such as Espinosa and Soto de Rojas, dealt with Granada's gardens and rivers. In the nineteenth century Pedro Antonio de Alarcón, Valera, Ganivet, and Salmerón (president of the first Spanish republic), are all associated with Granada. More important, the great Institución Libre de Enseñanza is also so linked, as Sanz del Río and Giner de los Ríos studied in Granada, and Giner's disciple and nephew Fernando de los Ríos made Granada his home in 1915 and was elected to represent it in the Republican legislature. Américo Castro, whose identifying the Semitic and especially Jewish elements in the Spanish nationality marks a watershed in Spanish intellectual history, was a graduate of the University of Granada. Both the influential Residencia de Estudiantes (Madrid), a descendent of the Institución Libre de Enseñanza, and the Centro Artístico y Literario (Granada), opened buildings in the Alhambra style in 1915.

In the early twentieth century Granada had the most important homosexual subculture in Spain. One of the first gay guidebooks in any language, Martínez Sierra's *Granada: Guía emocional*, with photos by "Garzón" ("an ephebe"), was published in 1911. With Manuel de **Falla**'s relocation to Granada in 1919, the city reached international status. Falla said that he felt in Granada as if he were in Paris, "at the center of everything." In Granada homophiles had a sympathetic newspaper, *El defensor de Granada* (the name suggests sympathy with the Moorish heritage), a bar, El Polinario, built on the site of a former Moorish bath, and in the Centro Artístico a sympathetic organization. The peak was the internationally famous festival of Cante Jondo in 1922, whose program appeared under the imprint of the Uranian Press. Subsequently the leading figure was De los Ríos' protegé, Federico García **Lorca**, executed along with many others in 1936. What homosexual life remained in Granada after the Civil War went underground.

See also **Jews, Sephardic.**

BIBLIOGRAPHY. María Soledad Carrasco-Urgoiti, *The Moorish Novel*, Boston: Twayne, 1976; Emilio García-Gómez, "Ibn Zamrak, el poeta de la Alhambra," in *Cinco poetas musulmanes*, Madrid: Espasa-Calpe, 1945, pp. 171-271; idem, ed., *Poemas árabes en los muros y fuentes de La Alhambra*, Madrid: Instituto Egipcio de Estudios Islámicos, 1985; James Monroe, *Hispano-Arabic Poetry: A Student Anthology*, Berkeley: University of California Press, 1974; José Mora Guarnido, "Granada, ciudad triste," in his *Federico García Lorca y su mundo*, Buenos Aires: Losada, 1958, pp. 35–49; Luis Rosales, "La Andalucía del llanto," *Cruz y Raya*, 14 (May 1934), 39–70.

Daniel Eisenberg

GRANT, DUNCAN (1885–1978)

English painter. In his youth Grant was the lover first of Lytton **Strachey** and then of John Maynard **Keynes**; all three were members of the **Bloomsbury** group of writers, artists, and intellectuals. After study in Italy and France, Grant participated in several English group exhibitions in the heady days before World War I, when the continental avant-garde was beginning to shake up Britain's relatively stodgy art scene. Together with Vanessa Bell, he headed the Omega Workshops, a modernist design studio (1913–19), where he created pottery, textiles, interior decoration, and stage flats. In 1916 Duncan Grant established a ménage à trois at the country house of Charleston in Sussex with David Garnett and Bell. Although Bell bore him a daughter, Angelica, in 1918, Grant's later sexual career seems to have been exclusively homosexual.

Despite much sophisticated proselytizing by the critic Roger Fry and others, the artistic achievements of Bloomsbury never attained the success of its literary productions. Grant tended to be dismissed as a tepid follower of Matisse, and his name scarcely figures in the standard histories of modern art. As in the case of such American artists as Charles **Demuth** and Marsden **Hartley**, his homosexuality may have hindered recognition. Despite neglect, Grant continued painting almost until the end of his life, accumulating an extensive oeuvre. Since his death, however, a more pluralistic approach to twentieth-century art has facilitated reevaluation of his work, and it can be seen that his best paintings are valid works in their own right.

BIBLIOGRAPHY. Paul Roche, *With Duncan Grant in Southern Turkey*, London: Honeyglen, 1982; Douglas Blair Turnbaugh, *Duncan Grant and the Bloomsbury Group*, Secaucus, NJ: Lyle Stuart, 1987; idem, *Private: The Erotic Art of Duncan Grant*, London: Gay Men's Press, 1989.

Wayne R. Dynes

GREECE, ANCIENT

Beginning with the **Romans**, every succeeding people in Western civilization has felt the attraction of ancient Greece. The adulation of Greece peaked in the eighteenth and nineteenth centuries. Ironically, just at this time the industrial revolution and the **Enlightenment** were working profound changes in the character of Western civilization; in the new context the values of Hellenic culture no longer seemed the eternal truths that the world had only to accept and revere. But in no aspect of its social order was the nineteenth century in Europe and the United States farther from the value system of the Greeks than in the matter of homosexuality. Accordingly, the study of same-sex behavior in ancient Greece is valuable not only for its own sake but for the contrast it points with our own society.

Basic Features. Although homosexual behavior was ubiquitous in ancient Greece, had an extensive literature, and was never seriously threatened either in practice or as an ideal (as it was to be in later times), it is not easy to appreciate just how the Greeks themselves conceptualized it. The specific function of homosexuality in their civilization was one which the modern world rejects, and which the homophile **movement** of the twentieth century has regarded as marginal at best to its own goals and aspirations. *Paiderasteia*, or the love of an adult male for an adolescent boy, was invested with a particular aura of idealism and integrated firmly into the social fabric. The *erastes* or lover was a free male citizen, often a member of the upper social strata, and the *eromenos* or beloved was a youth between 12 and 17, occasionally somewhat older. Pedophilia, in the sense of erotic interest in young children, was unknown to the Greeks and the practice never approved by them. An interesting question, however, is what was the average age of puberty for ancient Greek boys? For some men (the *philobupais* type), the boy remained attractive after the growth of the first beard, for most he was not—exactly as with the modern pederast. The insistence upon the adolescent *anthos* (bloom) and the negative symbolism of body hair that occur repeatedly in the classical texts leave no doubt that modern androphile (adult–adult) homosexuality was foreign to the Greek mentality, both in aesthetic theory and in the practice of male courtship.

When it emerges into the light of history in the archaic period, **pederasty** is the specific Greek form of a relationship that may have been institutionalized among some **Indo-European** peoples in prehistoric times. It formed part of the process of initiation of the adolescent into the society of adult males, of his apprenticeship in the arts of the hunter and warrior. The attachment of the lover to his boy eroticized the process of learning, making it less arduous and more pleasurable, while reinforcing the bond between the mentor and his pupil.

The homoerotic ties between the older male and the youth were, it is true, grounded in a biological universal—the physical beauty and grace of the adolescent that invest him with an androgynous quality soon lost when he reaches adulthood. The Greek form of pederasty institutionalized that bond of affection in a form that varied from one city-state to another, because Greece never had a unitary, homogeneous civilization. Each polis (city-state) preserved and used its own local dialect; each had its own constitution and laws. If periodic festivals such as the Olympic games were pan-Hellenic, they bore witness only to the sense that all Hellenes shared certain values in common which set them apart from the other peoples of the eastern Mediterranean.

The Greeks were at first barbarians invading a realm whose civilizations—Babylonian, Phoenician, Egyptian—were already old at the moment when the art of alphabetic writing reached the mainland (ca. 720 B.C.). The achievements of their own history necessarily rested upon the legacy of three thousand years of cultural evolution in the Semitic and Hamitic nations. In technology and material culture they—and their successor peoples—never went far beyond the accomplishments of the non-Indo-European civilizations of the East. It was in the realm of theory and philosophy that the Greeks innovated—and created a new model of the state and society, a new conception of truth and justice that were the foundations of Western civilization. Sir Francis Galton calculated in the late nineteenth century that in the space of two hundred years the population of Athens—a mere 45,000 adult male citizens—had produced 14 of the hundred greatest men of all time. This legacy—the "Greek miracle"—owed no small part of its splendor to the pederastic ethos that underlay its educational system and its civic ideal.

Pederasty was in each of the city-states a channel of transmission of its specific traditions and values from the older generation to the younger. In many states, it was virtually inseparable from preparation for the rights and duties of citizenship. The emphasis on outdoor athletic training and practice in the nude, and the concomitant eroticization and glorification of the adolescent male body, strongly reinforced the pederastic spirit.

Homoerotic behavior in either the active or passive roles in no way disqualified one for heterosexual activity. Marriage and fatherhood were part of the life cycle of duties for which the initiation and training prepared the *eromenos*. Needless to say, family life did not hinder a male from pursuing boys or frequenting the geisha-like *hetairai*. Down to the fourth century B.C., however, the really intense and reciprocal passion that the modern world calls romantic love was reserved for relationships between males. Only in the Hellenistic period (after 323 B.C.) was the additional possibility of love between man and wife recognized.

Misinterpretations. Some authors—including Christian apologists and historians influenced by them—have tried to maintain that while pederastic liaisons were intense enough, they rarely descended to the level of physical union and sexual release. This nonsense stems from a misinterpretation of the "double standard" that prescribed a modest and coy demeanor for the boy, who was to yield his person only to a worthy suitor and—above all—could never offer his body for money. Such mercenary conduct was unworthy of a free citizen and could incur the penalty of *atimia*, civic degradation. The misinterpretations have been reinforced by the strictures of the elderly **Plato** in the *Laws*, where an element of ressentiment toward the young and of embitterment at his own failures and disappointments as a teacher seems to have been at work. This text, however it may anticipate later Judeo-Christian attitudes and practices, was never typical of Greek thought on the subject. The evidence of the classical authors shows that as late as the early third century of our era the Greeks accepted pederasty nonchalantly as part of the sexual order, without condemnation or apprehension.

The greatest error of which modern commentators have been guilty has been to take the strictures of the Mosaic Code as if they were moral truths that had been decreed at the beginning of time, when in fact they are part of a text that was compiled by the Jewish priests living under Persian rule in the fifth century before our era. The Greeks knew nothing of the Book of Leviticus, cared nothing for the injunctions it contained, and scarcely even heard of the religious community for which it was meant down to the beginning of the Hellenistic era, when Judea was incorporated into the empire of Alexander the Great. On the other hand, there is evidence that in the **Zoroastrian** religion pederasty was ascribed to a demonic inventor and regarded as an inexpiable sin, as a vice of the Georgians, the Caucasian neighbors of the Persians—just as the Israelites identified homosexual practices with the religion of the heathen Canaanites whose land they coveted and invaded. However, the antagonism between the Greeks and the Persians precluded any adoption of the beliefs and customs of the "evil empire"—against which they won their legendary victories. The Greek spirit—of which pederasty was a vital component—stood guard over the cradle of Western civilization against the encroachments of Persian despotism. Only on the eastern periphery of the Hellenic world—where Greeks lived as subject peoples under Persian rule—could the Zoroastrian beliefs gain a foothold.

Sexual Mores. The bulk of the available evidence—and the universal grounding of male physiology and psychology—support the view that Greek pederasty was carnal in expression, and not restricted to intercrural intercourse but often involved complete penetration. Oral–genital sexuality seems not to have been popular, but this was probably for hygienic reasons specific to the ancient world. But again, it is a profound error to project modern attitudes shaped by Christian theology and the definitions of sodomy or ages of consent upheld by Anglo-American courts onto the social or legal setting of ancient Greece. It is important to bear in mind, however, that (1) the active--passive dichotomy was crucial for the ancient mind, rather than the heterosexual–homosexual one, (2) norms of sexual behavior were not uniform, but varied for different social classes, and (3) that while men and women could have sexual relations for procreation within marriage, men alone were allowed to pursue sexual pleasure outside of marriage. That is to say, some forms of homosexual behavior were proscribed for certain individuals on the basis of sex and social status, but there was no general taboo such as Christianity later formulated for its whole community of believers.

The career of **Sappho** suggests that lesbian relations in ancient Greece took the same pattern, that is to say, they were corophile—between adult women and adolescent girls who were receiving their own initiation into the arts of womanhood. But the paucity of evidence makes it difficult to assay the incidence of the phenomenon, especially as Greek sexual mores were entirely androcentric—everything was seen from the standpoint of the adult male and free citizen. The subordinate status of women and children was taken for granted, and the effeminate man was the object of ridicule if not contempt, as can be seen in the plays of Aristophanes and his older contemporary Cratinus. Such individuals were a liability in a society in which each city-state had constantly to field armies that would fight for its independence and hegemony.

The central opposition in the Greek mind was between the active (*ho poion*) and the passive (*ho paschon*) partner in the sexual encounter. The Greeks were concerned not with the *act* as a violation of a religious taboo (as in the Christian Middle Ages) or with the *orientation* as psychological substratum (the legacy of forensic psychiatry), but with the *role* as becoming or unbecoming particular actors. A man behaves appropriately when he penetrates boys or women (or even other men whom he has vanquished and captured on the battlefield). From this perspective, the dichotomous classification of men as heterosexual or homosexual makes no sense, although the ancient sources sporadically mention as an idiosyncrasy of character that particular historical figures loved only women or only boys. Disapproval—which could be intense, though it never took the form of imprisonment or death—was reserved for males who took the passive-effeminate role and for women who played the active-aggressive part in relations with men.

These two phenomena, then— the idealization of pederasty and the primacy of the active–passive dichotomy— made Greek homosexuality radically different from what the homophile apologists and forensic psychiatrists of the late nineteenth century defined by that name, leaving aside the evaluation of sexual contacts between members of the same sex in Judeo-Christian moral theology. It is true that the more abstract thinking of the Greeks ultimately recognized the parallel between male and female homosexuality, beginning with a passage in Plato's *Laws* (636b-c) in which both are stigma-tized as "against nature"—a concept which the Semitic mind, incidentally, lacked until it was adopted from the Greek authors translated in the Middle Ages.

In **Hellenistic** and Roman times a genre of **contest literature** emerged that debated the merits of boys versus those of women as sexual partners for men. The option falls to the adult male: adolescent boys or adult women, although there was usually an age disparity between husband and wife that was greater than customary in modern times. **Plutarch** was even willing to entertain the idea that an older woman might legitimately aspire to marry a teenaged boy. So in terms of age marked asymmetry is commonplace.

Greek attitudes toward homosexuality reflected the allocation of status and power in Greek society, and the goals which Greek education pursued. They were, furthermore, embedded firmly in the context of Greek religion and **mythology**, in which pederastic loves were ascribed to gods and heroes who in a sense furnished the sublime models which their admirers could follow and imitate. If the Greeks were less psychologically introspective than the heirs of their civilization have become, it was because they stood at an earlier stage of cultural development; they cannot be blamed for failing to anticipate what came only millennia later—often in a context of guilt and self-exculpation.

Historical Evidence. Modern archeology has determined that proto-Greek dialects were spoken in the southern area of the Balkan peninsula that later was called Hellas from about 2000 B.C., that is, during the whole of the Mycenean period. While material evidence has given scholars more information about this period than the Greeks themselves possessed, scarcely anything can be said with certainty about the sexual life of this prehistoric age. There is no basis whatever for the currently popular assumption that this was a matriarchal period. Toward the end of the second millennium the Mycenean era closed with a series of disasters, both natural catastrophes and wars—of which the Trojan war sung by Homer was an episode. During this period the Dorians invaded Greece, blending with the older stocks. One landmark paper on Greek pederasty, Erich Bethe's article of 1907, ascribed pederasty to the military culture of the Dorian conquerors, an innovation ostensibly reflected in the greater prominence of the institution among the Dorian city-states of history. More recently, however, Sir Kenneth Dover has shown that the evidence for specific links with the Dorian areas of Greece is weak. What may be worth exploring is the notion, stressed by Bethe, that the essence of the lover passes into the soul of the beloved through sexual union—a survival of archaic beliefs on the function of sexuality in initiatory rites.

As Greece emerged from the dark age of the heroic period into the light of history, one of the salient features is the relative insignificance of the priestly caste as compared with its predominance in the cultures of **Egypt** and **Mesopotamia**. This entailed the absence of sacral prostitution of members of both sexes as was found, for example, in the Ishtar worship of western Asia. The sexual lives of the Greeks were free of ritualistic taboos, but enacted in a context of comradeship in arms—the union exemplified in the devotion of Achilles and Patroclus, which foreshadowed the pederastic ideal of the Golden Age. The lyric poetry composed in the dawn of Greek literature was rich in allusions to male love, between gods and between mortals. In the art of this period the male nude—as seen especially in the monumental *kouros* figures of young men—was cultivated and perfected. The classic age (480–323 B.C.) produced the great dramatists and philosophers, and saw the rise of Greek science and medicine.

At the conclusion of this phase of tremendous creativity, the armies of **Alexander the Great** conquered the whole of the eastern Mediterranean littoral and the

western Asia hinterland. In a mere four centuries Greek civilization had matured into a force that intellectually and militarily dominated the world—and laid the foundations not just for Western culture, but for the entire global metasystem of today. What followed was the Hellenistic era, in which Greek thought confronted the traditions of the peoples of the east with whom the colonists in the new cities founded in Egypt and Syria mingled. The emergence of huge bureaucratic monarchies effectively crushed the independence of the city states, eroding the base of the pederastic institution with its emphasis on civic initiative. The outcome of this period, once Rome had begun its eastward expansion, was Roman civilization as a derivative culture that blended Greek and indigenous elements. Even under Roman rule the position of the Greek language was maintained, and the literary heritage of previous centuries was codified in the form in which, by and large, it has been transmitted to modern scholars and admirers.

Authors and Problems: The Early Epic. For nearly two hundred years scholars have argued the Homeric question: Did one, two, or many authors create the two great epic poems known as the *Iliad* and the *Odyssey*? What were the sources and techniques of composition of the author (or authors)? The current consensus favors a single author utilizing a traditional stock of legends and myths; the final redaction may have taken place as late as 640 B.C. A second question arises in connection with these epic poems: Did they recognize homoerotic passion as a theme, or was this an accretion of later times?

The central issue is the relationship of **Achilles** and Patroclus in the *Iliad*, which forms the real subject of the poem. Later Greek opinion in general judged their friendship to have been an erotic one (Aeschylus, Plato, Lucian), a judgment reversed by many modern scholars who would like to imagine the heroic age as free of the "decadence" of later periods, and point to the absence of explicit passages. Recently, however, opinion has veered about, identifying subtleties of the Homeric text that support the contention that Achilles and Patroclus were male lovers. This recognition makes still other verses in **Homer** even clearer: Telemachus' male bedmate in Pylos (*Odyssey*, 3, 397); Hermes' ephebic attractiveness to Odysseus (*Odyssey*, 10, 277); and the **Ganymede** story (*Iliad*, 5, 266; 20, 282: "godlike Ganymede that was born the fairest of mortal men"). Homer may not have judged the details of their intimacy suitable for epic recitation, but he was not oblivious to a form of affection common to all the warrior societies of the Eastern Mediterranean in antiquity. The peculiar resonance of the Achilles–Patroclus bond probably is rooted in far older Near Eastern epic traditions, such as the liaison between Gilgamesh and Enkidu in the Mesopotamian texts.

Hesiod, the other great epic poet of early Greece, left a much smaller body of work, but the *Shield of Heracles*, a work of his school, if not actually by him, depicts a pederastic relationship between the hero and his page Iolaus. Later poems in the epic genre devoted far more attention to mythological and legendary tales of homoeroticism.

The Archaic Lyric. Paiderasteia may not yet have become self-conscious, but in the seventh century a new lyric genre arose that marked an advance over the epic in that it recorded vivid fragments of experience tinged with personal emotion. The subjectivity of Greek lyric poetry is saturated with the vicissitudes of homosexual passion. Though none of these early writers is preserved in entirety, they come from the whole far-flung Hellenic world.

Archilochus of Paros, writing perhaps about 650 B.C., is generally recognized as the earliest major figure of the group. His sense of personal ambivalence strikes an almost modern chord. In admitting contradictory, unheroic, and at times

irrational feelings he invites comparison with the Roman **Catullus**. In fragment 85 he concedes to a male that "desire that loosens our limbs overpowers me." The famous Athenian lawgiver Solon was also a poet, and in two surviving fragments (13 and 14) he speaks of pederasty as absolutely normal (see also Plutarch's *Life of Solon*).

The isle of Lesbos, off the coast of Asia Minor, was the home of a school that brought Greek lyric poetry to its peak. Alcaeus is in fact the first poet whose surviving corpus takes pederasty as its major theme. Despite the mutilated and fragmentary state in which **Sappho**'s poetry has been transmitted, she was hailed in antiquity as the "tenth Muse," and her poetry remains one of the high points of lyric intensity in world literature. In the nineteenth century philologists tried to reconcile her with the Judeo-Christian tradition by dismissing the lesbian interpretation of her poems as libelous, and misinterpreting or misusing bits of biographical data to make her nothing but the strait-laced mistress of a girls' finishing school. The homoerotic intensity and candor of her poems has been vindicated by modern critics, who locate her entire career in the setting of the *eros paidagogikos*, the affection between teacher and pupil that was integral to Greek education. Again, not surprisingly the last book of her collected poems contained the epithalamia she had written for the weddings of the alumnae of her school. The corophile lesbianism of Sappho was part of the training that prepared a girl for her duties as mistress of a household, just as the boy's education prepared him for service to the polis. Over the centuries, her name has become a byword for the love of woman for woman, hence the earlier term "sapphist" and the modern "lesbian."

Anacreon of Teos, who flourished in the mid-sixth century, owes his fame to his drinking songs, texts composed for performance at the symposia, which inspired an entire genre of poetry: anacreontic. Though bisexual like most of the poets, he clearly preferred boys. **Theognis** of Megara is more serious and moralizing, and the second book ascribed to him (with less certainty than the first) presents pederasty in its ideal form, as it flourished for only some two centuries, from 600 to 400 B.C. **Ibycus** of Rhegium composed poems at the court of the tyrant Polycrates, where among other subjects he explored love in old age.

Pindar of Thebes (518–438) composed magnificent odes fusing the intensity of the new lyric trend with the monumental style of the earlier epic tradition, so joining the personal with the public. His poems celebrate youths of the aristocracy, above all the victors in the athletic contests that played a major role in Hellenic life. Changes in cultural expectations and assumptions have made his poetry more remote than that of other classical authors, but he still represents one of the giants of world literature, and he deals with themes integral to pederasty in its noblest form.

Athenian Politics and Art. Archaic Greece had many political and cultural centers, but among those of the mainland Athens emerged in the late sixth century as the dominant force in its culture—"the school of Hellas." A political power as well, Athens witnessed a shift from tyranny to democracy, a revolution in which homoerotic bonding played a catalytic role. In 514 B.C. Harmodius and Aristogiton, angered by the sexual harassment of one of the Peisistratid tyrants, slew him and opened the way for the family's downfall. Although they perished in the attempt, the heroes were thenceforth honored as major benefactors of the polis, honored by annual sacrifices and the performance of odes. Two statuary groups were successively commissioned to preserve their likenesses, the second of which (477 B.C.) is one of the first landmarks of the emerging classic style in art. Other civic leaders were renowned for their

homoerotic attachments: Solon, Themistocles, Xenophon, and **Alcibiades**.

Toward the end of the sixth century Athens took the lead in the style of **vase painting** with red figures, replacing the older black-figure style. Many of these ceramic works were inscribed with the names of the male beauties who enjoyed the favor of the Athenian (male) public and the word *kalos*: *Alkibiades kalos* meant "Alcibiades [is] handsome." These pederastic "calendar boys" were thus celebrated throughout the Hellenic world. Although some girls' names appear with the inscription *kale*, it is revealing that they are outnumbered by boys' names almost 20 to 1. In the field of sculpture the strapping *kouros* type of youth yielded to the more supple and graceful ideal of the classic type, beginning with the so-called Critian Youth (Athens, Acropolis Museum).

Drama and History. The fifth century saw Athenian drama reach its apogee in the work of the three great tragedians who all composed plays that dealt with one homoerotic aspect or another of Greek mythology: **Aeschylus** wrote *The Myrmidons* and *Laius*; Sophocles *The Lovers of Achilles*; and Euripides *Chrysippus*, all unfortunately lost save for a few surviving quotations. In comedy as well, lost plays of Cratinus, Eupolis, Timocles, and Menander, and the surviving masterpieces of Aristophanes dealt with the subject, often in subtle double entendre and other satiric word plays that the modern philologist must struggle to retrieve from the text.

In a different genre, Herodotus, the "Father of History," used the data that he gathered on his extensive travels to point up the relativism of moral norms. Among the phenomena that he reported was the **Scythian** institution of the Enarees, a shift in gender that puzzled the Greeks, who called it the *nousos theleia* or "feminine disease," but can now be identified as akin to the **shaman** and the **berdache** of the sub-Arctic and New World cultures. Profiting from the insights of the pre-Socratic thinkers, Herodotus anticipated the findings of modern anthropology in regard to the role of culture in shaping social norms. The consequence of his relativistic standpoint was to discredit absolutist concepts of "revealed" or "natural" morality and to allow for a pluralist approach to sexual ethics.

Law. The legal institutions of the Greeks were highly diverse owing to the particularism of the regions and city-states, and comparatively few of the laws and analyses of the political structure of the polis have survived. Thanks to a surviving oration of **Aeschines**, the *Contra Timarchum* of 346 B.C., we know of the restrictions that Athenian law placed on the homosexual activity of male citizens: the male who put his body in the power of another by prostituting himself incurred *atimia* or infamy, the gymnasia and those who had authority over youth were subject to legal control, and a slave could not be the lover of a free youth. There is no evidence for parallel statutes elsewhere, and certainly no indication that homosexual behavior per se was ever the object of legal prohibition, or more stringently regulated than heterosexual, which had its own juridical norms.

Philosophy. **Socrates** (469–399 B.C.) wrote nothing, but left disciples who have transmitted his teaching to later ages. He was undeniably a pivotal figure in the evolution of Greek philosophy, the one who reoriented it from the preoccupation of the Ionians with the physical cosmos to questions of ultimate human concern, such as the nature of knowledge and the critical scrutiny of ethical norms. In the writings of Plato and Xenophon, Socrates basks in a strongly homophile ambiance, as his auditors are exclusively male, even if he was no stranger to heterosexuality and had a wife named Xanthippe who has come down in history as the type of the shrewish wife.

His chief disciple, **Plato** (ca. 429–347 B.C.), whose thought cannot easily be disentangled from that of his teacher, never married, and left a record of ambivalence toward sexuality and homosexuality in particular that is one of the problematic sides of his thinking. His influence on Western civilization has been incalculable. One of the ironies of history is that the atypical hostility to pederasty in the elderly Plato, probably reflecting both personal resentment and envy and the decline of the institution in the fourth century (while anticipating later "puritan" attitudes), was often received with enthusiasm in later centuries, becoming a Hellenic source of Christian homophobia.

In one of Plato's most brilliant dialogues, the *Symposium*, the speaker Aristophanes explains the origin of differences in sexual orientation by means of a myth of Babylonian provenance: human beings as but the severed halves of three primitive entities: male-male, female-female, and male-female. Homosexuality is thus the yearning for reparation and wholeness of the first two types, heterosexuality the longing for physical union of the third. In this dialogue Plato also adumbrated the concept of sublimation, suggesting that the contemplation of male beauty should only be a stage in an upward path toward a spiritual ideal that is implicitly one of continence. Thus he inculcated the notion of sexual activity as ignoble and demeaning, which was integrated with the absolute prohibitions of biblical Judaism to form the ascetic ideal of complete asexuality which was to have fateful consequences for homosexuals in later centuries.

A completely negative approach to pederasty emerges in one of his last works, the *Laws*, the product of the pessimism of old age disappointed by Athenian democracy and the failure of his ambitions at statecraft in Sicily. In the first book (636) Plato calls homosexual acts "against nature" (*para physin*) because they do not lead to procreation, and in the eighth book (836b–839a) he proposes that homosexual activity can be repressed by law and by constant and unrelenting defamation, likening this procedure to the incest taboo. The designation of homosexual acts as "contrary to nature" found its way into the New Testament in a text that intertwined Judaic myth with Hellenic reasoning, Romans 1:18–32. This passage argues that "the wrath of God is revealed from heaven" in the form of the rain of water that drowned the Watchers and their human paramours and the rain of fire that obliterated the homosexual denizens of **Sodom** and Gomorrah. Later Christian thinkers were to insist that the morality of sexual acts was coterminous with procreation, and that any non-procreative gratification was "contrary to nature," but this view never held sway in pagan antiquity, so that Plato himself cannot be charged with the tragic aftermath of this belief and the attempt to impose it upon the entire population by penal sanctions and by ostracism. The attempt of modern Christian historians to prove that Plato's idiosyncratic later attitude corresponded to the mores of Athenian society, or of Greece as a whole, is unfounded.

Plato was succeeded by the almost equally influential **Aristotle** (384–322 B.C.), who sought to correct some of the imbalances in his teacher's work and bring it more in line with experience. Aristotle was more concerned with the empirical sciences and the match between theory and objective, multifaceted reality. Though known to have had male lovers, he also expressed some reservations about homosexual relations, but his work evaluating the **Cretan** form of pederasty has not survived. In the *Nicomachean Ethics* (1148b) he undertook to differentiate two types of homosexual inclination, one innate or constitutionally determined ("by nature") and one acquired from having been sexually abused ("by habit"). He stated categorically that no fault attached to behavior that flowed from the nature of the subject (thereby contradicting Plato's assertion that homosexuality per se was unnatural), while in the second type some moral fault could be imputed. In the thirteenth century Thomas **Aquinas** utilized this passage in arguing that sodomy was unnatural in general, but connatural in some human beings; yet in quoting Aristotle he suppressed the mention of homosexual urges as determined "by nature," so that Christian theology has never been able to accept the claims of gay activists that their behavior had innate causes. At all events, Aristotle can be cited in favor of the belief that in some forms, at least, homosexuality is inborn and unmodifiable.

The successors of Plato and Aristotle, the **Stoics**, are sometimes regarded as condemnatory of pederasty, but a closer examination of their texts shows that they approved of boy-love and engaged in it, but counseled their followers to practice it in moderation and with ethical concern for the interests of the younger partner. However, they lived in an age when the pederastic ideal was more and more fading into the past, as the aristocratic way of life of the ruling class in the Greek city-states gave way to a more sensual, more oriental type of pederasty in the Hellenistic world ruled by the successors of **Alexander the Great**.

Medicine. Greek medicine stands at the beginning of the Western tradition of the art of healing, both in theory and practice. **Medical theory** accomplished far less than other branches of Greek thought because of the limitations of technique and the restriction that Greek religion imposed on such practices as dissection. However, the Hippocratic corpus knew the term *physis* (nature) in the sense of "constitution, inborn trait," and recognized that there were innate differences in sexual orientation correlated with the secondary sexual characters. The ethical corollary of this distinction is that the individual is obliged only to act in accord with his own nature, not with any hypothetical unitary "human nature."

Also, the Greek physicians evolved a number of fanciful notions in regard to human physiology which, though now discarded by science, influenced later civilization. For example, the pseudo-Aristotelian *Problemata* (IV, 26) claims that the propensity to take the passive role in anal intercourse is caused by an accumulation of semen in the rectum that stimulates activity to relieve the tension. Another notion was *pangenesis*—the belief that the semen incorporated major parts of the body in microscopic form; yet another the belief that the male seed alone determines the formation of the embryo (only in the nineteenth century was the actual process of fertilization of the ovum observed and analyzed). Another major belief system was the theory of the four humors, which became the basis of four temperaments associated with the characterological ideas embraced by Simonides, Theophrastus, and the comic playwrights.

The **Hippocratic** treatise *On Airs, Waters, and Places* touched upon the effeminacy of the Scythians, the so-called *nusos theleia*, which it ascribed to climate—a view that was to recur in later centuries. The Greek adaptation of late Babylonian **astrology** created the individual horoscope—which included the factors determining sexual characterology. Such authors as Teucer of Babylon and Claudius Ptolemy of Alexandria named the planets whose conjunctions foretold that an individual would prefer his or her own sex or would be effeminate or viraginous. Because Greek religion and law did not condemn homosexual behavior, it fell into the category of an idiosyncrasy of temperament which the heavenly bodies had ordained, not of a pathological condition that entitled the bearer to reprieve from the severity of the law. Ptolemy taught, for example, that if the influence of Venus is joined to that of Mercury, the individuals affected "become restrained in their relations with women but more passionate for boys" (*Tetrabiblos*, III, 13). The astrological texts make it abundantly clear that the ancients were familiar with the whole range of sexual preferences—a

knowledge that psychiatry was to recoup only in modern times.

The Hellenistic Age. Beginning with the death of **Alexander the Great** in 323 B.C., the Hellenistic period saw many profound changes in Greek institutions such as had to attend the formation of a far more cosmopolitan culture shared by subject peoples of different races for whom the Greek language was a binding force. The instrument for its cultivation was the system known as *paideia*, or humanistic training grounded in the mastery of the classics. This new emphasis on teaching worked to promote a fusion between the person of the *paidagogos*, the instructor, and the ideals of *paiderasteia* bequeathed by the earlier part of the Golden Age of Hellenic civilization. **Alexandria** in Egypt, the capital of the kingdom of the Ptolemies, emerged as the intellectual center of the Hellenistic age. Two poets, both associated with the great library in that city, composed works that dealt with aspects of boy-love. Callistratus exhibits the Hellenistic penchant for recondite allusions to and quotations from older literature; a number of his surviving epigrams are pederastic in theme. **Theocritus** created the poetic convention later known as Arcadian pastoral that served as a model for much of later Western poetry. His idylls are tinged with homoerotic sentiment in a rustic setting.

However, the greatest single collection of the pederastic poetry of the Hellenistic period is the twelfth book of the **Greek Anthology**, the core of which was assembled by Meleager of Gadara about 80 B.C. The collection was several times enlarged, notably by Strato of Sardis in the middle of the second century. His anthology bore the name *Musa paidike* or Boyish Muse; its sparkling epigrams sound the whole diapason of emotions felt by the Greek lover of male youth: the fleeting radiance of his *anthos* doomed to perish as adulthood encroaches upon his charms; unresponsive or avaricious boys; the disappointment that awaits the boy himself when age overtakes him; and fear of the loss of the boy's affection, expressed in the mythological guise of Zeus' abduction of Ganymede.

Another literary innovation of the Hellenistic period was the romance of adventure or Milesian tale. Though most of the extant examples tell of the vicissitudes of heterosexual lovers, homoerotic episodes and characters often figure as secondary motifs. A good instance is *The Adventures of Leucippe and Clitophon* by Achilles Tatius (probably of the Roman period that followed the Hellenistic one). The chief homosexual component is a debate on the respective merits of love for women and love for boys—a subject that was to reappear in later centuries. Essays on pederasty were also written, the most notable being those ascribed to **Lucian** and to **Plutarch**. The latter composed the *Parallel Lives* in which the homosexual proclivities of Greco-Roman statesmen are frankly discussed, but also a humorous piece entitled *Gryllus* in which a talking pig argues that pederasty is unnatural because it is unknown among animals— an assertion that contradicted the observation of ancient naturalists. (*See* **Animal Homosexuality**.)

Perhaps the last major work in the Hellenistic tradition that deals extensively with pederasty is *Deipnosophistae* or Banquet of the Learned by **Athenaeus**, composed about A.D. 200. It treats the subject of love for boys with utter nonchalance, and preserves quotations from earlier works that have not survived in their entirety. The pagan culture of the Greco-Roman world accepted homosexual interests and relationships as a matter of everyday life, with no scorn or condescension. It was the growing influence of Christianity, and its adoption as the state religion of the Roman Empire, that sounded the death knell of this major era in the annals of homosexuality.

Conclusion. If we include its prolongation into the Roman period, the world of ancient Greece offers almost a millennium of evidence for homosexual behavior from poems, prose, inscriptions, and works of art. Many of these are not only documents of the occurrence of homosexual relations, but vivid capsules of personal feeling. The historian must, of course, be wary of anachronism—of the temptation to project back our own same-sex customs and judgments onto a very different era. Every allowance made, however, there remain notable similarities; the differences themselves set in relief the spectrum of homosexual expression of which human beings are capable.

BIBLIOGRAPHY. Erich Bethe, "Die dorische Knabenliebe: ihre Ethik und ihre Idee," *Rheinisches Museum*, 62 (1907), 438–75; Félix Buffière, *Eros adolescent: la pédérastie dans la Grèce antique*, Paris: Les Belles Lettres, 1980; Sir Kenneth Dover, *Greek Homosexuality*, Cambridge, MA: Harvard University Press, 1978; Hans Licht, *Sexual Life in Ancient Greece*, London: Routledge and Kegan Paul, 1932; William A. Percy, *Greek Pederasty*, New York: Garland, 1990; Bernard Sergent, *Homosexuality in Greek Myth*, Boston: Beacon Press, 1986.
Wayne R. Dynes and
Warren Johansson

GREECE, MODERN

A republic of ten million occupying the southern extremity of the Balkan peninsula and the adjacent islands, Greece today has a strong sense of national identity. Each year it is the goal of millions of tourists, some of them in quest of sexual experience.

History. The modern Greeks derived their sexual mores, like their music, cuisine, and dress, from their overlords the Turks rather than from ancient **Greece**. During the long Ottoman domination from the fall of Byzantium in 1453 to 1821 and in Macedonia and Crete until 1911, and in Anatolia and Cyprus even today, the descendants of the Byzantines who did not convert to Islam preserved their language and religion. Orthodox bishops were given wide political authority over their flocks whom they helped the Turks fleece. The black (monastic) clergy were forbidden to marry, and they were often inclined to homosexuality. Greeks, like Armenians, often rose in the hierarchy at the Sublime Porte, sometimes as eunuchs. Also they served as Janissaries in the Ottoman regiments which were taught to revere the Sultan as their father, the regiment as their family, and the barracks as their home. Forbidden to marry, they engaged in sodomy, particularly pederasty, and in such Ottoman vices as opium and bribery. Along with the Armenians, Greeks became the chief merchants of the Empire, especially dominating the relatively backward Balkan provinces where they congregated in the cities and towns as Jews did in the Polish-Lithuanian commonwealth.

After being inspired by the French Revolution and Napoleon, Greek nationalists sought to revive their ancient traditions. The war for independence, in which Lord **Byron** died fighting, began in 1821 and triumphed in 1829 with much support from Hellenophiles in Western Europe inspired originally by J. J. **Winckelmann**. The German art historian was murdered in Trieste while waiting for a ship to carry him to Venice on his return to Rome; he never reached Greece itself as he wished.

Byron visited Ali Pasha, a notorious Albanian Moslem pederast, and then Athens, where he went in search of boys for pederasty. Oscar **Wilde** was taken to Greece by his Dublin professor, Mahafy, probably influencing his later sexual proclivities.

Although Orthodox prelates like Makarios, Archbishop of Cyprus, contributed to the nationalist leadership and still exert a strong homophobic influence throughout modern Hellas, native homosexuals, often in contact with gay foreign tourists, and scholars such as Renée **Vivien** and Kimon Friar revived ancient concepts.

Homosexuality over the age of seventeen is not criminal in Greece, but public disapproval is sometimes expressed.

The socialist government headed by Andreas Papandreou engaged in some harassment of meeting places and organizations during the 1980s. Apart from Athens, gay tourists flock to Mykonos, while the island of Mytilene, home of **Sappho**, understandably attracts lesbians. Three gay magazines have been active: *Bananas* (now defunct), *Amphi* (1978–), and *To Kraksimo* (1984–), while the literary review *Odos Panos*, though not strictly gay, often publishes works of a homophile nature.

Since the Greeks generally reject the hybrid compounds formed by Western European scholars and scientists from classical roots, the Modern Greek term for "homosexuality" is *omophylophilia*, literally "same-sex-love," in contrast to *eterophylophilia*, "heterosexuality."

Literary Achievements. As in ancient Greek literature, homosexual themes figure prominently in the work of several twentieth-century writers. With his special linguistic gifts and his interest in both ancient and modern reality, the poet Constantine P. **Cavafy** (1863–1933), considerably influenced modern Greek verse. His specifically homoerotic themes have inspired such contemporaries as Dinos Christianopoulos. Born in 1931 in Salonika, Christianopoulos was abandoned by his parents at the age of one and a half, then adopted. In 1945 the poet began to use the pseudonym "Christianopoulos," which suggests "son of a Christian" or "little Christian." He studied literature at Aristotle University in Salonika, receiving his degree in 1954. In 1958 he founded the literary review *Diagonal* and in 1962 opened his own publishing firm under the same name. In his earliest poems, he began dealing with what was to become his major theme: homosexual love. His first collection, *Season of the Lean Cows* (1950), includes several historical poems in the Cavafy mode. The juxtaposition of situations and details from diverse periods and sensuality in conflict with Christian faith reveals T. S. **Eliot**'s influence. In *Knees of Strangers* (1954), *Defenseless Craving*

(1960), *Suburbs* (1969), and *The Cross-Eyed* (written between 1949 and 1970), Christianopoulos discards historical settings for *erotika piimata*, "erotic poems" or "love poems," which, although similar to Cavafy's in their directness and simplicity, being void of metaphor, move beyond them in their even greater boldness and contemporaneity. The poems commemorate emotions, corporal sensations, rendezvous, chance encounters, nights spent searching for love in city parks, evenings spent in a lover's embrace far beyond the city limits. In 1960 Christianopoulos began writing what he calls *mikra piimata*, "short poems," cryptic epigrams based on puns and psychological paradoxes. In his later work the poet deplores the influence of the American and European gay movement entailing the evanescence of the strict Middle Eastern division of roles into "active" and "passive." His previous collections of verse are now published in one large volume, *Poems* (1985), which is regularly updated and reprinted.

Andreas Angelakis (born 1940) has written a series of poems based on the life of Cavafy (*Cavafy on the Way*, 1984), several homosexual plays, and compiled and translated an anthology of American gay poetry (1982), the first such to appear in Greece. Also influenced by Cavafy, the poet Yiannis Ritsos (born 1909) in the several volumes of his fictionalized autobiography, *Iconostasis of Anonymous Saints*, has written more frankly of his own homosexuality than he had earlier. An early poet who wrote explicitly homoerotic poetry was Napoleon Lapathiotis; more discreet was Mitsos Papanikolaou. Two contemporaries are Loukas Theodorakopoulos and Yiorghos Khronas.

Kostas Taktsis' (1927–1988) novel *The Third Wedding Crown* (1963), now considered a classic of twentieth-century fiction, and a few stories in the collection *The Leftover Change* (1972) deal in particular (though as minor themes) with homosexual incest and transvestism. First shocked by the divorce of his parents and moved by his mother from Salonika to Athens where he was raised by a half-crazed grandmother, then settling by accident into a building inhabited by female prostitutes, he took some of their customers for himself. Influenced by **Rimbaud**, he won recognition in Greece after his works were translated into French and English. He was found strangled to death on his bed in Athens. Taksis discussed homosexuality in a long interview included in his *My Grandmother Athens and Other Texts* (1979).

Two other major writers on homosexuality are Yiorghos Ioannou (1927–1985) and Menis Koumandareas (born 1933), while Alexis Arvanitakis, Yiannis Palamiotis, Vassilis Kolonas, and Prodromos Savidis have also dealt with it. Themos Kornaros' novel *Mount Athos* (for which he was sent to prison) treated the initiation rites undergone by novice monks in monasteries. The ecclesiastic code of the Greek Orthodox Church has specific statutes dealing with the punishments to be inflicted (e.g., prayers to be said in atonement) for homosexual acts.

As for the vestiges, especially in colloquial speech and folksongs, of homosexual mores from the earlier periods of modern Greece, much work has been done by Elias Petropoulos (*The Bordello; Rebetic Songs; Kaliardá; The Underworld and Greek Shadow Theater*) and by Mary Koukoules in her continuing series *Neoelleniki Athyrostomia* (1984–). A play has also been staged dealing with the life of transvestites and homosexual prostitutes, Yiorghos Maniotis' *The Pit of Sin*.

Such writers depict traditional Greek (or Middle Eastern) or **Mediterranean homosexuality** in terms of strict role opposition: "active" counterposed to "passive" partners, as well as each writer's views on the coming to contemporary Greece of "European" homosexual mores—the "Gay Movement"—in which sexual roles are not so strictly defined, because "identity" has taken the foreground. Greek readers by no means consider the work of many of these writers, some of whom were or are major figures in Greek literature, to exemplify a specific literary genre designated "homosexual" or "gay" literature (though the more explicit work of certain contemporary writers may modify this situation). Whether eros is depicted in its homosexual or its heterosexual manifestation is secondary in importance to the literary power with which it is depicted.

BIBLIOGRAPHY. Kimon Friar, "The Poetry of Dinos Christianopoulos: An Introduction," *Journal of the Hellenic Diaspora*, 6/1 (Spring 1979), 59–83; Tom Horner, *Eros in Greece*, New York: Aegean Books, 1978; John Taylor, "The Poetry of Dinos Christianopoulos," *Cabirion*, 12 (1985), 11–13.

William A. Percy and
John Taylor

GREEK ANTHOLOGY

The Greek Anthology is another name for the Palatine Anthology preserved in a unique manuscript belonging to the Palatine Library in Heidelberg. It was assembled in the tenth century by the Byzantine scholar Constantine Cephalas on the basis of three older collections: (1) the Garland of Meleager, edited at the beginning of the first century B.C.; (2) the Garland of Philippus, which probably dates from the reign of Augustus; and (3) the Cycle of Agathias, collected in the reign of Justinian (527–535) and including only contemporary works. But in addition Cephalas incorporated in his anthology the *Musa Puerilis* or "Boy-love Muse" of Strato of Sardis, who probably flourished under **Hadrian** (second quarter of the second century). It is probable that the segregation of the poems on boy-love from the rest of the anthology (with the mistaken inclusion of some heterosexual pieces) reflects the Byzantine attitude, quite different from that of the pagan Meleager who indifferently set the two themes side by side.

These poems, assembled in the twelfth book of the Anthology (with others scattered elsewhere in the collection), are monuments of the passion of an adult male for an adolescent boy (never another adult, as some modern scholars have suggested; XII, 4 is the most explicit testimony on this matter) that was an integral part of Greek civilization. The verses frankly reveal the mores and values of Greek pederasty, exalting the beauty and charm of the beloved youth, sounding the intensity of the lover's attachment, and no less skillfully describing the physical practices to which these liaisons led, so that it is not surprising that the complete set of these poems was not published until 1764. They are realistic in that they deal with the rejection and frustration of the lover, the brief and ephemeral quality of the boy's prime (anthos), and the loss of his attractiveness once the coarseness and hairiness of the adult male make their appearance, even the gloating at the downfall of a youth who once could tease and reject his lovers with cruel impishness. The whole set of themes belongs specifically to the world of the boy-lover and his paramour, not that of the androphile homosexual of modern times, even if certain poems also profess an exclusively homosexual orientation that is indifferent to women's beauty. Some of the verses are little masterpieces of Greek literature whose euphony can scarcely be rendered into English; and when they were translated, until quite recently, often the sex of the subject or the addressee was falsified to conform to the mores of contemporary society. It has been said that if every other work of Greek literature had perished, the Anthology would make it possible to reconstruct the private life of Hellenic civilization down to the smallest detail, and this truism certainly applies to its image of the *paiderasteia* that informed the culture of Greece not just in its golden age, but even in later centuries, when the Hellenistic world embraced the whole of the Eastern Mediterranean. The most recent poems in the group are from the second century, showing that in pagan circles the old ethos was undimmed.

The prudery that persisted into modern times compelled scholars to treat this section of the Anthology only in the obscurity of Latin annotations, and just recently has it become possible to discuss the content of these poems in the clarity of the modern languages. Students of classical literature and apologists for pederasty alike have undertaken the task of analyzing and commenting this corpus of poems; in particular one may consult the works of J. Z. Eglinton, *Greek Love* (New York, 1964) and Félix Buffière, *Eros adolescent* (Paris, 1980), as well as the bilingual editions of the Anthology that have appeared in various countries, beginning with the Loeb Classical Library text in English (1918). No account of the homosexuality of the Greeks can be written without taking into account the abundant and express testimony of the Anthology on the facet of their civilization that marked the apogee of love and fidelity between males.

Warren Johansson

GRIERSON, FRANCIS (1848–1927)

American musician and essayist. Grierson was born Benjamin Henry Jesse Francis Grierson Shepard in England; until 1899 he was called Jesse Shepard. His family moved to frontier Illinois, where Jesse heard Lincoln debate Douglas in 1858, an incident incorporated in his *The Valley of the Shadows* (London, 1909; Boston, 1948). The family next moved to St. Louis, where the boy's beautiful singing voice attracted the attention of John Frémont (explorer, first Republican presidential candidate, and Civil War general). Frémont took thirteen-year-old Jesse as his page, but when the older man lost his command, the boy moved with his family to Niagara Falls and then to Chicago. Jesse early developed

his talent as a pianist and gave musical recitals along the Atlantic coast in 1868. He met Walt **Whitman** then and the two remained life-long correspondents and friends.

Not yet twenty, he went to Paris, where his singing and piano improvisations made him an international star. On March 25, 1870, he sang the lead part in Léon Gastinelle's mass at Notre Dame Cathedral. Inviting him to dinner, the elder Dumas predicted "With your gifts you will find all doors open before you." In 1874 he returned to the United States and in October conducted seances at Chittenden, Vermont, with Helena Petrovna Blavatsky, the founder of Theosophy. She, however, disapproved of Grierson because he had performed at Salle Koch, a St. Petersburg dancehall frequented, Blavatsky claimed, "by dissipated characters of both sexes." Jesse was not deterred in his career as a medium, which he combined with his music. He made his way to San Francisco and thence to Australia. In 1880 he was in London lecturing and in 1885 he met Waldemar Tonner, a German Jewish tailor in Chicago; the two remained lovers for forty-two years. Offered a city block in San Diego, the couple moved for a time to 20th and K streets, where they built the Villa Montezuma with contributions from spiritualists and theosophists.

With the collapse of their San Diego venture, the couple returned to Europe in 1890. Taking the name Francis Grierson, Jesse wrote a series of books: *Essays and Pen-Pictures* (Paris, 1889), *Pensées et essais* (Paris, 1889), *Modern Mysticism and Other Essays* (London, 1899), *The Celtic Temperament and Other Essays* (London, 1901), *Parisian Portraits* (London, 1910), *La Vie et les hommes* (London, 1911), *Some Thoughts* (London, 1911), and *The Humour of the Underman, and Other Essays* (London, 1911). His works denounced materialism, praised art and explored a cosmic consciousness. Grierson's sketch of Paul **Verlaine** details visits to the poet's garret and concluded that two lines of Verlaine were worth more than the whole of *Paradise Lost*.

Fearing the onslaught of war, Grierson returned to New York City in 1913. The New York *Evening Post* sent a reporter to interview him, who later wrote, "I had never seen a man with lips and cheeks rouged and eyes darkened. His hair was arranged in careful disorder over his brow, his hands elaborately manicured and with many rings on his fingers; he wore a softly tinted, flowing cravat." Grierson's writings on the German menace and the "yellow peril" show him at his weakest: *The Invincible Alliance, and Other Essays, Political, Social, and Literary* (London, 1913) and *Illusions and Realities of the War* (New York, 1918).

Grierson's fame in the United States faded with the years; he remained known only among spiritualist circles. His last two books were *Abraham Lincoln, The Practical Mystic* (New York, 1918) and *Psycho-Phone Messages* (Los Angeles, 1921); his lover never found a publisher for a poetry anthology and Grierson's autobiography, which were left in manuscript. Tonner and Grierson moved to Los Angeles in 1920 and soon took up with a Hungarian count, Michael Albert Teleki, and his mother; they all ran a dry-cleaning business together. In 1927, Tonner arranged a concert for Grierson; at the end of the performance, when he did not turn to the audience, Tonner checked and found his lover dead.

Having observed Queen Victoria's funeral, Grierson was no sexual liberationist. While he was flamboyant and enjoyed the airs of the aristocracy, he deeply loved and shared his life with a tailor. He lived his entire life like the grasshopper enjoying whatever prosperity showered upon him. When his funds ran low, he pawned his fur coat or ruby ring. More truly than his contemporary Oscar Wilde, Grierson could have said that he put his genius into his life and only his talent into his books.

BIBLIOGRAPHY. Harold P. Simonson, *Francis Grierson*, New York: Twayne's United States Authors Series, 1966.

Charley Shively

GRIFFES, CHARLES TOMLINSON (1884–1920)

American composer. Growing up in a middle-class home in Elmira, New York, the young Griffes early became aware of his musical talent as well as his "difference"—his lack of attraction to girls and dislike of contact sports. His ability as a pianist attracted the attention of an eccentric patron, Mary Selma Broughton, who arranged for him to go to Berlin to study (1903). There his acquaintance with the city's thriving gay subculture must have given him an insight into his own nature far richer than the hints that he been able to piece together in Elmira. He also acquired a "special friend" in an older student, Konrad Wölcke, who helped him to become acclimated in Germany. The two remained devoted to one another for a number of years. On the advice of his teacher, Engelbert Humperdinck, Griffes' professional goal shifted from piano performance to composing. His first compositions reflected the heavy, Germanic taste that he had learned; later, however, under the influence of French and Russian music, he acquired the lighter, more colorful accents that are characteristic of his mature work.

In 1907 Griffes returned to the United States, and the following year he accepted an appointment at the Hackley School for boys in Tarrytown, NY. Frequently complaining of overwork, he was to remain there until his death. During his trips to New York City he became a regular patron of the Lafayette Place Baths and the Produce Exchange Baths. Although he disliked some aspects of these establishments, he found them an indispensable resource for sexual contacts. Griffes' last years were illuminated by a deeply emotional friendship with a married New York policeman, Dan C. Martin, an arrangement recalling one effected some years later by the English novelist E.M. **Forster**. Always of a delicate constitution, Charles Tomlinson Griffes died of pneumonia in 1920. His papers passed into the hands of his younger sister Marguerite, who destroyed many of them, apparently because she feared their "compromising" nature. In this way precious material for the understanding of his inner life has been lost.

Griffes was the first important American composer to be fully conversant with the avant-garde, as represented by such figures as Claude Debussy, Ferruccio Busoni, and Edgard Varèse. He was also influenced by Indonesian and Japanese music. His *Symphony in Yellow* of 1912 bears a dedication to Oscar **Wilde**. The choral work *These Things Shall Be* employs a text by another English homosexual writer, John Addington **Symonds**. One of his last works, the experimental *Salut au Monde*, uses texts from Walt **Whitman's** *Leaves of Grass*. The general public, however, knows Griffes best for his sensual short pieces, *The Pleasure-Dome of Kubla Khan* and *The White Peacock*.

BIBLIOGRAPHY. Edward Maisel, *Charles T. Griffes: The Life of an American Composer*, rev. ed., New York: Knopf, 1984.

Ward Houser

GROSS INDECENCY

As a term of art for homosexual acts, "gross indecency" entered English law through the **Criminal Law Amendment Act** of 1885. An amendment, drafted by Henry Labouchère and retained as Section 11 of the Act, has the following language: "Any male person who, in public or private, commits, or is party to the commission of, or procures or attempts to procure the commission by any male person of, any act of gross indecency with another male person, shall be guilty of a misdemeanor. . . ." Earlier legislation, culminating in the 1861 Offenses Against the Person Act, directed against anal activ-

ity (buggery), required proof of penetration (down to 1828 the law was interpreted to require proof of penetration and emission). Ambitiously, the 1885 legislation enlarged the prohibition to include any homosexual contact whatsoever. As Havelock **Ellis** pointed out in 1897, it was illogical to include private acts, since no one would be present to record the indecency or be outraged by it. At all events, Oscar Wilde was convicted ten years later under the 1885 Act in a case that sent shock waves throughout the Western world.

"Indecency" has a broad connotation, suggesting anything held to be unseemly, offensive, or obscene. The 1861 Act had mentioned "indecent assault" against both females and males. Apparently wishing to leave no uncertainty that consensual acts, as well as coercive ones, fell within the scope of the prohibition, Labouchère seems to have deleted the noun "assault," adding the adjective "gross" by way of compensation. There is no crime of "petty indecency."

In 1921 a Scottish Conservative M.P. proposed to criminalize acts "of gross indecency between female persons." This legislation was not adopted, and in fact lesbian acts have never been against the law in the United Kingdom. The 1967 Criminal Offenses Act (England and Wales) removed private conduct between consenting adults from the scope of the criminal law, but left the expression "gross indecency" for public acts. If committed by members of the Armed Forces or Navy, even private acts remain a matter of gross indecency. It also remains illegal to "procure" an act of gross indecency; in a bizarre case, the director of a play, *The Romans in Britain*, was prosecuted in 1982 for a brief episode of simulated buggery.

Five New England states and Michigan imitated the British statute. As of 1988 Michigan still recognized "gross indecencies between males" and "gross indecencies among females." Generally, however, the expression has little currency in American law and is unlikely to acquire much, as it would be vulnerable to attack under the "void for vagueness" principle.

See also **Common Law.**

BIBLIOGRAPHY. Paul Crane, *Gays and the Law*, London: Pluto Press, 1982; H. Montgomery Hyde, *The Love That Dared Not Speak Its Name*, Boston: Little, Brown, 1970.

William A. Percy

GUIDES, GAY

In the nineteenth century various guides of limited circulation were published of the demimondes of Paris, London, Brussels and other cities, sometimes including directories of prostitutes; none is known to have had a homosexual emphasis. For some decades in our own century, it appears, homosexual men exchanged among themselves handlists of favorite haunts—bars, restaurants, hotels, baths and public meeting places. A few seem to have been duplicated in a kind of *samizdat* form, reproduced in carbon-copied or mimeographed sheets. These lists were distributed privately, and sold, if at all, clandestinely. This clandestinity served to protect the establishments listed from notoriety that might result in police harassment.

Out of the small handlists pamphlets and books emerged. The earliest surviving example seems to be *The Gay Girl's Guide* (69 pp.), a male-oriented publication with a directory of "where to make contacts," that apparently began publication in Boston in 1949. It was succeeded by the international *Guide Gris*, first published in San Francisco in 1958 with subsequent editions, which seems to be the first such collection to appear as a real book. In the 1960s, the *Incognito Guide*, published in Paris, enjoyed fairly wide circulation. In 1972, "John Francis Hunter" (John Paul Hudson) published a heroic one-man job of 629 pages, *The Gay Insider USA*. While these and other guides of those decades are now obsolete, they are useful for the historian who wishes to establish the "homo-geography" of the recent past.

Currently three well-established publications dominate the field: the *Spartacus Guide*, covering the world outside the United States; the Movement-oriented annual *Gayellow Pages*, blanketing North America, with one national and five regional editions; and the lesbian *Gaia's Guide*, edited by Sandy Horn. Gay guides have also been published for such cities as London, Paris, Amsterdam, Berlin, New York, San Francisco, and Los Angeles, with special telephone books ("yellow pages") appearing also for the latter two.

Wayne R. Dynes

GUYON, RENÉ CHARLES MARIE (1876–1961)

French jurist and sexual theorist. Guyon earned a doctorate in law from the University of Paris with his study *La Constitution australienne de 1900* (Paris: Chevalier-Marescq, 1902). This work and his *Ce que la loi punit: code pénal expliqué* (Paris: Larousse, 1909) brought him to the attention of the King of Siam, who appointed him in 1908 a member of the Code Commission and in 1916 chief of the Drafting Committee of the Siamese Code of Law. In 1919 the Siamese government published Guyon's *The Work of Codification in Siam* in both English and French editions. René Guyon developed early the principle of privacy, that law should never invade the bedroom. "The greatest charity you can render your neighbors," he wrote, "is keeping out of their private lives." In Siam (called **Thailand** after 1949), as the *Spartacus Gay Guide* notes, "The right to be homosexual has never been forbidden or restricted."

In his philosophy, Guyon developed a rationalism endebted to Epicurus and updated with Einstein, Freud, and modern science. He expounded his ideas in a series of works: *Essai de métaphysique matérialiste* (Paris: Costes, 1924); *Essai de biologie matérialiste* (Paris: Costes, 1926), *Reflexions sur la tolérance* (Paris: Alcan, 1930); *Essai de psychologie matérialiste* (Paris: Costes, 1931), and *La porte large* (Paris: Rieder, 1939). His belief in freedom, science, and reason was absolute: he vigorously opposed the irrationalities incorporated in Judaism, Christianity, and Islam.

From anthropology and from his own travels, Guyon found many superstitions but also sexual freedoms unknown to Europeans. With his brother he wrote an account of Brazil's emerald forest: *A travers la forêt vierge: aventures extraordinaires de deux jeunes Français au Brésil* (Paris: Gedalge, 1907). Guyon traveled extensively throughout Asia and Africa and closely studied the works of James Frazer (*The Golden Bough*), Paul Gauguin (*Noa Noa*), General A. H. Pitt-Rivers (*The Clash of Cultures and Contact of Races*), and Sigmund **Freud** (*Totem and Taboo*).

Most of the latter half of his long life was spent in Bangkok, where he died in 1961. Editing a two-volume *Anthologie bouddhique* (Paris: Crès, 1924), Guyon praised **Buddhism**, whose general ideas he found "logical, acceptable, and relatively practical" because "sexuality is not made an object of special odium of an unreasonable and almost pathological kind." In *La cruauté* (Paris: Alcan, 1927), he contrasted the Buddhist attitude toward animals with Christian cruelty.

In 1929, Guyon published the first volume of his monumental *Etudes d'éthique sexuelle*. Before World War II, six volumes appeared: *I. La légitimité des actes sexuels* (Saint-Denis: Dardaillon, 1929); *II. La liberté sexuelle* (Saint-Denis: Dardaillon, 1933); *III. Révision des institutions classiques* (Mariage: Famille) (Saint-Denis: Dardaillon, 1934); *IV. Politique rationnelle de sexualité, la reproduction humaine* (Saint-Denis, Dardaillon, 1936); *V. Politique rationelle de sexualité; le plaisir sexuel* (Saint-Denis: Dardaillon, 1937); and *VI. La persécution des actes sexuels I. Les courtisanes*

(Saint-Denis: Dardaillon, 1938). The first volume was translated into English in 1934 and the second volume in 1939 with introductions by Norman Haire.

A further volume which would have included homosexuality has never appeared, but Guyon's analysis of the topic emerges from his other volumes. He rejected all notions of perversion, abnormality, inversion, third sex, and the "woman's soul trapped in a man's body." Separating sexual gratification from human reproduction, he argued that any and all sexual pleasures are reasonable, natural, and legitimate. What he labeled "intersexual" (man and woman) intercourse is relatively uncommon (abnormal); masturbation, he argued, was the most common (normal) form of sexual activity. He rejected the idea of "genital" sexuality and argued that the mouth, anus, fingers, tongue, or other outlet was no less erogenous than the penis and vagina. For him bestiality, incest, festishism, talking dirty, exhibitionism, voyeurism, necrophilia, coprophilia, and other activities are equally joyful. "Every mechanical means of producing sexual pleasure," Guyon postulates, "is normal and legitimate; there is no room for moral distinctions between the various available methods: all are equally justifiable and equally suited to their particular ends."

His reservations were sadism, chastity, and love. The first, he argued, too often violated "the fullest respect for the liberty of others and the free consent (uncomplicated by any element of violence or deceit) of the sexual partner." Deliberate chastity to Guyon was an incomprehensible disease. Love was understandable, but too limited: "Individualized love is only sexual desire concentrated on a single person," which is unduly selfish and lasts at most a few years. Guyon was nearly unique among sexologists in recognizing that homosexual and incestuous love "enjoy exactly the same possibilities of passion, the same paroxysms of joy, the same jealousies and torments, in a word the same characteristics, as the most usual forms of intersexual love."

Guyon participated in the work of the World League for Sexual Reform on a Scientific Basis and supported Magnus **Hirschfeld** and the founding of a French chapter of the organization under Pierre Vachet. Guyon corresponded with Norman Haire in London and Sigmund Freud in Vienna. He himself became a practicing psychoanalyst, but Freud did not go far enough for him. Freud's *Three Essays on the Theory of Sex* (1905) identified the libido of the child but failed to reject censorship and repression. Guyon defended infant sexuality as natural and normal, but social conventions "as abnormal and undesirable." In his reply, Freud argued that homosexuality was not natural but "acquired." Guyon also rejected the idea of a death instinct advanced in Freud's *Beyond the Pleasure Principle* (1920); for Guyon, the conflict was not between thanatos and eros, but between eros and convention.

Guyon corresponded with Alfred **Kinsey** and warmly welcomed the appearance of *Sexual Behavior in the Human Male* (1948). Kinsey in turn studied Guyon closely and cited his six-volume *Etudes* in the notes and bibliography of *Sexual Behavior in the Human Female* (1953). Guyon's work has had a continuing influence among sexologists. In 1952 Milan's *Scienza e Sessualità* published Guyon's "L'istinto sessuale" as a supplement to their journal. "Chastity and virginity: the case against" appeared in the year of Guyon's death in the Albert Ellis-edited *The Encyclopedia of Sexual Behavior* (New York: Hawthorn Books, 1961).

Guyon is best known today for his teachings on childhood sexuality. He vigorously opposed all notions of innocence, chastity or virginity; he wrote: "nature is on the side of the child, and artificial convention on the side of the average adult." A year after his death, a group of seven intersexual adults formed the René Guyon Society in Los Angeles. Their motto—credited to Guyon—was "Sex before eight or it's too late," and they encouraged training children in the use of condoms. Tom O'Hare for some time issued the René Guyon Society Bulletin, but the organization suffered persecution and repression in the anti-sex climate of the eighties.

Guyon's unfinished *Etudes* resemble **Foucault's** unfinished *History of Sexuality* in the ambition of the authors. There is no evidence that Foucault ever studied Guyon, but Foucault's argument that sexologists invented the idea of homosexuality could be corrected by reading Guyon. Guyon's books were published in editions as small as a hundred copies. The Nazis who conquered France in 1940 and Charles DeGaulle, who took power after World War II, had an equal repugnance for sexual liberation. Guyon's work still remains to be discovered.

Charley Shively

GYMNASIA

The Greek sports ground, usually at first outside the city walls, was open to all citizens but not to slaves or foreigners. Gymnasia evolved from the Cretan *dromos* (simple running track) where in the seventh century B.C. boys and young men began to exercise together nude. The Greeks and those nations they influenced were the only civilized peoples ever to exercise regularly in the nude. As institutionalized **pederasty** spread to Sparta and the rest of Greece, so did gymnasia, some of which added covered tracks. The oldest in Athens date to the sixth century, probably established by Solon, who forbade slaves, as in Crete, to enter them: the Academy and the Lyceum, originally as elsewhere on the outskirts of the city, outside the walls and large enough for parades and riding lessons. Soon a third was added for metics, the Cynosarges. In the larger gymnasia special areas of the palestra were set aside for the teenagers, from which men were barred so that they would not cruise the boys while they were exercising. The principal supervisor, the paedotribe, had to be over 40.

That the gymnasia early became centers of plotting is attested by the fact that Polycrates, the tyrant of Samos (d. 521 B.C.), had them burned. The more pederasty became associated with tyrannicide as it did, the more tyrants opposed it. The Persians also opposed gymnasia, as did the tyrants they supported, and Ionia after the Persian conquest did not practice pederasty, as **Plato's** *Symposium* said.

Gymnasia had three principal subdivisions: (1) the track (*dromos*), where athletes practiced for contests of distance—running, javelin throwing, and the like; (2) the palestra, for physical exercise, wrestling, and ball playing, at times with a library attached; and (3) baths, swimming pools, and rooms for massage. As centers of recreation and leisure for the Greek male the gymnasia became the setting for *paideia* (educational instruction), as reflected in the Platonic dialogues, several of which are set in them. Philosophers, sophists, dialecticians and all kinds of other teachers frequented them, drawing audiences of boys and men to their lectures. Plato preferred the Academy and **Aristotle** the Lycaeum.

In the Hellenistic period gymnasia and pederasty spread to all the cities where Greeks settled or which became Hellenized. The gymnasiarchs appointed by the Ptolemies eventually acquired wide political and administrative powers in their *poleis*, under the Romans becoming the chief officials. Even Jerusalem briefly acquired a gymnasium near the Temple, where circumcised Jewish youths with simulated foreskins performed their exercises nude in the reign of Antiochus. The scandal helped provoke the Maccabean uprising, which destroyed the gymnasium in Jerusalem, though Herod the Great (d. 4 B.C.) later patronized ones in the Greek cities. Gymnasia also appeared in Rome and some Latin cities in the West, although most Romans disapproved of nudity and gymnastics, preferring hunting and war games. During the empire Roman baths, some of which had mixed patrons, often added exercise rooms and even libraries, thus coming to resemble the increasingly elaborate Hellenistic gymnasia, which even in the eastern provinces they rivaled and to some extent replaced.

No more is heard of gymnasia after A.D. 380, when the intolerant Christian Theodosius the Great began to persecute pagans. Ascetics, calling themselves "athletes for Christ," preferred to mortify the body, condemning not only pederasty and nudity but even bathing, and fulminating against gymnasia and baths, which declined especially in the Western provinces as cities shrank and became impoverished beginning with the disasters of the third century.

During the **Renaissance** Italian theorists like Guido di Montefeltro revived the Greek and Latin desideratum of a sound mind in a sound body and the English **public schools** established in the sixteenth century reimposed systematic exercise and games as part of the program for their students, but no one proposed nudity. The modern gymnasium thus grew up as an adjunct to the playing fields of Eton and Harrow. American schools and colleges imitated these English models. In the nineteenth century and even more in the twentieth gymnasia were established in European and American cities for the rich, often as clubs, and for the general public as the YMCAs. Some became centers of homosexual cruising and after the **Stonewall Uprising**, openly gay gymnasia appeared in most larger American cities. The Westernizing elites of the Third World also established gymnasia.

See also **Bathhouses.**

BIBLIOGRAPHY. Jean Delorme, *Gymnasion: Etude sur les monuments consacrés à l'éducation en Grèce*, Paris: Boccard, 1960.

William A. Percy

H

HAAN, JACOB ISRAEL DE (1881–1924)

Dutch novelist, poet, and scholar. De Haan was born in the small village of Smilde in the northern part of the Netherlands, where his father was a rabbi. In 1885 the family moved to Zaandam near Amsterdam. After preparing to be a schoolteacher in Haarlem, he moved to Amsterdam to work and study law. There he met Arnold **Aletrino**, a novelist and medical practitioner who had specialized in criminal anthropology and, though not himself homosexual, had written unambiguous defenses of homosexual love. The encounter inspired de Haan to write his first novel, *Pijpelijntjes* (1904), which was naturalist and clearly homosexual. It was a thinly veiled and rather sexual autobiography in which Aletrino figured prominently. The latter was instrumental in having the first edition destroyed because it seemed to imply that he himself was a homosexual.

De Haan was a member of the Socialist Workers' Party and wrote the children's column for its daily, *Het Volk* ("The People"). After publication of his novel, his column was terminated but he was not expelled from the party; he also lost his teaching job. Nevertheless, he wrote a second novel, *Pathologieën* (1908), which describes in even more explicit terms a homosexual sadomasochistic relationship. The protagonist is driven by his lover to commit suicide after a series of sexual degradations. The book is written in the spirit of literary decadence, which also dominated short stories of the period. In one of the latter, de Haan homosexualizes the Faust theme: the protagonist abuses Jesus sexually on Satan's instructions. Both novels received very little critical approval, not surprisingly, considering the times.

De Haan wrote no more novels. He married, received his doctorate with work on the problem of criminal responsibility (1915), and concentrated on poetry, publishing *Libertijnsche liederen* (1914, "Libertine Songs"), *Liederen* (1917), and *Kwatrijnen* (1924). Many of the poems have gay content, for example the life and sufferings of Oscar **Wilde**.

Before World War I, de Haan became an orthodox Jew, and after it he left Holland for Palestine. He joined the Zionist movement, but because he could not find his place there, he soon quit it. Then he supported Agudat Yisrael, the most important orthodox Jewish and anti-Zionist movement of the time, for which he immediately became an important spokesman with his Western intellectual background. From Jerusalem, he wrote articles for the Dutch daily *Algemeen Handelsblad* and the English *Daily Press* in which he ventured his anti-Zionist opinions. For the Dutch daily, he also described his attraction to Arab boys.

De Haan had maneuvered himself into a very strange situation: an unrepentant pederast with a socialist and "decadent" background, defending Orthodox points of view against Zionism. In the tumultuous early twenties in Palestine, his was a dangerous position; after defending the Orthodox case with the British as well as with King Hussein of Jordan, he was murdered by extreme Zionists of the Hagana movement who were never apprehended. Zionists spread the rumor that it was a homosexual murder by Arabs.

De Haan is now considered one of the most accomplished Dutch poets. A complete edition of his poems was published in 1952, and many of his works have been reissued in the 1980s.

BIBLIOGRAPHY. Jaap Meijer, *De zoon van een gazzen*, Amsterdam: Atheneum, Polak & Van Gennep, 1967.

Gert Hekma

HADRIAN (76–138)

Roman emperor from 117 to 138. Protected and adopted by the emperor Trajan, Hadrian had a military and political career before ascending the throne upon his protector's death. Hadrian traveled extensively throughout the Empire, undertook extensive administrative reforms, built cities, roads, public buildings, and aqueducts. He withdrew the Roman armies from Assyria, Armenia, and Mesopotamia to reduce the cost of maintaining the eastern frontier of the Empire, but fought a war against Bar Kochba's uprising in Palestine that ended with the devastation of the country and its decline as a center of Jewish cultural life.

Though married to Sabina, Hadrian is remembered most of all for his attachment to the youthful **Antinous** (ca. 111–130), whose beauty, perpetuated in countless busts and reliefs, won the emperor's affection. During a voyage up the Nile Antinous was drowned under circumstances that gossip enveloped in romantic legend, even to the point of asserting that the youth had sacrificed his life for his lover. In his grief Hadrian ordered the boy deified as god and hero, and even authorized the belief that Antinous had ascended to the firmament as a new star, though it was only in the Renaissance that Tycho Brahe confirmed the emperor's wish by assigning the name to a heavenly body.

In Egypt Hadrian founded a new city named after Antinous, and elsewhere in the empire the youth was commemorated by cult, festival, and statues. Surviving are numerous inscriptions in his honor, and Pancrates and Nicomedes composed poems to celebrate his qualities. Scandalized by these actions of the emperor, the early Christians contrasted their reverence for the saints and martyrs with this object of an "impure" passion.

A great patron of the arts, Hadrian brought the Roman revolution in architecture that had commenced under **Nero** to its fulfillment, as seen in the Pantheon, which still survives in the Eternal City. Outside Rome, at Tivoli, Hadrian's villa displays a series of innovative pavilions recalling places he had visited, so that he could revive the happy memories at his leisure. Hadrian may be deemed the archetype of the wealthy homosexual traveler and connoisseur.

Hadrian's reign was marked by the flourishing of the neo-Greek manner in art, one of whose most frequent themes was the Antinous type of male beauty, echoed in scores of coins and statues that can be seen today in museums. The aura of mystery that enveloped the death of Antinous has inspired modern literary treatments of the liaison, some explicit in their analysis of the homosexual motif, such as Marguerite **Yourcenar**'s *Hadrian's Memoirs* (New York, 1954). Antinous remains the archetype of the handsome youth protected by a noble lover that was the ideal of Greek *paiderasteia*, and the embodiment of the beauty of late adolescence immortalized by untimely death, while Hadrian stands out as one of the "good emperors" under whose enlightened rule Greco-Roman civilization flourished throughout the Mediterranean world.

BIBLIOGRAPHY. Royston Lambert, *Beloved and God: The Story of Hadrian and Antinous*, New York: Viking, 1984.

Warren Johansson

HAFIZ
(CA. 1320–CA. 1390)

Persian poet. Hafiz was the title of Shams al-Din Muhammad, whose tomb remains a pilgrimage site near Shiraz in southern Iran. While every detail of his life can be contested, no one can question his mastery of *iham*—Persian for ambivalence.

Politically, Hafiz lived in a troubled time. The Arab ascendency over Persia had broken and at the end of his life was replaced by Mongol rule. Hafiz never became a court poet, but neither did he suffer martyrdom, and, despite the changes in rulers, he was able to spend most of his life and to be buried in Shiraz, the city of his birth. The legend of his meeting with the Mongol Tamerlane (Timur) demonstrates Hafiz' subtle diplomacy. The conquerer challenged the poet's offering of two of Tamerlane's cities for a boy. (Emerson translates the verse: "Take my heart in thy hand, o beautiful boy of Shiraz! I would give for the mole on thy cheek Samarcand and Buchara!") Hafiz responded that "because of such generosity I now come before you a poor beggar." Tamerlane rewarded the poet, but the conquerer may not have shared the poet's love of roughs—in Persian *rends* or vagrants who loved wine, poetry, and boys. Muslims who, like Hafiz, favored rough trade found support in the tradition that Mohammed said, "I saw my Lord in the shape of a beautiful young man with his cap askew."

Religiously, Hafiz' name suggests **Islamic** orthodoxy: in Arabic, *hafiz* means "protector"; it was one of the names of Allah and was a title given those who had memorized the entire Koran. For a time Hafiz earned a living copying theological works; a copy in his hand of Sufi Amir Khusrau is dated 1355. Iranians now read Hafiz as a **Sufi** mystic; in 1979 the Ayatollah Khomeini (using the pseudonym "Hendi") published a collection of Hafizian verses. During his life Hafiz attacked the orthodox and praised Mansur al-Hallaj (d. 922), a Sufi martyr beheaded in Baghdad as a heretic. Hafiz spurned mosques in favor of taverns where he found men, who led him to ecstasy: "With mussed-up hair and sweating brow, bright lips, intoxicated smile, shirt torn open to the waist, singing a sonnet softly, his cup contains an overpowering joy." Legend held that at his

death the orthodox disputed Hafiz' right to burial, but he was granted honors after a youth by chance drew the following line from his work: "Dance joyfully by Hafiz' grave; buried in sin, he's carrying on in Paradise."

Poetically, Hafiz has endured many interpretations. In Urdu-, Turkish- and Persian-speaking societies, only his collected verses and the Koran are used for divination. His work has survived but not with any accepted canonical text; collected works range from 152 to 994 poems. But virtually no one questions that Hafiz is the greatest writer of Persian *ghazals*, a form which he perfected. Like the sonnet, the ghazal was often a love song. Among predecessors, **Sa'di** (also from Shiraz) had a strong influence; at least thirty of Hafiz' ghazals use the same end rhymes, metrical pattern and subject as Sa'di's. And Hafiz shared some of Omar Khayyam's love of the moment as well as **Rumi**'s intensity. Like Rumi, Hafiz paired divine beauty (*jamal*) with divine terror (*jalal*), nightingale (*bulbul*) with rose (*gul*). The complexity of his verse can be seen in his lines about the first letter of the Arabic alphabet (*alif*): "Only the *alif* [i. e., penis] of my lover standing scratches my heart slate." Here the blend between the body and a mystical monotheist are combined ingeniously in writing.

Pederasty, which lies at the center of Sa'di, Rumi, and Hafiz' work, is censored even today from English translations. Joseph von Hammer translated Hafiz into German in two volumes in 1812–13, with male–male lovers (as in the Persian) because he was "afraid of getting entangled in contradictions by praising girls for their green-sprouting beards." Friedrich Rückert published even finer translations of Hafiz in 1822 which were shared with his friend Count **Platen**. In 1908, Friedrich Veit wrote a thesis, "Des Grafen von Platen Nachbildungen aus dem Diwan des Hafis," which celebrated the homoerotic aspects of Hafiz. **Goethe**, Emerson, and Nietzsche were among the most famous who wrote poems from Hafiz based on German translations.

Contemporary Muslims like Khomeini angrily reject European interpretations of Hafiz as an unrestrained libertine, drunkard, and pederast. Europeans can be faulted for projecting their desires on people they have defined as aliens, but the rising nations of Asia have themselves been tricked into suppressing their own customs to please missionaries. In his own time Hafiz had to struggle against the Islamic proscription of drinking; he struggled to go beyond good and evil, God and Satan, the body and spirit by transcending dualities. In his quest he searched for boys who wore their caps askew.

BIBLIOGRAPHY. Annemarie Schimmel, "Hafiz and his Critics," *Studies in Islam* (January 1979), 1–33.

Charley Shively

HAITI

This French- and creole-speaking black republic of over six million people occupies the western third of the island of Hispaniola. Although handicapped by poverty and political discord, Haiti is a remarkable cultural amalgam, retaining many hallmarks of the African diaspora.

In the early 1980s claims were made that male homosexuality is such a tabooed topic in Haitian culture that dying **AIDS** patients would necessarily deny any homosexual involvements. Yet earlier observers such as the anthropologist Melville Herskovits, who studied rural Haiti, were able to elicit information about attitudes toward local homosexuals. The attitudes reported—bemused denigration—and the lack of any attempts to extirpate homosexual behavior do not differ from those known throughout Latin America. If anything, less prominent machismo in Haiti connects with greater toleration of homosexuals in *voudon* cults than is imaginable in any Spanish-speaking Latin American societies. Bahia, in one of the most Afro-American parts of **Brazil**, which

was similarly populated from Dahomey (now Benin), is the closest cultural analogue. There, cross-gender possession and homosexuality are prominent parts of Xango cults. The literature on *voudon* contains many mentions of possessions by *loas* (spirits) of a sex other than that of the person possessed. No particularly notable taboo on homosexuality was reported in pre-AIDS ethnographic literature. This claim would seem to have been concocted to protect tourism in Haiti. Explicit gender non-conformity in the folk religion, which was sanctioned by the Duvalier regime between 1957 and 1986, was notable; the homosexual taboo is not found there.

Any serious assertion that it is particularly difficult to elicit information about homosexuality from Haitians must be comparative, but no one has compared elicitation in Haiti with elicitation in the Dominican Republic (the Spanish-speaking other portion of the island of Hispaniola), Bahia, or any other point for comparison. In the United States itself, one observer has noted, "except for three cases of AIDS in admittedly homosexual Haitians, none of the other cases reported have admitted to homosexual activity despite intensive questioning in both French and Creole by both American physicians and by Haitians."

BIBLIOGRAPHY. Melville J. Herskovits, *Life in a Haitian Valley*, New York: Knopf, 1937; Stephen O. Murray and Kenneth W. Payne, "The Social Classification of AIDS in American Epidemiology," *Medical Anthropology*, *(1989)*, 115–28.

Stephen O. Murray

HALL, RADCLYFFE (1880–1943)

English novelist and poet. Born to a well-to-do family in Bournemouth, Hall was left a good deal to herself as a child, developing her own identity under her favorite name of "John." Throughout her life she was to affect a strikingly masculine appearance. At the age of 27 she fell in love with the 50-year-old Mabel Batten, whom she had met at the resort of Homburg. The two took up residence together and, influenced by her lover, Hall converted to Roman Catholicism. In 1915 the two women attended a tea party in London, where Hall met Una, Lady Troubridge, the wife of an admiral. When Batten died soon after, the way was clear for Hall and Troubridge to live together—much to the admiral's puzzlement. The two women were destined to remain together for thirty years.

Hall published several volumes of poetry during this period, but it was only with the appearance of her novel *Adam's Breed* in 1926 that she achieved popularity. In this work she transposed her own personality into that of a man, Gian-Luca. Two years later, however, she launched her bombshell, the openly lesbian novel *The Well of Loneliness*. This work, though it seems mild and lacking in explicitness today, was declared "obscene" and the British courts ordered all copies seized. After this point Hall and Troubridge judged it prudent to live abroad, retaining however the conservative political and social views characteristic of their class.

Inevitably *The Well of Loneliness* strikes readers today as a time-bound work, inasmuch as Hall subscribed to current theories of "sexual inversion," which she popularized. Indeed as a role model she may have led many women into an unnecessary cultivation of stereotypes. Nonetheless, the notoriety of her work helped to move lesbianism into the consciousness of a public which in the Anglo-Saxon world at least had managed until 1928 to ignore the phenomenon almost entirely.

BIBLIOGRAPHY. Michael Baker, *Our Three Selves: The Life of Radclyffe Hall*, New York: William Morrow, 1985; Gillian Whitlock, "'Everything Is Out of Place': Radclyffe Hall and the Lesbian Literary Tradition," *Feminist Studies*, 13 (1987), 555–82.

Evelyn Gettone

HANDBALLING

This sexual practice involves the insertion of one partner's hand—and sometimes much of the arm—into the rectum of the other. Before attempting such insertion the nails are pared and the hand lubricated. Sometimes alcohol and **drugs** are used by the receptive partner as relaxants. This practice acquired a certain popularity—and notoriety under the name of *fistfucking*—in a sector of the gay male leather/S & M community in the 1970s. A few lesbians have also reported engaging in it. A medical term, apparently uncommon, has been proposed for handballing: brachiproctic eroticism.

It need scarcely be stressed that handballing is dangerous in all its variations, as puncturing of the rectal lining may lead to infection and even death. Although handballing does not directly expose the passive partner to **AIDS** or to sexually transmitted diseases, by scratching or scarring the rectal wall it may create tiny portals for the invasion of microbes during a subsequent penetration. With the new emphasis on safe sex in the 1980s, handballing has greatly declined, and it will probably be relegated to history as one of the temporary excesses of the sexual revolution.

Historical precedents are elusive. It may be conjectured that the recent resort to the practice is due to medical knowledge of operations in which the anus is dilated, since the ordinary individual scarcely credits that such enlargement is possible or desirable. In a late Iranian version of the binding and riding of the god of darkness Ahriman by the hero Taxmoruw, the demonic figure breaks loose by means of a trick and swallows the hero; by pretending to be interested in anal intercourse the brother of Taxmoruw manages to insert his arm into Ahriman's anus and retrieve the body from his belly. The brother's arm—the one that entered the demon's anus—becomes silvery white and stinking, and the brother has to exile himself voluntarily so that others will not become polluted. The myth is interesting as linking the forbidden sexual activity with stigmatization and outlawry of the perpetrator.

There seems to have been no term for handballing in the Greek language, though *siphniazein* (from the island of Siphnos) has been defined as to "insert a finger in the anus." This harmless practice has long been known, and it may have served as a kind of modest precedent.

BIBLIOGRAPHY. Jack Morin, *Anal Pleasure and Health*, 2nd ed., Burlington, CA: Yes Press, 1986.

HARLEM RENAISSANCE

Harlem is a section of northern Manhattan originally developed as housing for the white middle class. As New York's blacks were gradually excluded from residing in the southern part of the island, however, from 1915 onward it became the chief Negro center of the city—and of the nation. New York City's black community was reinforced by thousands migrating from the South in search of freedom from discrimination and lynching. In the 1920s, sometimes termed the Jazz Age, Harlem's black culture and intelligentsia enjoyed a golden age. Harlem was the center of Marcus Garvey's nationalist movement, and also an entertainment mecca for blacks and whites alike.

Probably the most important achievement of the Harlem Renaissance was the emergence of new writers whose works could appear under the imprint of major publishers. The writings of the gay poet Countee Cullen (1903–1946) were to become widely known. Cullen's marriage to Yolanda Du Bois, daughter of the famed black scholar and journalist W. E. B. Du Bois, proved a disaster, but his homosexuality was hushed up. To this day conflicting opinions are heard on the possible homosexuality of Langston Hughes (1902–1967), one of the major figures of the group. Either he was particularly successful in covering up or repressing his homo-

sexuality, or it did not exist at all—though the latter seems unlikely. There is no doubt of the orientation of the experimental writer (Richard) Bruce Nugent (1906–), who lived into gay liberation days, when he gave informative interviews. Nugent wrote what may have been the first fictional account of American black homosexuality, the short story "Smoke, Lilies, and Jade," published in the little magazine *Fire!* (1926). The bisexual Wallace Thurman took a more sardonic view of the Harlem Renaissance, as seen in his novel *Infants of the Spring* (1932).

White enthusiasm for the achievements of black America's "talented tenth" was heavily laced with stereotypes—including the one that made the Negro the symbol of heterosexual virility. The creative contribution of blacks was still held to be circumscribed by their "more elemental" approach, in contrast to the cerebral logic attributed to the white tradition. This perception encouraged a stream of chic whites north of 110th Street, where they attended speakeasies and nightclubs. Here they could see a series of bisexual and lesbian entertainers, notably Ma Rainey, Bessie Smith, "Moms" **Mabley**, and Gladys Bentley. Carl Van Vechten, a blond gay novelist from Iowa, became the unofficial publicity agent for this side of Harlem. Other, more ordinary gays flocked to Harlem night spots where they found a more tolerant atmosphere. It was not just a Bohemia like Greenwich Village, it was a place where the homosexual visitor could be more relaxed and uninhibited. Huge drag balls were given at the Rockland Palace and the glittering Savoy Ballroom. This side of Harlem is sensitively reflected in Blair Niles' novel *Strange Brother* (1931).

The deepening Depression of the 1930s caused all these activities to fade. Until the black cultural revival of the sixties and seventies, the Harlem Renaissance was almost forgotten. Although even today its homosexual component tends to be slighted, the trend made a real contribution to American gay life and culture.

See also **Black Gay Americans;
New York City.**

BIBLIOGRAPHY. Eric Garber, "T'aint
Nobody's Business," *Advocate*, no. 342
(May 13, 1982), 12–13, 15; David
Levering Lewis, *When Harlem Was in
Vogue*, New York: Knopf, 1981.

Ward Houser

HARTLEY, MARSDEN (1877–1943)

American painter, poet, and essayist. Born Edmund Hartley in Lewiston, Maine, he was raised there and at his father's home in Cleveland. While working as a clerk in a marble quarry, he started formal study of art at the Cleveland School of Art. A scholarship sent him to New York City to complete his training. In 1904 he began an important friendship with Horace Traubel, the biographer of Walt **Whitman**. After producing a number of impressionist and neoimpressionist paintings, he launched his public career as an artist under the name of Marsden Hartley (Marsden was his step-mother's maiden name). Through Alfred Stieglitz, who gave him his first one-person show at his 291 gallery, Hartley gained entrée into New York's avant-garde.

After experimenting in the style of Picasso, Hartley went to Paris (1912), where he became an intimate of Gertrude **Stein**. He also absorbed Central European influences, including the abstractionism of Franz Marc and Vassily Kandinsky. In 1913 he settled in Berlin, entering into a love affair with Lieutenant Karl von Freyburg. His lover was killed in battle on October 7, 1914, and Hartley created several of his finest paintings to memorialize the relationship. These works, which feature regalia of the German officer corps, did not stand him in good stead when he returned to New York in 1915. In the fall of 1916 he began to share a house in Provincetown with Charles **Demuth**, an artist of a similar modernist style who was well acquainted with the gay scene of New York and environs. Hartley also was friendly with the lesbian writer Djuna Barnes.

In 1921 he returned to Europe, where his book *Twenty-Five Poems* was issued by Robert McAlmon's Contact Publishing Company in Paris. The Great Depression forced Hartley to return to the United States, though a Guggenheim Fellowship enabled him to spend 1932 in Mexico, where he became close friends with Hart **Crane**. After learning of Crane's suicide, Hartley painted *Eight Bells; Folly*. In the mid-thirties he supported himself in New York through participation in the Public Works of Art Project. He struck up a friendship with the Francis Mason family in Nova Scotia, and he was to live with them for much of the rest of his life.

Hartley's work is now seen to belong to a native American current of expressionism in which he was a pivotal figure. During his lifetime, however, his seeming shifts of style, combined with the relative immaturity of the American art world, prevented him from receiving full recognition. This neglect augmented a loneliness that his shyness about his homosexuality induced in him. In 1980, however, a full-scale retrospective at the Whitney Museum of American Art in New York restored his reputation.

BIBLIOGRAPHY. Barbara Haskell,
Marsden Hartley, New York: Whitney
Museum of American Art, 1980.

Wayne R. Dynes

HELIOGABALUS (ALSO KNOWN AS ELAGABALUS; 204–222)

Roman Emperor from 218 to 222. Born at Emesa in Syria as a descendant of the royal family of King Samsigeramus, he became priest of Elagabal in that city in 217. His grandmother Julia Maesa arranged to have him declared emperor by the Tenth Gallican Legion on April 14, 218. The legions sent against him deserted and killed their commanders, and as sole ruler of the

Empire he traveled to Rome in the winter of 218/19. Here he reigned in a style of luxury and effeminacy unprecedented even in the history of Rome. He sent out agents to comb the city for particularly well-hung partners for his couch, whom he made his advisers and ministers. His life was an endless search for pleasure of every kind, and he had his body depilated so that he could arouse the lusts of the greatest number. His extant portraits on coins suggest a sensual, even African type evolving through late adolescence. The refinements which he innovated in the spheres of culinary pleasure and of sumptuous interior decoration and household furnishing are mentioned by the historians of his reign as having survived him and found emulators among the Roman aristocracy of later times. For what Veblen called "conspicuous consumption" he set a standard probably unequaled until the Islamic middle ages.

His sexual personality cannot be reduced to a mere formula of passive-effeminate homosexuality, although this aspect of his erotic pleasure-seeking is the one stressed by his ancient biographers. He loved the role of Venus at the theatre and the passive role in his encounters with other men, yet he was married several times and even violated a Vestal virgin, but remained childless. This facet of his sexual life has enabled the more dishonest classical historians to write of him as if he were just another heterosexual ruler, when in fact he seems to have desired an operation that would gratify his fantasy not of changing into a member of the opposite sex (transsexual in the modern sense) but of becoming truly androgynous—having the functioning genital organs of both. As high priest of the Syrian deity Elagabal he sought to elevate the cult of the latter to the sole religion of the Empire, yet he did not persecute the Christians. Family intrigues ultimately cost him the favor of the soldiers who murdered him and his mother on March 11, 222. Unique as he was in the history of eroticism and of luxury, he has inspired writers from the third-century biographer Aelius Lampridius in the *Scriptores Historiae Augustae* through the later treatments of Jean Lombard, Louis **Couperus**, and Stefan **George** to Antonin Artaud and Alberto Arbasino.

BIBLIOGRAPHY. J. Stuart Hay, *The Amazing Emperor Heliogabalus*, London: Macmillan, 1911; Robert Turcan, *Héliogabale et le sacre du Soleil*, Paris: Albin Michel, 1985.

Warren Johansson

HELLENISM

This trend in Western civilization is part of a larger preoccupation with idealizing a privileged era of the past as a source of cultural norms for the present. Sometimes this idealization engenders **utopian** longings. In this case classical antiquity, or a portion of it, occupies the place of honor as model and guide. Examples of prescriptive precedents from ancient **Greece** include the three orders in architecture (Doric, Ionic, and Corinthian), Platonism in **philosophy**, and **Homer** as a pattern for epic poetry.

Permutations of the Hellenic Image. Although **Christianity** retained selected elements of Greek culture and philosophy, it tended to treat the whole phenomenon as part of the discarded pagan model of human development. Clearly unsalvageable, the institution of **pederasty** figured as one of the most reprehensible survivals of the Hellenic heritage. This rejection persisted for a thousand years after the adoption of Christianity as the state religion of the Roman empire in the fourth century of our era. Hellenism as a norm reemerged during the Italian **Renaissance**; although this word is modern, it captures the central notion of rebirth of classical ideals and standards of beauty. The Renaissance also saw the first tentative beginnings of an apologetic literature for homosexual behavior. The Florentine thinker Marsilio **Ficino** (1433–1499), who contributed to this apologetic endeavor, was interested not only in Greece but equally in Egyptian (or what he believed to be Egyptian) thought: the Hermetic corpus. Other humanists were more attracted to ancient Rome than to Greece.

A more exclusive focus on Greece began to emerge in the course of the eighteenth century, reflecting the consolidation of a Europocentric mentality that had become contemptuous of the cultures of other continents which colonialism was engaged in subduing. In 1752 the Göttingen scholar Johann Matthias Gesner (1691–1761) gave a lecture in which he cautiously explored the evidence for Socrates' homosexuality. The text, *Socrates Sanctus Paederasta*, was only published eight years after the author's death and not in Germany but in Utrecht in Holland with its much greater freedom of the press. In 1759 Johann Georg Hamann, the precursor of the Counter-Enlightenment, issued his *Sokratische Denkwürdigkeiten*, emphasizing the sensual element in true friendship between males. Toward the end of the century franker discussions were offered in the Netherlands by Frans Hemsterhuis and Cornelis de Pauw.

A new purified Hellenism triumphed in the artistic movement known as neo-classicism. The homosexual archeologist Johann Joachim **Winckelmann** (1717–1768), for example, rejected Egypt as a source of ideal beauty, saying that short, stocky people with snub noses could never inspire great figural art. Although he was not able to visit Greece in person, knowing it only from art and literature, he insisted that only the physical type of that country could serve as a paradigm. Winckelmann had a major influence not only over the rise of neo-classical painting and sculpture, with their emphasis on the male **nude**, but also over the trend toward "aesthetic paganism" in German literature. Greek ideals, though sometimes anachronistically conflated with Roman ones, played a major role in both the American and French Revolutions.

In the nineteenth century, cultural Hellenism found particular favor with English homosexuals, such as Walter **Pater** and John Addington **Symonds**. This ethos of **aestheticism** was grounded in part in the all-male **public schools** that combined the officially approved reading of Greek texts with a clandestine, but pervasive subculture of homosexuality. Matthew Arnold, though not himself homosexual, had posited a fundamental contrast between the stern morality of Hebraism and the more permissive and beauty-loving Hellenism. Toward the end of the century a group of minor pederastic poets appeared in England (sometimes termed the **Calamites**), who went back to the **Greek Anthology** for much of their inspiration.

In Switzerland Heinrich **Hoessli**, who published the first major modern work on homosexuality (1836–38), took much of his material from ancient Greece, as did his successor Karl Heinrich **Ulrichs**. In his *Birth of Tragedy* (1872), the philosopher Friedrich Nietzsche effected a major correction of the conventional wisdom about the Greeks. He showed that the ideal of "nothing in excess," of rule by reason and good sense, was but one aspect of the Greek ethos, which he termed the Apollonian side. Its complement was the **Dionysian** element, which was emotional, intuitive, and irrational. Beginning with the Göttingen professor Karl Otfried Müller (1797–1840), German philologists strove to distinguish separate strands of pederasty, as those of Sparta, Thebes, and Athens. The contemporary French scholar Bernard Sergent has sought to relate Greek homosexual traditions to a putative **Indo-European pederasty**. Although their findings have remained controversial in detail, the labors of these writers have served to show that Hellenic pederasty was not monolithic.

The great modern Greek poet Constantine **Cavafy** chose as his two central themes Greek history, though more the Hellenistic period than the Golden Age, and his own homosexual experiences in **Alexandria**, a city whose very existence attested to the expansive capacity of Hellenism. In the early twentieth century André **Gide** could still appeal (in *Corydon*, 1924) to Greek pederasty as his model, saying that it was hypocritical to honor the Greeks for their philosophy and art, while ignoring or condemning a central feature of their civilization. This approach lingered in J. Z. Eglinton's *Greek Love* (New York, 1964).

The fame of an ancient Greek poet, **Sappho** of Lesbos, assured that she was synonymous with female same-sex love: sapphism. Later that honor was transferred to the island on which she lived. In the twentieth century such writers as H. D. (Hilda **Doolittle**) and Natalie **Barney** made a cult of ancient Greece, striving to recapture qualities of purity and concision that they found in surviving texts. Significantly, Barney was known as "the Amazon," after that legendary women's tribe.

Outlook. The same-sex component of Greek culture has been subject to various procedures of censorship and emendation. Until recently, more popular treatments of "the Greek miracle" simply omitted any discussion of the prevalence of homosexuality. Some mentioned it only to chide the Greeks for their tragic flaw. In recent decades some homophile scholars have seen the Greeks in their own image—one of adult–adult love or **androphilia**—and neglected to acknowledge that the normative form of Greek same-sex love was pederastic, the love of a male adult for an adolescent youth. In keeping with the male-centered character of Greek society as whole, there was no generally accredited lesbian counterpart of the pederastic institution.

Today's rapid pace of social and technological change has dimmed the appeal of the Greek model. Feminists and others have flayed Hellenic civilization as sexist and elitist. More broadly, the contemporary mainstream, discounting the idea of inspiration from the past, has become present-minded and future oriented. In gay studies, the **social construction** trend has branded investigation of eras before the nineteenth century irrelevant, claiming that "homosexuality" is a recent innovation. Even disregarding this prohibition—as scholars should—more careful study of ancient Greece suggests that it was not as **sex positive** as earlier idealized views had claimed. Sexual freedom was hedged with formidable taboos of class and gender.

Acknowledging these restrictions and qualifications, there is no doubt that continued scrutiny of the well documented sexual behavior of the ancient Greeks can provide insights for the understanding of such distant societies as **Japan** and Melanesia. Ancient Greece was the focus of the last works of the influential French social philosopher Michel **Foucault**. Using both time-honored and distinctively modern techniques of investigation, other scholars are at work in a new effort to wring the full meaning from the extensive body of Greek texts on human sexuality. In the present context the enduring significance of ancient Hellas is that its civilization cherished an attitude toward the pederastic form of male homosexuality standing in diametric opposition to that of the Judaeo-Christian tradition. This chapter of the collective memory of mankind encapsulates a behavioral norm which institutionalized Christianity and other opponents could reject but never wholly suppress.

BIBLIOGRAPHY. E. R. Dodds, *The Greeks and the Irrational*, Berkeley, University of California Press, 1973; Henry Hatfield, *Aesthetic Paganism in German Literature*, Cambridge, MA: Harvard University Press, 1964; Richard Jenkyns, *The Victorians and Ancient Greece*, Cambridge, MA: Harvard University Press, 1980.

Wayne R. Dynes

HELLENISTIC MONARCHIES (323–31 B.C.)

Alexander the Great's generals, known in the first generation as *diadochoi* (successors), who presided over the new cultural synthesis, half-Greek and half-Oriental, founded by Alexander, seized the fragments of his empire. Ptolemy took **Egypt**, Antigonus Greece and Macedonia, and Seleucus Asia after the decisive battle of Ipsus in 301 ended the wars that broke out on Alexander's death. They established bureaucratic monarchies, with the Ptolemies becoming the wealthiest from irrigated agriculture and **Alexandria's** central position in world trade. The Seleucids recreated the Persian Empire with variegated ethnicities loosely supervised from Antioch and Seleucia—new foundations rivaling Alexandria—while the relatively poor Antigonids relied on Hellenic homogeneity.

Basic Character and Historical Development. Inspired by the examples of Philip of Macedon and Alexander, the Hellenistic monarchs and their Greek or Hellenized subjects in newly founded or Hellenized cities as far east as India and Bactria practiced **pederasty**, patronized **gymnasia**, secluded women, and held **symposia**. Eventually Pergamon, under the Attalids, and the island of Rhodes managed to secure independence as buffer states in the Aegean, where Ptolemaic navies contested Antigonid and Seleucid claims. In Alexandria, Ptolemy I established the Museum, subsidizing its learned symposia frequented by leading scholars, and the Library, created by Demetrius of Phaleron on the model of his teacher **Aristotle.** Aristotle had first systematized the collections of books begun by the sixth-century Polycrates of Samos and Hipparchus of Athens, both pederasts. Other cities, notably Pergamon, Beirut, and Athens, which also created libraries, took the lead in science, culture, and **philosophy.**

Weakened by internecine rivalries, the Hellenistic monarchies fell one by one to **Rome**—Macedonia in 147, Syria, its easternmost provinces in Parthia, Persia, and Mesopotamia long since independent, in 78, and Egypt in 30 B.C. at the death of Cleopatra, last of the Ptolemies. It was Hellenistic rather than Hellenic pederasty that the Romans absorbed, and this more often involved relations between masters and slaves or rich men and poor boys than the classical model of one aristocrat training another, younger one. Further, effeminate boys and transvestites of the type long popular in the East, even eunuchs like Bagoas, seized with the rest of King Darius' harem by Alexander, became fashionable in the Hellenistic cities even among Greeks. The Hellenic institutionalization of pederasty passed into Asia and Africa before it began to penetrate **Rome** during the middle and late Republic. In the East, as in Rome and in Greece itself, this later pederasty spread to the lower classes, which teemed in the urban slums, separated from families or village stability. The independent citizen hoplite (foot soldier) from the classes wealthy enough to afford their own heavy armor and hence able to fight in the phalanx was replaced by the mercenary recruited abroad or drawn from the lower classes. The new "volunteer" soldiers often regarded the barracks as their homes and the regiment as their family, and were hired by the monarchs who snuffed out the liberties of the Greek city-states.

Sexual Aspects. The following monarchs became famous for homosexuality: Demetrius Poliorcetes; his son Antigonus Gonatas; Antiochus I, who loved three boys at the same time; Ptolemy IV; Ptolemy VII, who kept a harem of boys; Ptolemy XIII; and Nicomedes of Bithynia, who paid the 16-year-old Julius **Caesar** to sodomize him.

Ptolemy II Philadelphus imitated the Pharaonic practice of marrying his sister as did some of his descendants such as Ptolemy XIII, XIV, and XV, each of whom in order married their sister Cleopatra. She was the last of the line and after their deaths Cleopatra became mistress of

Julius Caesar and then wife of Mark Anthony. Even members of the lower classes began to marry their sisters, but many in vast city slums and in the countryside were doubtless too poor to marry: like slaves unable to secure regular access to women they must have often turned to homosexuality. Poets such as **Theocritus** and Callimachus, scholars at the Library of Alexandria, testify to the ready availability of boys. Pederasty was a subject for Alexandrian as it had been for Athenian tragedians. Beginning with Rhianus of Crete (floruit ca. 275 B.C.), Aristides of Miletus (ca. 100 B.C.), Apollonius of Rhodes (ca. 295 B.C.), Diotimus (third century B.C.), Moschus (ca. 150 B.C.), Bion (ca. 100 B.C.), and Meleager of Gadara (ca. 100 B.C.) number among the pederastic poets. Phanocles (ca. 250 B.C.) composed his garland of elegies entitled *Love Stories of Beautiful Boys* (ca. 250 B.C.). The *Musa Paidike*, Book XII of the **Greek Anthology**, contains poems mostly composed in this era exhibiting a frankly sensual pederasty without even a pretext of *paideia* (education). This attitude continued in the Greek-speaking east until the Christian sexual counter-revolution of the fourth century, contemporaneous with the establishment of the **Byzantine Empire**.

Instead of recommending civic virtue as their classical predecessors had done, philosophers argued how one should best inure oneself against the changing fortunes controlled by the goddess *Tyche* or arbitrary despots. These philosophers included: **Epicurus**; **Zeno** of Citium, founder of **Stoicism**; Peripatetics, who continued **Aristotle's** tradition in the Lyceum; and members of the Academy of **Plato.** Jews, like **Philo**, especially in Alexandria, where their largest colony lived, and in Jerusalem, where under the Maccabees they revolted against Antiochus IV, condemned pederasty and some other aspects of Hellenism which they found morally repellent, while absorbing still others.

The lasting importance of the Hellenistic monarchies lies in the interface which they created between Judaic and Hellenic cultures; this setting fostered the new syncretistic religion of Christianity which was destined to embrace the entire Greco-Roman world—with tragic consequences for homosexuality.

BIBLIOGRAPHY. Claude Préaux, *Le Monde Hellénistique*, 2 vols., Paris: Presses Universitaires de France, 1978.
William A. Percy

HEMINGWAY, ERNEST (1899–1961)

American novelist and short story writer. Hemingway first achieved fame as a member of the "Lost Generation" in **Paris** in the 1920s. His trademark, a lean, almost laconic style, was widely imitated. Noted for his exploration of "supermasculine" subject matter—war, bullfighting, safaris, deep-sea fishing—Hemingway became a veritable icon of heterosexuality.

Yet careful readers could note hints of sexual unorthodoxy. The short story "Mr. and Mrs. Elliott" (1925) concerns lesbianism, and in fact Hemingway was fascinated with the expatriate world of lesbian Paris typified by Natalie **Barney**, Sylvia **Beach**, Gertrude **Stein**, and their associates. In *The Sun Also Rises* (1926) the hero is unable to consummate a sexual relationship because of impotence. The material for the novel derives from a trip to Spain financed by his traveling companion, the bisexual writer Robert **McAlmon.**

Hemingway's mother, Grace, who may have been a lesbian, dressed the boy in girl's clothes to make a twin sister of him for the older Marcelline. *The Garden of Eden*, a novel published in abridged form only in 1986, reveals homosexual and transsexual fantasies. Rumors that his suicide was the result of an unhappy gay affair have not been substantiated.

BIBLIOGRAPHY. Kenneth Lynn, *Hemingway: His Life and Work,* New York: Simon and Schuster, 1987.

HENRI III OF FRANCE (1551–1589)

French king, the son of Henri II and Catherine de' Medici. Elected to the throne of Poland in 1573, he left the country on the death of his brother Charles IX of France to ascend the throne at the age of 23. Because he refused to adopt the measures for extermination of the Protestants advocated by the Catholic party under the leadership of the Duc de Guise (which had in 1572 perpetrated the massacre of St. Bartholomew's Eve), he found himself at war with its supporters, and even Paris and other cities rebelled against him. He made common cause with the Protestant Henri of Navarre, but in his camp at St. Cloud he was assassinated by a fanatical Dominican monk and died at the age of 38.

Seldom has the homosexuality of a ruler been so public and undisguised, or have the favorites of a monarch been so clearly identified as in the life of Henri III. Though exhibiting many traits of the stereotypical homosexual, and that of the effeminate variety, he is indicated by reliable sources to have felt passionate attraction to women as well. If he remained childless, it was in the opinion even of his foes because an incurable gonorrhea had left him sterile. Many writers have tried to ascribe his homosexual leanings to a stay in Venice in 1574, where satiated with the charms of the opposite sex which he had known only too well, he succumbed to the pederastic vice so rampant in Italy, or to the syphilis which he contracted in the city on the Adriatic. The most that he could have learned was how many others shared his proclivities, and the moment Henri became king of France, he gave free rein to his homosexual urges and also to the fondness for luxury and extravagance which the ancients equated with effeminacy.

Henry was well-built, charming in looks, and gracious in manner; his hands were especially beautiful. His character was marked by the feminine traits of tenderness and religiosity. In 1583 an anxiety-provoking dream even caused him a crisis of piety in which he founded a brotherhood called the Penitents that staged processions in which the king, his mignons, and other dignitaries of the court participated in masks. Other feminine traits of his were a fondness for lapdogs, for childish games and toys, and for elegant costumes. He loved to wear women's clothing and even to appear at public events clad in the style affected by the ladies of his court. Not long after ascending the throne he surrounded himself with handsome young men in their early twenties—the mignons, who used all the feminine arts to ape the king's own proclivities in dress, speech and walk. Two categories of mignons can be differentiated: the *mignons de coeur,* who shared his pleasures and erotic passions—Quélus, Maugiron, Livarol, Saint-Mégrin and others, and the *mignons d'état,* who played a military and political role and acquired a real influence over the affairs of the reign—notably Joyeuse and d'Epernon. Henri cemented his ties with the mignons not just by showering them with favors and gifts of all kinds, but also by arranging marriages for them that were celebrated in a lavish and fabulous manner. He was not troubled by jealousy when they took an interest in the opposite sex.

A contemporary satire entitled *L'Ile des Hermaphrodites* (The Isle of the Hermaphrodites) depicts the life of the mignons and their protector in a quite perceptive manner. The author describes how entering the palace of the hermaphrodites he sees them beautifying their persons to enter the inner sanctum of their lord for sensual mysteries in which he cannot follow. The walls of one room are hung with tapestries depicting **Hadrian's** passion for **Antinous**, another with scenes from the life of **Heliogabalus**, a third chamber has a bed whose roof depicts the marriage of **Nero** and Pythagoras. The mignons join in the praises of their master and his fair hands. The significance of this work has not been fully appreciated, as it owes its title to the misunderstanding of the phenomenon of the **berdache** in accounts of the New World; the berdaches were mistaken for genuine hermaphrodites rather than as individuals who had adopted a culturally prescribed cross-gender role. Given the attitude toward homosexuality that had prevailed in Latin Christendom since the thirteenth century, the conduct of Henri and his mignons inevitably provoked enormous hostility and indignation, and a considerable literature defaming the king and his court was composed that formed the basis for later treatments of the period by historians who gave vent to their homophobia. Only in modern times has it been possible to form a truer picture of the virtues and foibles of a monarch whose public and private life was molded by the homosexual and effeminate in his personality.

BIBLIOGRAPHY. Maurice Lever, *Les bûchers de Sodome*, Paris: Fayard, 1985; Numa Praetorius (pseudonym of Eugen Wilhelm), "Das Liebesleben des Königs Heinrich III. von Frankreich," *Zeitschrift für Sexualwissenschaft*, 18 (1932), 522–531; L. S. A. M. von Römer, "Heinrich der Dritte, König von Frankreich and Polen," *Jahrbuch für sexuelle Zwischenstufen*, 4 (1902), 572–669.

Warren Johansson

HENRY, PRINCE (1726–1802)

Brother of **Frederick II** (the Great) of Prussia. Less distinguished than his brother, who occupied the throne for forty-six years, Henry was another homosexual member of the House of Hohenzollern. The portrait of him drawn by historians varies according to the degree of sympathy or aversion which they feel for him. A great lover of the military, Henry took an aggressive part in the Seven Years War and was particularly renowned for his role in the battle at Friedberg (October 29, 1762), which he won, ending the war. He retired early from active duty and lived thereafter as a dilettante in castle Rheinsberg, a few hours distant from Berlin. Like Frederick, he used the French language exclusively for his literary compositions. An enthusiastic admirer of **Voltaire** and of French philosophy, Henry loved uninhibited discussions of morality and metaphysics. He took particular pleasure in the theatre, while maintaining his own troupe of French performers. His friends fell into two categories: one group satisfied his intellectual and literary needs, the other his homoerotic passions and sensual cravings.

Henry's personality was profoundly masculine: reflective and calculating, endowed with firm will and extraordinary memory, real talent for literature, and outstanding ability as a military strategist. But with these qualities he combined a feminine sensitivity and antipathy to cruelty and brutality in any form, compassion for the weak, and nobility and generosity toward his foes, especially the French. Physically he was small, his face unattractive, his whole figure somewhat ill-proportioned, so that one author remarked that seldom has such a beautiful soul and great talent had such a wretched exterior. All authors who dealt with the sexual side of his character agreed that he felt no love for women, and the compulsion which his older brother exercised on him to marry only strengthened his aversion to the opposite sex. He scarcely concealed his passion for young men and effeminate homosexual types, and he even had a temple of friendship built whose walls were decked with French inscriptions glorifying friendship—which in his case often meant a sensual passion for his youthful adjutants. Some of his favorites were of quite inferior station in life and unworthy character, yet possessing a coarse male attractiveness which the prince could not resist. One of these, a Major Kaphengst, exploited the prince's interest in him to lead a dissipated, wasteful life on an estate not far from Rheinsberg. Others, such as the actor Blainville and the French émigré Count La Roche-Aymon, were better able to reciprocate his affection for them. Subsequently German novelists such as Theodor Fontane in *Stechlin* and Alexander von Ungern-Sternberg in *Der deutsche Gil Blas* alluded to the prince's character in works that indirectly furnish additional details about his private life.

Of interest is one detail of his political career: At the moment when Americans were considering the possibility of a constitutional monarchy, and George Washington had indignantly declined the honor, Henry's name was put forward as that of a cultured and liberal-minded soldier who would make an excellent king. On November 2, 1786 his old friend Baron von Steuben wrote to convey the support of his candidacy by many prominent Americans, but Henry waited until April 1787 to reply and then refused to commit himself until he could be assured of the sentiment of his future subjects.

If less renowned than his brother Frederick, Henry was still one of the homosexual members of the high nobility who, sympathizing with the ideas and ideals of the **Enlightenment**, put their rank and wealth at the service of the movement for political and ideological change in the closing decades of the Old Regime.

BIBLIOGRAPHY. Numa Praetorius (pseudonym of Eugen Wilhelm), "Die Homosexualität des Prinzen Heinrich von Preussen, des Bruders Friedrichs des Grossen," *Zeitschrift für Sexualwissenschaft*, 15 (1929) 465–76.
Warren Johansson

HERESY

Defined as willful and persistent departure from orthodox Christian dogma, heresy forced the church progressively to refine the formulation of its doctrines and to anathematize deviant theological opin-ions. At times heretical movements such as **Gnosticism**, the mystical belief that the elect received a special enlightenment, and Arianism, greatest of the Christological heresies, seemed almost to overshadow the universal church. From Constantine the Great (d. 337) onward, the church used state power to impose uniformity of belief. In both eastern and western halves of the Roman Empire law subjected pertinacious heretics to branding, confiscation of property, exile, and even death. The assumption that the church had the right to call upon the secular power to suppress heresy survived the Empire itself. In the early Middle Ages in the West, few heretics were noticed or prosecuted from the sixth through the tenth century. When prosperity returned after 1000, however, ecclesiastical and secular authorities noted and persecuted heretics who multiplied particularly at first in the reviving cities of southern France and Italy. The iconoclastic controversy of the eighth and ninth centuries nearly destroyed the **Byzantine Empire** where other heresies such as dualistic Paulicianism flourished continuously.

The Image of the Heretic. Modern hypotheses on the causes of heresy were foreign to the churchmen of late antiquity and the Middle Ages, who simply considered heresy the work of the devil. Author after author repeated stereotypical descriptions and denunciations and often applied such beliefs and practices with scant discrimination to later heretics. These clichés were assembled into a type-figure of the heretic with conventional traits: his pride, since he has dared to reject the teaching of the official Church; his superficial mien of piety, which must be meant to deceive, since he is in fact an enemy of the faith; and his secrecy, contrasted with the teaching of the Church, which is broadcast to the four winds. Most significantly, the heretic is often accused of counterfeiting piety while secretly engaging in **libertinism**—and the form of sexual libertinism most often imputed to him is homosexuality, or **sodomy**, as the term generally used from the end of the twelfth century onward.

Late Antiquity. Even before the end of antiquity, Western Christian controversialists, using a charge pagans had once leveled against them, had accused members of dissident sects of engaging in unmentionable orgies "for the sake of pleasure." Not satisfied with their promiscuous intercourse with women, some of them, in the words of the Apostle, "were consumed with their lust for one another." A sect called the Levites, after the members of the tribe who officiated in the Temple in Jerusalem, were reported by Epiphanius of Salamis not to have intercourse with women, but only with one another. It was these who were held in distinction and honor by other libertine Gnostics, because they "had sowed no children for the Archon," that is to say, had begotten no offspring whose souls would like theirs be trapped in the lower, material world and could not ascend to heaven. Such charges were also hurled against the **Manichaeans**, who derived from **Zoroastrianism** the dualistic doctrine that an evil god created matter and human reproduction in the sense of having more bodies to rule.

The Middle Ages. It was at the end of the eleventh century that the so-called Bulgarian heresy became known in Western Europe. It was also known as the Albigensian or Cathar heresy. This was a dualistic ideology that had flourished in the kingdom of Bulgaria, which some ascribed to a priest named Bogomil, who combined the beliefs imported from the Byzantine Empire (Paulician and Manichaean) into a new system. From the reign of Tsar Peter (927–969) onward these doctrines were propagated throughout Europe. The Bogomils believed that the Devil was the creator of the visible, material world and that Christ was a phantom who had no ordinary body, was not born of Mary, and did not truly suffer on the cross. They rejected the sacraments, including baptism and the eucharist, in favor of initiation rites that included the laying on of hands, and identified the Devil with the Jewish god, the demiurge whose revelation in the Old Testament they accordingly repudiated. In their rejection of the Greek Orthodoxy propagated from Byzantium, the heretics were as radical as one could imagine. They subjected the Gospel narratives to an exegesis that made all the miracle stories symbolic and allegorical.

From the "Bulgarian" Heresy to Buggery. Since the Bulgarian heresy was the religious deviation *par excellence* of the later Middle Ages, all heretics in Western Europe came indiscriminately to be labeled *bulgari*, which became *bougres* in Old French and **buggers** in Middle English. But in addition to heresy, the term gained the meanings of sodomite and usurer. It has been claimed that this was only the church's way of defaming unbelievers and provoking hatred for them. In fact, however, as Catholics claimed, they advocated chastity because they retained the dualist notion of the wrongfulness of procreation, and may have tolerated sterile promiscuity, at least in the lower ranks of their sect. It is also quite possible that their highest ranks, the so-called *perfecti*, included more than their share of homosexuals, given the affinity of a certain homosexual character type for leadership in religious communities. The anti-homosexual doctrines of the Catholic Church, grounded in the prohibitions of the Old Testament which the Cathari rejected, may have added to the alienation of such types from its fold. The oft-repeated allegations of homosexual conduct were not without foundation: a promiscuous sodomite, Arnold of Verniolle of Pamiers, was caught in a heretic hunt in 1323. After careful examination of the evidence most modern historians have concluded that the accusations of debauchery and sodomy against the Cathars had some justification and corresponded to the survival of the mores of pagan Mediterranean antiquity in the folkways of Provence.

The further association of buggery with **usury** stemmed from the fact that medieval economic doctrine held money to be sterile, so that the earning of interest was equated with "unnatural" = non-reproductive forms of sexual expression. But all these factors coalesced to make *bougre* and *bugger*, *Ketzer* and *ketter* mean not only heretic but also sodomite. German even distinguished the sodomite as the *Ketzer nach dem Fleisch*, while the heretic proper was the *Ketzer nach dem Glauben*. In texts of the thirteenth century, it is true, the general meaning of "heretic" still prevails. Then also, however, scholastic theologians such as Albertus Magnus and Thomas **Aquinas** defined the "crime against nature by reason of sex" as second only to murder in its heinousness, and the social intolerance of homosexual expression rose to a point where everyone under the authority of the church was obliged to profess heterosexual interests alone. Moreover, the ecclesiastical courts gained the authority to try persons suspected of sodomy, as a crime under canon law, and then to relax them to the civil authorities for execution. Contrary to the modern belief that the term **faggot** for "effeminate homosexual" drives from the practice of burning such offenders at the stake, in England the penalty for both sodomy and witchcraft was hanging. As the significance of the Albigensian heresy receded, the meaning *bugger* = "sodomite" remained, and in the statute 25 Henry VIII c. 6 (1533), the word **buggery** is attested for the first time in English in the unequivocal sexual meaning. In German such terms as *Bubenketzer* for "pederast" retain the same association of ideas. Some writers even brand sodomy as worse than murder, because the murderer kills only one human being while the sodomite aims at the death of the entire human race, which in line with dualistic thinking would perish if one and all ceased to procreate so as not to enslave their offspring in the bonds of matter.

Later Middle Ages. In Cologne Meister Johannes Eckhart (d. 1327) began a pantheistic mysticism that often became heretical among his Rhenish followers. Partly inspired by the Rhenish mystic, Beguines and Begards, lay groups living communally in celibacy, concentrated in the Flemish towns, were accused of lesbianism more often than of sodomy with males. The general disruption of order by famines, endemic after 1314, the Black Death, which returned every ten years for a century after 1347, and the Hundred Years War led to both flagellants and dissipation as well as anti-Jewish outbursts, witch trials, and intensified persecution of sodomites.

Aftereffects. Certainly the theological overlap of heresy and sodomy served to magnify the hatred and aversion with which homosexuality was regarded by the masses of the faithful in Western Europe from the late thirteenth century down to modern times. In later medieval law codes heresy and sodomy were both capital crimes, and the accusation of "unnatural vice" was one of the charges brought against the **Templars** in a series of trials the objective basis of which remains disputed among medieval historians. Again, there is a real possibility that sexual non-conformity was the initial impetus that distanced the heretic from the Church, both then and in later times, when skepticism and unbelief replaced heresy as the chief foes of Christian dogma. It is noteworthy that in Great Britain *bugger* has, apart from the slightly archaic legal usage, been an exceedingly obscene taboo word that could not be used in polite company because of the images and emotions which it evoked.

A final consequence of the association of heresy and sodomy was the positive one, that both crimes were ultimately seen as expressions of the religious intolerance decried by antitrinitarians in the seventeenth century and by deistic thinkers in the eighteenth. The antithesis of the doctrine of the medieval Church was the conviction that crimes against religion and morality, which included heresy and sodomy *par excellence*, should not be the object of criminal sanctions unless they harmed third parties or the interests of society in general. It is therefore all the more regrettable that in the English-speaking world, where freedom of conscience and toleration of sectarianism in religion came comparatively early, the place of buggery in the scheme of medieval intolerance was overlooked and the statutes adopted from canon law were perpetuated as bulwarks of morality.

See also **Christianity**; **Patristic Writers**.

BIBLIOGRAPHY. Michael Goodich, *The Unmentionable Vice: Homosexuality in the Later Medieval Period*, Santa Barbara, CA: ABC-Clio Press, 1979; Malcolm Lambert, *Medieval Heresy: Popular Movements from Bogomil to Hus*, London: Edward Arnold, 1977.

Warren Johansson

HERMAPHRODITE

The hermaphrodite, a human being fusing male and female characteristics, is the physical embodiment of the principle of **androgyny**. In mythology and art, hermaphrodites may be divided horizontally (where developed breasts may signal the female on top, with a complete penis below) or, more commonly, vertically (one side containing a breast and half of a vulva, the other side flat-chested with half of a penis). Sometimes hermaphrodites are regarded positively, standing for a desirable equality and balance between the sexes. Other traditions despise them as symbols of an unacceptable blurring of categories. In some instances the fusion seems relatively successful; in others, presenting a mere juxtaposition of forms, the result is grotesque. In behavior the hermaphrodite may be predominantly male or predominantly female. Cross-cultural data suggest that "male" hermaphrodites, who are likely to be viewed favorably, are much more frequent than "female" hermaphrodites, whose image is generally negative. With respect to their origin, some hermaphrodites result from the merger of a separate male and female person; others come into the world in a fused form, only splitting later into a separate male and female.

Scientific Research vs. Cultural Traditions. Early in the twentieth century the work of Franz Ludwig von Neugebauer demonstrated that in nature true human hermaphrodites, with fully developed male and female organs, are extremely rare—virtually nonexistent. What does occur is a situation where an individual is born with more or less complete organs of one sex and rudimentary or vestigial ones of the other. In other instances both sets may be undeveloped. For the first few weeks the human embryo is undetermined as to sex, and the hormones that effect the determination sometimes do not fully accomplish their task. Since our society dislikes the ambiguity of any anatomical intermediacy, the perceived flaw is usually surgically corrected and the individual takes his or her place as a "real" man or woman. In contrast with the sexual dimorphism of mammals, true hermaphroditism is the rule in many lower animal species, such as snails and worms, and in many kinds of flowers.

Cross-culturally there is no close link between physical and cultural hermaphroditism: the Greeks, who had a well-developed concept of the mythological hermaphrodite, were accustomed to kill hermaphroditic babies after birth. What is of greatest interest is in fact the cultural (that is imaginary) aspect of hermaphroditism, for it is a vehicle of feelings and speculation about gender, **gender** roles, and sexual **orientation.**

European Mythological Traditions. In Greek the word *hermaphroditos* stems from a fusion of the name of a male god, Hermes, with the goddess of love, Aphrodite. According to a story in Ovid's *Metamorphoses* (IV, 285–388), the god Hermaphroditos was in fact the son of the union of Hermes and Aphrodite, but he was originally male. The nymph Salmacis fell in love with him. Repulsed, she successfully beseeched the gods to unite her body forever with his. Immersion in the waters where this fusion took place reputedly turned the bather into a hermaphrodite.

In another myth Kainis was a maiden who formed a liaison with Poseidon. At her request he turned her into a powerful warrior, Kaineus. After his death, he became a woman once more.

Another case of serial hermaphroditism is that of the blind seer Teiresias. Chancing one day on a pair of coupling snakes, he disturbed them, wounding the female. He was punished by being turned into a woman. Seven years later he repeated the experience, and became a man once more. On being asked by the gods whether sex was more pleasurable as a man or a woman, he said that nine parts out of ten belonged to the woman.

In the *Symposium* **Plato** sets forth a myth in which human beings were originally double beings: the man-man, the woman-woman, and the man-woman. When split the last, the hermaphrodite, yielded heterosexual men and women who yearn to reunite with a "better half" of the opposite sex. According to homiletic commentators, the first man Adam in the Hebrew creation myth of Genesis was androgynous until Eve was extracted from his body. Since the creator made Adam in his own image, the implication is that Yahweh was himself androgynous.

Later Greek and Roman art shows many representations of hermaphrodites, most notably in monumental sculpture. These images stem ultimately from age-old concepts of fertility, but their enhanced popularity in the Hellenistic age (323–30 B.C.) probably reflects the fact that this was an age of changing sex roles. The androgynous features of these statues served to pose the question without offering a specific answer.

In medieval travel lore Hermaphrodites lived in their own country in Asia, where European visitors claimed to have observed them. Anatomically, these exotics were divided vertically, with one set of organs on the left and the other on the right, so that copulation face to face was an easy matter. This notion of a nation of a civilization of hermaphrodites has inspired some modern **science fiction** writers; the most notable example is Ursula Le Guin's *Left Hand of Darkness* (New York, 1969), which works out the cultural consequences in considerable detail.

Modern Visions. The hermaphrodite or androgyne became common in French nineteenth-century writing. Inspired by Emanuel Swedenborg, Honoré de **Balzac** wrote a novel, *Séraphita* (1835), about a double-sexed being. The most consistent theoretician of the androgynic vision was probably Joséphin **Péladan**, who influenced artists as well as writers. In fact the androgynous figure—usually depicted as an effeminate youth—is a recurrent figure in the iconography of the so-called decadent painters, from Simeon Solomon to Leonor Fini. In the twentieth century Carl Gustav **Jung**'s interest in the matter sparked a rediscovery of hermaphroditic beings in alchemical imagery of the sixteenth and seventeenth century.

Cross-dressing can sometimes give the impression that the wearer is a true androgyne, and in the popular imagination cross dressers and effeminate homosexuals are physically hermaphroditic. This confusion has probably been unwittingly abetted by the fashion of turn-of-the-century psychologists to refer to bisexuals as "psychosexual hermaphrodites," and more recently by some spokespeople for the gay movement who emphasize getting in touch with the "submerged" half of one's personality. The late twentieth-century fashion among men of wearing a single earring is probably a muted version of the vertical hermaphrodite.

Tribal Cultures. Among the North American Indians the Trickster is a figure of ambiguous sexuality. Primarily a male, he not only wears female dress but gives birth to children. He carries his detached penis in a box, and is thus self-castrating. When he wishes to have intercourse, he sends it separately to the woman. In real life the **berdache** type is sometimes called "he-she" or "man-woman" in Indian languages, but is not regarded as a true hermaphrodite but as a man who has abandoned the male gender role for the female.

Among the Dogon in West Africa, a mythical figure draws outlines of a male and a female on the ground before the newborn baby, who touches the outlines and is possessed by two souls. If the child retains the foreskin or the clitoris he remains two-souled and androgynous, with no inclination to procreation. In order to join the proper sex the male must be circumcised, the female must undergo a clitoridectomy. Among the Australian aborigines, subincision in the male achieves the opposite result: the creation of a "male vagina," which may be re-opened and bled in later life.

India. The mythology of **India** abounds in androgynous and hermaphroditic beings. The great Hindu deities usually have an accompanying female manifestation; thus in art Shiva is often shown partially fused with his female alter ego, Parvati. In some traditions a primordial hermaphrodite has been replaced by twins (e.g., Yami and Yama). Folklore abounds in tales of men who were made womanish by the curse of a god and of male child bearing. There are also legends of individuals were alternated from month to month as king and queen. In Tantrism the male adept or yogi must activate the female principle within himself that is personified by the dormant goddess Kundalini. Only by this means can he experience full wholeness, the internal union of the male and female divine principles. In Buddhism the male Bodhisattva Avalokiteśvara becomes a female, Kuan Yin, in China.

A central feature of the Hindu belief system is transmigration of souls, so that an individual can be reborn as a member of the opposite sex or an animal. This idea was already known to Plato who describes cowardly men being reborn as women in the *Theatetus.* Some Hindus today hold that male homosexuals are individuals whose immediately previous life was that of a woman.

In north India today there is a distinct social grouping of some 100,000 homosexuals known as Hijra or Hinjra. These men wear female dress and perform female tasks, including prostitution. They are commonly believed to be eunuchs or physical hermaphrodites. While medical data are lacking, it is unlikely that many qualify in the anatomical sense. Rather the Hijra myth of self attests to the persistence of the androgynous ideal in Indian civilization.

BIBLIOGRAPHY. Hermann Baumann, *Das doppelte Geschlecht: ethnologische Studien zur Bisexualität in Ritus und Mythus,* Berlin: Reimer, 1955; Marie Delcourt, *Hermaphrodite: Myths and Rites of the Bisexual Figure in Classical Antiquity,* London: Studio Books, 1961; Wendy Doniger O'Flaherty, *Women, Androgynes, and Other Mythical Beasts,* Chicago: Chicago University Press, 1980.
Wayne R. Dynes

HETEROSEXUALITY

The word *heterosexual* was invented by the same man who coined *homosexual:* the publicist and translator Károly Mária **Kertbeny**. The words appear for the first time (as far as is known) in Kertbeny's German-language draft of a private letter to Karl Heinrich **Ulrichs** of May 6, 1868. Although Kertbeny subsequently wavered in his choice of *heterosexual,* the contrasting pair was popularized some years later by Gustav Jaeger, supported by the analogy of such pairs as homogeneous/heterogeneous. At the close of the nineteenth century the terms migrated from German into other major European languages.

Sources of the Concept. While the word heterosexual may be relatively new, the ingredients of the concept are of venerable antiquity. The late coinage of the word reflects the fact that, until recently, "heterosexual norms" were silently assumed and discussion seemed superfluous. Hence the sources of the concept are sometimes elusive. Moreover, in the ensuing account one should bear in mind that the entrance of the pair homosexual/heterosexual into the dictionary presupposes a binary contrast—even a stark opposition—which may be absent in older approximations of the notion.

Historically, the core of the concept of heterosexuality has been linked with procreation and its consequence—the family. Whether we think in terms of the modern compact nuclear family or the extended family found in many societies, the members are typically related by lineage which is established by procreation. (While the custom of adoption is well attested historically, this procedure works by the assimilation of the adopted children to the dominant pattern established by those procreated by the "natural" parents.) Yet although all human beings come into the world by procreation, not all need practice it: many cultures have provided niches for individuals who wished to dedicate themselves to ritual celibacy or priestly homosexuality (as seen in the **berdache** and **ḳādēsh** traditions).

Plato. In hindsight we may detect a first attempt to give a theoretical formulation to the distinction between heterosexual and homosexual in *The Laws*, a late work (ca. 380 B.C.) of the Greek philosopher **Plato.** "When the male sex unites with the female for the purpose of procreation the pleasure so experienced is held to be according to nature, but when males unite with males or females with females, to be considered contrary to nature." (I 636b–C; cf. also VIII 836B–839A). From this passage

we can see that "according to nature" equates in effect with heterosexuality. In proposing that same-sex acts be labeled as unnatural, Plato also merges, for the first time in recorded history, male and female homosexual conduct, which up to this time had been categorized separately. The behaviors are combined because the overarching contrast **natural** vs. unnatural. No doubt Plato was influenced by a pervasive Greek tendency to look for purpose. What is the purpose of copulation? The only answer that appeared was the engendering of offspring.

Christianity. Reappearing in highly charged language in Paul's Epistle to the Romans (1:26), Plato's rejection of same-sex relations as unnatural echoed through the subsequent history of Christian ethics. Yet if Christian tradition agreed that homosexual behavior was unnatural per se, this exclusion did not mean that all *heterosexual* behavior was permitted. Fornication and rape, though "natural," were nonetheless sins. Logically, the Christian approach entails four categories: (1) marriage; (2) celibacy, which are both permitted; as against (3) illicit (heterosexual) copulation; (4) same-sex conduct, both forbidden. In this analysis what we would call heterosexuality appears on both sides of the ledger (1 and 3). In order to reach the modern contrast reclassification was needed, extracting two contrasted behaviors from the scheme and fusing them into a single positive concept: heterosexuality.

Another vexed question has recurred in many different guises over the centuries. Is it appropriate to discuss same-sex conduct exclusively in terms of behavior—same-sex acts—or are there persons whose identity or character is homosexual, regardless of the frequency of this or that act? In medieval times this ambiguity lurked in the term **sodomite**, which could refer either to a basically faithful "son of the church" who had fallen into such sins, but who could confess and be returned to the fold, or to one who was obstinately and seemingly irremediably immersed in such practices—the sodomite with a capital S. In the former view heterosexuality is in effect universal and can only be disregarded on an occasional basis; in the latter situation it has a nemesis—homosexuality.

The Enlightenment and the Rise of Modern Psychiatry. The eighteenth-century **Enlightenment** grappled with these problems by attempting to secularize the concept of the natural. But earlier confusions lingered. Nineteenth-century **psychiatrists**, however, took a more radical step with their doctrine of **perversions**, which implicitly defines what later came to be called heterosexual normality by contrasting it with the abnormal. The procedure might be compared to paring a cheese: the mouldy and inedible "abnormal" parts are stripped away revealing the nutrient substance within. What remains after the subtractions is that which is mandatory: sexual normality. Since this healthy core was by definition nonpathological, it was not a legitimate object of psychiatric concern. To vary the metaphor, shoe fetishism, coprophilia, necrophilia, and homosexuality are, so to speak, so many obscure bypaths ("deviations" or "perversions") from the great highway of normality. The majority, who are already traveling this main road, should simply continue to do so. As for the bypaths, closer inspection revealed a significant criterion of difference. Most of the perversions observed by **Krafft-Ebing** and others of his ilk did not involve persons as objects. Such behaviors as shoe fetishism and umbrella fetishism could be separated off from the rest; they were later to be dubbed "paraphilias."

This double sequence of separations left standing, when all was said and done, a fairly straightforward contrast between heterosexuality and homosexuality as forms of sexual conduct between two or more consenting adults. Moreover, increasing acceptance of birth control and abortion made it possible to begin to separate heterosexuality from procreation. Heterosexuality could in fact become more like homosexuality: an avenue of pleasure and personal fulfilment. So matters stood for decades. In the 1940s Alfred **Kinsey** attempted a new formulation in a seven-step scale from exclusive heterosexuality to exclusive homosexuality. Insisting that we speak of these patterns as behaviors rather than fixed character types, Kinsey looked forward to a dissolution of the binary contrast between heterosexuality and homosexuality in favor of a behavioristic approach, one inherently pluralistic and nonjudgmental. Whatever the other merits of Kinsey's work, which are considerable, this hopeful outcome has not been attained.

Doubleness of the Heterosexual Concept. For those who reject psychic **androgyny** (as most do reflexively) another problem looms. In keeping with the postulate of psychosexual dimorphism, *two* norms are needed: an aggressive, dominant one (male); a yielding, receptive, nurturant one (female). Thus contemporary traditionalists who defend obligatory heterosexuality must grapple with the fact that it articulates itself into two norms, according to the genitalia of the individual. If two, then why not three or four permitted patterns?

Gay Liberation Views. For the most part theorists of the gay **liberation** movement contented themselves with asserting the parity of homosexuality with heterosexuality: "gay is just as good as straight." The two were to be viewed simply as different **lifestyles**. In the early 1970s, however, some radical feminists argued that all heterosexuality signified complicity with male domination, and sought to persuade, with some (mostly temporary) success, even their straight sisters to abandon the questionable practice. Other voices, holding that feminism means empowerment, spoke in favor of the right of each woman to make her own choices, even if they be heterosexual.

In the 1970s some gay radicals adopted the term *heterosexism* (modeled on **sexism**). The new word apparently serves as a pejorative label for "straight chauvinism," an excessive prizing or favoring of heterosexual persons and values. The term had little success in the United States, but was taken up in the 1980s by some sectors of the British Labour Party. Unfortunately, the label heterosexism suggests hostility to heterosexuality itself, alienating many Britons who might otherwise have been sympathetic. The matter has been exploited by Conservatives as part of their campaign against the "loony left."

Conclusion. By and large normality (= "heterosexuality") remains an unspoken assumption underpinning much popular thinking. There are few considered explorations or defenses of heterosexuality as such; none seems required. Thus the suggestion of one Southern clergyman that libraries and bookstores contain "heterosexual sections" to help the public rally to its norms has not been taken up. Moreover, the **AIDS** crisis has probably given new life to the folk certainty that heterosexuality is best. Battered but unbeaten, this belief survives as part of the inherited social amalgam that makes up the deep structure of modern societies, the tacit body of unexamined postulates that form a kind of collective "operating procedure." But as many converging forces in modern international civilization push toward cultural pluralism, a more explicit analysis of the place of this pivotal yet still obscure concept is sure to appear, situating it within a constellation of ideas about sex and **gender**.

Wayne R. Dynes

HILLER, KURT (1885–1972)

German writer and political figure active both on the left and in the homosexual **movement**. In the published version of his doctoral dissertation (1908), Hiller formulated arguments for the control over one's body that were to become important for supporters of homosexual and women's rights. As a journalist, essayist, and poet he evolved an aphoristic style reflecting the strong imprint of Friedrich Nietzsche's work and possessing affinities with early Expressionism. A collaborator of Magnus **Hirschfeld**'s on the **Scientific-Humanitarian Committee** in Berlin, he also sought to influence socialist politics through his Activist Movement. At the close of World War I he pioneered in applying the topical notion of (national) **minorities** to homosexuals as a group. As an independent thinker and writer under the Weimar Republic, he represented almost the mean of opinion on the German left. In 1933 he was arrested by the Nazis and beaten almost to death in the Columbia Haus in Berlin. Escaping to Czechoslovakia and then to England in 1938, he returned to Germany after the war, where he settled in Hamburg and attempted without great success to revive the homophile movement and the famous petition for abolition of **Paragraph 175** of the Penal Code. His collected essays and articles brandish a style virtually untranslatable into English, so that his literary fame is confined to the German-speaking world.

BIBLIOGRAPHY. Lewis D. Wurgaft, *The Activists: Kurt Hiller and the Politics of Action on the German Left, 1914–1933*, Philadelphia: American Philosophical Society, 1977.

Warren Johansson

HIPPIES
See **Beatniks and Hippies; Bohemia.**

HIPPOCRATIC CORPUS
The Greek Corpus Hippocraticum is the collection of approximately 60 medical treatises ascribed to Hippocrates of Cos (460–circa 370 B.C), about whose biography little is known for certain, though in his lifetime and afterward he enjoyed the renown of a great physician. In

fact the Hippocratic writings are the legacy of two different schools of medicine, the Coan and the Cnidian, over several centuries. The former school had a generalized conception of disease with individual variations, while the latter preferred to localize specific diseases and then insert them in a fixed but comprehensive schema. The actual dates of composition of the various treatises range from 500 B.C. to the first century of our era; the early second century saw the beginning of editions of the Hippocratic corpus and of the writing of glossaries and commentaries.

Homosexual behavior appears only occasionally in the corpus, perhaps most notably in the original text of the Hippocratic oath, where the apprentice physician swears that in the course of his professional visits he will abstain from "sexual acts on the persons of women and of men, of freemen and of slaves." The causes of sexual characterology figure in the work *Peri diaites*, 28–29: If both father and mother secrete "male bodies," the offspring will be men "brilliant in soul and strong in body." If the secretion from the man is male and that from the woman is female, the former still dominates, so that the offspring turn out less brilliant, but still brave. But in case the man's secretion is female and the woman's is male, the fusion of the two creates a "man-woman" (*androgynos*), the equivalent of the modern notion of effeminate homosexual. The same is true of girls: if the man's secretion is female and the woman's male, and the female is predominant, the offspring will be "mannish." Hence by the fourth century B.C. the Hippocratic school saw factors of procreation as determining sexual constitution.

The treatise *On Airs, Waters and Places* discusses the infertility and impotence of the **Scythians** (21–22). "The men have no great desire for intercourse because of the moistness of their nature and the softness and coldness of their abdomen, which are the chief barrier to the sexual urge." Moreover, the vast majority of the male Scythians "become impotent and perform women's work and behave like women," a condition ascribed to their constant horseback riding, which causes swellings at the joints, in severe cases lameness and sores on the hips. To cure themselves they cut the vein behind each ear, but in so doing they cause the impotence from which they suffer. The author of the treatise deems this an attribute of class: the upper-class Scythians suffer from the disease but not the lower class, which does not ride horses.

The writers whose work was later ascribed to Hippocrates because of his general renown take no offense at homosexuality, but see it as part of the totality of sexual behavior on which, however, they acknowledge certain ethical limitations. The medical science of antiquity was aware of the problems posed by differences in sexual constitution and sought to explain them in its own theoretical terms.

See also **Medical Theories**.

Warren Johansson

HIRSCHFELD, MAGNUS (1868–1935)

Leader of the homosexual emancipation movement in Germany.

Life. Magnus Hirschfeld was born in Kolberg on the Baltic coast of Prussia (today Kołobrzeg in Poland) on May 14, 1868. His father, Hermann Hirschfeld, had distinguished himself by making the town a popular resort; for this service his fellow citizens erected a monument to him that stood until 1933. The son at first studied languages and philosophy at Breslau and Strasbourg, then medicine at Munich and Berlin, where he took his degree. After traveling in the United States and North Africa, he settled first at Magdeburg in Saxony and then in Charlottenburg, a district of Berlin.

The suicide of one of his patients, a young officer who ended his life on the eve of a marriage demanded by his family, awakened Hirschfeld's interest in the problem of homosexuality. The subject was also topical, as contemporary publications by **Carpenter**, Ellis and **Symonds**, **Krafft-Ebing**, Raffalovich, and **Aletrino** attest. Hirschfeld's first book, under the pseudonym Th. Ramien, was entitled *Sappho und Sokrates* (1896) and put forward a bold argument that the homosexual form of love is part of human sexuality, that both its causes and its manifestations should be the object of scientific investigation, and that the penal laws against homosexuality should be changed in society's own interest. In regard to the etiology of homosexuality Hirschfeld outlined a complex theory which he was to modify and expand over the next four decades without ever coming to a satisfactory formulation.

On his twenty-ninth birthday, May 14, 1897, Hirschfeld founded the Wissenschaftlich-humanitäre Komitee (**Scientific-Humanitarian Committee**), the world's first organization dedicated to the aim of ending the century-long legal intolerance and social opprobrium that homosexuals had suffered in Western civilization. Its first activity was to prepare a petition "to the legislative bodies of the German Empire" calling for the repeal of **paragraph 175** of the Imperial Penal Code of 1871 which imposed a maximum of five years' imprisonment for "lewd and unnatural conduct" between males. In the decades that followed this petition was to be signed by some six thousand individuals prominent in all walks of German life, including members of the high intelligentsia whose names are still world-famous.

In 1899 the Committee began the publication of the *Jahrbuch für sexuelle Zwischenstufen*, the world's first journal devoted to scholarship on all aspects of homosexual behavior. Edited by Hirschfeld, its 23 volumes are in some respects a still unsurpassed collection of materials of all kinds on the subject, from questionnaire studies and articles on homosexuality among primitive peoples to biographies of the great and near-great

and analyses of theoretical problems in law and biology.

Hirschfeld also composed a questionnaire with 130 separate items which was filled out by more than 10,000 men and women. The data which he thus assembled served as the basis of major articles and of the book *Die Homosexualität des Mannes und des Weibes* (1914), which summarized all that the Committee and its supporters had learned in the sixteen years since its founding, and remains one of the major works on the subject from the pre-1933 period.

In 1919, with film censorship temporarily abolished, Hirschfeld and the Committee accepted an offer from Richard Oswald to produce a film about homosexuality. The result was *Anders als die Andern* (Different from the Others), which had its premiere on May 24, 1919. It was a breakthrough in the dramatic presentation of an unorthodox subject, and as such provoked bitter controversy, as its express aim was to expose the injustice of paragraph 175. When censorship was restored in 1920, the film was promptly banned, in no small part because of the unfavorable judgment of Albert **Moll**, who had by then become Hirschfeld's bitter opponent.

No less critical was an article by Moll that appeared in the *Zeitschrift für Sexualwissenschaft* (1927) in the wake of the International Congress for Sexual Research held the previous year, to which Hirschfeld was pointedly not invited because Moll resented the propagandistic element in the latter's activity, and also because of conduct which Moll branded as unethical, such as publicly exhibiting individuals who suffered from various psychosexual abnormalities and unabashedly discussing them in the presence of an audience.

For his part, Hirschfeld presided at one conference after another of the World League for Sexual Reform on a Scientific Basis, the first in Berlin in 1921, the second in Copenhagen in 1928, the third in London in 1929, the fourth in Vienna in 1930.

These conferences featured papers on the whole spectrum of problems of sexual life, together with vigorous pleas for the abandonment of laws and practices inspired by the ascetic beliefs of the medieval church: on sex education, birth control, law reform, sexual perversions and abnormalities, and eugenics.

Hirschfeld's campaign on behalf of homosexual emancipation had far less success, although he did effectively persuade the district attorneys in the larger German cities to refrain from enforcing paragraph 175 where private, consensual adult behavior was concerned. Germany was the only country in the world with an extensive network of homosexual organizations and of bars, cafés, and other meeting places which individuals seeking partners of their own sex could casually frequent. However, the Committee itself never had more than 1500 supporters, and Hirschfeld was obliged to admit, toward the end of his life, that the vast majority of homosexuals were unwilling to fight for their legal and political rights, and that the bourgeois parties were unable or unwilling to reform the penal law to bring it into conformity with the findings of modern science.

Furthermore, Hirschfeld's propaganda for repeal of paragraph 175 so alienated the conservative and clerical elements of German society that he became the target of attacks by the Nazis even while they were a comparatively small party on the far right, and as their movement grew, they persecuted him relentlessly, terrorizing his meetings and closing his lectures, so that for his own safety and that of his audience, he could no longer appear in public. In November 1931 he left Germany for a lecture tour around the world, during which he collected material that he shipped to the Institute for Sexual Science in Berlin. The Nazi accession to power on March 7, 1933, was followed by the destruction of the Institute and its unique files and library, and the dissolution of the Scientific-Humanitarian Committee to preclude its banning by the new regime. Hirschfeld settled in France and attempted to recreate his research institute on a smaller scale, but the Depression and mounting dissension within the sexual reform movement limited what he could accomplish. He died in Nice on his sixty-seventh birthday, May 14, 1935.

Evaluation. Hirschfeld's less public behavior motivated severe criticism, not to mention outright scandal. He is reputed to have been not just homosexual but a foot fetishist who had male prostitutes perform a ritual that involved pressure on his toes. There is evidence that the accusations printed in the Berlin *Vorwärts*, the Social Democratic daily, which led to the suicide of the industrialist Alfred Krupp came from Hirschfeld himself, after he had unsuccessfully tried to extort the sum of 100,000 marks from him with the assistance of a young engineer. During the Harden-Eulenburg affair his expert testimony as to the homosexuality of Count Kuno von Moltke indirectly played into the hands of those who wished to label homosexuals in high places as a peril to the fatherland.

Worst of all, although Hirschfeld made the issue of blackmail central to his propaganda for repeal of paragraph 175, he sought to wrest monies from individuals who had in good faith furnished him with questionnaires and other material revealing the intimate (and incriminating) sides of their personal lives. His willingness to profit from his reputation as one of the world's leading experts on sexuality led him to endorse patent remedies of questionable value, such as aphrodisiacs and drugs for restoring potency.

In intellectual matters he was guilty of serious lapses from professional ethics that resulted in a complete breach with the school of thought represented by Benedict **Friedlaender** and Hans **Blüher**. The former led a "secession" from the Scientific-Humanitarian Committee that culminated in the formation of a rival group, the Gemeinschaft der Eigenen

(Community of the Exceptional), which united the virile, pederastic type of homosexual in contrast to the effeminate male and viraginous female which Hirschfeld was trying to palm off on the learned world as a biological "third sex." Blüher in turn accused Hirschfeld of falsifying the text of his work of 1912 *The Wandervogel Movement as an Erotic Phenomenon*, stressing as it did the role of male comradeship in mass organizations and public life.

Hirschfeld's life and work represent at best an ambivalent legacy for the homophile movement of today. He never succeeded in formulating a coherent scientific explanation of homosexuality, and the Nazi seizure of power in 1933 spelled the tragic end of the organization he had founded. His career presents in retrospect as many errors and failings to be shunned as achievements to be emulated.

BIBLIOGRAPHY. Magnus Hirschfeld, *Von einst bis jetzt: Geschichte einer homosexuellen Bewegung*, James Steakley, ed., Berlin: Verlag Rosa Winkel, 1986; James D. Steakley, *The Homosexual Emancipation Movement in Germany*, New York: Arno Press, 1975; Charlotte Wolff, *Magnus Hirschfeld: A Portrait of a Pioneer in Sexology*, London: Quartet, 1986.

Warren Johansson

HISTORY

The word history refers both to the events of the past and to the systematic study of them; the practice of the latter is sometimes termed *historiography*. The Greeks, who invented the word, used *historia* to refer to any sort of organized study or inquiry; under the Romans, however, the word assumed the meaning it has today. Examples of Roman history are the continuous narratives of Tacitus and the biographies of Suetonius.

During the Middle Ages history was largely subsumed under the category of sacred history, though there were national and local chronicles and biographies of rulers. The Middle Ages adopted the idea of progress, both as a narrative device and an ideology; the idea persisted in later secular historians of the Whig type, who emphasized the concomitant growth of technical, moral, and intellectual progress.

The Renaissance and the Rise of Historicism. The beginnings of modern historiography lie in the **Renaissance**, when a revival of models derived from classical antiquity combined with the idea of fame to foster local and national histories. Although classical scholars became familiar with homosexual aspects of ancient history and **mythology**, these were commonly discussed in learned volumes of Latin commentary rather than made available in narratives for the lay reader.

From about 1550 to 1750 European historiography was dominated by an ideal known as the Exemplar Theory. This approach concentrated on the commanding role of great figures, some of them deserving emulation and veneration, others meriting only scorn. In this perspective history was *magistra vitae*, the great compass of how we should live, linking the experiences of the reader to those of the great protagonists of earlier times. One of the favorite models of this mode of history writing was the *Lives of the Noble Greeks and Romans* of **Plutarch** which mentions homosexual behavior as an aspect of the lives of a number of heroic individuals. Needless to say, this feature was not imitated in the officially sanctioned writings of Christian Europe. Suitably updated, this was a preeminently "elevating" (and judgmental) view of the past, which was not only usable, but peremptory.

Moreover, as there have been good and bad people, there have been good and bad eras. Outstanding among the happy eras of human history were Periclean Athens, Augustan Rome, and Medici Florence. The supreme instance of a bad era was, of course, the Middle Ages, the "Dark Ages."

New ideas came to the fore in the historiographic revolution that occurred in Germany during the second half of the eighteenth century with such writers as Justus Moser, Johann Gottfried Herder, and J. W. von **Goethe**. When the standard bearers of the new view appeared in the second half of the eighteenth century, the Exemplar Theory was already fading—though it never completely died out, exacting tribute even today in journalistic treatments of "Great Men" of the past. The new view is often called Historicism (or in German *Historismus*). Its outlook stressed the fundamental difference between the phenomena of nature and those of history. Nature, in this view, is the theatre of the stable and eternally recurring, while history comprises unique and unduplicable human acts. In the summary of George G. Iggers, "The world of man is in a state of incessant flux, although within it there are centers of stability (personalities, institutions, nations, epochs), each possessing an inner structure, a character, and each in constant metamorphosis in accord with its own internal principles of development. . . . There is no constant human nature; rather the character of each man reveals itself only in his development."

In its emphasis on subjective uniqueness the new orientation of Historicism accorded in part with romanticism. Yet the individual was not seen as alienated and atomic, but was rather immersed in that ongoing stream that is Process. With regard to epochs it insisted that sympathetic understanding must always precede judgment.

The Emergence of Homosexual History. Building on these foundations the nineteenth century has been termed the age of history. Yet when Heinrich **Hoessli** and K. H. **Ulrichs** began their pioneering homosexual scholarship, they found little in the way of comprehensive historical data, except for material from ancient **Greece** and **Islam**. Some other information was added by the English scholars Richard **Burton** and Havelock **Ellis**. In German Albert **Moll** published a volume collecting lists of famous homosexuals. By the end of the century, however, when the Berlin **Scientific-Humanitarian Committee** was formed it was realized that a comprehensive bibliographical search must be undertaken. The results of this inquiry were incorporated into the volumes of the *Jahrbuch für sexuelle Zwischenstufen* and the monumental tome of Magnus **Hirschfeld**, *Die Homosexualität des Mannes und des Weibes* (1914). After World War I similar, though somewhat shorter attempts at synthesis were made in the Iberian peninsula, by Arlindo Camillo Monteiro (1922), Asdrúbal António d'Aguiar (1926), and Alberto Nin Frías (1932). The world Depression and the rise of Nazism put a stop to most serious homosexual research.

In 1950 the contemporary gay **movement** began in Southern California, at first with little consciousness of its European predecessor. Gradually a certain number of historical articles made their way into such movement periodicals as *The Ladder*, *Mattachine Review*, *One*, and *One Quarterly*. In France *Arcadie*, thanks to one of its editors, Marc Daniel (Michel Duchein), published a considerable amount of historical material. Almost without exception, university scholars were afraid to touch the subject—even under a pseudonym. As a result much of the work was done by autodidacts toiling under less than ideal conditions. Since most of this scholarship was done under movement auspices, it tended to reflect relevant concerns: compiling a brief of injustices (histories of oppression) and biographical sketches of exemplary gay men and women of the past.

In the 1960s this atmosphere began to change. The sexual revolution itself made human sexuality an appropriate object of research. Then a new emphasis on social and intellectual history appeared, stemming in large measure from the group around the French periodical

Annales. Yet standards for homosexual and lesbian history continued to be contested, as seen in the quarrel in the 1980s over the **Social Construction** approach. Although several useful syntheses of the world history of homosexuality have appeared, much material, especially from **Islam**, **China**, and other non-Western cultures has not yet been properly studied and published, so that undoubtedly these will be superseded.

Conclusion. Without attempting to forecast the content of particular future researches, it may be worthwhile to offer a tentative scheme of how this research will be allocated. Here is a five-level model for the investigations of sexual meanings and behaviors in historical context.

(1) The universal level grounded in biology. This most general level recognizes that in human beings the libido emerges forcefully in adolescence and is capable of direction to a single gender. Further investigation of biological parameters is not to be discouraged but encouraged. There is also the possibility of detection of universals that are not, in any obvious sense, biological, as the universals of language, some of which are governed by principles of logic which must also be observed by thinking machines, which are not biological. They are suprabiological.

(2) *Kulturkreise* (supraregional cultural entities). As employed by some Central European ethnologists, the Kulturkreis is a large complex of societies in which certain cultural constants can be observed. Examples would be the Bantu-speaking peoples of southern **Africa** and the **Paleo-Siberian peoples**. The **berdache** phenomenon, which is historically recorded not only in North America but also in Western Siberia and Madagascar, would be a good example of a same-sex Kulturkreis. Another is the **kadesh** (cult prostitute type), found in many cultures of classical antiquity. The possibility of "submerged Kulturkreise," where only a few islands survive of once much larger complexes, must be entertained. If Bernard Sergent is right, the institution of pederasty, known from the record for only a few **Indo-European** peoples, is the relict of a once-vast family.

(3) Migration of individual motifs across cultural boundaries. For example, the category of the "unnatural" was first applied to same-sex behavior by **Plato** and his circle in classical Greece. It found its way into the Pauline corpus of the **New Testament**, being transmitted by medieval Scholasticism to the present. Of course such "unit-ideas" undergo modification according to context, but continuity must also be recognized. If one is studying the unnatural in, say, nineteenth-century texts it does not suffice to limit one's horizon to that century, especially since reading of the classics was still widespread during that period. The history-of-ideas methodology developed many years ago by Arthur O. Lovejoy offers guidance in this approach.

(4) Cultural epochs. There are attitudes that are specific to particular periods, such as the later Western Middle Ages and the early Renaissance. In investigating these care must be taken not to overinsulate them from what came before and what followed after in the manner of Michel **Foucault**'s epistemes. One must also beware of a too-easy acceptance of economic and social determinism, where "superstructure" attitudes are simply derived from the supposedly all-determining base or *Unterbau*. The detection of a pervasive pattern of such determinisms is the holy grail of the historical materialists of the **Marxist** tradition. Without denying such relationships in this or that case, one must be sceptical of the overall validity of such a research program, especially in view of levels 1–3.

(5) Temporary fashions lasting only one or two generations. The "**beatnik**" organization of sexuality of the 1960s and 70s (though it has roots and successors like anything else) seems a relatively limited phenomenon. So perhaps was the **molly** subculture of early eighteenth-

century **England**, which was snuffed out before it had much chance to develop.

The advantage of such a scheme is that it encourages scholars to pursue investigations in all time frames, from the longest (humanity itself) to the shortest (a single generation). It does not anticipate constants, but allows one to correlate those that seem to be emerging, however tentatively.

See also **Typology.**

BIBLIOGRAPHY. Vern L. Bullough, *Sexual Variance in Society and History*, New York: John Wiley, 1976; Wayne R. Dynes, *Homosexuality: A Research Guide*, New York: Garland, 1987; David F. Greenberg, *The Social Construction of Homosexualities*, Chicago: Chicago University Press, 1989.

Wayne R. Dynes

HOBOES

The hobo subculture of the **United States** is now largely a thing of the past, as it flourished when the railway was the only means of travel over long distances, and began to decline when the automobile and the truck shifted America's transport to the roads and highways. The best studies of this marginal subculture were done at the end of the nineteenth century and in the first two decades of the twentieth. There seems to be no precise European counterpart, though the vagabonds known from late medieval times constitute an anticipation.

The hobo was a permanently unemployed vagabond who lived by begging and had mastered the art of life "on the road" with a variety of schemes and tricks. Characteristically the hoboes lived along the railway lines, taking refuge in unguarded freight cars or nestling in the grass near watering tanks. The hobo subculture originated in the western United States and spread eastward. Recruited at first from the ranks of Civil War veterans who could not adjust to peacetime existence, the hoboes were joined by adolescents who had left home in search of freedom and adventure, by unsuccessful crimi-

nals reduced to beggary, and also by alcoholics who had lost their jobs and families and had reached "the bottom of the heap."

In this society of the lower depths—vividly, though reticently recalled in Jack London's memoir *The Road* (1907)—homosexuality largely took the form of pederastic relations between adult hoboes and their teen-aged companions. The youth, known as a "prushun," was obliged by the unwritten law of the hobo fraternity to be the virtual slave of the "jocker," his protector. The "prushuns" were generally between 10 and 15 years of age, occasionally older or younger. In every town the pair visited the "prushun" had to beg for their keep, and lack of success brought him harsh punishment from the older male. The boy was periodically beaten by his protector in a manner that was but an exaggerated form of the discipline then customarily meted out to the young, though the modern observer would perceive sado-masochistic undertones in the liaisons.

The sexual aspect of the relationship usually consisted of interfemoral intercourse, sometimes of anal. The passive partner is described as enjoying the physical side of the contact. Men who engaged in these relations generally preferred a "prushun" to a woman. Those who had served in the army or navy and then made their way into hobo life are mentioned as likely to be exclusively homosexual in their preferences. A few hoboes are said to have adopted homosexuality because of the scarcity of women in their milieu, as they were outnumbered by men a hundred to one. The gruff masculinity of the older partner was usually matched by a femininity in the younger one—a phenomenon of the sexual culture of the lower class in general. The male hustler also appeared as a denizen of this underworld. The jails of the period reflected this side of hobo life, and boys incarcerated in them were forced to submit to the older inmates. When the boy grew old enough to fend for himself, he would be emancipated from the "jocker" and would then seek a boy of his own in turn. On the other hand, if a boy became a source of embarrassment or jeopardy for his protector, he could be abandoned or simply murdered.

The hobo subculture had its own argot, changing from year to year but always kept alive by the oral tradition of the "old timers" in its midst. This language was a colorful commentary on the mores of the hobo, and ignorance of it instantly betrayed the newcomer. So the novice would sit by the campfire, listening quietly while absorbing the unfamiliar words and expressions.

The onset both of the criminal subculture spawned by Prohibition and of the modern welfare state in America led to the end of the hobo as he was known before the 1920s. The casual young traveler was more likely to hitchhike by automobile, a mode of travel not exempt from sexual opportunity, but lacking the element of camaraderie that rail yards and freight cars had offered. Yet the homoerotic side of hobo society, as one part of the American underclass, was perpetuated in the mores and practices of the **prison** subculture, where forms of homosexual dependence and subordination thrive at the present day.

BIBLIOGRAPHY. Nels Anderson, *The Hobo: The Sociology of the Homeless Man*, reprint, Chicago: University of Chicago Press, 1961; Josiah Flynt (pseud.), "Homosexuality Among Tramps," in Havelock Ellis, *Sexual Inversion*, 3rd ed., Philadelphia: F. A. Davis, 1915, pp. 359–67; Godfrey Irwin, *American Tramp and Underworld Slang*, New York: Sears Publishing Company, 1931.

Warren Johansson

HOCQUENGHEM, GUY (1946–1988)

French gay liberationist, filmmaker, essayist, and novelist. Hocquenghem was born in suburban Paris and studied Greek epigraphy at the Ecole Normale Supérieure. Swept up in the May 1968 rebellion, he became a militant leftist, though the French Communist Party expelled him because of his homosexuality. Hocquenghem joined the Sorbonne gay activists and was one of the first males in the Front Homosexuel d'Action Révolutionnaire (FHAR), which was formed in March 1971 by a group of lesbians who split from **Arcadie** (Mouvement Homophile de France). In 1971 Hocqueghem created a sensation at a forum of *Le Nouvel Observateur* (a left mass-market weekly), which later interviewed him. He also participated in writing the manifesto "Trois milliards de pervers."

Hocquenghem's *Le désir homosexuel* (Homosexual Desire; 1972), followed by *L'Après-Mai des faunes* (1974) and *La dérive homosexuelle* (1977), provided a radical theory for French gay liberation. Like Mario Mieli in Italy, Hocquenghem attempted to bridge Marx's class and Freud's libido in understanding gay love. He did this through an analysis of the privatization of the anus, the foundation in his view of both capitalism and homophobia.

Like Jean **Genet**, Hocquenghem was an early defender of the Black Panther Party and vigorously opposed white supremacy and racism. His *La beauté du métis, reflexion d'un francophobe* (Immigrant Beauty; Francophobe Reflections; 1979) traces the hatred of foreigners (in France: Arabs) and of queers to the same cultural uptightness. He likewise attacked sixties radicals who joined the establishment in his stinging *Lettre ouverte à ceux qui sont passés du col Mao au Rotary* (Open Letter to Those Who've Gone from Chairman Mao to Rotary Clubs; 1986).

As a child of the sixties, Hocquenghem understood the importance of publicity. He attacked the mainstream media in a delightful *Minigraphie de la presse parisienne* (1981), an updated commentary on Honoré de **Balzac**'s nineteenth-century philippic. In 1977 he became a regular columnist for *Libération*, a leftist daily where he edited the television review supplement.

His writings attempted both to bring a gay perspective to the mainstream as in *Comment nous appelez vous déjà? Ces hommes que l'on dit homosexuels* (What Should You Call Us So-called Homosexuals?) with Jean-Louis Bory (1977), and also to articulate an authentic voice within the gay press as in *Le gay voyage, guide homosexuel des grandes métropoles* (Gay Cruise Guide to Hot Cities; 1980) and *Les Français de la honte* (The Shameless French). He wrote for *Gai Pied Hebdo*, appeared regularly on Fréquence Gaie (the French gay radio station), and on television.

Always ready to experiment, he produced with Lionel Soukaz a full length feature film in 1979; the script was published a year later as *Race d'Ep! Un siècle d'images de l'homosexualité* (1980). *The Homosexual Century* (as the film is called in English) tried to define twentieth-century gay history; the French censors attacked the film. Michel **Foucault**, among those protesting to the Ministry of Justice, wrote: "This documentary is based on historical research of great seriousness and interest. It seems strange that a film on homosexuality is penalized when it portrays the persecutions for which the Nazi regime was responsible—strange and disturbing."

In the aftermath of academic upheaval, Hocquenghem was appointed professor of philosophy at the University of Paris at Vincennes-Saint Denis, where he taught with his beloved colleague René Schérer. Together with Schérer he wrote *Co-ire, album systématique de l'enfance* (1976) demythologizing childhood sexuality. *Les petits garçons* (Boys; 1983) fictionalized the French government's witch hunt against the Corral, a boys' school in southern France.

In the eighties, Hocquenghem developed a **gnostic** outlook derived from first-century Alexandria. With Schérer he wrote *L'âme atomique, pour une esthétique d'ère nucléaire* (Atomic Sensibility, Toward a Nuclear Age Esthetic; 1986), wherein they explored a free, sensual epicurean vitality which would reawaken dandyism or *gravité dans le frivole* (Baudelaire: "seriousness inside frivolity"). *Fin de section* (End of Division; 1976), a collection of short stories, attracted little attention, but Hocquenghem's fiction soon won a large audience as he developed his epicurean and gnostic themes.

L'amour en relief (1982), translated as *Love in Relief*, follows the liaisons of a young Tunisian boy who is blind and never sees how beautiful he is. *La colère de l'agneau* (Wrath of the Lamb; 1985) pursues St. John the Evangelist through many revelations. *Eve* (1987) crosses science fiction with Genesis and the author's own physical changes with AIDS. *Les Voyages et aventures extraordinaires du frère Angelo* (Brother Angelo's Amazing Adventures), published the day after Hocquenghem's death in 1988, chronicles an Italian monk's travels with conquistadors in America. Like the monk, Hocquenghem never abandoned the joy of adolescent rebellion and sexual pleasure, which he honed on the fine stone of French philosophy.

Charley Shively

HOESSLI, HEINRICH (1784–1864)

Swiss-German pioneer of homosexual emancipation. Born in Glarus, he spent his childhood there, leaving it only at the approach of the Russian army commanded by General Suvorov in 1799, when he was sent to Bern. There he learned the trade of milliner by which, on his return, he later earned his livelihood. In 1811 he married and had two sons, both of whom emigrated to America. Endowed with a pronounced feminine taste, in the 1820s he was known as "the first milliner" of Glarus, and was also a talented interior decorator. Acquiring the nickname "Modenhoessli" as a maker of fashion, in business he led a prosperous life until 1851, when he retired and spent the rest of his days as a restless wanderer in Switzerland and Germany.

Hoessli's main contribution to the homosexual emancipation movement, of which he was truly a lonely forerunner, was the two-volume work entitled *Eros: Die Männerliebe der Griechen: Ihre Beziehungen zur Geschichte, Erziehung, Literatur und Gesetzgebung aller Zeiten* (Eros, the Male Love of the Greeks: Its Relationship to the History, Education, Literature and Legislation of All Ages), published in 1836–38. The idea of the work had entered Hoessli's mind in 1817 on the occasion of the execution of a citizen of Bern named Franz Desgouttes, who for having killed his lover Daniel Hemmeler was punished by being broken on the wheel. Two years later he approached the popular Swiss-German writer Heinrich Zschokke (1771–1848), asking him to treat the subject because he himself did not feel competent to compose a work of literature. Zschokke did in fact publish his own "Eros oder über die Liebe" (Eros or On Love) in the eighth issue of his *Erheiterungen* for the year 1821, which amassed a respectable quantity of material on the subject, but concluded by reaffirming the conventional beliefs of his time that this side of Greek civilization was a revolting aberration which no other country should follow.

Disappointed by Zschokke, Hoessli set about composing his own work and printing it at his own expense. It was promptly suppressed by the authorities in Glarus, who forbade him to sell the book within the canton or to publish any more of his manuscript. He did, however, bring out the second volume two years later in St. Gallen. The unsold portion of the work was destroyed by the great fire that devastated Glarus in 1861. A planned third volume remained in manuscript.

In the opening section of *Eros* Hoessli likened the prevailing condemnation of Greek love to the witchcraft delusion of the previous centuries. He next set out the differences between the Greek conception of love and that of his own time, with copious references to classical history and literature and a plea for the toleration of male love. The second volume repeated his theses on the naturalness of the passion and contained an anthology drawn not just from classical Greece, but also from the Arabic, Persian, and Turkish poetry which Romantic authors had translated into German. Last of all, he sought to refute the false ideas about the character of Greek love that ranged from making it merely a contemplation of male beauty to stigmatizing it as child abuse. Throughout *Eros* Hoessli insisted that this form of love had not vanished, and was as prevalent in modern times as it had been in antiquity.

In his lifetime Hoessli's work achieved no recognition, but was acquired and read by a small educated public. It contained among other things the germ of Karl Heinrich **Ulrichs'** notion of "a female soul trapped in a male body," and documented the universality of male homosexuality as no previous author had done. The composition of an amateur, not a professional writer, *Eros* ranks as the first sustained protest against the intolerance that homosexual love had suffered for centuries in Christian Europe, and as such was appreciated by later activists who quoted it and reprinted excerpts. It was the harbinger of the movement that was formed only at the close of the nineteenth century, when the interest in evolution awakened by the controversy over Darwin's theories set the stage for a biologistic rather than a merely antiquarian and literary approach to the subject.

BIBLIOGRAPHY. Ferdinand Karsch-Haack, *Der Putzmacher von Glarus, Heinrich Hössli, ein Vorkämpfer der Männerliebe*, Leipzig: Max Spohr, 1908.
Warren Johansson

HOLOCAUST, GAY

The genocide of Jews and Gypsies in Nazi-occupied Europe has overshadowed the persecution and murder of male homosexuals, which is only now beginning to be recognized and analyzed from the few surviving documents and memoirs. Regrettably, in the immediate postwar period most of those who wrote about the concentration and extermination camps, and even courts which dealt with the staffs and inmates of the camps, treated those sent there for violating the laws against homosexual offenses as common criminals deserving the punishment meted out to them by the Third Reich. The final insult to the victims of Nazi intolerance was the decision of the Bundesverfassungsgericht (Federal Constitutional Court) in Karlsruhe on May 10, 1957, which not only upheld the constitutionality of the more punitive 1935 version of **Paragraph 175** of the Penal Code because it "contained nothing specifically National Socialist" and homosexual acts "unquestionably offended the moral feelings of the German people," but even recommended *doubling* the maximum penalty—from five to ten years. If any other victims of National Socialism had been rebuffed in this manner by a West German court, there would have been outraged demonstrations around the globe; but this one went unprotested and ignored—above all by the psychiatrists who until recently never missed an opportunity to assert that "homosexuality is a serious disease"—for which ostracism and punishment were the best if not the only therapy. Until the late 1980s homosexuals, along with Gypsies, were denied compensation by the West German authorities for their suffering and losses under the Nazis.

The Background of Nazi Views. The National Socialist attitude toward homosexuality was and had to be ambivalent. Most pro-Nazi eugenicists had in the 1920s quietly if not enthusiastically accepted Magnus **Hirschfeld's** arguments that homosexuality was innate and unmodifiable. They therefore saw no need to interfere in the private lives of those who by nature if not choice were already marked for biological death. In fact, Hans F. K. Günther (1891–1968), professor of rural sociology and racial science first at Berlin and then at Freiburg im Breisgau, the chief authority on such matters in the Third Reich, held that the genetically inferior elements of the population should be given complete freedom to gratify their sexual urges in any manner that did not lead to reproduction because they would painlessly eliminate themselves from the breeding pool. Also, Reichsmarshal Hermann Goering (and his cousin Matthias Goering) were greatly interested in promoting psychotherapy and giving it an institutional base within the Reich, even if their protégés were forbidden to mention explicitly the Jewish contribution to the subject (Freudian psychoanalysis).

However, National Socialism in Germany, like Marxism–Leninism in Russia, was a conspiracy of the seventeenth and the nineteenth centuries against the eighteenth-century **Enlightenment**—against liberalism and its beneficiaries, which included homosexuals in those countries where legal reformers had stricken the medieval sodomy statutes from the books. National Socialism inclined even more than its totalitarian Soviet mirror image toward the assertion of traditional values and beliefs—of which the Judeo-Christian taboo on homosexuality and petty bourgeois antipathy toward it was emphatically one. Furthermore, Nazi leaders, preoccupied with the German birth rate, foresaw extensive German colonization of that part of Eastern Europe which they meant to annex. Some of them even cherished the belief that homosexuality was the harbinger of race suicide and wished to encourage it among inferior races.

The principal figures who determined or influenced Nazi policy in regard to homosexuals, apart from Hitler himself, were: Heinrich Himmler (1900–1945), the chief of the SS; his protégé Karl August

Eckhardt (1901–1979), who after the war devoted himself to editing early Germanic legal texts; Rudolf Klare, a student at the University of Halle, who under the supervision of Erich Schwinge (1903–) wrote a dissertation, *Homosexualität und Recht* (Homosexuality and Law); and the Munich psychiatrist Oswald Bumke (1877–1950). On October 15, 1932 Bumke wrote a letter meant for Hitler's eyes, urging him to remove Ernst **Röhm** from his entourage because of his Chief of Staff's "corrupting influence" on German youth and assuring him that "homosexuality has in all ages been one of the most objectionable phenomena of degeneration that we encounter among the symptoms of a declining culture with great regularity."

Rationale. The confused and illogical thinking of these homophobic policy-makers had certain common themes. In 1937 Eckhardt published an article in *Das Schwarze Korps*, the newspaper of the SS, which mentioned that documents seized by the Nazis after they came to power revealed that two million men had been involved in the homosexual organizations that flourished under the Weimar Republic, but that a mere 2 percent of these—40,000—represented a "hard core" that was responsible for infecting the others. To identify and extirpate this source of contagion would be the task of the NSDAP. Such an approach contradicted the rationale of the Wannsee conference of January 20, 1942, where, with Reinhard Heydrich (1904–1942) presiding, Nazi leaders determined upon the physical extermination of the eleven million European Jews. For them a "racial Jew" (*Rassenjude*) was defined by ancestry—a meaningless criterion when applied to homosexuals. Their ideological motive for wishing to liquidate Jews and Gypsies was that these nomadic peoples were trespassing on the *Lebensraum* of other nations— another conception that had no relevance to homosexuals, inasmuch as the latter had never constituted an ethnic group distinct from the one from which they

individually descended. So while the extermination of the Jews was Hitler's pet project from 1942 onward, there is no evidence that the Nazi leadership ever contemplated or undertook a mass screening of the German male population in order to identify even "hard core" homosexuals for imprisonment or execution.

Hence Nazi policy in regard to homosexuals consisted in making the penal laws more punitive, as was effected by a legal novella of June 28, 1935, altering Paragraph 175 by eliminating the definition that restricted the offense to "beischlafsähnliche Handlungen" (acts similar to coitus). The new wording opened the door to prosecution for the most trivial acts, but at the same time the novella amended the code of criminal procedure to allow the Staatsanwalt (equivalent to the district attorney) not to prosecute an individual whose sexual activity had subjected him to blackmail. This amounted to a recognition of Magnus Hirschfeld's tireless assertion that Paragraph 175 was a major source of blackmail and extortion. The motives for the new law were never consistently set forth; the most common justification was the lapinist argument that homosexuality diminished the German birth rate with which the leaders of the Third Reich were obsessed. Nazi indifference to lesbian activity—and the official commentaries specified that Paragraph 175 could not be extended by analogy to women— was motivated by the assertion that female homosexuality did not interfere with marriage and procreation or with the conduct of public life.

The fullest treatment of the subject was Klare's dissertation of 1937, which found that of ancient peoples the Jews alone had proscribed homosexual activity. After rejecting the "liberalistic" arguments for legal toleration, he concluded that the solution to the "homosexual problem" was the complete exclusion of homosexuals from society. Even so, the constitutional biologists in Nazi Germany, far from abandoning the position which Hirschfeld had argued for thirty years, voiced it openly on the pages of criminological journals. Paradoxically, Jewish figures such as Magnus Hirschfeld (1868–1935) and Kurt Hiller (1885–1972) prominent in the homosexual emancipation movement had linked this aspect of sexual reform with the hated "Semitic influence" that the Nazis determined to eradicate from German life. During World War II German military courts often dealt less severely with homosexual offenders than did the less sophisticated American counterparts. On the other hand, instead of giving homosexuals dishonorable discharges, as was the American practice, some German authorities preferred to send them to the eastern front—to die in battle.

Actions Against Homosexuals. Under the legal novella of 1935 the number of prosecutions for homosexuality grew enormously—but many of those convicted were not strictly speaking homosexual at all. Some were political opponents—leaders of youth organizations or Catholic clergy—against whom the Nazis knew how to bring perjured testimony; others were simply street hustlers whom the police had rounded up in Hamburg, Munich, and Berlin, particularly to clean up the capital before the 1936 Olympic Games. Eventually even the Chief of Staff General von Fritsch was charged to break the power of the Junkers. The memoirs of Rudolf Hoess (1900–1947), the commandant of the death camp at Auschwitz/Oświęçim, shows the wretchedness of homosexuals in the camps. Himself incarcerated under the Weimar Republic, Hoess had become familiar with the realities of homosexuality inside prison and took vigorous measures to prevent homosexual activity among his charges. He later calmly wrote that he imposed a regime upon wearers of the **pink triangle** so severe that few survived.

Administrators used two pink triangles sewed onto their uniforms to identify inmates as homosexual, part of a system to isolate groups that potential leaders and troublemakers might incite. A Communist, who normally wore red triangles, might instead be given a black triangle for asocial (habitual) criminals so that placed in the midst of such types he would be an outsider, unable to organize them for political struggle. Camp memoirs mention that although homosexual activity was rife among all groups, other inmates most ostracized prisoners with the pink triangle. In the 1970s gay activists discovered and adopted the pink triangle as a symbol of their movement.

The Question of Numbers. Just how many homosexuals died in the camps, much less elsewhere during the Holocaust, can never be ascertained. Not all those convicted under the penal codes of Axis and collaborationist governments such as Vichy France, which in 1942 raised the age of consent to 21, Italy, Hungary, Croatia, and Slovakia were homosexual. Like National Socialism, **fascism** also deployed the charge of homosexuality against political opponents. A small percent of those exterminated by the Nazis on racial or political grounds must also have been homosexual or bisexual. Compared with the ferocity that the Nazis exhibited against Jews and Gypsies, their treatment of homosexuals was for a while what could have been expected of certain authoritarian regimes. It was not much worse than what the Soviets actually inflicted on them after their law of March 7, 1934—symbolically on the first anniversary of the National Socialist seizure of power in Germany—which like the Nazi law of 1935, under which convictions mounted from 800 or 900 in 1933–34 to nearly 9000 in 1937, prescribed a maximum penalty of five years for male homosexuality but ignored lesbianism. However, homosexuals were among the first executed, as early as 1933, by Nazi doctors practicing euthanasia on inmates of asylums, and the killing accelerated before the war in camps that tried to "reform" homosexuals through hard labor. Many died there of abuse and others who failed to perform when provided with female prostitutes were executed as incorrigible. Once the war began, German males became so valuable that fewer were incarcerated or exterminated for homosexuality, from 8000 a year before 1940 to 3000 after it. Another figure that will never be precisely known is that of homosexuals who took their own lives to end the fear and misery into which the totalitarian state had plunged them. Among all modern states for which figures can be compiled, Nazi Germany offers the horrible example of suicides increasing rather than decreasing in wartime.

Richard Plant, following earlier documentation by Professor Rüdiger Lautmann of the University of Bremen, estimated that between five and fifteen thousand homosexuals were exterminated in Hitler's camps in the Reich because of their sexual orientation. He makes no attempt to count the pink triangles exterminated in the death camps, none of which was within the boundaries of Germany proper: they were all in Poland, in the General Government established in 1939. On the basis of the figures for those convicted under Paragraph 175, many estimate 50,000 killed, but many of those were actually released or "reformed." The Protestant Church in Austria had earlier arrived at the figure of 225,000 homosexual victims of the Third Reich. On the basis of Himmler's statements that there were 1,500,000 German homosexuals in 1938 and half a million in 1944, Jean Boisson believed that the Nazis killed one million, presumably all citizens of the Reich. This is a wide discrepancy, and both extremes are misleading. The regime's rhetoric encouraged violence against homosexuals inside and outside the Reich, in occupied territories as well as in German satellites. No one has yet estimated the numbers murdered in random acts of violence which collaborationist governments also encouraged. Of these measures Vichy's laws are the best documented and fully discussed by Boisson, who shows that Marshal Pétain, at the instigation of Admiral Darlan, in 1942 raised the age of

consent to twenty-one for the first time, thus creating an invidious distinction between homosexual and heterosexual acts. Giovanni Dall'Orto has shown that in 1938, because of his alliance with Hitler, Mussolini began to persecute not only Jews but homosexuals, of whom several thousand were exiled to island prisons or remote Calabrian villages, while Jews were merely deprived of their professional posts. Ironically, in 1930 Mussolini had intervened in a parliamentary debate to prevent the passage of a law criminalizing homosexual conduct on the grounds that it was rare among Italians and practiced only by decadent foreigners who even if homosexual should not be driven out of the country because they increased Italy's supply of foreign exchange.

Less information exists on repression in Croatia, Slovakia, Hungary, Romania, and Finland, but Pilsudski's decriminalization of 1932 may have become a dead letter in the General Government (Nazi-occupied Poland). The Plant school argues that because the Nazis were not interested in purifying other races and rather wished to limit their reproduction, no persecution occurred among them. However, even within the death camps other inmates ostracized the "pink triangles," as Boisson poignantly relates, so that as Lautmann proved by comparing them with the control group of Jehovah's Witnesses and political prisoners, they suffered the shortest life expectancies and highest death rate, belonging as they did to a "scapegoat group" unable to form a strong support network. Even in the occupied zones where no collaborationist government existed, one cannot imagine that homosexuals suffered less during than before the war.

Because the Nazis aimed to "cure" Germans they thought curable, many who could perform with women, such as hustlers who had merely been selling their bodies, were released from concentration camps and ordinary prisons. Probably the chief cause of death of German homosexuals was from being shipped to the eastern front, where acute suffering if not certain death awaited them, not only to the *Strafbataillonen* (penal units) but to regular ones that had to have replacements. The army continued to avoid arresting soldiers as it had in the pre-Hitler era, in spite of Himmler's orders to avoid amnesty and prosecute homosexual offenders (only a handful of executions in the military is known). Many officers, some inadvertently owing to their natural homophobia, disproportionately selected homosexuals from the misfits under their command for the ever more frequent replacements demanded from other units for service at the front. So to the figures in Plant, which play into the hands of homophobic apologists who would belittle the size and extent of the persecution of homosexuals, must be added not only those exterminated in the death camps outside of German soil but also: (1) those killed by random homophobic violence both inside Germany and outside it; (2) those sent to the eastern front; (3) those persecuted and killed by collaborationist governments; (4) those who ended their own lives by suicide. The overall figures, especially if one counts those who fell into two categories such as homosexual Jews or homosexual members of other persecuted groups, would be not five thousand but many times that, and would include all nationalities, not merely subjects of the Reich.

Scandalously, a world which protested the persecution of the Jews in the Third Reich and was horrified by its other crimes against humanity remained indifferent to the treatment of homosexuals by Hitler, denied compensation to survivors, and refused to allow the pink triangle to be inscribed on monuments to victims of inhumanity. Many of these historians and commentators, silent about the persecution of homosexuals, lose no opportunity to insult and defame the German people for their unwillingness to resist Hitler's policies, even though they were living in a country where everyone was at the mercy of the Gestapo and the rest of the Nazi terror apparatus. Such contrasts are a measure of the continuing dishonesty and **hypocrisy** of the Judeo-Christian world and of the liberals within Western society on the subject of homosexuality—actions that effectively give the lie to apologists who would claim that the Church and Synagogue were no more than "innocent bystanders," powerless to prevent the injustice which they saw and deplored. Indeed, if Hitler had only killed homosexuals, these exemplars of self-righteousness might still be applauding him for having done just that.

BIBLIOGRAPHY. Jean Boisson, *Le triangle rose: La déportation des homosexuels (1933–1945)*, Paris: Editions Robert Laffont, 1988; Rüdiger Lautmann, "The Pink Triangle: The Persecution of the Homosexual Male in Nazi Germany," *Journal of Homosexuality*, 6 (1980–81), 141–60; Richard Plant, *The Pink Triangle: The Nazi War Against Homosexuals*, New York: Holt, 1986.

Warren Johansson and William A. Percy

HOMER

Greek epic poet. Most Greeks believed that Homer was a blind bard from Chios or Smyrna (which the predominance of the Ionic dialect supports) who, at a date which they variously placed from the Trojan War (ca. 1200 B.C.) to the beginning of literacy (700 B.C.), composed both the *Iliad* and the *Odyssey*. Although dramatically dated to Mycenean times, the late second millennium B.C., the epics sometimes refer to things that cannot predate 650 or even 570, because interpolations existed in one form or another when seventh-century poets cited the epics.

Although the poems may have evolved over centuries orally, the final version suggests a unifying hand, even if the view of some Alexandrian critics that each poem was composed by a separate bard—the *Odyssey* forty years after the *Iliad*—has not been abandoned by all. The contrasts between the two have been explained by aging of the author and differences in topics: war and peace, the siege of Troy and the wanderings of Ulysses on his return voyage. In any event, the author or authors owed much to tradition.

It is difficult to detect all interpolations and changes, especially additions of Attic terms as high culture became increasingly centered in Athens, where the Peisistratids in the mid-sixth century had the epics recited annually at a festival, and many believe the first texts written well over a century after the latest possible date for Homer's death. A definitive text resulted only from the efforts of second-century editors in **Alexandria**. These texts became almost sacred to the Greeks, whose education was based on them even until the fall of Constantinople to the Turks in 1453.

Like Hesiod and all other poets and artists through the time of Archilochus (floruit ca. 660) and even later Tyrtaeus (floruit ca. 630), Homer failed to depict institutionalized pederasty, to which almost all subsequent writers referred, many making it central. Though poets and artists around 600 B.C. make the earliest unmistakable references to institutionalized pederasty, Homer mentioned **Ganymede** twice, "the loveliest born of the race of mortals, and therefore the gods caught him away to themselves, to be Zeus' wine-pourer, for the sake of his beauty, so he might be among the immortals" (*Iliad*, 20, 233–35) and Zeus' giving Tros, Ganymede's father, "the finest of all horses beneath the sun and the daybreak" (*Iliad*, 5, 265ff.) as compensation for his son. Sir Moses Finley concluded that "the text of the poems offers no directly affirmative evidence at any point; even the two references to the elevation of Ganymede to Olympus speak only of his becoming cup-bearer to Zeus." Sir Kenneth Dover denied that these passages implied pederasty: "It should not be impossible for us ... to imagine that the gods on Olympus, like the souls of men in the

Muslim paradise ... simply rejoiced in the beauty of their servants as one ingredient of felicity." However, the **Abrahamic religions'** taboo on homosexuality did not exist in Hellenic and Etruscan antiquity. Societies that had the formula "eat, drink, and be merry" held that banquets should fittingly issue in sexual revelry. Anachronisms such as those of Finley and Dover should therefore be dismissed, even though Homer's allusions to Ganymede may be pederastic interpolations like those ordered by the Peisistratids—successors of **Solon**, who introduced institutionalized pederasty into Athens—to antedate the cultural prominence of Athens.

Besides the love between **Achilles** and Patroclus, two episodes from the *Iliad* not involving Ganymede have been incorrectly related to pederasty. After Patroclus' death Achilles associated very closely with Nestor's son Antilochus, who thus may have replaced Patroclus as lover or, rather, perhaps as beloved now that Achilles had fully matured. Both relationships, however, really involved coevals. Second, later poets interpreted the close friendship between the Cretan king Idomeneus and his charioteer Meriones as pederastic, perhaps because of **Crete's** reputation as the birthplace of pederasty.

Achilles and Patroclus grew up together, the latter slightly older. Later authors, believing a pederastic relationship to have existed between the two, were in a quandary as to which must have been the older, as after 600 there was customarily a ten-year difference. Some assigned the role of mentor to Achilles, others to Patroclus, to impose the disparity essential to pederastic liaisons in their own time. Of course the fact that Homer implied that they were approximately the same age, adolescent companions, does not exclude their having been physically intimate when younger, but it shows their relationship not to have been the institutionalized pederasty of later centuries. The plot of the *Iliad*, with Achilles' boundless grief and dreadful revenge on the Trojans for killing Patroclus, is homophile, as is the language in which the hero addresses the dead Patroclus and Patroclus' spirit requests that their ashes be united in the same urn forever.

So if Homer (or the bards whose work is preserved under his name) did not anticipate the pederasty of the Golden Age, he created an imperishable monument of male love and fidelity on the battlefield that is one of the earliest, yet enduring classics of world literature.

BIBLIOGRAPHY. D. S. Barrett, "The Friendship of Achilles and Patroclus," *Classical Bulletin*, 57 (1981), 87–93; W. M. Clarke, "Achilles and Patroclus in Love," *Hermes*, 106 (1978), 381–96; Sir Kenneth Dover, *Greek Homosexuality*, Cambridge, MA: Harvard University Press, 1978; Sir Moses Finley, *The World of Odysseus*, 2nd ed., London: Penguin, 1962; Hans Licht, "Homoerotik in den homerischen Gedichten," *Anthropophyteia*, 9 (1912), 291–300.

William A. Percy

HOMOPHILE

A modern coinage from the Greek, etymologically the term means "loving the same." *Homophile* is, theoretically at least, broader in scope than **homosexual**, in that it includes nongenital as well as genital relations, but less broad than **homosocial**, which comprises all significant relations between members of the same sex. Although the term had some circulation in Germany in the 1920s (e.g., as *Homophilie* in the writings of the astrologically inclined Karl-Günther Heimsoth), it was first used systematically in the Dutch homosexual rights movement after World War II. It was internationally diffused through the advocacy of the International Committee for Sexual Equality (Amsterdam) in the early 1950s. In the following decade the word homophile was adopted as a self-designation by a number of middle-class organizations in the United States, and it seemed for a time that it might prevail. Homophile had the advantage of clearly including affectional, nonsexual

relations as well as sexual ones, thereby deemphasing the perceived genital emphasis of the term homosexual.

The new militant trend that arose in the wake of the 1969 **Stonewall Rebellion** rejected the word homophile as a euphemism, preferring **gay**. Histories of the gay **movement** sometimes refer to the years 1950–69, when the word was in vogue, as the "homophile period." This phase stands in contrast with the more radical one that ensued.

HOMOPHILE MOVEMENT
See **Movement, Homosexual**.

HOMOPHOBIA

Although precise definitions vary, this term usually refers to negative attitudes toward homosexual persons and homosexuality. Characterizing antihomosexual prejudice as a *phobia* has been criticized for several reasons, including the implication that such prejudice is an irrational fear and a manifestation of individual pathology rather than of cultural norms. Despite its limitations, "homophobia" is likely to enjoy increasingly widespread use in American English until a more suitable term is introduced. Care should be taken, therefore, to identify homophobia as a prejudice, comparable to racism and anti-Semitism, rather than an irrational fear similiar to claustrophobia or agoraphobia.

Institutional Homophobia. At the institutional and individual levels, homophobia can be observed both through explicit hostility toward lesbians and gay men and through failure to recognize the existence of gay people or the legitimacy of their concerns. Institutional homophobia manifests itself in part through anti-gay laws, policies, and pronouncements from legislatures, courts, organized religion, and other groups within society. It also is evident in the social processes that reinforce the general invisibility of lesbians and gay men in society (e.g., in mass media, through definitions of "family" entirely in heterosexual terms).

The complex evolution of institutional homophobia is revealed through historical and anthropological studies, which indicate that the development of Western definitions of sexuality and sexual orientation has for centuries been characterized by disapproval of homosexuality. Among the factors cited to explain this disapproval has been society's presumed need to define and maintain strict gender roles and to link sexual behavior with procreation. Both of these ideological factors often are presumed to be necessary for promoting heterosexual family units as sites for reproduction and the socialization of children into the economic and social system. Other explanations for institutional homophobia highlight intergroup conflicts in which hostility toward homosexuality has been utilized to one group's advantage (e.g., in power struggles by religious groups or in electoral politics).

Individual Homophobia. This is exemplified by many heterosexuals' open hostility toward gay people (ranging from deprecatory statements to physical attacks) and their maintenance of a completely heterosexual worldview (including, for example, the ongoing assumption that all of their friends and relatives are heterosexual).

National surveys and laboratory studies consistently have documented correlations between individual homophobic attitudes and various demographic and psychological variables. In contrast to heterosexual persons with favorable or tolerant attitudes, those with more homophobic attitudes also are more likely to subscribe to a conservative or fundamentalist religious ideology and to attend religious services frequently, to hold restrictive attitudes concerning sexuality and gender roles, and to manifest high levels of authoritarianism. Additionally, homophobic individuals are less likely than others to report having engaged in homosexual behaviors or to have had personal contact

with openly gay men or women. Homophobic persons tend to be older and less well-educated than nonhomophobic persons, and are more likely to live in areas where negative attitudes toward homosexuality are the norm (e.g., the midwestern and southern United States, and rural areas or small towns).

In many empirical studies, more anti-gay hostility has been observed among heterosexual males than among heterosexual females; the highest levels of homophobia often have been displayed by heterosexual males toward gay men. This sex difference has been found in laboratory studies more often than in national surveys, possibly because the former kind of study tends to assess deeply-felt emotion-laden reactions to homosexual persons while the latter tends to assess value-oriented responses to homosexuality (i.e., whether or not it is morally acceptable and whether civil rights protection should be extended to gay people).

Empirical research on homophobic behavior (e.g., acts of discrimination, assaults on lesbians and gay men) is sparse, although interest in the perpetration of "hate crimes" based on homosexuality is increasing among political groups and policy makers. Several nonrandom surveys conducted in the United States suggest that homosexual persons are much more likely than heterosexuals to be targets of verbal harassment, vandalism, physical assault, sexual assault, and murder. The incidence of such hate crimes may be increasing, fueled by societal reactions to the epidemic of Acquired Immune Deficiency Syndrome; as an epidemic closely associated in the United States with gay men, **AIDS** has been used by some heterosexuals as a justification for expressing preexisting homophobic attitudes.

Various explanations have been offered for the existence of individual homophobia. All of them implicitly acknowledge that individual attitudes are formed within a larger societal context that encourages prejudice against homosexual people. The goal of such explanations, then, is to explain why some heterosexuals manifest higher (or lower) levels of homophobia than is expected by society.

A psychodynamic explanation proposes that extremely homophobic individuals themselves have unconscious homosexual desires which, because of societal attitudes, cause them great anxiety; their homophobia serves as a psychological defense by disguising those desires. An alternative explanation is that individual homophobia reflects ignorance about homosexuality, owing to lack of personal contact with gay women and men. A third approach suggests that homophobia serves different social and psychological functions for different persons. For some it is a strategy for psychological defense; for others it is a way of making sense of past interactions with gay people; for others, expressing homophobic sentiments provides a means for gaining social approval or for affirming a particular self-concept through expressing values important to that self.

Internalized Homophobia (Self-Contempt). Lesbian women and gay men themselves are not immune from homophobia, since they are socialized into a culture where hostility toward homosexuality is the norm. Homophobia among gay people is termed "internalized homophobia" and is understood to involve a rejection of one's own homosexual orientation. This phenomenon is analogous to the self-contempt felt by members of stigmatized ethnic groups. Recognizing and rejecting the homophobic aspects of socialization are important parts of the coming out process.

Reducing Homophobia. Eliminating homophobia at the institutional and individual levels inevitably must be a dialectical process since individuals live within the social context created by institutions, while those institutions are shaped and populated by individuals. Among major successes in challenging institutional

homophobia have been the elimination of homosexuality as a diagnostic category from the Diagnostic and Statistical Manual (DSM-IIIR) of the American Psychiatric Association, recognition and acceptance of gay people by some liberal religious denominations, repeal or overturning of several state sodomy laws, and the passage of anti-discrimination legislation in one state (Wisconsin) and more than 40 municipalities.

Little empirical research has been conducted on the effectiveness of various strategies for reducing individual homophobia. To the extent that different heterosexuals have different motivations for their homophobia, multiple approaches are necessary. When expressions of homophobia function to reinforce an individual's self-concept as a good Christian, for example, appeals to other important values (e.g., compassion and love of one's neighbor, patriotism and support for civil rights) are more likely to change attitudes than are factual refutations of incorrect stereotypes about homosexual persons.

While no single strategy is universally effective in countering **prejudice**, personal contact with gay people appears to be the most consistently influential factor in reducing heterosexuals' homophobia. In national opinion polls, persons who say they know an openly gay man or lesbian consistently report more positive attitudes toward gay people as a group. This pattern is consistent with the social science finding that ongoing personal contact between members of majority and minority groups frequently reduces prejudice among majority-group members. Thus, disclosing one's homosexual orientation to family members, friends, and coworkers often is a potent means for challenging homophobia. This hypothesis highlights the importance of institutional changes (e.g., elimination of sodomy laws, passage of anti-discrimination legislation, protection from hate crimes) that will enable lesbian women and gay men to come out with fewer risks.

See also **Authoritarian Personality; Discrimination; Myths and Fabrications; Stereotype.**

BIBLIOGRAPHY. Gregory Herek, "Beyond 'Homophobia': A Social Psychological Perspective on Attitudes Toward Lesbians and Gay Men," *Journal of Homosexuality*, 10 (1984), 1–21; idem, "Violence Against Lesbians and Gay Men: Gaybashing, Public Policy, and Psychology," *American Psychologist*, 44 (1989), 948–55; Kenneth Plummer, *Sexual Stigma: An Interactionist Account*, London: Routledge & Kegan Paul, 1975; Jeffrey Weeks, *Coming Out: Homosexual Politics in Britain, from the Nineteenth Century to the Present*, London: Quartet, 1977.

Gregory Herek

HOMOSEXUAL (TERM)

For at least half a century *homosexual* has been the most generally accepted designation for same-sex orientation. The cognate forms enjoy a similar status in all the major Western European languages, and in others as well (e.g., Russian and Turkish). Etymologically, the word homosexual is a hybrid: the first part, homo-, being the Greek combining form meaning "same"; the second (late) Latin. (The mistaken belief that the homo-component represents the Latin word for "man" has probably contributed to resistance to the expression among lesbians.)

The term homosexual began its public life in two anonymous German pamplets published by Károly Mária **Kertbeny** in 1869. (He used the term in private correspondence a year before.) *Homosexual* probably owed its inspiration in part to the term **bisexual** that had been introduced into botany in the first decade of the nineteenth century with the meaning "having the sexual organs of both sexes" (of plants). Writing in opposition to a proposed extension of a Prussian antisodomy law to the whole of the North German Confederation, the writer was by no means a disinterested observer. A polyglot and translator (not a physician as usually claimed), Kertbeny contrasted *homosexual* and *normalsexual*. His coinage might have gone unnoticed had not Gustav Jaeger, a lifestyle reformer and professor of zoology and anthropology at the University of Stuttgart, popularized it in the second edition of his *Entdeckung der Seele* (1880). Thus the term homosexual was not born under the aegis of pure science as one might suppose, but was the creation of a closeted advocate of homosexual rights. It is a curious irony today that some gay liberationists of the second half of the twentieth century oppose the word homosexual as a label imposed on them by the enemy.

In the period of its introduction, Kertbeny's term had to compete with other German creations, notably Karl Heinrich Ulrichs' *Urningtum* and *Uranismus* (uranianism) and K. F. O. Westphal's *die conträre Sexualempfindung* (contrary sexual feeling). Given its obscure origins, why did the term homosexual ultimately prevail? **Uranian** and its congeners enjoyed currency for a time, but were too arcane for the ordinary speaker, while the antonym Dionian (= heterosexual) never achieved the slightest acceptance. Westphal's cumbersome expression was doubly isolated: it was usable only in German and lacked the matching terms of the series. By contrast, the set *homosexual/bisexual/heterosexual* that finally emerged seemed to encompass (and trisect) the semantic field. Moreover, the abstract nouns *Homosexualität/Homosexualismus* which Kertbeny also devised served to denote the condition. All these forms, being grafted onto the trunk of the Latin adjective *sexualis*, had no difficulty in gaining international currency. And so in the first decade of the twentieth century—in the course of reporting the Harden–**Eulenburg**–von Moltke–Städele affair in Wilhelmine Germany—journalism adopted the Greek–Latin hybrid *homosexual* and made it part of the everyday vocabulary, while the expression *sexual inversion* remained limited to psychiatric circles.

Thus it was under the name homosexuality that the subject became known to the general public at the time when the German sexual reform movement founded by Magnus **Hirschfeld** was beginning its long campaign to change the law and public opinion in favor of those whose sexual activity was still stigmatized and outlawed under the name of **sodomy** or crimes against **nature**. The tireless activity of Hirschfeld and his associates consolidated the status of the word among professionals (physicians, sexologists, psychiatrists, and psychoanalysts) and among the public at large.

In English-speaking countries some controversy has arisen over the question as to whether the word homosexual is both a noun and an adjective or an adjective alone. Behind the seeming pedantry of such grammatical quibbling lies a conflict between those who claim that homosexuals are a "people," or at least a stable minority, and others who insist that there are no Homosexuals, only homosexual acts, which individuals—who should not otherwise be labeled—elect from time to time. John Boswell has persuasively traced this difference back to the medieval philosophical dispute between the realists (or essentialists) and the nominalists. However this may be, the first position (homosexuals as a people) may lead to separatism, the second (individuals engaging in elective behavior) may counsel integration. If homosexuals really are profoundly different they should form separate institutions; but if, despite the negative stereotypes with which they have been burdened, those engaging in homosexual behavior remain in the last analysis "just folks," they may look forward to fitting in as lefthanders, say, have done. Here we enter the realm of the homosexual concept, on the one hand, and that of political strategy, on the other, with the battleground the sense of **identity**.

Whatever one may think of the battle of the essentialists and the nominalists, which has been much waged in con-temporary debates on **social construction**, it does not seem likely that the use of the word homosexual as a noun will be extirpated. The English language has no Academy to dictate such matters of usage. And in Romance languages any adjective may be used as a noun without special permission.

Existentially, for any human being to affirm "I am a homosexual" is both an act of courage and an acknowledgment that this attraction is a central element in one's personality. In other times and climes, sexual orientation seems to have been or is relatively labile and peripheral. In Western society, however, where the term engenders strong and often negative emotional responses from the general public and from those wielding power over homosexuals' lives, there are many who feel subjectively that homosexuality—or gayness—is a crucial personal attribute. What role words, as tools not invented by those to whom they refer but given to them and wielded against them, may play in the reinforcement of this perception is hard to determine, but one cannot deny the bearers of such sentiments the right to express them.

BIBLIOGRAPHY. Jean-Claude Féray, "Une histoire critique du mot homosexualité," *Arcadie* (no. 325), 11–21; (326), 115–24; (327), 171–81; (328), 246–58 (January–April 1981).

Wayne R. Dynes and
Warren Johansson

HOMOSEXUALITY

In the sense used in the present Encyclopedia, the term homosexuality embraces the entire range of same-sex relations and affections, male–male and female–female. Some writers prefer to restrict the terms homosexual and homosexuality to the male, while female–female relations are designated **lesbianism**. Since there are in fact significant phenomenological differences, a good case can be made for separating the two phenomena. In earlier times in the West and in other societies the equation of the two was not generally recognized, and it may be that at some future point research and public opinion will concur in effecting a separation. For present purposes, however, consideration of male homosexuality and lesbianism together seems to offer better prospects of attaining understanding, in particular of the social context of homosexuality.

One of the vexing problems with the homosexual concept is its ambiguity with regard to exclusivity of **orientation**: does it include **bisexuality** and **situational homosexuality**?

Another question is whether homosexuality should include deep **friendships** that are not genitally expressed: male bonding and female bonding. Some scholars place these phenomena under the general umbrella term of **homosociality**.

The Greeks and Romans focused on the phenomenon of **pederasty**, that is to say, age-graded relations between males governed by strong cultural tradition. Rarely did they attempt a synoptic view of the whole realm of same-sex relations. The modern Western world, by contrast, recognizes other types of age-graded relations (such as **ephebophilia**, the attraction to maturing youths, and **pedophilia**, the attraction to children) but then assimilates all male same-sex relations to ones between adults (**androphilia**), which are regarded as the norm.

The **Middle Ages** gave birth to the problematic concept of **sodomy**. While the abstract noun sodomy could cover almost the whole range of illicit sexual acts, the noun of agent, sodomite, tended to be restricted to the male homosexual. Sodomite then, allowing for significant cultural changes, foreshadows the modern term *homosexual*.

This expression arose out of an intense phase of discussion in the second half of the nineteenth century in Central Europe. Rival terms, such as **uranianism**, contrary sexual feeling, and **inversion**, were coined and canvased, but in the end the word homosexual won out.

See also **Typology**.

HOMOSEXUALITY (ORIGINS OF THE MODERN CONCEPT)

The German term *Homosexualität*, the original form of the word, points to a concept of homosexuality that crystalized in Central Europe in the sixties and seventies of the nineteenth century. With some changes, this concept is the immediate predecessor of the mainstream of present-day Western thinking about same-sex **orientation**. Familiarity has made the model seem simple and straightforward, almost a given of nature. It is none of these things. The notion that modern society has adopted is a hybrid that owes its existence to the interaction and fusion of three remarkable semantic innovations stemming from historically distinct cultural epochs, two of great antiquity and one of recent origin.

Three Conceptual Sources. First, there was the Judaic law (Leviticus 20:13) that treated the union of two individuals having male genitalia as a single offense. Other civilizations of antiquity had accepted as a matter of course a dichotomy between the **active and passive** sexual partners. The consolidation effected by the Judaic legislation boldly disregarded this tradition. Second, there was the equation of male–male and female–female relationships in the more abstract thinking of the Greeks. By contrast, the ancient Near Eastern mind had never identified the two, and—as shown by the Babylonian myth reported by Berossus and echoed in **Plato's** *Symposium*—had traced male–male and female–female attraction to separate origins. But the Greek drive toward logical parallelism made it possible to regard **pederasty** and **tribadism** as two aspects of a single entity. Third, modern Europe—specifically nineteenth-century Germany—attempted a quantification of psychic phenomena.

The German Forensics. The acceptance of a mathematical continuum (0 to 100) made it possible to distinguish individuals in whom sexual attraction to others of the opposite sex was completely absent [the zero degree of heterosexuality = H1] from those who merely experienced an attraction to their own sex that did not exclude the opposite one [H2]. The recognition of exclusively same-sex oriented individuals [H1]—known to the ancients but denied by Christian theology and Christian society for centuries—was crucial to the emergence of the concept of sexual **inversion** in **psychiatry** with the classic papers of Karl Friedrich Otto Westphal (1869), Richard von **Krafft-Ebing** (1877), and Arrigo Tamassia (1878).

The investigators—being forensic psychiatrists—did not limit themselves to a descriptive analysis, but also entered the realm of the prescriptive and judgmental. They concluded that those who were incapable of feeling any attraction to the opposite sex [H1] could not, by virtue of the involuntary and exclusive character of their orientation, be held legally responsible for their sexual conduct, but that the others who, though primarily attracted to their own sex, could nonetheless function on occasion with the other sex [H2] were by comparison morally blameworthy and legally responsible.

Nature and Implications of the German Concept. The nineteenth-century conceptual innovation did not arise spontaneously, as a direct product of psychiatric insight or of the interrogation of homosexual patients. The new formulation was the outcome of a dialogue between the psychiatric profession and the spokesmen for the inchoate homophile movement, Karl Heinrich **Ulrichs** and Károly Mária **Kertbeny**. The word homosexual was invented by the litterateur Kertbeny and not by the psychiatrists, so that contrary to the almost universal assumption within today's gay community it did *not* originate

as a **medical** term, though it was subsequently used as such. Rather the new concept was dialectical in origin and stemmed (in the case of the **homophile** apologists) from the polemic need to combat the deeply rooted theological-forensic tradition of the Christian world that stigmatized and penalized sexual activity between individuals having the genital organs of the same sex, and to exonerate those whom public opinion execrated as guilty of "unconditional self-surrender to the immoral." Only in this way could the burden of centuries of obloquy begin to be lifted. Yet few developments in human thought are completely new, and in this instance the new distinction was superimposed upon the two long-standing equations noted at the beginning of this article, the Levitical assimilation of the active and passive partners, and the Greek conflation of male–male and female–female attraction. The emergent concept was thus an "old wine in a new bottle," or perhaps more correctly a cocktail blended from three different vintages. The two older strata had abolished two antinomies (active vs. passive; male vs. female) to create the theological notion of "crime against nature by reason of sex"; conversely, the modern stratum created a new antinomy: exclusive [H1] vs. elective [H2], yielding the psychiatric notions of "homosexual" vs. "**bisexual**." The fact that the popular mind lumped both of the latter behavioral types together under the term "homosexuality" does not efface the historical reality that the concept arose out of the perception of duality.

The two authors of the concept themselves disagreed in that Ulrichs was more the spokesman for the [H1] category, while Kertbeny was concerned more with the rights of the [H2] group, since their behavior was equally culpable in the eyes of the law, yet he argued that they had the right to choose the same rather than the opposite sex for purposes of erotic gratification. In fact, to limit the application of the law to the [H2] category in practice would mean that the prosecution would have to prove that on other occasions the defendant engaged in heterosexual behavior which was perfectly legal—a logical impossibility from the standpoint of the law.

Problems. As the outcome of its complex pedigree, the new concept was fraught with ambivalence and ambiguity: a century of medical and biological investigation has failed to discover any common denominator among the individuals labeled homosexual. Success in such a quest was precluded from the start since H1 and H2 are typically treated as if they were one: the problem of the occurrence of homosexual attraction is not identical with the problem of the absence of heterosexual attraction. Yet until a relatively recent date many researchers wrote of "the homosexual" in the singular, as if they were describing a discrete species. Though this linguistic habit is not common now, its long prevalence served to reinforce the misapprehension that a single phenomenon was under study. To the extent that the researchers did follow more attentively the nineteenth-century model, which focused on this single psychological trait of ability or nonability to respond to heterosexual stimuli, they perforce neglected the tremendous range of variation in constitutional and personality type found within both H1 and H2. Of course, it cannot be excluded that at some future time a genetic basis for the absence of heterosexual desire or response will be discovered, but thus far biology has furnished no evidence for this.

It is not surprising that in its perplexity the general public wavers on the issue, unable to secure any authoritative guidance from the experts. On the one hand, homosexuality is thought to be exclusive and innate [H1], so that fathering or giving birth to a child is regarded as indisputable proof that the parent is *not* homosexual—a "true" homosexual could not manage such a fundamental shift. On the other hand, when homosexuals are

exhorted to enter therapy in order to change their orientation, by a sleight of hand the conceptualization moves over to pigeonhole H2, taken to imply that individuals who have been functioning homosexually should function heterosexually. In this way a claim is made that the first assumption had categorically denied.

Interference of Related Concepts. The ultimate source of the confusion lies in the fact that the new term was superimposed upon the already emotion-laden semantic fields of "pederasty/tribadism" and "**sodomy**," neglecting the crucial element of the exclusive and involuntary character of H1, which had so impressed the rational minds of the pioneering nineteenth-century investigators. This lingering afterglow of the older attitude of condemnation hindered the progress of the movement for gay rights for many decades. By confounding exclusive homosexual attraction [H1] with elective homosexual attraction [H2] it played into the hands of an opposition that clung to the notion that "homosexuality is only a new name for an old vice," insisting that "homosexuality is a disease" that can be cured if the homosexual will only "renounce his way of life." To be sure, the disease concept of homosexuality represents a modernization of the religious notion of sin. But the conversion from sin to sickness was made possible by the initial belief in the statistical rarity of H1, which suggests that homosexuality is a human variant outside the normal range: a biological anomaly. And yet the opposing H2 model underlies the notion of change of orientation through therapy. Thus at the present day one half of the inherited nineteenth-century concept is invoked to diagnose disease, the other half to insist on the possibility of cure.

Kinsey. In 1948 Alfred **Kinsey** and his associates were to retain the category of same-sex exclusives [H1] in the 6 of their 0–6 scale, but because of their approach as evolutionary biologists they stressed a spectrum of sexual response and attached no significance to the crucial line of demarcation that had so impressed the European forensic psychiatrists. The Kinsey "rainbow" has had considerable influence on the academic discussion of homosexuality, but comparatively little impact on the popular mind.

Conclusion. The intricacies of the formation of the concept of homosexuality illustrate the general principle in intellectual history that key ideas are not forged through a simple conjunction taking place at a single moment in history. That moment represents at most a phase of crystalization, not of creation ex novo. Moreover, concepts are not simply the product of an impartial evaluation of data, but rather take shape in human minds already equipped with semantic grids. As Blaise Pascal observed, "Chance smiles only on minds that are prepared." In the realm of thinking about sexuality the theories are almost inevitably contaminated with ideology, the strivings of interested parties, and the wish to preserve an existing value system or replace it with a new one. The world still awaits a conceptual system that overcomes the serious flaws of the one inherited from the nineteenth century.

See also **Typology.**

Warren Johansson

HOMOSOCIALITY

A neutral term, homosociality designates the patterns and relationships arising from gender-specific gatherings of all sorts. When men or women participate affectively in homosocial situations, one may speak also of male bonding and female bonding.

Basic Features. In the field of lesbian and gay studies, homosociality has become a methodological tool. In 1975 Carroll Smith-Rosenberg ("The Female World of Love and Ritual," *Signs,* 1 [1975]), and then Michel Foucault (interview in *Masques* [13], Spring 1982), outlined the concept of homosociality as a way of broadening the terrain of gay and lesbian studies. At the international conference "Among Men, Among Women" (Amsterdam 1983) it was stated thus: [With the concept of homosocial arrangements] "we hope to achieve several results at the same time. In the first instance, it can be illuminating to relate sexual relations between members of the same sex to other forms of homosociality, instead of continuing to compare them with sexual relations between men and women. Secondly, it can be a methodological improvement to use the notion of the 'recognitions of masculine and feminine relations' and avoid falling back on the stereotyped notion of 'homosexuality.' Our attempt here is to open perspectives on the enormous diversity in (and types of) masculine and feminine relations which have developed in the past 200 years alone. Thirdly, the study of the relations between members of the same sex can contribute to historical and sociological theory on the development of homosexual arrangements in particular, and homosocial arrangements and their relation to heterosocial arrangements in general."

Homosociality can exist at three levels. First, one finds it at the level of societies, e.g., when social life is sex-segregated with men operating in public and women in private spheres. In this sense, Western society of some centuries ago and many non-Western societies today can be described as strongly homosocial. Secondly, homosociality can exist at the level of institutions—the **military, prisons, monasteries,** merchant marine (*see* **Seafaring**), schools, **athletic** teams and clubs, scouting. Formerly most public bodies in western countries were organized along homosocial lines (law, politics, industry). Thirdly, personal relations can be homosocial, as in friendships, **circles,** or cliques.

Female Homosociality. The second and third forms have been thoroughly examined in lesbian and women's studies, because of the general interest in the separate spheres of women outside the realm of male dominance, and also because of the difficulty of finding explicit sexual material with regard to lesbianism. So, female bonding as the affective participation of women in separate spheres has become an important object of research (Smith-Rosenberg, Martha Vicinus, Lillian Faderman, Adrienne Rich).

A lively discussion has ensued on the sexual character of female friendships in history. In this debate is implicated the actual question of whether the sexualization of lesbian relations was a liberation or a new means of subordinating women. Here Radclyffe Hall's novel *The Well of Loneliness* (1928) is an important landmark witnessing the sexualization of women's separate spheres.

Problems of Methodology and Data. For male homosociality, an even more extensive literature exists than for its female counterpart, but it has some major problems. First of all, it scarcely ever focuses on the intimate relations of the men in bonding. Secondly, when male homosociality is discussed, it is mostly seen as an exceptional situation and less commonly as a fundamental structure of societies. Taking the latter viewpoint, however, Lionel Tiger analyzed it from a sociobiological perspective stressing the homoeroticism of male bonding, as did Thorkill Vanggaard from a historical perspective. Bernard Sergent and Eva C. Keuls did the same for classical Greece, for opposed reasons: Sergent to stress the institutional and ancient character of pederastic relations, Keuls to criticize the phallocracy of Athenian "democracy." The histories of soldiering, education, seafaring, and politics have hardly ever been discussed from this homosocial angle— just as women's emancipation is nowadays generally seen as going along heterosocial lines. More specific studies in which attention is paid to homoeroticism have been done on English **pirates** of the seventeenth century (B. R. Burg), on English **public schools** (J. Gathorne Hardy, J. R. de Symons Honey, and J. Chandos), on the military (P. Fussell and P. Parker) and on the eros tradition (G. Dall'Orto and T. Maasen).

The Socialization of Masculinity. In many cultures the standards of masculinity are learned in such all-male situations. For many tribal cultures, the men's houses are the centers for male initiation; in modern cultures sex-segregated schools, armies, sports groups, and student societies were until recently and sometimes still are the institutional sites of male socialization. Even where such homosocial sites still exist, they are more integrated into heterosocial society. The strictures governing such enclaves tend nowadays to be much looser, because of the better possibilities of transportation, the extension of free time, the abolition of corporal punishments, and the informalization of discipline in most institutions. Where in recent decades such institutionalized frameworks are declining, groups of pubertal boys become more important for sex-specific socialization and the youngsters define for themselves their norms of manliness outside institutional frameworks.

The norms of masculinity are thus purveyed, from the time of puberty onwards, in all-male situations. But it was also the environment in which men had their most intimate (sexual and non-sexual) relationships. In novels, letters, diaries, and book dedications written prior to World War I, the importance of male bonding was underlined: men had their most expressive, intimate and strong attachments from puberty up until marriage with other men. Adulthood meant mostly responsibility, respectability, and thus boredom. Old ties of friendship could be revived in men's clubs and pubs or on festive occasions, but they could not surpass the emotional bonds of a younger age.

This world of male bonding and male intimacies is in decline with the heterosocialization of society. The rise of explicit homosexual identities and communities can be seen as a byproduct of this process of declining homosociality. Whereas in former times much homosexual behavior existed under the cover of homosociality, with the decline of male bonding, homosexual situations are standing more apart and are thus becoming more visible (and as such, more threatening to the homosocial groups).

With the advent of the homosexual identity, the homosocial male (soldier, seaman, cowboy, outlaw, fireman, cop) became the typical object of desire for homosexual men, and when in the last decades this border traffic between gay and straight society diminished, some gay men in their "**clone**" stereotypes tried to realize these homosocial types in themselves.

Conclusion. The subject of homosociality, and more specifically, of female and male bonding, has great relevance for gay and lesbian studies. First, as a sphere where forms of homosexual pleasure are engendered, and secondly, because it broadens as well as changes the perspective of gay and lesbian studies. As a concept, it alerts researchers to the differences existing between gay and lesbian culture. Finally, it is an extremely rich field which is insufficiently studied, especially the male variants, and one in which **gay studies** can display its strengths.

See also **Friendship, Female Romantic; Friendship, Male.**

BIBLIOGRAPHY. Janet L. Barkas, *Friendship: A Selected, Annotated Bibliography*, New York: Garland, 1985; Lillian Faderman, *Surpassing the Love of Men: Romantic Friendship and Love between Women from the Renaissance to the Present*, New York: William Morrow, 1981; Thijs Maasen, *De pedagogische eros in het geding*, Utrecht, 1988; Peter Parker, *The Old Lie: The Great War and Public School Ethos*, London, 1987; Carroll Smith-Rosenberg, *Disorderly Conduct: Visions of Gender in Victorian America*. New York: Alfred A. Knopf, 1985; Lionel Tiger, *Men in Groups*, New York: Random House, 1969; Ernst Günther Welter, *Bibliographie Freundschaftseros einschliesslich Homoerotik, Homosexualität und die verwandte und vergleichende Gebiete*, Frankfurt am Main: Dipa Verlag, 1964.
Gert Hekma

HORACE (65–8 B.C.)

Latin lyric and satiric poet of the Golden Age. Quintus Horatius Flaccus was the son of a freedman who cared for his education. In Athens he studied philosophy and ancient Greek literature. As a supporter of Brutus he fought at Philippi, then returned to Rome, where in the spring of 38 **Vergil** and Varius Rufus introduced him to Maecenas, the great patron of Latin literature, who after nine months admitted him to his intimate circle. Horace thereafter lived withdrawn, dining out only at Maecenas' invitation. The friendship lasted to the end of their lives, and in 32 Horace received from Maecenas a Sabine estate.

As a poet Horace is remembered for his *Odes*, *Epodes*, and *Satires*. The *Odes* are modeled on the Greek poems of Alcaeus, **Sappho**, **Pindar**, and Bacchylides, with the added refinement which the Hellenistic era gave to the short poem. The *Satires* are inspired by Lucilius, but composed in hexameter verse, though freer than in epic poetry. The subject matter—as befitted the son of a freedman—was not ruthlessly personal and political, but apolitical and universal: the vices and follies of private life, stoic paradoxes, and his own friendship with Maecenas are the themes. The *Epistles* in verse are philosophical and literary discourses modeled on Lucilius, Mummius, and **Catullus**. The language of the poems ranges from the popular to the most literary and formal; it is rich in imagery and symbolism.

In his private life Horace was certainly bisexual, with a preference in the homosexual direction. The love poems to women—to Lalage, Chloe, Lydia, or Pyrrha—strike the modern reader as artificial and insubstantial, despite the severe grace of language and structure which the poet inscribed in them. The poet's account of his love for handsome boys and youths rings far more true and sincere. The very intensity of his affection for boys precluded his deeply loving any woman; all the women that he portrays or addresses seem lifeless, and really unhappy love for a woman never troubled him. In spirit Horace was never young, never knew the intensity of youthful passion, and as he grew older, he became more and more a spectator of life and love, counseling his reader to observe the golden mean, even if he can be momentarily enthralled by the beauty of a youth. The poet regarded the phenomena of sexual life with a wonderful humor that gave him a magic touch over them all, but maturity had distanced him from the spontaneous ardor of the lover. His ideal was that of the wise man who remains unperturbed in the face of every event, from sheer happiness to unrelieved sorrow.

BIBLIOGRAPHY. Otto Kiefer, *Sexual Life in Ancient Rome*, London: Routledge and Kegan Paul, 1934.

Warren Johansson

HOUSMAN, A[LFRED] E[DWARD] (1859–1936)

English poet and classical scholar. The son of a solicitor, he earned prizes for poetry at Bromsgrove School and won an open scholarship to St. John's College, Oxford, in 1877. He pursued his classical studies so single-mindedly that he neglected the rest of the Greats examination and failed his finals in 1881, but received a pass degree the following year. For some nine years he worked as a civil servant in the Patent Office in London, while publishing a series of papers in learned journals on such authors as Horace, Propertius, Ovid, Aeschylus, Euripides, and Sophocles. By 1892 his reputation was such that he could enlist seventeen top scholars in support of his application for the vacant Chair of Latin at University College, London. He held this post until 1911, when he was appointed Professor of Latin at Trinity College, **Cambridge**. As a Latinist Housman devoted himself to the arduous and painstaking editing of the *Astronomicon* of the poet Manilius (1903–1930), an austere subject that could interest only the specialist, not the general reader.

Housman's poetic output in his lifetime was limited to *A Shropshire Lad* (1896) and *Last Poems* (1922). *More Poems* appeared after his death in 1936. The Shropshire of the poems is a contrived pastoral setting which if idealized is scarcely Arcadian in that its youthful inhabitants are burdened by life's frustrations and disappointments. Time and happiness vanish; the young and beautiful die; the army and even the gallows take their toll. Housman's verse forms are simple, yet fashioned with classical precision and a fine balance of contrast and paradox. The underlying emotion of the poems is often homoerotic, though the implicit tensions, when present, are too subtle for the average reader to appreciate fully. The unforgettable phrases of the poems betray a melancholy over male love and male beauty forever lost, but still alive in dreams.

The personality of the scholar and poet was opaque to his contemporaries, whom he kept at a discreet distance by mannerisms that gave him the reputation of being frigid and unapproachable. Those who knew him suspected a deeply wounded and repressed personality, but in his lifetime the subject of his sexual orientation had to be whispered; it could not be discussed in print. While an undergraduate at Oxford he had been passionately in love with a tall, handsome young man, Moses Jackson, whom he lost to the latter's bride— a source of profound bitterness and emotional deprivation for him. Rejected by the man whom he loved, Housman had to accept the fact that not only was he homosexual, but that he loved someone who could never return his affection. The further burden that the Church condemned homosexual expression as sinful drove him into an absolute and rigorously maintained atheism. Housman's ambivalence about his homosexuality certainly shaped his inner, emotional life; he felt guilty because of his homosexual desires, yet believed them not utterly wrong. In one of his poems he described himself as "a stranger and afraid/In a world I never made" obliged to keep "These foreign laws of God and man."

Once he had crossed the English Channel and found himself in a country where "the laws of man" did not penalize homosexuality, he at once set about gratifying his forbidden cravings with male prostitutes, including sailors, ballet dancers and other inhabitants of the Parisian demimonde. He also frequented the Turkish baths of Paris, and gratified his fondness for haute cuisine which had been raised to its absolute peak by such master chefs as Ritz and Escoffier. Here, too, he could acquire pornographic writings in English, among them works on flagellation, as well as the French and German classics of sexual science. So his double life did afford him some relief from the frustrations of the façade that he carefully maintained while in London and Cambridge—a pattern not uncommon among homosexuals who cannot afford to compromise themselves in the community where they live, but at an appropriate distance lose most if not all of their inhibitions. On a visit to Constantinople Housman admired the features and complexions of the male Greeks and even more of the Turks, in whom he discerned traits of the British aristocracy.

In his lifetime Housman had an ambiance of repressed pederasty, simply because the society to which he belonged would not allow him to be open about his sexual feelings. Only some four decades after his death was the truth about his sexual orientation finally revealed to the world. It does not diminish his stature as a scholar or a poet, but reminds the reader of

his work of the tragedy inherent in the inability of human beings to express their inner feelings or to communicate with one another.

BIBLIOGRAPHY. Richard Perceval Graves, *A. E. Housman: The Scholar–Poet*, New York: Charles Scribner's Sons, 1979.
Warren Johansson

HUDSON, ROCK (ROY SCHERER FITZGERALD; 1925–1985)

American film actor. Becoming a major star with the release of *Magnificent Obsession* in 1954, Rock Hudson came to personify unproblematic heterosexual masculinity for millions of women. Ironically, for most of his life he was predominantly homosexual. His image was carefully nourished and protected by his agent Henry Willson, who gave him his screen name and identity. Hudson's lack of acting training and flair seemed to help in establishing an air of authenticity that history has revealed to be spurious. When the rumor mills began to grind, and it was feared that the truth about the actor's sexuality would surface in one of the popular Hollywood gossip magazines, Willson arranged for Hudson to court and marry his secretary Phyllis Gates in 1955. They were divorced three years later, and Hudson settled into a series of male affairs, the last of which was with Marc Christian, who went public in a dispute about the star's inheritance. Having been diagnosed with **AIDS** on June 5, 1984, Hudson first tried to keep the matter secret—to the subsequent distress of his unwitting co-stars and sex partners. As his condition grew worse, however, concealment became impossible, and before his death on October 2, 1985, Rock Hudson's condition and his homosexuality had exhaustively aired in the media.

BIBLIOGRAPHY. [Rock Hudson and] Sara Davidson, *Rock Hudson: His Story*, New York: William Morrow, 1986.

HUMBOLDT, ALEXANDER FREIHERR VON (1769–1859)

German scientist and explorer. The brother of Wilhelm von Humboldt, he studied engineering and natural history at Frankfurt an der Oder, Berlin, and Göttingen. He traveled through western Europe, and in 1792–97 held an official position in the mining enterprises of the Franconian principalities. From 1799 to 1804, together with the French botanist A. Bompard, he conducted studies in exact geography in several countries of Latin America, determining the course of the Casiquiare River and climbing Mount Chimborazo to a height of 5,400 meters. He also measured the temperature of the Humboldt Current (on the Pacific Coast of South America), as it was later named after him. From 1807 to 1827 he lived with brief interruptions in Paris. Here he conducted experimental studies on gases with J.-L. Gay-Lussac, and also evaluated the findings of his voyages in America in collaboration with other scientists. His major contribution to science is the 30-volume work *Voyage aux régions équinoxiales du nouveau continent* (1805–34).

Returning to Berlin in 1827, he delivered his renowned lectures on physical geography. Accompanied by G. Rose and C. G. Ehrenberg, in 1829 he undertook an expedition into Asiatic Russia (the Urals, the Altai, Dzungaria, the Caspian Sea) at the behest of Tsar Nicholas I, whose main outcome was a worldwide chain of magnetic observatories initiated by Humboldt and realized by the mathematician C. F. Gauss. He also published a two-volume "mineralogical-geognostic" account of his travels and a work entitled *Central-Asien* (1843–44). Settled once again in Berlin after 1830, he compiled a five-volume work that summarized all that was then known about the earth, *Kosmos: Entwurf einer physikalischen Weltbeschreibung* (Cosmos: Outline of a Physical Description of the World; 1845–62). It was the last attempt by a single individual to collect within the pages of a work of his own the totality of human knowledge of the universe; after his time the increasing specialization of the sciences and the sheer accumulation of data made such a venture impossible.

During his scientific expeditions Humboldt assembled enormous quantities of botanical specimens (some 60,000 plants) and geological ones as well. He recorded the fall in the strength of the magnetic fields from the Pole to the Equator and observed swarms of meteors. He prophetically foresaw the advantage of a canal through the Isthmus of Panama. He recorded isotherms and collected data on the languages and cultures of the South American Indians. Through the accounts of his findings—models for all subsequent undertakings—he made significant contributions to oceanography, meteorology, climatology, and geography, and furthered virtually all the natural sciences of his time; but above all else he was responsible for major advances in the geographical and geological sciences.

Magnus **Hirschfeld** preserved in his volume of 1914 the lingering reminiscences of Humboldt in the homosexual subculture of Berlin, where persons who had known him intimately were living as late as the first decade of the twentieth century, among them the homosexual dendrologist Karl Bolle. Humboldt is reputed never to have sexual relations with a woman. To a servant who was also his lover, Johann Seifert (1800–1877), he bequeathed his entire estate. He had many feminine traits of mind and body, and his homosexual personality revealed itself in a certain restlessness that led him to travel in remote areas of the globe and also to explore a whole range of scientific disciplines. He was the last universal intellect in Western civilization, who in the tradition of the Renaissance man took the entire world as his object of study. Humboldt is still remembered in Germany as one of the greatest scientists his nation has ever produced.

BIBLIOGRAPHY. Helmut De Terra, *Humboldt: The Life and Times of Alexander von Humboldt, 1769–1859,* New York: Knopf, 1955; Wolfgang Hagen-Hein, *Alexander von Humboldt: Leben und Werk,* Frankfurt am Main: Weisbecker, 1985.

Warren Johansson

HUMOR

Humor is that which gives rise to mirth or amusement, though the notion often eludes precise definition. The psychology of humor has elicited much theorizing, the common denominator of which is that the element of surprise, of shock, or of unexpectedness is a necessary (even if not sufficient) condition for the humorous experience. Humor interrupts the routine, familiar course of thought and action; it activates the element of play which (as Johan Huizinga stressed) is a component of culture. Acting as the personality's safety valve, humor seems to effect a release from constraint or excess tension. Floating nervous energy in search of an outlet activates the organs of speech and muscles of respiration in such a way as to produce laughter. At the same time humor can afford a sudden insight into the ridiculousness of a situation, or an opportunity to vent anger and aggression, as in the case of a joke or witticism directed at a personal foe or at an enemy in wartime that places him in a ridiculous light.

Erotic Aspects. Sexuality has been the subject of humor since the dawn of recorded history. This is in no small part because of the incongruity between the attraction or the pleasure felt by the actor in an erotic situation but invisible to the observer, who can only note the objectively graceless or even repellent behavior by which third parties procure sexual gratification. The sexual act in itself has nothing aesthetic, even if the pleasure obtained from the physical contact of two human bodies borders on the ecstatic. From this fundamental incongruity derives the piquancy of the countless jokes, anecdotes, tales, cartoons, and pictures in which sexuality is the central theme. At the same time sexual tensions in the subject—and fears of sexual aggression—can also be alleviated by the mechanism of humor.

Homosexuality and Humor. Homosexuality occupies a special place within the domain of sexual humor, both because of the intense taboo with which the very mention of it was once invested, but also because of the perceived incongruity of erotic attraction between two members of the same sex—its departure from the cultural expectation of heterosexuality. The individual who departs too markedly from the gender role norms of the culture is bound to be a target of disapproval, expressed at least in the form of humor. Moreover, homosexual activity itself, aimless and pleasureless as it is to the heterosexual observer, can be the object of rage and contempt but also of a humor that incorporates symbolic aggression. Humor in regard to homosexual activity can be an escape route or symbolic excuse for the inconsistent behavior, or can express absolution from the cultural taboo in the form of an expressive laugh or indirect approval of what cannot be explicitly acknowledged. As homosexuals have come to be recognized as a socially discrete element of Western society, "fag jokes" have taken their place beside ethnic jokes as facets of intergroup tension.

Humor in sexual matters may also reflect the tensions between the official norm of society, which condemns all sexual expression outside of marriage, and the unofficial admiration and envy accorded the individual who successfully violates the taboo and obtains the forbidden pleasure. There is also the implicit denigration of the passive partner, who is seen as being used for the pleasure of the active one while obtaining nothing in return. These dichotomies are intensified in the case of the doubly tabooed and intensely paradoxical homosexual experience, which demands an explanation and justification that Western society has thus far been unable to find to its own satisfaction. Humor in gay circles can also have the function of a defense mechanism that scores points at the expense of the hostile larger society, exposes its **hypocrisy** and inconsistency, affirms the values of the deviant subculture, and rejoices in every erotic success achieved in defiance of the taboos and the obstacles contrived by the social order to enforce them. The need of the outgroup to maintain its morale can also be served by the mechanism of humor that releases the accumulated tensions provoked by the constant need for psychological self-defense. This was especially true when nearly all except "obvious" homosexuals had to maintain a heterosexual façade by sundry and ingenious means calculated to deceive the outside world— with all the incongruous and embarrassing situations that ill chance could inflict on the closeted subject.

Humor as a Dimension of Personality. It is universally recognized that humor as a creative activity is a rare and highly specialized psychological trait. The editor of one of America's most popular humor magazines in the 1960s commented at a public lecture that although every day's mail brought his office letters with jokes, cartoons, suggestions for features and the like, still in the whole history of the periodical only a half dozen had ever been judged suitable for its pages. Children do not possess a sense of humor; it is the outgrowth of experience and education, of a mastery of the surrounding world. Humor is also a largely masculine affair: all the great humorists throughout history have been men, even if women have excelled in other literary genres, and even the image of the clown is a male, not a female figure. Arguably, the woman as comedienne is playing a male role.

Psychoanalytic studies of the humorist have brought out the importance of the oral-erotic element in character formation, and also of the manic-depressive personality. Humor entails a subtle dialectic of ability to laugh (from the hypomanic side) and depth of feeling (from the depressive one). The realist in literature who tinges his writing with humorous traits is able to face the harshness of life and yet erect a screen of defensive humor that shields him from its pain and sorrow. The humorist has an intensity and seriousness inherited from the father, but also a strongly developed superego with cheerful propensities derived from the mother. A student of the humorist as personality type has found aversion to marriage, a pronounced wanderlust, and lack of a regular profession as the outward signs, with a split personality, a tendency to self-reflection, to play fondly with the trivial and absurd, and indifference to the world's opinion as the inner traits of character.

This inventory suggests a marked overlap with at least certain facets of the homosexual personality. A specific alloy of the masculine and feminine foreign to the heterosexual mentality, a decided antipathy to marriage, satisfaction in an unattached, roaming lifestyle, a need to reflect upon one's fate in the midst of a hostile society, and a deep-seated indifference to its opinions and judgments are all traits of the homosexual in Western culture. Even the capacity for self-irony, the ability to accept the ridiculous in one's situation as a homosexual, can be positive, survival-enhancing qualities. Noted humorists who were homosexual were Edward **Lear,** "Saki" (Hector Hugh **Munro**), and Alexander Woollcott (the prototype of the hero in *The Man Who Came to Dinner*).

Homosexual Jokes. Jokes on the subject of homosexuality are legion. They are usually invented by people hostile to homosexuals and so are tinged with malice. They can turn on the double meaning of particular words: "What do gay termites eat? Woodpeckers." "Have you heard about the gay burglar? He couldn't blow the safe, so he went down on the elevator." "Is it better to be born black or gay? Black—you don't have to tell your parents." "What do you call a gay bar without any stools? A fruit stand." In the Deep South a gay man is a "Homo Sex You All." They can reflect hostility and violence directed against homosexuals: "A gay man was lying on the sidewalk with a broken arm and a bloody face. When passers-by asked what had happened, he said: 'Would somebody please tell that marine on the fifth floor that fairies can't fly.'"

A particular genre of homosexual joke turns upon the husband who finds his wife in flagrante delicto with another man but is indifferent to the insult to his honor or even focuses his attention upon some irrelevant detail of the situation. A modern variant of this motif is: "The husband of the wife raped by the Mexican bandit is in the meantime forced to hold the bandit's testicles up out of the hot sand. When the wife later complains that the husband has not acted the part of a man, he replies: 'Is that so? Why, twice when he wasn't looking, I let his balls drop in the hot sand.'" Another version of the tale ends with the lines: "Here's my bed, and that's my wife in it." "But who's that young man in bed with her?" "Oh, that's me when I'm not here." The implicit notion is that this is a homosexual "front marriage" of the sort meant primarily to deceive the outside world, but also for financial or social advantage.

Other jokes turn upon the real or assumed competition between homosexuals and women for the favors of the male sex: A worried, elderly clergyman arrived at a hotel lounge that was a rendezvous for prostitutes and their clients. He was searching for a son who had run away from home with funds embezzled from the church. A lady of the night swooped down on him and asked: "Are you looking for a naughty little girl?" "No," replied the clergyman, "I am looking for a naughty little boy." The woman threw up her hands in despair: "Lord knows what's to become of us women these days!" A brief joke is: Homosexual (passing whore in street): "Prostitute!" Whore (in rebuttal): "Substi-tute!" Another story turns upon a homosexual patronizing a brothel in Paris: "Would you like a lovely French girl?" "No, I'm tired of French girls." "How about a Swedish beauty then?" "No, I'm tired of Swedish girls. Do you happen to have a good-looking boy?" "Monsieur, I shall call a gendarme." "Don't bother. I've had enough of gendarmes too."

A particular type of joke turns upon not only the ability of homosexuals to recognize one another, but also the heterosexual's fear (quite intense, in the past) of being taken for one: A field boss at a steel mill calls the office and tells the brand-new clerk that he needs three men to be sent out at once as blowers on a hot job. The baffled clerk calls the main office and says: "Send three men here in a hurry for a hot blow job." The voice at the other end says: "Hold your horses. The supervisor's two assistants are both here, but we're not so sure of the stock-room clerk."

Camp. A variety of humor common to male homosexuals, but by no means their exclusive property, is **camp**. Camp is grounded in gesture, performance, and public display; it turns upon an inversion of values that trivializes the serious but takes the frivolous seriously. The targets of camp are the values of conventional middle-class society, but the barbs are never fatal, because a good measure of toleration for the unconventional is implied (and needed). Camp also entails an element of self-irony, an acknowledgement that one is only "clowning" and not to be taken at face value. The "no man's land" of the homosexual who is consciously departing from the masculine yet cannot be truly feminine belongs in the domain of camp, and is often the point of departure for its refined manifestations. Oscar **Wilde's** celebrated tour of the United States was one of the first media successes of high camp—of which the "**counter-culture**" of the late 1960s and after was to see many more.

AIDS Jokes. **AIDS** has produced its quota of topical jokes: "Do you know what GAY means? Got AIDS yet?" "What do they call a troupe of homosexual musicians? Band-AIDS." "What do they call gay lawyers? Legal AIDS." "How do homosexuals spell relief? No AIDS." "How do you know that the flowers in your garden have AIDS? When the pansies start dying." "What do near-deaf homosexuals carry? Hearing AIDS." "How did **Liberace** catch AIDS? He forgot to clean his organ between hymns." The circulation of such jokes shows how quickly a new repertoire can be created, and also how cruel and vicious public attitudes can be.

Conclusion. Humor emerges in anonymous forms as social commentary on the events of the day, in individualized forms as the expression of a personality with a gift for satire and wit. Until quite recently the gay subculture had only "word of mouth" as means of communicating, but today the leading gay periodicals carry cartoons, stories, and jokes meant to provoke mirth in their readership. The periodical *Christopher Street* began as a rival to *The New Yorker* with its urbane and sophisticated humor, but was never able to rise to the level of its model. Yet as the gay world becomes more emancipated, it should be able to laugh at its own foibles and those of straight society, to partake fully in the humanity defined by the saying: "Man is the only animal that laughs."

BIBLIOGRAPHY. Jeffrey H. Goldstein and Paul E. McGhee, *The Psychology of Humor: Theoretical Perspectives and Empirical Issues*, New York: Academic Press, 1972; Venetia Newall, "Folklore and Male Homosexuality," *Folklore*, 97 (1986), 123–47; Alfred Winterstein, "Contributions to the Problem of Humor," *Psychoanalytic Quarterly*, 3 (1934), 303–16.

Warren Johansson

HUSTLERS
See **Prostitution**.

HYDRAULIC METAPHOR
The idea that sexual energy accumulates in the body until sufficient pressure is generated to require an outlet has over the centuries had considerable appeal. The notion acquires plausibility through observation of the wet dream, which eventually occurs in males if the semen is not evacuated through intercourse or masturbation. A more banal (though less sexual) model is that of the bladder's periodic filling and consequent need to void urine.

The first statement of the doctrine is probably owing to the Roman philosopher–poet Lucretius who says that the semen gradually builds up in the body until it is discharged in any available body (*On the Nature of Things*, IV, 1065). In its later development this idea has the corollary of separating sexual desire from the object to which it may be directed, and this separation has done valuable service in freeing sexual science from normative notions specifying that some particular object-class (as one gender only) is the only appropriate goal. As a device for relieving erotic tension, a homosexual outlet stands on the same plane as a heterosexual one.

A curious attestation of the hydraulic concept comes from colonial America. In his reflections on an outbreak of "sodomy and buggery" in the Bay Colony, William Bradford (1590–1637) noted: "It may be in this case as it is with water when their streams are stopped or dammed up; when they get passage they flow with more violence and make more noise and disturbance, than when they are suffered to run quietly in their own channels. So wickedness being here more stopped by strict laws and more nearly looked into, so it cannot run in a common road of liberty, as it would and is inclined, it searches everwhere and at last breaks out where it gets vent."

Some Victorians defended prostitution as a necessary evil. Without this safety valve, they held, the pent-up desires of men would be inflicted on decent women, whose security depends, ironically, on their "fallen" sisters. The Nazi leader Heinrich Himmler even extended this belief by analogy to hustlers and male homosexuals.

With the rise of modern sexology more neutral and less judgmental versions of the hydraulic concept appeared. An influential notion of sexual energy occurs in the work of Havelock Ellis (1859–1939) who saw human existence as marked by an unceasing ebb and flow of tumescence and detumescence. Somewhat later the idea was adopted by the Freudo-Marxian Wilhelm Reich (1897–1957), who evidently found it in accord with his interpretation of materialism. In Freud's own thought the dammed-up energy is supposed to be capable of transformation into some creative endeavor (sublimation). Finally, the idea was adopted by Alfred Kinsey (1894–1956) in his behavioristic concept of "sexual outlets."

Despite its appeal, the metaphor is not unproblematic. The hydraulic idea rests upon materialist reductionism, identifying the accumulation of semen with the strengthening of sexual desire. Yet the two do not necessarily act in concert, as anyone knows who has visited some sexual resort such as a sauna and felt sexual desire far more frequently than the body is able to replenish its supply of semen. Conversely, one may go for long periods while the body is manufacturing semen without feeling sexual desire. The hydraulic concept of sexual desire seems one-sided: it does not take into account the key role of external stimuli in triggering desire—not to mention feelings and ideas not directly linked to simple organic processes.

Wayne R. Dynes

HYPOCRISY

Hypocrisy is a combination of malice with an external appearance of goodness whereby a human being deceives himself or others. The Greek word *hypokrites* used in the Gospels signified in profane Greek an actor, one who played a role on the stage that was not his true persona. The subject of hypocrisy merits particular attention in a work on homosexuality if only because many reference works (such as the three editions of the *Great Soviet Encyclopedia* and the new, multi-volume *Theologische Realenzyklopädie*) have no entry for it at all, and even some religious encyclopedias merely summarize Jesus' reproaches to the scribes and Pharisees, as if hypocrisy had indeed flourished among the Jews in New Testament times but vanished with the triumph of **Christianity**.

In general terms, the hypocrite feigns a morality and a virtue that are foreign to his inner self. In a religious context, he attempts to deceive God by outward compliance with his commandments that masks the inner unbelief of the soul. For Jesus the hypocrisy of Pharisaic circles lay in their minute observance of the ritual and ceremonial laws of **Judaism**, while neglecting and even violating the moral precepts of their religion.

Historical Considerations. In the high Middle Ages the Christian Church established itself as an absolute moral authority within a closed system. From the end of the thirteenth century onward, it imposed upon the homosexuals of Western Europe a regime of lifelong hypocrisy if they were to exist within a society that rigorously tabooed every form of homoerotic attraction and gratification. They were obliged to profess an exclusive interest in the opposite sex, to engage in courtship and other heterosexual rituals, and even to enter marriages which they had not the slightest inclination or wish to consummate. The art of masking his true interests and desires became part of the socialization of every homosexual, a crux of his "human condition," and a lifelong burden and torment.

Donald Webster Cory (pseudonym of Edward Sagarin) wrote in his landmark *The Homosexual in America* (1951): "Society has handed me a mask to wear, a ukase that it shall never be lifted except in the presence of those who hide with me behind its protective shadows. Everywhere I go, at all times and before all sections of society, I pretend. As my being rebels against the hypocrisy that is forced upon me, I realize that its greatest repercussion has been the wave of self-doubt that I must harbor. . . . And, though adamant, on an intellectual level, in my negative response [to this self-doubt], I find it difficult to reconcile self-pride with cowardice, abnegation, the wearing of the mask and the espousal of hypocrisy—in short, with an outward acceptance of the mores of the hostile society."

Canon Derrick Sherwin Bailey asserted in his *Homosexuality and the Western Christian Tradition* (1955): "It is not as if, throughout the last two millennia, reluctant legislatures had been forced by the spiritual authority to enact laws and to prescribe punishments which they secretly detested. . . . In the Middle Ages ecclesiastic and layman, Church and State, were in principle unanimous . . . about the recompense meet for indulgence in homosexual practices." But later in the same volume he pleads on behalf of the Church: "None of these enactments, as far as the evidence goes, seems to have been implemented by any vigorous campaign to suppress sodomy or to exterminate the pederast. . . . There is no proof that large numbers of persons were put to death simply and solely because they had committed some homosexual offence. Indeed, it is doubtful whether such delinquents were ever handed over by the Church to the civil power after conviction in the ecclesiastical courts. . . . In practice homosexual offenders only became liable to the severity of the law if their behaviour was attributable to heretical ideas, or if immorality in conduct was accompanied by grave error in belief."

In other words, medieval legislators unanimously held that the crime of Sodom—because it threatened the community with divine retribution—merited the penalty of death, but after enacting the appropriate laws enforced them only in rare and exceptional cases where the accused was guilty as well of heresy. A fuller confession of the hypocrisy of church and state in regard to homosexuality could hardly be imagined. And in fact, prosecutions were sporadic, often limited to brief periods during which the populace was excited by religious fanatics, and never succeeded in apprehending a majority of those engaging in such "unnatural" practices. But as a result of the policy of the Church, homosexuals were driven to the margin of Christian society to eke out a clandestine existence fraught with illegality and insecurity, the prey of police informers and blackmailers, and always exposed to extortion, robbery, and violence.

Contemporary Forms. On the subject of homosexuality cowardice and hypocrisy have long been second nature. The compulsion to play the hypocrite was a straitjacket that tore into the flesh of every homosexual in the Western world, yet was also the *Tarnhelm*, the cap that made him invisible to an uncomprehending and vindictive society. That this form of medieval intolerance should have survived into the last quarter of the twentieth century bears witness to the tenacity with which the church clings to its medieval beliefs, even in the midst of an otherwise enlightened political order.

The newest guise of hypocrisy has been the assertion of not a few theologians and church bodies that "the homosexual condition" is morally neutral, but that every expression of it is unnatural and immoral, that church and society should accept the homosexual but only on the condition that he refrain from his perverted behavior. But what practical value can such toleration have for the exclusively homosexual individual? It would accord him no more right to sexual expression than he had in the late Middle Ages; the difference is one of terminology, not of substance. Another argument is that "society should keep the laws against sodomy on the books but not enforce them" in order to express its disapproval of homosexual conduct. Such a policy violates elementary principles of jurisprudence, namely that the subject of the law should know his rights and obligations and that the law should be enforced uniformly, not sporadically or capriciously. Having seldom enforced statutes on the books invites random violence against victims who know that the law affords them no protection, while sanctioning arbitrary acts of police power and encouraging police harassment and corruption that in turn strengthen the grip of the underworld on the public life of the gay community.

Critique. Aleksandr Solzhenitsyn, in his *Letter to the Soviet Leaders* (1974), writes of the official ideology of Marxism–Leninism: "In our country today *nothing constructive rests upon it;* it is a sham, cardboard, theatrical prop—take it away and nothing will collapse, nothing will even wobble. . . . The ideology does nothing now but sap our strength and bind us. It clogs up the whole life of society—minds, tongues, radio and press—with lies, lies, lies. For how else can something dead pretend that it is living except by erecting a scaffolding of lies?" All this is true, *mutatis mutandis,* of the situation of the homosexual in Western society: nothing constructive rests upon the official ideology of obligatory heterosexuality; take it away and nothing will collapse or even wobble. The fiction of an ascetic morality does nothing but sap the strength of homosexuals and bind them; it clogs up their entire lives with lies, lies, lies. Acceptance of the principle that the individual should be forthright about his sexual interests and orientation—even while respecting the citizen's right to the privacy of his sexual acts—is the precondition for dealing honestly with the problems of sexual life and for promoting the legitimate goals of the state as they pertain to sexual activity and its consequences. The demand of the gay liberation movement for the right to "come out," to live one's sexual life truthfully and unashamedly, to end the regime of obligatory heterosexuality, parallels Solzhenitsyn's appeal to the Soviet leadership to end the anachronistic rule of unanimity and conformity in political life. This goal—the end of hypocrisy in sexual life—will serve a higher morality than the one which condemns every expression of the erotic impulse as "sinful" and strives for asexuality as a glorious ideal.

Warren Johansson

IBYCUS
(SIXTH CENTURY B.C.)

Greek lyric poet. Ibycus sprang from a noble family of Rhegium in Magna Grecia. His lyrical narrative poems liberally endowed myths with **pederasty**. Refusing to become a tyrant at home, he went to the court of the pederastic tyrant Polycrates. Wealthy from commerce and piracy, Polycrates raised Samos to the forefront of Hellenic art and literature. In fear of conspiracies, he burned the palestrae (**gymnasia**), forcing Pythagoras into exile, where he became one of the first homosexual **exiles and émigrés**. Soon thereafter the Persians crucified him in 522 and sent Ibycus and Simonides into exile, where Ibycus sang of love in his old age—especially of love for the tyrant's son.

The **Alexandrian** scholars collected his poems in seven books: choral poems and encomia, and a great many love poems, hardly any of which have survived because of the ravages of time and Christian disapprobation. Cicero deemed him more amorous than **Sappho**'s compatriot Alcaeus—perhaps the first pederastic poet, or even Anacreon—and the **Greek Anthology** described him as one who "culled the sweet bloom of Persuasion and of the love of lads." Because **Horace**, **Catullus**, and some poets of the *Greek Anthology* imitated him, one can derive a fair picture of his carefree, insouciant, promiscuous loves. To one of his eromenoi he wrote: "Euryalus, offshoot of charming graces, object of the fair-haired maidens' care, Cypris and mild-eyed Persuasion have reared you in the midst of rosy flowers" (fr. 6).

William A. Percy

IDENTITY

Individual identity may be defined as a sense of the unity and persistence of personality or core consciousness, an awareness of a stable framework of self, related to but separate from the surrounding environment. One of the pitfalls of the term is that the existence of a *sense* of identity as so described may be considered tantamount to proof that such a unitary, persistent, stable self is an actual fact. This last assumption has sometimes been rejected (e.g., by **Buddhists**). Psychologically, identity seems to be much more fluid objectively than subjectively. While the word is in common circulation, it remains an ambiguous term, and even to some **psychologists** a dangerously misleading one.

Basic Features. In 1690 the English philosopher John Locke wrote of identity in the psychological sense as "that sameness of rational being." By 1820 Washington Irving had posited the idea of loss of identity in the case of a character who was not sure whether he was himself or another person. In the 1960s the psychoanalyst Erik Erikson popularized the notion of an "identity crisis" as an "interval between youth and adulthood" when one seeks to achieve an inner and outer coherence following a break away from the parent-derived identity and the beginnings of a new adult sense of self.

In addition to the concept of an individual identity, there is the notion of a group-derived but individually self-applied social identity which may be lifelong (e.g., being a female or an Italian) or may change over time (e.g., being a football player or a stockbroker). Group-derived identities are seldom unitary in any sense, as each individual feels a part of more than one group. A modern phenomenon seems to be an increasing tendency to build social identities around **subcultures** rather than local geographic units, nations, classes, and occupations.

Sexual Aspects. Today, some gay **liberation** spokespeople perceive the process of **coming out** as one of forging a gay identity which supersedes or takes precedence over all other group-derived identity; others reject this view as reflecting an excessive separatism, regarding the homosexual element in personality as not radically sundered from the identity-deriving elements predominant in heterosexuals. The gay-identity position has also come under attack from a neo-nominalism that insists that scientifically there is no such thing as a "homosexual" as a noun, but rather the word can only be used as an adjective describing a kind of behavior open to any human being; the advocates of this position would not, however, deny the existence of a (sub)culturally-constructed sense of identity independent of scientific standing.

Some prefer to address the question in terms of self-concept. Yet is the self unitary; or a bundle of subselves; or lacking in substance altogether? The second and third formulations may explain some aspects of cognitive dissonance with respect to homosexuality, as seen in the case of the late Roy Cohn, a protagonist in the **McCarthy** hearings, who seemed both to deny and to affirm his homosexuality. This phenomenon may be also be explained if one thinks of the self as a mediator between public identity or persona ("normal") and the private identity (in some individuals, expressed only in **fantasies**). There are other individuals, such as the poet John Berryman (1914–1972), whose homosexual side emerges only in **alcoholic** bouts, but here it may be more properly said that it was his behavior which was otherwise repressed, not his identity. If Berryman had acted homosexually whether drunk or sober, but only felt himself to be gay when drunk, then one could speak of a repressed identity.

Homosexual behavior need not be related to identity at all, but may be seen as a casual or situational or revenue-producing activity only. To take a clear case, the macho **prisoner** who uses another male as a substitute female until he is released never deals with any sense of homosexual identity, peripheral or central, public or private. There seems to be a requirement for a socially mediated model of "homosexual identity" which an individual can conceive of applying to himself before the question can even arise. Perhaps relevant here is the question of a **"bisexual** identity" which has often arisen in individuals without reference to a group or **subculture** at all, but based on models provided by the general culture.

In the integrative process that occurs with the acknowledgement of one's homosexual identity and its management in the course of life, it may have varying degrees of centrality. How does homosexuality migrate from one personality region, say from a peripheral one to a central one and then out again? How does it achieve the status of a *master identity*, only perhaps to become less dominant later? Perhaps such questions must await answers to more preliminary enigmas such as how sexual **orientation** itself can change over the course of time.

Clearly many questions remain for further research. Since the matters discussed in this article are among the thorniest addressed by the human sciences, one cannot expect that perfect clarity will be soon achieved—and perhaps it never will.

BIBLIOGRAPHY. Vivienne C. Cass, "Homosexual Identity: A Concept in Need of Definition," *Journal of Homosexuality*, 9:2–3 (1983–84), 105–26; William Du Bay, *Gay Identity: The Self Under Ban*, Jefferson: McFarland, 1987; Jon Elster, ed., *The Multiple Self*, Cambridge: Cambridge University Press, 1986; Barbara Ponse, *Identities in the Lesbian World: The Social Construction* of Self, Westport, CT: Greenwood Press, 1978; Richard R. Troiden, *Gay and Lesbian Identity: A Sociological Analysis*, Dix Hills, NJ: General Hall, 1988; Thomas S. Weinberg, *Gay Men, Gay Selves: The Social Construction of Homosexual Identities*, New York: Irvington Press, 1983.

Stephen Donaldson

IMMATURITY THEORY

When confronted with a teenager's homosexuality or lesbianism, parents will often exclaim, "It's just a phase. S/he will grow out of it." While this view reflects popular ideas of personality growth, it also finds a learned prop in the **psychoanalytic** idea that human bisexuality is a halfway house along a path that is always directed toward a final goal of heterosexual maturity. In keeping with this premise the persistence of a homosexual pattern in adult life is ascribed to "arrested development."

The immaturity notion also accords with the folkloric view that a "little experimentation" is permissible, as long as it does not "become a habit." This motif borders on the concept of deviant sex as self-indulgence, a flight from the serious responsibilities imposed by raising a family. In clinical sessions **psychiatrists** have had recourse to the reproach of immaturity as a lever to induce young clients to give up their homosexuality.

Of course there are individuals who try a few homosexual acts in youth and, having then found that this is not where their major interest lies, come to live essentially heterosexual lives. Other young people, aware of the stigma that still attaches to homosexuality, cling to the immaturity notion as a device of denial, refusing to accept as long as they can their homosexual orientation. In the recent past, some of these persons would contract a heterosexual marriage in hopes of putting the "immaturity" behind them. Such expedients have rarely been successful. This denial can result in unhappiness both for those who embrace it and for others who are emotionally and socially involved with them.

Conceptually, the immaturity theory makes an incongruous contrast with its opposite, **satiation**.

IMMIGRATION

Today's world has become concerned with immigration, not only because millions have migrated but also because the rise of the modern state and its definition of nationality has made the matter fraught with complications. Homosexuals live in a certain degree of tension with the environing society and have fewer ties to keep them rooted in the communities where they grew up. For this reason, they tend to migrate, not just to large cities with their convenient anonymity, but even across national borders. In the past, conflict with the law often sent homosexual men in precipitous flight to escape long **prison** terms or even a lynch mob, while voluntary exile amounted to a commutation of a severe penalty: in either case the individual whose homosexual activity was exposed ceased to be a member of society. If he was fortunate, he might settle in another part of world where his past was unknown and could not easily be discovered; and here, too, he could resume the series of casual liaisons that had become part of his lifestyle.

A visit of few days as part of a vacation trip is technically an act of immigration, even if the foreigner has no intention of residing permanently or becoming a citizen of the host country; and many are the homosexuals who either prefer exotic sexual partners or, possessing discretionary income but without families to accompany them, enjoy **travel** abroad, even to distant lands, in search of erotic adventures or pleasures denied them in the communities where they reside.

The Evolution of American Law. Homosexuality as an issue for the authorities that control immigration, in the United States the Immigration and Naturalization Service (INS), did not arise until the second decade of the twentieth century, for the simple reason that in the nineteenth century homosexuality as a psychiatric entity was unknown to the general public. There were, however, laws that sought to bar the movement of prostitutes and particularly the white slave traffic which had assumed international dimensions on the eve of World War I. Inside the United States the Mann Act of 1910 made it a crime to transport a female across state lines "for immoral purposes," while the movement to restrict immigration from Europe gathered support in the hinterland which resented the growing clusters of new arrivals from eastern and southern Europe in the large cities.

The first comprehensive revision of the immigration laws came with the Immigration and Naturalization Act of 1917, which denied entry to persons certified by an examining physician as "mentally defective" or afflicted with a "constitutional psychopathic inferiority." However, because the concept of homosexuality as a psychological condition was still new, the Board of Immigration Appeals excluded only those aliens who confessed to committing, or had been convicted of, homosexual acts involving moral turpitude. In 1947 the Senate began an investigation into the entire immigration system, and in 1950, when Senator Joseph R. McCarthy had made "sex perverts in government" a political issue, Senator McCarran of Nevada and Representative Walter of Pennsylvania introduced a bill that added "homosexuals and other sex perverts" to the class of medically excludable aliens. The Senate Judiciary Committee dropped the phrase from the bill primarily because of the objection raised by the Public Health Service that some difficulty would be encountered in substantiating the diagnosis of homosexuality and sexual perversion. Its report did, however, state that the Public Health Service had asserted that "the provision for the exclusion of aliens afflicted with a psychopathic

or a mental defect" was "sufficiently broad to provide for the exclusion of homosexuals and sex perverts," and also specified that the "change in nomenclature" was "not to be construed in any way as modifying the intent to exclude all aliens who are sexual deviates." The revised bill was passed by Congress to become the Immigration and Nationality Act of 1952.

The new law was enacted, it should be stressed, not just because the American Psychiatric Association and a majority of the medical profession considered homosexuality a mental illness, but also because they had no objection to any measure that deprived homosexuals of rights in civil and administrative law. This is a classic instance of how religious sanctions were in the nineteenth and twentieth centuries rationalized as pseudo-**medical** or pseudo-biological norms so that a policy of discrimination and exclusion could be justified in the eyes of the public. It was only the advocacy of measures for greater toleration that provoked the ire and indignation of the **psychiatric** "experts" of that day.

The issue of whether the expression "psychopathic personality" included homosexuality was soon raised, and the courts in looking at the legislative history of the Immigration and Nationality Act reached a consensus that Congress intended to include homosexuals within the term "psychopathic personality" regardless of the medical profession's understanding of the term. However, in a 1962 case a Federal appellate court did hold that the expression "psychopathic personality" was void on account of vagueness as it did not provide a "sufficiently definite warning that homosexuality and sexual perversion are embraced therein." It subsequently set aside a deportation order on the ground that homosexual aliens could not be excluded as "persons afflicted with psychopathic personality."

The liberal Congress elected at the time of Lyndon Johnson's landslide victory in 1964 responded to this decision by amending the law to add the term "sexual deviation" to the roster of excludable medical afflictions, and the Supreme Court, in *Boutilier v. Immigration & Naturalization Service* (1967) ruled that Congress intended the expression "psychopathic personality" to exclude homosexual aliens, stating that Congress had used the expression not in any clinical sense, but as a term of art designed to achieve its goal of exclusion. Case law further established that an integral part of the statutory scheme is the issuance of a "class A" certificate—a medical determination of "sexual deviation," and the Supreme Court held that an order of exclusion could not be issued unless the alien had been labeled with the requisite Public Health Service certificate. It did not raise the procedural issue of whether the INS could simply bar homosexuals who had not been so certified.

The Legal Impasse. In the wake of the decision of the American Psychiatric Association to drop homosexuality from its nomenclature of mental illnesses, the United States Surgeon General in 1979 notified the INS that the Public Health Service would no longer furnish the medical certification required for the exclusionary procedure, and instructed Public Health Service medical officers that they should not certify homosexual aliens as psychopathic personalities or sexual deviates solely on the basis of their homosexual orientation. The INS, in response to legal advice from the Justice Department that it was still required by law to enforce the exclusion of homosexual aliens, adopted the practice of excluding only those aliens who are identified as homosexual by a third party arriving at the same time, or who offer an unsolicited, unambiguous admission of homosexuality and repeat that admission in a second interview. An affirmative answer at the second hearing will result in a formal exclusionary hearing that may result in a denial of entry. This procedure allows for exclusion in the absence of the medical examination and certificate.

Faced with a new situation in administrative practice, the appellate courts have split over the issue of whether Congress has the power to exclude homosexual aliens under the new, non-medical procedure. The ultimate solution of the dilemma rests with Congress itself, but when the issue of homosexual rights became clouded by the problem of AIDS, support for repeal of the measure denying admission to the United States of aliens suspected of being homosexual became politically far more difficult. In practice most immigration officials and consuls attempt to avoid any direct confrontation with a law that bars any and all homosexuals by ignoring it rather than excluding homosexual celebrities on the basis of an absurd statute.

In 1985 the Committee on Immigration and Naturalization Law of the Association of the Bar of the City of New York formally reported that "The United States, alone among all the nations of the world, statutorily excludes homosexual persons from admission into the country for any purpose whatsoever, from casual visitor to would-be permanent resident. It is now time to correct that anomaly by removing homosexuality as a ground for exclusion from the United States."

BIBLIOGRAPHY. Peter N. Fowler and Leonard Graff, "Gay Aliens and Immigration: Resolving the Conflict between *Hill* and *Longstaff*," *University of Dayton Law Review*, 10 (1985), 621–44; "Committee Report: The Exclusion of Homosexuals Under the Immigration Law," *Record of the Association of the Bar of the City of New York*, 40 (1985), 37–51.

Warren Johansson

IMPERSONAL SEX AND CASUAL SEX

"Impersonal sex" refers to intercourse between two or more human beings who, for the sexual act considered, treat each other simply as a means to the goal of sexual pleasure. What makes sex impersonal is not the individuals involved, nor their relationships outside the sex act. A sex act is impersonal when it omits any expression of the traditional romantic attraction and longterm commitment expected of such acts in conventional Western society. Outside the designated sexual activity, individuals involved in impersonal sex may range, in familiarity, from lifelong partners to mere acquaintances to absolute strangers. There may be special pleasure in impersonal sex with someone who, at other times, is an intimate friend. A number of slave–master scenarios revolve around play-acting that an intimate partner is to be treated purely as a sexual outlet.

Impersonal sex is not the same as "casual sex." The distinctive element of casual sex, as in casual labor (for instance, temporary office help), is uncertainty about whether there will be another encounter with the same partner, and if so when. Casual sex can be quite personal in the intimacy of encounter between personalities as well as bodies. Impersonal sex, by contrast, avoids intimate personal exchanges (e.g., conversation is minimal or nonexistent) and total bodily interaction (e.g., elaborate and affectionate foreplay).

Comparative Perspectives. Impersonal sex occurs in heterosexual relationships where there is no expression of endearment, commitment, or love, but merely the purpose of consummating marriage, conceiving children, or solidifying property, nobility and other social bonds. But its most frequent heterosexual occurrence is for the same purpose as among homosexuals: the attainment of sexual release. A couple married for years may no longer take any pleasure from sexual congress, yet continue it. Foreplay may be entirely absent, and intercourse resented, yet conceded as a marital duty.

The institutional facilities of both casual and impersonal heterosex range through history—from ancient Roman baths and Renaissance bordellos to the whorehouses of the American gold rush, mobile prostitution units of armies in World War I, and Plato's Retreat, operating in New York in the 1970s, where men and women could meet each other for sex. But both impersonal and casual sex occur with greater frequency, per capita, among homosexuals, for an obvious reason: there is no possibility of pregnancy. For almost all of human history, women have had few means or opportunities to prevent pregnancy. In addition, most religions have treated sex as primarily a way of "making babies," and some have even treated enjoyment of sexual activity for its own sake as a sin. The history of sexual mores would certainly be different if men got pregnant. Males have had to bear much less of the burden of third-party consequences (childbearing, child-raising, punishment by others for illegitimacy) arising from sex outside marriage.

Third-party consequences of sexual acts are significantly reduced in homosexual sex, so it can be enjoyed for its intrinsic pleasure, if allowed to go unpunished. Each participant may enter the activity with no desire for relationship beyond that required to enjoy and complete the sex act. These facts make many moralists determined to punish homosexual sex even more severely than heterosexual illegitimacy.

Wherever in history and society homosexual activity has been condemned as wrong, it has been sought in covert encounters among networks of those who are "wise" to the activity. Fear of detection has thereby discouraged long-term relationships among homosexuals. Thus, a combination of factors has in many western societies produced a type of homosexual activity in which each partner behaves, and expects the other to behave, in a noncommittal manner.

Lesbians, as women, are more likely to be socialized into the conventional morality that sex is for making babies in a lifelong, monogamous relationship.

Gay males are more likely to share the heterosexual double standard of sexual behavior, which requires male conformity to the conventional morality in marriage but tolerates (and in locker room talk, often encourages) casual and impersonal sex. Thus, more impersonal sex occurs among gay men than lesbians, and the remainder of this discussion applies largely to males.

Territorial Aspects. The development of specific gay territories in which homosexuals could locate each other also tended to facilitate both casual sex and impersonal sex, since participants would often be drawn there for sexual outlet, without expectation of meeting a partner for a longer relationship. In casual sex, anonymity is not necessary or facilitative, but for impersonal sex, anonymity is a safety element in participation, and the anonymity of sex partners obviously contributes to the impersonal quality of the sexual intercourse. Prior to **AIDS**, some gay **bars** and **bathhouses** included "orgy rooms" where patrons engaged in sex with numerous strangers in pitch-dark and crowded rooms.

Activities and Attitudes. Impersonal gay sex is more likely to include a higher proportion of activity of a less physically joining kind, such as oral sex and masturbation. Participants will often remain fully clothed, and physical barriers to body contact add to the impersonal quality: the **toilet** "glory hole" in a partition is a prime example. Danger of discovery often means that sexual outlet has to be reached quickly, with a minimum of foreplay and special preparation, and with postures least likely to prove compromising should discovery occur.

It is entirely possible for two (or more) people to have intimate and very pleasurable sexual intercourse without revealing anything about their social identities—and to repeat this pleasure again and again over time, while still remaining anonymous. Once a quality of personal encounter develops (conversation not directly related to intercourse, formal arrangements for the sexual locale) such a sexual relationship may continue to be casual but often ceases to be impersonal.

The 1960s and 1970s were the modern "golden age" of impersonal gay male sex, since they came after penicillin and before AIDS. With the possible exception of some instances of hepatitis there was no significant sexually-transmitted disease during those decades which could not be treated, and usually cured. The first scholarly study to use the term "impersonal sex" reflects an ethnography obtained in a gay bathhouse (Weinberg and Williams, 1975).

As this and subsequent studies have noted, impersonal sex requires both psychological and sociological structures. The participants must have sufficient self-direction to break free of sex-negative, sex-restricting mores. They must be capable of adopting the same attitude to the consumption of sexual pleasure which one would normally adopt to eating. No sane person expects to limit eating to one food source for a lifetime, to eat only in formal personal settings, and to eat only to avoid starvation. We often eat food quickly, casually and for sheer pleasure, not to reduce any real hunger. Adopting the same attitude to sex is not easy in our society.

We are conditioned to associate sex with romantic love and long-term relationship. Impersonal sex requires the detachment of sexual excitement from personal identification with others, especially if many partners are to be enjoyed and jealousy is to be avoided (it greatly spoils the fun). The pursuit of impersonal sex requires considerable knowledge about and concern for sexual health, if one is to avoid contracting and passing on sexually transmitted diseases, but conventional morality has often opposed "sex education."

Even if an individual acquires the necessary psychological and health information and attitudes, impersonal sex will not be enjoyed widely in the majority of North American commuties. Its practice by one community member would be regarded as threatening and immoral by other members, unless extremely discreet and covert, and therefore restricted in frequency. But in the modern era, and especially after the **Stonewall Rebellion** (1969), the gay male population of large urban centers became the base for development of a system of sexual marketplaces where impersonal sex was both welcomed and frequently facilitated.

These places offered relative safety from view and harassment by the forces of conventional morality, as well as opportunities for encounter on a basis of casual entry and exit, without the need to identify oneself or seek the permission of others (as would be required, for example, in a private heterosexual "swinger's club"). Preeminent among such social facilities were the gay bar and the gay baths, but these were soon joined by the gay disco, where dancing with strangers was a means of recruiting new partners for both casual and impersonal sex.

These and similar social institutions of the emerging gay community differed importantly from earlier facilities for impersonal sex such as the public toilet, **cruising** park, movie theatre back row, and highway rest area. The gay bar, disco, and bath are businesses with an economic base and linkages, thus providing an infrastructure with vested interest in the facilitation of impersonal sex, within an organized and institutionally complex gay community.

"Ideology." It was only a short step to the development of ideology arguing the legitimacy of such institutions, and of impersonal gay sex. But it should hardly be assumed that the voices for legitimation are only of modern origin. The first "handbook" for guidance of those seeking the right attitudes and favorable opportunities for casual and impersonal sex was published by **Ovid** in the year A.D. 1: *The Art of Love.*

The modern gay ideology of impersonal sex spilled over into the heterosexual culture, and even produced publications on "how to pick up men" for women readers. But casual heterosexuality was almost always linked with negative moral outcomes. Alfie and his male peers might seek sex merely for pleasure, but were condemned to the same fate as their patron saint, Don Juan. Women might pick up Mr. Goodbar, but were sure to be injured or murdered.

The social structures of impersonal sex have been affected dramatically by the onset of AIDS. Indeed, much of the moralistic sentiment that AIDS is a punishment of homosexuals can be traced to conventional morality's outrage at the earlier sexual liberation ideology of impersonal sex.

BIBLIOGRAPHY. John Alan Lee, "The Social Organization of Sexual Risk," in *Studies in the Sociology of S and M,* Kamel and Weinberg, eds., Buffalo: Prometheus, 1984, pp. 175–93; idem, *Getting Sex,* Toronto: General, 1977; Martin Weinberg and Colin Williams, "Gay Baths and the Organization of Impersonal Sex," *Social Problems* 23 (December 1975), 124–36.

John Alan Lee

INCARCERATION MOTIF

This term refers not to literal incarceration or confinement but to an aspect of gender **dysphoria**—the idea that a human body can contain, locked within itself, a soul of the other gender. In their adhesion to this self-concept, many pre- and postoperative transsexuals unknowingly echo a theme that has an age old, though recondite history.

The pioneer in the struggle for homosexual rights Karl Heinrich **Ulrichs** (1824–1895) formulated the notion that the Urning, as he called the male individual attracted to his own sex, was endowed with *anima muliebris corpore virili inclusa,* "a female soul trapped in a male body." He took the notion from *Eros: die Männerliebe der Griechen* (Glarus and St. Gall, 1836–38) by Heinrich **Hoessli**. This Swiss homosexual writer had in turn purloined it from an article in the *Beilage* to the Munich *Allgemeine Zeitung* that discussed the kabbalistic belief in the transmigration of souls (*gilgul naphshot*).

Foreign as this idea is to the rationalistic Jew of the twentieth century, and to the Biblical and **Talmudic** periods of Judaism as well, it is first mentioned by Saadiah Gaon (882–942), the spiritual leader of Babylonian Jewry, who rejected it as an alien doctrine that had found its way into Judaism from the Islamic cultural milieu. However, the belief in transmigration took firm hold in the earliest center of Kabbalistic thinking in Spain, Gerona in Catalonia, and the notion that a female soul might be reincarnated in a male body is first expressed by Jacob ben Sheshet Gerondi (about 1235) in a work entitled *Liqqūṭé shikhḥāh ū-phē'āh* [Gleanings of the Forgotten and Unharvested], printed at Ferrara in 1556. Later, Isaac ben Solomon Luria (1534–1572), the head of the kabbalistic center at Safed in Galilee, made it an essential part of his doctrine. His oral teaching was incorporated in a book written by his disciple Ḥayyim Vital between 1573 and 1576 entitled *Sha'ar ha-gilgūlīm* (The Gate of Transmigrations).

According to the Kabbalists, the absolute destiny of the soul is—after developing all those perfections the germs of which are eternally implanted in it—to return to the Infinite Source from which it first emanated. Another term of life must be vouchsafed to those souls that have not yet fulfilled their destiny in the nether world and have not been sufficiently purified for the state of reunion with the Primordial Cause. Hence the soul must inhabit one body after another until after repeated trials it is able to ascend to the "palace of the Heavenly King." In the second half of the thirteenth century the *Zohar* had declared: "All souls are subject to transmigration," and Luria further taught that in general, the souls of men transmigrate into the bodies of men, those of women into the bodies of women; but there are exceptions. The soul of the patriarch Judah was in part that of a woman, while Tamar had the soul of a man (a fanciful interpretation of the story in Genesis 38: 12–26). Tamar's soul passed into Ruth, so that the latter could not bear children until God had imparted to her sparks from a female soul. The transmigration of a man's soul into the body of a woman was considered by some Kabbalists a punishment for the commission of heinous sins, such as man's refusing to give alms or to communicate his own wisdom to others. The wide diffusion and reception of the Lurianic version of the Kabbala ensured that many Jews of a mystical bent would entertain the belief down to modern times.

Belief in metempsychosis, or the transmigration of souls, is a characteristic theme of **Indian** thought, from which the Jewish motif that has been discussed may ultimately derive. Some Hindus today explain male homosexuality by saying that the individual had previously lived as a woman.

Ulrichs' formulation, strictly speaking, applies only to the "subject homoerotic"—the individual who feels himself a member of the opposite sex and plays the female role in relations with members of his own sex. As a scientific theory such a notion, because of the mind–body dualism which it entails (not to mention the belief in reincarnation, which has been relegated to the realm of the occult), has no standing whatever. Yet the reiteration of Ulrichs' views in the work of later homosexual apologists kept them alive into the twentieth century, and may have contributed to the rise of the practice of transsexualism and its underlying belief system, which Magnus **Hirschfeld** (1868–1935) never encountered even in the enormous casuistic material that he assembled in his lifetime. Pre- and postoperative transsexuals cherish the belief that some quirk of nature has confined them in bodies of the wrong genital sex. In the Hollywood film *Dog Day Afternoon* (1975), which was based upon a real incident in Brooklyn a few years earlier, the character Leon asserts that "My psychiatrist told me I have a female soul trapped in a male body," and more recently even advertising has taken up the theme, as in a telephone company poster with a cartoon character declaring "I feel that I'm a 516 trapped in the body of a 212." So a doctrine of medieval Jewish mysticism has entered the **folklore** of the gay **subculture**, and thence passed into the mainstream of American popular culture as a metaphor for a profound state of alienation.

Warren Johansson

INCEST

Incest means sexual intercourse between closely related individuals, especially when they are related within degrees where marriage is prohibited by law or religious custom. Until recently the sexual abuse of sons by their fathers was considered rare, but in the later decades of the twentieth century a different picture emerged. Statistics drawn from child welfare agencies, hospitals, police reports, and general surveys indicate that considerable numbers of boys are involved in homosexual activity with their own fathers. David Finkelhor's analysis of data derived from 5,809 substantiated cases of child abuse reported by agencies in thirty-one states indicated that 57 percent of the 757 boys in the group were abused by their fathers. It is probable that the twin taboos attaching to homosexuality and incest result in the underreporting of such cases.

Problems of Interpretation. Clinical studies of father–son incest are few, and the reported case histories often lack sufficient data to develop descriptive models. Many cases significantly fail to describe the actual nature of the sexual contact, and the literature on incest equally fails to employ strict criteria. Is the mere touching of the child's genitalia a sexual act, or must the adult's contact with the child's body lead to sexual arousal and

then orgasm in one or both partners? The law often demands a more stringent definition of the act in order to justify conviction.

While sexual contact between fathers and daughters is now recognized as more frequent than most authorities had suspected, the line of demarcation between reality and fantasy remains difficult to draw. The same consideration applies to instances of alleged father–son incest. Several cases have been reported in which homosexual incest occurred in an apparently disorganized family situation where impulsive, phyically abusive behavior by the father was the norm. These fathers sexually exploited their children, often both sons and daughters. The age of the son at the time of the initial sexual contact was usually prepubertal.

In one reported case a father with a record of convictions for manslaughter, bootlegging, and sale of pornography promoted sexual relations between the two oldest children and himself and his stepdaughter for pornographic ends. In another, the eldest son in a family of six children confided to his therapist the family secret that his father has sexually molested all six children over a period of ten years. When the father was in a violent temper, the oldest son or daughter would offer his or her sexual favors to protect the younger children from cruelty.

The father's **alcoholism** is an outstanding feature in some cases. Though often appearing homosexual in orientation, these fathers often do not so define themselves. One reported case describes sexual involvements between a father and his fourteen-year-old son that ranged from genital fondling to anal penetration. The father initiated the sexual activity, each time in a state of intoxication. Both father and son denied any previous homosexual encounters or desires.

Another set of cases in the literature describes the father as having some positive emotional investment in the son with whom he has sexual contact. Aggression does not accompany the sexual act. The fathers in some instances deny the homosexual character of the relationship, maintain that it was only an expression of love, and express the usual contempt for homosexual men as weak and effeminate.

On the other hand, there are also reported cases in which the son is gradually drawn into the homosexual life style of the father, at times after having independent homosexual experience on his own. A remarkable account of three generations of father–son incest in one family where this behavior seemed to be accepted centered upon a father who was a professor and theatre director. Another case involved an eighteen-year old who began his homosexual career six years earlier, welcomed his father's advances, and even described him as his "best lover."

The clinical picture of the father in cases of homosexual incest does not offer the profile of a "symbiotic" relationship between him and his son. In the cases that describe the triadic relationship between father, mother, and son, the father's incestuous behavior appears unrelated to the quality of his marital relationship. The sexual needs of the father in sexual contact with his son are less those which the wife cannot fulfill than those which he is afraid to express outside the home or with strangers.

Social Response. Public welfare agencies receive far fewer reports of homosexual than of heterosexual incest. This disparity reflects cultural factors such as the male ethic of self-reliance joined with the child's fear that if he reveals an incident his own independence and activities might be restricted. Because all studies indicate that most abuse of male children is by a partner of the same sex, a double stigma emerges in the violation of the taboo against homosexuality as well as of the prohibition of sexual contact between adults and children.

Follow-up studies of homosexual incest are rare. Studies of prostitutes of both sexes often elicit the assertion that they had been physically and sexually abused in their childhood. A recent investigation has found that the predominance of psychopathology reported in cases of father–son incest was higher than in all other pairings with the exception of sister–sister incest. The association of father–son incest with serious psychopathology, however, appears to be the pattern in this type of liaison. During the period of victimization or shortly thereafter the son often displays behavior revealing serious emotional disorder.

The therapist dealing with father–son incest must allow his professional diagnosis and treatment to be guided by an understanding of interplay between the intrapsychic and environmental factors in the situation. The psychological history of the father is of paramount importance. Some fathers act on impulses that are pansexual, others are responding to homosexual urges. Non-judgmental professional assistance can enable males involved in homosexual incest to face their own sexual orientation and to manage in a socially less dysfunctional manner the erotic component of their interaction with other members of the family. Family therapy may also be needed to enable all members of the family to cope with the sequelae of the incestuous behavior. At the same time, it cannot be denied that some adults, even if they are heterosexual or bisexual, are not fit or desirable parents; they do not have the personality structures that make for successful parenthood. Marriage counseling that would dissuade such individuals from ever having offspring would better serve the interests of society than belated measures to repair harm already inflicted.

Cross-Cultural Parallels. The taboo on homosexual behavior promulgated by the **Abrahamic religions** has led researchers to overlook the fact that the primary core of prohibitions in Leviticus 18 included two that were specifically directed against sexual relations with one's father (18:7) and one's father's brother

(18:14), and Orthodox Judaism recognizes these as two distinct commandments of the traditional 613. If Leviticus 18:22 had already existed, these provisions would have been otiose. The story of Ham and Noah in Genesis 9:20–24 is a euphemistically worded account of father–son incest, of aggression by Ham, "the father of Canaan," who "saw the nakedness of his father." The narrator then deploys this primal violation of patriarchal morality—the first homosexual episode in the Bible—to justify the conquest and subjugation of the descendants of Ham by the invading Israelites; it is an erotic legend with a political tendency.

All human societies forbid incest, not for supposed biological reasons, but simply because the prohibition of sexual relations between kinsmen is part of the operational definition of the family. Family status includes both the right to have sexual intercourse with other members of the family and the rigorous denial of that right. The code of sexual morality in Leviticus 18 is a compact among the male members of the patriarchal family not to transgress one another's sexual rights and prerogatives, a code which the primitive Church ratified and made part of its own constitution (Acts 15:20, 29). Thus homosexual aggression and incest have been culturally defined as perennial problems for the social order.

BIBLIOGRAPHY. Mark Williams, "Father–Son Incest: A Review and Analysis of Reported Incidents," *Clinical Social Work Journal*, 16 (1988), 165–79.

Warren Johansson

INCIDENCE, FREQUENCY, AND THE KINSEY 0–6 SCALE

Soon after Alfred **Kinsey** began tabulating the sex data he was collecting in the 1940s it became obvious that several new modes of analyzing it would be necessary, both for clarity and to avoid confusion. For instance, to show how easy and feasible homosexual contacts are for "the human animal" as Kinsey liked to say, it was necessary to determine their *incidence*—that is, how many people's sex histories contained at least one such experience to the point of orgasm.

Likewise, an *accumulative incidence* figure was needed to indicate what percentage of the histories reflected at least one such homosexual experience by each age (a gradually rising curve since additional individuals each year either "come out" or try out such activity). These group data also made it possible to draw a curve that would accurately estimate how many subjects would eventually have at least one overt homosexual experience. As Kinsey put it (1948, p. 623), "at least 37% of the male population has some homosexual experience between the beginning of adolescence and old age. . . . This is more than one male in three of the persons that one may meet as he passes along a city street."

But of course, a single experience does not a homosexual make (even though a sizable portion of lay observers has always been ready to assume so). Nor, in any case, does an incidence figure reflect when and how often homosexual experiences may be repeated—thus the need for some measure of *frequency*. Frequency figures were determined by ascertaining in each history how many and how often homosexual contacts (to the point of orgasm) were experienced by or before age fifteen, as well as during each five-year period thereafter, through age 55.

However, since homosexuality can exist as a psychological response (sometimes in the absence of any kind of overt activity of the kinds noted by incidence or frequency figures), Kinsey also devised his famous Heterosexual–Homosexual scale from 0 to 6:

0 = entirely heterosexual.

1 = largely heterosexual, but with incidental homosexual history.

2 = largely heterosexual, but with a distinct homosexual history.

3 = equally heterosexual and homosexual.

4 = largely homosexual, but with distinct heterosexual history.

5 = largely homosexual, but with incidental heterosexual history.

6 = entirely homosexual. (Kinsey, 1953, p. 470)

As indicated, this scale not only takes into account differences in the balance between heterosexual and homosexual actions, but also allows an investigator to consider "psychologic reactions" in arriving at each rating. Thus two people might both be rated "6" for being exclusively homosexual, with one of them living out his or her experiences, while the other might have as little as no overt activity of this kind—for reasons ranging from moral inhibitions to simply a lack of opportunity.

Ordinarily, it is easy to arrive at a single rating for a person's mental and physical responses. But whenever the two are in sharp discord (such as when a man has most or all of his sexual activity with women, but requires homosexual **fantasies** to actually reach orgasm), there is much to criticize in the compromises implicit in the 0–6 Scale. (To such complaints Kinsey simply pointed out that while rating difficulties and imperfections are, indeed, apparent in some cases, it is nevertheless useful, the best rating device so far, and that more is gained by using than by ignoring it.)

The combination of applying these measures of incidence, of frequency, and of placement on the 0–6 Scale (tabulated yearly or for a lifetime) not only permitted the Kinsey Research to cast out oversimplified stereotypes long used in defining heterosexual and homosexual variations, but to offer a variety of samples of its white male population, among them

that:

58 percent of the males who belong to the group that goes into high school but not beyond, 59 percent of the grade school level, and 47 percent of the college level have had homosexual experience to the point of orgasm if they remain single to the age of 35.

13 percent of males react erotically to other males without having overt homosexual contacts after the onset of adolescence. (This 13 percent, coupled with the 37 percent who do have overt homosexual experience, means that a full 50 percent of males have at least some sexual response to other males after adolescence—and conversely, that only the other 50 percent of the male population is entirely heterosexual throughout life.)

25 percent of the male population has more than incidental homosexual experience or reactions (i.e., rates 2–6) for at least three years between the ages of 16 and 55.

18 percent of males have at least as much homosexual as heterosexual experience in their histories (i.e., rate 3–6) for at least three years between the ages of 16 and 55.

13 percent of the male population has more homosexual than heterosexual experience (i.e., rates 4–6) for at least three years between the ages of 16 and 55.

8 percent of males are exclusively homosexual (i.e., rate 6) for at least three years between the ages of 16 and 55.

4 percent of males are exclusively homosexual throughout their lives after the onset of adolescence. (Kinsey, 1948, pp. 650–51)

Here, as elsewhere, data concerning homosexuality are cited for males rather than for females, not out of "male bias" but mainly because equivalent female data often cannot be understood without extensive additional explanation. Orgasm, for instance, is fundamental to virtually all overt male sexuality, while with females, psychological arousal, overt sexual action, and actual orgasm are often disconcertingly apart. In fact, orgasm is reached in only about half of female homosexual contacts (and in a still smaller portion of female heterosexual contacts).

Moreover, female sexuality tends to be far more pliant, and thus more changeable, than equivalent male responses. Thus while the sexual revolution made no appreciable change in the male percentages cited above (Gebhard, 1969), certain changes in female responses, especially regarding homosexual try-outs, have been noted subsequent to Kinsey's 1953 findings (Bartell, 1971; Tripp, pp. 271, 272). The reasons for these and a host of other complex matters in both male and female sexuality continue to intrigue sex researchers, and continue to validate the Kinsey 0–6 Scale as a much needed and appreciated measuring and descriptive device.

BIBLIOGRAPHY. Gilbert D. Bartell, *Group Sex: A Scientist's Eyewitness Report on Swinging in the Suburbs*, New York: David McKay, 1971; Paul H. Gebhard, ed., *Youth Study*, unpublished manuscript, Bloomington, IN: Institute for Sex Research, ca. 1968; Alfred C. Kinsey, Wardell B. Pomeroy, and Clyde E. Martin, *Sexual Behavior in the Human Male*, Philadelphia: Saunders, 1948; Alfred C. Kinsey, Wardell B. Pomeroy, Clyde E. Martin, and Paul H. Gebhard, *Sexual Behavior in the Human Female*, Philadelphia: Saunders, 1953; C. A. Tripp, *The Homosexual Matrix*, new ed., New York: New American Library, 1987.

C. A. Tripp

INDIA

The Republic of India includes over 800 million people crowded onto the Indian subcontinent, an appendage of the Asian mainland which it shares with Pakistan, Bangladesh, Nepal, and Bhutan. Historically, the Indian cultural zone has included all of the subcontinent as well as the island of Sri Lanka, and at times large areas of Southeast Asia, though India's political boundaries have been a frequently shifting kaleidoscope.

Attitudes toward Sex. Indian history, geography, and demography all exhibit a rich diversity of traits, making generalizations hazardous. Sexual attitudes and practices also show considerable variation, ranging from the classic sex-affirming *Kamasutra* and the world-famous erotic sculptures of ancient temples to the extreme prudishness of ascetics who condemned all forms of seminal emission and a modern educated elite which still derives its inspiration from Victorian England.

Shakuntala Devi observed in 1977 that "any talk concerning homosexuality is altogether taboo" and that "serious investigations on this subject in India are almost nil." This taboo, which applies with somewhat less rigor to discussion of sex in general, can be traced back to at least the British colonial occupation of the eighteenth and nineteenth centuries. Independence, which came in 1947, has done nothing to loosen it.

The strength of this taboo is such as to lead noted Indologist Wendy O'Flaherty to describe India as "a country that has never acknowledged the existence of homosexuality." While Giti Thadani was right to call this observation "factually incorrect" in an unpublished paper, as a broad generalization it is not so far from the truth; one must search far and wide to find the exceptions.

Any discussion of homosexuality in India must be placed against the background of the Indian social system, which is centered on the extended family. The first obligation of any Indian is to his or her family, not to his own goals. Everyone is expected to marry (as arranged by the families) and procreate sons. Until the marriage takes place (often to a complete stranger), the modern Indian of either sex is expected to remain celibate and avoid masturbation, though some allowance is made for the involvement of males with female prostitutes. Nevertheless, there may be a significant amount of well-hidden homosexual activity among unmarried boys and young men.

Ancient India. The oldest surviving literature is the set of scriptures called the Vedas, the first of which (the *Rig-Veda*) is usually dated from 1500 to 1200 B.C. These texts were composed by the Aryans who invaded India from Central Asia. A common view is that of the Czech scholar Ivo Fiser, who reviewed their references to sex and concluded that "in the Vedic period . . . homosexuality, in either of the sexes, was almost completely unknown and if there were such cases, the Vedic literature ignores them."

Later, but still ancient legal and religious texts, however, starting with Buddhist codes going back at least to the third century B.C., seem to take homosexuality for granted as a rather minor part of common life. The Buddhist monastic code cites various instances of homosexual behavior among the monks (all of which, like heterosexual behavior, was prohibited).

Vatsyayana, writing the *Kamasutra* in the fifth century of our era, included a whole chapter on the practice of fellatio as performed by eunuchs. Other erotic manuals suggested that sodomy was common in Kalinga (southern Orissa state) and Panchala (in the Panjab). In general, sex for pleasure was explicitly validated (at least for males, and often, as with Vatsyayana, for females as well) and not necessarily linked to procreative function.

The Medieval Period. Indian medieval history (twelfth–eighteenth centuries) saw the North Indian cultural heartland dominated by **Islamic** conquerors, who did not succeed in converting most of the Hindu masses but did leave an indelible imprint on Indian life. Enough of their subjects became Muslims for large areas of India to become primarily Islamic in character (becoming the nations of Pakistan and Bangladesh in 1947 and 1971).

The Muslims brought with them the institution of pederasty, and forced the withdrawal of women from public life. The free and open Indian attitude toward (heterosexual) sex which had characterized the ancient period now gave way to Islamic semiprurience.

At the same time, the Hindu (and later the **Buddhist**) religion saw the rise of Tantrism, with its hospitality toward sex as a means of liberation and its explicit endorsement of cross-gender role-playing.

The Colonial Period. The British, who came first as traders and stayed to conquer the subcontinent (eighteenth and nineteenth centuries), were scandalized by the sexual customs of the Indians, but in keeping with their policy of minimizing interference in the local mores, they did little about them. The educational system they established, however, eventually created a new Indian elite which enthusiastically absorbed British ideas, including the more prurient attitudes of the Victorians toward sex. This elite, in turn, imposed their new antisexuality on the Indian middle class.

A jaundiced description of Indian Muslim sexuality was written by the Dutch Admiral John Splinter Stavorinus in the 1770s. Referring to the Islamic Bengalis, Stavorinus opined that "The sin of Sodom is not only in universal practice among them, but extends to a bestial communication with brutes, and in particular with sheep. Women even abandon themselves to the commission of unnatural crimes."

"I do not believe that there is any country upon the face of the globe," the Dutchman continued, "where lascivious intemperance, and every kind of unbridled lewdness, is so much indulged in, as in the lower provinces of the empire of Indostan. [This] extends likewise to the Europeans, who settle, or trade there."

According to Allen Edwardes, who based his book *The Jewel in the Lotus* (New York: Julian, 1959) largely on nineteenth-century sources, pederasty was rare among the Hindu majority, though "rampant" among the Muslims and Sikhs of the Panjab, Deccan, and Sindh. Sir Richard

Burton investigated the boy brothels of Karachi (in what is now Islamic Pakistan) and found them to outnumber by far the houses of female prostitution.

The Maharajas. The British kept extensive files (destroyed in June 1947) on the sexual peccadillos of India's native princes. Tipu Sultan, the late eighteenth-century "Tiger of Mysore," is today revered in India as one of the fiercest opponents of British expansion (he fought three wars with them and frequently defeated them in battle), but British accounts claimed that Tipu raped European boy captives and "set enormous black vulgarians upon them who, stark naked, held them down and unmercifully abused their bodies."

Other nineteenth-century princes whom the British described as known sodomites included Wajid Ali Shah (the Maharaja of Oudh, also known as a transvestite), Runjeet Singh (the Lion of Lahore), and Suraj-ud-Dowlah, defeated by Clive in 1757 at the epochal Battle of Plassey.

Regarding the twentieth-century princes, British files, now apparently destroyed, contained a number of revelations. According to them, Hari Singh, the maharajah of Kashmir, after being blackmailed in London between the world wars in a heterosexual context, abandoned females in favor of males. Hari Singh became an important historical figure when, in 1947, he opted to take his overwhelmingly Muslim state into India rather than Pakistan, touching off a territorial dispute which led to two wars and remains unresolved. Moreover, the maharaja of Alwar (a principality of a hundred thousand people near Rajasthan) was reputed to have used a casting couch for officer candidates. This prince was noted for staging orgies, some even supposedly culminating in sadistic murders.

Pederasty in the Schools. In the early 1930s there was a brief flurry of discussion of pederasty in Indian boarding schools, reported in Devi's book. No less a figure than Gandhi wrote in *Young India* that "'unnatural vice' . . . was on the increase practically all over India in public as well as in private schools. Personal letters received from boys have confirmed the information." Despite Gandhi's assertion, the subsequent discussion seems to have been primarily concerned with Muslim areas.

A retired Muslim Inspector of Schools, K. B. Khurshid Ahmed, wrote in 1932 that "the detection of the crime is a very difficult task. The connection in most cases takes the form of a love affair and neither of the parties concerned would like to disclose the secret. . . . Even in cases when compulsion has been used and the outraged son has taken his woeful tale to his parents, no action is taken, as it is feared it will tell on the reputation of the boy and of the family. The headmaster, too, if complaints come to him, would try to hush up to keep the fair name of the school from being soiled."

The Panjab minister of education reported in 1934 that there were 31 "cases of seduction amongst the secondary departments of the schools in the province during the last five years."

A Muslim college principal, P. N. Maulik, wrote that year that "the vice is quite widespread among students, and in most schools there are some teachers who are corrupters of the young. I have frequently found that many such teachers are otherwise very useful and sometimes really efficient workers [a rarity in India then as now]."

R. B. L. Kanwar Sain, later Chief Justice of Kashmir, wrote in 1934 that "The evil is not sporadic, nor is it confined to any particular locality, but is widespread and our province stands next only to Northwest Frontier Province [both heavily Islamic] in the gravity of the situation."

Indian Law. In ancient times, laws were not so much a matter of state promulgation as codified traditions, enforced by social pressure more than by courts. The oldest extant law codes, therefore, are not decrees by kings but sacred texts written by Brahmin-class priests. Often conflicting with each other, they were held in widely varying degrees of reverence by different communities and social groups; in many kingdoms they were not followed at all.

The earliest surviving text on Indian law is the *Arthashastra*, a manual on statecraft by Kautilya, a minister of the Mauryan Empire of the fourth century B.C. Kautilya set out fines of 48 to 94 panas for male homosexual activity and 12 to 24 panas for lesbian acts. These fines were much lower than those for many heterosexual offenses.

The *Code of Manu*, which dates from the first to third centuries of our era and is the best known of the sacred law texts, prescribes that an upper-class man "who commits an unnatural offense with a male . . . shall bathe, dressed in his clothes." The same purification ritual is prescribed for one who has intercourse with a female in the daytime. An expiation ritual is prescribed for a man who swallows semen. The members of the lowest of the four great classes, as well as outcastes, were not restricted at all, as they were not expected to uphold high standards of ritual purity.

Manu laid down more severe restrictions on women, prescribing a fine of 200 panas plus double her nuptial fee as well as ten lashes with a rod for a girl "who pollutes another girl"; if a woman pollutes a girl she is to undergo the humiliation of having her head shaved or two fingers cut off and be made to ride through the village on a donkey.

Some later sacred-legal writers held that oral sex was equivalent to the killing of a Brahmin, the worst imaginable crime as far as the Brahmins (who wrote the texts) were concerned, and could not be expurgated in less than one hundred life-cycles.

When Britain took control of India, British sexual law was imported by the colonial administration. The 1861 legislation which changed the British penalty for sodomy from hanging to life imprisonment became Section 377 of the Indian Penal Code after independence. This law prohibits "carnal intercourse against the order of nature" and continues to prescribe imprisonment up to life as well as whippings and fines. Any sexual act involving penetration of the anus or mouth by a penis, whether homosexual or heterosexual, makes both partners criminal, according to Indian courts. In addition, intercrural (between the thighs) sex has been held by Indian courts to be banned by this law. Lesbian activities, and heterosexual cunnilingus, however, are legal.

Indian legal tradition justifies this law with the argument that "the natural object of carnal intercourse is that there should be possibility of conception of human beings, which in the case of unnatural offence is impossible." Indian legal scholars, however, trace it to English beliefs that "all emission other than *in vas legitimum* was considered unchristian because such emission was supposed ultimately to cause conception of demons."

Under a 1925 court decision still cited in legal texts, fellatio (called "the sin of Gomorrah") is "less pernicious than the vice of Sodom. . . . It has not been surrounded by the halo of art, eloquence and poetry. It is not common and can never be so. It cannot produce the physical changes which the other vice produces."

Evidentiary standards are rigorous, however, in that penetration "must be strictly proved" and corroborating testimony is normally required. According to Devi, prosecutions are "very rare." All the Indian cases cited in the legal manuals involve boys.

Following the British law reform of 1967, attempts were made in the Indian courts to challenge Section 377. In 1983, the Supreme Court (in *Fazal Rab Chaudhary* v. *State*) declared that "Neither the notions of permissive society nor the fact that in some countries homosexuality has ceased to be an offense has influenced our thinking." Having said that, the court, dealing with a case involving sex between a man and a "young boy" but without force, upheld the law but reduced the sentence to six months.

Lesbianism. Female homosexuality is not discussed in modern Indian law, reflecting its invisibility in society at large. The harems of the rulers of various Indian states are said to have been "hotbeds of lesbianism." In the realm of legend, however, we find mention of *strirajya* or female-ruled ancient kingdoms in which "women were said to have group congress with their own sex, and more rarely with men." No historical evidence has survived for such kingdoms.

Hindu Traditions. As with most everything else in that amorphous collection of religious traditions loosely called "Hinduism," there is a wide variety of attitudes displayed toward gender identity and homosexuality. In keeping with general Hindu attitudes, however, there is little attempt to impose religious views on sexuality on those who do not share them.

Apart from the previously mentioned writings of the Brahmin legalists, there are not many references to homosexuality in the enormous corpus of mainstream Hindu scriptures and sacred texts. The yogic tradition, however, has maintained a morbid concern that any emission of semen is debilitating and has thus taken a relentlessly hostile stance toward any male sexuality.

Throughout Indian history, the only acceptable escape from marital duties has been "renunciation" (*sannyas*), leaving family and caste behind to take up the unattached religious life as a monk, guru, teacher, or wandering holy man. It is not difficult to imagine that many Indians who had no heterosexual inclinations must have followed that route, which had the further advantage of placing them in the company of other members of their own gender.

Shiva, the most popular of all Hindu gods, has from the most ancient of times been worshipped primarily in the form of a *lingam* or erect phallus; in the most common ritual milk is poured over the tip of the lingam and flows down on all sides. The lingam is worshipped by males as well as by females, suggesting the existence of a sublimated homoerotic element.

Perhaps the only record of something approaching homoeroticism in Hindu mythology is part of the myth of Shiva, who engaged in intercourse with his wife Parvati for a thousand years without ejaculating. Interrupted by a delegation of other deities, he withdrew from Parvati and then ejaculated. The semen was swallowed by Agni, a male god connected with fire and ritual sacrifices, but it proved too hot for him to handle and he vomited it up; eventually the sperm turned into Shiva's son Skanda ("The Ejected"), without any contribution from Parvati. Skanda became the god of youth, beauty, and warriors.

Indian mythology shows many examples of sex changes, which Thadani considers to be covers for male homosexuality. Vishnu, Shiva's main rival for the devotion of Hindus, turned himself into the stunningly beautiful Mohini in order to distract the demons at a critical moment. Shiva was so taken with Mohini that he copulated with her and impregnated her so that she bore him a son. In some versions of the myth the son is Harihara, but in South India, where the act is described as a rape, the son is Ayappa, focus of a rapidly growing cult.

Androgyny has long been considered a divine attribute, and many of the leading deities have been pictured as **hermaphrodites**, half male, half female, reflecting the Hindu belief that godhead contains within itself all the elements of the cosmos, including both male and female. The most notable example of this, however, is Shiva, who is often shown with the left side female, the right male, and in this form is called "Ardhanarishvara."

Devotees of androgynous deities have occasionally sought to further their approach to God by emulating this divine quality, giving a sacred aura to androgyny. Thus the famous nineteenth-century Hindu reformer Ramakrishna went about for some time wearing women's clothes.

The Sakibhava cult, which worships Krishna (an incarnation of Vishnu), holds that only Krishna is truly male and that all other creatures are female in relation to him. Male followers of the cult dressed like women and even imitated menstrual periods. Vern Bullough, citing R. B. Bhandarkar in his *Sexual Variance in Society and History* (New York: John Wiley, 1976), says they "all were supposed to permit the sexual act on their persons (playing the part of women) as an act of devotion. Usually, the male members did not show themselves much in public, in part because of public hostility." Benjamin Walker confirms this account in his encyclopedic *The Hindu World*. For comparison, see the Hijra sect below.

Separate from such small sects is a wide religious movement which swept through India, affecting both Hinduism and Buddhism, in the late ancient and early medieval period, though it has become unrespectable since British Victorian prudery became dominant. This "left-handed" esoteric Tantrism utilizes ritual sexuality as a sacred technique. Though mostly heterosexual, numerous Tantric texts do advocate the desirability of a male follower developing his opposite (female) traits and visualizing himself as female; sometimes this has taken the form of participating in homosexual acts.

Walker, in his discussion of sexual "perversions" in Hinduism, considers these to be "aspects of antinomianism thought to be favored by the gods, and regarded as methods of achieving degrees of 'intensity,' which ... release a stream of vital power which if rendered to the service of the deity is returned multifold to the giver."

Anal intercourse, called *adhorata* or "under-love," involves the anus as one of the most significant *chakras*, or energy-centers, in the body, and thus has been held to energize the artistic, poetic, and mystical faculties. "Some medieval writers speak of it as quite common and do not regard it as perverse," according to Walker.

Maukhya, or fellatio, has also been given sacred significance in connection with the Shiva-Agni legend cited above. "Certain Hindu writers on erotics have held that 'the mouth is pure for purposes of congress,'" Walker writes.

The Hindu–Buddhist doctrine of reincarnation has been used to explain the phenomenon of homosexual orientation by depicting it as a transitional state following a change of gender from one lifetime to the next, on the theory that long-acquired ingrained habits (such as sexual interest in men) are slower to change than the physical body, which is replaced at death/birth. Noteworthy about this rationale is the absence of negative overtones.

Homosexuality in Contemporary India. Indian male friends are very affectionate with each other and do not hesitate to demonstrate this in public (something they would never do with their wives). Men and boys can easily be seen sleeping on the pavement in each other's arms. This has given many Western visitors the mistaken idea that homosexuality is rampant.

The legal scholar Ejaz Ahmad noted in 1975 that "there seems to be a widespread tendency of [Indian] males to experiment in homosexual activities, although most do not become pure homosexuals." Ahmad's observation, which may reflect his Islamic background, has found little support from other Indian writers, though that may have more to do with taboos on discussion—as Devi puts it, "Even today, people in India find it difficult to conceive of the very idea of homosexuality"—than with the accuracy of his remark.

Devi paints a picture of Indian (Hindu) homosexuals leading very cautious, hidden lives, meeting primarily through private cliques while fulfilling their expected marital duties. A lack of privacy which is pervasive in this extremely overcrowded country seems to be the major handicap, along with an absence of clubs, bars, and similar meeting places. Devi states that "boy brothels are very common in the bigger cities" employing boys as young as eight.

Other reports indicate that big-city bus terminal toilets seem to be the major sites for anonymous non-reciprocal sex, while some urban parks serve as meeting places. No gay-oriented organizations are known to be functioning in India.

Among the hundred million Muslims still remaining in India after partition, it may be speculated, ancient practices such as pederasty which were more congenial to Islamic culture may continue to survive, but there are few or no data.

While there is almost no modern Indian literature on homosexuality, according to Devi two Hindi films have touched on the topic: *Dosti* and Raj Kapoor's *Sangam*.

The Hijras. No discussion of contemporary homosexuality in India can ignore a religious sect, the Hijras, whose numbers have been estimated between fifty and five hundred thousand. This all-male group, divided into those who surgically remove the penis and those who remain intact, worships the Mother Goddess and seeks to identify with her by becoming as feminine as possible.

While their traditional role in North Indian society is as entertainers, and they theoretically uphold an ideal of chastity, many Hijras function as prostitutes, taking the passive role for Indian male insertors who look upon the transvestite Hijras as substitutes for females and do not consider themselves homosexual or unmasculine. In this their customers reflect an inarticulated belief that "sexual object choice alone does not define gender." Serena Nanda, in her study of the Hijras, points out that this sect welcomes many teenage homosexuals who are cast out of their own families and have no other niche in a communal-oriented culture.

The level of tolerance experienced by the Hijras appears to vary considerably, so that one must question blanket assertions that their behavior is condoned by Indian society. Nevertheless, they seem to provide the only open social status for homosexuals, transvestites, and transsexuals in a culture which otherwise provides it only through marriage and the family, and which can hardly conceive of an individual not attached to a communal group as well as a family.

Conclusion. The forces of modernization, while slow by Western standards, are accompanied by social changes in India which seem rapid to this very old, tradition-bound culture. Some young people are rebelling against the institution of the family-arranged marriage with its dowries, and educated professional women are beginning to make dents in the rigid social roles prescribed for females. One of the consequences of these changes are that the taboo on discussion of sex is slowly beginning to weaken, along with the devotion of the Indian educated elite to the values of Victorian Britain. Eventually, this candor is bound to open up the subject of homosexuality as well.

Urbanization is starting to loosen the grip of family and caste and beginning to provide the anonymity which seems necessary for homosexuals to develop independent lives. Whether Western notions of homosexuality take root in India (apart from the small English-educated professional class) remains to be seen— Indian mores have already proven their capacity for astonishing resistance to foreign influence. Perhaps a model of pre- and extra-marital experimentalism by "normal" males keeping to insertor roles with a small number of effeminate passives (and boys and foreign tourists) along more Mediterranean or pederastic lines will develop.

Apart from caste and family obligations, however, Indian society is remarkably tolerant of individual eccentricities, and it is quite possible that when the curtain finally lifts on Indian sexuality one may find the patterns of homosexuality in India distinctively Indian.

BIBLIOGRAPHY. Ejaz Ahmad, *Law Relating to Sexual Offenses*, 2nd ed., Allahabad: Ashoka Law House, 1975; J. P. Bhatnagar, *Sexual Offenses*, Allahabad: Ashoka Law House, 1987; Shakuntala Devi, *The World of Homosexuals*, New Delhi: Vikas Publishing House, 1977; Serena Nanda, "The Hijras of India: Cultural and Individual Dimensions of an Institutionalized Third Gender Role," in Evelyn Blackwood, ed., *Anthropology and Homosexual Behavior*, New York: Haworth Press, 1986, pp. 35–54; Wendy Doniger O'Flaherty, *Women, Androgynes, and Other Mythical Beasts*, Chicago: University of Chicago Press, 1980; Benjamin Walker, *The Hindu World*, London: George Allen & Unwin, 1968.

Lingānanda

INDIANS OF NORTH AMERICA

Like many societies around the world that accepted homosexual behavior as a common and normal activity, North American Indian aboriginal cultures often incorporated same-sex activity into their way of life.

Underlying Cultural Attitudes. This acceptance was owing to several factors, especially the fact that sex was not seen as sinful in their religions. With some exceptions, sex was not restricted to its reproductive role, but was seen as a major blessing from the spirit world, a gift to human beings to be enjoyed freely from childhood to old age. Among the matrilineal tribes, women were particularly free in their behavior, since their child's family status depended on the mother's relatives rather than on the father. In general, North American Indian religions emphasized the freedom of individuals to follow their own inclinations, as evidence of guidance from their personal spirit guardian, and to share generously what they had with others.

Children's sexual play was more likely to be regarded by adults as an amusing activity rather than as a cause for alarm. This casual attitude of child-rearing continued to influence people as they grew up, and even after their marriage. Yet, while sex was certainly much more accepted than in the Judeo-Christian tradition, it was not the major emphasis of Indian society. The focus was instead on two forms of social relations: family (making ties to other genders) and friendship (making ties within the same gender). Since extremely close friendships were emphasized between two "blood brothers" or two women friends, this allowed a context in which private homosexual behavior could occur without attracting attention. Simply because this role of sex in promoting bonds of friendship was so accepted, there is relatively little information about this kind of casual same-sex activity. It demonstrates that the role of sex in promoting close interpersonal ties is just as important for a society as the role of sex as a means of reproduction. While Christian ideology emphasizes that the purpose of sex is only for reproduction, that is clearly not the view of many other religions.

Institutional Forms. Beyond its role in same-sex friendships, homosexual behavior among many aboriginal tribes was also recognized in the form of same-sex marriages. However, the usual pattern among North American Indians (as well as in many areas of the Caribbean, Central and South America) focused not on two masculine men getting married, or two feminine women, but to have a typical man or woman marry an androgynous person who takes on a different gender role. Traditionally in many tribes, the feminine male had a special role as a **berdache** and the masculine female took on an **Amazon** role.

These androgynous roles were different and distinct from the regular roles of men and women. Some scholars suggest that this pattern is "gender mixing," while others see such roles as forming their own unique "alternative genders," but almost all specialists currently doing research reject the older notion that berdaches and Amazons were hermaphrodites, transsexuals, transvestites, or "gender-crossers," for the simple reason that Indian cultures allowed more than two gender options. Though the early sources are incomplete and unclear, probably most cultures that recognized such alternative genders assumed that such a person would have sex with a person of the same biological sex. While there are isolated examples of heterosexual marriage, the usual assumption is that a feminine male berdache would marry a man, while a masculine female Amazon would marry a woman. The complementary advantages of persons filling different genders, meant that two hunters would not get married, nor would two plant-gathering/farming women. In aboriginal economies, a husband–wife team needed to do different labor roles to provide the household with a balanced subsistence.

Accordingly, the husband of a berdache was not defined as a berdache, merely because he had sex with a male. The community defined him on the basis of his gender role as a "man," being a hunter and/or warrior, rather than on his sexual behavior. Likewise, the wife of an Amazon was not defined as a lesbian, but continued to be defined as a woman because she continued to do women's labor roles of plant-gathering, farming, cooking, and craftwork. This gender-defined role did not categorize people as "heterosexual" versus "homosexual," but left a certain fluidity for individuals to follow their sexual tastes as they were attracted to specific individuals of whichever sex. In tribes that accepted marriage for the berdache or the Amazon, the clan membership of one's intended spouse was much more important than their sex.

This fluidity also meant that a person who had married a berdache or an Amazon was not stigmatized as different, and could later easily marry heterosexually. In fact, many tribes that accepted same-sex marriages did considerable kidding to the husband of the berdache, and the wife of the Amazon, which likely had the function of helping to break up these marriages after a time, so that the person would be heterosexually married at some point in his or her life. With the exception of the berdaches and Amazons, who were relatively few in number in a tribe, social pressure emphasized for most people that they should beget children. After they had done so, to help insure the continued population of the society, the sex of the lover did not matter much. Indeed, even the berdaches and Amazons contributed toward population growth through their important role as adoptive parents for orphaned children.

In many tribes' conceptions of spirituality, the person who was different was seen as having been created that way by the spirit world. Berdaches and Amazons were respected, even though they were recognized as different from the average tribal member. They were considered to be exceptional rather than abnormal.

The Encounter with Europeans. This view changed drastically, however, after the arrival of the Europeans. Bringing with them their homophobic Christian religion, Spanish conquerors in Florida, California, and the Southwest, as well as in **Latin America**, emphasized the Indians' acceptance of "sodomy" as a major justification for European conquest and plunder of the New World. Likewise, the English settlers brought a similar condemnation, and the United States and Canadian governments followed a policy of suppressing Indian peoples' sexuality as well as their native religions. The berdache and Amazon traditions went underground, and sex became a secret matter as it was persecuted by reservation officials and Christian missionaries.

In the twentieth century, while European condemnation of homosexuality has had an influence on many modern Indians, those who have retained their traditions continue to respect berdaches and Amazons even today. This attitude had a significant impact on the white founders of the homophile and gay **liberation** movements in the United States and Canada. With a recent renaissance in Indian culture, younger gay and lesbian Indians have in turn been influenced by the gay community to stand up openly and take pride in their accepting Indian traditions. Like traditionalist Indians, they feel an appreciation for the strength and the magic of human diversity, and they accept people as they are rather than expect everyone to conform. This respect for the different gifts that gay people can provide as a benefit for society, and a respect for women and for androgynous men, is having an impact on Western culture as a whole.

BIBLIOGRAPHY. Will Roscoe, "Bibliography of Berdache and Alternative Gender Roles Among North American Indians," *Journal of Homosexuality*, 14:3/4 (1987), 81–171; Walter L. Williams, *The Spirit and the Flesh: Sexual Diversity in American Indian Culture*, Boston: Beacon Press, 1986.
Walter L. Williams

INDO-EUROPEAN PEDERASTY

Indo-European is the name given to a family of languages extending from Old Irish and Old Norse on the northwestern periphery of Europe to Old Persian and Sanskrit in the Middle East, together with the modern descendants of these tongues. The discovery by western European scholars that this set of languages was interrelated in the same way as the members of the Semitic family led to the hypothesis of a primordial anthropological (ethnic) unity of the speakers of the proto-language, often designated as Aryans in opposition to the Semites and Hamites of the Near East. Further study of the original common vocabulary of Indo-European pointed to a cultural and institutional legacy of the preliterate past which some investigators sought to reconstruct in meticulous (though often speculative) detail.

Sergent's Thesis. Recently Bernard Sergent has claimed that Indo-European warriors practiced initiatory pederasty until after their dispersion in the second millennium B.C. Before a youth proved his manhood by a feat of valor, he was feminized and reduced to the passive sexual role. Sergent thus went beyond the nineteenth-century German scholars who ascribed pederasty to the Dorian tribesmen invading **Greece** ca. 1200 B.C., after the Achaeans and other Greeks who had no such institution had arrived there from their *Urheimat* (primitive homeland) on the Eurasian steppes (or wherever else a particular hypothesis located it).

Nothing, however, proves that pederasty was institutionalized among the *kshatriyas* (warrior caste) of **India**, the ancient Persians, or the grave *patres* of early **Rome**. Just as the theory of "Dorian invasions" and of their transformation of the material culture of Greece by introducing iron and other innovations has been discredited by twentieth-century archeology and linguistics, the whole concept of the dispersion of an Indo-European speech community by nomadic conquerors during the second millennium B.C. has also been called into question. Colin Renfrew argues that the Indo-Europeans dispersed as early as 6000 B.C. as peaceful farmers. The institutionalization of pederasty in Greece belongs to historic time, not to prehistory.

The Greeks. Although Erich Bethe argued in a celebrated 1907 article that the Greeks believed that they transferred their manliness to their boys through their semen, many would still like to claim that the original "Dorian" pederasty was "pure," i.e., devoid of overt sexuality. Like most of the ancients, Cicero viewed Spartan mōres with a grain of salt, even though they claimed not to soil even the thighs of their boys: "The Lacedemonians, while they permit all things except outrage in the love of youths, certainly distinguish the forbidden by a thin wall of partition from the sanctioned, for they allow embraces and a common couch to lovers" (*De Republica*, IV 4). **Vase painting, graffiti,** and literary allusions leave no doubt that intercrural and even anal intercourse were frequent and expected. Black-figured vases portray sexual contact more explicitly, with youths having larger virile members and more mature bodies, than the red-figured ones that replaced them after ca. 520 B.C. Even if Zaleucus, the earliest colonial lawgiver who copied much from **Crete,** may have introduced pederasty to Locri in 664 B.C., the pederasty of Phalanthus, Spartan colonizer of Tarentum in 706 B.C., was just another founder's myth. The attempts of Sergent's mentor Georges Dumézil to name the god or hero who established pederasty in every *polis* shows that its origin had to be justified in each, as Bethe realized long ago when he claimed that the practice spread to the other city-states from Sparta. The institutionalization of pederasty followed rather than preceded the rise of the city-states during the eighth century B.C. One should not conclude with Sergent that Greek *paiderasteia* was "not started by the influence of the Dorians or of any others." It began in Crete in the seventh century B.C. and was popularized by **Sparta's** military and athletic prowess before spreading to most of the rest of Hellas during the sixth century B.C.

Other Peoples. Inadequate also is the documentation that any other Indo-European peoples ever practiced initiatory pederasty. It has been claimed that **Tacitus** depicted the Germans as drowning "passive homosexuals" in bogs; recent scholarship has demonstrated that Tacitus' expression meant "cowards and shirkers in combat." Two other historians, however, Ammianus Marcellinus, writing ca. A.D. 380 and, more ambiguously, Procopius, writing ca. 550, expressed disgust that Germanic tribes, Taifales and Heruls, practiced pederasty. In the early Middle Ages Germanic law also failed to mention homosexual acts, except under Christian influence in Visigothic Spain. While Sergent omitted evidence from the Irish **penitentials** for Celtic pederasty, he implausibly rationalized Caesar's silence in the *Gallic Wars* by claiming that the Roman general feared criticism of his own proclivities.

A recent effort at demolishing the Indo-European theory is Martin Bernal's thesis in *Black Athena* (New Brunswick, 1987) that the Greeks did not bring with them from the Eurasian heartland the genius, the ideas, and the institutions from which Western civilization evolved, but borrowed them from the Hamitic and Semitic peoples of the eastern Mediterranean. It was only the racism and anti-Semitism of nineteenth-century Germany that invented the "Aryan model" of Hellenic greatness. It is true that Greek civilization began in the south and east—the interface with the far older cultures of **Egypt,** Syria, and **Mesopotamia**—and that in the sphere of material culture the Greeks and Romans and even their successor nations did not innovate; they merely adopted the heritage of the Near Eastern peoples. But in politics, in science, and in **philosophy** the Hellenes were supremely original: the Near East simply had no counterpart to their democratic city-states or to their achievements in speculative thought. Moreover, it may be argued that the pederastic spirit guarded the cradle of Western civilization, shielding it well from the despotism and servility of the Persians and their client-peoples—with religions that rejected and condemned homosexual expression as an abomination in the sight of their deities. Though suggestive, the notion of a common Indo-European tradition of initiatory pederasty long antedating the rise of Hellenic civilization remains essentially hypothetical.

BIBLIOGRAPHY. Erich Bethe, "Die dorische Knabenliebe: ihre Ethik und ihre Idee," *Rheinisches Museum*, 62 (1907), 438–75; Karl Otfried Müller, *Die Dorier* [1820–24], vols. 2 and 3 trans. as *The History and Antiquities of the Doric Race*, London: John Murray, 1830; Colin Renfrew, *Archaeology and Language: The Puzzle of Indo-European Origins*, Cambridge: Cambridge University Press, 1988; Bernard Sergent, *L'homosexualité initiatique dans l'Europe ancienne*, Paris: Payot, 1986; *Homosexuality in Greek Myth*, trans. by Arthur Goldhammer, Boston: Beacon Press, 1986.

William A. Percy

INDONESIA

This island nation shares with its Southeast Asian neighbors a heritage of acceptance of homosexual behavior in its traditional cultures. Though little is known about the same-sex practices of many of the tribes of the East Indies, there is information from early explorers about several cultures. Among both the Dayak (Iban) of Kalimantan, and the Bugis (Makasar) of Sulawesi, there was a socially-recognized "half-man/half-woman" androgynous role for males similar to the **berdache** tradition among American Indians. Such individuals were often sacred religious leaders of great spiritual power, wore a mixture of men's and women's clothes, combined masculine and feminine aspects in their character, and had sex with men. Among the Bugis, such *bisu* individuals traditionally resided at the courts of local rulers, where they took care of the sacred royal ornaments.

Melanesian Cultures. In contrast, the eastern part of Indonesia is Irian Jaya, which is a totally different culture area from the rest of the nation. Irian is the western part of the island of Papua New Guinea, where the tribes share the **Pacific** Melanesian way of life. Melanesian cultures emphasize super-masculinity for males, who are grouped together in warriorhoods. In these societies, feminized males are looked down upon, and boys are pressured to adopt the masculine warrior lifestyle. One means of gaining masculinity, in the lifestyle of many of these Melanesian cultures, is for a boy to absorb masculine characteristics through sex with a man. Accordingly, every boy is expected to go through a stage of growth, in which he either orally ingests or anally receives semen. It is believed that he cannot mature into manhood without gaining this sperm through homosexual acts, even though he will marry heterosexually after he matures. Homosexual relations, often done in a ritual context, provide a major means for transmission of masculine values from one generation of males to another.

Javanese Culture. The major culture of Indonesia is Javanese, and only in the Ponorogo area of eastern Java is homosexuality institutionalized in man–boy relationships. Here, however, boys are valued for their feminine characteristics, and men will take a boy as a *gemblakan*. Traditionally, gemblakans were kept by a *warok*, a spiritually and physically powerful masculine adult man. Waroks would gain social status by the lavish wealth they could display on their beautiful gemblakan. A man would arrange with the boy's parents to keep him for one or two years, and would present the parents with gifts and financial support during the time in which he kept the boy. Some gemblakans were as young as seven years old, but most were in their teens, and some were loved so much by their man that they stayed together until the boy was in his twenties.

In recent decades, however, it has become too expensive for most men to support a gemblakan, so in the traditional villages of Ponorogo where the practice still continues, several men will combine their resources to share a boy. The group of men is usually either young and unmarried or a royal dance troupe, where the boy performs in androgynous dress and heavy makeup. The boy spends a few days in the house of each group member, before being shared with another member. Married men will sleep with the boy rather than with their wife while the gemblakan is visiting, but the wife usually does not mind because of the social prestige that the gemblakan brings. Often, after the boy matures, he continues to regard the man's family as extended kin, and he will sometimes even marry the daughter of the man he had formerly slept with.

Islam. Indonesia today is mostly Islamic in religion, and the attitudes of **Islam** toward homosexuality are ambivalent. Among fundamentalist *santri* followers of Islam, sex of any kind outside heterosexual marriage is discouraged, but it is an open secret that adolescents in Muslim boarding schools are often involved in homosexual relationships. Usually Islam has adapted itself to local customs, and in areas like Ponorogo where homosexual behavior was common, the religion did not oppose this practice. However, in recent decades as Islam has reacted against the European stereotype that all Muslim men are pederasts, and as a more fundamentalist wave has swept through the Middle East, Islam in Indonesia has taken a more negative view of homosexuality. Fundamentalist Muslims today do not seem as intent on inducing guilt over homosexuality as fundamentalist Christians are, but they come close.

Modern Homosexual Life. Nevertheless, among those Indonesians who are not so strict on religion, popular acceptance of homosexuality continues. One popular form of entertainment in eastern Java is *ludruk*, a form of theatre in which female roles are traditionally played by transvestite males. The actors in these traveling troupes are often homosexual, and serve as sexual partners for married men who come and visit them after the ludruk performances.

With traditions like this, it is not surprising that transvestite homosexuality is well known in modern Indonesia. The term for such individuals is *banci*, which is similar in meaning to the gay vernacular term "drag queen." Bancis are often employed in beauty salons or other fashion-related businesses, but many of them make their living by prostitution.

Gay men in Indonesia are a separate social group, quite distinct from bancis, even though some gay males will sometimes dress in drag and will joke among themselves that they are banci. Although gay men are active in every field of labor, they are most noted as models, dancers, tourist guides, hair stylists, and fashion designers.

An open gay scene exists in all Indonesian cities, but many remain secretive. There is very little social contact between gay men and lesbians, who are usually quite secretive about their sexuality. The main fear of those in the closet is that their family will find out, which is an indication of low self-acceptance. Nevertheless, there is not much pressure on gays outside of the family. Employment discrimination against gays is not often a problem, and homophobic violence against gays is quite rare. Police are not known for their anti-gay activities, and government policy in general is not discriminatory. Some top ministers of the government are commonly known to be gay, yet this does not lead to calls for their dismissal.

As a result of this lack of discrimination, few gays see a reason to become politicized, and they tend to integrate more into general society rather than establishing their own separate subcultural institutions. For example, since same-sex couples are free to dance together in discotheques, and gays can associate comfortably with each other in these dance places alongside heterosexuals, there are not many strictly gay bars. The one great social inhibitor for gays is that their family will confront them about their sexuality, and many of them seem resolved to become heterosexually married in their later years. Otherwise, gay people in Indonesia seem to have an accepted place in society generally.

It is ironic that the position of gay people in the democratic nations is often more repressed than it is in an authoritarian regime like Indonesia. Indonesian values such as social harmony, non-violence, responding to the voice of the people, and unity in diversity seem to protect gays more effectively than traditions of majority rule and individual rights. Still, as Indonesians are becoming more westernized, some "progressive" elements are bringing western homophobic attitudes into society.

BIBLIOGRAPHY. Penelope Graham, *Iban Shamanism*, Canberra: Research School of Pacific Studies, 1987; Gilbert Herdt, ed., *Ritualized Homosexuality in Melanesia*, Berkeley: University of California Press, 1984; Justus M. van der Kroef, "Transvestism and the Religious Hermaphrodite in Indonesia," *University of Manila Journal of East Asiatic Studies*, 3 (April 1954), 257–65; James Peacock, *Rites of Modernization: Symbolic and Social Aspects of Indonesian Proletarian Drama*, Chicago: University of Chicago Press, 1968.
Walter L. Williams

INFAMY

This term, which now connotes an evil reputation in a general sense, formerly had a range of sexual connotations. Under the term *infâmes*, with the abstract noun *infamie*, eighteenth-century French designated all those "addicted to unnatural pleasures," thus not exclusively homosexuals, but those who engaged in any category of nonprocreative sex. But for a short period—the second quarter of the century—*infâmes* and *infamie* applied almost entirely to male homosexuality.

The notion of infamy derived from Roman law where it served to designate a person as civilly unworthy or disgraced as a result of a judgment against him (*infamia juris*, infamy of law), or even without such a judgment (*infamia facti*, infamy of fact). The first was a matter of law, the

second of public opinion. Feudal and **canon law** from the fourth century onward extended the concept of infamy to heretics, whom this stigma excluded from communion with believing Christians. William Eden, an English criminal jurist of the **Enlightenment**, explained the penal effect of civic degradation in his *Principles of Penal Law* (1771) by saying that "virtue, though of a social nature, will not associate with infamy." Although the concept of infamy was never received into the common law tradition, Jeremy **Bentham** in his work on the subject enumerated some thirty-three English synonyms for the expression.

For an individual to suffer the penalty of infamy, his misconduct had to be publicly known; the canon lawyers even upheld the principle *Ecclesia de occultis non judicat*, "The church renders no judgment on hidden matters." On the other hand, infamy of law could be established by a tribunal in accordance with received rules of evidence, while infamy of fact depended upon one's loss of reputation. It was the latter rather than the former that plagued homosexuals over the centuries, as actual prosecutions and convictions for sodomy were rare, even under the Old Regime, and were more often than not show trials intended to impress the multitude with the gravity of the offense and potential wrongdoers with the dreadful penalties to which they might expose themselves. Sodomy between laymen was punishable with excommunication, and when convicted by a tribunal, the culprits, if clerks, were permanently deprived of benefit of clergy, and then both classes were relaxed to the secular authorities, who would carry out the sentence by burning them at the stake, from the mid-sixteenth century onward in accordance with two constitutions of pope Pius V, *Cum primum* (April 1, 1566) and *Horrendum* (August 30, 1568). Conviction for the crime entailed *infamia juris*, notoriety *infamia facti*. Further, the overlap of sodomy with heresy and to a lesser extent with witchcraft in the medieval mind and in the texts of canon law darkened the penumbra of infamy that enveloped sins "against the order of nature."

French usage of the eighteenth century employed such expressions as *goût infâme, vice infâme, commerce infâme, moeurs infâmes* to designate homosexual relations; **Voltaire** in the *Dictionnaire philosophique* (1764) could even speak of the *amour infâme*. The records of the Paris police even use these expressions as technical terms for sodomy and those addicted to it when recording the activities of the vice squad in its surveillance of the homosexual underworld of the capital. Occasional lingering examples of the word in this meaning are found as late as the nineteenth century, in Pierre Proudhon and, somewhat ironically, in the "decadent" bisexual poet Paul **Verlaine**.

Cesare **Beccaria**, in his treatise *Dei delitti e delle pene* (1764), attacked the concept of infamy in the Roman law of late feudal and early modern Europe, and the favorable reception of his work in the early Republic accounted for the reference to "a capital, or otherwise infamous crime" in the Fifth Amendment to the American Constitution. However, although Beccaria's principles were enacted into law in the Bill of Rights in 1791, the criminal penalties for sodomy, and the infamy of fact attaching to the homosexual in public opinion, remained in the United States and generally in the Protestant countries of northern Europe, whose religious tradition had discarded the notion of infamy of law. Down to the second half of the twentieth century the overt, known homosexual continued to be a criminal and an outcast in the eyes of his fellow Americans.

Thus the Old Regime survived among a people who believed that its forefathers had left such intolerant practices behind when they set foot in the new land. The gay rights movement of today carries on the struggle against this survival of medieval infamy by combatting the defa-

mation which the church had practiced for centuries—and in many instances continues to practice in the face of the modern understanding of homosexual behavior and of twentieth-century norms of personal freedom and self-determination.

BIBLIOGRAPHY. Claude Courouve, *Vocabulaire de l'homosexualité masculine*, Paris: Payot, 1985; Mitchell Franklin, "The Encyclopédiste Origin and Meaning of the Fifth Amendment," *Lawyers Guild Review*, 15 (1955), 41–62; Benno Löbmann, *Der kanonische Infamiebegriff in seiner geschichtlichen Entwicklung*, Leipzig: St.-Benno-Verlag, 1956.

Warren Johansson

INGLE

This word is now obsolete in English, but in the late Elizabethan era and afterward it designated a **catamite** or kept boy. The earliest quotation is from Thomas Nashe, *Strange News* (1592): "I am afraid thou wilt make me thy ingle." J. Z. Eglinton has suggested that the word may derive from Medieval Latin *angelus* through one of the Celtic languages, Irish or Scots Gaelic, which has the word *aingeal* meaning "angel." The depiction of the angels in Christian art as beautiful, epicene creatures of the sort desired by the boy lover would have motivated the semantic transition. Ben Jonson, in the play *Epicene* (ca. 1609), has one character voice envy for another's luxury, including the option of "his mistress abroad and his ingle at home." The term was also used as a verb, attested by John Florio in *A World of Wordes* (1598), an Italian-English dictionary with the entry: *Cinedulare*, to bugger . . . to ingle; while *ingler* designated the **active** partner: *pedicone*, a buggrer, an ingler of boys.

The word should not be confused with the homophone *ingle*, "fire," which is derived from the Scots Gaelic *aingeal* (a homophone of the first *aingeal*) in the same sense, but of unknown origin; it is probably cognate with Old Prussian *an-*

glis, Lithuanian *anglis*, Russian *ugol'*, Polish *węgiel*, Albania *thëngjill*—all with the primary meaning "glowing coal." The second English word figures in *inglenook*, "the nook or corner beside the hearthfire, chimney corner"; however, influenced by the erotic associations of the homonym, *inglenook* itself acquired the meaning "female pudendum."

Warren Johansson

INJUSTICE COLLECTING

The Vienna, then New York, **psychoanalyst** Edmund **Bergler** (1899–1962) developed the theory that the basic neurosis is psychic masochism, and that homosexuals are neurotic "injustice collectors." In Bergler's view the provocative behavior observed in his patients arises in the following manner. They create a situation in which some substitute for the mother of early childhood is perceived as "refusing." Not realizing that they are themselves to blame, they become aggressive in righteous indignation and self-defense alternating with self-pity, while "unconsciously enjoying psychic masochism." Under the façade of pseudo-aggression are hidden deep self-damaging tendencies. The psychic masochist in the homosexual "habitually transforms conscious displeasure into unconscious pleasure," so that he can resign himself to the punishments resulting from the humiliation and insult heaped on him by an intolerant society. Instead of learning to avoid punishment, the homosexual actually enjoys it, and by turning displeasure into pleasure he "takes the sting out of the pain and defeat of his tormented existence." Such were Bergler's idiosyncratic views.

While it is true that a homosexual with self-damaging tendencies (and such people do exist) is likely to encounter reprisals from a society permeated with Judeo-Christian **homophobia**, only a shrinking minority of homosexuals are of this type. Moreover, early writers denying the pathological character of homosexuality pointed to the success with which many **closeted** homosexuals deceive intolerant heterosexuals in their entourage with the skill of an accomplished undercover agent or spy. But the "injustice collector" mentality may also have had the function of preserving the individual's self-esteem in the face of society's condemnation and rejection. Instead of internalizing the values of the homophobic culture, he can in effect say: "You are the wrongdoer, and I am the one to whom the injustice is being done." The alternative would be to accept the stigma of being a sinner, a criminal, and a monster—which a rational subject could scarcely do without a total loss of self-respect. Whatever therapeutic results Bergler scored with his homosexual analysands seem to have been with individuals whose superego had been unable to ward off society's castigation of their behavior and the ensuing guilt and self-reproach. Then his very success with them attracted ever more to his couch, so that his "patient universe" became skewed in the direction of such guilt-ridden personalities.

BIBLIOGRAPHY. Edmund Bergler, "The Myth of a New National Disease: Homosexuality and the Kinsey Report," *Psychiatric Quarterly*, 22 (1948), 66–88; idem, *The Basic Neurosis: Oral Regression and Psychic Masochism*, New York: Grune & Stratton, 1949; Edmund Bergler and Joost A. M. Meerloo, "The Injustice Collector," in *Justice and Injustice*, New York: Grune & Stratton, 1963, pp. 20–35.

Warren Johansson

INQUISITION

During the **Middle Ages** the Roman Catholic church established special ecclesiastical courts to detect and punish heretics, blasphemers, witches, and sorcerers. Stemming from the Latin for "investigation," inquisitions may be divided into the episcopal phase, which began informally by 312, the papal phase, which began in 1232, and the royal phase, which lasted in Spain from 1478 to 1834. It was the royal Spanish Inquisition which was responsible for most of the burnings at the stake which posterity associates with the Inquisition.

Episcopal Inquisitions. In the early centuries, Christians usually punished **heresy** by excommunication, exclusion from the community of the faithful. **Patristic** writers generally disapproved of physical sanctions, though after **Christianity** became the official religion of the Roman empire, rulers often chose to regard heresy as a kind of *lèse-majesté*, an offense to the imperial dignity worthy of loss of property or even death. The collapse of the Roman Empire in the west, in 476, made a uniform imposition of such severity impractical. On the whole, the early medieval church itself kept to a relatively restrained attitude, which lingered in the twelfth century in the precept "Faith is to be secured by persuasion, not by force" of St. Bernard of Clairvaux.

Shortly after the year 1000, however, the western church was threatened by the inception of a new wave of heresy. In due course the new dissidents, who threatened not only the principles of faith but also the prerogatives of the church as an institution, rallied behind the dualism of the Cathars (or Albigensians), which in parts of Europe, notably in southern France, took on the character of a full-fledged counter-church. St. Dominic and his preaching friars tried in vain to win back the heretics to the church. Although the Cathars claimed that their elect members must be strictly celibate, the Catholics regularly accused them of sexual licence, as they had certain heretics before the fall of Rome. That such licence did occur and could be homosexual is shown, among others, by the detailed record of an investigation of sodomy in Pamiers in the south of France. The Cathars were subjected to a bloody crusade called by Pope Innocent III in 1208 and lasting until 1229, which succeeded in driving them partly underground but not extirpating them.

The Papal Inquisition. The establishment of a papal mechanism to combat heresy was gradual. One key step occurred in 1232 when Emperor **Frederick II**, himself accused of heresy, charged state officials of the Holy Roman Empire with the task of ferreting out and burning heretics. Fearing Frederick's ambitions, but more to suppress the Albigensians, whom the Crusade had failed entirely to exterminate, Pope Gregory IX (1227–1241) claimed this office for the church, appointing papal inquisitors. These were chosen, not from the retinue of the bishops who had hitherto dealt with heresy and were now enjoined to cooperate, but from members of the newly-formed mendicant orders, especially the Dominicans and Franciscans.

Torture Introduced. At first the inquisitors mainly admonished the guilty to confess voluntarily and accept penance. The obdurate were, however, imprisoned under harsh conditions. Influenced by the revival of Roman law, in 1252 Innocent IV authorized the use of torture to break the resistance of the accused. Penalties were confiscation of property, imprisonment either temporary or perpetual, and surrender (relaxation) to the secular arm, which meant death by burning at the stake. The proportion who suffered the supreme penalty was relatively small; out of 613 cases he prosecuted, the famous inquisitor Bernard of Gui "relaxed" 45.

Detection of sodomy per se was not a goal of the papal inquisition, though this prohibited behavior was not infrequently uncovered in the course of investigations conducted on other grounds, and appropriately punished—though rarely with death. The modern notion that the vernacular expression **faggot** derives from a supposed common practice of using male homosexuals as kindling for the burning of witches is fantasy, but English **bugger** comes from *Bulgarus*, the generic designation for adherents of dualistic heresies such as the Bogomils of Bulgaria and the Cathars of Provence.

As late as 1179, the Third Lateran Council decreed only degradation and confinement within a monastery for sodomitical clerics, the penalty prescribed by canon law, and excommunication for laymen. Secular **laws, feudal and royal,** were harsher: the thirteenth-century Castilian law ordering castration and stoning was in 1497 altered by Spanish King Ferdinand and Queen Isabella, *los reyes católicos* ("their Catholic Majesties"), to burning with confiscation of property, no matter what the rank or order of the condemned. Sodomy was *mixti fori*, subject to secular as well as regular ecclesiastical courts and after the decree of Pope Nicholas V in 1451 also to the papal Inquisition.

Spanish and Portuguese Inquisitions. In 1478 Ferdinand and Isabella created the Spanish Inquisition under royal sponsorship with papal approval. In 1524–30 pope Clement VII authorized the Inquisitions of Aragon, Saragossa, Valencia, and Barcelona to pursue sodomites. The Suprema in Madrid, the new capital after 1560, which allowed the accused to choose an "advocate" from members or familiars of the Inquisition as an illusory protection, sold exemptions at very high prices from its penalties such as prison, the galleys, or wearing the *sanbenito* (penetential costume). The grand inquisitor Tomás de Torquemada (1420–1498), of *converso* origin, even proceeded against bishops, who were usually exempt, and a successor did so against the archbishop of **Granada**, primate of Spain. After 1660 even the Jesuits, exempt from all ordinary authority, became subject to the Inquisition.

The Spanish Inquisition, though more avaricious, contributed less to royal centralization than had the one in France against the Albigensians. It was extended to the Italian provinces in the Spanish empire—Sicily, Sardinia, Naples, and Milan, as well as the Canaries, Mexico, Peru, and New Granada. The rumor that Philip II intended to introduce the Spanish Inquisition to the Netherlands in the 1560s contributed to the outbreak of the Dutch revolt against Spain, then the most powerful country in the world.

The Spanish Inquisition was all-pervasive: It was organized hierarchically—district inquisitors, *comisarios*, and *familiares* (local informers). In the province of Valencia in 1567 the number of *familiares* peaked at 1638 or an average of 1 per 42 inhabitants; they were particularly dense in the smallest hamlets so that social control was well-nigh complete. Spanish inquisitors applied tortures commonly used by contemporary ecclesiastical and secular tribunals: the pulley, water torture, and the rack.

In 1506 at Seville the Inquisition made a special investigation into sodomy, causing many arrests and many fugitives and burning 12 persons, but in 1509 the Suprema in Castile declared that crime not within the jurisdiction of the Inquisition. But after a fiery sermon preached by Fray Luis Castellioli attributing the pestilence then raging in Valencia to God's wrath against sodomites, the townspeople found four who confessed and were burnt at the stake by order of the court, while a fifth, given a more lenient sentence (*vergüenza*), was torn from the jailers, garroted and burnt by the mob. Alleging that the crime of sodomy had been introduced to Spain by the Moors, the Spanish Ambassador to Rome obtained from Pope Clement VII in 1524 a special commission for the Holy Office to curb its spread by investigating laymen and clergy in Aragon, Catalonia, and Valencia and proceeding according to local, municipal law in spite of the resistance by local bishops to this usurpation of their authority. In Castile, however, in 1534 and 1575, and in Peru in 1580 and again toward the end of Philip II's reign, royal inquisitors were barred from deciding cases involving only sodomy, but they nevertheless often ordered arrests. Moreover, Castilian secular courts prosecuted sodomites even more vigorously than the Inquisition in Aragon: between the 1580s and the 1650s between 100 and 150 sodomites were executed in Madrid alone. In 1568 Philip II ordered death for all sodomites in all his realms but Sicily successfully resisted. There the authorities inflicted surprisingly lesser penalties in a large number of cases: imprisonment or banishment for life or for a number of years or fines and degradation from office.

The papal Inquisition refused cognizance of sodomy and in 1638 Dr. Martí Real claimed that throughout Italy leniency inadequate to the enormity of the offense prevailed. In fact, in 1644 some Franciscans praised the practice.

In Portugal John III obstinately pursued jurisdiction for his Inquisition, which the reluctant papacy granted only in 1562 after his death and as in Aragon only provided that judges proceed according to municipal law. By 1640 the offense was tried like heresy and punished by scourging and the galleys or relaxation. As a result of complaints by the Cortes, the Concordat of 1646 recognized the principle of *mixti fori* so that whichever court proceeded first gained jurisdiction. In all the regions under the Spanish crowns, which included Portugal between 1580 and 1640, squabbles over jurisdiction, procedure, and penalties continued, but torture tended to be freely used even upon the testimony of but one accomplice.

Valencia. There were two peak periods of prosecution in Valencia: 1571–90 and 1621–30. The first sodomite was burned by the Inquisition in Valencia in 1572. The accused included 19.5 percent clergy, 5.6 percent nobles and other upper-class groups, 36.7 percent workers and artisans, 18.6 percent slaves and servants, 17.6 percent soldiers, sailors, and vagabonds, and 2.3 percent other groups. Poor boys leaving home to seek their fortunes beginning as early as 8 to 10 were the most frequent objects of desire, but as passives and minors they received much lighter if any sentences than their older and active seducers. Of those brought to trial, 29.1 percent were between 12 and 19 years old and 43.2 percent were under 25. Of the 347 cases of "crimes against nature" between 1566 and 1775, 259 involved homosexuality; minus bestiality the proportion rises from 74.6 percent to 99.2 percent. Prior to 1570 the records show between 10 and 20 cases; from 250 to 260 were found between 1570 and 1700, and only 50 or 60 cases in the eighteenth century. Thus from 320 to 350 cases occurred between 1566 and 1775, of which 50 to 60 resulted in burnings.

A growing reluctance to convict those who, unlike heretics, could not escape by confession and penance led after 1630 to greater leniency and more commutations. Torture decreased: in Valencia 21.4 percent of sodomites were tortured prior to 1630, but only 4.2 percent afterwards. Priests held that only incorrigibility should lead to relaxation, and sodomy was held to be a sin or vice, not a fixed characteristic. The subjects of inquisition then in theory could not be tortured until the church failed after repeated attempts to reform them, for torture should only be used when conviction could lead to death. In the trial of Fray Manuel Sánchez del Castellar y Arbustán in 1684 with two accomplices testifying to consummated acts and others—solicitation, lewd and lascivious acts, and a foul reputation—continual cross-examination, so rarely allowed in such tribunals, revealed inconsistencies, discrepancies, contradictions, jealousies, and enmities; this trial led only to exile and silencing of the distinguished clerk, who had already lingered three years in prison. By the early eighteenth century, greater mildness in regard to those found guilty of sodomy was on the rise.

Portugal. The records of the Portuguese Inquisition, which are complete for sodomy from 1567 to 1794, have been carefully studied by Luiz Mott, a leading Brazilian scholar. During this period 4,419 persons confessed to, or were accused of, sodomitical crimes, but of these fewer than ten percent were arrested and tried. Only thirty sodomites were actually burned by the Portuguese Inquisition, so that it seems milder than persecutions in other countries. Throughout western Europe, however, the strategy of social control of homosexual behavior seems to have been much the same: since there could be no possibility of blanket surveillance, the authorities severely punished in public a few signal cases of sodomy to intimidate others. The accused included a disproportionate number of blacks and mulattoes, reflecting the popular belief that sodomy had been imported from overseas. As in Aragon, in Portugal the persecution of sodomites peaked in the period 1620–34, when as many cases were tried (94) as those recorded for the previous century. In the eighteenth century sodomy trials became uncommon, and the Portuguese Inquisition concentrated on persecuting heretics and libertines.

Overseas. Cardinal Jiménez had given bishops inquisitorial power in the Indies in 1516–17. Philip II established tribunals in Lima (1570) and Mexico City (1571). The first auto-da-fé (public burning) took place at Mexico City in 1547, the year of Cortes' death. The Inquisition in America was less active than in Spain, with only some 100 executions in the 250 years of its existence; only 30 were executed in Lima, for example. The Portuguese Inquisition made Goa its overseas capital and in 1571 Philip II had the pope create an "Inquisition of the galleys . . . of fleets and armies." Protestants, even English and French ones, were burned.

Much work needs to be done in evaluating the records of the Iberian Inquisition. However, a glimpse of their treatment of sodomites is afforded by a scene in Seville in 1585. The authorities decided to make an example of a black man who had been accused of sodomy and procuring young boys. They painted his face, adorned him with a lace ruff and a big curled wig, and marched him through the streets to the stake.

How Many Victims? Estimates of the total number of victims of the Inquisition vary enormously, and modern critical scholarship has corrected some of the exaggerations of earlier Protestant and anti-

clerical historians. Stanley Paine, in his *History of Spain and Portugal* (Madison, WI, 1973), concluded that in the first century of the Iberian Inquisition (1478–1578), 50,000 conversos were condemned, but that the Spanish Inquisition executed a total of some 3,000 (including a small number of Protestants) over a span of three hundred years (1478–1778). A few executions are recorded from the eighteenth century, and the last hanging occurred in 1826. By contrast, between 1562 and 1684 3,200 individuals were executed for witchcraft in Southwest Germany alone.

Henry Kamen, in *Spain 1469–1714* (New York, 1965), states that about 5.4 percent of those arrested by the Inquisition were accused of Judaizing and 7 percent of Protestant sympathies. Most of the Protestants were foreigners. In all of Spain after 1562 fewer than half a dozen individuals were burned at the stake for Protestantism. In Aragon, Granada, Saragossa, and Valencia most of the accused were moriscos (Moors forcibly converted to a nominal Christianity). Executions amounted to no more than 10 percent a year of those arrested. In much of this period the total number of executions by order of the Inquisition came to only 2 or 3 a year in all of Spain and its American colonies. Kamen further notes that as many as one-third of those arrested in Toledo were accused of extra-marital sexuality—fornication, adultery and the like—over which secular tribunals also had jurisdiction.

The anti-clerical Napoleonic-era historian Juan Antonio Llorente concluded that 31,912 condemned persons were relaxed to the secular authorities and 17,659 were relaxed in effigy because they had already fled, while 291,450 persons were given penitential sentences, thus assigning the Spanish Inquisition a total of 341,021 victims in its three-and-a-half century history.

Conclusion. The principle of toleration proclaimed by the **Enlightenment** caused the Inquisition in Spain first to be abolished in 1808 by Joseph Bonaparte and although restored by the reactionary Ferdinand VII in 1814, it was abolished by the liberals after they came to power in 1820, and definitively abolished by royal decree in 1834. Its crimes are still remembered as a high-water mark of the attempt to impose uniformity of belief by systematically prosecuting and punishing all who were guilty of "error," and it has served as a sad precedent for totalitarian states of the twentieth century that have demanded the same sort of ideological unanimity from their subjects. The mass purges and atrocities of Soviet Russia, Nazi Germany, and other dictatorships that explicitly rejected the legal doctrines of the Enlightenment have revived these horrendous practices of the Old Regime. The Holy Office, responsible for the conduct of the papal Inquisition since 1542, was replaced by the Congregation for the Doctrine of the Faith in 1965.

In retrospect, it must be conceded that the number of homosexual victims of the Inquisition, even at its fiercest, was but a small percent of the whole. Marranos (nominal Christians of Jewish descent), Nicodemites, sundry heretics, and other offenders outside the sexual realm made up the bulk of those persecuted by the inquisitors, while a minority—perhaps only a fifth—of those convicted of sodomy were actually burnt at the stake. The object of the show trials and executions was to intimidate other, potential offenders, not to exterminate an entire segment of the population, since the modern notion of the "exclusive homosexual" did not exist at this time.

It is clear from the historical record that even in that era a few thinkers did everything in their power to calm the irrational panic unleashed by credulity and superstition, so that the peak of intolerance was always followed by a decline in the number of prosecutions and in the severity of the sentences. The Iberian peninsula seems to have reached the height of persecution of sodomy first, in the earlier half of the seventeenth century; France (without the device of Inquisition) in the second half under Louis XIV; Holland in the first half of the eighteenth century, and last of all Protestant England in the eighteenth and early nineteenth century. By the time such Continental reformers as **Beccaria** and **Voltaire** began their attack on the criminal practice of the Old Regime, mass trials and executions for sodomy were largely a thing of the past, and an enlightened public opinion was preparing for the abolition of all offenses motivated by superstition and fanaticism—a step finally taken by the Constituent Assembly during the French Revolution, some time before the persecution of sodomites was to reach its peak in England.

BIBLIOGRAPHY. Rafael Carrasco, *Inquisición y represión sexual en Valencia: historia de los sodomitas (1565–1785)*, Barcelona: Laertes, 1985; Henry C. Lea, *A History of the Inquisition of Spain*, 4 vols., New York: Macmillan 1906–07; Luiz Mott, "Pagode português: a subcultura *gay* em Portugal nos tempos inquisitóriais," *Ciência e Cultura*, 40 (1987), 120–39.

William A. Percy

INSANITY, MORAL

Moral insanity, defined as "madness consisting in a morbid perversion of the natural feelings, affections, inclinations, temper, habits, moral dispositions, and natural impulses, without any remarkable disorder or defect of the intellect or knowing and reasoning faculties, and particularly without any insane illusion or hallucination," was a widespread **psychiatric** concept in the nineteenth century. In the English-speaking world it was particularly propagated by James Cowles Prichard (1786–1848), whose fame, however, rests upon his work as an anthropologist and comparative linguist. Educated at Cambridge and then at Oxford, in 1811 he became a physician at Saint Peter's Hospital in Bristol and in 1814 at the Bristol Infirmary, besides which he developed a substantial private practice.

In the *Cyclopaedia of Practical Medicine* Prichard published an article "Insanity," which he afterwards expanded into a separate treatise that became a classic in this branch of medical literature. Its outstanding contribution was the definition of the form of mental derangement that gained the name of "moral insanity." The subject had earlier been broached by Philippe Pinel (1745–1826), the founder of modern psychiatry, and then by his pupil, Jean Etienne Dominique Esquirol (1772–1840), who wrote extensively on the moral causes of insanity, which even more than his predecessor he considered to predominate over the physical ones in a ratio as high as 4 to 1, as in a memoir which he presented to the Society of Medicine in 1818. In the eyes of his contemporaries Prichard's merit was that of proving for the first time the existence of insanity "without marked intellectual aberration."

In *A Treatise on Insanity and Other Disorders Affecting the Mind* (1835), Prichard only incidentally touched upon what were later to be called sexual perversions or parhedonias. For him the fundamental criterion of the pathological was quantitative, so that he could write of instances "in which the unusual intensity of particular passions or emotions has been thought to constitute mental illness" and add that "a series of compound epithets has been invented for the purpose of affording names to such states of the mind and its affectations. Nostalgia [here meaning a longing for an absent lover] and erotomania have been considered as disorders of sentiment; satyriasis and nymphomania of the physical feelings. The excessive intensity of any passion is disorder in a moral sense; it may depend physically on certain states of the constitution; but this does not so clearly constitute madness as the irregular and perverted manifestation of desires and aversions." Prichard concludes with the pertinent remark that "this species of insanity has been the real source of moral phenomena of an anomalous and unusual kind, and of certain perversions of natural inclination which excite the greatest disgust and abhorrence."

Prichard further conceded that courts and medical writers in England recognized no such disorder as moral insanity, where insanity was held coterminous with mental illusion, with what German writers called *Wahnsinn*. "English writers . . . know nothing of moral insanity either as requiring control in the exercise of civil rights, or as destroying or lessening culpability in criminal ones." Thus from both the medical and the forensic standpoints Prichard's thinking never reached the insight which psychiatrists from the late 1860s onward were to achieve—but only after reading the work of the pioneer homosexual apologists **Ulrichs** and **Kertbeny**. He could not go beyond the concept of a quantitative change in the sexual drive, as did his successors, who recognized and defined a set of qualitative ones which they classified as perversions of the sexual instinct and held that they limited, if not entirely abolished, the responsibility of the subject in criminal cases.

Another concept propagated by Prichard was that of *monomania*, which had been introduced by Esquirol in 1814. The British author defined this as "partial insanity, in which the understanding is partially disordered or under the influence of some particular illness, referring to one subject, and involving one train of ideas, while the intellectual powers appear, when exercised on other subjects, to be in a great measure unimpared." This notion did influence early psychiatric authors on sexual inversion such as Julien Chevalier, who in his dissertation of 1885 classified the phenomenon as an "instinctive monomania," that is to say, an illness affecting only one aspect of the instinctive life while leaving all the others sound and normal. Individuals suffering from instinctive monomanias could even possess great intellectual gifts, could be "dégénérés supérieurs" (superior degenerates). The abandonment of the whole concept naturally invalidated this particular application of it as well.

Discarded also was Esquirol's emphasis on moral rather than physical causes of mental illness, which Prichard had dutifully echoed in his work of 1835. On the eve of Westphal's discovery, a paper was published in an American psychiatric journal which analyzed recent statistics to show that all cases were now ascribed either to physical or to "unknown" causes. in other words, that the notion of moral causality had been abandoned. This triumph of materialism in psychiatry paved the way for the acceptance of the concept of *psychopathia sexualis* by **Krafft-Ebing** and later authors. It is instructive that Westphal's immediate predecessor in the psychiatric division of the Charité (Berlin's general hospital), Wilhelm Griesinger (1817–1868), actually had a male homosexual patient under examination, but dismissed his sexual proclivities as a "revolting aberration." Only when armed with the insights furnished by the early homosexual apologists could the new generation of psychiatrists overcome the narrow vision—and spontaneous aversion—that had hobbled such investigators as Prichard and Griesinger.

Warren Johansson

INTERMEDIATE STAGES, SEXUAL

Homosexuality has sometimes been regarded as a type of sexual intermediacy, part of a continuum that stretches between the male and female poles. The notion stems from the propensity of the early investigators of sexual abnormality to devise conceptual schemes that would embrace larger categories of psychopathology, and also fit their new discoveries into the evolutionary framework that had been popularized by Charles Darwin and Ernst Haeckel. Richard von **Krafft-Ebing**, in his *Psychopathia sexualis* (first edition 1886), carried this schematizing tendency to inordinate lengths, even classifying delusion of change of sex as the last degree of abnormality of which sexual inversion was the first.

Magnus **Hirschfeld** followed his lead by changing the original title of the scholarly organ of the **Scientific-Humanitarian Committee**, *Jahrbuch für homosexuelle Forschungen*, to *Jahrbuch für sexuelle Zwischenstufen* (Yearbook for Sexual Intergrades), which first appeared in 1899 and lasted, with some interruptions, until 1923, when catastrophic inflation deprived the Committee of financial resources. Hirschfeld, with propaganda for repeal of **Paragraph 175** of the Penal Code of the German Reich as his aim, for years endeavored to prove that homosexuals belonged to an "intermediate sex" that fell on the continuum between the male and the female and was characterized by a whole set of traits that were located on the statistical mean between the norms for the opposite sexes. He laid great stress on subjects who displayed marked inversion of the secondary sexual characters (pronounced effeminacy in men or masculinity in women), conveniently ignoring those homosexuals and lesbians who, while being exclusively attracted to their own sex, in no way depart from its normal physical type. Commensurate with the *Zwischenstufentheorie*, the pages of the *Jahrbuch* carried articles on transvestism, hermaphroditism, and androgyny from the standpoint of cultural history as well as material on all aspects of homosexuality proper.

This notion of sexual intergrades, confusing the orientation of the sexual drive with the anatomical traits of the sexes, stemmed in part from the classical notion of the **hermaphrodite** as combining male and female, and also from the notion that *natura non facit saltus*, "Nature makes no sudden leaps," but rather all phenomena are arranged along a continuum within which a certain group may be legitimately so defined. Sigmund **Freud** rejected the whole notion, maintaining that it was absolutely incorrect to set the homosexual apart as a special type or variety of human being, and that all human beings are capable of a homosexual object choice and have already made one in the unconscious. The popularity of **psychoanalysis** caused the intermediate stage idea to be abandoned, even if it continues to figure in the reprints of the English translation of the twelfth edition of Krafft-Ebing and similar works from the first decade of the century.

If, in its original form, the idea of sexual intermediate stages no longer enjoys currency, it reflects a broader conceptual tendency that is found in other realms. Many are dissatisfied with the rigidity that they detect in such binary oppositions as good and bad, kind and cruel, extrovert and introvert, male and female, and would prefer to replace them with a scale admitting gradations between the two poles. In their first *Report* (1948) Alfred **Kinsey** and his associates proposed to abandon the dichotomy between heterosexual and homosexual, and to replace it with a seven-point scale. More recent gender studies have tended to emphasize states of **androgyny** between the male and female. Although these approaches may raise problems of explanation in terms of underlying biological mechanisms, they reflect an enduring feature of the modern mind: the quest to overcome dualism.

Warren Johansson

INTERTESTAMENTAL LITERATURE

This term designates a body of Jewish religious writings which in the main fall between the last writings of the **Old Testament** (mid-second century B.C.), on the one hand, and the closing of the **New Testament** and the creation of the Mishnah (late second century), on the other. Traditionally these texts are distinguished from the Old Testament Apocrypha, a relatively privileged group which, though not part of the Bible proper, is accorded deuterocanonical status by some Christian groups. As cultural documents the intertestamental writings—though rarely consulted by the general public today—are of incalculable value in helping to trace the multifaceted evolution of **Judaism** in **Hellenistic** and **Roman** times.

Among other points these texts bear witness to the continuing Jewish rejection of homosexual behavior. The Testaments of the Twelve Patriarchs contain repeated condemnations of fornication and sexual immorality, and the Testament of Naphtali (3:4–5) notes that the people of **Sodom** changed the order of their **nature**, a key concept that recurs in the Pauline discussion in Romans 1:26–27. The Book of Jubilees asserts that the Sodomites "were polluting themselves and they were fornicating in their flesh and they were causing pollution upon the earth. And thus the Lord will execute judgment like the judgment of Sodom on places where they act according to the pollution of Sodom" (Jubilees 16:5–6). This is the first specific mention of Sodom as an example of sexual depravity whose punishment will be repeated in the future. The passages in the Second Book of Enoch are interpolations found only in a manuscript written in Poltava in 1679, but the Testament of Isaac contains a description of the torments of the Sodomites in Hell. As is well known, the Old Testament itself contains no explicit indication of infernal punishments.

The Sibylline Oracles condemn homosexual activity in numerous passages, such as 3:185: "Male will have intercourse with male and they will set up boys in houses of ill-fame," while in 3:596–600 the Jews are praised because "they do not engage in impious intercourse with boys, as do" many other nations, "transgressing the holy law of God immortal." This passage establishes that for the Jews of the Hellenistic diaspora the taboo on male homosexuality had become one of the distinctive mores of their religion that set it apart from all others in its claim to possess a higher morality. For the proto-Christian community it was to be a norm of moral purity as well. Thus the intertestamental texts repeat and amplify the Biblical injunctions against homosexual behavior, even in the neighborhood of host peoples who tolerated such activity and knew no religious taboo against it. While the exclusiveness of the Jews and their disdain for the polytheism of the other peoples of the Hellenistic world precluded general adoption of their laws, **Christianity** was to retain the sexual provisions of the Mosaic code after it seceded from Judaism in a bid to become the universal religion of the Greco-Roman world.

Warren Johansson

INVENTOR LEGENDS

In some traditions, the introduction of homosexual conduct to human society has been ascribed to a single individual. Some Greek writers held that same-sex relations among men had been devised and spread by **Orpheus**, perhaps as a result of his disappointment over the loss of Eurydice. In this story homosexual behavior is not regarded as a misfortune, but as a gift on a par with Orpheus' celebrated musical accomplishments. **Pederasty** in fact had a divine archetype in Zeus' love for **Ganymede**. Other Greek sources attribute the invention of human homosexuality to King Laius, who kidnapped Chrysippus, the beautiful son of his host Pelops, during his exile from Thebes. It was this outrage that set in motion the tragic fate of his son Oedipus, a fact rarely cited by interpreters of Sophocles' trilogy or by those who adhere to the psychoanalytic construct known as the "Oedipus complex." The Chrysippus story was the subject of a lost play by Euripides. Apollodorus ascribes pederasty to yet another figure, the singer Thamyris.

Among the Arabs a curious reversal occurred in that Lot, urged by God in the Hebrew Bible to flee **Sodom** because of its devotion to vice (*Genesis* 19), was actually made responsible for the practice itself, so that in Arabic homosexuals may be called *ahl Lūṭ*, "the people of Lot."

Did homosexuality, as an aspect of human culture, in fact have an inventor, or at least a phase of introduction to human society? Any answer to this question, like that of the appearance of human language, would have to be hypothetical. To the extent that homosexuality is found among **animals**, it would not seem to be a human discovery at all. Yet historical sequences show that homosexual behavior has undergone changes in social organization—as from the Greeks to the Romans, through the Middle Ages, and down to modern times. Where these changes can be monitored, as in this sequence, they seem to be the result of the gradual shift of ideological, economic, familial, and other factors, which could not readily respond to the suggestion of any single individuals. Thus while the inventor question is useful to raise social elements in the origins of particular forms of homosexual behavior, in its literal sense it seems to be a false quest.

Wayne R. Dynes

INVERSION

Since the end of the nineteenth century some **medical** and other writers have equated homosexuality with inversion. For some, the term meant simply the reversal of the current of attraction from the opposite to one's own sex. Others believed that inversion entails also an adoption of patterns of thinking, feeling, and action that are characteristic of the other sex. In this broader sense it amounts to **effeminacy** in the male, and viraginousness in the female, but it would not include the majority of male homosexuals and lesbians who do not show these traits. Studies of **androgyny** have also suggested that there is a continuum rather than a sharp separation between the two poles of male and female, so that inversion in the sense of a complete volte-face does not seem to occur. In any event, the terms *inversion* and *invert* have acquired a negative, clinical aura, and for this reason they are less commonly used today.

An examination of the history of these terms is helpful in understanding the connotations they carry today. In 1878, in a professional article in the *Rivista di freniatria, di psichiatria e di medicina legale*, the Italian alienist Arrigo Tamassia introduced the term *inversione*, which was quickly adopted into other languages as well as Italian to render the cumbersome German expression *die conträre Sexualempfindung* which Karl Westphal had used in 1869. The new coinage owed its success not only to its grammatical malleability—yielding the noun *invert* and the adjective *inverted*—but also to the fact that while the word itself was new, the ideas on which it drew were deeply rooted in Western consciousness.

The byways of the history of ideas reveal many episodes of the use of the spatial metaphors of "backwards-to-forwards" and "upside down" to symbolize social abnormality. Sometimes the inversion procedure is temporal rather than spatial, as in reciting the alphabet or some ritual formula backwards to produce a magical spell.

In Euripides' play *Medea* (fifth century B.C.), the social disturbance of role reversal catalyzed by the heroine's assumption of masculine qualities is evoked by the image of rivers running backwards in their course. And **Orpheus**, who according to some Greek sources invented pederasty, was supposed to have made wild oaks migrate from their mountain habitat to the seashore, and to reduce savage beasts to lamb-like docility, thus altering the natural order by switching things to their opposites. In Hellenistic times, the poet Sotades (third century B.C.) invented a kind of verse which was innocuous when read forwards, but obscene backwards.

The sexual predilections of the Romans for the "posterior Venus" (anal receptivity) were held to be revealed in the very name Roma, which is a backwards spelling for *amor* ("love"). In the Koran, God turns the sinful cities of **Sodom** and Gomorrah literally upside down. Medieval texts, such as the *Roman de la rose*, speak of sodomites doing things *à rebours* ("in reverse"), an expression that served Joris-Karl Huysmans in 1884 as the title for his novel of aristocratic perversion. Sixteenth- and seventeenth-century Europe witnessed the popularity of a genre of popular prints known as *Le Monde à l'Envers* or The World Upside Down, whereby alongside such outlandish things as fish nesting in trees and men plowing the sea, we find the wife going out to hunt while the husband stays home to mind the baby, and similar instances of sex-role reversal.

As used by late nineteenth-century writers, the word inversion often had an application that went beyond sexual **orientation**. The medical authorities who studied "inversion" were fascinated by gender-role reversal—masculine women and feminine men—positing such purportedly biological tendencies as the root cause of "inverted" sexual object choice, rather than vice versa. Certain writers preferred to restrict the term to the narrower meaning of the reversal of the secondary sexual characters as distinct from the sexual orientation proper; thus only the effeminate homosexual and the viraginous lesbian were "inverts" in this sense.

The idea was used in a number of creative ways by Marcel **Proust** in his great novel sequence *A la recherche du temps perdu* (1913–27) which shows that it need not always be negative. One of his homosexual characters, Robert de Saint-Loup, seeks out danger in battle instead of fleeing it, while Baron Charlus becomes more pro-German rather than less so as war nears. In a larger sense the novel's goal— the gradual recovery of more and more layers of memory—is a process of inversion or retrogression. This great enterprise is mirrored in Proust's fascination with musical techniques, including the device of melodic inversion.

Wayne R. Dynes

IRAN

Formerly known to the West as Persia, the name Iran was selected by the modern Pahlevi dynasty as a sign of the country's "Aryan," or Indo-European, heritage. This ethnically diverse land contains large numbers of Persians, Turks, nomadic tribesmen, and smaller numbers of Jews, Assyrians, and Arabs. The national language (Farsi) is **Indo-European**, not Semitic; Iran is not an Arab country.

The Pre-Islamic Period. The history of homosexuality in Iran has been both influential and contradictory. **Zoroastrianism**, the teachings of Zarathustra, is the most homophobic ancient faith known to modern scholarship. The fateful Zoroastrian doctrine (that all homosexuals, active or passive, are inherently demonic, and must be put to death when detected) was to make its way into the religious tradition of the Jews, who escaped their Babylonian captivity under Persian rule in 538 B.C.

This condemnation seems to have made its way but slowly against the much older Iranian traditions of polytheism and initiatory pederasty, traditions similar to those of the Greeks and probably inherited from a common ancestral Indo-European behavior pattern. During the Achaemenid period (sixth and fifth centuries B. C.), these two Iranian religious cultures were in conflict, as were two similarly warring faiths in the Palestine of the **Old Testament**. The Mazdaist/Zoroastrian cult reached its zenith of social control under the Sassanids (second to seventh centuries of our era). The only surviving Zoroastrian documents date from this time, when factions urged the Mazdaist clergy to a formal codification in the Pahlevi language.

The Sassanian church was a cruel persecutor of other religions, which included by this time Jews, Christians, **Manichaeans**, and even Buddhists toward the east. The battle with the Christians was especially fierce, and it is a minor irony of history that Christianity seemed destined to triumph over Mazdaism in Iran, when the Arab whirlwind of conquest decisively overcame both of them.

Islam. The Persians were conquered by the Arabs in A.D. 637. The Mazdaist faith was cast out and replaced by **Islam**, and the first three fourths of the oldest Pahlevi Avesta perished during the conquest. (The older religion now survives chiefly among the Parsees of India, who fled Iran during this epoch.)

The Arabs were only superficially intolerant of homosexuality, and certainly the Koran specified no earthly punishment for such behavior (it did, however, repeat the Sodom story in various places, most notably Sura 6, "The Heights," 80–84, where homosexual behavior is specified as the unique reason for the destruction of **Sodom**). The Islamic *hadith*, or oral traditions of Muhammad, held only that homosexuality was a sin greater than *zina*, or fornication, and specified no earthly punishment. The devout Muslim was expected to know that God would be displeased, and this knowledge (added to the desire for paradise) would be enough to control his behavior.

The outcome was a toleration and even celebration of pederasty in classical Islam, and much of the Arab poetry of this time (e.g., that of **Abu Nuwas**) is devoted to boys and their beauty. As a result, over a period of time the people of Persia once again moderated or reversed their earlier position. The most famous Persian poets were familiar with the love of young men— **Hafiz**, **Rumi**, **Sa'di**, and the astronomer– poet Omar Khayyam. The oft-cited lines "A Loaf of Bread beneath the Bough, A Flask of Wine, a Book of Verse—and Thou / Beside me singing in the Wilderness" are addressed to a young man. The matched themes of wine and boys became staples of Arabic and Persian poetry of the classic period, and echoed down the centuries into the gardens of Moorish **Granada**.

The conquered Persians did, however, formalize their anger at the Arab conquest into the Shiite schismatic movement. (The mainstream of Islam is Sunni.)

The Shiite faction has, from the beginning, been innately mystical, revolutionary, and capable of extreme sadism, masochism, and puritanism. It has hosted the whirling dervishes and the poetry of wine and boys; but it has also been the school of the Old Man of the Mountains, the fanatic who drugged his murderers with hashish and duped them into the belief that he held the keys to paradise on earth. (The term "assassin" derives from the hashish used by this group of thugs, who would risk anything for a return to the paradise they had glimpsed.)

In more recent times, this historical confusion about the subject has produced a sort of schizophrenia in the Iranian mind. Travelers from the nineteenth century report a man executing his son in the town square for the "crime," yet clearly many Iranians were and are devotees of pederasty, the Farsi term *bachebazi* (lit. "boyplay") being the equivalent of the ancient Greek *paidika*. In modern times under the Shah, Teheran had open gay bars and male hustlers were available. (These tended to come from the south of Teheran, particularly the impoverished suburb of Rayy, often under the guidance of tough *lutiyy* [brawling, folk-hero types] as their pimps and protectors.)

The overthrow of the Shah and the installation of the Khomeini regime saw another abrupt reversal. Basing their legitimacy on "Islamic fundamentalism," the mullahs (religious teachers) soon began executing homosexuals en masse in town squares—acting like Zoroastrians while citing Islam. They were also executing the few remaining Iranian Zoroastrians, which should come as no surprise to anyone who has been following this singularly erratic government.

The Iranian Baha'i sect, which claims to integrate all the great religions, also suffered at the hands of the mullahs. The Baha'i had never made any formal statement about homosexuality, finding this question difficult to solve, but unofficially held that homosexuality was a "curable disease," which shows they had gathered elements of psychiatry into their ecumenical mixture.

An ironic sidelight on the new regime is the fact that, for centuries, the Iranian people had regarded the mullahs themselves as generic homosexuals, and respectable Persian fathers would routinely warn their sons to guard their chastity during religious instruction.

Geoff Puterbaugh

IRELAND

In the first millennium B.C. the ancient **Celts** of the European continent were noted for their initiatory and military homosexuality. Yet as the mists of prehistory lift in Ireland in the fifth century of our era, no trace of these institutions is recorded. This absence (or silence) undoubtedly reflects the thoroughness of the process of Christianization, initiated by the quasilegendary St. Patrick. Yet the Irish Church pioneered in a new system of **penitentials**, a procedure that allowed sinners to "work off" their infraction with specified periods of restriction. The penalties for homosexual conduct found in these documents reveal a more lenient attitude toward homosexual conduct, while at the same time initiating the bureacratic approach that was to eventuate, centuries later, in the confessional system of the Roman Catholic Church. Irish missionaries active in remote areas of the British Isles and the European continent were sometimes linked by bonds of intense affection, a **homosocial** (if not homosexual) pattern that was to recur among the later medieval **clergy** ("particular friendships").

Beginning in the ninth century devastation by foreign invaders, first the Vikings and then the English, complicated the history of Ireland. In the present state of our knowledge we can only point to a few homosexual episodes before recent decades. In 1640 John Atherton, bishop of Waterford and Lismore, was convicted of sodomy and hanged. There is some indication that his execution occurred because he had offended both the powerful Earl of Cork and the still significant Roman Catholic party of the country. Two centuries later another high ecclesiastic became notorious throughout Europe. Jocelyn Percy, Bishop of Clogher, was in 1811 involved in a homosexual case in Dublin, for which he was not prosecuted. In 1822, however, he was apprehended in London, and only managed to escape serious punishment by fleeing to Scotland, where for some years he made his living as a servant.

Unlike the tragedy of Oscar **Wilde**, which was enacted entirely outside the emerald isle, that of Roger **Casement** is closely connected with Irish politics. Casement, an Irish patriot, was arrested in Ireland in 1916, after disembarking from a German submarine. On his person the British found a diary which recorded his homosexual activities in some detail. During his subsequent imprisonment and trial the London government "leaked" portions of the diary to erode sympathy for Casement, who was then executed for treason. For decades defenders of Casement disputed the authenticity of the diary, but it is now generally conceded to be genuine.

The preeminence of the Roman Catholic church in the new Irish Free State (1922–) meant repressive attitudes with regard to family and sex. The new republic retained the English laws of 1861 and 1885 against homosexual conduct. Pubs (bars) in Dublin were discreetly "mixed," and many Irish gays and lesbians undoubtedly joined the waves of immigration to Britain and America. During World War II and after, the country benefited from economic and social development that culminated in its joining the European Common Market. Efforts to unify the island by ending British sovereignty in the northern six counties proved unsuccessful. Sexual restrictions were slow to fall, though Ireland felt the impact of the American and European gay liberation movement after 1969. Homosexuality was decriminalized in Northern Ireland as a result of a favorable decision handed down by the European Court of Human Rights (Strasbourg) in the Jeff Dudgeon case in 1982. Yet the Catholic preamble to the Republic's constitution was quoted by the Dublin Chief Justice in his 1983 opinion dismissing the suit of David Norris to have the laws against gay men struck down. Continuing control of educational, medical, and social services gives the Roman Catholic church power to mold consciousness throughout the Republic of Ireland—but not in the larger world of the European Community to which Ireland belongs. Norris, the country's only openly gay legislator, appealed the case, and on October 26, 1988, the European Court of Human Rights ruled that the Republic's sodomy laws violate Article 8 of the European Charter of Human Rights.

The National Gay Federation established a noteworthy premises in Hirschfeld Centre in Dublin, and telephone "hotlines" were set up and successfully maintained. Unfortunately fire destroyed the Centre in 1987, but organizational work continues. For a time the Irish capital was also the headquarters of the International Gay Association. Despite some problems with violence, today gay life flourishes in the cities of Dublin and Cork, and, in Northern Ireland, in Belfast.

BIBLIOGRAPHY. Dublin Lesbian and Gay Men's Collectives, *Out for Ourselves: The Lives of Irish Lesbians and Gay Men*, Dublin: Women's Community Press, 1986.

Wayne R. Dynes

IRRUMATION
See **Oral Sex.**

ISHERWOOD, CHRISTOPHER (1904–1986)

Anglo-American novelist. Born in upper-middle-class circumstances, Isherwood became acquainted with W. H. **Auden**, his life-long friend and occasional collaborator, during their English **public** school days. In 1930–33 Isherwood lived in Berlin, where he gathered the material for some of his most effective writing. After Hitler's rise to power, he moved from country to country in an effort to stay together with his young German lover Heinz. He described this period with considerable frankness in his later memoir *Christopher and His Kind* (1976). During this period he worked with Auden (who had emerged as a major poet) on three plays, and they traveled to China together in 1938. Isherwood then settled in Southern California where in 1953 he took another young lover, Don Bachardy, who remained with him until Isherwood's death. Bachardy acquired some renown as an artist, creating many portraits of the writer and his friends.

Isherwood first found his footing as a writer in the material written in the 1930s and later collected in *The Berlin Stories* (1954). In these sketches of expatriation and sexual eccentricity, of poverty and political turmoil, he introduced the naturalistic method he called "I am a camera." Through several stage and screen metamorphoses this material came to play an important part in the post-War fascination with Weimar **decadence**.

Homosexuality, which was only one of several themes in his earlier novels, became increasingly prominent with the passage of time. *The World in the Evening* (1954), though later dismissed by the author as unsuccessful, contains what may be the first satisfactory explanation of **camp**. *A Single Man* (1964) is the portrait of a lonely, but not despairing Los Angeles gay man, while *Down There on a Visit* (1966) offers a portrait of Denny Fouts, said to be the most expensive hustler in the world. In Southern California Isherwood became interested in mysticism under the influence of a fellow expatriate, Gerald Heard, who later emerged as something of a philosopher of the homophile movement. For several years the novelist was a devoted disciple of Swami Prabhavananda, a Vedantist who had settled in Hollywood

(see *My Guru and Myself*, 1980). Isherwood was also active in the homophile rights organization, **ONE**.

Isherwood's writing has a spare elegance, but he declined to participate in the avant-garde experiments of his time. In all likelihood, his works will continue to be read for their candid picture of the life trajectory of a gay man in a time that saw enormous social and sexual changes.

BIBLIOGRAPHY. Brian Finney, *Christopher Isherwood: A Biography*, New York: Oxford University Press, 1979; Claude J. Summers, *Christopher Isherwood*, New York: Frederick J. Ungar, 1980.

Geoff Puterbaugh

ISLAM

A major world religion, Islam stems from the preaching of the Prophet Muhammad in Arabia in the seventh century. It is based on the principle that the believer (or *muslim*) surrenders (Arabic: *islam*) to the will of the one and only God (Allah). God's will is expressed in Islamic law, consisting of a system of duties which every Muslim has to submit to by virtue of his belief. Islamic law, also known as the *Shari'ah* (path), forms a comprehensive code of behavior, a divinely ordained path of conduct that guides the Muslim in the practical expression of his religious conviction toward the goal of divine favor in paradise. Law is based on the *Koran*, the word of God as revealed to his Prophet, on the *Hadith*, which is a collection of the words and deeds attributed to the Prophet which are used as precedents, and on the interpretations of the Islamic jurists (*Ulama*).

Basic Features. A central theme is Islamic law and its theoretical attitude toward male homosexual behavior, and how this attitude relates to the way Muslims generally deal with such behavior in practice. It is difficult to speak of Islamic law in general, however, because of the differences of opinion among various Islamic law schools and sects (such as the

Shi'a), while the same can be said of Islamic attitude in practice, as it varies in specific historical periods and regions. Even with a focus on material from the contemporary Middle East, an emphasis adopted in this article, general conclusions must be tentative

Islam considers sexuality an absolutely normal and natural urge of every human being. Symbolic of this positive attitude is the important place sex is accorded in paradise, which will be the fulfillment of the spiritual and bodily self. Islamic representations of paradise depict a height of delights, with, among other things, girls whose virginity is continually renewed, immortal boys as beautiful as hidden pearls, perpetual erections and infinite orgasms. On earth, however, because of human imperfection, sex has a problematic side, which makes regulation necessary. Unregulated sex threatens the social order and leads to anarchy and chaos, and therefore has to be restricted to marriage. Marriage is a social obligation, and forms the basis of orderly society, giving expression to the divine harmony consisting of the complementarity of men and women. An essential and sacred part of marriage, sex is considered to be a tribute to divine will, an acknowledgement of God's kindness and generosity, and a foretaste of the joys of paradise, which will sometimes lead to a renewal of his creation. Social order and the God-given harmony of life are threatened by the suppression of sexuality in celibacy and by sexual acts outside of marriage, heterosexual as well as homosexual. Celibacy is regarded as boring and unnatural, and rejected because it would inevitably lead to sinful feelings and to a knocking on forbidden doors. Sexual activity outside of marriage, adultery, is sharply condemned by Islamic law as a crime against humanity, which opens the door to many other shameful acts, and affects the reputation and property of the family, thereby disrupting the social fabric.

Homosexual behavior (*liwat*), i.e., sexual acts between members of the same sex, is considered to be adultery, being sex with an illicit partner. A person who performs such actions (*luti*) is regarded as extraordinarily corrupt, because he challenges the harmony of the sexes and topsyturvies God's creation: "Cursed are the men who behave effeminately, and cursed are the women who behave in a masculine way." Homosexual behavior is actually considered a revolt against God which violates the order of the world, and would be a source of evil and anarchy. The only remedy against such unnatural and sinful feelings is to fight and suppress them: "He who falls in love, conceals his passion, is chaste and patiently abstains, is forgiven by God and received into Paradise." Those who stubbornly persist in their behavior, however, await severe punishments, at least theoretically.

The Koran and the Hadith. In the Koran, homosexual behavior is explicitly condemned: "And as for the two of you who are guilty thereof, punish them both. If they repent and mend their ways, let them be. God is forgiving and merciful." (4:16). Homosexual behavior is further mentioned in the parable of the apostle Lot, which is repeatedly told in the Koran, and relates of the corrupted and evil-minded people of Lot's village, who transgressed consciously against the bounds of God. The behavior of these unbelievers was considered evil in general, their avarice led to inhospitality and robbery, which in turn led to the humiliation of strangers by mistreatment and rape. It was their homosexual behavior, however, which was seen as symptomatic of their attitudes, because it was regarded as "an abomination such as none in all the world has ever committed before." Obstinately refusing to accept God's message brought by Lot, the villagers were punished by God raining upon them "stones of heated clay" which killed them all and left their village ruined as a sign of the power of God for all to see. "The doings of the people of Lot" even became

616

proverbial, alluding specifically to homosexual behavior, while the Arabic words for homosexual behavior and for a person who performs such actions both derive from Lot's name.

In the Hadith, homosexual behavior is condemned harshly: "Whenever a male mounts another male, the throne of God trembles"; the angels look on in loathing and say: "Lord, why do you not command the earth to punish them and the heaven to rain stones on them?" God replies: "I am forebearing; nothing will escape me." Beside dreadful torments and humiliations in the world to come, homosexual behavior had to be punished on earth: "If you see two people who act like the people of Lot, then kill the active and the passive."

Legal Sanctions. The punishment which the Islamic jurists generally prescribe for adultery, and therefore also for homosexual behavior, is stoning to death for married people, and one hundred lashes for unmarried people. Persons who are married are punished more harshly because their behavior had severe consequences in regard to property and reputation, and would disrupt the family and the institution of marriage, both so important for the social order. The extravagant punishments which are prescribed are meant to have a deterring effect, and for that reason punishments are even carried out publicly.

Discouragement and repentance are considered more important than punishment, therefore the following conditions have to be met before condemnation is possible: Four adult Muslims of the male sex, of unblemished integrity of character, have to swear that they have been eye-witnesses to the carnal act itself. Less than four witnesses will lead to a punishment of the witnesses themselves, while the false accuser will receive eighty lashes, because of slander. Perpetrators can only be condemned when adult, Muslim, sane, and acting out of free will. A confession is sufficient for condemnation, if four times repeated. Before it is accepted, however, the judge has to point out to the accused the consequences of his confession, and the fact that repentance before the giving of testimony will be punished less harshly.

The fulfillment of all these conditions seems almost out of the question, leading to the conclusion that in practice it is only in very exceptional circumstances that persons are convicted and punished for adultery, and thus for homosexual behavior.

Theory and Practice. Theoretically homosexual behavior is sharply condemned by Islam, but in practice it is at present, and has been in the past, for the most part tolerantly treated and frequently occurring in countries where Islam predominates. The established societal norms and morals of Islam are accepted as unchangeable and respected by the majority of Muslims, which does not imply however that they will or can conform to them in practice. Human beings are considered by Islam as imperfect, and are expected to make mistakes and consequently to sin. God is understanding of man's weaknesses, and when a person is sincere in his shame and shows repentance of his sinful behavior, he will be mercifully forgiven by God. In practice it is only public transgression of Islamic morals that is condemned, and therefore Islamic law stresses the role of eye-witnesses to an offense. The police are not allowed to go in search of possible sinners, who can only be caught red-handed, and not behind the "veil of decency" of their closed doors. In a way, concealment is advised, because to disclose a dreadful sin would be a sin in itself.

But it is not only condemnation by the law which can be avoided by secrecy, the same can be said of shame, a concept which plays an important part in the social role pattern of Islamic countries. Shame is engendered by what an individual thinks that others might think of him, and arises when public behavior is not according to the prescribed role, and therefore improper and disgraceful, bringing obloquy on the individual and tarnishing the reputation and standing of his family.

This emphasis on externals in Islamic law as well as in the social concept of shame, with its connivance in theoretically forbidden and shameful behavior, could be deemed hypocritical. But such a judgment would be beside the point, missing the essence of the entire matter, which is that in principle the validity of Islamic morals and of the social role pattern is confirmed by not openly resisting it, and it is just that which maintains the system as it is.

Kicking at the boundaries of permissibility by telling obscene and shocking anecdotes, sometimes expressed in literature but mostly in the conversation and speech of the people, has always been popular, but as long as it did not give rise to publicly unlawful behavior or to open resistance to morality, it posed no serious problem for the social order.

The generally tolerant attitude toward homosexual behavior in practice can partly be explained by the fact that it will usually take place discreetly. Moreover it does not have serious personal consequences such as, for example, heterosexual adultery would have. There is no question of abuse of possession (which a wife is of her husband) or of loss of honor and face of husband and family, while there fortunately exists no danger of pregnancy, with all its consequences.

Practical tolerance therefore is the rule with respect to discreet homosexual behavior, but what about homosexuality?

Islamic law in theory only condemns homosexual acts and does not express itself on the subject of homosexuality. This is not in the least surprising, however, if we bear in mind that homosexuality is a western concept, crystalizing in the nineteenth century and stemming from the notion that sexual behavior is characteristic of someone's personality and identity, and therefore influences his behavior in general, leading to a certain lifestyle. Such a concept is essentially foreign to countries where Islam predominates, because there (sexual) behavior is not so much determined by personal preferences or someone's personality, as by a person's role and the circumstances in which he finds himself. Generally speaking, a person behaves in a particular situation as much as possible according to the social role pattern that prescribes whether a certain kind of behavior in that situation is proper or not. He conforms to this, because otherwise he would bring shame on himself and his family, and lose face and honor. For that reason it is, for example, not particularly important if a sexual act is homo- or heterosexual, but rather which role is performed (active, as is proper for a man, or passive, like a woman), and if the act has social consequences or not. Therefore concepts like homo- and heterosexuality make no sense in cultures like these. Such contemporary western principles as "I am a homosexual, and thus I do not marry" are laughed at, because a person has to comply with his role, and therefore is expected to marry and beget children. As long as he maintains his role in public, his private preferences and idiosyncrasies are nobody's business but his own, that is if he is discreet about them, and harms no one.

The Repression in Iran. What, then, of the executions of homosexuals in Iran betwen 1979 and 1984? The problem here is a confusion of terms, because the "homosexuality" meant in **Iran** is far different from the western concept of it. In Iran "homosexuality" has become a negative label, as it has in other Islamic countries, but fortunately with less extreme consequences. The label "homosexuality" refers to behavior which clashes with the God-given order of society and with the social role pattern; it is behavior which violates public decency, and is moreover seen as a typical example of western **decadence.** "Homosexuality" refers specifically to passive homosexual behavior, which is considered particularly objectionable, because it turns God's creation topsyturvy, and threatens the God-given harmony between men and women, which is reflected in the social role pattern. A man who plays the active, penetrator role in a homosexual act, behaves like a man, and is therefore not considered "homosexual." Passive homosexual behavior, however, implies being penetrated like a woman, and is considered to be extremely scandalous and humiliating for a man, because it is feminine behavior. Deviant behavior like this was in olden times viewed as abnormal and unnatural, and sometimes even characterized as an illness, because it was incomprehensible that a man could voluntarily choose to be dishonored and debased in the role of a woman. More common is the belief that sexual behavior that deviates from the norm causes illness, a notion soon to be confirmed by the appearance of AIDS.

Another myth that influences the negative labeling of "homosexuality" is that of the foreignness of sexually deviant behavior. In past centuries the Arabs ascribed homosexual behavior to Persian influence, and nowadays it is mostly regarded as originating from the West—a rather paradoxical viewpoint, because it used to be the other way around. Western society is viewed as shameless and depraved, permissiveness making license public and ultimately leading to social chaos. "Homosexuality" epitomizes this western decadence, this "unbridled riot of wantonness."

Finally, "homosexuality" also refers to the public transgression of morals, the conscious refusal to hide behind the veil of secrecy, and thus openly challenging established norms and values. As in the story of Lot, it is today "homosexuality" that has become symptomatic of evil behavior in general. "Homosexuality" would inevitably lead to chaos and decay, and therefore "homosexuals" are considered as antisocial, and as a threat to social order. Ayatollah Khomeini (who died in 1989) alluded to this idea, asserting that "homosexuals" had to be exterminated because they were parasites and corruptors of the nation by spreading the "stain of wickedness." "Homosexuality" not only is seen as evil in itself, but provides a convenient label for stigmatizing bad people in general. This broad-gauge definition underpinned what happened in Iran, where "homosexuality" was often deployed as a generic label to be applied at will to persons adjudged criminals, whether rightly or wrongly. It did not matter much what they did, it was enough to know that they were antisocial and therefore evil. In this way, for example, political opponents could be eliminated without any legal justification. In times of crisis especially, when the need for security is strong, public morals tend to become more severe, and deviant behavior that was once ignored is repressed. Moreover, in a period of political, economic, and social instability, internal chaos will often be blamed on outsiders and foreigners.

But what occurred in Iran is certainly not typical of the attitude toward homosexual behavior in the whole spectrum of Islamic countries. Even in Iran it may be regarded as exceptional. The executions of "homosexuals" took place in an atmosphere of revolutionary turbulence, with strong reactionary and antiwestern accents that led to excesses and an overall atmosphere of terror. Yet the foundation of such extremes is probably present in all Islamic countries, and stems from a negative attitude toward passive homosexual behavior, coupled with a rejection of western morality and condemnation of public indecency. Therefore "homosexuality" is rejected. In practice homosexual behavior is usually treated tolerantly as long as it is discreet and harms no one. This tolerance was well characterized by the words of an unknown Arab poet: "As the boy looked at it, my thing moved, and he whispered: 'It is splendid! Do let me try its love making.' I answered 'Such an act is reprehended, in fact many people call it unlawful.' He said: 'Oh them; oh them! With me all things are lawful.' And I was too polite to disobey."

Lesbianism. Of female same-sex behavior (*musahaqa*) almost nothing is known. Islamic law considers it sex outside of marriage and therefore as adultery, with all the consequences already described. Yet because no penetration takes place, punishment is theoretically limited to one hundred lashes. In practice lesbian behavior is regarded as relatively unimportant, because it usually takes place discreetly.

See also **Abu Nuwas; Africa, North; Mujun; Rumi; Sa'di; Sufism; Turkey.**

BIBLIOGRAPHY. Abdelwahab Bouhdiba, *Sexuality in Islam*, trans. A. Sheridan, London: Routledge & Kegan Paul, 1985; G. H. Bousquet, *L'éthique sexuelle de l'Islam*, Paris: Maisonneuve, 1966; Madelaine Farah, *Marriage and Sexuality in Islam: A Translation of al Ghazzali's Book on the Etiquette of Marriage*, Salt Lake City: University of Utah Press, 1984; Gabrielle Mandel, *Islamische Erotik*, Fribourg: Liber, 1983; Basim F. Musallam, *Sex and Society in Islam: Birth Control before the Nineteenth Century*, 1983; A. L. al-Sayyid Marsot, *Society and the Sexes in Medieval Islam*, Malibu, CA: Undena, 1979.

Maarten Schild

ITALY

Apart from classical antiquity, there are two eras in which Italy has a salient interest for the study of homosexual behavior. The first stretches from approximately 1250 to 1650 (the **Renaissance**, broadly interpreted); the second from World War II to the present.

Italy has a particular attraction for the historian because of its vast archives of material from the premodern period—archives which have not yet been much tapped. For the curious layperson, present-day Italy offers a lively homosexual subculture which sprang up after World War II, accelerating notably after the birth of the country's gay **movement** in 1971.

The Classical Heritage. Contrary to what has often been stated, there was no direct continuity on Italian soil between the homosexuality of Greco-Roman stamp and that which arose after the barbarian invasions. "Greek love" in Italy is in fact a later invention of northern European **travelers** of the nineteenth century, invented to lend dignity to the type of sex that they came to the country to enjoy.

In reality, at the time of the fall of the **Roman** empire there were recurrent foreign invasions. Over the centuries Italian soil was occupied by the most disparate peoples—Goths, Langobards (Lombards) and other Germanic tribes, Byzantines, Slavs, Arabs and Berbers, Normans, and Albanians. In addition it would be a mistake to discount the profound effects of the implantation of **Christianity**. All these factors could not help but disturb the characteristic features of the Greco-Roman world.

To cite an example of how complex the amalgam produced by the introduction of the customs of foreign peoples, one need only recall that the laws of the Lombards, a Germanic people, displaced Roman law in vast regions of Italy down to the thirteenth century. In fact the last remnants of Lombard law, confined to a few districts of southern Italy, disappeared only with the Napoleonic regime at the start of the nineteenth century. (*See* **Law, Germanic.**)

The Latin heritage was significant in the history of Italy (and not solely in that country) as an ideal image of a golden age which must be recaptured through a "revival." In the **Middle Ages** this aim took concrete form in the institution known as the Holy Roman Empire, and it was to have later avatars.

This theme is found in jurisprudence, having come about through the rediscovery and renewed study of Roman law (as concretized in the Corpus Juris Civilis of Justinian) conducted by the great Bolognese jurists of the twelfth and thirteenth centuries. This rediscovery is responsible for the West's adoption of the penalty of burning at the stake for sodomites, originally stipulated by the fourth-century Christian emperors of Rome. (The first such burning of which we have documentary evidence dates only from 1266.)

The literary revival, which was accomplished by the labors of philologists and the renewed circulation of surviving ancient texts, was a later task—that of the Renaissance proper.

The process of rediscovery, restoration, and reelaboration of classical antiquity continued in Italy until the sixteenth century, constituting the backbone of the Renaissance, which was one of Italy's most important contributions to Western civilization. This revival, which in some circles assumed the guise of a real idolatry of the antique, influenced in one way or another the most varied realms of old Italy, from philosophy (as seen in the work of Marsilio **Ficino**), through language, the arts, and law, to religion itself.

One should not be surprised then if a substantial portion of the evidence on homosexuality in premodern Italy "speaks classically," in the sense that it allows one to see behind it a classical model that gave it inspiration. Of course the same phenomenon is to be seen to some degree in the other European countries.

Before the Renaissance. The first homosexual poem of Italy after the classical age is the song, "O admirabile Veneris ydolum" ("Oh, splendid image of love") of the ninth century. It is in fact suffused with classical—even pagan—reminiscences. Evidently the author was a cleric, that is a member of the only social class that could engage in cultural pursuits before the arrival of the new lay-bourgeois culture after the year 1000.

From the religious sphere comes the first (condemnatory) treatise on homosexuality in Italy, the harsh *Liber Gomorrhianus* of ca. 1050 by St. Peter **Damian** (1007–1077), a violent invective against the sodomitical clergy, as well as the revealing *Sermones subalpini*, written in the vernacular at the end of the twelfth or the beginning of the thirteenth century.

Yet a real body of homoerotic poetry, such as that produced in France and the northern countries of Europe in the eleventh and twelfth centuries (*see* **Medieval Latin Poetry**), has not come to light.

One cannot ignore the appearance of laws against sodomy in the statute books of the Italian city states. At first mild, then ever more severe, they began about the middle of the twelfth century.

Only at the end of the twelfth century does Italy show a literary interest in the theme of homosexuality. The course of the thirteenth century is illuminated by a whole constellation of poetry of love and moralizing which directly confronts the subjects of same-sex affection and love, with such well known names from Italian literature as Brunetto Latini (ca. 1211–1294, who was placed by Dante among the sodomites in the *Inferno*), Rustico di Filippo (second half of the thirteenth century), and Guido Cavalcanti (1255–1300).

Special note must be taken of the circle of Perugia love poets of the thirteenth and fourteenth centuries (major figures are Cecco Nuccoli and Marino Ceccoli), as well as of the Sienese burlesque poets of the fourteenth century, who treat homosexual love with the greatest freedom of expression and naturalness—whether they are approving or condemning.

A special place belongs to the treatment of homosexuality by **Dante** Alighieri (1265–1321), the "father of the Italian language," in his *Divine Comedy*.

It should be noted that the whole period was deeply marked, as Michael Goodich has shown, by the ascendency of the Dominican St. Thomas **Aquinas** (1225–1274), and by the growth of a moralizing trend calling for the reform of customs among certain sectors of the bourgeoisie. The convergence of these two factors led, toward the middle of the fourteenth century, to the enactment of severe laws against sodomy in most of the Italian city states.

The Coming of the Renaissance. As a result of these developments Renaissance Italy confronted homosexuality with a much more hostile attitude than that which had prevailed several centuries before. The source of this hardening was not so much the Catholic church, which did indeed have a reinforcing role, as those urban strata that in a struggle that stretched over the centuries had pursued a policy of moral reform.

And yet, if in the fourteenth century homosexual love disappeared from love poetry, the figure of the sodomite lingered, often described in a light-hearted way, in vernacular short stories. The best known author is of course Giovanni Boccaccio (1313–1375), but alongside him are numerous short story writers and chroniclers—too many to be cited here—who were not averse to recounting in explicit fashion the diverting adventures of this or that sodomitical character. In some instances the classical model becomes dominant (for example Apuleius' *Golden Ass* in Boccaccio), in others the pure anecdote prevails.

The fact is that it is just at the start of the fourteenth century that one can detect the first signs pointing to the existence of a sodomite subculture in the great mercantile cities of Italy, including **Venice**, Siena, Bologna, and **Florence**. It would be interesting to know to what degree the legislative hardening constituted simply a reaction to the perceived menace of a "deviant" underground which seemed to be proliferating.

Literary documentation and the trial records reveal how homosexual behavior enjoyed a certain margin of tolerance and protective silence among the citizens; paradoxically, silence was greater where legal sanctions were most severe, as in Venice, than where they were milder, as in Florence.

Nonetheless it is important not to commit the error of viewing this **subculture** as a kind of prefiguration or rough sketch of the gay "ghettoes" of American cities of our own day. Fourteenth-century sodomites formed a subculture with certain recognizable features, but which was strongly marked by a type of relationship which was regarded as "normal" even by the heterosexual population of the day, though not necessarily by us: the adult–adolescent bond (**pederasty**). The denizens of this subculture, though accustomed to meeting one another, did not have sexual relations one with another, but rather with boys who came into their orbit from time to time (money usually served to facilitate consent). One must never lose sight of this fundamental characteristic when one speaks of the homosexual subculture of former times.

During the major phase of the Renaissance, with its characteristic showcasing of classical texts, Italian society entered into a period of enlightened tolerance of homosexual conduct. This tolerance, to which the so-called **libertine** current contributed, fostered a flowering of cultural expression in which homosexuality appeared in the forefront.

This efflorescence, noteworthy also in the field of the visual **arts**, began to lose strength with the coming of the Counterreformation, which imposed a return to a more moralistic climate, and above all an iron discipline over sexual themes.

The Counterreformation. In Italy the Catholic Counterreformation coincided with the inception of a period of decline that lasted until the nineteenth century. This decline was not merely economic, stemming in large measure from the shift of trade routes away from the Mediterranean to the Atlantic (to which Italy had no direct access), but also political.

In a changed European climate it was particularly disastrous that Italy saw the persistence of a pattern of many small states (some minuscule) which hindered the creation of any unified nation. The most determined opponent of such unification was the **papacy**, which until 1870 held a large-sized state that cut the peninsula in two at the center.

In this atmosphere of stasis the bourgeois stratum became "feudal," permitting itself to be absorbed by the nobility and becoming a parasitic class that was more concerned with preserving the status quo than with keeping up with the times.

The Counterreformation set the seal on these trends of ideological and political conservatism. The treatment of the scientist Galileo Galilei (1564–1642) by the Holy Office is symptomatic of the fate of Italian intellectuals during this period. In this way Italian civilization suffered a blow that could not be easily remedied afterwards.

In accordance with the trends, the "enlightened" tolerance toward homosexuality that was typical of the Renaissance gradually disappeared as the generation born before 1550 died off.

In Italian literature evidence is found until about 1650, one example being the book *Alcibiade fanciullo a scola*, which defended pederasty, but these manifestations become ever rarer and more isolated. In the same period historical evidence on homosexual behavior in Italy diminishes to a trickle, while at the same time it increases in countries like **France** and **England**, which in a fairly short time became as loquacious on homosexuality as Italy had been up until that point. One must add, however, that the historical period that precedes the Risorgimento, the Italian national revival of the nineteenth century, has not been sufficiently studied. Recent scholarship shows that under the conformity imposed by the Counterreformation there continued to flow, like underground streams, currents of heterodox thought, such as the libertine one that has been cited.

This fact means that, in order to unearth the indications of nonconformist thought of this period, special attention must be directed to the recovery of unpublished manuscripts—*samizdat*, in effect—created for internal circulation among private circles of enlightened intellectuals.

As regards the working class, the persistence of a homosexual cultural pattern that has been designated **Mediterranean** made possible the de facto tolerance of same-sex conduct, provided that it conformed to a rigid and prescribed model of behavior.

The Age of Enlightenment and Positivism. A number of preliminary inquiries pursued by the present author have shown that it is probable that in the seventeenth and eighteenth centuries there arose the first prototypes of the insidious type of "repressive tolerance" still practiced today in Catholic countries. Even though in the initial phases of the Counterreformation there were new outbreaks of persecution, with the passage of the decades one notes an ever greater reluctance to impose the death penalty for sodomy.

An underground debate, the dimensions of which we are not now in a position to determine, must have taken place. Otherwise one cannot explain the appearance in 1764 of *Dei delitti e delle pene* (On Crimes and Punishments) by Cesare **Beccaria** (1738–1794). A book that captured the spirit of the times, which influenced legislation throughout Europe, and which called for the abolition of the death penalty for sodomy—such a book cannot have come out of a void.

Nonetheless the fanatical censorship that was imposed during those centuries, combined with a certain reluctance by Italian historians to enter "obscure zones of a special character," has served to keep us from learning much of homosexual life of the epoch.

The only certainty is that in this period the homosexual subculture took shape and began to come out of hiding, as shown by several studies completed by scholars in the field. We still lack, however, a precise analysis of what happened in eighteenth- and nineteenth-century Italy; from what is known it seems that Italian conditions were not very different from those of other Catholic countries, such as France, which have been better studied.

Italy Today. Two main factors characterize Italian gay life today: its situation overlapping the two main paradigms of homosexual culture—the central and northern European type, which predominates in northern Italy, and the Mediterranean type, which rules the south—and its acceptance of a kind of "social pact," typical of Latin and Catholic countries, between the homosexual community and the state.

The first factor means that homosexual lifestyles in Italy are not homogeneous. In the north the foreign observer, even though he does not fail to register the difference between Italian gay culture and his own, still recognizes the links with central and northern European gay life. Southern Italy, however, follows a completely different model, that of the abovementioned "Mediterranean homosexuality."

Situated astride the boundary of two different cultures, Italian homosexual life lacks homogeneity, embracing as it does lifestyles which are profoundly different and even contradictory.

The second characteristic element is the "social pact" which the political authorities have tacitly conceded the homosexual minority since the nineteenth century, when sodomy was decriminalized thanks to the Napoleonic reforms. In exchange for the renunciation of homosexual militancy and advocacy of the right to be different, the state has agreed to respect the abrogation of all specifically antihomosexual laws.

This concession does not mean that homosexual conduct is exempt from stigma, but simply that the task of "social control" in the realm of sexual repression has been left to the Catholic church. Consequently, the state authorities need only intervene when the informal system of social control is not felt to be adequate. This occurred during the **fascist** period

when scores of homosexuals were sent into exile on small islands for periods from some months to several years. Despite this policy, there is no known case of a homosexual deported as such to a concentration (extermination) camp or of anyone executed for his homosexuality.

These contradictory factors explain how it was possible that from 1800 to 1950 Italy was a "wonderland" for foreign gays, who saw in the country a paradise where everything was allowed (hence it was an obligatory stop for every aristocratic Anglo-Saxon gay tourist), while at the same time it remained a country in which homosexuals, with rare exceptions, were reluctant to seek affirmation of their own identity, or to proclaim it through fiction and essays.

For generations Italian gay people declined to speak up on a vital question, understanding that repression would be deployed only in response to an attempt to create an "alternative lifestyle" in competition with that of the heterosexual family. In exchange they have benefited from a climate in which, though homosexuality officially did not exist and it was forbidden to mention it even in condemnation, scandals were systematically hushed up, the authorities dispensed with any "witch hunts," and the common people refused to make an issue of it. Italy has never had an Oscar **Wilde** scandal.

Moreover, the Mediterranean culture of homosexuality has long permitted a certain phase of homosexual experimentation to young heterosexuals in order to safeguard the virginity of nubile girls. Italian homosexuals took advantage of this situation—until the arrival of the "sexual revolution" which, by facilitating premarital sexual relations, has progressively reduced the viability of this erotic ploy.

Residues of this legacy of compromise persist even today in Italian politics—on the one hand in the considerable integration that the gay community has achieved with society in general (no Italian cities have gay ghettoes, the ghetto being a reaction to a society that leaves no other space to the minority than the ghetto itself), on the other, in the absence, thus far, of phenomena such as the antigay crusades of an Anita Bryant or a Jerry Falwell, or the witch hunts occasioned by hysteria over AIDS.

Also a product of this tradition are the lesser strength of the Italian gay movement in comparison with the Anglo-Saxon countries, as well as the reluctance of homosexual intellectuals to "come out." There are no laws to defy, no clearly definable immediate objectives, so that the average Italian gay man can hardly grasp the need for an affirmation that, in this context, is more a political choice than a lifestyle choice. This last factor explains the high degree of politicization of the Italian gay movement, which often surprises foreign visitors.

This situation should not obscure the fact that the period after World War II has seen the appearance of a generation of intellectuals more or less willing to discuss homosexuality not only in the lives of others, but at times in their own. In recent years there has arisen a new generation with ideas influenced by the gay movement and more receptive to a "transgressive" vision of homosexuality.

Among the most important names of the first generation are the novelists Giovanni Comisso, Umberto Saba, Carlo Coccioli, and Alberto Arbasino; the poet-novelists Piero Santi, Dario Bellezza, Elio Pecora, Giampiero Bona; the poets Sandro Penna, Nico Naldini, Mario Stefani; the directors Luchino **Visconti** and Franco Zeffirelli; the playwrights Giuseppe Patroni Griffi and Giovanni Testori (also a poet); the painters Filippo De Pisis, Aligi Sassu, Ottone Rosai, Mario Schifano, and Renzo Vespignani; and the composer Sylvano Bussotti. To these must be added the complex personality of the poet, novelist, playwright, and filmmaker Pier Paolo **Pasolini**. Other creative figures whose sexual orientation is known are omitted because

their work does not reflect any commitment to homosexuality.

Among the most important personalities of the new generation who can be defined without any hesitation as gay (apart from a few who claim the status of bisexuals) are Aldo Busi (unquestionably one of the most important living Italian writers), Piervittorio Tondelli, Dario Trento, Corrado Levi, Riccardo Reim, Giancarlo Rossi, Stefano Moretti, Gino Scartaghiande, Ciro Cascina, and the director Marco Mattolini.

In the last few years theatre, **film**, music, and the entertainment world in general have experienced a flowering of interesting talent that is openly gay.

The new climate of intellectual openness means that it is now possible to speak of the homosexuality of major figures of the Italian litterature of the past, such as Carlo Emilio Gadda, an innovative Roman writer, and Aldo Palazzeschi, not to mention the nineteenth century patriot Luigi **Settembrini** and even the great Giacomo Leopardi (1798–1837).

Today's Italian gay scene is notable particularly in the great industrial cities of the north; tourism has also stimulated the appearance of a leather scene in Florence. The south and Rome see, by contrast, the prevalence of a more "Mediterranean" mode: cruising takes place mainly outdoors so that many cities lack locales, such as bars and bathhouses, that are directed at a gay clientele. As a whole the Italians—except for those in Milan and Turin—are still little accustomed to **bathhouses** as places of gay encounter.

The Italian gay movement dates only from 1971, but it grew rapidly. Today it is organized on a national scale in the Arci-gay confederation, with its seat in Bologna, where there is a gay center (Il Cassero) and an archive-library. In 1988 there were twenty-two groups affiliated with Arci-gay, which also issues publications.

Turin and Milan boast their own gay archives linked to centers of gay initiative: one of these, the Fondazione Sandro Penna in Turin, publishes a high-quality annual of gay culture, *Sodoma*. There is also a gay Catholic movement, active only in the north.

Closely related to the gay movement is the informative Milanese monthly *Babilonia*, the only non-pornographic gay magazine in Italy. *Babilonia* publishes an annual gay guide in pocket-book format, bilingual in Italian and English and known as *Italia Gay*.

BIBLIOGRAPHY. Arci-gay Nazionale, ed., *Omosessuali e stato*, Bologna: Il Cassero, 1987; Giovanni Dall'Orto, *Leggere omosessuale: bibliografia*, Turin: Gruppo Abele, 1984; idem, "L'omosessualità nella poesia volgare italiana fino al tempo di Dante," *Sodoma*, 3 (1986), 13–37; idem, ed., *La pagina strappata*, Turin: Gruppo Abele, 1987; Gianni Delfino, ed., *Quando le nostre labbre si parlano*, Turin: Gruppo Abele, 1986; Fondazione Sandro Penna, ed., *Orgoglio e pregiudizio*, Turin: Fondazione Sandro Penna, 1983; Michael Goodich, *The Unmentionable Vice*, Santa Barbara: Ross-Erikson, 1979; William Ruggiero, *The Boundaries of Eros*, New York: Oxford University Press, 1985.

Giovanni Dall'Orto

J

JACOB, MAX (1876–1944)

French poet. Jacob came to Paris from his native Brittany at the age of twenty-two, determined to become a poet and painter. In the capital he gravitated to the bohemian avant-garde circle around Guillaume Apollinaire. When he was twenty-five Jacob met Pablo Picasso, then unknown; the two quickly formed a pair bond and became roommates. The aggressively heterosexual Picasso tried to "correct" his friend's homosexuality, but without success. In 1915 Jacob, who had been born a Jew, converted to Catholicism with Picasso as his sponsor. The poems he wrote at this time are a rich amalgam of puns and parody, and mixtures of high and low subjects, all shot through with a hermetic complexity that was analogous to Picasso's Cubism.

In 1921 Jacob retired to live in the ancient monastery of Saint-Benoît-sur-Loire. His mysticism, heightened by the Catholic revival orchestrated by Jacques Maritain and others at the time, began to play an increasingly important part in his poetry. Another feature was reminiscences of Brittany, a region in France known not only for its traditional Celtic ways, but also for its association with the modernist primitivism of Paul Gauguin and his school. Despite his religious vocation, Jacob would make extended visits to Paris where he saw his old friends and enjoyed the sexual scene. In due course a bout of guilt would drive him back to the monastery.

In 1944 Max Jacob was arrested at Saint-Benoît-sur-Loire and deported to the notorious concentration camp at Drancy. Jean **Cocteau** and other friends attempted to intervene on his behalf, but Picasso refused. Although they are difficult, the poems of Max Jacob retain an important place in avant-garde French literature. A better understanding of the linkage of his life and work will be the task of a major biography, which has not yet been written.

Ward Houser

JAHNN, HANS HENNY (1894–1959)

German novelist and dramatist. Jahnn was born in Stellingen near Hamburg. Raised in a bourgeois milieu, Jahnn made his first literary efforts at the age of fourteen. In 1911, in high school, he met his friend and later life companion Gottlieb Harms, with whom he quite early made several attempts to break out of his repressive bourgeois environment.

Jahnn's diaries offer an effusive record of the love affair linking him with Harms, who was one year older. After the outbreak of World War I the friends as self-proclaimed pacifists emigrated to Norway. There in great seclusion Jahnn wrote among other things the drama *Pastor Ephraim Magnus*, which was published by the Fischer firm after his return to Germany in 1919; winning the prestigious Kleist Prize, this work made Jahnn famous (and notorious).

Sharply rejecting Christian beliefs and morality, Jahnn and Harms founded (together with Franz Buse) the "Ugrino" commune, whose members shared living quarters and common beliefs. This home-spun utopia, for which the multitalented Jahnn designed buildings for everyday use and for worship, was to be realized on a large plot of land south of Hamburg—acquired specifically for the purpose—and was to afford a free life for a community of artists. The ambitious plan consumed all of Jahnn's energy and ultimately failed because it required immense sums beyond the ability of even wealthy benefactors to raise. Nonetheless, Jahnn embodied his ideas in the fragmentary novel *Ugrino und Ingrabanian*. In actual fact, of the whole project there came only the Ugrino-Verlag, which published several of Jahnn's own works and undertook the reprinting of forgotten composers of the early baroque period (Buxtehude, Scheidt, Lübeck). What remained was a small, bohemian clique of living artists, from whose circle Jahnn and Harms in 1926 married the sisters Ellinor and Monna Philips. Jahnn's daughter Signe was born in 1929.

Alongside his scandalous literary production Jahnn earned international recognition as an expert in historic organs, in particular by his work on the restoration of the Jacobi organ in Hamburg.

In February 1931 Gottlieb Harms died. Jahnn composed an incomparable monument to his memory in the novel trilogy *Fluss ohne Ufer* (River Without a Shore), published in 1949–61.

At the beginning of the National Socialist regime Jahnn once again went into Scandinavian exile. He purchased an estate on the Danish island of Bornholm, managed it, and devoted himself—always alongside his literary activity—to extensive research on hormones.

In 1950 Jahnn finally returned to Hamburg and there founded the Free Academy of Arts, whose first president he became. As General Secretary of the Pen Club he passionately strove to prevent the emerging split between East and West. To the very end of his life he fought first against the rearming of Germany and later above all against atomic weapons. In 1956 he received the Lessing Prize of the city of Hamburg.

Hans Henny Jahnn died on November 29, 1959; in accordance with the provisions of his will he was buried in a grave alongside his friend Gottlieb Harms.

Jahnn, whose collected works fill eleven volumes, ranks alongside Hermann Broch and Robert Musil as one of the most important German writers of the twentieth century. In his extensive narrative and dramatic work male homosexuality was a central theme. In at times excessive, sensual-erotic language Jahnn describes virtually without exception relationships between males—with all their utopias and fantasies, their moments of happiness and failures, with all the constructive and destructive traits of human beings. A striking feature of all his pairs of friends in the great novels is the inequality of the partners: the sexually inhibited, markedly intellectual type is always counterposed to a sensual, handsome "nature boy" for whom homosexual love is self-evident and in the direct meaning of the word natural. Jahnn's whole oeuvre proclaims the need for harmonizing human feeling and action with nature. Starkly, Jahnn shows that the creatures of nature are cruel; they devour one another and are devoured in turn; only man is capable of pity—a capacity that Jahnn elevates to a moral imperative.

Jahnn cannot be fitted into existing categories on the basis either of his literary style or of the philosophical currents of his lifetime. The same is true of his attitude toward homosexuality and his literary treatment of it: Jahnn is far removed from **Hirschfeld**'s theory of a "third sex" and other justification paradigms of the Weimar era. Jahnn was one of the first to propagate, with sovereign self-understanding, the belief that homosexuality is but one variant of human sexuality.

BIBLIOGRAPHY. Thomas Freeman, *Hans Henny Jahnn: Eine Biographie*, Hamburg: Hoffmann und Campe, 1986; Elsbeth Wolffheim, *Hans Henny Jahnn: Monographie*, Reinbek: Rowohlt, 1989.

Dietrich Molitor

JAHRBUCH FÜR SEXUELLE ZWISCHENSTUFEN

The *Jahrbuch* (whose title literally means "Yearbook for Sexual Intergrades") was the world's first homosexual periodical, with articles by experts in the relevant fields covering all aspects of the subject as it was then conceived. Edited by Magnus **Hirschfeld** in Berlin, it appeared in 23 volumes between 1899 and 1923, when its publication was halted by the economic collapse of Weimar Germany that undermined the financial base of the sponsoring institution, the Wissenschaftlich-humanitäre Komitee (**Scientific-Humanitarian Committee**).

Along with major articles, each volume included an annual review of the literature, fiction and non-fiction, pertaining to homosexuality, as well as comments on current events and the progress of the legal-political struggle for repeal of the notorious **Paragraph 175**. Some of the articles were illustrated with plates or photographs, a few even in color. The bibliographical sections were conducted by Eugen Wilhelm, a judge in Strasbourg, under the pseudonym of Numa Praetorius: they cover the German, French, and Italian (but not English) literature of the first two decades of the century. Scattered foreign contributions to the periodical were in French and English.

Magnus Hirschfeld himself wrote several pieces, the longest of which was entitled "Ursachen und Wesen des Uranismus" (Causes and Nature of Homosexuality, 5, 1903). Eugen Wilhelm also composed articles on the legal side of the problem, in particular "Die strafrechtlichen Bestimmungen gegen den homosexuellen Verkehr" (The Penal Statutes against Homosexual Intercourse, 1, 1899). Gustav Jaeger published the materials that he had obtained in 1879 from Károly Mária **Kertbeny** under the heading "Ein bisher ungedrucktes Kapitel uber Homosexualität aus der Entdeckung der Seele" (A Hitherto Unpublished Chapter from *The Discovery of the Soul*, 2, 1900).

Richard von **Krafft-Ebing** revised his earlier views on homosexuality in "Neue Studien auf dem Gebiete der Homosexualität" (New Studies in the Area

of Homosexuality, 3, 1901). The same volume contained a study by Friedrich Karsch-Haack on "Uranismus oder Päderastie und Tribadie bei den Naturvölkern" (Uranism or Pederasty and Tribadism among Primitive Peoples), which formed the basic core of his great 1911 monograph on ethnography. The Warsaw physician Franz Ludwig von Neugebauer contributed a whole series of not wholly relevant articles on pseudo-hermaphroditism. The Dutch writer L.S.A.M. von Römer contributed an excellent biographical study of "Heinrich der Dritte, König von Frankreich und Polen" (Henri III, King of France and Poland, 4, 1902), a book-length survey "Über die androgynische Idee des Lebens" (On the Androgynous Idea of Life, 5, 1903), which remains an unparalleled, if uncritical treatment of the subject from distant antiquity to modern times, and a long historical essay, "Der Uranismus in den Niederländen bis zum 19. Jahrhundert, mit besonderer Berücksichtigung der grossen Uranierverfolgung im Jahre 1730" (Homosexuality in the Netherlands until the Nineteenth Century, with Special Reference to the Great Homosexual Persecution of 1730, 8, 1906), which began an inquiry that has been resumed more recently in the **Netherlands**. **Kertbeny**'s legal polemic of 1869 that introduced the term *homosexuality* was reprinted in full (7, 1905). Paul Brandt, who used the pseudonym Hans Licht, composed a two-part article on "Der *paidon eros* in der griechischen Dichtung" (The *paidon eros* in Greek Poetry, 8, 1906; 9, 1908). I. Leo Pavia did a perceptive series on "Die männliche Homosexualität in England mit besonderer Berücksichtigung Londons" (Male Homosexuality in England with Special Reference to London; 11, 1909; 13, 1911).

Shorter pieces were biographies of famous homosexuals, critiques of arguments for retaining the paragraph against homosexuality in drafts of a new penal code, and presentations of the theory of the innate character of sexual inversion. A large part of the material that had been published in the *Jahrbuch* was utilized in Hirschfeld's 1914 magnum opus, *Die Homosexualität des Mannes und des Weibes* (Male and Female Homosexuality). After 1914 the contributions became somewhat shorter and more trivial, while others were devoted to wartime happenings of relevance to the subject. Hirschfeld went so far as to list any element of "male character" in women as part of the general theme of "intersexuality."

On the whole, the articles in the *Jahrbuch* rallied to Hirschfeld's belief that homosexuals represented an evolutionary **intermediate stage** or intergrade between the male and the female, and that their condition was inborn and unmodifiable by any form of therapy or any accident of environment or experience. This stance was the bedrock for the Scientific-Humanitarian Committee's plea for toleration for an "unjustly persecuted variety of human being," as Kurt **Hiller** later phrased it. However, it led to an open break with Benedict **Friedlaender** and others who looked to the classical model of **pederasty** as the practice of a bisexual male population, not of exclusive inverts and effeminates. The supporters of this view later seceded to form the Gemeinschaft der Eigenen (Community of the Exceptional) with its journal *Der Eigene*.

Ignored by official science and scholarship in Wilhelmine Germany and later, the *Jahrbuch* remains a unique collection of materials for the study of all aspects of homosexual behavior and cultural attitudes toward it. While it scarcely paid attention to such problems as "gender," "role playing," "lifestyles," and the like, it treated the subject as defined by contemporary psychiatry and jurisprudence in a thorough and serious manner not equaled by much later apologetic writing on behalf of homosexual liberation. Its contributors surveyed all the literature that appeared in both the learned and the popular press of the day, discussed the homosexual sides of cultures remote in time and space, and scoured the writings of the past for the light that they might shed. If these early studies were sometimes uncritical, amateurish or biased, they at least were a starting point for investigation of a field that had been almost totally excluded from academic scholarship, dependent as that was upon the control of the state and of respectable opinion. Surviving in complete sets in a few medical and university libraries and in private collections, as a resource for the serious investigator the *Jahrbuch* has not been superseded even today.

Warren Johansson

JAILS
See **Prisons and Jails.**

JAMES I (1566–1625)

King of Scotland and England. The son of Lord Darnley and Mary Queen of Scots, he became James VI of Scotland upon his mother's forced abdication in 1567. Studying under various teachers, notably George Buchanan, he acquired a taste for learning and theological debate. During his minority the king was the pawn in a complicated struggle between the Catholic and Protestant factions within the clergy and nobility. His personal rule began in 1583; three years later he allied himself with the childless Queen Elizabeth of England to improve his prospects for succeeding to the throne, breaking with the party of his mother, whose execution in 1587 he accepted calmly. In 1589, this time against Elizabeth's wishes, he married Anne of Denmark. In 1603 he succeeded to the English throne by virtue of his descent from Margaret Tudor, the daughter of Henry VII.

Though welcomed in his new domain, James brought little understanding to its parliament or its problems. At the Hampton Court Conference he displayed an uncompromising anti-Puritan attitude in face of the request of the Puritan clergy for status within the established church. Out of this conference came the project for revision of the Bishops' Bible of 1566 that produced the so-called King James Version of 1611, which on its merits won a firm place in the Protestant churches and in English literature. Although it is a Renaissance translation that could not go beyond the store of learning available in its time, fundamentalist Protestants have invested it with an almost sacred and revealed character, even refusing to abandon it for more recent English renderings such as the Revised Version (1881–95) or the Revised Standard Version.

The private life of James I impinged upon his public life in a manner that betrayed his erotic proclivities. He relied upon favorites whose qualifications consisted more in physical charm than in talent for government. His adolescent passion for Esme d'Aubigny, and his friendship for Patrick Gray, Alexander Lindsay, and others had already provoked comment. But because the resources of the Scottish exchequer were skimpier than those of the English, these friendships had no real impact on the regime in Edinburgh. Three favorites have left their names in the chronicles of the time, James Hay, John Ramsay, and the Englishman Philip Herbert. Of these the first enjoyed James' indulgence the longest; he was heaped with honors and benefitted from a marriage with the daughter of the Earl of Northumberland; the third was married to the daughter of the Earl of Sussex, and on the occasion of the festivities the dramatist Ben Jonson composed a masque entitled *Cupid Pursued*. The Englishman had a shorter period of royal grace than the others because of his faults of character.

More important than any of these was a young Scotsman named Robert Carr, who managed to break a limb in front of James at a tourney in March 1607. At the sight of this blond athlete James' heart quivered, and in no time the handsome young man was on the rise. He was named Gentleman of the Chamber, then Viscount Rochester and later Earl of Somerset (in this capacity he was the first Scot to sit in

the House of Lords). As the leading personality of the court, he was a force with whom ambassadors and even Robert Cecil had to reckon. That their liaison was homosexual was not doubted by James' contemporaries, but the young man was something more than a lover to him, he was also a spiritual heir. On the negative side, the courtier was extravagant and insolent, and his behavior contributed no little to the decline of James' popularity. In 1615 Carr was disgraced, and in the following year he and his wife were convicted and sent to prison, where they remained until 1622.

James' choice then fell upon George Villiers, Duke of Buckingham after 1617. Of a distinguished family, the handsome and cultivated youth knew that what the sovereign wanted was an adopted son—a role that he had no difficulty in playing. The aging king may not have had a physical relationship with him, and was not jealous of his female interests; but the two were recognized by their homosexual contemporaries as a classic pair: a king and an all-powerful favorite. The life of James I illustrates how the general opprobrium attached to "sodomitical" relationships did not interfere with the passion of a ruler who occupied the throne and conferred his favors upon young men of his choosing, who by their privileged estate and position were exempt from the death penalty that threatened the rest of his subjects.

BIBLIOGRAPHY. Michel Duchein, *Jacques Ier Stuart: Le roi de la paix*, Paris: Presses de la Renaissance, 1985; David Harris Willson, *King James VI and I*, London: Jonathan Cape, 1956.

Warren Johansson

JAMES, HENRY (1843–1916)

American novelist, playwright, and critic. His father, Henry James senior, was a writer on theology influenced by the mystical works of Emmanuel Swedenborg; his brother William became a distinguished professor of psychology and philosophy at Harvard University.

Finding the study of law not to his liking, Henry James began to contribute reviews and short stories to American periodicals. For a number of years his fiction showed a decided debt to the conventions of popular works of the time, a tutelage from which he gradually emancipated himself so as to become sui generis: "the Master." He chose to reside mainly in Europe, at first in France and Italy, but increasingly in England. A novel of the middle period, *The Bostonians* (1886), portrays a close emotional relationship between the wealthy feminist Olive Chancellor and her acolyte Verena Tarrant, which is spoiled by the intervention of a selfish young lawyer. James' most characteristic works of this period, however, focus on the "international theme," the encounter of callow but innocent Americans with European sophistication. In what is probably the most poignant of these works, *Daisy Miller* (1870), a young American girl dies of a fever after an encounter at the Colosseum in Rome.

Related to male homosexuality are "The Pupil" (1891), which concerns a mentoring relationship, and the ghost story, "The Turn of the Screw" (1898). In the latter novella, a young governess is given charge of two young children, a boy and a girl, in a remote country house. She finds that the deceased figures of her own predecessor and of the sinister valet Peter Quint have returned to possess them. The boy Miles dies at the hands of Quint, who—it is intimated—had corrupted him during life. James left the story deliberately ambiguous so that it is always possible that the occurrences are hysterical fantasies on the part of the governess.

James's last three major works, *The Wings of the Dove* (1902), *The Ambassadors* (1903), and *The Golden Bowl* (1904), return to the "international theme," but on a level of complexity and abstraction that makes them entirely different from his earlier treatments of it. More than any

others, these late works have attracted both devotion and hostility—the latter stemming from their highly wrought literary style and baffling elusiveness. Their fascination lies in part in the sense that James has glimpsed truths that are ultimately inexpressible, and has gone as far as he could to make them at least mystically present. It may be, however, that the novelist was unconsciously aware that he had other themes that he might have dealt with, but in the repressive climate of the age in which he lived did not dare to attempt.

The question of James' sexuality remains puzzling. He never married and, though he cherished many friendships with women, no heterosexual genital relations are recorded. His letters reveal an infatuation with a macho sculptor, Hendrik Andersen, whom he met, however, only in 1899. It has also been asserted that the writer was in love with his brother, William James. It is of interest that their sister, Alice James, an invalid who died young, was inclined toward lesbian feelings.

Whether James simply had a very low sexual drive or a formidable capacity to repress the homosexual feelings that surely visited him from time to time will probably never be known. Certain features of his personality are characteristic of upper-class homosexuals of the period: fastidiousness and horror of "vulgarity," sensitivity to art (albeit limited by dilettantism), extraordinary attention to social nuances, social climbing (akin to Marcel Proust's), and aestheticized cosmopolitanism.

BIBLIOGRAPHY. Leon Edel, *The Life of Henry James*, 5 vols., Philadelphia: Lippincott, 1953–72.

Wayne R. Dynes

JAPAN

Japan is an island nation of about 125 million people on the northwestern rim of the Pacific Ocean, heavily influenced by **Chinese** culture but politically independent since the beginning of historical records in the fifth century.

Present-day Japanese attitudes toward homosexuality are a complex blend of modern and traditional ideas about love and sex. Homosexual behavior is accepted in some circles and stigmatized in others, but in general it is looked upon more as an eccentricity than a perversion. Sex of whatever variety tends to be thought of as playful and pleasurable, but, even so, sexual behavior is held to strict standards of social decorum that require it be enjoyed with discretion and propriety. Japanese men and women share a great amount of social and non-sexual physical contact with their own sex and as a result most Japanese experience and are more comfortable with close emotional friendships with members of the same sex. To a remarkable degree, social definitions of appropriate sexuality have not excluded homosexuality or declared it a social heresy, and homosexuality does not inspire the level of horror and disgust it has sometimes received in the Judeo-Christian West, largely because no native Japanese religious tradition has ever singled it out for condemnation.

Marriage Duties. Homosexual preference becomes a problem for Japanese men and women when it threatens marriage. In the Confucian philosophical scheme, which still exerts great power in Japanese and East Asian social life, the refusal to marry represents not just a repudiation of the past (one's ancestors) but a denial of future unborn generations and one's place in the familial continuum. Exclusively homosexual individuals are expected to sublimate their personal feelings, regarded as selfish, for the sake of the "family," the historically ongoing line of generations from the obscure past into the future of which every person is considered a part. Refusal to marry and raise a family makes it difficult for an individual to assume his or her rightful place as a mature member of adult society, since it is marriage that confers social respectability.

Homosexual men and women are nevertheless able to form socially acceptable marriage-like relationships through adoption. In general, adult adoption is far more common in Japan than infant adoption, and for gay men and lesbians this means they have a legal means to make a commitment to their partners. When the popular young actor Oki Masaya committed suicide in 1983 at what seemed the peak of his career, it was his adoptive "father" who was interviewed, weeping, on Japanese television.

Due to the emphasis placed on marriage in Japanese society, homosexual relations are usually conducted in a context of bisexuality. This is ideal for men and women with a bisexual orientation, but for those having an exclusively homosexual orientation who marry for the sake of their family, such "enforced" bisexuality is a psychological and emotional strain. The frequency and nature of extramarital homosexual relations varies from person to person, ranging from continence, to brief encounters, to life-long extramarital commitments. Such commitments may have the spouse's blessing, particularly if the public "form" of the marriage is maintained. This seems to have been the case with the Japanese novelist **Mishima** Yukio (1925–1970) and his wife Yoko. She has continued to maintain the public propriety of their marriage since her husband's death by censoring all media discussion of his homosexuality. (The 1985 film *Mishima* was banned in Japan because of its explicit depiction of his affairs.) In this and similar cases, the media generally practice self-censorship to prevent embarrassment to the bereaved survivors, even though the person's homosexual activity may already be public knowledge, as with Mishima.

Aesthetics. **Androgyny** is the traditional ideal of sexual aesthetics in Japan. A boy or man is deemed most beautiful when he is desired by both men and women; a woman or girl is likewise most beautiful when both men and women desire her. The handsome "masculine" woman and the beautiful "feminine" boy are favorite stereotypes in Japanese **theatre**, finding expression in the traditional all-male kabuki theatre and in the newer all-female Takarazuka Opera Company, where handsome women act men's roles opposite beautiful heroines. Fans of both Takarazuka and kabuki may develop a serious "crush" tinged with homoeroticism for their favorite actor or actress.

Modern Gay Life. Hierarchy and clear separation of roles are important elements in sexual relations in Japan, and homosexual relations are no different. Usually, one partner is clearly the "man," the other the "woman" in the relationship, although more egalitarian partnerships are increasingly common.

Gay publications are more widespread than lesbian and are rarely censored for content. If the publication is pornographic, censorship will eliminate pictures of genitalia and pubic hair, just as in straight pornography. A recent Japanese gay guide identifies bars in terms of the clientele they attract, whether students (high school and college), young and middle-aged businessmen, or laborers. Gay bath houses exist in most major cities and male homosexual prostitution is legal. In recent years, both official health policy and public opinion have become less tolerant toward male extramarital sex, including homosexual, owing to its association with the spread of **AIDS**. Lesbians have not been identified with AIDS, however, and remain relatively unaffected by it.

The Meiji Repression. The origins of Japan's modern sexual constructs can be traced to the Meiji Period (1868–1912), when Japan's leaders were striving to achieve social, political and technological parity with the "enlightened" West. They quickly perceived the stigma attached to homosexuality and went about discouraging it in order to bring Japan's sexual behavior into line with that of nineteenth-century Europe. Homosexuality was temporarily outlawed with the adoption of the Prussian legal code in the 1870s, but the ban was soon dropped. Anti-homosexual morals were taught in public and missionary schools and in Japan's "Higher Schools" (universities), which students entered in their mid-teens. Male homosexual activity persisted there, however, as attested in Mori Ogai's (1862–1922) *Vita Sexualis* in which he details his narrow escape from the sexual advances of upperclassmen.

Daily newspapers of the late nineteenth century reported incidents in which roving bands of students abducted handsome boys and seduced them; the papers bemoaned such goings on as a social problem unbecoming to a new, modernized Japan, but there was no moralistic hysteria surrounding the censure. In girls' schools and women's universities, "S" clubs were formed in which women calling themselves "sisters" (using the English word) met secretly to discuss their lesbian feelings. The Meiji government's attempt to marginalize and pathologize homosexuality by the adoption of nineteenth-century western social constructs was never entirely successful, probably because there was no urgent indigenous imperative for eradicating a form of sexual behavior that probably struck most Japanese as harmless, but it seems to have created the conditions for a separate homosexual identity, the need for which had not previously existed in Japan.

Ancient Literature. Stories about male homosexuality abound in the literature and lore of pre-modern Japan. *The Chronicles of Japan* (720) mentions two young male courtiers who loved each other and were buried in the same tomb when they died. Several exchanges of erotically-charged poems in the *Manyoshu*, compiled late in the eighth century, were apparently sent from one male courtier to another. Japan's eleventh-century masterpiece of classical literature, Lady

Murasaki's *Tale of Genji*, includes a scene in which Prince Genji spent a night with the young brother of a woman who refused his advances, and the narrator states that Genji found the boy's physical charms quite pleasing.

Yoshida Kenko (1283?–1352?), a fourteenth-century courtier–monk and aesthete, wrote in *Essays in Idleness* about his sexual attraction for boys. In the thirteenth and fourteenth centuries, sermon-like stories called "acolyte tales" (*chigo monogatari*) were written about **Buddhist** monks who fell in love with their temple acolytes and as a result became enlightened as to the illusory nature of emotional attachment. Samurai men and boys who died for the sake of male love were idealized in the sixteenth century in accounts of contemporary historical events.

Kabuki. Seventeenth-century literature depicted boy actors in kabuki theatres who were patronized for prostitution by merchant and samurai men. The primary writer about male homosexual love in the seventeenth century was Ihara **Saikaku** (1642–1693), who wrote peripherally about it in several works including *The Man Who Loved Love* and *Five Women Who Loved Love*, and devoted an entire book to the topic in *The Great Mirror of Male Love*. The latter work is virulently misogynistic and seems to have been designed to appeal to an urban male readership that thought of itself as exclusively homosexual. Many woodblock prints survive from this era depicting men and boys in sexual embrace. Besides stories about male homosexual love, there were also guides to the kabuki theatre that had a frankly homoerotic appeal, and many etiquette books were published that advised men and boys how to dress, groom, and attract male lovers.

Not much can be said with certainty about homosexuality among the men and women of the lower classes in pre-modern times, but history and legend give ample testimony to its popularity among their social superiors. One legend states that male homosexuality was introduced to Japan from China in the ninth century by Kukai (774–835), the revered founder of Esoteric Buddhism in Japan. Certainly, homosexual love seems to have been an important element of life in many of Japan's Buddhist temples and monasteries. The Zen temples of the Five Mountains (*Gozan*) are said to have asserted their control over the Ashikaga shoguns during the fourteenth century in part by making handsome boys available to them whenever the shoguns visited.

Noh. The third Ashikaga shogun, Yoshimitsu (1358–1408), observed a performance of Noh in 1374 when he was 16 that featured a beautiful 12-year-old boy, Zeami (1363–1443), who became the founder of classical Noh. Yoshimitsu's homosexual attraction for Zeami changed the history of Noh theatre by giving it the shogunal patronage that would allow Noh to reach levels of artistry and spiritual power it could not otherwise have obtained. Zeami's Noh represented the first major influence of plebeian culture on an aristocratic tradition that had been isolated from low culture for centuries.

In the sixteenth century, Oda Nobunaga (1534–1582) began the process of unifying a war-torn Japan, but was assassinated before he could complete his task. His page and reputed male lover, Mori Rammaru (1565?–1582), died by his side in the same attack. A recent year-long television series produced by the Japan Broadcasting Company (NHK) on the history of this period depicted the final moments of Nobunaga and Rammaru accurately but without explanation.

The Tokugawa Period. Japan was finally unified under Tokugawa Ieyasu (1543–1616) in 1603, and he and his descendants ushered in a 250-year period of peace. The Tokugawa shoguns most famous for their love of boys were Ieyasu's grandson, the third shogun Iemitsu (1604–1651) and Iemitsu's son, the fifth shogun Tsunayoshi (1646–1709). Tsunayoshi caused considerable scandal by giving fiefs and promotions to his male lovers and was rumored to have had a harem of boys recruited from throughout Japan whence he summoned his favorites to his chamber at night. His taste for young men was apparently shared among the upper level leadership of the day, but his behavior drew criticism from contemporaries for its excess.

Lesbianism. The history of female homosexuality is much more obscure, largely because women's sexuality was not taken seriously except in relation to men. This is true both in literature by women in the Heian period (794–1185) and in later literature dominated by male perspectives. One exception is a twelfth-century tale called *The Changelings*, about a brother and sister who switched roles and lived as if they were the opposite sex. The story is told primarily from the perspective of the sister living as a man, and reveals the spirit of a woman who finds her society's definition of the female role too confining for her taste. In the seventeenth century, Ihara Saikaku wrote in *Life of an Amorous Woman* of an affair the heroine had with the mistress of an all-female household. Though such literary depictions are rare, pictorial representations of two or more women engaged in sex are much more common from the seventeenth century, when erotic woodblock prints became popular. It is not known whether these pictures catered to a male or female audience.

In modern Japanese literature, Nobel laureate Kawabata Yasunari (1899–1972) often depicts lesbian relationships, particularly in a triangular competition with a man, such as in *Beauty and Sadness*. The third volume of Mishima Yukio's *Sea of Fertility* tetralogy, called *Temple of Dawn*, uses both male and female homosexuality as a symbol of decadence. He wrote about male homosexuality as a source of adolescent confusion in *Confessions of a Mask*, and as a sadistic force in *Forbidden Colors*. A short story called "Onnagata" shows homosexual desire as a petulant force in the personality of a kabuki actor of female roles. Japan's most highly acclaimed modern gay poet has been Takahashi Mutsuo, whose strange blend of Christian symbolism and gay sensibilities is captured for English readers in a collection called *Poems of a Penisist*. The title poem is reminiscent of Walt **Whitman**'s *Leaves of Grass*, of which it may be a conscious imitation.

BIBLIOGRAPHY. Ian Buruma, *Behind the Mask: On Sexual Demons, Sacred Mothers, Transvestites, Gangsters, and Other Japanese Cultural Heroes*, New York: Pantheon Books, 1984; Margaret H. Childs, "*Chigo Monogatari*: Love Stories or Buddhist Sermons?" *Monumenta Nipponica*, 35:2 (1980), 127–51; Thomas B. Hare, *Zeami's Style: The Noh Plays of Zeami Motokiyo*; Stanford: Stanford University Press, 1986; Donald H. Shively, "Tokugawa Tsunayoshi, The Genroku Shogun," in Albert M. Craig and Donald H. Shively, eds., *Personality in Japanese History*, Berkeley: University of California Press, 1970.
Paul Gordon Schalow

JARRY, ALFRED (1873–1907)

French dramatist, novelist, and humorist. After an obscure apprenticeship in literary avant-garde circles in Paris, Jarry achieved sudden and stunning celebrity with the 1896 production of his knockabout drama *Ubu Roi*. Ubu, the violent and aggressive antihero, becomes king of Poland through guile and fraud. This farce, a reworking of a collaborative effort undertaken with two schoolmates when Jarry was fifteen, anticipates the Theatre of the Absurd. His 1902 novel *Le Surmâle*, which concerns a machine that falls in love with its creator, has a proto-surrealist character. Although Jarry garnered a cult following, his other works failed to earn him a living. Once his meagre inheritance was exhausted, increasing poverty and alcoholism brought on his early death.

In his personal life Jarry had very few intimate relations. No heterosexual affair has ever been documented. His one close female friend, the novelist Rachilde (Marguerite Aymery Vallette), was known for her own interest in sexual ambiguity. The only serious treatment of sex in Jarry's work appears in the short play *Haldernablou* (*Oeuvres complètes*, Paris: Pléiade, 1972, pp. 214–29), based on his relations with the bisexual poet Léon-Paul Fargue. Whether he and Jarry were lovers in the physical sense is uncertain, though the play suggests that they were. The hero, Haldern (Jarry), seeks a partner who is "neither man nor woman nor monster at all, a devoted slave and one who could speak without breaking the harmony of his sublime thoughts."

Unable to resolve his personal conflicts, Jarry transformed them into the paradoxes of his art. In the 1920s the Surrealists took him up, together with his predecessor **Lautréamont**; today he is regarded as a major (though perplexing) French writer.

BIBLIOGRAPHY. Keith Beaumont, *Alfred Jarry: A Critical and Biographical Study*, Leicester: Leicester University Press, 1985.

Ward Houser

JESUS (D. CA. 29)

A Galilean Jewish teacher who lived during the reigns of the Roman emperors Augustus and Tiberius, Jesus was, if not the founder of **Christianity**—the point can be debated—certainly the inspiration for it. Hence any discussion of this faith, which has persecuted homosexuals, must begin with his pronouncements and examples, insofar as they can be ascertained. Franciscans, for instance, look to his ideal of poverty, while the Amish emphasize his style of simple living. Gay men and women have principally found his pronouncements on homosexuality curiously missing and taken this absence of condemnation as tantamount to tacit approval. Because no word from him favors it, critics of homosexuality have judged the silence to signify his endorsement of other Scriptural condemnations, thereby attesting emphatic disapproval.

Problems of Source Evaluation. Both sides take as primary sources the gospels of Matthew, Mark, Luke, and John, the first four books of the **New Testament**. The numerous apocryphal gospels, among other supplementary sources, becloud the issue, as does the meaning of the word "gospel" (*euangelion*) itself. With a long history, by the first century it meant simply "good news." Thus, the Good News According to Mark, the earliest surviving gospel, does not claim to be a life of Jesus but a proclamation or testimonial about him. Testimonials of faith are not biographies; it is misleading to use them as such. Above all, they are not history. The four endorsed by Christian orthodoxy as canonical were written between 40 and 80 years after the Crucifixion, and whatever sources, if any, they are based upon cannot be clearly identified. Besides, they not infrequently contradict one another as in the instance of how many witnessed the Resurrection and when and where they did so. Yet it can be argued that the gospels do convey the spirit of a person—relatively liberal, iconoclastic, somewhat political, certainly charismatic—who made a powerful impression on his followers.

How much of the record was changed to suit later circumstances? There is every reason to believe that if other facets of the tradition, different from those we now have, did exist at the time when James, the pious brother of Jesus, came to be head of the church, these facts would have been changed to suit the clean-cut image that James wanted to project. This "brother" (if indeed he was one in blood, for Roman Catholics deny that the perpetual Virgin Mary produced any other offspring), who had not even been a part of the movement during Jesus' lifetime, was beheaded about the year 44, which was approximately a quarter of a century before the first gospel, Mark, was composed. The non-canonical gospels, generally known as gnostic because they claim to contain *gnosis* or special knowledge, come from an even later time than the "synoptic" account of Mark-Matthew-Luke (all with similar perspectives) and the more philosophic, somewhat later John. But again, how far back do the traditions of **gnosticism** go, or do they represent only special interest groups of the mid-second century and later?

Gleanings. The canonical gospels indicate that Jesus was single in his early thirties, contrary to the Jewish tradition that made marriage and fatherhood the norm even for the religious elite. Moreover, they show that he had attracted an entourage of men and women—mostly men—who followed him closely, and that they wandered throughout Galilee, Judea, and the surrounding countryside (areas impoverished and oppressed by Roman and upper-class Jewish and Greek exploiters), preaching repentance and the forgiveness of sins. John the Baptist, an ascetic whom Jesus encountered, preached a similar message, but Jesus was more successful, perhaps because he was also a miracle worker and healer. After his death a final element was added, the notion of an eternal life that believers could share, the poor having a much better chance of salvation than the rich.

The gnostic Secret Gospel of Mark (see Morton Smith, *The Secret Gospel*, pp. 113f.) suggests that Jesus may have had physical union with certain initiates who came to him at night for a secret baptism. They were naked except for a linen cloth around their waists. Mark 14:51–52 records that a young man was with Jesus but ran away on the night that he was arrested by the brook Kidron, a place and time that meet the requirements of such a baptism as described by Smith. This special treatment for members of Jesus' inner circle only accords with the gnostic idea of concentric circles—the inner circle, of course at the center, knowing all secrets; the members of the second circle having only a more general knowledge and baptism administered to them; and a third circle consisting of potential candidates and all outsiders. Jesus told members of his inner circle that certain secrets were reserved only for them, that is, he preached an esoteric gospel for initiates, the *teleioi*. But other aspects of this "Secret Gospel," if there was one, may have been only what later factions wanted to believe.

Jesus appeared when the Qumran sect that produced the Dead Sea Scrolls was at its peak, yet the gospels never mention the sect nor do its writings contain so much as one reference to Jesus or his Nazarene followers. Nor does the New Testament name the enigmatic Essenes, known only from **Philo**, Pliny the Elder, and Flavius Josephus—a sect that is described as leading a monastic life that generally excluded women. Other sectarians lived in their own homes throughout Judaea and Galilee, but if married both partners abstained from sexual relations after their initiation into the order. Like the monasteries, these were enjoined to give hospitality to other Essenes who were traveling, and it has been suggested that this custom explains in part how Jesus and his group found accommodations while on the road. Often associated with this sect is John the Baptist, an ascetic whom Jesus visited and honored, who was quite close to this group—but Jesus was no conventional ascetic, and nothing in the canonical gospels and the Book of Acts suggests that the first Christians lived as hermits or in monastic communities, Christian **monasticism** commencing only in Egypt in the third century.

Jesus was also a younger contemporary of the revered Jewish leader Hillel (flourished ca. 30 B.C.–A.D. 10), who fostered a systematic and liberal interpretation of Hebrew Scripture, but again neither Jesus nor any New Testament author cites Hillel in any connection. The similarities with Jewish teaching that have been so extensively analyzed in this century in order to reconstitute a Judeo-Christian tradition probably stem from the use of common sources: sayings that far from being original had already found their way into folk tradition.

What did Jesus think of homosexuals and bisexuals, given the lack of any specific pronouncements? He raised no issue about a Roman officer who loved a boy-slave so much that he came pleading with Jesus on the sick boy's behalf and was granted his request (Matthew 8:5–13 has *pais*, "boy," but Luke 7:1–10 uses *doulos*, "slave"). The symbolic meaning of this passage is instructive: the centurion represents the military power of **Rome** and at the same time the Roman pederastic tradition in which the servant was also the bed partner of his master. The story reflects Jesus' (or the early church's) acceptance of the Roman state as open to its its preaching and conversion—an accommodation which culminated in Constantine the Great's adoption of Christianity in 313. Moreover, and contrary to Jewish tradition, Jesus held eunuchs in high regard. In directing his closest disciples about the place where his last supper should be kept, he told them to go into the city and follow a man who would be carrying a pitcher of water, which was women's work and most likely performed by an effeminate male. The instances of a **beloved disciple**, recorded only in John's gospel, can be explained both in ordinary (Near Eastern custom) and in allegorical terms; thus we should not make too much of this favoritism as evidence for a sexual preference, though the last supper incident shows a typical dinner with exclusively male company. In Jewish tradition the guests at the Passover meal are supposed to recline in the manner of the **symposia** where the ancients dined while stretched out on couches.

Finally, in the context of his time, Jesus' actions and teachings reveal a highly positive attitude toward women, a stance that is generally at odds with the Jewish (and Northwest Semitic) traditon of a totally androcentric religious culture, but more compatible with Roman customs in this sphere.

See also **Racha.**

BIBLIOGRAPHY. Rudolf Augstein, *Jesus Son of Man*, New York: Urizen Books, 1972; John Boswell, *Christianity, Social Tolerance and Homosexuality*, Chicago: University of Chicago Press, 1980; A. Powell Davies, *The Meaning of the Dead Sea Scrolls*, New York: New American Library, 1956; W. D. Davies, *Invitation to the New Testament*, Garden City, NY: Doubleday, 1969; Tom Horner, *Jonathan Loved David*, Philadelphia: Westminster Press, 1978; Paula Frederiksen, *From Jesus to Christ: The Origins of the New Testament Images of Jesus*, New Haven: Yale University Press, 1989;William Phipps, *Was Jesus Married!* New York: Harper & Row, 1970; Morton Smith, *The Secret Gospel*, New York: Harper & Row, 1972.
Tom Horner

JOHN, APOSTLE
See **Beloved Disciple.**

JONATHAN
See **David and Jonathan.**

JOSEPHUS, FLAVIUS (37–CA. 105)
Jewish priest of aristocratic descent, Pharisee, and historian. Though a zealous defender of the Jewish religion, he sympathized with the Romans and discounted the militant nationalism that plunged Judaea into war with Rome in the year 66. Appointed commander of the forces in Galilee by the Sanhedrin, he capitulated to the Romans when besieged in Jotapata, winning the favor of Vespasian by prophecying that he would become emperor. Upon the fulfillment of the prophecy, he was released from captivity but remained with Titus until the destruction of Jerusalem in 70.

As a protégé of Vespasian and Titus, he settled in Rome and composed not only the classic history of the Jewish War, but also the *Jewish Antiquities* in 20 books, published in 93/94. In this work (I, xi, 1, 3) he endorsed a homosexual interpretation of the sin of **Sodom**, alleging that the inhabitants had tried to violate the angelic visitors because of their youthful beauty. As a believing Jew he wrote in the apologetic work *Contra Apionem* (2, 199) that "the Law recognizes no sexual connection save the natural union of husband and wife, and that solely for the sake of begetting children. The sexual union of males with males it abhors, and punishes with death whoever is guilty of such an assault." In other words, even in a polemic addressed to gentile readers in imperial Rome, Josephus already voiced the moral principle that sexuality is legitimate only for purposes of procreation; in this respect there was nothing left for St. Paul or St. **Augustine** or the scholastic philosophers of the thirteenth century to invent. His writings, preserved in Greek and translated into Latin, became part of the Judaic heritage of the **intertestamental** period that influenced Christianity; they continued to be copied and read during the Christian **Middle Ages** as an appendix to the Biblical history proper and a "proof" of its veracity.

Warren Johansson

JOUHANDEAU, MARCEL (1888–1979)

French novelist, short-story writer, essayist, and diarist. Scarcely known outside France, Jouhandeau compares with André **Gide**, François Mauriac, and Julien Green in his passionate concern with the relations between God and man—especially where sexuality is concerned.

Brought up in a strict Catholic family in the provincial town of Guéret, Jouhandeau steeped himself in mystical literature. After completing his studies in Paris, in 1912 he took a job at a preparatory school for boys in Passy, where he was to teach until 1949. In 1914 he had his first passionate homosexual relationship. His first novel, *La Jeunesse de Théophile* (1921), began a multivolume chronicle focused on the imaginary town of Chaminadour.

The novel *Chronique d'une passion* (1949) is a striking example of Jouhandeau's use of personal subject matter. The narrator Marcel becomes the lover of the artist Jacques, whom he had long admired. So intense is his passion that Marcel compares his love with that for God. But his wife Elise (based on Jouhandeau's real spouse, Elizabeth), who had at first tolerated the affair, becomes intensely jealous and resolves to kill Jacques—a plan she abandons only when Marcel agrees to renounce him. Although for most of its length the novel seemed to point to the breakup of the marriage, it ends by reaffirming it. *Chronique d'une passion* is a paradoxical mixture of homosexuality, religion, and conjugality.

Many of these themes recur in Jouhandeau's vast diaries or *Journaliers*, which achieved 26 volumes from 1961 to 1978. The essay *Ces messieurs: Corydon résumé et augmenté* (1951) reexamines in the post-World War II period the considerations that André Gide had laid before the French public in his original defense of homosexuality, *Corydon*, of 1924.

BIBLIOGRAPHY. Frank Paul Bowman, "The Religious Metaphors of a Married Homosexual: Marcel Jouhandeau's *Chronique d'une passion*," in G. Stambolian and E. Marks, eds., *Homosexualities and French Literature*, Ithaca: Cornell University Press, 1979, pp. 295–311; Jean Gaulmier, *L'univers de Marcel Jouhandeau*, Paris: Nizet, 1959.

Ward Houser

JUAN II OF CASTILE (1405–1454); ENRIQUE IV OF CASTILE (1425–1474)

The most famous homophile relationship in Spanish history is that between Juan II and his older lover Álvaro de Luna (ca. 1390–1453), who shared a bedroom for years. The king is remembered as a great patron of literature, who sponsored the birth of Castilian lyric poetry, which until that time was missing from the culture. He is also remembered for his choice of Álvaro de Luna to take over the tiresome business of running the country. Luna has long been recognized as one of the best administrators Spain ever had, and because of his dramatic fall from favor and public execution he became a well-known figure in both popular poetry and drama.

The story of the love between Juan and Álvaro, for which there are many sources, is worthy of a novel. The relationship began when the king was three, with the appointment of Álvaro as his page (*doncel*). The bond which quickly emerged between them was so strong that those hostile said the king was victim of an *hechizo* or enchantment; this in fact became a euphemism in Spain for "inappropriate" sexual desire. When the young king was seven, his mother exiled Álvaro and kept the king virtually a prisoner, a period that ended only with her death six years later. Juan and Álvaro were immediately reunited, and Álvaro, a brilliant conversationalist, was the favorite of many court ladies. He is also the author of one of the earliest and most balanced Spanish defenses of women against misogynist charges.

Save for a later period when the king was again prisoner and Álvaro exiled, which was intended to end their relationship, Juan and Álvaro remained together for thirty-five eventful years. They struggled together against a hostile aristocracy, sometimes fleeing together from superior force. The end came with Juan's remarriage after his first wife's death; his new wife, mother of the prudish Isabella the Catholic, was able to force the dismissal and then the execution of Álvaro. The king died a year later.

The homosexual tastes of Juan's son Enrique IV have been dealt with more openly. His reign was much more chaotic, and he seems to have suffered from a disease which affected his personality. Enrique did not have a governor with the talent of Álvaro de Luna and was unable to meet the challenges from the aristocracy. His marriage with his first wife Blanca was unconsummated and annulled; Enrique's impotence was explained as enchantment. After remarriage, a major successorial and political issue arose concerning the legitimacy of his daughter Juana, widely believed to be the daughter of the court favorite Beltrán de la Cueva. Enrique was dethroned in effigy as "puto," and during the latter part of his reign was almost without authority. A kind, cultured, but sick and weak man, like his father he enjoyed hunting expeditions, which apparently served as cover for homosexual activity. Juan II and Enrique IV stayed on comparatively good terms with both their Jewish subjects and the Islamic kingdom of **Granada**. Enrique in particular had a Moorish guard—the last Spanish ruler to do so until Franco—and gave other evidence of sympathy toward Spain's non-Christian cultures.

BIBLIOGRAPHY. Daniel Eisenberg, "Enrique IV and Gregorio Marañón," *Renaissance Quarterly*, 29 (1976), 21–29; Didier T. Jaén, *John II of Castile and The Grand Master Álvaro de Luna* , Madrid, 1978; Nicholas Round, *The Greatest Man Uncrowned: A Study of the Fall of Don Álvaro de Luna*, London: Támesis, 1986.

Daniel Eisenberg

JUDAISM, POST-BIBLICAL

As Julius Wellhausen stated in his *Prolegomena to the History of Israel* (1883), Judaism is the religious community that came into being on the ruins of the kingdom of Judah after the exiles were repatriated as part of the minorities policy of the Persian Empire in the year 536 before the Christian era. Biblical Judaism in the form in which we know it from the canonical scriptures of the Hebrew Bible (commonly known as the **Old Testament**) was created in the middle of the following century by a group of scholars and notables under the leadership of Ezra the Scribe. The apodictic commandments in the book of Leviticus (18:22 and 20:13) leave no doubt that homosexual relations between males were judged worthy of the death penalty, though female homosexuality went unmentioned. This condemnation paralleled the one in the Zoroastrian state religion of the Persians themselves.

The Hellenistic Period. With the spread of the Jewish diaspora from the territory of Persia into the **Hellenistic** world following the conquests of Alexander the Great, the Jewish attitude toward homosexual behavior came into conflict with the tolerant and even approving customs of the Greeks and the other peoples of the Eastern Mediterranean. The apocryphal and pseudepigraphal writings reveal that Judaism did not mute its disapproval, but reinterpreted the Sodom legend so that it became a tale not merely of divine retribution for inhospitality, but of the punishment of a city where homosexual activity was practiced (Book of Jubilees, 16:5–6).

The writings of the opinionated and eccentric **Philo Judaeus** (notably *De specialibus legibus*, 3, 37–42), and even of the ideologically colorless Flavius Josephus (*Contra Apionem*, 2, 199), indicate that during the first century of the Christian era Hellenistic Judaism categorically condemned sexual relations between males, so that on this subject nothing remained for **Christian** theologians to invent; the primitive Church simply ratified the eighteenth and twentieth chapters of Leviticus as received and interpreted in the contemporary Synagogue and made them part of its own constitution. What was left for Christianity to elaborate was a comprehensive definition of "unnatural" (= nonprocreative) sexual activity that classed all of it as the "sin of the Sodomite" (*peccatum sodomiticum*), that is to say, it fused a Greek philosophical concept with a Jewish legend. This Judaism proper never did, just as it never fully abandoned the older notion of **Sodom** as a place where the conventions of hospitality were grossly violated and the norms of justice literally reversed. It is this side of the legend that is expanded and illustrated with narrative vignettes in the traditions recorded in the **Talmud** and the Midrashim during the first millennium of the Christian era.

Subsequent History. There is a further development of the prohibition on homosexuality in the Mishnah and the Gemara. The commandments prohibiting male homosexual activity were associated (b. Sanhedrin 53a) with two groups of statutes, one aimed at breaches of patriarchal authority and power, the other forbidding idolatry and magic. The penalty was death by stoning, as in other sexual offenses. Both the active and the passive partners were held culpable, in contrast to the relative indifference to the active male homosexual in many other cultures (b. Sanhedrin 54a–55a). All these provisions may have been of limited import once the Jewish authorities were deprived of the power to impose the death penalty after the Kingdom of Judaea lost its independence, which occurred with finality in the year 70. Thereafter the Jews were doomed to be a client people living under foreign domination, with a diaspora that extended to the very ends of the known world, and subject to the varying and divergent legal codes of the states on whose territory they resided, albeit as a protected community with formally recognized privileges.

With rise of Christianity and then Islam and their acquisition of the state power, the Judaic taboo on homosexuality was adopted by the host peoples, so that the authority of Talmudic law became superfluous. But even where the Jewish communities had not the power to execute one of their members, they could always ostracize him and in effect exile him from their midst. It is thus all the more remarkable that in the Islamic cultural milieu the pederastic tradition should have revived, and that poems extolling the beauty of adolescent boys should have been composed in Medieval Hebrew, naturally in imitation of Arabic models. The "gazelle" (*ṣĕbhī*) of these lyrics is the beloved youth with his charms and caprices, just as in contemporary **Islamic** poetry. These poems thus constitute the sole body of homoerotic literature in the Hebrew language to the present day, as the theme did not figure in writings in neo-Hebrew of the *Haskalah* (Enlightenment) and then of the revival of Hebrew as a spoken language that accompanied the Zionist movement and the resurrection of the state of Israel.

The treatment of homosexuality in the Rabbinic writings of the Middle Ages is limited to: (1) commentaries on the Hebrew Bible, such as those of Solomon ben Isaac of Troyes, which were transmitted to the Christian world in the Latin glosses of Nicholas de Lyra on the Vulgate; (2) commentaries on the Talmud, of which Rashi's is the classic; (3) responsa in answer to questions of criminal law (the so-called *halakhah*); and (4) codifications and restatements of Talmudic law, such as the *Mishneh Torah* of Musa ibn Maimun (Maimonides) in the thirteenth century and the *Shulhan Arukh* of Joseph Karo in the sixteenth.

No such interweaving of Biblical and classical (Platonic–Aristotelian) thought as was effected by Thomas **Aquinas** could occur in Jewish theology, which retained the tradition of a simply formulated and wholly praxis-oriented Oriental code of law. Above all, never in all of its history did Judaism institutionalize an ascetic tradition with a celibate clergy and monastic communities, leaving no room for a religious order with crypto-homosexual overtones and even an unspoken norm of deviant sexuality that stealthily lurked beneath the surface of Greek Orthodoxy and Roman Catholicism. The medieval rabbi and scholar was a husband and the father of a numerous family, unlike his Christian counterpart. And the want of any parallel to the study of Greek and Latin literatures perpetuating a culture in which overt homosexuality flourished precluded the imitation or revival of the pagan customs of antiquity.

Thus the legacy of Judaism down to modern times has been a negative one, even more so than that of official Christianity, which was always undercut by the persistence of Greco-Roman paganism—the other source of European civilization which the Christian Church could never disavow.

Jewish Contributions to Sex Reform. But despite the absence of a positive homosexual tradition in Judaism, many "emancipated" and assimilated Jews were to play an enormous role in the sexual reform movement and as pioneers in the study of human sexuality in general and of homosexuality in particular. The leader of the world's first homosexual rights organization was Magnus **Hirschfeld** (1868–1935), the son of a Jewish physician from Kolberg (now Kołobrzeg) on the Baltic coast of Prussia. One of his early collaborators was Kurt **Hiller** (1885–1972), who even claimed descent from Rabbi Hillel. It was Hiller who in the spring of 1918, in the wake of the discussion of the minority problem in Central Europe provoked by Wilson's Fourteen Points, conceived the notion of the homosexual as a member of a minority deserving of protection instead of the persecution and ostracism that it had suffered under the Old Regime. Two other figures, Marc-André Raffalovich, the brother of a banker from Warsaw, and Arnold **Aletrino**, a Sephardic Jew of Amsterdam, were also among the early defenders of homosexual rights and in particular of the homosexual as a healthy, normal human being, albeit with an idiosyncratic sexual orientation.

The scientific study of sexual behavior early attracted many Jewish figures such as Iwan **Bloch** (1868–1922), a polymath whose writings cover vast areas of anthropology and history, and Sigmund Freud (1856–1939), whose psychoanalytic interpretations stressed the homoerotic component in the thinking and behavior not just of homosexuals, but of all human beings—to whom he ascribed a fundamental bisexuality. On the other hand, not a few of his disciples have been doggedly insistent in the belief that homosexuality is a mental illness, often with clear overtones of moral condemnation that amounted to a pseudo-medical rationalization of the earlier religious taboo. The **psychoanalytic** profession has remained largely Jewish in its membership, even after Hitler's rise to power scattered the original followers of Freud from their homes in Central Europe into exile in England and the United States. Despite their shortcomings, these analysts deserve credit for examining questions of sexuality, and indeed the popular mind typically equates psychoanalysis with the science of sexuality itself. Just because Judaism never branded sexuality as intrinsically obscene and unmentionable, the Jew in modern times has been able to achieve a certain measure of detachment and objectivity when dealing with matters which the Christian mind had dismissed as unthinkably obscene.

Until 1948 Jewish religious rejection of homosexuality lacked access to state power. Although the Turkish penal code in force since 1858 had penalized homosexual acts only when committed with a minor under the age of nine, the new nation of Israel inherited, along with the rest of the **common law** tradition, the criminal law of Mandate Palestine, which followed that of England itself in punishing male homosexuality with a maximum of ten years of imprisonment. However, in practice the Israeli authorities were clearly influenced by the sexual reform movement in Central Europe and did not prosecute consensual adult homosexual acts. After two attempts to repeal the law from the Mandate period foundered on the opposition of the Orthodox parties, in 1988 the Knesset, the Israeli parliament, passed a bill abrogating Section 351 of the Penal Code. Homosexuals are not excluded from military service which is obligatory in the garrison state that Israel has been forced to become, but homosexuals are transferred to non-security posts.

Israel's homophile organization, the Society for the Protection of Personal Rights, was founded in 1975. In 1988 an independent gay magazine, *Maga'im* (Contacts) began to publish, with text in Hebrew and an English summary for foreign subscribers.

Gay Synagogues. With the emergence of the gay liberation movement in the 1970s, the gay churches found their counterpart in gay synagogues such as Beth Simchat Torah in New York and Sha'ar Zahav in San Francisco—another instance of how modern Judaism has been profoundly influenced by its Christian environment. Under the wing of the Reform movement in modern Judaism, these foundations have obtained a measure of acceptance, and several international congresses of Jewish homosexuals have been held in major cities of the world. Moreover, public opinion polls in the United States show assimilated Jewish respondents as far more willing to abandon the traditional negativity toward homosexual behavior and gay rights than Christians of similar class backgrounds. The gay synagogues, like their Christian brethren, struggle to gain acceptance and understanding from the House of Israel in the face of the condemnation in the Torah and the long tradition of rejection and exclusion from the religious life of the Jewish community. For their members they serve to reaffirm links with an ethnic identity that they do not wish to renounce.

BIBLIOGRAPHY. Raphael Patai, *Sex and the Family in the Bible and the Middle East*, Garden City, NY: Doubleday, 1959.
Warren Johansson

JUDAISM, SEPHARDIC

The splendor of the Jewish culture of medieval **Spain** ("Sepharad," in Hebrew) would be hard to exaggerate. In a symbiotic relationship with Muslim and then Christian rulers, Jews enjoyed from the eighth through the tenth centuries (in Andalusia) and from the eleventh through the fourteenth centuries (in Christian Spain) as much stability and legal protection as they had ever known. They prospered economically and demographically, and made up a larger proportion of the population than in any other European country. During some periods Jews considered Spain a historically Jewish country, and their new homeland.

Spain as a Center of Medieval Jewish Culture. Jewish intellectual life and the Hebrew language were reborn in Spain. There was the greatest flowering of Hebrew poetry since Biblical times, and Hebrew was used for the first time for secular poetry. Pioneering work was done in Hebrew grammar, lexicography, and comparative Semitic linguistics; Spanish Jewry produced philosophers and scientists; Jews participated in government as nowhere else in Europe. Except for the Ashkenazi Jews of central Europe, Spain was quickly recognized by all but the most isolated Jews as their intellectual and religious leader. Although the history is complicated, and during the twelfth through the fifteenth centuries most of the Jewish population lived in Christian rather than Islamic territory, the fate of the Jews in the Iberian peninsula was linked with that of Islam. The decline saw Kabbalistic mysticism reach its greatest development, and an influential intellectual contribution to *aliyah* (the return of Jews to Israel) in the Zionist poetry and travels of Judah ha-Levi. The legacy of this cultural hothouse survived within Judaism into the seventeenth century, and the Judeo-Spanish identity and the Hasidic offshoot of Kabbala to the present. Much of Spain's great Catholic culture of the sixteenth and seventeenth centuries has also been revealed to be the work of converts or descendants of converts. Before idealizing the era, however, one must remember that Spanish Jews were no less intolerant than their contemporaries of other religions, and perhaps more so; they dominated the slave trade from Khazaria to Moorish Spain in the eighth to tenth centuries, among other things producing eunuchs for export to the rest of the Islamic world. Also, Spanish Judaism was very misogynistic, at times more than the often quite misogynist Islamic culture. Sometimes (as with the Almoravids) there are suggestions of a protofeminism in Spanish anti-Semitism, as there are at other times in the Christian campaign to expel Islam from the peninsula.

Homosexuality. A link between Spanish Jews and homosexuality is suggested by circumstantial evidence; it is also a common theme of Spanish anti-Semitism. The first known condemnations of homosexuality in the peninsula, in the seventh century, coincide with harsh penalties against Jews. The well-documented Jewish role in the introduction of Islamic rule to Spain, and the thriving of Jews in that culture, where homosexuality was tolerated and sometimes openly encouraged, is itself circumstantial evidence of Jewish sexual behavior. Under Christian rulers who were tolerant of homosexuality, such as **Juan II** and Enrique IV, Jews thrived; under those intolerant, such as Ferdinand and Isabella, Jews suffered. Those hostile to Judaism spoke of it as a contagious condition or as an incurable disease, a charge familiar from homophobic literature of many periods. Jews were accused of having introduced homosexuality to Spain (through the Moors); after they were expelled from Spain in 1492 and briefly took refuge in Portugal, Jews were blamed for having introduced homosexuality into that country. The countries in which they finally settled after the expulsion were more tolerant of homosexuality: the Ottoman empire and to a lesser extent Italy. Satirical poetry of the thirteenth through fifteenth and seventeenth centuries frequently associates Jewishness with sexual perversion. In the twentieth century, "Jew" was used in Spain as an epithet meaning "homosexual," and homosexuals were often referred to as a "sect."

Poetry. What has taken the matter out of the realm of coincidence and anti-Judaic fantasy has been the recovery of secular Hispano-Jewish poetry, much of which is refined, sensual, and unabashedly hedonistic. This body of work was virtually unknown a century ago, and some has been saved only by chance in the famous Cairo *genizah* (storeroom of old manuscripts). It is far from being completely translated or assimilated, although some Hebrew texts have been known, and seemingly discussed in some circles in Spain, for over fifty years. In it pederasty is widely found, and while male–female love is by no means absent, it is less prominent than in Hispano-Arabic poetry. There are scores of pederastic poems, written by the greatest Jewish authors of the period: Ibn Gabirol, Samuel ha-Nagid, Moses Ibn Ezra, Judah ha-Levi, and others. In addition, strong love between adult males, such as Moses Ibn Ezra and the younger Judah ha-Levi, is found in the poems. Male–male love was used as a religious metaphor; Israel's love for God was expressed as love of a male. In different poems Israel takes sometimes a male, at other times a female role.

These poems are frequently mentioned by later Sephardic poets, and one must conclude that they circulated widely at the time, and were not viewed as something which needed to be kept secret from other Jews. (Being in Hebrew, they were of course unknown to non-Jews.) The conclusion seems unavoidable that they reflect widespread homosexual behavior among Sephardic Jews, at least until they moved to Christian territory in the late eleventh century, after which the pederastic poetry tapers off. As homosexuality was treated much more secretively by Jews living in Christian Spain, by the converts and descendents of converts who were to dominate Spanish intellectual life in the fifteenth through seventeenth centuries, and by Sephardic Jews who chose exile from Spain over conversion in 1492, its extent is impossible to determine. It is probably reflected in the androgyne of the Kabbala, and in the power and mystery surrounding the Hebrew language and even more the pseudo-Aramaic of the *Zohar*, which guarded access to secret, untranslated texts. Among the converts there are occasional suggestions of sympathy with

what may have been considered a heritage, even if it was no longer expressed in sexual activity and only known through vague oral transmission, the pederastic poetry having been lost or forgotten.

Scholarship. The poets and intellectual leaders of Sepharad were also Biblical scholars, indeed those who founded modern Biblical scholarship. Besides compiling the first dictionaries of Biblical Hebrew, they examined the chronology of the Bible, detecting for the first time the two Isaiahs and identifying the Pentateuch as post-Mosaic. As they saw the Bible as their national as well as poetic and religious source, their views on Biblical homosexuality (to which Biblical chronology is very relevant) are worthy of reconstruction, though not yet studied in any Western language. That Samuel ha-Nagid claimed descent from and identified with King **David**, however, suggests that he perceived David, Israel's great poet–king and symbol, as predominantly homosexual. The Song of Songs, traditionally interpreted as portraying love of God from a symbolic female viewpoint, and whose role in the Kabbala is well-known, was of course taken as the work of David's son Solomon. Although modern archeology does not support it, Sephardic Jews dated their presence in Spain from the time of David and Solomon, when Jews accompanied the Phoenician seafarers; the Phoenician king Hiram was a friend of David and Solomon.

These Biblical experts must have noted the homosexual temple prostitution which reached its peak during the reigns of David and Solomon (Deut. 23:17–18; 1 Kings 14:24, 15:12, 22:24; 2 Kings 23:7; all references to the kādēsh). Ha-Nagid never tired of talking of his Levitic origin, to which he ascribed his talents as a poet, and Judah ha-Levi ("the Levite") also chose to emphasize that fact; it is possible that they saw a link between homosexuality and the Levitical priesthood, which figured prominantly during the times of the two great kings. When one finds verse claiming that "If Moses could have seen . . . my friend, . . . he would not have written in his Torah 'Do not lie with mankind as thou liest with women,'" one can be sure that Biblical homosexuality was seen somewhat otherwise than it commonly is today.

Granada. No part of Hispano-Jewish history is more fascinating than is that of **Granada.** Early Arabic writers repeatedly called it a Jewish city, "Garnata al-Yahud" (Granada of the Jews). The Zirid kingdom of Granada emerged as an independent entity after the breakdown of centralized Islamic authority in Córdoba, and insecurity in that city led distinguished Jews to move to Granada. Granada was in the eleventh century the center of Sephardic civilization at its peak, and from 1027 until 1066 Granada was a powerful Jewish state. Jews did not hold the client (*dhimmi*) status typical of Islamic rule. Samuel Ibn Nagrilla, recognized by Sephardic Jews everywhere as the quasi-political ha-Nagid ("The Prince"), was king in all but name. As vizier he made policy and—much more unusual—led the army. In his poetry, the main source for his military career, there is found a disturbing joy in gory combat in the name of the lord of Israel. It is said that Samuel's strengthening and fortification of Granada was what permitted it, later, to survive as the last Islamic state in the Iberian peninsula.

All of the greatest figures of eleventh-century Hispano-Jewish culture are associated with Granada. Moses Ibn Ezra was from Granada; on his invitation Judah ha-Levi spent several years there as his guest. Ibn Gabirol's patrons and hosts were the Jewish viziers of Granada, Samuel ha-Nagid and his son Joseph. One cannot avoid the conclusion, for which there is also evidence in the memoirs of the last Zirid king, that homosexuality and pederasty were the norm in aristocratic Jewish and Muslim circles in Granada.

In a startling thesis, Frederick P. Bargebuhr has argued that the Alhambra in Granada was begun during this period.

On the basis of a poem of Ibn Gabirol first published in 1941, plus architectural evidence, he has proposed that the Fountain of the Lions was part of a Jewish temple-palace, whose foundations can still be seen. According to Bargebuhr, it was undertaken by Samuel ha-Nagid's son and successor Joseph, 1000 years after the destruction of the Second Temple in Jerusalem. Joseph did not have his father's political skills, however, and was assassinated in 1066 during the only anti-Jewish pogrom in Islamic Spain. While the Jewish community of Granada reestablished itself for some years, this marked the beginning of the end, and a turning point in Sephardic history. Judah ha-Levi's Zionism has the fate of Zirid Granada as its immediate background.

The final period of independent Granadine history, the Nasrid kingdom of the thirteenth to fifteenth centuries, is very imperfectly known. Estimates of the size of its Jewish community vary greatly, and little is known about its intellectual life, nor is it known to what extent the Alhambra we know, with an esthetic called homosexual, reflects the putative original Jewish temple-palace, although it might. Some Jews and involuntary converts to Christianity fled to Granada from the newly hostile Christian Spain; they were warmly received by the Jewish community there. After conquering the city Ferdinand and Isabella had the Jewish quarter razed as a site for the cathedral, and Jewish inscriptions obliterated. They left nothing (other than the Fountain of the Lions) to remind one that Granada was once a major Jewish city, even briefly a new Jerusalem. Their unexpected decision to expel all Jews from Spain was at the behest of the fanatic Torquemada taken in Granada only three months after its conquest.

BIBLIOGRAPHY. Frederick P. Bargebuhr, *The Alhambra,* Berlin: De Gruyter, 1968; David Gonzalo Maeso, *Garnata al-Yahud,* Granada: Universidad de Granada, 1963; Rudolph Kayser, *The Life and Time of Jehudah Halevi,* New York:

Philosophical Library, 1949; Helen Leneman, "Reclaiming Jewish History: Homo-erotic Poetry of the Middle Ages," *Changing Men*, 18 (Summer/Fall 1987), 22–28; Stanley Rose, "Anti-Semitism in the Cancioneros of the Fifteenth Century: The Accusation of Sexual Indiscretions," *Hispanófila*, 78 (May 1983), 5–6; Norman Roth, "'Deal Gently with the Young Man': Love of Boys in Medieval Hebrew Poetry of Spain," *Speculum*, 57 (1982), 20–51; idem, "'My Beloved is Like a Gazelle': Imagery of the Beloved Boy in Religious Hebrew Poetry," *Hebrew Annual Review*, 8 (1984), 143–65; idem, "Satire and Debate in Two Famous Medieval Poems from al-Andalus: Love of Boys vs. Girls, The Pen and Other Themes," *Maghreb Review*, 4 (1979), 105–13; Jefim Schirman, "The Ephebe in Medieval Hebrew Poetry," *Sefarad*, 15 (1955), 55–68.

Daniel Eisenberg

JUDEO-CHRISTIAN TRADITION

After World War II Christian theologians were horrified and conscience-stricken by the revelation of the **Holocaust** and by the bitter realization that the mass murder of millions of men, women, and children in the gas chambers was in some respects the logical and inevitable consequence of everything that the Christian Church had taught in regard to the Jewish people almost since the beginning of its existence. The Church had stigmatized the Jewish people as deicides and Christ-killers, as exiles rejected by God and fated to wander homeless across the face of the earth, as guilty of host profanation and ritual murder, had decreed that they be marked with the Jew badge and confined behind the walls of the ghetto. Small wonder then that Christians had remained silent in face of the mounting wave of **anti-Semitism** in the 1930s and finally of the deportation of their Jewish neighbors to destinations from which they never returned.

Hence in the postwar period liberal theologians undertook to find a common ground between Judaism and Christianity which they labeled the "Judeo-Christian tradition." This movement required a great deal of soul-searching, since it implied a renunciation of the exclusive claim to possess the truth of revelation which all the **Abrahamic religions** uphold. The condemnation of Judaism by Christian thinkers and scholars in the past, it must be acknowledged, was not a conscious and deliberate injustice, but rather the consequence of deep-seated prejudices inherited from generation, and in many, of the unconscious wish to convert the Jews and to justify the policy of the Church in their regard. When Christian scholars exposed to rabbinic literature realized that their negative judgment of Judaism was false and untenable, they sensed that they had either to abandon it or to continue perpetrating an injustice. In the latter case they would be violating the principles of their own conscience; and in the former, they would have to conclude that there was no motive for seeking the conversion of the Jews or for rationalizing the treatment meted out to them by the Church and Christian legislators in the Middle Ages.

Much debate within the context of the "Judeo-Christian tradition" has turned upon the question of whether there are one, two, or many covenants between God and his people. But whatever the answer, it is clear from the historical record that all forms of Judaism and Christianity, however much or little they had in common, regarded the code of sexual morality formulated in Leviticus 18 as part of their covenant, their fundamental law. Even in the centuries before the rise of Christianity, Judaism had accepted the principle that its adherents should suffer death rather than engage in sexual immorality.

Hence for homosexuals the Judeo-Christian tradition has meant nothing but ostracism and punishment, exile and death. It has spelled rejection by close friends and relatives, denial of employment and economic opportunity, violence at the hands not just of the authorities but also of the criminal underworld, legal penalties ranging from fines and confiscation of property to castration and death. To find anything positive in this tradition would be an arduous task; but the analogy in the relationship between Judaism and Christianity merits comment.

The Church and Synagogue have never been able to accept homosexual love as on a par with heterosexual, yet that is the precondition for any reconciliation with the gay community. To admit that the attachment of two persons of the same sex can be as selfless, as devoted, as positive in its effect on society, as the love of members of the opposite sex would have major repercussions for the theology of sexual relations. Jewish and Christian moral theologians would have to concede that the attempt to "convert" homosexuals forcibly to heterosexuality was as cruel and unjust as forced conversions in the religious sphere; and that the moral condemnation and legal prohibition of homosexual behavior, particularly since the thirteenth century, was as wrong as the anti-Judaic measures adopted by the Church from the Fourth Lateran Council (1215) onward. The effort to exclude homosexuals—a stable minority of the population—from Christian society never reduced their numbers, but produced only a vast and needless amount of human misery. It undoubtedly contributed to the persecution and killing of homosexuals in Nazi Germany which—unlike the Jewish Holocaust—went unnoticed and unprotested by Christian theologians while it was happening, and has gone uncondemned and unrequited since 1945.

A genuine new beginning in the relationship between homosexuals and the church and synagogue requires such an act of reflection and contrition on the part of the religious groups whose past record has been one of condemnation and rejection. Acquaintance with the writings of homosexual men and women across the centuries, with the record of their feelings and aspirations, of their struggle to survive

within an implacably hostile society, is a precondition for insight and understanding. Only on this basis will the Judeo-Christian tradition be able to come to terms with the biological and psychological reality of homosexual love.

Warren Johansson

JUNG, CARL GUSTAV (1875–1961)

Swiss depth psychologist. One of a number of major thinker–therapists who became active at the beginning of the twentieth century, he and his work have received the accolade of a special adjective, "Jungian."

Life. Born in Basel into a family both sides of which had members gifted with ESP powers, Jung was the son of a pastor in the Swiss Reformed Church. Reading the textbook of psychiatry written by Richard Freiherr von **Krafft-Ebing** convinced him that this should be his future specialty, and he took his medical degree from the University of Basel in 1902. He worked at the Burghölzli Hospital under Eugen Bleuler from 1900 to 1907. He established his reputation with a book on *The Psychology of Dementia Praecox* in 1906.

In the following year he first encountered Sigmund **Freud** during a trip to Vienna, and for six years the two actively corresponded and collaborated. In 1909 Jung renounced his hospital appointment in favor of his growing private practice, and also traveled with Freud to lecture at Clark University in Massachusetts. The two thinkers increasingly diverged, particularly after Jung published his own ideas in a book entitled *The Psychology of the Unconscious* (1912), later renamed *Symbols of Transformation*. At the first meeting of the International Psychoanalytic Association in Munich in 1913, the rift between Jung and Freud turned to open hostility, and the two never met again. In April 1914 Jung resigned as President of the Association.

Between 1913 and 1917 Jung went through a period of deep and intensive self-analysis; he now asserted that he had never been a Freudian, and set about creating his own school, which he dubbed analytical psychology in contrast to psychoanalysis. He devoted himself fully to his private practice, to research, and to writing; his *Collected Works* amount to eighteen volumes. He treated not only psychology and psychotherapy, but also religion, mythology, social issues, art and literature, and such occult and mystical themes as alchemy, astrology, telepathy and clairvoyance, yoga, and spiritualism. He lived and worked at his home in Küsnacht, by the lakeside of Zurich, interrupting his routine with travels to India, Africa, the United States and other parts of the world. His theory of the collective unconscious led him to anthropological study of African peoples and the Navajo Indians of the Southwest United States. He outlived nearly all of his early associates in the psychoanalytic movement, dying at the age of eighty-five in 1961.

Distinctive Elements of Jung's Thought. At least part of the incompatibility between Freud and Jung stemmed from their differences in psychological endowment and clinical background. Freud was committed to rationalistic and materialistic explanations, had little experience of paranormal psychic phenomena, and had never worked in a hospital or confronted psychotic patients. Jung was repelled by the emphasis which Freud had placed on the sexual (the "libido"), but at the same time sought to probe the deepest layers of the unconscious. In Jungian psychology, the whole personality is designated the psyche, which has three components: the conscious *ego*, the *personal unconscious* and its *complexes*, and the *collective unconscious* and its *archetypes*. Major dynamic concepts are *psychic energy* or *libido*, *value*, *entropy*, and *equivalence*. The persona is a mask adopted by an individual in response to the demands of social convention. The purpose of the mask is to make an impression upon others and often to conceal one's true feelings and thoughts. The *anima* refers to the feminine side of a man's nature, and the *animus* refers to the masculine side of a woman's nature. The *shadow-archetype* consists of the animal instincts that man inherited in the process of evolving from lower forms of life. The shadow typifies the animal side of the psyche, while the *self* represents the individual's striving for unity, wholeness, and completeness.

Jung's actual influence upon psychiatry has been slight, but he has contributed to the practice of **psychotherapy** by the flexibility and variety of his technique, which included painting, modeling, and writing as well as dialogue. Since Jung's death, some followers have found support in his teachings for concepts of feminism and **androgyny**, but these interpretations presuppose an element of revisionism.

Jung and Homosexuality. Jung never developed a major theory of homosexuality, but five general positions emerge from his writings.

The first is that homosexuality ought not to be a concern of the legal authorities, and that, barring the social stigma, homosexuality does not diminish the "value of the individual as a member of society," while laws against homosexuality as a criminal offense are useless, inhumane, and in fact promote crimes such as blackmail. Thus Jung, like Freud, ratified Magnus **Hirschfeld**'s arguments for legal toleration of homosexual expression; and it is probably not by chance that when in 1938 Switzerland adopted a federal penal code replacing that of the cantons, there was no provision making homosexual acts criminal. The second position is that homosexuality is best understood when set in a historical and cultural context. Ancient **Greece**, in which pederasty served a social and political function, was a constant point of reference for Jung in dealing both with individual cases and with larger issues of theory.

A third point is that Jung did identify homosexuality with "primitive" societies, and by analogy reasoned that homosexuality is a result of psychological immaturity and therefore abnormal and disturbed. This interpretation is maintained in both the theoretical and the casuistic portions of his work.

Fourth, Jung distinguished an individual's homosexuality from other aspects of his personality. In the case histories Jung went beyond the patient's homosexual behavior, scrutinizing other aspects of his psychological development. In theoretical discussions he posited that a mother complex resulting in homosexuality could also foster other personality traits, positive and negative.

The last and most characteristically Jungian attitude is that an individual's homosexuality has its own meaning specific to the individual in question, and that psychological growth consists in becoming conscious of that meaning. The search for that meaning led Jung to elaborate a two-stage process of examination; he first discerned how the homosexuality finds expression in the patient's life, then examined the repercussions of this expression on the patient's entire personality. This culminated in the insight that homosexuality can have both positive and negative meanings for any individual. Underpinning this whole approach to homosexuality is the characteristic "individuality" of Jung's psychology, in which the unit of study is the individual soul. Thus homosexuality varies from one subject to another and contains seeds of growth and of deformation for each individual. Hence his teaching implies that every homosexual must examine his sexual interests with the goal of deeper self-understanding.

BIBLIOGRAPHY. Robert H. Hopcke, "Jung's Attitudes Toward Homosexuality: A Review," *Spring: An Annual of Archetypal Psychology and Jungian Thought*, 1987, pp. 154–61.

Warren Johansson

JUVENAL (67–CA. 140)

The last extant Roman satirist. The facts of his personal life are elusive, as his work contains almost no autobiographical material. The unreliability of the Life compiled only in late antiquity makes reconstruction of the events of his life impossible. His *Satires* in 16 books (the last of them mutilated) castigate the moral corruption and hypocrisy of contemporary **Roman** society, particularly its upper strata, which are contrasted with the sober virtues of an idealized Roman past. The bitter indignation of his work may have been the result of his personal fortunes. The publication of his verse satires began in the reign of Trajan and reached its high point under Hadrian. After Juvenal's death his works were little read, quoted, or studied, since the vices and literary fashions which he excoriated became increasingly fashionable at the Imperial court; but interest in him revived at the close of the fourth century, when the authoritative, commented edition of his *Satires* was published. The Christians, however, relished his denunciation of contemporary pagan cults, and the Middle Ages appreciated his writings far more as a textbook of ethics, as hundreds of manuscripts and commentaries attest.

Juvenal observed and judged the cosmopolitan city of Rome with all its domestic and foreign vices and roundly condemned them, from the man equally ready to give children to a woman and sexual pleasure to another man to the virago brandishing her spear in the arena. In the second satire he spends his ire on several types of homosexual male, particularly the effeminate and the transvestite: hypocritical philosophers, affected moralists, members of secret societies and orgy clubs, and mincing noblemen. In the ninth satire he voiced his disdain for adult hustlers. Witnessing and denouncing all the byways of sexual expression in frank and unequivocal language, he (unlike **Martial**) never resorted to obscenity. Yet he went so far as to urge his readers, if they really want to "burn the candle at both ends," to seek sensual pleasure from a boy rather than from a woman—advice that betrays a strong element of homosexuality in his character. Juvenal was a convinced misogynist; he detested and despised not the women of his own corrupt age, but women in general. However, there are favorable references to boys as love objects, which would imply that his own preferences were those of the pederast.

Juvenal was basically a member of the **Stoic** and aristocratic opposition to the empire who painted its life and manners in the blackest possible hues. Moralizing Christian commentators, and even modern scholars such as Gilbert Highet, have seized upon certain of his satiric thrusts as anticipating and confirming their own attitudes, but his work merits a more detached approach to its ethical complexities. Juvenal undeniably represents a major source of information about homosexual life in Rome in the first half of the second century, and is also a classic of the satiric genre in antiquity.

BIBLIOGRAPHY. E. C. Courtney, *A Commentary on the Satires of Juvenal*, London: Athlone Press, 1980; Otto Kiefer, *Sexual Life in Ancient Rome*, London: Routledge & Kegan Paul, 1934.
Warren Johansson

JUVENILES
See **Youth.**

KĀDĒSH

Ḳādēsh (pl. *ḳĕdēshīm*) is a Biblical Hebrew word that literally means "holy or consecrated one," and is rendered "sodomite" or more accurately "male cult prostitute" in various translations of the scriptures. It is a key term for understanding the **Old Testament** references to homosexuality. It occurs as a common noun at least six times (Deuteronomy 23:18, I Kings 14:24, 15:12 and 22:46, II Kings 23:7, Job 36:14). It can also be restored on the basis of textual criticism in II Kings 23:24 (= Septuagint of II Chronicles 35:19a) and in Hosea 11:12. They all ostensibly designate foreigners (non-Israelites) who served as sacral prostitutes (hierodules) in the Kingdom of Judah and specifically within the precincts of the first Temple (ca. 950–622 B.C.). That these men had sexual relations with other males and not with women is proven by Hosea 4:14, which castigates the males exclusively for "spending their manhood" in drunken orgies with hierodules, while their wives remained at home, alone and unsatisfied, and by the reading of Isaiah 65:3 in the Qumran manuscript: "And they (m. pl.) sucked their phalli upon the stones." Their involvement in the Ishtar–Tammuz cult—an obvious rival of the monotheistic Jahweh religion—is responsible for the Biblical equation of homosexuality with idolatry and paganism and the exclusion of the individual engaging in homosexual activity from the "congregation of Israel," which persists in the fundamentalist condemnation of all homosexual expression to this day.

The Cultural Setting. To understand that the condemnation of the *ḳādēsh* was a cultic prohibition and the self-definition of a religious community, not a moral judgment on other acts taking place outside the sphere of the sacral, it is necessary to see the *ḳādēsh* or male hierodule (with the *ḳĕdēshāh* as his female counterpart) in his historical and cultural setting, as a part of Northwest Semitic religion on the territory of the Kingdom of Judah down to the reforms of King Josiah (622 B.C.). The commandments forbidding male homosexual activity on pain of death in the Holiness Code (Leviticus 18:22 and 20:13) were added only in the Persian period (first half of the fifth pre-Christian century specifically). Critical scholarship generally dates the Holiness Code to the beginning of that period, but Martin Noth in his major commentary *Leviticus* (Philadelphia, 1965) ascribes this part of Leviticus to a time slightly after 520 B.C., when the new and reformed Jewish religion set about throwing off all the associations believed responsible for the catastrophe of 586, the destruction of the first Temple and the exile of the population of Judah to Babylon. The proof of the later origin of the verses indicated above is the prophetic reading ("*haphṭarāh*") for the portion of the Torah including Leviticus 18, namely Ezekiel 22:10–11, a comparison of which shows that Ezekiel was alluding to a text which in the final years of the First Commonwealth began with Leviticus 18:7 and ended with 18:20, as if to say "You have committed every sexual sin in the book." While there are those who maintain that the Levitical references condemn all male homosexual acts, the character of the Holiness Code suggests that it had the sacral aspect of the sexual liaison in mind.

Derrick Sherwin Bailey, in his *Homosexuality and the Western Chris-*

tian *Tradition* (London, 1955), argued that the *kedeshim* "served the female worshipper" and so would translate the word as "male cult prostitute" but not "sodomite." However, it is unlikely that women were admitted to the Temple, then or later, and all parallels from the religious life of antiquity, from Cyprus to Mesopotamia, involve male homosexual connection. Designations for the male prostitute in Hebrew and Phoenician are "dog" (*kelebh*) and "puppy" (*gur*), notably in Deuteronomy 23:17, where the *kelebh* is set in parallel to the *zonah* "(female) prostitute." In Isaiah 3:4 the word *ta'alulim* is rendered *effeminati* by St. Jerome; it means "males who are sexually abused by others," = German *Schandbuben*. Another likely reference is Isaiah 2:6, the closing hemistich of which Jerome translated *et pueris alienis adhaeserunt*, while the Aramaic pseudo-Jonathan Targum euphemistically renders the text "And they walked in the ways of the gentiles," in which the Hebrew verb has an Arabic cognate that means "they loved tenderly." In Hosea 11:12 a slight emendation, together with comparison again of the Arabic meaning of the verb in the first half of the parallel, yields the meaning "And Judah is still untrue to God/but faithful to *kedeshim*."

How could male prostitutes fit into the scheme of Northwest Semitic—specifically Canaanite—religion during the First Commonwealth? Foreign as the notion is to the modern religious consciousness, the worship of Ishtar and Tammuz was a fertility cult in which union with the hierodule consecrated to the service of the goddess was thought to have magical functions and powers. Such hierodules could be either male or female, and the singular *kadesh* in I Kings 14:24 is to be taken as a collective, meaning "hierodules as a professional caste" who were "in the land," practicing their foreign rites. The males may even have been eunuchs, though the context of Job 36:14 "Their soul dieth in youth, and their life at the hierodules' age" suggests that they were adolescent prosti-

tutes no different from the bar or street hustler of today. Furthermore, place names containing the element *Kadesh*, such as the one in Genesis 14:7, which also was called *En-mishpat* "Spring of Judgment" indicate the locales of shrines whose personnel had both erotic and mantic functions. This is independently confirmed by the glosses on the Septuagint renderings of *kadesh* and *kedeshah* in Deuteronomy 23:18, and by the fourth-century work of Firmicus Maternus, *De errore profanarum religionum*, which ridicules the pretensions of the effeminate pagan priests to foretell the future. This aspect of the professional activity of the *kedeshim* parallels the homosexual associations of the shaman in primitive cultures and of the medium in the occult underworld of modern times.

Aftermath and Parallels. The taboo on homosexuality in Western civilization is thus a legacy of the religious rivalries and conflicts in Ancient Israel, and of the formation of the Jewish community after the Babylonian captivity as a client-ethnos of the Persian monarchy—the "evil empire" against which the Greeks fought their heroic wars.

Female and male temple prostitution is known in a wide range of civilizations in the ancient world from Cyprus to India. Further comparative study is needed to clarify the place of the institution within the overall conspectus of same-sex relations.

BIBLIOGRAPHY. Michael Astour, "Tamar the Hierodule," *Journal of Biblical Literature*, 85 (1966), 185–96; Tom Horner, *Jonathan Loved David: Homosexuality in Biblical Times*, Philadelphia: Westminster, 1978, chapters 5–6.

Warren Johansson

KADESH BARNEA

This Biblical place first appears in Genesis 14:7, where it has the alternate name *En-mishpat* ("Spring of Judgment"), implying that it was a cultic shrine renowned both for a theophany and as the site of an oracular spring. The following discussion is necessarily tentative and speculative, but the material cited in it has been so largely ignored in the standard reference works published by the religious establishment that it needs to be better known, if only as a starting point for further investigation. The authors whose opinions are summarized below enjoy international reputations, and their interpretations cannot simply be dismissed as the tendentious construction of a prejudiced amateur.

Modern archeologists identify the locale as En Qdes, first discovered by Rowlands in 1842, an extensive oasis with many springs lying some 80 kilometers south-southwest of Beersheba. The first component of the name, Kadesh, clearly means that the shrine housed a retinue of hierodules, male and female, who had both erotic and mantic functions. Virtually every standard religious reference work conceals this elementary fact by explaining the name simply as "holy," which is indeed the primary meaning of the Semitic root, but in the sense of cult personnel consecrated to the worship of Ishtar, the goddess of love. Very likely because of these pagan reminiscences, the Targumim (the Aramaic translations of the Old Testament), suppress the name Kadesh Barnea, replacing it with Rekem or Rekem Gea. As for the second activity of the kědēshîm, the role of homosexuals as **shamans** and seers is too well documented to need further comment.

Site of the Revelation. It was the historian Eduard Meyer (1855–1930) who first emphasized the importance of Kadesh Barnea as the site of the primitive revelation to Moses in his book *Die Israeliten und ihre Nachbarstämme* (1906), and later in the second half of the first volume of his *Geschichte des Altertums* (1909). This locale cannot be identical with the Mount Sinai of today, since the latter has no trace of the volcanic activity which Exodus 19:16–18 unmistakably describes as the prelude to the giving of the Law. The primitive account in Exodus showed Moses leading the Israelites from bondage in Egypt to Kadesh Barnea in northwestern Arabia with its volcanic districts (the so-called *harras*). Elsewhere in the sacred narrative Jahweh reveals himself as a fire god, like the Greek Hephaistus and the Roman Vulcan, in particular in a late interpolation into the legend of **Sodom and Gomorrah** in Genesis 19:24, where he rains brimstone and fire on the twin cities—that is to say, causes a volcanic eruption rather than the earthquake alone possible in Palestine proper which the earlier version describes in Genesis 19:21 and 25.

The Levites. Kadesh Barnea also belongs to the tribe, or more correctly the brotherhood of Levi, which figures in the patriarchal era as a neighbor of the tribe of Simeon in the account of the raid on Shechem in Genesis 34 and 49:5–7. Moses as a member of the tribe of Levi receives from Jahweh at Kadesh Barnea the revelation of the Law and the mysteries of the priesthood. In later centuries the Levites evolved from a warrior into a priestly caste with a covert tradition of male bonding that may have included homosexual activity, because Epiphanius of Salamis (ca. 315–403) could report in his *Panarion* (I, 2, 13, written between 375 and 377) that a Barbelognostic sect called the Levites had no intercourse with women, but only with one another. One is inclined to see analogies with the medieval **Templars** persecuted by the French crown with accusations of sodomy whose truthfulness remains moot. It is also relevant that Sigmund **Freud**, in his last major work, *Moses and Monotheism* (1938), speculating upon Meyer's findings and also upon a book by the Old Testament scholar Ernst Sellin (1876–1946), *Mose und seine Bedeutung für die israelitisch-jüdische Religionsgeschichte* (1922), claimed that there was a secret tradition stemming from the primal revelation at Kadesh that was transmitted within the inner circles of the priesthood to later centuries, when Judaism assumed its historic form. Layman that he was in Biblical matters, Freud was still guided by a remarkable intuition, so that the question remains open for students of the Old Testament.

God and Moses. In addition, the philologist Franz Dornseiff (1888–1960), in an article rather daringly published in *Zeitschrift für die alttestamentliche Wissenschaft* in 1935, hence in Nazi Germany, likened the Levites of Exodus 32:26–29 to the SS of his own time and the slaughter of the three thousand "enemies of Jahweh" to the German St. Bartholomew's Eve, the **Röhm** purge of June 30, 1934. He further equated the dialogue of Moses with Jahweh in Exodus 33:11 with the intercourse of the legendary Cretan legislator Minos with Zeus mentioned in **Homer's** Odyssey 19, 179–80, a comparison that had already been drawn in antiquity by **Clement** of Alexandria in his *Stromata*, II, 5. Dornseiff also interpreted the curious passage in Exodus 33:20–24, which caused so much merriment to Victorian skeptics because Jahweh tells Moses: "Then I will take away mine hand, and thou shalt see my back parts," as the euphemistic account of a liaison in which God is the *erastes* and Moses the *eromenos*, thus as a parallel to other ancient myths in which sexual union with the god or goddess is the medium of revelation. The verb "to see" would have the same meaning as in the account of homosexual **incest** in Genesis 9:22. The *Zohar*, the classical repository of Kabbalistic lore (written in Christian Spain between 1268 and 1290), ascribes to Moses a love affair with the Shechinah, the divine presence (conceived as feminine), a theme which may be a later heterosexualizing reflex of the primitive tradition.

Conclusions. All these considerations point to the existence in the early centuries of Israel's history (from the *Landnahme* beginning about 1300 B.C. to the end of the First Commonwealth in 586 B.C.) of a homoerotic and even pederastic tradition (with the *eros paidagogikos*) in the warrior and the priestly castes, not too different from the analogous phenomena in ancient **Greece** and other cultures of the eastern Mediterranean. Its traces could not be wholly expunged from the older narratives even by the strong Zoroastrian influence in the fifth century, when Ezra the Scribe and the men of the Great Assembly, in formulating the laws of normative **Judaism**, suppressed these customs and institutionalized a homophobic tradition that became the common property of the **Abrahamic religions**.

BIBLIOGRAPHY. Franz Dornseiff, "Antikes zum Alten Testament. 2. Exodus," *Zeitschrift für die alttestamentliche Wissenschaft*, new series, 12 (1935), 153–71; Sigmund Freud, *Moses and Monotheism*, New York: Knopf, 1939; Eduard Meyer, *Die Israeliten und ihre Nachbarstämme*, Halle am Saale: Max Niemeyer, 1906, pp. 60–82; idem, *Geschichte des Altertums*. I:2. *Die ältesten geschichtlichen Völker und Kulturen bis zum sechzehnten Jahrhundert*, second ed., Stuttgart: J. G. Cotta, 1909, pp. 376–83; Edwin M. Yamauchi, "Cultic Prostitution: A Case Study in Cultural Diffusion," *Orient and Occident: Essays presented to Cyrus H. Gordon on the Occasion of His Sixty-fifth Birthday*, Kevelaer: Verlag Butzon & Bercker, 1973, pp. 213–22.

Warren Johansson

KALIARDÁ

Kaliardá is the most common term for Modern Greek homosexual argot, specifically the argot used by the "passive" homosexual (the *kinaidhos* or, pejoratively, the *poustis*), but not by his "active" sexual partner, the *kolombarás*. Synonyms of Kaliardá include *Kaliardí, Kaliardo, Tsinavota, Liardo, Doura Liarda, Latinika* ("Latin"), *Vathia Latinika* ("Deep Latin"), *Etrouska* ("Estruscan"), *Loubinistika*, and *Frangoloubinistika*. The argot may also be divided into a "common" Kaliardá and a much more esoteric Kaliardá, *Doura Liarda* (also "Deep Latin" or "Etruscan"), the latter known only to a select few. The language was first studied by the folklorist Elias Petropoulos in his book *Kaliardá: An Etymological Dictionary of Greek Homosexual Slang* (1971). For this at first privately printed dictionary Petropoulos served a seven-month prison term in 1972. The etymology of the term Kaliardá is to be derived, according to Petropoulos, from the French word *gaillard*; Gordon M. Messing has suggested, however, that the term may derive from a common Romany term meaning "Gypsy."

The great flexibility of the Greek language, the facility with which foreign words are assimilated and compounds formed, as well as the conscious wordplay carried on by the gay Greek while speaking the argot, explain in part why Kaliardá is a rich conglomerate of several languages. Besides words deriving directly from Modern Greek and phonetically transformed, many English, French, Italian and Turkish words are employed, as well as terms borrowed from Romany. A Kaliardá compound can indeed be an alloy of two or three roots from two or three different languages. Sometimes foreign-sounding endings are attached to a Greek (or foreign) root-word. Onomatopoeias are also common. Among the grammatical curiosities of the argot is the fact that nearly all nouns and adjectives are used in the feminine form. As opposed to other Greek argots (such as underworld slang) which grammatically are Modern Greek but with slang terms inserted, Kaliardá is nearly a language in itself: only a few Greek words are necessary, along with two particles required in the construction of verbal tenses. Articles are generally not used in Kaliardá where they would be in Greek. Kaliardá nicknames, proverbs, curses, and place-names also exist.

BIBLIOGRAPHY. Elias Petropoulos, *Kaliardá: An Etymological Dictionary of Greek Homosexual Slang*, 4th ed., Athens: Nefeli, 1984.

John Taylor

KAMPMANN, CHRISTIAN (1939–1988)

Danish novelist. At the age of twenty-one he fled the stifling atmosphere of his family and went to Paris to study French, at the same time seeking to come to terms with his homosexuality. In 1973 he published *Visse hensyn* (Certain Considerations) the first in a series of four novels exploring social changes in Denmark from the 1950s to the 1970s through the lens of five children (one of them gay) in a well-to-do Rungsted family. The other novels in the quartet are *Faste forhold* (Firm Relationship, 1974), *Rene Linier* (Straight Lines, 1975), and *Andre nader* (Other Ways, 1975). With *Fornemmelser* (Feelings, 1977) he initiated an autobiographical sequence, showing how he first tried to go with women and even married, but later had to admit that he was gay; his growing self-understanding led him into the Gay Liberation Front. This novel was followed by *Videre trods alt* (Onwards in Spite of All, 1979) and *I glimt* (In a Flash, 1980).

For the last thirteen years of his life Kampmann lived with a fellow writer, Jens Michael Schau. Their relationship was stormy, characterized by insecurity on both sides; Schau was plagued with chronic depression. On September 12, 1988, at their retreat on the island of Laeso, Schau beat Kampmann to death only hours before the premiere of Schau's Danish television drama, *Perhaps Next Month*. The play dealt with a bisexual married man who was infected with the AIDS virus by his friend.

Stephen Wayne Foster

KANTOROWICZ, ERNST (1895–1963)

German-American historian. Scion of a Prussian family of liquor producers, Kantorowicz served as an intelligence officer on the Turkish front in World War I. Returning to Germany, he became active in the Freikorps, a rightist paramilitary organization that fought the left before he joined the elitist Stefan **George** circle. Under its auspices his first masterpiece, *Frederick the Second* (1927), conceived in the grand manner of monumental history as recommended by Friedrich Nietzsche, presented not only the facts but the mythical elements of the medieval emperor's personality and times. Although sharply criticized for being almost erotically engaged with his nearly superhuman subject, Kantorowicz vindicated himself with the supplementary volume of 1931 that showed his thorough mastery of the sources. The mystical and nationalistic fervor that enlivens some pages of the biography appealed to the National Socialists, despite Kantorowicz's Jewish origins.

After serving briefly as a professor of history at Frankfurt am Main, Ernst Kantorowicz fled the Nazis, going first to Oxford and then to the United States. He taught at Berkeley from 1939 to 1951, where he fitted into the gay scene, notably befriending the poet Robert **Duncan** and one of Duncan's many lovers, Werner Vordtriede, a fellow ex-member of the Stefan George circle. One of the few brave enough to refuse to sign the loyalty oath required of all employees in the state of California as a result of the **McCarthyite** agitation, he was invited (like the physicist Robert Oppenheimer, who also refused) to join the Institute for Advanced Study in Princeton. As a homosexual immigrant he might, of course, have been deported.

After the war, Kantorowicz welcomed a fellow German gay medievalist Theodor Mommsen, Jr., grandson of the most famous German classical historian and nephew of the sociologist Max Weber and of the classical philologist Ulrich von Wilamowitz-Moellendorff. Having taught during the war at Groton, Mommsen came to Princeton University and unselfishly contributed to Kantorowicz' second masterpiece. Composed at Princeton, *The King's Two Bodies: A Study in Mediaeval Political Theology* (1957), peerlessly commands a vast range of disciplines from law to art history. Like their colleague in French Maurice Coindreau, who translated Faulkner and Hemingway, Kantorowicz and Mommsen did what they could to counter the **homophobia** and discrimination that still routinely resulted in the expulsion of undergraduate and graduate students, as well as the firing or refusal to grant promotion or tenure to suspected gay teachers at Princeton, but they had to be discreet. Parting sadly from his colleague the gay art historian A. M. Friend, Mommsen left for Cornell University, where he joined the most distinguished professor in the history department, the gay M. L. W. Laistner. In 1958 Mommsen committed suicide.

Kantorowicz was succeeded at the Institute for Advanced Study, which sheltered so many brilliant **exiles and émigrés**, by the grandson of the composer Mendelsohn, Felix Gilbert, whose autobiography in 1988 splendidly memorialized his close friends Kantorowicz and especially Mommsen. Gilbert's distant cousin Clara née Mendelsohn had been the wife of Karl Friedrich Otto Westphal (1833--1890), the author of the first, epoch-making psychiatric article on sexual inversion (1869).

In his later work Kantorowicz showed how the strict philological training that he had received in Europe could be combined with an interdisciplinary approach to shed light not only on the past but on the present as well. Combining precision and scope, his work might well guide today's gay scholars, who are seeking to emerge from advocacy and provincialism to a fuller understanding of their infinitely ramified subject.

William A. Percy

KEROUAC, JACK (1922–1969)

American novelist. Born to a working-class French-Canadian family in

Lowell, Massachusetts, Kerouac entered Columbia University on a football scholarship in 1941. His early friendships on Morningside Heights with William Burroughs and Allen Ginsberg nourished his leanings toward experimental literature. Kerouac's first published novel, however, the sprawling *The Town and the City* (1950), was couched in a somewhat elegiac mode deriving from Thomas Wolfe. Then the writer entered a footloose period that took him to Mexico, Tangier, France, and San Francisco. He forged a buddy relationship with the goofy but charismatic Neal Cassady, who in turn was loved by Ginsberg.

Through the influence of oriental literature, jazz, and a liberal infusion of mind-altering drugs, Kerouac formed an ideal of literary spontaneity: one should write as quickly as possibly and revisions should be eschewed as reducing the freshness. Revised or not, his first major work, *On the Road* (1957) records his wanderings, his friends, and his aesthetic ideals. Under different names, the characters reappear in such novels as *The Subterraneans* (1958), *Dharma Bums* (1958), and *Vanity of Duluoz* (1968). However, some critics believe the early work *Visions of Cody* (written in 1951–52) is his masterpiece.

In the Eisenhower years the media focused upon Kerouac, Ginsberg, Burroughs, and their friends as something new, dubbing them "the **beat generation**," heralds of the full-fledged **counterculture** that was to entrance millions a few years later. Kerouac, however, never completely fit the mold, and in his later years he even became an ally of William Buckley's conservative *National Review*. Kerouac also stood apart from his two major confreres—in public estimation at least—as the purely heterosexual balance to his two gay associates, Burroughs and Ginsberg. Accumulating evidence, however, shows that Kerouac's own homosexual experience was more than casual, though it usually occurred while he was (conven-

iently for later excuses) high or otherwise *non compos*. In contrast with his iconoclasm in other spheres, sexually he clung to an almost stereotypical straight image. The one great love of his life was surely Neal Cassady, his straight buddy, and being unable to express his feelings, he gradually sank into alcoholism and despair. Despite major flaws in his writing, Kerouac nonetheless succeeded in capturing the spirit of an America that was on the move, and he may even have succeeded in shifting its course somewhat.

BIBLIOGRAPHY. Barry Gifford and Lawrence Lee, *Jack's Book: An Oral Biography of Jack Kerouac*, New York: Penguin, 1979; Gerald Nicosia, *Memory Babe: A Critical Biography of Jack Kerouac*, New York: Grove Press, 1983.
Wayne R. Dynes

KERTBENY, KÁROLY MÁRIA (KARL MARIA BENKERT; 1824–1882)

German-Hungarian writer, translator, and journalist. He bore the surname Benkert until 1847; then the police of his native city of Vienna authorized him to use the Hungarian noble name of his family as his sole name. Kertbeny is considered the inventor of the words *homosexuality* and *heterosexuality*. The draft of a private letter to Karl Heinrich **Ulrichs** of May 6, 1868 contains for the first time the expressions *homosexual* and *heterosexual*.

From 1869 to 1875 Kertbeny lived in Berlin, and here in 1869 he wrote two pamphlets that were published anonymously, demanding freedom from penal sanctions for homosexual men in Prussia and the Prussian-dominated North German Confederation. They were entitled *§143 des Preussischen Strafgesetzbuchs und seine Aufrechterhaltung als §152 des Ent-wurfs eines Strafgesetzbuchs für den Norddeutschen Bund* (Paragraph 143 of the Prussian Penal Code and its Maintenance as Paragraph §152 of the Draft of a Penal Code for the North German Confederation) and *Das Gemeinschädliche des §143 des Preussischen Strafgesetzbuches . . .* (The Social Harm Caused by Paragraph 143 of the Prussian Penal Code . . .). Here for the first time the word *Homosexualität* is found as a substitute for the designation *Urningthum* that Ulrichs had introduced in 1864. Instead of *Urninge* Kertbeny used the word *Homosexualisten*; instead of *Urninden* (lesbians), *Homosexualistinnen.*

The book by the professor of zoology and anthropology Gustav Jaeger (1832–1917) of Stuttgart contains parts of a text that Kertbeny had written on the sexual instinct, in which the expression *Heterosexualität* occurs for the first time. A continuation of this text, which Jaeger had at first thought too offensive, he published only in 1900 in **Hirschfeld**'s *Jahrbuch für sexuelle Zwischenstufen* without mentioning Kertbeny's name. Jaeger designated the author only as "Dr. M.," a pseudonym that probably contributed to the oft-repeated but erroneous belief that Kertbeny was "a Hungarian doctor." A bibliography of his works printed in a doctoral dissertation at the University of Szeged in 1936 shows that he never received a doctorate in any subject and wrote nothing on medicine or the natural sciences.

Kertbeny's arguments for the emancipation of the homosexuals correspond roughly to those employed by Ulrichs, but his chief emphasis lies less on the assertion that homosexuality is natural and inborn than on the demand that the modern constitutional state extend to homosexuals its principle of non-interference in the private life of its citizens. That is to say, instead of focusing on the claim of exclusive homosexuals to be free of legal hindrances, he asserted the right of all human beings to engage in homosexual activity on the basis of the liberal doctrine that the state itself has no right to interfere in such a private matter as sexual behavior. In this respect he continued the line of reasoning that had begun with the crimi-

nal law reformers of the eighteenth century and was further elaborated by thinkers such as John Stuart Mill.

Kertbeny repeatedly claimed that he himself was a *Normalsexualer*, hence not homosexual. However, there is no proof of that assertion, or for the hypothesis of his homosexuality or bisexuality. The collection of Kertbeny's manuscripts in the Hungarian National Library in Budapest does contain evidence for Kertbeny's authorship of the aforementioned texts, so that alongside Heinrich **Hoessli** and Ulrichs he ranks as one of the most important advocates of homosexual emancipation in the nineteenth century.

Kertbeny died in Budapest in 1882, supposedly in consequence of the late stages of a syphilitic infection.

BIBLIOGRAPHY. J.-C. Feray, "Une histoire critique du mot homosexualité," *Arcadie* (1981), 325: 11–21, 326: 115–24, 327: 171–81, 328: 246–58; Manfred Herzer, "Kertbeny and the Nameless Love," *Journal of Homosexuality*, 12 (1985), 1–25; idem, "Ein Brief von Kertbeny in Hannover an Ulrichs in Wüzburg," *Capri*, 1 (1987), 25–35.

Manfred Herzer

KEYNES, JOHN MAYNARD (1883–1946)

British economist. A polymath, Keynes cultivated many interests, from book collecting to probability theory. His real importance, however, stems from the epistemic break he achieved with the classical theory of economics, changing the landscape of that discipline for all time. Keynes was no ivory-tower theorist, and the thirty-year boom in Western industrial countries (1945–75) has been called the Age of Keynes.

Born into an academic family in **Cambridge**, Maynard Keynes' parents carefully groomed him to be a member of the upper echelon of Britain's elite. After attending Eton, where he won many prizes, it was a foregone conclusion that he should attend King's College, Cambridge. There he blended effortlessly into the idealistic atmosphere of the "higher sodomy," which attained its most rarified form in the secret society known as the Cambridge Apostles, to which he was almost immediately elected. In the Apostles he met his lifelong friends Lytton **Strachey** and Leonard Woolf. Believing himself ugly, Keynes tended to be shy in the presence of the undergraduates he admired. In 1908, however, he began a serious affair with the painter Duncan **Grant**, whom he later said to be the only person in whom he found a truly satisfying combination of beauty and intelligence.

After leaving Cambridge, Keynes launched his career in the India Office in London, where he made many useful professional contacts. He also joined the nascent **Bloomsbury** group, participating with relish in its merry-go-round of intellectual, social, and sexual contacts. In 1908, however, he obtained a lecturership in economics at King's College, and the courses he gave there were the foundation of his later writings in the field. As editor of the *Economic Journal* he actively promoted new trends in the discipline outside of Cambridge. Yet he did not turn immediately to the core of the subject, as he spent a number of years writing a challenging *Treatise on Probability*, which was published in 1921.

The outbreak of World War I caught Keynes and his Bloomsbury friends, ensconced in their own corners of Edwardian comfort, initially unawares. Although most his associates became conscientious objectors, Keynes elected to enter the Treasury where, despite the chronic disapproval of the Prime Minister, David Lloyd George, he worked wonders in managing the wartime economy. During this period the homosexual members of Bloomsbury (Keynes included) found their supply of eligible young men cut off, and began to engage in flirtations and even liaisons with women. After the end of the war Keynes spent a frustrating period as an adviser at the Paris peace conference, trying to limit

voracious Allied demands for reparations from defeated Germany. Returning to London, he set down his pungent reflections on the event in what became his most widely read book, *The Economic Consequences of the Peace* (1919), which eroded the resolve of the Allies to enforce the Treaty of Versailles, at least in its financial provisions.

In 1925 Keynes, now famous, married the noted ballerina Lydia Lopokova. He became an adviser to government and business, consolidating his practical knowledge of economic affairs. These experiences contributed to his great book, *General Theory of Employment, Interest and Money* (1936). He held that money was not only a medium of exchange but also a store of value. Believing that unregulated capitalism had proved to be its own worst enemy, he sought to explore ways whereby state intervention could stimulate productive capacity, while forestalling anarchic effects. By "fine tuning" the economy, the state could ward off unemployment and the noxious effects of downturns in business cycles. Because of the stubbornness of traditional forces, Keynes' ideas were largely ignored during the great Depression, which they might have alleviated. Their more general utilization after World War II has been credited with a major role in the extraordinary prosperity of that period, though the full extent of this effect remains uncertain. Economic difficulties after 1975 subjected Keynsian views, which had become orthodoxy, to contemporary reassessment.

In 1940 Keynes again became an adviser to the Treasury. Through taxation policies he sought to limit the ravages of inflation in wartime Britain. In 1944 he was leader of the British delegation at the Bretton Woods Conference in Washington, DC, which set the terms for the emerging economic structure of the postwar world. He also coordinated the Lend Lease program, which was vital to the Allied war effort. In 1942 Keynes was raised to the peerage. Returning from the United

States in April 1946, he was near collapse, and died at his home in Sussex on Easter Sunday, April 12, 1946.

Keynes' family background and elite education prepared him for a leading role in England's ruling class which, after some permutations, he duly obtained. Yet he participated equally in the genteel adversary cultures of the Cambridge Apostles and Bloomsbury. Surprisingly, in the decades after the conviction of Oscar Wilde, his numerous affairs with young men never caused the slightest legal or even social trouble. This charmed life can be explained only by his combination of extreme personal brilliance, family and professional connections, and remarkable self-confidence. Although Keynes married he never had children. The economic historian Joseph Schumpeter has noted that his economic theory, which concentrated on short-term effects, was compatible with a mentality that had given no "hostages to fortune" through offspring.

BIBLIOGRAPHY. Charles H. Hession, *John Maynard Keynes: A Personal Biography*, New York: Macmillan, 1984; Robert Skidelsky, *John Maynard Keynes*, vol. 1: *Hopes Betrayed, 1883–1920*, New York: Viking, 1983.

Wayne R. Dynes

KINSEY, ALFRED C. (1894–1956)

American entomologist and sex researcher. When Kinsey died at the age of sixty-two, "he was one of the most widely known scientists of this century, a household name in the United States and a familiar figure in the rest of the civilized world.... Kinsey's two landmark volumes, *Sexual Behavior in the Human Male* (1948) and *Sexual Behavior in the Human Female* (1953) raised one of the most violent and widespread storms since Darwin, not only in the scientific community but among the public at large" (Pomeroy). No doubt part of the uproar derived from Kinsey's plain, straight-out way of reporting on sex and sexual variations. Loud disapproval was registered by moralists, not only by priests and preachers, but also by psychiatrists, clinicians of many stripes, parts of the legal profession, and still others who for various reasons chose to defend the mores; often they seemed to feel their provinces had been invaded with contradictory, possibly destabilizing information.

To many, the Kinsey revelations were alarming not only because of the surprisingly high figures on premarital, extramarital and particularly on homosexual sex, but also because of the auspices of the work. From this conservative professor in a respected midwestern University came countless alarming sexual facts and surprises—all obtained with direct backing from Indiana University, the National Research Council, the Rockefeller Foundation, and the list of close consultants read like a cross-section of American men of science.

Intrinsic Value of the Kinsey Research. Of course, the substance of the Kinsey Research lay elsewhere than in what seemed sensational. Then, as now, its great value was the establishment of reliable baseline data. In the past it had been easy enough for the prudish and uninformed to warn of dire consequences from sex, even from **masturbation**. But such a judgment was suddenly made untenable by the realization that masturbation is practiced by at least 95 percent of males (with no indication of blindness or depleted male virility). Likewise, it had been easy to attribute homosexuality to various flaws in nature or to some illness when it was thought rare; but it was quite another matter to account for its occurrence in over a third (37 percent) of males, or for the fact that fully 50 percent of adult males admit having been sexually attracted at least sometimes to other males, or that 10 percent of married males in their twenties make overt homosexual contacts *after* being married, and so on.

Could these and other "Kinsey figures" have significantly changed in the intervening years as a result of the sexual revolution and other social forces? Some certainly have. The average age-at-first-intercourse is clearly down from age 17 where it once was, just as the amount of premarital intercourse is decidedly higher than it was in Kinsey's time. The frequency of homosexuality, which Kinsey found to be stable for five generations, has probably remained so. At least, judging from several subsequent studies (e.g., Gebhard; Bell), nothing indicates it has either increased or decreased.

Kinsey's Background. The marked originality of Kinsey's work, his easy readiness to avoid conventional concepts, and to examine every sexual event on its own merits frequently raise the double question of how Kinsey came to sex research, and then arrived at such a fresh start. In 1938 Indiana University instituted its first marriage course, and Kinsey was elected to teach it. When his students asked far-ranging questions about sex, he would try to answer them, or look them up in the existing literature—literature he found appalling by its general lack of evidence and rigor. He quietly decided to collect his own data. He began to interview people, to ask basic questions about their sex lives, and to polish and greatly expand his questions. Out of both generosity and wanting to extend his own knowledge of "the reality" as he used to call it, he did a good deal of private counseling of students and of married couples from his course (conducting some 280 of these personal conferences during the spring semester of 1939 alone).

Born into a rigidly religious family, Kinsey had a father who refused to allow his family to ride to church on Sunday, even with the minister. The father also taught Sunday school and demanded a triple Sabbath for the whole family—Sunday school, church, and evening prayer meeting. Part of this moralism stayed with young Kinsey until at least his first year in college where, as he later recalled with amusement, a classmate once came to him and confessed he was masturbating excessively, as he thought, and had to tell someone. Kinsey took his friend back to the dormitory and knelt down beside him to pray for God to help the boy stop.

Although Kinsey soon rejected religion, in other respects it seemed for some time as if he would continue on a conventional path. As a young zoologist he accepted an appointment at Indiana University as an assistant professor, got married, fathered four children, and pursued a career of teaching, writing, and fieldwork in entomology. In fact, a theme never to reverse itself was Kinsey's life-long fascination with nature, and with its effect on his interpersonal relations.

As a boy he was entranced by the out-of-doors, by going it alone on long hikes over the countryside, everywhere noticing the plants and animals, and particularly the differences and similarities between individuals of the same species. He was fascinated, too, by the sorts of people he found on every side—farmers and country folk from a generally less educated background than his own, but whose permission he often needed to cross their land or to camp out. Everywhere he learned to meet strangers very different from himself, to tune into their views and attitudes, to establish rapport quickly, and to gain their cooperation in whatever he was doing.

Field Methodology. These abilities were greatly in use and perfected during 20 years of "bug hunting" as he called it—hiking thousands of miles in search of gall-wasps in the 48 states, in Guatemala, and especially in the mountainous back-regions of Mexico. He quickly overcame the initial suspicion of the Indians, getting them to scour the hillsides searching for oak trees with the galls on their leaves that contained the tiny wasps, bringing them back by the hundreds to his tent. From such experiences he formulated certain cardinal principles that were to stand him in good stead in sex research. "Try never to move forward or back, especially in dangerous situations, be they dealing with the mafia, interviewing prostitutes, or getting 'round the nervousness of ordinary people." (Moving forward can seem intrusive, moving backwards can look defensive or rejecting.) "Be considerate and thoughtful, never selfish in your own pursuit; let people know what you want, then allow them to bring it to you"—and many others.

From his boyhood hiking days, and from his many new experiences in dealing with the sorts of anxieties people feel about sex, Kinsey learned whole new modes of dealing with it and of making people comfortable. He could almost instantly put strangers at ease and win their confidence with his kindly, never judgmental quality, and even his simple language. As he always reminded his college-bred interviewers: "The lower-level individual is never ill or injured, though he may be sick or hurt. He does not wish to do something, though he wants to do it. He does not perceive, though he sees. He is not acquainted with a person, though he may know him. . . ." Everywhere in his approach it seemed that even plainness and politeness were powerful stuff, part of his respect for each person's makeup and right to be who they are, regardless of their current position or predicament. He insisted that anyone generous enough to give a history deserves to be treated as a friend or guest, "The tottering old man who is a victim of his first penal conviction appreciates an interviewer's solicitation about his health and that he is provided with tobacco, candy, or other things the institution allows one who has sufficient funds. The inmate in a woman's penal institution particularly appreciates those courtesies which a male would extend to a woman of his own social rank, in his own home."

Sex Research. Early on he realized a need for a far broader knowledge of what sex is like in special and diverse contexts; he wanted to see behind the curtains of privacy that people use to dis-guise or to hide entirely what they do from others, and sometimes from themselves. By July 1939, Kinsey had collected some 350 sex histories, and from this material he realized he needed more information on homosexuality. From a student whose history he had taken he heard of "someone in Chicago who could introduce him to homosexuals and show him how they live." Acting on this tip with a trial visit to meet that contact in Chicago, he soon began weekly trips. (He would leave Bloomington after his last class on Friday, drive the more than 200 miles to Chicago, work through the weekend, and drive back in time for his 8:30 class Monday morning.)

Within two months he had collected scores of homosexual histories, and was astonished at the countless variations he had seen for himself on every side. (The Chicago groups he met did, indeed, constitute valuable urban samples, although he was later amused at how naive he had been about "the homosexual" and the miles he had traveled to find the sorts of histories which, had he known more at the time, he could have had in abundance within walking distance of his Bloomington office.)

On other occasions, too, he traveled far and wide to find and explore particular groups: prisoners and prostitutes and paragons of virtue from religious sects. Nothing he saw ever diverted or defeated him, for as a colleague put it, "he was always able to look through the ugliness to something lovely beyond." Whenever he ran into anything unique, he immediately tried to investigate it. Once when a man said he could come to orgasm in ten seconds from a flaccid start, the man was asked if he could demonstrate this (he could and did, on the spot). Deep in rural Kansas, Kinsey searched out a community where, remarkably, *all* the women were easily able to reach orgasm in ordinary intercourse. (It turned out that their prevailing style of pacifying small children involved a particular patting and stroking technique that soon induced sleep; unbeknownst to the mothers it was first and accidentally bringing the babies to orgasm, thereby leaving traces in the sexual substrate which made them "easy responders" for life.) Other special cases (tabulated separately to keep from biasing the averages) involved such things as the sexual responses of people who had had brain surgery, others who for religious reasons had struggled all their lives against *any* sexual expression, members of nudist colonies, and groups of paraplegics.

Besides many investigations of plain and special people, Kinsey pursued literally dozens of subprojects. He and his coworkers made an extensive study of the differences between the sexes that so affect their psychology and compatibility. (A central finding was that male sexuality tends to be genitally focused, while females are more "peripheral" i.e., tend to place more value on the stimulations, the moods, and the ambience *around* sex than on genital stimulations.) There were separate studies of fourteen mammalian species, extensive studies of human neurology and physiology, as well as ancient and modern cross-cultural surveys, including a detailed investigation of sex practices in pre-Columbian civilizations, and another to trace the shifts in Japanese mores for 400 years. Legal experts were brought in to help trace the relationship between a man's education and how he is treated by the courts. And a bevy of translators worked to bring into English the first accurate record of important classical literature, and so on and on.

The Fate of the Kinsey Research. But nothing was more important to the fate of the Kinsey Research than was homosexuality. For while it was only one of the six basic forms of sex examined, and represented only a fraction of the research effort, nothing disturbed the critics more, nor brought them to such a fever pitch of hate as did the homosexual findings. As A. H. Hobbs (associate professor of sociology, University of Pennsylvania) charged, "There must be something wrong with Kinsey's statistics, which [coupled with] the prestige of the Rockefeller Foundation, give unwarranted weight to implications that homosexuality is normal, and that premarital relations might be a good thing." Others insisted "homosexuality just can't be that prevalent"—and, anyway, "by talking about it you encourage it."

Similar sentiments came from Congressmen, from a handful of anthropologists and psychoanalysts, and more stridently from Union Theological Seminary's Henry Van Dusen (also on the board of the Rockefeller Foundation). The hue and cry cast aspersions on the Kinsey data, causing the National Research Council to request the ASA (American Statistical Association) to examine the work in detail. Kinsey was well prepared for this challenge but not for the delay it entailed, during which his financial backing began to evaporate. Only years later came the ASA's report; it rated Kinsey's research as the best ever done in the field, and characterized it as "a monumental endeavor." (Here too, homosexuality was a central issue and the only form of sex dealt with in the Committee's 338-page report.) But by then the battle with reaction was lost.

Heartsick at losing support for his "right to do sex research" as he always put it, and exhausted by great efforts at seeking new support, Kinsey, in failing health, died on August 25, 1956. Numerous researchers have since stepped in to continue his work, with success in a few areas, but nothing has come close to the quality and detail of Kinsey's Male and Female volumes. These endure as standard reference works on what people did and mostly still do sexually. In particular, Kinsey's considerations on "Interviewing" and on "Homosexual Outlet" in the Male volume, his "Psychologic Factors in Sexual Response" in the Female volume, and a unique separate essay, "Concepts of Normality and Abnormality," are unlikely to be surpassed.

BIBLIOGRAPHY. Alan P. Bell, Martin S. Weinberg, and Sue Kiefer Hammersmith, *Sexual Preference: Its Development in Men and Women*, Bloomington: Indiana University Press, 1981; Cornelia V. Christenson, *Kinsey: A Biography*, Bloomington: Indiana University Press, 1971; William G. Cochran, Frederick Mosteller, John W. Tukey, and W. O. Jenkins, *Statistical Problems of the Kinsey Report on Sexual Behavior in the Human Male*, Washington: American Statistical Association, 1954; Paul H. Gebhard, ed., *Youth Study*, unpublished manuscript, Institute for Sex Research, Bloomington: ca. 1969; Alfred C. Kinsey, Wardell B. Pomeroy, and Clyde E. Martin, *Sexual Behavior in the Human Male*, Philadelphia: Saunders, 1948; Alfred C. Kinsey, Wardell B. Pomeroy, Clyde E. Martin, and Paul H. Gebhard, "Concepts of Normality and Abnormality," in Paul H. Hoch and Joseph Zubin, eds., *Psychological Development in Health and Disease*, New York: Grune & Stratton, 1949; Alfred C. Kinsey, Wardell B. Pomeroy, Clyde E. Martin, and Paul H. Gebhard, *Sexual Behavior in the Human Female*, Philadelphia: Saunders, 1953; Wardell B. Pomeroy, *Dr. Kinsey and the Institute for Sex Research*, New York: Harper & Row, 1972; C. A. Tripp, *The Homosexual Matrix*, second ed., New York: New American Library, 1987.

C. A. Tripp

KLEIST, HEINRICH VON (1777–1811)

German playwright and short story writer, whose *The Broken Pitcher* is esteemed as possibly the greatest of (and among the few) German comedies. Overshadowed by his contemporary, Johann Wolfgang von **Goethe**, Kleist's significance came to light only after his suicide at age 34, a secretive joint pact made with a terminally ill female friend.

Kleist's slim literary production (eight plays and eight short stories) vividly and violently captures the historical break between Enlightenment rationalism and Romantic mysticism, often framed as either a psychological conflict (*Das Käthchen von Heilbronn, Penthesilea*) or a political one (*Prinz Friedrich von Homburg, Die Hermannsschlacht*). A profound sense of the irrational and absurd permeates Kleist's works. In stories such as "Michael Kohlhaas" or "Earthquake in Chile," individuals stand powerless before arbitrary circumstances. Kleist's remarkable heroines, who bear uncanny resemblance to Kleist psychologically, act from the unconscious, for example when "The Marquise of O" places a newspaper ad in hopes of discovering the gentleman responsible for her pregnant condition, or when Penthesilea's confusion between love and war leads her, while intending to kiss her lover Achilles, instead to tear him from limb to limb with her bare hands and teeth.

Kleist's personal life was as bizarre and fascinating as his works. His love of secrecy and disguise has, for example, left us with no explanation for his mysterious trip to Würzburg in 1800 with a male friend. Debate over this trip has established a sexual dysfunction at the root of the matter, but it remains unresolved whether Kleist was a compulsive masturbator, suffered a phimosis, was bisexual or homosexual. His passionate attachment for men (unusual even for his society), the inconclusive engagement to Wilhelmine von Zenge, his periodic suicide notes, and his famous "Kant crisis" (if eternal truths cannot be conclusively established through human faculties, then reality can never have any meaning) unequivocally reveal a sensitive and dramatic nature. Kleist's striking mental imbalance, at times penetratingly insightful but at other times oblivious to the obvious, has long obscured the debate on his homosexuality.

The only document which seems to reveal Kleist's true feelings is a letter, dated January 7, 1805, to his friend Ernst von Pfuel: "You reawakened in my heart the age of the Greeks, I could have slept with you, you sweet youth; thus did my entire soul embrace you. Often I looked upon your beautiful body with truly *girlish* feelings whenever you waded into the lake at Thun before my eyes. . . . Come with me to Ansbach and let us enjoy our sweet friendship . . . accept my proposal. If you do not do this, then I shall feel that no one on earth loves me."

BIBLIOGRAPHY. Diethelm Bruggemann, *Drei Mystifikationen Heinrich von Kleists*, Frankfurt am Main: Peter Lang, 1985; Joachim Maass, *Kleist: A Biography*, transl. by Ralph Manheim, New York: Farrar, Straus and Giroux, 1983; William C. Reeve, *In Pursuit of Power*, Toronto: University of Toronto Press, 1987.

Leslie K. Wright

KOREA

The civilization of Korea, the "land of the morning calm," cannot be understood in isolation. Having received major influences from **China**—including **Buddhism**, Confucianism, and the bureaucratic form of state organization—the peninsular nation transmitted them in turn to **Japan**.

Old Korea had three classes of **shamans**, of whom two were the Mootangs and the Paksoos. The Mootangs are women who while shamanizing always wear the outer dress of a man; they outnumber a hundred to one the Paksoos, who in turn wear the outer dress of a woman. This practice was styled "change of sex" by some anthropologists, "change of dress" by others, but it possesses some mystical significance and is far more than a simple change of garments. Modern Koreans do not know the origin of the custom, but adhere to it meticulously. It is no doubt a legacy from their ancestral home, as shown by the fact that the name for the female shaman is practically the same in all the languages of Siberia, from Mongolian to Kirgiz.

Before the introduction of Buddhism in the Kogoryu period (which began about the time of Christ) elite youth, distinguished by their beauty and known as *hwarang*, seem to have been involved in shamanistic practices. During the Silla period (from ca. A.D. 350 onwards) the *hwarang* were turned into a military elite formed by austere training. After their period of service, many became officials and landowners. Although full information is not available, they seem to have been bound by homoerotic loyalties, recalling the Sacred Band of Thebes, the Ottoman Janissaries, and the Japanese **Samurai**.

Even as late as the period just before the Japanese conquest in 1895, the palace rejoiced in handsome pages. The Buddhist priesthood was said to be given to pederasty.

The Korean **theatre** employed only men, and vestiges of homoerotic traditions survive in this context to this day. As a type of indigenous performing theatre in Korea down to 1920, the *Namsadang* troupes roamed the country with a program of six variety entertainments. This troupe seems to have been a homosexual commune, composed of 40 to 50 single homeless males, with some 14 senior performers and a number of novices. According to a native source, they were divided into groups of *Sutdongmo* ("butch") and *Yodongmo* ("queen"); all newcomers had to be *Yodongmo*. Homosexuality was highly immoral in the view of Confucianism. In a society permeated by strong Confucian influence for hundreds of years, the *Namsadang* performers were probably treated simply as outcasts and ignored by the educated class, but their homosexuality was ignored by the common people whose voice they were. Hatred of the ruling class and exceedingly subtle parody were the traits in which their performances surpassed those of other varieties of folk theatre. Although independent Korea attempted to preserve the *Namsadang* tradition as part of its folk heritage, the performing skills are in a process of extinction, as the authentic actors are too old and few are interested in mastering their art.

The authoritarian government of the early 1980s used the **AIDS** crisis as an excuse to harass gay bars, and to stifle an emerging gay movement. Given insufficient information about the disease, many people in South Korean society assume all gay men are AIDS carriers. The older tendency to think of homosexuals as feminine or even transvestites persists, and the media do little to educate the public. In the words of one Korean activist: "Under the guise of protection from AIDS gays are treated like cheap bargain sale material. For the seed of gay liberation to grow again, the mass communications will have to stop their anti-gay pronouncements."

BIBLIOGRAPHY. Young Ja Kim, "The Korean Namsadang," *Drama Review*, 15 (1981), 9–16; Richard Rutt, "The Flower Boys of Silla (Hwarang)," *Transactions of the Korean Branch of the Royal Asiatic Society*, 38 (1961), 1–66.

Ward Houser

KRAFFT-EBING, RICHARD VON (1840–1902)

German-Austrian psychiatrist, forensic authority, and writer of medical treatises on psychiatry and sexual psychopathology. A leading figure in the history of psychiatry, his works were the starting point for the treatment of "abnormal" sexuality by Freud and Jung, to cite only two of the major figures who came after him. During his career he held professorships at Strasbourg, Graz, and Vienna— then the world's leading medical school.

Krafft-Ebing's speculations on homosexuality reveal the influence of Karl Heinrich Ulrichs' concept of the "Urning" and Karl Westphal's discovery of "contrary sexual feeling" (1869). He began to develop his theories on the manifestations and etiology of homosexuality in the wake of a survey of the recent publications on the subject of sexual psychopathology that he compiled in 1876. In the following year he published an article in which homosexuality was defined as "an absence of normal sexual feeling, with compensatory attraction to members of the same sex." His proclivity for schematization on the basis of the current Darwinian notions of evolution led him to insert every known variety of abnormality of sexual attraction, gender, and constitution into a global framework that later inspired Magnus **Hirschfeld**'s concept of "sexual intermediate stages." Krafft-Ebing did recognize that these subjects were basically happy with their lot and that their distress stemmed from society's laws and attitudes. He even placed their love—as an emotion—on a footing with those of "normal feelings." However, he clung to the belief in "degeneration" as a cause of such mental illnesses, and it was with disturbed individuals in prisons and insane asylums that, as a forensic psychiatrist, he mainly came into contact.

Krafft-Ebing's classic work, *Psychopathia sexualis* (1886), focused attention on four subgroups: "psychosexual hermaphrodites" (= bisexuals), homosexuals, effeminates and "viraginites" in whom the psychic disposition corresponds to that of the opposite sex, and androgynes. His etiological scheme differentiated sharply between "inborn" and "acquired" homosexuality in line with the forensic bias of his work.

After studying Hirschfeld's writings at the turn of the century, Krafft-Ebing revised his views in 1901, stating in an article in the *Jahrbuch für sexuelle Zwischenstufen* that homosexuality was not a manifestation of degeneracy or pathology, but could occur in otherwise normal subjects. But this retraction written shortly before his death could do little to alter the tremendous impression made on the public by the many editions of *Psychopathia sexualis* (12 in his lifetime), which was translated into other languages and achieved an authority no previous volume on abnormal sexuality had ever enjoyed; and his definition of "every expression of the sex drive that does not correspond to the purposes of nature, i.e., reproduction" as "perverse" (= unnatural, hence immoral) greatly shaped the notion of "abnormal" sexuality.

Krafft-Ebing's legacy solidified the category of "sexual **inversion**" in psychiatry. It was the clinical psychiatrist and depth psychologist who now undertook the treatment and analysis of those to whom this definition attached.

BIBLIOGRAPHY. Albert Caraco, *Supplément à la Psychopathia sexualis*, Lausanne: Edition L'âge d'homme, 1983; Klaus Pacharzina and Karin Albrecht-Désirat, "Die Last der Ärzte," in J. Hohmann, ed., *Der unterdrückte Sexus*, Lollar: Achenbach, 1977, pp. 97–113.

Warren Johansson

KUPFFER, ELISÀR VON (1872–1942)

Baltic German painter, writer, and thinker. The son of a physician who was a hereditary nobleman, Elisàr von Kupffer—or as he later called himself, Elisarion—inherited a labile constitution which he ascribed to his father's dependence on tobacco and opium. In 1891 he went to St. Petersburg, where later he attended courses in Oriental languages at the University. He also studied in Switzerland and Bavaria and composed his first dramatic work, *Die toten Götter* (The Dead Gods). In the following years he wrote other plays, now and then encountering his friend Eduard von Mayer. The beginning of the homosexual emancipation movement in 1897 had a profound effect on Elisarion. Living in Berlin in the winter of 1898–99, he compiled an anthology of *Lieblingsminne und Freundesliebe in der Weltliteratur* (Love of Comrades and Friends in World Literature), inspired by the writings of **Krafft-Ebing** and by the debates that followed the trial of Oscar **Wilde** in London. The publication of the anthology by Adolf **Brand** in 1900 brought the author as much rejection as approval. His uncle Hugo von Kupffer, the editor in chief of the *Berliner Lokalanzeiger*, tried vainly to keep it from appearing; an attempted confiscation of the book was rescinded thanks to the intervention of Ulrich von Wilamowitz-Moellendorff, Franz von Liszt, and Rudolf

von Gottschall. Benedict **Friedlaender** later declared that Elisarion's anthology marked a "new phase in the emancipation movement," while *Meyers Grosse Enzyklopädie* stressed that for the first time since Plato Elisarion had presented "a cultural and ethical appraisal of the phenomenon of pederasty."

In 1902 Elisarion and Eduard von Mayer moved to **Florence**, where they lived until the outbreak of war in 1915. Like **Winckelmann**, he felt the aesthetic attraction of the Mediterranean culture of Italy, and here his life's work in painting and philosophy matured. A product of these studies is the 1908 monograph on the Renaissance painter **Sodoma**, perhaps the first full-length study of an artist to reflect the ideals of the homosexual **movement**. In 1911 the two founded in Munich the "Klaristische Verlag Akropolis"—later moved to Leipzig—whose task it was to communicate his ideas to a larger public, but in fact no one outside a narrow circle of followers ever shared them. They amounted to a "confessionless Christianity" and a comprehensive social, aesthetic, and political program that was intended to lead to a renaissance. In the same year he published the two basic works of the "claristic" movement: the *Hymnen der Heiligen Burg* (Hymns of the Holy Citadel) and *Ein neuer Flug und eine Heilige Burg* (A New Flight and a Holy Citadel).

The war obliged Elisarion to move to Muralto in Switzerland, and in 1922, following the Russian Revolution, he became a citizen of the canton of Ticino. In 1925 the companions acquired a property in Minusio on which over the years he constructed a temple that reflected his ideals. Elisarion gave this Sanctuarium a remarkable, if somewhat academic complement of frescoes that depict male friendship in idyllic-arcadian terms. Elisàr von Kupffer died in Minusio in 1942, his last work—a revision of *Ein neuer Flug*—appearing a year later under the title *Heldische Sicht und froher Glaube* (Heroic Vision and Joyous Faith). Now the property

669

of the municipality, the Sanctuarium has since his death undergone some modifications.

BIBLIOGRAPHY. Ekkehard Hieronimus, *Elisàr von Kupffer (1872–1942)*, Basel: Kunsthalle, 1979.

Warren Johansson

KUZMIN, MIKHAIL ALEKSEEVICH (1872–1936)

Russian poet and short story writer. Although 1875 is usually given as the year of his birth, recent investigation has shown that Kuzmin was born in 1872 at Yaroslavl on the Volga River into a family of Old Believers. His interest in the theatre was kindled by attending operettas at nearby Saratov. In 1885 the family moved to St. Petersburg. A major influence on the young Kuzmin was the future Soviet diplomat (and homosexual) Georgii Vasil'evich Chicherin (1872–1936). Among the arts Kuzmin's first love was music, and in August 1891 he enrolled in Rimsky-Korsakov's composition course at the St. Petersburg Conservatory, but remained for only three years out of the full seven. Even among writers of a remarkably erudite period, Kuzmin was outstanding for his knowledge of languages, and when Soviet literary policy had made it impossible for him to publish his own work, he was still able to earn a living by translating from Greek, Latin, French, German, Italian, and English. The wide thematic range of his poetry and its allusion to recondite **Gnostic** matters also attest to the vastness of his learning.

In 1895 he accompanied his mother to Egypt, and settled in Alexandria, where he remained until early in 1896. His *Alexandrian Songs* reflect his real experience in the Levantine milieu, where he endured a religious crisis and a tragic love affair. Wholly independent of his contemporary Constantine **Cavafy**, he created his own myth of **Alexandria**, where refined eroticism rubbed shoulders with

Gnostic mysteries. In March 1897 he left for Italy, another foreign country whose ambiance was to pervade his later work; the Italian episode of *Wings* is mainly autobiographical. There followed an exceedingly mysterious period of his life in which he traveled through northern Russia, searching for his familial and religious roots by living with Old Believer monastic communities in northern Russia, an episode reflected in the second part of *Wings*, where the young hero Vania lives with an Old Believer family.

On his return to St. Petersburg Kuzmin was in 1904 introduced by Chicherin to the circle that had formed in the penumbra of the journal *Mir iskusstva* (World of Art), edited by Sergei **Diaghilev**. This milieu he found immensely sympathetic, and to boot several of its members shared his sexual orientation. The revolution of 1905, by putting an end to Tsarist censorship, gave Russian literature its brief (and only) taste of true freedom. Kuzmin's *Wings* appeared in the symbolist journal *Vesy* (The Scales) in November 1906, and created the great literary scandal of its day; edition after edition sold out. The same periodical also published twelve of Kuzmin's *Alexandrian Songs*. In 1907, however, the authorities confiscated the little volume *Three Plays*, because one of the three, *The Perilous Precaution*, was an adroit minuet of sexual identities that poked fun at conventional morality. In 1906 Kuzmin also began his association with the theatre, whose atmosphere gave him an ideal opportunity to play roles which expressed his contradictory nature—the decadent dandy with the made-up eyes or the bearded, long-robed Old Believer. He also attended the Wednesday evening salon of the poet Viacheslav Ivanov and his second wife, Lydia Zinovieva-Annibal, who was incidentally the author of the first lesbian work in Russian, *Tridtsat' tri urodstva* (Thirty-three Freaks).

The Bolshevik Revolution Kuzmin greeted with warm optimism, and during the bitter years of the civil war participated in the enterprise for translating classics of world literature which Gorky and Lunacharsky had created to keep the literary intelligentsia from literally starving. During the NEP period he was still able to publish, but the themes and the style of his writing were so alien to the Soviet scene that Leon Trotsky in *Literature and Revolution* dubbed him an "internal émigré." As late as 1927 he was able to place a few poems in various periodicals, but after that lapsed into silence. In 1928 he gave his last public reading, a touching occasion marked by the invasion of a throng of Leningrad homosexuals many of whom showered him with flowers during the ovation that followed. By 1929 Kuzmin was reduced to scraping together a living by translations, turning into Russian an enormous set of Western classics, Shakespeare above all. All this work was lost during the Stalinist terror when much of the Kuzmin archive was destroyed. He himself escaped execution only by dying of pneumonia in a Leningrad hospital on March 1, 1936.

After his death, Kuzmin's status was that of a non-person, because he had been a homosexual, and not a "closet case," but openly and defiantly gay. In fact, the word *gay* even in its primary meaning would have fitted Kuzmin perfectly. Although homosexual fiction was by then appearing in Germany, for a Russia that had not escaped the yoke of Tsarist censorship until the October Manifesto of 1905, the shock value of *Wings*—essentially a frank defense of the homosexual way of life—was tremendous. He even dared to present homosexuality as a liberating force of the personality. *Wings* gave the journalists of his day endless matter for debate, parody, and innuendo. Homosexuality remained a major component of Kuzmin's poetry and fiction, and even slips into his theatre, in which the motif of male dyad endangered by a female interloper occurs with obsessive frequency, even if rarely with a tragic denouement. Kuzmin also belonged to a group of homosexuals at the heart of the Russian cultural scene of his day, among them Konstantin Andreevich Somov (1869–1939), a leading Russian painter of the period, who did a fine portrait of the writer. Dismissed by official criticism in the Soviet Union as an example of "bourgeois decadence," Kuzmin awaits rediscovery and appreciation in the homeland whose literature he magnificently enriched.

BIBLIOGRAPHY. Mikhail Kuzmin, *Selected Prose & Poetry*, edited and translated by Michael Green, Ann Arbor, MI: Ardis, 1980.

Warren Johansson

L

LABELING

In social practice labeling is the habit of categorizing individuals with a descriptive epithet, generally negative, as "thief" or "shrew." The relevance of this concept to homosexuality stems from the argument that publicly labeling someone as a delinquent can result in the person's becoming the very thing he is at the outset perhaps fortuitously described as being. Naming has a powerful effect on the impressionable minds of young people—so much one can readily acknowledge. But the question can be pressed further: is the acquisition of a homosexual identity conditional upon being labeled **queer** (or whatever the abusive term is in the local idiom), or can it develop independently even before the individual is aware of the label that is affixed to his behavior? The internalization of a label that is repeatedly attached to an individual by one's peers certainly occurs, but there are other cases in which a future homosexual becomes aware of his orientation before he has learned that there are such people as "homosexuals." He may even think of himself as unique in the whole world. When the first writings on sexual **inversion** began to appear in the 1880s, their authors received letters from subjects who had reached middle age believing until then that their sexual orientation was shared by no one else, so effective had been the taboo on public discussion or even oblique mention of the subject of sexual activity between members of the same sex.

Sociological studies have shown how intimately men or boys can be involved in a specific homosexual **subculture** (to be sure, one with little or no political consciousness) without considering themselves in the category of "queers." The preponderance of married men in Laud Humphreys' study of sexual contacts in **toilets**, *Tearoom Trade* (Chicago, 1970), and celebrated cases in which highly conservative public figures have been compromised, bear witness to this split between objective behavior and the subject's self-concept. Moreover, "homosexual" is an ambiguous term: it can be applied to a wide range of individuals, including ones who have had but a single overt same-sex experience, or limited to those who have never had heterosexual experiences or even feelings. Even "bisexual" may be disavowed as a label by individuals who have had more than incidental experience with both sexes, but nonetheless perceive their "identity" as heterosexual or homosexual.

Homosexuality has been studied in **anthropology** and **sociology** as an ascribed status which in turn provides a complex of culturally prescribed roles and behavior which individuals are expected to learn and perform. Because homosexual roles and behaviors are conceived as inappropriate to the individual's genital sex, they have been theoretically defined as deviant. Allison Davis stated in 1941: "Sex-typing of behavior and privileges is even more rigid and lasting in our society than is age-typing. Indeed, sexual status and color-caste status are the only life-long forms of rank. . . . Whereas sexual mobility is somewhat less rare today than formerly, sex-inappropriate behavior, social or physical, is still one of the most severely punished infractions of our social code." In a society that judges such behavior immoral, individuals labeled homosexual are frequently denied the social, economic, and legal rights of so-called normal human beings; they may be the objects of scorn, ridicule, aversion, and fear, and suffer denial of employment or interrogation and harassment by the **police**.

Labeling can be triggered by an individual who is observed to behave in a manner deviating from the behaviors held in common by members of the group to which he belongs. There are differences between the sexes in this regard: unlike stereotypically **effeminate** appearance and gestures in boys (sissihood), "masculine" appearance in girls (tomboyishness) is less likely to be interpreted as predictive of homosexuality. But when a youngster is so labeled, then even the slightest deviation from the norm can be noticed and magnified in the image that others hold of him. Another class of evidence is overt sexual propositions, which may consist of a series of verbal or physical cues that are deemed progressively inappropriate. Retrospective reinterpretation of the deviant behavior then reinforces the label as every departure from the norm is fitted into a **stereotype**.

Conversely, the individual who perceives himself as homosexual may believe that he must act out all the features of the stereotype connected with the label, no matter how repellent or alien they may have been to him in the past. Such behavior is most common among working-class homosexuals who live in a milieu where sex roles are rigidly prescribed, so that the individual who has become accustomed to behaving sexually "like a woman" must, so he feels, act in other ways like a caricature of the female. This provokes the question asked by the teenager who is just "coming out": "Do I have to be like that?" with the implication that he perceives the stereotype as alien, even if he accepts the sexual orientation as consonant with the rest of his inner self. The internalization of the identity implied by the label is sometimes designated as "secondary deviance," in contrast with the "primary deviance" which is the overt activity that initially motivated the label.

BIBLIOGRAPHY. John I. Kitsuse, "Societal Reaction to Deviant Behavior: Problems of Theory and Method," *Social Problems*, 9 (1963), 247–56; Stephen O. Murray, *Social Theory, Homosexual Realities*, New York: Gay Academic Union, 1984.

Warren Johansson

LAMBDA

In the early 1970s, in the wake of the **Stonewall Rebellion**, New York City's Gay Activists Alliance selected the Greek letter lambda, which member Tom Doerr suggested from its scientific use to designate "kinetic potential," as its emblem. (Curiously, in some ancient Greek **graffiti** the capital lambda appears with the meaning "fellate," representing the first letter of either *lambazein* or *laikazein*.) Because of its militant associations, the lambda symbol has spread throughout the world. It sometimes appears in the form of an amulet hung round the neck as a subtle sign of recognition which can "pass" among unknowing heterosexuals as a mere ornament. Such emblems may reflect a tendency among homosexuals toward "tribalization" as a distinct segment of society, one conceived as a quasi-ethnic group.

LANGUAGE AND LINGUISTICS

The history of the study of language, which in the Western tradition goes back to the ancient Greeks, has two main phases: the prescriptive era, when most linguists were in alliance with schoolmasters in seeking norms of correctness, and the descriptive era, which began with the discoveries of the neo-grammarian school in the early nineteenth century in Germany. Taken as a whole, neither tradition has had much to say about the vocabulary and semantics of sex and their development. Three branches of linguistics have however made some contribution. **Etymology**, the science of the origin of words, can cast light on changing ideas about sexuality. Unfortunately one must beware of many false and misleading etymologies, such as the absurd claim that the word **faggot** in the meaning "homosexual" derives from the burning of sodomites at the stake. Then the study of **slang**, where sex vies with intoxication for the title of the most productive realm, has also produced considerable material. Finally, the recent development of sociolinguistics offers some material on the pragmatics of gay male and lesbian social encounters.

Words and Concepts over the Centuries. Study of the origins of words pertaining to sexuality show that many—probably most—expressions in current use have pedigrees stretching back over centuries and even millennia. Such backgrounds are characteristic not only of "scientific" words, such as **deviation** and **orientation**, but also of such slang or street words as *chicken* or *rocks*. Folklorists have shown that notions in circulation, say, in the Ozarks in the first half of this century have ultimate origins in opinions expressed by Greek thinkers seventy or more generations before. For this reason, and also because of scholarly habit, our language preserves a number of terms going back to the ancient Greeks, the oldest significant source. Interestingly, however, the Greeks had no single term encompassing same-sex conduct as a whole, only more specialized terms for what we would regard as aspects of homosexuality. The absence of the idea derived from the fact that the Greeks concentrated on one particular form of male same-sex behavior, pederasty; also, their semantic grid classified sexual activity from standpoints that did not admit a high level of generalization. Carefully employed, then, the study of words can reveal not only ideas that were current but also ideas that were absent.

In addition to lack of development of words and concepts, there is also active deletion as a result of taboo. From earliest recorded history we have evidence that certain names were not to be uttered because of the dangers that surrounded them. With regard to homosexuality this factor has entered in through the Judeo-Christian proscription of sodomy. Thus we encounter such expressions as "the nameless sin," "the Cities of the Plain" (for **Sodom** and Gomorrah), "the crime against **nature**," "**gross indecency**," and so forth. There is also a common garden variety of deletion, as when a suburbanite will ask another: "Is he *that way*?" or "Is she one of *them*?" Such evasive verbal ploys belong to the realm of euphemism, which in addition to neutral terms can resort to foreign words because their impact is less harsh than that of the native ones learned in childhood.

Against this background the open use of hostile street language gains, by contrast, a particular aggressive edge. Thus for one teenager to call another **queer** or *faggot* may be particularly damaging to the self image of the one so styled. This phenomenon has been studied by social scientists under the name of **labeling**—though the role such incidents are likely to play in the emerging self-concept of the young gay or lesbian person remains problematic.

Not to be neglected are the contributions of generations of homosexuals themselves. While the distinction of the wry gay wit known as **camp** has been generally recognized, the writings of homosexual theorists—particularly in Germany—have played a major role in forming the learned vocabulary. Down to 1897 the experts who wrote on homosexuality felt obliged to use such expressions as "this disgrace to human nature" or "these dark crimes," but after the **movement** had devised its own terminology a neutral phraseology gradually became standard. More difficult to investigate are nondenotative levels—particular arrangements of ordinary words and such paraverbal aspects as lilt and pitch, not to mention the **gestures** that accompany particular expressions. In the past these gestures and intonations were often the obligatory passport to acceptance in some circles and situations; their absence was thought to betray the undercover agent or would-be robber or blackmailer. What is ultimately needed is a semiotics of gay and lesbian communication, which would embrace both verbal and nonverbal elements.

Sources of Words. At one time a strict separation was made between "scientific" terms, on the one hand, and slang or taboo expressions, on the other. As a rule, the latter have flourished among the folk as emotion-laden epithets, while the former were ostensibly coined to foster a more dispassionate and "objective" tone of discussion. Today these boundaries are eroding, and one can use **gay** or **dyke** in respectable discourse, while some learned terms, such as *androgyny* and *sadomasochism*, are fairly widely understood in the vernacular. Also, terms such as "deviation," originally introduced because of their strict neutrality, filtered down into the technical language of the law, so that some jurisdictions adopted statutes penalizing "deviant sexual conduct." Yet a problem persists with terms coming from the slang vocabulary: they are sometimes confusingly polysemous, as *hustler* (male prostitute or pool-hall pro?) and *straight* (heterosexual or drug free?).

The sources of our words may be classified as follows: (1) *classical* (from Greece and Rome: fellatio, ganymede, hierodule, tribade); (2) *theological* (buggery, the unnatural, the unnamable vice); (3) *medical* (constitutional homosexuality, inversion, masochism); (4) *literary euphemism* (posterior, maleness, titillation); (5) *slang* (butch, cornholing, nellie). A possible sixth category is the law, yet study of legal usage shows that its terms, in this realm at least, have generally been borrowed-above all from theology (sodomy, crime against nature). Some coinages come from a gray area or interface between these main spheres, notably *homosexual*, which was invented by Károly Mária **Kertbeny**, a closeted homophile apologist, and then taken up by medical and scientific writers, some of them too, of course, homosexual.

On occasion the ultimate field of origin is surprisingly remote, e.g., **bisexuality** (from botany) and **orientation** (from church architecture).

Some scholars have been interested in an ambitious project to correlate the strata of word use with successive stages of conceptualization. This endeavor is usually regarded as part of the sociology of knowledge. In the case of words pertaining to sexuality, particular care is needed so as not to make this parallel too mechanical. Thus the meaning of a single word **sodomy** has varied considerably over the centuries; a single bottle has held various contents, so to speak. Conversely, when the term (sexual) **inversion** was introduced in 1878, it was made to contain various older ingredients. The invention of new words does not necessarily signal the appearance of new meanings.

Sociolinguistics. Assisted by new techniques, including electronic monitoring and analysis, the emerging subdiscipline of sociolinguistics has begun to study oral language usage in actual encounter situations. For example, in gay cruising the classic opening gambits are the pro forma questions, "Do you have the time?" or "Do you have a match?" The sociolinguist studies the context of such exchanges and their characteristic patterns. Another situation is the use of coded language to reveal one's homosexuality to another person thought to be gay. This procedure may be fairly subtle, as in the use of ordinary words in an ambiguous context or reference to "in" places and events. Then there is a more flagrant manifestation, formerly termed "dropping pins," in which the speaker abandons all caution and "camps up a storm."

A subject of continuing interest is the difference between men's and women's use of language, as seen, for example, in intonation. Study has found that women are more likely to end a sentence with a rising inflection, as if it were a question. More generally, the pitch of women's speech in our culture has a broader range than the more monotonic texture of the macho male—which is "straight" with regard to pitch. Like women's speech, that of gay men has more range or animation. But there is also an aggressive, "bitchy" form of gay male intonation that has no precise equivalent among women. This intonation may sometimes be heard when a gay man tells a joke; the same joke may take on a different coloration owing to a different tonic rendition on the part of the speaker. Older gay men will remember that "tunes" which were once common have disappeared to be replaced by others. In these realms clearly much more study is needed.

BIBLIOGRAPHY. J. N. Adams, *The Latin Sexual Vocabulary*, London: Duckworth, 1982; Claude Courouve, *Vocabulaire de l'homosexualité masculine*, Paris: Payot, 1985; Wayne R. Dynes, *Homolexis: A Historical and Cultural Lexicon of Homosexuality*, New York: Gay Academic Union, 1985; Joseph Hayes, "Language and Language Behavior in Lesbian Women and Gay Men: A Selected Bibliography," *Journal of Homosexuality*, 4 (1978–79), 201–12; 299–309.

Wayne R. Dynes

LATENT HOMOSEXUALITY

Psychiatric writings of the 1940s and 1950s commonly distinguished between overt and latent homosexuality. The latter in turn has two forms: in the first, conscious homosexual desires are present but are controlled by the subject; and in the second, homosexual drives are unconscious. The popularity of the notion stems from two themes of Sigmund **Freud**. In human psychosexual development, Freud held, the *latency period* begins at the time of the decline of infantile sexuality in the fifth or sixth year and lasts until the onset of puberty. During this phase sexual development essentially marks time, and does not undergo any fundamental reorganization, albeit the capacity for repression becomes marked. Although Freud used the term in a nonpathological

sense, most analysts, having had medical training, would recall the older definition of "latent period" among physicians: the period of the incubation of a disease. The other Freudian theme was the idea of universal **bisexuality**. In this perspective all human beings have a capacity to experience same-sex attraction, but for most of them this option is not exercised during adulthood.

A process of abstraction from these two sources yields two distinct models of latent homosexuality: as dormant, and as potential. In the first model (dormant), latent homosexuals are thought of as a discrete body of individuals whose same-sex dimension is pre-overt. They are set off from the rest of the population in that they are "on track" to becoming practicing homosexuals—though this goal may not be achieved in every instance. In the second model (potential), a much larger segment of the population is involved—possibly everyone, if the hypothesis of universal bisexuality is accepted. The first model is selective, and assuming adequate methods of diagnosis—constituting a kind of "early warning system"—it would permit the psychiatrist to predict the likelihood of an individual's becoming an overt homosexual. The second model has no diagnostic or predictive value, being merely "philosophical." The difference seems clear, yet rarely were the two models distinguished in psychiatric literature and practice. Moreover, as has been indicated, hovering in the background was the assumption that latent conditions are pathological. Hence repetition of the phrase helped to reinforce the prejudice that homosexuality was a disease. Finally, since latent homosexuality could be present in the unconscious, some individuals began to worry that, though they felt no identifiable symptoms, somehow their homosexuality was simply waiting to burst into full flower. Thus the spread of the notion helped to foster homosexual **panic**, and numbers of individuals—sometimes labeled "pseudohomosexuals"—sought clinical help for a problem which was not theirs. To be sure, their panic was real, and this distress the clinician sought to treat.

Because of these complications, the idea of latent homosexuality has come to be generally regarded as heuristically unsound, and the expression has begun to disappear from both psychiatric and lay discourse.

BIBLIOGRAPHY. Leon Salzman, "'Latent' Homosexuality," in J. Marmor, ed., *Sexual Inversion: The Multiple Roots of Homosexuality*, New York: Basic Books, 1965, pp. 234–47.

Wayne R. Dynes

LATIN AMERICA

The conquests of the Spanish and the Portuguese in the New World laid the basis for colonial and post-colonial societies that show a number of common features. It is customary to associate with them the French-speaking republic of **Haiti**, but this country is so distinct that it will not be considered here.

The Basic Underlying Sexual Ideology. Today the former Iberian colonies in the New World provide the prototype of the gender-defined organization of homosexuality. Across the whole culture area, ideal norms distinguish masculine insertors (*activos*) not considered *homosexuales* from feminine insertees (*pasivos*) who are. The typological system is very simple, but in messy reality behavior and identity are more complex. Over time (in a "sexual career") or with different partners, a man's behavioral repertoire may diverge from the clearcut dichotomy. The imaginary undifferentiated phallic supremacy of the *hombre* supposedly common to Iberian and former Iberian colonies in the New World is overly neat. Certainly there are individuals who impersonate these ideal types (essences), but the sexually omnivorous hombre who has no preferences in "object choice"—the man who "fucks anything that moves"—is more a fantasy of the *maricón*, the stereotypical homosexual who aspires to his attentions, than a plausible empirical observation. Projection of this fantasy is undoubtedly flattering to the other who may be insecure about his masculinity and not likely to contradict flattering maricón claims about how masculine he is.

The pretence is carefully maintained by the activo's endless stream of sexual remarks which proclaim an insatiable sexual appetite but may not signify any actual sexual expectations or even interest in the targets of the remarks. Latin American men must show that they are interested in phallic activity—especially if they do not have regular sexual opportunities—by talking about what they would like to do to any imaginably penetrable object. Particularly in cities, there are not many ways to demonstrate "traditional" masculinity: only a few have physically demanding jobs.

The dearth of women who are available for actual sex and the general lack of privacy for sex with willing partners—along with cultural pressure on men to have sex regularly and on women to maintain the honor of their fathers, brothers, or husbands by resisting sexual involvement with anyone except a husband—lead to flamboyant verbal sexual posturing. Foreign observers may mistakenly interpret such talk as indicating that Latino men are hypersexual. It is easy to play the role of a *lobo listo* (literally, "ready wolf") when few demands are likely to be made: the Latino male is rarely if ever going to be pressed to demonstrate that he is ready.

Some observers have claimed that a fear of enjoying being anally penetrated is a salient concern for Latino males. The danger (not of being penetrated, but of coming to desire it) has been reported to be part of Islamic sexual ideology and may have a circum-**Mediterranean** diffusion carried to the New World by Iberian conquerors. Still, the feared anal penetration does not turn everyone who has experienced it into a maricón, and masculine deportment and self-conception are not necessarily compromised or jettisoned even by insertee homosexual activity, especially with aliens.

Within the culture, among natives, sexual receptivity does not necessarily lead to enacting a maricón role or building a gay identity. Even when obtainable, the luxury of privacy is not as safe with peers as with foreigners. Thus, to say that it does not matter what a Latino male does as long as no one finds out does not say much, because of the necessary caveat "hardly ever does no one find out." Some things remain hidden (*escondido*), but guarantees of eternal silence are dubious. Homosexuality can be compartmentalized—in space or time. According to Goode (1960), compartmentalization of **roles** is a common response to role strain, not just to managing masculine self-presentation while engaged in homosexual behavior in Latin America. In Latin America, as in Anglo North America, homosexual involvement of some persons is an open secret, homosexual involvement of others is genuinely escondido. Despite the reticence about discussing homosexuality in regards to one's self or peers or family, there is essentializing pressure to tie up sex and gender, even though the nuances of technical distinctions of sex, sexuality, gender (and possible variations of each) can be illustrated. There are certainly masculine-appearing males who are insertees, and effeminate-appearing males who are exclusively insertors, but the clear, simple masculine/feminine division is paramount in Latino views of gender and sex. Behavioral variance is irrelevant to this organizing principle. The actual flux and uncertainty of sexual expression is ignored "by the culture," or, rather, by Latino males who do not want to know, talk about, or think that masculine appearances do not necessarily validate untainted masculine essence. Behavioral variance corrodes certainty in the ideal norms, but these ideal norms are carried in many media, including primary socialization. Credence in and approval of the machismo complex channel behavior to conformity. How and what sexual norms and behaviors mean for natives is only beginning to be explored. Major obstacles exist in Latin America to community-formation and public self-identification as both masculine and homosexual. These will be surveyed in the remainder of this article.

Obstacles to an Autonomous Gay Culture. The Latin American family retains economic functions. The family as a production unit is particularly significant in Mesoamerica—less so in the "southern cone" nations of Argentina and Chile. Even urban families that are not production units provide social security in countries far from being welfare states. In societies experienced by most as capricious and heartless, the family provides more than merely psychological shelter. If one is struck down by illness or injury and has no family to support him or her, s/he will be reduced to begging in the streets. Examples of this horrific danger are readily visible.

Latin Americans cannot, and had better not, take for granted minimum security being supplied against disability, as citizens of welfare states can. The insurance against disability offered by the family is an economic system, not any perverse, pathological passivity deriving from an obsession with fertility on the part of individuals, the culture, or the Roman Catholic Church. "Familial orientation" as well as high Mesoamerican fertility can better be explained by examining the family as an economic unit than by looking to individual-level values.

Because revelation of homosexuality is a basis for expulsion from the home and the economic as well as psychological security provided by the family, homosexually active Latin Americans cultivate family relations to a greater extent than do those who can take it for granted. In some cases, they exercise the right of males who have reached sexual maturity to come and go from home at will less than do their brothers. Moreover, behavior must be particularly circumspect in the presence of one's siblings, and particularly on the subject of sex. Reticence is essential if many people live in a small space *juntos pero no revueltos* (together, but not scrambled).

Though homosexually active Mesoamericans who do not build their own families live at home longer than those who start families of their own, and also show somewhat greater concern with maintaining the support of relatives, these relations often involve no intimacy. The popular psychoanalytic obsession with mothers, projected onto the etiology of homosexuality, is useless in explaining homosexuality in Mesoamerica, because the veneration of martyr (Madonna/saintly) mothers is ubiquitous, while homosexuality is not. Regardless of sexual orientation, persons continue to live at home, not just "mother-fixated" homosexual men. Taking prospective sexual partners to where one lives is rarely possible in Mesoamerica. For the affluent, there are visits to resorts, repair to hotels in their own city, automobiles, and trysting apartments (*puterías*). For those who are not affluent, there is the dark. There are also public baths, varying in how predominantly they are patronized by those in search of homosexual encounters. As elsewhere in the world, secure privacy for lovemaking is a luxury. The pattern of residence pushes pre- and extramarital intercourse (heterosexual as well as homosexual) into the streets. This fact does not prevent quick sexual encounters (*fichas*), but is a major obstacle to ongoing relationships. Those who wish "to walk in the realm of love" (*amblar en el plan del amor*) do not have the easy path—moving in together—open to norteamericanos. Even families which accept a relationship within the family circle (treating the *amante* as another son) do not want outsiders to know that they have produced and are harboring *un raro* (a queer one). In gratitude for this (infrequently granted) minimum of acceptance, few couples are willing to demand more, such as the chance to be alone together

sometimes. Some couples do manage to carry on long-term relationships without any place in which they can be together in private, but this is quite a difficult achievement.

Collective Consciousness. Gay consciousness is no more automatic a product of homosexual behavior than class consciousness is of "objective class position" or ethnic consciousness of genealogy. In a population of persons with such a characteristic, some will not consider themselves defined in any way by it, and others will deny the characteristic altogether. The existence and importance of a characteristic must be realized if there is to be a consciousness of kind: characteristics are only potential bases.

In Anglo-America such a realization was facilitated by the congregation into "gay **ghettoes**" after World War II. Such residential concentration of homosexually-inclined men is precluded where the unmarried indefinitely continue to live at home. The specific pattern of historical development of gay communities in Anglo-America need not be assumed to constitute the only possible route to the rejection of pariah status. On the other hand, provision of sex will not in itself produce a sense of peoplehood. **Cruising** areas and social networks of homosexually-inclined men exist and have existed with varying degrees of visibility in cities everywhere, while a sense of belonging to a community of those whose identity is based on shared sexual preferences has not. Something more than sexual acts in "the city of night" is needed to provide a conception of a shared fate.

A Mesoamerican cannot learn about the common experiences of those with homosexual desires from print media, any more than he can discuss them with those with whom he lives. There is de facto censorship of anything remotely interpretable as legitimating homosexuality. Police and judges exercise wide discretion in interpreting what is immoral and declaring publications as *apologías de un vicio* (apologies for vice). Military dictatorships in particular find publications advocating unconventional behavior threatening—more threatening than homosexual behavior which may be tolerated as long as gender conventions are maintained.

Nonetheless, association with like others is also limited. For fear of having their reputation "burned" (*quemada*) and their security thereby endangered, many persons involved in homosexual behavior avoid being seen with or being acknowledged by males who might be judged effeminate, and also avoid places where homosexuals are known to congregate. The same pattern existed among homosexual Anglo-Americans, although there it was fear of losing jobs more than Mesoamericans' fear of the family's learning of stigmatizing association. The lack of positive literature and the fear of guilt by association were obstacles overcome by gay liberation movements in Anglo-America, so there is evidence that such obstacles are surmountable. Indeed, the demonstration that change is possible is an advantage gay movements in their early development today have. In post-war North America, without any known historical precedent, the possibility of change was difficult to conceive. On the other hand, in a welfare state in which there was no economic necessity to stay with one's family, a critical mass developed in a visible territory. The growth and metamorphosis of recreational facilities within an area of increasing residential concentration of homosexuals facilitated the sense of shared experience that led gay North Americans to reject negative attitudes toward homosexuality and to demand full acceptance. Whether there are functional alternatives to residential concentration is at this point open to question. Although a sense of community is easier to instill if there is a visible territory, distinct gay facilities and services might develop without a residential concentration. Continued residence with families scattered

throughout cities is a considerable obstacle to the formation of gay consciousness, culture and community as these have developed in Anglo North America. Only time will tell if there are other routes to similar—or to other—developments.

BIBLIOGRAPHY. Joseph M. Carrier, "Cultural Factors Affecting Urban Mexican Male Homosexual Behavior," *Archives of Sexual Behavior*, 5 (1976), 103–24; idem, "Family Attitudes and Mexican Male Homosexuality," *Urban Life*, 5 (1976), 359–75; William J. Goode, "Role Strain," *American Sociological Review*, 25 (1960), 483–96; Stephen O. Murray, *Male Homosexuality in Central and South America*, New York: Gay Academic Union, 1987 (Gai Saber Monograph 5).
Stephen O. Murray

LAUTRÉAMONT, COMTE DE (PSEUDONYM OF ISIDORE DUCASSE; 1846–1870)

French writer, author of *Les chants de Maldoror* (1868), a book-length poem in prose. It is a fantasy and meditation in which the title character addresses the reader, sometimes reporting things said to him or switching to the third person. Maldoror's narration is a unique revel in the horrible and macabre, as he delights in sadism and gloats over human wickedness, weakness, and cruelty. The disgusting, repulsive, and painful are stressed. The work contains murder, torture of children and animals, and bestiality (intercourse with a female shark, his "first love"). God, whom Maldoror sees as an inferior, sits on a throne of excrement and gold and eats men. The poem is seemingly a study in hatred and self-loathing, but it is actually a work of self-affirmation and even innocence, and Maldoror is a powerful example of a Romantic hero. Though he despises himself and is disgusted by the universe, Maldoror at least recognizes and admits what he and it are, and this is his claim to moral stature. It is a statement that one is human and that one accepts that. He faces death and annihilation as a pagan, without sorrow or fear.

The homosexual theme of the book is central. Male homosexuality is presented positively, and women are rejected. Homosexuals are "crystallizations of a superior moral beauty," whose "prostitution to any chance comer exercises the logic of the deepest thinkers." What tenderness and compassion is found in the work is directed toward beautiful, angelic boys, although Maldoror tortures and kills them. Compared with the violence, sodomy is made to seem positively benign. Maldoror wishes the universe were an "immense celestial anus," through which, with his penis, he would "discover the subterranean spot where truth lies slumbering."

The relationship between the narrator Maldoror and the author Lautréamont is of course ambiguous. The reader cannot help but speculate about the author's personality, but little biographical information is available, which adds to the work's allure. Born in Uruguay of French parents, Ducasse attended school in France, and died in obscurity at the age of 24. His only other work is a less interesting *Poésies* (1870). None of the few biographical details laboriously unearthed long after his death explains the work in the slightest. The reader is left with speculations. Ducasse certainly shows more strongly the influence of Baudelaire and Sade than does any other writer. Like **Sade**, he is rarely studied in universities.

Lautréamont had a great influence on the **decadent** and Surrealist writers of the late nineeenth and early twentieth century. In the case of Surrealism, this influence is somewhat ironic inasmuch as André Breton, the leader of the movement, was openly homophobic.

BIBLIOGRAPHY. Lautréamont, *Maldoror (Les Chants de Maldoror)*, translated by Guy Wernham, New York: New Directions, 1943; Wallace Fowlie, *Lautréamont*, New York: Twayne, 1973; Guillermo de Torre, *Historia de las literaturas de vanguardia*, Madrid: Guadarrama, 1971, II, 65–72.

Daniel Eisenberg

LAW (MAJOR TRADITIONS IN THE WEST)

Those who reject homosexual behavior as abhorrent often suppose that legal prohibitions against it are universal—the product of some instinctive human rejection of the "unnatural" or "abominable." Examination of the historical and cross-cultural evidence discloses no such universal prohibition. Even the Mediterranean–Northwest European traditions discussed here have no consistent uniformity of condemnation. Yet some patterns emerge: the criminal statutes of late medieval Europe and their successors stem from a single source—the Biblical prohibitions of the Mosaic Law.

The Ancient Near East. The law codes of the ancient Near East took notice of homosexuality only when incest or the use of force was involved, or when a male individual was falsely accused of taking the passive role in homosexual relations (slander). This is all that the Hittite, Middle Assyrian, and early Israelite legal texts have to say on the subject. However, a quite old statute forbade the male Israelite to be a ḳādēsh, a hierodule in the service of the Ishtar-Tammuz cult, and for that reason the ḳĕdēshîm mentioned in the books of Kings of the **Old Testament** are foreigners who "were in the land" until expelled by the reforming monarchs who favored the religion of Jahweh.

The laws of Leviticus 18:22 and 20:13 are the first in the ancient world to formulate, albeit awkwardly, a global prohibition of homosexual acts between males, though not between females. These laws were not part of the original Holiness Code, but belong to a novella of the Persian period, in any case no later than 458 B.C. It is likely that they were influenced by a similar prohibition of male homosexuality in the **Zoroastrian** religion of the Persian Empire, under whose domination the

Jewish community lived for more than two centuries. But by the time the conquests of **Alexander the Great** initiated the Hellenistic period of Jewish history, the prohibition had become a distinctive feature of Judaic sexual morality, and from this source it passed into the other **Abrahamic religions**, **Christianity** and **Islam**, though with different consequences in each. Significantly, none of the sacred texts of these three religions—the Old Testament, the **New Testament**, and the Koran—makes any mention of lesbianism, which was invisible to their ethical consciousness.

Classical Antiquity. The Athenian law punished only the male citizen who prostituted himself to another male, as **prostitution** was a calling only of slaves and aliens—not of full-fledged citizens. This law formed the background of **Aeschines'** accusations against Timarchus, which have been misread as a global condemnation of pederasty in Athenian society. What ancient Mediterranean culture did maintain was a sharp dichotomy between the active and passive roles in homosexual (and even heterosexual) relations; for an adult male to take the passive role in sexual union with another man degraded and dishonored him in the eyes of society. Contrariwise, the woman who proved too aggressive in heterosexual relations was equally stigmatized in that culture. This mentality created the background for Paul's strictures in Romans 1: 25–27: the women who "changed the order of nature" were the "daughters of men" who are accused of seducing the "sons of the gods" in Genesis 6: 1–4. The men who "burned in their lust toward one another" are the Sodomites of Genesis 19 who are reproached for passive homosexuality. As an early commentator remarked, "what their worst enemies would have liked to do to them, they did to themselves."

Under the **Roman** republic, the *Lex Scatinia* or *Scantinia* from the third century B.C. seems to have directed against the use of force or authority to compel a free man to submit to what was in Roman eyes a degrading act; its full import and application remain obscure. Jewish apologists boasted that in the Mediterranean world at the beginning of the Roman empire, their own people alone remained untainted by the vice of pederasty which all other nations practiced. In fact, the defeat of the Jews in the war against Rome which ended with the destruction of the Second Temple (A.D. 66–70) was felt by them to be a particular humiliation because the Romans engaged in pederasty.

It was with the dynasty of Constantine the Great (305–337) that the first statutes penalizing male homosexuality enter the Roman law codes. Victorious Christianity had ratified the code of sexual morality embodied in Leviticus 18 and made it part of its own constitution. Even so, the first legal texts are couched in the language of Roman virtue and of condemnation of men who "have changed their sex" rather than that of the Latin renderings of the Old Testament. It is with the **Byzantine** Emperor Justinian (527–565) that allusions to the destruction of **Sodom** enter the logic of Novellae 77 and 141, which prohibit the crime that had caused "whole cities to be destroyed together with their inhabitants." Since the *Corpus Juris Civilis* became the foundation of legal thinking in Western Europe, these texts were the motivation for the criminalization of sodomy through later centuries.

The Middle Ages. With the collapse of the Roman Empire, its codes were replaced by barbarian legal traditions that know little of homosexual behavior as a crime. It was in **Canon Law**, therefore, that the religious condemnation of homosexual expression was perpetuated and made a part of popular morality, although centuries of indoctrination were needed to instill the belief in the mass mind that sodomy was a "crime against nature" and the sodomite a criminal on a par with heretics and witches.

The full force of the church's teaching arrived only in the thirteenth century, when the scholastic theologians Albertus Magnus and Thomas **Aquinas** taught that sodomy was a crime against the order of nature because it denied the procreative function of sexuality, and held it second only to murder in gravity. The close of that century saw not merely legal enactments prescribing the death penalty, but also records of capital punishment. Although executions were never numerous, they served to impress upon the popular mind the horror of "unnatural" sexual conduct. The defamation of sodomy also offered a convenient alibi to the church whenever any misfortune struck: since there was always a reservoir of unpunished sexual immorality within the community, divine wrath at these unexpiated sins became the explanation, and the "sodomite" the scapegoat upon whose head all the ills of society could be blamed. From the end of the thirteenth century until the close of the eighteenth the homosexual was everywhere in Western Europe a criminal and an outcast who had to hide his sexual activity and identity from a vindictive Christian society.

Modernity and the Foundations of Reform. With the **Enlightenment** the legal thinkers of Western Europe began the secularization of the criminal law. **Beccaria**, **Voltaire**, and their followers, arguing that the crime of sodomy belonged to canon and not to civil law, convinced the educated public that offenses against religion and morality were matters for confession and expiation rather than concerns of the state. It was against the background of these beliefs that the penal code adopted by the Constituent Assembly of Revolutionary France in 1791 for the first time in modern history omitted the crime of sodomy from the list of punishable offenses, and the *Code Napoléon* of 1810 retained this innovation. Following the French example, a large number of countries, mainly Roman Catholic ones, reformed their own penal codes in the course of the nineteenth century. In other legal systems, however, the sole change was to replace the death penalty with life imprisonment or some other punishment that fell just short of it.

Most significant, however, was the change in the motivation of the laws. While medieval legislators had only to refer to the Bible as the inspired word of God, modern lawmakers have had to rationalize their condemnation with the pseudo-utilitarian claim that homosexual acts "undermine the moral fibre of the nation" or would reduce the birth rate so drastically as to raise the spectre of race suicide, or with some quasi-democratic allusion to the "moral feelings of the people" that are purportedly offended by homosexual behavior. What reveals the alleged motives as rationalizations is the simple fact that wholly different arguments are cited in official or semi-official commentaries on the same law. This has been true particularly in the authoritarian states of the twentieth century that restored the earlier laws (the Soviet Union) or even made the existing ones more punitive (Nazi Germany). By contrast the American court decisions that allude to the book of Leviticus as the starting point of the legal tradition have an almost naive and old-fashioned ring. The cumulative effect of the sundry changes in the law down to the 1950s and later resulted in a situation where—in some jurisdictions—consensual sodomy carried more severe penalties than armed robbery, theft of funds from a charitable institution, or beating or neglecting a small child.

Phases of Reform. The modern sexual reform movement began at the end of the nineteenth century. Its efforts were directed at the legal plight of homosexuals because the latter still bore the brunt of legal and social intolerance that had survived the middle ages. The **Scientific-Humanitarian Committee**, founded in Berlin in 1897, took as its primary goal the repeal of **Paragraph 175** of the Penal Code of the German Reich, a stance ratified by the World League for Sexual Reform on a Scientific Basis in the 1920s. However, even in such democratic countries as England and the United States, a still uninformed and puritanical public opinion frustrated the attempt to create similar movements until the 1950s.

The new era commenced after the Second World War with the **Kinsey** Reports of 1948 and 1953, and the Report of the **Wolfenden** Committee in 1957. The extent of the tabooed sexual activity became known to the public as never before, and a committee appointed by parliament after weighing the evidence concluded that private, consenting homosexual behavior was "not the law's business," while sociologists argued that "victimless crimes" harmed no one and their prosecution was detrimental rather than beneficial to society. Further, the notion of privacy in sexual matters as a right of the individual found its way into legal discourse, so that the European Court of Human Rights in 1981, in response to an appeal brought by a citizen of Northern Ireland, held that laws penalizing private consensual homosexual behavior violated the right of privacy guaranteed by the European Convention on Human Rights (1950).

Informed opinion has veered almost totally to the side of decriminalization of homosexual activity, and in a few jurisdictions the first steps have been taken toward guaranteeing homosexuals the civil rights enjoyed by the rest of the population but denied them because of the social intolerance that still thrives in circles that regard the Old Testament as the inspired word of God. In the 1980s the issue of Acquired Immunodeficiency Syndrome (**AIDS**) unhappily raised the specter of a "threat to public health," gleefully brandished by the enemies of law reform to reinforce their never-ending citations from Leviticus and Romans when arguing before the courts and legislatures. But the secular trend is toward the abolition of the penal statutes that echo the canon law of the medieval church, as even more and more heterosexuals depart from the Christian ideal of "lifelong, indissoluble, mo-nogamous heterosexual marriage." Consequently, the legislators and appellate courts of the future will have the task of defining intimate relationships between members of the same sex (and members of opposite sexes) so as to do justice to the realities of social life and the interests of the community.

See also **Common Law; Criminal Law Amendment Act; Law, Feudal and Royal; Law, Germanic; Law, Municipal.**
Warren Johansson

LAW, BRITISH
See **Common Law.**

LAW, CANON
See **Canon Law.**

LAW, COMMON
See **Common Law.**

LAW, FEUDAL AND ROYAL
Between 1050 and 1300 scholars of ecclesiastical or **canon law** and scholastics and other theologians had defined sodomy as tantamount to murder, both sins contrary to reason, nature, and the will of God. The rebirth of the study of Roman law occurred after 1100 with the discovery of Justinian's Digest or Pandects (compiled during the early phase of the **Byzantine Empire**). This legal revival gave renewed currency to the provision condemning sodomy as an infamous crime deserving of the death penalty. Doctors of civil law from the University of Bologna—which also awarded degrees in canon law, often to the same candidate, so that he became *Doctor utriusque iuris*, "Doctor of both laws"—cited the *Corpus Iuris Civilis*, which contained in addition to the Digest, the Code, Institutes and Novellae, to demand capital punishment in secular law and severer penalties in canon law. In his *Commentary on the Codex*, ca. 1230, Accursius briefly noted the distinction the Romans made between *stuprum* (forcible rape of a female or a boy) and consensual sodomy, for which there had been no penalty before 342. Accursius correctly

commented that *stuprum* referred to rape of boys as well as females. Peter the Chanter (d. 1197) equated homosexual acts with murder and the Third Lateran Council in 1179 ordered guilty clerics defrocked or confined to monasteries and laymen excommunicated. Moslems were accused of raping men and boys and even sodomizing a bishop to death. The Germanic law codes of the early Middle Ages had made no reference to homosexual offenses. Charlemagne, shocked by monkish sodomy, threatened penalties against the offenders, but the only part of a capitulary of Charlemagne (in 779) condemning homosexual acts that survives is a forgery. In 966 in Rome the Emperor Otto I promulgated an edict that prescribed strangulation and burning for sodomy between males, as it were epitomizing Theodosius' edict of 390.

Crusaders were accused of importing effeminate Moslem customs to Europe. This charge underlay the suspicion of the Templars. Thirty years after the First Crusade, the Latin Kingdom of Jerusalem drafted the first secular laws during the high Middle Ages prescribing burning for sodomites. "When Saracens see boys, they lust for them and like mad dogs race to buy the (Frankish) boys," declared William of Ada.

Before the end of the twelfth century, other civil authorities began to assume jurisdiction over sodomy. Hitherto the clergy had meted out penances for it and continued to do so, though it soon became "reserved" so that only bishops could absolve it, in part because it had become associated with **heresy**. In 1215 the Fourth Lateran Council called for secular help against heretics, with whom sodomites were classified. When the episcopate failed, the Papal inquisitors increasingly took charge after 1220. The **Inquisition** associated the Cathari of Southern France, also called "Bougres" because their sect was identified with the Bogomils of Bulgaria, with sodomy. Inquisitors supported by the crown tortured and burned the sodomites in Toulouse and throughout the South along with the Albigensians. The Holy Roman Emperor **Frederick II** promulgated the Constitutions of Melfi in 1231, which conspicuously omitted sodomy, of which he himself was accused. Likewise silent were the German Sachsenspiegel and Schwabenspiegel compiled in Frederick's reign. However, Alfonso X of Castile, St. Louis of France, and Edward I of England all used Roman law to create a national law to override local customs and centralize their realms, and claimed jurisdiction over capital crimes such as sodomy and the property of those convicted thereof. The Guelph Charles of Anjou, king of Sicily from 1266 to 1285, regularly paid papal inquisitors from his royal coffers.

Individual Countries. As Boswell argues, "between 1250 and 1300 in most Catholic countries laws which had previously ignored homosexual acts prescribed the death penalty for them." But these laws were inspired by the church as when Gregory IX sent the Dominicans to extirpate sodomy in Germany "so ridden with unnatural vice . . . that some parts, especially Austria, are thought of as infected with the foulness of leprosy." About 1250 the English legal author Fleta prescribed burning for sodomites, to whom the earlier collections of Glanville and Britton or those known as the "Laws of Henry I" had made no reference.

Alfonso X of Castile (ca. 1226–1284) prescribed castration and then stoning, and his *Siete Partidas* considered sodomy "infamous" so that it dishonored the offender's clan and deprived them of their inheritance. In 1497 Ferdinand and Isabella, *los reyes católicos*, ordered confiscation of goods and burning alive, no matter what class the offender, treating such cases as *mixti fori*, belonging to both secular and ecclesiastical courts. The Spanish Inquisition gained jurisdiction in Aragon, but not in Castile or Sicily.

Pope Nicholas II had empowered the papal **Inquisition** to investigate sodomy in 1457. In 1506 at Seville inquisitors arrested a great number of suspects, though many more fled, and burnt 12. When in Valencia in 1519 a Friar preached that the pest infecting the city was caused by sodomites, the mob found four culprits who confessed and were burnt by the justiciary, and a fifth who given a lesser sentence was seized by the populace, garroted, and burnt.

Philip II in 1569 ordered rigid enforcement by royal officers of the death penalty in Sicily, the informer receiving a bounty from the estate of the sodomite, but since there were not many convictions, jurisdiction reverted to the Inquisition in 1597.

At the urging of João III (1502–1557), but only after his death, the Papacy agreed to have the Inquisition in Portugal deal with sodomy. In 1562 Pope Pius IV ordered that Portuguese inquisitors punish sodomy, but as in Aragon according to the laws of the municipality in which the offense occurred, with punishment either burning or scourging and the galleys.

The *Coutumes* of Touraine-Anjou were reflected in the *Etablissements* of St. Louis. Noting that his action was in accord with papal decretals, Louis ordered confiscation of property and burning of sodomites, as did Philippe de Beaumanoir in *Les Coutumes de Beauvaisis* (1283). A collection of statutes made in 1260 at Orléans prescribed confiscation of property by the crown and mutilation, castration, and burning for the first, second, and third offense for women as well as for men. Philip IV (1285–1314) solved all questions of jurisdiction between canon, municipal, and royal courts by reserving them all for the crown. In the trial of the **Templars**, Philip dominated the pope, the inquisitors readily cooperating with the king.

The Norwegian law of Gulathing ca. 1250 permanently outlawed sodomites.

Conclusion. The revival of Roman law and its reception by the legislators and jurists of Western Europe, completed in Germany in the sixteenth century, meant the virtually unanimous adoption of the death penalty prescribed by the book of Leviticus and the Christian Roman Emperors. Backed by the hallowed traditions of Roman justice, the intolerance of homosexual expression lasted until **Beccaria**, **Voltaire**, and the thinkers of the **Enlightenment** put an end to what they considered part of the barbarity of the **Middle Ages**.

BIBLIOGRAPHY. John Boswell, *Christianity, Social Tolerance, and Homosexuality*, Chicago: Chicago University Press, 1980; Michael Goodich, *The Unmentionable Vice: Homosexuality in the Later Medieval Period*, Santa Barbara, CA: ABC-Clio, 1979.

William A. Percy

LAW, GERMANIC

The law codes of the Germanic tribes that overran the Western half of the Roman Empire in the fifth century are known collectively as the *Leges barbarorum* or Germanic law. Recorded in Medieval Latin at various times between the fifth and ninth centuries, they imitated Roman law in codifying what until then had been an oral tradition of customary law. They departed from the geographical uniformity which the Empire had gradually and somewhat imperfectly imposed upon legal status and legal practice in that they were *Stammes- und Standesrechte*, sets of legal norms that depended upon the tribal membership and social status of the juridical subject, not upon where he lived. Their adoption contributed to the particularism of the early **Middle Ages** that ended only with the triumph of codes applicable to the entire territory of nation-states and embodying the principle of the equality of all citizens before the law which the **Enlightenment** achieved at the close of the eighteenth century.

Frequently cited as evidence that the primitive Germanic tribes punished male homosexuality with death is the passage in the twelfth chapter of the *Germania* of **Tacitus** which tells how the Germans drowned *ignavos et imbelles et* *corpore infames* in swamps with a basket of wickerwork over their heads. The last of the three Latin terms has usually been taken to mean "sodomites." However, close philological analysis of the entire passage and of the phrase in question shows that Tacitus was describing a violation of military discipline, cowardice or failure to perform one's soldierly duty, and not a sexual offense. This three-part Latin expression renders the Old Norse word *argr*, with the notion of passivity and lack of courage associated with the passive-effeminate male rather than sexual behavior per se. In any case Tacitus was exaggerating Germanic virtue, bravery, and sexual continence to condemn Roman vice, cowardice, and licentiousness. Ammianus Marcellinus and Procopius, on the other hand, testify that Germanic warriors enjoyed pederastic acts with impunity and commonly indulged in them.

The Germanic codes generally omit discussion of penalties for homosexual behavior, and the Icelandic sagas show that such conduct was a purely private matter entailing, to be sure, frightful ignominy for the passive adult partner, but no penal retribution on the part of the tribe or local community. Among the Germanic peoples the imposition of sexual morality was exercised entirely by the family as an internal matter. Most experts writing on this question agree that intolerance in sexual matters stems from the Judaic influence on ecclesiastical law, fundamentally alien to Germanic mentality and custom. The introduction of criminal sanctions against sodomy was the work of the Christian church. In citing Tacitus to justify the death penalty for homosexual "degenerates" and "race defilers," National Socialist writers of the 1930s were guilty of monumental anachronisms characteristic of the confused and irrational thinking by which they validated the sodomy delusion in seemingly contemporary terms.

It is true, however, that Germanic peoples associated passive homosexuality with cowardice and also with the practice of *seiđr*, sorcery, for which they could on occasion exact drastic penalties. According to an account in *Historia Norwegiae*, Rognvaldr Rettilbeini, a wizard versed in magical lore, was drowned in Hadaland at the command of his father King Harald because of the disgrace that he had incurred by busying himself with an art that stamped him an as *argr* (in the Latin original *ob usitatem inertissimae artis ignominiam infamatus*).

A separate matter is the so-called *Moorleichenfrage*, the problem posed by human remains found in bogs and marshes in a condition supporting the belief that these are the corpses of individuals either sacrificed or executed. The full range of motives and circumstances behind their deaths remains obscure because written evidence for the practice is slim. However, it is clear that the victim was meant to disappear from sight and never return as a malevolent ghost, hence the custom of sinking him in morasses and bog holes that were imagined as a fathomless abyss.

The actual texts of the codes from the early Middle Ages contain no such provisions. The *Codex Euricianus* for the West Gothic subjects of King Euric (475–76), the *Breviarium Alaricianum* (a summary of Roman law for the "Roman" subjects of the Visigoths, not a compendium of Germanic custom), the *Lex Visigothorum* of the sixth and seventh centuries, the *Edictum Theoderici* (supposedly before 507), the *Lex Burgundionum* (after 480), the *Pactus Legis Salicae* (ca. 507), the *Pactus Legis Ribvariae* (seventh century), the *Pactus Legis Alamannorum* (seventh century), and the *Edictus Rothari* (643) make no mention of homosexual offenses. The last, the *Lex Baiuvariorum*, *Lex Thuringorum*, and *Lex Saxonum* were all completed before 900. New redactions of most of these laws were promulgated under the Carolingians. The Anglo-Saxon dooms from Aethelbert of Kent (560–616) to the Danish King Canute the Great (1016–1038) are the greatest collections of Germanic laws and were written in Anglo-Saxon rather than in Latin; not one specifically refers to sodomy.

The Visigothic Law, which alone among Germanic laws treated prostitution in detail, provided that a woman could divorce her husband if he committed sodomy with another male or forced her into adultery against her will. The significant point is that *tale nefas fieri nequaquam inter Christianos oportet*, "such wrongdoing ought nowhere to occur among Christians," revealing the foreign and churchly origin of the sanction.

Penitentials, the decisions of church councils, and decrees of local bishops do not belong under this subject, as they derive from Biblical and canon law and not from Germanic custom. The very language in which they are couched reflects at every point the influence of the Latin text of the Scriptures and of **Patristic** thought. In this vein King Reccesvinth ca. 654 had imposed the penalty of castration on sodomites, and the Visigothic king Egica (687–701), in a message to the sixteenth Council of Toledo (693), urged the assembled dignitaries to "extirpate that obscene crime committed by abusers of themselves with mankind, whose fearful conduct defiles the charm of decent living and provokes from heaven the wrath of the supreme Judge." Upon receiving the statement of the council he reinforced it with an edict of his own prescribing not only castration but also the death penalty for all found guilty of the crime.

Codes in the Germanic languages from the later Middle Ages that condemn homosexual practices use terms such as **sodomy** and **buggery** that stem from Christian legend and belief, not from native tradition. That medieval lawmakers had to employ such exotic expressions (the one of Semitic, the other ultimately of Turkic origin) shows how foreign the very notion of the offense was to the Germanic culture of antiquity. The ultimate acceptance of the taboo among Germanic folk must be ascribed to Christian indoctrination, even if underlying pagan attitudes linking passive male homosexuality with cowardice and sorcery to some extent reinforced the disapproval. Accusations of homosexuality did not figure notably in the **witchcraft** delusion of the sixteenth and seventeenth centuries, even in Germanic lands where it raged the most fiercely.

BIBLIOGRAPHY. Vern Bullough, *Sexual Variance in Society and History*, New York: John Wiley, 1976; Hermann Conrad, "Das Wehrstrafrecht der germanischen und fränkischen Zeit," *Zeitschrift für die gesamte Strafrechtswissenschaft*, 56 (1937), 713–15; Rudolf His, *Geschichte des deutschen Strafrechts bis zur Karolina*, Munich and Berlin: Oldenbourg, 1928; Folke Ström, *On the Sacral Origin of the Germanic Death Penalties*, Stockholm: Wahlstrom & Widstrand, 1942, pp. 48–57, 171–88; Josef Weisweiler, "Beiträge zur Bedeutungsentwicklung germanischer Wörter für sittliche Begriffe. I. Germ. *arga-*," *Indogermanische Forschungen*, 41 (1923), 16–29.

Warren Johansson and William A. Percy

LAW, MUNICIPAL

Municipal ordinances against sodomy were first enacted in **Italy** in the later **Middle Ages** as the slackening of imperial power produced a situation of de facto local autonomy.

The Ecclesiastical Background. The **papacy** accused of sodomy the imperial forces it was fighting in Italy. In 1233 the Curia enlisted the religious enthusiasm of the newly founded mendicant friars (Franciscans and Dominicans, who were directing the **Inquisition** in Southern France). Manipulated by the popes and the Guelph (pro-papal) bankers and merchants, the friars denounced the sexual laxity of the Ghibelline nobles who supported the Holy Roman Emperor **Frederick** II and his sons, and insisted upon the execution of heretics, sodomites, and other offenders against morality. At Ancona, Bologna, whose university had revived the study of Roman law, and Perugia, lay confraternities of the orders of friars received authority to prosecute sodomites.

Although falling into disuse or repealed following the Ghibelline victory at Cortenuova in 1237, the statutes were reenacted after the Guelph triumph at Benevento in 1266. Inquisitors branded noble Ghibellines as pederasts and adulterers, while other mendicants defamed heretics and Jews, the latter with the accusation of ritual murder. In 1255–61 Humbert of Romans, the Dominican general, advised brothers in Bologna, Mantua, and Faenza to suppress that "evil filth," sodomy. A Dominican brother, a Guelph, introduced statutes in Bologna in 1265–66 ordering state assistance in prosecuting heretics and sodomites. Burning replaced mild penalties in Perugia in 1309, and its code of 1342 ordered that eight men be chosen from each of the five quarters of the city to denounce sodomites. Most Italian communes, as in Sicily, enacted the penalty of burning for sodomites and confiscation of their property, sometimes as at Ascoli Piceno offering a bounty to informers and collaborators in prosecution. Pisa fined those harboring sodomites 100 lire and at Bologna the building in which sodomy occurred could be burnt along with its inhabitants. Every important city-state persecuted sodomites throughout the Italian **Renaissance**, including **Leonardo** da Vinci and Benvenuto **Cellini**.

Although secular, these codes referred frequently to Scripture, the **Patristic writers**, papal decretals, **Canon law**, the Decretum of Gratian, and Thomas **Aquinas**. On the other hand, there is no allusion whatever in them to the "feelings of the people"; they appealed to no plebiscite or democratic process for their justification. Modern apologists for the Church, who claim that these laws were enacted because "the way people felt was utterly different from what it is now," are simply inventing a rationale that in medieval times would not have interested, let alone persuaded anyone who held power.

Municipal Ordinances Proper. Siena, Perugia, and Florence enacted the longest ordinances against sodomy. In 1305

Fra Giordano condemned **Florence** as a veritable Sodom where fathers encouraged sons to prostitute themselves, and in the next century Matteo ascribed the floods that destroyed one-third of the city to the widespread practice of sodomy. In 1325 the Podestà graduated penalties according to the age of the culprit and the frequency of his offenses: pederasty was punished by castration. A boy who submitted voluntarily to the act was beaten, driven through the city naked, or fined 50 lire. The panderer, his accomplice, or a habitual criminal suffered a fine of 500 lire; if unable to pay the sum, he had his hand cut off; if he had no hand, then his foot. A father who induced his son to commit the act was punished likewise. The dwelling, field, or other premises in which the act was committed with the owner's consent was to be destroyed or laid waste. Any man found in suspicious circumstances with a boy to whom he was not related was presumed guilty of the offense and punished accordingly. "Rogues," "imposters," and foreign criminals, of which Florence was notoriously full, received particularly severe punishment, and boxes were placed about the city to receive anonymous denunciations. In 1403 the Signoria created the Questa to protect public morality and especially to suppress sodomy, though favoring female prostitution, and in 1432 established the Official of the Curfew and the Convents to suppress sodomy. Siena in 1421, and other Italian cities during the same period, took similar measures. In the 1490s the Dominican Savonarola ordered exposure for the first offense, tying to a pillar for the second, and burning for the third.

Linking sodomites with heretics and Patarenes (a mob of hyperenthusiasts who had flourished in eleventh-century northern Italy), in 1262 and 1270 Siena expelled those who did not confess within a week and a day and confiscated their goods, and on the first Sunday in every month expelled members in every category. In 1309–10 the commune ordained a fine of 300 lire for the first offense, the culprit being hung by his virile member in the town square if he did not pay within a month. In 1324 it ordered men to track down sodomites "in order to honor the Lord, ensure the peace, maintain the good morals and praiseworthy life of the people" and quoted Ephesians 5:6 that the crime if not punished would bring God's ire down upon the town. Bologna punished sodomites with burning or perpetual exile in 1259.

Venice. The Adriatic city's illicit sexual culture, in which even some of the most distinguished citizens occasionally participated, included prostitutes, mistresses, street people, and sodomites. The state increasingly interfered with sexual conduct after the oligarchy took charge by closing the Grand Council to new members in 1297. Rhetoric and prosecutions for sodomy grew during the fourteenth and fifteenth centuries as Jews were being confined to the periphery. In 1458 the Council of Ten tightened surveillance and increased the number of patrolers, explaining that "God . . . detesting the sin of sodomy . . . brought down his wrath upon the cities of Sodom and Gomorrah and soon thereafter flooded and destroyed the whole world for such horrible sins; [hence] our most wise ancestors sought with all their laws and experts to liberate our city from such a dangerous divine judgment." God had not punished any other sin so harshly!

Records of the night police, which began in 1348, mention prosecution in that year of two servants who shared the same bed. Having confessed under torture to taking the active role in "unnatural intercourse," one was burnt alive between the columns of justice before the Doge's palace. After the discovery of a circle involving at least fifteen nobles in 1406, the Council of Ten, which in one case held that sodomy on board would cause God to destroy the fleet, took over jurisdiction of this most dangerous crime from the night police. In 1497 the Doge heard a Francis-

can monk ascribe the plague to blasphemy, usury, selling justice, and "the societies of sodomy" and convents of nuns that were really "whorehouses and public bordellos." The Ten labeled sodomy "the most foul crime," "the most infamous sin," and "a diabolical desire."

The Ten, which offered 2,000 lire to anyone making a denunciation that resulted in conviction, uncovered groups of up to twenty, several of which in the early periods involved Florentines or people who had been in Florence. By the fifteenth century Venice had a widespread subculture, centering around apothecary shops; schools of gymnastics, singing, music, dance, and the abacus; pastry shops; and certain dark areas. The authorities regularly distinguished between actives, who were burned, and passives (pathics), often young following the immemorial **Mediterranean** pattern, who normally received lashes, fines, and imprisonment. *Pueri* (who might be as young as ten) were seldom even prosecuted in the fourteenth century, 14 years being considered adult, but after 1424 those under 14 were "not to be freely absolved as in the past . . . but . . . subject to a minimum penalty of three months in jail and in addition ought to receive from 12 to 20 lashes in the torture chamber." Occasionally boys were prosecuted as actives and older males as passives. For capital sentences in the early fifteenth century decapitation and then burning supplanted burning alive. One jailed individual had undergone brutal prolonged torture that damaged his genitals and other bodily parts; the doctor advised amputating his arms to save his life.

Between 1326 and 1359 five individuals were prosecuted; 1351–75, 8; 1376–1400, 3; 1401–25, 87; 1426–50, 81; 1451–75, 134; and 1476–1500, 196. Between 1326 and 1500 514 individuals, including 66 nobles, were prosecuted, in 279 cases of which 78 involved boys, 34 females, and 33 nobles. The Ten complained to the pope that clerical sodomites, escaping persecution by secular courts, were not being sufficiently punished by courts canon, merely being banished from Venetian territory by the Council. Sexual immorality was commonly ascribed to those accused of heresy.

Elsewhere in Europe. Communes in Northern Europe also punished sodomites. The first documented burning occurred in Ghent when on September 28, 1292 John, a local knifemaker, was burned near the pillory. The same source documented the banishment of an adulteress and the burning of her house. The last previous documented execution had taken place in 521, shortly before the reign of Justinian. In the fourteenth century the legal school of Orléans synthesized the *Fuero real* and the *Siete Partidas* of Alfonso the Wise in a code punishing the first sodomitical offense by castration, the second by dismemberment, and the third by burning. In Portugal as in Aragon in the sixteenth century the Inquisition tried and punished sodomites according to the statutes of the municipalities in which the trial occurred, but in Castile the municipalities themselves did so.

In Germany, where the Magdeburg Law had ignored it, sodomy entered the law codes in the sixteenth century with the Bamberger Halsgerichtsordnung (Constitutio Criminalis Bambergensis) of 1507, evidently inspired by the Italian jurists of the preceding century and the Italian municipalities. The provisions of this code became Article 116 of the Peinliche Gerichtsordnung Kaiser Karls V (Constitutio Criminalis Carolina), enacted by the Imperial Diet in Regensburg on July 27, 1532. This article decreed death for *Unkeusch wider die Natur* [unchastity against nature] "in accordance with the common law." Exceedingly influential as was the Carolina as far east as Russia and down to the French Revolution, it found no reception in England or its colonies. England with its strong crown saw no municipal ordinances and no Inquisition. In 1533, the year following the Carolina

but apparently independent of it, Parliament enacted the statute 25 Henry VIII c. 6 ordering death by hanging for the crime of "buggery with mankind or beast." Despite much discussion of the origins of this enactment, the precise reasons for its adoption in 1533 remain unknown.

Conclusion. The particularism of medieval law allowed for local variations in the punishment for sodomy after the lawlessness of the Dark Ages, but never toleration. Public exposure and humiliation of the offender and even the obliteration of the site of his crime expressed late medieval society's fanatical campaign against "unnatural" forms of sexual expression. While the statutes were abolished long ago, their enforcement left in the popular mind into the twentieth century a legacy of fear and loathing.

See also **Police; Sixteenth-Century Legislation.**

BIBLIOGRAPHY. Michael Goodich, *The Unmentionable Vice: Homosexuality in the Later Medieval Period*, Santa Barbara, CA: ABC-Clio, 1979.

William A. Percy

LAW, ROMAN
See **Rome, Ancient.**

LAW, UNITED STATES

Homosexuality is relevant to a number of aspects of American law. Historically, the criminal offense of **sodomy** has been pivotal for the legal situation of homosexuals in post-Classical civilization. The sexual negativism enshrined in Europe's sodomy laws, a type of condemnation which is scarcely a cultural universal, came to North America in colonial times as part of the heritage of English **common law**. New themes emerged, however, during the second half of the twentieth century as decriminalization spread among the most populous and important American states, in keeping with a trend evident throughout the industrialized world. As elsewhere, sodomy law reform proved not the end of the road, but the beginning, for ancillary problems stemming from old prejudices remained.

The Criminal Law. In the English-speaking world, the subject of homosexuality and the law was placed on the agenda by the Report of the **Wolfenden** Committee in Britain in 1957. Until then it had been tacitly assumed, if not explicitly stated, that homosexual activity (characterized as "sodomy," "buggery," or "the infamous crime against **nature**") was immoral and illegal, and that the individual engaging in such conduct had no rights which the law or society needed to recognize in any way—apart from the rights accorded to all defendants in criminal cases, though reputable lawyers often refused to defend individuals accused of homosexual offenses.

The Wolfenden Report had considerable impact in the United States. Yet its reception occurred in the context of an important fact: the American states are sovereign in the sense that each has its own criminal code and civil code and its own regulations governing state employees, together with a court system that hears cases arising under state law and appeals from the decisions of courts of first instance. To be sure, no state law can stand if found in conflict with the United States Constitution, and this principle of review of legislative acts by courts whose members serve for long terms or even for life has served several minority groups seeking to affirm their rights. The American Constitution is the outcome of the fusion of French and Italian political and legal theory with British and colonial law and administrative practice. Hence in the United States the Constitution limits the power both of Congress and of the individual state legislatures, and the state constitutions do the same for their respective jurisdictions. By contrast, in Great Britain the power of Parliament is absolute: there is no plea of "unconstitutionality." Although the United Kingdom has adhered to the European Convention on Human Rights, providing for the hearing of cases

by a tribunal in Strasbourg, the decisions of the tribunal are not absolutely binding on member states. In the United States, as indicated, the Constitution is supreme. With reference to homosexuality, however, the federal law codes and the federal judiciary are chiefly significant for such issues as federal employment, military service and the rights of service personnel, and immigration and naturalization.

The first efforts at sodomy law reform in the United States were influenced by English thinking. The Wolfenden Report of 1957 made a classical liberal case for repeal of the criminal laws against private homosexual activity between consenting adults; ten years later Parliament acted on its recommendations, decriminalizing homosexual conduct between consenting adults in England and Wales. About half the American states have followed suit, though in several major instances the law was struck down by the decision of a state appellate court rather than by the action of the legislature. In the other half of the states nearly all forms of homosexual intimacy involving penetration are still criminal, though prosecutions (which were never common for the full offense of sodomy) are today ever rarer. The decision of the Supreme Court of the United States in *Bowers v. Hardwick* (1986) upheld the constitutionality of the Georgia sodomy law, ruling that there was no right of privacy in regard to homosexual behavior. Nonetheless, the constitutionality of sodomy laws may still be tested in regard to other issues such as the establishment of religion clause of the First Amendment and the equal protection clause of the Fourteenth. Canada (1969) and New Zealand (1987) have repealed the criminal laws on their entire territory, while in Australia the individual states still vary in their legal norms.

If prosecutions for the act of sodomy were uncommon even in the past, charges of loitering or solicitation for indecent purposes were frequently brought against homosexual men, often as the result of entrapment by plainclothesmen of the vice squad who accosted them in known cruising areas. Minor as the actual charge may have been, if the facts became known to an individual's employer or family, the outcome could be a ruined career and a personal tragedy. Also, the attorney who was willing to represent the defendant in such a case was often concerned only with extracting from him as large a fee as possible. Lesbians ran afoul of the criminal law principally through statutes against cross-dressing in public, as most of the repressive activity of the state in regard to the female was aimed at the prostitute with a male clientele. Historically, the sodomy laws—the ultimate linchpin of all legal discrimination against homosexuals—are grounded in religious horror of sexual activity between males.

Gay Couples. The union of man and woman is consecrated in law and custom by the act of marriage, which conveys legally specified rights and duties to both partners. Until quite recently, **couples** of the same sex lived outside the law, which was not a protector but an oppressor. The property rights of the couple languished in a legal limbo; if there was a dispute between them, neither party could venture to bring the matter to court, as both would have been exposed to prosecution and imprisonment, or at the very least to social ostracism and economic ruin. But with the end of the criminal laws and the onset of the movement for the recognition of gay rights, cases involving gay couples began to reach the courts.

The landmark decision was the one rendered in the case of a heterosexual couple, *Marvin v. Marvin*, decided by the California Supreme Court in 1976. The court first declared that marital property laws do not apply to persons who are not legally married, but recognizing that unmarried couples had become a fact of American social life, the court held that the parties to such unions "may order their economic affairs as they choose." The fact that a couple is living together

outside of wedlock does not invalidate such agreements by mutual consent. A gay couple living together is free to enter a contract to divide income, property, and all other assets as the two see fit, just as if they were partners in a business or any two competent adults conducting a business transaction. In states that have adopted the *Marvin* ruling, such a contract is legally binding and enforceable. Yet the question remains open as to what behavior, circumstances, and conduct have created an implied agreement to share property.

A couple seeking to guard against unforeseen problems and conflicts in the future will, therefore, formulate a contract which may be as broad or as specific as the parties choose. The contract will be enforceable in court only to the extent that it concerns personal and real property. Provisions for the support and custody of children will be enforced by a court only if the judge finds that the provisions reflect "the best interests of the children." A contract may also refer to financial obligations assumed by the couple on a specified basis over a future time span.

Under the law of intestate succession, if one member of a gay couple dies without having willed his property to the other, the estate passes to the relatives of the deceased, who, if they disapprove of the relationship or actively resent the presence of the partner, can simply dispossess him and treat him as a perfect stranger with no claims whatever, even if he has been intimate with the lover for many years.

Child Custody. The custody of children conceived in a heterosexual union is commonly the most difficult problem a previously married homosexual or lesbian faces. If there is a court battle over custody, the heterosexual partner to the marriage will try to use facts, accusations, and insinuations about the deviant lifestyle, identity, and behavior of the rival party to win his case. The defense is that one's sexual identity is irrelevant to being a good and devoted parent. If the spouses agree on the custody of the children, the court will almost certainly ratify the decision without prying into the details of the parents' private life. Court battles arise when the parents cannot agree, and particularly when the heterosexual parent wants to deny the bisexual or homosexual one virtually all custody rights. The latter faces a difficult uphill battle in court, especially if he or she is living openly with a lover. In the last few years, however, some courts have renounced the practice of automatically denying custody to the homosexual parent. Even where custody is not granted, the parent may have visitation rights, which means that he or she can see and spend time with the child under specified conditions. During most of the twentieth century, the mother was almost always awarded custody unless she was found to be an "unfit" parent—as lesbians usually were in disputed cases. In practice, the judge has almost complete discretion in awarding custody where the parents are in conflict, and even in restricting visitation rights by forbidding the mere presence of the homosexual parent's new lover. Because of the moral stigma still attaching to homosexual behavior, the odds are still against the unconventional parent in a custody dispute.

Employment. There is no federal legislation to protect homosexuals in employment. In the absence of local or state protections, employers may refuse to hire, decline to promote, and even demote or dismiss a homosexual employee solely on the grounds of "immoral conduct" or a similar accusation. Fellow workers may complain to an employer that they resent the presence of a homosexual in their midst. For many gay people the open acknowledgement of their orientation spells the likelihood of the loss of employment or of opportunity for promotion. Beginning with World War II, "fair employment practices" statutes and regulations of various kinds were enacted at the federal and state levels which at first prohibited discrimination

on the basis of race, religion, or national origin, but not of sexual orientation (or "affectional preference"), which became an issue only when it was raised by gay rights organizations in the 1970s. Since then some 50 towns, cities, and states have enacted laws extending the protection of these anti-discrimination measures to homosexuals. The homosexual who is most exposed to prejudice is one who works with children in any capacity, not only because of fear of child molestation but also because such an individual is deemed an unsuitable role model for the young. Nevertheless teachers' unions have fought for the inclusion of anti-discrimination clauses in their contracts, and the devotion and frustration tolerance which the homosexual teacher or counselor is able to bring to his or her work speak for rather than against fairness in such cases.

Housing. This matter poses a special problem for the homosexual, because most housing is oriented toward families, and the permanently single individual is often marginalized by society's assumption that the status is merely transitory. Landlords can, where no legal protection exists, refuse to rent an apartment to an individual or to a pair of individuals whom they believe to be homosexual, again on the grounds that their presence would be "morally offensive" to the other tenants, to families with children, and the like. Also, if one member of a gay couple dies, the survivor may find himself with no rights comparable to those of a heterosexual widow or widower and liable to be evicted from the premises at the landlord's whim. In cities where gentrification is proceeding apace, the landlord may find it very much in his own interest to expel the partner and then raise the rent enormously. On the other hand, cases involving refusal to admit a homosexual as a guest in a hotel, motel, or restaurant, in contrast with the type of discrimination formerly practiced on religious or racial grounds, are quite rare.

Military. The unfitness of homosexuals for **military** service was taken so much for granted in the past that the Senate Subcommittee of 1950 that investigated Senator Joseph McCarthy's charges of "sex perverts in government" could only congratulate the military for its aggressiveness in "ferreting out sex perverts." Only in the 1970s did a few brave servicemen and women dare to challenge the long-standing policy of exclusion, usually with no legal success. The courts repeatedly upheld the right to the armed services to discharge known homosexuals, as in the well-publicized cases of Leonard Matlovich in the Army and Vernon Berg in the Navy. The upper echelons of the military are reputed to be virtually paranoid on the subject of homosexual activity in their midst. Those who were separated from the military for homosexual behavior often received undesirable or dishonorable discharges that handicapped them for life, making certain kinds of employment unobtainable because of the moral stigma with which they had been branded. In individual cases it was possible to have the official record of the discharge altered in favor of the ex-serviceman, particularly if the rest of his conduct had been exemplary. The federal courts continue to hear appeals from military personnel who acknowledge their homosexual orientation but claim that it does not impair their fitness to serve.

Immigration and Naturalization. This area was the first in which the law actually took notice of homosexuality as a condition recognized by psychiatry. Until the twentieth century the courts everywhere acted on the assumption that homosexual conduct stemmed from willful depravity, not from an abnormal mental state. A law of 1917 had excluded prospective immigrants with "constitutional psychopathic inferiority," and the Walter McCarran Act of 1950, adopted at a moment when **McCarthyism** had raised the issue of "sex perversion," specified that homosexuality was grounds for denial of **immigration** and naturalization. The United States is virtually unique among the nations of the world in seeking to exclude foreigners from its territory solely on grounds of homosexuality, but despite severe criticism of the law, it has not been repealed, though some federal courts have decided in favor of homosexual plaintiffs in particular instances.

AIDS and the Law. The discovery in 1981 of Acquired Immunodeficiency Syndrome (**AIDS**) as a condition particularly affecting homosexual men created a whole new series of legal issues with which the American legal system has had to contend. Despite the data accumulated by medical investigators as to the specific modes of transmission of AIDS, the general public quickly gained the false notion that the condition was highly contagious and could be spread even by casual and indirect forms of contact. The pervasive fear of contagion, anxiety about casual transmission, and the stigmatization of the AIDS carrier in the public mind has led to a demand for measures to protect public health at the expense of civil liberties, particularly the liberties of persons diagnosed as having AIDS or falling into "high risk" categories. Traditional public health practices—screening, testing, reporting, contact tracing, isolation, and quarantine—have all been invoked. At the same time organizations defending the rights of people with AIDS have vehemently opposed most if not all of these measures. A further problem is AIDS-Related Complex (ARC) and even the test finding of seropositivity, which can become grounds for discrimination and exclusion.

The American courts have dealt with AIDS in the context of statutes protecting victims of disease and handicap from discrimination—statutes that ironically are far more widespread than ones protecting the rights of homosexuals. So a homosexual diagnosed as having AIDS can appeal to the courts for the protection of rights that are not extended to his sexual orientation. However, it is a fact that even within the ranks of health workers there is such intense fear of contracting AIDS through repeated contact with patients that some physicians, dentists, and hospital employees have refused to treat such individuals. The common law does not impose any duty upon even a qualified physician to treat a patient unless a contractual relationship exists. Here the legal obligation is narrower than the ethical tradition, as it has been enshrined in the Hippocratic Oath.

Claims for public assistance to people with AIDS fall into the sphere of social policy, but where a state has created the right of indigent persons to support in case of illness, this right applies to the penniless individual diagnosed with the condition. The special problem arises of the ability and willingness of municipal governments to provide the facilities (hospices, intensive care units, and the like) required to cope with the mounting number of AIDS cases. Here AIDS activist organizations have labored mightily to bring the issue before the legislative bodies and the general public to secure funding for such facilities.

Individuals in "total institutions" such as prisons, military units and the like can be subjected to forms of involuntary screening and isolation, with minimal concern for confidentiality, as medical records are frequently accessible to a whole range of authorities—and even to office staff in the institution. While the armed services have the option of promptly separating personnel found to be carriers of AIDS, prisons for obvious reasons cannot find such an easy solution. Prison officials are required under the terms of the Eighth Amendment to protect inmates from infection and to care for those who develop the disease. The social order of the prison entails a considerable amount of coerced homosexual behavior in which weaker inmates are subjected to sexual penetration of a kind that exposes them to high risk for AIDS, and although Federal courts have held that a prisoner has the right to

protection from such abuse, enforcing that right within the context of the informal power system of the prison is exceedingly difficult.

A wider area of the concern is the wish of insurance companies to exclude real and potential AIDS carriers from access to coverage—which in practice means measures aimed at identifying and excluding homosexual men, or demanding higher premiums for policies that cover death from AIDS-related illness. Here traditionally influential insurance companies have crossed swords with gay rights activists in seeking to gain favorable actions from the courts and legislatures.

Immigration and travel are also issues impacted by the AIDS crisis, as one country after another has adopted measures calling for obligatory testing of visitors or of foreign nationals remaining more than a specified time on its territory. Such policies fall within its competence as a sovereign state and could be challenged, if at all, only in its own courts, where the foreigner does not enjoy the rights of a citizen.

The greatest threat to homosexual rights posed by the AIDS crisis has been the new relevance given to clauses in the various charters of human rights that allow any right to be abridged in the interest of "public health and morals." While the latter obstacle was still in vigor as late as the beginning of the 1960s, it was beginning to fade away when the threat of AIDS gave immediacy to the former one. The public health issue has been the perfect pretext for advocates of a traditional religious morality to claim that homosexuals should be denied equal rights because "their sexual activity spreads AIDS." This is, strictly speaking, true only of male homosexuals, not of lesbians, who are virtually immune to venereal disease because of the obvious anatomical differences in their mode of sexual union, but the ignorant and fearful have extended the discrimination to them as well. So AIDS has spawned a new handicap, in current practice if not in ultimate accomplishment, for those advocating full legal equality for homosexual men and women in contemporary society.

Conclusions. In keeping with the European origin of the defining traits of American civilization, the legal problems facing homosexuals emanate from the sodomy legislation of late medieval and Renaissance Europe. Yet the range of topics covered in this article points to a second important determinant: in a context suffused with age-old popular prejudice, the excision of these laws does not in and of itself resolve all difficulties. Permanent change can be achieved only through manifold and patient efforts toward legal reform combined with the spread of more accurate knowledge of human sexuality. Nonetheless, citizens of the United States are fortunate to enjoy not only the common law traditions of individual liberty, but also such distinctively American possessions as the Bill of Rights and the principle of judicial review. These resources offer protections and opportunities lacking—it scarcely needs remarking—not only in Third World and Communist countries, but even in Britain itself. The struggle for gay rights legitimately belongs to the ongoing effort to realize the inherent promise of American democracy.

BIBLIOGRAPHY. Roberta Achtenberg, ed., *Sexual Orientation and the Law*, New York: Clark Boardman, 1985; Hayden Curry and Denis Clifford, *A Legal Guide for Lesbian & Gay Couples*, Reading, MA: Addison-Wesley, 1980; Harlon L. Dalton, Scott Burris, and the Yale AIDS Law Project, *AIDS and the Law: A Guide for the Public*, New Haven: Yale University Press, 1987; Richard D. Mohr, *Gays/Justice: A Study of Ethics, Society, and Law*, New York: Columbia University Press, 1988; Thomas B. Stoddard, E. Carrington Boggan, et al., *The Rights of Gay People*, revised ed., New York: Bantam Books, 1983.

Warren Johansson

LAWRENCE, DAVID HERBERT (1885–1930)

English novelist, poet, critic, and painter. Born in a mining area of Nottinghamshire, Lawrence derived much of the problematic of his work from the tension between his coalminer father, representing for him the physical and the elemental, and his mother, a former schoolteacher, who stood for the world of higher culture, politeness, and civilization. Having attended a two-year teacher training course in Nottingham (his only higher education), Lawrence wrote two early novels, *The White Peacock* (1911) and *The Trespasser* (1912), while teaching at Croydon. In 1912 he eloped with the German-born Frieda von Richthofen Weekley, and the two led a bohemian life of wandering on the continent until the outbreak of World War I. During this period he wrote and published his first masterpiece, *Sons and Lovers* (1913), an intensely autobiographical novel.

The war years were ones of exceptional strain for the Lawrences, whose patriotism was challenged. In 1914 he published a short story entitled "The Prussian Officer," which dwells on the sado-masochistic potential of a relationship between an older male and his subordinate in the context of a mood that blamed "Prussian militarism" for the conflict. During this period the novelist interacted with the **Bloomsbury** circle, and found the sexual nonconformity of the group disturbing. Nonetheless, Lawrence became acquainted with the draft of E. M. **Forster's** homosexual novel *Maurice* (written in 1913, but not published until 1971), and on it he later modeled his own heterosexual novel of erotic frankness, *Lady Chatterley's Lover* (1928), which for a considerable time was available to the general public only in an expurgated version. Lawrence had been earlier influenced by the homosexual theorist Edward **Carpenter**, and by Walt **Whitman**, one of Carpenter's major sources.

Women in Love (1921) has, despite the title, an extraordinary emphasis on the male love affair (though it is non-genitally expressed) between the wealthy Gerald Crich and the schoolteacher Rupert Birkin. These aspects were further explored in the "Prologue" to the book, which Lawrence withheld from publication. The theme of male bonding is treated in a less satisfactory political context in *Kangaroo* (1923), which is set mainly in Australia.

Throughout Lawrence's later wanderings in Italy, Mexico, and New Mexico he struggled to achieve what he regarded as a proper balance in his relation with Frieda. The sexual theories presented in his prose writings reveal the impress of Sigmund **Freud**, though mingled with remnants of Victorian prudery. As late as 1929 he asserted that "masturbation is the deepest and most dangerous cancer of our civilization." In his paintings, however, he strove to capture images of "phallic consciousness." Having lived a life that was consistent in its intense productivity, Lawrence died of tuberculosis at the age of 44.

After World War II the eloquent advocacy of the critic F. R. Leavis brought the reputation of D. H. Lawrence to its zenith. A number of his works were filmed in a richly colored style that created the image of Edwardian opulence for the later twentieth century. Some have noted that the admiration for the primitive and irrational in Lawrence's work sometimes borders on fascism, and that he seems in some respects to have been an intellectual who turned on the intellect itself because of his failure of self-acceptance and integration. Although Leavis and others have hailed him as a model of sexual sanity, his inability to come to terms with the strong homosexual component in his essentially bisexual makeup renders his example problematic.

BIBLIOGRAPHY. Paul Delany, *D. H. Lawrence's Nightmare: The Writer and His Circle in the Years of the Great War*, New York: Basic Books, 1978.

Wayne R. Dynes

LAWRENCE, THOMAS EDWARD (1888–1935)

British soldier and writer. His friends remembered his boyish looks, impish sense of humor, and many-sided geniality. He was famous for his legendary military activities in the Middle East during World War I, which earned him the sobriquet "Lawrence of Arabia," and for his account of those activities in *Seven Pillars of Wisdom: A Triumph*.

Lawrence was born in Tremadoc (Wales) and educated at Oxford. After he finished his history study, he worked as an archaeologist in Carchemish (Syria) until war broke out. He then served as an intelligence officer, first in Cairo and later with the Arab army, which was allied with the British against the Turkish overlord. His strategic insight and his inspiring example helped make the Arab revolt a success. While serving colonial interests, he tried to help the Arabs politically at the Peace Conference of Versailles (1919) and worked as an advisor to the Colonial Secretary (1921–22). In the meantime he had become a folk hero as "the Uncrowned King of Arabia," an ascription he in part liked, but mostly hated because he felt unworthy of it.

Lawrence's torture and **rape** by the Turks in Dar'a (Syria) in November, 1917, when he was imprisoned for a short time, was an intense personal humiliation, even more traumatic because it made him aware of hidden desires within himself. The writing of the epic confession *Seven Pillars* (1919–22) made it absolutely clear to him that it had not been "a triumph" at all. His integrity had been "irrevocably lost" personally and politically, for which he could only feel indescribable shame and guilt. In this and other respects, Lawrence demonstrated reactions now known to be typical of male rape trauma syndrome. His boyish romantic idealism ("a man on his tip-toes trying very hard to fly") yielded to a fatalistic and even nihilistic realism ("men on their very flat feet stumbling over a ticky and noisome earth"). Unclean like the leper, he felt forgiveness was impossible, which made him foreswear decent living. Afraid of himself, of his obstinate will, he chose the path of degradation and the shackling of his soul, looking for security in submission. He went into the armed forces (1923–35) as a kind of mental suicide, in the hope of becoming an ordinary man. Colonel Lawrence enlisted as a private in the Royal Air Force as John Hume Ross and later as T. E. Shaw. But publicity followed him, which led to reclusive intervals, transfers, and a two-year stay in the Tank Corps. Unfortunately he could not escape himself: he remained "a unicorn strayed amongst sheep." Aimless and failing to find rest, because he could not reach the ideal standard which was an absolute in his life, he was killed in a motorcycle accident just two months after he left the RAF.

Lawrence's life can be seen as a continuous battle between mind and body. Thanks to puritan upbringing by his dominating mother, sexuality became associated with guilt and sin, humiliation and pain, and with a loss of integrity. Everything bodily had to be suppressed, a belief that led him to **asceticism**. His obsessive self-control was shattered in pain and fear when he was tortured and raped by the Turks, and led to a loss of his "citadel of integrity" and his "crown of manhood." The desire he felt at that time was like an inner demon which had betrayed him, and this made penance necessary. Chastisement by young men was the humiliating punishment he inflicted on himself, but this was probably also the only way to release his sexuality without loss of integrity, because pain neutralized the enjoyment and purified the soul ("only our pain is never masquerade"). Distrust and fear of himself and others made real intimacy almost impossible.

Instead there were many male friendships. Men were less emotional and possessive than women, and therefore more trustworthy and facile as company, and also their bodies appealed more to his sense of beauty. He idealized Middle Eastern intimate friendships between men, which in his eyes showed perfect love because they were spiritual relations above all, even if sexuality entered: "friends quivering together in the yielding sand with intimate hot limbs in supreme embrace, found there hidden in the darkness a sensual co-efficient of the mental passion which was souls and spirit in one flaming effort." The only time he came close to a friendship like this was with Dahum (1896–1918), an Arab boy he met at Carchemish, with whom he had a very intimate, but probably nonsexual, relationship for three years. But Dahum died of typhus at the end of the war, just before Lawrence had a chance to see him again, "and now not anywhere will I find rest and peace." After the rape at Dar'a it became even more difficult to open himself for another, and, like many others in the army, he spent life "in the enforced celibacy of their blanket's harsh embrace."

BIBLIOGRAPHY. Malcolm Brown, ed., *T. E. Lawrence: The Selected Letters*, New York: W. W. Norton, 1989; H. Montgomery Hyde, *Solitary in the Ranks: Lawrence of Arabia as Airman and Private Soldier*, New York: Atheneum, 1978; John E. Mack, *A Prince of Our Disorder: The Life of T. E. Lawrence*, London: Weidenfeld & Nicolson, 1977; Jeffrey Meyers, *T. E. Lawrence: A Bibliography*, New York: Garland, 1974; idem, *The Wounded Spirit: A Study of the Seven Pillars of Wisdom*, London: Martin Brian & O'Keeffe, 1973; Thomas J. O'Donnell, *The Confessions of T. E. Lawrence: The Romantic Hero's Presentation of Self*, Athens: Ohio University Press, 1979.

Maarten Schild

LEADBEATER, CHARLES WEBSTER (1854–1934)

English clergyman and occultist. Although in later life he liked to romanticize his early circumstances, Leadbeater was born to ordinary lower-middle-class parents in Stockport. Unable to attend university, he nonetheless obtained orders in the Church of England through a family connection. He then became curate of a village church, attending to the usual everyday round of parish duties. Chafing under the limitations of his appointment, he turned for stimulation to the High **Anglican** tradition (which appealed through its colorful liturgy and vestments) and to the then fashionable enthusiasm for spiritualism and the occult. He also showed an interest in several parish boys, instructing them in spiritualist practices.

In 1883 Leadbeater took the decisive step of joining the London lodge of the Theosophical Society, in whose ranks he rose rapidly. The following year Helena Petrovna Blavatsky, who had founded the society in 1875, invited him to travel with her to India, necessitating his resignation from his parish post. During the voyage, the imperious Blavatsky found the shy excurate an apt pupil, and she awakened interests in him that were the foundation for his later claims of clairvoyance, spirit communication with the "Masters," knowledge of past lives of himself and others, and even the ability to see the inner structure of atoms.

For the following few years, he toiled at the hard work of gaining converts to Theosophy in Sri Lanka and south India. After Blavatsky's death in 1891, Leadbeater linked up with her heir, Annie Besant, one of the most powerful personalities of the later Victorian age, and the two formed a durable, though Platonic partnership. Besant's eloquence and resourcefulness were several times severely tested when she found herself called upon to extricate her associate from scrapes resulting from his adventures in teaching sexual magic to boy pupils. The most notable incident of this kind was Leadbeater's 1909 proclamation that an attractive Brahmin boy, Krishnamurti, was destined to become the future Maitreya (world savior). But the boy's father, who failed to appreciate this great honor, sued to get his son back and a major court battle followed.

In the meantime Leadbeater, always a prolific writer, had composed a series of popular books explaining the principles of Theosophy to lay people. Perhaps the most influential of these was *Thought-Forms* (1901; written in collaboration with Besant). This little book was illustrated with colored diagrams of auras and "thought-forms," many of which are in fact abstract paintings executed by assistants following Leadbeater's instructions. The images had a catalytic effect on such artists as Vasily Kandinsky and Piet Mondrian, so that Leadbeater may justly be regarded as the godfather of abstract art.

By the outbreak of World War I a senior Theosophist, but ever restless, Leadbeater spent most of his later life in Australia, where he turned first to Freemasonry and then, surprisingly, back to Christianity. In Sydney in 1916 he founded the Liberal Catholic Church, an institution that claimed apostolic succession through consecration from an associate who had in turn obtained his orders from an Old Catholic bishop. What engaged Leadbeater in this enterprise was not so much its theology, but the chance to work out elaborate rituals and to design rich vestments. Ever loyal, Besant gave her blessing, and Bishop Leadbeater now had a little religious kingdom all his own.

Claiming that his weak heart required constant monitoring, he insisted on having a boy with him at all times, even in the bath, so that a signal for help could be given. Increasingly reclusive in his later years, the Bishop gained a reputation among the residents of Sydney as the "swish bish." Although the Liberal Catholic Church subsequently acquired more conventional leadership and atmosphere, the original foundation has a claim to the honor of the first gay church.

Leadbeater's religious odyssey was marked by many unexpected twists and, some would say, a strong admixture of charlatanism. Unbeknownst to himself, however, he constitutes a link in a chain that leads back to the tribal **berdache** and **shaman** figures, and forward to the involvement of gay men and lesbians in "new age" religion with its interest in channeling, new rituals, and discovery of special powers. More broadly, Leadbeater's popularization of such ideas as auras, vibrations, and reincarnation played a significant role in the Aquarian revival of the occult that began in the 1960s.

BIBLIOGRAPHY. Gregory Tillett, *The Elder Brother: A Biography of Charles Webster Leadbeater*, London: Routledge & Kegan Paul, 1982.

Wayne R. Dynes

LEAR, EDWARD (1812–1888)

English painter, humorist, and travel writer. A delicate child, Lear was raised by his older sisters who tended to inculcate in him feminine rather than masculine pursuits and hobbies. At the age of five or six he had his first attack of epilepsy—the "Demon" as he called it—an affliction which was then little understood and not yet controllable by drugs. This ever-present problem, which he never avowed even to his closest friends, caused him to be cautious and reclusive in his relations with others.

In his teens Lear found employment as an ornithological illustrator; his achievements in this field are still admired today. In 1837, however, he went to live in Rome, where he supported himself by painting landscapes and giving drawing lessons to members of the English colony. In Rome he began a series of close friendships with fellow artists and visiting aristocrats. In 1846 Lear published his first *Book of Nonsense*, under the pseudonym of Derry Down Derry. In 1848 he began two decades of travel in Greece, Palestine, and Egypt, settling finally in San Remo, Italy (1870). He tried unsuccessfully to persuade a teenager, Hubert Congreve, to come and live with him in his villa in the Italian resort. In his last years Lear became almost a total recluse, his society consisting of his manservant and his beloved cat Foss.

Although Lear's paintings have recently gained renewed appreciation, it is for his nonsense limericks and songs that he is best remembered. Recoiling from the earnest atmosphere of evangelical Christianity in which he had been raised, Lear sought to puncture its pretensions with gentle spoofery. The nonsense also served to create a kind of utopian retreat, which was important for a man who felt that he must conceal both his epilepsy and his homosexuality.

Lear never married—and his one effort to do so was managed in such a way as to guarantee failure. He cherished passionate friendships with men, but his ardor was seldom returned with the intensity that he wished. Upon his death, one of his closest friends, his literary executor Franklin Lushington, destroyed many of his papers, apparently because they contained compromising material. Awkward, asthmatic, and retiring, Lear was aware of his social deficits. "Some think him ill-tempered and queer," he wrote of himself. Although he did not mean the last adjective in its current sense, its full range probably applies to him. Out of the depths of his afflictions, however, Lear was able to generate the writings that have made him immortal.

BIBLIOGRAPHY. Susan Chitty, *That Singular Person Called Lear*, London: Weidenfeld and Nicolson, 1988; Vivien Noakes, *Edward Lear, 1812–1888*, London: Royal Academy of Arts, 1985.

Wayne R. Dynes

LEE, VERNON (1856–1935)

Pen name of Violet Paget, short story writer and essayist dealing with aesthetics, art history, and travel. Long neglected, her work is being revived in the 1980s, with reprints of her greatest short stories anticipated in the near future.

Lee was a child prodigy with a good background in European languages.

As a child in Italy she was a close friend of John Singer Sargent, and throughout her life she continued to have significant encounters with prominent figures of her day. Not a great success at keeping friends, Lee was shunned by members of the British aesthetic movement after the publication of her novel, the satirical and feminist *Miss Brown* (1884). Later she had a major falling out with Henry **James**, who felt he was satirized in her story "Lady Tal." Bernard Berenson discussed aesthetics with her in **Florence**, but this also led to a major misunderstanding. A friend and follower of Walter **Pater**, she wrote stories that combined decadent themes, aestheticism, and a concern for morality in a striking blend, enriched by an excellent sense of style. A pacifist during World War I, she took an unpopular stand that lost her readers in her last two decades.

Lee's voluminous papers have become available to scholars in recent years. One can now read her letters to her companion (1887–98), Kit Anstruther-Thomson. As Lee had not made her private life public, investigation of her papers may aid scholars trying to relate aesthetic formalism, decadence, and homosexuality in the 1880–1914 period.

Lee's best work is found in her approximately two dozen short stories, some of which are collected in *Hauntings* (1890), *Vanitas* (1892), *Pope Jacynth* (1904), and *For Maurice* (1927). Her truly remarkable fantastic tales include "Prince Alberic and the Snake Lady," "The Virgin of the Seven Daggers," "Dionea," "Amour Dure," "A Wicked Voice," and "Oke of Okehurst."

BIBLIOGRAPHY. Vineta Colby, *The Singular Anomaly*, New York: New York University Press, 1970; Peter Gunn, *Vernon Lee: Violet Paget, 1856–1935*, London: Oxford University Press, 1964; Phyllis Mannocchi, "Vernon Lee and Kit Anstruther-Thomson: A Study of Love and Collaboration between Romantic Friends," *Women's Studies* 12 (1986), 129–48.

Peter G. Christensen

LEFT, GAY

It is widely believed that there is a special affinity between the political left and homosexuality, more particularly between the left and the organized gay **movement.** Gay leftists have promoted the notion that capitalism has been especially homophobic, so that gay people as one of many oppressed strata of the population can only benefit from its overthrow. Yet this hope for improvement through revolution is belied by the status of homosexuals in Communist countries, which is generally worse than in the West; the gay communities there are denied the right to have organizations and periodicals of their own, even under the strict control of the Party. Moreover, **homophobia** is scarcely a special creation of capitalism but goes back to the first millennium B.C.—to the slave-holding societies of Near Eastern antiquity. And paradoxically enough, the militant atheism and the blanket condemnation of feudalism in Communist ideology did not lead to what might appear a logical conclusion: that the sanctions against homosexual behavior are the anachronistic legacy of the role of the church as arbiter of morality under the Old Regime, and as such should be repudiated by the new. Be this as it may, in day-to-day experience the gay/left affinity has been underlined by the high visibility of left-based gays and lesbians in the movement—actual numbers are fairly small—and by some undeniable theoretical contributions, especially from Marxism.

Main Trends. The roots of the modern left lie in the eighteenth century: in the anthropocentric materialism of **Enlightenment** thought and in the radical practice of the French Revolution. From the Enlightenment, the "party of humanity," the left inherited a commitment to fight oppression and injustice wherever they may appear. Moreover, concern with human happiness must be universal rather than directed to one nation or segment of society. That these ideals have, as often as not, been honored more in the breach than in the observance, does not make them less worthy of respect. The Revolution that began in 1789 remains the archetype of the massive transformation that many leftists assume is the only remedy for society's ills. It was the French Revolution that abolished France's sodomy laws in 1791. Yet the full range of leftist thought does not emerge until the nineteenth century, when three strands may be discerned.

The first strand is the **utopian**, which looked to the creation of new communities in which social harmony and cooperation would replace competition as the motor of human association. The Scottish philanthropist Robert Owen (1771–1858) attempted to set up model communities, but his principal legacy is the cooperative movement. The eccentric Charles Fourier (1772–1837), who also designed model communities, was one of the few thinkers of this formative period to emphasize sex. Indeed, his utopian phalansteries were to provide for homosexual as well as heterosexual relations. The chief bequest of the utopian trend to today's gay movement is the commune, though this also absorbed elements of the ecology and "New Age" spirituality movement.

The second strand is **anarchism**, which has several aspects. There was the individualist anarchism of Max Stirner (1805–1856), which was later promoted by the boy-love thinker John Henry **Mackay** (1864–1933). The Russian Mikhail Bakunin (1814–1876) advocated violent overthrow of the state, and became a principal competitor of Marx, while his fellow Russian Peter Kropotkin (1842–1921) emphasized cooperation and mutual aid. Probably the chief legacy of anarchism to the modern gay movement lies in the gay participation in the **libertarian** movement.

The final strand is socialism proper, which may in turn be divided into **Marxism** and **Social Democracy**. Marx and Engels rarely gave much sustained thought to sexuality, a matter which they seem to have regarded as distinctly subordinate to the question of the relations of production, the economic base that for them represents the grounding of all other sociocultural phenomena. Their occasional pronouncements on same-sex love are homophobic, and in any event only in the twentieth century did an organized sexual reform movement emerge, some of whose theoreticians sought to create syntheses of Marxism and feminism, Marxism and gay liberation. The Social Democratic trend owes much to the English tradition of gradual and measured change. An outstanding figure in this tradition is Edward **Carpenter** (1844–1929), who created a kind of gay commune at his farm in Milthorpe. His writings drew upon a number of sources, including Walt **Whitman** and **Indian** thought. They were widely read not only in the English-speaking world, but also in translation on the European continent. In Germany Social Democracy gained a strong footing in the Reichstag (Parliament), and its leaders, beginning with August Bebel (1840–1913), threw their support behind the campaign for homosexual law reform. Although they were not successful at that time, it is significant that most of the reforms of the sodomy laws in Western Europe since 1930 have been achieved under Social Democratic regimes.

Toward the Present. The acute crisis signaled by the world depression of the 1930s caused many to seek solutions either in socialism or in Soviet-style communism. Because of pressing material problems, as well as actual persecution in the Nazi **holocaust**, the thirties were a period of occultation of the gay movement. When the American homosexual rights **movement** emerged in Southern California in 1950, a number of its founders had Communist party backgrounds. The rise of **McCarthyism** forced this trend underground, and leftist affiliations in the gay movement were to surface later in a very different guise, under the aegis of the counterculture and the New Left. Some theorists saw the gay movement as forming part of a "rainbow alliance" of oppressed groups, especially women and peoples of color. In leftist politics, however, the gay movement did not receive a uniformly cordial welcome. The factions oriented toward Moscow, Peking, and Havana all rejected gay liberation just as the parties to which they looked for guidance had in their own countries maintained or even intensified the traditional sanctions against homosexuality. In Western countries much leftist activity amounted to little more than "statementism," the issuing of ringing manifestoes and the passing of whole laundry lists of demands. When this rhetoric failed to lead to action, as was usually the case, adherents began to wonder whether those issuing the statements really wished to achieve meaningful change.

As hopes for revolution—or even radical incremental change—faded in the 1970s, most politically oriented gay men and lesbians sought to "work within the system." In the United States this meant participation not only in the Democratic party, with its traditional though sometimes problematic policy of welcoming minorities, but also in the Republican party. The excitement of the New Left phase of gay politics had obscured a fundamental fact: the political affiliations of gay men and lesbians, distributed as they are all across the socio-economic spectrum, generally mirror those of the society at large. Also, in practice the candidate who stands too far to the left—who embraces both economic and social radicalism—is likely to find himself cut off from any major constituency, while the centrist in economic matters can more easily embrace such a cause as gay rights in sections of the country where much of the population is conservative in religion or simply clings to the traditional prejudices. The need of any aspiring movement in the United States to win over the center in order to gain majorities at the polls precludes a political strategy grounded solely in the patronage of the left.

These problems were underscored by experiences in Britain in the 1980s, where sectors of the Labour Party were tarred in the media as the "loony left," in large measure because of their principled support for gay rights. Unfortunately this Labourite support has involved denunciations of "heterosexism," and such critiques are easily misconstrued as put-downs of heterosexual persons. Not surprisingly, the situation has been opportunistically exploited both by those against the left and those (some of them within the left itself) opposed to homosexual rights.

In all likelihood the best strategy for homosexuals and lesbians in any pluralistic society is to function as an interest group, contracting alliances according to a realistic assessment of advantages, and disclaiming any permanent attachment to any one political grouping.

Wayne R. Dynes

LEGAL PROCEDURE

Over the years lawyers in the American system of justice have come to recognize that it is best to observe certain procedures in serving gay and lesbian clients. At the outset of a prosecution for sodomy or some other homosexual offense, bailment or release on one's own recognizance should be sought to avoid persecution and rape in jail. If no dismissal is obtained, no demurrer filed, and no continuance requested, the defendant or his attorney must enter a plea at the arraignment. A plea of guilty or *nolo contendere* (no contest) ends the process that a plea of innocence would continue to a trial. Often the judge indicates his intended sentence and the prosecutor his recommendation before the plea so that the defendant and his counsel may determine the consequences of the plea. Also the sealing of the arrest records, changing an arrest to a detention, or the expungement of the judgment might be negotiated in advance. The attorney tries to shop for a favorable forum though continuances and waiving rights for a speedy trial, to pick a judge known for clemency, and to select by challenges a sympathetic jury. The defendant's excellent character, community contributions, and good prior record should be emphasized to combat homophobia, prejudice, and biases. To secure a plea bargain the defendant must waive, often in writing, his constitutional rights and protections, including a speedy public trial with counsel before a judge or jury, the right to remain silent without self-incrimination, to confront, cross-examine, and subpoena witnesses, among others. Popular amended pleas bargained for include misdemeanors or mere infractions such as disorderly conduct, disturbing the peace, and trespassing.

The differences in the maze of U.S. jurisdictions, municipal as well as state, render all precedents problematic and emphasize the need for experienced and erudite counsel. Often convictions under municipal ordinances do not appear on the criminal record of the defendant, such as a small fine satisfying a prosecutor of public nudity, remaining in a public place after closing time, and the like. Continuance for six months or some other period of time in contemplation of dismissal in view of good conduct is more common in eastern than in western states. Some prosecutors allow "office hearings" instead of court appearances. Diversion from the courts to therapy or rehabilitation programs such as Alcoholics Anonymous is often allowed. Prior convictions and probation violations, demonstrable only by a preponderance of evidence, render alternative processes more difficult. Paroles stipulating that the defendant stay out of public restrooms or avoid social contact with homosexuals may, however, be overturned as too sweeping.

Reviewing the police report, interviewing witnesses, visiting the scene of the crime, assessing the facts about location and action to demonstrate the impos-

sibility of particular allegations, and enticement and entrapment with the vice squad member's entreaties often result in a winning defense. For a gay client, however, it is often difficult to prove lack of predisposition. A discovery motion or its alternative the subpoena *duces tecum* seeks to obtain evidence and knowledge in the possession of the prosecutor or his witnesses, such as previous abuse and brutality by the vice squad member or other evidence of his prejudice to discredit his testimony or to indicate discriminatory enforcement. Codes and freedom of information acts aid in gaining such defenses. Destruction of evidence may allow dismissal.

Change of venue, refusal of a certain prosecutorial office or a bill of particulars alleging the ambiguity of a statute, suppression of illegally obtained evidence, a forced confession, or improper identification in a lineup, double jeopardy, disqualification of a particular prosecutor or judge are among the many legitimate ploys. Current normal practices within the jurisdiction, old common law remedies, and creative arguments all justify such motions. Independent witnesses such as psychiatrists and sociologists, independent investigators, and visual aids help the court understand the homosexual's situation.

Waiving the right to trial by jury gives away the possibilities of a hung jury, the defense attorney's plea to the jury, and the judge's misinstructing the jury. In the *voir dire* process an attorney can not only challenge prospective jurors "for cause" but educate the ones selected about law and justice, and at times even suggest that favorable ones stick to their guns and not go along with majority pressure in the hope of getting a hung jury. Judges, however, are at times less biased and more acute than juries, and waiving of them saves time and money. All these items must be considered in response. Motions *in limine* limit in advance the nature and extent of questions that may be put to certain witnesses, thus diminishing the need for objections, for example, about the sexual orientation or preference of the defendant, his prior offenses, and prior complaints about him.

Instruction to the jury should include reasonable doubt, presumption of innocence, burden of proof, specific intent, and credibility of witnesses. The judge's refusal to instruct properly per request of the defense constitutes an irreversible error and hence allows an appeal. An effective summation in the closing argument weaving together the case by use of notes taken throughout the trial to prove the theory of the defense and rebutting the prosecution often wins acquittal.

After the trial many jurisdictions require the defense attorney to have the court correct any error in a pre-sentencing or pre-judgment motion, while failure to do so may result in the waiving of the alleged error and thus the loss of an opportunity to appeal. Evidence in support of a plea for a mild sentence should be proffered. Probation officers, usually overworked, should be won over to recommend clemency, especially in view of the overcrowded jails and their negative effects on inmates. Alternate sentencing should be sought, such as work furloughs, weekend incarceration, and community service. Obligation to register as a sex offender should be resisted.

See also **Law, United States.**

BIBLIOGRAPHY. Roberta Achtenberg, ed., *Sexual Orientation and the Law,* New York: Clark Boardman, 1985.

William A. Percy

Leonardo da Vinci (1452–1519)

Italian painter, sculptor, architect, scientist, inventor, and thinker. One of a little band of truly universal men of the Renaissance, Leonardo's multiple creativity, in all its vastness and intricacy, still offers a stunning challenge to modern interpreters.

Born in Vinci, the illegitimate son of a Florentine notary, Leonardo was taken away from his mother shortly after birth and given to his paternal grandparents to bring up. He was then apprenticed to the Florentine painter Andrea del Verrocchio, whom he seems to have quickly surpassed—to the point that Verrocchio is said to have given up painting in disgust. In 1476, while he was still living at Verrocchio's house, he had an anonymous accusation of homosexuality lodged against him. He was said to have had, along with three others (one a Medici), active homosexual relations with a seventeen-year-old model. Eventually the prosecution was dropped, but not until after the accused had become frightened. This evidence shows that the young Leonardo was well acquainted with the flourishing "sodomite" **subculture** of quattrocento **Florence.**

In the 1470s his insatiable curiosity led him to investigate the fundamentals of art, as seen in his studies of drapery and oil painting. Such early works as the *Madonna* in Munich and the portrait of *Ginevra de' Benci* in Washington astonished contemporaries with their naturalism.

The year 1493 found Leonardo in Milan, where he did a portrait of the mistress of duke Lodovico il Moro. He then did the two versions of *Virgin of the Rocks,* showing his remarkable mastery of detail. In the field of sculpture he made studies for a huge equestrian statue of the previous duke, Francesco Sforza, but the group was never executed. His major work in Milan is the celebrated *Last Supper* mural in Santa Maria delle Grazie, which sums up more than a century of efforts by Italian artists to come to terms with this complex problem in composition, psychology, and iconography. Unfortunately Leonardo executed the work in an experimental fresco technique and, despite the efforts of generations of restorers, today the mural is only a ruin, though an exceedingly eloquent one. His work in Milan inspired a host of imitators, including the gifted **Sodoma.**

After the French invasion of Milan in 1499 Leonardo returned to Florence, where he found employment as a military engineer for Cesare Borgia. He also took great interest in dissection and anatomy, attending (among other things) to the mechanisms of coitus and reproduction. His major fresco project of this period, a state commission to commemorate a victory which pitted him against the young **Michelangelo**, was never completed—again because he insisted on using an experimental medium that could not be continued beyond the central group (1503–05). He also grappled with the compositional problem of the Madonna and Child with Saint Anne, which resulted in several works, notably the cartoon in the National Gallery in London. One of his few finished works of this period is his portrait, known as the *Mona Lisa*, now in the Louvre in Paris, which owes its enduring fascination in large measure to Leonardo's mastery of the *sfumato* technique, permitting him to envelop sitter and background in an air of impenetrable mystery.

In 1507 Leonardo entered the service of the French king Louis XII—at first in Milan and in Rome, and then in France itself. He spent much of this last period of his life in scientific pursuits and architectural designs, liberally supported by the French court. He also revised and extended his voluminous writings—8,000 manuscript pages have survived—including a treatise on painting, which was only published in 1651. His last work was the androgynous *St. John* now in the Louvre. Venerated by everyone who knew him, he died at Cloux near Amboise in a chateau bestowed by the king.

Over the centuries Leonardo's genius has attracted a variety of interpreters. In a controversial study of 1910 Sigmund **Freud** tried to throw light on the artist's homosexuality through a recollection of childhood in which Leonardo imagined his mouth assaulted by the wings of the bird. Misled by an error of translation, Freud believed the bird to have been a vulture, rather than the kite (*nibbio*) of Leonardo's description. This and other errors vitiate Freud's essay, and his failure has discouraged others from venturing much further. Although Leonardo was devoted to a scamp-like assistant, Salai, and later to a young aristocrat, Francesco Melzi, whom he adopted, not much is known about his emotional life. His practice of making his notes in a mirror writing that casual snoopers could not read shows that his instinct for concealment was well developed. In an age in which artists—and many others—were relatively forthright about their sexual tastes, Leonardo felt an instinctive need to guard his privacy. Grounded in his illegitimacy, as it surely is, this reclusiveness has other wellsprings that cannot now be gauged. In this realm, as in others, Leonardo transcended his own age, producing endless food for thought and study on the part of each generation of scholars. In addition, Leonardo has captured the attention and affection of the general public, which he is surely destined to keep through all subsequent shifts of the whirligig of fashion.

BIBLIOGRAPHY. Serge Bramly, *Léonard de Vinci*, Paris: Editions Jean-Claude Lattes, 1988; Carlo Pedretti, *Leonardo da Vinci: A Study in Chronology and Style*, Berkeley: University of California Press, 1973.

Wayne R. Dynes

LESBIAN SEPARATISM
See **Separatism, Lesbian.**

LESBIANISM
What is lesbianism: a predetermined state, a preference, affectional and/or sexual in nature, a political choice? Moreover, is it an aberration, a playing out of male/female roles by men-hating women, an adolescent or immature phase?

Serious research in the field of lesbian behavior is relatively recent and remains uneven in coverage. Nonetheless, studies in the **United States** have yielded a relatively comprehensive description. For this reason, the present article limits itself to that country. Future research, it is hoped, will provide data affording a more global perspective on lesbianism.

Varying Definitions. At various points in the development of thought on this topic, experts, advocates and opponents alike have used some of the above descriptions. For some, lesbianism remains a state of awareness of self experienced at an early age: one realizes a difference, an attraction to women. Proponents of this view say that they always knew that they were lesbians. For them, there was no choice: they were lesbians and they had to follow their inclination.

For others, lesbianism is a political choice, a conscious rejection of the patriarchy, of traditional roles for women, of limitations placed on women's control of their own lives. It is a conscious embrace by women of women as their primary emotional, erotic, and spiritual attachments. For these lesbians, their involvement with women may have begun at a later age, stemming from a feminist consciousness, or it may have, in fact, started much earlier and been reinforced through activity in the women's movement.

Regardless of the definition of "born lesbian" or "political lesbian," lesbianism has both emotional and sexual components. There are those who would attribute these characteristics according to gender roles within a lesbian couple. If the lesbian couple mimics heterosexual couples, the reasoning goes, one woman must be "fem" or more emotional/feminine in nature, and the other "butch" or more sexual/masculine in nature. Research has shown that less than twenty percent of lesbians engage in role playing of this kind.

Those who adhere to the belief that homosexuality is an "arrested stage of development" are greatly influenced by **Freud** and Victorian mores. Because of this background, homosexuality was classified as a mental illness until 1973, when psy-chiatrists and other mental health professionals supported by the work of lesbian and gay **activists** fought to have homosexuality (as an illness) removed from the *Diagnostic and Statistical Manual of Mental Disorders* (DSM). Etiological studies had shown that experts could not prove what made the homosexual different and that, therefore, he/she had no scientifically diagnosable sickness or deviance.

Detractors will always find an authority to validate the claim that lesbianism is an aberration. Some religious leaders and biblical scholars have found "proof" for the condemnation of homosexuality. Just as many scholars have retranslated and reinterpreted the same quotations to show that it was the acts (hetero- and/or homosexual) of adultery, jealousy, inhospitality, and so forth, that were being condemned and not homosexuals. Likewise, **sodomy** remains a crime in many American states.

Lesbian History. Why has there been such a great effort to define lesbianism as a crime or a sickness? And why is there an effort to trivialize it as only a sexual liaison or, in fact, to blot out its mention totally? Given the paucity of material available on lesbianism, is lesbianism just a product of twentieth-century America, surfacing more rampantly since the 1960s and in certain **bohemian** urban centers?

There has been an almost total obliteration of the lesbian in history. Those who study Greek civilization and culture learn about **Sappho** and the women on the isle of Lesbos. Yet few strong women, independent of men, and attached to other women, stand out in our historical texts. When such a figure does appear, she is never identified as a lesbian. This "conspiracy of silence" has kept role models and the potential threat to patriarchy under control. Only when intimate friendship between women was combined with women's growing financial independence toward the beginning of the twentieth century was this age-old bonding condemned. What mention remains is that of a stereotypical, lonely, lewd, man-like woman who frequents seedy bars and seeks to seduce nubile girls.

The **Kinsey** Report on female sexuality (1953) helped somewhat to dispel this notion. No longer was the homosexual so foreign and remote from the heterosexual. The report found that the sexuality of those sampled lay on a continuum ranging from completely heterosexual through somewhat homosexual to completely homosexual. Accordingly, ten percent of the population could be assumed to be essentially homosexual, with a possibility of a considerably higher proportion of the population having engaged in homosexual behavior at one point or another.

Despite this beginning "normalization" of homosexuality, some lesbian theorists still referred to "pre-1950s" and "post-1950s" lesbians. Those of the earlier period are classified as less political, lacking role models, and committed to role playing. One dressed "butch" or "fem" and frequented bars which tolerated homosexuals. Socializing took place in private clubs or among friends, homosexual men and lesbian women. "Post-1950s" lesbians tended to be more open, politicized, and not involved in role playing. Moreover, as of 1969, a new legitimacy was being claimed by gay men and lesbians. The contemporary struggle for gay rights was begun by gay men at the **Stonewall** bar in New York. Furthermore, feminism supplied the philosophical base to lesbianism.

In light of this absence from history, an effort is being made to write and preserve lesbian history. Lesbian history groups exist; individual lesbians record and exhibit/present their stores of information; archives preserve books, articles and photographs. Lesbians are at work retracing their roots, finding in history a visible reference group.

Lesbian Identity. It is this group of strong, independent women which re-

flects a positive **identity** for the lesbian and the world to see. Where stigma is removed from a minority group, the group becomes a viable functioning part of society. It also represents a real choice as opposed to the illusion of choice which many lesbian theorists claim is inherent in the "heterosexual preference." If there are no positive images of lesbianism, no role models, no mention of homosexuality, then "heterosexual" women do not have to ask themselves if they are lesbians. If there is nothing but a stigmatized stereotype, then heterosexual women do not dare question a preference. This assumption of **heterosexuality**, unless one announces one's lesbianism, is what theorists label "heterosexism." It reinforces the absence of lesbianism and eliminates the need for any choice while leaving the illusion of choice of sexual preference. In essence, heterosexism is the way a patriarchal system has of preserving itself.

It is just this stigma and heterosexism which make it difficult for lesbians to know who they are, to come to a healthy sense of identity. This is what is known as **coming out**, reaching an awareness and an acceptance of self as a lesbian and, as a result, letting others know about this lesbian identity.

Coming out is a lengthy process involving one's inner and outer reality. Some lesbians are merely aware of a feeling of difference at an early age. Some know that it is an attraction to women. Either way, it entails a comparison of oneself to images of lesbians and to known lesbians, along with an attempt at putting together the way one sees oneself with these external images. Most often, the lesbian struggles against the stereotypical view of a lesbian. Frequently, she attempts to hide her feelings and inclinations because she is "not like them." In order to accept oneself as normal, it is necessary to recognize oneself in other lesbians by getting to know the variety of types within the lesbian world. The lesbian may have already entered into sexual relations with another woman during this process, or she may have refrained from actual physical involvement until she felt more comfortable. Total comfort with one's lesbian identity usually comes after involvement in one or more relationships. The ability to totally disclose one's lesbian identity generally signifies that one has fully accepted this identity. Some would say that along with this acceptance comes a generalized sensitization to one's oppression and alienation at the hands of a patriarchal society.

How does the lesbian view herself? Is she first and foremost a lesbian and then an amalgam of different personality traits that constitute her person? Does her difference lie solely in her sexuality or in her spiritual bonding with other women?

It is often difficult for a lesbian to establish a healthy balance between her "lesbian identity" and her "personal identity." As a member of a stigmatized minority group, she needs the security of the community, the reference group, in order not to feel isolated. Yet, among lesbians there is a tendency to internalize stigma, the self-hate and the powerlessness inherent in minority groups and, then, seeing this stigma mirrored in her equals, a tendency to reject them.

The fear of rejection by the group is very strong and creates a conflict for a lesbian. If she is being accepted in the lesbian world exclusively because of her lesbian activity, must she, therefore, subordinate her personal identity to this lesbian identity? Whereas, in the heterosexual world, she will be rejected exclusively because of her lesbian identity. The lesbian must, therefore, constantly assert her personal identity to avoid its being assumed into a group identity. Without this, individuality suffers, and one can become merged with the group.

While maintaining a healthy balance of her personal and her lesbian identity, and thereby, of autonomy and merger with the lesbian community, the lesbian struggles to integrate the various facets of her lesbianism. In her interaction with others, she draws together the affectional and sexual. Her difference from heterosexuals does not lie solely in her sexuality. Nor can one deny her sexuality and see only emotional bonding. Both perspectives have been promulgated by the heterosexual world to trivialize the way the lesbian relates as an integrated person to another woman.

Minorities Among Lesbians. The balance of personal and lesbian identity is all the more complicated for lesbians who are non-white, working class, aging, young, differently-abled ("handicapped"), or rural. Here, the lesbian also belongs to another group where she may have the additional conflict of whether to assert herself first as a black person, for example, and then as a lesbian. Many lesbians of color and Third World lesbians feel they must subordinate their lesbian identity to their racial/ethnic identity. Many non-white groups who view homosexuality as white society's disease see it as a form of genocide of their ethnic/racial group. In many of these groups, then, there exists a greater conservatism which would call for ostracizing the lesbian from the community. Therefore, the lesbian of color may deny her lesbianism to survive in her reference group.

On the other hand, racism reflective of macrosociety pervades some lesbian communities. Here, the lesbian of color does not feel welcome. On the contrary, she may feel forced to remain in her ethnic/racial community and deny her lesbianism. Some have sought to separate themselves into all black, all Asian, and similar lesbian groups. Among those who define themselves as progressives, many hold that the struggle for lesbian rights can only advance the struggle for the rights of blacks, Asians, Latinas, native Americans, and so forth, and vice versa.

The struggle for lesbian youth, aging lesbians, and differently-abled lesbians is similar. These groups also face discrimination at the hands of the heterosexual world and the lesbian community. Aging lesbians may blend in among senior citizens or the differently-abled and then, not be seen as lesbians. Within the lesbian community, they may feel oppressed because of their "difference." A lesbian senior citizen, for example, can be denied access to nursing homes and retirement centers. If she is admitted, the administration will not accept her lover. To avail herself of services for senior citizens, in essence, she will probably be forced to deny her lesbianism or her lover.

Within the lesbian community, aging lesbians are often stereotyped as grandmothers or mothers to younger, more attractive lesbians. Activists attack the existence within the lesbian community of ageist attitudes prevalent in the heterosexual world. Ageism perpetuates the patriarchal attitude that only the young, attractive female is of use to society. Aging lesbians fear being cut off and pushed aside as are aging heterosexual women.

Similarly, lesbian **youth** do not have access to the rights and privileges of older lesbians. More than this, though, they remain on the outside of their heterosexual peer group since very often the "gayness" stands out vividly when youth tends to exaggerate stereotypes. Deprived of role models, many lesbian youth copy the negative images seen in the media. They face ostracism, harassment, and violence because of their difference. On the other hand, older lesbians are often loath to offer support, friendship, and shelter to lesbian youth because of the legalities involved owing to their status as minors.

Lesbian youth face even greater risk if they have run away or have been thrown out by their families. This happens frequently to rural youth. Foster homes and shelters will usually not accept openly lesbian youth. If forced out onto the street, they often turn to prostitution to survive. Here, too, they are subject to violence.

Differently-abled lesbians must, likewise, deal with a double oppression.

They too may feel as if they must "choose their oppression." If they disclose their lesbianism within their differently-abled group, they risk being rejected because of their sexuality. Some able-bodied lesbians do not view differently-abled lesbians as sexual at all, thereby rejecting them. In other communities, an insufficient effort is made to accommodate the differently-abled at functions and centers.

Thus, for the lesbian who is not white, middle class, of average age, the oppression experienced as lesbian women in the heterosexual world is unfortunately also reflected in the lesbian community. When lesbians have been raised in an oppressive society and surrounded by stigma, there remains a residue of this stigma. One must constantly be aware of this internalized stigma and realize that the phenomena of oppression display similar patterns. In this, the lesbian community is beginning to make inroads in speaking out against all forms of oppression: racism, classism, ageism, and able-ism.

Who, then, is this individual lesbian? She is a woman who identifies herself with and as a woman for friendship, spirituality, erotic love. She is a member of a stigmatized minority with no officially accepted rights, no societal validation, no role models, no societally mirrored identity—in brief, with no officially sanctioned existence.

She is a woman of strengths despite her deprivation. Independent by the very nature of her choice to identify with women, she has had to stand up for her rights as an activist, a leader, or as a survivor. Coping with stigma, she has developed the skills to deal with prejudice and oppression and has learned to recognize social control in the multi-oppressive policies surrounding her.

Oppression. Yet what is the actual manifestation of the stigma surrounding the lesbian? Of what is she deprived, and how does it take its toll on her well-being? What is homophobia, and is it only heterosexuals who are homophobic?

Homophobia lies at the root of the harassment, the violence, and the exclusion from the "protection under the law" experienced by lesbians and gay men. It is an exaggerated fear of homosexuality in oneself and in others. Because of this fear of one's potential "conversion" to homosexuality, the heterosexual directs his/her hostility outward onto homosexuals. It is a fear so abject that it would threaten one's belief in the family and in Western capitalism. As a result, atrocities, including murder, have been committed falsely using the name of god, law, and science as justification.

Yet, lesbian theorists have argued that homophobia is better examined as heterosexism. This is the assumption that every woman wants to be attached financially and emotionally to a man. Accordingly, everyone and everything is heterosexual and heterosexuality is a preference. This silencing of lesbianism arises from the fear of woman-bonding and woman's spirituality which, because of their power, pose a threat to man's power. Hence, capitalism must be protected by insuring patriarchal privilege through heterosexism.

The resulting oppression of lesbians (and gay men) begins with their civil rights—rights generally guaranteed to all Americans by the Bill of Rights and reiterated more specifically by the Civil Rights Act of 1964. Yet there is no federal guarantee of rights to homosexuals, and fewer than sixty municipalities have ordinances of protection. Even as "liberal" a state as New York has no "gay rights" bill. Moreover, those gay rights bills which do exist merely prohibit discrimination in housing and employment on the basis of "sexual preference." Other gay rights bills have set up a body to investigate claims of discrimination on the basis of "sexual preference" with no power to prosecute.

With so few structures in place to monitor or guarantee rights, instances of **oppression** run rampant. Lesbians are most at risk in the areas of work, custody, and health. Here, they experience discrimination both as women and as lesbians.

Work. Work for the lesbian is vital for her survival. Depending on self as the sole means of support, she must exercise vigilance concerning her lesbianism. In a traditional domain of male privilege, sexist advances may be one thing. However, a woman may be suspected of being a lesbian for as much, and supervised more stringently and found incompetent. Few companies or corporations have anti-discrimination policies, and if one does not work in a city with a gay rights bill, one has no recourse.

Work, however, plays a double role for a lesbian. The place of employment is also a social arena where it is, perhaps, easier than in other social situations to get to know other women. There is great risk involved here, since the lesbian may lose a potential friend, face harassment and ostracism once she discloses her lesbianism to her colleague. The friend may be heterosexual and fear that the lesbian is trying to seduce her. Then again, the friend may be a lesbian and both must seek a way of discovering the other's sexuality without alienation in case she is not a lesbian.

Certain types of employment are riskier than others. The military is a traditional area where one can be dismissed for homosexuality. Regardless of the type of work, lesbians have been discriminated against widely. Studies indicate that between twenty and twenty-four percent of the lesbians sampled have actually experienced discrimination on the job, and over sixty percent anticipate being fired, not employed, or passed over for promotion if their lesbianism is suspected. As a result, many lesbians experience higher levels of work-related stress. Working under conditions where one fears overzealous scrutiny, suspicion, and ultimately, the loss of one's job, the lesbian may be forced to deny any hint of her lesbianism. Inner conflict and lowered self-esteem often result.

713

In conjunction with work, insurance is also an area of discrimination. No provision is made for a partner in a long-term relationship. Medical benefits, for example, cannot be extended to cover a lover or a child one is co-parenting. Some forward-looking corporations and unions are attempting to have insurance companies extend coverage to "spouse equivalents."

Custody. Another area where lesbians face almost total discrimination is child custody. The lesbian is virtually placed on trial for being an unfit woman and for challenging her ex-husband's custodial rights. In custody law, judges are charged with examining the "best interests of the child." What, in fact, is under scrutiny is the mother's lesbianism. Most custody cases have resulted in the denial of custody to lesbian mothers or severe limitations to visitation rights: the mother's lover may not be present, the child may not spend the night, and so forth. Despite expert witnesses, judges have consistently ruled in favor of the father or even for placement in institutions. The mother's lesbianism is seen as utterly detrimental to the child.

Expert witnesses attempt to demonstrate the emotional and psychological well-being of the child. They focus their attention on the mothering received and the development of gender and sex roles. In studies, researchers have consistently found that there is no significant difference in the general emotional and psychological well-being of the children of lesbians as compared with those of heterosexual mothers. They urge the courts to look at the quality of the mothering involved, the relationship between mother and child, and the mother's ability to foster growth in the child.

Concerning conflict over sexual identity, children of lesbians do not demonstrate sexual confusion. Researchers question how, if it were the mother's intention to "convert," "androgynous" features could be induced. These features include: self-assertiveness, independence, an ability to stand up for rights, leadership, and ambition. They agree that the acquisition of sex and gender roles is influenced by the total environment, including television and peers, rather than solely by the mother.

Actually, the studies have shown that children of lesbians may, in fact, be more flexible, independent, and aware of greater options in life. Moreover, they may profit from greater nurturing and support if they grow up in a household where the mother's lesbian lover is present (as opposed to a male lover).

Since custody struggles have resulted in so few victories for lesbians, most progressive lawyers urge the lesbian mother to try to settle out of court. If, however, this is not possible, she is encouraged to retain a lawyer well-versed in this type of case. Decisions must be made concerning publicity and the presence of the mother's lover in the house. Questions of visibility are important since judges often rule on the basis of the lesbian's degree of notoriety.

Notoriety proves one of the stumbling blocks in the struggle for rights of lesbian mothers. Many lesbian activists and legal groups hesitate to take on custody causes because they might have to publicize the case in order to raise funds. Moreover, given the lack of precedence-setting in custody law and, therefore, the great degree of discretion with which judges rule, a success for an activist group is limited to that one case. A successful case may serve as a consciousness-raiser, but it will not influence future decisions.

Other legal struggles include custody of children by artificial insemination, legal guardianship, and will. To date, in most cases where a lesbian lover has been named upon the death of her partner, inheritances, custody, and rights of guardianship have been challenged. Many gay and lesbian lawyers volunteer their time to instruct gay men and lesbians in the use of the law.

714

Health. Similar to the legal world, the world of medicine has been the domain of men. Here, again, the lesbian must fight against discrimination to maintain her physical and emotional health. Many lesbians avoid using traditional physical and mental health facilities because of the inevitability of disclosing one's sexuality. Traditionally, lesbians have faced abuse at the hands of the mental health industry. Despite the removal of lesbianism as a disease from the standard manual in 1973, many mental health professionals continue to treat lesbianism as pathological.

Likewise, many physicians have either made the assumption that the lesbian is heterosexual or offered poor service upon discovering she was not. Gynecologists will often treat the lesbian as ignorant because she is not using birth control or unhealthy because she is not having intercourse with a man. Service is geared to women heterosexually active.

Because of this ignorance on the part of the doctor, medical mishaps have been known to happen. In one instance, a lesbian, wheeled into an emergency room, was assumed to be suffering from an ectopic pregnancy. If the treating physician had been aware of her lesbianism, he/she could have ruled out pregnancy and avoided a near-fatal delay in diagnosing a ruptured appendix. Similarly, less time would be spent examining for venereal disease (virtually non-existent in lesbians) and vaginal infections (less common).

Given the potentially hazardous situations resulting from the lack of a "sexual history," more appropriate service could be provided by the taking of just such a history. Lesbians, however, must feel comfortable and safe enough to give this history. In this, the choice of a physician is of utmost importance.

Additionally, other documents are necessary to prevent undue stress during illness. These would include physician's rights of attorney and living wills. Because of discriminatory policies in hospitals and in the medical arena, in general, the lover of a lesbian is barred from taking an active role in her partner's recovery or death. Intensive care units limit visitation to immediate family members. The lover's only guarantee of being allowed to visit and to share in decision-making is through the above-mentioned documents. Here, with the knowledge of the physician, the lesbian gives the lover the power to make medical decisions for her should she be incapacitated.

Alcoholism. Inappropriate or inadequate service by the medical world is a general symptom of homophobia. Yet, one witnesses the full impact of oppression and stigma when one examines the **alcoholism** and the need for psychotherapy among lesbians. The general silence surrounding these issues speaks more to a community's fear of further stigmatizing its members by admitting its vulnerabilities, than of denial.

Alcoholism stands out as a major health concern among lesbians. Statistically, between thirty and thirty-five percent of the lesbian community is troubled by alcohol abuse. This is about three times the national average for heterosexuals. Part of this high incidence may stem from the centrality of the **bar** within the lesbian community. Meeting place and center of entertainment, the bar has also served as a political focus and a hub of activity within the community.

However, the prime factor in viewing the lesbian as vulnerable to alcohol would seem to be her status as a member of a doubly stigmatized minority: she is a woman *and* a lesbian. Lowered self-esteem, anxiety, paranoia, spiritual and social alienation often characterize the emotional make-up of members of a minority group. Moreover, the lesbian has had to cope with her family's and society's denial of lesbianism or their portrayal of lesbianism as deviant and sinful. She has had to pretend that her feelings for women did not exist, or adapt to the stereotype of the isolated, role-playing deviant who could only find acceptance in seedy bars. She has learned to pretend everything is all right, denying over a long period of time that she lives with stigma and alienation. Out of the resulting tendency to seek relief or instant gratification, the lesbian may come to trust in the security of the bottle.

Furthermore, the lesbian possesses many of the characteristics of those at high risk for chemical dependency. Research shows these individuals to be deficient in one or more of the following: identification with a viable role model, identification with responsibility for family processes, low faith in miraculous solutions to problems, adequate inter- and intra-personal skills, skills to deal with systems, and judgment skills. Thus, lesbians seem at greater risk because they experience lack of coping skills and competence, since they are often isolated from family, institutions, and people responsible for inculcating those same coping skills.

Participation in the lesbian community provides the means to bridge the isolation and the stigma. Responsible for the well-being of its members, the lesbian community offers alcohol-free spaces, alcohol education, and recreational opportunities which do not require alcohol. Perhaps its greatest act of responsibility lies in the breaking through of its own denial (that alcoholism is a major health problem in the lesbian community) to take an active role in combatting alcoholism.

More and more consciousness-raising groups and rap groups are addressing the issue of alcoholism. Lesbian Alcoholics Anonymous and Adult Children of Alcoholics groups exist. Moreover, many lesbian (and gay) community centers have hired alcoholism counselors and have set up programs within the centers, while gay alcohol rehabilitation centers have already been established.

While the community can undertake some of the responsibility for service to its own members, society cannot be excused from its role. Programs sensitized to the needs of lesbians are still necessary. This need is especially felt in the area of psychotherapy. It is here that lesbians seek out insight into and healing for the stress related to living as a stigmatized minority in a hostile world.

Psychotherapy. Perhaps one of the most basic issues in psychotherapy for lesbians revolves around coming-out and self-image. Successful resolution reinforces a strong sense of self and a healthy identity. Lack of resolution would entail a form of identity crisis: self-hatred, withdrawal and underachievement, depression, self-victimization, and/or suicidal ideas.

Treatment focuses on self-definition. This process explores the feelings, images, needs, and roles involved in being a lesbian from the client's perspective. The therapist would also help the client mourn the loss of the former (non-lesbian) self, working through the denial of lesbianism and repression of feelings for women, and then, reconcile the negative stereotype of lesbians with the image one has of self. Building of coping mechanisms and empowering the client to deal with minority stress are also therapeutic interventions. The lesbian is particularly vulnerable in her self-esteem since she has been socialized as a woman, and therefore, traditionally undervalued and disempowered.

In a similar vein, couples composed of two people socialized as women will also face characteristic problems. Trained to self-efface and to put a partner's needs before her own, a woman involved in a relationship with another woman can become enmeshed in a dance of mutual self-effacement or an inverted power struggle. A lack of self-definition and therefore, an ignoring of one's own needs, leads to frustration, resentment, and anger, and often, hostility. The resulting power struggle can lead to a cycle of abuse where victim becomes victimizer.

Within lesbian couples, there may be a tendency to bond too closely or to "merge." Once again, this is a question of self-effacement or a lack of self-definition. Female children, nurtured by the mother, a same-sex parent, never have to separate from the same sex or turn away from the mother as do male children when they begin to side with the father. As a result, women tend to bond more closely on an emotional level, and two women together, then, can fall into a symbiotic relationship. Furthermore, society's lack of validation of the lesbian couple also tends to force the couple to turn inward on itself and to close itself off.

This false sense of intimacy or merger will usually result in a reaction in the opposite direction or distancing. When couples merge, their sense of themselves as individuals is lost. Clothing may be shared, friends held in common, all activities engaged in together. The end result can be stifling, and the only escape, a fight or a break-up.

Therapy with couples addresses the issue of self-definition again. This work enables one to self-assert, to work through conflict, and to step out of victim/abuse cycles. It also strengthens both individuals who can come together as integrated, autonomous partners. They are now capable of true intimacy since there is difference between them, and sharing, not merger, is possible.

Families of Lesbians. Given the range of oppression and the resultant vulnerability to alcoholism and to weakened coping skills, what has enabled lesbians to overcome stress and remain healthy? Are lesbians limited to marginal lives of social isolation and alienation? Is therapy the only answer?

Research has shown that lesbians are aging better than heterosexual women. If this is so, what are the factors involved? What societal features enable the lesbian not only to survive, but to prosper and to continue to come out and remain out in public?

While many lesbians have been rejected by their families of origin, others have disclosed to their families and found there a base of true support. Those lesbians whose families have accepted their lesbi-

anism have this traditional resource as a grounding factor in their lives.

Coming out to one's family plays a major role in one's self-definition. Yet, the family, very often, goes through the same type of struggle as the lesbian herself. Questions arise as to how the family now views itself and the "new" lesbian member; how to put together a stereotypical image of a lesbian with the image of the family member; how to deal with the stigma this will bring to the family; how to fight the stigma, and in its place, project a love and pride in the lesbian family member.

The family mourns the "loss" of the "old" (non-lesbian) daughter and becomes resocialized as a different family. Dreams of a marriage and grandchildren are lost, perhaps; fears of the daughter being oppressed are very real; religious conflicts arise. The struggle for the family parallels that of the lesbian, and for this reason, support groups exist for **parents** and families to deal with coming-out.

Just as the lesbian goes through a process of denial and slow acceptance, so too, the family experiences denial, guilt, isolation, and anger. Parents and family members may suffer a loss of self-esteem, depression, fears of not having modeled appropriate roles, of having "homosexual traits" themselves. The family may actually bargain with the lesbian to remain silent about her lesbianism, so things will be all right. Eventually, its members begin to explore feelings related to the daughter's lesbianism and gain knowledge affirmative of lesbians so as to break the myths and to confront stereotypes. It is only after this mourning process that integration can occur as a life-long possibility of communication which promotes self-actualization, as well as the means for the system to reconstruct itself and come to a full acceptance of the lesbian member.

Thus, a lesbian who is assured of her family's love during this time of struggle can better cope with the general fear and guilt she experiences in disclosing to them. She is also empowered to confront stress in her environment.

Lesbian Couples. Another source of strength and validation for the lesbian is her primary relationship. Contrary to popular belief, lesbians do form committed, long-term relationships. These **couples** are commonly characterized by stability, an absence of role playing, and satisfaction.

The values of relationships expressed by lesbians resemble those of heterosexual women rather than those of either hetero- or homosexual men. They focus on equality of power, emotional expressiveness, and self-disclosure. Compared to heterosexual women, lesbians seem to favor more sexual openness and a greater similarity of beliefs between partners. Moreover, being less bound by traditional roles, lesbians seem to profit from a greater range of choices and individual freedom in the lesbian couple and better coping skills from having overcome stigma.

Stigma, then, would seem to be the factor which most differentiates lesbian from heterosexual couples. No markers, rites, or documents sanctify or protect the coming together of two lesbians. Families and friends often transgress boundaries by attempting to "fix up" one of the partners with a male date, or they fail to invite the partner to functions. It is no uncertain tribute to the resiliency and commitment of women to women that lesbians, pitted against this stigma, do succeed in maintaining relationships.

Parenting. As lesbian couples remain together longer, many consider becoming a family by adopting a child or by giving birth. Artificial insemination by donor has enabled many lesbian couples to form lesbian families and to co-parent. Some couples choose a gay male, others a relative of the partner to donate sperm. Along with this growing practice comes an emphasis on legalities concerning limitations of fathering rights and the inclusion of the rights of the lover of the biological mother in a nomination of guardianship. Cases already exist where, upon the death of the biological mother, her parents fought and won custody from the "psychological" parent (with whom the child naturally wanted to continue to live).

Lesbians are likewise adopting and fostering children. This is a more difficult procedure. Given the stereotype of lesbians as child molesters and seductresses, great care must be given to the personal and psychological examination and inspection of the residence in which the child will live.

More common than "new" lesbian families, though, are those families of procreation issuing from the earlier marriage of the lesbian. While potentially at risk because of the lesbianism of the mother (and custody challenged by the father), these families can provide much stability and validation of the lesbian mother and her lover. In this family, too, all members pass through a coming-out process. Herein lies the deciding factor controlling the degree of acceptance by the children and the ability to continue as a family unit.

Coming out as a lesbian to one's children involves great risk. The younger the children are, the more easily they can accept that there is love between their mother and another woman. This is all the more true when the mother's partner is seen as nurturing and giving. Children usually respond appropriately when the information given is in accord with their age and ability to understand.

Teen-agers present a more difficult situation. Here, the fear of "contamination" enters into the picture. Adolescents, so engrossed in their own sexuality, may fear that the mother's lesbianism is genetic, or that they will be "turned into lesbians." The anger involved in their mother's stigmatizing them, by making them "different," sometimes creates great rifts in families.

The lesbian mother's task, then, is complex. She must convince her children of her continued love, of her continued identity as "their" mother and not a "different" person, and of her ability to continue as a healthy model for them. This task is complicated by the mother's usual resulting guilt over her choice.

Because of this guilt and the fear of losing her children, the lesbian mother may deny herself access to a potential source of support: other lesbians, mothers and non-mothers, as well as other heterosexual mothers. To lesbians, she may appear to be a heterosexual woman; to heterosexual mothers, she may not be able to disclose her lesbianism.

Working through the guilt enables the mother to parent more effectively and to model emotional strength and stability for her children. Lesbian mothers who have dealt successfully with intolerance communicate their resiliency to their children and are more likely to foster tolerance for difference of every kind and self-actualization in their own children, male or female.

Friends. In addition to biological families and partners, lesbians garner their support from their friends. In many cases, friends have become the "kinship network" for the lesbian whose family has rejected her. Friends often include past lovers; lovers are usually considered friends as well as sexual and romantic partners.

This network of friends provides an emotional and concrete support system which is held responsible for many "advantages" that lesbians would appear to have over non-lesbian women in certain areas. It is said that lesbians age better than heterosexual women. This advantage over heterosexual women in the aging process is attributed to the fact that lesbians are less likely to be "left alone" by a partner's desertion or death. Since men are usually outlived by women, many wives find themselves alone at an early age and somewhat isolated from a social network. This also holds true for newly separated and divorced women. Lesbians have never really distanced themselves from their women friends upon becoming involved in a couple. Therefore, they remain in touch with a range of friends, companions, and potential partners should a partner leave or die. Moreover, the lesbian community tends to represent women of all ages, thereby providing a circle of companions who are not likely to "disappear" or die within a short period of time of one another.

Community and Culture. It is just this circle of friends, acquaintances, and co-participants in lesbian activities who make up the lesbian **community**. "Community" bears with it not only the sense of solidarity as in "the women's community," but also conveys the image of all those establishments, institutions, activities, and media which provide an environment for lesbians.

This environment is both concrete and abstract. On one hand, figure the lesbian (and gay) community centers, the therapy institutes, groups, bookshops, the bars, shops, hotels, coffee houses, and alcohol treatment centers. On the other, the term "lesbian culture" can be abstracted from the combined workings of all of these establishments and women.

Lesbian culture does not simulate heterosexual or "straight" culture; nor does it merely complement straight culture. It has its origins in the homophile movement of the 1950s. Yet, it is distinct from the gay male culture. This discrete nature was expressed in the founding of the Daughters of **Bilitis** in 1955, the beginning of *The Ladder* in 1956, the first lesbian magazine, and the gradual politicization of the Daughters of Bilitis and of lesbianism in general during the 1960s and 1970s. Lesbian culture has as its core a philosophy of feminism and embraces therefore, an analysis of society, sometimes radical, sometimes not.

From this political base, where one is reminded that one's personal undertakings are political, emanates a full range of cultural representations, the most widely publicized of which is lesbian writing. While there are publishing companies, novels, essays, plays, poetry, magazines, journals, and newspapers which are known as "lesbian," for example, this label may imply that their value is marginal. On the contrary, lesbian women are producing work which is universal. The frame of reference, however, is lesbian.

Periodicals address a range of interests. Major cities and regions have lesbian magazines focusing on issues of concern to the lesbian community, as well as an analysis of broader issues. Calendars list local events and provide activities almost every day/night of the week (in larger cities and university towns). Magazines and journals feature areas of specific interest: for example, women's music, country lesbians.

In the world of **art**, lesbians are also represented. Collectives exist for the purpose of encouraging and supporting the work of lesbian photographers, filmmakers, and artists. Some remain grass roots operations, while others have incorporated and are producing "commercially competitive" work.

Lesbian music or women's music, as it was once called, is perhaps the form which succeeds in assembling the whole gamut of tastes, ages, styles, and politics among lesbians. Originally, one company, Olivia, a woman-owned company, represented all the lesbian-identified musicians. Now, many labels produce quality music of all styles. However, the pull of lesbian music goes beyond the record or tape to the lesbian concert.

Concerts have been a celebration for and of lesbians. There are several regional two-day festivals which bring together lesbian musicians, comedians, theorists, healers, book dealers, and so forth in a ritual of lesbian culture. A type of "Woodstock" event, festivals give lesbians "women-only" or "lesbian-only" space with camping, dancing, communal living for a weekend. Other concerts, such as that of Cris Williamson and Meg Christian in 1982 at Carnegie Hall in New York, helped to mark over ten years of women's music. Now, even "straight" clubs host lesbian musicians and draw large crowds, both straight and gay.

Conclusion. There is a lesbian button which was distributed in the 1970s. Its message reads: "We Are Everywhere." As the years pass, this may be even truer than before. Statisticians tell us that lesbians represent at least ten percent of the female population, but intimate that the actual figure is closer to twenty percent. More and more gay rights bills and ordinances are being passed despite right-wing politics. Some legislators and other prominent figures are making known their lesbianism and standing up publicly to advocate for gay rights. Lesbian families are thriving, and parents of lesbians march alongside them in Gay Pride marches.

These are changing times. The description above no longer seems to portray a stigmatized minority. Rather, a group emerging from its political infancy and adolescence appears to be closer to taking its full space. Like other minorities, lesbians have been fragmented and divided from one another or lumped together in a "seen one seen them all" type of focus. Their growing unity in diversity signifies a "no turning back" forward march.

This march of a diversified, strengthened people enhances the richness of all cultures. Lesbian culture reflects more and more diversity, and the manifestations of talent, skill, and excellence have grown proportionately. Just as ethnic lesbians bring back to their particular racial or ethnic community a more varied perspective, lesbians add another facet to the pluralism which characterizes American society.

Lesbians may remain outside the mainstream of society, through the continued oppression that is homophobia. Or, they may be gradually assumed into society through a desensitization of the "lesbian issue" and a political liberalization. Whichever turn things take, whichever stance lesbian theorists put forth as more desirable to avoid cooptation, the presence of lesbians still delivers a clear message. The message remains: We Are Everywhere, and, as such, lesbians stand as a critique of society and provide an alternative to the traditional limiting role and identity accorded to women. Lesbians have self-defined: therein lies the power and promise of a discrete people.

See also **Butch-Fem Relationships; Friendship, Female Romantic; Separatism, Lesbian.**

BIBLIOGRAPHY. Boston Lesbian Psychologies Collective, *Lesbian Psychologies: Explorations and Challenges*, Urbana: University of Illinois Press, 1987; Virginia Brooks, *Minority Stress and Lesbian Women*, Lexington, Massachusetts: Lexington Books, 1981; *Catalyst: A Socialist Journal of the Social Sciences* 12 (1981), special issue on homosexuality; Margaret Cruikshank, ed., *Lesbian Studies: Present and Future*, Old Westbury, NY: Feminist Press, 1982; Trudy Darty and Sandee Potter, eds., *Women-Identified Women*, Palo Alto, CA: Mayfield Press, 1984; Josette Escamilla-Mondanaro, "Lesbians and Therapy," in *Psychotherapy for Women: Treatment Toward Equality*, Edna Rawlings and Diane Carter, eds., Springfield, IL: Charles C. Thomas, 1977; Estelle B. Freedman, Barbara C. Gelpi, Susan L. Johnson, and Kathleen M. Weston, eds., *The Lesbian Issue: Essays from Signs*, Chicago: University of Chicago Press, 1985; *Journal of Homosexuality*, 7 (Summer 1982), special issue on alcoholism; Sarah Lucia Hoagland, *Lesbian Ethics: Toward New Values*, Palo Alto, CA: Institute of Lesbian Studies, 1988; Dolores Maggiore, *Lesbianism: An Annotated Bibliography and Guide to the Literature, 1976–1986*, Metuchen, NJ: Scarecrow Press, 1988; Barbara Ponse, *Identities in the Lesbian World: The Social Construction of Self*, Westport, CT: Greenwood Press, 1978; *Resources for Feminist Research*, 12 (March 1983), special issue on lesbianism; Barbara Sang, "Psychotherapy with Lesbians: Some Observations and Tentative Generalizations," in *Psychotherapy for Women: Treatment Toward Equality*, Edna Rawlings and Diane Carter, eds., Springfield, IL: Charles C. Thomas, 1977; Ginny Vida, ed., *Our Right to Love*, Englewood Cliffs, NJ: Prentice-Hall, 1978; Natalie J. Woodman and Harry R. Lenna, *Counseling with Gay Men and Women: A Guide for Facilitating Positive Life-Styles*, San Francisco: Jossey-Bass, 1980.

Dolores J. Maggiore

LEWDNESS, OPEN OR PUBLIC

This is the American legal designation for a sexual touching in view of someone who might be offended thereby, in statutes often selectively enforced against homosexuals. It is often successfully argued that a vice officer used to the sight of such behavior, in fact trained to seek out observation of it and inured to it by frequent experience, cannot conceivably be shocked or offended by it. However, if he himself is touched, then battery, often a recommended conviction in plea bargaining, is committed. "Battery," non-consensual touching, often of a plain-clothes member of the vice squad, is a non-sexual misdemeanor not requiring registration with the authorities as a "sex offender," thereby having no automatic credentialing, licensing or employment disabilities. It is not a sex crime or one of moral turpitude and does not constitute a felony on the second offense as does loitering.

Statutes often fail in their language to make clear that the conduct to be punished is *public*, not private, as appears to have been the intention of framers who entitled it "open lewdness." The omission of clear language limiting the scope to public conduct is disturbing and the wording of the statute should run as follows:

A person commits a disorderly offense if, *in a place exposed to public view*, he commits any flagrantly lewd and offensive act which he knows is likely to be observed *by members of the public* who would be affronted or alarmed.

[Proper phraseology indicated by italics does not alter the meaning in any way.]

The whole history of statutes of this kind is against criminalizing lewd conduct when it occurs in private. The common law punished conduct such as indecent exposure, not because of its sexual character, but because it threatened a breach of the peace. This is reflected in many of the older penal laws such as the one in New York, replaced in 1965 by the present code. Section 722(8) of the old New York law punished such conduct only when it took place "with intent to provoke a breach of the peace, or whereby a breach of the peace may be occasioned." The same concept is involved in Section 2C:34-1, which penalizes the conduct only when other persons are affronted or alarmed. Where people are so offended, a clear risk of breach of the peace exists. This fortifies the conclusion that the drafters of such provisions had in mind only conduct exposed to public view, since by definition, a breach of the peace is something that affects the public. To punish conduct which is not exposed to public view, such as that occurring within the home or family, even if it be there observed by others, would extend the criminal law into areas where it has not generally intruded and would contradict the entire thrust of modern statutes that protect sexual **privacy**.

Open or public lewdness became a common law offense not because it was immoral but because it constituted a threat to public order. The common law did not punish lewd or lascivious behavior in private; fornication, unlike adultery, was no crime. But adultery, originally cognizable in ecclesiastical rather than royal courts, was punished as a criminal offense whether it took place in public or in private.

It can be argued that forms of "engaging" constitute "lewd, lascivious, or dissolute conduct." The law is also vague as to the meaning of "public place," a "place open to the public" and "exposed to public view." The analogies to **solicitation** are obvious, and in jurisdictions where **sodomy** is decriminalized, should the kissing or hugging of same-sex partners in public be defined as less legal or more lewd than similar activities by heterosexual

couples? "Indecent exposure" would proscribe conduct so gross as to deserve criminalization. This refers to intentional, sexually motivated attracting of attention to one's exposed genitalia. Unlike solicitation, it is often offensive to the general public and reported by it to the authorities. In some jurisdictions it may be a felony on second or subsequent convictions. It often overlaps in certain respects with the non-provable misdemeanor "public lewdness." In fact, the modern penal codes of some jurisdictions combine the crimes of indecent exposure and public lewdness into a single statute. Though elimination of "public lewdness" would make it more difficult for police to build up their arrest records easily, it would lessen the burden of the courts and hardly cause more embarrassment or offense to the vast majority of the public.

See also **Law, United States**.
William A. Percy and Arthur C. Warner

LEZAMA LIMA, JOSÉ (1910–1976)

Cuban novelist and poet. The son of an artillery officer, Lezama Lima was impressed by military parades and gala events, images which often recur in his work. He suffered, like Marcel **Proust**, from asthma attacks that caused him to be separated from playmates. After his father died when he was nine, Lezama Lima lived with his mother, his two sisters, and his grandmother. His studies were brought to an end in 1930 when the Machado government closed the University of Havana. In 1936, however, he met the Spanish poet Juan Ramón Jiménez, who encouraged him to embark on a literary career. Alongside his own poetic production, he edited the journals *Verbum* (1937), *La Espuela de plata* (1939–41), *Nadie parecía* (1942–44), and *Orígenes* (1945–56). For these periodicals he translated the work of many French- and English-speaking writers, including Proust and Camus, Yeats and T. S. **Eliot**.

In 1944 Lezama Lima began his masterwork, the novel *Paradiso*, which was not to be published until 1966. In its reminiscences from his childhood, marked by illness and attachment to his mother, the novel recalls Proust's *A la Recherche du temps perdu*. The descriptions of the narrator's homosexuality surpass, however, this model in frankness. Other comparisons—to **Dante's** *Divine Comedy*, Thomas **Mann's** *Magic Mountain*, and even Joyce's *Finnegans Wake*—reveal the monumental status of the work. Upon its Havana publication, even in a defective first edition, the novel immediately assumed its place at the forefront of the "boom" of Latin American prose. Its linguistic innovations and breadth of consciousness were hailed by such peers as Julio Cortázar, Mario Vargas Llosa, and Juan Goytisolo. Although the book has been translated into the major European languages, its difficult prose style and anchoring in the Latin American scene have thus far denied the author the world recognition that he deserves. Lezama Lima intended to publish two sequels, but completed only one fragment, *Oppiano Licario*.

After the death of his mother in 1964, he lived in seclusion. Although he was never officially denounced by Castro's government, his homosexuality and his Catholicism were known to be the subject of disapproval in the bureaucracy. His work has remained an example of artistic integrity and refusal to bow to political pressures.

BIBLIOGRAPHY. Mechtild Straussfeld, ed., *Aspekte von José Lezama Lima "Paradiso,"* Frankfurt am Main: Suhrkamp, 1979.

Wayne R. Dynes

LIBERACE, WLADZIU VALENTINO (1919–1987)

American popular entertainer. Liberace first attained local success by performing schmaltzy, abbreviated versions of piano classics at restaurants in his native state of Wisconsin. After appearances in the vaudeville circuit, he found a perfect match with American **television** as it emerged as the dominant mass medium in the 1950s. His flamboyant costumes and props helped to generate the adulation that made him one of the highest paid entertainers of all time. Many of his most faithful fans were older women, who apparently accepted at face value his public protestations that he was not homosexual .

In his West Milwaukee high school he already showed a fondness for drag, but apparently remained uninterested in sex until the 1940s, when he began to explore his taste for men. In 1956 Cassandra, an acidulous columnist for the London *Daily Mirror*, reviewed a Liberace concert, calling him "the summit of sex—the pinnacle of masculine, feminine and neuter. Everything that he, she, and it can ever want." Then the American gossip tabloid *Confidential* joined in with a cover story entitled "Why Liberace's Theme Song Should Be 'Mad About the Boy.'" Unabashed, Liberace sued both publications, and won.

Rumors continued to circulate. Although he claimed to be devoted only to his pet dogs, Liberace's mansions were home to a succession of handsome young men. In 1982 an ex-lover brought a palimony suit. Although Liberace was diagnosed with **AIDS** five months before he died, the fact was continually denied. Only a mandatory coroner's autopsy revealed the truth. Liberace's image as an entertainer had been a highly artificial creation, and so it remained until the end.

BIBLIOGRAPHY. Bob Thomas, *Liberace*, New York: St. Martin's Press, 1988; Scott Thorson, *Behind the Candelabra: My Life with Liberace*, New York: Dutton, 1988.

LIBERALISM

Liberalism is generally regarded as a distinctively modern political credo. As such it has implications for **sexual liberty**, but these must be understood against a broader background of political controversy.

Formative Influences. Liberalism arose in a civilization profoundly shaped by Greek **philosophy**, by Roman law, and by **Protestant** religion affirming the closeness of man's relationship with God. Nonetheless, the liberal idea of freedom was a novelty in the formative period of modern European civilization; it arrived only with the ascription of rights to the individual against those in authority over him, or against the collective embodied in tribal custom or in the state power. The rights posited by liberalism are significant, universal, and allotted to every human being endowed with the minimum of competence to govern his own affairs.

Liberalism undertook to restrict or even abrogate the power of the state and the church in favor of the individual, who was invested with a sovereignty in his own right, as the one best capable of judging his own needs and interests. In the Western European countries of Latin **Christianity** it was the church rather than the state that bore the responsibility for defending as well as teaching the true faith, and the temporal power was but the auxiliary summoned to smite those whom the church had condemned as heretics and reprobates. Hence the West—as compared, say, with Byzantium, Islam, or China— could more easily accept the notion that matters of faith and conscience lie beyond the jurisdiction of the state, that the spiritual and temporal powers must never be joined in one, and that the state should have the minimal function of preventing harmful and antisocial behavior, rather than serving as the primary upholder of religious and ethical truths.

The Role of Major Thinkers. The doctrine of the social contract, fashionable among political theorists in the sixteenth and seventeenth centuries, was first used to support the claims of religious minorities, and of churches and sects anxious to assert their independence of the civil power. This doctrine postulates an individual whose rights and wants precede the establishment of a government whose assigned task is to protect the rights and supply the wants. John Locke (1632–1704), in his *Second Treatise of Civil Government* (1690), argued that government exists to protect the life, liberty, and property of its subjects, who are obliged to obey it only so long as it protects them adequately and does not abuse its powers. Eventually, the defense of property was extended to one's own body, providing a powerful argument for sexual liberty. Political power, Locke maintained, is legitimate only when those holding it exercise it with the consent of the governed, who may take steps to prevent abuses of power. In France Montesquieu (1687–1755) further argued that it is expedient to separate the judicial from the executive and legislative powers, and in the twelfth book of *The Spirit of the Laws* (1748), he discussed principles and practices to ensure that no one be punished except for breaking the law, that accused persons receive a fair trial, and that citizens can exercise their rights effectively against both public officials and other citizens.

Edmund Burke (1729–1797), though an unrelenting champion of democracy, was concerned with another aspect of freedom that liberalism has seen fit to defend: the need to protect the rights of the individual from radical demagogues and popular dictators who seek to crush everyone who opposes the "will of the masses." The sovereignty of the people had to be dammed up by constitutional forms and legal procedures that would thwart unjust and oppressive measures, no matter how strongly they were desired by the majority. This doctrine, sometimes termed counter-majoritarianism, was later to prove important for the defense of unpopular minorities, including homosexuals. In essence, classical liberalism saw the rights of the individual as standing in opposition to the claims of the state, whether the latter derived its power from divine sanction or from the will of the electorate.

The modern idea of freedom has also had to confront the problem of the relation between man and society. In his *Discourse on the Origins of Inequality among Men* (1754), Jean-Jacques Rousseau (1712–1778) argued that man acquires distinctively human skills and needs only by leaving the state of nature, and that these social needs can be satisfied only by civil institutions such as government. Rousseau also introduced the notion that insofar as man is "corrupted" by society he can be motivated to act in a manner harmful to himself and to others. He can acquire wants and ambitions that are insatiable, inconsistent with one another or with his future well-being, or such that the means to satisfy them will always be lacking.

Immanuel Kant (1724–1804) made a sharper distinction than did Rousseau between morality and legality. The task of the state is to make and enforce laws in the common interest; the freedom that lies in obedience to self-imposed laws belongs to a sphere with which the state is not directly concerned. This principle was later to be invoked as an argument that there is a sphere of moral choice which should be left to private conscience and not to the intervention of the state with its police power.

One nineteenth-century thinker stands out, the English utilitarian John Stuart Mill (1806–1873). In his widely read paper, "On Liberty" (1869), Mill held that no one has the right to interfere with the freedom of action of another competent adult, unless the action causes harm. Moreover, Mill linked this principle of liberty of action with liberty of expression. One should hesitate to repress opinions because it is very difficult to tell which opinions are false, and even if this could be determined, silencing them will cause more harm than good.

In 1911 L. T. Hobhouse (1864–1929) created a new model of welfare liberalism, incorporating some elements from Fabian socialism and advocating vigorous government intervention. Although this version of liberalism is the most familiar form today, it is of less significance for homosexuals than classical liberalism, since the economic and social issues addressed by the welfare state are not pertinent to gay people as such.

Applications. Homosexual advocates, from the 1860s to the present day, have appealed to one strand or another of the classical liberal tradition in their effort to sway public opinion. The basic argument has been that the individual should have the same right to seek happiness in the sexual sphere as in any other, that the state should no more intervene in the bedroom than it does in the marketplace. Crucial to the logic of this position is the assertion that true homosexuality is inborn, or at least environment-stable, and not modifiable by conditioning or experience. The inference is that homosexual men and women should have the same right to sexual expression as their heterosexual counterparts, and that it is unjust to penalize any segment of the population for engaging in conduct which it finds pleasurable and which causes no harm to others. The opposition has often countered with a version of Rousseau's belief that the child and adolescent are exposed to a corrupting environment which can cause them to be fixated in a homosexual orientation.

The separation of church and state—which, it should be emphasized, has not been achieved in many countries where liberalism triumphed in the political and economic spheres—has been a cornerstone of the arguments for homosexual emancipation in the **United States**. It might be thought that the formal separation of the spiritual and temporal powers realized by the First Amendment to the American Constitution would have ended all laws whose object is to impose the ascetic morality of the Christian church upon the citizenry by penal sanctions. That this did not occur at the end of the eighteenth century and in many jurisdictions has not occurred until now must be regarded as the greatest single failure of liberalism in the English-speaking world. While other areas of criminal law and procedure underwent drastic changes as a consequence of liberal criticism of the practices of the Old Regime, by standing still the penalties for consensual homosexual behavior between adults became relatively even *more* severe: in not a few states, as late as the 1960s, they were three or four times the maximum that could be imposed for armed robbery, theft of funds from a charitable institution, or beating or neglecting a small child.

A conservative argument for retaining the penal sanctions is that they are actively desired and approved by a majority of the electorate. To this the liberal reply is that the individual—including the homosexual individual—should be protected in his personal rights and freedoms against an intolerant majority, in this case a majority incited by fundamentalist and tradition-minded religious bodies who openly appeal to their members to oppose legislation on behalf of homosexuals. However, referenda sponsored by right-wing churches have in numerous cities succeeded in repealing gay rights bills enacted by a majority of the city council; and the very same courts that have ruled in favor of other minority groups have balked at extending the protection of the First and Fourteenth Amendments to the gay minority.

Classical liberalism addressed itself mainly to political and economic issues, leaving the topic of sexual morality and the legitimacy of sexual acts strictly alone. It was too preoccupied with reform of the commonwealth, with the winning of political rights and economic freedoms for the individual, to be concerned with so sensitive an area of private life as the sexual. Its sole accomplishments in this sphere were an exceedingly gradual relaxation of the laws on divorce that expanded the admissible grounds for terminating a marriage, and a similar attenuation of the statutes against birth control and pornog-

raphy. Also, liberal reforms required an organized interest group, a constituency that could bring pressure to bear on the executive and legislative branches of government—and because of the social stigma attaching to homosexuality no such formal organization was possible until quite recently. On the other hand, the exceedingly **authoritarian personality** types who detest homosexuals are often self-excluded from the political arena because they cannot follow the grammar of politics which liberalism has formulated, including the need to unite around a single issue with allies who hold divergent views on other issues.

Liberalism never extended the notion that enlightened self-interest is a legitimate motivating principle for human actions to the realm of sexual pleasure, except in the work of a handful of thinkers such as Jeremy **Bentham** who were well in advance of their time. Many of the revered authors of the liberal school, when they discussed sexual matters at all, felt obliged to treat traditional views as beyond criticism. Furthermore, although prior **censorship** of printed matter had been abolished in England in 1694, through the offense of blasphemy which was retained the notion of obscenity crept into the common law, with the definition that a book was obscene if it tended to corrupt anyone "into whose hands it might fall." In practice this ruling meant that it was impossible even to publish works that sought to enlighten the public on the subject of homosexuality.

The consequence of this liberal failure of nerve was that postmedieval attitudes toward homosexual individuals and homosexual behavior persisted well into the middle of the twentieth century, even in countries where almost every other vestige of the inequality and intolerance of the Old Regime had been relegated to the "dustbin of history." It was only in 1954, 57 years after Magnus **Hirschfeld** founded the **Scientific-Humanitarian Committee**, 90 years after Karl Heinrich **Ulrichs** began his lonely campaign for homosexual emancipation, 190 years after Cesare **Beccaria** published his treatise *On Crimes and Punishments*, that the Moral Welfare Council of the Church of England finally "took the initiative" to call for reform of the archaic laws.

The Report of the **Wolfenden** Committee that was published three years later utilized many of the arguments of classical liberalism to justify its decision to recommend law reform, yet one critic of the document noted that it seemed to stand outside time—that far from being novel, it appealed to notions which victorious liberalism had by then made commonplace and self-evident in all other spheres of life.

Relevance. Since the struggle for homosexual liberation is far from ended, it is well to consider how the fundamental notions of the liberal creed apply to the issue. Liberalism denied the role of the state as a coercive guardian of the morals of the citizen; instead it defended his right to autonomy and to freedom in his private life. It demanded the separation of the state from the church, and an end to the use of the police power of the state to enforce religious teaching. It held the rights of the individual sacrosanct against the tyranny of the majority as much as against the arbitrary whim of a crowned sovereign. The laws and customs that stand in the way of homosexual liberation are an anachronistic legacy of the Europe of absolutist monarchies that the liberal credo was to transform into a set of constitutional states with laws and institutions meant to safeguard the freedom and dignity of the individual. Despite its shortcomings, the liberal tradition is an indispensable resource for the gay rights **movement** of today.

BIBLIOGRAPHY. John Gray, *Liberalism*, Milton Keynes, England: Open University Press, 1986; Richard D. Mohr, *Gays/Justice: A Study of Ethics, Society, and Law*, New York: Columbia University Press, 1988; Ronald D. Rotunda, *The Politics of Language: Liberalism as Word and Symbol*, Iowa City: Iowa University Press, 1986.

Warren Johansson

LIBERATION, GAY

In 1969, almost immediately after the **Stonewall Rebellion**, the Gay Liberation Front (GLF) sprang up in **New York City**. The choice of name reflects the fame of several movements to overthrow foreign domination that had arisen after World War II in Europe's remaining colonies, especially in Vietnam and Algeria where the insurgent forces both adopted the name National Liberation Front. Such models became attractive in North America because of the widespread opposition to the Vietnam war, and the analogy that was at that time discerned between the colonized in the Third World, on the one hand, and blacks and other ethnic minorities in North America (e.g., the Québecois), on the other.

A major source of ideas and inspiration for gay liberation has been the women's movement. Betty Friedan recalls first hearing "women's liberation" in 1967, two years before the Stonewall Rebellion. The expression apparently originated among women of SNCC, a civil rights group, and Students for a Democratic Society (SDS), who had grown tired of being assigned the demeaning roles of coffee makers and secretaries in their own organizations. Thus women's liberation meant not only freedom from the **oppression** of society in general, but also from the **sexism** rampant in movements for social change as they were then constituted.

All the same, the Gay Liberation Front in New York City and its namesakes elsewhere were inspired by the New Left analysis which viewed the plight of the minorities as the result of deep, systemic flaws in society. In the turbulent days of the early seventies the GLFs faded, in part because of their lack of strong organizational structure, which made them vulnerable to factional strife, internal opportunism from inadequately screened re-

cruits from the "street people," and FBI
infiltration. Also, with the end of the
Vietnam war in January 1973 the wave of
radicalism that had swept over North
America came to an end, and the multi-
issue organizations of the late 1960s could
no longer rally large followings. These
volatile groupings yielded to more structured and "respectable" single-issue bodies, such as the Gay Activists Alliance and
the National Gay Task Force, which sought
to advance the cause of gay rights within
the existing political and economic framework of American society. In Britain and
Europe the greater strength of older radical
traditions made the multi-issue model—
in alliance with the left, even the extreme
left—more long-lived, but eventually it
faded everywhere.

What remained was the idea of
liberation, the definition of which varied
of course from one tendency to another.
An early statement of the liberationist's
aims was Carl Wittman's "A Gay Manifesto" of 1969, which lashed out against
the mimicry of "straight" society, oppression, self-oppression, and role dichotomies,
while favoring gay ghettoes (if reorganized
as "liberated zones"), together with coalitions with women, blacks, Hispanics, and
radicals. Wittman had been active in the
paramount New Left organization, SDS,
and he later acknowledged that the oppression he felt as a gay person in that group
both hindered and shaped the emergence
of his consciousness.

Thoroughgoing true believers
invidiously contrasted gay liberation with
gay emancipation, which was stigmatized
as a collage of mere cosmetic, reformist
pseudosolutions designed to "mystify" and
obstruct the revolutionary project. Others, with less flaming rhetoric, viewed that
matter as a two-stage process. In the first
stage there is a primarily legal and legislative struggle to secure basic gay rights.
This phase then gives way to the more
creative and difficult construction of gay
liberation as part of a program of universal
human liberation. Such utopianism,
though probably not destined to disappear
altogether, became less salient in the 1980s.

The sexual liberation movement
inspired many GLF groups. The New York
GLF paper Come Out carried pictures of
the staff in the nude as did Rosa von
Praunheim's German film It Is Not the
Homosexual Who is Perverse But the
Society in Which He Lives (1971). Boston's
Fag Rag and San Francisco's Gay Sunshine, together with Washington's Furies
and Boston's Amazon Quarterly, explored
themes of phallic imperialism and new
forms of sexual liberation. Herbert
Marcuse's widely read Eros and Civilization, Wilhelm Reich's works, and Shu-
lamith Firestone's Dialectics of Sex all
provided early clues to a new direction.
Consciousness-raising groups based on the
Chinese cultural revolution spread to the
women's movement and then to gay liberation. In the 1980s they were largely
replaced by psychotherapists who favored
accommodation more than fundamental
social change.

Although many adherents of the
"revolutionary" program of gay liberation
would be loath to admit it, there probably
lingers in the background of their program
the kernel of a Judeo-Christian theological
notion, that of deliverance, in the sense of
a rebirth or total transformation of the
spirit. The Exodus experience—simultaneously an escape from bondage and a
summons to build a new life for the community in the Promised Land—is the most
important single precedent. Another significant religious tradition is medieval
millenarianism, which yoked demands for
radical social change ("the last shall be
first") to expectations of apocalyptic upheavals. These ideas fed into nonconformist Christian traditions of various stripes.
Protestant churches have preserved memories of separation from ties to a Roman
Catholicism accused of having lost the
ideal of primitive Christianity, in order to
build a new Jerusalem. In the 1980s a group

of Radical Faeries purchased land in Wolf Creek, Oregon, where they seek to build both a refuge and a new kingdom.

These traditions, and others not cited that may also be relevant, share universal themes: the slave losing his shackles; release from prison; and escape from the arbitrary power of a despot. Yet as gay men and lesbians more and more take their place in the mainstream, these images of radical change seem less persuasive. By the 1980s—when the insurrectionary turbulence of gay radicalism was only a memory—while the expression "gay liberation" was still heard, it had lost the almost messianic fervor with which it was once invested, to become part of the everyday language of political entitlement. The mandate of separatist charisma had yielded to the more immediate rewards of mainstreaming.

BIBLIOGRAPHY. Dennis Altman, *Homosexual: Oppression and Liberation*, New York: Outerbridge and Dienstfrey, 1971; Joseph A. McCaffrey, ed., *The Homosexual Dialectic*, Englewood Cliffs, NJ: Prentice-Hall, 1972 (contains Wittman's "A Gay Manifesto," pp. 157–71); Toby Marotta, *The Politics of Homosexuality*, Boston: Houghton Mifflin, 1981; Mario Mieli, *Homosexuality and Liberation*, London: Gay Men's Press, 1980.

Wayne R. Dynes

LIBERTARIAN PERSPECTIVES

In the strict sense libertarianism is a political trend that emerged in the **United States** in the 1960s. Its ideas stem not only from the **anarchist** tendency that views the state as the enemy, but also from Anglo-American traditions of individual liberty, private property, and classical **liberalism**. Libertarians see the expansion of state power as the principal source of the ills of modern society, as it tends to restrict the rights of the individual, choke economic development, and foster international intervention and conflict. Libertarians can claim to combine features from both the radical and conservative traditions, and they have attracted followers from both groups. In an era of computerization and nuclear weapons, their ideas are often dismissed as anachronistic. If the goal is abolition of the state or even reduction of its role to that of a "night watchman" offering only the most limited services (the minimal state), libertarian ideals may seem chimerical. Yet as the histories of the abolitionist and prohibition movements show, the function of such projects is not to supplant existing political parties, but to place issues on the agenda. Feasibility studies of individual sectors of the economy, such as garbage collecting and fire protection, suggest that these tasks can be performed more efficiently by private industry. As the appeal of state socialism has faded throughout the world, such diverse countries as France, Mexico, and Singapore have embarked on privatization campaigns. Libertarians have also been strongly in favor of deregulation in industries that already are private.

The defense of individual rights—which is, of course, not conducted exclusively by libertarians—has appealed strongly to mainstream gay men and lesbians. To be sure, the libertarian insistence on preserving the realm of personal privacy goes against the radical slogan "The personal is the political," but this principle no longer seems a categorical imperative. Deployment of privacy strategies has been an effective strategy for lawyers seeking to defend gay rights. Libertarians consistently favor abrogation of all **sodomy** laws as unwarranted intrusions into the private sphere. In this instance they are following the classical liberal principle that the state has no right to prohibit acts committed by competent adults that do not harm others. However, libertarians oppose new legislation banning discrimination against homosexuals in employment, housing, and public accommodation. This opposition stems from the principle that freedom *of* association is also freedom *from* association. As a general rule, libertarians are against efforts to achieve equality by governmental intervention. This stand alienates not only socialists but many liberal Democrats. At the same time the libertarian critique of adventurism in foreign affairs appeals to these same groups. As indicated, the libertarian program straddles both left and right, making it difficult for it to present a clear electoral image. Not surprisingly, libertarians have not done well at the polls in the United States, though considerably better than the miniscule **Marxist** parties.

Roots. It is tempting to dismiss libertarianism as a minor bubble in the political profile of the late twentieth century. However, its key ideas have deep roots, and two of these have consequences for sexual freedom. The first theme is the idea of reexamining the laws, one by one, to see if they truly contribute to human happiness. In many instances laws are found to have been created for, or captured by special interest groups. The second key theme is the idea of the individual's right to control his or her own body. "Get your laws off my body" turns out to be a new version of an old idea.

Focus on unjust and unnecessary laws was part of the **Enlightenment** critique of the Old Regime. **Voltaire** succeeded in mobilizing public opinion by focusing on particular atrocities. One such was the execution of the Protestant Jean Calas in 1762 on a false charge of having murdered his own son. Voltaire showed that Calas' punishment reflected more hatred of his deviant religious faith than any concern for the impartial administration of justice. Later he was to make much of cases of blasphemy and witchcraft.

An overarching theory of legal reform was created by the Italian Enlightenment thinker, Marquis Cesare **Beccaria**, whose treatise of 1764, *On Crimes and Punishments*, was received with almost rapturous enthusiasm throughout Europe. As a utilitarian, Beccaria held that the state's right to punish must be subordinate to the overarching imperative of human happiness. Hence there can be no excuse for torture or excessive punishment. Moreover, unless punishment can be certainly demonstrated to be efficacious, it should be renounced. Wherever possible, social ills should be avoided by treating the root causes in a preventative manner. Thus sodomy (which Beccaria certainly did not favor) has persisted for centuries despite draconian legislation. It should be dealt with, he held, by reforming the places in which it is fostered, such as same-sex boarding schools.

These continental trends supported a comprehensive overhaul of the legal system with a view to radical pruning of bad laws. Before this program could be accomplished, as a consequence of the French Revolution, the European continent had received two important motifs of British origin. One is the notion, developed over several centuries of dispute between king and parliament, that the power of the state must be constantly monitored to see that it does not encroach upon the rights of the individuals and groups that comprise society. Then John Locke and others in his tradition had stressed that private property is closely connected with personal liberty. From this link one can deduce that as one owns one's body, the state has no justification in seeking to control it in the absence of harm to others.

The Nineteenth and Twentieth Centuries. The early socialist writers tended to emphasize the collective at the expense of the individual. One among them, however, the visionary Charles **Fourier** (1772–1837), stands apart. The guiding feature of Fourier's system is the law of attraction he derived from astronomy. Through this concept he anticipated the libertarian idea of spontaneous order arising from individual needs as against artificial order imposed from above. Among the needs Fourier recognized was sexual expression, including that of same-sex love, and his ideal communities were organized to provide a place for the whole range of sexual expression.

Seminal for the libertarian tradition is the German Max Stirner (1806–1856), the individualist anarchist. Stirner rejected every type of collectivism, and all theories which purported to discern a single, abstract essence of humanity. At the center of his vision stands the human individual, of whom alone one can have certain knowledge. Stirner, who taught in a girl's school, was not bold enough to develop the corollary of sexual freedom which follows from his theory of absolute individualists. Perhaps his caution was justified. Even at the end of the century, when John Henry **Mackay** (1864–1933)—an anarchist who was also a boy lover—revived Stirner's theories, he did not dare to state frankly their implications for sexual freedom.

The anarchist thinkers are generally reproached for overlooking the organic unity of society as a collective, rather than a mere aggregate of individuals. No such objection can be made to the thought of the utilitarians Jeremy **Bentham** (1748–1832) and John Stuart Mill (1806–1873). Unfortunately Bentham's incisive critiques of the criminalization of sodomy long remained in manuscript and were not published until the twentieth century, by which time the ideas had in some respects become dated. Mill, though not concerned with sexual variation, defended a fundamental principle of liberty that has continued in honor in the English-speaking world. In "On Liberty" (1859) he affirmed that "the sole end for which mankind is warranted, individually or collectively, in interfering with the liberty of action of any of their number, is self-protection." With this defense of competent adults to do anything they wish provided they do nothing to harm others, he combined a powerful advocacy of freedom of expression. "We can never be sure," he insisted, "that the opinion we are endeavoring to stifle is a false opinion; and if we were sure, stifling it would be an evil still."

A number of these strands were drawn together and stated in a strikingly modern way in the unfortunately little known 1908 Heidelberg doctoral dissertation of Kurt **Hiller**, *Das Recht über sich Selbst* (The Right over Oneself). This work concerns a broad front of topics: suicide, self-mutilation, duelling, incest, homosexuality, bestiality, and abortion. Marshalling a dense body of argumentation in a historical perspective reaching back to classical Roman law, Hiller provided a kind of unified-field theory of offenses that he held should not be criminalized because they pertain to self-ownership. The case for decriminalizing deviant sexual behavior—incest, homosexuality, and bestiality—gains force from the analogous (and probably more easily acceptable) arguments for nonsexual deviation. Hiller believes that almost all the rationalizations that have accumulated in favor of criminal sanctions in the categories he surveys have a religious or mystical origin. As such, they are arguments that cannot pass unchallenged in a modern secular state. In this contrast of religion and secularism Hiller admits himself a child of the Enlightenment. Ultimately, however, the solution lies in recognizing that the criminalization of all these matters interferes with the right to control one's own body.

In conclusion, it should be emphasized that the libertarian opposition to the state is founded not only upon anarchism, with its visceral distrust of authority, but on a kind of universal sundown principle: which laws—and there are probably many—do not deserve to remain on the books? They should be struck down because they fetter human liberty and creativity and serve no other useful social purpose. However, the abolition of private property, advocated by many leftists and some anarchists, must not be countenanced, for this will undermine one's right to own one's body. Not only does this principle of self-sovereignty lie at the heart of the libertarian social philosophy, it makes possible its particular contribution to the cause of sexual liberty.

BIBLIOGRAPHY. Robert Nozick, *Anarchy, State, and Utopia*, New York: Basic Books, 1974; Ralph Raico, *Gay Rights: A Libertarian Approach*, Washington: McBride for President Committee, 1976; Murray Rothbard, *Ethics of Liberty*, Atlantic Highlands, NJ: Humanities Press, 1982.

Wayne R. Dynes

LIBERTINISM

This current of sixteenth- and seventeenth-century European thought, which was imbued with ancient skeptical philosophy (Pyrrhonism), offered a materialist approach to reality. It reflected also the "polemic of the three imposters" (Moses, Jesus, and Mohammed) and the heterodox Aristotelianism of the later Middle Ages.

Basic Features. What passes under the name of libertinism today is in fact a heterogeneous amalgam of beliefs and ideas, which are philosophical in the broad sense, and moral as well. Despite the diversity of the phenomena grouped under the umbrella of the label, all the variants of libertinism share a family resemblance; they all have at least one of its constituent elements (e.g., belief in the mortality of the soul, the theory of religion as imposture, moral relativism, and skepticism).

Not having coalesced into a school, libertinism never created a dogmatic system; it is rather a climate of thought and an overall approach. It was often more a matter of problems than specific solutions. Thus in response to the problem of the existence of **God** the libertines oscillated between atheism and deism, and some were even Christian believers.

The plasticity of libertinism is also shown by the presence of libertine elements in the religious polemics of the sixteenth and seventeenth centuries—especially when Christian sects accused one another of being the creations of imposters. Not surprisingly skepticism in relation to religion provoked a vast campaign by religious defenders, both Catholic and Protestant, against libertinism. These attacks lingered in the tendency to equate libertinism with dissolute license: even today, in common parlance the libertine is simply a rake.

With respect to genuine libertinism, a typical claim is that all religions are the carapaces of cunning imposters, who have taken advantage of popular credulity to terrorize the ignorant with fables so as to keep them submissive to those who would manipulate them. This premise yields the conclusion that there can be no "revealed" moral code, but only what the educated man succeeds in fashioning for himself through the application of Reason in search of virtue and truth.

Libertinism does not accept prohibitions on conduct that are based solely on the revelation of holy scriptures of any sort. Thus its morality is intended to be strictly rational, and as such secular. Moral imperatives and laws come not from the dictates of religion but from comprehension of the need for rules in order to obtain a well-ordered civil society.

A last major component of the sensual morality of the libertines was the widespread belief in the mortality of the soul. This doctrine was taught at Padua, a major center of the trend, by Cesare Cremonini (1550–1631), who based his thought on that of Pietro Pomponazzi (1462–1525).

Sexual Aspects. Libertines held that, as a loving and benign mother, not a cruel one, Nature has provided men with sexual organs so that they may use them. Man is not born to suffer, but to enjoy the pleasures which he might seek, provided that others are not harmed. Since each man may only expect a single life, the earthly one, there is no profit in suffering in exchange for a nonexistent heavenly reward.

These are the reasons why the libertine thinker could not fail to place a positive value on human sexuality—including its homosexual aspects. For him homosexual relations have, on the moral plane, the same dignity as heterosexual ones; morally they are indifferent. For the libertine the Biblical condemnation of sodomy is the ultimate absurdity; an illustration of this view is the pederastic text *L'Alcibiade fanciullo a scola*. Here too there can be no wrong in making use of one's genitals to obtain the pleasure that Nature herself has made possible. Nothing can be "against nature" that occurs through Nature's grace.

The famous declaration attributed to the Elizabethan playwright Christopher **Marlowe**—"all they that love not tobacco and boys [are] fools"—synthesizes the libertine approach to the question; one has to be a fool not to appreciate the pleasures that life offers.

Also typical of libertinism is the lowering of the whole supernatural dimension to a human level through the attribution of human defects and desires (including sexual ones) to the personages of sacred history. Thus there emerged those terrible "blasphemies" which so convulsed the church. In the homosexual realm a typical libertine affirmation is one that can be documented several times across the centuries—in a Venetian Inquisition trial of 1550 against one Francesco Calcagno, in the 1593 accusation against Christopher Marlowe, in a Lisbon **Inquisition** trial (1618) of one Manuel Figuereido, and in the *Essai sur la peinture* of Denis Diderot (1713–1784)—namely that Jesus and St. John (the **beloved disciple**) were lovers.

Sexual heterodoxy was quickly taken advantage of by the adversaries of the libertines to present them as monsters of vice, and immoral individuals capable of any evil in order to obtain carnal pleasure. In actual practice libertines respected human laws as far as possible. Convinced that they belonged to an elite of a few enlightened persons in a world dominated by ignorance and stupidity, they had no intention of creating scandal among the masses who were too obtuse to grasp the reasons for their behavior.

In fact libertinism was an intrinsically conservative attitude: it is not an accident that Antonio Rocco (1586–1652), author of the *Alcibiade fanciullo a scola* just cited, was one of the most determined opponents of Galileo Galilei. The libertine held that the ignorant masses, incapable of curbing their animal passions through Reason, needed the restraints offered by religion and superstition. For this reason the libertine attitude toward religion is one of amused indulgence—yielding at most to mocking blasphemy—but refraining from outright and sustained attack. In this perspective superstition, though an evil, was a necessary evil.

Historical Vicissitudes. Initially strong in Italy in the sixteenth and seventeenth centuries, libertinism attracted the determined persecution of Counterreformation society which succeeded in driving it underground. The shrinkage of Italian libertinism nonetheless did not mean its end, while in seventeenth-century France and England it enjoyed a noteworthy flowering. One need only mention the figure of John Wilmot, Earl of **Rochester** (1647–1680), the witty Restoration rake whose writings heralded the liveliness and license of eighteenth-century England.

Nonetheless, the seeds of decline were sown in the seventeenth century when Western thought cut away its ground of scientific speculation, which was rooted in Aristotelianism. René Descartes (1596–1650) proposed an approach to materialism that was more productive. Only in the moral field did the libertine trend succeed in remaining alive until the rise of the Enlightenment, of which it constituted one of the sources.

Arguments and attitudes typical of libertinism reemerged in the writings of the thinkers of the **Enlightenment**: one of the most radical sequelae of their thought was the work of the Marquis de **Sade**.

Yet this author marks the last stage of libertinism, for in him it becomes what the adversaries of the trend reproached it for being: the search for pleasures (reserved for the elite) which stopped at nothing, the sufferings of others being of no account. This attitude is very far from the equilibrium and urbanity of the beginnings of libertinism. With Sade the principle of maximizing the enjoyment of the single existence of man, and hence of a positive and joyous attitude to life, becomes a search for pleasure that can lead to suffering and death—as seen in the *120 Days of Sodom*.

Having reached this stage of intellectual no return, libertine thought became moribund. The French Revolution tore asunder the social fabric in which libertinism had sheltered its last adherents, and after this point it must be regarded as extinct.

BIBLIOGRAPHY. Alan Bray, *Homosexuality in Renaissance England*, London: Gay Men's Press, 1982; Giovanni Dall'Orto, "Antonio Rocco and the Background of His 'L'Alcibiade fanciullo a scola,'" in *Among Men, Among Women*, Amsterdam: University, 1983, pp. 224–32; René Pintard, *Le libertinage érudit dans la première moitié du dix-septième siècle*, 2 vols., Paris: Boivin, 1943.

Giovanni Dall'Orto

LIBRARIES AND ARCHIVES

Because of the clandestine or marginal origins of so many publications dealing with nonconforming sexuality, their representation in public and university libraries is thin. Sometimes librarians reject donations of erotic items (even scholarly books), or relegate them to special collections, the existence of which may be unknown even to sophisticated and well-qualified users. At the British Museum (now the British Library), the books in the Private Case were not entered in the main catalogue until the end of the 1960s. As such items are often stolen, there may be good reason to keep them secure, but such precautions are quite different from concealing their existence altogether.

Some Basic Features of Research Libraries. With the lessening of taboos such books are now more commonly accessioned and catalogued, but they remain restricted to a small number of libraries, from which, however, they may usually be borrowed through interlibrary loan. In the case of brochures, articles, or selections from books photocopying is a good alternative. Bearing in mind the limitations of its several editions, the *National Union Catalogue* should be consulted in checking locations. It is also worthwhile to examine the printed catalogues of the British Museum/Library in London and the Bibliothèque Nationale in Paris. Determined researchers prepare lists of rare sources so that in visiting the cities in which they are found, they can consult them.

Anecdotal evidence suggests that in North America at least a high proportion of male librarians are homosexual. Only in 1971, however, was the Gay Task Force of the American Library Association formed. Under the leadership of Barbara Gittings, this group has created a number of short bibliographies, which have been distributed to librarians and patrons in a successful effort to improve the scope of books on homosexuality in the average public library. It is here, after all, that many young and closeted gay men and lesbians go to seek information about themselves; in earlier decades they were likely to find only judgmental accounts under the category of "abnormal psychology."

In view of their rarity and inherent interest, books in the realm of "erotica" have appealed to well-to-do collectors, and a specialized book trade has grown up to meet the demand. We have a detailed record of the contents of one such private holding produced by the collector himself, the Victorian Henry Spencer Ashbee ("Pisanus Fraxi") in three volumes in 1877–85, and reprinted as *Bibliography of Forbidden Books* (New York, 1962).

In order to compensate for difficulty of access elsewhere, research institutions and gay organizations have sought to build up their own libraries. The Berlin Institute of Sexual Science, headed by Magnus **Hirschfeld**, had 20,000 volumes, together with a large picture collection, and a unique archive of sexual histories. Following Hitler's accession to power, a campaign of bookburning was begun to rid the German people of "unhealthy" influences. The Institute was one of the first targets, and on May 10, 1933, the bulk of its collections were destroyed in a public ceremony. Although no catalogue of this library has survived, many of the printed items contained were noted in the lists published annually in the *Jahrbuch für sexuelle Zwischenstufen* (until 1923). A contemporary, though smaller Dutch library, assembled by Jacob van Schorer, was catalogued. Today, the library of the Kinsey Institute for Sex Research on the campus of Indiana University at Bloomington is unquestionably the largest collection devoted to all types of sexual expression.

Gay and Lesbian Archives. As the American gay movement emerged in the 1950s a need for specialized libraries began to be felt, not only for research but also for the convenience of members who could not find even fairly innocuous gay and lesbian novels at their tax-supported public libraries. Modest budgets restricted acquisitions so that only in rare instances was it possible to obtain the classic European studies of the subject; in practice these organizational collections consisted mainly of pulp paperbacks donated by members. For want of security the collections were sporadically pilfered, and when the organizations folded, the materials that had been assembled were usually dispersed.

To deal with the problem a new institution, the gay and lesbian archive, emerged. Appropriately, the largest of these is located in **Los Angeles**, where the modern American movement began. The International Gay and Lesbian Archive (IGLA) comprises some 25,000 books, together with clippings, photographs, artworks, and gay/lesbian ephemera and memorabilia (flyers, banners, buttons, etc.). The IGLA core derives from the private collection started by the curator, Jim Kepner, in 1943; it was opened as a public institution in Hollywood in 1979. Also in Southern California is the Baker Memorial Library of **ONE**, Inc. The holdings of the Homosexual Information Center, formerly in Hollywood, have been transferred to Shreveport, Louisiana. These institutions are rivaled by the Canadian Gay Archives, which began in Toronto in 1973 as an offshoot of the monthly *The Body Politic*. This collection concentrates on, though is not limited to, Canadian material, and has issued a number of useful publications. The Thesaurus, or detailed subject listing, created by the Canadian group is probably the best available. In New York the Lesbian Herstory Archives, restricted to women's materials, is the largest collection of its kind. Bibliographical information is provided by the *Lesbian Herstory Archives News*, which began in 1975. Smaller archives flourished in a number of other North American cities, and others are being developed in Europe and Australia. Some European scholars take the position, however, that it is better to integrate holdings into public collections where they are less exposed to attacks of the kind that destroyed the Berlin collection.

While some archives have been forced to shut down owing to lack of funds, personnel, and user interest, and others have gone into temporary storage for similar reasons, enough stability has been achieved to permit the formulation of some basic operating principles. At the outset it is important to determine the scope of the archive and the public that it is intended to serve. These definitions will reflect in part the presence or absence of complementary institutions in the region, so that the existence of a first-class university library would make superfluous the acquisition of some mainstream items. Securing adequate premises, not only for present collections but for future growth, is a major consideration. Self-owned buildings are the ideal but this is rarely attainable. It may be possible to share quarters with a cognate institution, thus reducing costs. Installation in a private home can only be considered a temporary measure, as access tends to be restricted. Materials should not simply be received on a passive basis, but an outreach must be made to secure categories that are not adequately represented. Scholars and movement figures can often be persuaded to give their papers to the archive, benefitting from a tax write-off. During the period in which the facility is being established, some donors may prefer to "loan" materials with a view to deeding them over later when they are satisfied that stability has been achieved. Increasingly archivists need to extend their horizons beyond "hard copy" (print and manuscript materials on paper) to embrace films, tape recordings, video tapes, and other electronic modes of data storage. For day-to-day work copiers and word processors are essential.

As regards the organizational papers donated by groups, it may be desirable to keep these together as a subcollection in order to preserve their integrity, rather than mingling them with related items of different provenance. The issuance of a newsletter is a major desideratum, not only to make a larger public aware of the collection, but also as a way of stimulating donor interest. Cataloguing depends on the existence of a thesaurus of categories, which may be self-generated or adopted from another archive. Needless to say, funding is a perennial problem, since governmental assistance usually cannot be obtained, even if wanted. Development of a dedicated and harmonious corps of volunteers is essential, together with "angels" to provide regular financial subsidy. Most archives reject charging user fees, but such policies must be reviewed if they spell the difference between continuing and shutting down.

BIBLIOGRAPHY. James A. Fraser and Harold A. Averill, *Organizing an Archives: The Canadian Gay Archives Experience*, Toronto: Canadian Gay Archives, 1983.

Wayne R. Dynes

LIFESTYLE

In current usage the term lifestyle refers to the ensemble of choices that an individual may make in employment, leisure activities, dress, and self-presentation that serve to link him with a larger group in society (e.g., the hippie, jetset, and yuppie lifestyles). The element of choice is central: although an individual may have been raised in one lifestyle, he may elect to join another. (Income is usually the limiting factor.) This usage contrasts with the meaning of the term when first introduced in English in translations (from 1929 on) of the writings of the depth psychologist Alfred **Adler**, for whom it denotes an individual's basic character as formed in childhood, after which it cannot be changed. (In German *Lebensstil* had been used by Georg Simmel as early as 1900.) The shift in meaning may have been assisted by the somewhat similar expression "way of life."

Problems of Definition. Lifestyle is currently a journalistic rather than a social science term. For this reason its definition and boundaries are not always easy to determine. In theory everyone has a lifestyle, but in practice the word attaches to those who have departed from mainstream conventionality. This departure occurs either through upward or downward mobility. The yuppie and "fast lane" lifestyles can only be supported through a good deal of discretionary income, while the hippie or dropout exults in his flight from middle-class respectability (though these individuals may not be as poor as they seem). It may be, however, that the unreconstructed "square," who retains the habits and mores of the environment in which he was brought up, is also following a lifestyle; as José Ortega y Gasset remarked in a different context, not to choose is also to choose. All the same, the square may decry "trendy" pursuers of lifestyles, who he feels are eroding the moral fabric of society. Similarly, leftists have attacked "lifestylism" as mere self-indulgence, a hedonistic disregard of the call to make a revolution. Then lifestyles may overlap: a motorcyclist may participate both in the leather gay **subculture** and the biker subculture. Finally, on closer inspection what appears to be one lifestyle, may break up into a bundle of related phenomena. Although the gay lifestyle may be discussed in a unitary fashion, one should bear in mind that it has many subcomponents, so that (e.g.) the lifestyle of a lesbian businesswoman is very different from that of a lesbian S & M adept. Neglect of these very real differences has sometimes hobbled the effectiveness of gay and lesbian activist organizations, which tend to assume a greater social homogeneity than actually exists.

What remains is a sense of pluralism. Here the second component, "style" is important. As in the case of the Gothic, the Mannerist, and the Baroque styles in art history, one can recognize diversity without insisting that any one manifestation be honored as the norm.

Lifestyles and the Consumer Society. All these caveats aside, the rise of a plurality of lifestyles seems to presuppose the existence of a relatively wealthy consumer society. Amazon tribesmen do not have a choice of lifestyles. The affirmation of a lifestyle entails conspicuous consumption and conspicuous leisure. Moreover, this pattern cannot be simply treated in class terms, for it reflects a symbolic mode of existence that goes beyond mere socioeconomic status. Adopting a lifestyle proclaims one's value system and one's personal self-definition to the world at large. Hence the term "alternative lifestyle," which connotes that its bearer dissents from the conventional wisdom of society's mainstream. In this sense a lifestyle may

be a new form of heresy, one expressed in conduct rather than formal belief system.

A lifestyle includes modes of behavior, speech, dress, thought, and social attitudes that define a segment of the population and serve as a model for those who seek acceptance by the peer group. At the same time it may have an individual aspect that serves to distinguish the subject from others of his social class and ethnic group; this phenomenon is seen, for example, in some types of teenage rebellion. Having a lifestyle is regarded as a major undertaking, requiring a huge investment of the subject's resources of time, energy, and money; it is the outcome of a process of selection from the multitude of consumer goods and cultural activities offered to the citizen of an industrial country by the marketers of such commodities. The lifestyles of celebrities, publicized as they are by the mass media, become the models imitated by the less rich and famous. The media, especially television, films, and glossy magazines, play a decisive catalytic role in launching new trends. And since sexual activity is an important part of adults' leisure, homosexuality is a determining factor in the lifestyle of many, though not all, participants in the gay subculture of the United States and Western Europe.

The Gay Lifestyle. Attainment of increased leisure and of greater discretionary income undoubtedly furthered the emergence of the contemporary gay lifestyle. The earlier part of this century witnessed a clandestine homosexual subculture in the big cities of the Western world, but it was the gay liberation movement of the late 1960s that created a self-conscious public with its own media and its own social identity. The rejection of heterosexuality with all that it implied—including participation in activities traditionally defined as appropriate for male–female couples—was matched by the growth of a new set of values and standards shared by the emerging gay world of metropolitan

America. A characteristic style of dress, patronage of particular **bars**, **bathhouses**, and resorts, subscription to the gay mass media, and participation in community events of a more or less political content were the criteria of a gay lifestyle. At the same time a lifestyle could also be symbolic behavior aimed at attracting sexual partners of one's preference.

The hallmarks of the gay lifestyle of the 1970s were: living as a single adult, or in a casual union with a partner of the same sex that could be terminated at will; freedom from the obligations of conventional heterosexual marriage; fashions of dress and coiffure that marked the subject as part of the gay subculture; a level of discretionary income considerably above the norm for a heterosexual couple; acceptance of sexual experimentation and promiscuity if not as the norm, at least as behavior to be accepted in others without criticism; and periodic attendance at demonstrations, rallies, meetings, and similar events that brought together diverse strata of the gay community on specific occasions such as the annual Gay Pride Day marches in major cities.

A given lifestyle may be a slavish copy of behavior which the individual has been led by the media to deem appropriate for himself, or it may be an expression of an individuality that approaches the realm of the creative in private life. The media produced in the metropolitan areas and the celebrities whose fame extends beyond the gay subculture into the larger society of contemporary America serve as foci of lifestyle values that radiate into the hinterland and across national boundaries. Publications such as the *Advocate* in the United States and *Gai pied* in France disseminate the values of the gay lifestyle throughout their respective countries, usually to an upscale readership. It is significant that although the United States developed a homosexual movement well after Germany and the Netherlands, it was the American popular culture of the 1960s (disdainfully termed "cocacolonization"

by some European intellectuals) which proved the vehicle for the spread of a worldwide gay lifestyle patterned on the American example. The reception of this subculture was part of the continuing Americanization of Western Europe and the Third World in the 1970s, and of the spread of a consumption-oriented, pleasure-seeking way of life. Abatement of fears of venereal disease and of legal prosecution for one's sexual activity contributed to the tacit acceptance of a markedly hedonistic lifestyle, which includes drug usage, frequent change of sexual partners, and a restless search for new diversions and gratifications. In this respect the gay subculture perpetuated the tradition that had originated in the bohemias of the nineteenth century, as well as the "alternative lifestyles" that came into vogue with the radical wave of the Vietnam War era.

Recent Changes. Only with the threat of AIDS in the 1980s did a monogamous homosexual lifestyle gain in popularity and achieve for a certain part of the gay community the status of a norm. Also, as conservative values displaced the liberal or even radical ones of the late 1960s, the forces shaping Western social attitudes began to affect the behavior of the denizens of the gay subculture. But the consciousness of being part of a minority— one whose conduct differs significantly from that of the heterosexual majority; whose sexual activity is still strongly tabooed in the eyes of many; and whose values deviate markedly from the traditional norm—continues to shape the lifestyle of the homosexual.

To be sure, the homosexual lifestyle is not monolithic, and shows contrasts between coupled and single individuals, between leather adepts and those who prefer "vanilla sex." As the foregoing discussion has indicated, the relative importance of these "sublifestyles" in the mix has shifted over time, and further changes may be expected.

Conclusion. The choice of a lifestyle is one of the freedoms that modern society accords to its members. Premodern societies often prescribed the behavior of an individual on the basis of social class, family position, and age so rigorously as nearly to obliterate the personality of the subject. The atomization of society, the emancipation of the adult from the tutelage of the extended family, and the constant drive of the global economic system to find markets for new objects of consumption—all these have contributed to the emergence of variegated lifestyles as behavioral options for the citizen of the contemporary world. The gay lifestyle owes its viability in turn to the freeing of sexual morality from the narrow limits of previous centuries, and to the emergence from clandestinity of an "alternative culture" that could openly disdain many of the norms of the still intolerant larger society.

BIBLIOGRAPHY. Michael E. Sobel, *Lifestyle and Social Structure: Concepts, Definitions, Analyses,* New York: Academic Press, 1981.

Warren Johansson

LLANGOLLEN, LADIES OF

The Irishwomen Lady Eleanor Butler (1739–1829) and Sarah Ponsonby (1755–1831) enjoyed a relationship that lasted over fifty years, during which time they became celebrities whose fidelity was deeply admired. Lady Eleanor, who came from a noble family that had retained its Catholicism, was educated in a convent in France, at a time when "particular friendships" were easily tolerated. Returning to Ireland, she showed no interest in heterosexual marriage and immersed herself in books. In 1768, however, she met Sarah Ponsonby, a member of a well-to-do Dublin family, who was then only thirteen. Over the years their friendship ripened through visits and correspondence. Finally, in 1778, they decided to elope. After a first attempt failed, they succeeded in making their way to Wales. After inspecting the splendid Welsh landscapes together, they settled the following year in a rustic cottage (Plas Newydd) near Llangollen, which was to remain the site of their "retirement" for the rest of their lives.

The ladies immediately set themselves a program of regular life patterns and self-improvement—their "system" as they termed it. In an era before mass communications they bought books voraciously, and read to each other daily. Literature, languages, and geography were among the subjects they addressed. Their favorite author was Jean-Jacques Rousseau, who influenced their romantic cult of nature and the sublime. Attentive observation of the changing seasons was combined with astute management of the farm. In fact, it was probably the attachment of the ladies to the cult of nature, a dominant trend of late eighteenth-century sensibility, that served to validate their relationship in the eyes of contemporaries. Although lesbianism was known (and usually condemned) in this period, it tended to be associated with racy urban environments, especially the world of the theatre. Because of their birth and exemplary life style, a mantle of respectability protected the ladies of Llangollen for all their lives.

They carried on an enormous correspondence, and could be sharp with their friends if replies were not immediately forthcoming. In time they attracted such visitors as Lady Caroline Lamb and Josiah Wedgewood. William Wordsworth and Robert Southey wrote poetry under their roof. In addition to the letters, the lives of the ladies are recorded in diaries. In these they referred to each other as "Beloved." In modern terms theirs was a "butch-fem" relationship, inasmuch as Lady Eleanor was somewhat masculine in appearance and usually took the initiative in decision making, while the younger Sarah sweetly followed her lead. Disputes were rare. The surviving writings contain no hint of genital relations, but this lack of direct evidence does not necessarily mean that they sublimated their "passion" (a term they were not afraid to use). In an era before the medically inspired "morbidification" of romantic **friendship** between women, theirs was a true marriage of the mind, spirit, and affections. Ever steadfast in their observance of the principles that they had adopted, they had a friendship that captured the imagination of their contemporaries in a way never before achieved, at least in the English-speaking world. In an age of transition, the art of living of the Ladies of Llangollen may offer an object lesson.

BIBLIOGRAPHY. Elizabeth Mavor, *The Ladies of Llangollen*, London: Michael Joseph, 1971.

Evelyn Gettone

LOITERING

American law has tended to criminalize loitering with intent to commit a lewd or lascivious act or loitering with the purpose of soliciting or engaging in sexually deviant conduct. If such conduct constitutes a crime, as in the 25 states in which sodomy laws have not been repealed, the First Amendment does not protect solicitation for the purpose of a criminal act.

States that proscribe loitering with intent of solicitation do not require the uttering of the forbidden words. "Prior restraint" may thus cause people not to linger in certain places to talk to someone out of fear of having their conduct misinterpreted by a vice officer. Such a law is too broad to be constitutional and unconstitutionally limits free speech. Thus a demurrer, a challenge to the constitutionality of the law, can often prevail against this inchoate charge. It is frequently the case that repeated demurrers are required over many years before judges begin seriously to examine the constitutionality of the law.

BIBLIOGRAPHY. Roberta Achtenberg, ed., *Sexual Orientation and the Law*, New York: Clark Boardman, 1985.

William A. Percy

LOMBROSO, CESARE (1836–1909)

Italian criminologist. A descendant of a Sephardic Jewish family, Lombroso was a physician who became the founder of modern criminology. Following contemporary thinking which stressed the evolutionary and innate factors in human behavior, Lombroso developed the theory of the born criminal (*delinquente nato*), an atavistic throwback to earlier stages of human evolution. In line with the belief propagated by the German biologist Ernst Haeckel (1834–1919) that ontogenesis recapitulates phylogenesis, Lombroso believed that the born criminal, like the savage, lacks the higher nervous centers that restrain the lower animal instincts, so that he freely engages in mutilation, torture, promiscuity, pederasty, tattooing of the body, and similar practices abhorrent to civilized human beings; such individuals could be identified by the stigmata of degeneration on their bodies.

The school of criminal anthropology created by Lombroso, with journals in Italian, French, and German, reached the peak of its influence just at the time when sexual **inversion** became a topic of controversy in psychiatric and legal circles. Although Lombroso had read Arrigo Tamassia's paper of 1878 at the time of its publication and approved its conclusions, in the debate over homosexuality he proved a bitter foe of toleration. At the International Congress of Criminal Anthropology in Amsterdam in 1901, he was one of those who, outraged by Arnold **Aletrino**'s paper on "The Social Situation of the Homosexual," denounced the invert as a degenerate who should be thrown into prison if he acts out his diseased urges. His colleague in Vienna, Moritz Benedict, even urged that homosexuals who would not abstain from their criminal practices be castrated. In later controversy Lombroso was opposed by the German psychiatrist Paul Näcke (d. 1913), who calmly answered all his arguments on the basis of his own far greater familiarity with the subject. Also, in France the *Archives d'anthropologie criminelle* published a series of articles by Marc-André Raffalovich and others who combatted the notion of homosexuality as a disease.

Long decried by the environmentalist school, Lombroso remains a disputed thinker in the history of criminology and constitutional biology. Since the Mendelian laws of heredity were unknown until the very end of his lifetime, his own pioneering work was often impressionistic and based on phenotypes rather than genotypes. In the 1970s and 1980s Lombroso's views attracted new interest, suggesting that something of value may be retrieved from his otherwise time-bound conceptual scheme.

BIBLIOGRAPHY. Renzo Villa, *Il deviante e i suoi segni: Lombroso e la nascita dell'antropologia criminale*, Milan: Angeli, 1985.

Warren Johansson

LONDON

The capital first of **England**, then of the United Kingdom and of the British Empire, London has played a major role in the history of homosexuality in Western Europe. The establishment of a unified monarchy in the wake of the victory of William the Conqueror (1066) laid the foundations for London's supremacy. Although it was never a major center of university life or of the church, London still had the court, the great merchants, and later the press and the coffee houses, the publishers and the theatre that were the basis of English cultural and literary life. As England emerged from the backwardness and insignificance, as well as the internecine strife, of the medieval period and created its merchant fleet and overseas empire, London grew into a world-class city. The dialect of London became the literary norm of modern English, which after England's victory in the Seven Years War (1763) achieved the status of a world language and a medium of international discourse.

The Middle Ages. Richard of Devizes' *Chronicle of the Times of King Richard the First* includes an account of the underworld **subcultures** of London in 1192 that mentions at least four classes of individuals who certainly or probably engaged in homosexual activity: *glabriones*, "smooth-cheeked, pretty, effeminate boys," *pusiones*, "little hustlers, kept boys," *molles*, "effeminates," *mascularii*, "man-lovers," a term found only in this passage in all of Medieval Latin, through plainly deriving from the *masculorum concubitores* of 1 Corinthians 6:9. Thus even in the early Plantagenet period London had its erotic subculture frequented by those who ignored or defied the official norms of the Church in the sphere of sexual morality.

The Renaissance. The Tudor era saw the enactment of the first statute against homosexual behavior, 25 Henry VIII c. 6, which ordained the death penalty—by hanging, *not* by burning at the stake—for "the detestable and abominable Vice of Buggery." It is interesting to note that English is the only modern language in which *buggery* has remained the legal term for the crime in question; the idioms of the Continent all discarded a word that smacked too much of medieval intolerance. But the Renaissance, which brought the cultural life of the capital to unsurpassed heights, saw the revival of the homoeroticism that had inspired much of classical literature. The theatres at which the plays of **Marlowe**, **Shakespeare**, and the lesser dramatists of that time were performed had all-male casts, and by tradition the roles of women were taken by boys, so that an ambiance of sexual ambiguity and double-entendre hung over an institution that was constantly assailed for "immorality." Christopher Marlowe wrote one play, *Edward the Second* (1594), about a homosexual king of England, and another, *The Massacre at Paris* (1590), which inserts the French king Henri III and his minions into the episode of the St. Bartholomew's Eve slaughter of the Huguenots. He even ascribed to Jesus Christ an erotic interest in John, the **beloved disciple**. Shakespeare composed several plays with the motif of the boy actor who appears first as a woman and then in the guise of his own sex, is courted by a man and by a woman, and finally won by the former. The court of **James** I, after whom the fundamentalists' favorite translation of the Bible is named, had a homoerotic atmosphere owing to the king's fondness for male favorites who achieved positions of wealth and influence thanks to their royal patron.

The Restoration. The Civil War and the Commonwealth were followed by the Restoration, during which the first signs of a modern homosexual subculture emerge. The social stratification and anonymity of the metropolis facilitated the growth of a clandestine network of meeting places for individuals with unconventional desires. Restoration drama, the novels of Henry Fielding and John Cleland, and the prints of William Hogarth have given the London of that era a reputation for sensuality that contrasted with the sober life of the English countryside. In the late 1720s London was scandalized by the discovery of homosexual clubs, **molly houses**, in which some men would don women's clothing and even go through mock marriages. In 1717 the Swiss entrepreneur John James Heidegger introduced fashionable masquerade balls where men dressed as women, women as men; at such affairs it was possible to engage in same-sex amorous dalliance which could be disguised as mistaking the true gender of one's partner. Also, wealthy Englishmen began to travel abroad in search of erotic pleasures, in particular to Venice, which had become the Las Vegas of late seventeenth-century Europe, and which may have supplied the name of the *condom* (from Italian *guantone* "gauntlet"), first mass produced and sold in London from 1705 onwards.

Renewed Intolerance. Although burning at the stake was never the penalty for buggery in England, a fate in some ways even worse lay in wait for the convicted sodomite. Such culprits were exposed in the pillory to abuse and assaults of the mob, which could freely pelt the guilty parties with filth and missiles of every kind. The belief that **Sodom** and Gomorrah had been destroyed because of the sexual depravity of their inhabitants justified these cruel penalties in the eyes of the populace. The Napoleonic wars saw a renewed outburst of intolerance, which resulted in numerous prosecutions. In 1810 a homosexual rendezvous on Vere Street in London was raided by the police, and nine men were subsequently convicted and placed in the pillory, where the commons vented their wrath on them in a manner that bespoke the intensity of popular hatred for those guilty of "unnatural crimes." Even when Sir Robert Peel asked Parliament to reform the archaic criminal laws of England in 1828, he urged that the proofs of the offense of buggery be made fewer to facilitate conviction, while the death penalty was not reduced to life imprisonment until 1861.

The Victorian Era. But homosexual life persisted beneath the surface of London's commercial and industrial life and the Victorian respectability of the capital of a great empire "on which the sun never set." Homosexuals of the upper social strata rubbed shoulders with hustlers from the depths of the criminal underworld, a phenomenon so aberrant from the standpoint of a class society that as late as the middle of the twentieth century the police could be moved to an investigation merely by evidence of associations of this kind. In 1889 a scandal occurred in which a house in Cleveland Street was discovered to be a place of assignation for homosexual clients and telegraph boys who served them as prostitutes. Oscar **Wilde**'s ruin was also caused by his involvement with this criminal milieu when it was revealed by his arch-enemy, the Marquess of Queensbury, in 1895.

The Twentieth Century. The hypocrisy with which English culture enveloped the phenomenon of homosexuality long obscured the facts of this subculture in the London of the twentieth century. Although English law was as punitive as German, no organized gay movement analogous to the one in Berlin could develop in the British capital, even if circles like the **Bloomsbury** one could quietly cultivate a homosexual ethos in a rarified milieu inaccessible to the British masses. The **theatre** and other cultural institutions were enclaves of homosexual influence, but they always had to defer publicly to the conventional norms of sexual morality. The conviction of Sir John Gielgud for public importuning in 1953 lifted the lid for once on this covert phenomenon.

The campaign for adoption of the recommendations of the **Wolfenden** Report was too limited in its scope and the roster of its supporters to affect the life of the average homosexual in London, which after the austerity of the immediate postwar period changed into the center of a vibrant, influential mass culture. The Beatles and the Rolling Stones were symbols of the world-wide impact of this new wave, which was paralleled by legalized gambling and Carnaby Street fashions that shaped the image of "swinging London." The plays of Joe **Orton** (who was, however, murdered by his lover in 1967) caught much of the wit and nonchalant cynicism of this era. During this decade a commercial gay subculture arose, with its base in the roaring pubs of South Kensington and Hampstead. The police continued even after the law reform of 1967 to harass individuals whom they caught in public places such as parks and "cottages" (toilets).

The **Stonewall Rebellion** in New York in 1969 created American political models such as Gay Activists Alliance which were then imported into the mother country, crystalizing first in a national gay organization, the Campaign for Homosexual Equality (CHE). Those who saw this group as too conservative and middle-class set up more radical formations, at first under anarchist and then increasingly under **Marxist** auspices. During the 1970s the London-based *Gay News* (now defunct) ranked as one of the world's three or four leading gay newspapers.

The economic setbacks experienced by the country caused rising social tensions, marked by racial disturbances in London and elsewhere. While several London boroughs gave direct financial aid to gay and lesbian organizations, a rising tide of homophobia was abetted by manipulation of the AIDS crisis through sensational articles in the tabloid newspapers. The new political situation—including a solid Conservative majority in Parliament—led to the passage of Clause 28 of the Local Government Act (1988), which forbade local governments to do anything to "promote" homosexuality, yet technical errors in the drafting of the bill rendered it at least partly inoperative. With all the ambivalence of its history, contemporary London is firmly established as a major center of homosexual life.

BIBLIOGRAPHY. Michael Elliman and Frederick Roll, *The Pink Plaque Guide to London*, London: Gay Men's Press, 1986; H. Montgomery Hyde, *The Love That Dared Not Speak Its Name: A Candid History of Homosexuality in Britain*, Boston: Little, Brown, 1970.
Ward Houser

LORCA, FEDERICO GARCÍA (1898–1936)

Poet and dramatist, **Spain**'s most famous author after Cervantes. Born in the southern province of **Granada** and influenced by the Andalusian revival of the early twentieth century, Lorca lived from the age of 20 in Madrid. In the famous "Residencia de Estudiantes," he met and collaborated with such future celebrities as Luis Buñuel and Salvador Dalí, with the latter of whom he had an amorous relationship of several years' duration.

An emotional and literary crisis in 1928 led to an extended visit to New

York and Cuba in 1929–30. With the birth of the liberal Spanish republic in 1931, Lorca moved from intellectual to mainstream circles. The government sponsored his traveling theatre troupe, "La Barraca," which took Spanish classics to isolated small towns. His own plays were produced with success, and he began to receive a significant income from royalties.

The revolt against the Spanish republic in 1936 brought Lorca's assassination by a semi-official death squad. An extensive literature exists concerning the mechanics of and motives for his death, which immediately became an international incident and a symbol of fascist stupidity and anti-intellectualism. Lorca's leftist sympathies, friends, and relatives would be sufficient to explain his execution, but much evidence suggests that his sexual orientation, activities, and writings were at least as important.

Lorca is an exceptional case of an author subject to self-censorship and, after his death, to deliberate manipulation and "cleansing" of his image by surviving family members. As a result his works and thought have been inaccurately discussed, and they remain imperfectly known and in some cases all but unknown. At the time of his death Lorca was best known for his *Gypsy Ballads*, still his most popular and accessible, yet somewhat unrepresentative book. Lesser-known volumes of poetry, and those dramas found unoffensive by his heirs, were published or reprinted in 1938. His central but difficult *Poet in New York*, incorporating an *Ode to Walt Whitman* privately published in 1933, first appeared in 1940; *The House of Bernarda Alba*, suppressed by his family, in 1945. In 1954 his family "rediscovered" the early but important drama *The Butterfly's Evil Trick* ("butterfly" is a Spanish slang term for homosexual). Only in 1974 was the long-unavailable *Impressions and Landscapes* reprinted. The overtly pederastic and Pirandellian *The Public* was published from an incomplete draft MS, over his relatives' opposition, in 1976; the final

text is still unavailable. (The play was very well received when premiered in Spain in 1987; its title has been borrowed for a major Spanish theatrical magazine.) The *Sonnets of Dark Love* were withheld by his family and published clandestinely in 1983. Important juvenilia are only slowly being made available, and of his extensive correspondence only that part without reference to sexual themes has been published.

Lorca was given to discussing works in advance of or during composition. Among those he mentioned are *The Destruction of Sodom*, in which frustration of homosexual desire causes incest, *The Blackball*, "the tragedy of a homosexual in conflict with society," and *The Beautiful Beast*, a treatment of zoophily. These exist only as tiny fragments or in the published recollections of his friends.

It is difficult and risky to outline Lorca's thought without full access to his works, but it is known in part. Central to his writings is the power, universality, and goodness of the sexual and reproductive instinct, and opposition to forces—especially the Catholic church—which repress and frustrate it. In his plays, many of which have female protagonists, he treats the frustrated desire for offspring; a long religious poem presents a beautiful crucified Christ as a figure of sexual liberation. A second current in his thought is the need for spiritual, cultural, and economic reform of Spanish and world society. Finally, there is the theme of isolation and melancholy. He explores poetically problems of self-acceptance and relating to a hostile world, the difficulty of transcending isolation through love, and a general existential and irresolvable anguish.

BIBLIOGRAPHY. Paola Ambrosi and Maria Grazia Profeti, *F. García Lorca: La frustrazione erotica maschile*, Rome: Bulzoni, 1979; Daniel Eisenberg, "Reaction to the Publication of the *Sonetos del amor oscuro*," *Bulletin of Hispanic Studies*, 55 (1988), 261-71; Ian Gibson, *Federico García Lorca: A Life*, London: Faber, 1989; idem, "Lorca's

'Balada triste': Children's Songs and the Theme of Sexual Disharmony in *Libro de poemas*," *Bulletin of Hispanic Studies*, 46 (1969), 21–38; Dennis Klein, "*Así que pasen cinco años*: A Search for Sexual Identity," *Journal of Spanish Studies: Twentieth Century*, 3 (1975), 115–23; Rafael Martínez Nadal, *Federico García Lorca and "The Public,"* New York: Schocken, 1974; idem, *Cuatro lecciones sobre Federico García Lorca*, Madrid: Juan March-Cátedra, 1980; Angel Sahuquillo, *Federico García Lorca y la cultura de la homosexualidad*, Stockholm: Akademitryck, 1986; Mario Socrate, "Studio critico" accompanying his translation of *Sonetti dell'amore oscuro e altre poesie inedite*, Milan: Garzanti, 1985, pp. 249–69; Joseph Velasco, "La poesía erótica del primer Lorca," *Hommage à Jean-Louis Flecniakoska*, Montpellier, 1980, II, 445–61; Luis Antonio de Villena, "La sensibilidad homoerótica en el *Romancero gitano*," *Campus* [Granada], December 1986, pp. 27–30.

Daniel Eisenberg

LOS ANGELES

Today the Los Angeles metropolitan area is believed to be the twelfth most populous conurbation in the world. The growth leading to this concentration is the result of several factors, notably the mild Mediterranean climate, which attracted immigration as well as certain industries not dependent on proximity to raw materials, such as motion picture production and aircraft manufacture.

A number of elements account for the emergence of Los Angeles as one of the leading urban foci of a homophile subculture by the mid-twentieth century. The long stretches of fine beach on the Pacific Ocean, coupled with long summer seasons of good, sunny weather eventually incubated a subculture of bodybuilders and physique photographers that became well-known around the country. Another factor appears to have been a spinoff from the **film** industry: like the theatre from which it in part derived, Hollywood used the talents of costume and set designers, makeup artists, and hairdressers—all vocations in which the homophile is believed to be represented in disproportionately high numbers. Another factor may have been religious diversity. Large numbers of Christians affiliated with a great diversity of Protestant denominations, as well as a number of Jews, and some immigrants from Asia who were adherents of Buddhism and other faiths, flocked to California in the latter half of the nineteenth century. As a result, no one denomination established such a hegemony as to be able to dictate moral standards. While same-sex relations were generally anathema to the various denominations for many years, the foundation was laid for increasing tolerance on the part of several of them.

Los Angeles developed its port of San Pedro beginning at the turn of the century, and facilities for maritime commerce emerged at the same time as those to serve the needs of the United States Navy. While many **seafarers**, whether civilian or military, sought out prostitutes or girlfriends during their time on shore, Los Angeles and its port district of San Pedro and maritime suburb, Long Beach, were no different from similarly situated communities in the development of opportunities for same-sex encounters involving sailors.

Victorian and Pre-World War I Periods, 1848–1917. The annexation of California to the United States pursuant to the Treaty of Guadalupe Hidalgo of 1848 led to the formation of state government in 1849 and admission to the Union the following year. One of the first acts of the new State's Legislature was to pass "An Act Concerning Crimes and Punishments" on April 16, 1850. Section 48 stated: "The infamous crime against nature, either with man or beast, shall subject the offender to be punished by imprisonment in the State Prison for a term not less than five years, and which may extend to life." This was derived from Field's Draft New York Penal Code. The 1880 Federal Census found three persons incarcerated in California for "crimes against nature." In an important case, *People v. Boyle* (1897), the California Supreme Court held that a sexual assault in the "victim's" mouth was insufficient to support a conviction. In 1915 this perceived defect was remedied by criminalizing fellatio and cunnilingus.

In 1914, the City of Long Beach, a Los Angeles suburb, hired undercover detectives who arrested over thirty men in the restrooms of the local plunge and elsewhere on "vagrancy" charges. This charge has been used in California, since a 1903 amendment to the "vagrancy" law, to prosecute same-sex activity where actual intercourse sufficient for "crime against nature" could not be proven. Most interestingly, two defendants pled not guilty, obtained jury trials, and were acquitted after testimony suggested entrapment or even perjury on the part of the police. The *Los Angeles Times* editorialized against "sodomites," but showed startling familiarity with the work of Edward **Carpenter**, mentioned historical figures such as Julius **Caesar**, King James I, and Oscar **Wilde**, and used the word "homo-sexuality"—possibly one of the earliest appearances of the term in the American mass media.

The World Wars and Interwar Period, 1917–1945. During the interwar period, same-sex cruising locales became clearly identified; the two best known in Los Angeles were Pershing Square, a park occupying a city block in the center of downtown Los Angeles, and Westlake Park (renamed General Douglas MacArthur Park during World War II), four to six times as large, a mile and a half to the west. These urban parks presented an ideal setting for casual pickups as well as prostitution, same-sex and otherwise. Pershing Square, in particular, was conveniently located to bars and cheap hotels where management was not so choosy about their clientele, and homosexuals would be tolerated when vice enforcement was not intense (by the thirties, the first identifiably "gay" bars can be noted). For the more affluent, one or more private clubs in Hollywood facilitated diverse sexual ac-

tivity. Other venues for same-sex encounters included the San Pedro and Long Beach entertainment districts which attracted sailors and those who were interested in meeting them. Both World Wars took men away from small towns to larger cities, such as Los Angeles, where social pressures to conform diminished and same-sex environments multiplied.

The Postwar Period, 1945–1969. The social turmoil resulting from World War II included the throwing together in same-sex environments of large numbers of servicemen and servicewomen, with the inevitable development of physical and emotional relations. Many who "came out" in this way during the war never returned to their home towns, but settled in large cities where they could live a life more compatible with their sexual orientation.

The late forties saw the first known lesbian periodical in America, *Vice Versa*, edited by "Lisa Ben," the pseudonym of Edyth Eyde. In 1950 and 1951, the **Mattachine Society** was organized in Los Angeles, the country's first large-scale homophile organization. It organized numerous discussion groups and struck a radical blow for civil rights in the spring of 1952 when it organized a legal defense for one of its members, Dale Jennings, who had been arrested by a vice officer for solicitation; Jennings got off. Internal politics led to a reorganization of Mattachine in 1953; later, it was based in **San Francisco**. Meanwhile, **ONE**, Inc. was founded in Los Angeles in late 1952, with a primary goal of publishing. *ONE Magazine* first appeared in January of 1953, and was the first successful American magazine by and for the homophile.

Gay bar life was facilitated by a California Supreme Court decision establishing the right of an establishment to operate, even if its clientele was predominantly or even exclusively homosexual. Sex itself was legally anathema; "crime against nature" was punishable by one year to life in prison after 1952. **Bath-**

houses catering to a gay trade were subject to harassment; an appellate decision of the mid-fifties upheld the Los Angeles Police Commission's closing of the Sultan Baths, a few doors from Pershing Square, citing numerous arrests and convictions of male patrons for sexual activity. During the sixties, organizing increased. The Council on Religion and the Homophile, opening lines of communication with religious leaders, presaged the later founding in the Los Angeles area of the Metropolitan Community Church and groups within existing religious denominations. The *Advocate* began in 1967 as the newsletter of the Los Angeles homophile group, PRIDE.

After Stonewall. The period marked by the **Stonewall Rebellion** in New York was one of continued building on past activity in Los Angeles. A Gay Community Services Center was organized. The Homophile Effort for Legal Protection was formed to help in the courts, and the California legislature legalized private, noncommercial, consensual sex between adults in 1975.

The seventies featured continued growth of traditional meeting places such as bars and baths, but opportunities for socializing in less sexually-charged contexts also burgeoned, including groups formed to enable businesspeople, or members of specific professions or occupations to congregate. Athletic, sports, and musical organizations proliferated. These were national trends, but they manifested themselves in Los Angeles at least as early as anywhere else. Political organizations, Democratic, Republican, and nonpartisan, appeared. The eighties would become known as the decade of **AIDS**, and Los Angeles was not far behind New York and San Francisco in being a target of this disease. Community organizations were soon mounting a strong response to the challenge, however.

Scholarly pursuits were not neglected; ONE Institute celebrated thirty years of work on a 3 1/2-acre campus, granting the world's first Master's and Doctoral degrees in Homophile Studies.

David G. Cameron

Louis XIII (1601–1643)

King of France at the time of the Thirty Years War. The question has been argued whether or not Louis XIII was homosexual. He was, remarkably enough, the son of Henri IV, known as "le Vert-Galant" because of his passion for women, and father of the equally heterosexual Louis XIV. Physically Louis was sickly and subject to insomnia, in character he was sulky, fretful, selfish, and obdurate to the point of cruelty. His childhood environment was not one that would have turned him toward heterosexuality. His father and mother quarreled constantly. The spectacle of his father's unceasing debauchery, the presence of bastard half-brothers whom he hated, and their mothers—his father's former mistresses—combined with the heavy burden of power shared with an ambitious mother, Marie de Médicis, did not make for a model to emulate. As a consequence the child's sensibilities were repelled by the lasciviousness of the court, but at the age of ten he developed a passionate attachment for a young nobleman, Charles d'Albert de Luynes, keeper of the king's hunting birds. Luynes was a handsome man of twenty-three, virile and athletic, and the passionate attachment of the boy for an older servant was a classic homoerotic liaison which lasted for ten years and reached the point where the sovereign could make no decision without consulting his friend. The only unanswered question is whether the ambitious and self-centered Luynes took advantage of the king's affection.

An arranged dynastic marriage with the Spanish Infanta, Anne of Austria, was a matter of political expediency and of amorous failure: Luynes had to carry him against his will to the bridal chamber where he had to "force himself" twice, and for more than twenty years the marriage remained without issue—this at a time when contraceptive devices were uncommon. The celebrated Cardinal Richelieu, since 1623–24 the Prime Minister, understood his sovereign's character perfectly, as befitted a statesman of his caliber, and so favored the friendship that sprang up between Louis and François de Barradas, an equerry of the royal stables, stupid and otherwise meritless, but handsome, athletic, and virile. According to Tallement des Réaux, the king was accused of "countless indecencies with him." After a break caused by the marriage of his favorite, the king found solace with Claude de Saint-Simon (father of the author of the *Memoirs*), and then in 1638, with an eighteen-year-old boy, Henri de Cinq-Mars, who within a few months rose from captain in the guards to Grand Master of the Wardrobe and Grand Equerry of France. For a time it was an idyllic love affair—but it proved one-sided, as Cinq-Mars saw in the king only a source of endless favors and gifts. So followed three years of jealous turmoil and heartbreak for Louis, which ended only when Cinq-Mars made the fatal error of plotting against Richelieu, who presented the monarch with written proof of his treason. Cinq-Mars was beheaded in September 1642 in the Place des Terreaux in Lyon. The king, neurasthenic and melancholy, lived but a year longer.

A puritan by natural rigidity and by the religious training which he received in the era of the Counterreformation, Louis XIII was also homosexual, and his sexual orientation is the key to his character. His passionate submission to the virile Luynes was a prelude to the domination which Richelieu by other means was to exert over him. He had many effeminate traits: weakness of character, the need to be dominated, jealousy, and pettiness. His love for women was never attended by sexual desire, a circumstance that led to his being named "Louis the Chaste"—an example of what V. V. **Rozanov** called "the psychological 'I cannot' masquerading as the moral 'I will not.'" But if he lacked the qualities of a true head of state and a great king, Cardinal Richelieu made up for these failings in his role as Prime Minister, and controlling Louis XIII as he did, he used his position to bring France to the height of its power in European affairs under the Old Regime.

BIBLIOGRAPHY. Marc Daniel, "A Study of Homosexuality in France during the Reigns of Louis XIII & Louis XIV," *One Institute Quarterly*, 4/3 (1961), 77–93; A. Floyd Moote, *Louis XIII, the Just*, Berkeley: UC Press, 1989.

Warren Johansson

LOVE

Unstintingly, modern philosophers and novelists have analyzed love, while creators of high and popular art never tire in their celebration of it. It goes without saying that the bulk of these discussions concern heterosexual love. Yet the ancient Greeks, from whom all our thinking in the matter ultimately derives, were as interested (if not more so) in homosexual love as in the heterosexual variety.

The Greek Contribution. The Greek language makes a sharp distinction between love as affection (*philia*) and love as desire (*eros*). Philia is directed mainly toward family members and friends, while eros is the more intense form, which would include, in our terms, both romantic love and lust. **Homer** describes eros as a kind of appetite, to be assuaged in much the same manner as thirst and hunger are slaked by drinking and eating. Although this notion of love as appetite survives even today, most of those who have experienced love would be unwilling to leave the matter there. Nor did the Greeks. The archaic lyric poets of the seventh and sixth centuries B.C., who were the first to portray subjective emotional life in all of its bittersweet intensity, presented a concept of love as a piercing experience that transformed the very core of one's being. As the Lesbian poet **Sappho** sang, "Some say that the most beautiful thing on the black earth is an army of horsemen, others an army of footsoldiers, others a fleet of ships; but I say it is the person you love." The poets understood that love could be a mania, depriving the lover of food and sleep and making him tear his hair and garments. In **pederastic** love a dynamic of reversal often occurred in which the superior partner, the *erastes*, became the slave of his beloved, the *eromenos*. Hence the theme of the tyranny of love. Pederasty also focused on love's transience, for the beloved speedily lost his attractiveness at the first growth of beard.

In the *Symposium* **Plato** presents the myth of human origins from double beings of which living men and women are but sundered halves. The longing to return to this primal unity is "the desire and pursuit of the whole." The ultimate impossibility of this quest is an apt metaphor for the unrealizability of love's final goals. But human love may be the starting point for an intellectual and spiritual endeavor which carries us up through a "ladder of being" to the ultimate contemplation of the good. Plato's concept (which is not identical with the later notion of "Platonic love") is the starting point of the whole tradition of idealization in love. Although later commentators tend to gloss the matter over, it is clear that in his discussion of the wonders of eros Plato and his colleagues have in mind exclusively the love of boys.

Rome and the Middle Ages. Reacting perhaps against Platonic idealization, the Roman poets Lucretius and Ovid advocated a down-to-earth concept of love as practical satisfaction. Lucretius saw human love as an extension of animal copulation, even of agricultural activity.

The writers of the **New Testament** abhorred what they regarded as the excessively carnal concept of love among the Greeks and Romans, even preferring the vulgar word *agape* for divinely sanctioned love. *Agape* could not include homosexual love, which was henceforth to be outlawed. In any event, however, the new concept did not oust the Greco-Roman

one, and the two competed in subsequent centuries. In medieval Europe the ancient concept, as transmitted by Ovid, enjoyed a revival, and this revival is one of the chief ingredients of the "courtly love" of the Provençal troubadours and those who came after them. A curious feature of the Provençal lyrics is the masculine form of address to the beloved—*midons* instead of *madonna*. If it is true that troubadour poetry was influenced by Moorish poetry from **Spain**, this address may be a relic of the conventions of the pederastic poetry that flourished in all the Islamic lands. There is also a considerable body of medieval pederastic poetry in Latin, including debates as to the respective merits of male and female love objects.

The Renaissance and After. The Italian **Renaissance**, permeated with **neo-Platonism** and the revival of **astrology**, saw love as the product of cosmic forces. In human affairs its actions could be compared to magic and sorcery; hence the "Circean" concept of love as a matter of charms, spells, and enchantments. In Renaissance plays and epic poems (such as Ariosto's *Orlando Furioso*) cross-dressing scenes permitted some exploration of same-sex love.

In the eighteenth and nineteenth centuries, romantic poets and novelists saw love under the sign of illusion, but a fruitful illusion that brings the lover into contact with the infinite and transcendental. In Freudian **psychoanalysis** the sense of illusion persists, but without the ennobling idealization.

One of the most profound twentieth-century analysts of love was the French homosexual novelist Marcel **Proust**. Working his way through the still predominately negative concepts of homosexuality that he inherited, he saw much commonality between homosexual and heterosexual love. The imperfect match between the lover's concept of the love object and the actuality of him made for complexity, as did changes over time.

With the implementation of the "sexual revolution" in the 1970s romantic love seemed to take second place to lust, but the AIDS crisis has helped it to make a comeback. With the relentless propagation of the common coin of love through the mass media, gay men and lesbians have inevitably internalized much of the sentimental lore of heterosexual love, so that there is now a genre of "romance" novels aimed specifically at this market. The popular psychologist Dorothy Tennov attempted to introduce a new term, *limerence*, but it is unclear that this word represents any conceptual advance; it is simply romantic love once again. Love, it seems, is a perennial theme, and one which retains much of its mystery intact.

BIBLIOGRAPHY. Edith Fischer, *Amor und Eros: Eine Untersuchung des Wortfeldes "Liebe" im Lateinischen und Griechischen*, Hildesheim: H. A. Gerstenberg, 1973; David M. Halperin, "Platonic *Eros* and What Men Call Love," *Ancient Philosophy*, 5 (1985), 161–204; J. E. Rivers, *Proust and the Art of Love*, New York: Columbia University Press, 1980; Irving Singer, *The Nature of Love*, 3 vols., Chicago: Chicago University Press, 1984–87.

Wayne R. Dynes

LOVER

In today's homosexual usage the term "lover" designates one's long-term partner. If one is invited to a social event, it would seem reasonable to ask "May I bring my lover?" just as others would say "May I bring my spouse?" Some have objected to the word as placing too much emphasis on the sexual side. Interestingly, a similar problem of designation occurs among unmarried heterosexual **couples** who need a word to describe their opposite number in the dyad.

In former times heterosexuals recognized a pattern of relationship between *lover* and *mistress* for a bond not sanctioned by the law and without implying absolute fidelity. Neither homosexuals or lesbians ever seem to have adopted the word mistress, which has retained exclusively heterosexual connotations of amorous arrangements.

Dissatisfaction with the term lover in its current sense suggests several alternatives, but these seem scarcely happier. *Fiancé* seems too old-fashioned, and the implication that marriage will follow is not appropriate for gay men and lesbians. *Paramour* has acquired the negative, judgmental connotation of a temporary partner with purely physical interests. An expression derived from **sociology**, *significant other*, seems too long and pretentious, while *partner* may imply a business relationship, or conversely, a chance participant in a one-night stand. Some have therefore proposed *life partner*, an expression now making its way into obituaries as they increasingly disregard the taboo on mentioning the survivor of a homosexual couple arrangement.

Latin recognized both *amator*, "lover, paramour, devoted friend," and *amans*, "loving one, sweatheart." In English usage, French-derived *amateur* has become specialized in the sense of a lover of things (not persons), or a dilettante.

LOWELL, AMY LAWRENCE (1874–1925)

American poet. Born into a distinguished and wealthy family in Brookline, Massachusetts, Lowell was educated privately. For a brief period she was associated with Ezra Pound, but broke with him to go her own way. In fact her imagist poetry is quite different from that of Pound's circle.

Lowell described herself in her adolescent diary as "a great, rough, masculine, strong thing." Lacking beauty in her own perception, she confessed in that same diary that "I cannot help admiring [sic] and generally falling in love with, extreme beauty." Although she had very strong crushes on young males during that adolescent period, it was her crushes on her female friends that appear to have first led to her writing poetry; one of her earliest extant poems came out of her adolescent crush on her girlfriend, "Louly W."

Amy Lowell's first published volume of poems, *A Dome of Many Coloured Glass* (1912), contains a number of seemingly homoerotic poems, addressed to two women. But the most significant body of her experiential love poems was written to and for the actress Ada Russell.

Amy Lowell first encountered Ada Russell in 1909 when the actress was traveling on a New England tour of *Dawn of a Tomorrow*. The two met again in Boston, in 1912, when Russell, playing the lead in *The Deep Purple*, appeared as a guest of honor at the Lunch Club, to which Lowell, then half-heartedly living the life of a Boston society woman, belonged. They spent part of the summer of 1912 together, and for the next two years the poet tried to convince the actress to live with her. This courtship is reflected in approximately 20 poems of *Sword Blades and Poppy Seed* (1914). Ada finally yielded to Amy's pursuit in the spring of 1914. She quit the stage and went to live with the poet in her Brookline mansion, Sevenels, ostensibly as her paid companion, but in fact as her mate. The two lived together until Amy's death in 1925.

Several of Lowell's later volumes contain love poems about the relationship between the two women, such as *Pictures of the Floating World* (1919) and two posthumous volumes, *What's O'Clock* (1925) and *Ballads for Sale* (1927). The 43 poems in the "Two Speak Together" section of *Pictures of a Floating World* are the best and most complete record of the love relationship between Amy Lowell and Ada Russell.

The usual critical observation that Lowell was overweight and unmarried, and that her work is a "knell of personal frustration . . . an effort to hide the bare walls of the empty chambers of her heart . . ." (Harvey Allen, *Saturday Review of Literature*, 1927) and the exposure of the heart of "a girlish, pathetic, and lonely woman, underneath [whose] . . . bumptious manner lies disappointment" (Winfield Townley Scott, *New England Quarterly*, 1935), is not borne out by the body of Lowell's poetry. The preponderance of her experiential poems suggest a life and a relationship that were extremely happy and productive. Typically, in "Thorn Pierce" Lowell talks about the world being dark and glazed, but another woman gives to her "fire,/And love to comfort, and speech to bind,/And the common things of morning and evening./And the light of your lantern." In "Christmas Eve" she tells the other woman, "You have lifted my eyes, and made me whole,/And given me purpose, and held me faced/ Toward the horizon you once had placed/ As my aim's grand measure." "A Decade," the poem that celebrates the first ten years of their acquaintance, concludes "I am completely nourished." Lowell admitted to her acquaintances, such as John Livingston Lowes, that such love poems were about Ada.

In a scurrilous study published one year after Amy Lowell's death, Clement Wood argued that Lowell was not a good poet because many of her poems were homosexual; therefore, they did not "word a common cry of many hearts." Lowell, he concluded, may qualify "as an impassioned singer of her own desires; and she may well be laureate also of as many as stand beside her," but non-lesbian readers will find nothing in her verse (*Amy Lowell*, 1926).

BIBLIOGRAPHY. Lillian Faderman, "Warding off the Watch and Ward Society: Amy Lowell's Lesbian Poetry," *Gay Books Bulletin*, 1:2 (Spring 1979), 23–27; Amy Jean Gould, *The World of Amy Lowell and the Imagist Movement*, New York: Dodd, Mead, 1975.

Lillian Faderman

LUCIAN
(CA. 120–CA. 185)

Greek writer. From Samosata on the Euphrates, Lucian traveled widely as a tutor and professional lecturer, delivering set pieces in Greek, though his native tongue was Aramaic. He was surnamed "the blasphemer" according to Suda for telling absurd tales of the gods. At about the age of 40 he settled in Athens and gave up rhetoric to write philosophic *Dialogues.* Eventually, perhaps under Commodus, he became an imperial official in Egypt. He borrowed from Cynic wit, Menippean satire, mime, Old Attic Comedy, and (for his later *Dialogues*) from **Plato.** Practicing successively law, sculpture, and rhetoric, he exposed the charlatan in *Alexander* and the religious fanatic in *Peregrinus,* who becoming a Christian grew wealthy by donations from his duped coreligionists but abjured Christianity when he was released from prison where he was confined for fraud and ended by immolating himself at the **Olympic games.** Anticipating the concerted attack that would be organized by later imperial families, he characterized Christ as "that crucified sophist" and his followers as "unhappy men (who) have persuaded themselves that they will be immortal and live forever; wherefore they despise death and willingly sacrifice themselves" (*Peregrinus,* 13).

His *Life of Alexander of Abonuteichos* satirized a Pythagorean divine who, having become rich and famous through fraud in middle age, kept a harem of pretty young priests. Born about 105 in that Hellenized Black Sea port, Alexander, a tall, handsome, quick-witted youth, became the beloved of a quack physician from Tyana who had once followed Apollonius. Having learned and gotten all he could from the doctor, the unscrupulous youth joined an itinerant entertainer "practicing quackery and sorcery." He claimed descent from Perseus and mesmerized credulous audiences as a prophet of Asclepius, whose snakes, Alexander's pets, answered in verse questions submitted in writing for one drachma and two obols. Marcus Aurelius granted a new name to his native city (Ionopolis), which issued coins showing Alexander wearing his grandfather Asclepius' fillets.

Lucian questioned his contemporaries' received beliefs and without great originality proffered sound comments on art, literature, and history. He satirized Zeus and **Ganymede,** poking gentle fun at the Greek gods' pederastic loves. In pamphlets Lucian often accused even innocent men of homosexual acts, a tactic by his time standard in Greek (and Roman) oratory. Peregrinus, he charged, paid the poor parents of a youth he had corrupted three thousand drachmae to escape being hauled before the governor of Asia.

The ironically entitled *True History* is possibly the first gay **science fiction.** On a voyage into the Atlantic, the narrator is suddenly enveloped by a typhoon, which sweeps him up to the moon. Earth's satellite is inhabited by men only, and is engaged in a war with the sun. After distinguishing himself in combat, the hero returns to the moon, where the king magnanimously gives him his son the prince in marriage. Since there are no women, male babies are born in two ways: by parturition from the thigh (presumably after having been inseminated anally) or by planting the left testicle in the ground, whereupon the child grows out of the ground as part of a plant. Shorn of its homoeroticism this romance inspired Swift's *Gulliver's Travels,* the fantasies of Cyrano de Bergerac (1619–1655), and many later European tales of interplanetary flight.

The romance *Lucius,* based on the work of Lucius of Patrae, may be among Lucian's authentic works, but rather appears to be a gross summary of his elaboration of Lucius' work. On a visit to Thessaly, the protagonist witnesses the drug-induced transformation of his hostess into a bird. Taking a draught himself, he becomes an ass and undergoes various sexual abuses, being buggered by a randy master and having to copulate interminably with a nymphomaniac. Lucian indicated that some Greeks abhorred lesbianism: "Citing monstrous instruments of lust . . . the *tribade* [lesbian] will become rampant" (*Loves*). Lucian attests to the widespread practice of pederasty in the Roman period, and also the range of public opinion on the subject.

BIBLIOGRAPHY. R. Bracht Branham, *Unruly Eloquence: Lucian and the Comedy of Traditions*, Cambridge, MA: Harvard University Press, 1989.

William A. Percy

LUDWIG II (1845–1886)

King of Bavaria during the period of German unification. Born at Nymphenburg Palace near Munich, he ascended the throne at the age of 18. In his early youth he was not only handsome but also intelligent and kind-hearted. The death of his father and his premature accession kept him from attending a university. One of his first acts was to invite the financially desperate Richard Wagner to Munich, promising him every favor, including the rebuilding of a theatre so that his operas could be performed. Despite opposition by officials and the public to the enormous sums that Ludwig devoted to the composer's projects, the king remained loyal to him throughout his life, supporting the construction of the opera house in Bayreuth where Wagner at last saw all his work performed.

In the Austro-Prussian War of 1866 Bavaria unwisely sided with Catholic Austria and was easily defeated; the peace treaty served to make Bavaria dependent upon Prussia and ensured its involvement in the Franco-Prussian War of 1870–71, which culminated in the creation of the German Empire with Prussia at its head. Ludwig was pressured by Bismarck to copy in his own hand a letter inviting the Prussian king to become emperor—an act which he himself regarded as disgraceful.

Toward women Ludwig was completely indifferent, and attempts to arrange a marriage for him came to naught. He had at least fleeting homosexual relations with Paul of Thurn and Taxis, and a more enduring liaison with Richard Hornig, who exerted such influence over him that in official circles the favorite was called "the secret Chancellor of Bavaria." Their love had its crises, but at other times Hornig was the only one who had access to the king, and his decision to marry was experienced by Ludwig almost as treason. But the king found a successor, a certain Hesselschwerdt, who later, after his death, gave frank and revealing testimony to a secret committee of the Bavarian Parliament: that Ludwig had a weakness for simple country boys, youths with muscular arms and legs whom he could observe stripped to the waist while they tilled the fields. For men in uniform he had far less fondness and never cared to wear uniforms himself. When he had to appear in uniform, he wore a fanciful adaptation of the costume of the uhlans that bordered on masquerade. Ludwig also had a love affair with a Viennese actor named Josef Kainz whom he watched perform as the sole member of the audience. But the actor had too great a need of a genuine public and tired of the liaison.

The psychological idiosyncrasies and peculiarities of the king gave rise to what Thomas Szasz has called "the first psychiatric assassination committed successfully and in broad daylight on an important peronality." In fact, the death of Ludwig II on the evening of June 13, 1886, is shrouded in mystery. His body was found floating on the surface of the Starnberger See along with the body of the psychiatrist Bernhard von Gudden, the Director of the Insane Asylum in Munich, who was part of a commission appointed to take the king into custody when the lavish expenditures on his new castles became impossible for the state. The castles themselves were expressions of the royal fantasy, executed in a series of derivative styles anticipating the interior decoration that was later to be recognized as a homosexual specialty. The death of the king was commemorated in literary works composed by nearly all of the great contemporary homosexual writers. As an eccentric on the throne, Ludwig of Bavaria was the last of the crowned monarchs who—untroubled by regard for "public opinion" or the prying and insinuation of the media—could freely indulge their homoerotic and other whims.

BIBLIOGRAPHY. Curt Riess, *Auch Du, Cäsar . . . Homosexualität als Schicksal*, Munich: Universitas Verlag, 1981; Louis II de Bavière, *Carnets secrets 1869–1886*, Préface de Dominique Fernandez, Paris: Grasset, 1987; Wolfgang Schmidbauer and Johannes Kemper, *Ein ewiges Rätsel will ich bleiben mir und anderen: wie krank war Ludwig II. wirklich?*, Munich: Bertelsmann, 1986.

Warren Johansson

LULLY, JEAN-BAPTISTE (1632–1687)

French operatic composer. Born in Florence, he originally had the name Giovanni Battista Lulli. A self-taught violinist, he went to France in 1648 and four years later entered the service of the young Louis XIV. He became chamber composer and conductor of one of the king's orchestras. Until 1672 he composed numerous ballets, then he obtained a patent for the production of opera and established the Académie Royale de Musique, where he enjoyed a virtual monopoly on the operatic stage. Through lucky, sometimes unscrupulous speculations he amassed a fortune from his opera productions. By adapting the Italian opera to French taste, he set the style for French opera down to the late eighteenth century.

Among his contemporaries Lully inspired as much hatred as admiration. The hallmark of his character was impudence, which went so far as to submit to the king and queen of France a marriage contract in which he styled himself "son of a Florentine gentleman," when his father was still living as a humble miller. Thanks to his powerful protectors and to the King, who closed his eyes to the composer's conduct, Lully could enjoy relative immunity from the legal consequences of his scandalous behavior, which in the late seventeenth century could still be punished by death at the stake. He seems to have been homosexual throughout his life, even though when compromised in 1661 he chose to marry, and for a decade behaved like a model husband of the epoch, siring a child each year by his wife and otherwise living like an "honest bourgeois of Paris."

Yet on becoming director of the Opera in 1672, he abandoned himself entirely to his homosexual inclinations. His reputation was so well established that his enemies lost no occasion to castigate him in malicious verses that circulated in manuscript. A document of 1676 written by one Henri Guichard, whom Lully had accused of trying to poison him, referred explicitly to his "infamous debauches and acts of libertinism" with which, however, he did not "wish to soil the ears of the magistrates." The fiasco of a fireworks display that Lully had arranged in 1674 provoked the sarcastic comment that he might soon be on a pyre in the Place de Grève, the locale where sodomites were burned at the stake. Once again Lully erected a façade of heterosexuality by taking as mistress one Mademoiselle Certain, a talented harpsichordist. However, the affair ended badly for him when in 1684 he fell in love with a page named Brunet and was not ashamed to expose the liaison to the eyes of his wife and children, and out of jealousy Mlle Certain denounced him to Louis XIV. His anger provoked, the king had the page arrested, imprisoned at Saint-Lazare and given a good flogging, in the course of which he allegedly denounced several great nobles of the Court. Lully received a formal reproof from the Marquis de Seignelay and was warned that if he ever reverted to such practices, the king would make a striking example of him. This episode too gave rise to burlesque verses satirizing the composer's fall from grace, but by June of 1685 he regained the royal favor, and once more threw his detractors off the scent by pursuing an affair with a noble widow, the Duchess de la Ferté. At the same time, however, he resumed his homosexual adventures, now in a manner that brought him to the consulting room of Dr. Jeannot, a specialist in venereal diseases. It is possible that his mysterious death in consequence of a minor wound on his foot that became infected and gangrened, despite the best efforts of the physicians, had this as its cause. Beyond a doubt, the life of dissipation which Lully had led hastened his end. His death was hailed with an outcry of joy by his enemies, and a controversy ensued between them and his admirers who defended his homosexual passion on the ground that it had been shared by "the greatest heroes and noblemen."

Even with his failings, Lully was a composer whose genius was acknowledged by all his contemporaries, friend and foe alike. His homosexual escapades reveal him as a man of intense sensuality who enjoyed life to the fullest and boldly took risks in his ceaseless search for pleasure.

BIBLIOGRAPHY. Henry Prunières, "La vie scandaleuse de Jean-Baptiste Lully," *Mercure de France*, 115 (May 1, 1916), 75–88.

Warren Johansson

LYNES, GEORGE PLATT (1907–1955)

American photographer. One of the more significant figures in American photography between 1930 and 1955, Lynes was born in East Orange, New Jersey, and educated in private schools. He visited Paris in 1925, the first of several summers he spent there. In Paris he was associated with André Gide, Pavel Tchelitchew, Jean Cocteau, and Gertrude Stein, the last two of whom were subjects for early portraits. He began to teach himself photography in 1927. In 1933 Lynes decided he had enough mastery to begin a new career, and opened a commercial studio in New York. He rapidly became a successful fashion photographer, contributing to *Harper's Bazaar* and *Vogue*.

In 1935 he was commissioned to record the work of the American Ballet, which he continued to do until his death, compiling a noted body of dance photography. Despite his prominence, in 1945 he closed his studio and moved to California; three years later he returned to New York, but was unable to repeat his earlier success. Declared bankrupt in 1951, he spent the four years before his death from cancer in obscurity.

Lynes was closely associated with such homosexual artists as Marsden Hartley (with whom he shared a studio in the 1940s), the circle around Paul Cadmus and Jared French (both of whom he photographed), the American homoerotic artist Neel Bates, and British photographer Cecil Beaton.

His work is an important expression of two artistic currents of his day. In the 1920s, photography turned away from the pictoralists' soft-focus aesthetic; Lynes' male nudes present the reality of men's bodies for our precise observation, almost as objects of reverence. In Paris he was influenced by Tchelitchew, Man Ray, and surrealism; his "mythological" subjects employ its concepts. All of his work shows a sense of theatrical staging and dramatic effects achieved by his use of lighting.

While his mythological works—safe because their ostensible subject was myth, not men—and some of his dance photographs are strongly homoerotic, Lynes felt he could not openly express his homosexuality in his art without threatening his career. He did, however, circulate overtly homoerotic photographs among his friends, and between 1951 and his death he published homoerotic images under the pseudonym Roberto Rolf and Robert Orville in the Swiss homophile journal *Der Kreis*. The conflict he felt is illuminated by the fact that, before his death, he destroyed two bodies of work in his archives: his nudes and explicitly sexual images, and his fashion work.

BIBLIOGRAPHY. *George Platt Lynes: Photographs 1931–1955*, Pasadena, CA: Twelvetrees Press, 1980.

Donald Mader